Trees and Shrubs

HARDY IN THE BRITISH ISLES

Volume III

N – Rh

Trees and Shrubs

HARDY IN THE BRITISH ISLES

W. J. BEAN
CVO, ISO, VMH

Eighth Edition Revised

CHIEF EDITOR
D. L. CLARKE
VMH

GENERAL EDITOR
SIR GEORGE TAYLOR
DSc, FRS, VMH

VOLUME III
N–Rh

JOHN MURRAY

First Edition (Vols I & II) 1914
First Edition (Vol. III) 1933
Seventh Edition 1950

Eighth Edition Revised (Vol. III) 1976
*Published in collaboration with
The Royal Horticultural Society
Revisions and additions for Eighth Edition*
© *M. Bean and John Murray (Publishers) Ltd 1976*

*Printed in Great Britain by
Butler & Tanner Ltd, Frome and London*

0 7195 2427 X

CONTENTS

v

PREFACE TO VOLUME III

Three years have passed since the publication of Volume II. It had been hoped that Volume III might follow rather sooner, but early on it appeared that the problems raised, especially by *Rhododendron*, were of quite a different order than those presented by earlier volumes. The task of revision has involved much research to ensure adequate review of all available information. Volume IV, which will complete the sequence, is now well advanced and should appear considerably quicker.

It is my privilege as general editor to acknowledge once more the unremitting zeal of Mr Desmond Clarke who has been responsible, apart from attributed articles, for the bulk of the new text of Volume III which includes treatments of 114 genera, many of which posed difficult taxonomic problems. His aim to present balanced treatments acceptable to botanists and horticulturists for such major critical groups as *Rhododendron*, has, I believe, been fully realised and the new 'Bean' clearly bears the stamp of his authority and industry. His involvement has been and remains crucial to the advancement of the work.

Mr J. Robert Sealy had continued to give generous help with taxonomic and nomenclatural matters. It is a pleasure to express sincere thanks to Professor J. Heslop Harrison who freely allowed access to the Herbarium and Library at Kew and who also approved the participation of several members of the Kew staff; Mr P. S. Green and Mr C. Jeffrey were responsible for revising the genera of the Oleaceae and Compositae respectively; Mr A. D. Schilling provided useful information from Kew's satellite garden at Wakehurst Place in Sussex and Mr David Hunt has been most helpful.

Mr J. Jobling of the Forestry Commission has contributed the section on the cultivation of poplars, besides supplying other information on this group. Mr Alan Mitchell's tree measurements are a vital element in these volumes.

Mr F. P. Knight has written the part on propagation of rhododendrons and Mr G. D. Waterer has provided an epitomised history of the two Waterer firms responsible for so many hardy Rhododendron hybrids described in this volume.

It is with great regret that note must be made of the deaths since Volume II was published of two gardeners who have always been most generous of advice and encouragement. They are Lord Talbot de Malahide who contributed extensive notes on olearias and Lt. Cdr T. A. Dorrien-Smith whose remarkable garden at Tresco afforded extremely interesting material. It is also sad for the same reason to record that Volume III will be the last occasion on which new photographs by Harry Smith will be included. He was one of the outstanding plant photographers of the last twenty years and we relied upon him greatly.

To help with revision of *Rhododendron*, and in particular the section on hybrids, specimens have been provided by several gardens, among them The Royal Horticultural Society's garden at Wisley, Surrey; Borde Hill, Sussex; Exbury, Hants; Grayswood Hill, Surrey; Knap Hill Nurseries, Surrey; The High Beeches, Surrey. The following are thanked for their help in this and other matters:

The Hon. and Mrs E.
  Boscawen
Mr C. D. Brickell
Miss Audrey Brooks
Mr R. N. S. Clarke
Mr P. H. Gardner
Mr A. F. George
Mr J. Grant
Mr H. J. Grootendorst
Mr G. A. Hardy
Mr H. G. Hillier
Mr M. Haworth-Booth
Mr J. K. Hulme
Capt. Collingwood Ingram

Mr Will Ingwersen
Mr J. Keenan, formerly of the
  Royal Botanic Garden,
  Edinburgh
Mr R. Lancaster
Major E. W. M. Magor
Mr C. G. Nice
the late Mr G. Pilkington
Mr. A. D. Schilling
the late Mr L. S. Slinger
Mr Frederick Street
Mr G. S. Thomas
Mr Donald Waterer
Dr P. F. Yeo

It would be appropriate while on the matter of *Rhododendron* to pay tribute to the work of Mr H. Davidian and the late Dr J. M. Cowan on the revision of this genus and to the excellence of the Year Books of the Royal Horticultural Society in which much of their work was published. Information has been freely drawn from these sources.

Finally, Miss Margaret Bean, Mr J. R. Sealy and Mr C. D. Brickell must be warmly thanked for their meticulous proof-reading, and Miss Mary Grierson for her drawings.

GEORGE TAYLOR

1976

APPROXIMATE METRIC EQUIVALENTS

INCHES TO MILLIMETRES

$\frac{1}{32}$ in	= 0·8 mm	$\frac{5}{8}$ in	= 15·9 mm	4 in	= 101 mm
$\frac{1}{16}$	= 1·6	$\frac{3}{4}$	= 19·1	5	= 127
$\frac{1}{8}$	= 3·2	$\frac{7}{8}$	= 22·2	6	= 152
$\frac{3}{16}$	= 4·8	1	= 25·4	7	= 178
$\frac{1}{4}$	= 6·4	$1\frac{1}{4}$	= 31·8	8	= 203
$\frac{5}{16}$	= 7·9	$1\frac{1}{2}$	= 38·1	9	= 229
$\frac{3}{8}$	= 9·5	$1\frac{3}{4}$	= 44·5	10	= 254
$\frac{7}{16}$	= 11·1	2	= 51	11	= 279
$\frac{1}{2}$	= 12·7	3	= 76	12	= 305

FEET TO METRES

2 ft	= 0·61 m	12 ft	= 3·66 m	60 ft	= 18·3 m
3	= 0·91	15	= 4·57	70	= 21·3
4	= 1·22	20	= 6·10	80	= 24·4
5	= 1·52	25	= 7·62	90	= 27·4
6	= 1·83	30	= 9·15	100	= 30·5
7	= 2·13	35	= 10·67	110	= 33·5
8	= 2·44	40	= 12·20	120	= 36·6
9	= 2·74	45	= 13·72	130	= 39·6
10	= 3·05	50	= 15·2	140	= 42·7
11	= 3·55			150	= 45·7

ALTITUDES TO METRES

500 ft	= 152 m	4,000 ft	= 1,219 m
1,000	= 305	5,000	= 1,524
1,500	= 457	10,000	= 3,048
3,000	= 914	15,000	= 4,572

TEMPERATURES: °F TO °C

0 °F	= −17·8 °C	45 °F	= 7·2 °C
10	= −12·2	50	= 10·0
20	= −6·7	55	= 12·8
32	= 0·0	60	= 15·6
40	= 4·4	65	= 18·3
		70	= 21·1

TREE MEASUREMENTS

All measurements of girth were taken at 5 ft (1·52 m) unless otherwise stated.

LIST OF DRAWINGS IN THE TEXT

Those marked with an asterisk were drawn by Miss E. Goldring: the remainder are by Miss Mary Grierson.

SOURCES OF PLATES

LIST OF PLATES

1 NANDINA DOMESTICA

2 NEILLIA THIBETICA

3 NYSSA SYLVATICA

4 NOTHOFAGUS PROCERA

5 OLEARIA MACRODONTA

6 OSMANTHUS
× BURKWOODII

7 Paeonia lutea var. ludlowii

8 Paeonia suffruticosa cultivar

9 PARROTIA PERSICA at
Westonbirt

10 PARTHENOCISSUS
HENRYANA

11 PASSIFLORA CAERULEA

12 PENSTEMON DAVIDSONII in Washington State, USA

13 PENSTEMON RUPICOLA

14 PERNETTYA FURIENS

15 Pernettya mucronata

16 Philadelphus 'Belle Étoile'

17 Philadelphus 'Erectus'

18 Philadelphus 'Manteau d'Hermine'

19 Philadelphus 'Norma'

20 Philadelphus 'Virginal'

21 PHILESIA MAGELLANICA

22 PHLOMIS FRUTICOSA

23 Phormium tenax

24 PHYGELIUS CAPENSIS

25 PHYLLODOCE ALEUTICA

26 PHYLLODOCE EMPETRIFORMIS
in Olympic National Park,
Washington State, USA

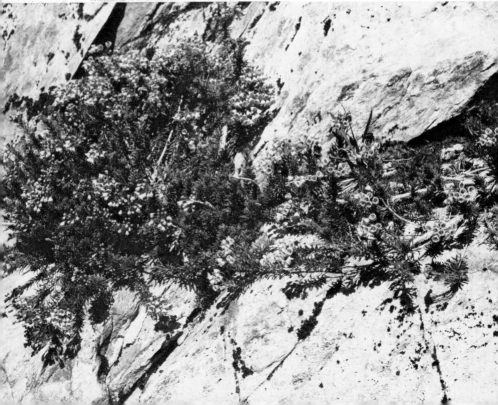

27 Picea glauca 'Conica'

28 Picea breweriana
at Westonbirt

29 Pieris formosa in Bhutan

30 PIERIS JAPONICA

31 PILEOSTEGIA
VIBURNOIDES

32 Pinus mugo

33 Pinus FLEXILIS
in N. Wyoming,
USA

34 Pinus PATULA
at Saltram,
Devon

35 PINUS MONTEZUMAE at Mt Usher

36 Pinus sylvestris in Wester Ross

37 Pinus pinea at Kew

38 Piptanthus
LABURNIFOLIUS

39 Pittosporum
TOBIRA

40 Pittosporum tenuifolium

41 A London plane in winter

42 PLATANUS ORIENTALIS
at Corsham Court,
Wilts

43 POPULUS TRICHOCARPA in Bath Botanic Garden

44 PRUNUS 'AMANOGAWA'

45 PRUNUS CERASIFERA

46 Prunus incisa

47 PRUNUS SERRULA

48 PRUNUS 'SHIMIDSU'

49 PRUNUS SUBHIRTELLA
'AUTUMNALIS'

50 PRUNUS 'OJOCHIN'

51 PRUNUS 'TAI HAKU'

52 PSEUDOTSUGA MENZIESII
'FLETCHERI'

53 Pseudotsuga menziesii in Washington State, USA

54 Pterocarya fraxinifolia

55 Pyracantha coccinea 'Lalandei'

56 QUERCUS × HISPANICA
'LUCOMBEANA' at Kew

57 QUERCUS CASTANEIFOLIA
at Kew

58 QUERCUS ROBUR
at Hazlegrove House,
Sparkford, Somerset,
known traditionally as
the King John Oak

59 QUERCUS RUBRA

60 QUERCUS PETRAEA
in Herefordshire, to show
straight growths

61 QUERCUS ILEX, fruits

62 Quercus suber, Killerton Gardens, Devon

63 A red oak hybrid (? QUERCUS RUBRA × QUERCUS PALUSTRIS)

64 RHAPHIOLEPIS UMBELLATA

65 Rhododendron
ALBIFLORUM,
Olympic Mts,
Washington, USA

66 Rhododendron
AUGUSTINII, St Paul's,
Walden Bury, Herts

67 RHODODENDRON
   BAILEYI in Bhutan

68 RHODODENDRON
   CALOPHYTUM

69 RHODODENDRON
CAMPANULATUM

70 RHODODENDRON
CAMPYLOGYNUM
var. MYRTILLOIDES

71 Rhododendron
   CEPHALANTHUM

72 Rhododendron
   CHARITOPES

73 Rhododendron
CILIATUM in Bhutan

74 Rhododendron
HODGSONII

75 RHODODENDRON EDGEWORTHII in Bhutan

76 Rhododendron
GLAUCOPHYLLUM in Bhutan

77 Rhododendron
GRIFFITHIANUM

78 Rhododendron LANATUM and Primula ELONGATA in Bhutan

79 Rhododendron LEUCASPIS

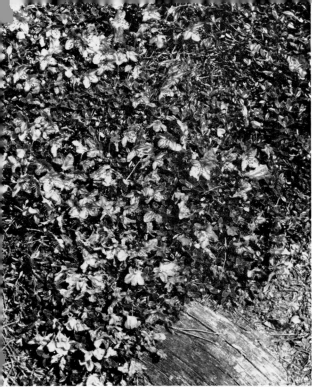

80 Rhododendron
KELETICUM

81 Rhododendron
LINDLEYI in Bhutan

82 RHODODENDRON LUDLOWII on alpine moorland in S.E. Tibet

83 Rhododendron
LUTESCENS
'BAGSHOT SANDS'

84 RHODODENDRON
MEGERATUM

85 Rhododendron
MUCRONULATUM

86 Rhododendron
OCCIDENTALE
at Seattle, USA

87 RHODODENDRON PUMILUM

88 RHODODENDRON RHABDOTUM in Bhutan

89 Rhododendron
ROXIEANUM, Rock 59589

90 Rhododendron
SCHLIPPENBACHII

91 RHODODENDRON SOULIEI
at Sandling Park, Kent

92 RHODODENDRON
TRICHOCLADUM
aff. in the wild

93 Rhododendron sinogrande

94 Rhododendron williamsianum

95 Rhododendron
YAKUSHIMANUM

96 Rhododendron yunnanense

97 RHODODENDRON
ALISON JOHNSTONE

98 RHODODENDRON ANGELO

99 RHODODENDRON
'BETTY WORMALD'

100 RHODODENDRON
CINNKEYS

101 RHODODENDRON
CORNISH CROSS

102 RHODODENDRON
'DR STOCKER'

103 Rhododendron
'Furnivall's Daughter'

104 Rhododendron
Lady Chamberlain

105 Rhododendron Loderi
'Pink Coral'

106 Rhododendron
'Prof. Hugo de Vries'

107 Rhododendron
'Sappho'

108 Rhododendron
(deciduous azalea)
'Ribera'

109 Rhododendron (evergreen azalea) 'Maxwellii'

110 Rhodothamnus chamaecistus

NANDINA BERBERIDACEAE

A genus of a single species in E. Asia. Although usually placed in the Berberidaceae, it is considered by some botanists to be sufficiently distinct and taxonomically isolated to rank as a separate family—the Nandinaceae —differing from the Berberidaceae in having flowers with numerous spirally arranged sepals and anthers opening by longitudinal slits.

The Japanese name for this species is 'Nanten'—hence *Nandina*.

N. DOMESTICA Thunb. [PLATE I

An evergreen shrub, with erect, unarmed, and unbranched stems, 6 to 8 ft high in this country, even taller in warmer ones, the lower part covered with the bases of fallen leaves. Leaves 1 to 1½ ft long, much divided (doubly or trebly pinnate), composed of numerous, linear-lanceolate leaflets, which are 1½ to 4 in. long, long-pointed, quite glabrous, tinged with red when young, becoming purplish in autumn. Flowers in an erect panicle, 8 to 15 in. long, borne at the top of the stem, each flower ¼ to ⅓ in. across, white, with large yellow anthers. Berries two-seeded, globular, ⅓ in. in diameter, bright red normally, but in some forms more purplish red; the stigma persisting, as in barberry fruits.

Introduced in 1804 from Japan, where it is much cultivated, but really a native of China. Its chief merit in this country is its elegant bamboo-like form, for its flowers are not very showy, nor are its fruits freely produced. It needs a good, moist soil and a warm, sunny position sheltered from the wind. Given these conditions it should succeed in all but the coldest gardens. There is a plant 6 ft high and over twenty-five years old on the rock garden in the Royal Horticultural Society Garden at Wisley. Another almost as tall, planted in 1938, grows at Belhaven House near Dunbar in East Lothian. It is best propagated from seeds, which, however, do not, as introduced, germinate freely. Cuttings put in a mild heat will root in time, but they too are slow. The young plants should be grown under glass for a year or two.

cv. 'NANA PURPUREA'.—Of dwarf habit, with leaves tinged with purple throughout the summer.

cv. 'PYGMAEA'.—A variety of dwarf, close habit, making a leafy mound up to about 2 ft high.

White- and yellow-berried forms are known.

NEILLIA ROSACEAE

A genus which, as now interpreted by most botanists, comprises some twenty species of shrubs and subshrubs, natives of E. and S.E. Asia and

Malaysia. For other species included in *Neillia* in previous editions, see
PHYSOCARPUS.

Leaves alternate, simple, with toothed lobes; stipules large, deciduous.
Flowers in racemes or panicles. Petals five, rounded, often pink, inserted
on the rim of the shortly five-lobed calyx-tube (receptacle). Stamens
in one to three whorls of ten each. Carpels one or two, enclosed within
the calyx-tube but not adnate to it, each developing into a follicle splitting
down one side only. Seeds several, unwinged, with copious endosperm.
In *Spiraea* stipules are absent and the seeds have little or no endosperm.

The genus was named by David Don in honour of his friend Patrick
Neill (1776–1851), a well-known Scottish naturalist.

The principal works on the genus are: J. Vidal, 'Le Genre *Neillia*',
published in *Adansonia*, n.s., Vol. 3 (1963), pp. 142–66, and J. Cullen, 'The
Genus Neillia (Rosaceae) in Mainland Asia and in Cultivation', published
in *Journ. Arn. Arb.*, Vol. 52 (1971), pp. 137–58.

N. SINENSIS Oliver

A deciduous shrub 5 or 6 ft high, with glabrous, brown, peeling bark. Leaves
ovate, 2 to 4 in. long, 1¼ to 2½ in. wide, the apex long drawn out, the margins
set with coarse teeth or small lobes which are again sharply toothed; there is

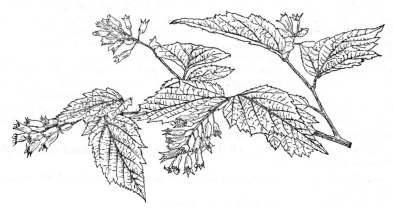

NEILLIA SINENSIS

down on the main veins and in their axils at first, but both surfaces become almost
or quite glabrous. Flowers nodding, produced in a slender, terminal raceme 1
to 2½ in. long, carrying twelve to twenty flowers; pedicels ⅛ to $\frac{5}{16}$ in. long. The
main feature of the flower is the smooth cylindrical white calyx-tube, ½ in.
long and ⅛ in. wide, dividing at the end into five narrow triangular lobes. Petals
small, broadly ovate, about as long as the calyx-lobes.

Native of Central China; discovered by Henry, and introduced to cultivation by Wilson in 1901. It is a shrub of elegant habit allied to *N. thibetica* but not so decorative, the racemes being usually shorter and fewer-flowered, though the individual flowers are larger.

var. RIBESIOIDES (Rehd.) Vidal *N. ribesioides* Rehd.—Flowers shorter-stalked (pedicels up to $\frac{3}{16}$ in. long), with a shorter calyx-tube (up to $\frac{1}{4}$ in. long). Described by Rehder (as a species) from specimens collected by Wilson in W. Szechwan, and also occurring in Yunnan. The only authentic plant recorded by Dr Cullen (op. cit.) grows in the Liverpool University Botanic Gardens. It is of unknown origin.

N. THIBETICA Bur. & Franch.   [PLATE 2
N. *longiracemosa* Hemsl.

A deciduous shrub 3 to 6 ft high (occasionally taller); young shoots slender. downy. Leaves ovate, sometimes indistinctly three-lobed, irregularly toothed, slender-pointed, rounded to heart-shaped at the base, $1\frac{1}{2}$ to 4 in. long, 1 to $2\frac{1}{2}$ in. wide, more or less downy on both surfaces, especially beneath and on the midrib; stalk up to $\frac{1}{2}$ in. long; stipules about $\frac{1}{4}$ in. long, entire or slightly toothed. Racemes terminal, 2 to 6 in. long, slender, bearing up to sixty rosy-pink flowers, opening in May and June; pedicels downy, up to $\frac{3}{16}$ in. long. Receptacle (calyx-tube) cylindrical-campanulate, $\frac{3}{16}$ to $\frac{1}{4}$ in. long, downy on the outer and inner surfaces, and becoming glandular-bristly on the outside in the fruiting stage; calyx-lobes erect, lanceolate. Petals rounded, only showing between the calyx-lobes. Ovary hairy at the top. *Bot. Mag.*, n.s., t. 3.

Native of Szechwan, China; discovered by A. E. Pratt near Tatsien-lu in 1890, and described by Hemsley in 1892 under the name *N. longiracemosa*, by which it has long been known in gardens. A few weeks before Pratt left Tatsien-lu for England, the French explorer Prince Henri d'Orleans (then twenty-three years of age) arrived with his companions after their adventurous journey from Siberia through Chinese Turkestan and the High Plateau of Tibet. Here they added to their botanical collections, all of which they entrusted to Pratt, who conveyed them as far as Shanghai. Among the specimens was a neillia, collected near Tatsien-lu, which the French botanists Bureau and Franchet described as a new species in the following year, 1891. This they called *N. thibetica*. It has long been suspected that Pratt's species and the Prince's were really one and the same, and they were united by Vidal in 1963, under the name *N. thibetica*, which has a year's priority. But the credit for the discovery belongs to Pratt, who had spent two summers studying the flora and fauna of the Tatsien-lu area.

N. thibetica was introduced by Wilson when collecting for the Arnold Arboretum in 1908 (as *N. longiracemosa*) and again in 1911 (as *N. thibetica*). It is a pretty, elegant shrub and the commonest of the genus in gardens. It received an Award of Merit in 1931.

N. thibetica is allied to *N. sinensis*, which is distinguished from it by its glabrous calyx-tube and fewer-flowered inflorescence.

N. THYRSIFLORA D. Don

A low deciduous bush of neat, rounded habit, about 3 ft high; young shoots angular, glabrous, sometimes reddish. Leaves 1½ to 3 in. long, two-thirds as wide, three-lobed (most markedly so on the barren shoots), ovate with a long, narrow point, sharply, often doubly, toothed, the base mostly heart-shaped, dark green and glabrous above, the bright green undersurface downy on the chief veins; stalk ¼ to ½ in. long. Flowers in a downy raceme, terminating the shoot, or springing from the axils of the uppermost leaves. Each flower is about ⅓ in. long; the calyx-tube bell-shaped, silky hairy, the lobes lance-shaped and pointed; petals roundish ovage, white. Fruits consisting of one 'pod' enclosed by the persistent calyx, and containing four to eight seeds.

A species of wide range in E. Asia, from Nepal eastward and south-eastward to S. China, Burma, and Malaysia. It was in cultivation as early as 1855, but has always been rare in gardens.

NEMOPANTHUS AQUIFOLIACEAE

A genus of a single species from north-eastern N. America, differing from *Ilex*, to which it is closely allied, in the much reduced calyx and linear petals.

N. MUCRONATUS (L.) Trel.

Vaccinium mucronatum L.; *N. canadensis* (Michx.) DC.; *Ilex canadensis* Michx., not West.

A deciduous shrub 3 to 10 ft high, with glabrous young wood. Leaves alternate, oval, oblong or ovate, thin, not (or very slightly) toothed, tapered more abruptly towards the base than the apex, quite glabrous, 1 to 2½ in. long, ½ to 1⅛ in. wide; stalk ¼ to ½ in. long. Flowers often unisexual, small, of no beauty; produced from the leaf-axils usually singly, occasionally a few together on a thread-like stalk ½ to 1 in. long. Fruit a globose berry, ¼ to ⅓ in. wide, pale crimson, containing four or five hard bony nutlets.

Native of eastern N. America; introduced in 1802. Although introduced so long ago, this shrub never appears to have obtained much recognition in this country. Unless it bears its fruits freely it is of no garden value, and our summer sun is probably not hot enough to develop its best qualities in that respect. I have never seen it in Britain bearing fruit anything like so freely as it does in N. America.

Some plants have flowers of both sexes as well as perfect flowers, others have those of one sex only.

NEOLITSEA   LAURACEAE

A genus of about sixty species of evergreen, dioecious trees or shrubs in E. Asia and Indo-Malaysia. Leaves alternate, usually three-veined from near the base. Inflorescence umbellate. Flowers with four perianth-segments, the males usually with six, rarely eight, stamens. Fruit a berry.

N. SERICEA (Bl.) Koidz.

Laurus sericea Bl.; *Litsea glauca* Sieb.; *Neolitsea glauca* (Sieb.) Koidz.

A small evergreen dioecious tree with silky young stems. Leaves leathery, three-veined from near the base, oblong-elliptic or broadest slightly below the middle, 3 to 6 in. long, 1¼ to 2¾ in. wide, acute to acuminate at the apex, cuneate at the base, young leaves covered with silky, golden-brown hairs, when mature the upper side glabrous, the lower one glaucous and usually with traces of the juvenile hairs; petioles about 1 in. long. Flowers produced in autumn in axillary clusters. Fruits red, ellipsoid, about ½ in. long, only borne on female plants.

Native of Japan, Korea (Cheju Do Island), and China; date of introduction uncertain. It is quite a handsome evergreen with remarkable young foliage, very uncommon but apparently hardy.

A plant at Wakehurst Place in Sussex, identified as *N. sericea*, but perhaps wrongly, bore black fruits and had the undersurface of the year-old leaves still closely covered with a coating of silky, silvery or pale bronze hairs and appearing as if burnished. The young foliage was hairy as in *N. sericea* and was not produced until quite late in the summer. This plant died in 1975.

NEVIUSIA   ROSACEAE

A genus of a single species in the south-eastern USA, not closely related to any other American member of the rose family. Flowers without petals. Carpels two to four, enclosed within the calyx-tube, each developing into a drupe-like achene. It was named by Asa Gray after its discoverer, the Rev. R. D. Nevius.

N. ALABAMENSIS A. Gray

A deciduous shrub 4 to 6 ft high, with erect stems and spreading branches, making a rounded bush, wider than it is high; branchlets at first covered with fine down. Leaves alternate, ovate-oblong, 1 to 3½ in. long, those of the barren shoots shallowly lobed, finely double-toothed; downy on the veins beneath; stalk up to ⅛ in. long, downy. Flowers produced in a cluster at the end of short leafy side-shoots in April and May. Each flower is borne on a slender, downy stalk $\frac{3}{4}$ to 1 in. long; it has no petals, but a conspicuous bunch of white stamens $\frac{1}{4}$ to $\frac{1}{3}$ in. long, and a calyx about $\frac{3}{4}$ in. across, with leaf-like, toothed lobes. *Bot. Mag.*, t. 6806.

Native of Alabama, where, apparently, it is only known in one or two spots. It was found on the cliffs of Black Warrior River, at Tuscaloosa, in 1858, by the Rev. R. D. Nevius. It is quite hardy in England, and is easily increased by fairly soft cuttings placed in heat. Its beauty in some parts of N. America is so great that it has been called the 'Alabama Snow-wreath', owing to the snowy whiteness and profusion of its feathery blossom. But out-of-doors in England it is never really pure white but of a dull greenish white. Forced early into blossom under glass, its colour is much purer, and it is then very elegant and beautiful. In March 1907, about fifty years after its discovery, a letter was received at Kew from Mr Nevius, then at Tacoma, Washington, from which it appears that this shrub is not always a success in its native land. He says: 'I have had it growing in many places in the open, but it does not do well. Even at Tuscaloosa, where I discovered it, a hedge I planted of it in the churchyard flowered but sparingly.'

NICOTIANA   SOLANACEAE

A genus of about seventy species of annuals, herbaceous perennials and subshrubs (but the species described here and a few others almost completely woody), natives of the New World, Australia and some of the Pacific islands. Named after Jean Nicot, who introduced the tobacco plant to France.

N. GLAUCA R. Graham

A semi-evergreen or deciduous shrub of erect, thin habit, 10 ft and upwards high in this country; branches slender, at first only semi-woody; perfectly glabrous. Leaves alternate, variable in shape, usually ovate and tapered towards both ends, sometimes heart-shaped at the base, pointed, quite entire, 1½ to 4 in. long, 1 to 3 in. wide, sometimes much larger, glaucous and perfectly glabrous on both surfaces; stalk slender and about as long as the blade. Inflorescence a lax terminal panicle bearing numerous flowers. Corolla bright yellow, tubular, 1½ in. long, $\frac{1}{6}$ in. wide, five-lobed at the mouth where it is $\frac{3}{8}$ in. wide, downy outside, glabrous within; calyx green, tubular, $\frac{1}{2}$ in. long, with five pointed triangular teeth, glabrous; stamens five, 1 in. long. *Bot. Mag.*, t. 2837.

Native of the Argentine, Brazil, and other parts of S. America; introduced in 1827. Although an ally of the common tobacco plant this is very different in general appearance, being an almost tree-like shrub of lax growth. It flowers from June onwards and is quite ornamental, the yellow flowers contrasting well with the vividly glaucous foliage. It was cultivated for several years in a sheltered sunny nook at Kew, but was not genuinely hardy there, being killed in hard winters. Even so, it is well worth cultivating, especially in the warmer counties.

In the warmer parts of the world it frequently escapes from cultivation and has even become naturalised.

NOTHOFAGUS   Southern Beeches   FAGACEAE

The northern beeches, of which *Fagus sylvatica* is the type, form a very homogeneous group of invariably deciduous trees with broad leaves; they are confined to the temperate latitudes of the northern hemisphere. The beeches of the southern hemisphere are mainly evergreen and are a larger, more varied group, with almost forty species (against ten in *Fagus*). Of these nine are natives of temperate S. America (Chile and bordering parts of Argentina); three occur in Tasmania and Australia; five in New Zealand. It has quite recently been discovered that southern beeches dominate in some of the remote mountain forests of New Guinea, and sixteen species were described from this region in 1952–3. There are also five species in New Caledonia, two of which were described by Baillon in 1874, but in a new genus—*Trisyngyne*—which he believed to belong to the Euphorbiaceae.

As remarked above, the southern beeches are mainly evergreen. But seven are deciduous, all of them from Chile and Argentina except the Tasmanian *N. gunnii*. It is interesting that these deciduous species resemble the northern beeches in having the leaves plicately folded in the bud, i.e., concertina-wise; in the evergreen species they are folded along the midrib. The leading characters of *Nothofagus* are: male flowers solitary or in pairs or threes, sessile or shortly stalked (in *Fagus* they are borne in globose, many-flowered, stalked inflorescences); female flowers usually three in each involucre (two in *Fagus*), normally each flower producing a nutlet, of which the two outer ones are three-winged or three-angled and the middle one flattened; styles short, not elongated as in *Fagus*. The valves of the involucre are essentially the same as in *Fagus* but are often obviously composed of several scales (lamellae) and the processes are more varied in form. Sometimes, too, they are much narrower than the nutlets and do not fully enclose them.

The name *Nothofagus* means 'false beech' or 'resembling the beech'; but *Notofagus*, meaning 'southern beech', would have been more appropriate, and it has even been suggested that Blume, who first published the name *Nothofagus*, inserted the letter 'h' inadvertently.

There is no monograph on the genus *Nothofagus*, but a valuable key, which includes the S. American and Australasian species, was published by C. G. G. J. Van Steenis as part of a study mainly devoted to the species recently discovered in New Guinea (*Journ. Arn. Arb.*, Vol. 34 (1953), pp. 328–38).

All the southern beeches so far introduced are hardy or nearly so in the woodland gardens of mid-Sussex, with the exception of *N. moorei*, which thrives only in the mildest parts. The deciduous species now in cultivation should grow satisfactorily over most of the British Isles (though *N. procera* is tender in some forms). The hardiest evergreen species is *N. betuloides*. Unlike the common beech, the southern beeches are not suitable for calcareous soils. They are poor wind-resisters in this country, possibly because they grow too fast and make top-growth out of proportion to their root-system.

N. ANTARCTICA (Forst. f.) Oerst.   Ñirre

Fagus antarctica Forst. f.; *N. montagnei* (Hombron & Jacquinot) Reiche

A small deciduous tree with a slender trunk usually under 50 ft high in the wild and often occurring as a low, dense shrub in exposed places; bark scaly; young shoots very downy. Leaves $\frac{1}{2}$ to 1 in. long (occasionally up to $1\frac{1}{2}$ in.), broadly ovate or somewhat triangular, heart-shaped or truncate at the base, rounded at the tip, sometimes slightly lobed, always irregularly and minutely toothed, glabrous on both sides except for minute down on the midrib beneath (or the blade downy on both sides in var. *uliginosa* (A. DC.) Reiche); stalk downy $\frac{1}{12}$ to $\frac{1}{6}$ in. long. Flowers produced during May, the males singly, in pairs or in threes in the basal leaf-axils of small twigs, pendulous, each about $\frac{1}{6}$ in. across; perianth of male flowers usually five-lobed. Husk of fruit four-valved, about $\frac{1}{4}$ in. long, each valve with a few transverse, entire scales; nutlets three.

A native of temperate S. America from Cape Horn northward to the Andes east of the Chilean town of Chillan (*c.* 36° 30′ S.). It is common as a 'subalpine' tree above the evergreen beech forests, but sometimes occurs below them in frosty valleys, and occupies large tracts east of the Andes, on the margins of the Patagonian steppe.

The date of the first introduction of *N. antarctica* is uncertain (see *N. betuloides*). But it was certainly uncommon in the last century, and even now is rarely met with in gardens. Some of the oldest trees now in cultivation derive from seeds collected by H. J. Elwes near Lake Meliquina in Argentina, in 1902, and no existing tree was planted before that date, so far as is known.

N. antarctica is perfectly hardy and deserves to be more widely planted, for few trees have greater distinction and elegance when young. It makes unbranched shoots as much as 3 ft long in a season, furnished the whole length with closely set leaves. The habit is thin and open, with the branchlets arranged more or less in one plane, as in so many of the southern beeches. In some forms the leaves are deliciously honey-scented when young, and even in late summer the fragrance can still be detected. Some young plants produce stamen-clusters in such abundance that they could almost be classed as flowering shrubs. It needs an open, sunny position.

N. antarctica has attained 50 × 4 ft at Dawyck in Peeblesshire (1966), and at Crarae, Argyll, a tree planted in 1936 is already 40 × 4$\frac{1}{2}$ ft (1969). At Wakehurst Place, Sussex, a tree which is probably from the Elwes seed introduction of 1902 measures 42 × 4 ft (1968). At Rowallane, Co. Down, there is a remarkable specimen with nine main stems and a wide spread.

Fertile seed is produced in this country, perhaps more frequently than is realised, for the fruits, being so small, might not be noticed. Self-sown seedlings have appeared at The High Beeches, Handcross. Layering is an alternative means of increase.

var. BICRENATA A. DC.—See *N. pumilio.*

var. ULIGINOSA A. DC.—This differs from the typical state of the species only in having the leaves on both sides covered with a very fine, short, erect down. The Elwes introduction mentioned above belongs to this variety and is also rather larger-leaved than normal. But typical *N. antarctica* may have leaves just as large, and some specimens of the var. *uliginosa* have small leaves. Judging from the material available, this variety is confined to the northern part of the range of the species, but is certainly not found only in boggy habitats, as the varietal epithet *uliginosa* would imply.

N. BETULOIDES (Mirbel) Blume

Fagus betuloides Mirbel

An evergreen tree or shrub of dense, leafy habit, said to attain a height of almost 100 ft in valleys where it is sheltered from the Pacific winds, but more common under 50 ft high and often a shrub on the coast. Young shoots sticky, minutely downy. Leaves set about ¼ in. apart on the twigs, ovate, wedge-shaped or rounded at the base, ½ to 1 in. long, ¼ to ¾ in. wide, margins edged with small usually bluntish teeth, upper surface dark varnished green, lower surface paler, finely net-veined, often sprinkled with minute dark glands, glabrous on both sides; petiole about ⅛ in. long. Male flowers solitary, shortly stalked, with ten to sixteen stamens; anthers red. Valves of husk four, narrower than the nutlets, with short tooth-like processes.

Native of the coasts of Chile from Valdivia province to Cape Horn, also occurring in Argentina on Tierra del Fuego and in Santa Cruz province. The date of introduction of this species, and of *N. antarctica*, is usually given as 1830, though Loudon, the authority for this statement, merely gave it as the reputed date and mentioned no specimens. It was in this year that Capt. King's surveying expedition to the Magellan region returned to Britain, and it may be that they brought with them plants or seeds of both species. Thirteen years later, J. D. Hooker sent to Kew a Wardian case containing plants of both *N. betuloides* and *N. antarctica*, but whether these survived the reversal of seasons is not recorded. It is, however, certain that *N. betuloides* was established in cultivation in the second half of the 19th century, and available in the trade.

N. betuloides is hardy except in the coldest parts, though it is unlikely to stand exposure to cold, drying winds. It is a sombre but impressive tree of dense habit, its dark green leaves closely crowded on the branchlets. Its relative *N. dombeyi* is of more open habit, with usually paler, more widely spaced leaves, which are sharply toothed and mostly lanceolate (at least at the tips of the shoots); in *N. betuloides* the leaves are stubby even at the ends of the shoots and the toothing blunt. There is the further difference that in *N. betuloides* the male flowers are solitary, whereas in *N. dombeyi* they are mostly borne in threes.

At Grayswood Hill, Haslemere, there is a fine specimen of this species, planted in 1882. In 1906 it measured 34 × 2¼ ft; a recent measurement is 50 × 6¾ ft (1969). In previous editions of this work a tree at Pencarrow, Cornwall, was mentioned; this was planted in 1847 and measured 36 × 4¼ ft in 1903; it died and was cut down in 1925; another in the collection there, planted several decades later, measures 46 × 7 ft (1957). Another old specimen of which the planting date is known grows at Hafordunas, Denbigh; planted in 1855 it is 46 ft high and has three stems, the largest 8½ ft in girth (1960); its size is given by Elwes and Henry as 36 ft × 5 ft 2 in. in 1904.

Some other specimens recorded recently are: Wakehurst Place, Sussex, in Heather Garden, 33 × 4½ ft (1965); Kitlands, Leith Hill, Surrey, 45 × 8 ft. (1965); Bulkley Mill, Conway, 49 × 3½ ft (1960); Muncaster Castle, Cumberland, 72 × 5¼ ft (1971); Powerscourt, Co. Wicklow, Eire, 52 × 6½ ft (1966); Mount Usher, Co. Wicklow, 85 × 8¾ ft (1966).

N. CUNNINGHAMII (Hook.) Oerst.

Fagus cunninghamii Hook.

An evergreen tree attaining a large size in the wild; bark scaly, vertically furrowed on old trees; young shoots wiry, covered with short, dark down. Leaves glossy green, mostly triangular with a truncate base, some broadly ovate or rhombic, a few almost orbicular, ¼ to ⅝ in. long, from half to quite as much wide, apex bluntly pointed, margins (except at the base of the blade) bluntly and irregularly single-toothed, both surfaces glabrous; petiole downy, very short. Male flowers solitary, with an irregularly six-lobed perianth. Husk of fruit dividing into four narrow valves about ¼ in. long, bristled over with short decurved scales each of which is terminated by a globular gland which hardens as the fruit ripens; nutlets three, the centre one flattened.

Native of Tasmania, where it varies from an enormous timber tree to a shrub, according to rainfall and altitude; also of Victoria. It was in cultivation as early as 1860 but has never been common and is not reliably hardy. The recorded specimens are: Wakehurst Place, Sussex, 26 × 1¾ ft (1966); Caerhays, Cornwall, 46 × 3¼ ft (1971); Stonefield, Argyll, 53 × 3¾ ft (1969); Mount Usher, Co. Wicklow, Eire, 53 × 3½ ft (1966); Rowallane, Northern Ireland, 45 × 4¼ ft (1966).

N. cunninghamii is closely allied to *N. menziesii* of New Zealand (q.v. for the marks of difference).

N. DOMBEYI (Mirbel) Blume   COIGÜE

Fagus dombeyi Mirbel

An evergreen tree of very large size; young shoots clothed with very minute down. Leaves of firm texture, ovate or ovate-lanceolate, rounded or broadly wedge-shaped, pointed, finely and unevenly toothed, ¾ to 1½ in. long, ⅜ to ⅝ in.

wide, dark glossy green above, paler bright green beneath, sometimes specked when older with minute blackish glands on both surfaces, but more densely beneath; chief veins inconspicuous; stalk $\frac{1}{12}$ in. long. Male flowers mostly in threes; stamens bright red. Valves of husk with short, tooth-like appendages; nutlets three.

Native of Chile and Argentina. It is a common and characteristic tree of the Chilean forests in their most developed form, and the most beautiful, assuming when old a cedar-like habit. In the northern part of its range it often occurs with one or other of the two main deciduous species—N. *obliqua* and N. *procera* —and occasionally all three can be found growing in the same stand. But it ranges farther to the south than either (to about 46° S.).

N. *dombeyi* was introduced to Britain by F. R. S. Balfour of Dawyck, who presented a large quantity of seeds to Kew in 1916. Of these only four germinated, but thanks to later importations, and the ease with which plants can be raised from cuttings, the species is now well established in cultivation. It has proved to be scarcely less hardy than N. *betuloides*, though it may suffer slight damage in severe winters.

As the following statistics show, N. *dombeyi* is well represented in southern England, though it does not attain such a large size as in the Atlantic zone, where the rainfall is higher and the climate more equable: Kew, near the Victoria Gate, *pl.* 1922, 45 × 3¾ ft (1967), and several younger trees elsewhere in the collection; Winkworth Arboretum, Surrey, *pl.* 1937, 45 × 4½ ft (1969); The Grange, Benenden, Kent, *pl.* 1922, 56 × 4¾ ft (1972); Borde Hill, Sussex, by The Tolls, 59 × 3½ ft (1968); Nymans, Sussex, 67 × 5½ ft (1970); Little Kingsmill Grange, Bucks, 58 × 3½ ft (1968); Pylewell Hall, Hants, 57 × 3¼ ft (1970); Minterne, Dorset, 62 × 6 ft (1967); Sidbury Manor, Devon, 57 × 5 ft (1959); Caerhays, Cornwall, 65 × 5½ ft (1965); Trewithen, Cornwall, 60 × 6 ft (1971); Bodnant, Denbigh, 58 × 8¼ ft at 1 ft (1966); Muncaster Castle, Cumb., four trees, the largest 75 × 6 ft (1971); Castle Kennedy, Wigtons., 70 × 7½ ft (1967); Rowallane, Co. Down, 66 × 7¼ ft and 55 × 6 ft (1966). The following were measured in Eire in 1966: Mount Usher, Co. Wicklow, 72 × 8½ ft; Powerscourt, Co. Wicklow, 58 × 4 ft; Headfort, Co. Meath, 60 × 8½ ft.

N. NITIDA (Phil.) Krasser *Fagus nitida* Phil.—This species, allied to N. *betuloides* and N. *dombeyi*, is little known and probably not in cultivation. It is an evergreen with coarsely toothed leaves, which are triangular-ovate or rhombic, up to 1⅜ in. long and 1 in. wide. The male flowers are borne in threes as in N. *dombeyi*, but are said to have fewer stamens. It occurs in the coastal region of Chile from as far north as the Cordillera Pelada near Valdivia to at least as far south as Capo Tres Montes at the northern end of the Golfo de Penas, and is common on the coast of Chiloe Island. A peculiarity of this species is the clear brown colour of the leaves in herbarium specimens.

N. FUSCA (Hook. f.) Oerst.

Fagus fusca Hook. f.

An evergreen tree of the largest size, described as 100 ft high in the wild; young shoots minutely downy, and in cultivated specimens very zigzagged.

Leaves broadly ovate to roundish, $\frac{3}{4}$ to $1\frac{1}{2}$ in. long, glabrous except on the coarsely toothed margins, which are ciliate, especially on the notches, wedge-shaped to truncate at the base; leaf-stalk downy, about $\frac{1}{8}$ in. long; veins in usually three or four pairs. Husk of fruit nearly $\frac{1}{2}$ in. long, four-lobed, containing three nutlets.

Native of New Zealand in both islands, from 37° southward. The small tree in the Coombe Wood nursery of Messrs Veitch mentioned in previous editions was about thirty years old in 1906 and may have represented the first introduction. The two largest extant trees—at Nymans in Sussex and Castlewellan in Northern Ireland—were both planted in the 1890s. This species is easily recognised by its deeply and sharply toothed leaves, which are also larger than in any other cultivated evergreen species, except *N. moorei*. The old leaves turn red before falling.

NOTHOFAGUS FUSCA

The following measurements suggest that *N. fusca* could be safely planted in all except the coldest and driest parts of the country: Grayswood Hill, Haslemere, Surrey, 40 × 4 ft (1968); Wakehurst Place, Sussex, 75 × 5¾ ft (1965); Nymans, Sussex, 70 × 7 ft (1966); Exbury, Hants, 68 × 5½ ft (1968); Garnons, Heref., *pl.* 1941, 48 × 2¾ ft (1969); Caerhays, Cornwall, *pl.* 1920, 60 × 5½ ft (1971); Trewithen, Cornwall, 62 × 5¼ ft (1971); Edinburgh Botanic Garden, *pl.* 1927, 28 × 1½ ft, and another, *pl.* 1938, 36 × 1¼ ft (1967); Castlewellan, Co. Down, N. Ireland, 53 × 8 ft (1966); Rowallane, Co. Down, 40 × 5¼ ft at 2 ft (1966); Mount Usher, Co. Wicklow, Eire, 56 × 5¼ ft (1966).

N. TRUNCATA (Col.) Ckn. F. *truncata* Col.; F. *fusca* var. *colensoi* Hook. f.— This species, which is probably not in cultivation, is closely allied to *N. fusca*, differing in the more leathery leaves with eight to twelve pairs of teeth, which are shallower and blunter than in its relative. It is a native of the North Island of New Zealand mainly, but also occurs in South Island as far south as 42° 30′ S.

In the wild, *N. fusca* and *N. truncata* cross with *N. solandri* and its var. *cliffortioides*, giving rise to hybrid swarms which in some places make up a substantial part of the forest or may even dominate. *N. blairii* (Kirk) Ckn. is now considered to be part of such a swarm, with the parentage *N. fusca* crossed with *N. solandri* var. *cliffortioides*. In its typical form this hybrid resembles the second parent in its entire leaves tomentose beneath, but they are larger, apiculate at the apex and the indumentum of the lower surface is rust-coloured. *N. apiculata* (Col.) Krasser, which, like *N. blairii*, was recognised as a species by Cheeseman in his *Manual*, is also now considered to be of hybrid origin, the parents being *N. truncata* and *N. solandri*.

N. MENZIESII (Hook. f.) Oerst.

Fagus menziesii Hook. f.

An evergreen tree 60 to 80 ft (occasionally 100 ft) high in the wild state, with a trunk 6 to 16 ft in girth and silvery white when young; young shoots clothed with yellowish-brown down. Leaves roundish ovate to diamond-shaped, broadly wedge-shaped at the base, rounded or pointed at the apex, doubly round-toothed, $\frac{1}{3}$ to $\frac{5}{8}$ in. long, $\frac{1}{4}$ to $\frac{1}{2}$ in. wide, glabrous on both surfaces except for one or two pits in the blade near the base beneath, which are lined with brown hairs; stalk $\frac{1}{16}$ in. long, downy. Male flowers solitary. Husks $\frac{1}{4}$ to $\frac{3}{8}$ in. long, with four or five rows of gland-tipped appendages on each valve. Nutlets three, their wings prolonged at the apex and ending in gland-tipped points.

Native of New Zealand on both islands, up to 3,500 ft above sea-level. It is allied to *N. cunninghamii*, but that species has singly (not doubly) toothed leaves, and the curious hairy pits seen in *N. menziesii* are absent. Also in *N. cunninghamii* the wings of the nutlets are not prolonged at the apex.

Although not a success at Kew, *N. menziesii* is hardy enough in mid-Sussex in a sheltered position, as is shown by the tree at Nymans, which was planted before 1917 and measures 57 × 6$\frac{1}{4}$ ft (1970). Others are: Caerhays, Cornwall, 62 × 8$\frac{3}{4}$ ft at 1 ft, dividing into five stems at 3 ft (1971) and another of 64 × 6$\frac{3}{4}$ ft (1971); Trewithen, Cornwall, 54 × 3$\frac{3}{4}$ ft (1971); Galloway House, Wigtons., a bush 40 ft high (1967); Castlewellan, Co. Down, N. Ireland, 30 × 2$\frac{3}{4}$ ft (1966); Mount Usher, Co. Wicklow, Eire, 39 × 3$\frac{1}{4}$ ft at 3 ft (1966).

Although some specimens of *N. menziesii* in this country have a whitish bark, as is said to be usual in young trees in New Zealand, they more commonly have a bark resembling that of the common gean, dark in colour with horizontal bands of lenticels.

N. MOOREI (F. v. Muell.) Krasser

Fagus moorei F. v. Muell.

An evergreen tree up to 100 ft high in the wild, occasionally taller; young twigs covered with brownish down. Leaves glossy dark green, ovate-lanceolate to ovate, 1$\frac{1}{2}$ to 3 in. long, $\frac{3}{4}$ to 1$\frac{1}{2}$ in. wide, base wedge-shaped, apex taper-pointed, margins sharply toothed, glabrous on both sides, except for some hairs on the midrib above; lateral veins prominent, in nine to fifteen pairs; petiole very short, downy.

A rare native of the rain-forests of E. Australia, with its main distribution in north-eastern New South Wales, from the headwaters of the Manning River north to the Macpherson Range, on the borders between New South Wales and Queensland. It was discovered by C. Moore, Curator of the Sydney Botanic Garden and described in 1865; introduced to Kew in 1892 and grown there in the Temperate House. Among the cultivated southern beeches it is easily distinguished by its large, finely toothed evergreen leaves recalling those of *Camellia saluenensis*. It is too tender to be grown outdoors in Britain except in the mildest parts, where it is represented at Caerhays, Cornwall, by two specimens, the larger measuring 52 × 2¾ ft (1971). Smaller trees grow in Eire at Fota, Co. Cork, and Mount Usher, Co. Wicklow.

N. OBLIQUA (Mirbel) Blume   ROBLÉ

A large deciduous tree up to 100 ft high in the wild, occasionally taller; bark of cultivated trees greyish, split into plates by vertical and horizontal fissures; on mature wild trees oak-like except in its ruddy tinge; young shoots glabrous. Leaves arranged alternately in two opposite rows, ovate to oblong, mostly blunt at the apex, rounded or broadly wedge-shaped at the base, unequal sided, 1½ to 3 in. long, ¾ to 1½ in. wide, irregularly set with small, triangular teeth, and usually more or less lobulate, at least in the lower half, dark green above, pale and rather glaucous beneath; veins commonly in eight or nine pairs, occasionally up to eleven; stalk ⅛ in. long. Male flowers produced singly in the leaf-axils, with thirty to forty stamens. Fruits about ⅜ in. long, with the usual three nutlets, the centre one flattened; valves of involucre with simple, gland-tipped processes.

N. obliqua is the most warmth-loving of the S. American beeches. Its equatorward limit actually lies in the zone of Mediterranean climate, where it occurs in shrubby form on the Campana de Quillota between Santiago and Valparaiso. Its southern limit is around 41° S. Before the colonisation of the forest region it formed extensive forests in the central valley of Chile from about 38° S. as far south as the northern end of Lake Llanquihue, but these have long since given way to arable and pasture, with isolated trees and copses here and there. But full roblé forest still exists in the remoter parts of the Andes. In Argentina, it occurs near the Chilean frontier in Neuquen province.

The roblé yields when mature a durable reddish timber, comparable to oak in the uses to which it is or has been put (shipbuilding, interior joinery, furniture, etc.)—hence, no doubt, the common Chilean name, which is simply the Spanish word for oak. The native names *pellin* and *hualo* are also used by Chilean foresters, the former for mature trees and heartwood, the latter for young trees and for the sapwood, which is soft and white.

It is usually stated that *N. obliqua* was introduced by the Veitchian collector William Lobb in 1849, which is actually the year of publication of an article in *The Gardeners' Chronicle*, mentioning plants grown under the name *Fagus obliqua* in Veitch's nursery. But this account, and another published two years later in the *Journal* of the Horticultural Society, are so confused that it is impossible to determine what species was involved; the plants may have been a mixture, consisting of an evergreen species and another which was perhaps *N. procera*. In any case, Elwes and Henry, writing early this century, knew of no specimens in this country, and all the oldest trees in cultivation were raised from seeds brought back by the former from S. America in 1902. Later introductions of which there is record are: by F. R. S. Balfour in 1910, who distributed plants from 1914 onward; and by Harold Comber in 1926.

N. obliqua succeeds remarkably well in the British Isles. It is hardy, grows well on a wide range of soils (though not on chalk), sets good crops of seed and even self-sows itself. It is also fast-growing and makes an elegant specimen. The ugly cracked bark is a defect, but in time this should give way to the handsome furrowed, richly coloured bark of maturity.

The following list of specimens from A. F. Mitchell's records includes most of the older trees and all those of which the planting date is known: Kew, west of Azalea Garden, from Elwes introduction of 1902, 83 × 6¼ ft and 72 × 5½ ft (1965), and two others in the same area, *pl.* 1911, 81 × 6¼ ft and 70 × 4½ ft (1965); Valley Gardens, Windsor Great Park, *pl.* 1947, 85 × 4¼ ft (1969); Sunningdale Nurseries, Berks, *pl.* 1905 (Elwes introduction?), 66 × 7¾ ft (1958); Grayswood Hill, Surrey, 75 × 8¼ ft (1968); Nymans, Sussex, *pl.* 1928 (Comber introduction), 67 × 6 ft (Magnolia Garden) and 75 × 6 ft (Wilderness, one of several) (1970); Borde Hill, Sussex, 93 × 6¼ ft (1971); Tilgate Forest Lodge, Sussex, 80 × 7 ft (1961); Sheffield Park, Sussex, 80 × 6 ft (1968); Wakehurst Place, Sussex, in West Wood, 75 × 6½ ft (1965); National Pinetum, Bedgebury, Kent, *pl.* 1930, 67 × 3¾ ft (larger of two) (1965); The Grange, Benenden, Kent, *pl.* 1920, 74 × 5¾ ft (1972); East Bergholt Place, Suffolk, 62 × 5 ft (1972); Holkham, Norfolk, *pl.* 1918, 68 × 5¾ ft (1968); Hergest Croft, Heref., *pl.* 1917, 60 × 7½ ft (1969); Westonbirt, Glos. (all from Balfour introduction) in Wigmore Bottom, *pl.* 1924, when 12 ft high, 60 × 4 ft (1966), in Silkwood, *pl.* 1922, 57 × 5¾ ft (1967), in Victory Glade, 60 × 3¾ ft (1969); Killerton, Devon, 70 × 6¾ ft (1970); Trewithen, Cornwall, *pl.* 1928 (Comber introduction), 67 × 4¾ ft (1971); Caerhays, Cornwall, 84 × 9 ft (1971); Bodnant, Denbigh, 98 × 6½ ft (1966); Muncaster Castle, Cumb., *pl.* 1925, 72 × 5¾ ft and 80 × 4¼ ft (1971); Crarae, Argyll, *pl.* 1936, 60 × 5 ft (1969); Benmore, Argyll, 75 × 5¼ ft (1970); Blairquhan, Argyll, *pl.* 1933, 70 × 6¼ ft (1970); Glendoick, Perths., *pl.* 1922, 60 × 6½ ft (1970).

The following specimens were measured in Eire in 1966: Glasnevin Botanic Garden, 81 × 6 ft; Mount Usher, Co. Wicklow, 75 × 6¾ ft; Ashbourne House, Co. Cork, 70 × 6½ ft; Birr Castle, Co. Offaly, *pl.* 1934, 59 × 4 ft.

For the use of *N. obliqua* in forestry, see under *N. procera*.

N. GLAUCA (Phil.) Krasser *Fagus glauca* Phil.—Although sometimes included in *N. obliqua*, this is a very distinct species, differing most noticeably in its papery bark and in its shortly stalked leaves truncate or slightly cordate at the base, glaucous beneath. There are also important differences in flower- and fruit-characters. It is known in Chile as 'roblé del Maule', and still dominates in the forest that stretches some way northward along the coast from the port of Constitucion, at the mouth of the river Maule. It was once the basis of a flourishing shipbuilding industry, and it is said that small craft made from its timber are still in use in Polynesia.

N. LEONII Espinosa is believed to be a natural hybrid between *N. glauca* and *N. obliqua* (Van Steenis, op. cit., p. 336).

N. ALESSANDRII Espinosa RUIL.—This Chilean species is very rare and local in the wild state, and is not closely allied to any other southern beech. Leaves deciduous, ovate, 2¼ to 5¼ in. long, 1⅜ to 3 in. or slightly more wide, with eleven to thirteen pairs of parallel veins, each vein running unbranched to a small, sharpish tooth. The best known stand of this remarkable species is near the village of Empedrado, a few miles inland from Constitucion (see above), and south of the river Maule. According to Van Steenis it is the most primitive of living species of *Nothofagus* in having seven fruits in each involucre. Judging from the small tree planted by the parish priest outside the church at Empedrado, it is certainly distinct from all the cultivated species in its foliage. It is figured in C. Muñoz, *Sinopsis de la Flora Chilena*, t. XCIV.

N. PROCERA (Poepp. & Endl.) Oerst.   RAULI   [PLATE 4

Fagus procera Poepp. & Endl.; *N. nervosa* (Phil.) Dimitri & Milano; *F. nervosa* Phil.

A large deciduous tree 80 ft and upwards high in the wild; young shoots clothed with small brownish hairs; winter-buds ¼ in. long, slender, pointed. Leaves oblong or narrowly oval, blunt or rounded at the apex, rounded or broadly wedgeshaped at the base, very finely toothed, 1½ to 4 in. long, ¾ to 1½ in. wide, yellowish green above and downy, especially on the midrib and on the raised part of the blade between the sunken veins; paler green beneath and downy on the midrib and veins; stalk $\frac{1}{12}$ to $\frac{3}{16}$ in. long, hairy. Veins fourteen to eighteen each side of the midrib, parallel, sunken above, prominent beneath. Husks about ⅜ in. long, the four valves ornamented with conspicuous toothed or fringed glandular appendages.

Native of the Chilean Andes from 35° 30' S. to just south of 40° S.; it also occurs in the coastal range and has a few stands in Argentina near the Chilean frontier. It was introduced to Britain in 1910 by F. R. S. Balfour of Dawyck, who distributed plants from 1914 onwards. There was also an introduction to Kew in 1913, in which year W. J. Bean received a share of the seeds imported by the Dendrological Society of France.

The rauli is perhaps the most valuable of Chilean forest trees, ready for felling when seventy to ninety years old and yielding a timber not unlike that of the common beech. Unfortunately it has the smallest natural area of the deciduous species (apart from the local endemics *N. glauca* and *N. alessandrii*) and this has been much reduced by over-exploitation. The best stands are now confined to the Andes between 38° S. and 40° S., where it forms forests with the evergreen *N. dombeyi* or sometimes with *N. obliqua*. For the most part, however, it grows at higher altitudes than *N. obliqua*, and seems to be at its optimum in cooler and moister conditions than that species demands.

N. procera is distinct from all the other deciduous southern beeches in its large, conspicuously ribbed leaves, which resemble those of a hornbeam or

Alnus firma. It is a quick-growing tree in the rainier parts of the British Isles, remarkable in its early years for its mast-like stem evenly tapered from the base and its slender, ascending branches. The tree in the Winkworth Arboretum, only thirty-six years old, shows what a fine specimen it makes when grown on its own, and how quickly. The leaves often turn to shades of yellow, orange, and red in the autumn. There have been casualties among young trees in exceptionally severe winters, but on the whole the rauli can be considered as hardy in this country. Good crops of seed are occasionally produced by trees over twenty years of age, and afford the best means of increase. It can also be propagated by means of cuttings put into gentle heat in July or August.

The following is a selection from the older trees in this country, none of which, it should be borne in mind, can have been planted before 1914: Kew, 47 × 3¾ ft and 36 × 3½ ft (1957); Wakehurst Place, Sussex, 56 × 8¾ ft (1968); Leonardslee, Sussex, 88 × 6¾ ft and 70 × 6¼ ft (1970); Borde Hill, Sussex, 75 × 7¼ ft in Lullings Ghyll (1967) and 63 × 4¾ ft in Little Bentley Wood (1968); Winkworth Arboretum, Surrey, *pl.* 1937, 65 × 6½ ft (1969); Westonbirt, Glos., in Victory Glade, *pl.* 1915, 85 × 6½ ft (1969); Exbury, Hants, 56 × 5½ ft (1968); Caerhays, Cornwall, *pl.* 1920, 74 × 6¾ ft and 66 × 8½ ft (1971); East Bergholt Place, Suffolk, *pl. c.* 1915, 85 × 9¼ ft (1972); Muncaster Castle, Cumb., *pl.* 1923, 82 × 8¼ ft (1971); Edinburgh Botanic Garden, 54 × 5¾ ft (1970); Brodick, Isle of Arran, 60 × 9¼ ft (1965); Castle Kennedy, Wigtons., 73 × 6¾ ft (1967); Benmore, Argyll, 75 × 7 ft (1970); Glendoick, Perths., *pl.* 1929, 74 × 6¾ ft (1970).

The following measurements show the rapid growth of young trees: Queenswood, Heref., *pl.* 1960, 38 × 2¼ ft (1970); Tavistock Woods, Devon, *pl.* 1961, 51 × 1¾ ft (1970, measd. by Lord Bradford); Rheidol, Cards., *pl.* 1956, 60 × 3 ft (1971).

N. procera is of great promise as a forestry tree in Britain, but its use is still limited by scarcity of seed, which is exceedingly difficult to procure from Chile. Home-raised seed is available in very small amounts but should become more plentiful when the plots planted in 1955 and 1956 start to bear fruit. At present only six plots are more than twenty-eight years old. The total area of existing plots in England, Scotland, and Wales is 28 acres (1971, excluding private estates). The rauli succeeds best where the rainfall is 30 in. and over, and should not be planted in valley bottoms and lower slopes, nor on sites exposed to cold winds.

N. obliqua also has a future as a plantation tree, though its timber is slightly inferior to that of the rauli, and it does not have the slender, lightly branched and perfect stem-development of its sister species. On the other hand, it succeeds in eastern England where the rainfall is too low for the best development of rauli, and has the ability to thrive on a wide range of soils, including the poor sandy soil of the National Pinetum at Bedgebury, Kent. The trial plots cover 34 acres (1971). Home-raised seed is relatively abundant, and has given results superior to that from wild-source seed.

For further information, see: M. Nimmo, *Nothofagus Plantations in Great Britain* (For. Comm. For. Rec. No. 79, 1971), on which the above note is based.

N. ALPINA (Poepp. & Endl.) Krasser *F. alpina* Poepp. & Endl.—This species was described simultaneously with *N. procera* and is very probably a small-leaved form of it. The two have in fact been united by the Chilean botanist Dr Muñoz Pizarro under the name *N. alpina*, and this name would have to be accepted if indeed only one species is involved. It has, however, been suggested that *N. alpina* is a natural hybrid between *N. procera* and *N. pumilio* and is therefore best kept separate from *N. procera*, at least for the time being.

N. PUMILIO (Poepp. & Endl.) Krasser   LENGA

Fagus pumilio Poepp. & Endl.; *F. antarctica* var. *bicrenata* A. DC.

A deciduous tree up to 70 ft high and occasionally even taller, but becoming a small, dense, thicket-forming shrub at high altitudes and in exposed places; stems covered with short, erect hairs persisting two or three years. Leaves broadly ovate to broadly elliptic, ¾ to 1¼ in. long, ½ to ⅞ in. wide, obtuse to rounded at the apex, the base usually obliquely cuneate, sometimes rounded or even cordate, upper surface medium green, slightly glossy, almost glabrous, underside paler, lustrous, with appressed hairs on the midrib and main veins, margins ciliate, bluntly double-toothed; lateral veins in five or six pairs, straight and parallel, raised beneath, each running out to a sinus; leaf-stalk ⅛ to ¼ in. long. Male flowers solitary. Nutlets one only in each involucre, three-angled, clasped by two linear valves.

Native of temperate S. America, ranging from Tierra del Fuego as far north as the Chillan Andes around 36° 30′ S. It is the commonest nothofagus in Argentina, where it covers vast tracts east of the Andes at 3,000 to 6,000 ft; at the southern end of its range it descends to sea-level. It is frequently associated with *N. antarctica* and the two have been confused. But *N. pumilio* may attain a considerable size, and yields a useful timber, while *N. antarctica* is always a minor tree or shrub. The two are very distinct in their foliage, for whereas the latter has irregularly serrated leaves, the lenga has two large blunt teeth between each pair of veins (but usually three smaller ones between the lowermost pair). There is also a marked difference in the female inflorescence: in the lenga there is only one flower (or only one develops) and the fruit consists of a single nutlet clasped by two linear valves. In the ñirre (*N. antarctica*) there are the normal three flowers each developing into a nutlet, and the involucre is four-valved.

Although so common in the wild, there seems to have been no recorded introduction of the lenga until the late 1950s and early 1960s, when there were three or more importations of seed. It is too early to judge whether this species will prove superior to *N. antarctica* as an ornamental tree, but it is certainly handsomer in foliage and grows faster. It is likely to be completely hardy.

N. GUNNII (Hook. f.) Oerst. *Fagus gunnii* Hook. f.—This species, not yet introduced to Britain, is of interest as the only deciduous southern beech in the Australasian region. It is a shrub or small tree endemic to Tasmania, where it occurs in the mountains of the centre and west. In its foliage it is not unlike *N. pumilio*, but the leaves are relatively broader, often almost orbicular, and there is only one blunt tooth between each pair of veins.

N. SOLANDRI (Hook. f.) Oerst.

Fagus solandri Hook. f.

An evergreen tree said to be 40 to 80 ft high in the wild, with a trunk 2 to 5 ft in diameter; young shoots clothed with a dense fine down. Leaves oval, sometimes rather ovate, not toothed, broadly wedge-shaped at the base, blunt at the apex, ¼ to ⅝ in. long, ¼ to ⅜ in. wide, glabrous and glossy above, covered

NOTHOFAGUS SOLANDRI

with a close down beneath; stalk $\frac{1}{16}$ in. long; veins usually four or five each side of the midrib. Male flowers produced one to three together in the leaf-axils. Husk of fruit usually three-valved, ¼ in. long; valves with three or four entire transverse plates. Nutlets usually three, winged.

Native of New Zealand on both North and South Islands, in lowland and montane forests. The date of introduction is uncertain, but there was a young tree at Nymans in Sussex by 1917, probably the one that still grows there, and the tree at Wakehurst Place in the same county is of about the same age. In those two gardens it is hardy but all the other recorded specimens are in the milder parts. On young trees the leaves are glabrous on both sides and according to Kirk they may remain so in quite tall trees, if these are shaded by the forest canopy.

The tree at Nymans mentioned above measures 59 × 4 ft (1970) and the Wakehurst specimen, in a more open position, 37 × 4¼ ft (1965). Others are: Caerhays, Cornwall, *pl.* 1928, 54 × 5 ft (1971) and Castle Kennedy, Wigtons., 55 × 4½ ft (1967).

var. CLIFFORTIOIDES (Hook. f.) Poole *F. cliffortioides* Hook. f.; *N. cliffortioides* (Hook. f.) Oerst.—In its typical state this beech is distinct from *N. solandri* in its ovate leaves, acute at the apex, rounded at the base, but intermediate shapes occur. Since there is no other reliable character by which the two beeches can be distinguished, *F. cliffortioides* was reduced to the status of a variety of *N. solandri* by Poole in 1958.

The var. *cliffortioides* ascends to a higher altitude than the typical variety and in places forms a low scrub at the tree-line. Even at lower elevations it is said to make on the average a smaller tree than the typical variety, not usually exceeding 50 ft in height. The date of introduction is not known, but the tree at Nymans in Sussex, which has the largest girth so far recorded in the British Isles, was 26 ft high in 1917 and was probably planted in the 1890s. The beech at Castlewellan, mentioned in *Journ. R.H.S.*, Vol. 27, p. 417, was not *N. cliffortioides*, as there stated, but *N. fusca*, and the trees at Enys in Cornwall, mentioned in 'Elwes and Henry' may have been the hybrid *N. × blairii.*

The tree at Nymans in Sussex mentioned above measures 53 × 5½ ft (1966). Two others in Sussex are: Leonardslee, 68 × 3½ ft (1962), and Wakehurst Place, 40 × 4½ ft at 3 ft (1969). In the Edinburgh Botanic Garden there is a small tree planted in 1945, measuring 38 × 2 ft (1967). The following have been recorded in the western parts of the British Isles: Muncaster Castle, four trees, the largest 57 × 4¾ ft (1971); Crarae, Argyll, *pl.* 1936, 44 × 3¼ ft (1969); Rowallane, Co. Down, 50 × 3¼ ft (1966); Mount Usher, Co. Wicklow, Eire, 46 × 2¾ ft (1966).

NOTHOPANAX *see* PSEUDOPANAX

NOTOSPARTIUM   LEGUMINOSAE

A genus of three species, all endemic to the South Island of New Zealand. From the leafless species of *Carmichaelia* (and from *Chordospartium*), it is distinguished by its linear, jointed pods.

N. CARMICHAELIAE Hook. f.

An almost leafless shrub 4 to 10 ft high in the wild, with slender, rush-like, mostly arching or pendulous branches, which are slightly flattened and grooved. Leaves (only seen on young plants) simple, roundish or orbicular, often notched at the apex, ¼ in. long. Racemes downy, 1 to 2 in. long, axillary, carrying from twelve to twenty flowers. Each flower is ⅓ in. long, pea-shaped, purplish pink; calyx densely covered with silky down, five-toothed; teeth triangular; flower-stalk hairy, ⅛ in. long. Pods ¾ to 1 in. long, slender, three- to eight-jointed, with one seed to each joint. It blooms in July.

Native of New Zealand, in the South Island, where it is said to be rare and local. This species grows and flowers well on the Temperate House Terrace at Kew, but is not absolutely hardy there in the open ground. Young plants are better with some protection during winter for the first few years of their existence, and may be grown in pots, for although not killed entirely the branches are so badly cut back that the progress of the plant is very slow. When once a firm woody base has been formed, they weather ordinary winters quite well. Seeds afford the best means of increase. The best soil is a light one, and the position should be well drained and sunny. It has no objection to chalk. So lovely a plant deserves special care.

N. GLABRESCENS Petrie

A round-headed tree 15 to 30 ft high in the wild; young shoots flattened, slightly grooved, not much spreading, glabrous, finally terete. Leaves reduced to triangular scales, scarcely visible. Flowers in a crowd of axillary racemes, 1½ to 2 in. long towards the end of the shoot, each raceme carrying fifteen to twenty-five blossoms. Standard petal nearly ½ in. across, erect, oval, notched at the tip, white with a conspicuous purple blotch at the base and with similarly coloured nerves radiating upwards from it; wing-petals and keel much smaller, oblong; calyx bell-shaped with ciliate, triangular lobes. Pods ¾ to 1 in. long, carrying about six seeds. *Bot. Mag.*, t. 9530.

Native of the South Island of New Zealand, in the valley of the Clarence River, first flowered in this country in 1933. A very attractive tree described as resembling in habit a weeping willow, its lower branches being more or less pendulous but the upper ones ascending. It blossoms quite freely, however, as a shrub and is evidently as hardy as *N. carmichaeliae*, to which it is closely related, and needs the same conditions. But its flowers are less crowded, more purplish, the pods are larger and the axis of the racemes is glabrous.

Like *N. carmichaeliae*, this species is represented on the Temperate House Terrace at Kew. It flowers just as freely but is not so elegant.

NYSSA   TUPELO   NYSSACEAE

A genus of about ten species in eastern N. America, N. Mexico, the Himalaya, and western Malaysia, of which only *N. sylvatica* is commonly grown in the British Isles. Leaves alternate, without stipules. Flowers small, unisexual, both sexes often occurring on the same tree. Male flowers numerous, in slender-stalked heads or racemes, females in fewer-flowered clusters, or solitary. Fruit a drupe, with a one-seeded stone. The family Nyssaceae is allied to the Cornaceae, in which Nyssa was once placed.

Propagation is by seeds or by layers. The nyssas transplant badly and should be given a permanent place as early as possible.

N. AQUATICA L. COTTON GUM, WATER TUPELO

N. uniflora Wangenh.; *N. tomentosa* Michx.; *N. grandidentata* Michx.

A tree up to 100 ft high in the wild; young stems downy at first, later glabrous except at the tips and reddish brown. Leaves oblong-ovate or elliptic, acute or acuminate at the apex, 4 to 7 in. long, 2 to 4 in. wide, entire or quite often angular-toothed, dark green above, undersurface paler, finely downy at first, sometimes glabrous later; leaf-stalks up to 2½ in. long. Female flowers solitary. Fruits ellipsoid, about 1 in. long, purple, with a thin flesh, borne on slender stalks; stone deeply and sharply ridged.

A native of the south-eastern USA, in the coastal plain and the lower reaches of the Mississippi, said to attain its best development in Louisiana and E. Texas; cultivated by Peter Collinson in 1735, but very uncommon in Britain. It grows mainly in swampy ground which is inundated except in summer, often to a depth of 6 ft. In such situations the trunk becomes remarkably swollen at the base. In the absence of flower or fruit this species can easily be distinguished from *N. sylvatica* by its winter-wood, its lateral buds being very small and roundish, but conspicuous and ovoid in *N. sylvatica*.

N. OGECHE Marsh. *N. candicans* Michx.—This species, confined to southern S. Carolina, Georgia, and Florida, has more than once been introduced to Kew but has never become established and is very probably tender. It is remarkable for its red fruits, which are pleasantly flavoured and have been used as a substitute for limes—hence the popular name 'ogeechee lime'.

N. SINENSIS Oliver

A deciduous tree 20 to 50 ft high, with downy young shoots. Leaves thin, narrowly oval, tapering at both ends, 4 to 6 in. long, 1½ to 2 in. wide, hairy at the margins and on the midrib, dull dark green above, pale and lustrous beneath; stalk ¼ in. long, hairy. Male flowers produced in a rounded head ½ in. across at the end of a slender, downy stalk 1 to 1½ in. long; females few on longer stalks, neither of any beauty. Fruits oblong, ½ in. long, bluish.

Native of Central China, where it was originally discovered in 1888 by Henry, who describes it as a rare tree occurring in mountain woods. Seeds were sent to Messrs Veitch by Wilson in 1901–2, but only one plant was raised. During his first expedition for the Arnold Arboretum he collected fruiting specimens in Kiangsi and most probably seeds also. At any rate, the Chinese tupelo is in cultivation in the USA and available in commerce in Britain, though it is very rare here. The leaves colour red or yellow in the autumn.

N. SYLVATICA Marsh.   BLACK GUM, TUPELO, PEPPERIDGE
N. multiflora Wangenh.; *N. villosa* Michx.   [PLATE 3

A deciduous tree occasionally 100 ft high in the wild, with a trunk up to 5 ft in thickness and a furrowed bark. Leaves of variable shape, but oftenest obovate or oval, with a tapering base, 3 to 6 in. long, 1½ to 3 in. wide, entire, usually perfectly glabrous in this country except on the young stalks and midrib, which are slightly hairy; stalk ½ to 1 in. long, frequently reddish. Flowers appearing in June, males and females on separate heads, ½ in. or less across, greenish, produced on a slender downy stalk about 1 in. long in the axils of the scales or lowermost leaves of the young shoots; male flowers numerous, female ones usually two to four in a head; they have no beauty. Fruits usually in pairs, each one ⅓ to ⅔ in. long, egg-shaped, bluish black.

Native of eastern N. America, chiefly found in swamps and ill-drained land; introduced some time in the first half of the 18th century. It was, until lately, quite scarce in cultivation, and few trees of any size exist in Britain. But Arthur Soames of Sheffield Park raised some four hundred plants from seed, many of which are now scattered about the grounds, vigorous and healthy. There is a curious diversity in the leaves of this species, not only in shape, but in lustre. Of two healthy trees at Kew growing within a few yards of each other, one has dull-surfaced leaves, the other has larger shining ones. The chief value of the tupelo in gardens, over and above its great interest, is the brilliant red and yellow of its autumnal foliage. Like many other American trees growing in wet situations at home, it thrives best in ordinary good loam when transplanted to our gloomier climate.

Loudon mentioned a tupelo in the Duke of Wellington's grounds at Stratfield Saye, Hants, 30 ft high (*Arb. et Frut. Brit.* (1838), Vol. 3, p. 1317). This tree measured 74 × 5½ ft in 1897 and was the only specimen of great size known to Elwes (*Tr. Gr. Brit. & Irel.*, Vol. 3, p. 511 and plate 145). Still by far the largest in Britain, it now measures 80 × 7½ ft (1968). The tree at Munden, Watford, which Elwes also mentions, is only 20 ft high, having lost its leader some time in the last century, but has a huge spread and is 6¼ ft in girth (1968). The largest example at Kew is 55 × 5¼ ft (1967). Of the many fine trees at Sheffield Park, mentioned above, one, planted in 1909, measures 48 × 3¾ ft (1968). At Chatsworth, Derb., the larger of two specimens measures 65 × 6¾ ft (1971).

var. BIFLORA (Walt.) Sarg. *N. biflora* Walt. SWAMP TUPELO.—This distinct variety, often treated as a separate species, occupies wetter situations than the typical variety and is confined to the coastal plains of the south-eastern USA. Botanically it differs in the relatively narrower leaves, which are mostly oblanceolate or oblong-elliptic and obtuse or rounded at the apex, and in having the female flowers mostly in pairs. It is probable, as suggested by Elwes and Henry, that the cultivated trees mentioned by Loudon under *N. biflora* were really the typical variety of *N. sylvatica*. On the other hand, it is not unlikely that some of the seed imported from America in the 18th and 19th centuries was of the swamp tupelo, and this might in part explain the rarity of old trees of *N. sylvatica* in Britain, since the variety needs warmer conditions and a longer growing season than the type and would not be so well adapted to our climate.

OCHAGAVIA   BROMELIACEAE

A genus of four or five species of subshrubs, natives of Chile, with the habit of the species described below. Flowers pink or yellow, clustered in a dense sessile or shortly stalked head. Sepals three. Petals three, erect, without ligules at the base. Stamens six. Ovary inferior. Style slender, longer than the petals, with three stigmas. Fruit fleshy, with numerous small seeds.

The related genus FASCICULARIA, also Chilean, consists of a few species of mostly epiphytic, stemless herbs. It is represented out-of-doors in this country mainly by F. PITCAIRNIIFOLIA (Verl.) Mez, with grey-green spiny leaves up to 18 in. long and dense clusters of blue flowers in autumn. At the time of flowering the short inner leaves become, partially or wholly, bright red. *Bot. Mag.*, t. 8087. This species has grown for many years on the rock garden by the pond at Wakehurst in Sussex, and flowers there. There was once a patch 10 ft wide at the Ludgvan Rectory, Corn-wall.

O. LINDLEYANA (Lem.) Mez

Bromelia lindleyana Lem.; *Rhodostachys andina* Phil.; *Bromelia carnea* Beer; *Rhodostachys carnea* (Beer) Mez; *Ochagavia carnea* (Beer) L. B. Smith & Losser

A short-stemmed evergreen 1 to 1½ ft high, the crowded leaves forming a kind of rosette 18 in. or so wide, in the manner of the pineapple plant. Leaves 1 to 1¾ ft long, 1 to 1½ in. wide at the base, tapering gradually thence to a long fine point and regularly armed on each margin with stiff incurved spines $\frac{1}{12}$ in. long; very much recurved, channelled on the upper surface; scurfy and grey below, ultimately of a rather bright green above, and of hard, rigid texture. Flowers very numerous and densely packed in a pyramidal or globose mass 2½ to 4 in. wide and high, proceeding from the centre of the plant on a stout main-stalk 4 to 8 in. high. The outer bracts of this inflorescence are tinged with red, the flowers themselves bright pink; petals three, 1 in. long, erect, of linear shape; stamens six, anthers yellow, conspicuous. *Bot. Mag.*, t. 7148.

Native of Central Chile; introduced to cultivation by Hendersons, formerly nurserymen of St John's Wood, and exhibited at a meeting of the Horticultural Society on August 5, 1851, under the name "*Tillandsia carnea*". It used to grow well in the garden at Ludgvan, near Penzance, where there was a dense patch of closely packed growths several feet across. At Kew, in the most sheltered nook that can be found for it, it is quite healthy out-of-doors, although suffering somewhat in hard winters. There are many places towards, and on, the south coast where it should succeed very well if given the sunniest possible place and perfect drainage. Canon Boscawen grew it on a stony mound. It appears usually to flower in the autumn.

OLEA OLIVE OLEACEAE

A relatively limited number of small or medium-sized evergreen trees from tropical or warm temperate regions of the Old World. The leaves are simple and opposite. The flowers are white, borne in axillary, decussate, and opposite-flowered or paniculate inflorescences. The calyx and corolla are four-lobed, the lobes of the corolla valvate and rolled inwards in the bud stage. Stamens two. Fruit an ovoid or spheroid drupe, usually dark blue or black when ripe.

Of the members of the genus only *O. europaea* is hardy in Britain, and then only in the most favourable situations. The genus is closely allied to *Osmanthus* and *Phillyrea*, differing only in minor characters.

NOTELAEA LIGUSTRINA Vent. of Tasmania and southern Victoria, a privet-like shrub occasionally grown in Britain, is allied to *Olea*. It has little horticultural value. For the species once known as *Olea excelsa*, see PICCONIA.

O. EUROPAEA L. COMMON OLIVE

An evergreen tree of rugged, much-branched habit and slow growth, generally 15 to 30 ft high, with grey-green foliage. Leaves opposite, narrowly obovate or oval, 1½ to 3 in. long, ⅓ to ¾ in. wide, glaucous or silvery beneath, leathery. Flowers white, ⅕ in. diameter, in axillary racemes 1 to 2 in. long, the corolla with four ovate lobes; stamens two. Fruit an oval, oily drupe, ¾ in. long, containing a bony seed.

Probably with an origin in S.W. Asia and largely cultivated all over the Mediterranean region. In many parts of Italy, as in the environs of Florence, its grey tints give the prevailing tone to the landscape. In Britain it can only be cultivated out-of-doors in the mildest parts. It has borne fruit in several places in the south-west. At Kew it has lived for a good many years on a south wall, but in such a place is only worth growing for its interest and associations. In the Chelsea Physic Garden, London, there is an example in the open ground, on three stems and about 20 ft high. It was bearing a few almost ripe fruits in January 1975.

OLEARIA* DAISY BUSH COMPOSITAE

A genus of over 100 species of evergreen shrubs or small trees, confined to the Australasian region. Leaves alternate or opposite, usually tomentose beneath. Flower-heads resembling those of *Aster*, with yellow, white, or purplish disk-florets and white, purplish, or bluish ray-florets. The bracts of the involucre are imbricate in several series, and by this character *Olearia* can be distinguished from *Senecio*, some shrubby species of which

* Revised by C. Jeffrey of the Herbarium, Royal Botanic Gardens, Kew.

superficially resemble some olearias in habit; in *Senecio* the bracts are in one row (apart from sometimes a few smaller outer ones).

There is no monographic treatment of the genus. Unpublished studies by Caroline Haycock show that the species fall into three distinct series of which probably only the first should properly be referred to the genus *Olearia*. This comprises all the species with T-shaped, stellate, or peltate leaf-hairs, and includes the majority of the cultivated species. The second series is Australian and includes here only *O. ramulosa* and the species dealt with under it. The third series is made up of the large-headed New Zealand species *O. chathamica, O. colensoi, O. semidentata*, and their allies. These are but distantly related to the true olearias, and perhaps would better be referred to the genus *Pleurophyllum*. If they are to be retained in *Olearia*, it is illogical to recognise the genus *Pachystegia*, which differs from the true olearias in comparatively minor characters. The species concerned is accordingly restored to *Olearia* in the present work (see *O. insignis*).

The late Lord Talbot de Malahide in *Journ. R.H.S.*, Vol. 90, pp. 207–17 and 245–50 (1965), discusses the relative hardiness of the cultivated species and hybrids, and confirms that *O.* × *haastii* alone is generally hardy. Nevertheless, over sixty species and hybrids have been in cultivation outdoors in the British Isles and of these about twenty-five are hardy enough to survive the average winter in all but the coldest parts. The olearias are particularly useful for shelter in the maritime areas of the west and south-west, being resistant to sea winds (see W. Arnold-Forster, *Shrubs for the Milder Counties*, pp. 22–3 and Chapter XII). Horticulturally the majority are undemanding. A light loamy or peaty soil suits most of them. Almost all root quite readily from cuttings made of moderately ripened wood and placed in a cold frame.

The following works will be found useful for identification of olearias: H. H. Allan, *Flora of New Zealand*, Vol. 1, pp. 657–74 (1961); A. L. Poole and N. M. Adams, *Trees and Shrubs of New Zealand*, pp. 186–97 (1963); N. C. W. Beadle, O. D. Evans and R. C. Carolin, *Flora of the Sydney Region*, pp. 454–5 (1972); W. M. Curtis, *The Student's Flora of Tasmania*, Vol. 2, pp. 300–9 (1963); and J. H. Willis, *A Handbook to Plants in Victoria*, Vol. 2, pp. 685–98 (1972).

O. ARBORESCENS (Forst. f.) Ckn. & Laing

Solidago arborescens Forst. f.; *O. nitida* (Hook. f.) Hook. f.

An evergreen shrub up to 12 ft high; young shoots grooved, clothed with fine, close, pale brown down. Leaves alternate, slightly leathery, ovate to roundish-ovate, pointed, usually rounded (sometimes broadly tapered) at the base, wavy or indistinctly toothed at the margins, $1\frac{1}{2}$ to $3\frac{1}{2}$ in. long, $\frac{3}{4}$ to 2 in. wide, dark shining green above and either glabrous or with appressed whitish hairs when young, clothed beneath with a silvery, satiny, closely appressed down; stalks about $\frac{1}{2}$ in. long. Flower-heads in corymbs opening in May and June, from the end of the shoots and the terminal leaf-axils, the whole forming a cluster 4 to 6 in. wide, the main-stalks 2 to 3 in. long, grooved and downy like the young shoots, secondary stalks more downy. Each flower-head is

¼ to ⅜ in. wide, aster-like, the seven to ten ray-florets being white, the disk-florets yellowish. Outer scales linear-oblong, clothed with short brown hairs. Cheeseman, *Ill. New Zeal. Fl.*, t. 88, as *O. nitida;* Salmon, *New Zealand Flowers and Plants in Colour*, t. 111.

Native of New Zealand from sea-level to 4,000 ft altitude and from 38° S. to Stewart Island. It was cultivated at Kew for at least seventy years, but was killed during the severe winter of 1946–7. Although it is moderately hardy near London it is really at its best in the milder parts, where it grows fast and makes a bush up to 12 ft high and more in width. It is well distinguished by the satiny sheen of the undersurface of the leaves, and is quite pretty in bloom. It grows well on chalky soil.

There is a variegated clone in cultivation.

O. × EXCORTICATA Buchan. *O. arborescens* × *O. lacunosa.*—Intermediate between the parents; leaves resembling those of *O. lacunosa* but comparatively shorter and broader, elliptic, with whitish tomentum beneath, up to 4 in. long and 1 in. wide. Davies, *New Zealand Native Plant Studies*, t. 125.

A natural hybrid.

O. ARBORESCENS × O. AVICENNIIFOLIA.—Leaves 1½ to 3 in. long, ½ to 1 in. wide, tapering at both ends, dark green above, dull white tomentose beneath, margin remotely and irregularly toothed; stalk about ¼ in. long. Ray-florets about seven, pure white.

A natural hybrid, also said to have arisen spontaneously in the garden of Sir John Ross at Rostrevor, Co. Down.

O. ARGOPHYLLA (Labill.) Benth.   MUSKWOOD
Aster argophyllus Labill.

An evergreen shrub or small tree up to 45 ft high in the wild; young shoots slightly ribbed and clothed with a closely appressed silvery down. Leaves alternate, leathery, oblanceolate or oval, tapered about equally towards both ends, pointed, toothed unevenly, 2 to 6 in. long, 1 to 2½ in. wide; grey green and slightly downy above when young, especially on the midrib, clothed permanently beneath with a close, fine, silvery, glistening felt; stalk grooved, ¼ to 1 in. long. Flower-heads produced very numerously in June in corymbs 3 or 4 in. wide at the end of the shoots of the previous year's growth, the whole forming a hanging cluster 8 in. or more wide. Ray-florets three to five, narrow, scarcely ¼ in. long, creamy white; disk-florets six to eight, yellow. *Bot. Mag.*, t. 1563, as *Aster argophyllus.*

Native of New South Wales, Victoria, and Tasmania; introduced in 1804. Although not particularly attractive in its flowers, this is a handsome foliage plant on account of its silvery appearance. It has also a very pleasant musky scent which may be detected by rubbing the leaves, and which is also perceptible in the atmosphere near a bush after a shower. It has been grown against a wall at Kew, but that amount of protection is insufficient to keep it alive permanently. At Rossdohan, Co. Kerry, Eire, there are two large plants which seed themselves widely; the larger is almost 40 ft in height and the largest of its stems is 4¼ ft in girth (1966).

cv. 'VARIEGATA'.—Leaves margined with yellow.

O. VISCOSA (Labill.) Benth. *Aster viscosus* Labill.—A shrub 3 to 6 ft high, distinguished by its thin, lanceolate, opposite leaves, silvery white beneath; young shoots and involucral bracts viscid. Ray-florets one or two, creamy white. Disk-florets three to five. Native of Victoria and Tasmania.

O. AVICENNIIFOLIA (Raoul) Hook. f.

Shawia avicenniifolia Raoul

An evergreen shrub or small tree varying from 8 to 20 ft in height in the wild; young shoots ribbed and clothed with a close, white, scurf-like down. Leaves alternate, oval-lanceolate, tapered towards both ends, pointed or bluntish at the apex, entire, 2 to 4 in. long, ⅞ to 1¾ in. wide, greyish green and glabrous above, the undersurface furnished with a close, thin, white or yellowish white felt; stalk ¼ to ¾ in. long, grooved and downy like the young shoots. Flower-heads produced in erect, rounded corymbs from the terminal leaf-axils in August and September, each corymb 2 to 3 in. wide and borne on a slender stalk 2 to 3 in. long, grooved and downy. Each flower-head is ¼ in. long, cylindrical, white, the outer bracts erect; there are usually two or three florets in each head, one or two (or sometimes none) of which are ray-florets. Salmon, *New Zealand Flowers and Plants in Colour*, tt. 109–10.

Native of New Zealand in the South Island, and Stewart Island, up to 3,000 ft altitude. It is one of the hardiest of the olearias, surviving all but the severest winters near London, provided it is given a sheltered position. At Kew it has lived for many years in the outside recesses of the wall of the Temperate House. In the milder parts it has attained a height of 15 ft.

cv. 'WHITE CONFUSION'.—A form differing but slightly from the type, with large, slightly wavy leaves. Flowers in June.

O. 'TALBOT DE MALAHIDE' *O. albida* Hort., not Hook, f.—Differs from *O. avicenniifolia* in its blunter leaves with more rounded bases and larger flower-heads with three to six ray-florets instead of none to two.

Not known in the wild, and perhaps of hybrid origin, involving *O. avicenniifolia* and an unknown parent. It is much confused in horticultural literature with *O. albida* (see below), the true *O. albida* being a much more tender species. This plant, hitherto nameless, is designated in memory of the late Lord Talbot de Malahide, whose interest in, and regard for, the genus is so well known.

Although damaged in some gardens in the severe winters of 1961–3, this olearia is one of the hardiest, and will withstand full exposure to Atlantic winds.

O. ALBIDA Hook. f.—A shrub or tree to 15 ft high, resembling *O. avicenniifolia*, but with undulate leaves, shorter flower-stalks, and flower-heads with one to five ray-florets. Salmon, *New Zealand Flowers and Plants in Colour*, t. 126.

Confined to the North Island of New Zealand, in coastal forests. Not known to be in cultivation in the British Isles except at Tresco Abbey in the Isles of Scilly.

O. CHATHAMICA Kirk

An evergreen shrub 3 to 7 ft high; young shoots stout, furrowed, and like the undersurface of the leaves and flower-stalks, clothed with a soft white felt. Leaves alternate, $1\frac{1}{2}$ to 5 in. long, $\frac{1}{2}$ to $1\frac{1}{2}$ in. wide, thick, leathery, oblanceolate or oblong-lanceolate, pointed, the margins set with rather regular blunt teeth, tapering at the base to a short broad stalk; green and glabrous above; the midrib is raised beneath and at each side of it are one or two similarly prominent veins running lengthwise. Flower-heads aster-like, $1\frac{3}{4}$ to $2\frac{1}{4}$ in. wide, solitary on stalks 4 to 6 in. long. Ray-florets numerous, usually white, sometimes tinged purplish, $\frac{5}{8}$ in. long, linear, pointed. Disk-florets dark violet-purple, forming a conspicuous centre to the flower-head $\frac{3}{4}$ in. wide. Outer bracts linear, pointed, $\frac{1}{3}$ in. long, woolly towards the top. *Bot. Mag.*, t. 8420.

Native of the Chatham Islands; introduced by Major A. A. Dorrien-Smith in 1910. It was successfully grown in the Rectory garden at Ludgvan, near Penzance, planted in peat, leaf-soil, and grit. It flowers in May and June. Among cultivated olearias *O. chathamica* most resembles *O. semidentata* and is equally beautiful, though more tender. It differs from that species in its larger, broader, more conspicuously toothed leaves with prominent veins beneath.

O. ANGUSTIFOLIA Hook. f.—Like *O. chathamica*, but of larger stature, with stouter peduncles bearing leaf-like bracts, narrower lanceolate leaves, and consistently pure white ray-florets. Kirk, *Forest Flora of New Zealand*, t. 138.

A native of New Zealand (South and Stewart Islands), not certainly known to be in cultivation in the British Isles.

O. OPORINA (Forst. f.) Hook. f. *Arnica oporina* Forst. f.—Differs from *O. chathamica* in its yellow disk-florets; ray-florets white. Native of New Zealand (South Island). Hall-Jones, *Fiordland National Park*, t., p. 62.

O. CHEESEMANII Ckn. & Allan

O. arborescens var. *angustifolia* Cheesem.; *O. cunninghamii* Hort., not (Hook. f.) Hook. f.; *O. rani* Hort., not (A. Cunn.) Druce

An evergreen shrub up to 12 ft high; young shoots covered with a dense, buff down. Leaves alternate, slightly leathery, elliptic to lanceolate, usually pointed, tapered at the base, indistinctly wavy at the margins, 2 to $3\frac{1}{2}$ in. long, $\frac{1}{2}$ to $1\frac{1}{4}$ in. wide, dark green above with appressed white hairs when young, buff or silvery below with fine very closely appressed down; stalks about $\frac{1}{2}$ in. long. Flower-heads in corymbs, arising from the uppermost leaf-axils, forming large clusters, on slender densely downy stalks. Ray-florets white. *Journ. R.H.S.*, Vol. 90, fig. 98, as *O. rani*; Salmon, *New Zealand Flowers and Plants in Colour*, t. 283.

A native of New Zealand. A very floriferous shrub, flowering in April and

May, tolerant of wind and site, and as hardy as *O. avicenniifolia;* during the severe winter of 1961–2, it was only slightly injured in a west border at Kew and not injured at all at Knightshayes Court near Tiverton in Devon.

O. CAPILLARIS Buchan. *O. arborescens* var. *capillaris* (Buchan.) Kirk—A densely branched shrub up to 8 ft high. Leaves elliptic to suborbicular, more or less entire, ¼ to ¾ in. long, silvery white beneath. Flower-heads in corymbs; ray-florets white.

A native of New Zealand, on montane forest margins. Flowers in June. There is a fine specimen at Wakehurst Place, Sussex, about 8 ft high and 12 ft across.

O. COLENSOI Hook. f.

An evergreen shrub 10 to 16 ft high. Leaves of very leathery texture, usually obovate to obovate-lanceolate, pointed or occasionally bluntish at the apex, tapering at the base to a stout stalk ½ to ¾ in. long, toothed (often doubly so) at the margin, 3 to 8 in. long, half or less than half as much wide; dark shining green above except when young, clothed permanently beneath with a thick white wool; veins netted, prominent beneath. Racemes clustered at ends of the branches, each 4 to 8 in. long and bearing five to eight or more flower-heads which are up to 1 in. wide and dark brownish purple. There are no ray-florets. Salmon, *New Zealand Plants and Flowers in Colour,* t. 460.

Native of New Zealand, where it is regarded as one of the most handsome of the daisy bushes. It was discovered on Mt Hikurangi by Colenso at altitudes up to 5,000 ft, so hardy forms must exist. But the garden stock probably came from Stewart Island, where it forms an important part of the vegetation near the sea, and attains the dimensions of a small tree. This form is tender, and rare in the British Isles, though it flourishes at Tresco Abbey in the Isles of Scilly, where there are several plants about 15 ft high. At Kew it needs the protection of a cool greenhouse.

O. × TRAILLII Kirk *O. angustifolia* × *O. colensoi.*—Differs from *O. colensoi* in its narrower leaves and in the presence of white ray-florets. It is a shrub or small tree and grows 10 to 20 ft high. It was discovered by T. Kirk in 1883 and among the localities where it is found are Puysegue Point, South Island, and Stewart Island, whence seeds were sent to this country in 1932 by Mr Stead.

O. LYALLII Hook. f.—This differs from *O. colensoi* in its larger stature, being a shrub or tree up to 30 ft high, and in its broadly elliptic leaves 4 to 10 in. long. It is known only from the Snares and Auckland Islands to the south of New Zealand, and would certainly be tender in this country.

O. ERUBESCENS (DC.) Dipp.

Eurybia erubescens DC.; *O. myrsinoides* Hort., not (Labill.) F. Muell. ex Benth.

An evergreen shrub 3 to 5 ft high; young shoots often long and slender, covered like the undersurface of the leaves with a pale, brownish, shining down. Leaves alternate, scarcely stalked, stiff and leathery, narrowly oval or oblong, pointed, tapered or rounded at the base, conspicuously toothed; ½ to 1½ in. long, ¼ to ¾ in. wide, dark glossy green and glabrous above. Inflorescence branched, up to 3 in. long and carrying several flower-heads, or often unbranched and only one. Flower-heads 1 in. wide, with three to five pure white ray-florets and six to eight yellow disk-florets in the centre. They open in May and June. The inflorescences come from the leaf-axils of the previous year and form altogether an elegant, densely flowered, cylindrical panicle 1 to 1½ ft long. *Gard. Chron.*, ser. 3, Vol. 45 (1909), fig. 92, as *O. myrsinoides*.

Native of Tasmania, Victoria, and New South Wales; already cultivated at Kew in the 1840s. It needs wall protection there although, in a well-sheltered spot like the foot of a house wall facing south, it may pass through several winters without serious injury. When seen at its best it is a charming shrub and is admirable for the south and west. It has been much confused in gardens with *O. myrsinoides* (q.v.), but is more ornamental and is quite distinct in its much larger, pointed, more conspicuously toothed leaves and its larger flower-heads with as many as five spreading pure white florets, plus six to ten yellow disk-florets. It is mainly represented in cultivation by the following variety:

var. ILICIFOLIA (DC) Bean *Eurybia erubescens* var. *ilicifolia* DC.—Leaves less spiny than in the type, larger, 3 in. long, 1 in. wide. The inflorescence is larger and bears more numerous flowers, and the plant is more vigorous.

O. MYRSINOIDES (Labill.) Benth. *Aster myrsinoides* Labill.—A low and straggling or densely bushy shrub; young shoots angled, silvery, with a scale-like covering like the undersurface of the leaves. Leaves alternate, mostly obovate, sometimes narrowly oval, tapered at the base, rounded at the apex, toothed; ¼ to ½ in. long, ⅛ to ¼ in. wide, shining green and glabrous above. Flower-heads three to five together in axillary clusters, borne on stalks up to 1 in. long; ray-florets white, two or three to each head; disk-florets two to five, yellow. Labill., *Nov. Holl. Plant. Specim.*, Vol. 2, t. 202, as *Aster myrsinoides*.

Native of Tasmania and Victoria. In shape and size the leaves often resemble those of *Myrsine africana*. It is possible that the true plant is not in cultivation. What has been grown under the name is *O. erubescens*, a very distinct thing.

O. PERSOONIOIDES (DC.) Benth. *Eurybia persoonioides* DC.—A shrub up to 10 ft high. Leaves elliptic to obovate, blunt, leathery, entire, shining green above, white or pale fawn with silky tomentum beneath, ½ to 2 in. long, ¼ to 1 in. wide. Flower-heads in small pedunculate groups from the axils of the upper leaves, forming terminal clusters. Ray-florets three to four, white. Curtis, *Endemic Fl. Tasmania*, Part I, No 13.

A species endemic to Tasmania. It has been introduced recently, but is not yet established in cultivation and may prove to be of little value as an ornamental.

O. OBCORDATA (Hook. f.) Benth. *Eurybia obcordata* Hook. f.—A straggling shrub, distinguished at once by its small, cuneate leaves with entire margins and truncate, bluntly three- to five-toothed apex, ¼ to ⅜ in. long. Curtis, *Endemic Fl. Tasmania*, Part I, No 17.

An endemic of the mountains of Tasmania. Of recent introduction and still untested.

O. SPECIOSA Hutch.—A straggling shrub 3 to 4 ft high. Leaves alternate, stout and leathery, narrow-oblong or oval, margins recurved and toothed, sometimes coarsely and irregularly, up to 4½ in. long and 1½ in. wide, brown felted beneath. Flower-heads borne about midsummer in rather lax corymbs 4 to 8 in. wide, each head about 1 in. wide, borne on a stalk up to 2 in. long. Ray-florets five or six, white, ⅙ in. long, tapering towards both ends, disk-florets about twice as many, yellow. Outer bracts woolly, forming an involucre ⅓ in. wide. *Bot. Mag.*, t. 8118.

Native of Australia (Victoria); introduced to Kew shortly before 1883. It is very tender, but is cultivated outdoors at Tresco in the Isles of Scilly.

O. TASMANICA W. M. Curtis   *O. alpina* (Hook. f.) W. M. Curtis, not Buchan.; *O. persoonioides* var. *alpina* Hook. f.—This closely resembles *O. persoonioides*, but is a smaller, bushier shrub up to 3 ft high, with the leaves reddish brown on the lower surface and the flower-heads borne singly in the axils of the upper leaves; ray-florets five to six, white. Curtis, *Endemic Fl. Tasmania*, Part I, No 15, as *O. alpina*.

An endemic of Tasmania, found, according to Dr Curtis, at altitudes of around 3,500 ft, but lower near the west and south-west coasts. The late Lord Talbot de Malahide considered this to be probably the best of the endemic olearias of Tasmania, judging from the wild plants, but it was introduced too recently (around 1965) for any assessment to be made of its value in gardens.

O. FROSTII (F. v. Muell.) J. H. Willis

Aster frostii F. v. Muell.; *O. stellulata* var. *frostii* (F. v. Muell.) Ewart

A rather straggling evergreen shrublet. Leaves alternate, obovate, entire or bluntly sinuate-toothed in the upper part, densely covered with stellate hairs on both surfaces, paler beneath, ½ to 1 in. long, ¼ to ½ in. wide. Flower-heads solitary, terminal, or two or three together from the axils of the upper leaves, pedunculate, ¾ to 1½ in. across. Disk-florets numerous, yellow; ray-florets forty to fifty, pale mauve or lilac. *Bot. Mag.*, n.s., t. 521.

An endemic of Victoria, Australia, where it grows in the Mt Hotham–Mt Bogong area at about 4,500 ft. It first came to notice in this country in 1966, when it was shown from Inverewe by the National Trust for Scotland at the R.H.S. Show on July 26, under the name *O. gravis*. How and when it was introduced to Inverewe is not known for certain. It is a comparative new-comer to the genus *Olearia*, for although described, as *Aster frostii*, in 1890 it was not transferred to *Olearia* until 1955.

O. frostii is a most ornamental species, with neat, sage-green leaves and large, delicately coloured flower-heads. Although of untested hardiness, it is likely to be very tender outside the mildest parts.

O. FURFURACEA (A. Rich.) Hook. f.

Aster furfuraceus A. Rich.; *Eurybia furfuracea* (A. Rich.) DC.

An evergreen shrub of bushy habit, sometimes a small tree up to 20 ft high; young shoots covered with a whitish soft down, which persists to the second year and becomes brown. Leaves alternate, very leathery, mostly ovate or inclined to oblong, abruptly pointed or blunt at the apex, rounded or broadly tapered and often unequal at the base, margins undulate, entire or remotely and shallowly toothed, 2 to 4 in. long, 1½ to 2½ in. wide, glabrous and dark glossy green above, lustrous beneath with a closely appressed down; leaf-stalk ½ to 1 in. long. Flower-heads numerously produced in axillary, much-branched corymbs 3 to 5 in. wide, the main-stalk up to 6 or 8 in. long. Each head is ⅓ to ½ in. wide, carrying two to five ray-florets and three to seven disk-florets, the former white, oblong, ⅛ to ¼ in. long; the latter yellow. March and April. Salmon, *New Zealand Flowers and Plants in Colour*, t. 108.

Native of the North Island, New Zealand. In its shining green foliage—in size and colouring rather like that of a Portugal laurel, only stiffer and shining grey-white beneath—this olearia is quite handsome, and its flowers are abundant enough to give a pleasing effect. It survives cold winters in a sheltered spot at Kew, but is, of course, happier farther south and west. Among cultivated olearias it comes nearest to *O. arborescens*, but that species has thinner, less leathery leaves, whose margins are usually more conspicuously wavy and toothed and whose flowers each carry fifteen to twenty disk-florets.

O. FURFURACEA × O. PANICULATA—Tree with elliptic, entire, blunt, wavy-margined leaves up to 3 in. long and 1¼ in. wide, with the dark midrib of *O. furfuracea*. Flower-heads in terminal corymbs, sweetly fragrant, white, each composed of two disk-florets. Ray-florets absent.

A hybrid of unknown origin, in cultivation at Tresco Abbey in the Isles of Scilly.

O. PACHYPHYLLA Cheesem.—A shrub up to 10 ft high. Leaves ovate to oblong-ovate, leathery, 3 to 5 in. long, 2 to 2½ in. wide, without purple midrib. Involucral bracts very numerous (thirty-five or more) in four or five series. Salmon, *New Zealand Flowers and Plants in Colour*, t. 105.

Native of the North Island of New Zealand.

O. × HAASTII Hook. f.

An evergreen shrub of bushy, rounded habit 4 to 9 ft high; young branches covered with a close, greyish-white down. Leaves crowded on the branches, alternate, oval or ovate, ½ to 1 in. long, about half as wide, not toothed, rounded or blunt at the apex, thick and leathery, dark shining green and glabrous above, white-felted beneath; stalk about ⅛ in. long. Flower-heads produced during July and August in a series of axillary corymbose clusters standing out beyond the leaves, the whole forming a flattish cluster 2 to 3 in. across at the end of each twig. Ray-florets white, disk-florets yellow; each flower-head is ⅓ in. across. *Bot. Mag.*, t. 6592.

A natural hybrid, native of New Zealand, rare in the wild, of which the parents are *O. avicenniifolia* and *O. moschata*. It was described by the younger Hooker from a specimen collected by Haast in Canterbury province, 'near the glaciers of Lake Ohau' at 4,000 to 4,500 ft altitude, and was introduced by Veitch of Exeter in 1858. This is the only olearia at Kew of proved hardiness. I have never seen it killed outright by cold, although in February 1895 it was cut to the ground, but sprang up again freely a few months later. It flowers when there are few shrubs in blossom, and its abundant white flowers show up well against the dark green leaves; they have besides the charm of a sweet hawthorn-like fragrance. The flower-heads in the seeding state are covered with brown-grey down, which some people object to and cut off, as it persists through the winter. This shrub is admirable for maritime districts. In the late Sir Herbert Maxwell's garden at Monreith some years ago I saw a specimen 9 ft high and 15 ft in diameter. I believe it thrives extremely well in the Orkneys. Pruning, which it bears well, should be done in early spring. It should consist merely of a shortening back of plants that have become lanky or too large for their place.

O. 'WAIKARIENSIS' *O. waikariensis* Hort.; *O. waikensis* Hort.; *O. oleifolia* Hort., not (?) Kirk—A compact shrub, 5 to 8 ft high; leaves elliptic, blunt, 2 to 3 in. long, silvery white beneath.

A hybrid of unknown origin, introduced from New Zealand in the 1930s. In aspect it recalls *O.* × *haastii*, but has longer leaves. It may in fact be, like *O.* × *haastii*, the result of a cross between *O. avicenniifolia* and *O. moschata*, and thus, strictly speaking, a nothomorph of *O.* × *haastii*. However, since its parentage is uncertain and it is horticulturally distinct, it is more convenient to leave it with a separate name. It is sometimes called *O. oleifolia* Kirk, which is said to be *O. avicenniifolia* crossed with *O. odorata*, but it is by no means certain that the plants in cultivation are identical with Kirk's type, and the parentage ascribed to the latter is open to doubt.

O. ILICIFOLIA Hook. f.
Eurybia dentata var. *linearifolia* Hook. f.

An evergreen bush of spreading habit up to 10 ft or more high; young shoots rather downy. Leaves alternate, hard and leathery, linear-oblong to lanceolate, pointed, rounded or truncate at the base, margins conspicuously wavy and sharply and coarsely toothed, glabrous and green at maturity above, clothed beneath with a close whitish felt, 2 to 4 in. long, $\frac{1}{2}$ to 1 in. wide; stalk $\frac{1}{2}$ to $\frac{3}{4}$ in. long. Flower-heads fragrant, produced during June in branched, rounded corymbs 2 to 4 in. wide from the end of the previous year's growths on a main-stalk 3 to 6 in. long. Each flower-head is daisy-like, about $\frac{1}{2}$ in. wide, with ten or more white ray-florets. *Bot. Mag.*, n.s., t. 654.

Native of New Zealand on both North and South Islands extending to 4,000 ft altitude. It is closely related to *O. macrodonta* and is somewhat similar in general appearance. Both have the same musk-like odour. The leaves of *O. ilicifolia* are more oblong in shape, usually narrower, more wavy at the margin, and the veins stand out from the midrib at right angles (pointing forward in *O. macrodonta*). The whole plant in this country is smaller and less vigorous.

It is about as hardy as *O. macrodonta* or even hardier, and has thrived for many years outdoors at Wakehurst Place in Sussex. It received an Award of Merit when exhibited from there by the Director of Kew Gardens on July 11, 1972.

O. × MOLLIS (Kirk) Ckn. (*not* of gardens) *O. ilicifolia* var. *mollis* Kirk—A natural hybrid between *O. ilicifolia* and *O. lacunosa*, intermediate between them. Leaves resembling those of *O. lacunosa* but comparatively shorter and broader, lanceolate, with a thick white or yellowish-white tomentum beneath, rounded at the base, with small scarcely spinous marginal teeth.

O. × *mollis* was originally described (as a variety of *O. ilicifolia*) from specimens collected in the South Island of New Zealand. But the following is of garden origin:

O. × *mollis* 'ZENNORENSIS'.—A shrub to 6 ft high. Leaves narrow, pointed, sharply toothed, about 4 in. long and ½ in. wide, dark olive-green above, white-tomentose beneath.

This olearia was distributed by W. Arnold-Forster, who had a notable collection of olearias in his garden at Zennor in Cornwall. It is a beautiful foliage plant, fairly readily propagated by cuttings, and tolerant of maritime exposure. It is not reliably hardy near London, but should survive all but the severest winters in a sheltered position.

O. ILICIFOLIA × O. MOSCHATA *O. mollis* Hort., not (Kirk) Ckn.—A small, compact, rounded shrub; leaves elliptic, 1 to 1½ in. long, silvery grey, with wavy margins; flower-heads in corymbs. This is the olearia cultivated under the name '*O. mollis*', which properly belongs to the hybrid between *O. ilicifolia* and *O. lacunosa* described above. *Journ. R.H.S.*, Vol. 90, fig. 97, as *O. mollis*.

Although killed or badly damaged during the severe winters of 1961–3, this is reckoned to be one of the hardiest of the olearias.

O. ILICIFOLIA × O. NUMMULARIFOLIA.—Like the above, but leaves shorter and flower-heads solitary. A plant possibly of this parentage is grown at Tresco Abbey in the Isles of Scilly.

O. INSIGNIS Hook. f.

Pachystegia insignis (Hook. f.) Cheesem.

A low, spreading, evergreen shrub, described as growing 6 ft high in the wild; young shoots thick and, like the undersurface of the leaves, leaf-stalks and flower-stalks, clothed with a white or pale brown woolly felt. Leaves crowded at the ends of the shoots, very stout and leathery, entire, oval or obovate, tapered, rounded, or slightly heart-shaped at the base, blunt at the apex, 3 to 7 in. long, about half as wide, upper surface at first woolly, ultimately dark glossy green and glabrous except on the midrib and margins; stalk stout, ½ to 2 in. long.

Flower-heads produced from the end of the shoot or in the terminal leaf-axils; each solitary on a slender stalk 4 to 8 in. long. Each flower-head is 1½ to 2½ in. wide; the ray-florets very numerous in two or more rows, white, linear, toothed at the end, ½ in. long. Disk-florets very crowded, forming a yellow centre to the flower-head 1¼ in. wide. Outer scales small, overlapping, woolly, arranged in many rows. *Bot. Mag.*, t. 7034.

Native of New Zealand on the South Island up to 4,000 ft altitude; discovered by Capt. Rough about 1850. A very handsome species, distinct from most olearias by reason of its large leaves; its large, white and yellow, long-stalked flower-heads; and large egg-shaped involucre of very numerous scales beneath the flower-head. As many as five heads may be borne on one shoot and they open in summer. It is not really happy out-of-doors at Kew although it survives at the foot of a warm wall. It is well worth cultivation wherever it can be grown. Blooms about August.

var. MINOR Cheesem.—A dwarf plant, with leaves up to 4 in. long and smaller flower-heads on more slender peduncles.

O. MEGALOPHYLLA (F. v. Muell.) F. v. Muell. ex Benth. *Eurybia megalophylla* F. v. Muell.—A shrub to 3 ft high; leaves opposite, elliptic to oblong, leathery, reticulated above, grey- or brown-felted beneath, 2 to 4 in. long, ½ to 2¾ in. wide. Flower-heads rather large and numerous in terminal corymbs; ray-florets seven to twelve, white. *Bot. Mag.*, n.s., t. 665.

A native of Victoria and New South Wales. It is grown on a wall at Wakehurst Place, Sussex, but is still untested for hardiness.

O. LACUNOSA Hook. f.
O. *alpina* Buchan., [not (Hook. f.) W. M. Curtis]

An evergreen shrub 5 ft or more high (in the wild sometimes a small tree •15 ft high); young shoots, undersurface of leaves, leaf-stalks, and flower-stalks all densely clothed with a pale greyish or rust-coloured down. Leaves of leathery texture, linear to linear-oblong, obscurely or not at all toothed, pointed, very shortly stalked, 3 to 7 in. long, ⅓ to 1 in. wide, margins recurved, upper surface glabrous, the veins conspicuously sunken above, very prominent beneath, proceeding from the midrib to the leaf margins at almost right angles; midrib yellow on the upper surface. Panicles terminal and several together, forming a group of flower-heads 4 in. or more wide. Flower-heads 3/16 to ⅜ in. wide, each carrying from eight to twelve florets, four or five of which have rays about ⅛ in. long. *Bot. Mag.*, n.s., t. 645.

Native of North and South Islands, New Zealand, up to 5,000 ft altitude; discovered by W. T. L. Travers in 1864 on the mountains near Rotoroa. It was grown at Kew, but although it survived mild winters out-of-doors in sheltered spots, it was not genuinely hardy there. Like most of the olearias it will only be seen at its best in the milder parts. The leaves make it one of the most distinct at the genus; the midrib is very prominent beneath, and the veins, leaving it in right angles, divide the lower surface into a long series of roughly rectangular hollows. It grows well at Wakehurst Place in Sussex, where there is a plant about 10 ft high above The Slips, which sheds its bark in large strips. *O. lacunosa* rarely flowers in this country and the Wakehurst plant has never done so. It is also exceedingly difficult to raise from cuttings. But a hardwood cutting taken in October was rooted recently at Wakehurst in a cold frame and produced in inflorescence when four years old and still in a pot. (The plant above The Slips died in 1975.)

OLEARIA LACUNOSA

O. LEDIFOLIA (DC.) Benth.
Aster ledifolius A. Cunn. ex DC.

A low shrub, forming rounded clumps 1 to 2 ft high. Leaves alternate, crowded, sessile, oblong-linear, blunt or rounded at the tip, $\frac{3}{8}$ to $1\frac{1}{4}$ in. long, leathery, with revolute margins, green above, silvery or rusty tomentose beneath. Flower-heads solitary in the axils of leaves near the ends of the branches, on short peduncles. Involucral bracts narrow-oblong, tomentose. Ray-florets ten to twelve, white. Curtis, *Endem. Fl. Tasmania*, Part I, No 16.

An endemic of Tasmania. Seeds of this species were sent by Harold Comber during his expedition to Tasmania 1929–30. In his Field Notes he wrote: 'Common at 3,500–4,000 ft in most exposed places on moors, rocky forests or hill-sides. Will be rather slow growing, but good on the rock garden. Probably will appreciate some peat. Should be perfectly hardy.' Comber rated it highly, but it has never become established in cultivation.

O. PINIFOLIA (Hook. f.) Benth. *Eurybia pinifolia* Hook. f.—A rigid shrub 3 to 9 ft high, in aspect like a small pine; leaves linear, with revolute margins,

up to 1¾ in. long, with sharp pungent tips. Flower-heads rather larger than in
O. ledifolia, with eight to twelve ray-florets. Curtis, *Endem. Fl. Tasmania*,
Part I, No 14.

An endemic of Tasmania, introduced in 1930 by Harold Comber.

O. MACRODONTA Baker   [PLATE 5

O. dentata Hook. f., not Moench

An evergreen shrub up to 20 ft high, or even a small tree in the wild, with
bark peeling in long strips; young shoots angled, downy. Leaves alternate,
firm and leathery, ovate to narrowly oval, rounded or tapering at the base,
pointed at the apex, 2 to 5 in. long, 1 to 2 in. wide, the margins wavy and
furnished with coarse sharp teeth, the hollows between them rounded; upper
surface dark glossy green, downy only when quite young, lower surface covered
with a close, silvery-white felt; leaf-stalk ½ to ¾ in. long. Flower-heads produced
in one or more branched clusters 3 to 6 in. across, at the termination of the
previous season's growth, each cluster on a silvery-white, downy stalk 3 to
6 in. long. The flower-head is ½ in. across, with ten or more white ray-florets
and a few reddish disk-florets. *Bot. Mag.*, t. 7065.

Native of New Zealand up to 4,000 ft. It is one of the finest olearias, almost
hardy if sheltered from cold winds. The leaves are musk-scented when crushed.

cv. 'MAJOR'.—A form with larger leaves and flower-heads. There is an
example at Rowallane, Co. Down, 22 ft high and 48 ft across.

cv. 'MINOR'.—A dwarf, compact form, smaller in all its parts.

The status of *O. macrodonta* is uncertain; it is perhaps of hybrid origin, from
O. arborescens crossed with *O. ilicifolia*. Forms which are said to be hybrids
between *O. arborescens* and *O. macrodonta* are also in cultivation, as *O.* 'ROWAL-
LANE HYBRIDS'; they have the toothed leaves of the latter and the hanging
flower-heads of the former, but are perhaps no more than variants of the very
variable *O. arborescens*.

O. 'ROSSII'.—A strong-growing shrub of medium size; leaves up to 4 in.
long and 1½ in. wide, tapered at the base, often obliquely, more sharply tapered
at the apex, at first pilose above, becoming glossy green, persistently yellowish-
white tomentose beneath, coarsely toothed at the margins.

A hybrid which arose spontaneously in the garden of Sir John Ross of
Bladensburg at Rostrevor, Co. Down. It is supposed to be *O. macrodonta*
crossed with *O. argophylla*, but this parentage is in need of confirmation.

O. MACRODONTA × O. MOSCHATA.—A plant which appears to be this
hybrid has been offered in recent years by Hillier and Sons as '*O. rani*'. It is
neither the true *O. rani* (A. Cunn.) Druce nor the species properly known as
O. cheesemanii, which has also been grown as '*O. rani*'. Leaves elliptic, tapered
at the base and apex, up to 2 in. long and 1 in. wide, green above, closely
white-tomentose beneath, coarsely but rather bluntly toothed and slightly
revolute at the margins; stalk up to ½ in. long.

O. MOSCHATA Hook. f.

An evergreen shrub of dense, bushy, much-branched habit, 3 to 6 ft high, with a distinct musk-like scent and slightly viscid; young shoots, flower-stalks, involucres and undersurface of leaves covered with a close white felt. Leaves of leathery texture, alternate, closely set on the branches, oval inclined to obovate, rounded at the apex, tapered at the base to a very short stalk, quite without teeth, $\frac{1}{3}$ to $\frac{3}{4}$ in. long, $\frac{1}{5}$ to $\frac{3}{8}$ in. wide, greenish grey and scurfy above. Corymbs axillary, made up of twenty to thirty flower-heads produced on a slender main-stalk up to 2 in. long, the stalks of the individual flower-head much shorter. There are twelve to twenty florets in a head; ray-florets white, usually seven to nine, linear, giving each flower-head a diameter of $\frac{1}{3}$ to $\frac{1}{2}$ in.; disk-florets yellow. Salmon, *Field Guide to the Alpine Plants of New Zealand*, t. 7.

Native of the South Island, New Zealand; discovered by Sir Julius von Haast in 1862. This daisy bush is very distinct on account of its silvery-grey colour, its musky scent, small leaves, and close compact habit. When in bloom the leaves are almost hidden by the wealth of blossom. It needs winter shelter at Kew, but farther south succeeds well in the open air.

O. MOSCHATA × O. NUMMULARIIFOLIA.—A natural hybrid, resembling a small-leaved *O.* × *haastii*, with closer tomentum on the lower surface of the leaves and larger, fewer flower-heads. It is not known for certain to be in cultivation.

O. NUMMULARIIFOLIA (Hook. f.) Hook. f.

Eurybia nummularifolia Hook. f.

An evergreen bush of dense growth up to 10 ft high; young shoots thinly downy or almost glabrous. Leaves alternate, thick and leathery, closely set on the branchlets (twelve or more to the inch), oval or obovate to almost round, tapering at the base to a very short stalk, rounded at the apex, toothless, the margins recurved, $\frac{1}{4}$ to $\frac{1}{2}$ in. long, from half to nearly as much wide, glossy green above, clothed beneath with a very close, yellowish-white felt. Flower-heads solitary, produced from the axils of the terminal leaves, beyond which they stand out slightly. Each flower-head is $\frac{1}{3}$ to $\frac{1}{2}$ in. long and each has three to five creamy-white or yellowish ray-florets. The scales of the involucre are erect, in several rows, often nearly glabrous except at the points and margins. Salmon, *Field Guide to the Alpine Plants of New Zealand*, t. 4.

Native of New Zealand on the North and South Islands, ascending to altitudes of 4,500 ft. It is one of the hardier olearias and survives ordinary winters at Kew, but still cannot be relied on there like *O.* × *haastii*. It is usually seen as a rather low bush in this country, distinct in its crowded, small, thick leaves and is well worth growing in the milder counties. The flowers are heliotrope-scented and borne in July.

var. CYMBIFOLIA Hook. f. *O. cymbifolia* (Hook. f.) Cheesem.—Leaves slightly longer and relatively narrower, with the margins revolute almost to the midrib. Salmon, *Field Guide to the Alpine Plants of New Zealand*, t. 4a.

O. CORIACEA Kirk—A shrub up to 10 ft high; leaves broadly ovate to suborbicular, ⅜ to ¾ in. long, up to ½ in. wide, very thick and leathery, green above, brownish-white tomentose beneath. Flower-heads corymbose, discoid, one-flowered. Davies, *New Zealand Native Plant Studies*, t. 115.

A native of the South Island of New Zealand; not known for certain to be in cultivation in the British Isles.

O. ODORATA Petrie

A shrub up to 12 ft high, of thin, sparse habit, with wiry, terete, little-branched stems. Leaves opposite, spathulate, ½ to 1½ in. long, ⅛ to ¼ in. wide near the rounded apex, bright green and glabrous above, silvery beneath with appressed, white hairs, tapering at the base, almost sessile. Flower-heads ¼ in. across, in opposite fascicles of two to five, borne on short, arrested, bud-like branches, which usually also carry a pair of leaves; they are scented and dull greyish brown; the bracts of the involucre brown and viscous glandular. Ray-florets up to twenty, white. Salmon, *New Zealand Flowers and Plants in Colour*, t. 455.

Native of the South Island of New Zealand, where it is very common in the lake district of Otago. It is a curious, not particularly ornamental shrub introduced in 1908 and put into commerce as 'O. virgata'. The true O. virgata has four-angled instead of terete stems.

O. HECTORIS Hook. f.—This differs from *O. odorata* in its deciduous habit, broadly elliptic leaves more than ⅜ in. wide, and yellowish flower-heads produced before the leaves. Salmon, *New Zealand Flowers and Plants in Colour*, t. 106.

A native of the South Island of New Zealand, distinct in the genus by its deciduous habit and precocious fragrant flowers.

O. FRAGRANTISSIMA Petrie—This differs from *O. odorata* in its dark reddish-brown bark, elliptic to obovate alternate leaves (opposite in *O. odorata*), and flower-heads in sessile or subsessile alternate clusters of up to twelve flower-heads; involucral bracts tomentose.

Native of the South Island of New Zealand.

O. PANICULATA (J. R. & G. Forst.) Druce

Shawia paniculata J. R. & G. Forst.; *Eurybia forsteri* Hook. f.; *Olearia forsteri* (Hook. f.) Hook. f.

An evergreen shrub or a small tree up to 20 ft high in its native country; young shoots ribbed and furnished with a dark brown scurf, as are also the leaf-stalks and flower-stalks. Leaves alternate, leathery, ovate or oval, rounded or slightly heart-shaped at the base, mostly blunt at the apex, the margins entire but conspicuously wavy, 1½ to 3½ in. long, 1 to 1¾ in. wide, shining green and without down above, clothed beneath with a grey-white, closely appressed felt; stalk ⅓ to ¾ in. long, grooved. Flower-heads dull white, produced in small, pyramidal, axillary panicles in October and usually about 2 in. long; each flower-head is cylindrical, ¼ in. long, composed of a solitary tubular floret enclosed by erect, slightly downy, dull white scales. Salmon, *New Zealand Flowers and Plants in Colour*, t. 104.

Native of both the main islands of New Zealand, up to 1,500 ft. It is not hardy near London except against a wall, but is grown outside in several parts of the British Isles, especially in the west, where it makes an excellent hedge, resistant to sea winds. It has no beauty of flower, but the blossoms are fragrant and continue to open during November and December.

O. PHLOGOPAPPA (Labill.) DC.

Aster phlogopappa Labill.; *Eurybia gunniana* DC.; *O. gunniana* (DC.) Hook. f. ex Hook.; *O. stellulata* Hort., in part, not (Labill.) DC.

An aromatic evergreen shrub 5 to 10 ft high, naturally much-branched; young shoots covered with a close white felt. Leaves alternate, oblong or narrowly obovate, ½ to 2¼ in. long, about one-fourth as wide, roundish at the apex, tapering towards the base, the margins sinuously or very shallowly toothed, dark dull green above, white or ashen grey, obscurely veined and closely felted beneath; very shortly stalked. Flower-heads 1 to 1¼ in. across, produced in erect, loose, slender-stalked corymbs. Ray-florets ten to sixteen, white, some-times pink, mauve or blue. *Bot. Mag.*, t. 4638, as *O. gunniana*.

Native of Tasmania, Victoria, and New South Wales; introduced to Kew about 1848. *O. phlogopappa* is the earliest olearia to flower (late April and early May). The form originally introduced has white flowers and survives most winters near London in a sheltered position. But in recent years it has given way in gardens to *O.* × *scilloniensis* (q.v.) and to the cultivars described below.

O. phlogopappa 'SPLENDENS' GROUP *O. gunniana* var. *splendens* Comber; *O. stellulata* 'Splendens'—During his expedition to Tasmania (1929–30), Harold Comber found some forms of *O. phlogopappa* with flowers ranging in colour from white, pale pink, deep pink, mauve, purple to blue. The seed he sent home germinated freely and these olearias are now well established in cultiva-tion. They may be referred to collectively as the 'Splendens' group of cultivars; they differ from the white-flowered plants of the old introduction not only in their flower-colour but also in their generally smaller leaves, up to 1½ in. long. They are also, unfortunately, less hardy and less vigorous. Mature plants should be lightly pruned after flowering.

var. SUBREPANDA (DC.) J. H. Willis *Eurybia subrepanda* DC.—An alpine variant with short, more or less obovate leaves, up to ½ in. long, very short leafy peduncles and often quite solitary flower-heads. Morcombe, *Australia's Wildflowers*, t., p. 22.

Native of Victoria and Tasmania. Of denser habit than the type and hardier.

O. LIRATA (Sims) Hutch. (in error as "*lyrata*") *Aster liratus* Sims—Very distinct from *O. phlogopappa* in its larger, lanceolate (not oblong) leaves, 3 to 5 in. long, ½ to 1 in. wide, light green and shiny above, densely felted beneath.

OLEARIA PHLOGOPAPPA

Flower-heads about ¾ in. across, in rounded terminal clusters; ray-florets twelve to fifteen, white. *Bot. Mag.*, t. 1509, as *Aster liratus*.

Native of Australia (Victoria and New South Wales), also of Tasmania. It was cultivated by Loddiges of Hackney as a greenhouse plant in 1813, but has never been common. It is hardy only in the mildest parts, and is not so well worth cultivation as its nearest allies.

O. NERNSTII (F. v. Muell.) F. v. Muell. ex Benth. *Aster nernstii* F. v. Muell.—A viscid shrub; leaves oblong-lanceolate, narrow, 1 to 3 in. long, pointed, rather thin, smooth and shining green above, loosely stellate-tomentose beneath. Flower-heads in terminal clusters; ray-florets fifteen to twenty, white.

A native of New South Wales and Queensland. Probably only hardy in the mildest districts.

O. STELLULATA (Labill.) DC. *Aster stellulatus* Labill.—This resembles

O. phlogopappa in leaf-shape, but the leaves are larger, 2 to 4 in. long, ¼ to ½ in. wide, distinctly veined and with a fuzzy yellowish tomentum beneath.

A native of E. Australia, from Queensland to Tasmania. It is taller and less compact than *O. phlogopappa*. Most references to "*O. stellulata*" in horticultural literature refer not to this species but to *O. phlogopappa*.

O. RAMULOSA (Labill.) Benth.

Aster ramulosus Labill.; *O. ramulosa* var. *communis* Benth.

A much-branched evergreen shrub 3 to 5 ft high, with graceful, very slender, arching shoots, which are usually more or less bristly, also often cottony and glandular. Leaves alternate, linear to linear-obovate, $\frac{1}{16}$ to ⅜ in. long, $\frac{1}{12}$ in. wide, margins recurved, dark green and at first slightly woolly or minutely warted above, permanently woolly beneath; stalk ¼ in. or less long. Flower-heads ⅝ in. wide, solitary on very short leafy twigs; ray-florets pure white or sometimes blue, three to fifteen in number, linear; disk-florets white, with yellow anthers. *Bot. Mag.*, t. 8205, as var. *communis*.

Native of Tasmania and Australia. It has long been cultivated, having flowered in a garden near Paris as long ago as 1822. It was treated as a cool greenhouse plant at Kew where it flowered from February onwards. It is grown out-of-doors in specially favoured places in the south-west, but must be regarded as one of the tenderest of the olearias. The flowers stand erect on the arching shoots and make very elegant sprays. H. F. Comber found it in dry, open pastures in Tasmania, fully exposed to the sun. In flower, he observes, the plant became simply a white mass.

O. ALGIDA N. A. Wakefield—This differs from *O. ramulosa* in having leaves only $\frac{1}{12}$ to ⅛ in. long, borne in dense, lateral clusters, and in its slender, never bristly but usually slightly cottony branches. Leaves grey-green or glaucous, triangular, broadest at the base, thick, with revolute margins. Ray-florets three or four, white. Murray, *Alp. Fl. Kosciusko State Park*, t. 8, as *O. floribunda*.

Native of New South Wales, Victoria, and Tasmania.

O. CILIATA (Benth.) F. v. Muell. ex Benth. *Eurybia ciliata* Benth.—A small, non-glandular shrub with roughly hairy stems; leaves in fascicles, heath-like, linear, sharp-pointed, ⅓ to ⅔ in. long; flower-heads solitary on slender 2 to 5½ in. long peduncles. Involucral bracts pointed, ciliate; ray-florets about twenty, white or blue. *Bot. Mag.*, t. 8191.

A native of temperate Australia, including Tasmania; introduced from Western Australia in 1899, by Sgt Goadby of the Royal Engineers, 'who whilst stationed in that State collected specimens and seeds of many interesting plants for Kew'.

O. ERICOIDES (Steetz) N. A. Wakefield *Eurybia ericoides* Steetz; *O. ramulosa* var. *communis* Benth., in part—Like *O. ramulosa*, but leaves and stems very viscid and the leaves closely revolute. It is a small shrub up to 3 ft high; leaves ⅛ to ¼ in. long, lower surface woolly but obscured by recurved margin and a viscid yellow secretion. Flower-heads solitary, about ¾ in. across, terminal on branches and short laterals; ray-florets about twelve, bluish or white. Curtis, *Endemic Fl. Tasmania*, Part I, No 18.

An endemic of Tasmania, not yet established in cultivation.

O. GLANDULOSA (Labill.) Benth. *Aster glandulosus* Labill.—An aromatic shrub 3 to 7 ft high, distinguished by the glandular tubercles on the young shoots and along the margins of the narrowly linear leaves, which are otherwise glabrous and ¾ to 2¼ in. long. Flower-heads small, in terminal corymbose panicles; ray-florets twelve to twenty, white or bluish.

A native of temperate Australia, including Tasmania. A swamp-loving species, flowering in August. It was introduced early in the 1960s by the late Lord Talbot de Malahide, but according to him its flowers do not make much show and it is likely to be tender.

O. FLORIBUNDA (Hook. f.) Benth. *Eurybia floribunda* Hook. f.—Like O. *ramulosa* but branches and lower surface of the leaves cottony, never bristly; from O. *algida* it differs in the bright to dark green, oblanceolate or oblong leaves, $\frac{1}{12}$ to ⅛ in. long, in loose lateral clusters, with almost flat or only narrowly recurved margins. Flower-heads solitary and sessile on very short laterals, numerous, forming large compound panicles; ray-florets three to four, white. Hooker, *Fl. Tasman.*, Vol. 1, t. 45, fig. B.

A native of S.E. Australia and of Tasmania, whence H. F. Comber sent seeds during his expedition in 1929–30. It is an interesting and attractive shrub, with foliage that has been likened to that of *Fabiana imbricata*, bearing its flowers in plume-like panicles. It is rather tender and said to be short-lived in cultivation, but cuttings strike readily. It received an Award of Merit when shown from Nymans, Sussex, on May 21, 1935.

O. HOOKERI (Sond.) Benth. *Eurybia hookeri* Sond.—A slender, viscid shrub up to 3 ft high, glabrous except for microscopic glands. Leaves alternate, narrow-linear, ⅛ to ¼ in. long, rounded at the tip. Flower-heads solitary, sessile on the ends of leafy branches; ray-florets eight to ten, conspicuous, bluish purple. Curtis, *Endem. Fl. Tasm.*, Pt. IV, No. 124.

An endemic of Tasmania, not yet established in cultivation.

O. ROTUNDIFOLIA (Lessing) DC.

Diplopappus rotundifolius Lessing; *Aster dentatus* Andr.; *Olearia dentata* Hort., not Moench nor Hook. f.; *O. tomentosa* Hort., not (Wendl.) DC. ex Steud.; *O. ferruginea* Hort. ex Gard. Chron.

A stout, much-branched evergreen shrub; young shoots clothed with a felt of rusty-brown, forked hairs. Leaves alternate, oval, ovate, pointed or blunt, mostly tapered at the base but sometimes rounded or slightly heart-shaped, with four to six shallow teeth on each margin or almost entire, 1 to 2½ in. long, about half as wide, dark green and rough to the touch above, clothed beneath with a felt of forked hairs similar to that which covers the branchlets; stalk ¼ to ⅝ in. long. Flower-heads in a terminal panicle of sometimes nine to a dozen, each head 1 to 1½ in. wide. Ray-florets numerous, linear, often notched

at the end, pale rose-coloured. Disk-florets forming a compact yellow centre
$\frac{1}{3}$ in. wide. Outer scales of flower-head linear, pointed, clothed with a red-
brown felt like that of the other parts, very numerous in several rows and
forming an ovoid involucre nearly $\frac{1}{2}$ in. wide. Achenes pilose. *Bot. Mag.*,
t. 5973, as *O. dentata.*

Native of E. Australia, and suitable only for the milder parts of our islands.
It has long been cultivated and was raised in Lee and Kennedy's nursery at
Hammersmith in 1793 and flowered there a few years later. It has been grown
at Tresco Abbey in Scilly since the middle of last century and Sir Joseph
Hooker records the existence of a fine bush there in 1872. The true plant is
now very rare. It is certainly one of the most beautiful of the olearias, for
few of them have flower-heads combining size, pretty colouring, and number
to such an extent. The flowering season is apparently an extended one and I
have seen specimens collected in March and July. Andrews, who figured the
plant in his *Botanist's Repository*, t. 61, gives the flowering season as extending
from December to August.

This species has been the subject of a great deal of nomenclatural confusion.
It was first described as *Aster dentatus* Andr., but the epithet could not be used
for this plant in *Olearia* because of the previous existence of *O. dentata* Moench,
itself a superfluous name for *Aster tomentosus* Wendl. The plant so named by
Wendland is the olearia *O. tomentosa* (Wendl.) DC. ex Steud., an allied species
distinguished from *O. rotundifolia* by its glabrous (not pilose) achenes. Unfortunately, the name *O. tomentosa* has long been erroneously applied to the
present plant, for which *O. rotundifolia* appears to be the correct name.

The very different *O. dentata* Hook. f. (not of Moench) is now correctly
known as *O. macrodonta* Baker (q.v.).

O. × SCILLONIENSIS Dorrien-Smith

A hybrid between *O. lirata* and *O. phlogopappa*, resembling the latter parent
but not aromatic. Leaves oblong-elliptic, up to $4\frac{1}{2}$ in. long, blunt, sinuate at
the margins, deep green and reticulate above, pale whitish green and closely
felted beneath, stalks up to $\frac{1}{4}$ in. long. Flower-heads in numerous stalked
corymbs, rather larger than in *O. phlogopappa*, with longer, more densely
tomentose involucral bracts; ray-florets ten to fifteen, pure white. *Gard. Chron.*,
Vol. 129 (1951), fig. 94.

This very floriferous hybrid arose spontaneously at Tresco Abbey in the
Isles of Scilly around 1910. 'It makes a solid, rounded bush 5 ft high or more,
grey-green; and every shoot becomes so covered with white daisies in May
that the leaf almost disappears. It is wind-hardy, strikes readily, grows fast,
and requires no attention except the removal of flowered shoots after flowering,
(W. Arnold-Forster, *Shrubs for the Milder Counties*, p. 267). Although not
reliably hardy, it should come through most winters uninjured in a sunny,
sheltered position and flowers freely when quite young. Award of Merit 1951.

O. SEMIDENTATA Decne.

An evergreen bush of rounded habit 6 to 12 ft high and as much or more in diameter; young shoots slender, clothed with a white, woolly felt. Leaves alternate, linear to lanceolate, pointed, tapered slightly to a stalkless base with a few shallow teeth at the upper half, 1½ to 3 in. long, ⅙ to ⅜ in. wide, upper surface dark green, wrinkled, lower one clothed with soft, silvery white wool. Flower-heads solitary at the end of the twigs, each one about 2 in. wide, aster-like in form, the numerous spreading or slightly decurved ray-florets pale purple and about ¾ in. long by ⅛ in. wide; disk-florets of a darker, more violet-purple, forming a conspicuous circular centre to the flower-head ½ to ¾ in. wide. The outer scales of the involucre are linear, pointed, closely set in about three rows, and almost hidden by a white cottony down. *Bot. Mag.*, t. 8550.

Native of the Chatham Islands; introduced to England in 1910 by Major A. A. Dorrien-Smith, who gives a very interesting account of a visit made to the native habitat of this beautiful shrub in the *Kew Bulletin*, 1910, p. 120. On this occasion he found a white form, var. *albiflora* Dorrien-Smith. Since its introduction, *O. semidentata* has spread in cultivation and become, in the milder parts of the British Isles, one of the most popular of the genus, which it well deserves to be. It first flowered at Tresco Abbey in Scilly in July 1913.

In colour beauty of blossom this surpasses all other olearias I have seen in cultivation. It is not adapted for the open air in places with a climate similar to that of Kew, only surviving there the mildest winters and even then not unscathed. It likes a light, well-drained or even stony soil. Closely related to *O. chathamica* (q.v.).

The clone grown in the British Isles from Major Dorrien-Smith's introduction, illustrated in the *Botanical Magazine*, and described above, differs from typical *O. semidentata* in several ways, especially in its larger, less clustered flower-heads and much more woolly involucral bracts. In these differences it approaches *O. chathamica* and it is possible that the plants known in cultivation as *O. semidentata* are of hybrid origin (*O. semidentata* × *O. chathamica*) and not the pure species. The introducer is likely to have picked out an especially striking and floriferous variant for introduction and a plant of hybrid origin would be likely to exhibit vigour and thus also these desirable garden qualities.

O. SOLANDRI (Hook. f.) Hook. f.
Eurybia solandri Hook. f.

An evergreen shrub up to 15 ft high in the wild, of erect habit, branches broom-like; young shoots angled, clothed with yellowish down. Leaves opposite or in opposite clusters, about ¼ in. long, $\frac{1}{20}$ in. wide (twice as long on quite young plants), linear inclined to obovate, rounded or bluntish at the end, tapered at the base to a very short stalk, dark green and glabrous above, the midrib deeply sunken, clothed beneath with a yellowish-white felt; margins recurved. Flower-heads solitary from the centre of the leaf-clusters, stalkless, yellowish, ¼ to ⅓ in. long, each containing eight to twenty florets. Outer scales of involucre in four rows, bright tawny yellow, rather downy.

Native of New Zealand on both the North and South Islands up to 1,500 ft altitude. It is distinct amongst cultivated olearias in its rather heath-like foliage and habit and its clusters (fascicles) of leaves. In general aspect it resembles *Cassinia fulvida*. It can be grown in a sheltered spot near a wall at Kew and has made healthy bushes there 6 ft high, apt nevertheless to be severely injured in hard winters. The whole plant has a yellowish tone due to the colour of the

OLEARIA VIRGATA

down on the shoots, underneath the leaves, and on the involucral scales. It blooms from August to October, but on the whole is a dull shrub.

O. TRAVERSII (F. v. Muell.) Hook. f.

Eurybia traversii F. v. Muell.

An evergreen shrub or small tree from 15 to 35 ft high in the wild; young shoots four-angled, clothed with a silvery-white, closely appressed felt as are also the leaves beneath, the leaf-stalks, and the flower-stalks. Leaves opposite, obovate or oval, tapered at both ends, but usually more abruptly towards the mucronate apex, quite untoothed, leathery, 1½ to 2½ in. long, ¾ to 1½ in. wide, at first furnished with appressed silky hairs above, but ultimately quite glabrous and bright dark green; stalk ⅛ to ¼ in. long. Panicles 1 to 2 in. long, produced during June in the leaf-axils and carrying usually five to twelve flower-heads, each ¼ in. long. From five to fifteen florets occur in each head, the outer ones of which are female. There are no ray-florets and the dull greyish flowers have little beauty. Kirk, *For. Fl. New Zeal.*, t. 34.

Native of the Chatham Islands, where it was discovered in 1840. Although this olearia has so little flower beauty to recommend it, the fine silvery sheen beneath the leaves is quite attractive. It is a free grower where the conditions suit it, and it has proved hardy at Kew but not on other inland sites. It thrives in the milder counties and is especially adapted for the seaside. At Castlewellan in Co. Down there is a specimen measuring 34 × 4¼ ft (1966). Even on the east coast as far north as Scarborough, it succeeds in exposed situations if planted close to the sea. It is well distinguished by its short-stalked, opposite leaves, numerous short axillary panicles, and squarish twigs.

O. VIRGATA (Hook. f.) Hook. f.

Eurybia virgata Hook. f.

An evergreen shrub up to 10 or 15 ft high and as much wide, often forming dense tangled bushes; young shoots very slender, wiry, usually four-angled and glabrous. Leaves opposite or in opposite clusters, narrowly obovate, $\frac{3}{16}$ to $\frac{3}{4}$ in. long, $\frac{1}{8}$ to $\frac{3}{8}$ in. wide, rounded or abruptly narrowed to a point at the apex, tapered at the base, upper surface usually glabrous and dark green, lower surface clothed with white felt; stalk very short or absent. Flower-heads in opposite clusters, each about $\frac{1}{6}$ in. long and wide and borne on very short downy stalks. Florets in each head five to twelve; ray-florets three to six, yellowish white. Outer scales of the involucre in about three rows, linear-oblong, usually silky-downy. Cheeseman, *Ill. New Zealand Fl.*, t. 91; Salmon, *New Zealand Plants and Flowers in Colour*, t. 107.

Native of New Zealand in the North and South Islands, from sea-level up to 3,000 ft altitude. This curious shrub has no great beauty and is chiefly interesting for its long, slender, wire-like branches furnished with small leaves and clusters of short flower-heads which open during May and June in this country.

O. virgata and *O. odorata* are closely related, but the latter has terete branchlets, broader leaves, many more (20 to 25) florets in each head, and the outer scales of the involucre are viscid and glandular. *O. virgata* itself is a very variable species. Allan in *Flora of New Zealand* recognises seven named varieties.

var. LINEATA Kirk *O. lineata* (Kirk) Ckn.—This variety differs in the more slender and pendulous branchlets, which are often downy when young. Still more does it differ in the opposite leaf-clusters being set farther apart, and in the narrowness of the leaves themselves, which are only $\frac{1}{24}$ to $\frac{1}{16}$ in. wide, but from $\frac{1}{2}$ to 2 in. long. The ray-florets are about twice as many in each head as in the typical state of the species, and number from eight to fourteen. Native of the South Island of New Zealand and of Stewart Island. This variety is more commonly met with in cultivation than the type. There is an example at Wakehurst Place in Sussex about 20 ft high. A plant at Messrs Hilliers' West Hill Nursery, Winchester, was 27 ft high in 1967.

ONONIS   LEGUMINOSAE

Of this genus—to which belongs the common 'rest-harrow' (*O. repens*) of our waysides and fields—only two or three species can be included amongst hardy shrubs, the majority being herbaceous or only slightly woody. They are natives of S. Europe. The leading characteristics of the genus are the alternate, trifoliolate, toothed leaves, the five long, narrow divisions of the calyx, the pea-shaped flowers, the stamens united in one bundle, and the slightly swollen seed-pods. The undermentioned are useful in flowering later in the season than the bulk of hardy shrubs, and are easily cultivated in moderately good soil in a sunny spot. Propagated by seeds, or, failing them, cuttings. Besides the three here described, O. NATRIX L. (*Bot. Mag.*, t. 329), is sometimes included in lists of shrubs. It is a rather showy plant with yellow flowers, the standard petal 1 in. across, but it is only partially woody and not long-lived. A native of S. Europe and popularly called 'Goat-root'. O. ARVENSIS L., closely allied to the common rest-harrow, is also sometimes cultivated for ornament.

O. ARAGONENSIS Asso

A deciduous bushy shrub 1½ to 2 ft high, of sturdy habit, with crooked branches and pale greyish young shoots. Leaves from ½ in. long on the flowering twigs, to 1½ in. long on the stronger flowerless shoots of the year; leaflets three, glossy green, roundish, irregularly toothed, glabrous, from ⅓ to ⅝ in. wide, the middle one stalked and larger, the side ones stalkless, or nearly so. Flowers yellow, ½ in. long, produced often in pairs along a crooked, hairy, terminal raceme, 3 to 6 in. high. The standard petal is ⅓ in. across, and the calyx consists of five-pointed, awl-shaped lobes covered with glandular hairs. Pods glandular-hairy, with the calyx persisting at the base.

Native of the Pyrenees southward into Spain, and of N. Africa; introduced in 1816. This is a pretty dwarf shrub, flowering from mid-May onwards. It bears its erect racemes very freely, the larger ones carrying ten or twelve pairs of blossoms. It does not ripen seed freely here, but can be increased by cuttings of half-ripened wood. It must have a sunny position, and the soil should be light loam. Suitable for the rock garden. It is perfectly hardy.

O. FRUTICOSA L.

A deciduous shrub of spreading habit, 2 or 3 ft high, with pale, crooked branchlets. Leaves trifoliolate, short-stalked, clasping the stem by the stipule at the base; the stipule is terminated by four slender teeth—two long and two short; leaflets narrowly obovate, ½ to 1 in. long, ⅛ to ¼ in. wide, not downy, but wrinkled, unevenly toothed, all stalkless. Flowers ¾ in. long, pale pinkish purple, borne (usually three on a stalk) on a short terminal panicle 2 to 3 in. long.

TAS—C

ONONIS ARAGONENSIS

Pods ¾ to 1 in. long, stout, covered with bristly hairs, and containing two to five seeds. *Bot. Mag.*, t. 317.

Native of S. Europe, especially in the Dauphiné Alps; also of N. Africa; known in our gardens since 1680. It flowers from June to August, and should only be propagated by seeds, which it ripens in plenty. Well distinguished from the other two by the shape of the leaflets, and by all three of them being stalkless.

O. ROTUNDIFOLIA L.

A deciduous half-shrubby species 1½ to 2 ft high, with very glandular-hairy, zigzag stems; the leaf-stalk, flower-stalk, and calyx are also glandular-hairy. Leaves trifoliolate, 1 to 3 in. long; leaflets roundish, sometimes obovate, the terminal one the largest, stalked, and ¼ to 1¼ in. long, side ones half to two-thirds as large, stalkless; all are toothed and hairy, especially below and on the margins. Flowers ¾ in. long, pink, produced from the axils of the leaves, three together towards the end of a stalk ½ to 2½ in. long. Pods very hairy, 1 to 1¼ in. long. *Bot. Mag.*, t. 335.

Native of S. and Central Europe; cultivated for more than three hundred years in England. Increased by seeds.

OPLOPANAX   ARALIACEAE

A genus of three closely related very prickly deciduous shrubs, with simple, lobed leaves, natives of western N. America and N.E. Asia.

O. HORRIDUS (Sm.) Miq.

Panax horridum Sm.; *Echinopanax horridus* (Sm.) J. G. Cooper; *Fatsia horrida* (Sm.) S. Wats.

A deciduous shrub up to 10 ft high in the wild, its stems, leaf-stalks, leaf-veins, and inflorescence all armed with slender needle-like prickles. Leaves 7 to 10 in. wide, palmately veined, cordate at the base, shallowly seven- or nine-lobed, doubly serrated; leaf-stalks about as long as the blade. Flowers very shortly stalked or almost sessile, borne in dense umbellate heads, which are arranged in elongated racemes or panicles up to 10 in. long. Fruits red. *Bot. Mag.*, t. 8572.

Native of north-western N. America, in the moister types of forest, where it forms dense entanglements; discovered by Menzies on Nootka Sound during Vancouver's voyage 1790–5. The date of introduction is uncertain.

If one judged from the climate in which this species is naturally found, it ought to thrive in this country. But owing to the warm soft weather we frequently experience in the early New Year, it starts into growth too soon, and is almost invariably cut by frost when grown in the open, and might succeed better in moist woodland.

Very similar plants occur in Japan, and were for a long time included in *O. horridus*. They differ from the American plants chiefly in leaf-characters, the blades being smaller, with narrower, long-acuminate lobes, which are themselves acuminately lobulate, while the inflorescences are more weakly spiny. However, at least one N. American specimen in the Kew Herbarium is very similar to those from Japan in these respects, which throws doubts on the validity of these characters. If separated from *O. horridus*, the Japanese plants would take the name O. JAPONICUS (Nakai) Nakai.

OPLOPANAX HORRIDUS

Korean plants have been separated from the American species as O. ELATUS (Nakai) Nakai. In this the leaves have broader lobes, which are not lobulate; they are toothed as in *O. horridus*, but the teeth are bristle-tipped, so that the margin appears notably ciliate; in addition the spines in *O. elatus* are everywhere much shorter than in *O. horridus*. So far as is known, neither the Japanese nor the Korean species is in cultivation in Britain.

ORIXA RUTACEAE

A genus of one species in E. Asia, allied to *Euodia* and *Zanthoxylum*, but distinguished from the latter (and from cultivated species of the former) by its simple leaves.

O. JAPONICA Thunb.

Evodia ramiflora A. Gr.; *Celastrus japonica* (Thunb.) K. Koch

A deciduous shrub of graceful, spreading habit, with long slender branches, and 6 to 8 ft high. Leaves aromatically scented, obovate or oblanceolate, 2 to 5 in.

long, 1 to 2 in. wide, dark green, quite entire, and glabrous except on the nerves of the young leaves. Flowers unisexual, the parts in fours, males in short racemes produced from the joints of the previous year's wood, green, scarcely ¼ in. across, with downy stalks. Female flowers on separate plants, solitary. Fruits about ¾ in. across, brown, and composed usually of four compressed, one-seeded carpels.

Native of China and Japan. As this pleasing and elegant shrub bears its male and female flowers on different plants, its fruits are only obtainable when both sexes are grown. According to Wilson, who saw them in China, they have the curious and interesting faculty when ripe of shooting out the seed a distance of several feet in the same way as *Impatiens* does. The leaves have a pleasant, spicy odour when crushed and turn pale yellow in the autumn. This shrub is said to be largely used by the Japanese as a hedge plant.

cv. 'VARIEGATA'.—Leaves margined creamy white, shading through grey to the normal green. Introduced to Britain by Messrs Hillier, who received it from M. Robert de Belder of Kalmthout, Belgium.

ORPHANIDESIA   ERICACEAE

A genus of a single species, confined to a small area in N.W. Anatolia and bordering parts of Russia. It is very closely allied to *Epigaea* and should perhaps be united with it. It has been stated that the anthers in *Orphanidesia* open by apical pores; in fact they dehisce by longitudinal slits, exactly as in *Epigaea repens*. In his note accompanying the plate in the *Botanical Magazine* the late Dr Turrill wrote: 'The shape of the corolla seems to give the best gross morphological difference between the two genera, if they be retained as such. In *Orphanidesia* the corolla is widely shallow-campanulate in its upper expanded portion; in *Epigaea* it is more or less urn-shaped (urceolate) or salver-shaped (hypocraterimorph). Whether the two genera should best be kept distinct or be united must be left for a decision of a monographer of the family.'

O. GAULTHERIOIDES Boiss. & Bal.

Epigaea gaultherioides (Boiss. & Bal.) Takhtadjan

A prostrate evergreen shrub, forming mats in the wild several feet across and 6 to 9 in. deep; stems, leaves (especially the margins and upper surface), petioles, inflorescence rachis, and bracts all bristly. The leaves are mostly oval or elliptic-oblong, acute to slightly obtuse at the apex, rounded to cuneate at the base, 3¼ to 4¾ in. long, dark green above, paler beneath, rather conspicuously net-veined on both sides; petiole about ½ in. long. Inflorescence a short, slightly zigzagged spike, bearing one to three sessile flowers; bracts narrow-lanceolate;

bracteoles two. Sepals five, appressed to the corolla, lanceolate-elliptic. Corolla pale pink, bowl-shaped but narrowed abruptly at the base into a short tube, five-lobed, slightly frilled, 1½ to 1¾ in. wide at the mouth, hairy inside towards the base. Stamens ten, filaments hairy at the base. Flowering time April. Ovary oblong, glabrous; style slender, glabrous, about ½ in. long. Capsules oblong, about ⅜ in. long, shortly stalked, containing numerous brown seeds. *Bot. Mag.*, n.s., t. 14.

ORPHANIDESIA GAULTHERIOIDES

O. gaultherioides occurs wild in a very small area in the mountains of N.E. Anatolia, near the Russian border, beyond which it extends for a short distance. It was discovered by Balansa, in fruit, in July 1866, and described nine years later. The enterprising Dr Dieck of Zoschen offered it in his catalogues for 1891 and 1892, but it was probably not introduced to Britain until 1934. In August of that year, the plant-collector E. K. Balls, accompanied by Dr W. Balfour Gourlay, found it again near the type-locality, growing at 3,000 to 4,000 ft on a torrent that flows into the Black Sea just west of Rize. Here it was associated with *Rhododendron ponticum* and *Vaccinium arctostaphylos*. The species has also been found farther inland near Artvin, growing with *Rhododendron ungernii* and *R. smirnowii*.

Seeds received from Dr Balfour Gourlay germinated in Dr Fred Stoker's garden in 1937, and he gave the first full illustrated account of the species three years later, in *Journ. R.H.S.*, Vol. 65, pp. 210–11 and figs. 55–6. One of his plants provided the material for the plate in the *Botanical Magazine*, cited above.

O. gaultherioides needs a moist, peaty soil and a shady position, but in some gardens it has proved shy-flowering and not altogether hardy. It received an Award of Merit on March 3, 1953, when shown from the R.H.S. Garden at Wisley. This was a potted plant from the Alpine House, but it is also grown there successfully in the open ground. Being so scarce in commerce, it is best grown under glass until a stock has been raised. Seed is the best means of increase, but it has been found at Wisley that the capsules are usually eaten by slugs before they can be harvested. It can also be propagated by layers.

OSMANTHUS*   OLEACEAE

A small group of evergreen shrubs and small or medium-sized trees. Two species (perhaps reducible to one) inhabit the southern USA, the rest are from Asia and the Pacific region. The cultivated species are from China and Japan, but one, *O. decora*, is from western Asia. They are closely akin to the olive (*Olea*), and have opposite leaves. Flowers white or yellowish, sometimes unisexual, in small axillary or terminal clusters. Calyx and corolla four-lobed; stamens two. Fruit an oval drupe, usually dark blue or violet. In *O. americanus* and the other American species, not treated here, the inflorescence is paniculate.

These shrubs are handsome evergreens with a holly-like appearance. They are sometimes propagated by grafting on privet—an undesirable method, for they are healthier and better on their own roots. Cuttings taken about the end of July strike readily if given a little bottom heat. They grow well in any good garden soil, and have no objection to chalk.

O. ARMATUS Diels

An evergreen shrub or small tree 8 to 15 ft high; young shoots stiff, at first clothed with minute down, turning greyish white by autumn, slightly warted. Leaves very leathery, oblong-lanceolate, 3 to 6 in. or even more long on young specimens, ¾ to 1½ in. wide, abruptly narrowed to the rounded or slightly heart-shaped base, taper-pointed, coarsely toothed, with up to about ten teeth per side, the teeth triangular, ⅛ to ⅓ in. long, and with spiny points, or entire, dark dull green, prominently net-veined and quite glabrous, minutely dotted beneath; stalk ⅛ to ¼ in. long, reddish. Flowers produced during autumn in clusters in the leaf-axils, creamy white, ¼ in. in diameter, fragrant; each on a slender glabrous stalk ¼ in. long. Fruits dark violet, egg-shaped, ¾ in. long. *Bot. Mag.*, t. 9232.

Native of W. China; introduced for Messrs Veitch by Wilson in 1902, and strikingly distinct in the length of the leaf from the other hardy species. Although the spine-tipped teeth are a prominent feature of the leaves of young plants, they are often quite absent in adult specimens. According to Wilson, it grows on humus-clad cliffs and boulders, either in dense shade or fully exposed to sunshine.

* Revised by P. S. Green of the Herbarium, Royal Botanic Gardens, Kew.

O. × BURKWOODII (Burkwood & Skipwith) P. S. Green   [PLATE 6
× *Osmarea burkwoodii* Burkwood & Skipwith

This hybrid between *O. delavayi* and *O. decorus* was raised by Messrs Burkwood and Skipwith of Kingston-on-Thames. It is an evergreen with downy young shoots and shortly stalked, oval to ovate leaves 1 to 2 in. long, slightly toothed, glabrous, leathery, dark, rather glossy green. Flowers white, fragrant, borne in terminal and axillary clusters of six or seven, opening in April. Tube of corolla about $\frac{3}{16}$ in. long, with lobes nearly as long as the tube.

Until one of the parent species, *O. decorus*, was recently transferred from the genus *Phillyrea* to *Osmanthus*, this plant was treated as a bigeneric hybrid with the generic name *Osmarea*.

O. × *burkwoodii* is very hardy, rather slow in growth, but dense and bushy, and as such is a useful and attractive evergreen and hedge-plant.

O. DECORUS (Boiss. & Balansa) Kasapligil
Phillyrea decora Boiss. & Balansa; *P. vilmoriniana* Boiss.; *P. laurifolia* Hort.

A rigidly branched shrub 5 to 10 ft high, more in diameter; young shoots slightly warted, but not downy. Leaves pointed, narrowly oval or oblong, 2 to 5 in. long, $\frac{1}{2}$ to $1\frac{3}{4}$ in. wide, tapering at the base, of firm, almost hard texture, very dark, glossy green above, paler below. They are (usually) quite entire, or there are a few scattered teeth on the margins of leaves of vigorous shoots; stalk $\frac{1}{3}$ in. or less long. Flowers about $\frac{1}{3}$ in. across, pure white, crowded in dense, axillary clusters, produced during April. Fruits oval, $\frac{1}{2}$ in. long, borne on slender stalks $\frac{1}{2}$ in. long, ripe in September, first reddish, then blackish purple. *Bot. Mag.*, t. 6800.

Native of Lazistan, near the south-eastern coast of the Black Sea; discovered in 1866 by Balansa, and introduced to France by seeds the same year. The first record of its flowering in this country is in the nursery at Knap Hill, in April, 1883. Owing to its being grafted on privet (an evil practice) in the early days of its cultivation, many of the plants were short-lived, and the reputation of the plant suffered. Raised from seeds or cuttings, it is quite satisfactory. It is very hardy. There is some variation in the foliage, one form being much narrower in leaf.

O. DELAVAYI Franch.
Siphonosmanthus delavayi (Franch.) Stapf

An evergreen shrub reaching 6 to 20 ft in height; branches spreading, stiff, downy when young. They are densely clothed with stiff leathery leaves that are dark glossy green above, dotted with tiny dark spots beneath, ovate or oval, tapered about equally at both ends, toothed, $\frac{1}{2}$ to 1 in. long, half as wide, shortly stalked. Flowers fragrant, pure white, in terminal and axillary clusters of four to eight; corolla with a cylindrical tube $\frac{1}{2}$ in. long, spreading at the mouth into four reflexed oblong lobes, and about $\frac{1}{2}$ in. across. Fruits roundish egg-shaped, blue-black. *Bot. Mag.*, t. 8459.

Native of Yunnan and Szechwan, China. It was introduced by seeds sent to Maurice de Vilmorin by the Abbé Delavay in 1890. These were distributed to several gardens, but only one germinated, at the School of Arboriculture of the City of Paris (*Frut. Vilm.*, p. 185). By grafting on privet and phillyrea a commercial stock was soon built up and the species appeared in several French nursery catalogues in 1911. Three years later it received an Award of Merit when shown by Vicary Gibbs from Aldenham. It was later reintroduced to Britain by Forrest.

OSMANTHUS DELAVAYI

This charming shrub is very distinct from the well known *O. heterophyllus* in having terminal as well as axillary flower clusters that open in April; in the long tubed corolla; and in the small leaves. It has proved itself to be one of the most beautiful of white flowered evergreens. In most parts of the country, one sees it every April almost hidden by its wealth of scented blossoms.

South of London *O. delavayi* will attain a height of about 10 ft, and more than that in width. In some Cornish gardens it is slightly over 20 ft high. Fertile fruits have been borne in several gardens and self-sown seedlings occur at Werrington Park in Cornwall.

O. × FORTUNEI Carr.

Olea japonica Sieb., *nom. nud.*; *Osmanthus aquifolium* var. *ilicifolius latifolius* Hort.;
O. ilicifolius var. *latifolius* Hort.

An evergreen shrub of rounded, bushy habit, rarely more than 6 ft high in inland counties, but 15 to 20 ft high in Cornwall, the whole plant devoid of down. Leaves leathery, 2½ to 4 in. long, 1½ to 3 in. wide, oval or slightly ovate, broadly wedge-shaped at the base, taper-pointed and spine-tipped, the margins armed like one of the large broad leaved forms of common holly with up to ten or twelve triangular, spine-tipped teeth on each side, ⅛ in. long. Some of the leaves, however, especially those at the base of the twig, are not toothed at all. Flowers about ⅓ in. across, white and delightfully fragrant, produced in clusters in the leaf-axils during autumn.

A hybrid of Japanese origin between *O. heterophyllus* and *O. fragrans*; introduced by Fortune in 1862. It is apparently known in this country only in the male state. It is quite hardy at Kew, and has only once been seriously injured in my recollection, which was in the great frosts of February 1895, when the temperature fell to nearly zero on three successive nights. It does not flower profusely except in such places as Cornwall. It is easily distinguished from *O. heterophyllus* by its larger, broader leaves, with more numerous teeth on either margin. For the history of this shrub and the elucidation of its confused naming, see *Kew Bulletin*, 1911, p. 177.

This hybrid has been re-made in California and the offspring is known under the name 'SAN JOSÉ'.

O. FRAGRANS Lour. *Olea fragrans* Thunb.—This species, mentioned above as a parent of *O.* × *fortunei*, is too tender for general cultivation outdoors. It has large, broad, entire, or finely toothed leaves, and white flowers so strongly fragrant that one or two of them, tiny though they are, will fill a fair-sized conservatory with sweet perfume. The Chinese use them for perfuming tea. In *Bot. Mag.*, t. 9211, is figured f. AURANTIACUS (Mak.) P. S. Green, which has pale to deep orange-coloured flowers.

O. HETEROPHYLLUS (G. Don) P. S. Green

Ilex heterophyllus G. Don; *Osmanthus aquifolium* Sieb.; *O. ilicifolius* (Hassk.) Carr.; *Olea ilicifolia* Hassk.

An evergreen shrub of rounded, dense, bushy habit, 10 ft or more high near London, twice as high in milder localities; young shoots minutely downy. Leaves oval, 1½ to 2½ in. long, 1 to 1½ in. wide, with two to four large spine-tipped teeth down each side, the largest teeth ½ in. long, triangular. In the adult stage the leaves on the top of the plant become oval or ovate, and quite entire at the margins, like a myrtle. The upper surface is of a dark, very glossy green, the lower one paler, both quite glabrous; stalk ¼ to ½ in. long. Flowers white, fragrant, ¼ in. across but with reflexed petals, borne during September and October, four or five together on short stalks, in axillary clusters. Fruits oblong, ⅝ in. long, ⅜ in. wide, blue, not often seen in this country.

Native of Japan, where it is described by Sargent as attaining the dimensions

OSMANTHUS HETEROPHYLLUS

of a tree sometimes 30 ft high, with a trunk 1 ft or more in diameter; also of Formosa. It was introduced by Thomas Lobb in 1856. In foliage it is one of the handsomest of evergreens. Its leaves are very like those of the holly, and the shrub is often mistaken for one, but it can, of course, even without flower or fruit, be at once distinguished by its opposite leaves. It has been used with success as a hedge plant. It has a number of varieties, of which the following are the most important:

cv. 'ARGENTEOMARGINATUS'.—See 'Variegatus'.

cv. 'AUREOMARGINATUS' ('Aureus').—Leaves margined with yellow.

cv. 'LATIFOLIUS VARIEGATUS'.—Leaves rather broader than in 'Variegatus'.

cv. 'MYRTIFOLIUS'.—As stated above, when O. *heterophyllus* gets to the adult stage the upper part of the shrub bears quite entire leaves, 1 to 2 in. long, narrow oval, and unarmed except for the sometimes spine-tipped apex. A similar transformation in the shape of the uppermost leaves is seen in the holly. Cuttings of these uppermost branches take root easily, and as they do not revert to the spiny-leaved type, they are known as the "myrtle-leaved osmanthus". On its own roots this state of O. *heterophyllus* is dwarfer and more spreading than the type with toothed leaves.

cv. 'PURPUREUS'.—In this variety, which was raised at Kew in 1880, the young leaves are of a black-purple shade; they and the very young shoots, in their black glossiness, have much the aspect of having been dipped in tar. It is the hardiest of all the forms of this osmanthus. The frosts of February 1895 left it quite unaffected, whilst all the others here mentioned were more or less seriously injured at Kew.

cv. 'Rotundifolius'.—A dwarf, very slow-growing shrub, with rigid, leathery leaves, 1 to 1½ in. long, half to two-thirds as wide, more or less obovate, with a marginal vein, wavy at the margins.

cv. 'Variegatus' ('Argenteomarginatus').—Leaves margined with creamy white.

O. serrulatus Rehd.

An evergreen shrub 6 to 12 ft high; young shoots minutely downy. Leaves oval-lanceolate to oblong or narrowly obovate, slender-pointed, wedge-shaped at the base, sharply toothed with up to thirty to thirty-five teeth per side or entire, 2½ to 4½ in. long, ⅝ to 1½ in. wide, of leathery texture, dark shining green above, paler and dotted beneath; stalk about ¼ in. long. Flowers fragrant, produced in spring from four to nine in a cluster from the leaf-axils; corolla white, deeply four-lobed, ½ in. wide; flower-stalk ⅓ to ½ in. long, slender. Fruits ⅜ in. long, oblong, blue-black.

Native of W. China; discovered by Wilson in 1904, introduced to the Arnold Arboretum in 1910 and to Kew in 1912. It is hardy at Kew and has grown into a dwarf stiff bush 4 ft high, but gives the impression that it would prefer a warmer locality.

O. suavis C.B. Cl.

Siphonosmanthus suavis (C.B.Cl.) Stapf

An evergreen shrub up to 12 ft high, sometimes a small tree; young shoots greyish, minutely downy. Leaves lance-shaped inclined to oblong, wedge-shaped at the base, more or less slender-pointed, sharply toothed to almost entire, 1½ to 3½ in. long, ½ to 1¼ in. wide, dark glossy green above, paler and minutely dotted beneath; stalk ⅛ to ¼ in. long. Flowers white, fragrant, produced in axillary clusters of up to as many as eight; corolla ¼ to ⅜ in. wide, with four roundish-ovate, spreading lobes and a tube ¼ in. long; calyx bell-shaped, four-lobed, the lobes edged with minute hairs; flower-stalk ⅛ to ¼ in. long, minutely downy. Fruits roundish egg-shaped, ⅖ in. long, bluish black. *Bot. Mag.*, t. 9176.

Native of the Himalaya from Sikkim to Assam and thence eastward to south-westernmost Yunnan, China; discovered by Griffith in 1838, but little known until Forrest sent seeds from Yunnan.

O. suavis is hardy south of London in a sheltered position but is more effective in the milder parts of the country. The flowering branch figured in the *Botanical Magazine* came from Headfort in Eire, where the species flowers in midwinter, though spring is the normal time.

An examination of a full range of specimens of this species and *O. delavayi* shows that in all characters the two converge, but the plants in cultivation are quite distinct.

O. YUNNANENSIS (Franch.) P. S. Green

Pittosporum yunnanense Franch.; *O. forrestii* Rehd.

An evergreen shrub to 30 ft or more high, with a spreading crown; young shoots yellowish grey. Leaves of firm hardish texture, dull green, ovate-lanceolate to oblong, wedge-shaped to rounded or heart-shaped at the base, 3 to 8 in. long, 1 to 2¼ in. wide, mostly slender-pointed, sometimes quite entire, sometimes conspicuously spiny-toothed, with up to thirty teeth per side, the teeth ⅛ in. long, glabrous, prominently net-veined and sprinkled thickly with minute black dots on both surfaces; stalk ⅛ to ⅜ in. long. Flowers creamy white to pale yellow, sweetly fragrant, produced numerously in clusters from the leaf-axils in spring, each flower on a slender stalk ⅜ in. long; corolla ⅜ in. wide, deeply four-lobed; lobes oblong; anthers yellow, attached near the base. Fruits egg-shaped, ½ to ⅝ in. long, 'deep blue-purple with a heavy waxy bloom much resembling the ripe fruits of *Prinsepia utilis*' (Forrest).

Native of N.W. Yunnan, China; introduced by Forrest in 1923. It occurs at altitudes of 6,000 to 11,000 ft and has proved hardy in a sheltered corner at Kew, but it needs the conditions of the southern and south-western counties to develop its best qualities. It is 20 ft high in the Royal Horticultural Society's Garden at Wisley and 30 ft at Exbury on the Solent. At Wayford Manor, Som., there is a specimen 20 ft high and 25 ft in spread. In Cornwall it has attained a height of 39 ft at Caerhays.

× OSMAREA *see* OSMANTHUS

OSMARONIA   ROSACEAE

A genus of one species in western N. America, allied to *Prunus* but differing in having up to five free pistils in each flower (one in *Prunus*). The name *Nuttallia*, by which this genus was long known, is invalid, having been used for other genera before it was applied to the present species. The name *Osmaronia*, which has supplanted it, is itself invalid, since (as discovered quite recently) there is an earlier name for this genus—*Oemleria*. But, to avoid further confusion, the name *Osmaronia* has been proposed for conservation.

O. CERASIFORMIS (Torr. & Gr.) Greene   OSO BERRY
Nuttallia cerasiformis Torr. & Gr.

A deciduous shrub, usually 6 to 8 ft (occasionally more) high, with the habit of a black currant, the stems springing erect from the ground in great numbers, and forming ultimately a dense thicket several feet through; branchlets glabrous, bright green. Leaves alternate, narrow-oblong or lance-shaped, 2 to 3½ in. long, ¾ to 1¼ in. wide, of thin texture, green and quite glabrous above, greyish beneath; margin entire; narrowed at the base to a stalk ¼ in. or less long. Male and female flowers usually on different plants; both borne on stiff, pendent, copiously bracted racemes 1½ to 2 in. long. Each flower is about ¼ in. across, the five petals

OSMARONIA CERASIFORMIS (in fruit)

white; the calyx green, bell-shaped, five-lobed. Male flowers have fifteen stamens; females five carpels. Fruits plum-like, oval, ¾ in. long, purple when ripe, usually not more than two of the carpels of each flower developing. *Bot. Mag.*, n.s., t. 582.

Native of California; introduced in 1848. In gardens the Oso berry is useful for its early, almond-scented blossoms, which are usually fully open by the third week in March, being produced from the leafless shoots of the previous year. The female plant is of coarser habit than the male and not so pretty nor so free in blossom, but it is worth associating with the male for the sake of its abundant fruits. The species is very hardy and thrives in a well-drained, loamy soil. It is easily propagated by taking off small pieces from old plants, also by seeds. The fruits are very bitter and strongly almond-scented.

OSTEOMELES ROSACEAE

A small genus of trees and shrubs ranging from E. Asia to Polynesia. Two species are in cultivation, both evergreen shrubs of very distinct appearance, with unequally pinnate leaves, white flowers, and haw-like fruits containing five seeds. From other genera of the pomaceous group of Rosaceae with pinnate leaves, they are distinguished by the entire-margined, bristle-tipped leaflets of small size.

O. SCHWERINIAE Schneid.

O. anthyllidifolia of some authors, in part, not Lindl.

An evergreen shrub growing probably 6 to 8 ft high in the open, considerably more against a wall; the long, slender, flexible branchlets covered with short grey hairs. Leaves pinnate, 2 to 4 in. long, composed of eight and a half to fifteen and a half pairs of leaflets, covered, more especially beneath, with grey down; main-stalk hairy, channelled above. Leaflets oblong-oval or obovate, with a short abrupt point, stalkless, ¼ to ⅝ in. long, about one-third as wide. Flowers white, ½ to ⅔ in. wide, produced in June in branching corymbs 1½ to 3 in. across, terminating lateral twigs; calyx-lobes ovate-lanceolate, hairy outside, glabrous within. Fruits egg-shaped, ¼ to ⅜ in. long, at first dark red, blue-black when ripe, glabrous, crowned by the persistent calyx; five-seeded. *Bot. Mag.*, t. 7354.

Native of Yunnan and other parts of W. China, originally raised in the Jardin des Plantes at Paris from seed which had been sent from Yunnan by the Abbé Delavay in 1888; introduced to Kew in 1892. Forms nearly allied to this Chinese plant occur through the south-east Pacific region as far as the Sandwich Islands. The whole were at first included under O. ANTHYLLIDIFOLIA Lindl., but the west Chinese plant has been separated on the strength of its glabrous fruit, less hairy calyx-lobes, and usually but not always narrower leaves, thus leaving Lindley's name for the tropical and subtropical woolly-fruited plants. They are extremely closely allied, but perhaps the latter could not be grown out-of-doors with us.

O. schweriniae is a shrub of distinct appearance, its foliage very suggestive of some of the Leguminosae; it is also very elegant in habit and attractive in blossom. But we do not find it hardy in the open, although it survives mild winters. It makes a very delightful wall plant. It can be increased by cuttings made of moderately ripened wood placed in gentle heat. Seed only ripens in favourable years.

var. MICROPHYLLA Rehd. & Wils.—This variety is distinguished from the type by its smaller, less downy leaves, glabrous calyx, and denser habit. Introduced by Wilson from W. China in 1908, under W.1016. Many of the plants cultivated in Britain belong to this variety, which is linked to the type by intermediates and perhaps hardly worth distinguishing.

O. *schweriniae* is a characteristic member of the vegetation of the hot, dry, river valleys of W. China and needs a very sunny position in well-drained soil. The Wilson introduction (var. *microphylla*) is hardy in such a position, even without the protection of a wall.

O. SUBROTUNDA K. Koch

O. anthyllidifolia f. *subrotunda* (K. Koch) Koidz.

A dwarf, slow-growing, evergreen shrub, the tortuous branches covered with silky down when young. Leaves pinnate, ¾ to 1½ in. long, composed of four and a half to eight and a half pairs of leaflets, the main-stalk hairy and grooved above. Leaflets obovate or oblong, ⅛ to ¼ in. long, stalkless, the apex broad and rounded; lower surface silky-hairy, the upper one less hairy and shining. Flowers white, ½ in. across, borne in axillary leafy corymbs.

Native of the Bonin Islands and the Ryukyus; first introduced to the Jardin des Plantes at Paris from Japan, thence to Kew in 1894. Botanically this species is, no doubt, closely allied to *O. anthyllidifolia* (see preceding species), but its stunted branches, slow growth, and obovate smaller leaflets amply distinguish it. Increased by cuttings. Not very hardy in the open.

Although the true *O. subrotunda* is still in cultivation, it is possible that some of the plants grown under this name are really *O. schweriniae* var. *microphylla*. That, at any rate, is the identity of a plant received by Kew in the 1930s under the name *O. subrotunda*.

OSTRYA   HOP HORNBEAM   CARPINACEAE

A genus of about ten closely related species, natives of the northern hemisphere, including Central America as far south as Guatemala and Costa Rica. They are medium-sized trees, with deciduous, alternate, parallel-nerved leaves, quite closely related to the hornbeams (*Carpinus*), and in the foliage especially similar. The chief botanical differences are in the female flowers and fruits. In both genera the female flowers are borne on slender catkins, and in pairs at the base of deciduous scales. In *Ostrya*, however, each flower is set in a bag-like husk (involucre), which at first is open at the top, but closes up after fertilisation takes place. The husk afterwards grows very considerably, and is the pale, membranous, ovate, flattish, bladder-like organ which, congregated and overlapping in hop-like clusters, and completely enclosing the nutlet, gives the trees of this genus their popular name. In *Carpinus* this involucre remains open and does not enclose the nutlet.

The four ostryas described here should be raised from seed; they thrive in any soil of good or moderate quality, all being perfectly hardy.

O. CARPINIFOLIA Scop.   HOP HORNBEAM
O. vulgaris Willd.; *Carpinus ostrya* L., in part

A tree 50 to 60 ft high, with a short, stout trunk covered with greyish, ultimately rough, bark, and a rounded head of branches; young shoots covered with short hairs (not gland-tipped). Leaves ovate, sometimes inclining to oval, rounded at the base, pointed and tapered at the apex, $2\frac{1}{2}$ to 4 in. long, half as wide, prettily double-toothed, dark green and glossy above, with appressed hairs mostly between the ribs, paler beneath and sparsely hairy, chiefly on the midrib and veins, and in the axils of the latter; veins in twelve to fifteen pairs; stalk about $\frac{1}{4}$ in. long, hairy. Male catkins nodding, $1\frac{1}{2}$ to 3 in. long, $\frac{1}{4}$ in. wide, scales finely and abruptly pointed. Fruit cluster $1\frac{1}{2}$ to 2 in. long; the nutlets (commonly called 'seeds') $\frac{1}{8}$ in. long, stalkless, enclosed at the base of an ovate, hairy, flat, bladder-like husk, $\frac{1}{2}$ in. long.

Native of S. Europe with a western limit in S.E. France; and of Asia Minor and the Caucasus; introduced early in the 18th century. This tree has very much the aspect of *O. virginiana* but is distinguished by never having any glands on the hairs of the twigs. It is pretty and rather striking when furnished with the pendent hop-like fruit clusters in autumn. The timber has the same bony texture and hardness as hornbeam.

The following specimens have been recorded: Kew, *pl.* 1878, 36 × $3\frac{1}{2}$ ft and another, *pl.* 1911, 47 × 3 ft (1968); Syon House, London, 54 × 4 ft (1968); Albury Park, Surrey, 42 × 4 ft (1968); Bulstrode Park, Bucks, 43 × 10 ft, grafted on hornbeam at 3 ft (1967); University Botanic Garden, Cambridge, 48 × 5 ft (1969); Killerton, Devon, 63 × 5 ft, with other stems of smaller girth (1970); Edinburgh Botanic Garden, 54 × $4\frac{3}{4}$ ft (1967).

O. JAPONICA Sarg.

A tree occasionally 80 ft high in nature, trunk 18 in. in diameter; winter-buds ovoid, shining; young shoots clothed with soft pale hairs, which persist through the winter. Leaves ovate or ovate-oblong, 3 to 5 in. long, $1\frac{1}{2}$ to 2 in. wide, rounded or slightly heart-shaped at the base, tapered at the apex to a long slender point, coarsely, sharply, and irregularly toothed; dark green and hairy above, paler, more downy and velvety to the touch beneath. Fruit clusters $1\frac{1}{2}$ to $1\frac{3}{4}$ in. long, $\frac{3}{4}$ in. wide.

Native of Japan, where it is said to be somewhat uncommon, and of China and Korea; introduced to Kew by Prof. Sargent in 1897. It is easily distinguished from the European and American species by the veins each side the midrib (nine to twelve) being fewer and farther apart, and by the more uniformly downy, softer, more velvety surfaces of the leaves.

The tree now at Kew was planted in 1947 and measures 37 × 2 ft (1967).

O. KNOWLTONII Cov.

A small deciduous tree 12 to 30 ft high; young shoots downy, greenish brown, becoming grey at two years old; buds cylindrical, very downy. Leaves ovate to oval, toothed, tapered, rounded or slightly heart-shaped at the base, pointed or bluntish at the apex, 1 to 2½ in. long, ¾ to 1¼ in. wide, downy on both surfaces; veins in five to eight pairs; stalk ⅛ to ¼ in. long. Male catkins 1 to 1¼ in. long, with downy stalks and scales. Fruit clusters 1 to 1¼ in. long, ¾ in. wide; the membranous husks or involucres that enclose the nutlets ½ to ¾ in. long, oval. Nutlets ¼ in. long, hairy towards the apex.

Native of Arizona and Utah; discovered by F. H. Knowlton in 1889 on the southern slope of the Grand Canyon of the Colorado river; introduced to cultivation in N. America in 1914. It differs from the hop hornbeam of the eastern United States (*O. virginiana*) by its much smaller size, its more abruptly pointed or round-ended leaves with about half as many pairs of veins.

O. VIRGINIANA (Mill.) K. Koch   IRONWOOD

Carpinus virginiana Mill.; *Carpinus ostrya* L., in part; *O. virginica* Willd.

A round-headed tree 30 to 50 ft high, similar in habit to *O. carpinifolia*; young shoots furnished with gland-tipped hairs. Leaves 2 to 4½ in. long, 1 to 2 in. wide, oval-lanceolate, rounded or sometimes slightly heart-shaped at the base, taper-pointed, sharply toothed (not so markedly double-toothed as in *O. carpinifolia*); dark green and hairy on the midrib and between the veins above, paler and more downy beneath; stalk ¼ in. long, glandular downy. Male catkins 2 in. long. Fruit clusters 1½ to 2½ in. long, ⅔ to 1½ in. wide. Nutlet ⅓ in. long, the pale bladder-like membranous bag enclosing it being ovate, ¾ to 1 in. long, hairy at the base.

Native of eastern N. America; introduced by Compton, Bishop of London, in 1692. Cultivated specimens differ from the closely allied *O. carpinifolia* in the glandular hairs on the twigs and leaf-stalks, in the usually fewer ribs of the leaf, and in the larger nut. The timber, as the common name denotes, is very hard and durable, and is used for mallets, handles of tools, etc. Although not very common in English gardens, this interesting tree thrives well.

The following specimens have been recorded: Kew, Pagoda Vista, 45 × 3¾ ft (1963), by the Main Gate, 40 × 3½ ft (1965); University Botanic Garden, Cambridge, 40 × 2 ft (1969); Westonbirt, Glos., 47 × 3¾ ft (1965); Edinburgh Botanic Garden, 36 × 2½ ft (1967); East Bergholt Place, Suffolk, 33 × 4 ft (1972).

OSTRYOPSIS   CARPINACEAE

A genus of two species of deciduous shrubs, natives of China. Involucre of fruit leafy, tubular, not membranous and bladder-like as in *Ostrya*, to which it is allied. The second species, *O. nobilis* Balf. f. & W. W. Sm., was discovered by Forrest in Yunnan in 1913 but is probably not in cultivation.

O. DAVIDIANA (Baill.) Decne.
Corylus davidiana Baill.

A deciduous shrub of bushy, rounded habit, 5 to 10 ft high, suckering from the base like a hazel; young shoots downy. Leaves alternate, broadly ovate, heart-shaped at the base, short-pointed, 1 to 3 in. long, ¾ to 2 in. wide, sharply, irregularly, and often doubly toothed, upper surface dull green with scattered hairs, lower surface much more downy; stalk ¼ in. or less long. Flowers unisexual, both sexes on the same bush. Male catkins ½ to ¾ in. long, slender, nodding, produced from the joints of the old wood. Female inflorescence terminal on the new shoot of the year, erect, very short. Fruit a conical nut enclosed in an outer covering or husk (involucre), which is also narrowly conical, ½ to ¾ in. long, downy, terminating in three slender points. At first this husk completely encloses the nut, but finally liberates it by splitting down one side. The fruits are crowded eight to twelve together in a cluster at the end of the twig.

Native of N. China and Mongolia; discovered by the Abbé David, after whom it is named. It was introduced from the mountains near Peking to Kew, in 1883, by Dr Bretschneider. It is an interesting little shrub, with the habit and foliage of a hazel, to which it is closely akin, but differs much in the shape of the nut. It has no particularly ornamental qualities to recommend it, but is interesting and quite hardy.

OVIDIA THYMELAEACEAE

Ovidia is a genus of some four species closely akin to *Daphne*, both having four-parted flowers with eight stamens and very supple young shoots. *Daphne* differs from *Ovidia* in its cylindrical perianth and in its style being very short or even absent. Neither of the species described here has any value as a garden plant.

In naming the genus after the poet Ovid, Meissner had in mind the famous passage in which he describes the metamorphosis of Daphne into a laurel.

O. ANDINA (Poepp. & Endl.) Meissn.
Daphne andina Poepp. & Endl.

A deciduous shrub, often of spare habit, up to 7 ft high; shoots downy when quite young. Leaves oblanceolate to narrowly elliptical or oval, bluntish or rounded at the apex, tapered to a stalkless base, 1 to 5 in. long, ½ to 1 in. wide, dull grey green and glabrous above, glaucous and furnished with appressed hairs beneath. Flowers produced in July along with and terminating the young shoots, crowded thirty or more together on a solitary umbel which is 1 to 1½ in. wide, and has a stout, downy main-stalk ¾ to 1 in. long. Each flower is about ¼ in. wide, white to creamy white with red anthers, the calyx (perianth) funnel-shaped, downy, dividing at the mouth into four oval or obovate lobes. Fruits pure white, egg-shaped, ¼ in. long, with the stigma persisting at the end. Individual flower-stalks very slender, ¼ to ½ in. long.

Native of Chile up to 5,000 ft altitude; introduced by H. F. Comber during his Andean expedition, 1925–7; it has also been collected by Clarence Elliott, who found it in flower in January 1928. It is a dioecious shrub. The female flowers are smaller than the males and shorter-stalked. Comber observes that he found it in semi-shady situations where the soil was moist and varying from peaty to loamy in character.

O. PILLOPILLO (C. Gay) Meissn. *Daphne pillopillo* C. Gay—This species was also introduced by Comber from Chile in 1927. It is closely related to *O. andina*, but is described as 10 to 30 ft high. It can be distinguished from that species by the glabrousness of its leaves, which are stalkless, oblanceolate, 1 to 3 in. long, ¼ to ½ in. wide, dull, pale, rather glaucous green. Judging by wild specimens the young shoots are mostly very downy. Flowers white, very downy outside, ½ in. wide; fruit reddish and purple when ripe. "Pillo-pillo" is the Indian name for this shrub.

OXYCOCCUS   CRANBERRIES   ERICACEAE

Only three species of *Oxycoccus* are known, which, although closely allied to *Vaccinium*, are very distinct in their long, slender, wiry, creeping stems, clothed with alternate leaves, and still more in the corolla, the four parts of which are so deeply divided that they become practically separate petals.

The cranberries like a moist or semi-boggy, peaty soil, and can be increased by seed or by layers. They have little garden value, although a broad patch of either kind forming a dense mass of interlacing stems is interesting and unusual. The berries are used for making tarts and in confections of various kinds.

O. MACROCARPUS (Ait.) Pursh   AMERICAN CRANBERRY
Vaccinium macrocarpon Ait.

A creeping evergreen shrub of prostrate habit, with long, thin, wiry stems. Leaves oval or oblong, ⅓ to ⅔ in. long, ⅛ to ⅙ in. wide, rounded at both ends, entire, very short-stalked, pale or bluish white beneath, usually recurved at the margins. Flowers produced during the summer in a raceme about 1 in. long, beyond which the leaf-bearing shoot continues to grow; each flower is borne on a curving, slightly downy stalk, but is itself drooping. Petals pink, $\frac{1}{4}$ in. long, rolled back so as fully to reveal the eight stamens, which stand up in a close cluster. Calyx with shallow, triangular lobes. Berry red, acid, $\frac{1}{2}$ to $\frac{3}{4}$ in. diameter, globose. *Bot. Mag.*, t. 2586.

Native of eastern N. America from Newfoundland to N. Carolina, generally inhabiting boggy ground. It has much the same general appearance as our native cranberry, but differs in its larger, rounder-tipped leaves and larger berries, in having a leafy shoot above the raceme, and in the stalk of the stamens being shorter in comparison with the anthers. This shrub is now being largely cultivated in the United States for its fruit. Hundreds of acres have been specially adapted for it by means of a water-supply which admits of the land being flooded at will. On well-prepared ground a crop of 500 bushels per acre has been gathered in a single season.

O. PALUSTRIS Pers.   SMALL CRANBERRY
Vaccinium oxycoccos L.; *O. quadripetala* Gilib.

A prostrate, evergreen shrub with long, thin, wiry stems. Leaves ovate, $\frac{1}{4}$ to $\frac{3}{8}$ in. long, pointed, dark green above, very glaucous beneath. Flowers nodding, produced during summer in a terminal cluster of up to four, each flower on a slender downy stalk, $\frac{3}{4}$ to 1 in. long. Petals rosy pink, bent backwards, $\frac{1}{4}$ in. long. Berries red, globose, $\frac{1}{3}$ in. across.

Native of N. and Central Europe, N. Asia, and N. America; widely spread in the British Isles, but most abundant in the north of England and the south of Scotland. At one time the gathering of cranberries was a considerable industry for women and children of that part of Great Britain, and in some of the markets of the northern towns (at Longtown in Cumberland, near the Solway Firth, for instance), £30 worth of cranberries would be sold in a day. But the draining and enclosing of boggy land induced by the high prices for corn during and after the Napoleonic wars destroyed many extensive and favourite haunts of the cranberry, and the plant is much less abundant than in former times. The berries are perhaps the most pleasantly flavoured of wild fruits.

O. MICROCARPUS Turcz. ex Rupr.
Vaccinium oxycoccos var. *microcarpum* (Turcz.) Ashers & Graebn.—Allied to the preceding, but with smaller, triangular-ovate leaves $\frac{1}{8}$ to $\frac{3}{16}$ in. long, glabrous flower-stalks and the fruits oblong or inversely pear-shaped. The total distribution of this species is not known for certain; it appears to be mainly confined to Siberia and N. Europe (including Scotland), but has been reported from a few localities in the mountains of Central Europe.

OXYDENDRUM ERICACEAE

A genus of a single species in eastern N. America. In its flowers it bears a marked resemblance to *Pieris*, to which it is allied, but in that genus all the species are evergreen and the anthers are awned.

O. ARBOREUM (L.) DC. SORREL TREE
Andromeda arborea L.

A deciduous tree, occasionally 50 to 70 ft high in the wild state, the slender trunk 1 to 1½ ft in diameter. In this country it is occasionally 25 to 30 ft high, but is more often a tree-like shrub under 20 ft high; young shoots quite glabrous. Leaves alternate, oblong-lanceolate, with a long, tapering point, 4 to 8 in. long, 1½ to 3½ in. wide, almost or quite glabrous, midrib sometimes bristly beneath, entire or minutely toothed, thin in texture, dark green, turning red in autumn; leaf-stalk ½ to 1 in. long. Flowers white, ¼ in. long, cylindrical, but narrowing towards the mouth, borne in late summer or autumn in a lax panicle 6 to 10 in. long, composed of several slender racemes from the end of the shoot or the terminal leaf-axils; flower-stalks, calyx, and corolla downy, the two latter five-lobed; stamens ten, enclosed within the corolla. Fruit a dry, woody, five-celled capsule, many-seeded.

Native of eastern N. America; introduced in 1752. Belonging to the heath family, this tree thrives under the same conditions as azaleas and rhododendrons. It is usually propagated by seed obtained from the United States. The leaves have a pleasant acid taste, to which its popular and scientific names refer. A beautiful late-blooming tree, turning scarlet in autumn, provided it is not planted in too dense shade. It thrives well near London as the following measurements show: Osterley Park, London, 40 × 2¾ ft (1965); Royal Horticultural Society Garden, Wisley, Surrey, 42 × 2¾ ft (1964); Leonardslee, Sussex, 49 × 2¾ ft (1962); Borde Hill, Sussex, 48 × 2 ft (1968). There is a fine group in the Winkworth Arboretum, Surrey. In Eire there is an example at Fota, Co. Cork, measuring 42 × 4¼ ft (1966).

OZOTHAMNUS* COMPOSITAE

A genus of about fifty species of evergreen shrubs or weakly woody perennial herbs, confined to the Australasian region. Leaves alternate, often heath-like. Flower-heads resembling those of *Helichrysum*, usually small, often in dense corymbs. Involucral bracts with dry papery appendages, often conspicuously radiating and simulating the ligules of ray-florets, then usually white; usually a few outer florets female, the rest

* Revised by C. Jeffrey of the Herbarium, Royal Botanic Gardens, Kew.

bisexual, all discoid (ray-florets nil); receptacle without scales. Closely related to *Cassinia* (from which it differs by the absence of receptacular scales) and *Helichrysum*, from which no one technical character serves to distinguish it, and in which it is often included as a subgenus.

There is no monographic treatment of the genus, and its taxonomic status is still in need of clarification. The Australian species may be identified by reference to: N. T. Burbidge, 'A Monographic Study of Helichrysum subgenus Ozothamnus', in *Austr. Journ. Bot.*, Vol. 6, pp. 229–84 (1958); and those of New Zealand to: H. H. Allan, *Flora of New Zealand*, Vol. 1, pp. 715–21 (1961).

O. ANTENNARIA (DC.) Hook. f.

Helichrysum antennaria (DC.) F. v. Muell. ex Benth.; *Swammerdamia antennaria* DC.

An evergreen shrub of dense leafy habit up to 10 ft high; young shoots glutinous, angled, they and the undersurface of the leaves not downy but covered with a close grey or tawny scurf. Leaves oblanceolate or obovate, tapered to the base, broad and rounded at the apex, set from $\frac{1}{8}$ to $\frac{1}{4}$ in. apart on the twigs; $\frac{1}{2}$ to $1\frac{1}{4}$ in. long, $\frac{1}{8}$ to $\frac{5}{8}$ in. wide, glabrous and dark green above; leaf-stalk very short. Flowers produced in June and July in dense clusters terminating short axillary shoots; each flower-head consists of twenty or more florets and is $\frac{1}{4}$ in. wide, dullish white, the most conspicuous feature being the pappus, which is really the calyx converted into a ring of silk-like hairs surmounting the ovary. Scales of the involucre and main flower-stalk downy. *Bot. Mag.*, t. 9152.

Native of Tasmania, especially on Mt Wellington and the Western Mountains. This shrub has proved hardier than it was first thought to be. For nearly twenty years a plant grew outside at Kew and remained in perfect health without any shelter other than that given by the wall of the Temperate House, which protected it from north and east winds. It was killed, however, during the severe winter of 1946–7. One collector records that he found it in May on Mt Wellington where the ground was covered with three feet of snow. The foliage when crushed has a slightly acrid although not unpleasant odour.

O. LEDIFOLIUS (DC.) Hook. f.

Helichrysum ledifolium (DC.) Benth. subsp. *ledifolium*

An evergreen densely leafy shrub up to 3 ft high, of rounded habit, densely branched; young stems downy. Leaves oblong-linear, blunt, spreading, leathery with strongly revolute margins, $\frac{1}{4}$ to $\frac{9}{16}$ in. long, $\frac{1}{20}$ to $\frac{1}{12}$ in. wide, glabrous or with a few hairs above, downy and, like the stems, covered by a sweetly aromatic yellowish exudate beneath. Flower-heads in dense terminal corymbs; involucral bracts downy, more or less sticky, pale yellow-brown to yellow or red, the inner ones with white, spreading tips; florets seven to fifteen.

An endemic of Tasmania, where it occurs on mountains above 2,500 ft; introduced in 1929–30 by Harold Comber, who collected the seed at 3,500 to

4,000 ft. It is perhaps the hardiest member of the genus. The yellow colouring of the young shoots and the undersurface of the leaves is suggestive of *Cassinia fulvida*. It derives from an aromatic secretion that renders the plant highly inflammable in the wild—whence the popular name 'kerosene bush'.

O. ERICIFOLIUS Hook. f. *Helichrysum ledifolium* (DC.) Benth. subsp. *ericifolium* (Hook. f.) N. T. Burbidge; *Helichrysum ericeteum* W. M. Curtis—This resembles O. *ledifolius*, but is of more columnar habit, up to 10 ft tall. Leaves smaller, ⅛ to ¼ in. long; exudate yellowish, sweetly aromatic. Flower-heads in dense corymbs terminal on the main and numerous short lateral branches, forming very long floriferous sprays; involucral bracts pale brown, the inner with white spreading tips; florets five or six.

An endemic of Tasmania, in montane heaths on the central plateau. A plant at Wakehurst Place, Sussex, about 4 ft high, is intermediate between this species and O. *ledifolius*, but nearer to the latter. The true species may not be in cultivation; see further below.

O. PURPURASCENS DC. *Helichrysum ledifolium* (DC.) Benth. subsp. *purpurascens* (DC.) N. T. Burbidge; *Helichrysum purpurascens* (DC.) W. M. Curtis; O. *rosmarinifolius* var. *ericifolius* Rodway—Very similar in habit to O. *ericifolius*, from which it differs in the sharply, not sweetly, aromatic smell, the longer (¼ to ¾ in.) leaves, the lack of yellowish colouration of the exudate, the usually purplish-pink involucral bracts, and the more numerous (eight to ten) florets.

An endemic of Tasmania, in dry open places from sea-level to 800 ft. The date of introduction is uncertain, but seeds were sent by Comber in 1929–30 and were distributed as O. *rosmarinifolius* var. *ericifolius*, which may explain why it has been grown erroneously as O. *ericifolius*. It has also been confused with O. *rosmarinifolius*, and the species portrayed in *The Endemic Flora of Tasmania*, Part I, No 20, as *Helichrysum purpurascens*, is not this species but O. *rosmarinifolius*.

O. *purpurascens* is inferior to O. *rosmarinifolius* and O. *thyrsoideus* as an ornamental, and not reliably hardy. The foliage has a harsh, curry-like odour.

O. ROSMARINIFOLIUS (Labill.) DC.

Helichrysum rosmarinifolium (Labill.) Steud. ex Benth.; *Helichrysum purpurascens* Hort., in part, not (DC.) W. M. Curtis; *H. rosmarinifolium* var. *purpurascens* Hort.

An evergreen shrub 3 to 10 ft high, with slender erect branches, more or less woolly when young. Leaves crowded, linear, mucronate, with closely revolute margins, ½ to 1½ in. long, up to $\frac{1}{12}$ in. wide, rough on the upper surface with small projecting points (muricate), woolly beneath. Flower-heads numerous in dense corymbs at the ends of the main and upper lateral branches. Involucral bracts sparsely hairy, light brown with usually a marked crimson-red tinge, especially in bud, the inner with small white radiating tips; florets five to seven.

Native of New South Wales, Victoria, and Tasmania, on wet peaty heaths and along watercourses; seeds were collected by H. Comber during his expedition to Tasmania in 1929–30, but it may have been introduced earlier. Although not reliably hardy, it should survive most winters and has grown for many years in sunny positions at Wakehurst Place in Sussex. Its most striking feature is the rich red colouration of the involucral bracts as the inflorescences begin to expand around midsummer. Award of Merit June 18, 1968, when exhibited by Lord Talbot de Malahide.

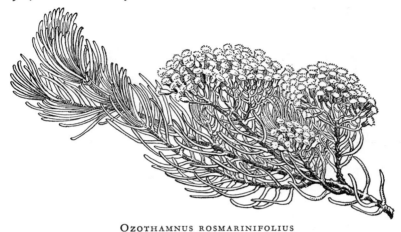

OZOTHAMNUS ROSMARINIFOLIUS

O. rosmarinifolius has been confused with the more tender *O. purpurascens*, which differs in being strongly aromatic, with much shorter leaves (rarely much more than ½ in. long), with a smooth upper surface. It should also be pointed out that until recently the name *Ozothamnus rosmarinifolius* or *Helichrysum rosmarinifolium* was used in gardens for the species properly known as *O. thyrsoideus*.

O. DIOSMIFOLIUS (Vent.) DC. *Helichrysum diosmifolium* (Vent.) Sweet—An erect evergreen shrub to 10 ft; branches shortly rough-hairy, also woolly when young. Leaves linear, closely revolute, up to ¾ in. long, usually rough on the upper surface with small projecting points, woolly beneath. Flower-heads in terminal corymbs; involucral bracts milky-white, the outermost often with a pinkish tinge, opaque, stiff, incurved and of more or less uniform texture, without distinct radiating tips, at length spreading but not reflexed; florets twenty to thirty.

A native of south-eastern Queensland and New South Wales, doubtfully hardy in Britain, and not known for certain to be in cultivation at the time of writing. The name (or *Helichrysum diosmifolium*) has been used in gardens for *O. thyrsoideus* and for *O. purpurascens*.

O. SELAGO Hook. f.
Helichrysum selago (Hook. f.) Kirk

An evergreen shrub much branched and 6 to 15 in. high; young branchlets arching or pendulous, about $\frac{1}{12}$ in. thick, with a cypress-like appearance due

to the leaves being closely appressed to the stem. Leaves overlapping, ovate
to triangular, $\frac{1}{10}$ to $\frac{1}{8}$ in. long, pointed or bluntish, dark polished green and
convex outside, covered inside with a white wool which shows slightly at the
edges and at the base of the leaves. With age they become markedly keeled
or ridged at the back. Flower-heads produced singly at the end of the shoot,
stalkless, the chief feature being the bracts of the involucre which are linear-
oblong, $\frac{3}{16}$ in. long, dull white or yellowish, and with membranous tips.

Native of New Zealand, where it occurs in mountainous districts of the
South Island up to 4,500 ft altitude. Its chief claim to notice is in its curious
cypress-like growth and the outlining of each leaf when young with a thin
fringe of white wool escaped from the otherwise hidden inner surface. The
description above is made from a plant that has grown for almost half-a-century
on the rock garden at Wakehurst Place in Sussex. The species is, however,
variable. The New Zealand specimens preserved at Kew show that. One of
them has shoots fully $\frac{3}{16}$ in. thick and they vary also in the amount of wool
they display.

O. GLOMERATUS (Raoul) Hook. f. *Helichrysum glomeratum* (Raoul) Kirk—
A curious evergreen shrub up to 8 ft high, with long, slender, thong-like
shoots covered with white down, and sparse roundish leaves 1 to 1¼ in. long,
also covered with white down beneath. Flower-heads in small, short-stalked,
axillary or terminal, globose clusters, ½ in. across. Native of New Zealand. It
is of little merit and tender.

O. THYRSOIDEUS DC.

Helichrysum thyrsoideum (DC.) Willis & Morris; *H. rosmarinifolium* Hort., not (Labill.)
Benth.; *O. rosmarinifolius* Hort., not (Labill.) DC.; *H. diosmifolium* Hort., in part, not
(Vent.) Sweet

An evergreen shrub 6 to 9 ft high, with ribbed, glutinous young branches.
Leaves narrowly linear, alternate, closely set on the branches, ½ to 2 in. long,
dark green and resinous above, paler beneath with fine appressed down,
except for the conspicuous green midrib and margins, which are narrowly
recurved. Flower-heads crowded in dense rounded corymbs ½ to ¾ in. across,
produced from June to August at the ends of short side-shoots; each flower-
head is about ⅙ in. wide, with the innermost bracts with white, radiating tips
which impart a snowy whiteness to the inflorescence, the outer bracts papery,
pale brown; florets ten to sixteen.

Native of New South Wales, Victoria, and Tasmania, widespread; introduced
to Britain early in the 19th century. It is not reliably hardy, and near London
is safer with the protection of a wall, though some gardeners in south-eastern
England have found it hardy in the open ground. Plants from the seeds collected
by Comber in Tasmania in 1929–30 at 1,500 ft are perhaps hardier than the
older forms, and have withstood 20° F. of frost without protection.

Where it thrives, this is a beautiful shrub. About midsummer every little
twig is terminated by its cluster of blossoms, which as a whole almost hide
the plant in a snow-white sheet. It is popularly known as 'snow in summer'.
The flowers are practically everlasting; I have specimens collected, dried, and

pressed over thirty years ago, which are still pure white. For room decoration long sprays should be cut, hung upside down in a place as free as possible from dust, and allowed to become dry and rigid. After a few weeks they may be taken down and arranged in the ordinary way in vases, where the flowers will remain white and beautiful for many months, no water of course being needed.

O. *thyrsoideus* received an Award of Merit when shown by Sir William Lawrence of Burford Court, Dorking, on June 23, 1925, under the name O. *rosmarinifolius*, by which it was once commonly known in gardens; it has also been called *Helichrysum diosmifolium*, but both names properly belong to other species.

O. SECUNDIFLORUS (N. A. Wakefield) C. Jeffrey, *comb. nov. Helichrysum secundiflorum* N. A. Wakefield in *Vict. Nat.* 68: 49 (1951)—This species, like the preceding, differs from O. *ledifolius* and its immediate allies in its flatter leaf-blades, with only narrowly recurved margins. It is an evergreen shrub to 6 ft high, with white-woolly branches. Leaves oblong-linear to narrowly wedge-shaped, up to $\frac{7}{16}$ in. long, sparsely downy above, densely woolly beneath. Flower-heads very numerous in clusters on the short lateral branches, facing outwards, forming very long floriferous sprays, sweet-scented; involucral bracts brownish red, the inner with conspicuous radiating white tips; florets about fifteen.

Native of the mountains of New South Wales and Victoria. It is related to O. *thyrsoideus* but is not resinous and is much more hairy. A plant of unknown origin is in cultivation at Kew on the Australian House terrace.

PACHYSANDRA BUXACEAE

A group of four or five species of curious semi-woody plants of tufted habit, allied to *Buxus*, but very distinct in general appearance, being in habit low and more or less prostrate. Leaves dullish green, alternate, mostly aggregated near the apex of the season's growth. Flowers uni-sexual on erect spikes, the males numerous, the females solitary or few; both sexes on the same spike, the females at the base. Petals none; sepals and stamens four in the male; sepals four to six, and ovary three-celled in the female. Fruit a two- or three-celled capsule, with the styles per-sisting at the top like three curved horns. The generic name is in allusion to the thick stamens.

The pachysandras thrive in any moist soil, and do not mind shade; they make neat tufts, but are of only moderate decorative value, though useful as ground-cover. Easily increased by summer cuttings.

P. AXILLARIS Franch.

An evergreen, semi-woody plant with prostrate root-stocks, from which rise the young stems 4 to 10 in. high, at first minutely downy. Leaves three to six near the summit of each stem, ovate, broadly wedge-shaped or rounded and entire at the base, coarsely toothed at the upper part, 2 to 4 in. long, 1¼ to 2¼ in. wide. Flowers white, produced in April in erect spikes ¾ to 1 in. long, from the axils of the leaves. Fruits about the size of a pea, with two or three long, curly-ended styles persisting at the top.

Native of China; discovered in Yunnan by the Abbé Delavay; introduced by Wilson in 1901. Of little beauty, it may by lovers of curiosities be given a place in some shady corner of the rock garden.

P. PROCUMBENS Michx.   ALLEGHENY SPURGE

A semi-herbaceous plant forming low masses, with stems 6 to 12 in. high, springing unbranched from a root-stock, downy, bearing the leaves in a cluster at the top. Leaves broadly ovate, obovate, or somewhat rhomboidal; 2 to 3½ in. long, often almost as wide, the upper part usually very coarsely toothed, the lower part entire and tapering to a stalk ½ to 1½ in. long. The lower leaves are the largest and longest stalked; all are furnished with minute, scattered hairs. The unisexual flowers are borne at the base of the stem (between the flowers and the leaves the stem is bare), crowded on several erect, cylindrical spikes 2 to 4 in. high; female flowers few, and confined to the base. The most conspicuous part of the spike is the stamens, with their pale, flattened stalk ⅛ in. long; the sepals are greenish or purplish. *Bot. Mag.*, t. 1964.

Native of the south-eastern United States from Virginia and Kentucky southwards; introduced in 1800. It grows vigorously in sheltered shady places. The inflorescence is formed in autumn, and expands in spring. Flowers unpleasantly scented.

P. TERMINALIS Sieb. & Zucc.

An evergreen, semi-woody plant 6 to 10 in. high; stems glabrous, the lower portion procumbent and matted. Leaves diamond-shaped, 1 to 2¼ in. long, ½ to 1¼ in. wide; coarsely and bluntly toothed on the upper half, entire and tapering below, glabrous, prominently three-veined at the base; stalk ¼ to ¾ in. long. The leaves persist two or three years, and each year's crop is produced in a whorl-like cluster at the end of its growth, being separated from the previous one by several inches of naked stem. Flowers green tinged with purple, produced in spring at the end of the previous year's shoot in a spike about 1 in. long.

Native of Japan. Not so striking a plant as the American *P. procumbens*, from which it is readily distinguished by its terminal spikes and smaller leaves, but hardier. It ultimately forms a dense low mass several feet across.

cv. 'VARIEGATA'.—Leaves bordered and striped with white.

PACHYSTIMA *see* PAXISTIMA

PAEONIA PAEONY PAEONIACEAE

A genus composed mainly of herbaceous perennials, but including the four woody species treated here. These constitute the section *Moutan*, which is confined to W. China and S.E. Tibet.

The genus *Paeonia*, long included in the family Ranunculaceae, is now placed in a separate family, of which it is the only genus. Leaves alternate, deeply divided. Flowers large and showy; sepals five, persistent; petals normally five, sometimes ten (and often very numerous in garden varieties); stamens very numerous, the anthers dehiscing centrifugally, i.e., the innermost shedding their pollen first (in the Ranunculaceae it is the other way about); carpels fleshy, up to five in number, free from one another, each developing into a follicle containing a few large arillate seeds. In *Paeonia* (but not in the Ranunculaceae) a disk is present at the centre of the flower. In *P. suffruticosa* this is very developed, forming an envelope round the carpels, while in other species of the section *Moutan* it forms a lobed, fleshy structure at the base of the carpels.

For the propagation of the garden varieties and hybrids see p. 83. Division is the best means of increasing *P. potaninii*, while *P. lutea* and its variety, and *P. delavayi* are usually propagated by seeds. If these are sown as soon as they are ripe in early autumn, there is a good chance that they will germinate the following spring, without artificial heat or any special treatment. The seed is otherwise best kept cool and dry, and sown in the spring or early summer; it will then germinate in the spring following. The explanation for this procedure is that root-germination takes place in warmth, but the embryonic shoot remains dormant until the seed has undergone a period of low temperature, which is only effective *after* the period of warmth.

The standard work on the taxonomy of the paeonies is: F. C. Stern, *A Study of the Genus Paeonia* (1946). Other useful works are: M. Haworth-Booth, *The Moutan or Tree Paeony* (1963); J. C. Wister, 'The Moutan Tree Peony', in *Peonies: The Manual of the American Peony Society* (1928); J. C. Wister and H. E. Wolfe, 'The Tree Peonies', in *Nat. Hort. Mag.* (1955), Vol. 34, pp. 1–61.

P. DELAVAYI Franch.

A deciduous shrub 3 to 6 ft high, devoid of down in all its parts. Leaves doubly pinnatifid, the ultimate divisions lanceolate, slender-pointed, 2 to 4 in. long, dark green above, glaucous beneath. The entire leaf with its stalk is from

6 to 18 in. long and it persists in its dead condition through the winter. Flowers one to three on a stalk, each 2½ to 4 in. wide, cup-shaped, rather drooping, opening in June. Each flower has an involucre of leafy bracts set close against the five greenish sepals. Petals five to ten, rounded, incurved, overlapping, of a rich, almost blood red, their beauty heightened by the clustered golden anthers in the centre. Seed-vessels ⅜ to 1¼ in. long, glabrous.

Native of China; originally discovered by the Abbé Delavay in 1884; introduced by Wilson about 1908. It is related to *P. lutea*, differing mainly in the colour of the flowers. Still, Forrest records that he found numerous plants in W. China with flowers of an indeterminate colour between red and yellow, sometimes orange-brown, which gave him the impression that they might be hybrids between the two species. Some of this mongrel type reached cultivation, but they are very inferior to the type described above. *P. delavayi* is a handsome shrub seen at its best, although it has the defect when small of hiding the face of its flowers. It likes a rich soil with occasional dressings of manure and succeeds well in chalky districts. Unlike *P. suffruticosa*, it does not appear to suffer from late spring frosts.

In the USA some hybrids with dark red flowers, deriving from *P. delavayi*, were raised by Prof. A. P. Saunders, and are classified by American growers with the Lutea hybrids (see under *P. lutea*). Of these, 'BLACK PIRATE' received a First Class Certificate in 1959 when shown by Sir Frederick Stern, but is scarce in this country. The flowers are single, maroon-crimson (*Journ. R.H.S.*, Vol. 88 (1959), fig. 118).

P. POTANINII Komar. *P. delavayi* var. *angustiloba* Rehd. & Wils.—This differs from *P. delavayi* in its smaller flowers, which lack a foliaceous involucre, in its much more dissected leaves with narrower segments, and in its suckering habit. Native of W. Szechwan and N.W. Yunnan. It was introduced by Wilson in 1904 and first flowered in Veitch's Coombe Wood nursery in June 1911. A handsome shrub in regard to its foliage but inferior to *P. delavayi* in its flowers, which are about 2 in. wide. It grows to about 2 ft in height and spreads by underground stolons.

f. ALBA F. C. Stern *P. delavayi* var. *alba* Bean—Flowers creamy white; stamens with green filaments.

var. TROLLIOIDES (Stapf ex F. C. Stern) F. C. Stern *P. trollioides* Stapf ex F. C. Stern; *P. forrestii* Hort.—This has yellow, trollius-like flowers and is of more erect growth than typical *P. potaninii*, with the flowers held above the leaves. Introduced by Forrest from Yunnan in 1914 (F.13195). It flowers end-May.

P. LUTEA Franch.

P. delavayi var. *lutea* (Franch.) Fin. & Gagnep.

A dwarf, subshrubby deciduous plant with a short woody stem; entirely glabrous. Leaves leathery, 12 to 15 in. long, strongly nerved, deep green above, glaucous beneath, ternate, with the three divisions pinnatifid and deeply cut at the margin. Outer sepals narrow-lanceolate, acuminate, inner ones roundish, concave, yellowish green. Petals six to ten, golden yellow, roundish concave, with usually crenate margins and sometimes with a carmine stain at the base. The flower is 2½ in. across, and is sometimes slightly 'double', both in the wild state and the cultivated. Seed-vessels three or four, glabrous. *Bot. Mag.*, t. 7788.

Native of the mountains of S.W. China; discovered in Yunnan by the French missionary Delavay, who also introduced it to Europe by means of seeds sent to the garden of the Paris Museum in 1887. A plant obtained from France flowered in the Temperate House at Kew in 1900 and from this the figure in the *Botanical Magazine* was made. Three years later *P. lutea* received a First Class Certificate.

P. lutea, in the form originally introduced, is not so decidedly a shrub as *P. suffruticosa*, but forms a short, woody stem up to 3 ft high (sometimes slightly taller). It is a beautiful paeony, though in some forms the flowers are apt to be hidden by the foliage. They are borne in June. It is now rare in gardens, having been displaced by the more vigorous var. *ludlowii*.

Only three plants were raised from the seeds sent by Delavay. One of these differed from the others in its more robust habit and in having flowers up to 3½ in. wide, with nine to eleven petals, reddish maroon stamens, and bronzy young foliage. This was propagated by Lemoine and named 'SUPERBA'.

var. LUDLOWII Stern & Taylor—This differs in its larger flowers up to 4 or 5 in. across, with more spreading petals, and with only one or two fertile carpels. It is also of larger stature, attaining in cultivation a height of 6 to 8 ft and as much in width. It flowers in May, three weeks or so before typical *P. lutea*. So far as is known, it is confined to a small area of S.E. Tibet near the Tsangpo gorges, at 9,000 to 11,000 ft. It was introduced by Ludlow and Sherriff in 1936 and reintroduced on later expeditions to the same area. At first it was known in gardens as the Tibetan or Ludlow and Sherriff form of *P. lutea* and was first distinguished botanically in 1953, in the article accompanying the plate in the *Botanical Magazine* (n.s., t. 209).   [PLATE 7

The var. *ludlowii* makes a splendid foliage plant, always of symmetrical and dense habit if not crowded. But on some plants the flowers are sparsely borne or concealed by the foliage. These may be growing in a too rich or too moist soil; or seedling variation may be the explanation, for this variety is always increased by seeds. At its best it makes a fine display. A.M. 1957.

P. × LEMOINEI Rehd.—Here belong hybrids between *P. lutea* and the moutan, *P. suffruticosa*. The first, and still the best known of these, were raised by Louis Henry in the garden of the Paris Museum, and by Messrs Lemoine of Nancy. Many others were raised later in the USA by Prof. A. P. Saunders. The following are available in commerce or have received awards from the Royal Horticultural Society:

'ALICE HARDING'.—Flowers lemon-yellow, fully double.

'ARGOSY'.—Flowers 7 in. across; petals primrose-yellow blotched carmine at the base. This is one of the Saunders hybrids and was considered by Sir Frederick Stern to be the best of the single yellows. It received a First Class Certificate when shown by him on June 6, 1956, but seems to be scarce in commerce.

'Chromatella'.—A sport from 'Souvenir de Maxime Cornu' with pure sulphur-yellow flowers.

'La Lorraine'.—Flowers yellow, double.

'L'espérance'.—Flowers 6 to 8 in. wide; petals pale yellow with a crimson stain at the base, arranged in two rows. F.C.C. 1931.

'Mme Louis Henry'.—Flowers 6 to 7 in. wide; petals about thirteen, creamy yellow suffused with red. A.M. 1955.

'Souvenir de Maxime Cornu'.—Flowers very fragrant, excessively double; petals yellow tinged brownish orange and red. The stems flop over under the weight of the flowers.

For culture, etc., see under *P. suffruticosa*. The flowering time is late May and early June.

P. lutea × P. delavayi—Hybrids of this parentage have been made deliberately in gardens and may also occur among seedlings where both species are grown. They (or at least the best of them) have flowers of a brighter red than in *P. delavayi*, and larger, but there is considerable variation. P. 'Anne Rosse' is the result of a deliberate cross between *P. delavayi* and *P. lutea* var. *ludlowii*, raised by The Earl of Rosse and given an Award of Merit when shown by him in 1961. The flowers are lemon yellow, 4 in. wide, with red streakings on the back of the petals.

P. suffruticosa Andr.   Moutan   [Plate 8
P. moutan Sims; *P. arborea* Donn ex K. Koch

A stiff-branched, deciduous shrub, of rather gaunt habit when in the leafless state, but of luxuriant aspect when in full leaf, rarely more than 6 ft high in this country, but said to be twice that height in China. Branchlets thick, soft with abundant pith. Leaves doubly pinnate or doubly ternate, 9 to 18 in. long, the leaflets deeply divided into acute lobes or teeth, glabrous above, slightly hairy beneath. Flowers borne in May or June, up to 12 in. or even more across in garden varieties, but about half that width in wild plants; the latter have up to ten petals, and the colour is apparently either white with a maroon-purple blotch at the base of each petal, or in some shade of red, but in the garden varieties the petals are often very numerous, and the range of colouring wider. In the wild plants the flowers are fragrant, at least when they first expand, but this is not true of all the garden sorts, some of which have unpleasantly scented flowers. Stamens numerous, mostly converted into petals in the fully double garden varieties; anthers yellow. Carpels five, enclosed at first in a leathery outgrowth of the disk.

The moutan paeony, in its primitive state, is a native of northern China, in the provinces of Shensi, Kansu, and perhaps Szechwan, but has become rare in the wild (see further below). Its history, as a domesticated plant, goes back to the 7th century A.D., when the Tang dynasty had its capital at Changan, in what is now Shensi province. The first plants to be cultivated were brought into the imperial gardens from their native hills. As its popularity spread, it came to be raised from seed, and garden varieties arose, which at first were propagated by grafting on wild stocks, later on the roots of herbaceous paeonies. The first treatise on the moutan was written in the 11th century, by which time the centre of cultivation had shifted east to Loyang. In later centuries its culture spread southwards, and when Fortune visited China in the 1840s there were nurseries at Shanghai. But at Canton, whence came the early introductions to Europe, the winters are too warm to give the moutan the period of dormancy it needs. The thousands of plants that decorated the houses and gardens of the city early in the year were imported from the north and thrown away after flowering (Li, *Gard. Fl. China* (1959), Chap. 3; Fortune, *Gard. Chron.*, Vol. 1 (1880), pp. 179–80). The name 'moutan' has a quite prosaic meaning—'male red'—which probably dates back to a time when it was valued more for its roots than its flowers (W. Gardener, *Gard. Chron.*, Vol. 160 (1966), p. 12). But it became known, from its sumptuous appearance and its association with the great days of the Tang dynasty, as the Hua Wang, the King of Flowers.

The moutan was introduced to Britain by Sir Joseph Banks, who 'engaged Mr Duncan, a medical gentleman attached to the East India Company's service, to procure a plant for the royal garden at Kew, where it was first received, through Mr Duncan's exertions, in 1787' (Loudon, *Arb. et Frut. Brit.*, Vol. I, p. 252, but the date given by Aiton is 1789). The original plant remained at Kew until 1842, when, owing to building operations, it had to be removed. This importation—'BANKSII' (*P. suffruticosa* var. *banksii* G. Anders.)—is double, with a varying number of petals, purplish red at the base fading to almost white at the tips. The plant in Sir Joseph Banks' garden at Isleworth was 6 or 8 ft high and between 8 and 10 ft wide in 1825. The type of the name *P. moutan* is probably the same as 'Banksii' (*Botanical Magazine*, t. 1154). The type of *P. suffruticosa* is not the Banksian introduction but a double, uniformly pink variety—'ROSEA PLENA' —introduced in 1795. Of some historic and botanical interest is 'PAPAVERACEA' (*P. papaveracea* Andr.), introduced in 1806, which was a more or less single white, very like Rock's paeony discussed below. On the other hand, 'ANNESLEI', named in 1826 after the Earl of Mountnorris, seems to have been near to *P. suffruticosa* var. *spontanea*.

These early introductions came, *via* Canton, from somewhere in the moutan country of the north. The next set, sent by Fortune to the Horticultural Society during his first expedition to China in 1843–5, came from Shanghai, where the winters are cold enough for the moutan to thrive. Here there were several nurseries devoted to its culture, and the varieties grown were different from those sold by the Canton florists, being mostly darker in colour and more double. They were probably also newer and, one suspects, less vigorous. The Fortune introductions flowered in the Society's garden and were given botanical epithets by Lindley, but seem to have died out. During his second expedition (1848–51) Fortune sent another set of thirty varieties from Shanghai to the firm of Standish and Noble, together with a supply of the herbaceous paeony used by the Chinese for grafting. In 1854 the plants were still growing in the containers in which Fortune had shipped them, but a special garden was planned for them, to be dug to a depth of 6 ft. Writing in 1880, the year of his death, Fortune lamented that the fine varieties he introduced had mostly been lost, but some seem to have found their way to the continent and been named, or renamed, there.

T A S—D.

The moutan was carried to Japan by the Buddhists and became there, as in China, a favourite garden plant. Numerous varieties were introduced to Europe by Siebold in 1844 from the Imperial gardens at Yedo (Tokyo) and Miyako (Kyoto), all single or semi-double and grafted on moutan stock. Judging from the descriptions in his catalogue of 1856, some of these varieties must have been very fine, but they seem to have suffered the same fate as most of Fortune's. Siebold also introduced the moutan stock used by the Japanese, which was of suckering habit and easily propagated by division. This he named 'Germania' and described the flowers as scented, 'd'un cramoisi vif'. If he used this stock for his own propagations, the loss of his varieties is understandable, since it throws up so many suckers that the variety grafted on it is apt to be smothered. It was not until late in the century that Japanese varieties began to be imported in quantity. Today, the majority of the moutan paeonies in cultivation are of Japanese origin.

In the last century, many varieties were raised on the continent, and there were no doubt further importations from China. In the 1860s and 1870s some nursery-men listed a hundred or more sorts, very few of which have survived. So far as Britain is concerned, a study of the horticultural literature of the last century gives the impression that the moutan was never a common plant in gardens, and certainly does not confirm the notion that the Victorians were more successful with it than we are today. The choice of tree paeonies available in commerce in Britain now is not wide, but it includes what are acknowledged to be the best of the European varieties, such as the double pinks 'ELIZABETH' ('Reine Elisa-beth'), 'COMTESSE DE TUDER', 'JEANNE D'ARC' and 'LOUISE MOUCHE-LET', and the famous white 'BIJOU DE CHUSAN', also double. The Japanese varieties, even when double, mostly have fewer petals than the Chinese and European sorts and a central boss of fertile stamens and pistils; the flowers are consequently less heavy and better poised. In the United States, one leading grower lists some 300 varieties. In Britain, the number regularly available is very limited and those imported from Japan are often not true to name, so to give a selection would be pointless.

In the wild, *P. suffruticosa* appears to be an uncommon plant, and little is known about it. The fact that its roots were valued by the Chinese as medicine, and the stems cut for firewood, may help to explain its present scarcity. At the end of the 17th century, according to a Chinese work, the moutan was so abundant on the Moutan-shan in Shensi that 'the whole hill appears tinged with red, and the air round about for a distance of ten *li* is filled with fragrance' (Bretschneider, *Eur. Bot. Disc. China*, Vol. I, p. 426). Yet when Purdom visited the mountain in 1912, he could find no trace of it. However, in 1910 he collected a specimen in Shensi, near Yennan, during his expedition for the Arnold Arboretum and Messrs Veitch (no. 338), from which Rehder described var. SPONTANEA. In this the flowers were said to be rose-coloured, 4 to 5 in. wide, with ten petals. The foliage differs from that of most garden varieties in that the terminal leaflet is bluntly lobed and the lateral leaflets roundish in outline and more or less tridentate at the apex (Stern, op. cit., pp. 41–2). Purdom sent a few seeds, but all the plants raised were lost save one, which grew in Professor Sargent's garden at Harvard. The Purdom introduction is said to be of suckering habit, and seems to be very like the moutan used at one time by the Japanese as stock for grafting the garden varieties. Purdom also found a wild moutan in S. Kansu, south of Minchow, where it is more abundant than in Shensi (*Gard. Chron.*, Vol. 54 (1913), p. 230). He did not state the colour of the flowers he had seen, but apparently it was dark magenta crimson.

Despite the epithet *spontanea*, Purdom's variety cannot be regarded as the sole or even the main ancestor of the garden varieties. A plant nearer to these, and of great beauty in itself, was found by Farrer in S. Kansu in 1914, during his journey with Purdom. This discovery grew near the border with Shensi about 40 miles north-east of Wutu (Kaichow). Farrer had seen 'white blobs' from afar and pushed through the thorn-scrub for a closer look. 'Nor did I need near approach to discover what it was that I was hunting, for there, balancing rarely amid the brushwood, shone out at me the huge expanded goblets of Paeonia Moutan, refulgent as pure snow and fragrant as heavenly Roses. It grew tall and thin and stately, each plant with two or three thin, upstanding wands tipped by the swaying burden of a single upright bloom with heart of gold, each stainless petal flamed at the base with a clean and definite feathered blotch of maroon.' (*Gard. Chron.*, Vol. 56 (1914), p. 213; see also Farrer, *On the Eaves of the World*, Vol. I, pp. 110–13, 162.)

Farrer did not introduce his find, nor even collect a specimen. But eleven years later the American collector Dr Joseph Rock spent a year in the great Choni Lamasery in S.W. Kansu (Farrer, who had visited it with Purdom, spells its name 'Jo-ni'). There he found a paeony very like Farrer's, growing in the garden of the Yamen, which, according to the monks, had come from somewhere in Kansu (*Journ. R.H.S.*, Vol. 64 (1939), pp. 550–2 and fig. 130). He sent seeds to the Arnold Arboretum, which were further distributed, but the date of this introduction is usually given as 1932, seven years after his stay at Choni. A young plant, received by Sir Frederick Stern in 1936 from Canada, flowered in his garden at Highdown, Worthing, in 1938 and by 1959 was 8 ft high and 12 ft across (*Journ. R.H.S.*, Vol. 84 (1959), fig. 104). Rock's tree paeony is so near to typical *P. suffruticosa* in its essential characters that a distinguishing botanical epithet is scarcely needed, but it could reasonably be placed under *P. suffruticosa* var. *papaveracea* (Andr.) L. H. Bailey, a name founded on the early introduction that Andrews named *P. papaveracea* (see above). Sir Frederick Stern pointed out that the only significant difference is in the colour of the sheath enclosing the carpels, which was described as purple in 'Papaveracea', whereas in the Rock introduction it is white. Rock's tree paeony received a First Class Certificate in 1944.

CULTURE AND PROPAGATION.—In many parts of the country the tree paeony is very unsatisfactory. At Kew it grows too early in the spring, and the young growths and flowers are almost invariably destroyed by late frosts. It is this, not genuine winter cold, that is to be feared. In the colder and bleaker parts of the country, where it is not excited into growth so easily, the moutan grows to a size that it will rarely attain in low-lying districts near London. And no doubt some of the highly bred varieties now in commerce are more delicate than the old sorts first imported from China. The practice of grafting the garden varieties on the herbaceous paeony is responsible for many failures, but it is the customary method, and the best means of producing plants at a reasonable price. Provided it is planted so that the union between stock and scion is about three inches below the level of the soil, a tree paeony will in two or three years develop its own roots. It is then advisable to lift the plant and remove the herbaceous stock altogether, though this is not essential.

The tree paeony is seen to best advantage as an isolated specimen, and is less likely when grown thus to be attacked by the dreaded paeony blight than when crowded in by other shrubs. Warm, sheltered corners, where it may be excited into early growth, are not the best place for it. North-facing positions suit it well, and some shade is desirable, provided it does not come from overhanging branches. It will grow in any good garden soil, but thrives best on a calcareous or slightly acid loam. The ground should be deeply dug, and good drainage is essential. The tree paeony is a gross feeder and should be liberally mulched with leaf-mould or well-rotted manure (almost all experts counsel against the use of fresh manure). If an artificial fertiliser is used at planting time or as a top dressing, it should be one with a high proportion of phosphate and potash.

The worst enemy of the moutan is the paeony blight *Botrytis paeoniae*, a grey mould which causes the young shoots to wilt and die, and also kills the flower-buds. So virulent has this disease become in recent years that old plants have succumbed even in parts of the country where the moutan thrives best. Infected shoots, and all snags of dead wood, should be cut out as soon as noticed and burned. The disease can be controlled by spraying with captan, dichlorofluanid, thiram or zineb. Systemic fungicides such as benomyl and thiophanate methyl are also said to give a good control, but too frequent use of these fungicides might lead to the development of tolerant strains of the fungus. The threat of paeony blight is an additional reason for giving the plants an open, airy position, since the disease is fostered by damp, stagnant conditions.

The usual commercial method of propagating the moutan varieties is by grafting on the roots of an herbaceous paeony. As already remarked, this need not be a cause of failure if the plant is placed with the junction between scion and stock some three or four inches below soil-level. Most of the Japanese varieties set seed, which probably offers the best means of propagation for the private gardener (see further in the introductory note). Although the varieties will not breed true, a fair proportion of the seedlings will be worth keeping, provided the parent has well-formed flowers of a pure colour. A plant that is on its own roots, and has formed a stool, can be propagated by division during the winter; the rooted pieces should be potted-up and, when established, should be grown on in a cold frame until large enough to be moved into the garden. Layering is also a possibility, but owing to the brittleness of the branches of the tree paeony is not a very satisfactory method. Little is known about propagation by cuttings, since this method has never been used commercially to any extent, being too chancy. But some varieties can be increased in this way, using cuttings taken after flowering with a heel of the previous year's wood (see *Journ. R.H.S.*, Vol. 88 (1963), pp. 449–50). The young plants would have to be grown on in pots or a frame until strong enough to be planted in their final positions. For further details on propagation see the works by Haworth-Booth and Wister and Wolfe, cited in the introductory note.

PALIURUS RHAMNACEAE

A genus of about eight species of spiny shrubs, ranging from S. Europe to E. Asia, allied to *Zizyphus*, which is a much larger and more widely distributed genus with fleshy fruits.

P. SPINA-CHRISTI Mill.   CHRIST'S THORN
P. aculeata Lam.; *P. australis* Gaertn.

A deciduous shrub or small tree up to 20 ft high in this country, with shoots downy when young, and armed at each joint with a pair of spines, one straight and pointing more or less upwards, the other shorter, curved, and pointing downwards. Leaves alternate, 1 to 1½ in. long, broadly ovate, three-nerved, and entire or slightly toothed; stalk ½ in. or less long. Flowers very numerous, and produced in a short branching umbel from each leaf-axil of the current year's shoots; the individual flowers small, greenish yellow, but rather striking, wreathed as the shoot is with them, the parts in fives. Fruits ¾ to 1 in. wide, consisting of a three-celled, roundish body, developing at the top a curious flat wing which runs all round, giving the whole fruit the aspect of a low-crowned, wide-brimmed hat.

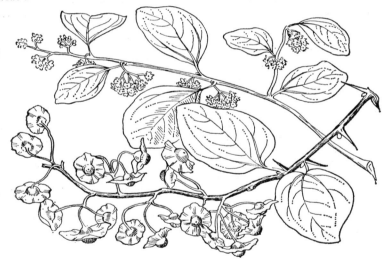

PALIURUS SPINA-CHRISTI

Native of S. Europe eastwards to W. Asia; cultivated in this country for over three hundred years. In some of its native places it is used as a hedge plant. I remember seeing it put to this use on the road between Spalato (Split) and Salona (Solun), in Dalmatia. It is perfectly hardy at Kew, and I have never seen it even touched by frost there. It grows very well in ordinary loam, and although the flowers have no great beauty they are pretty, and abundantly produced in rows of umbels on the upper side of the shoot. The flat, disk-like, greenish yellow fruits, too, have an interesting appearance, quite distinct from that of any other hardy shrub. The branches are pliable and excessively spiny, and the tree has a legendary interest as the one of whose branches the Crown of Thorns was believed to have been made. It flowers in July and August. Well worth cultivation. There is an ancient specimen at Ham House, Petersham.

PARAHEBE SCROPHULARIACEAE

A small genus of dwarf shrubs and subshrubs (one species herbaceous), allied to *Veronica* and *Hebe* and mainly or perhaps wholly confined to New Zealand. They are less woody than the true hebes, but the main difference is that the capsules are laterally compressed, whereas in most hebes they are dorsally compressed (as if by pressure acting from the bract towards the inflorescence-rachis). There is also a difference of chromosome number. The genus is nearer to *Veronica* than is *Hebe*, and the resemblance is particularly marked in the species described here, with their speedwell-like flowers.

P. CATARRACTAE (Forst. f.) W. R. B. Oliver

Veronica catarractae Forst. f.; *Hebe catarractae* (Forst. f.) Wall; *Veronica diffusa* Hook. f.; *Parahebe diffusa* (Hook. f.) W. R. B. Oliver; *V. lanceolata* Benth.

A deciduous shrub or subshrub up to 12 in. high; young shoots purplish, slender, often with a line of down extending upwards from the axil of each leaf. Leaves ovate-lanceolate to lanceolate, pointed, tapered at the base, coarsely saw-toothed, $\frac{1}{2}$ to $1\frac{1}{2}$ in. long, $\frac{1}{4}$ to $\frac{1}{2}$ in. wide, dark green above, paler below, glabrous; stalk $\frac{1}{12}$ to $\frac{1}{4}$ in. long. Racemes slender, erect, 3 to 9 in. high, produced in late summer from leaf-axils at the upper part of the shoots. Flowers white with rosy-purple lines, $\frac{1}{3}$ to $\frac{1}{2}$ in. wide; flower-stalks downy, the individual ones about $\frac{1}{4}$ in. long, very slender.

Native of New Zealand. This is a variable species and specimens with stems 2 ft long and leaves 4 in. long are included under it. The form described above and cultivated at Kew is the same as Forster's type on which he based the name in 1786. On some wild plants the leaves are linear-lanceolate, six or seven times as long as wide. Such plants were given specific rank by Bentham as *V. lanceolata*, but they are part of the variation of this species. In the plants that the younger Hooker named *V. diffusa* the habit was decumbent and diffuse, the racemes glandular and the leaves ovate and acute, but Miss Ashwin has pointed out that this shape of leaf is not always associated with the other characters of Hooker's species (*Fl. N.Z.*, Vol. 1 (1961), p. 879).

At the present time P. *catarractae* appears to be mainly represented in cultivation by a hardy form resembling the one described above from a Kew plant, but usually offered as "*Hebe lyallii*". There is also in commerce a form listed by Messrs Ingwersen as *Hebe catarractae* 'Of Gardens', which differs from wild plants in having flowers of a deep purplish blue.

P. *catarractae* flowers from late summer into early autumn.

P. LYALLII (Hook. f.) W. R. B. Oliver *Veronica lyallii* Hook. f.; *Hebe lyallii* (Hook. f.) Allan—This is a near relative of the above but smaller in all its parts. It is of prostrate habit, the branches taking root in the ground. Young shoots with usually two lines of down as in *P. catarractae*. Leaves thick and leathery, ovate to orbicular, $\frac{1}{4}$ to $\frac{1}{2}$ in. long, with a few coarse teeth on each margin. Flowers white, veined with rose, $\frac{1}{3}$ in. wide, produced in late summer and autumn on erect racemes 2 to 6 in. high; anthers blue. Native of the South Island of New Zealand up to 4,500 ft. It is hardy.

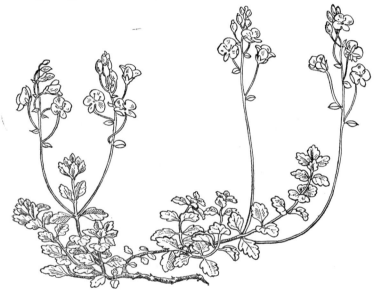

PARAHEBE LYALLII

Although there has been confusion between them, *P. lyallii* and *P. catarractae* are, for the most part, clearly distinguishable. In the former the leaves are obtuse to rounded at the apex, and the teeth are rather wide and blunt. In *P. catarractae* the leaves are acute and sharply serrated, and are also generally much larger than in *P. lyallii*. In the wild, plants occur in some areas which are intermediate, but so far as is known these have not been introduced to cultivation.

P. DECORA M. B. Ashwin

Veronica, Hebe or *Parahebe bidwillii* of most authors, not *Veronica bidwillii* Hook.

A prostrate shrub, wide-spreading and rooting at the nodes, the main stems giving off rather short, leafy branchlets, all downy. Leaves rather thick, glabrous, $\frac{1}{16}$ to slightly over $\frac{1}{8}$ in. long, ovate to broad-elliptic or almost orbicular, entire or with a lobule on each side near the base, broadly rounded to almost truncate at the apex, cuneately narrowed at the base to a short petiole. Racemes axillary with mostly six to ten flowers, up to 9 in. long including the peduncle, which is as long or longer than the flower-bearing part; pedicels slender, up to $\frac{3}{4}$ in. long; they, and the peduncles, may be glabrous or sparsely downy; lowermost pedicels paired or in a whorl of three, rather distant from the others, which are alternately arranged. Corollas white or pale lilac, usually veined with pink, about $\frac{3}{8}$ in. wide, the tube very short. Capsules glabrous, longer than the calyx.

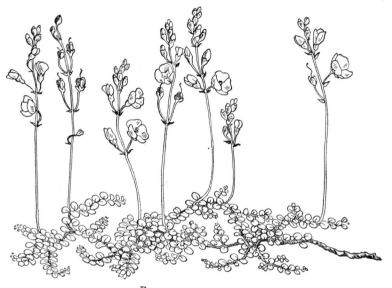

PARAHEBE DECORA

A native of the South Island of New Zealand, in river shingles, screes, etc. Although known for well over a century, this species was, until recently, confused with *P. × bidwillii*, its hybrid with *P. lyallii*, and remained without a name until Margot Ashwin provided the name *P. decora* for it in *Flora of New Zealand*, Vol. 1 (1961), pp. 877 and 974.

The date of introduction of *P. decora* is not known, but the plant which Farrer discusses as the 'true' *Veronica bidwillii* is certainly *P. decora* (*The English Rock Garden* (1919), Vol. 2, p. 440). The oldest cultivated specimen in the Kew Herbarium is dated 1922. The species was rare in Farrer's time and still is, but there is a plant on the rock garden by the lake at Wakehurst Place, which flowered well in 1972 (it does not do so every year). The most striking feature of this species is the disproportion between the leafy and flowering parts of the plant. On a specimen from the Wakehurst plant a shoot 1½ in. with leaves about ⅛ in. long bears a pair of racemes almost 8 in. long (including the leafless peduncles).

P. × BIDWILLII (Hook.) W. R. B. Oliver *Veronica bidwillii* Hook.; *Hebe bidwillii* (Hook.) Allan—A natural hybrid between *P. decora* and *P. lyallii*, which occurs occasionally in South Island. Specimens of this hybrid were collected by Bidwill in the valley of the Wairau river and from them the elder Hooker described *Veronica bidwillii* as a species in 1852. Until Miss Ashwin established the true nature of these plants, *P. decora* (see above) was confused with this hybrid, though the two are really very distinct. In *P.* × *bidwillii* the influence of the other parent *P. lyallii* shows in the larger leaves, with often two pairs of lobules, and the shorter peduncles (up to 2½ in. on the type specimens, against up to almost twice that in *P. decora*.) It is not certain whether *P.* × *bidwillii* is in cultivation. The plants grown under the name *Veronica bidwillii* seem to have been either *P. decora* or *P. lyallii*.

P. LINIFOLIA (Hook. f.) W. R. B. Oliver
Veronica linifolia Hook. f.; *Hebe linifolia* (Hook. f.) Allan

An evergreen, subshrubby plant, 2 to 4 in. high, of tufted habit; branchlets slender, woody at the base only, glabrous, with leaves set twelve to sixteen to the inch. Leaves linear, ⅛ to 1 in. long, 1/16 to ⅛ in. wide, not toothed, bluntish at the tip, tapered at the base to a broad, membranous, flattened stalk, which clasps the stem and is margined with pale hairs. Flowers white, up to ½ in. wide, produced in May and June several together close to the ends of the shoots, each on a slender stalk ¼ to 1 in. long. Corolla-tube very short, with four broad, spreading, veined lobes. Calyx deeply four-lobed.

Native of the South Island of New Zealand, up to altitudes of 4,500 ft. This is a charming dwarf plant for the rock garden, very hardy and covering itself with white flowers in May and June. The lower branches are procumbent and self-rooting. Although both Hooker and Cheeseman describe it as a herb, it is certainly woody at the base. The racemes are very distinct from those of the type common to the New Zealand hebes, the flowers being rarely more than four to a raceme, which may be 1 to 2 in. long, each blossom on a slender glabrous stalk which springs from the axil of a leaf-like bract and is one-third to half as long as the entire raceme.

PARASYRINGA   OLEACEAE

A genus of a single species, intermediate between *Ligustrum* and *Syringa*, but perhaps more nearly allied to the former.

P. SEMPERVIRENS (Franch.) W. W. Sm.

Syringa sempervirens Franch.; *Ligustrum sempervirens* (Franch.) Lingels.

An evergreen shrub 6 to 10 ft high, of bushy shape; young shoots minutely downy. Leaves oval, suborbicular, broadly ovate, or obovate, not toothed, widely tapered at both ends, pointed or bluntish, ½ to 2½ in. long, ⅜ to 1¾ in. wide, dark glossy green above; dull, paler and with numerous black dots beneath; of thick leathery texture; stalk 1/12 to ¼ in. long. Flowers creamy white, fragrant, produced in August and September in mostly terminal, pyramidal or cylindrical panicles 2 to 4 in. long. Corolla-tube about ¼ in. long, the oblong rounded lobes half as long; calyx cup-shaped, indistinctly toothed. Fruits oval, ¼ in. long, black, at first juicy, ultimately splitting downwards into two halves, unless, as frequently happens in cultivation, they are abortive. *Bot. Mag.*, t. 9295.

Native of Yunnan, China, where it was discovered by the French missionary, Delavay; also of Szechwan; introduced by Forrest in 1913. We apparently owe its existence in British gardens to J. C. Williams, who raised it at Caerhays Castle from Forrest's seeds. It was originally described as *Syringa sempervirens* in 1886 by Franchet from Delavay's specimen, on account of its splitting fruit, but it has a much greater resemblance to the privets, especially in flower and mode of growth. It is very healthy, grows freely, and appears to be perfectly hardy at Kew in a sheltered position but without artificial protection. In the warmer counties it is a really good evergreen of shapely form and the leaves become larger and more leathery than in colder places, resembling those of *Ligustrum coriaceum*. It can also be regarded as one of the best flowering shrubs of the privet tribe and may prove to be a useful evergreen hedge plant. It was given an Award of Merit at Westminster in September 1928, when exhibited in flower by Mr Armytage-Moore from Northern Ireland. Easily grown in ordinary soil and easily propagated by cuttings. I have not seen the fruits split on cultivated plants, and judging by them one would never regard this shrub as anything but a ligustrum.

PARROTIA HAMAMELIDACEAE

A genus of a single deciduous species with alternate leaves and small flowers crowded in terminal, globose heads, subtended by several bracts. The flowers have no petals, but numerous stamens, which furnish their chief attraction. The nearest allied genera are *Parrotiopsis* (q.v. for the marks of distinction), *Sycopsis*, which is evergreen, and *Fothergilla*, which has no bracts beneath the head of flowers. The genus is named after the German F. W. Parrot, who made the first ascent of Mt Ararat in 1829.

P. PERSICA (DC.) C. A. Mey. [PLATE 9

Hamamelis persica DC.

A deciduous tree 30 to 40 ft high in the wild (occasionally taller), or a shrub, with a smooth grey bark which comes away in flakes, as in the plane; young twigs at first furnished with stellate hairs. Leaves ovate, oblong or obovate— 2½ to 5 in. long, 1 to 2½ in. wide—rounded or tapering at the base, coarsely, shallowly and unevenly toothed, or merely wavy towards the apex, almost glabrous above, sparsely furnished beneath with stellate hairs; stalk ¼ in. long, downy. Flowers produced during March in short clusters ½ in. across, often terminal on short leafy twigs, and only conspicuous for their numerous red stamens. Bracts brown and hairy outside, green within, ¼ in to ⅓ in. long, ovate. Seed-vessels nut-like, opening at the top; seeds ⅜ in. long, bright brown, pointed at one end. *Bot. Mag.*, t. 5744.

Native of the forest region south and south-west of the Caspian Sea (N. Persia and the Lenkoran region of Russia); introduced to Kew from St Petersburg in 1841. The great charm of this tree is in the beautiful tints of gold and crimson its foliage assumes in autumn. Few trees are more effective then. In the early spring, too, when in flower, the numerous red-anthered stamens and rich brown bracts give to the still leafless branches a hazy effect of red which is very pleasing in sunshine. It is perfectly hardy.

In the wild, *P. persica* is sometimes a shrub, forming thickets of stout, enmeshed stems which often become grafted to their neighbours; or it may be a slender-stemmed tree, growing slowly to a height of 45 ft or so, but reported to attain 80 ft occasionally. In gardens, it is usually seen as a spreading shrub up to 20–30 ft high and considerably more in width. It should be trained up in its early stages, and the lower branches pruned away, but it is doubtful whether this form could ever be made into more than a short-trunked shrubby tree.

At Syon House, London, there is a specimen with scarcely any trunk, but 45 ft high. At Kew, the largest plant has a bole 8 ft in height and measures 30 × 4¼ ft and there is another of about the same size at Wakehurst Place at Sussex, with a bole 10 ft high (1967–8). A specimen at Abbotsbury in Dorset is a definite tree measuring 50 × 3½ ft with a bole of 20 ft (1972).

P. persica is usually propagated by layers or even by grafting onto American witch-hazel. But cuttings should strike under mist.

PARROTIOPSIS   HAMAMELIDACEAE

A genus of a single species allied to *Parrotia* and included in it in previous editions of this work. Although allied to that genus, it differs in its flowers, which have up to twenty-four stamens with upright filaments and oval anthers; in *Parrotia* the stamens are less numerous, the filaments pendulous, and the anthers linear. A less essential, but more obvious, difference is that the involucral bracts in *Parrotiopsis* are white and conspicuous. It is also allied to *Fothergilla* and the species often appears in old works of Himalayan botany under the name *Fothergilla involucrata*; but in *Fothergilla* involucral bracts are lacking.

P. JACQUEMONTIANA (Decne.) Rehd.

Parrotia jacquemontiana Decne.; *Fothergilla involucrata* Falconer; *Parrotiopsis involucrata* (Falconer) Schneid.

A deciduous tree, ultimately 15 to 20 ft high, with a smooth grey trunk and a much-branched bushy head; sometimes a shrub; young twigs covered with clustered (stellate) hairs. Leaves roundish or very broadly ovate, 2 to 3½ in.

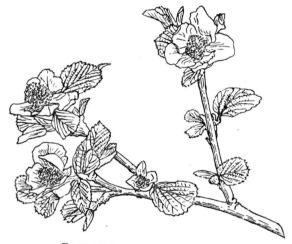

PARROTIOPSIS JACQUEMONTIANA

long and nearly as wide; margins set with broad open teeth; both surfaces furnished with stellate hairs, the upper one thinly so and finally almost glabrous, the lower one densely on the nerves; stalk ¼ to ½ in. long. Flowers stalkless, produced from April to July, about twenty together in a shortly stalked globose head about ⅝ in. across, the chief feature of which are the numerous yellow stamens. Beneath the head of flowers are four to six conspicuous petal-like bracts of the same shape as the leaves, but only ½ to 1 in. long, and white; they constitute the chief feature of the inflorescence. Seeds shining, oblong, ¼ in. long. *Bot. Mag.*, t. 7501.

Native of the western Himalaya, especially in Kashmir; where it was discovered by Dr Falconer in 1836. It does not appear to have reached cultivation until 1879, when seeds were sent to Kew. It has no claim to a place among showy plants, but belongs to a family of exceptional interest, and when well furnished with its flower-heads it is at least pretty. The leaves remain long on the tree after those of *Parrotia persica* have fallen. The largest inflorescences, with the surrounding bracts, are sometimes 2 in. across, especially those that open late. The main crop is borne in April and May, but flowers continue to open intermittently through the summer. The twigs are very rough and are largely used for making rope bridges in the western Himalaya. The wood, too, is useful in being hard and close-grained.

There is an example at Kew near the Pagoda, which is quite hardy and flowers annually. Propagation is by cuttings or layers.

PARTHENOCISSUS   VITACEAE

A genus of about ten species of deciduous (rarely evergreen) climbers, natives of N. America, E. Asia, and the Himalaya. Tendrils branched, twining or equipped with adhesive pads. Leaves alternate, palmately compound, sometimes simple and three-lobed, or unlobed. Flowers in cymose panicles. Petals four or five, spreading (hence differing from *Vitis*, in which the petals are united in a cap which falls without expanding). Ovary included in the disk (in *Ampelopsis* the disk is cup-like and free from the ovary). Fruit a dark blue or black berry, with one to four seeds.

The generic name, meaning 'Virgin Vine', derives from the French name for the Virginia creeper—*vigne-vierge*.

P. HENRYANA (Hemsl.) Diels & Gilg   [PLATE 10
Vitis henryana Hemsl.; *Psedera henryana* (Hemsl.) Schneid.

A vigorous deciduous climber, with sharply four-angled stems free from down; tendrils forked, ending in disks by which it adheres to flat surfaces. Leaves composed of three to five leaflets borne on a stalk 1½ to 4½ in. long. Leaflets obovate, oblanceolate, or narrowly oval, slender-pointed, tapered at the base to a short stalk, coarsely toothed except near the base, 1½ to 5 in. long, one-third to one-half as wide, dark velvety green, variegated with silvery white and pink along the midrib and primary veins, which are slightly downy beneath. The green part turns red in autumn. Inflorescence a terminal leafy panicle of cymes up to 6 or 7 in. long.

Native of Central China; discovered by Henry about 1885; introduced by Wilson for Messrs Veitch in 1900. It is a remarkably handsome vine closely allied to the true Virginia creeper, and having the same power of attaching itself to walls, etc., by means of its adhesive disk-tipped tendrils. It thrives quite well against a wall or where it gets a little shelter, but fully exposed in the open it is not quite hardy. Its variegation is better defined on a north-west or even north wall, than when the plant is fully exposed to the sun.

P. HIMALAYANA (Royle) Planch.

Ampelopsis himalayana Royle

A vigorous deciduous climber, with semi-woody, glabrous young stems; the tendrils terminated by clinging disks. Leaves composed of three leaflets, each shortly stalked and borne at the end of a slender, common stalk 2 to 5 in. long. Central leaflet ovate, oval, or obovate; the side ones very obliquely ovate (two or three times as much blade on one side of the midrib as on the other), and often somewhat heart-shaped at the base on one side only. They are all abruptly tapered at the apex, toothed, dark green and glabrous above, paler, slightly glaucous beneath, with a few short hairs on the midrib only; 2 to 6 in. long, 1¼ to 4 in. wide. Fruits globose, ¼ in. wide, in loose clusters several times forked.

Native of the Himalaya up to 11,000 ft. It is a rather tender species, and only thrives well on a wall. Its leaves change to rich red in autumn.

P. SEMICORDATA (Wall.) Planch. *Vitis semicordata* Wall.; *V. himalayana* var. *semicordata* (Wall.) M. A. Lawson—This is perhaps not specifically distinct from *P. himalayana*, but it has smaller leaves and its young shoots and the undersurface of the leaves are bristly. It is perhaps a form from higher altitudes.

P. INSERTA (Kerner) Fritsch

Vitis (Ampelopsis) inserta Kerner; *Parthenocissus vitacea* (Knerr) Hitchc.; *Ampelopsis quinquefolia* var. *vitacea* Knerr; *Vitis vitacea* (Knerr) Bean; *Ampelopsis* or *Parthenocissus quinquefolia* Hort., in part

A deciduous climber closely allied to the true Virginia creeper, *P. quinquefolia* (q.v.). The best and most obvious distinction between it and that species is the absence of disks at the ends of the tendrils, on account of which it is unable to attach itself to flat surfaces. It supports itself, as most vines do, by twining its tendrils round whatever is available or by inserting them into crevices. It has the same five, obovate-lanceolate leaflets radiating from the end of a long, slender common stalk as in *P. quinquefolia*, but it differs in their being larger, greener beneath, brighter green above, and in the deeper, sharper teeth; the inflorescence is cymose and flatter.

P. inserta is widely spread in eastern, central, and south-western N. America. It was in cultivation by 1824, when it was figured in the *Botanical Magazine* (t. 2443) as *Cissus quinquefolia* and believed to be of Brazilian origin, but it may well have been introduced much earlier. It is so closely allied to the true Virginia creeper, *P. quinquefolia*, that it was not separated from it specifically until late in the 19th century, and judging from gardening literature of the period 1840–1880 no distinction was made between the two species, both being called Virginia creeper, of which it was sometimes said that it was self-clinging (this was the true *P. quinquefolia*), sometimes that it needed to be nailed to the wall (this was probably *P. inserta*). Confusion was probably made worse by the existence of hybrids between them.

When a self-supporting climber is not needed, *P. inserta* is a better and more handsome vine than either the true Virginia creeper or *P. tricuspidata,* and colours just as well in the autumn.

var. LACINIATA (Planch.) Rehd. *P. quinquefolia* var. *laciniata* Planch.; *Vitis vitacea* var. *laciniata* (Planch.) Bean; *V. quinquefolia incisa* Hort.—Leaves very deeply, sometimes doubly, toothed, some of the teeth being ½ in. deep, with a roughness on the surface due to scattered minute hairs; the main stalk of the leaf and the stalks of the leaflets are both longer than in the type. The variety is found wild in the western and south-western United States.

f. MACROPHYLLA (Lauche) Rehd. *Vitis quinquefolia* var. *macrophylla* Lauche; *Vitis quinquefolia* var. *major* Hort.—Leaflets very large, 6 to 8 in. across, 3 to 4½ in. wide.

P. QUINQUEFOLIA (L.) Planch.   VIRGINIA CREEPER

Hedera quinquefolia L.; *Vitis quinquefolia* (L.) *Lam.*; *Vitis hederacea* Ehrh.; *Ampelopsis hederacea* (Ehrh.) DC.

A tall, deciduous climber, reaching to the tops of lofty trees, free from down in all its parts; stems slender, reddish at first, clinging to its support by means of a disk at the end of each branch of the tendril. Leaves composed of five leaflets (sometimes three) radiating from the end of a common stalk 1 to 4 in. long. Leaflets oval to obovate, 1 to 4 in. long, ⅓ to 2½ in. wide, slenderly pointed, tapered at the base to a stalk ⅕ to ½ in. long, coarsely toothed except at the base; dull green above, pale and rather glaucous beneath. Inflorescence several times forked, the final subdivisions terminated by an umbel of three to eight flowers. Fruits globose, about ¼ in. wide, blue black.

P. quinquefolia (including its varieties) is widespread in eastern and central N. America as far south as Florida and Texas. It was in cultivation in 1629, and by the early part of the 18th century had become, according to Miller, 'as common as if it were a Native of the Country'. It is one of the finest of all climbers, its leaves turning a rich crimson before they fall. As it clings of itself to walls and tree trunks it is very useful. At Kew, without artificial support, it has climbed the naked trunks of lofty pine trees and reached the tops. Towards the end of the last century it became quite scarce in cultivation, having been replaced mainly by the Japanese creeper *P. tricuspidata,* but partly by *P. inserta,* a species without the sucker disks on its tendrils, and therefore not able to attach itself to flat surfaces. But at the beginning of this century various forms of it were reintroduced, and no doubt the old Virginia creeper could still be found (though nowadays the Japanese creeper is much commoner).

From the above, and from the accounts of *P. inserta* and *P. tricuspidata,* it will be seen that three species bear the name Virginia creeper. The present plant, *P. quinquefolia,* is the true Virginia creeper, but the name has also been used for *P. inserta,* and not altogether wrongly, for it is at least American, and closely allied to *P. quinquefolia.* But there can be no excuse for using the name Virginia creeper for *P. tricuspidata,* which is a native of Japan.

P. quinquefolia appears to be a variable species, but the published accounts do not give a clear picture of the variations and their geographical distribution

f. ENGELMANNII (Rehd.) Rehd. *Ampelopsis quinquefolia* var. *engelmannii* Rehd.; *Vitis engelmannii* Dieck; *Ampelopsis engelmannii* Spaeth—This differs botanically only in its smaller leaflets. But the plants distributed commercially, possibly from seeds collected by Engelmann, were said to differ in their blue-green leaflets and good autumn colouring.

var. HIRSUTA (Pursh) Planch. *Cissus hederacea* var. *hirsuta* Pursh; *Ampelopsis graebneri* Bolle; *A. quinquefolia* var. *graebneri* (Bolle) Rehd.—A distinct variety with hairy shoots, leaf-stalks, leaflets (both surfaces), and inflorescence. The culti-vated plant originally named *Ampelopsis graebneri*, which belongs here, was also distinguished by its intense autumn colouring.

var. MURORUM (Focke) Rehd. *Ampelopsis hederacea* var. *murorum* Focke; *Parthenocissus radicantissima* Koehne & Graebn.; *Ampelopsis muralis* Hort.— According to Rehder, this is the more southern form of the species, with ten-drils that have shorter, more numerous branches, and with usually broader leaflets. Some at least of the cultivated plants belonging to this variety are characterised by a very close, self-clinging habit.

var. SAINT-PAULII (Koehne & Graebn.) Rehd. *P. saint-paulii* Koehne & Graebn.; *Vitis quinquefolia* var. *saint-paulii* (Koehne & Graebn.) Bean—Young shoots, leaf-stalks, and under-surface of leaflets as well as midrib above clothed with down of a finer nature than in var. *hirsuta*, from which it also differs in the sharper, deeper teeth. This variety was described from plants distributed by Saint-Paul-Illaire of Fischbach, which were said to make good wall-climbers. It also occurs in the wild.

P. THOMSONII (M. A. Laws.) Planch.

Vitis thomsonii M. A. Laws.; *Cissus thomsonii* (M. A. Laws.) Planch.; *Cayratia thomsonii* (M. A. Laws.) Suessenguth; *P. henryi* var. *glaucescens* Diels & Gilg

A slender, deciduous climber; young stems slightly downy at first, ribbed. Leaves composed normally of five leaflets, borne on a slender downy stalk $1\frac{1}{2}$ to $4\frac{1}{2}$ in. long. Leaflets oval or obovate, 1 to 4 in. long, $\frac{1}{2}$ to $1\frac{1}{2}$ in. wide; slenderly pointed, the upper half shallowly but sharply toothed, the base entire and tapered to a stalk, $\frac{1}{8}$ to $\frac{3}{4}$ in. long; undersurface sparsely downy on the midrib, glossy. The entire leaf, leaf-stalk, and young shoots are of bright claret purple when young, becoming greenish purple later, changing finally to deep reddish purple. Flowers in cymes on a slender stalk.

A native mainly of W. and Central China, but described from a specimen collected in the Khasia Hills, Assam; introduced by Wilson from China in 1900, when collecting for Messrs. Veitch. It was awarded a First Class Certificate three years later and is, indeed, one of the most charming of the vines. It appears to be most nearly related to *P. henryana*, but is decidedly hardier.

P. TRICUSPIDATA (Sieb. & Zucc.) Planch.   JAPANESE CREEPER,
                        BOSTON IVY

Ampelopsis tricuspidata Sieb. & Zucc.; *Ampelopsis veitchii* Hort.; *Parthenocissus tricuspidata* f. *veitchii* (Carr.) Rehd.; *Cissus veitchii* Carr.; *Vitis inconstans* Miq.; *Psedera tricuspidata* (Sieb. & Zucc.) Rehd.

A lofty deciduous climber reaching the tops of trees over 60 ft high; young shoots glabrous, attaching themselves to their supports by means of viscous disks terminating the tendrils. Leaves extremely variable, but of three main types: 1, broadly ovate with a heart-shaped base, shallowly or coarsely toothed, but not, or very slightly, lobed; 2, composed of three distinct, stalked leaflets, the middle one obovate, the side ones obliquely ovate; 3, conspicuously and deeply three-lobed, the side lobes erect or spreading. The two first types are characteristic of young plants and young shoots, and the leaves average from 2 to 5 in. across; the last are found on old plants that have reached the flowering and fruiting stage, and the leaves are large and coarse, 8 in. or even more across. In all forms they are glabrous above, finely downy on the veins beneath. Flowers yellow-green, produced in cymes mostly on short two-leaved shoots. Fruits dull, dark blue with a bloom, flattish, $\frac{1}{4}$ in. to $\frac{1}{3}$ in. wide. *Bot. Mag.*, t. 8287.

Native of Japan and China; introduced by John Gould Veitch about 1862. No climbing plant ever introduced has secured so important a place in British horticulture. Owing to its abundance, it is now becoming the vogue to decry it. It certainly requires watching, and should never be allowed to grow over and shroud beautiful architectural detail. On the other hand, the stark ugliness of innumerable brick walls in urban districts has been hidden by it. It is really one of the least troublesome of climbers, being self-supporting and attaching itself readily and securely to walls, etc., by means of the viscid tips of the tendrils, and spreading with remarkable rapidity. The leaves of the young climbing branchlets are at first pressed to the wall. In autumn the foliage turns one of the loveliest of crimsons. The large leaves that appear on old plants near the base are coarse in appearance, and the plant then loses much of its charm. It does not bear fruit except during hot summers. Cuttings made of firm pieces of young branchlets, 3 or 4 in. long, and put in gentle heat about August strike root readily. The young plants should be grown in pots until planted out permanently, as they dislike transplanting.

P. tricuspidata (still better known in Britain as "*Ampelopsis veitchii*"), is very often, and quite wrongly, referred to as Virginia creeper. The explanation no doubt is that the true Virginia creeper from America (*P. quinquefolia*) was once very common as a wall-covering. But from the early 1870s the Japanese creeper gradually usurped its place on walls and at the same time took over its popular name. The two species are superficially similar, both being deciduous pad-climbers and both colouring in the autumn. But the Japanese creeper bears three kinds of leaf as described above; in the true Virginia creeper all the leaves are compound.

cv. 'LOWII'.—A seedling form raised by Messrs Low of Enfield and first exhibited by them in 1907. It has small three- to seven-lobed leaves, at least when young, very elegant, and colouring as well as the type.

PARTHENOCISSUS TRICUSPIDATA 'LOWII'

cv. 'PURPUREA'.—Leaves reddish purple all through the summer. Raised by H. Collyer and Co. of Tunbridge Wells and introduced in 1887.

PASSIFLORA   PASSION FLOWER   PASSIFLORACEAE

A large genus of more than 500 species, mostly climbers and almost wholly confined to the New World. The genus *Tacsonia* is now usually included in it. Only the two species described below are known to be reasonably hardy in the British climate, but there are several others which might be tried in the mildest parts, notably *P. antioquiensis*.

The name of 'passion flower' by which the following and all passifloras are known, was given originally by the Spanish priests in S. America, because of the resemblance their piety led them to detect between the various parts of the flower and the instruments of Christ's Passion. Dr Masters, the historian of the family, has pointed these out to be as follows: The three stigmas represent the three nails, two for the hands and one for the feet; the five anthers represent the five wounds; the corona represents the crown of thorns or the halo of glory; the five sepals and five petals stand for ten apostles—Peter and Judas being absent; the hand-like leaves and whip-like tendrils represent the hands and scourges of His persecutors.

P. CAERULEA L. PASSION FLOWER [PLATE 11

A climbing plant of great vigour and more or less evergreen, attaching itself to its supports by tendrils; devoid of down in all its parts. Leaves palmate, five- or seven-lobed, 4 to 7 in. across; lobes oblong with rounded ends; green above, somewhat glaucous beneath. Flowers borne on long, slender stalks from the leaf-axils of the young growing shoots; flat and open, fragrant, 3 to 4 in. across, the five sepals and five petals whitish. Between the petals and the stamens is a conspicuous ring of thread-like, purplish growths 2 in. across, known as the 'corona'. Fruits ovoid, up to $1\frac{3}{4}$ in. long, with a tough, orange-coloured rind and numerous seeds inside, embedded in pulp. *Bot. Mag.*, t. 28.

Native of S. Brazil; introduced, according to Aiton, in 1609. It is not genuinely hardy near London, but will often survive several winters on a sheltered wall. As it grows very rapidly and is easily propagated from seeds or cuttings, it is worth growing for its beautiful and remarkably constructed flowers, which start to appear in June, and continue until the end of September.

cv. 'CONSTANCE ELLIOTT', first shown by Messrs Lucombe, Pince, & Co., of Exeter, in 1884, has ivory-white flowers (see *Gard. Chron.* (1884), i., p. 701).

P. UMBILICATA (Griseb.) Harms
Tacsonia umbilicata Griseb.; *P. ianthina* Mast.

A vigorous glabrous climber, attaining at least 25 ft in cultivation, climbing by means of tendrils which are borne singly in the leaf-axils. Young stems slender, green, ribbed. Leaves deeply three-lobed with the lateral lobes spreading almost at right-angles to the terminal, the whole blade $1\frac{1}{4}$ to 2 in. long and $1\frac{5}{8}$ to 3 in. wide; lobes oblong, rounded and shortly mucronate at the apex, entire except for a small mucronate tooth on each side, terminal lobe $\frac{5}{8}$ to $1\frac{1}{4}$ in. long, $\frac{7}{16}$ to $\frac{7}{8}$ in. wide, the laterals a little shorter and narrower, upper surface deep bright green, lower surface paler; petioles $\frac{5}{8}$ to $1\frac{1}{4}$ in. long; stipules leafy, broadly ovate to roundish, up to $\frac{1}{2}$ in. long, undulately and widely toothed. Flowers on stout pedicels $2\frac{1}{4}$ to $3\frac{1}{4}$ in. long; bracteoles rich mauve-purple, borne close to the perianth, broadly cordate and up to $\frac{3}{4}$ in. long. Perianth rich mauve-purple or amethyst, 2 to $2\frac{1}{2}$ in. long, with a broad tube swollen to $\frac{3}{4}$ in. wide at the base; sepals and petals oblong-lanceolate, tapered to a narrow, acute apex, $\frac{3}{4}$ to $1\frac{3}{8}$ in. long, and about $\frac{1}{4}$ in. wide at the base; corona of numerous filaments about $\frac{3}{16}$ in. long arising near the mouth of the perianth-tube and standing erect above it. Androgynophore $1\frac{3}{8}$ in. long; stamens with filaments up to $\frac{3}{8}$ in. long. Ovary ellipsoid, about $\frac{1}{4}$ in. long; styles three, diverging a little, $\frac{1}{4}$ in. or slightly more long; stigma globose.

Native of central Bolivia and adjacent Paraguay to N. Argentina, at 8,000 to 9,500 ft. The above description is made from a plant that once grew in the Temperate House at Kew, raised from seeds received in 1954 from the late Norman Hadden, which had been collected in Bolivia by Miss W. M. A. Brooke. All the plants now growing in Britain are believed to be of this origin. The hardiness of this species is not yet fully tested, but it survived the very hard winters of 1961–3 at Porlock in Somerset, and grows vigorously there.

PAULOWNIA   SCROPHULARIACEAE

A small genus of deciduous trees, natives of China, Korea, Indochina, and Formosa, in which six species are recognised by Dr S.-Y. Hu in her monograph (*Qtly Journ. Taiwan Mus.*, Vol. 12 (1959), pp. 1–54). The leading characters are: Bark smooth, branchlets pithy; leaves opposite, entire or lobed; flowers in three- or five-flowered stalked or almost sessile cymes in the axils of the fallen leaves, produced in spring from buds developed in the previous autumn; calyx fleshy, five-lobed; corolla between tubular and funnel-shaped, obscurely two-lipped, the upper lip two-lobed, the lower three-lobed; stamens four; style one, with a small stigma; capsules ovoid to ellipsoid, with numerous winged seeds.

Dr Hu follows Pennel in retaining *Paulownia* in Scrophulariaceae as a monotypic tribe. Other botanists have placed it in the Bignoniaceae and indeed it bears a very close resemblance to *Catalpa*, which certainly belongs to the latter family. However, the Bignoniaceae and Scrophulariaceae are closely allied, and it has been suggested that *Catalpa* and *Paulownia* are near to the ancestral stock from which the two families have branched. The most obvious differential character of the catalpas is that their trunks are rugged and that the flowers are borne in summer at the ends of the seasonal growths; they also differ markedly from any paulownia in their long, cylindrical fruits.

The genus was named by Siebold in honour of Anna Paulowna, Hereditary Princess of the Netherlands.

For propagation and cultivation, see under *P. tomentosa*.

P. FORTUNEI (Seem.) Hemsl.

Campsis fortunei Seem.; *Paulownia duclouxii* Dode

A tree reported to attain 85 ft in S.E. China, but usually only half that height or less. Leaves ovate, mostly 5½ to 10 in. long, 2¾ to 5 in. wide, acuminate at the apex, cordate at the base, but those subtending the flower-buds much smaller and usually rounded or cuneate at the base, all densely woolly beneath; leaf-stalks 3 to 4½ in. long. Cymes mostly three-flowered, shortly stalked, arranged in the form of a narrow panicle. Calyx funnel-shaped, about ¾ in. long. Corolla

funnel-shaped, lavender-purple in the bud and retaining that colour on the outside, but white or creamy white inside and heavily spotted with dark purple,
3½ to 4 in. long, about 2 in. wide at the mouth. Capsules oblong-ellipsoid, 2
to 3 in. long, woody.

A native of S. and S.E. China, Formosa, and Indochina; described from a
specimen collected by Fortune in China but not introduced by him. Young
plants (of unrecorded origin) were at Kew in 1934, of which two were given
in that year to Neil McEacharn of the Villa Taranto, Pallanza, Lake Maggiore,
and are now one of the chief glories of the famous garden he created there. So
far as is known, all the examples of *P. fortunei* now growing in Britain (including those at Kew) are seedlings from the Pallanza trees. A note on this
species by Dr Herklots will be found in *Journ. R.H.S.*, Vol. 89 (1964), p. 300.

P. LILACINA Sprague
P. fargesii Hort., not Franch.; *P. tomentosa* cv. *Lilacina* Hu

A deciduous, sparsely branched tree up to 60 or 70 ft high; young shoots
pale green, clothed with viscid gland-tipped hairs; brown and warted the
second year. Leaves opposite, broadly ovate with a heart-shaped base, slender-
pointed, 6 to 12 in. long, 4 to 7 in. wide, dull green, nearly glabrous above,
downy beneath, especially on the veins and midrib when young; stalk thick,
2 to 4 in. long, covered with sticky hairs similar to those of the young shoots.
Panicles terminating the growths of the previous year, erect, pyramidal, 12 to
18 in. high, two-thirds as much wide. Corolla 3 in. long, tubular, divided
at the mouth (where it is 2½ in. wide) into five large rounded spreading lobes;
downy outside; pale lilac with a large yellowish stain in the throat. Calyx bell-
shaped, ½ in. long, with five deep recurved lobes covered with felt that is
fawn-coloured inside, dark brown outside. Ovary and style glutinous; flower-
stalk ¼ to ½ in. long, felted like the outside of the calyx. Fruits ovoid, 1½ to
1¾ in. long, ¾ to 1 in. wide, tapering at the top to a short slender point, brown.
Bot. Mag., t. 8926–7.

Native of China (probably western). It was sent to Kew in 1908 by Maurice
de Vilmorin and flowered there in June 1928. Judging by the behaviour of this
tree it would seem better fitted for our average climate than *P. tomentosa*. It
was sent to Kew as *P. fargesii* and seeds of it were distributed under that name.
When it flowered and was figured for the *Botanical Magazine* Dr Sprague found
it to be quite distinct from that species and gave it the above name. It received
a First Class Certificate when shown from Exbury on May 16, 1944.

From the commoner *P. tomentosa* this species differs in unlobed leaves, in the
more shortly hairy calyx and in the paler corolla with a widely expanded mouth.

The true P. FARGESII Franch. was described in 1896 from a specimen collected by Père Farges in N.E. Szechwan, and may not be in cultivation. It has an
oblong, spike-like inflorescence, with almost sessile cymes, and the leaves green
and almost glabrous beneath.

P. TOMENTOSA (Thunb.) Steud.

Bignonia tomentosa Thunb.; *Paulownia imperialis* Sieb. & Zucc.; *P. imperialis* var. *lanata* Dode; *P. tomentosa* var. *lanata* (Dode) Schneid.; *P. recurva* Rehd.

A round-topped, deciduous tree 30 to 50 ft high, with thick, stiff branches and rather open habit; all the parts more or less downy. Leaves opposite, the small ones ovate, the larger ones three- to five-lobed, the lobes pointed but shallow, the base deeply notched, the dimensions are very variable; in adult trees they are 5 to 10 in. long and wide, dark green, and with scattered hairs above, covered beneath with a soft, greyish wool; stalk nearly as long as the blade. Panicle terminal, up to 1 ft long, the flowers forming in autumn but not opening until the following May. Corolla blue-purple, fragrant, 1½ to 2 in. long, shaped like a huge foxglove; calyx woolly, ½ in. long, bell-shaped, with five ovate teeth. Seed-vessel an ovoid, pointed capsule, 1½ to 2 in. long, containing numerous winged seeds.

Native of China, but introduced from Japan to France in 1834 by means of seeds given to Neumann, director of the hothouses at the Jardin des Plantes, Paris. Only one plant was raised, which was 12 ft high in 1840 and flowered in the following year. In 1842 it was estimated that the total stock of plants raised from this single individual by seeds and vegetative propagation was between 20,000 and 30,000. There was a direct importation of seeds from Japan to Britain in 1838, which was distributed to private gardens, but some at least of the plants distributed commercially came from the Paris tree. In 1843, F. and A. Smith of Hackney were asking 7s 6d each for plants in 3-in. pots, a moderate price for a novelty (*Gard. Chron.* (1843), p. 81). It first flowered at Hampton Court in 1846 or 1847, and the first general flowering in Britain was in 1858 (*Gard. Chron.* (1849), pp. 387 and 405; op. cit., 1858, many references).

Few more beautiful flowering trees than this exist, but although the tree is fairly hardy and sets its flowers, they often do not develop in this country, owing to its curious habit of exposing them in bud through the winter. Perhaps they do not derive sufficient stamina from our dull summers, but more likely the unrest of our winters, with their alternate frosts and mild spells, prevents their proper development.

But whilst many gardens in Great Britain are denied the blossoms of this tree, it may, by another mode of cultivation, be made to provide a fine feature anywhere but in the coldest parts. This is to treat it simply as a fine-foliaged plant. To get the best effect the plants should be set out 3 or 4 ft apart in a group of at least twenty, and be kept to a single stem, the object being to obtain leaves as large as possible. In spring the stem is cut back to within 2 in. of the older wood. From the crowd of young growths that then push out the two strongest are selected, the rest rubbed off. Two are left for fear of accident only, and after they are fairly established the weaker one is removed. It then only remains to water when necessary and to feed the plants with manure. Well-grown plants will have huge pentagonal leaves 2 to 3 ft across, and the sturdy erect stems will grow over 12 ft high in the season. Paulownias need a rich soil and are best propagated from seed, which is produced in plenty on the Continent. Root-cuttings may also be used. Young plants, being almost herbaceous, are very tender and should pass their first winter under glass.

The tree at Westonbirt mentioned below is by far the tallest paulownia so far recorded in Britain and one of the largest in girth. Other notable specimens are: Linton Park, Kent, 35 × 5½ ft (1972); Botanic Gardens, Bath, 40 × 7½ ft (1962); Paignton Zoo, Devon, 40 × 7 ft (1969); Hergest Croft, Heref., 38 × 3½ ft (1969); Shelton Abbey, Co. Wicklow, Eire, 36 × 6 ft (1968); Birr Castle, Co. Offaly, Eire, 44× 4 ft (1966).

An old paulownia at Ashridge Park, Herts., is portrayed in *Gard. Chron.*, Jan. 26, 1957, p. 98. In the accompanying letter, Maynard Greville gave its dimensions as 56 × 7¾ ft. He also mentioned a tree at Elsenham Hall, Essex, 5¾ ft in girth, which had been completely bored out by woodpeckers to within 3 ft of the ground, but was still alive.

During his first expedition for the Arnold Arboretum in 1907–9, Wilson found *P. tomentosa* growing wild in W. Hupeh and sent seeds under W.769. This form was generally referred to as *P. tomentosa* var. *lanata* or as *P. recurva* and a note on a tree at Exbury under the former name will be found in *Journ. R.H.S.*, Vol. 68 (1943), p. 235. There is no significant botanical difference between the Wilson introduction and the common form, but the plants are reported to have grown faster. Also, judging from the tree in the Specimen Avenue at Westonbirt raised from the Wilson sending, this form also grows taller; in 1972 it measured 86 × 6¾ ft, a remarkable height for this species, and is still in good health. H. J. Elwes had a tree from the Wilson seeds at Colesbourne, suckers of which he distributed to a number of gardens.

PAXISTIMA   CELASTRACEAE

Two North American, low, glabrous shrubs, with small evergreen opposite, leathery leaves and tiny inconspicuous flowers. They have four petals, four stamens, and a two-celled ovary; the fruit is small; oblong, white. These two shrubs thrive best in a soil that is partly peat, partly sandy loam, and are, perhaps, best adapted for a nook in the rock garden, where, however, their interest will be chiefly botanical. They need only be recommended to people who love rare, out-of-the-way plants, irrespective of their beauty. At the same time the paxistimas make neat, rather dainty tufts. Both are easily increased by cuttings.

Rafinesque originally called this genus *Pachistima*, from the Greek παχύς (pachys), 'thick', and 'stigma'. But he did not validly publish this name, and when he established the genus in 1838 he used the spelling *Paxistima*. It may well be that Rafinesque inadvertently wrote the Greek symbol χ instead of *ch*, and that this was printed 'x' in which case it would be in order to treat *Paxistima* as a misprint for the original *Pachistima*. But Rafinesque was a strange figure, and a law unto himself so far as the coining of names is concerned. In the light of his other oddities, the possibility cannot be ruled out that he deliberately altered *ch* to 'x', for some reason that is not now apparent. Both spellings appear in modern works. The rendering *Pachystima*, also sometimes used, is definitely not allowable.

P. CANBYI A. Gray

A low evergreen shrub up to 1 ft high, with linear or narrow-oblong leaves, ½ to 1 in. long, $\frac{3}{16}$ in. or less wide, shallowly toothed towards the apex, the margins decurved; quite glabrous. Flowers very small, greenish, borne on very slender-stalked cymes ½ in. long in the leaf-axils. Fruits $\frac{3}{16}$ in. long, white.

Native of steep rocky slopes in the mountains from Virginia westward as far as south-east Ohio and north-east Kentucky; introduced to Kew in 1893, where it has proved hardy. It is of no beauty of flower, and its only merit as a garden shrub is its neat low habit, for it does not bear fruit freely with us. It is also of scientific interest because of its restricted geographical distribution. It is mainly confined to W. Virginia and is said to be found only on calcareous soils. It blooms from May to August.

P. MYRTIFOLIA (Nutt.) Wheeler

Myginda myrtifolia Nutt.; *Ilex? myrsinites* Pursh, *nom. prov.*; *Paxistima myrsinites* (Pursh) Raf.

An evergreen shrub 6 to 18 in. high, ultimately spreading in habit. Leaves oblanceolate to narrow-oblong or ovate, from ½ to 1¼ in. long, from $\frac{1}{16}$ to ¼ in. wide, toothed towards the tip. Flowers ⅛ in. across, reddish, produced singly, or two or three together in the leaf-axils. Fruit white, ⅛ in. long.

This is the western representative of the genus, being found in woods on the north-western coast of N. America, and in the valleys of the Rocky Mountains. It is much more widely spread and abundant than its eastern ally, but has no more value in the garden. If differs from *P. canbyi* in its freer, more robust growth, its wider, larger leaves not so much decurved at the margins, and in its shorter flower-stalks. It blossoms in April and during the two or three succeeding months.

PENSTEMON   SCROPHULARIACEAE

This genus is almost purely N. American and consists of some 150 species, most of which are perennial herbaceous plants. The shrubby species are mostly native of California. The leaves are opposite; the corolla tubular, two-lipped; stamens five, as the generic name indicates, but one of them is always sterile. The shrubby species are easily increased by cuttings of moderately ripened wood; they like a sunny position and a lightish well-drained soil. A very beautiful genus.

P. CORDIFOLIUS Benth.

An evergreen shrub of straggling loose habit; young shoots opposite, very downy. Leaves heart-shaped, pointed, coarsely toothed, $\frac{1}{2}$ to 2 in. long and about two-thirds as wide, glossy dark green, minutely downy on both sides; stalk $\frac{1}{4}$ in. or less long. Flowers produced in a large terminal pyramidal panicle as much as 12 in. long and 9 in. wide. Corolla $1\frac{1}{2}$ in. long, scarlet, glandular-downy, with a cylindrical tube, two-lipped; upper lip hooded, the lower one decurved and divided into three linear lobes. Calyx very glandular, downy, $\frac{1}{4}$ in. long, cut deeply into five lanceolate lobes; flower-stalk glandular; anthers yellow, finally whitish. *Bot. Mag.*, t. 4497.

Native of California; discovered by David Douglas in 1831; introduced by Hartweg in 1848 through the Horticultural Society. The sterile stamen is conspicuously bearded on one side with pale hairs. Like most of the shrubby penstemons this is not very hardy, but when grown at Kew on a south wall, it makes a fine display from late June until August or even later. It is undoubtedly one of the finest of the shrubby species.

P. CORYMBOSUS Benth.—This species is allied to the preceding, but less common in gardens. It is a dwarf shrub in the wild, usually less than $1\frac{1}{2}$ ft high and often mat-forming. Leaves variable in shape from ovate to elliptic or oblong, up to $1\frac{1}{4}$ in. long and $\frac{3}{8}$ in. wide, entire or finely toothed, tapered at the base, never cordate as in *P. cordifolius*. Flowers scarlet, borne after midsummer in terminal corymbs (not in a leafy panicle as in *P. cordifolius*).

P. DAVIDSONII Greene [PLATE 12

P. menziesii Hook., *nom. illegit.*; *P. menziesii* subsp. *davidsonii* (Greene) Piper; *P. davidsonii* subsp. *menziesii* Keck; *P. davidsonii* var. *menziesii* (Keck) Cronquist

A creeping, mat-forming shrub with erect flowering stems 2 to 6 in. high, downy. Leaves on the prostrate stems rather thick, glabrous, not glaucous, $\frac{3}{16}$ to $\frac{3}{8}$ in. long, variable in shape from elliptic to obovate or roundish, entire or more or less saw-toothed, usually obtuse to rounded at the apex, shortly stalked; the leaves on the flowering stems below the flowers reduced in size and often bract-like. Racemes glandular-downy, few-flowered. Calyx $\frac{5}{16}$ to $\frac{7}{16}$ in. long, the sepals lanceolate to ovate-lanceolate. Corolla lavender- to violet-coloured, 1 to $1\frac{1}{2}$ in. long, between tubular and funnel-shaped, two-lipped, the upper lip two-lobed, the lower one three-lobed and hairy near the base. Anthers densely bearded; staminode much shorter than the fertile stamens, hairy at the tip.

Native of western N. America from the southern end of the Sierra Nevada, California, north to southern British Columbia (including the southern part of Vancouver Island); it also occurs in Alaska and extends east into Nevada. It was discovered by Menzies during the Vancouver expedition 1790–5 and described by the elder Hooker under the illegitimate and confused name *P. menziesii* (on this name see further below). The specimen was said to have been collected in Nootka Sound (on the Pacific coast of Vancouver Island), where the species is still to be found. But J. C. Bennett has pointed out that these sea-level plants are robuster and larger-leaved than the plant found by Menzies, which matches those that occur high in the mountains of Vancouver Island. Yet Menzies cannot have visited these high-level locations, which would in his time have been inaccessible owing to the dense forests and the hostility of the Indians (*Journ. R.H.S.*, Vol. 59 (1934), p. 353). A possible explanation is that at the end of the 18th century the small-leaved very dwarf form still existed at sea-level as a relict from a cold and wet climatic phase of the post-glacial epoch, but has since disappeared.

P. davidsonii was described in 1892 from a plant collected in the Yosemite region of California. In this plant the leaves are quite entire, as they are on all plants from California, while in the type of *P. menziesii* they are toothed. Judging from the plants in the Kew Herbarium the presence or absence of teeth is not correlated with any other character, but the combination *P. davidsonii* var. *menziesii* (Keck) Cronquist is perfectly valid, and could if necessary be used to distinguish plants with toothed leaves from those with entire leaves.

The name *P. menziesii* appeared in garden literature around the middle of the last century, and the name *P. davidsonii* early in the present century. Yet curiously enough the species to which these names properly belong did not come into cultivation until the 1930s. This introduction was at first known as *P. menziesii microphyllus* and is believed to have come from the Selkirk mountains of British Columbia. This is a high-mountain form, growing only an inch or two high, with leaves ⅜ in. or less long with scarcely noticeable toothing, of a dark, glossy green. The flowers, borne May and June, are of a remarkable size for such a small-leaved plant.

For the plant distributed by the Six Hills nursery as *P. davidsonii*, see *P. rupicola*, treated under *P. newberryi*. The plant known to Farrer as *P. davidsonii* was probably a form or hybrid of *P. newberryi*. It had stems that ended 'in baggy bugles of a ferocious aniline red-mauve most terrible and breath-taking to look upon in the sun' (*The English Rock Garden*, Vol. 2, p. 49).

NOTE. Although Hooker's description of *P. menziesii* is based on the Menzies specimen from Nootka, he cited as a synonym *Gerardia fruticosa* Pursh, which is the type of *Penstemon fruticosus* (Pursh) Greene. This citation renders the name *P. menziesii* illegitimate, for if Hooker considered the Menzies specimen to belong to the same species as the penstemon which Pursh named *Gerardia fruticosa*, then he should have used the epithet *fruticosus*. This may seem a pettifogging reason for suppressing a long-established name, but there is the further consideration that Hooker's *P. menziesii* is a confused species, in effect compounded of two distinct species, namely *P. davidsonii* and *P. fruticosus*. This in part explains how *P. menziesii* came to be used in such a wide sense.

P. FRUTICOSUS (Pursh) Greene

Gerardia fruticosa Pursh; *P. douglasii* Hook.; *P. menziesii* var. *douglasii* (Hook.) A.Gr.; *P. fruticosus* var. *douglasii* (Hook.) Schneid.; *P. lewisii* Benth.; *P. crassifolius* Lindl.

An erect subshrub with glabrous or slightly downy stems, 6 in. to 2 ft high. Leaves variable in shape from obovate to elliptic-oblong or lanceolate, acute or obtuse at the apex, entire or saw-toothed, shortly stalked, up to 2¼ in. long and ⅝ in. wide, those at the base of the flowering shoots smaller than on the sterile shoots. Flowers arranged oppositely in short racemes, the main axis and pedicels glandular-hairy. Calyx-lobes glandular-hairy, lanceolate to lanceolate-ovate, acute to acuminate at the apex. Corolla lavender or light purple, funnel-shaped, two-lipped, the upper lip two-lobed, the lower three-lobed and hairy, $1\frac{1}{4}$ to $1\frac{3}{4}$ in. long. Stamens not exserted from the mouth of the corolla; anthers densely woolly.

Native of western N. America from southern British Columbia to Oregon, east to Montana and Wyoming; discovered by Lewis and Clark during their pioneering overland journey to the Pacific and back in 1803–6. David Douglas collected a specimen in the Blue Mountains of Oregon in 1827 and also introduced it to cultivation. The form he found had small, rather thick, entire leaves and was given specific rank as *P. douglasii* by the elder Hooker and as *P. crassifolius* by Lindley; the two names were published in the same year, the former based on the specimen he collected, the latter on plants raised from his seeds. The Douglas introduction and other plants of a similar nature are now considered to be part of the normal variation of the species.

var. SCOULERI (Lindl.) Cronquist *P. scouleri* Lindl.; *P. menziesii* var. *scouleri* (Lindl.) A. Gr.; *P. fruticosus* subsp. *scouleri* (Lindl.) Pennel & Keck—*P. fruticosus* is mainly represented in cultivation by this variety, which really differs from the typical state of the species only in its relatively narrower leaves, which are 1 to 2 in. long but never more than $\frac{1}{4}$ in. wide; they are always finely toothed, except for the smaller basal leaves of the shoot, but the toothing is irregular and not always conspicuous. *Bot. Mag.*, t. 6834.

This variety occurs within the area of the typical state of the species, but has a more restricted distribution. It was discovered by Douglas on the Columbia River near the Kettle Falls and introduced by him in 1828. It is hardy in a sunny position in well-drained soil and flowers in May and June. There are white- and pink-flowered forms in cultivation.

The plant portrayed in *New Flora and Sylva*, Vol. 3, fig. 96, as *P. lyallii* and discussed on p. 265 of that issue, is really a form of *P. fruticosus* var. *scouleri*. The true *P. lyallii* is a much taller plant and scarcely shrubby.

P. BARRETIAE A. Gray—An ally of *P. fruticosus*, but quite distinct. It is an erect subshrub 1 to 2 ft high, with glabrous leaves and stems. Leaves on the sterile shoots and at the base of the flowering stems $1\frac{1}{4}$ to 3 in. long and up to 1 in. wide, tapered at the base into an indistinct petiole, entire or faintly toothed, rather thick and distinctly glaucous; leaves at the base of the flowering stems shorter and relatively broader, sessile. Flowers in racemes, or sometimes the peduncles two-flowered. Calyx about $\frac{1}{4}$ in. long, the sepals ovate. Corolla lilac-purple, about $1\frac{1}{2}$ in. long. This species was discovered by a Mrs Barret and described in 1886. It has a limited distribution in the Cascade mountains, in Klickitat Co., Washington, north of the Columbia River, and in Mount Hood and Wasco Cos., Oregon, to the south of it. It was in cultivation in Britain as early as 1889 but may not have been in cultivation continuously since then. Plants raised at Kew in the 1930s from seeds received from commercial sources in California and British Columbia were not the true species but forms of *P. fruticosus*. But J. Elliott had what seems to have been the true species (see *Gard. Chron.*, Vol. 120 (1946), p. 135 and fig. 63).

P. CARDWELLII Howell *P. fruticosus* var. *cardwellii* (Howell) Krautter;

P. fruticosus subsp. *cardwellii* (Howell) Piper—Very closely allied to *P. fruticosus*, differing in the always toothed leaves obtuse or rounded at the apex, and the darker, sometimes red-purple flowers. It occurs in Oregon on the western side of the Cascade mountains and in the coastal range, and extends into S.W. Oregon. It was introduced to Kew in the 1930s by means of seeds received from Lester Rowntree of California.

P. HETEROPHYLLUS Lindl.

A subshrub usually under 1½ ft high, the stems, leaves, and inflorescences either glabrous or slightly downy. Leaves opposite, sessile, linear or lanceolate, 1 to 4 in. long, ⅛ to ¼ in. wide, sessile, green or more rarely glaucous. Flowers lavender-blue at the mouth, purplish red at the base, 1 to 1¼ in. long, borne in the axils of reduced leaves at the ends of the season's shoots singly or in twos; tube narrow, somewhat inflated and expanded at the apex. Anthers hairy on the margin; sterile stamen glabrous. *Bot. Mag.*, t. 3853.

Native of California; discovered by Douglas and introduced by him in 1828. It is a beautiful species in its best-coloured forms but rather tender and intolerant of winter wet.

P. ISOPHYLLUS B. L. Robinson

A semi-shrubby plant of bushy habit, 2 to 3 or more ft high; young shoots densely leafy and very minutely downy. Leaves opposite, elliptic-ovate, 1 to 2½ in. long, ⅓ to 1 in. wide, pointed or blunt, rather fleshy, dark green, minutely warted and glaucous beneath, sessile or scarcely stalked. Flowers scarlet-crimson with pale lines in the throat, borne on loose, erect racemes 8 to 15 in. long, corolla tubular, 1½ to 1¾ in. long, ⅔ to 1 in. across, two-lipped, the upper lip two-lobed, the lower one three-lobed, the lobes rounded; fertile stamens four, white, two attached to the bottom of the corolla-tube, the other pair amalgamated with the corolla for the lower half-inch. The flowering season is late summer and autumn. *Bot. Mag.*, t. 9482.

Native of Mexico, introduced in 1908. It is a plant of great beauty but not quite hardy, although it may survive several mild winters in a sheltered position. If merely cut back to the base it will spring up again. It is an admirable plant for the milder parts.

P. NEWBERRYI A. Gray

P. menziesii var. *newberryi* (A. Gr.) A. Gr.; *P. menziesii* var. *robinsonii* Mast.

This species is mainly represented in gardens by the following form:

f. HUMILIOR Sealy *P. roezlii* Hort., not Reg.—An evergreen, mat-forming subshrub 4 to 6 in. high; young stems clad with fine, spreading down. Leaves broad-elliptic to almost orbicular, $\frac{5}{16}$ to ¾ in. long, ¼ to $\frac{7}{16}$ in. wide, rounded to obtuse at the apex, cuneate at the base, bluntly toothed, dull green, leathery, glabrous; petioles $\frac{1}{16}$ to $\frac{1}{4}$ in. long. Flowering stems 3 to 5 in. long, with several pairs of reduced leaves in their lower part and terminated by two to eight flowers rather densely crowded together; pedicels $\frac{3}{16}$ to $\frac{3}{8}$ in. long, clad, like the upper part of the flowering stem, with fine glandular down. Calyx about $\frac{3}{8}$ in. long, with bluntly acute to acuminate lobes. Corolla tubular-funnel-shaped, with scarcely spreading lips, bright cerise-crimson on the outside, about 1$\frac{1}{4}$ in. long. Filaments of stamens glabrous; anthers densely bearded. Staminode (infertile stamen) hairy. Ovary glabrous, tapered into the style. *Bot. Mag.*, n.s., t. 4.

The origin of the plant described above is unknown, but it was originally distributed earlier this century under the name "*P. roezlii*", which properly belongs to a quite different plant. Under this erroneous name it received an Award of Garden Merit in 1931, and even today is still offered under it by some nurserymen. It is perhaps the commonest of the dwarf shrubby penstemons in gardens and one of the most decorative, bearing a profusion of vividly coloured flowers in May and June. It is hardy, provided it is planted in full sun and a well-drained soil, and is easily propagated by tip-cuttings in June, or even as late as September.

P. newberryi, in its typical state, resembles the plant described above in all essentials, but is more robust, with leaves up to 1 in. or slightly more long, and usually taller-growing, to about 1$\frac{1}{2}$ ft. It is a native mainly of California, in the Sierra Nevada, from Tulare Co. northward; also farther north, in south-west Oregon. It was discovered by the geologist J. S. Newberry, who accompanied a railroad survey expedition in northern California and southern Oregon in the middle of the last century. It was in cultivation in Britain by 1872.

P. RUPICOLA (Piper) Howell *P. newberryi* var. *rupicola* Piper; *P. davidsonii* Hort., in part, not Greene—This species is near allied to *P. newberryi* and was originally described as a variety of it, from a specimen collected on Mount Rainier. It differs in its prostrate, creeping habit; in its markedly glaucous, thick leaves, which usually have short, inconspicuous hairs on the midrib and main veins; in the fewer-flowered inflorescence; and in the more ventricose shape of the corolla. In the cultivated plant the colour of the flowers is pinker than in *P. newberryi*. *Bot. Mag.*, t. 8660.   [PLATE 13

P. rupicola has a limited distribution from Washington to N. California. It was introduced to cultivation around 1910 and was distributed by Clarence Elliott's Six Hills nursery as "*P. davidsonii*", a name that belongs to a different, though related, species. It is hardy in a sunny place in well-drained soil.

The hybrid 'SIX HILLS' was the result of a cross between *P. rupicola* and *P. eriantherus* (*cristatus*), the second parent being an almost herbaceous species not treated here.

P. PINIFOLIUS Greene

A dwarf, spreading shrub 4 to 12 in. high (up to 2 ft high in the wild), 3 ft or more wide. Leaves needle-like, $\frac{3}{8}$ to 1 in. long, sharply pointed, narrowed at the base to a short indistinct petiole, glabrous. Flowers borne in August in terminal racemose or narrowly paniculate inflorescences 2 to 4$\frac{1}{2}$ in. long, on pedicels $\frac{1}{8}$ to $\frac{3}{16}$ in. long, densely glandular-downy. Calyx about $\frac{3}{16}$ in. long, divided to about half-way into five narrow, trianguiar-acute or ovate, long-apiculate lobes, glandular-downy. Corolla about 1 in. long, scarlet, narrowly tubular at the base, divided at the top into five oblong lobes rounded at the apex, three of them narrow, the other two broader. Stamens exserted from the throat but overtopped by the lobes. Ovary glabrous; style slender, exserted beyond the stamens.

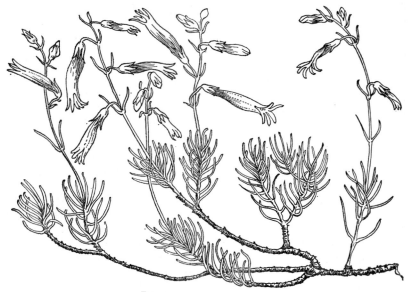

PENSTEMON PINIFOLIUS

Native of the S.W. United States in Arizona and New Mexico, extending into Mexico; introduced to Britain by Mrs Crewsdon, who received seeds from Dr Worth of the USA shortly before 1951. It is perfectly hardy in full sun and a well-drained soil.

PENTACTINA   ROSACEAE

The species described below is the only member of this genus, which is allied to *Spiraea* but differs from it in its linear petals and its carpels with only two ovules. The inflorescence resembles that of *Stephanandra*, which genus differs in having stipules.

P. RUPICOLA Nakai

A deciduous shrub 2 to 2½ ft high; young shoots angled, glabrous, reddish; winter-buds silky. Leaves without stipules, alternate, very shortly stalked, mostly oblanceolate to obovate, wedge-shaped at the base, with usually three or five lobes or large teeth towards the apex, the lobes fine-pointed, often toothed, ¾ to 1½ in. long, ⅓ to ¾ in. wide, glabrous above, more or less furnished with silky hairs beneath. Flowers small, white, produced in June and July on slender terminal pendulous panicles 1½ to 3 in. long. Petals five, linear, ⅕ in. long; sepals five, triangular, persisting to the fruiting stage when they become much reflexed; stamens twenty, white, exposed. Each flower has five dry seed-vessels about $\frac{1}{16}$ in. long.

Native of the Diamond Mountains of Korea and the only species known; introduced to the Arnold Arboretum in 1918 by Wilson, who found it common on cliffs. It is a graceful dwarf shrub with clustered stems, usually found wild growing in the crevices of rocks, but with more beauty in leaf and habit than in flower. It is quite hardy.

PERAPHYLLUM   ROSACEAE

A genus of one species in western N. America, closely allied to the amelanchiers, but differing in the narrow entire leaves, longer calyx-tube and rounded petals.

P. RAMOSISSIMUM Nutt.

A deciduous shrub 6 to 10 ft high in some of its native haunts, of spreading habit; branchlets at first downy, ultimately glabrous and bluish grey. Leaves 1 to 2 in. long, about ¼ in. wide, narrowly oblanceolate, entire, tapering to a short stalk at the base, rather more abruptly to the point; downy beneath when young, becoming glabrous. On the young shoots the leaves are alternate; on one-year-old shoots they are in tufts. Flowers in short-stalked corymbs, produced in April and May with the leaves from the joints of the previous summer's wood; there are from one to three flowers in the cluster, each ⅝ in. in diameter; calyx and flower-stalk silky; petals white, orbicular. Fruit a berry, ⅓ to ½ in. in diameter, globose, yellow with a reddish cheek, edible. *Bot. Mag.*, t. 7420.

Native of western N. America on dry hillsides; introduced to Kew in 1870. In English gardens it must be regarded more as a curiosity (being the only species of its genus) than as an ornamental shrub, for it flowers indifferently and rarely bears fruit. It comes from regions (Colorado, Utah, California, etc.) where the summers are infinitely hotter and brighter than ours, and this summer heat, no doubt, is what it misses here. It is, however, quite hardy, and can be increased by layers.

PERIPLOCA   PERIPLOCACEAE

A small genus of twining or laxly-stemmed shrubs, ranging from W. Africa and the Canary Islands through S. Europe and the Near East to China. Eleven species are recognised by the Polish botanist K. Browicz in his monograph on the genus (*Arb. Kornickie*, No. XI (1966), pp. 5–104, in English).

Leaves opposite, entire (though some species, not treated here, are almost leafless). Inflorescence a terminal or lateral cyme. Calyx five-lobed. Corolla with five spreading lobes, the inner surface of which is heavily marked in some shade of brown or purple and more or less viscid except at the paler margins. Stamens five, free from each other. Corona-lobes five, linear, each springing from the base of a stamen and arching inward at the apex. Styles two, stigmas united. Carpels two, each developing into a many-seeded follicle ('pod'). For the remarkable pollination mechanism see: Willis, *Dict. Fl. Plants & Ferns*, ed. 7, p. 852, ed. 8, p. 874.

P. GRAECA L.   SILK VINE

A deciduous climber of vigorous, twining habit, reaching 20 to 30 ft in height; stems brown, quite glabrous, exuding a milky juice when cut. Leaves opposite, mostly oval or ovate, 2 to 4 in. long, about half as wide, not toothed, pointed at the apex, rounded or wedge-shaped at the base, with prominent

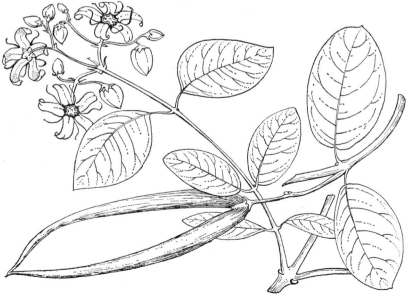

PERIPLOCA GRAECA

parallel veins merging into a marginal one; stalk $\frac{1}{4}$ to $\frac{1}{2}$ in. long. Cymes 2 or 3 in. across, terminating short lateral shoots, produced in July and August, and consisting of eight to twelve flowers. Flowers 1 in. across, the corolla composed of five narrow, oblong segments, $\frac{3}{16}$ in. wide, rounded at the end and downy, especially at the edges, brownish purple inside, greenish yellow outside; calyx $\frac{1}{4}$ in. across, with five ovate lobes. Seed-pods in pairs, cylindrical, 5 in. long, $\frac{1}{4}$ in. wide, tapering to a point where they are usually united; full of seeds, each with a remarkable tuft of silky hairs at the end $1\frac{1}{4}$ in. long.

Native of the Balkans, the coasts of the Black Sea, and the Near East; also of Italy, where it is rare and local; cultivated since the 16th century. It thrives in any soil of moderate quality, and requires a sunny position. Best propagated by division of the root in spring. It is a free-growing, hardy climber, interesting in its curious flowers, and may be used for pergolas, etc. The milk that exudes from the broken stems is poisonous, and in the south of Europe it is believed to be injurious to health to inhale the heavy odour of the flowers.

P. LAEVIGATA Ait.

An evergreen shrub with lax, mostly non-twining stems; young shoots glabrous. Leaves leathery, densely arranged, mostly elliptic, 1 to 2 in. long, $\frac{3}{16}$ to $\frac{5}{8}$ in. wide, bright green above, paler beneath, glabrous on both sides, tapered at the base to a short, stout petiole. Inflorescence terminal and lateral, about 1 in. to almost 3 in. long, with up to fifteen flowers. Corollas about $\frac{1}{2}$ in. across, lobes violet or brownish violet on the inside, linear. Follicles horizontal, or spreading at a very wide angle, 3 to 4 in. long, tapered evenly from the base to an acute apex.

Native of the Canary Islands; described in Aiton's *Hortus Kewensis* (1789), from a plant introduced by Francis Masson.

P. ANGUSTIFOLIA Labill. *P. laevigata* var. *angustifolia* (Labill.) Fiori; *P. laevigata* subsp. *angustifolia* (Labill.) Markgraf—Closely allied to *P. laevigata*, differing mainly in its narrower leaves, $\frac{5}{8}$ to $1\frac{1}{8}$ in. long, about $\frac{1}{8}$ in. wide, densely clustered on the lateral spurs. Native mainly of N. Africa, but extending into S.E. Spain, Malta, and some of the smaller islands of the central Mediterranean. It is also found in one locality in Syria, and it is from this that Labillardière described the species. As in *P. laevigata*, the follicles spread horizontally or almost so.

P. SEPIUM Bunge   CHINESE SILK VINE

A deciduous climbing shrub 6 to 10 ft (perhaps more) high; young shoots glabrous. Leaves opposite, lanceolate to narrowly oval, not toothed, mostly slenderly pointed, tapered at the base, $1\frac{3}{4}$ to 4 in. long, $\frac{1}{2}$ to $1\frac{1}{4}$ in. wide, shining green, glabrous on both surfaces; stalk $\frac{1}{8}$ to $\frac{1}{2}$ in. long. Flowers fragrant, about $\frac{3}{4}$ in. wide, produced two to nine together in axillary and terminal cymes during June and July; main flower-stalk 1 to 2 in. long. Corolla greenish outside, dark purple inside, five-lobed, the lobes revolute and woolly towards the margin.

T A S—E.

Seed-pods in pairs, slenderly cylindrical, tapering at the end where they are con-nected, 4 to 6 in. long, $\frac{3}{16}$ in. wide; seeds furnished with a tuft of silky white hairs.

Native of N. China; introduced to America in 1905. It differs from *P. graeca* in its narrower, often lanceolate leaves, more slender stems and somewhat hardier constitution. A further distinction given by Dr Browicz is that the corolla-lobes have a prominent glandular patch on the inner surface near the midpoint, absent in *P. graeca*.

PERNETTYA   ERICACEAE

This genus commemorates Antoine Joseph Pernetty, the historian of Bougainville's voyage to the Falkland Isles, the Straits of Magellan, and other parts of S. America (1763–4). He was born in 1716 and died at Avignon in 1801. *Pernettya*, represented in Tasmania and New Zealand as well as in Central and S. America, is closely allied to *Gaultheria*. In that genus, however, the ovary develops into a dehiscent capsule, while in *Pernettya* it becomes fleshy and does not dehisce. In *Gaultheria* the calyx becomes fleshy and enlarged, almost enclosing the capsule and united with it; in *Pernettya* too the calyx becomes fleshy in the majority of species, but it does not enlarge so much as in *Gaultheria* and is not united to the fruit. However, the difference, such as it is, is not very clear cut, and the two genera are likely to be united before long, under the name *Gaultheria*, which has priority.

The distribution of sexes in wild plants has not been studied in detail. So far as the cultivated species are concerned, Dr Stoker found that those with fleshy calyces, namely *P. tasmanica*, *P. macrostigma*, *P. prostrata*, and *P. furens*, bear bisexual flowers and produce fruits even if only one indi-vidual is grown, while *P. mucronata* *P. leucocarpa*, and *P. pumila* are func-tionally dioecious and will not set fruit without a pollinator. But see further under *P. mucronata*.

P. FURENS (Hook.) Klotzsch   [PLATE 14
Arbutus furens Hook.; *Gaultheria furens* (Hook). Hook. & Arn.

An evergreen shrub 2 to 4 ft high; young shoots hairy at first, becoming brown and glabrous. Leaves ovate to ovate-lanceolate, up to 2 in. long by $\frac{1}{2}$ to $\frac{3}{4}$ in. wide, pointed, tapering to a very short red stalk, sparsely toothed, ciliate when young, dark green. Flowers crowded in axillary racemes $1\frac{1}{4}$ in. long, nodding; corolla waxy white, ovoid-globose, $\frac{1}{4}$ in. long, spreading at the apex into five quite short, broad, reflexed lobes, opening from April to June; calyx with five short, spreading lobes; stamens ten, downy at the base. Fruits brownish red, with a fleshy calyx. *Bot. Mag.*, t. 4920.

Native of the coastal region of Chile from Concepcion to the region of Puerto Aisen; introduced by Standish and Noble about the middle of the last century, but always rare. It is a rather anomalous species, agreeing best with *Pernettya*, but differing from all the other species in its racemose inflorescence, and with unusually large leaves for a pernettya. Its rarity in cultivation is due partly perhaps to its slight tenderness, and partly, perhaps, to the dullness of its fruits. As a flowering shrub it is the most decorative of the pernettyas, though not superior in this respect to the hardier and commoner × *Gaulnettya* 'Wisley Pearl'.

P. LEUCOCARPA DC.

P. andina Meigen; *P. gayana* Decne.

A low, creeping evergreen shrub up to 6 or 8 in. high, spreading much wider by underground stems and of dense habit. Leaves mostly ¼ to ⅜ in. long, elliptic, oblong-elliptic, or oblong-lanceolate, roundish at the apex, dark shining green, glabrous, lateral veins beneath not visible, margins entire or very faintly crenate-toothed. Flowers white, sometimes tinged with pink, solitary in the leaf-axils, pedicels equalling or shorter than the leaves. Fruits globose, white, edible; calyx not fleshy.

Native of the Andes of Chile and bordering parts of Argentina, from the latitude of Santiago at least as far south as 42° S., common on the volcanoes, where it reaches to the snow-line; described by de Candolle from a specimen collected by Poeppig on the Antuco volcano; introduced by Harold Comber in 1926 under C.501.

P. leucocarpa is closely allied to *P. pumila*, but is of more open habit and the leaves are not so densely arranged.

P. COMBER 591   *P. leucocarpa* Hort.; *P. leucocarpa* var. *linearis* Hort.— From specimens preserved in the Kew Herbarium it is clear that the plants raised from the seeds sent by Comber under 591 and distributed as *P. leucocarpa* var. *linearis*, do not in fact belong to *P. leucocarpa*, and are most probably hybrids between it and *P. prostrata* subsp. *pentlandii*. This could also be true of the wild plant from which Comber gathered the seeds, since the dried specimen he collected does not agree well with *P. leucocarpa*. Of the cultivated plants under C.591 some resemble *P. prostrata* subsp. *pentlandii*, but have unusually narrow leaves. Thus the plant at Nymans which received an Award of Merit as "*P. leucocarpa*" when shown in 1929 has linear-oblong or linear-elliptic leaves up to ½ in. or slightly more long and about ⅒ in. wide, slightly toothed and with the lateral veins raised beneath. Other specimens from the same batch of seeds are nearer to *P. leucocarpa*, but none agrees well with it. The wild plant named *P. leucocarpa* var. *linearis* by Reiche could well have been a hybrid also; the name is given by Dr Sleumer as a synonym of *P. prostrata pentlandii*.

P. MACROSTIGMA Col.

Gaultheria perplexa Cheesem.; *G. antipoda* var. *microphylla* Hook. f.; *G. depressa* var. *microphylla* (Hook. f.) Cheesem.

A low evergreen sometimes prostrate shrub, the branches wiry, flexuous and often interlaced. Leaves linear, pointed, $\frac{1}{4}$ to $\frac{1}{2}$ in. long, $\frac{1}{16}$ in. wide, often recurved, inconspicuously bristle-toothed, quite glabrous, very shortly stalked. Flowers solitary in the leaf-axils towards the end of the shoot, each on a glabrous stalk $\frac{1}{12}$ to $\frac{1}{6}$ in. long; corolla white, urn-shaped, $\frac{1}{8}$ in. long; calyx-lobes linear-lanceolate, minutely downy on the margins. The seed-vessel is usually enclosed in the enlarged succulent calyx, the whole forming a rosy-red, berry-like fruit $\frac{1}{2}$ in. across.

Native of the North and South Islands, New Zealand, where it has a wide range of habitats, but is commonest at elevations of 1,500 to 3,000 ft; first discovered about 1847. It is a curious shrub of no great beauty, being remarkable for the often intricate interlacing of the slender branches and the small narrow leaves which are distinct from those of any other species in cultivation.

Natural hybrids occur in the wild between *P. macrostigma* and various species of *Gaultheria*. Some of these resemble *P. macrostigma* but are more erect, or have fruits in which the calyx remains dry and unenlarged.

P. MUCRONATA (L.f.) Gaud.   [PLATE 15
Arbutus mucronata L.f.

An evergreen shrub 2 to 5 ft high, spreading freely by suckers and forming ultimately a dense, low thicket; young branches thin and wiry, sometimes furnished with a few appressed, forward-pointing bristles or short down, but usually becoming glabrous in a short time. Leaves alternate, dense upon the branches, ovate to oblong, very shortly stalked, $\frac{1}{3}$ to $\frac{3}{4}$ in. long, $\frac{1}{8}$ to $\frac{1}{4}$ in. wide, toothed and spiny-pointed, hard in texture, lateral veins scarcely visible on the underside. Flowers produced singly in the leaf-axils near the end of the shoot, in May. Corolla white, nodding, cylindrical, about $\frac{1}{4}$ in. long, five-toothed. Calyx five-lobed, green; stamens ten; flower-stalk $\frac{1}{4}$ in. long. Fruit a globose berry $\frac{1}{3}$ to $\frac{1}{2}$ in. diameter, containing many very small seeds; it varies in colour from pure white to pink, lilac, crimson, and purple, or almost black; calyx not fleshy.

Native of Chile and bordering parts of Argentina from Cape Horn northward to around 40° S.; introduced in 1828, from the region of the Straits of Magellan. This is one of the hardiest of S. American shrubs, and is rarely severely injured by frost in the neighbourhood of London. Certainly it is one of the finest ornamental berry-bearing shrubs we have. Its berries attain their colour by early autumn, and remain on the branches through the winter and following spring. (See further below, in the note on the garden varieties.)

P. mucronata and its garden varieties need a light, peaty soil and like full sunshine.

var. RUPICOLA (Phil.) Reiche *P. rupicola* Phil.—Leaves rather thinner than in typical *P. mucronata*, more or less elliptic, $\frac{3}{8}$ to $\frac{1}{2}$ in. long, scarcely $\frac{3}{16}$ in. wide.

Native of the island of Chiloe and of the bordering mainland. Probably introduced in the 1830s.

P. mucronata was for long strangely neglected in gardens, but a great fillip to its cultivation was given by an exhibit in London made about 1882 by the Irish nurseryman T. Davis of Hillsborough in Co. Down, who showed a number of remarkably beautiful varieties he had raised during the previous thirty years. According to his own account the original parent was 'the hardiest and most free-flowering variety of *P. mucronata*, namely var. *angustifolia*'. Whether this plant was really the true *P. angustifolia* Lindl. it is impossible to say. According to Davis, among the original seedlings from this plant were several that varied considerably from the 'type' in foliage as well as in colour of berries.

The plants shown in 1882 ranged in colour from white through shades of pink and red to almost black, and some were given distinguishing epithets in Latin. The plants offered in commerce at the present time as Davis's Hybrids appear to be seedlings or later selections, some of which have been given cultivar names. One of the best known clones is 'BELL'S SEEDLING', raised in Ireland, with large, long-persisting fruits of a bright carmine-red. But many others are listed by nurserymen. Seven named varieties raised in Holland were given awards at Boskoop in 1968 (*Dendroflora*, No. 6, p. 56).

It may be mentioned here that many if not all of the plants of *P. mucronata* have been found to be functionally, if not structurally, unisexual, and that to get the best results they should be planted in groups, with a few certified male plants mixed with named female clones, at the rate of about one male to five or at the most ten females. This statement is based on the researches of the Dutch botanist Dr B. K. Boom, carried out in the 1930s on behalf of the Boskoop nurserymen, who had found that their varieties of *P. mucronata* were producing less and less fruit every year. The explanation was, of course, that by selecting the best fruiting varieties they had eliminated most of the pollinators. Male clones are now offered by most nurserymen who list *P. mucronata*.

A very distinct form of *P. mucronata* is offered by Messrs Hillier under the cultivar-name 'E. K. BALLS'. It has stout, erect branches densely set with imbricated, ovate or triangular-ovate leaves about ⅜ in. long, with pronounced terminal spines. Its origin is unknown.

P. ANGUSTIFOLIA Lindl. *P. mucronata* var. *angustifolia* (Lindl.) Reiche— This pernettya was described by Lindley in 1840 from plants raised from Chilean seed (*Bot. Reg.*, Vol. 26, t. 63). He did not compare it with *P. mucronata*, from which it differs obviously in the shortness or virtual absence of the terminal spine. Some of the specimens in the Kew Herbarium originally referred to *P. angustifolia* belong to *P. prostrata* subsp. *pentlandii*. Others agree with *P. mucronata* but have narrowly elliptic leaves. Some appear to be intermediate and might be hybrids, as *P. angustifolia* itself possibly is. The Chilean pernettyas occurring from the latitude of Chiloe island northward appear to be very variable and are in need of further study.

P. PROSTRATA (Cav.) Sleum.

Andromeda prostrata Cav.

This species (in the broad sense) is extremely variable and has a wide range in S. America from Costa Rica to Chile. In his monograph, Dr Sleumer divides it into a number of varieties, while admitting that these are linked by intermediates or perhaps by hybrids and scarcely merit the status of variety. In his article accompanying *Bot. Mag.*, n.s., t. 127, B. L. Burtt suggests that *P. prostrata* is best divided into two subspecies, 'each containing a considerable range of minor variation'. Of the two subspecies, the typical one (i.e., containing the type of *P. prostrata*) is discussed later in this entry. The cultivated plants belong mainly to the subsp. *pentlandii*:

subsp. PENTLANDII (DC.) B. L. Burtt *P. pentlandii* DC.; *P. purpurea* subsp. *pentlandii* (DC.) Ktze.; *P. angustata* Benth.; *P. purpurea* subsp. *subsetosa* Ktze. var. *angustata* (Benth.) Ktze.; *P. prostrata* var. *angustata* (Benth.) Sleum.; *P. prostrata* var. *pentlandii* (DC.) Sleum., *nom. illegit.*; *P. poeppigii* (DC.) Klatt; *Gaultheria poeppigii* DC.—A dwarf evergreen shrub, sometimes prostrate; young shoots downy and sparsely bristly. Leaves shortly stalked, oblong-ovate, pointed, rounded or tapered at the base, bristly toothed, ½ to ¾ in. long, ⅛ to ¼ in. wide, dark glossy green and glabrous above, pale green and either glabrous or with a few dark bristles on the midrib beneath; there may be ten or more leaves to the inch. Flowers solitary in the leaf-axils, nodding, opening in June. Corolla ovoid-globose, white, ⅓ in. long, contracted towards the mouth and there dividing into five pointed, recurved lobes. Stamens ten, with downy stalks swollen at the base; anthers with four short bristles. Calyx-lobes ovate, pointed, becoming, at any rate sometimes, swollen at the fruiting state and turning blue-purple. This is the colour also of the globose berry, which is ¼ to ⅜ in. wide, nodding, with the remains of the stigma at the top and the usually fleshy lobes of the calyx at the base.

The subsp. *pentlandii* has broadly the same range as *P. prostrata* as a whole. It was originally described by de Candolle (as a species) from a specimen collected by Pentland in Bolivia. The description given above is made from a form which still grows at Wakehurst Place in Sussex, and is perfectly hardy. There is another slightly differing form in cultivation which appears to have been distributed originally under the name "*Pernettya nigra*". It is a more robust plant than the one described, with trailing or arching branches and leaves up to 1 in. or slightly more long. This is the form figured in *Bot. Mag.*, n.s., t. 127, from a plant in the late Sir Frederick Stern's garden at Highdown in Sussex. The plants there were killed in the severe winter of 1946–7, but similar plants at Borde Hill, also received as "*P. nigra*", were completely hardy and made a thicket about 1 ft high and 15 ft wide.

In the plants considered above, the fruits are almost black when ripe. But in some at least of the Chilean plants they are pink or even white. A pink-fruited form was introduced by Comber under his number 1113 and makes at Wakehurst Place an erect shrub about 2½ ft high. A low-growing form of the subsp. *pentlandii*, with white fruits, received an Award of Merit when shown from the R.H.S. Garden at Wisley in September 1957. It was stated, erroneously, to have been raised from seeds collected by E. K. Balls in Mexico.

The typical subspecies of *P. prostrata* (subsp. *prostrata*) differs from the subsp. *pentlandii* in its relatively broader and shorter leaves. It is figured in *Bot. Mag.*, t. 6204, from a plant introduced by Anderson-Henry from the Andes of Quito, Ecuador. This proved to be hardy and bore fruit.

P. CILIATA (Cham. & Schlecht.) Small *Gaultheria ciliata* Cham. & Schlecht.; *P. pilosa* (Graham) G. Don; *Arbutus pilosa* Graham; *P. buxifolia* Mart. & Gal.; *P. hirsuta* (Mart. & Gal.) Camp; *P. mexicana* Camp—Closely allied to *P. prostrata*, which it replaces north of the equator between 15° and 20° N., and, like it, is very variable. According to Sleumer it is not separable from *P. prostrata* by any one character, but in some forms the branchlets are densely bristly and the leaves ciliate. Although introduced early in the last century (*Bot. Mag.*, t. 3177) the cultivated plants mostly derive from seeds collected by E. K. Balls in Mexico in 1938, on Mt Malinche and Popocatepetl (*Bot. Mag.*, n.s., t. 66).

P. *ciliata* appears to be quite hardy in cultivation. It occurs in Mexico at altitudes of 7,000 to 10,000 ft.

P. PUMILA (L.f.) Hook.

Arbutus pumila L.f.; *P. empetrifolia* (Lam.) Gaud.; *Andromeda empetrifolia* Lam.

A low, often prostrate evergreen shrub frequently only a few inches high, easily distinguished from *P. mucronata* by the smaller ovate or ovate-lanceolate leaves having no mucro at the apex; often they are blunt or even rounded there; they are $\frac{1}{8}$ to $\frac{1}{4}$ in. long and have cartilaginous, very minutely toothed margins. Flowers white, nodding, bell-shaped, $\frac{3}{16}$ in. wide, with five shallow reflexed lobes. Fruits globose, $\frac{3}{16}$ in. wide, white or pink; calyx not fleshy.

Native of the Falkland Islands and of the Magellan region; known since the second half of the 18th century, but not introduced, so far as is known, until the 1920s or 1930s. It makes an interesting plant for the rock garden and is quite hardy, but the fruits are only borne if plants of both sexes are grown. In the wild state it bears fruit very abundantly; one collector states that they could be gathered by the bushel and cooked like huckleberries.

P. TASMANICA Hook. f.

A dwarf, prostrate, evergreen shrub, forming large, dark green mats or carpets only a few inches high; branches much forked, slender and slightly downy when young. Leaves alternate, leathery, shortly stalked, oval-lanceolate, pointed, margins often wavy, $\frac{1}{4}$ to $\frac{1}{3}$ in. long, half as much wide, shining. Flowers $\frac{1}{8}$ in. wide, solitary on a short stalk in the upper leaf-axils; corolla white, bell-shaped, five-lobed; stamens ten, anthers not awned. Fruit a globose red berry $\frac{3}{8}$ in. wide, the persistent calyx in which it is seated often becoming fleshy and coloured also.

Native of Tasmania, where, according to Hooker, it occurs on all the mountains, especially on a granite soil, forming large green cushions there. He records that the fruits, normally red, are sometimes yellow or cream-coloured. H. F. Comber found it only 2 in. high in 1930 on an exposed moor at 4,000 ft altitude.

It is a pleasing little evergreen for the rock garden where it can have a moist, preferably peaty soil.

PERNETTYA TASMANICA

P. NANA Col. *P. tasmanica* var. *neozelandica* Kirk—In most of its botanical characters this species is very near to *P. tasmanica*, in which it was included by the younger Hooker. However, it differs in one important respect, namely that the anthers are awned, as is usual in this genus, whereas in *P. tasmanica* the awns are lacking. As a garden plant *P. nana* seems to be less easy to grow than the Tasmanian species, and is certainly no better.

PEROVSKIA   LABIATAE

A genus of seven species of subshrubs ranging from Central Asia to N.E. Persia, Afghanistan, the N.W. Himalaya, and Baluchistan. Leaves opposite, toothed or pinnately divided. Inflorescence paniculate, with numerous spike-like branches, on which the flowers are arranged in whorls. Corolla two-lipped, the upper lip four-lobed, lower lip entire. Fertile stamens two, with contiguous anther-cells. Nutlets four, oblong-ovoid.

The name (sometimes spelt "*Perowskia*") commemorates V. A. Perovski, Governor of the Russian province of Orenburg at the time when Karelin founded the genus (1841).

P. ATRIPLICIFOLIA Benth.

A deciduous, semi-woody plant 3 to 5 ft high, with a sage-like odour; branches long, stiffly erect, covered with a white, close down. Leaves opposite, 1 to 2 in. long, $\frac{1}{3}$ to 1 in. wide, rhomboidal or slightly obovate, tapered at both ends, coarsely toothed, grey-green and slightly downy; stalk $\frac{1}{12}$ to $\frac{1}{3}$ in. long. Panicles terminal, 9 to 12 in. long, produced in August and September, and composed of numerous slender, opposite, leafless spikes, 2 to 5 in. long. Flowers beautiful violet-blue, $\frac{1}{3}$ in. long, produced in whorls; corolla two-lipped, tubular at the base with a five-lobed spreading limb $\frac{1}{3}$ in. across; calyx shaggy with white hairs.

The whole inflorescence is covered like the stem with a white, powder-like down, which brings the colour of the blossoms into greater prominence. *Bot. Mag.*, t. 8441.

Native of the W. Himalaya and Afghanistan. It covers large areas in the Chitral Valley, to the exclusion of other vegetation. Although woody at the base, the stems made during the summer die back considerably during winter. It should be planted in good soil, in a group of at least half a dozen plants, and makes a pretty effect in late summer. A heat-lover, it should have the sunniest position available. The plants should be pruned over in spring, cutting off the dead portion and perhaps a little more. It is easily propagated by cuttings in early June by taking young shoots when they are 2 or 3 in. long. Seed is rarely produced in this country.

There is a group of *P. atriplicifolia* in the R.H.S. Garden at Wisley, on the dry wall by the entrance.

cv. 'BLUE SPIRE'.—A particularly fine variant of *P. atriplicifolia*, with distinct foliage. The uppermost leaves are narrowly elliptic-oblong and pinnately lobulate, the lower ones up to 2 in. long, cut more than half-way to the midrib into lobes which are themselves lobulate. It is of upright habit, to about 3 ft high, and bears its flowers in large panicles. It has been suggested that 'Blue Spire' is a hybrid between *P. atriplicifolia* and *P. abrotanoides*. But in the Kew Herbarium there are specimens from Kashmir and Lahul (where *P. abrotanoides* does not occur) which, though they lack the lower leaves, seem to agree quite well with 'Blue Spire'. It was distributed under its present name by Messrs. Notcutt and received an Award of Merit when exhibited by them on August 28, 1963. It came originally from Germany as *P. atriplicifolia erecta*.

P. ABROTANOIDES Karelin *P. atriplicifolia* sens. Hook. f. in *Fl. Brit. Ind.*, Vol. IV, p. 652, not Benth.—Allied to *P. atriplicifolia* but stems with a thinner indumentum which tends to wear off, leaves deeply incised, often to the midrib, the segments sometimes linear and entire, more often themselves pinnately dissected. Native of Russia (Turkmenia and Tianshan), Iran, and Baluchistan; introduced to Kew before 1935 from Iran. It can be grown in situations that suit *P. atriplicifolia*, but really needs more summer heat. It is much less common in gardens.

PERSEA   LAURACEAE

A genus of evergreen trees mainly confined to tropical and warm temperate regions, but extending as far north as Japan, S. Korea, and central China. Leaves alternate, pinnately veined. Flowers bisexual, in axillary inflorescences. Perianth segments six; stamens twelve in four rows, the innermost set reduced to staminodes. Pistil one, with a single style. Fruit a fleshy berry, usually with the perianth-segments persistent at the base, one-seeded. The species treated below is, so far as is known, the only one truly hardy in the open air in the British Isles. It was originally described in *Machilus*, but this genus has been included in *Persea* by Kostermans (*Reinwardtia*, Vol. 6, pp. 189–94). P. BORBONIA (L.) Spreng. of the south-eastern USA, and P. LINGUE Nees of Chile, could probably be grown outdoors in the mildest parts. The latter is a valuable but rare timber tree, with very handsome fruits.

The best known species of *Persea* is P. AMERICANA Mill. (*P. gratissima* Gaertn. f.), the fruit of which is the avocado of commerce. Cultivated in the warmer parts of the New World since pre-Columbian times, its distribution as a wild tree is not known for certain, but it is probably native from southern Mexico to northern South America. It is now grown as an orchard tree in many of the warmer parts of the world, including the Mediterranean region. There are many named varieties, propagated by budding, which differ in the size of their fruits, in the texture of the skin, which varies from leathery and smooth to shell-like and warted; and in their season of fruiting. The common name derives from the Mexican 'ahuacatl' through the Spanish 'aguacate'.

P. ICHANGENSIS (Rehd. & Wils.) Kostermans
Machilus ichangensis Rehd. & Wils.

A small evergreen tree: young growths angled at first, soon becoming terete, light green, remaining green and smooth for several years, lenticels very sparse; buds large, the outer scales oblate, indented, the inner ones enlarging into bracts, broadly spathulate to oblanceolate. Leaves leathery, glossy, narrow-oblanceolate, narrowly oblong-oblanceolate or narrowly oblong-elliptic, gradually or abruptly acuminate at the apex, tapered to an acute base, 5 to $9\frac{1}{2}$ in. long, $\frac{3}{4}$ to $1\frac{1}{2}$ in. wide, light green above, paler, somewhat glaucous green beneath, glabrous on both sides when mature, but finely downy when quite young; petiole $\frac{3}{4}$ to $1\frac{1}{2}$ in. long, channelled above. Flowers produced in narrow panicles, arising in the axils of deciduous bracts at the base of the young shoots; peduncles and pedicels finely silky, the former up to 3 in. or so long. Flowers described as white but greenish yellow in the cultivated plant; perianth segments about $\frac{3}{16}$ in. long. Ovary subglobose, with a very short style. Fruits subglobose, with the perianth persisting at the base, about $\frac{1}{4}$ in. wide.

Native of central and S.W. China, also of S.E. Tibet; described from specimens collected by Wilson in W. Hupeh. It is represented in cultivation by a fine tree at Wakehurst Place in Sussex, the provenance of which is unknown. It may be from seeds sent home by Wilson, but the species was also collected by Forrest in Yunnan on numerous occasions. The description of the foliage given above is drawn from the Wakehurst plant, in which the leaves are predominantly very slender, with a ratio of length to breadth of about 6 : 1 or slightly more, rarely 5 : 1. This tree is remarkably vigorous and occasionally flowers and produces ripe fruits and even self-sown seedlings. It measures 38 × 3 ft + 2 ft at 3 ft (1969).

PERTYA COMPOSITAE

A genus of a few species of herbs and shrubs ranging from India to Japan. Flower-heads solitary or arranged in racemes or panicles; florets all tubular, the corollas deeply divided into five segments. Involucres with numerous imbricate membranous or leathery bracts. Named in honour of J. A. Maximilian Perty, Swiss naturalist, 1804–84.

P. SINENSIS Oliver

A deciduous bush 4 to 6 ft high, with glabrous, slender, ribbed branches. Leaves alternate on the shoots of the year, ovate-lanceolate, long and taper-pointed, 2 to 3 in. long, ¾ to 1 in. wide, deep green, usually with one to three sharp teeth on each margin, but sometimes not toothed. On the year-old branches they are produced four to six together in rosette-like clusters from each joint, and are only half or less than half the size of the others, and without teeth. The leaves are either glabrous or have some small bristles on the midrib; stalks ⅛ in. or less long. Flower-heads pinkish purple, ½ in. across, surrounded by a series of oval, membranous, overlapping bracts; about a dozen are produced from the centre of each leaf cluster on the year-old shoots, each on a slender, slightly bristly stalk about ¼ in. or more long. It flowers in June and July.

Native of Hupeh, China; discovered by Henry in 1889, and introduced by Wilson in 1901 for Messrs Veitch. It is a neat shrub, but perhaps of more botanical than garden interest. The leaves have an intense, quassia-like bitterness. The chief interest of this shrub is in its being an addition to the few shrubby composites that are hardy in cultivation.

PETROPHYTUM ROSACEAE

A genus of three dwarf subshrubs in western N. America, allied to *Spiraea*, from which they differ in their entire, evergreen leaves and in having follicles which split down both sides.

P. CAESPITOSUM (Torr. & Gr.) Rydb.

Spiraea caespitosa Nutt. ex Torr. & Gr.

It is, perhaps, stretching the term 'shrub' somewhat to include mention here of this species, but its base is purely woody and as it occurs in nature the main stem may be half an inch or more in diameter. The plant is a low, prostrate evergreen forming a close, compact tuft or mat an inch or two high. One writer describes it in the state of Idaho as making dense and perfectly flat mats of tough woody branches growing over rocks, in the cracks of which the seed had originally germinated. Leaves oblanceolate, not toothed, $\frac{1}{4}$ to $\frac{1}{2}$ in. long, $\frac{1}{8}$ in. or less wide, tapering gradually to the base, bluntish at the apex except for a minute tip; grey-green covered with silky hairs. Flowers white, very small, produced during July and August densely packed in cylindrical racemes 1 to $2\frac{1}{2}$ in. long, the racemes being borne at the top of an erect stalk 1 to 4 in. long. The stamens (about twenty to each flower) are conspicuously exposed.

Native of the S.W. states of N. America, where it often occurs on limestone formations. It is hardy even in the eastern United States and is grown successfully in Scotland. It is adapted only for the rock garden, or moraine, where there is perfect drainage and unobstructed sunshine. Very distinct in its dwarfness, its narrow entire leaves, and the close packing of the small flowers near the top of a quite erect spike.

P. HENDERSONII (Canby) Rydb. *Eriogynia hendersonii* Canby; *Spiraea hendersonii* (Canby) Piper—Judging from wild specimens, this species differs from *P. caespitosum* in its larger more broadly spathulate leaves $\frac{1}{4}$ to $\frac{3}{8}$ in. long and up to almost $\frac{1}{4}$ in. wide, often with two veins springing from the base on each side of the midrib; they are also only sparsely villose on both sides. The flower-spikes are rather short, up to $1\frac{3}{4}$ in. or so long.

An endemic of the Olympic Mountains, Washington, USA, where it inhabits talus-slopes and the crevices of cliffs and rocks at 5,000 to 7,500 ft; introduced by Jack Drake and Will Ingwersen from Mt Angeles in 1936. It is perfectly hardy, flowers from midsummer onwards, and grows well on the rock garden in a scree or crevice. It also makes a good pot-plant for the alpine house, and some gardeners have found that it flowers much more freely when grown that way than in the open ground. Propagated by cuttings taken in spring or after flowering, by layers, or by seed. A.M. 1963. Wild plants are illustrated in *Qtly Bull. A.G.S.*, Vol. 6, p. 216 and Vol. 15, p. 248.

PETTERIA LEGUMINOSAE

A genus of a single species allied to *Laburnum*, from which it differs in the more tubular calyx, the upper lip of which is divided almost to the base. The racemes are erect, a character that also serves to distinguish it from the two best known species of *Laburnum*.

The genus is named after Franz Petter, a Dalmatian botanist who died in 1853.

P. RAMENTACEA (Sieber) Presl   DALMATIAN LABURNUM

Cytisus ramentaceus Sieber; *C. weldenii* Vis.

A deciduous, tree-like shrub of sturdy habit, 6 or 8 ft high. Leaves trifoliolate, with a slender stalk 1 to $1\frac{1}{2}$ in. long; leaflets oval or obovate, very shortly stalked,

1 to 2 in. long, half as much wide, rounded at the apex, glabrous, entire. Racemes terminating short twigs of the year, erect, 1½ to 3 in. long; flower-stalks short, hairy. Flowers fragrant, densely arranged, yellow, ¾ in. long, resembling those of a broom; calyx tubular, downy; standard petal erect. Seed-pod 1½ to 2 in. long, pointed at the end, dark brown when ripe, containing five or seven seeds.

A native of W. Yugloslavia from the region of Split southwards, mainly near the coast but extending inland into Hercegovina and Montenegro; also of northern and central Albania. It can be seen growing on the sides of the beautiful road that climbs from Kotor to Cetinje, the old capital of Montenegro. It was introduced in 1837 but is not common. It is perfectly hardy and flowers regularly in May and June, and ripens seeds which (like those of *Laburnum*) are poisonous.

PHELLODENDRON   RUTACEAE

A small genus of deciduous trees found in N.E. Asia, with opposite, pinnate leaves which give off a rather aromatic odour when crushed, and whose leaf-stalks, swollen at the base, completely hide the bud. The inner bark is yellow. Male and female flowers appear on different trees, but both are inconspicuous; the fruits are roundish, about the size of large peas, juicy and aromatic, with a black, tough skin. The chief attraction of the phellodendrons is in their foliage and often picturesque habit. When seeds are not available, cuttings taken from the tree in July may be rooted in gentle heat; they should be made of short twigs with a 'heel' of older wood. Root-cuttings taken in December are also used. These trees are gross feeders, and like a deep rich soil.

The name is derived from the Greek *phellos* (cork) and *dendron* (tree) given in reference to the corky bark of *P. amurense*, the species first described by Ruprecht in 1853. The species have but little beauty of blossom.

P. AMURENSE Rupr.

A deciduous tree 20 to 40 ft high, with a rugged, corky trunk and spreading branches; winter-buds coated with silvery hairs; young shoots glabrous. Leaves pinnate, 10 to 15 in. long, with five to eleven leaflets which are 2½ to 4½ in. long, ovate or ovate-lanceolate, long-pointed, hairy only on the margin and at the base of the midrib, glossy green above. Panicles erect, 3 in. high, 1½ to 3 in. wide; few-branched. Flowers small, yellow-green, ¼ in. long. Fruits about ½ in. in diameter, black.

Native of the Amur region, Manchuria, etc. Although the most handsome of the phellodendrons where the climate is suitable, it is a failure here. Like so many other trees from the mainland of N.E. Asia, it is very liable to have its young shoots injured by late frosts. This induces excessive branching and an unnaturally dwarfed, bushy habit. It thrives well in the Arnold Arboretum, Massachusetts, which has a more decided winter than ours, and a later spring. There it has developed the corky trunk to which the genus owes its name. However, it is now considered that typical *P. amurense* also occurs in Japan, and it might be that trees of this provenance would succeed in Britain.

var. LAVALLEI (Dode) Sprague *P. lavallei* Dode; *P. amurense* Hort., in part, not Rupr.; *P. japonicum* Hort., in part, not Maxim.—Bark corky, though less so than in typical *P. amurense*. Leaflets oval-lanceolate, seven to eleven, with long slender points, obliquely rounded at the base, or sometimes abruptly narrowed to an acute wedge, dullish green above, midrib and chief veins beneath furnished with white hairs, margins ciliate. Panicles downy. *Bot. Mag.*, t. 8945.

Native of Japan; introduced to cultivation in 1865 or 1866 by means of seeds collected by Tschonoski and distributed from St Petersburg by Regel; reintroduced by Wilson in 1918. It was at first grown as *P. amurense* or *P. japonicum*, and was separated as a species in 1909 by Dode, who drew up his description from a tree grown by Lavallée in the Segrez Arboretum (see further in Dr Stapf's note accompanying the plate in the *Botanical Magazine*). *P. japonicum* differs from this variety in the soft down which covers the whole of its much more rounded leaflets beneath; typical *P. amurense* has only a little down near the base of the midrib and the upper surface is dark, glossy green.

P. amurense var. *lavallei* succeeds very well under cultivation and grows vigorously at Kew, where there is a specimen planted in 1899, measuring 40 × 3½ ft (1967). This tree fruits and produces fertile seeds, although the nearest male phellodendron is at a considerable distance. This is also true of a tree at Borde Hill in Sussex, younger than the Kew tree, which measures 35 × 3½ ft at 4 ft (1968); it fruits abundantly, although the nearest possible pollinator is a small tree more than 100 yards away. The leaves turn bright yellow before falling.

var. SACHALINENSE F. Schmidt *P. sachalinense* (F. Schmidt) Sarg.—This variety differs from typical *P. amurense* in its non-corky bark. Also the leaflets are not ciliate, or scarcely so, and the inflorescence is almost glabrous. Other differences noted by Sargent from the trees in the Arnold Arboretum are that the leaflets are dull above, and that the winter-buds are covered with a rusty down (silky in typical *P. amurense*).

Native of Japan, Sakhalin, and Korea; introduced from Japan to the Arnold Arboretum, USA, in 1877. A tree at Kew, received from the Arnold Arboretum in 1904, is probably a seedling from one of the originals there, and possibly a hybrid. It grows near the Victoria Gate and measures 43 × 5 ft (1965).

P. CHINENSE Schneid.

A deciduous tree 20 to 35 ft high, with young shoots at first thinly downy, brown and glabrous the second year. Leaves pinnate, up to 15 in. long, with seven to thirteen leaflets, main stalk downy. Leaflets 3 to 5 in. long, 1 to 1¾ in. wide, oblong-lanceolate, furnished with pale hairs beneath, especially on the midrib. Flowers small, yellowish green, crowded on a short, very downy panicle; ovary downy. Fruits black, globose, ⅖ in. wide, aromatic, closely packed in a panicle 2 to 3½ in. long and half as much wide.

Native of Central China; introduced by Wilson from W. Hupeh in 1907, when collecting for the Arnold Arboretum, and perhaps earlier, on one of his expeditions for Messrs Veitch. It is most closely akin to *P. japonicum* and has similar though less downy leaves, but the fruits are larger, and their close, compact arrangement distinguishes the species well. It first bore fruit at Kew in 1920, and the specimen in the collection now measures 30 × 2¾ ft (1967). There is another in the University Botanic Garden, Cambridge, measuring 30 × 1¾ ft (1969).

var. GLABRIUSCULUM Schneid. *P. sinense* Dode—This differs in having the down on the leaves confined almost to the midrib and main veins. It is probably part of the normal variation of the species. An example at Borde Hill in Sussex, received from the Aldenham Collection under this name, measures 30 × 3¼ ft (1968).

P. JAPONICUM Maxim.

P. amurense var. *japonicum* (Maxim.) Ohwi

A deciduous, bushy-headed tree, of stiff habit, 20 to 35 ft high, its trunk 1 to 2 ft in thickness. Leaves 10 to 15 in. long, pinnate, with seven to fifteen leaflets, which are very downy beneath, dull green, and soon nearly or quite glabrous above, broadly ovate, pointed, oblique at the base, 2 to 3 in. long, with a short stalk. Panicle of male flowers about 4 in. long, and 2 in. wide, erect; the female one more slender. Flowers ¼ in. across, yellowish green. Fruits orange-shaped, black, each nearly ⅓ in. across, borne on an erect downy panicle.

Native of Japan; introduced about 1870. It is distinguished from the other species by the thick, greyish down beneath the leaflets, and by their broader proportions. A well-grown tree is handsome when in full leaf and fruit. It flowers in July.

The example at Kew measures 35 × 5 ft (1967) and there is another in the Edinburgh Botanic Garden of the same size, planted in 1898.

PHILADELPHUS   PHILADELPHACEAE

A genus of deciduous shrubs most nearly related to *Deutzia*, from which they chiefly differ in having four petals and four calyx-lobes, and twenty to forty stamens, whilst in *Deutzia* the petals and the calyx-lobes are in fives and the stamens ten; the hairs in *Deutzia*, too, are stellate, in *Philadelphus* they are simple. Leaves opposite, stalked, often three- or five-nerved. Flowers often strongly scented, mostly pure white, occasionally yellowish or blotched with purple at the base of the petals. The inflorescence is always terminal, but varies from a solitary flower to a raceme or panicle. Fruit usually four-valved, dry, and woody, splitting lengthwise to liberate the numerous seeds. Flowers are not infrequently seen with the flower-parts in fives. In the majority of species the leaf-buds on the young shoots are completely hidden by the base of the leaf-stalk.

Perhaps no genus of shrubs presents so many difficulties in the differentiation of its species as this. A few of them are well marked, like *P. microphyllus*, with small entire leaves; *P. hirsutus*, with exposed leaf-buds and united stigmas; and *P. mexicanus*, with similar leaf-buds but divided stigmas; but the majority offer no really distinctive characters. The difficulty is further increased by free hybridisation under cultivation, so that now a large proportion of cultivated plants are not species at all, but garden hybrids.

These beautiful shrubs, commonly known as "Syringa"—a name which properly belongs to the lilacs—need no recommendation. They contribute to our gardens their most attractive pictures during June and July, when the great flowering time of shrubs is rapidly waning. They are useful in shrubberies where the vigorous ones can take care of themselves in competition with most things, and they also make very charming objects isolated on lawns. They grow best in a loamy soil, in a position at least moderately sunny, and are easily increased by cuttings made of softish young wood placed in bottom heat. They flower on short lateral twigs which spring from the shoots made the previous year, so that whatever pruning has to be done should consist of taking out old branches that have flowered and leaving the long, vigorous shoots of the current year to provide the succeeding crop of blossom. No mere shortening back should be done unless from considerations of space.

The main work on the genus is: S.-Y. Hu, 'A Monograph of the Genus Philadelphus', *Journ. Arn. Arb.*, Vol. 35 (1954), pp. 275–333; Vol. 36 (1955), pp. 52–109, 325–68; Vol. 37 (1956), pp. 15–90.

P. ARGYROCALYX Wooton
P. ellipticus Rydb.

A deciduous shrub of graceful spreading habit 6 to 8 ft high; young shoots slender, downy, pinkish at first, becoming black-brown the second year. Leaves ovate, up to 2 in. long by 1 in. wide on the virgin shoots, smaller and narrower on the flowering ones, not toothed, pointed, tapered at the base, glabrous above, hairy on the midrib and veins and paler beneath, three-veined; stalk ⅛ in. or less long, downy. Flowers solitary or in threes, terminating leafy twigs 1 to 2 in. long, white, 1¼ in. wide. Calyx-tube hemispherical, the four lobes ovate, about ¼ in. long, covered with silvery-grey down; petals obovate; anthers greenish; styles united, stigmas free; ovary quite glabrous.

Native of New Mexico; discovered in 1892, introduced in 1922. This charming philadelphus is related to *P. microphyllus* and the flowers have a similar fruity fragrance, but that species has a nearly glabrous calyx whilst in this it is silvery grey with down; *P. argyrocalyx* has also larger flowers and a more vigorous growth. It is very pretty in bloom, the flowers showing in two rows on the upper side of the previous year's (usually arching or drooping) shoots. Flowering in late June and July, being perfectly hardy and of a convenient size, it deserves to be more widely planted.

P. CALIFORNICUS Benth.

P. lewisii var. *parvifolius* Torr.; *P. lewisii* var. *californicus* (Benth.) Gray; *P. lewisii* subsp *californicus* (Benth.) Munz

An elegant, pendulous-branched shrub up to 10 ft high, the young shoots glabrous, the year-old bark peeling. Leaves three-nerved, ovate, 1½ to 3 in. long, ¾ to 2 in. wide, shortly and broadly toothed, or nearly entire (especially on the flowering twigs), either glabrous or slightly downy beneath. Flowers 1 in. or less wide, pure white, slightly fragrant, produced numerously in panicles at the end of the shoot, often over twenty flowers in each. Petals oblong-obovate; calyx glabrous outside the lobes, downy on the margins, and near the apex inside; styles united, stigmas separated.

Native of California. Although much confused with *P. lewisii,* and sometimes regarded as a variety of it, this is really one of the most distinct of American species. On weak shoots its inflorescence may be only a simple raceme, but normally it is composed of several racemes, thus forming a true panicle. Flowers small and crowded. The base of the leaf-stalk does not hide the axillary bud, as it does in *P. lewisii.*

P. CORONARIUS L.   MOCK ORANGE

P. pallidus Hayek ex Schneid.

A shrub up to 12 ft high, with erect stems, the year-old bark brown and peeling; young shoots ribbed. Leaves ovate to oval-lanceolate, broadly wedge-shaped or nearly rounded at the base, distantly toothed, 1½ to 4 in. long, ⅝ to 2 in. wide; glabrous except for a few hairs on one or both surfaces and on the leaf-stalk, which is ⅛ to ⅓ in. long. Flowers yellowish white, heavily scented, about 1 in. across, produced in terminal racemes of five to nine blossoms. Petals oval, ¾ in. wide; calyx-lobes downy at the margins, the tube and flower-stalk either glabrous or slightly downy; styles separated at the upper third.

Native of S.E. Europe and Asia Minor; cultivated in Britain since the 16th century, probably before. It flowers in early June. This is the best-known species of mock orange in gardens, but is not in the first rank. The fragrance of its flowers is pleasing out-of-doors, but may become too insistent if the plants are numerous or near sitting-room windows. The odour is too strong for the flowers to be enjoyed in a cut state indoors. Over three hundred years ago Gerard, the herbalist, wrote:

'They have a pleasant sweete smell, but in my judgment troubling and molesting the head in very strange manner. I once gathered the flowers and laid them in my chamber window, which smelled more strongly after they had lain together a few howers, but with such a pontick and unacquainted savor that they awaked me from sleepe, so that I could not take rest till I had cast them out of my chamber.'

cv. 'AUREUS' ('FOLIIS AUREIS').—Leaves bright yellow, and very effective in spring, becoming duller after midsummer.

cv. 'NANUS' ('DUPLEX').—This 'is of humble growth, seldom rising above three feet high; the leaves are shorter . . . and approach near to an oval form; they are but little indented on their edges. The flowers come out singly from the side of the branches, and have a double or treble row of petals . . . this sort flowers very rarely, so is not much esteemed' (Miller, *Gard. Dict.*, ed. 1768). In the earlier editions of his *Dictionary*, Miller also mentioned a form of normal growth which produced a mixture of single and double flowers, but mostly single. 'DEUTZIIFLORUS', of more recent origin, is also a double-flowered variety of dwarf habit, but it flowers more freely.

cv. 'VARIEGATUS'.—Leaves with an irregular border of creamy white.

P. 'SALICIFOLIUS'.—A plant of uncertain status, usually considered as a variant of *P. coronarius*, distinct in its leaves, which are 2 to 4 in. long, $\frac{1}{2}$ to $\frac{3}{4}$ in. wide, sparsely toothed. Dr Hu points out that its flowers are abnormal but show that the plant does not belong to *P. coronarius*.

P. DELAVAYI L. Henry

A shrub up to 10 or 15 ft high; shoots glabrous or sometimes hairy. Leaves ovate, rounded at the base, slender-pointed, toothed, up to 4 in. long and $1\frac{3}{4}$ in. wide on the flowering twigs, but 6 to 7 in. long, 3 to $3\frac{1}{2}$ in. wide on the sterile growths, dark green and sparsely hairy above, rather densely coated with loosely appressed hairs beneath (but sparsely so in var. CALVESCENS Rehd.). Flowers fragrant, 1 to $1\frac{1}{2}$ in. or slightly more wide, produced in racemes of seven to eleven. Petals pure white, roundish oval, often deeply toothed or undulated at the margins. Calyx glabrous outside, often tinged with purple and

PHILADELPHUS DELAVAYI

wholly plum-purple in f. MELANOCALYX (L. Henry) Rehd. Style glabrous, divided only at the apex.

Native of W. China, S.E. Tibet, and N. Burma; discovered and introduced by the Abbé Delavay in 1887. It first flowered in the Jardin des Plantes, Paris, in 1891. However, most of the plants now in British gardens were raised from seeds collected by George Forrest in W. Yunnan. Of these the best known is the 'NYMANS VARIETY', in which the calyx is coloured an almost uniform plum-purple, and on this account would be referable to f. *melanocalyx*. It received an Award of Merit when shown from Nymans on June 18, 1935. Identical plants were, however, raised in other gardens from the seeds sent by Forrest, for example at Wakehurst Place, whence came the material figured in *Bot. Mag.*, t. 9022. In this plant, as in those now in commerce as 'Nymans Variety' or var. *calvescens*, the leaves are sparsely hairy beneath, but the species varies in the degree of hairiness of the undersides of the leaves even in the same locality and, indeed, 'typical' plants with the undersides densely hairy and others with hairs of the same type but more sparse, have been raised from one and the same batch of wild seed.

P. *delavayi*, as represented in commerce, is a vigorous plant with strikingly large leaves. The flowers, borne from end-May or early June, are beautifully formed, saucer-shaped at first, becoming almost flat, their pure white petals contrasting with the richly coloured calyx.

P. PURPURASCENS (Koehne) Rehd. *P. brachybotrys* var. *purpurascens* Koehne —This species is closely allied to *P. delavayi* and perhaps not separable from it. The best distinguishing character is provided by the leaves, which in wild material of *P. purpurascens* are scarcely more than 1 in. long on the flowering twigs and up to only 1⅝ in. long on the sterile shoots (but slightly larger on some cultivated plants); they are almost glabrous above, and sparsely hairy beneath. The flowers are smaller (not much over 1 in. wide), and the petals are relatively narrower and moré erect. The calyx is green or slightly tinged with purple. *P. purpurascens* was introduced by Wilson from W. Szechwan when collecting for Messrs Veitch and was figured in *Bot. Mag.*, t. 8324, as *P. delavayi*.

P. 'FALCONERI'

P. falconeri Sarg.

A shrub up to 10 or 12 ft high, forming a dense mass of slender, arching branches, which become a dark purplish brown the second year; young shoots nearly free from down, slightly ribbed. Leaves ovate to ovate-lanceolate, broadly wedge-shaped at the base, slender-pointed, distantly and minutely toothed, 1¼ to 3½ in. long, ½ to 1⅝ in. wide, glabrous except for a few hairs on the margins and ribs beneath when young. Flowers delicately scented, pure white, 1½ to 2 in. across, produced at the end of twigs 2 to 4 in. long in racemes of three to seven flowers. Petals oblong-lanceolate, ¼ in. wide, slender-pointed; calyx glabrous, except for minute down at the margins of the lance-shaped lobes; styles separated half-way down.

The origin of this mock orange is not known; it was first distinguished in Parson's nursery at Flushing, Long Island, USA, and is probably a hybrid. It is not one of the best of the genus, and although elegant in habit is shy-flowering, at least in this country. Its long, narrow petals make it one of the most easily distinguished of the genus.

P. HIRSUTUS Nutt.

A shrub up to 6 or 10 ft high, of thin habit; young shoots covered with pale bristles; axillary buds not hidden by base of leaf-stalk. Leaves three-nerved, ovate (broadly so on the barren shoots), rounded or tapered at the base, taper-pointed, margins set with irregular, coarse, outstanding teeth, ¾ to 3 in. long, ½ to 1¾ in. wide, downy and dull green above, shaggy beneath; stalk ⅓ in. or less in length. Flowers 1 to 1¼ in. across, sometimes solitary, often in threes on lateral twigs 1 in. or less long, bearing as a rule one pair of leaves. Petals creamy white; calyx shaggy, with triangular lobes; stigmas united. *Bot. Mag.*, t. 5334.

Native of the south-eastern United States; introduced in 1820. Although one of the most easily recognised of a confusing genus, this species is one of the least attractive. Its flowers are scentless, and comparatively few. Its distinguishing marks are its exposed axillary buds, its short one- or three-flowered twigs, its dull shaggy leaves, etc., and united stigmas.

P. INCANUS Koehne

A shrub up to 8 ft or more high; young shoots more or less hairy. Leaves ovate or oval, broadly wedge-shaped or almost rounded at the base, slender-pointed, finely toothed, 2½ to 4 in. long, 1¼ to 2¼ in. wide on the barren shoots; those of the flowering twigs mostly 1 to 2 in. long; upper surface set with sparse minute hairs, the lower one thickly covered with appressed pale, stiff hairs giving it a dull grey hue; stalk 1/12 to ½ in. long, bristly. Flowers white, fragrant, about 1 in. across, produced five to nine (usually seven) together on downy racemes about 2 in. long, at the end of leafy shoots of about the same length. Petals roundish; style about the average length of the stamens, glabrous, divided quite half-way down; disk glabrous. Calyx and flower-stalk shaggy, like the undersurface of the leaves. Fruits top-shaped, ⅜ in. long.

Native of W. Hupeh and Shensi, China; discovered by Henry about 1887 and introduced by Wilson in 1904. It flowers late—from middle to late July or even into August—and the species is desirable on that account. It is also charmingly fragrant with an odour like that of hawthorn.

P. SUBCANUS Koehne *P. wilsonii* Koehne; *P. subcanus* var. *wilsonii* (Koehne) Rehd.—This species is very closely allied to *P. incanus* and was first separated from it in 1904. It differs in having the calyx and the underside of the leaves more sparsely hairy; also the disk and the lower part of the style are downy (glabrous in *P. incanus*). Native of W. Szechwan. Wilson may have introduced it while collecting for Messrs Veitch, but it is mainly and perhaps wholly represented in cultivation by Wilson's introduction during his first expedition for the Arnold Arboretum. The plants (sometimes labelled *P. wilsonii*) flower earlier than *P. incanus*, in late June or early July.

At Wakehurst Place in Sussex there are plants of unknown origin, the largest 15 ft high and as much wide, which agree with *P. subcanus* except that the style and disk is glabrous, as in *P. incanus*. The best is very free flowering, with racemes of up to eleven flowers, usually the lower two pairs in the axils of normal leaves.

P. INODORUS L.

A shrub of compact habit 4 to 6 ft high, usually more in diameter; bark glabrous, peeling the second year, of a chestnut-brown colour. Leaves ovate, with a rounded base and a fine point, 1½ to 4 in. long, ¾ to 2 in. wide, sparsely and inconspicuously toothed, dark glossy green, with pale, appressed hairs above; paler, also glossy beneath, with only a few hairs on the veins. Flowers solitary, not scented, produced at the end of short twigs, pure white, 2 to 2¼ in. across, petals overlapping, making the flower square in outline, with rounded corners. *Bot. Mag.*, t. 1478 (var. *carolinus*).

Native of the south-eastern USA. The date of introduction to Britain is uncertain, but plants under the name *P. inodorus* were in commerce in the second half of the 18th century and the true species (and also the var. *carolinus*, see below) were in cultivation early in the succeeding century. Miller raised a plant from seeds received from Carolina in 1738, but this died two years later.

The plant described above, which came from the Arnold Arboretum early this century, should, strictly considered, be distinguished as var. CAROLINUS S. Y. Hu, since the species is typified by the plate in Catesby's *Natural History of the Carolinas*, which shows a plant with leaves tapered at the base and flowers of cruciform shape with oblong petals. Plants which match this plate still exist in the wild and are in cultivation in the United States.

P. inodorus var. *carolinus* is one of the finest and most striking of the genus. It is distinguished by its glossy dark green leaves, and solitary, large, squarish flowers.

var. GRANDIFLORUS (Willd.) A.Gr. *P. grandiflorus* Willd.; *P. speciosus* Schrad.—Leaves sharply toothed, usually with tufts of hairs in the vein-axils and bristles along the main veins. As in all forms of *P. inodorus* the flowers are white and scentless; they are solitary or in threes, but occasionally the two lateral flowers are replaced by cymes of three or four flowers each. The flowers are cup-shaped when first expanded and occasionally (in f. QUADRANGULATUS Hu) they have four distinct corners (a feature also of the Lemoine hybrid 'Belle Étoile'). This variety was introduced in 1811 and has usually been known as *P. grandiflorus*, but some of the plants grown under that name are really *P. pubescens* (q.v.).

var. LAXUS (Schrad.) Hu *P. laxus* Schrad.; *P. grandiflorus* var. *laxus* (Schrad.) Torr. & Gray; *P. humilis* Hort.—Leaves narrower than in *P. inodorus*, lanceolate or elliptic-lanceolate, up to 2¼ in. long and 1 in. wide, tapered at the base or almost entire. A small, laxly branched shrub, native of the south-eastern USA. Introduced 1830.

P. 'SPLENDENS'.—A hybrid of uncertain parentage, possibly deriving from *P. inodorus* var. *grandiflorus* crossed with *P. lewisii* var. *gordonianus*. Although little known in this country, it is valued in the USA, where it originated, as it makes an excellent specimen about 8 ft high, of rounded habit, branched to the ground. The flowers are white, single, faintly fragrant, flat, with rounded petals, about 1½ in. across, borne in clusters of five or sometimes more. Calyx glabrous. Leaves resembling those of the first putative parent. (Hu, *Journ. Arn. Arb.*, Vol. 37, p. 57; Wyman, *Shrubs and Vines for American Gardens* (1969), pp. 326–7, with fig.)

P. INSIGNIS Carr.
P. billiardii Koehne; *P. 'Souvenir de Billiard'*

The origin of this handsome mock orange is not known, but it is probably a hybrid. It is a vigorous bush up to 10 or 12 ft high; young shoots glabrous or nearly so; bark of year-old ones not peeling. Leaves ovate or sometimes heart-shaped, 1½ to 3½ in. long, 1¼ to 2½ in. wide, minutely and sparsely toothed, glabrous and glossy green above, shaggy with pale hairs beneath. Flowers faintly perfumed, pure white, cupped, a little over 1 in. across, produced during late June in leafy terminal panicles of fifteen to over twenty blossoms. Petals roundish, ¾ in. long, overlapping; calyx and flower-stalk hairy; style shorter than the stamens, united just below the stigmas.

Although cultivated since before 1870, this is not much grown in gardens, although certainly one of the most attractive of mock oranges. It is distinct in its many-flowered inflorescences, combined with its glossy green leaves, its cupped flowers, and overlapping petals, and is useful in flowering well into July.

Rehder considered that *P. insignis* is a hybrid between *P. pubescens* and either *P. californicus* or *P. cordifolius* (an ally of *P. californicus* not treated here). Dr Hu, however, points out that matching plants occur wild in California and accepts *P. insignis* as a Californian native, allied to *P. californicus* (*Journ. Arn. Arb.*, Vol. 37, p. 40).

P. LEWISII Pursh

A shrub up to 12 ft high, of graceful, pendulous habit; year-old branches with greyish-brown, non-peeling bark. Leaves broadly ovate to ovate-lanceolate, 1½ to 4 in. long, 1 to 2½ in. wide, coarsely and distinctly toothed or, especially on the flowering twigs, entire, with scattered hairs beneath, still fewer above. Flowers five to nine, in racemes, scentless, white, 1⅓ in. across; petals oval; calyx smooth outside like the flower-stalk, downy at the margins, and near the apex of the lobes inside; styles divided half-way down.

Native of western N. America from British Columbia to Oregon; introduced about 1823. It is one of the most elegant and floriferous of all the taller species.

var. GORDONIANUS (Lindl.) Jeps. *P. gordonianus* Lindl.—Leaves downy beneath all over the blade. Flowers (at least in Lindley's type) up to almost

2 in. across. British Columbia to California. A handsome and very hardy variety, introduced by David Douglas in 1825, and described (as a species) from a plant raised from the seeds he sent.

P. *lewisii* is a variable species. The var. *gordonianus* and others recognised by Dr Hu, intergrade with each other and with the type. The plant described above under P. *lewisii* does not perfectly match the type of P. *lewisii*, but neither does it fit into any of the named varieties. The species seems to vary in the fragrance of its flowers.

P. MAGDALENAE Koehne

P. *subcanus* var. *magdalenae* (Koehne) S. Y. Hu

A shrub of bushy habit up to 12 ft high; young shoots downy; year-old bark peeling, glabrous. Leaves ovate-lanceolate or narrowly oval, tapered at both ends, finely toothed except towards the base, 1 to 2½ in. long, ½ to ⅞ in. wide, furnished both above and below with pale, bristle-like, minute, appressed hairs, but especially dense and grey with them beneath. Flowers white, ¾ to 1 in. in width, borne during early June in racemes of three to eleven; flower-stalk and calyx hairy, purplish; style downy towards the base, shorter than the stamens; stigmas separate. Fruits top-shaped.

Native of Szechwan, China, and bordering parts of N.E. Yunnan; introduced to France by the missionary Farges in 1894 and described from plants in the collection of Maurice de Vilmorin, and thence to Kew in 1897. It is one of the prettiest of the species, and one of the first to come into flower, in late May or early June. It is closely allied to P. *incanus* and P. *subcanus*.

P. MEXICANUS Schlecht.

A shrub up to 6 ft high, with hairy young shoots; axillary buds not hidden by base of leaf-stalk. Leaves ovate-lanceolate, rounded at the base, slenderly pointed, sparsely toothed, three-nerved, 1 to 2½ in. long, ½ to 1 in. wide, with appressed pale hairs on both surfaces, but more abundant beneath. Flowers cupped, solitary (rarely in threes) at the end of short, leafy shoots; 1½ to 2 in. across, strongly fragrant, yellowish white; petals roundish, overlapping; calyx hairy, the lobes sometimes toothed; flower-stalk very short hairy; style about as long as the stamens; stigmas separate. *Bot. Mag.*, t. 7600.

Native of Mexico; introduced by Hartweg in the late 1830s. It is a handsome and distinct species with rose-scented flowers, not hardy outside the mildest parts unless grown against a warm wall. It seems to be mainly represented in gardens by the blotched variety discussed below.

cv. 'ROSE SYRINGA'.—Petals mostly with a purplish-pink mark at the base (P. *coulteri* Hort., not S. Wats.; P. *mexicanus* var. *coulteri* Burbidge).

This philadelphus first came to botanical notice in 1891, when F. W. Burbidge, Curator of the Trinity College Botanic Garden, Dublin, sent a specimen to Kew. In the accompanying letter he wrote: 'Can you kindly give me the name of the enclosed? I cannot find it in the books. It exists in one or two old gardens here, where it is called Rose Syringa. Its sweet fragrance and purple-centred flowers are remarkable.' What reply he received is not known, but writing some years later in *The Gardeners' Chronicle* he referred to this plant as *P. mexicanus coulteri* and it is by this name, or as *P. coulteri*, that this philadelphus has been grown for the past seventy years. In fact, it is not *P. coulteri* S. Wats.; nor is it *P. maculatus* (Hitchc.) S. Y. Hu, as has recently been suggested (see below). Burbidge quite rightly referred to it as a variant of *P. mexicanus*, and was wrong only in identifying it with *P. coulteri* S. Wats.

Since this philadelphus lacks a valid distinguishing name, it seems reasonable to take up the traditional garden name and call it 'Rose Syringa'. The old plant at Tresco Abbey in the Isles of Scilly agrees in every detail with the example at Kew, except that the leaves are larger (up to 3 in. long), but this discrepancy can be explained by its greater size and vigour. These plants in turn agree with the Irish specimens in the Kew Herbarium. The origin of 'Rose Syringa' is not known, but it may well have been introduced by Hartweg at the same time as normal *P. mexicanus*. It agrees well with a specimen of this species collected by him and preserved in the Kew Herbarium, in which the flowers have a dark stain at the base, possibly indicating that they were blotched as in 'Rose Syringa'. It is, however, very likely that the plants cultivated as *P. coulteri* are not the old variety of Irish gardens but a similar, perhaps indistinguishable, clone, distributed by Lemoine under that name (see further below).

This variety is grown at Kew on the Temperate House Terrace and also in the University Botanic Garden, Cambridge, in a sheltered bay outside the greenhouses. In both gardens it makes a small plant, but would grow taller if there were room to train it.

P. COULTERI S. Wats.—This species, which is probably not in cultivation, differs from *P. mexicanus* in its acute or obtuse, not acuminate leaves, and in having the calyx and pedicels densely covered with white hairs. Native of Mexico. For *P. coulteri* Hort., see *P. mexicanus* 'Rose Syringa'. A plant grown under the name *P. coulteri* was used by Lemoine in creating the hybrids of the Purpureo-maculatus group and was distributed by him commercially. The Irish gardener W. H. Gumbleton received a plant from Lemoine under the name *P. coulteri* in 1893. This flowered in 1896, and from his description it would seem that Lemoine's *P. coulteri* was, like 'Rose Syringa', a blotched form of *P. mexicanus*. Gumbleton added: 'I believe M. Lemoine has used this new Philadelphus for crossing with other varieties . . . but none of his seedlings from these crosses has yet flowered'. (*Gard. Chron.*, Vol. 19 (1896), p. 752.)

P. MACULATUS (Hitchcock) S. Y. Hu   *P. microphyllus* subsp. *maculatus* Hitchcock—This species or natural hybrid is probably not in cultivation and is only mentioned because Dr Hu, in her monograph on *Philadelphus*, states positively that the Rose Syringa of Irish gardens belongs to *P. maculatus*. In fact, this plant differs from *P. maculatus* in every way that *P. mexicanus* does.

P. MICROPHYLLUS A. Gray

A deciduous shrub of densely bushy, rounded habit, ultimately about 4 ft high; branchlets slender but rigid, downy; bark shining brown the first year, peeling and almost black the second. Leaves ovate, pointed, not toothed, $\frac{1}{2}$ to $\frac{3}{4}$ in. long, $\frac{1}{4}$ to $\frac{1}{3}$ in. wide, bright green and almost glabrous above, grey and covered with pale, appressed hairs beneath; stalk $\frac{1}{16}$ in. long. Flowers very fragrant, pure white, about 1 in. across; produced in June, usually singly, at the end of lateral branches 1 to 2 in. long, which spring from the joints of the previous year's shoots.

PHILADELPHUS MICROPHYLLUS

Native of Colorado, Arizona, etc.; introduced by Prof. Sargent to Britain about 1883. It is quite distinct from all other cultivated species of philadelphus in its small entire leaves and low, compact habit. The leaves on wild plants are much more hairy than with us. The flowers have a strong pineapple-like odour, very pleasant in the open air. Coming from such a hot and sunny climate, it succeeds best in eastern and south-eastern England and tends to be shy-flowering, though quite hardy, in cool gardens.

P. PEKINENSIS Rupr.

A shrub up to 8 ft high; young shoots glabrous, the bark peeling off the year-old branches. Leaves ovate to ovate-lanceolate, slender-pointed, toothed, $1\frac{1}{2}$ to $3\frac{1}{2}$ in. long, $\frac{3}{4}$ to 2 in. wide; three-nerved, glabrous or nearly so; stalk and veins beneath purplish. Flowers yellowish, about 1 in. across, slightly fragrant, produced in racemes of five to nine (sometimes eleven). Petals oval, rounded at the top; calyx glabrous outside, downy towards the points of the lobes inside; styles separated at the top only; flower-stalk glabrous.

Native of N. China and Korea. It flowers in late May and June and is distinct in its yellowish flowers, glabrous leaves with purplish stalks, and glabrous flower-stalks; but it is not one of the best, although free-flowering.

P. BRACHYBOTRYS Koehne   P. *pekinensis* var.   *brachybotrys* (Koehne) Koehne—This species is near to P. *pekinensis* and sometimes made a variety of it. It, too, has yellowish flowers, but smaller, and the young shoots and leaf-undersides are furnished with a few stiff hairs. It was introduced to the Vilmorin collection in 1892 by one of the French missionaries in China and the seeds are believed to have been collected in Kiangsi. It forms a rounded, dense-habited bush.

There is a philadelphus in cultivation under the name P. *pekinensis* var. *brachybotrys* which is probably a hybrid and does not in the least resemble P. *brachybotrys*. It most probably acquired the name through mislabelling of a stock plant many years ago—it has been in cultivation under its erroneous name since the 1930s at least.

P. PUBESCENS Loisel.

P. *grandiflorus* var. *floribundus* Gray; P. *latifolius* Schrad. ex DC.; P. *grandiflorus* Hort., in part, not Willd.; P. *verrucosus* Schrad.

A robust shrub 10 to 20 ft high, as much or more in diameter; young shoots glabrous, green; the year-old shoots grey, not peeling. Leaves of the barren shoots oval or ovate, broadly tapered or rounded at the base, pointed, sparsely and irregularly toothed, 2 to 5 in. long, about half as wide, dull and almost glabrous above, downy beneath; with three or five prominent veins. Leaves of the flowering twigs smaller. Flowers pure white, 1¾ in. wide, not much scented; produced in June at the end, and in the uppermost leaf-axils of lateral twigs, usually seven or nine each. Calyx-lobes ⅖ in. long, lanceolate, and, like the individual flower-stalks, downy.

Native of the S.E. United States; introduced early last century. It is a fine free-flowering shrub, not uncommon in gardens, distinguished chiefly by the year-old bark not peeling, the numerous flowers in each raceme, and the downy calyx. One of the finest and noblest of mock oranges.

P. INTECTUS Beadle   P. *pubescens* var. *intectus* (Beadle) A. H. Moore; P. *latifolius verrucosus* Hort.—This philadelphus resembles P. *pubescens* in size, bark, foliage, and inflorescence, and is usually considered to be a variety of it, differing in the glabrous leaf-undersides, pedicels, and calyx-tube, but Dr Hu considers it to be a distinct species, more closely allied to P. *lewisii* than to P. *pubescens*. It is reported from Kentucky, Tennessee, and Oklahoma. Some of the tall-growing mock oranges found in older gardens may belong here rather than to P. *pubescens*.

P. × NIVALIS Jacques   P. *verrucosus* Hort., not Schrad.—A hybrid of P. *pubescens*, differing from it chiefly in the peeling second-year bark. The other parent is thought to be P. *coronarius*, from which it differs in having the leaves sparsely toothed or almost entire, as in P. *pubescens* and in the usually hairy calyx. Such plants have been in cultivation since the middle of the last century and were grown as P. *verrucosus* and perhaps under other names. In P. × *nivalis* 'PLENUS' the flowers are double.

P. SATSUMI Lindl. & Paxt.

P. *satsumanus* Sieb. ex Miq.; P. *acuminatus* Lange; P. *coronarius* var. *satsumi* (Lindl. & Paxt.) Maxim.; P. *chinensis* Hort.

An erect shrub 6 to 8 ft high; young shoots glabrous; bark of the previous year's shoots dark greyish brown, more or less split lengthwise, but not peeling off. Leaves ovate or oval, with long drawn-out points; those of the barren shoots 2 to 6 in. long, half as wide, toothed, usually five-nerved, glabrous above, downy in the vein-axils beneath; the leaves of the flowering shoots are smaller and proportionately narrower, and often quite or nearly entire. Flowers slightly scented, white, about 1¼ in. across, produced in erect racemes of five to eleven flowers; petals oval, rounded; style rather shorter than the stamens, the stigmas separate; calyx-lobes ovate, glabrous outside or nearly so.

Native of Japan; introduced in 1851. P. *satsumi* is a variable species; the calyx-tube, pedicels, and style may be downy or glabrous, and the leaves are downy beneath in f. NIKOENSIS (Rehd.) Ohwi. In var. LANCIFOLIUS (Uyeki) Murata (P. *shikokianus* Nakai) the styles are downy at the base (Ohwi, *Fl. Japan* (1965), p. 512; Hara, *Fl. E. Himalaya*, 2nd report, p. 47).

P. SCHRENKII Rupr.

P. *mandschuricus* Nakai

A vigorous deciduous shrub up to 12 ft high; young shoots brown, slightly hairy; bark peeling the second year. Leaves ovate, sparsely toothed, slender-pointed; 1½ to 4½ in. long and about half as much wide on the virgin shoots, smaller on the flowering ones; slightly downy beneath, less so above. Flowers about 1½ in. wide, in five- or seven-flowered racemes; style usually hairy at the base; calyx-tube and flower-stalks hairy.

Native of the Amur region, Korea, and N. China; introduced in 1874. This vigorous shrub is one of the earlier flowering species of philadelphus. A fine bush 12 ft high in Col. Stern's garden, near Worthing, flowers in late May and early June. In the summer of 1930 I noticed the ground beneath it was freely sprinkled with seedlings that had sprouted from the seeds of 1929. It is quite an ordinary philadelphus, with no strongly marked qualities or characteristics; but the racemose inflorescence, the peeling bark of the year-old shoots, and the style being hairy at the base are the more distinctive ones.

The plant in the garden of the late Sir Frederick Stern, mentioned above, was raised from seeds collected by Reginald Farrer in Kansu.

P. SERICANTHUS Koehne

A shrub 6 to 12 ft high, shoots glabrous, becoming reddish brown the first year, ultimately peeling. Leaves ovate to oval-lanceolate, tapered to both ends, especially to the slender acuminate apex, coarsely toothed with up to eleven pairs, 1½ to 4 in. long by 1 to 2½ in. wide, sometimes entire, sparsely hairy or glabrous above with a few hairs at the back and tufts in the vein-axils. Flowers about 1 in. wide in racemes of up to eleven, not scented; petals pure white, rounded-oval to nearly orbicular; calyx and stalks densely covered with appressed, stiff, white hairs; style glabrous. *Bot. Mag.*, t. 8941.

Native of Hupeh and Szechwan, China; discovered by Augustine Henry in 1888–9 and introduced to France in 1897, when M. de Vilmorin received seeds from the Abbé Farges. To Britain it was introduced by Wilson in 1900, when collecting for Messrs Veitch. It is quite hardy and flowers freely in June.

P. TOMENTOSUS G. Don

A shrub 6 or 8 ft high; young shoots glabrous, or slightly hairy when quite young only. Leaves 1½ to 4 in. long, ¾ to 2 in. wide; oval or ovate, with long slender points and a rounded or tapered base, unevenly toothed; dark green and hairy above, especially when young, grey and felted beneath; stalk ⅕ to ⅖ in. long. Petals oval, rounded at the end; calyx glabrous outside, downy inside; style about as long as the stamens; stigmas separate at the top.

Native of the Himalaya; introduced, according to Loudon, in 1822. It is often regarded as a variety of *P. coronarius*, but is amply distinguished from it by the grey-felted undersurface of the leaves. It is more nearly related to *P. delavayi* (q.v.).

f. NEPALENSIS (Koehne) Hara *P. nepalensis* Koehne; *P. triflorus* Wall. ex Hu—Leaves glabrous beneath.

f. LANCIFOLIUS (Koehne) Hara *P. lancifolius* Koehne—Styles downy.

P. ZEYHERI Schrad. ex DC.
P. coronarius var. *zeyheri* (Schrad.) Hartw. & Ruempl.

A deciduous shrub of very vigorous spreading habit up to 8 ft high, considerably more in width; bark deep brown, slightly peeling; young shoots glabrous. Leaves broadly ovate to lanceolate, tapered at the base, slender-pointed, varying from coarsely toothed to nearly entire, 2½ to 4 in. long, ¾ to 2 in. wide, glabrous above, downy beneath along each side of the midrib and chief veins, with occasional hairs between. Flowers pure white, 1½ to 1¾ in. across, produced during June in a terminal corymb of three to seven blossoms (sometimes solitary). Petals oval; style distinctly longer than the stamens; calyx glabrous, with slender lobes ½ in. long.

This philadelphus, of unrecorded origin, was in cultivation early in the 19th century and reputed to have come from N. America. It was compared by de Candolle to *P. coronarius*, differing in its leaves being rounded at the base and in its fewer, larger and scentless flowers. It is treated by Dr Hu as a variety of *P. coronarius*, but some authorities consider it to be a hybrid between that species and *P. inodorus* var. *grandiflorus*.

It is very distinct in its comparatively low, spreading habit, but its flowers are scentless, it blossoms poorly and is of inferior quality. The young shoots are apt to be killed back in winter, which may be due to their sappy vigour.

The Lemoine and other Modern Hybrids

In the 19th century various hybrids arose spontaneously in gardens between the species then in cultivation, notably the Old World *P. coronarius* and the American *P. inodorus* and *P. pubescens*. Some of these are treated with the species. The hybrids described below are of more recent origin and are mostly the result of deliberate crossing. Except where otherwise stated, they are the creations of the great French plant-breeder Victor Lemoine of Nancy (1823–1912) or of his successors, and it would be no exaggeration to say that these still represent three-quarters or more of the philadelphus hybrids grown in gardens, even though the newest of them are almost half a century old.

The history of the Lemoine hybrids goes back to 1883, the year in which Lemoine received from the USA a plant of *P. microphyllus*. Crossing this with garden varieties of *P. coronarius* he obtained 'Lemoinei' (1888), 'Erectus' (1892), 'Avalanche' (1896), and 'Manteau d'Hermine' (1898). These are the best known members of the Lemoinei group (*P. × lemoinei* Rehd.), characterised by the rather small, very fragrant flowers and by the small, smooth, sparsely toothed or almost entire leaves. The later hybrids are of more complex ancestry. Those with double flowers arranged in a determinate raceme and with hairy calyces are thought to be crosses between 'Lemoinei' or its allies and the double form of *P. × nivalis* (see p. 138). The best known of these is 'Virginal' (1909), which is the type of *P. × virginalis* Rehd. Other hybrids in this group are 'Girandole', 'Argentine', and 'Enchantement'.

In many of the Lemoine hybrids the inflorescence is a cyme or a reduced panicle, suggesting that *P. inodorus* or *P. insignis* enters into their parentage. Those which also have a glabrous calyx have been classified by Rehder as *P. × cymosus*, a group which has 'Conquête' as its type. Others in this group are (to name only those treated here) 'Rosace', 'Norma', 'Albâtre', and 'Voie Lactée'. But there seems to be no very clear-cut distinction between this group and Rehder's *P. × polyanthus*, which has a similar inflorescence but hairy calyces. The type of this group is 'Gerbe de Neige', which is apparently not in commerce in Britain. 'Boule d'Argent' belongs to it, and perhaps 'Favorite'.

Some of Lemoine's finest hybrids have a pinkish or purplish blotch at the base of the petals and derive from a plant received by him as *P. coulteri*. The plant grown in British gardens under this name is a form of *P. mexicanus* (q.v.) and Lemoine's plant, judging from its offspring, must have been similar, if not the same. The first of these bi-coloured hybrids was 'Fantaisie' (1900), which is believed to be a cross between "*P. coulteri*" and 'Lemoinei'. This had indistinctly marked flowers, but in 'Purpureo-maculatus' (1902) the blotch is more pronounced. Both seem to be now rare in gardens, and the same is true of many others in this group. These were put into commerce by Lemoine during the first world war and may never have been introduced to Britain. But it is doubtful if any of these could be better garden plants than 'Sybille' (date of origin uncertain) and 'Belle Étoile' (1923). The researches of Dr Janaki Ammal have shown that both these clones, and also 'Bicolore', are triploid (*Journ. R.H.S.*, Vol. 76 (1951), p. 273).

'ALBÂTRE'.—Flowers 1½ in. wide, fragrant, double, but with a few fertile stamens. Inflorescence racemose, with jointed pedicels, or the lower peduncles branched and two-flowered. Calyx almost glabrous. Leaves on the flowering shoots narrow-ovate, up to 1½ in. long, sparsely toothed. 4 to 5 ft. Early July.

'ARGENTINE'.—Flowers fragrant, about 2 in. wide, very double, borne mostly in threes. Sepals often six instead of the usual four. 3 to 4 ft.

'ATLAS'.—Flowers slightly fragrant, single, cup-shaped, 1½ in. wide, in racemes of five or seven. Calyx sparsely hairy. Leaves on flowering shoots sparsely toothed, up to 2½ in. long, 1 in. wide. 4 to 6 ft. A.M. 1927.

'AVALANCHE'.—Flowers fragrant, cruciform, ¾ to 1 in. wide, borne in racemes of mostly seven. Leaves elliptic, acute at both ends, glabrous, entire Hu, *Journ. Arn. Arb.*, Vol. 37, p. 64). Of arching and very spreading habit, as shown in *Gard. Chron.*, Vol. 18 (1897), p. 89. A.G.M. 1936. Although the true 'Avalanche' must be in cultivation, it appears to have become confused with 'Erectus' (q.v.).

'BEAUCLERK'.—Flowers fragrant, white with a slight pinkish flush in the centre, up to 3 in. wide, saucer-shaped at first, becoming flat, solitary or in clusters of three or four (occasionally up to seven); petals roundish oblong, irregularly toothed. Stamens spreading, with conspicuous bright yellow anthers. Leaves on the sterile growths broad-ovate, acute, with a few mucronate teeth on each side, up to 2½ in. long, those on the flowering twigs smaller and less toothed. It attains 6 ft in height, more in width. Raised by the Hon. Lewis Palmer from a cross made in 1938 between 'Sybille' (seed-parent) and 'Burfordensis'. A.M. 1947, F.C.C. 1951, A.G.M. 1957.

'BELLE ÉTOILE'.—Flowers very fragrant, with a conspicuous reddish blotch in the centre; petals broadly oblong, at first spreading-erect and slightly folded down the centre, so that the flower is rather angular, later spreading more widely. Inflorescence variable, in its complete form a compound cyme of nine flowers. Leaves on the flowering twigs narrow-ovate, long-pointed, scarcely toothed or entire, but those immediately under the inflorescence bract-like. Leaves on the sterile growths ovate, acuminate, up to 3½ in. long, with a few large teeth on each side. A lovely, deliciously scented philadelphus usually 5 to 6 ft high, more in width, very free-flowering. A.M. 1930, A.G.M. 1936. [PLATE 16

'BICOLORE'.—Flowers fragrant, single, cup-shaped, about 1¾ in. wide, mostly solitary; petals creamy white with a flush of purple at the base. Leaves on the flowering shoots entire or sparsely toothed, ovate, mostly 1¼ in. long, ¾ in. wide, uniformly covered with appressed silky hairs beneath. Of dwarf habit.

'BOULE D'ARGENT'.—Flowers 1¾ in. wide, scarcely fragrant, more or less double, borne five to seven together in a cymose cluster. Calyx-tube slightly hairy, sepals long-acuminate, glabrous. Leaves up to 2½ by 1⅞ in., broad-ovate, with five to seven teeth on each side. Of bushy habit, to about 4 ft high. F.C.C. 1895.

'BOUQUET BLANC'.—There appears to be some confusion between this variety and 'Albâtre' and the two are treated as synonymous by Dr Hu (*Journ. Arn. Arb.*, Vol. 37, p. 60). A plant under the name 'Bouquet Blanc' has not been seen, but a photograph reproduced in *Journ. R.H.S.*, Vol. 38 (1912–13), fig. 116, shows a plant with semi-double to almost single flowers (with some petaloids), whereas 'Albâtre' has almost fully double flowers. A.M. 1912.

'BURFORDENSIS'.—Flowers 2½ to 3 in. across, not fragrant, in racemes of five to nine, stamens with conspicuous yellow anthers. Calyx-tube glabrous, sepals very sparsely hairy. Leaves up to 4½ in. long by 2 in. wide, coarsely toothed, often deeply so. A very vigorous, free-flowering hybrid, attaining 10 ft in height, but less in width. It is difficult to believe that this philadelphus is the true 'Burfordensis', which received an Award of Merit when shown by Sir W. Lawrence of Burford Court, Dorking, in 1921. This was said to be a sport of 'Virginal', whereas the plant now grown under the name does not even belong to the Virginalis group, but bears some resemblance to 'Monster'. It was, however, raised at Burford Court.

'BURKWOODII'.—Flowers very fragrant, about 1¾ in. wide; petals relatively narrow, acute, not overlapping, stained purplish pink at the base. Inflorescence cymose, with three to five flowers, or the flowers solitary. Calyx-tube and sepals sparsely hairy. Leaves on the flowering shoots ⅝ to 1½ in. long, up to ⅝ in. wide. Raised by Messrs Burkwood and Skipwith shortly before 1931; the parentage is said to be 'Étoile Rose' crossed with 'Virginal'.

'CONQUÊTE'.—Flowers shaped rather as in *Clematis montana*, very fragrant, about 2 in. wide, single or with a few petaloid stamens, borne in compound cymes of three or five, the lateral peduncles jointed. Calyx-tube and outside of sepals glabrous, the latter long-acuminate. Leaves on flowering shoots lanceolate, up to 4 in. long, entire. A low-growing shrub, 3 to 4 ft high. It is the type of the Cymosus group. 'ROSACE' is similar, but the flowers are semi-double and it is taller growing.

'COUPE D'ARGENT'.—Flowers solitary or in twos or threes, rose-scented, at first saucer-shaped, becoming flat, about 2¼ in. wide; the petals broadly rounded and overlapping, so that the flower is squarish in outline. Leaves entire or slightly toothed, narrow-ovate, up to 2½ in. long, 1¼ in. wide. Weak-growing but very beautiful. The description is of the plant in commerce here, but it is doubtful if the name is correct. According to the earliest description that can be traced, Lemoine's 'Coupe d'Argent' had long arching branches and pure white flowers of perfect form 1 in. wide (*Le Jardin*, Vol. 30, no. 749 (1921), p. 36).

'DAME BLANCHE'.—Flowers slightly fragrant, broad-campanulate, about 1 in. wide, double or semi-double, up to nine in a raceme. Leaves dark green, smooth and almost glabrous above, slightly hairy beneath, narrowly to broadly ovate, 3¾ to 6 in. long, 1½ to 2⅝ in. wide, with a few distant, shallow teeth. A very attractive philadelphus of moderate growth. The description is from a plant at Wisley, which belongs to the Virginalis group. 'Dame Blanche', as described by Dr Hu in her monograph, is evidently different and belongs to the Lemoinei group.

'ENCHANTEMENT'.—Flowers faintly fragrant, double, ¾ to 1¼ in. wide, up to eleven crowded in a short raceme (about 2 in. long); outer petals rounded at apex. Calyx and pedicels hairy. Leaves on the extension growths about 2½ by 1½ in., with three or four coarse teeth on each side. It is a vigorous shrub with arching branches, attaining 7 ft, very free flowering. A.M. 1966.

'ERECTUS' ('Lemoinei Erectus').—Flowers fragrant, creamy white, cruciform, 1 in. or slightly more wide, borne in threes or fives. Leaves on the flowering shoots ovate-lanceolate, acuminate, rounded or broad-cuneate at the base, ⅞ in. long, ⅜ in. wide, entire or with a few sharp teeth; on extension shoots up to 1⅜ in. long, ⅝ in. wide. Of erect, close habit, to about 4 or 5 ft; on young or heavily pruned plants the habit may be more lax. Some plants distributed as 'Avalanche' belong here.   [PLATE 17

'ÉTOILE ROSE'.—Flowers fragrant, solitary or in twos or threes, saucer-shaped at first, becoming flat, 1½ to 1¾ in. wide; petals stained rose at the base, broad-oblong; sepals caudate, the tails ¼ in. long. Leaves narrow-ovate, entire or with a few mucronate teeth, up to 3 in. long, 1⅛ in. wide. Of dwarf habit.

'GIRANDOLE'.—Flowers milky white, fully double, 1 to 1½ in. wide, up to nine crowded in a roundish, racemose cluster. Calyx sparsely hairy. Leaves on the extension growths up to 2 in. long, 1¼ in. wide, with four or five well-defined teeth on each side. 4 to 6 ft. A.M. 1921.

'GLACIER'.—Flowers fully double, fragrant, only 1¼ in. wide, borne in racemes of five to nine. Leaves mostly less than 1¾ in. long, toothed. Calyx hairy. 4 to 5 ft high.

'INNOCENCE'.—Flowers single or with a few petaloid stamens, about 1½ in. wide, five to seven in a cluster. Leaves mottled with yellow, up to 2 in. by 1 in., with fairly numerous small teeth.

'LEMOINEI'.—Flowers pure white, very fragrant, 1 in. or slightly more wide, produced at the ends of short lateral branches, three to seven in each. Leaves on the sterile growths ovate, rounded at the base, slender-pointed, with usually three to six coarse teeth on either margin, 1 to 2½ in. long and about half as wide, dull green and with scattered hairs above, glossy and more hairy beneath. Leaves on the flowering shoots about 1 in. long, narrowly ovate, almost entire.

This hybrid, the type of the Lemoinei group, was raised by Lemoine around 1883, by crossing some garden form or hybrid of *P. coronarius* with *P. microphyllus*. See further in the introductory note above. It makes a round-topped bush 6 ft or more high, but seems to have become uncommon. A.M. 1898.

'MANTEAU D'HERMINE'.—Flowers creamy white, fragrant, ¾ to 1½ in. wide, borne mostly in threes, sometimes in fives. Leaves almost entire, those on the flowering shoots mostly less than 1½ in. long. Of dwarf, compact habit. A.M. 1956.   [PLATE 18

'MINNESOTA SNOWFLAKE'.—Flowers white, fragrant, fully double, in racemes of up to nine, about 1¾ in. wide, the inner petals mostly narrow and acute. Sepals narrowly triangular or lanceolate, slightly hairy. Raised in the

USA by G. D. Bush of Minneapolis, Minnesota, and patented in 1935. Of mounded habit, up to 8 ft high. 'FROSTY MORN' is a newer hybrid from the same raiser, smaller growing. Both are available in commerce in Britain but their chief value is their great hardiness, which permits them to be grown in the colder parts of the USA and Canada, where most philadelphus cannot survive the hard winters.

'MONSTER'.—Flowers single, about 2 in. wide, cup-shaped at first, flatter when fully expanded, up to nine in a raceme. Calyx sparsely hairy. Leaves large even on the flowering shoots, where they may be 6 in. or so long, half as wide. A coarse, vigorous shrub, quickly growing to 10 ft and eventually much taller. It is near to *P. pubescens* and was apparently named and distributed by Messrs V. N. Gauntlett of Chiddingfold. It reached a height of 25 ft at Nymans in Sussex (*Gard. Chron.*, Vol. 120 (1946), p. 219). It is possibly a form of *P.* × *monstrosus* (Spaeth) Rehd., believed to be a hybrid between *P. pubescens* and *P. lewisii* var. *gordonianus*, though it differs from Rehder's description in having more strongly toothed leaves.

'NORMA'.—Flowers fragrant, saucer-shaped, about 1¾ in. wide, single or occasionally with a few petaloid stamens, borne in fives or threes in a cymose cluster. Calyx almost glabrous; sepals long-acuminate. Leaves ovate, toothed, up to 2 in. long on the flowering shoots. One of the finest of the single-flowered hybrids, with arching branches and 4 to 5 ft high. A.M. 1913, A.G.M. 1949. [PLATE 19

'PATRICIA'.—Flowers single, fragrant, about 1¼ in. wide, in racemes of five or seven. Leaves remarkable for their dark green colouring and rather leathery texture; they are almost entire, ovate, acute, glabrous beneath except for axillary tufts, up to 2¾ in. long, 1½ in. wide. Raised by the well-known Canadian plant-breeder F. L. Skinner. In cultivation in the Royal Horticultural Society Garden at Wisley.

'PURPUREO-MACULATUS'.—Flowers fragrant, 1½ in. across, solitary at the end of a short lateral branchlet; petals white with a blotch of purplish rose at the base, opening in mid-June. Leaves on the sterile shoots broadly ovate or roundish, the base slightly heart-shaped, up to 1¾ in. long, 1½ in. wide, with one to three teeth each side, dull dark green; leaves on the flowering twigs 1 in. or so long, with usually one tooth or entire. *Bot. Mag.*, t. 8193. A dwarf shrub, 2 or 3 ft high. It is the type of the Purpureo-maculatus group, see further in introductory note.

'ROSACE'.—See under 'Conquête'.

'SILVER SHOWERS' ('Silberregen').—Flowers 1¼ in. wide, fragrant, single, mostly solitary at the ends of the twigs, flat, with four or sometimes five petals. Leaves slightly hairy, ovate, up to 1½ in. long, acute, with two or three teeth on each side. 3 ft or slightly more high, making a rounded bush. A promising hybrid of German origin, recently introduced, It is near to the Lemoinei group.

'SYBILLE'.—Flowers fragrant, saucer-shaped, up to 2 in. wide, solitary or in two or threes (occasionally an extra one or two flowers are produced lower down in the leaf-axils). Petals fimbriated, marked purplish rose at the base, or sometimes with a broad stain of that colour extending half-way to the apex.

Leaves broad-ovate, sea-green when mature, up to $1\frac{3}{4}$ in. long on the flowering twigs. Young stems pinkish, hairy. A lovely philadelphus, very free-flowering and graceful, one of the best for small gardens. It is rarely more than 4 ft high, 6 ft wide. A.M. 1954.

'Velleda'.—Flowers saucer-shaped, about 2 in. wide, very sweetly rose-scented, mostly solitary at the ends of the lateral twigs; petals rounded. Leaves up to $2\frac{1}{4}$ by $1\frac{1}{8}$ in., mucronate-toothed or entire. Of fairly dwarf habit. A beautiful, little-known hybrid of uncertain position. Despite the unblotched flowers it seems to derive from the Purpureo-maculatus group.

'Virginal'.—Flowers white, fragrant, cup-shaped, 2 in. wide, double or semi-double, the true petals and outer petaloids rounded. Calyx rather densely hairy. Leaves ovate, up to $1\frac{3}{4}$ in. long, 1 in. wide on the flowering twigs, twice as large on the sterile growths, coarsely toothed, but the smaller leaves with obscure, mucronate teeth. This is perhaps the most widely planted of the hybrids and one of the most beautiful in flower, but it is of gaunt habit; height 6 to 8 ft. F.C.C. 1911, A.G.M. 1926. It is the type of the Virginalis group, see introductory note above.   [Plate 20

'Voie Lactée'.—Flowers slightly scented, saucer-shaped at first, becoming flat, with the petals then slightly reflexed, 2 in. or slightly more wide, solitary or in cymose clusters of three or five; petals occasionally five or six instead of the usual four. Calyx almost glabrous. Leaves on the flowering shoots up to $2\frac{7}{8}$ in. long, $1\frac{1}{4}$ in. wide, slightly toothed. One of the most beautiful of the single-flowered hybrids. Height 4 to 5 ft. A.M. 1912.

× PHILAGERIA   PHILESIACEAE

An intergeneric hybrid between *Philesia* and *Lapageria*, of which only the one cross described here is known or indeed possible, since both genera consist of a single species.

× P. veitchii Mast.

A hybrid between *Lapageria rosea* and *Philesia magellanica* which was raised by Messrs Veitch at Chelsea, and flowered in their nursery there in 1872. It was named, described, and figured that year in *The Gardeners' Chronicle*, p. 358, fig. 119. The lapageria was the seed-bearer. It is a scrambling shrub with leathery, dark green, shining leaves about $1\frac{1}{2}$ in. long and $\frac{1}{2}$ in. wide, with three prominent veins running lengthwise and converging at the apex. Flower pendulous, about 2 in. long, $\frac{1}{2}$ to $\frac{3}{4}$ in. wide, with a rosy purple calyx of three oblong, pointed fleshy sepals about 1 in. long; and a corolla of three bright rose-coloured overlapping petals twice as long; anthers $\frac{1}{2}$ in. long, yellow; flower-stalk $\frac{1}{4}$ in. long. *Bot. Mag.*, n.s., t. 92.

This interesting hybrid bears more resemblance to the lapageria in habit, in the stamens and in the colour of the flower, than it does to the philesia. It is hardy in Cornwall and similar places but is now very rare.

The plate in the *Botanical Magazine* depicts a flowering stem from a plant growing in the cool Fern House at Kew in July 1948. If grown under glass (as it must be over much of the country) it should be planted in a border where it can remain undisturbed. Propagation is by layers.

PHILESIA   PHILESIACEAE

A genus of a single species, closely allied to *Lapageria*, with which it has been successfully hybridised (see × *Philageria*). But the lapageria is a true climber, with lax, twining stems, and has much wider, larger leaves which are three- or five-veined from the base. The flowers are essentially the same, though smaller in *Philesia*. In both genera the fruit is a berry, but in *Lapageria* it is three-celled, one-celled in *Philesia*.

P. *magellanica* was discovered by the French naturalist Philibert Commerson in the Magellan region during de Bougainville's voyage round the world. He was accompanied on his explorations by his mistress Jeanne Baret, disguised as a manservant, and by the young Prince of Nassau-Siegen. The charming generic name *Philesia*, chosen by Commerson though published by de Jussieu, comes from the Greek verb *philein*, to love.

P. MAGELLANICA Gmel.   [PLATE 21
P. *buxifolia* Lam.

An evergreen suckering shrub forming thickets of stems up to 3 or 4 ft high, but sometimes a climber, growing up tree trunks or mossy rocks to a considerable height; branchlets alternate, angled, glabrous. Leaves alternate, stiff and hard, dark green above, glaucous white beneath, about 1½ in. long, ¼ to ⅜ in. wide, but made narrower by the reflexed margins, quite glabrous, midrib prominent beneath; stalk ⅛ in. long. Flowers solitary, nodding, terminal, 2 to 2½ in. long, rich rosy crimson, produced mainly from mid- to late summer; petals three, oblanceolate, pointed, not expanding, and thus giving a tubular form to the flower. Calyx of three oblong sepals about ¼ to ¾ in. long, appressed to the petals. Fruit a roundish red berry. *Bot. Mag.*, t. 4738.

Native of Chile from Valdivia province to the Straits of Magellan; introduced by William Lobb in 1847. It grows wild only in those types of forest where the rainfall and atmospheric humidity is high and is sometimes found in boggy soils. Although by nature a suckering shrub rather than a climber, it attains a considerable height in the wild by growing up the trunks of trees such as

Fitzroya cupressoides, to which it clings by adventitious roots. At Inverewe on the west coast of Scotland it has climbed up the trunk of a Chusan palm, an ideal host because of its fibrous bark, and no doubt it could be grown in this way anywhere in the mildest and rainiest parts of the Atlantic zone. The largest known plant of the commoner suckering habit grows at Rowallane in Co. Down at the foot of a cliff-like rock. This is 4 ft high and 14 ft across. In Cornwall, Canon Boscawen had one almost as large in the rectory garden at Ludgvan. A plant at Trehane, near Probus, in the same county was 3 ft high, 5 ft across, and needed four strong men to carry it when it was lifted and sold after the owner's death (*Journ. R.H.S.*, Vol. 75 (1950), p. 330).

PHILESIA MAGELLANICA

Contrary to what has sometimes been said, *Philesia magellanica* is hardy in all but the coldest parts of the country but, being a moisture lover, it is less likely to succeed in the driest parts of the country, or in positions where it suffers the competition of greedy tree-roots. In the south of England the best place for it is perhaps at the foot of a north-facing wall, where it will receive plenty of light but no direct sun; or at any rate in a position which is cool but not too shaded. It needs a moist soil rich in humus and may be propagated by taking suckers; for propagation by cuttings see *Journ. R.H.S.*, Vol. 70 (1945), p. 327.

PHILLYREA* OLEACEAE

A group of evergreen shrubs or small trees, natives of the Mediterranean region. They are nearly related to *Osmanthus*, and have opposite leaves, toothed or entire, and small white or greenish flowers borne in clusters in the leaf-axils of the previous year's growths. Calyx and corolla four-lobed; stamens two. Fruit a roundish oval, mostly one-seeded drupe.

They are all easily cultivated, and thrive in any soil that is of average quality. They bear clipping well, and cuttings made of the current season's wood in July take root readily.

P. ANGUSTIFOLIA L.

A shrub of dense habit up to 10 ft high, and occasionally more in diameter; branches minutely downy and slightly warted. Leaves linear or linear-lanceolate 1 to $2\frac{1}{2}$ in. long, $\frac{3}{16}$ to $\frac{3}{8}$ in. wide; tapering towards both ends, rarely toothed, dark dull green; glabrous on both surfaces. Flowers fragrant, dull greenish white, produced during May and June in short axillary clusters $\frac{1}{2}$ in. or less long; flower-stalks minutely downy. Fruits blue-black, roundish-oval, $\frac{1}{4}$ in. long.

Native of Portugal, N. Africa, and of the Mediterranean region as far east as Dalmatia; cultivated in England before 1597. It is a neat, quite hardy evergreen, without any striking features, but easily distinguished from all the rest by its entire, long, narrow leaves.

f. ROSMARINIFOLIA (Mill.) Schelle *P. rosmarinifolia* Mill.—Leaves narrower and smaller than those of the type, $\frac{1}{8}$ to $\frac{3}{16}$ in. wide, and of a greyer, rather glaucous shade.

P. LATIFOLIA L.

(incl. *P. media* L.)

An evergreen shrub or small tree up to 15 or even 30 ft high; young branchlets and flower-stalks minutely downy. Leaves variable in size and shape, ovate or elliptic-ovate to lanceolate or elliptic-lanceolate, $\frac{1}{2}$ to $2\frac{1}{2}$ in. long, $\frac{3}{8}$ to $1\frac{1}{2}$ in. wide, more or less dentate to serrate, serrulate, or entire, pointed at the apex, broadly tapered, rounded, or slightly heart-shaped at the base. Flowers dull greenish white, in short axillary clusters. Fruits blue-black, roundish or orange-shaped, $\frac{1}{4}$ to $\frac{3}{8}$ in. long.

Native of the Mediterranean regions of S. Europe, N. Africa, and Asia Minor; cultivated in Britain since the 16th century.

f. SPINOSA (Mill.) Rehd. *P. spinosa* Mill.; *P. latifolia* var. *ilicifolia* DC.—A form with strongly toothed leaves, 1 to $1\frac{1}{2}$ in. long, ovate and rounded at the base.

Two species, *P. latifolia* L. and *P. media* L., were recognised in the past but it is generally agreed that specific separation within this variable entity is not

* Revised by P. S. Green of the Herbarium, Royal Botanic Gardens, Kew.

possible. Some plants previously named *P. media* represent the adult stage of *P. latifolia.* Numerous forms have been described under *P. media* and that known as f. *buxifolia* (Ait.) Schelle has small, almost entire leaves.

PHLOMIS   LABIATAE

A genus of about 100 species of herbs, subshrubs, and shrubs, ranging from the Mediterranean region to China; one species (*P. tuberosa,* a herb) extending into Central Europe. Flowers yellow, purple, pink, or white, arranged in whorls. Calyx equally five-toothed. Corolla with a hooded upper lip, the lower lip spreading, three-lobed. Stamens four. Style-branches unequal. Nutlets three-angled.

P. FRUTICOSA L.   JERUSALEM SAGE   [PLATE 21

A vigorous evergreen shrub; branchlets soft, herbaceous, stout, square, thickly covered with grey, branched hairs. Leaves opposite, dull green, wrinkled, and with prominent veining like common sage, 2 to 5 in. long, 1½ to 1¾ in. wide, ovate-lanceolate, covered with branched hairs, sparsely above, thickly beneath; stalks ¼ to 1 in. long. Flowers stalkless, bright yellow, crowded at the leaf-bases in two dense clusters which together form a circular tier 2 in. across. Corolla 1¼ in. long, two-lipped, the upper lip hood-shaped; calyx green, funnel-shaped, hairy, with five projecting narrow teeth at the top. *Bot. Mag.,* t. 1843.

Native of the Mediterranean region, with its western limit in Malta, Sicily, and Sardinia; cultivated in England since the 16th century. The flowers develop in late summer and autumn, and are very bright and interesting, forming curious, short, crowded clusters. The foliage is like that of a giant sage, but is weakly scented. Easily propagated by cuttings. The Jerusalem sage should have some sunny sheltered spot, such as a house corner facing south, or a dryish, sunny bank.

The clone cultivated under the name *Phlomis* 'E. A. BOWLES' appears to be no more than a robust form of *P. fruticosa* with flowers of a paler yellow. The leaves are up to 6 in. long and 3in. wide, on petioles up to 5½ in. long.

The following subshrubby species are also cultivated, though much less commonly than *P. fruticosa:*

P. CHRYSOPHYLLA Boiss.—A low subshrub. Leaves broadly elliptic to oblong-elliptic or oblong-ovate, up to 2¼ in. long and 1½ in. wide, obtuse to roundish at the apex, base mostly truncate to cordate and abruptly decurrent onto the petiole, sometimes cuneate, densely stellate-hairy on both sides, all the veins impressed above, raised beneath; petioles ½ to 1 in. long. Flowering stems

1 ft or more long, with one or two distant whorls of yellow flowers; calyx-teeth shortly spine-tipped. Native of the Lebanon, etc. It is sometimes cultivated for the golden-green tinge of the young leaves, which comes from the colouring of the hairs. On dried specimens the indumentum on the younger leaves soon becomes a deep, vivid yellow, whence the specific epithet *chrysophylla*, which the living plants scarcely merit.

P. ITALICA L. *P. rotundifolia* Mill.; *P. balearica* Chodat—Leaves oblong or oblong-lanceolate, up to 2 in. long, ⅝ in. wide, clad on both sides with a wool of stellate hairs, but more densely so beneath, shallowly crenate-toothed. Flowers about six in each whorl; bracts awl-shaped to linear-lanceolate, shorter than the calyx, which, like the bracts, is densely hairy, the hairs concealing the five, short, roundish, mucronate teeth. Corolla about ¾ in. long, pink or pale lilac. Despite its name, this species is an endemic of the Balearic Islands; it was probably introduced in the 17th century and was certainly in cultivation by the middle of the 18th century. *Bot. Mag.*, t. 9270.

P. PURPUREA L.—This species is closely allied to *P. italica*, but the floral bracts are broader, acuminate at the apex, and the teeth of the calyx sharply pointed. Also, the leaves are rather thinly coated with hairs on the upper

PHLOMIS PURPUREA

surface. Native of S. Portugal and of southern and central Spain, common in the Ronda region. *Bot. Mag.*, n.s., t. 518. Introduced in the 17th century. Rather tender. In the wild it grows to a height of 3 or 4 ft, but in cultivation is usually of sprawling habit.

PHORMIUM AGAVACEAE

A genus of two species formerly included in the Liliaceae, but at present residing in the Agavaceae, where in Hutchinson's classification *Phormium* is placed in the monotypic tribe Phormiae. Its proper taxonomic position remains a matter of dispute.

The phormiums are not woody but are so frequently included in nurserymen's lists of trees and shrubs that perhaps their anomalous inclusion here may be excused.

The phormiums are clump-forming plants, spreading by stout rhizomes. The leaves are evergreen and bear a resemblance in shape and arrangement to those of the flag irises. Flowers bisexual, borne in long-pedunculate inflorescences, the lower part of the peduncle clothed with sterile bracts, the upper bracts subtending flowering laterals. Corolla of six segments, connate at the base. Ovary superior, developing into a loculicidal capsule containing numerous small, winged seeds.

The phormiums were killed or badly damaged in many gardens in the exceptionally severe winter of 1962–3, but should come through most winters unharmed except in the coldest and driest parts of the country. They thrive in a good garden soil, but are not very particular in their requirements, and have been found to succeed well in peaty soil and even in boggy moorland. They are propagated by division.

The phormiums are as out of place among tall shrubs as they are in the herbaceous border. They are best treated as architectural features near buildings, and also look well when rising out of a ground-work of low-growing shrubs and herbaceous plants.

P. COOKIANUM Le Jolis   MOUNTAIN FLAX
P. colensoi Hook. f.; *P. hookeri* Gunn ex Hook. f.

This is, in general aspect, similar to the better known *P. tenax* described below, but its leaves are usually only 2 to 5 ft high, less stiff and often drooping. So far as the cultivated plants are concerned, there is the further difference that the leaves are lighter green, rarely glaucous, and without the orange-coloured or red line on the leaf margins that is commonly seen in *P. tenax* (but not a distinctive character of that species as a whole). The flowers, too, are paler than in *P. tenax*, the inner segments being yellow or greenish yellow, the outer ones yellow or yellowish red. The seed-vessel is twisted (not so in *P. tenax*). *Bot. Mag.*, t. 6973.

Native of New Zealand, from the North to Stewart Island; described by Le Jolis in 1848 from a plant brought direct from New Zealand to a garden at Cherbourg, and named by him after Captain Cook. Although it may share some habitats with *P. tenax*, it occurs most commonly on sea-cliffs and in mountain 'fell-fields'.

cv. 'TRICOLOR'.—Leaves 2 to 2½ ft long, variegated with stripes of white and edged with red. Put into commerce by Messrs Duncan and Davies of New Zealand, who received their original stock from the Maoris.

cv. 'VARIEGATA'.—Leaves with marginal stripes of white. First Class Certificate when shown by the nurseryman William Bull in 1869.

P. TENAX J. R. & G. Forst.   NEW ZEALAND FLAX   [PLATE 23

Leaves erect, of hard tough texture, rigid except at the points, up to 6 or 9 ft long and 4 or 5 in. wide, tapering near the top to a fine point, green inside, glaucous outside, with a red or orange-coloured line on the margins and midrib; they are stalkless, sheathing at the base, keeled, and V-shaped farther up, flattening out more towards the apex which is slit on old leaves. Flowers produced in summer on a panicle 5 to 15 ft high, each flower 1 to 2 in. long, with the six dull red segments separate but assuming a tube-like arrangement. *Bot. Mag.*, t. 3199.

Native of New Zealand, including Stewart Island, the Chatham Islands, and Auckland Island; also of Norfolk Island. It was discovered during Cook's first voyage (1769–70), but the seeds collected by Sir Joseph Banks and brought home failed to germinate. It was successfully introduced to Kew in 1789.

Although said to ascend to 4,000 ft, it is in the main a plant of the lowlands, common in coastal and swamp associations. It is a very variable species, and the description given above is of a cultivated example and is not intended to represent the species as a whole. According to Moore and Edgar, in *Flora of New Zealand*, Vol. 2, the leading characters of *P. tenax* are the stiff more or less erect leaves up to 10 ft long, the usually dull red flowers, the straight carpels and the erect, straight, dark coloured seed-vessel. For cultivation, hardiness, etc., see introductory note.

cv. 'PURPUREUM'.—Leaves purplish, up to 6 ft high. The name should probably be taken to indicate a group rather than a single clone, since this form comes more or less true from seed.

cv. 'VARIEGATUM'.—A tall-growing variety, the leaves of which are striped with creamy yellow. Put into commerce by Messrs Veitch in 1870.

cv. 'VEITCHII'.—A fairly dwarf variety with narrowish leaves, variegated with stripes and bands of creamy yellow, some leaves wholly of that colour except at the margin; ground-colour rich green. Put into commerce by Messrs Veitch in 1866.

For other garden varieties, available in New Zealand, see the R.H.S. Year-book *Lilies and other Liliaceae* (1973), pp. 82–5 and L. J. Metcalf, *The Cultivation of New Zealand Trees and Shrubs* (1972), pp. 208–12.

The leaves of *P. tenax* yield one of the finest fibres known. The Maoris put it to many uses, and recognised numerous races and local varieties, which they distinguished according to the quality of the fibre. An interesting account of these was published in Hector, *Phormium tenax as a Fibrous Plant*, 2nd ed. (1889), pp. 76–80.

PHOTINIA ROSACEAE

A genus of about sixty woody species in E. and S.E. Asia, extending westward into the Himalaya; one species in western N. America. It belongs to the same group of the Rosaceae as *Malus*, *Sorbus*, *Crataegus*, etc., in which the fruits consist of up to five carpels, surrounded by, and more or less merged with, the fleshy calyx-tube. Leaves evergreen or deciduous, alternate, simple. Flowers white, in corymbs or panicles; petals five, spreading; stamens up to twenty; styles mostly two; carpels united with the calyx-tube for most or all of their length. Fruits small, red, fleshy, with persistent calyx-lobes.

The photinias like a warm soil, not too heavy and close. The evergreen species grow well on chalky soils, and some are particularly valuable for that reason (see *P. × fraseri*, p. 156); but the deciduous species need a neutral or acid soil. Propagation is by seed or by cuttings of half to nearly ripened wood in gentle heat. The practice of grafting the photinias on hawthorn can only be condemned.

P. ARBUTIFOLIA Lindl.

Crataegus arbutifolia Dryander, *nom. illegit.*; *Heteromeles arbutifolia* (Lindl.) M. Roem.; *Photinia salicifolia* Presl

An evergreen tree occasionally 30 ft high, or in cultivation more often a shrub, with downy young bark. Leaves stiff and leathery, 2 to 4 in. long, ¾ to 1½ in. wide, oblong, lanceolate or obovate, tapering at the base to a thick downy stalk ½ to ¾ in. long, the margins set with stiff teeth, each tipped with a small black gland. Flowers produced very numerously in a large, flattish panicle, composed of corymbose clusters terminating the shoot, and in the axils of the uppermost leaves. Each flower is from ¼ to ⅜ in. diameter; petals pure white; calyx-tube with glabrous, triangular lobes; stamens ten. Fruits about the size of holly berries, bright red, tasting like common haws.

Native of California; introduced by Menzies in 1796. It is a handsome evergreen, but unfortunately not reliably hardy. It may be grown on a wall, but is, of course, at its best in the open where the climate is suitable. In California the fruit-covered branches are used for Christmas decorations as we use holly.

P. BEAUVERDIANA Schneid.

A deciduous tree up to 30 ft high, devoid of down in all its parts; young wood purplish brown, marked with very pale lenticels. Leaves lance-shaped to narrowly obovate, long and slenderly pointed, narrowly wedge-shaped at the base, finely and sharply toothed, the teeth frequently tipped with a small dark gland, 1½ to 5 in. long, ½ to 1¾ in. wide, of thin firm texture with some ten or twelve pairs of veins conspicuously raised beneath. Flowers in corymbs 1½ to 2 in. wide, terminating short leafy twigs which spring from the previous season's growth. Each flower is scarcely ½ in. wide, white; petals roundish, tapering to a claw; sepals triangular. Fruits deep red, rather egg-shaped, nearly ¼ in. wide.

Native of W. China; discovered by Henry, introduced to the Coombe Wood nursery in 1900 by Wilson, who describes it as a small, slender tree common in woods and copses. It has been cultivated at Kew since its introduction, is quite hardy and bears fruit regularly and usually freely enough to make it quite ornamental. A distinguishing character is the conspicuous veining, almost ribbing, of the leaves beneath. It flowers in May.

There is a specimen at Westonbirt, Glos., 30 ft high, planted in 1933.

var. NOTABILIS (Schneid.) Rehd. & Wils. *P. notabilis* Schneid.—Easily distinguished from the type by the larger and especially broader leaves, which are up to 5. in. long, and the larger, looser inflorescences 3 to 4 in. wide. Fruits orange-red. Superior to the type. Introduced by Wilson in 1908 from W. Hupeh, where he found it 30 ft high. Award of Merit as a hardy fruiting shrub when shown from Nymans, Sussex, on November 29, 1960.

P. DAVIDSONIAE Rehd. & Wils.

An evergreen tree 20 to 45 ft high, the young shoots reddish, appressed-downy; buds minute; short branches somewhat spiny. Leaves leathery, oblanceolate to narrowly oval, tapered towards both ends, usually more gradually towards the base, 2 to 6 in. long, ¾ to 1¾ in. wide, finely toothed, dark glossy green above, pale beneath, soon quite glabrous; stalk ¼ to ½ in. long. Flowers numerous, in terminal corymbs 3 or 4 in. across; each flower scarcely ½ in. wide, white. Petals roundish, spreading; calyx-tube funnel-shaped, with triangular lobes, downy like the flower-stalks. Fruits roundish, orange-red, glabrous, about ⅓ in. long, the calyx-lobes persisting and incurved.

Native of W. Hupeh, China; discovered in 1900 by Wilson, who describes this as one of the handsomest evergreen trees in Central China, where it is frequently planted round shrines and tombs. It is most closely allied to *P. serrulata*, but is well distinguished by its shorter-stalked leaves and downy inflorescence; the fruit and flowers are larger than in *P. serrulata*. Although not completely hardy at Kew, it is damaged only in severe winters.

P. GLABRA (Thunb.) Maxim.

Crataegus glabra Thunb.; *Sorbus glabra* (Thunb.) Zab.

A glabrous evergreen shrub up to 10 ft high. Leaves bronzy when young, becoming glossy dark green, narrowly oval, sometimes slightly obovate, 1½ to 3½ in. long, one-third to half as wide, pointed, tapered at the base, regularly and shallowly serrate; stalk ¼ to ½ in. long, glabrous. Flowers in loose, terminal, much-branched panicles 3 to 5 in. across, scented like hawthorn, each about ⅜ in. wide with five narrowly oval petals, white tinged with pink, hairy on the inside at the base, opening in June. Fruits globose, ⅛ to ¼ in. wide, red, ultimately black.

Native of Japan, whence Wilson introduced it in 1914, but it may have appeared previously; it also occurs in China. It is a pleasant evergreen without any outstanding merits. The related *P. serrulata* is a much larger shrub or small tree, with larger, oblong or oblanceolate leaves, leaf-stalks hairy when young and longer than in *P. glabra* (up to 1¾ in. long), and glabrous petals.

cv. 'RUBENS'.—Young leaves bright bronzy red. A very striking garden variety, in cultivation in New Zealand since the 1930s, but of fairly recent introduction to Britain.

P. × FRASERI Dress—A group of hybrids between *P. glabra* and *P. serrulata* of which the first to be identified and described was raised by the Fraser Nurseries, Birmingham, Alabama, USA. It was found around 1940 among seedlings raised from the seeds of *P. serrulata*, which grew in the nursery in close proximity to *P. glabra*. All of the batch agreed with the seed-parent except this one outstanding plant, which was propagated, and the first plants put into commerce in 1955. According to W. J. Dress, who described this hybrid in *Baileya*, Vol. 9 (1961), pp. 101–3, it is intermediate in its characters between the two parents in the size and shape of its leaves and in the length of the petioles, which are hairy as in the seed-parent. The inflorescence is intermediate in width and the petals are downy on the inside at the base as in *P. glabra*, though less densely so. The original clone, which has been named 'BIRMINGHAM', is notable for the bright bronzy-red young growths, produced from spring until quite late in the summer.

Two other photinias probably belong to this group, namely 'ROBUSTA' and 'RED ROBIN'.

These hybrids, which are scarce at present, will in time become valued ornamental evergreens, especially in gardens on chalky soils, where *Pieris formosa* 'Wakehurst' and similar clones cannot be grown. The young growths are less frost-tender than in the pieris, and in character over a much longer period—up to almost four months.

P. PARVIFOLIA (Pritz.) Schneid.
Pourthiaea parvifolia Pritz.; *Photinia subumbellata* Rehd. & Wils.

A deciduous shrub 6 to 9 ft high, with dark red, glabrous young shoots. Leaves oval, ovate, or somewhat obovate, slenderly pointed, broadly wedge-shaped or almost rounded at the base, finely toothed, 1¼ to 2½ in. long, ½ to 1⅓ in. wide, dark bright green and soon quite glabrous; stalk ⅛ in. or less long. Corymbs 1 to 1½ in. wide, terminating short leafy twigs and carrying few (rarely more than eight or nine) flowers; flower-stalks ½ to 1 in. long, slender, glabrous. Flowers about ½ in. wide, white; petals roundish with a few hairs inside the claw; calyx-tube top-shaped, with small, ovate, pointed lobes. Fruits oval, ⅓ in. long, not so much wide, dullish red or orange-red, crowned with the persistent sepals.

Native of Hupeh, China; introduced by Wilson to the Arnold Arboretum, Mass., in 1908. It is perfectly hardy at Kew, but neither in flower nor in fruit has it proved very ornamental up to the present. It blossoms in May.

P. PRIONOPHYLLA (Franch.) Schneid.

Eriobotrya prionophylla Franch.

An evergreen shrub of stiff habit; young shoots covered with greyish down. Leaves of leathery texture, obovate or inclined to oval, wedge-shaped at the base, rounded or with a short point at the apex, sharply, almost spinily toothed; 1½ to 3 in. long, 1 to 2 in. wide, finely downy above when quite young, becoming glabrous and dark green later, persistently downy and strongly veined beneath; stalk up to ½ in. long. Flowers white, ⅓ in. wide, produced in summer in flattish corymbs 2 to 3 in. across. Petals obovate, incurved; stamens about twenty with yellow anthers. Calyx-tube woolly, the short triangular lobes downy or glabrous towards their tips where there is a small gland. Fruits globose, ¼ in. wide, crimson, woolly at the apex where the calyx remains. *Bot. Mag.*, t. 9134.

Native of Yunnan, China, where it was discovered on limestone hills by the Abbé Delavay in 1888, and since collected by C. K. Schneider and Forrest, to the latter of whom we owe its introduction to cultivation. It was originally placed in the genus *Eriobotrya* by Franchet. It is distinguishable amongst the cultivated photinias by the sharp, often coarse toothing of the hard-textured obovate leaves. The species appears first to have flowered with E. J. P. Magor at St Tudy, Cornwall, in July 1922. It needs the protection of a wall away from the south and south-west of the country.

P. SERRULATA Lindl.

Crataegus serratifolia Desf.

An evergreen shrub, or a tree ultimately 30 to 40 ft high in favoured situations; branchlets stout, glabrous. Leaves oblong, very firm and leathery, reddish when young, 4 to 8 in. long and from 1½ to 3½ in. wide, rounded or tapering at the base, shallowly toothed, perfectly glabrous on both surfaces; the stalk, however, which is from 1 to 1½ in. long, is clothed with whitish hairs which also extend up the midrib when young. Flowers white, ⅜ in. in diameter, produced in April and May in large, terminal corymbose panicles 4 to 6 in. through; petals glabrous. Fruits about the size of common haws, red. *Bot. Mag.*, t. 2105.

Native of China; first introduced by Captain Kirkpatrick of the East India Co., in 1804. Where it thrives, this is undoubtedly one of the finest evergreens ever introduced. At Kew it is hardy in all but exceptional winters, but it is only seen at its best farther west (see below). It is most beautiful in spring, when the white flowers are associated with the rich brownish-red, shining young leaves, but near London the latter are apt to be spoilt by late spring frosts.

The following specimens have been recorded in recent years: Killerton, Devon, by the Chapel, 44 × 3¼ ft (1970); Pylewell Park, Hants, 26 × 2½ ft (1970); Bath Botanic Garden, 30 × 3¼ ft (1962); Luscombe Castle, Devon, 45 × 4¾ ft at 3 ft (1970); Trewithen, Cornwall, 50 × 3 ft (1971); Derreen, Co. Kerry, Eire, 30 ft high on two stems (1966).

f. ROTUNDIFOLIA (Mouillef.) Rehd.—Leaves shorter and proportionately broader.

NOTE. Although this is not the place to make an important nomenclatural change, it should be pointed out that the name *P. serrulata* Lindl. is illegitimate, since Lindley cited *Crataegus glabra* Thunb. as a synonym. This is a different species (see *P. glabra*) but if Lindley considered his species to be the same as Thunberg's he should have taken up the epithet *glabra* for it. The earliest legitimate epithet would seem to be *serratifolia*, from *Crataegus serratifolia* Desf.

P. VILLOSA (Thunb.) DC.

Crataegus villosa Thunb.; *Pourthiaea villosa* (Thunb.) Decne.;
P. variabilis Hemsl.

A deciduous shrub or a small tree. Leaves obovate, or ovate-lanceolate, $1\frac{1}{2}$ to $3\frac{1}{2}$ in. long, $\frac{3}{4}$ to $1\frac{1}{2}$ in. wide, the apex drawn out into a long fine point, tapered at the base, finely and regularly toothed, each tooth gland-tipped. Flowers white, in corymbs 1 in. long and $1\frac{1}{2}$ in. wide, produced in May; stalks conspicuously warted; each flower about $\frac{1}{3}$ in. in diameter. Fruit the size and shape of common haws, red.

Native of Japan, China, and Korea. It is a variable plant especially in the amount of down on the leaves, young shoots, and flower-stalk. In the typical *P. villosa* the leaves are, as a rule, more obovate, and all the younger parts of the plant hairy; the flower-stalk is felted with grey down, and the fruit is about $\frac{1}{3}$ in. long. In var. LAEVIS (see further below), the leaves are usually longer-pointed and, like the branchlets and flowers, are glabrous or only slightly downy; the brilliant red fruits are $\frac{1}{2}$ in. long. These two varieties, while distinct enough in themselves, are united by various intermediate forms, and it is doubtful if the distinction need be recognised in gardens. Indeed it never has been, since most of the plants grown as *P. villosa* belong strictly to the var. *laevis*. It was introduced to Europe by Siebold around 1865, but did not reach this country until later in the century.

Although not in the first rank as an ornamental, *P. villosa* makes an elegant shrub of large size and is very reliable both in its fruiting and in its red autumn colouring. It is not suitable for chalky soils.

var. LAEVIS (Thunb.) Dipp. *Crataegus laevis* Thunb.; *Pourthiaea arguta* Lav., not Decne.—This variety has been discussed above. Figured in *Bot. Mag.*, t. 9275.

f. MAXIMOWICZIANA (Lévl.) Rehd. *Pyrus sinensis* var. *maximowicziana* Lévl.; *Photinia maximowicziana* (Lévl.) Nakai, not *P. maximowiczii* Decne.—Leaves almost sessile, rounded and abruptly acuminate, sometimes almost truncate, at the apex, cuneate at the base; veins deeply impressed above. Autumn colour of cultivated plants yellow. R. L. Lancaster considers that this photinia is distinct enough to merit specific rank and has proposed for it the name *P. koreana* in the *Manual* of Messrs Hillier & Sons.

var. SINICA Rehd. & Wils.—This variety, which represents the species in Central and Western China, was discovered by Henry and introduced by Wilson about 1901. It is a slender deciduous tree 18 to 25 ft high, with downy young shoots. Leaves oval to oblong, sometimes rather obovate, pointed, usually tapered but sometimes rounded at the base, finely and sharply toothed, $1\frac{1}{2}$ to $3\frac{1}{2}$ in. long, $\frac{1}{2}$ to $1\frac{1}{2}$ in. wide, bright green and soon glabrous above, paler beneath and downy especially on the midrib and veins, becoming glabrous by late summer; stalk $\frac{1}{12}$ to $\frac{1}{5}$ in. long, downy. Flowers produced in May on racemose corymbs 1 to 2 in. wide with downy stalks. Each flower is about $\frac{1}{3}$ in. wide, with white rounded petals, a woolly bell-shaped calyx with triangular teeth and twenty stamens. Fruits egg-shaped, $\frac{1}{2}$ in. long, orange-scarlet; the fruit stalks conspicuously warted.

This variety, which replaces typical *P. villosa* in W. China, is distinct in its mostly elliptic leaves and in its larger fruits, borne in racemes rather than corymbs. It, too, colours well in the autumn.

PHYGELIUS   SCROPHULARIACEAE

A genus of two species of subshrubs, natives of S. Africa. Leaves opposite or the upper ones alternate. Flowers showy, on recurved stalks, in terminal panicles. Calyx with five lobes. Corolla-tube elongated, curved in *P. capensis*; limb with five rounded lobes. Stamens four, exserted.

P. CAPENSIS Benth.   [PLATE 24

An evergreen shrub a few feet high; shoots erect, four-angled, very pithy, glabrous. Leaves opposite, glabrous, ovate, $1\frac{1}{4}$ to 5 in. long, about half as wide, shallowly toothed, rounded or shallowly heart-shaped at the base, tapered to the bluntish apex; stalk $\frac{3}{4}$ to 2 in. long, deeply channelled. Flowers nodding, borne on terminal erect panicles 6 in. to $1\frac{1}{2}$ ft tall, loosely pyramidal, up to 6 in. wide at the base. Corolla tubular, 1 to $1\frac{1}{4}$ in. long, $\frac{1}{2}$ in. wide at the five-lobed mouth, scarlet, yellowish in the throat. Stamens four, attached beneath the mouth of the corolla. *Bot. Mag*, t. 4881.

Native of S. Africa, introduced about 1850. As a shrub for the open ground *P. capensis* succeeds only in the milder parts, where it will reach 6 or 7 ft in height. Elsewhere it can be treated as an herbaceous perennial and should prove hardy provided the soil is well drained. But the best place for it is a sunny wall, where it will attain a height of 20 ft or more in the most favoured localities. In colder gardens its soft shoots will be cut back in winter, but this is really of no account, as some trimming is always necessary. The shade of red in the flowers varies considerably in depth, and is brightest in 'COCCINEUS'. Easily increased by cuttings.

P. AEQUALIS Hiern—This is the only other species known and is not often seen in cultivation. Lady Byng of Vimy obtained an Award of Merit for it at Vincent Square, September 15, 1936. It is a subshrub, woody below, more or less herbaceous above, 2 to 3 ft high, shoots quadrangular. Leaves opposite, stiff in texture, 1 to 4 in. long, about one-third as wide, ovate to lanceolate, bluntly toothed. Flowers quite pendulous on terminal panicles 6 to 9 in. high;

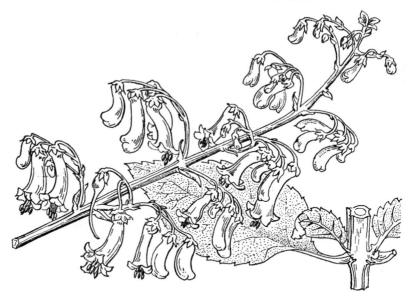

PHYGELIUS CAPENSIS

corolla slender, tubular, 1 to 1½ in. long, buff-pink outside, the mouth yellow with a bright red margin. On wild plants the blossoms are shorter-stalked and much more closely set on the panicles than in *P. capensis*, but this distinction is not shown so clearly by cultivated plants. A more important difference is that the corollas are narrower and almost straight, with the mouth of the tube quite regular and the lobes spreading only slightly; in *P. capensis* the corolla is curved, the mouth of the tube is oblique, and the lobes spread widely (*Bot. Mag.*, n.s., t. 214). Native of S. Africa; flowers from August to October. At Kew it is cut to the ground in most winters. Increased by cuttings.

PHYLLOCLADUS   PODOCARPACEAE

This curious genus of trees and shrubs is related to *Podocarpus*, although they are very different in outward aspect. Of the species that are, or have been, in cultivation, one is native of Tasmania and three of New Zealand. Two tropical species grow in Borneo and the Philippine Islands. They are evergreen and are chiefly remarkable because the branchlets are flattened out to resemble leaves and perform the functions of leaves, after the fashion of several acacias and the butcher's broom; they are known as phylloclades. The true leaves are small and linear or scale-like—scarcely noticeable except on young seedling plants. Flowers unisexual; both sexes occurring on one tree in some species, on separate trees in others.

The four species here described succeed in a good, open soil but need a copious rainfall and warmer conditions than our average climate affords. Propagation can be done by cuttings put in gentle heat in summer, but plants raised from imported seeds are preferable.

P. ALPINUS Hook. f.   CELERY PINE

An evergreen shrub or small tree from 8 to 25 ft high, but in exposed alpine localities, according to Cheeseman, often reduced to a bush 3 to 6 ft high. The 'leaves' are usually very crowded and vary much in shape and size. On scrubby bushes growing on the mountains at 5,000 ft elevation the 'leaves' are small and narrow, $\frac{1}{2}$ to $\frac{3}{4}$ in. long and $\frac{1}{8}$ to $\frac{1}{4}$ in. wide. But at lower elevations and growing under more favourable circumstances they are as much as $1\frac{1}{2}$ in. long and $\frac{3}{4}$ in. wide, ovate to rhomboid in shape, sometimes pinnately lobed, often merely irregularly toothed. Nuts produced a few together, each nut about the size of a radish seed, the apex exposed.

Native of the North and South Islands of New Zealand, most abundant at elevations of 1,500 to over 5,000 ft. It differs from the other two New Zealand species (*P. glaucus* and *P. trichomanoides*) in the irregularly disposed branchlets and 'leaves', those two species having them pinnately arranged. It is more closely related to the Tasmanian *P. asplenifolius*. Although the hardiest of the genus, its rather congested growth and crowded 'leaves' make it the least elegant and effective. It has attained a height of 11 ft in the National Pinetum at Bedgebury, Kent.

cv. 'SILVER BLADES'.—'Leaves' (phylloclades) silvery blue. Raised by Messrs Hillier and put into commerce in 1968. They state that the colour is best developed under glass.

P. ASPLENIFOLIUS (Labill.) Hook. f.
Podocarpus asplenifolius Labill.; *Phyllocladus rhomboidalis* L.C. & A. Rich.

An evergreen tree up to 60 ft high at low elevations but dwarfed and bushy at high altitudes; trunk usually slender; all the parts glabrous. 'Leaves' irregularly arranged on the branchlets and resembling in this respect those of *P. alpinus*, but differing from the pinnately arranged ones of *P. trichomanoides* and *P. glaucus*; nor are the branchlets strictly whorled as in these two species, although often clustered. The 'leaves' have the usual rhomboid or diamond shape seen in this genus, being wedge-shaped and entire at the base, the upper part also tapering to the apex but always toothed and often lobed as well—sometimes deeply so; they vary from $\frac{3}{4}$ to $2\frac{3}{4}$ in. in length and from $\frac{1}{3}$ to 1 in. in width, dark dull green.

Native of Tasmania where it is described as being a 'beautiful tree, growing to a great height but not attaining any great size of trunk; found in rich, humid situations, and abundant on the Hampshire and Surrey hills'. It has long been cultivated in England. A fine tree once grew in the pinetum at Bicton in S. Devon, a shapely, slender pyramid 32 ft high. It was probably the most admirable example of phyllocladus ever seen in the British Isles, but it died many years ago. This species is most nearly allied to the New Zealand P. *alpinus*, especially in the irregularly arranged, not pinnate, branchlets, but is a finer, free-growing tree with larger foliage.

P. GLAUCUS Carr.   TOATOA

An evergreen tree 20 to 30 ft, sometimes more, high, of slender tapering habit, even somewhat fastigiate; branchlets stout, whorled. 'Leaves' (phyllo-clades) arranged on branchlets 4 to 10 in. long in two opposite rows, very leathery, diamond-shaped to roundish ovate, the lower part entire and tapered to a short stalk, the upper part with often three to five shallow lobes on each side, 1 to 2¼ in. long, ⅝ to 1¼ in. wide, glaucous when young, becoming dark dull green. Male flowers in cylindrical spikes ¾ to 1 in. long, produced at the tips of the branchlets. Nuts about the size of radish seeds, ten to twenty of them stuck on one egg-shaped receptacle about ½ in. long, the nuts half exposed; these take the place of phylloclades towards the base of a branchlet.

Native of New Zealand on the North Island up to 3,000 ft above sea-level. Although most closely akin to P. *trichomanoides*, especially in the thick whorled branches and frond-like arrangement of the 'leaves', this is very distinct. It has the largest 'leaves' of any of these cultivated phyllocladuses and they are glaucous when young. As this tree is confined to the North Island, it is likely to be more tender than the other New Zealand species; still it should be hardy in the south-west. It has long been cultivated in the Temperate House at Kew and as far back as 1881 bore fruit there. It is described as a very elegant tree in the wild, but is only one-third the height of its relative, P. *trichomanoides*.

P. *glaucus* is certainly very tender. The only specimen recorded by A. F. Mitchell is one of 19 ft × 10 in. on Garinish Island, Co. Cork (1966).

P. TRICHOMANOIDES D. Don

An evergreen tree of graceful habit from 50 to 70 ft high in the wild, with a trunk 3 to 9 ft in girth; devoid of down; branchlets in whorls. 'Leaves' (phylloclades) arranged in opposite rows on short branchlets only 2 to 4 in. long so as to resemble a pinnate leaf or certain fern fronds. Each 'leaf' is ¼ to 1 in. long, not so much wide, obovate to diamond-shaped, the lower half entire, the upper half cut into several shallow lobes, dark dull green. Flowers of both sexes on the same plant, the males in cylindrical clusters ⅓ to ½ in. long at the tips of the branchlets, the females at the margins of small modified phylloclades and usually solitary. Nut (seed) solitary and seated in a cup-shaped receptacle.

Native of New Zealand on the North and South Islands ascending from sea-level to 2,500 ft. The wood is white, close-grained, and is much valued in New Zealand for building purposes. The Maoris obtain a red dye from the bark. It is hardy in Cornwall, the south of Ireland, and in similar places. It is easily recognised from the other species except *P. glaucus* by the whorled arrangement of the branches combined with a pinnate arrangement of the phylloclades; from *P. glaucus* it is well distinguished by the much smaller average size of the phylloclades which have a reddish-brown tinge when quite young.

There is an example of *P. trichomanoides* at Mount Usher, Co. Wicklow, Eire, measuring 22 × 1¼ ft (1966), and another at Fota, Co. Cork, of the same height but slightly smaller in girth, planted in 1941. In England there are smaller examples at Leonardslee and Wakehurst Place, Sussex.

PHYLLODOCE   ERICACEAE

A small group of some six or seven species of dwarf evergreen shrubs, similar in habit to the heaths, but with stouter stems and larger leaves. Leaves alternate, linear. Flowers bell-shaped or pitcher-shaped, slender-stalked, produced in terminal racemes, umbel-like clusters, or even solitary. Corolla and calyx five-parted; stamens usually ten; seed-vessel a dry, subglobose, five-celled capsule, carrying numerous small seeds.

The genus has by some botanists been united with *Bryanthus*, but the general practice now is to keep them apart and to confine *Bryanthus* to one species, *B. gmelinii* D. Don, on which that genus was originally founded.

With the exception of *P.* × *intermedia* these little shrubs require rather special care in the south of England. They inhabit cool, moist altitudes and latitudes, and dislike dryness in the air or at the root. A cool, moist nook on the lower levels of the rock garden, where the soil is peaty, is as good a place as any. Propagation is effected in the same way as recommended for *Erica*.

There is an excellent study of the genus by Fred Stoker in *New Flora and Sylva*, Vol. 12, pp. 30–42 (1940).

P. ALEUTICA (Spreng.) Heller   [PLATE 25

Menziesia aleutica Spreng.; *Bryanthus aleuticus* (Spreng.) A. Gray;
Phyllodoce pallasiana D. Don

A dwarf evergreen shrub 5 to 9 in. high, the young shoots entirely hidden by the leaves. Leaves linear, tapered at the base, bluntish at the apex, finely toothed, ⅜ in. long, 1/16 in. wide, bright green above, yellowish-green beneath with a white line down the centre; very shortly stalked. Flowers nodding, each on a downy glandular stalk ½ to 1½ in. long, several of them produced in May near the top of the shoot. Corolla yellowish white, corrugated, pitcher-shaped, ¼ in. wide, contracted at the top to an orifice 1/16 in. wide; stamens enclosed in the corolla, their stalks white, glabrous; anthers pink; ovary globose, glandular;

style glabrous. Sepals five, lanceolate, pointed, $\frac{1}{8}$ in. long, pale at the margins, very hairy where they join the stalk. *Bot. Mag.*, n.s., t. 496.

Native of Japan, Sakhalin, the Kuriles, the Aleutians, and W. Alaska; described in 1825, but always rare in cultivation. It is allied to *P. glanduliflora*, which takes its place in north-western N. America. Suitable for a cool damp spot in the rock garden and a pretty plant, though scarcely equal in beauty to *P. breweri*, *P. nipponica* or *P.* × *intermedia*. It received an Award of Merit when shown by Messrs Marchant in 1939. A plant in their nursery near Wimborne, Dorset, attained a width of 2½ ft in only five years.

P. BREWERI (A. Gray) Heller

Bryanthus breweri A. Gray

A dwarf evergreen shrub 6 to 12 in. high, of tufted habit; young shoots erect, very leafy. Leaves almost stalkless, linear, blunt, $\frac{1}{2}$ to $\frac{3}{4}$ in. long (shorter immediately beneath the raceme), $\frac{1}{16}$ to $\frac{1}{12}$ in. wide, dark glossy green. Flowers produced during May in a terminal raceme 2 to 4 in. long, each flower on a slender, glandular stalk about $\frac{1}{2}$ in. long, from the axil of a short, leaf-like bract. Corolla bright purplish rose, $\frac{1}{2}$ in. in diameter, saucer-shaped, the five lobes ovate and rounded at the apex; stamens protruded. Calyx half as wide as the corolla, with five ovate, pointed, ciliate, but otherwise glabrous loves. Seed-vessel globose, $\frac{1}{6}$ in. in diameter. *Bot. Mag*, t. 8146.

Native of California, and found on the Sierra Nevada at 9,000 to 10,000 ft altitude; first discovered by W. H. Brewer about 1862. In some places it is said to cover extensive areas. It is a charming rock garden plant, delighting in a moist, peaty soil and a cool spot. The racemes vary considerably in length and in the density of the blossoms. The expanded corolla, elongated raceme, and protruded stamens distinguish it from the other three cultivated species, and bring it nearer than any to the true *Bryanthus* (*B. gmelinii*).

P. CAERULEA (L.) Bab.

Andromeda caerulea L.; *Bryanthus taxifolius* A. Gray

A dwarf, much-branched evergreen shrub about 6 in. to 9 in. high, of tufted habit. Leaves linear, blunt, much crowded, $\frac{1}{4}$ to $\frac{1}{2}$ in. long, $\frac{1}{16}$ in. or less wide, minutely toothed, dark glossy green. Flowers produced in June and July singly on a slender, glandular stalk up to 1½ in. long, or in an umbel of three or four flowers. Corolla bluish purple, pitcher-shaped, nodding, five-toothed, $\frac{1}{3}$ in. long. Calyx with five lance-shaped, downy lobes; stamens ten, and, like the style, included within the corolla.

Native of high alpine summits and high latitudes in Europe, Asia, and N. America. It is found in Scotland in a few localities on the border between Perthshire and Inverness-shire (Forest of Atholl and Badenoch), but had, and may still have, a wider distribution. There are old specimens at Kew from near Aviemore and the Isles of Shiant. Under cultivation it succeeds better in the north of England and in Scotland than in the south, where the summers are too dry and hot for it, and cause its foliage to drop prematurely. It is, consequently, uncommon. In the Botanic Garden of Edinburgh it thrives very well. It should be planted in peat and sphagnum moss mixed, and have a surfacing of the latter also. One of the most interesting of British plants, and distinct in this genus because of its colour. It is figured in: Ross-Craig, *Draw. Brit. Pl.*, Pt. XIX, t. 29.

Two forms of *P. caerulea* were exhibited by R. B. Cooke in 1938, one from Japan with red-purple flowers, the other, with paler flowers, from Norway. Both received an Award of Merit.

P. EMPETRIFORMIS (Sm.) D. Don [PLATE 26

Menziesia empetriformis Sm.; *Bryanthus empetriformis* (Sm.) A. Gray

A low mat-forming shrub up to 12 or 15 in. high; stems downy when young. Leaves linear, $\frac{3}{16}$ to $\frac{5}{8}$ in. long, usually blunt at the apex, margins minutely glandular-toothed. Flowers purplish pink, borne in umbel-like clusters from the upper leaf-axils on downy-glandular stalks; calyx-lobes ciliate, otherwise glabrous, obtuse; corolla widely bell-shaped, glabrous, about $\frac{1}{3}$ in. long, with recurved lobes; stamens included; style exserted. Capsule globose-ellipsoid. *Bot. Mag.*, t. 3176.

Native of western N. America from Alaska to California, fairly frequent in open places near and above the tree-line, sometimes in association with the yellow-flowered *P. glanduliflora*, with which it hybridises. The plant once generally grown in gardens as *P. empetriformis* is not the true species but one of these hybrids (see *P.* × *intermedia*).

P. GLANDULIFLORA (Hook.) Cov.

Menziesia glanduliflora Hook.; *Bryanthus glanduliflora* (Hook.) A. Gray

An evergreen shrub 4 to 8 in. high (sometimes 12 in.) with erect branchlets. Leaves numerous, covering the twig, linear, rounded at the end, $\frac{1}{4}$ to $\frac{1}{2}$ in. long, $\frac{1}{20}$ in. wide, minutely toothed, dark green with a white line beneath. Flowers produced several together in a cluster at the end of the shoot in April and May, each flower on a stalk $\frac{1}{2}$ to 1 in. long thickly furnished with glandular hairs, as are also the calyx and (to a lesser degree) the corolla. Corolla yellowish, pitcher-shaped, scarcely $\frac{1}{4}$ in. long, downy outside, narrowed at the top to a small orifice where are five tiny, glabrous, reflexed lobes. Stamens with downy stalks and purple anthers. Ovary downy; style longer than the stamens, glabrous. Sepals lanceolate, pointed, $\frac{1}{6}$ in. long, very glandular.

Native of western N. America, from Oregon to Alaska and on the Rocky Mountains, often just below the perpetual snow line. Of the group of phyllodoces with the corolla contracted to a narrow orifice at the top (as distinct from those with an open bell-mouthed corolla) this is distinguished by its downy stamens and very glandular flower-stalks, sepals, and corolla. It is perhaps most closely akin to *P. aleutica*, but that has glabrous stamens—and corolla.

P. × INTERMEDIA (Hook.) Rydb.

Menziesia intermedia Hook.; *P. hybrida* Rydb.; *P. pseudoempetriformis* Stoker, *nom. prov.*

A low evergreen shrub 6 to 9 in. high, of tufted habit, densely furnished with leaves. Leaves $\frac{1}{4}$ to $\frac{5}{8}$ in. long, $\frac{1}{16}$ to $\frac{1}{12}$ in. wide; linear, rounded at the tip, very shortly stalked, minutely toothed on the margin, dark glossy green. Flowers solitary, on slender, glandular-hairy stalks $\frac{1}{2}$ to $\frac{3}{4}$ in. long, produced during April

PHYLLODOCE × INTERMEDIA

from the leaf-axils near the end of the twigs. Corolla pitcher-shaped, bright reddish purple, $\frac{1}{4}$ in. long, scarcely so wide; with five rounded teeth at the orifice. Calyx-lobes five, ovate, $\frac{1}{8}$ in. long, glabrous; style exposed.

A variable natural hybrid between *P. empetriformis* and *P. glanduliflora*, which occurs frequently in the wild where the two species grow together. The plant described above is the commonest form of the hybrid in cultivation and was for long grown as *P. empetriformis*, though it clearly differs from that species (q.v.) in its urn-shaped corolla and bushy habit. The error was pointed out by Dr Fred Stoker in *New Flora and Sylva*, Vol. 12, pp. 38–41 (and see Dr Camp's article in the same volume, pp. 207–11). The wild hybrids are said to combine the characters of the parents in various ways, but their usual corolla-shape is cylindric-campanulate, i.e., narrower than in *P. empetriformis*, but not urn-shaped as in the other species. The plant described above, which is of unknown origin, inclines to *P. glanduliflora* in having the corolla more or less urn-shaped, though not so constricted at the mouth, while the influence of *P. empetriformis* shows in the colour of the corollas and in their being almost glabrous outside.

The common form of *P*. × *intermedia* was given the clonal name 'FRED STOKER' by Dr Camp, to distinguish it from other forms of the cross. It is perhaps the most satisfactory of the phyllodoces, being easy to grow in peaty soil. It received an Award of Merit when shown by Messrs Marchant under the name *P*. × *hybrida*.

P. NIPPONICA Makino

P. amabilis Stapf; *P. empetriformis* var. *amabilis* (Stapf) Rehd.; *P. nipponica* var. *amabilis* (Stapf) Stoker

An evergreen shrub about 4 to 9 in. high (occasionally to 2 ft), forming compact tufts of erect, stiff branches; young stems minutely downy, with erect, gland-tipped bristles interspersed. Leaves closely set on the branches (about twenty to the inch), linear, toothed, rounded at the end, $\frac{1}{4}$ to $\frac{3}{8}$ in. long, $\frac{1}{16}$ in. or

PHYLLODOCE NIPPONICA

less wide, glabrous and glossy dark green above, midrib white beneath with minute down. Flowers on slender, erect, often reddish, glandular-downy stalks $\frac{1}{2}$ to 1 in. long, which are produced singly in from three to seven of the terminal leaf-axils in early May. Corolla open bell-shaped, about $\frac{1}{4}$ in. long, rather more wide, with shallow, rounded lobes; white tinged with pink on the lobes; sepals about $\frac{1}{12}$ in. long, pointed, ciliate, glabrous on the back, often reddish. Stamens and style enclosed within the corolla. Seed-vessel globose, depressed at the top where it is roughened with short, hardened glandular hairs. *Bot. Mag.*, t. 8405.

This delightful little shrub, one of the daintiest of the heath family, is a native of Japan. It flowered at Kew in 1911, but owing to some misplacement of labels its history was lost, and it was described as a new species by Dr Stapf. It received a First Class Certificate in 1946.

var. OBLONGO-OVATA (Tatewaki) Toyokuni *P. tsugifolia* var. *oblongo-ovata* Tatewaki; *P. tsugifolia* Nakai; *P. nipponica* var. *tsugifolia* (Nakai) Ohwi—This variety has a more northern distribution than the typical state of the species, from which it differs chiefly in the much longer flower-stalks (1 to 1⅜ in. long). The leaves are somewhat longer and wider. This phyllodoce and typical *P. nipponica* are figured in Takeda's *Alpine Flora of Japan in Colour* (1960), Plate 20.

P. × ALPINA Koidz. *P. hybrida* Nakai, not Rydb.—The phyllodoce described by Koidzumi as *P. alpina* is now considered to be a hybrid between *P. nipponica* and *P. aleutica*. It resembles the former in its foliage, and in having the calyx-lobes glabrous on the outside, but the corollas are contracted at the mouth and slightly larger. In colour they are said to be pink. Figured in Takeda (loc. cit. supr.), Plate 20.

PHYLLOSTACHYS   GRAMINEAE

For a general discussion of the bamboos belonging to this genus, see *Arundinaria*. The distinctive characters of *Phyllostachys* are in the stems, which are always more or less zigzag and flattened on each side alternately above the joint; and in the two or three branches only at each joint, those at the base of the stem developing first.

It is a genus of about thirty-five species in Japan, China, and the Himalaya.

The following revised account of the cultivated species is based on the article by Dr C. E. Hubbard in the Royal Horticultural Society's *Dictionary of Gardening*, Supplement 1969, pp. 449–50; and on the nomenclatural notes by F. A. McClure in *Journ. Arn. Arb.*, Vol. 37, pp. 186–96.

P. AUREA (Carr.) A. & C. Riv.

Bambusa aurea Hort. ex Carr.; *P. bambusoides* var. *aurea* (Carr.) Mak.

Stems pale yellowish green, 10 to 15 ft high in this country, stiffly erect, growing in tufts and spreading slowly, the joints often 5 or 6 in. apart, except at the base, where they are crowded. Beneath each joint there is a curious swollen band, about ¼ in. wide, which distinguishes this from all other hardy bamboos. Leaves 2 to 4½ in. long, ⅛ to ⅞ in. wide, broadly tapered at the base, slenderly pointed, dark green above, glaucous beneath, glabrous on both surfaces, minutely toothed on the margins; secondary nerves four or five each side the midrib; stalk ⅛ in. or less long; the leaf-sheath surmounted by two tufts of bristles at the summit.

Native of China, cultivated in Japan, whence it was introduced to Europe in the 1870s. It flowered at Bitton in 1876 and again in various parts of the British Isles and overseas in 1904–5, 1919–21, and 1935–7, giving it a life cycle of about fifteen years. It is a pleasing bamboo if planted in a goodly sized mass, although not so graceful as the majority. It is only likely to be confused with P. *pubescens* which is, however, a taller bamboo without the crowded joints at the base of the stem, and without the swollen band beneath the joint, which is so distinctive a character in P. *aurea*.

P. BAMBUSOIDES Sieb. & Zucc.   MADAKE

P. quiloi A. & C. Riv.; *P. reticulata* Hort., not Rupr.

Stems 10 to 18 ft high in this country, ¾ to 1¼ in. thick at the base, deep green. Branches long; stem-sheaths pinkish when young, conspicuously mottled with deep purple. Leaves varying from 2½ to 6 in. long, ½ to 1¼ in. wide (occasionally they are even larger), bright green above, glaucous beneath, glabrous except for some down at the base of the midrib beneath; one margin toothed; secondary veins five to seven each side the midrib; leaf-sheath with a conspicuous tuft of bristles at the top, ¼ to ½ in. long.

Native of China; introduced to France by Admiral Du Quilio in 1866. It is one of the finest of hardy bamboos, very hardy and free-growing. P. *viridi-glaucescens* is the only species with which, in the adult state, it is likely to be confused, and from that species it is distinguished by the mottled leaf-sheaths (in P. *viridi-glaucescens* they are simply striated or tinged with purple), by the larger leaves and longer branches.

cv. 'ALLGOLD' ('Sulphurea').—Stems bright yellow, sometimes slightly striped with green, becoming deep golden yellow (P. *sulphurea* (Carr.) A. & C. Riv.; *Bambusa sulphurea* Carr.).

McClure suggests that this bamboo may be a mutant from 'Castillonis'. He has proposed for it the cultivar-name 'Allgold', to avoid confusion with another bamboo to which the name P. *sulphurea* has been misapplied.

cv. 'CASTILLONIS'.—Stems 8 to 10 ft high (more no doubt in warmer climates) very hollow; bright yellow except on the flattened portion which extends from joint to joint either side alternately, and that is dark green. Leaves 2 to 5 in. long as a rule, and ⅜ to ¾ in. wide, but occasionally up to 8 or 9 in. long and 1½ in. wide, usually striped with creamy yellow lines, but not uniformly so; sometimes they are more yellow than green, sometimes wholly green (P. *castillonis* Mitf.; P. *bambusoides* var. *castilloni* (Marliac) H. de Lehaie; *Bambusa castilloni* Marliac).

This is the most beautifully coloured in its stems of all hardy bamboos. The curious alternation of green and yellow, together with the often variegated leaves, makes it very distinct. Although better known as P. *castillonis*, it is a garden variety of P. *bambusoides*, introduced from Japan in 1886. It flowered in 1903–4 and again in 1963–8. At Kew all the flowering plants have died.

cv. 'MARLIACEA'.—This bamboo is distinguished by a curious wrinkling of the stems, especially towards the base. It is not so vigorous, nor so hardy, as typical *P. bambusoides* (*P. marliacea* Mitf.; *P. quilioi* var. *marliacea* (Mitf.) Bean).

cv. 'VIOLASCENS'.—A cultivated form of *P. bambusoides*, very distinct in having the young stems of a deep violet, almost black, changing the second year to yellowish brown. The sheaths are also violet. There was a plant of this at Shrublands, near Ipswich; but frequently it is not a success, growing late, and having its summer growth cut back during the ensuing winter (*P. violascens* A. & C. Riv.).

P. FLEXUOSA (Carr.) A. & C. Riv.
Bambusa flexuosa Carr.

A bamboo of elegant but compact, rounded habit, rarely exceeding 6 or 8 ft in height, but up to 30 ft in warmer parts; stems at first bright green, becoming darker with age, sometimes almost black like those of *P. nigra*. Leaves 2 to 4 in long, ⅓ to ⅝ in. wide, dark green and glabrous above, glaucous beneath and downy at the base of the midrib, secondary nerves four to six each side the midrib; one margin toothed.

Native of China; introduced to France in 1864. In the characters of leaf and stem this bamboo bears much resemblance to *P. viridi-glaucescens*, but it is much dwarfer and more compact, and the change of the old culms to black does not, so far as I have observed, occur in that species. The stem-sheaths also differ, as pointed out under *P. viridi-glaucescens*. *P. flexuosa* is a pleasing bamboo of the middle size, graceful and very hardy.

P. NIGRA (Lodd.) Munro   BLACK BAMBOO
Bambusa nigra Lodd.

Stems varying from 10 to 20 ft high in different parts of the country, and from ½ to 1¼ in. in diameter, very hollow; at first green, they become with age quite black; the branchlets usually mottled. Leaves in plume-like masses, usually 2 to 3½ in. long, ¼ to ⅝ in. wide (sometimes larger), of thin texture, dark green above, rather glaucous beneath, glabrous on both surfaces, the margins roughened with minute teeth; secondary veins three to six each side the midrib. When quite young there is a slight downiness at the base of the midrib beneath. The leaf-sheath is terminated by a few erect bristles. *Bot. Mag.*, t. 7994.

Native of China, and one of the most elegant of bamboos; very distinct because of its black stems. It is a quite hardy species when once established, although it grows much larger in hotter climates. It flowered in many parts of the world including Britain between 1931 and 1935 and has probably a very long life cycle. It is the oldest of *Phyllostachys* in English gardens and, according to Loudon, was 7 ft high in the Horticultural Society's gardens in 1837. It was introduced by the nurseryman Loddiges around 1825, probably from Canton.

cv. 'BORYANA'.—The bamboo known as *P. boryana* (Marliac) Mitf. is a minor variant of the var. *henonis*, with stems becoming yellow when mature. It flowered in this country in 1905, and is now rare.

cv. 'FULVA'.—A garden form of the var. *henonis*, in which the stems become yellow in their second year (*P. fulva* Mitf.)

var. HENONIS (Mitf.) Rendle *P. henonis* Mitf.; *P. puberula* (Miq.) Munro; *Bambusa puberula* Miq.—A very graceful and luxuriant bamboo, reaching in favourable situations 14 ft in height, laden when in good health and well established with heavy plumose masses of foliage, which make the outer stems arch outward; stems bright green at first, very hollow. Leaves rather uniform in size, and from 2 to 3½ in. long and ¼ to ⅜ in. wide, tapering at the base to a well-developed stalk ⅛ in. long, slender-pointed; dark lustrous green above, glaucous and downy at the base of the midrib beneath; secondary veins four to seven.

Although long cultivated in Japan, this variety is a native of China and probably represents the normal wild state of the species. It was introduced about 1890. In the richness of its verdure combined with a remarkable elegance of form this bamboo is probably the loveliest of all its kind. From about 1894 to 1900 it made perhaps the most delightful feature of many gardens from October to January. In 1900 it commenced to flower all over the country, and by 1905 nearly every specimen was either dead or very severely crippled. A proportion of them recovered, and from these, as well as from plants imported afresh from Japan, it is now getting re-established in gardens. It has a long life cycle.

cv. 'PUNCTATA'.—More robust than typical *P. nigra*, and differing in the stems not being wholly black, but mottled. It flowered all over Europe 1900–8 and many plants died in consequence (*P. nigra* var. *punctata* Bean; *P. puberula* var. *nigro-punctata* H. de Leh.).

P. PUBESCENS H. de Lehaie   MOSO-CHIKU

P. mitis Hort.; *P. edulis* H. de Lehaie, not *Bambusa edulis* Carr.; *Bambusa mitis* Hort.

Stems reaching sometimes nearly 20 ft high in this country and bent somewhat stiffly, 1½ in. in diameter, deep yellow when mature. Leaves 2 to 5 in. long, ¼ to ¾ in. wide, tapering or rounded at the base, slender-pointed, dark green above, glaucous beneath, glabrous except at the base of the midrib beneath, and toothed—especially on one margin; stalk ⅛ in. or less long; leaf-sheath with a tuft of bristles at each side near the top; secondary nerves three to six each side the midrib.

Native of China, long cultivated in Japan; introduced about 1890. In foliage it resembles *P. aurea*, under which the distinctions are pointed out. It requires a sheltered spot and abundant sunshine to develop its best qualities, and does not recover from injury by cold so rapidly as *P. aurea*. The stems are never truly erect, but are bowed, with usually also an inclination to twist. The stems when young grow with great rapidity, sometimes nearly 1 foot in twenty-four hours in this country—more in hotter ones. They are the stoutest among our hardy bamboos. In Japan the young shoots are cooked and eaten; according to Lord Redesdale they are flavourless, but have a crisp and pleasant consistency.

cv. 'HETEROCYCLA' ('KIKKO-CHIKU') TORTOISE-SHELL BAMBOO.— Although this curious bamboo has been given specific rank as *P. heterocycla* (Carr) Matsum., it is simply a cultivated form of *P. pubescens*. It is distinguished by the joints of the stems near the base not circling them in the ordinary way, but taking diagonal directions, the normal space between the joints being suppressed at each side alternately. Thus the scars join at opposite sides alternately for 1 or 2 ft up the stem, when it assumes its normal form and the scars become horizontal rings. The plant is not well adapted for this country, and I have never seen a single characteristic stem produced here. The popular name—of Japanese origin—refers to the humped appearance of the space between the joints. This distortion is a freak of nature, and is not, as was once believed, due to the handiwork of Japanese gardeners. Introduced from Japan to France about 1877, and to England in 1893.

P. VIRIDI-GLAUCESCENS (Carr.) A. & C. Riv.
Bambusa viridi-glaucescens Carr.

Stems 14 to 18 ft long, about ¾ in. in diameter, very hollow, yellowish green, except at the joints, which are purplish; the outer stems of vigorous plants growing in the open arch outwards and downwards to the ground. Stem-sheaths striped with close lines of purple and suffused with purple when young. Leaves 2 to 5 in. long, ⅓ to ⅞ in. wide, abruptly tapered at the base, slender-pointed, bright green above, glaucous beneath, downy only at the base of the midrib beneath; toothed on one margin; secondary veins four to seven each side the midrib; leaf-sheath purplish, with two clusters of bristles at the top.

Native of China; introduced to France about 1846, and a very elegant, vigorous, and useful bamboo. It is liable to be confounded with *P. bambusoides* and with *P. flexuosa*, but the former is well distinguished by its mottled stem-sheaths, its stouter stems, and larger leaves, whilst *P. flexuosa* is altogether a smaller plant whose old stems are often almost black. There are also two little, fringed, ear-like projections at the top of the stem-sheath that are missing in *P. flexuosa*. *P. viridi-glaucescens* requires an isolated position, when it will in time form a graceful mass at least 25 ft in diameter, with pendulous plumes of foliage. It spreads at the root with some freedom, and is easily propagated by offsets. It never appears to have flowered under cultivation.

× PHYLLOTHAMNUS   ERICACEAE

A genus of intergeneric hybrids between *Phyllodoce* and *Rhodothamnus*, in which only the cross described below is known. These two genera are outwardly very dissimilar, the flowers in *Phyllodoce* being campanulate or urn-shaped, salver-shaped in *Rhodothamnus*. In fact they are quite closely allied, both belonging to the tribe *Rhododendreae*.

× P. ERECTUS (Lindl.) Schneid.

Bryanthus erectus Lindl.; *Phyllodoce erecta* (Lindl.) Drude

A dwarf evergreen bush 6 to 10 in. high, with numerous erect, very leafy branches, minutely downy when young. Leaves alternate, ½ to ⅝ in. long, linear, tapering towards each end, recurved slightly at the margins, finely toothed, deep glossy green, crowded on the branchlets. Flowers solitary on slender, downy, glandular stalks ½ to ¾ in. long; produced in April in a cluster of four to ten at the end of each twig. Corolla delicate rose, broadly funnel-shaped, ½ in. across, with five triangular, pointed lobes. Calyx-lobes ovate, ⅓ in. long, glabrous; style protruded.

A hybrid raised about 1845 in the nursery of Messrs Cunningham & Fraser at Comely Bank, Edinburgh, between *Rhodothamnus chamaecistus* and, so its raisers stated, *Phyllodoce caerulea*. The general belief is, however, that *P. empetriformis* was the other parent. It is a very pretty shrub, but requires considerable care to keep it in permanent health in the south, where the dry heats of July and August cause it to suffer. A cool, moist spot in the rock garden where the soil is peaty may be recommended for it.

PHYLLOTHAMNUS ~~~~ PHYSOCARPUS ROSACEAE

A genus of about twenty species in N. America, Mexico, and N.E. Asia. allied to *Neillia*, in which it was included in previous editions of this work. It differs in its valvate calyx-lobes (imbricate in *Neillia*) and in having inflated follicles that open down both sides. Also the inflorescence is usually corymbose (racemose or paniculate in *Neillia*). They need a moist soil and should be grown in full sun.

P. AMURENSIS (Maxim.) Maxim.

Spiraea amurensis Maxim.; *Neillia amurensis* (Maxim.) Bean

A deciduous shrub 6 to 8 ft high, the larger branches covered with a loose peeling bark. Leaves three- or five-lobed, up to 4 in. long by 3 in. wide, more or less downy beneath, the lobes pointed, margins double-toothed. Flowers white, ⅓ in. across, produced each on a slender downy stalk in corymbs 1½ to 2 in. across, terminating short twigs. Calyx with five thickly downy, triangular lobes. Stamens about forty, purple; petals downy on the outside. Fruits downy.

Native of the Russian Far East, Korea, and N.E. China; much resembling *P. opulifolius*. The leaves appear generally to be larger, more downy beneath and more distinctly five-lobed; the downy pods too are distinctive, and much shorter in proportion to the calyx.

P. BRACTEATUS (Rydb.) Rehd.

Opulaster bracteatus Rydb.; *Neillia bracteata* (Rydb.) Bean

This is a shapely deciduous shrub up to 6 ft or more high and more in width, of free and elegant growth, with grey, flaky bark; young shoots glabrous, yellowish. Leaves 1½ to 3½ in. long, nearly or quite as wide, roundish ovate in main outline, often heart-shaped at the base, usually three- sometimes five-lobed, the lobes doubly toothed; both surfaces are free from down, the lower one pale; stalk about one-third as long as the blade. Flowers white, ⅓ in. wide, opening in June, closely packed in rounded clusters 1½ to 2 in. wide which come on short leafy twigs from the previous season's growths, thus forming handsome sprays. Calyx with five-pointed ovate lobes; flower-stalks slender, ½ to 1 in. long; both densely covered with starry down.

Native of the mountains of Colorado, at altitudes of 5,000 to 6,000 ft. It was introduced in 1904 under the specific name of "Ramaleyi", but subsequently seems to have disappeared. It was reintroduced in 1930. It is most nearly akin to *P. malvaceus* and *P. monogynus*, having, like them, only two carpels to each fruit which are united half their length, whereas in the common *P. opulifolius* there are three to five carpels united only at the base. It differs from them in the obovate or spatulate floral bracts being more persistent.

P. CAPITATUS (Pursh) Greene

Spiraea capitata Pursh; *Neillia capitata* (Pursh) Greene

A deciduous shrub 6 to 10 ft high (in the wild over 20 ft). Leaves three-lobed, broadly ovate, 2 to 4 in. long, doubly toothed, downy beneath. Flowers white, produced in a corymb, each flower on a downy stalk about ½ in. long; calyx very downy. Fruits glabrous or nearly so, composed of three to five inflated pods ⅓ in. long, containing usually two obliquely pear-shaped seeds.

Native of western N. America from British Columbia to California, where it is said to have stems often more than 20 ft long interlaced with willow branches, and forming impenetrable thickets on the banks of streams (Greene). It is really a western form of *P. opulifolius*, from which it differs chiefly in the more downy leaves and in the pear-shaped seeds. Introduced in 1827.

P. MALVACEUS (Greene) O. Kuntze

Neillia malvacea Greene; *N. torreyi* of *Bot. Mag.*, t. 7758, not S. Wats.

A deciduous shrub 3 to 5 ft high, with erect stellately downy stems. Leaves three-lobed, sometimes obscurely five-lobed on the non-flowering shoots, from 1½ to 3 in. wide, scarcely so long; usually roundish or broadly oval in general outline; variable in the amount of down on the lower surface. Flowers ⅓ in. wide, white, produced in corymbs 1½ in. wide; calyx downy. Fruits composed of two or three pods, each one- or two-seeded. *Bot. Mag.*, t. 7758.

Native of western N. America, reaching from Oregon and Idaho through Utah and Nevada to W. Texas. It is allied to *P. monogynus*, which has a more eastern distribution, differing chiefly in the more robust habit, larger leaves, and sometimes more numerous carpels. Introduced to Kew in 1897. The pods are described as indehiscent, until after falling.

P. MONOGYNUS (Torr.) Coult.

Spiraea monogyna Torr.; *Neillia monogyna* (Torr.) Greene; *N. torreyi* S. Wats.; *Physocarpus torreyi* (S. Wats.) Maxim.

A dwarf deciduous bush about 2 ft high in the wild, with erect, much-branched stems. Leaves ¾ to 1½ in. long, roundish ovate, three-lobed, the lobes irregularly and doubly toothed, sometimes very downy beneath, sometimes only slightly so. Flowers ¼ in. in width, of a clear or slightly rose-tinted white, produced in early June in few-flowered corymbs ¾ to 1¼ in. across. Fruits downy, usually composed of two pods cohering for more than half their length, but sometimes only one; each contains one obovoid seed.

Native of the Rocky Mountains of Colorado up to elevations of 9,000 ft. It is a pretty little shrub with small leaves often lobed and toothed, like a ribes. Its dwarf habit, small leaves, and few downy seed-vessels well distinguish it.

P. OPULIFOLIUS (L.) Maxim.

Spiraea opulifolia L.; *Neillia opulifolia* (L.) Brewer & Watson

A deciduous shrub 6 to 10 ft high, occasionally much more in diameter; bark glabrous, peeling. Leaves usually broadly ovate and three-lobed, sometimes only very slightly lobed or not at all, doubly toothed, 1½ to 3 in. long and from half to fully as wide, glabrous; stalk ¼ to ¾ in. long. Flowers numerous, in hemispherical corymbose clusters 2 in. wide, produced in June at the end of leafy twigs from the previous year's branches. Each flower is white tinged with rose, ¼ to ⅓ in. across, and borne on a slender downy or glabrous stalk. Stamens about thirty, purplish. Fruits consisting of three to five pods ¼ in. long, which are inflated, glabrous or nearly so, and usually carry two egg-shaped seeds.

Native of eastern N. America; introduced, according to Aiton, in 1687, and a common shrub in gardens. The largest I have seen was in Sir A. Buchan Hepburn's garden at Smeaton, Scotland, which was 30 ft across and 10 ft high. The shrub is a handsome one in blossom, and useful for rough shrubberies where plants are left largely to take care of themselves.

cv. 'LUTEUS'.—Leaves of a beautiful golden yellow when young, but soon becoming green and almost of the same shade as the type. Once popular, this, like others of its class of golden-leaved shrubs, is being superseded by varieties which retain their colour until autumn. *Bot. Mag.*, n.s., t. 459.

PICCONIA* OLEACEAE

A genus containing two species of small evergreen trees or shrubs native to Macaronesia: *P. excelsa* (Ait.) DC. from Madeira and the Canary Islands and *P. azorica* (Tutin) Knobl. from the Azores. It lies within the *Olea/Osmanthus* complex of genera and may be distinguished by a combination of characters: the decussate racemose inflorescence with characteristic large deciduous, concave, floccose-ciliolate, pale green bracts, the extremely short corolla tube and petals imbricate in early bud.

P. EXCELSA (Ait.) DC.
Olea excelsa Ait.; *Notelaea excelsa* (Ait.) Webb & Berth.

Small evergreen tree or shrub to 40 ft (or even 60 ft) high. Leaves stiff, leathery, elliptic or broadly elliptic, acute at both ends or very slightly acuminate at the apex, slightly decurrent onto the petiole, mostly 3 to 4 in. long and 1 to 2 in. wide, entire, glabrous, dark green and slightly lustrous above, paler and duller beneath, petiole ¼ to ½ in. long. Inflorescence axillary, decussate racemose 1 to 2 in. long lengthening rapidly at anthesis, sometimes two or three borne above one another, bracts in decussate pairs, ¼ in. long, somewhat membranous, glabrous except for a minutely floccose-ciliolate margin, light green, early deciduous. Flowers white, sometimes sweetly scented; sepals four, small; petals four, imbricate in early bud, about ⅛ in. long, joined in pairs by the bases of the two filaments and between pairs only at the very base, irregularly notched, or rounded and shallowly bilobed or trilobed; stamens two about equal to petals. Fruit a dark blue ellipsoid drupe, ⅝ to ¾ in. long, with a fine bloom, flesh very thin, stone shallowly ribbed.

Native of Madeira and the Canary Islands, introduced in 1784. It is marginally hardy in Britain, even in the south, and is not widely grown. Where, however, local conditions allow it to do so it can develop into a handsome and impressive evergreen tree, as in the case of the notable examples at Abbotsbury on the coast of Dorset, which flower well and fruit. The larger of these measures 55 × 8½ ft (1972); at Caerhays, Cornwall, there is a two-stemmed tree 30 ft high.

The wood is reported to be extremely heavy and hard and has been much used in its native areas. In 1868 the Rev. R. T. Lowe writing in his *A Manual Flora of Madeira* remarks about 'the yearly increasing scarceness of the tree, which indeed seems likely soon to become extinct altogether'.

PICEA SPRUCE PINACEAE

A group of evergreen trees found in most of the cool temperate regions of the northern hemisphere, of pyramidal form, especially in a young

* Contributed by P. S. Green of the Herbarium, Royal Botanic Gardens, Kew.

state, with branches in tiers. Leaves linear or needle-like, mostly four-sided, arranged spirally on the shoots, but the undermost ones usually twisted at the base, so as to crowd them more on the upper side of the twig than on the lower. Each leaf is seated on a slight cushion which, if the leaf be gently pulled off downwards whilst fresh, it brings mostly away. When, however, the leaf falls naturally, or the twig is dried for herbarium purposes, it leaves at the base a peg-like stump. These leaf-stumps thickly studded on the shoot are extremely characteristic of the spruces, and well distinguish them from the firs (*Abies*). Flowers uni-sexual, both sexes produced on the same tree at or near the end of the twigs; the males solitary, stalked, composed of numerous anthers. Female cones nearly always pendulous, their scales persisting until they fall. Seeds winged.

Some botanists divide *Picea* into three sections, but in Pilger's view a subdivision into two sections only is more natural. These are:

sect. PICEA (sect. *Eupicea* Willk.; sect. *Cassicta* Mayr, *pro max. part.*)— Leaves with four faces and four angles, rhombic in cross-section, with rows of stomata on all four surfaces. In some species the stomata are more numerous on the downward-facing (ventral) surface. To this section be-long all the species except those listed below.

sect. OMORIKA—Leaves flattened, with stomata usually on the ventral surface only, so that there is a marked contrast between the green, ex-posed surface and the bluish or whitish inner or downward-facing sur-face. The species belonging to this section are: *P. omorika* (the only European member); *P. breweriana* and *P. sitchensis* (N. America); and the Asiatic *P. spinulosa*, *P. brachytyla*, and *P. jezoensis*.

In the last century, the spruces were almost always called "*Abies*" in Britain, whilst the true silver-firs (*Abies*) were called "*Picea*". This in-version of names dates from Loudon's time and should be borne in mind when consulting his great work. But it has its source in Linnaeus' *Species Plantarum* (1753), in which he named the common spruce *Pinus abies* and the European silver fir *Pinus picea*. This incidentally explains how it has come about that the common spruce is correctly called *Picea abies* (L.) Karsten. The name of the European silver fir would be *Abies picea* (L.) Bluff & Fingerhut (1825) were it not that Philip Miller used that name earlier for the common spruce (in his *Dictionary*, ed. 1768).

The confusion over the names *Abies* and *Picea* is now a thing of the past, but the following distinctions between the two genera may still be useful:

PICEA (Spruces)—Leaves inserted on peg-like stumps (see first para-graph); mostly they are rhombic in cross-section and, if flat, then the lines of stomata are concentrated on the ventral side, i.e., that which is morphologically the upper side of the leaf, since it faces towards the apex of the shoot. But the appressing or forward leaning of the leaves on the upper side of a horizontal shoot exposes the green back (dorsal side) of the leaf without the need for any twisting at the base; the same is also true of a vertical leading shoot, where the primary leaves are closely appressed. Further, in *Picea* the cones are pendent, with persistent scales, and fall in one piece.

ABIES (Silver firs)—Leaves nearly always flat, not falling away in drying, nor leaving the peg-like stumps of *Picea*. In marked contrast to that genus, the stomata are concentrated on the dorsal side of the leaf, i.e., on the morphologically lower side of the leaf (facing towards the base of the shoot), which is the normal arrangement in flowering plants. Consequently, an appressed leaf in *Abies* would expose its white under-side but for the fact that the base of the leaf is twisted through about 180°, as can be seen by examining the upper central leaves on a shoot of, say, *Abies nordmanniana*. In *Abies* the cones are erect, and break up on the tree, i.e., the scales fall away from the central axis, which remains on the branch.

The spruces have scarcely the garden value of the firs, but the following are handsome and effective: *P. brachytyla*, *P. breweriana*, *P. jezoensis* var. *hondoensis*, *P. likiangensis*, *P. omorika*, *P. orientalis*, *P. polita*, *P. pungens* (silver and glaucous forms), *P. smithiana*, and *P. spinulosa*.

The species of *Picea* should always be raised from seed if this is available. The dwarf garden varieties are propagated by cuttings taken in July or August. Grafting is used to increase varieties abnormal in habit and those with coloured leaves, notably the various blue and silver forms of *P. pungens*; some species have to be propagated in this way, if seed is not available or scarce, but such plants are not so fine or long-lived as those raised from seed. The spruces like abundant moisture at the root; if rainfall is deficient it may be compensated for by planting in a deep moist soil. *P. pungens* is one of the best in a dry climate. Few conifers withstand town conditions worse than the spruces, and they are not really at home on shallow, chalky soils. Many of them produce a useful timber, especially *P. abies* in Europe. *P. glauca* is cultivated in some of the northerly regions of Scandinavia too inclement for any other tree to thrive.

The measurements of cultivated trees, as throughout this revised edition, have been provided by Mr A. F. Mitchell of the Forestry Commission. Much fuller information will be found in his recently published work *Conifers in the British Isles* (Forestry Commission Booklet 33, publ. 1972). This contains descriptions of all coniferous species cultivated in the British Isles, and keys based on field characters.

P. ABIES (L.) Karsten   NORWAY OR COMMON SPRUCE
Pinus abies L.; *Picea excelsa* Link; *Abies picea* Mill.

A tree 100 to 120, sometimes 150 ft, high, of tapering, pyramidal form densely clothed with branches and leaves; bark thin and scaling; branchlets pale brown, usually more or less downy, sometimes glabrous. Leaves mostly arranged in two sets in or near the horizontal plane, ⅛ to ¾ in. long; very deep glossy green, quadrangular, with a few faintly defined lines of stomata on each face. Cones cylindrical, tapered at the top, usually about 5 in. long and 1½ to 2 in. wide; light shining brown; scales bluntly triangular at the apex, the end jagged as if bitten off.

P. abies has its largest and most continuous area in Scandinavia and N.W.

Russia, but also occurs wild in mountainous regions from southern Poland and the Carpathians of Rumania to S.E. France. From the rest of France it is absent, as it is from the Italian and Iberian peninsulas. In Britain it was apparently in cultivation by the 17th century, but the accounts are so confused that its early history remains obscure. In 'Hunter's Evelyn' (1776) it is stated that the spruce is a native of Scotland, an error that no doubt springs from the vague use of the word fir for the Scots pine, the Norway spruce, and the silver fir.

Although handsome as an isolated tree and imposing in its height, it is known rather as a forest tree with us than in the garden. It is by nature a slender tree in this country, rarely over 10 ft in girth, but attaining a height of 130 ft or slightly more. Most of the finest trees are to be found in Scotland. The Norway spruce is still an important forestry tree, both in the Commission forests and on private estates, though it is not suitable for chalky or poor acid soils nor, except in moist soils, for areas where the rainfall is less than 30 in. The total area under Norway spruce in 1965 was 263,000 acres, and the annual planting rate by the Forestry Commission is 3,000 acres.

cv. 'ACROCONA'.—A monstrosity in which all or most of the leaves of some leading shoots are converted into cone-scales. It is of shrubby habit and does not develop a leader.

var. ALPESTRIS (Bruegg.) Kruessm. *P. alpestris* Bruegg.; *P. obovata* var. *alpestris* (Bruegg.) Henry—An interesting local race found here and there in the central Alps at high altitudes. Leaves glaucous; twigs densely hairy; cone-scales rounded and entire at the apex. Henry, and other authorities, consider that this variety belongs to *P. obovata* (q.v.).

cv. 'ARGENTEOSPICA'.—Young shoots of a clear creamy white, approaching afterwards the normal colour; very striking and ornamental. Raised by Messrs Hesse of Weener, Hanover.

cv. 'AUREA'.—Leaves yellowish white at first, later green or green streaked with yellow. In cultivation 1855. There are examples 60 to 90 ft high at Vernon Holme, Harbledown, Kent; Nymans, Sussex; Westonbirt, Glos.; and Hergest Croft, Heref. Probably not a clone.

cv. 'CLANBRASSILIANA'.—A variety of low, dense, rounded habit, usually wider than high. A plant thirty years old will be under 3 ft in height. Annual growths very short. Leaves bright green, up to ⅜ in. long, forward pointing, two-ranked or more or less radially arranged. It is said to have been found originally on the Moira estate near Belfast towards the end of the 18th century. It was introduced to cultivation by Lord Clanbrassil of Tullymore Park, Co. Down, and what is believed to be the original plant still grows there, presumably moved there after its discovery. In 1956 it was 16¾ ft high with a rounded crown borne on several bare stems about 7 ft high, but cuttings from it growing at the Slieve Donard Nursery were only 6 to 8 in. high when fifteen years old (letter from Alistair Simpson in *Gardening Illustrated* (Feb. 1956), p. 40).

f. COLUMNARIS (Jacques) Rehd.—Of columnar habit, with short more or less horizontal main branches. Fairly frequent in the wild.

cv. 'CRANSTONII'.—See under f. *virgata*.

cv. 'FINEDONENSIS'.—Young foliage and shoots pale yellow, darkening to yellowish brown but finally becoming the normal green. Raised at Finedon Hall, Northants.

cv. 'Gregoryana'.—A very dwarf variety making a hummock rarely more than 2 ft high. Leaves greyish green, up to $\frac{1}{2}$ in. long, radially arranged, pointing at right angles to the shoot or slightly forward. It was raised at Gregory's Royal Nurseries, Cirencester. Hornibrook gives 1860 as the date, but the firm was wound-up in 1850, after Gregory's death in that year. 'Gregoryana Veitchii' is similar but more vigorous, and the leaves on the side-branches are often pectinately arranged (Hornibrook, *Dw. and Sl. Gr. Conif.*, Ed. 2, p. 150).

cv. 'Inversa'.—See under f. *pendula*.

cv. 'Maxwellii'.—According to Hornibrook, the true variety, which was raised in the USA, makes a low, rounded cushion, with thick, very short branches; radially arranged, roundish leaves up to $\frac{1}{2}$ in. long, terminated by a long, hair-like point; and stout, ovoid, obtuse buds. The plants cultivated under this name in Europe he called 'Pseudomaxwellii'. They bear some resemblance to the true variety when young, but become of more open habit; the buds are conical and acute, the leaves are flattened, and the hair-like tip is very short or wanting (op. cit., pp. 140–1).

cv. 'Ohlendorfii'.—A medium-dwarf shrub of pyramidal form, eventually 6 ft high, leaves yellowish green, up to $\frac{1}{2}$ in. long, those on the upper side of the shoot forward pointing and slightly appressed.

f. pendula (Laws.) N. Sylven—A very variable and confused group. Some wild plants dubbed *pendula* have drooping branches. At the other extreme is 'Inversa', with the main and secondary branches quite pendulous and appressed to the trunk.

cv. 'Procumbens'.—A low, flat-topped shrub, 2 or 3 ft high, much wider.

cv. 'Reflexa'.—A pendulous variety which does not develop a leader and is usually grown on the flat or trailing down a bank, and eventually covers a wide area with its trailing branches.

cv. 'Remontii'.—A semi-dwarf variety of dense, conical habit, 6 ft or more high.

cv. 'Repens'.—A low bush with short, radially arranged leaves, with the branches prostrate or arching up and then spreading, eventually a foot or so high.

f. viminalis (Alstr.) Lindman *Pinus viminalis* Alstr.—Main branches more or less horizontal, secondary branches pendulous, almost devoid of laterals and much elongated. This variant is reported to be fairly frequent in Sweden, and was described by Baron Alströmer, a friend of Linnaeus, in 1777.

f. virgata (Jacques) Rehd. *Abies excelsa* var. *virgata* Jacques; *Picea excelsa* var. *denudata* Carr.—An abnormality, found occasionally in the wild and among garden-raised seedlings, in which the main branches bear very few lateral buds, so that the energy of the plant is concentrated in the leading growths and the sparse laterals, which become snakily elongated. The leaves resemble those borne on leading shoots in being long and thick. A clone of this, perhaps the typical one, is fairly common in cultivation, but is no more than a grotesque curiosity, of no beauty. In f. MONSTROSA (Loud.) Rehd. the reduction of branching is carried to its extreme, the plant consisting of a single stem with a bud at the top, the only foliage being of the kind found on leading shoots. The variety 'CRANSTONII', raised in Britain in the last century, is intermediate between this and the f. *virgata*.

P. ASPERATA Mast.

According to Wilson this spruce attains 100 ft in height in Western China and closely resembles in general outline the common European spruce (*P. abies*) but is more glaucous in colour; young shoots pale, yellowish, changing to grey, and either glabrous or more or less downy. Leaves ½ to ¾ in. long, four-angled in cross-section, stiff, pointed, with a few lines of stomata on all four surfaces; the uppermost ones of the twigs point forwards, those at the side and underneath standing out at right angles; the pegs left by the fallen leaves are very stiff, large and prominent. Cones cylindrical, up to 4 in. long, 1¾ in. wide, 'fawn-grey when ripe, changing to chestnut-brown with age and retained on the tree six months after they mature' (Wilson); cone-scales variable in shape, obovate, rounded or truncate at the top.

Native of W. China; named from specimens collected by Wilson in 1903 but introduced to cultivation by seeds he sent home in 1910. He describes it as the common quadrangular-leaved spruce of N.W. Szechwan, especially in the region of Sungpan in the Upper Min valley, where he collected the type-specimen and some of the seeds sent in 1910 (W. 4061). His other sendings of typical *P. asperata* were from farther south.

⊦   *P. asperata* is slow-growing when young, and subject to damage by late spring frosts. But it is well represented in collections by trees from the seeds sent by Wilson and later by Dr J. Rock. Examples are: Wakehurst Place, Sussex, *pl.* 1919, 45 × 4 ft (1969); Westonbirt, Glos., *pl.* 1936, 60 × 4¼ ft (1974), and several others, one from Rock 15042; National Pinetum, Bedgebury, Kent, *pl.* 1925, 50 × 4 ft (1974); Hergest Croft, Heref., *pl.* 1916, 59 × 3¾ ft (1961); Bicton, Devon, 58 × 3½ ft and 50 × 4¼ ft (1968); Birr Castle, Co. Offaly, Eire, 49 × 4 ft (1966). The cultivated trees vary in colour from grey-green to glaucous.

Wilson found a large-coned form of *P. asperata* in the Pan-lan-shan (some 200 miles to the south of the type-locality of the species); this was introduced under W.4068 and named var. PONDEROSA Rehd. & Wils. Another variety described from the same area is var. NOTABILIS Rehd. & Wils., in which the cone-scales are acute; seeds of this were sent under W.4067. But typical *P. asperata* also occurs in the Pan-lan-shan, and it is probable that these varieties are only minor fluctuations, comparable to those that occur in the common spruce (*P. abies*). In var. HETEROLEPIS (Rehd. & Wils.) Rehd., the cone-scales are emarginate. More distinct is:

var. RETROFLEXA (Mast.) Boom *P. retroflexa* Mast.—Bark grey, shed in large thin plates. Shoots usually golden yellow. Leaves stout, pungently pointed. Cones with acute scales. According to Wilson, this is the common spruce in the neighbourhood of Tatsien-lu (Kangting). It is in cultivation from W.4083.

P. BICOLOR (Maxim.) Mayr

Abies bicolor Maxim.; *Abies alcocquiana* Veitch ex Lindl., in part; *Picea alcockiana* Carr.

A tree up to 80 ft in the wild, with horizontal or slightly ascending branches, forming a broad crown; bark grey or grey-brown, scaly; buds broadly ovoid, obtuse, not or only slightly resinous; young shoots pale brown, glabrous or sometimes downy in the furrows. Leaves pointing forward on the upper part of the shoot, the lower ones more or less horizontal, a few downward pointing, $\frac{3}{8}$ to $\frac{5}{8}$ in. long, rather stiff, apex bevelled, acute with a pale horny tip, four-angled, with lines of stomata on all four surfaces, but these are rather more numerous on the lower surface, which is bluish or whitish green, in contrast to the upper (exposed) surface, which is greyish green—hence no doubt the epithet *bicolor*. Cones 2 to 4 in. long, cylindrical or slightly tapered from the middle, the scales toothed, variable in shape even on the same cone, some broad and rounded, some tending to a triangular outline.

Native of Japan, where it is confined to the mountains of the central part of the main island (Honshu); introduced by J. G. Veitch in 1861. Veitch procured the seeds, and specimens, when he visited Mt Fuji as unofficial botanist on an excursion to the summit led by the British Minister to Yedo (Tokyo), Rutherford Alcock (see *Gard. Chron.* (1861), pp. 49–50). From the specimens Lindley described *Abies alcocquiana*, but it later proved that only the cones belonged to the species described here; the leaves were from *P. jezoensis*, which grows with *P. bicolor* on the mountain. The seeds too were mixed and produced both species. The confusion was cleared up by Masters in 1880, but in the meantime species described here had been validly named *Abies bicolor* by Maximowicz. *P. jezoensis*, the other party to the confusion, is a quite distinct species belonging to the *Omorika* or flat-leaved section.

P. bicolor is hardy, but rare and of no ornamental merit. Among the largest examples 'are: Wakehurst Place, Sussex, 71 × 3 ft (1973); Bicton, Devon, 74 × $7\frac{1}{2}$ ft (1968); Melbury, Dorset, 75 × $5\frac{1}{4}$ ft (1971); Scone Palace, Perth, 52 × 6 ft (1970).

var. ACICULARIS Shirasawa & Koyama—This variety was described from trees growing in the Yatsuga range, and was said to differ from the typical state in having more densely crowded, longer, linear leaves, bluish white on the concealed side; and in its entire cone-scales. A tree at Borde Hill, Sussex, of unknown provenance, is grown under this name but does not agree with the original description. The var. *reflexa*, described by the same authors from the Shirane-san in the Akaishi range, was said to have reflexed cone-scales. Wilson considered that both varieties were part of the normal variation of the species.

P. BRACHYTYLA (Franch.) Pritz.

Abies brachytyla Franch.; *P. ascendens* Patschke; *P. pachyclada* Patschke; *P. sargentiana* Rehd. & Wils.; *P. complanata* Mast.

A tree 40 to 80 ft high with a usually greyish scaly bark, the main branches horizontal, the branchlets more or less pendulous; young shoots glabrous or downy, creamy white or yellowish, becoming pale reddish brown in the second year; buds pale brown, ovoid, resinous, the terminal ones almost concealed on strong shoots by tufts of leaves. Leaves flattened, acute, mostly $\frac{1}{2}$ to $\frac{5}{8}$ in. long, those on the upper side of the shoot appressed, the lateral leaves pointing forward and slightly downward, those on the underside directed downward and forward (i.e., not pectinately arranged); the leaves are medium green on the exposed side, darkening in the second year, and the underside is conspicuously white-glaucous, even the midrib being usually covered with a pruinose bloom. Cones $2\frac{1}{2}$ to 5 in. long, 1 to $1\frac{3}{4}$ in. wide, tapering towards both ends but more abruptly towards the base; cone-scales dull brown, the exposed part broadly rounded (f. LATI-SQUAMEA Stapf) or tapered to a broadly triangular, wavy apex. (f. RHOM-BISQUAMEA Stapf). *Bot. Mag.*, t. 8969.

Native of Central and W. China; described from specimens collected by the French missionaries Delavay and Farges; introduced by Wilson in 1901. It is a variable species, as may be judged from the synonyms cited above, and it is now regarded as including the whole of the flat-leaved spruces of Central and Western China. Wilson's first sending was from W. Hupeh (W.1282), but he sent seeds again on later expeditions. W.1530, from W. Szechwan, was collected during his second expedition for Veitch and distributed as *P. complanata*. The plants originally grown as *P. ascendens* and *P. sargentiana* are from seeds collected in W. Szechwan during his second expedition for the Arnold Arboretum in 1910.

P. brachytyla is one of the most ornamental of the spruces, with leaves of an unusually cheerful shade of green, contrasting with the vividly glaucous undersurface. It grows well and, coming into growth late, does not suffer damage from spring frosts. Some of the largest specimens are: Warnham Court, Sussex, 63 × 5½ ft (1971); Wakehurst Place, Sussex, *pl.* 1914, 72 × 7¾ ft (1973); Westonbirt, Glos., in Morley Ride, *pl.* 1933, 82 × 5¾ ft (1973); Hergest Croft, Heref., *pl.* 1912, 79 × 6¼ ft (1969); Stourhead, Wilts, 84 × 5½ ft (1970); Bicton, Devon, *pl.* 1920, 73 × 5¼ ft and 72 ft × 5¼ ft (1968).

P. BREWERIANA S. Wats.   [PLATE 28

A tree up to 120 ft high in the wild, the trunk 2 to 3 ft in diameter, the branches ultimately pendulous, with the final ramifications slender, whip-like, and often 7 to 8 or even 12 ft long, but no thicker than a lead pencil, and hanging perpendicularly; pyramidal and stiffly branched when young. Leaves pointing forwards, and arranged about equally all round the shoot, $\frac{1}{2}$ to 1 in. long, $\frac{1}{20}$ to $\frac{1}{12}$ in. wide, blunt at the apex, somewhat tapered at the base; one side dark glossy green without stomata, the other grey with stomatic lines. Cones cylindrical-oval, about 3 in. long, purple, the scales rounded and entire at the margins. *Bot. Mag.*, t. 9543.

Native of the Siskiyou Mountains of California and Oregon, where it occurs in comparatively small numbers in a few places at about 7,000 ft altitude; discovered by W. H. Brewer, the Californian botanist. A single plant was sent by Prof. Sargent in 1897 to Kew, where it thrives very well but grows slowly in height. It first bore cones in 1920 and measures 36 × 2 ft (1963). Fourteen seedlings collected in the wild reached Dawyck in Peeblesshire in 1911 (see *Conifers in Cultivation* (1932), p. 198) and there were probably other introductions at about the same time or slightly earlier.

With its curtained branches, *P. breweriana* is one of the most striking and ornamental of conifers, and only its scarcity in commerce prevents it from being more widely planted. It is many years before seedling plants begin to develop the characteristic branching, but they are still to be preferred to grafted ones. Among the oldest specimens in the country are: Vernon Holme, Kent, 53 × 5 ft (1973); National Pinetum, Bedgebury, Kent, *pl.* 1926, 30 × 4 ft (1968); Sheffield Park, Sussex, *pl.* 1910, 46 × 4¼ ft (1974); Leonardslee, Sussex, 44 × 3¾ ft (1969); Wakehurst Place, Sussex, *pl.* 1915, 46 × 4 ft (1970) and another in the Valley, 52 × 3¾ ft (1973); Exbury, Hants, 39 × 4½ ft (1968); Hergest Croft, Heref., *pl.* 1916, 42 × 3¾ ft (1963); Dawyck, Peebles., *pl.* 1911, the best 51 × 5¾ ft (1974).

P. ENGELMANNII (Parry) Engelm.

Abies engelmannii Parry; *Picea glauca* subsp. *engelmannii* (Parry) T.M.C.Taylor

A tree 80 to 100, occasionally 150 ft high, assuming as a young tree in cultivation a pyramidal form, with slightly ascending branches; young shoots pale yellowish brown, clothed with stiff, erect down. Leaves arranged all round the twig, but thinly beneath; they are ¾ to 1⅛ in. long, quadrangular, bluntish at the tips, flexible, dull, slightly glaucous-green, with three or four lines of stomata on all four surfaces. Cones 1½ to 3 in. long, ¾ to 1 in. in diameter; tapered towards the top, pale shining brown when mature; scales with a truncate apex and jagged margins.

Native of the mountains of western N. America from Alberta and British Columbia (where it attains its greatest size), south to New Mexico and Arizona. This handsome spruce is very hardy, and thrives better in N. Continental Europe and New England, where the winters are severe, than it does in places with a mild climate and late spring frosts. It is comparatively rare in gardens, the tree grown under the name being frequently the glaucous form of *P. pungens*. The two species, although so much confused, are really very distinct. *P. engelmannii* is easily recognised by its downy shoots; its soft and flexible, not spine-tipped leaves; also by its shorter cones.

The finest specimens of *P. engelmannii* grow at Dawyck in Peeblesshire; they were collected as seedlings in the Rocky Mountains by F. R. S. Balfour in 1902 and the taller of the two measures 89 × 7¼ ft (1974).

f. GLAUCA Beissn.—Leaves with a pronounced glaucous hue. There is an example at Dawyck, measuring 63 × 4¼ ft (1966). F. R. S. Balfour considered that this form would be more suitable for Scotland than the much commoner glaucous forms of *P. pungens*, which grow best in a hot, dry climate.

P. GLAUCA (Moench) Voss   WHITE SPRUCE

Pinus glauca Moench; *Picea alba* Link; *Abies canadensis* Mill.

A tree usually 60 to 70 ft high; young specimens with much the habit of the common spruce, but of a greyer green; branchlets very pale brown, not downy; buds with ciliate scales. Leaves mostly on the upper side of the branches; they are ½ to ¾ in. long, pointed, but not prickly, four-angled, grey-green, with two to five lines of stomata on each face. Cones cylindrical, 1½ to 2 in. long, pale shining brown when mature; scales very thin and flexible, broad and rounded, nearly entire at the margins.

Native of N. America; introduced about the end of the 17th century. It is very widely spread in the wild, reaching, according to Sargent, from Labrador to Alaska, extending southwards along the eastern side of the Rocky Mountains to Montana, and to New York, Michigan, etc. It reaches a higher latitude than any other evergreen tree, and nearly to the Arctic Sea, on ground which only thaws 3 or 4 ft down in summer. It possesses little merit as an ornamental tree in Britain, especially in the south, but on the vast 'Danish heaths and dunes of Jutland which are continually swept by the gales of the North Sea it has been extensively planted, especially as a shelter tree. It serves this purpose so well that no other known tree could take its place there' (Rafn). In the catty smell of its foliage it resembles *P. engelmannii*, but that species has longer leaves and more tapered cone-scales, and it, as well as the more nearly allied *P. mariana* and *P. rubens,* are further distinguished by their downy shoots.

The finest trees of *P. glauca* grow in the Rhinefield Drive in the New Forest. Planted in 1861, the best is 90 × 5¾ ft (1970). Other examples are: National Pinetum, Bedgebury, Kent, *pl.* 1929, 43 × 2¾ ft (1970); Speech House, Glos., *pl.* 1916, 64 × 3¼ ft (1968); Hergest Croft, Heref., *pl.* 1911, 60 × 3½ ft (1969); Bicton, Devon, 54 × 4 ft (1968); Eridge Castle, Kent, *pl.* 1880, 69 × 8 ft (1971).

var. ALBERTIANA (S. Brown) Sarg. *P. albertiana* S. Brown—This variety occurs at the western end of the range of *P. glauca*, in parts of Alberta, British Columbia, etc., and is believed to be the result of crossing between this species and *P. engelmannii*. It is said to grow taller than typical *P. glauca* (to 160 ft), but there seems to be no constant botanical character by which it could be identified with any certainty. Elwes distributed seeds in 1906.

cv. 'CONICA'.—This is one of the most distinct and pleasing of dwarf spruces. It makes a slender, cone-shaped bush, very closely and densely branched, resembling the old-fashioned candle extinguisher in shape. The young shoots are slightly downy, pale creamy yellow, the leaves bright green, very slender, ¼ to ½ in. long, slenderly pointed, with one to three broken lines of stomata on each face (*P. albertiana* var. *conica* Bean; *P. glauca* var. *albertiana* f. *conica* Rehd.). Award of Merit 1933.   [PLATE 27

This variety was found by Dr Alfred Rehder and J. G. Jack near Lake Laggan in Alberta in 1904, and distributed by the Arnold Arboretum. A plant was received at Kew in 1909 and in twenty years it got to be 6 ft high and made a perfect cone 3 ft wide at the base. It can be increased by late summer cuttings. The discoverers collected four plants, but presumably only one was propagated.

cv. 'CAERULEA'.—Of dense habit, with conspicuously glaucous leaves.

cv. 'ECHINIFORMIS'.—A dwarf, slow-growing bush with glaucous foliage, forming a flat-topped hummock. Leaves stout, rigid, usually incurved, about $\frac{3}{16}$ in. long.

P. GLEHNII (F. Schmidt) Mast.
Abies glehnii F. Schmidt

A tree up to 130 ft high in the wild; young shoots reddish, densely downy in the grooves; buds ovoid, resinous, brown, the terminal ones with a ring of subulate scales at the base. Leaves arranged as in the common spruce, $\frac{1}{4}$ to $\frac{3}{8}$ in. long, quadrangular, dark green on the exposed side, whitish on the ventral side. Cones oblong, $1\frac{1}{2}$ to $2\frac{1}{2}$ in. long, dark or bluish when young, changing to brown; scales broadly rounded, entire or more or less erose. *Bot. Mag.*, t. 9020.

Native of the northern island of Japan (Hokkaido) and of S. Sakhalin; discovered by Glehn in 1861. Maries collected specimens in 1877 during his expedition for Messrs Veitch, but it was apparently not introduced to Britain until some twenty years later. It is rare in Britain and of no great ornamental value. There are four trees at Murthly Castle, Perths., *pl.* 1897, the largest 69 × 4¼ ft (1970). The material portrayed in the *Botanical Magazine* came from Headfort in Co. Meath, Eire, where there are two trees received from Veitch's Coombe Wood nursery in 1912. The larger of these measures 57 × 7 ft (1966).

P. JEZOENSIS (Sieb. & Zucc.) Carr.
Abies jezoensis Sieb. & Zucc.; *Picea ajanensis* Fisch.

This species seems to be represented in the British Isles almost wholly by the following variety:

var. HONDOENSIS (Mayr) Rehd. *P. hondoensis* Mayr; *Abies alcocquiana* Veitch ex Lindl., in part.—A tree up to 90 ft high in the wild, with a greyish scaly bark; young shoots yellowish, glabrous, becoming reddish brown in the second year; buds shining, resinous, broadly conical-ovoid. Leaves flattened, confined to the upper side of the shoots, the lower ones pectinately arranged, mostly $\frac{3}{8}$ to $\frac{5}{8}$ in. long, obtuse and bevelled at the apex, dark green and without stomata at the apex, the ventral surface blue-white, almost covered with stomatic lines, but the two bands separated by the green midrib. Cones cylindric, 2 to 3 in. long, about 1 in. wide, crimson when young; scales narrowly oblong, with jaggedly toothed margins. *Bot. Mag.*, t. 6743.

Native of the main island of Japan (Honshu, formerly Hondo); introduced by J. G. Veitch from Mt Fuji in 1861. As noted under *P. bicolor*, the cones of these two species were mixed by Veitch's collectors, with the result that both were at first grown under the name *Abies alcocquiana*. In clearing up the confusion in 1880, Masters adopted for it the name *P. ajanensis* Fisch., by which it was generally known until well into the present century (see further below). At the present time it is usually known as *P. jezoensis* simply, and not incorrectly, since it is debatable whether it is really distinct enough from typical *P. jezoensis* to merit distinction even as a variety. The main differences would appear to be that in the var. *hondoensis* the leaves are somewhat shorter than in the typical state, never mucronate at the apex, and that the shoots turn brown in their second year, whereas in typical *P. jezoensis* they remain yellowish.

The Honshu spruce grows well in Britain and is represented in most collections. Details of over forty specimens will be found in A. F. Mitchell's *Conifers in Great Britain*, of which the following is a selection: Eridge Castle, Kent, *pl.* 1877, 75 × 10 ft (1971); Leonardslee, Sussex, *pl. c.* 1905, 85 × 8 ft (1969); Tregrehan, Cornwall, 100 × 8 ft (1971); Benmore, Argyll, *pl.* 1880, 80 × 10¾ ft (1970).

Typical *P. jezoensis* is of wide distribution in N.E. Asia, from the northern island of Japan (Hokkaido, formerly Yezo), to Sakhalin and the S. Kuriles, and on the mainland from Korea and Manchuria through the mountains of the Russian Far East as far north as about 58° N. It was originally described from specimens of a tree growing in a garden near Tokyo, said to have come from the northern island; the synonymous name *P. ajanensis* is founded on a specimen collected near Ayan on the Sea of Othotsk. J. G. Veitch introduced this species from near Hakodate, the port of Hokkaido, in 1861 and Maries, the Veitchian collector, sent seeds again eighteen years later, but the first introduction was a failure, and the second, which probably came from the same area, is unlikely to have been any more successful. A third introduction was by Wilson from Korea in 1917, but whether any trees were raised from the seeds sent to Britain is not known. All the thriving trees of *P. jezoensis* in this country appear to be of the Honshu provenance, i.e., the var. *hondoensis*.

P. KOYAMAE Shirasawa

A tree 40 to 60 ft high in Japan, with a slender trunk and of densely branched, pyramidal habit, with a dark brown or blackish bark peeling off in paper-like flakes; young shoots brown, stronger leading shoots glabrous or slightly glandular, the lateral ones always more or less glandular-bristly; buds conical, light brown or purplish brown, resinous. Leaves ¼ to ⅝ in. long, rigid, four-sided, dark green or grey-green, those on the upper side of the shoot pointing forward and upward (i.e., not appressed to the shoot), the under ones pectinately arranged. Cones cylindrical (smaller ones ovoid-cylindrical), 2 to 4 in. long, 1¼ to 1½ in. wide, shining pale brown; scales broad and rounded, with slightly jagged margins.

This spruce was discovered in the Shinano province of Central Japan by Koyama, on Yatsugatake, at elevations of 5,000 to 6,000 ft; afterwards found in Korea, where Wilson collected it in 1917. It was introduced by him from Japan in 1914 to the Arnold Arboretum and thence to Kew in the following year; seed from the Korean expedition was distributed in Britain in 1918. According to Wilson, who visited its Japanese habitat in company with its discoverer in 1914, this spruce is only known to exist there in a grove of about one hundred trees. He described it as shapely and decidedly ornamental.

P. koyamae is hardy in Britain but only to be seen in a few collections. Among the largest specimens are: National Pinetum, Bedgebury, Kent, *pl.* 1928, 57 × 5 ft

(1970); Warnham Court, Sussex, 60 × 4 ft (1971); Borde Hill, Sussex, 70 × 4¼ ft (1973); Stanage Park, Radnor, 66 × 4 ft (1970). There is a tree measuring 44 × 2½ ft in the Pinetum of the Royal Horticultural Society at Wisley (1969).

P. LIKIANGENSIS (Franch.) Pritz.

Abies likiangensis Franch.; *P. yunnanensis* Hort.

A tree up to 150 ft high in the wild; bark grey or purplish grey, fissured; buds ovoid, resinous; young shoots usually pale brown or yellowish grey, more or less hairy; leaf-pegs unusually long. Leaves four-angled, slightly broader than high in cross-section, ⅔ to ⅝ in. long, acute and bevelled at the apex, those on the upper side of the shoot pointed forward, the lower leaves more or less pectinately arranged, grey-green or dark green on the exposed side, glaucous or silvery on the ventral side. Cones ovoid, 2 to 2½ in. long, 1¼ to 1¾ in. wide; cone-scales flexible, the upper part ovate, rounded, wavy, spreading outward after ripening.

P. *likiangensis* is of wide range in Western China and extends into Tibet; discovered by the French missionary Delavay in the Lichiang range of Yunnan in 1884. Forrest sent seeds from this area in 1910 (F.6746), but the first introduction was by Wilson six years earlier, from W. Szechwan (W.1834), when collecting for Messrs Veitch. Even from a single seed collection P. *likiangensis* varies considerably in the colour and degree of hairiness of the shoots, colour of the leaves, etc.

Although subject to damage by late frosts when young, this spruce grows well in the British Isles and deserves to be more commonly planted; at present it is rarely seen outside collections. The young cones and male flower-clusters are brilliant red. Some examples are: Wakehurst Place, Sussex, 56 × 5¼ ft (1969) and 59 × 5 ft (1968); Warnham Court, Sussex, from W.1834, 69 × 5½ ft (1971); Borde Hill, Sussex, from F.6746, 56 × 5¼ ft (1968); National Pinetum, Bedgebury, Kent, *pl.* 1926, 48 × 6¼ ft (1968); Stanage Park, Radnor, *pl.* 1910, 71 × 6 ft (1970); Edinburgh Botanic Garden, from F.6746, 46 × 4¾ ft (1970); Powerscourt, Co. Wicklow, Eire, 68 × 6¼ ft (1966).

var. BALFOURIANA (Rehd. & Wils.) E. H. Hillier *P. balfouriana* Rehd. & Wils.—This variety was described, as a species, from specimens collected by Wilson west of Tatsien-lu (Kangting) in 1910, during his second expedition for the Arnold Arboretum, but was not recognised as even varietally distinct from the type by A. B. Jackson. A. F. Mitchell has noted that the cultivated trees are really nearer to var. *purpurea* than to the type. These may be from W.4065, collected in the Pan-lan-shan, of which Rehder and Wilson remarked: 'In general appearance this number suggests P. *purpurea.*' There are trees in a few collections.

var. PURPUREA (Mast.) Dall. & Jacks. *P. purpurea* Mast.—Bark divided into rather thin, scaly plates; shoots very densely clad with long hairs. Leaves shorter than in the type, about ½ in. long, dark green on the exposed side, more closely appressed to the shoot. Cones mostly smaller, about 2 in. long (but occasionally up to 3 in.), violet-purple when young. Native of Kansu and N.W. Szechwan; discovered by Wilson in 1903 and introduced by him in 1910–11 from near Sungpan; it was reintroduced by Joseph Rock from Kansu. Some examples are:

Wakehurst Place, Sussex, 70 × 3¼ and 56 × 4½ ft (1974); Borde Hill, Sussex, Pinetum, 60 × 3¼ ft (1974); Vernon Holme, Kent, 60 × 4¼ ft (1973); Weston-birt, Glos., *pl.* 1931, 62 × 3½ ft (1969).

P. MONTIGENA Mast.—A little-known species, possibly a hybrid between *P. likiangensis* and *P. asperata*; discovered by Wilson in 1903 in W. Szechwan. He may have sent seeds in the same year, and anyway did so in 1910–11, during his second expedition for the Arnold Arboretum (W.4084; this number is wrongly dated 1908 in *Pl. Wils.*). Some plants distributed under the name *P. montigena* proved to be a stunted form of *P. asperata*.

P. MARIANA (Mill.) Britt., Sterns and Poggenburg   BLACK SPRUCE
    Abies mariana Mill.; *Picea nigra* (Ait.) Link; *Pinus nigra* Ait.

A tree 20 to 30 ft (occasionally twice or thrice as) high, of close, pyramidal habit as seen in cultivation, branches densely twiggy; young shoots abundantly furnished with reddish down; terminal bud with a few downy awl-shaped scales at the base. Leaves arranged all round the twig, but thinly beneath, ¼ to ⅝ in. long, slightly curved, quadrangular, with a bluntish, bevelled point; more or less glaucous in hue, with two to five lines of stomata on each surface. Cones egg-shaped, ¾ to 1¼ in. long, brownish purple when young; scales rounded or somewhat bluntly triangular at the apex, and slightly jagged at the margin.

Native of N. America, where it covers an immense tract from Labrador and Alaska in the north to Virginia and Wisconsin in the south; introduced to the Fulham garden about 1700 by Bishop Compton. This is not one of the most ornamental of spruces, but is still pleasing in its dense furnishing of leaves and its large crops of rich purple young cones. It is nearly allied to *P. rubens*, but differs in its blue-green foliage and in the long persistence of its cones upon the branches—twenty to thirty years, according to Sargent.

Among the few specimens of the black spruce in this country are: Nymans, Sussex, 63 × 5¾ ft (1970), and another of about the same size; Wakehurst Place, Sussex, 53 × 4 ft (1964); Rhinefield Drive, Hants., 69 × 4½ ft (1971); Caerhays Castle, Cornwall, 62 × 6¾ ft (1971).

cv. 'DOUMETII'.—A small densely branched tree growing slowly to about 10 ft in this country. Leaves blue-green, slender, crowded, mostly under ½ in. long. Branchlets bright orange-brown. This variety was described by Carrière in 1855 from a plant growing at the Château de Balaine near Moulins, where there was (and still is) a fine collection of American trees planted by Aglaé Adanson, daughter of the French botanist Michel Adanson (1727–1806). The original tree was planted about 1835; when Elwes visited La Balaine early this century it was dead, but still standing and about 30 ft high.

cv. 'ERICOIDES'.—This is a pigmy form of the black spruce, and is a rounded bush with very slender leaves never more than ⅜ in. long, almost heathlike, young shoots thin, much branched, downy the first two or three years. It has been known since the second half of the last century but is extremely rare and is only mentioned here because the earliest description of it appeared in the first edition of this work.

P. MAXIMOWICZII Reg. ex Mast.

P. obovata var. *japonica* (Maxim.) Beissn.; *Abies obovata* var. *japonica* Maxim.

The leading characters of this little-known spruce appear to be: young branchlets glabrous, reddish brown; buds ovoid, acute, resinous, about $\frac{3}{16}$ in. long; leaves $\frac{3}{8}$ to $\frac{1}{2}$ in. long, four-angled, concolorous, rigid, pungent, arranged radially round the shoot as in *P. polita*. Cones up to 2 in. long, with scales rounded and entire at the apex.

P. maximowiczii was described by Masters in 1880 from a small, stunted bush at Kew, raised from seeds distributed by Regel from St Petersburg in 1865. Plants from the same batch throve better in some continental collections, but grew slowly. The original seeds were collected in Japan by Tschonoski and came either from Fujiyama or from Shinano province (there are coning specimens in the Kew Herbarium from both localities, gathered by Tschonoski). No spruce resembling *P. maximowiczii* has since been found on Fujiyama, but in 1911 what is supposed to be this species was found by Koyama on Yatsugadake, near the borders between Shinano and Kai provinces. According to Wilson, who saw the stand a few years later, adult trees bear a strong resemblance to *P. polita*, but really large specimens were rare and mostly confined to temple gardens. He said it was fairly common, however, as a small, bushy, densely branched tree, growing on open moorland between 4,000 and 5,500 ft, and scattered in mixed woods, where it attains 65 ft. Adult trees have a thick, deeply fissured bark.

If the radial arrangement of the leaves is a permanent character of this species, it is doubtful if it is any longer in cultivation in this country. But some authorities consider it to be a juvenile phase, or a characteristic of plants growing at high altitudes. Beissner, for example, considered *P. maximowiczii* to be nothing but a subalpine variety of *P. obovata*. A tree at Nymans in Sussex, planted as *P. maximowiczii*, bears some resemblance to *P. obovata*, and is of very dense habit. On the other hand, a vigorous tree at Borde Hill in Sussex, believed to have been planted as *P. maximowiczii*, and said to resemble what is grown under that name in Germany, seems to be near to *P. rubens* or *P. glehnii*, and could be a hybrid.

P. MORRISONICOLA Hayata

A slender lofty tree, sometimes quite 150 ft high, but usually under 100 ft, with a trunk girthing from 10 to 20 ft, bark grey, coming away in round thin scales. Young shoots glabrous, pale brown. Leaves very slender, $\frac{1}{4}$ to $\frac{2}{3}$ in. long, quadrangular but flattish. Cones cylindrical or ovoid-cylindrical, $1\frac{1}{2}$ to $2\frac{1}{2}$ in. long, 1 to $1\frac{1}{2}$ in. wide, tapering at top and bottom; cone-scales roundish obovate with slightly uneven margins.

Native of Formosa; discovered on Mt Morrison in 1900; introduced to cultivation in 1918 by Wilson, who found that it constituted pure forests in precipitous country up to 9,000 to 10,000 ft. The leaves are dark green and the aspect of the tree 'decidedly sombre'. Hayata considers it to be related to *P. glehnii*, but that species is easily distinguished by its downy shoots. It seems to resemble

P. wilsonii in its pale, slender, glabrous twigs, and more especially in the very slender leaves. It is growing in the Bedgebury Pinetum, but is not particularly happy there, probably requiring, like most Formosan trees and shrubs, a somewhat warmer climate.

A tree at Borde Hill, Sussex, 3½ ft high in 1932, measures 50 × 2½ ft (1968), and there are two of about the same height and girth at Wakehurst Place in the same county. The present tree at Bedgebury, planted 1937, is 36 × 2 ft (1970).

P. OBOVATA Ledeb.   SIBERIAN SPRUCE
P. abies subsp. *obovata* (Ledeb.) Hulten

The Siberian spruce is allied to *P. abies*, the most reliable difference being the smaller cones (up to about 3 in. long) with the scales entire at the apex, not jagged as in *P. abies*. Also, the shoots are densely covered with a short, glandular down and the leaves are somewhat shorter, up to about ⅝ in. long. It is usually stated that the leaf-arrangement is similar to that of the common spruce, but in cultivated trees (of unknown provenance) the leaves are more appressed to the shoot and the lower ones are not strictly pectinate as in *P. abies* but directed slightly downwards. Another character noted by A. F. Mitchell is that the leaf below a lateral bud is displaced so as to point out vertically from the shoot.

P. obovata has a very wide range, from N.W. European Russia through Siberia to the Russian Far East. Spruces intermediate between the common and Siberian spruce occur in Finland, Norway, and N.W. Russia, which are usually included in *P. obovata* as var. FENNICA (Reg.) Henry. Cultivated trees with sparsely downy shoots may belong here. See also *P. abies* var. *alpestris*.

The Siberian spruce is rare in cultivation. A specimen at Dawyck, Peeblesshire, measures 62 × 4 ft (1974), and there are others of about the same size at Wakehurst Place, Sussex, and Blackmoor, Hants. Smaller trees, planted in 1926, grow in the National Pinetum at Bedgebury, Kent.

P. OMORIKA (Pančić) Purkyně
Pinus omorika Pančić

A narrow, short-branched tree, described as occasionally attaining over 100 ft in height, with a remarkably slender trunk, 3 to 5 ft in girth; juvenile trees assume a very slender, tapering, and elegant form; shoots covered with stiff down, persisting several years. Leaves mostly disposed in or above the horizontal plane, but with a few standing out beneath; those on the upper side appressed, pointing forwards and hiding the branch; they are ½ to 1 in. long, $\frac{1}{16}$ to $\frac{1}{12}$ in. wide; abruptly and sharply pointed on young trees, rounded on old ones; dark glossy green, and without stomata on the uppermost side; greyish beneath, with stomatic lines. Cones egg-shaped, tapered at the top, 1¼ to 2 in. long; scales broad and rounded, with jagged margins. *Bot. Mag.*, t. 9163.

P. omorika, or a species closely allied to it, was widely distributed in Europe before the Ice Age, but is now confined to a few stands in the limestone mountains on either side of the upper Drina in Yugoslavia, most of them located from north-west to north-east of Višegrad. A distribution map by Prof. Fukarek will be found in *Int. Dendr. Soc. Ybk.* (1968), p. 32. It was described in 1876 by Dr Pančić, who had received specimens in the previous year, and visited the stands in 1877. It was introduced to cultivation in 1881, by Froebel of Zurich, who received seeds from Dr Pančić. Kew received seeds direct from Belgrade in 1889.

P. *omorika* is of considerable scientific interest as the only flat-needled spruce in Europe and an undoubted relict from the tertiary epoch. It is, besides, one of the finest spruces introduced to this country. Near London it thrives better than any other, remaining well furnished with its dark green leaves, growing rapidly, and retaining a slender, very elegant form. As it starts into growth late, it is not damaged by spring frosts, and will grow well on acid as well as calcareous soils.

The largest tree at Kew from the introduction of 1889 measures 62 × 2¾ ft (1970). Two trees at Murthly Castle, Perths., a few years younger, measure 90 × 6¼ ft and 85 × 6¼ ft (1970). Others are: Wakehurst Place, Sussex, Bloomer's Valley, 80 × 4¾ ft (1973); Leonardslee, Sussex, 79 × 4¼ ft (1968); Sheffield Park, Sussex, *pl.* 1910 (?), 78 × 5 ft (1968). The following were measured in Eire in 1966: Headfort, Co. Meath, *pl.* 1913, 54 × 6 ft; Ashbourne House, Co. Cork, 62 × 5¾ ft.

cv. 'NANA'.—A slow-growing variety of dense, irregular habit, eventually 10 ft or so high. Leaves closely set, about ⅜ in. long, more or less radially arranged. One of the best small conifers, raised in Holland around 1930.

P. ORIENTALIS (L.) Link   ORIENTAL OR CAUCASIAN SPRUCE
Pinus orientalis L.

A tree over 100 ft high in the wild, forming in a young state a densely branched, very leafy, pyramidal tree, with the shape of the common spruce, but smaller-leaved and more slenderly branched; branches stiffly horizontal; young shoots furnished with short, erect, bristle-like hairs. Leaves arranged mostly at and above the horizontal plane, the upper ones appressed to and hiding the twig; they are dark shining green, ¼ to ⅓ in. long, bluntish at the apex, quadrangular in section, with one to four lines of stomata on each surface. Cones of a beautiful purple when young, ultimately brown, 1½ to 3 in. long, ¾ to 1 in. wide; cylindrical, slender, and pointed when young; scales entire at the margin.

Native of the Caucasus and N.E. Anatolia; introduced in 1839. This is undoubtedly one of the most attractive of all the spruces, its foliage being of a brilliant dark green, the habit neat and dense. It has the shortest leaves of all spruces, except, perhaps, some of the pigmy forms of other species. Near London, and in localities with a deficient rainfall, it is much to be preferred to P. *abies*, although slower-growing. In a small state it is one of the daintiest looking of spruces; and older, when bearing a crop of its richly coloured cones, it is very ornamental.

The largest specimens in Britain are slightly over 100 ft high, and the largest girths 10 to 11 ft. But Alan Mitchell notes that the oldest trees, which are mostly 100 or slightly more years old, have ceased to grow or are dying back.

cv. 'AUREA'.—Young shoots golden yellow, very handsome. Raised in Germany, before 1873. There are examples in the National Pinetum at Bedgebury. A tree at Vernon Holme in Kent reached 60 ft but is dying back at the top.

P. POLITA (Sieb. & Zucc.) Carr.   TIGER-TAIL SPRUCE
Abies polita Sieb. & Zucc.; *Abies torano* Sieb.; *Picea torano* (Sieb.) Koehne

A tree over 100 ft high in Japan; in cultivation a small pyramidal tree of very stiff habit; branches rigid and densely clothed with leaves; young shoots not downy, pale and yellowish the first year; terminal buds conical, shining brown, with closely appressed scales. Leaves set all round the shoot except for an open V-shaped groove beneath; they are 1¾ in. long, 1/12 in. wide; diamond-shaped in cross-section, very rigid, somewhat curved, spine-tipped; dark glossy green, with four to seven faint lines of stomata on all four surfaces. Cones 2½ to 4 in. long, 1¼ to 1¾ in. wide before opening; brown when mature; scales minutely toothed.

Native of Japan; introduced by J. G. Veitch in 1861. This spruce is decidedly one of the most distinct and striking in the genus, especially in the comparatively long, thick, rigid, spine-tipped leaves standing out at almost right angles to the shoot. It is also one of the handsomest, and in a young state forms a shapely tree suitable for an isolated position on a lawn. It is a very hardy spruce, but not quick-growing. The pegs, or persisting bases of the leaves, left on the shoot are unusually large and prominent.

One of the oldest and largest specimens of *P. polita* grows at Stourhead, Wilts. Planted 1871, it measures 83 × 7½ ft (1970). The largest in the Home Counties is a tree at Petworth House, Sussex, measuring 80 × 7¼ ft (1971).

P. PUNGENS Engelm.   COLORADO OR BLUE SPRUCE
P. parryana Sarg.; *Abies parryana* Hort. Angl.

A tree 80 to 100, occasionally 150 ft, high; pyramidal as a small tree in cultivation with stiff horizontal branches; young twigs not downy; buds brownish yellow. Leaves arranged all round the branchlets, more thinly beneath, the upper ones pointing forward; they are ¾ to 1¼ in. long, stiff, quadrangular, spine-tipped, dark green in the type, with three or four lines of stomata on all four faces. Cones cylindrical, shining, straw-coloured when ripe; 3 or 4 in. long, about 1¼ in. wide; scales wavy, oval, blunt and jaggedly toothed at the apex; seeds ⅛ in. long, with a wing ¼ in. long.

Native of the Rocky Mountains, mainly in Colorado, E. Utah, E. New Mexico, and N. Arizona, but with scattered stands as far north as Montana; discovered by Dr Parry in 1862. It was in commerce in Britain by 1875, probably from seeds sent by the commercial collector Roezl, though some of those collected by Parry in 1865 may have been sent to Britain. Typical trees, with dark blue-green leaves, are very rare in gardens, where the species is almost wholly represented by the glaucous forms. There is an example at Westonbirt in Willesley Drive, measuring 56 × 4 ft (1969), and another at Leonardslee in Sussex.

P. pungens is allied to *P. engelmannii*, differing in its glabrous shoots, and in its bluer, more pungently pointed, leaves. Its bark becomes thick and furrowed on old trees, whereas in *P. engelmannii* it remains comparatively thin, and scaly.

PICEA PUNGENS

f. GLAUCA (Reg.) Beissn. and f. ARGENTEA Beissn. BLUE SPRUCE.— *P. pungens* varies much in the more or less glaucous hue of its foliage; many shades may be selected in any batch of seedlings, and the most striking, with blue or silvery leaves, have been perpetuated by grafting. The oldest known clone descends from a tree that grew in Prof. Sargent's garden at Harvard, where it had been raised from the seeds sent by Parry in 1865. Cuttings from this were taken by Anthony Waterer during a visit to America in 1877 and plants distributed by his Knap Hill nursery under the name *Abies parryana glauca*. This clone, which has never received a distinctive name, received a First Class Certificate in 1890. Probably many of the older trees are of the Knap Hill clone, though some may be seedlings. One of the original propagations still grows in the Knap Hill Nursery and measures 65 × 5¾ ft (1974). Two of the finest specimens are: Westonbirt House, Glos., 73 × 5½ ft (1967) and Tring Park, Herts, 65 × 6 ft.

To those who admire silvery trees the blue spruces may be recommended as some of the most handsome. This applies more to young specimens; with age they are apt to become rusty and thin of foliage at the bottom, especially those selected forms that have been grafted on common spruce.

The following are the more important named selections:

'ENDTZ'.—Of dense, conical habit, with horizontal branches. Leaves blue, silvery in winter, slightly falcate. Ultimate height at least 30 ft. Raised by L. J. Endtz of Boskoop, Holland.

'ERICH FRAHM'.—Leaves deep blue throughout the year. Of conical habit, attaining 30 ft at least. Raised by Timm & Co. of Elmshorn, Germany.

'GLAUCA GLOBOSA' ('GLOBOSA').—A dwarf, rounded, flat-topped bush, attaining 3 ft or so in height, more in width. Leaves bluish white, more or less radial. Raised in Holland.

'GLAUCA PROCUMBENS' and 'GLAUCA PROSTRATA'.—Of spreading or prostrate habit. It is uncertain whether these names really represent clones, since, as pointed out by Dr Krüssmann, similar plants can be raised from any of the varieties of blue spruce, by using lateral shoots as scions. The tree forms are always propagated from leading shoots.

'KOSTER'. KOSTER'S BLUE SPRUCE.—According to Den Ouden and Boom, this name does not represent a clone. The plants originally sent out by Koster towards the end of the last century were grafted from a number of selected seedlings with glaucous foliage. Later the firm of C. B. van Nes & Son made a re-selection of ten plants, uniform in habit and in their silvery-glaucous foliage, and the present commercial stock derives from these (*Man. Cult. Conif.* (1965), p. 283).

'MOERHEIM'.—Of slender, conical habit, ultimately 30 ft or more high. Leaves bluish white in both summer and winter. Raised by Ruys at the Moerheim nursery, Holland.

'MONTGOMERY'.—A dwarf bush, forming a broad cone. Leaves grey-blue. Raised in the USA.

P. RUBENS Sarg.   RED SPRUCE
P. rubra (Du Roi) Link, not A. Dietrich

The red spruce is a close ally of *P. mariana*, but appears to be extremely uncommon in cultivation. It is, apparently, on the average a considerably larger tree than *P. mariana*, being usually 70 to 80 ft high; it has similar although less persistently downy young shoots. The leaves are quadrangular, ½ to ¾ in. long, with stomatic lines on all four surfaces; they differ from those of *P. mariana* in being of a dark yellowish, rather than glaucous, green, and somewhat more slender. Cones reddish brown, up to 2 in. long and thus larger than those of *P. mariana*; the scales, too, are entire, or only slightly toothed at the apex. But the most marked distinction between the two is in the duration of the cones on the branches. In *P. rubens* they begin to fall as soon as the scales open, but in *P. mariana* they persist sometimes twenty or thirty years. In the wild *P. rubens* has a much more restricted distribution than *P. mariana*, being confined to eastern

N. America, where it extends from Prince Edward Island southward to the mountains of N. Carolina. Introduced in 1755. It has not much to recommend it for gardens beyond its interest. *Bot. Mag.*, t. 9446.

The oldest known examples of *P. rubens* grow in the Rhinefield Drive near Lyndhurst in the New Forest; they were planted in 1861 and the best measures 83 × 5¾ ft (1971). Others are: National Pinetum, Bedgebury, Kent, *pl.* 1925, 50 × 4¼ ft (1970), and several others slightly smaller; Wakehurst Place, Sussex, 59 × 3¾ ft (1970); Bicton, Devon, 60 × 4 ft (1968).

P. SCHRENKIANA Fisch. & Mey.

P. obovata var. *schrenkiana* (Fisch. & Mey.) Carr.; *P. tianschanica* Rupr.

A tall tree in the wild, of very slender habit; the branchlets are greyish white, glabrous or nearly so; the leaves arranged all round the twig, spine-tipped in young trees, blunter in adult ones, ¾ to 1¼ in. long, quadrangular, dark green, with two to four very indistinct lines of stomata on all four surfaces. Cones 3 to 4 in. long, cylindrical; scales rounded, and not toothed at the apex.

Native of Central Asia in the Djungarski Alatau and Tianshan (S.E. Kazakhstan), extending into Chinese Turkestan and said also to occur as far east as Kansu; discovered by Schrenk in 1840 and introduced to cultivation in western Europe around 1878. It was at first considered to be near to *P. obovata*, but Kent noted that the trees in Veitch's nursery, raised from the original seed, bore a very strong resemblance to *P. smithiana* of the Himalaya, and that is now considered to be the nearest ally of Schrenk's spruce. But the leaves of the latter are shorter than in *P. smithiana* and the radial arrangement is not so marked. Also, in cultivated trees of *P. schrenkiana* the branchlets are not pendulous, though they are said to be so quite frequently on wild trees. A tree at Bayfordbury, Herts, *pl.* 1907, measures 50 × 3½ ft (1973).

P. SITCHENSIS (Bongard) Carr.   SITKA SPRUCE

Pinus sitchensis Bongard; *Abies menziesii* Lindl.

A tree already over 150 ft high in Great Britain, occasionally 250 ft in its native state, bark scaling; young shoots very stiff, not downy, yellowish. Leaves standing out stiffly all round the branchlet, but thinnest underneath; ½ to 1¼ in. long, 1/12 to 1/20 in. wide, prickly pointed, green, mostly without stomata on the supper surface, silvery, with two bands of stomata beneath. Cones blunt, cylindrical, shortly stalked, 2½ to 4 in. long, about 1¼ in. wide, pale brown; scales oval-oblong, ½ to ⅝ in. long, rounded and toothed towards the apex; seeds ⅛ in. long, with a wing thrice as long.

Native of western N. America, near the coast, from Alaska to California; discovered in 1792 by Menzies; introduced by Douglas in 1831. The Sitka spruce is, above all, a moisture-loving tree, thriving best where the soil is permanently on the wet side. It grows admirably in the wet valleys of Scotland, forming in the open a broad pyramid. As an isolated tree it has, even in Scotland, the defect of retaining its inner branches and twigs after they are dead, and these the outer fringe of living growth is not dense enough to hide. Under such conditions it will make growths 4 ft long in a season, and attain a height of 100 ft in thirty years.

In commercial forestry, Sitka spruce has come to be of more importance than any other conifer, being well adapted to the cool, humid climate of the north and west, where most of the land available for afforestation now lies. The area under Sitka spruce amounted in 1965 to 612,000 acres, and was then being extended at the rate of 36,000 acres each year, which is far more than the annual planting of all other forest trees combined. Its timber equals that of Norway spruce in quality, and is produced rather more quickly.

Virtually all the notable specimens of Sitka spruce are in Scotland, and the oldest of these are mostly from the reintroduction by Jeffrey for the Oregon Association in 1851. These are now well over 100 ft high and a few have reached 150 ft or even more, and the girths are in the range 15 to 20 ft for the most part.

P. SMITHIANA (Wall.) Boiss.

Pinus smithiana Wall.; *Picea morinda* Link; *Abies khutrow* Loud.

A tree 100 to 120, sometimes 200 ft high, with horizontal branches, but perfectly pendulous branchlets; young shoots stiff, pale grey, shining, not downy; buds conical, often resinous, up to ½ in. long. Leaves arranged all round the twigs (rather more thinly beneath), standing out at an angle of about 60°; they are quadrangular, rigid, needle-like, with prickly points, 1½ in. long, often slightly curved, green with a few stomatic lines on each of the four faces. Cones cylindrical, tapered towards the apex, 4 to 7 in. long, 1½ to 2 in. wide, brown when mature; scales broadly rounded and entire at the margin.

Native of the W. Himalaya; introduced to Scotland in 1818 by Dr Govan of Cupar, who received cones from his son in India, which he gave to the Earl of Hopetoun; it is named after Sir James Smith, first President of the Linnean Society. It is distinct from the other spruces in the great length of leaf, and is also one of the most striking from the weeping character of its branchlets, which, perhaps, give it a somewhat funereal aspect. It is subject to injury by spring frost especially in the young state, and will thrive best in a situation shaded from early morning sun. It likes a moist, loamy soil.

An original tree still grows at Hopetoun in West Lothian, Scotland; it measures 90 × 10½ ft (1971), and there are several others in Scotland, slightly younger and of about the same size. A fine example at Taymouth Castle, Perths., measures 112 × 13¼ ft (1974). Some of the largest in southern Britain are: Cuffnels, Lyndhurst, Hants, 118 × 10¼ ft and 113 × 11 ft (1970); Melbury, Dorset, 108 × 12¼ and 111 × 11¼ ft (1970); Bicton, Devon, 107 × 10¼ ft (1968); Redleaf, Kent, 99 × 10¼ ft (1963); West Dean, Sussex, 105 × 9 ft (1973); Bowood, Wilts, 105 × 11¼ ft and 106 × 10½ ft (1968); Boconnoc, Cornwall, 100 × 12 ft (1970); Nettlecombe, Somerset, 100 × 9 ft (1971); Bolderwood, New Forest, 111 × 8½ ft (1970).

P. SPINULOSA (Griff.) Henry

Abies spinulosa Griff.; *Picea morindoides* Rehd.

A tree of large size, over 200 ft high, branches pendulous at the ends; young shoots pale, yellowish, without down. Leaves arranged all round the shoot most thinly underneath, the upper ones appressed to the branch and pointing forward; they are needle-like, ½ to 1⅓ in. long, sharply pointed; green and without stomata on the uppermost side, glaucous, with stomatic lines beneath. Cones cylindric, 2½ to 3½ in. long, 1 to 1¼ in. wide; purple when young, pale brown when mature; scales blunt at the apex, the margins jagged. *Bot. Mag.*, t. 8169.

A native of the E. Himalaya from Sikkim to Assam (and probably of Upper Burma also); discovered by Griffith in N. Bhutan and shortly described by him in 1848; introduced by Sir George King, Director of the Calcutta Botanic Garden, who sent seeds to a number of European gardens and botanical institutions around 1878, probably collected in the Chumbi area of Sikkim (Elwes and Henry, *Tr. Gt. Brit. & Irel.*, Vol. 6, p. 1393). The oldest one in the British Isles, at Castlewellan in Co. Down, is from seeds received from Calcutta about ten years later. At that time this very distinct spruce was scarcely known, and thought to be the same as *P. smithiana* (*morinda*). The first full description was drawn up by Dr Alfred Rehder in 1903 from a tree growing in M. Allard's famous collection at Angers. He believed it to be a new, undescribed species, naming it *P. morindoides*.

P. spinulosa grows well in the south and west, but develops a sparsely branched, open crown. With its pendulous shoots it bears some resemblance to *P. smithiana*, but in that species each branch is curtained, whereas in *P. spinulosa* the pendulous shoots are confined to the end of the branches. The two species are quite different in their leaves. Those of *P. smithiana* are quadrangular, with a few stomatic lines on all four surfaces. *P. spinulosa* belongs to the flat-leaved Omorika group.

The oldest specimen of *P. spinulosa* grows at Castlewellan in Co. Down. It was planted around 1890 and measures 84 × 10 ft. Some other examples are: Wakehurst Place, Sussex, *pl.* 1916, 64 × 4¾ ft (1970); Borde Hill, Sussex, 88 × 8 ft (1974); Melbury, Dorset, *pl.* 1899, 85 × 6½ ft (1971); Bodnant, Denb., *pl. c.* 1915, 88 × 6½ ft (1974). In Eire, there is a fine tree at Fota, Co. Cork, *pl.* 1914, measuring 71 × 4¾ ft (1966).

P. WILSONII Mast.

P. watsoniana Mast.

A tree 70 to 80 ft high of shapely pyramidal form, with short horizontally spreading branches. Young shoots quite glabrous, pale, greyish, becoming whitish the second year; 'pegs' left by the fallen leaves quite small. Leaves stoutish, quadrangular, sharply pointed, up to ⅝ in. long, densely set and pointing forwards on the upper side, those beneath spreading laterally at right angles to the shoot in two sets. Cones ovoid to cylindrical, 1½ to 3 in. long; cone-scales thin, broadly rounded, slightly jagged at the margin. Wilson observes that the cones are very freely produced and remain on the tree for a year or more after they are ripe. *Bot. Mag.*, n.s., t. 107.

Native of China, where it is common in the mountains of N.W. Szechwan and N.W. Hupeh and extends northward to Kansu and Shansi. A sterile specimen was collected by Augustine Henry in 1888, but the species was first described from fuller material collected by Wilson, and was introduced by him in 1901 for Messrs Veitch (Seed No. 1309).

PICRASMA   SIMAROUBACEAE

A genus of about six species in E. Asia and the S.W. Pacific, mostly tropical or subtropical in distribution. It belongs to the same family as *Ailanthus*, differing in the axillary inflorescences and fleshy fruits. The specific epithet of the species described here refers to its resemblance to *Quassia amara*, which is the source of the intensely bitter quassia wood.

P. QUASSIOIDES (D. Don) Bennett
Simaba quassioides D. Don; *P. ailanthoides* Planch.

A slender, deciduous tree 20 to 40 ft high, with very handsome young bark of a reddish brown, conspicuously marked with yellow spots. Leaves alternate, pinnate, 10 to 15 in. long, glabrous, consisting of nine to thirteen leaflets, which are glossy green, 1 to 4 in. long, ovate, unequal at the base, round or pointed at the apex, sharp-toothed at the margin, and with a very short stalk. Flowers green, $\frac{1}{3}$ in. across, in a lax, branching corymb 6 to 8 in. long, and often nearly as wide; stalks downy. Fruit a berry, about the size of a pea, red, rather obovoid, with the calyx still attached. *Bot. Mag.*, n.s., t. 279.

This tree is widespread in the wild state, from Japan and Korea through China to the Himalaya. The above description is based on trees growing at Kew which were introduced from Japan in 1890. They have flowered and borne fruit several times, and young plants have been raised from the seed. They have no beauty of flower or fruit, but of the foliage in autumn Sargent observes, 'few Japanese plants I saw are as beautiful as this small tree'. The leaves turn first orange then scarlet. The whole tree is permeated by a singularly bitter principle.

P. quassioides is rare in cultivation, the following being the only sizeable ones on record: Kew, near the Stone Pine, 29 × 5 ft at 6 in. (1967); Wakehurst Place, Sussex, a many-stemmed plant 20 ft high; University Botanic Garden, Cambridge, *pl.* 1923, 18 × 1$\frac{1}{2}$ ft at 3 ft (1969); Westonbirt, Glos., Mitchell Drive (East), *pl.* 1919, 26 × 1 ft (1967).

PIERIS ERICACEAE

A genus of about ten species, the hardy ones of which are found in N. America, Himalaya, Japan, and China. They are evergreen or deciduous shrubs, sometimes tree-like, with alternate leaves; flowers in terminal or axillary racemes or panicles, formed in autumn, but not opening until the following spring. Corolla more or less pitcher-shaped, five-toothed; calyx five-lobed and persistent; stamens ten. Seed-vessel a globose capsule.

All the pierises are handsome shrubs of neat habit, and great freedom in blossoming. They need the same conditions and treatment as rhododendron; that is, either a peaty soil or a light lime-free loam improved by the addition of decayed leaves. They are also moisture-lovers at the root. Propagation is effected by seed, by layering, or late summer cuttings.

P. FLORIBUNDA (Pursh) Benth. & Hook. f.
Andromeda floribunda Pursh ex Sims

An evergreen shrub from 3 to 6 ft high, of bushy, rounded habit, and when in good condition furnished right to the ground, the branches rather stiff; shoots and leaf-stalks furnished with dark bristles appressed to the stem, and pointing forwards. Leaves ovate, $1\frac{1}{2}$ to 3 in. long, $\frac{1}{2}$ to 1 in. wide, pointed, rounded or tapering at the base, slightly toothed, bristly at the edges, dark glossy green above, paler beneath, sprinkled with very short black hairs on both surfaces; stalk $\frac{1}{4}$ to $\frac{3}{8}$ in. long. Flowers produced in March and April in erect terminal panicles 2 to 5 in. high, each consisting of several slender, downy racemes; corolla pure white, pitcher-shaped, $\frac{1}{4}$ in. long, calyx-lobes ovate; flower-stalk decurved so as to bring all the flowers to the lower side, and furnished with two linear bracts. *Bot. Mag.*, t. 1566.

Native of the south-eastern United States; introduced in 1800. This is one of the most beautiful and hardy of flowering evergreens, slow-growing and of neat bushy habit, admirable for planting in groups.

cv. 'ELONGATA'—A very fine form from Keeper's Hill Nursery, given an Award of Merit at Vincent Square, April 5, 1938. Some of the racemes were 8 in. long.

P. FORMOSA (Wall.) D. Don [PLATE 29
Andromeda formosa Wall.; *Lyonia formosa* (Wall.) Hand.-Mazz.

A large evergreen shrub 8 to 12, or sometimes up to 25 ft, high, spreading half as much more in diameter; young wood glabrous. Leaves oblong-oblanceolate or oblong-elliptic, 3 to 7 in. long, 1 to $2\frac{1}{4}$ in. wide; pointed, tapering at the base, finely toothed to the base, glabrous, and dark glossy green, of firm leathery texture. Flowers produced during May in a cluster of panicles, terminating the shoots of the previous year, and from 4 to 6 in. long and wide. Corolla pendent, white, pitcher-shaped, $\frac{1}{4}$ to $\frac{5}{16}$ in. long, contracted at the mouth, where are five shallow, rounded teeth; calyx-lobes $\frac{1}{8}$ in. long, green, narrowly ovate; flower-stalk $\frac{1}{4}$ in. or less long, with a pair of bracts. *Bot. Mag.*, t. 8283.

P. *formosa* is a wide-ranging species, from Nepal through the eastern Himalaya, Assam, upper Burma to south-west and parts of central China at 6,000 to 11,000 ft; the date of introduction is not known, but it was cultivated at Lamorran in Cornwall in 1881. This shrub is perfectly hardy and reaches a large size in the woodland gardens of southern England, though the finest specimens are to be found in Cornwall, where it attains a height of 25 ft. As in P. *japonica* and P. *taiwanensis*, the panicles are produced in autumn, and it has been suggested that when they drop prematurely the cause is dryness at the root rather than frost.

In China, P. *formosa* appears to be more variable than in the Himalaya, which is the source of all the older plants. In addition to the forms represented in cultivation, and discussed below, there are some with remarkably small leaves, suggesting P. *japonica* rather than P. *formosa*—indeed two specimens collected by Forrest in Yunnan during his first journey were originally identified as that species.

P. *formosa* received a First Class Certificate when shown from Caerhays on April 29, 1969.

At Wakehurst Place in Sussex there is a plant of typical P. *formosa* raised from Forrest 8945, collected in Yunnan on the Shweli–Salween divide in 1912 at 9,000–10,000 ft. It has made a dense many-stemmed bush about 15 ft high, with leathery, rather stiff, slightly undulated leaves very rugulose above, elliptic to broadly so or slightly ovate, relatively rather broad for the species, $2\frac{3}{4}$ to $3\frac{1}{2}$ in. long, $1\frac{1}{8}$ to $1\frac{5}{8}$ in. wide, dull brownish red when young; in Forrest's original material under this number the leaves are similar, though rather smaller. The flowers are produced in large panicles about once every three years; corolla about $\frac{5}{16}$ in. long; calyx pale green. There is a matching plant at Borde Hill which was planted before 1935 as *Pieris* species F.8945, and is believed to have come from Messrs Marchant. Flowering material from the Wakehurst plant was exhibited by Sir Henry Price on March 20, 1957, and received an Award of Merit. Unfortunately the award was given to it under the cultivar-name 'Wakehurst', which traditionally belongs to a clone of P. *formosa* var. *forrestii* (see below). The application of the same cultivar-name to two quite different plants has been the source of much confusion and should be rectified. The plant discussed here is inferior to the true 'Wakehurst', and slow-growing and tender when young.

A late-flowering form of P. *formosa* was exhibited by Mrs Warren, The Hyde, Handcross, Sussex, on June 23, 1964, under number Forrest 29002. The flowers are about the normal size for the species but the leaves are unusually narrow, $2\frac{5}{8}$ to $3\frac{1}{4}$ in. long, $\frac{5}{8}$ to 1 in. wide. There are plants at Borde Hill, Sussex, of unknown provenance, with the same narrow leaves and also late-flowering. The young foliage is bronzy, and the flowers are borne in stiffly branched panicles; calyx white, sometimes tipped with green. They are very hardy and flower every year.

var. FORRESTII (Harrow) Airy Shaw P. *forrestii* Harrow; *Gaultheria forrestii* Hort., not Diels—This variety was described in 1914, as a species, from a plant raised from seeds collected by Forrest. There is no specimen from the original wild plant, but according to Forrest the seeds came from the Tali range in Yunnan. There can be little doubt that they were collected during his first expedition for A. K. Bulley (1904–6), not the second (1910). In 1914 the only plants in cultivation were those growing in the Royal Botanic Garden at Edinburgh and in the nurseries of Messrs Bees (of which firm Mr Bulley was the founder and proprietor). The description was made from a plant at Edinburgh, then some 3 ft high, and was probably drawn up by W. W. Smith, though the name is attributed to R. L. Harrow, who was Principal Gardener there at the time. In the original description it was said that *P. forrestii* was very near to *P. formosa*, differing in a number of minor points,'the sum of which is beyond mere varietal divergence'. These were, notably, the more pendent habit, the slenderer pedicels with more narrow bracts, the whitish sepals, the rounder, longer corolla, more constricted at the mouth, which had 'straight-cut pentagonal edges' and shorter, more erect lobes; and the longer and slenderer style. No mention was made of the colour of the young foliage.

A different view of *P. forrestii* was taken by the Kew botanist H. K. Airy Shaw, in an article accompanying the plate in the *Botanical Magazine*, t. 9371. He wrote: 'Examination of the ample . . . material of *P. formosa* and *P. Forrestii* in the Kew Herbarium shows that the latter constitutes what may be termed the "*grandiflora*" end of a long series, between the members of which no hard and fast lines can be drawn. Although it is possible that a monographer might feel inclined to sweep the subject of our plate into the oblivion of total synonymy, the middle course of according it varietal rank has been adopted, as being possibly the best compromise between scientific conscientiousness and horticultural expediency.'

P. formosa var. *forrestii* is represented in commerce mainly by the following clone, which should not be confused with the plant which received an Award of Merit in 1957 under the name 'Wakehurst' (see above):

cv. 'WAKEHURST'.—A shrub up to 18 ft high. Leaves oblong-elliptic to oblanceolate, apex acute or acuminate, sharply pointed, base cuneate to narrowly rounded, margins serrated, brilliant red when unfolding in March or April, fading to crimson pink, then almost colourless for a while before turning chlorotic green and eventually the normal deep green. Flowers in large trusses, profusely borne in some years; calyx white; corolla broad-urceolate, about ⅜ in. long. It is hardy and vigorous, but the young growths may be killed by spring frost.

'Wakehurst' received a First Class Certificate on May 20, 1930, as *P. forrestii*, when exhibited by Gerald Loder of Wakehurst Place, Sussex. There are still several plants in the garden, and larger ones at Nymans and Borde Hill in the same county, both known to have come from Wakehurst. The history of this clone is not known. According to previous editions of this work, the Wakehurst plant was raised from F.8945, but it differs so much from Forrest's original specimen, and from plants known to have been raised from this batch of seed, as to suggest that Loder inadvertently misinformed the author about its origin. But for this statement it would never have been doubted that 'Wakehurst' derived from the original introduction of var. *forrestii*. It certainly bears a strong resemblance to the type, i.e., the plant to which the name *P. forrestii* was originally given.

Six years before the Wakehurst plant received the First Class Certificate, A. K. Bulley exhibited the var. *forrestii* at the Chelsea Show, when it was given an Award of Merit (May 27, 1924, as *P. forrestii*). The foliage was said to be salmon-pink—the colour 'Wakehurst' would have at that season. There is at the present time a large plant of the var. *forrestii* in what was once Mr Bulley's garden, now the Botanic Gardens of the University of Liverpool, at Ness in Cheshire, which has young foliage of a brilliant red. Mr J. K. Hulme, the Director, tells us that one of the old gardeners there remembers having helped to move this plant to its present position in 1919, when it was already a good size. This plant bears a strong resemblance to 'Wakehurst'; so too does the material figured in the *Botanical Magazine*, the source of which was a plant at Headfort, raised from a cutting received from Edinburgh in 1920. That the Ness plant is an original from Forrest's seeds is almost beyond doubt, and it is very likely, though perhaps unprovable now, that the original commercial stock sold as *P. forrestii*, including the Wakehurst plant, derives from this.

The form of Forrest's variety that most impressed the collector himself was found by him in April 1925. The note attached to his flowering specimens (F.26518) reads: 'In every sense a most exceptional species. Habit good, foliage and flowers most attractive, the latter finer than anything I have yet seen of this class, large and purely coloured and produced most freely. A finer thing than even the type.' He found it on the Burma–Yunnan frontier on the western flank of the Nmai Hka–Salween divide at 10,000 ft, as a shrub 5 to 6 ft high. He introduced it the same autumn (F.27401, which is the duplicate in fruit of F.26518).

In cultivation, this introduction has proved to be very unlike the var. *forrestii* as generally known. The flowers are of a remarkable size, sometimes not much less than ½ in. long, borne in stiff, upright panicles, and the young foliage is bright green. Material of F.26518 in the Kew Herbarium is from Borde Hill in Sussex and from Fota, Co. Cork, Eire. There is a similar specimen from Trewithen, Cornwall, without number. Plants at Caerhays in the same county, one now 20 ft high, were raised from seed under F.27765 and F.27165, but these numbers are wrong, the first belonging to a *Vaccinium* species and the latter to a *Camellia* species. The clone 'CHARLES MICHAEL' derives from the Caerhays plant under F.27765, and is available in commerce. The panicles are upright, about 8 in. long, 4 in. wide, and the corollas ½ in. long. The young growths are bronze-coloured. A.M. 1965.

P. 'FOREST FLAME'.—Leaves oblanceolate or oblong-oblanceolate, acute at the apex, narrowly tapered to the base, up to 5 in. long by 1 in. wide, margins with close, shallow serrations. This clone arose at the Sunningdale Nurseries as a self-sown seedling at the foot of a plant of *P. japonica*. It is near to this species in the shape and toothing of its leaves, but their colouring when young and their size, as well as the vigour of the plant, suggests that *P. formosa* var. *forrestii*, or possibly *P. formosa* F.8945, was the other parent. It comes into growth somewhat earlier than 'Wakehurst'. The foliage is not quite so vivid when young, but is more elegant, and the habit of young plants is more compact and symmetrical. Award of Merit May 1, 1973. Similar to this, and also a hybrid, is 'FIRECREST', put into commerce by Messrs Waterer, Sons and Crisp. It was originally distributed as '*Pieris* species F.8945', and presumably a plant under

that number was the seed-parent. The other parent was probably *P. japonica.*
'Firecrest' received an Award of Merit on May 1, 1973.

P. JAPONICA (Thunb.) D. Don   [PLATE 30

Andromeda japonica Thunb.

An evergreen shrub, ultimately 9 or 10 ft high, of bushy habit, and clothed
to the ground with branches; young shoots usually glabrous. Leaves leathery,

PIERIS JAPONICA

oblanceolate or narrowly oval, usually widest above the middle, tapering
towards both ends, 1¼ to 3½ in. long, ⅓ to ¾ in. wide, shallowly toothed, dark
glossy green above, paler beneath, glabrous on both surfaces. Flowers in a
terminal cluster of slender pendulous racemes each 3 to 6 in. long; corolla
white, pitcher-shaped, ¼ to ⅜ in. long, narrowed towards the mouth, where are
five shallow, rounded teeth; calyx-lobes lanceolate, scarcely half as long as the
corolla; flower-stalk ⅛ in. long, glabrous.

Native of Japan. This shrub is not so hardy as *P. floribunda*, from which it is
easily distinguished by the leaves being narrower and more tapering at the
base, by the pendulous inflorescence, and by the absence of hairs on the young
wood and flower-stalks. It flowers in March and April, and is often injured by
frost. At its best it is a very beautiful shrub. It should be given a sheltered
spot, with a western exposure.

cv. 'BERT CHANDLER' ('Chandleri').—Young leaves at first bright salmon-pink, paling through cream to white and becoming the normal green by mid-summer. A seedling raised by the Australian nurseryman Bert Chandler around 1936 (*Gard. Chron.*, Vol. 167 (1970), p. 4).

cv. 'DAISEN'.—Flowers deep pink in the bud, paling as they open. The original plant was found on Mount Daisen in Japan and put into commerce by Mr K. Wada (see his article '*Pieris japonica* and its Future' in *Journ. R.H.S.*, Vol. 92 (1967), pp. 26–8). According to him, the colour is best developed in shade. 'CHRISTMAS CHEER' is a seedling of this and of the same character, but it opens some of its flowers in winter, whence the name. Raised by Mr Wada.

cv. 'PURITY'.—Flowers pure white, unusually large. A Japanese variety reputed to have come from Yakushima, and originally distributed as *P. yakusimana*, though Mr Wada suggests that it may be a 'natural sport' (loc. cit.). It appears to be intermediate in foliage between *P. japonica* and *P. taiwanensis*, but according to Mr Wada, no plant known to have come from Yakushima resembles 'Purity'.

f. PYGMAEA (Maxim.) Yatabe *Andromeda japonica* lusus *pygmaea* Maxim.—This was described by Maximowicz from a plant of Japanese gardens, about 1 ft high, with linear-lanceolate leaves about one-third of the usual size, and with more sparsely flowered, sometimes unbranched, inflorescences. A similar plant has been found growing wild on Mount Daisen in Japan (Wada, loc. cit.).

It may be mentioned here that prostrate plants only 10 in. high and a yard across were found by M. Robert de Belder on Mt Miyanoura, Yakushima, in November 1970, from which seeds were collected (*Int. Dendr. Soc. Ybk* (1972), p. 29).

cv. 'VARIEGATA'.—This has narrower leaves than the type, edged, espec-ially towards the apex, with yellowish white. Well grown, it is one of the most attractive of variegated evergreens. It is slow-growing at first, but has reached a height of 12 ft at Grayswood Hill, Haslemere, and is almost as tall at Nymans in Sussex and at the Sunningdale Nurseries, Berks.

P. NANA (Maxim.) Makino

Andromeda nana Maxim.; *Cassiope oxycoccoides* A. Gray; *Arcterica oxycoccoides* (A. Gr.) Cov.; *Arcterica nana* (Maxim.) Makino

An evergreen shrub of prostrate habit growing only 3 or 4 in. high; young shoots finely downy. Leaves leathery, arranged in whorls of three or occasion-ally in pairs, oval with recurved margins, $\frac{1}{4}$ to $\frac{3}{8}$ in. long, rounded at the base, terminated by a gland at the apex, not toothed, quite glabrous on both surfaces, dark glossy green above; stalk very short. Flowers fragrant, white, roundish urn-shaped, $\frac{1}{16}$ in. long, contracted at the mouth to five short teeth; they are in terminal clusters or racemes of three or four flowers, and open in late April or May. Sepals ovate, persisting through the fruiting stage; flower-stalks downy, the main-stalk $\frac{1}{4}$ in. or so long, the individual stalks very short, each bearing one or more bracts.

Native of middle and N. Japan to Kamchatka, also of Bering Island. It is very hardy and flowers freely, but needs a cool position and a moist, peaty soil. It received an Award of Merit when shown by Messrs Reuthe in 1924.

This species is usually placed in *Arcterica*, a genus created for it by Prof. F. Coville in 1901. It was transferred to *Pieris* by the Japanese botanist Makino in 1894 but he later came to accept Coville's view that it represented a distinct genus. It is certainly very distinct in appearance from any other pieris (except perhaps from pygmy forms of *P. japonica*).

P. TAIWANENSIS Hayata

A compact evergreen shrub usually not more than 6 ft high in cultivation, with yellowish green, perfectly glabrous young shoots. Leaves oblanceolate or oval, tapered towards both ends, bluntish at the apex, shallowly toothed at the upper half only, 2 to 5 in. long, $\frac{1}{2}$ to 1 in. wide, stout and leathery, deep glossy green above, pale green beneath, quite glabrous. Flowers in a cluster of racemes or in panicles at the end of the shoot, each one of which is 3 to 6 in. long, the stalks minutely downy, the flowers nodding. Corolla pure white, urn-shaped, $\frac{3}{8}$ in. long, $\frac{1}{4}$ in. wide, with five small, slightly reflexed lobes at the much contracted mouth. Sepals normally five, but sometimes reduced apparently to three or four through one or two pairs being united, green, glabrous outside, tipped with down inside, ovate, $\frac{1}{8}$ in. long. Stamens white, $\frac{1}{10}$ in. long, thickened towards the base, slightly downy except at the top; anthers brown, with two awns at the back; style $\frac{1}{5}$ in. long. Flowers in April. *Bot. Mag.*, t. 9016.

Native of Formosa, where it inhabits open places in the mountains from 6,000 to 11,000 ft; introduced by Wilson in 1918. Grown under glass, it flowered at Kew when only two years old, raised from seed. It received an Award of Merit when shown by Lord Headfort in 1922, and a First Class Certificate in the following year. In the article accompanying the plate in the *Botanical Magazine*, Dr Stapf remarked that *P. taiwanensis* is variable in the posture of its inflorescences, from upright to drooping, adding that the variation is independent of external conditions, 'both extremes occurring indeed in the same sowing'. In the form usually seen in cultivation, the inflorescence branches are more or less horizontal, not drooping as in *P. japonica*. To that species *P. taiwanensis* is certainly very closely allied. The difference given by Dr Stapf is that in *P. japonica* the leaves are smaller and thinner, more finely crenulate from the base, the raceme-spindles and pedicels more slender and the flowers smaller. But whether these differences would hold good if a large amount of material were available for study is not certain. See also *P. formosa*.

P. taiwanensis is hardy, perhaps rather more so than *P. japonica*, and at least under woodland conditions its flowers and young growths are rarely cut by spring frost and self-sown seedlings often appear around the parent plant. It received an Award of Garden Merit in 1964.

PILEOSTEGIA HYDRANGEACEAE

A genus of probably only two species in temperate E. Asia, closely allied to *Schizophragma* and perhaps to be included in it. Apart from the immaterial difference that the species of *Pileostegia* are evergreen against deciduous in *Schizophragma*, there is really nothing to separate the two genera except that in the latter some flowers are sterile and bear large showy sepals, whereas in *Pileostegia* all the sepals are normal. But as Dr Stapf pointed out in the article accompanying *Bot. Mag.*, t. 9262, some species included without question in *Hydrangea* lack the showy ray-flowers shown by the majority of the species (e.g. *H. hirta* and *H. serratifolia*). If the presence or absence of this character in *Hydrangea* is not considered to be of generic value, it is scarcely justifiable to use it to separate *Pileostegia* from *Schizophragma*. Dr Stapf accordingly transferred *P. viburnoides* to *Schizophragma*, which was the first of the two genera to be described.

P. VIBURNOIDES Hook. f. & Thoms. [PLATE 31]
Schizophragma viburnoides (Hook. f. & Thoms.) Stapf

An evergreen prostrate or climbing shrub described as from 10 to 20 ft high, in the wild growing over trees and cliffs; young leaves and shoots at first scurfy, afterwards quite glabrous. Leaves opposite, leathery, entire, narrowly oblong, obovate or oval, pointed, tapered at the base, 2½ to 6 in. long, ¾ to 2½ in. wide, dark, dullish green, strongly veined and minutely pitted beneath; stalk ⅓ to 1 in. long. Flowers milky white, usually densely crowded in a terminal panicle 4 to 6 in. wide and high, opening in September and October. Each flower is about ⅜ in. wide, with four or five petals and twice as many stamens; the latter are ¼ in. long, white, and make the most conspicuous feature of the inflorescence. Calyx cup-shaped at the base with four or five short lobes. Fruit a small, dry, top-shaped capsule, rather like that of a hydrangea, to which genus *Pileostegia* is nearly akin. *Bot. Mag.*, t. 9262.

Native of the Khasi Hills, India, also of China and Formosa. The plants in cultivation were introduced by Wilson, who sent seed to the Arnold Arboretum which he had collected in 1908. This, the only species of the genus as yet described, makes an excellent evergreen climber for a wall, covering it densely with its foliage and clinging of itself by aerial roots. Grown on a west wall at Kew, it has shown no sign of tenderness there. The late Hon. Vicary Gibbs first showed it at Westminster in bloom during September 1914, and sixteen years later Lord Wakehurst exhibited fine flowering sprays during the same month. It likes a good soil and is easily propagated by cuttings.

PIMELEA THYMELAEACEAE

A genus of about eighty species of evergreen shrubs and subshrubs, ranging from the Philippines to Australia, Tasmania, and New Zealand. Leaves usually opposite and often decussate. Flowers in terminal heads. Corolla, as in *Daphne*, consisting of a four-lobed perianth. Stamens two, inserted in the throat of the perianth. Ovary one-celled. Fruits small, dry or fleshy, containing a single stone.

The genus contains many decorative shrubs, not hardy with us. The species described here seems to be the only one grown out-of-doors, but P. TRAVERSII might not be too tender and seems worthy of trial (see Philipson and Hearn, *Rock Garden Plants of the Southern Alps*, pp. 104–5).

P. PROSTRATA (J. R. & G. Forst.) Willd.

Banksia prostrata J. R. & G. Forst.; *Pimelea laevigsta* Gaertn.; *P. coarctata* Hort.

A dwarf shrub of variable habit, with the main branches prostrate and mat-forming, or semi-erect, or tortuous and congested; bark dark brown ageing to grey or almost black; branchlets covered with short down or sometimes with longer, spreading hairs. Leaves opposite, rather closely spaced, more or less four-ranked, spreading or deflexed, sometimes very crowded and overlapping, $\frac{1}{8}$ to $\frac{1}{4}$ in. long, one-third to one-half as wide, variable in shape, sessile or almost so, rather leathery, more or less concave beneath, the upper surface dull green, sometimes grey-green, the margins often tinged with red. Flowers perfect or unisexual, white, fragrant, clustered at the tips of the short side branches. Perianth-tube swollen at the base, hairy on the outside, $\frac{1}{16}$ to $\frac{1}{8}$ in. long, the female flowers rather smaller than the staminate and perfect ones. Fruits fleshy, or sometimes dry, usually white, about $\frac{1}{12}$ in. long. *Bot. Mag.*, t. 9010.

Native of both islands of New Zealand, where it occurs in a variety of open habitats from the coast up to about 4,500 ft. Although not completely hardy, it is of easy cultivation in the rock garden, in a sunny position, but prefers a deep, cool root-run. The fragrant flowers, though individually inconspicuous, are borne in great profusion in summer, and the small fruits, like grains of rice, are produced by hermaphrodite plants. It is, in the wild, a species of the greatest complexity; for a discussion of its variations see *Flora of New Zealand*, Vol. 1 (1961), pp. 295–6.

P. prostrata received an Award of Merit in 1955 and again in 1965, the second award being to a form known in gardens as *P. coarctata* or *P. prostrata* var. *coarctata* (*Bull. A.G.S.*, Vol. 23 (1955), p. 367 and Vol. 33 (1965), p. 354).

PINUS   PINACEAE

Among coniferous trees the pines constitute by far the most important
group, regarded either from the point of view of number of species or
that of economic value. As timber trees they easily predominate over any
other genus in the northern hemisphere. They are evergreen, and range
from trees over 200 ft high to mere shrubs; very resinous, producing
their branches in tiers.

The leaves of pines are nearly always produced in clusters or bundles
of from two to five, occasionally there are six, and in *P. cembroides monophylla* they are solitary. Each bundle is really a much reduced lateral
spur, which bears at the base a few scale-like bracts (the sheath), followed
by leaves in the number characteristic of the species, after which the growing point of the spur aborts. The seedling leaves of all pines are solitary,
the adult condition commencing to appear in the second and third years.
The individual leaf or 'needle' is long and narrow, mostly finely toothed
at the margin, and always more or less conspicuously lined with rows of
minute white, or whitish, dots called stomata. Where the leaves are in
bundles of two the transverse section of each is semicircular, in the bundles
of three to five they are three-sided. Each bundle of leaves, whatever their
number, forms in the aggregate a slender cylinder. At the base of each
bundle is a sheath, whose varying length and duration give very useful
indications of the identity of the species. The leaf-bearing shoots of each
season are always to a greater or less extent naked at the base, being
furnished there with 'scale-leaves' only—small, thin, membranous bodies,
often fringed, and usually falling away quickly. The terminal winter-bud
is an important differentiating character according to its shape and size,
the character of the scales by which it is covered, and whether it be
resinous or not, although in some species the last character is variable.

The flowers of pines are unisexual and borne in conical clusters, the
males at the base, the females at the apex of the year's growth; the female
inflorescence develops the second year into a woody fruit often of great
size and weight, commonly known as a cone, and of egg-shaped, cylindrical, or tapered form. These cones are composed of a number of woody
scales which vary in length, in thickness, and in the character of the scar or
boss at the end, and in the presence or absence of spines. When the cone
is ripe (most frequently at the end of the second year), the scale opens and
allows the two seeds at its base to escape; but some species take longer, and
several appear never to release their seeds at all unless through some outside agency such as fire (in the West American forests), or squirrels, or
birds. Some species have small seeds which are furnished with a large
membranous wing whose object is to assist in their dispersion. The larger,
edible seeds have only rudimentary wings or none at all.

As garden or park trees the pines are of varying merit, but the best of
them are amongst the noblest of evergreens. They do not need a rich soil
so much as an open, well-drained one. The hardier ones, like *P. banksiana,
P. uncinata* and *P. sylvestris,* grow in some of the most inclement parts
of the globe. On chalky soils *P. nigra, P. brutia, P. halepensis, P. pinea*

and others succeed very well. For spots exposed to sea-gales and in maritime situations generally *P. nigra, P. radiata, P. muricata, P. pinaster,* and *P. thunbergii* are extremely useful in building up the first line of protection against sea-winds. The genus has given rise to many valuable dwarf varieties, suitable for the rockgarden or as specimens in small gardens, and some species are naturally dwarf, e.g., *P. pumila* and *P. mugo.*

The garden varieties have to be increased by grafting on the types to which they belong, but all other pines must be grown from seed. With few exceptions it is desirable to get them planted in their permanent places as young as possible.

P. ALBICAULIS Engelm.   WHITEBARK PINE
P. flexilis var. *albicaulis* (Engelm.) Engelm.

A shrub 10 to 20 ft high, rarely a tree twice as high; in the smaller state usually with two or three main stems. Young branchlets yellowish brown, minutely downy or glabrous, becoming grey the second or third year, finally whitish. Leaves in fives, persisting five to seven years, 1 to $2\frac{1}{2}$ in. long, green with whitish stomatic lines on all three surfaces, stiffly pointed; not toothed at the margins; leaf-sheaths $\frac{5}{8}$ in. long, soon falling. Cones indehiscent, $1\frac{1}{2}$ to 3 in. long, and nearly as thick; scales very thick, with a spine-tipped boss. Seeds about $\frac{1}{2}$ in. long, with little or no wing, sweet, edible.

Native of western N. America at high elevations, becoming in cold bleak sites reduced to dwarf scrub. It was introduced by Jeffrey in 1852, but subsequently disappeared from cultivation, and is still scarcely represented in Britain. The only recorded specimen is one at Kew 18 ft high, raised from seeds received early this century. It is closely allied to *P. flexilis* and the two species occupy similar habitats. But *P. albicaulis* has a more northern distribution, and is very different from *P. flexilis* in its cones. The popular name (and the specific epithet) refer to the whitish bark of very old trees.

P. ARMANDII Franch.   DAVID'S PINE
P. mastersiana Hayata; *P. armandii* var. *mastersiana* Hayata

A medium-sized tree in the wild, with very much the aspect, in a young state, of *P. wallichiana;* young shoots greyish green, often covered at first more or less densely with translucent glands. Leaves in fives, mostly falling the second year, 4 to 6 in. long, white with stomata on two sides, glossy green on the third, pointed, minutely toothed on the margin; leaf-sheath soon falling away. Cones 4 to 8 in. long, $2\frac{1}{2}$ to 3 in. wide before expanding, tapering slightly from the base. Scales thick, broadly triangular, about $1\frac{1}{4}$ in. long. *Bot. Mag.,* t. 8347.

Native of western and central China, particularly common in the south-west, where it extends into Burma; it also occurs in Formosa and (according to some authorities) in Korea. A closely related species (not further mentioned) is found in the Japanese islands of Yakushima and Tanega-shima—P. AMAMIANA

Koidz. *P. armandii* is named after the great French missionary-naturalist Père Armand David, who discovered it in Shensi in 1873. It was introduced to Britain by Augustine Henry, who sent seeds to Kew from Mengtsz in S. Yunnan in 1897. But two years previously seeds had reached Maurice de Vilmorin at Les Barres from the French missionary Père Farges.

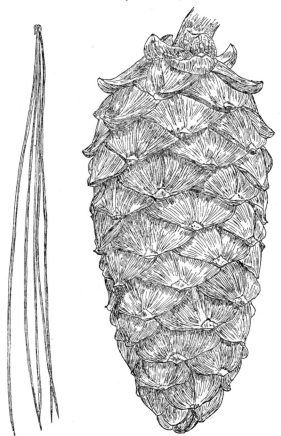

PINUS ARMANDII

The trees at Kew raised from the seeds sent by Henry grew quickly when once established, and first bore cones (infertile) in 1909. Two of these trees still exist; they are 52 and 60 ft high respectively, and about 3¾ ft in girth (1971).

P. *armandii*, although of interest as one of the very few pines of China, is of no value as an ornamental tree and does not thrive so well as the Himalayan five-needled pine—*P. wallichiana*. From this it is easily distinguished by its relatively broad scarcely tapered cones with thick scales.

P. armandii was reintroduced by Wilson for Messrs Veitch in 1900 and again for the Arnold Arboretum in 1908. Probably most trees in private collections are from this source or from seeds collected by Kingdon Ward in Yunnan. A specimen at Wakehurst Place, Sussex, *pl.* 1914, measures 60 × 4¾ ft (1970).

P. ATTENUATA Lemm.   KNOBCONE PINE
P. tuberculata Gord., not D. Don

A tree 20 to 80 ft high in this country, occasionally up to 100 ft in the wild; young shoots glabrous, bright brown; buds cylindrical, ¾ to 1 in. long, ⅛ to ¼ in. wide, resinous. Leaves in threes, falling the third or fourth year, 4 to 7½ in. long, slender, bright green, finely pointed, minutely toothed; leaf-sheath ⅓ to ½ in. long, persistent. Cones slenderly conical, usually 4 to 5 in. long, 2 in. wide at the oblique base, deflexed, with the scales near the base on the upper side developing the conical, spine-tipped knobs or prominences referred to in the popular name; the cones are produced in whorls of three or more, and persist on the branches for sometimes thirty or forty years, or until the death of the tree. At first they have a stalk ¾ in. long, which gradually becomes enclosed in the thickening branch. *Bot. Mag.*, t. 8717.

Native mainly of California, but extending north into Oregon, south into the Mexican state of Baja California; discovered and introduced in 1847 by Hartweg. It has no special merits as an ornamental tree, although on account of its long-persisting cones it is a very interesting one. On a piece of branch, 4 ft long, from a tree grown at Bayfordbury and now preserved at Kew, there are over forty cones. It is botanically allied to *P. radiata*, but differs in the larger, stiffer, grey-green leaves and narrower cones. It is also a hardier tree, and according to Jepson, inhabits the most desolate and inhospitable stations for tree growth in the Californian mountains. As may be judged from the life-history of its cones, it is admirably adapted to survive as a species on fire-swept zones. (See also *P. muricata.*)

A tree at Bodnant, Denb., *pl.* 1902, measures 80 × 10½ ft (1974). Two trees at Borde Hill, Sussex, are of about the same age; they measure 75 × 6½ ft (Pinetum) and 76 × 5¾ ft (Warren Wood) (1974).

P. AYACAHUITE Ehrenb.   MEXICAN WHITE PINE

A tree attaining 100 ft or slightly more in the wild; trunk grey, smooth on young trees, becoming shallowly furrowed and reddish brown with age; terminal buds brown, resinous, about ½ in. long, the scales with free, acuminate tips. Young branchlets usually covered with a short, brown down. Leaves in fives, very slender, falling the third year, 4 to 7 in. long, three-sided, the outer side green, the two inner surfaces each with three or four white lines of stomata, margins toothed; leaf-sheaths ¾ in. long, soon falling away. Cones 6 to 12 in. long, 1 to 2½ in. wide before expanding, cylindrical, with a tapered, slightly curved apex; they are pendulous, shortly stalked, and borne in twos or threes, or sometimes singly; scales about 1 in. wide, with a blunt, resinous, sometimes reflexed apex, but the basal scales always strongly reflexed. Seeds with a relatively narrow wing 1 in. or even more long, the body of the seed about ⅜ in. long.

Native of Guatemala and of southern and central Mexico, from 8,000 to 10,000 ft, in sheltered valleys or on the slopes of the moister mountain ranges, where even in the dry season there is frequent low cloud and drizzle. It was introduced to Britain by Hartweg, who sent cones to the Horticultural Society from Guatemala in 1840. But the existing trees probably all derive from later introductions and some belong to the following variety:

var. VEITCHII Shaw *P. veitchii* Roezl, *nom.*; *P. bonapartea* Roezl ex Gard. Chron.; *P. loudoniana* Gord.—Body of seed relatively larger, about ½ in. long, wing shorter and relatively broader, about ½ in. long. Cones sometimes as long as 15 in., with scales 1⅛ to 1¼ in. wide. According to Martinez there is the further difference that the scales are thicker and stronger than in the typical state of the species. This variety is apparently confined to central Mexico, where intermediate forms also occur (Martinez).

P. ayacahuite and the var. *veitchii* are both likely to vary in hardiness, according to provenance. The famous tree at Westonbirt is now decrepit and no longer bears cones, but at one time it coned freely and many seedlings were raised from it (some of which proved to be hybrid; see *P. × holfordiana*). This tree certainly belongs to the var. *veitchii*; Shaw, who saw cones from it in the Herbarium of the Arnold Arboretum, actually cites it in his description of var. *veitchii*. The statement by Elwes and Henry that var. *veitchii* is tender probably refers to the original introduction by Roezl (as *P. veitchii*).

Among the largest or oldest specimens of *P. ayacahuite* (some may be var. *veitchii*) are: Kew, *pl.* 1873, 54 × 3½ ft (1974) and another, possibly a seedling of the Westonbirt tree, *pl.* 1904, 49 × 4½ ft (1966); R.H.S. Pinetum, Wisley, Surrey, 62 × 7¼ ft (1969); Hergest Croft, Heref., *pl.* 1916, 60 × 6 ft (1968); Bicton, Devon, 88 × 7½ ft and 78 × 8¾ ft (1968); Bodnant, Denb., *pl.* 1902, 64 × 10¾ ft and 71 × 10½ ft (1974); Fota, Co. Cork, Eire, *pl.* 1902, 60 × 7¼ ft (1966).

The Westonbirt specimen of var. *veitchii*, mentioned above, has lost its top; it measured 62 × 6¾ ft in 1909 and is now 8½ ft in girth (1971).

var. BRACHYPTERA Shaw *P. strobiformis* Engelm.—Seed about ½ in. long, the wing reduced to a mere rim or absent. Native of N. Mexico, commonest in the states of Coahuila and Durango. Probably not in cultivation, but worthy of introduction, as it should succeed in eastern England.

P. BALFOURIANA Oreg. Comm. ex Balf.   FOXTAIL PINE

A small tree 20 to 40, rarely over 50 ft high, forming in a small state a very densely branched, bushy tree; young shoots covered with minute but scarcely visible down, so closely packed are the leaf-bundles. Leaves mostly in fives, sometimes in fours, persisting as long as twelve or fifteen years, very stiff and sharply pointed, about 1½ in. long, three-angled, two surfaces at first white with stomata, becoming nearly green like the third with age; margins not toothed. The scales of the leaf-sheath curl back and make a sort of rosette surrounding the base of the leaf cluster, and persist in that shape. Cones 2½ to 5 in. long, each scale armed with a minute, incurved prickle.

Native of California, where it occupies two widely separated areas. One is in the northern part of the coastal ranges, where it was discovered by Jeffrey in the mountains between the Scott and Shasta rivers in 1852, when collecting for the Oregon Association, and introduced by him from the same locality. The other area is in S. California, in the Sierra Nevada. The species was named by the Oregon Committee in honour of Prof. J. H. Balfour, Regius Keeper of the Edinburgh Botanic Garden from 1845 to 1880, who also described it, in a report to members of the Association.

P. balfouriana is one of the most distinct and attractive pines for limited spaces. It grows very slowly, but its long-retained, closely packed leaves give it a healthy, vigorous aspect. It is exceedingly rare in gardens, however. The two largest examples grow in the Edinburgh Botanic Garden, both a little over 30 ft high and about 2¼ ft in girth (1970). It, and its immediate allies (see below), differ from the other five-leaved pines in their short needles, and in having the sheaths in the form of a rosette.

P. ARISTATA Engelm. *P. balfouriana* var. *aristata* (Engelm.) Engelm. BRISTLECONE PINE.—This is very closely allied to the above, but is always distinguishable by conspicuous exudations of whitish resin on the leaves, giving them very much the appearance of being infested with some scale insect. The branches are more drooping, the young shoots more distinctly downy, and the cones of *P. aristata* are armed with considerably longer, slender prickles. Introduced in 1863 from Colorado, where it grows on the outer range of the Rocky Mountains, also in New Mexico and Arizona. It is better represented in cultivation than *P. balfouriana*, but rare none the less. Among the recorded specimens are: Kew, *pl.* 1908, 20 × 1½ ft (1969); Royal Horticultural Society Garden, Wisley, 20 × 1½ ft (1968); National Pinetum, Bedgebury, Kent, *pl.* 1932, 13 ft × 8 in. (1971); Leighton Hall, Montgom., 27 × 1¼ ft (1960).

P. BANKSIANA Lamb. JACK PINE

P. hudsonica Poir.; *P. divaricata* (Ait.) Dum.-Cours.; *P. sylvestris* var. *divaricata* Ait.

A plant varying in height from a scrubby bush to a tree 20 to 45 ft high in this country, but said sometimes to become 70 to 90 ft high in N. America; young shoots without down; terminal buds egg-shaped, ⅓ in. long, encased in resin. Leaves in pairs, persisting two to four years, 1 to 1¾ in. long, flat on one side, convex on the other, dark green, much curved; leaf-sheaths about ⅙ in. long. Cones pointing forward, slender, conical, but very much curved at the tapered point; about 1½ in. long, ¾ in. wide at the base before opening; yellow when ripe.

Native of Canada and the N.E. United States. It is the most northerly of pines, and is spread over a vast region, usually in poor soil; introduced early in the 18th century. It appears to be very well adapted for poor sandy soil, and has been planted in great numbers in Germany on that account. It has not much to recommend it for gardens. Among pines with short leaves in pairs and with resinous buds, this is to be distinguished by its slenderly tapered cones, curiously curved like a bent little finger at the apex.

P. *banksiana* grows in a few British collections, where the oldest trees are up to 70 ft in height and 3 to 4¼ ft in girth (5¼ ft at Blairquhan, Ayrs.).

P. BRUTIA Ten.
P. *halepensis* var. *brutia* (Ten.) Henry; P. *pyrenaica* of some authors, in part

Although by some authorities regarded as a variety of P. *halepensis*, this seems to be a distinct, though closely related, species. The tree is of thin, ungainly habit; its leaves (in pairs) are 4 to 6 in. long, its young shoots are green, and more flexible than in P. *halepensis*; finally, its cones point forwards instead of backwards, and are thicker (2 in.) at the base. It is rather lacking in

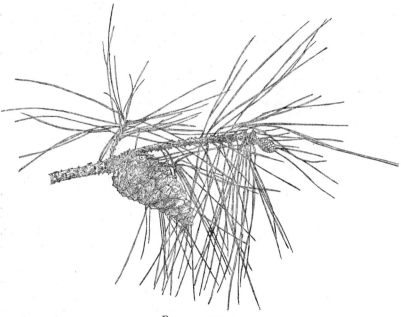

PINUS BRUTIA

attractive qualities, being thin in branch and leaf and inferior in this respect to P. *halepensis*. It was described by Tenore in 1811 and was said by him to occur wild in western Calabria, though it has not been rediscovered there since. Its main distribution is in Asiatic Turkey and the Near East, as far east as Kurdistan; it also occurs in the Aegean and Cyprus.

P. *brutia* is rare in cultivation, the only large specimen recorded being one at Kew, which measures 44 × 6 ft (1971).

This species was by some 19th-century botanists confused with *P. nigra* var. *cebennensis* under the name *P. pyrenaica*.

P. PITYUSA Stev.   *P. halepensis* var. *pityusa* (Stev.) Gord.—This interesting conifer occurs along the north-eastern coast of the Black Sea from Anapa to Pitsunda. It is closely related to *P. brutia*, differing mainly in its shorter leaves.

P. BUNGEANA Zucc.   LACEBARK PINE

A tree sometimes forming a rounded, bushy head, but frequently branching near the ground and forming several stems which grow erect to a height occasionally of 80 to 100 ft. The bark is smooth and peels off the trunk like that of a plane; in young specimens it is brown, but in old ones becomes quite white and gives to this pine its most remarkable character. Young shoots perfectly glabrous, shining, greyish green. Leaves in threes, persisting four or five years, about 3 in. long, two-edged, stiff, sharply pointed, bright green, very minutely toothed, marked all round with faint stomatic lines; leaf-sheath $\frac{1}{2}$ to $\frac{3}{4}$ in. long, soon falling. Cones 2 to $2\frac{1}{2}$ in. long, $1\frac{1}{4}$ to $1\frac{1}{2}$ in. wide, shortly stalked, the scales terminated by a decurved, triangular spine; seeds $\frac{1}{3}$ in. long, with a short wing. *Bot. Mag.*, t. 8240.

P. bungeana was described from a specimen collected by Bunge near Peking in 1831. In that region, and elsewhere in China, it was widely cultivated for its beautiful white bark, especially in the grounds of Buddhist temples. It is wild in the mountains west of Peking and thence south-eastward to Kansu and southward to Hupeh. It was introduced by Robert Fortune around 1846 to Glendinning's nursery, but during that journey to China he only saw young nursery plants. But fifteen years later, in the mountains west of Peking, he found a tree with a thick trunk only 3 or 4 ft high, from which 'some eight or ten branches sprang out, not branching or bending in the usual way, but rising perpendicularly, as straight as a Larch, to the height of 80 or 100 feet. The bark of the main stem and the secondary stems was of a milky-white colour, peeling like that of the Arbutus . . .' He must have arranged for a further supply of seeds to be sent, for in 1864 he advertised seeds at 25 shillings an ounce, recently arrived from Peking 'by the Overland Mail' (*Gard. Chron.* (1864), p. 195).

P. bungeana is perfectly hardy, though rather slow growing. The bark on cultivated trees is not milky-white, and perhaps may never reach that stage in our climate. But it is beautifully marbled in various colours, yellowish when freshly exposed, darkening to greyish green or purplish brown. The oldest tree at Kew grows near the northern end of the Palm House; it is short-trunked, $4\frac{3}{4}$ ft in girth at the base, and a little over 30 ft high (1969). There is a group of taller trees, with well-developed main stems, growing in the Pinetum at the S.W. corner of the Lake, about 40 ft high. In the Pinetum of the Royal Horticultural Society at Wisley a tree *c.* 45 ft high is of very slender habit.

P. CANARIENSIS C. Smith   CANARY ISLAND PINE

A tree upwards of 80 ft high and 10 ft in girth of trunk, of conical shape, with somewhat pendulous branches; young shoots yellowish, not downy; winter-buds ovoid, pointed, ¾ in. long, ½ in. wide; bud-scales reddish brown, free and reflexed at the top, but matted together lower down by a fringe of whitish bristles. Leaves in bundles of three, very slender, minutely toothed, averaging 8 or 9 in. in length (sometimes 12 in.) with two to four lines of stomata on each surface; basal sheath persistent, ½ to ¾ in. long. Cones solitary or several together, more or less deflexed, 5 to 8 in. long, 3 in. wide, the exposed part of the scales of rhomboid outline and pyramidal shape, altogether resembling those of *P. pinaster*. Seeds with a wing over 1 in. long. The leaves remain on the shoots for two seasons.

Native of the Canary Islands and once very plentiful there, but now becoming restricted to the higher altitudes and less accessible places. It is most abundant on Tenerife and Grand Canary. At one time the islands contained many giant trees, most of which have been felled.

This pine is only hardy in our mildest localities. The largest of the very few examples is at Tresco Abbey in the Isles of Scilly, and measures 85 × 7½ ft (1970). A tree at Mount Usher, Co. Wicklow, Eire, is 39 × 2½ ft (1966). It makes a fine tree on the Riviera, where it succeeds on calcareous soil, and is grown in other parts of the world with a warm temperate climate, both as an ornamental and for its timber, which is exceedingly durable and ranks with the best types of pinewood.

P. ROXBURGHII Sarg. *P. longifolia* Roxb. ex Lamb., not Salisb. CHIR PINE.—This is one of the finest of Indian pines. It is described as attaining 150 to 180 ft in height and a trunk-girth of 20 to 35 ft. The winter-buds are ovoid, not resinous; the leaves in threes, 8 in. to over 12 in. long. Cones elongated, ovoid, 5 to 8 in. long, 2½ to 3½ in. wide. It is the chief resin-producing pine of India. Tender, although capable of being grown in Cornish gardens.

P. CEMBRA L.   AROLLA PINE

A tree varying in height from 60 to over 100 ft, usually of pyramidal form, especially when young; young shoots clothed with a thick coat of brownish down. Leaves in fives, very densely packed on the shoots, persisting three to five years according to vigour; pointing forward, fragrant in summer, 1½ to 4½ in. long, rich green; triangular, with three to five lines of stomata on two faces; margins toothed except near the point; leaf-sheaths ¾ to ⅞ in. long, soon falling away. Cones egg-shaped, 2 to 3 in. long, scarcely as wide; the scales do not expand, and the seeds fall with the cones and are either released by birds or animals or by the decay of the scales.

Native of the Alps, from France to Lower Austria, and of the Tatras and Carpathians, rarely descending below 5,000 ft. In the Alps it occurs in the inner ranges, where it is often associated with the common larch and forms with it the highest limit of tree growth. Visitors to the high valleys of the Mont Blanc area, the Engadine, the Valais, and the inner Tyrol will have noted picturesque old veterans that have braved the storms, doubtless for hundreds of years.

The Arolla pine was in cultivation in Britain as early as 1746, when the Duke of Argyll had it at Whitton near Hounslow. In 1903 there was still a tree there which must have been planted in the Duke's lifetime, i.e., before 1761. It makes a very handsome small tree, pyramidal, densely branched and very leafy, especially from 8 to 20 ft high. It does not appear to be long-lived nor produce cones freely in southern England, although there are trees between 60 and 70 ft. The oldest is a leaning tree at Dropmore, Bucks, *pl.* 1795, measuring 65 × 7¾ ft (1970). Others in the south are: Lythe Hill, Haslemere, Surrey, 70 × 6 ft (1970); Leonardslee, Sussex, 60 × 4¾ ft (1960); Waddesdon, Bucks, 62 × 7½ ft (1973). *P. cembra* grows best, however, in the cooler and rainier parts of the country. Examples in these areas are: Powis Castle, Montgom., 71 × 8 ft and 60 × 9 ft (1970); Taymouth Castle, Perths., 90 × 11 ft (1970); Dawyck, Peebl., *pl.* 1840, 58 × 8½ ft (1974); Murthly Castle, Perths., 80 × 8 ft (1970).

P. SIBIRICA Du Tour *P. cembra* var. *sibirica* Loud.—This Russian species is very closely allied to *P. cembra*, and is by some botanists included in it without differentiation. The main differences are that in the Siberian tree the leaves are longer, the cones longer and relatively narrower, with thinner scales. Its distribution in Russia is vast, from about 55° E. to an eastern limit around 125° E. Its name in Russian is *kedr*—a word of the same parentage as ancient Greek *kedros* and Latin *cedrus*. In English translations of Russian works this is usually misleadingly rendered as 'cedar'.

P. PUMILA (Pall.) Reg. *P. cembra* var. *pumila* Pall. DWARF SIBERIAN PINE.—Botanically this species is near to *P. cembra*, although of different aspect. It is a dwarf, mostly prostrate shrub rarely over 10 ft high in the wild, the shoots downy, the leaves usually 1½ to 2¾ in. long, hence shorter than in *P. cembra*, and are usually less toothed or entire (finely toothed almost throughout in *P. cembra*). Male flowers deep red. Cones and seeds smaller than in *P. cembra*, the former about 1½ in. long. It is a native of the colder parts of N.E. Asia, including Japan, often forming extensive thickets above the tree-line or in other exposed places. It was in cultivation early last century, but appears to have been lost sight of until the beginning of this century, when Admiral Clinton Baker collected plants in Japan and sent them to the Bayford-bury collection.

In cultivation *P. pumila* varies in size and habit, but is usually under 4 ft in height. It associates well with the heaths.

Selections are: 'DWARF BLUE', with glaucous leaves and of spreading habit; and 'JERMYNS', of slow growth and compact habit, raised by Messrs Hillier.

P. × HAKKODENSIS Makino—A natural hybrid between *P. pumila* and *P. parviflora*, occurring in the northern part of the main island of Japan, and originally described from Mt Hakkoda. Near to *P. pumila*, but with longer, thicker, twisted needles (Krüssmann, *Handb. der Nadelgehölze* (1972), plate 97). It is said to be of promise as an ornamental plant.

P. CEMBROIDES Zucc.   MEXICAN NUT PINE, PINYON

P. llaveana Schiede

A bushy tree usually 15 to 20 ft high, sometimes 40 or 50 ft, the young branches slender, glaucous. Leaves mostly in threes, sometimes in pairs, persisting for about three years, 1 to 2 in. long, dark green; in each cluster the inner faces of the leaves are pressed together, especially when young; margins not toothed; leaf-sheath at first ¼ to ⅜ in. long, the scales afterwards becoming reflexed and forming a rosette round the base of each cluster. Cones roundish, egg-shaped, 1½ to 2 in. long, 1 to 1½ in. wide, with very few scales. Seeds ½ in. long, edible.

Native of Mexico (including northern Baja California) and of bordering parts of Arizona, New Mexico, and Texas; introduced by Hartweg in 1839, but very rare in collections. The seeds are sold in Mexican markets as 'piñones'. The nut pines of the south-western USA are now included in *P. cembroides* as varieties by most botanists. These are:

var. EDULIS (Engelm.) Voss   *P. edulis* Engelm.—Leaves chiefly in pairs instead of threes and rather thicker; otherwise scarcely differing from typical *P. cembroides*. Native mainly of Colorado, Utah, Arizona, and New Mexico, but also occurring in northern Mexico. It is a pleasing small tree of neat dense habit, but very rare in gardens.

var. MONOPHYLLA (Torr. & Frem.) Voss   *P. monophylla* Torr. & Frem. SINGLELEAF NUT PINE.—Leaves solitary and terete (circular in cross-section), or occasionally in pairs and then semi-terete. It has a more westerly distribution than var. *edulis*, mainly in Utah, Arizona, Nevada, and S. California, and often forms pure stands of considerable extent. It is one of the main sources of pinyons (pine nuts). The best known and largest specimen in Britain grows in the University Botanic Garden, Cambridge; planted shortly before 1900, it measures 33 × 3½ ft (1969); when young it gained an average of 8 in. in height per annum (*Journ. R.H.S.*, Vol. 41 (1915), p. 7 and fig. 8). There are smaller trees at Edinburgh and Kew. This pine deserves to be more widely planted, especially in the drier parts of the country.

var. PARRYANA (Engelm.) Voss   *P. parryana* Engelm., not Gord.; *P. quadrifolia* Sudw. FOURLEAF NUT PINE.—Leaves mostly in fours. Native of S. California, extending into the Mexican state of Baja California. Probably not in cultivation. The *P. parryana* of Gordon is *P. ponderosa*.

P. NELSONII Shaw—A small tree with pale glaucous or whitish shoots. Leaves in threes, usually adhering and apparently single in wild plants, slender, up to 2½ in. long (occasionally longer), three-sided, light green on the outer side; sheaths persistent, about ¼ in. long, not reduced to a rosette. Cones cylindrical or oblong-ovoid, up to 5 in. long, pendulous from the downward curving of the stout peduncle, which is 1 to 2 in. long; scales relatively few, the exposed part rhomboidal, the transverse diameter much the larger, with wide, prominent umbos; seeds large, wingless, edible (*Gard. Chron.*, Vol. 36 (1904), p. 122, fig. 49).

Native of N.E. Mexico. A tree at Kew, planted in 1910, is considered to belong to this species. It measures 32 × 2¼ ft (1969).

P. CONTORTA Loud.   BEACH PINE

A tree 20 to 30 ft in the wild, but taller in cultivation; bark of mature trees thick, roughly fissured; young shoots often curiously twisted, glabrous; terminal buds narrowly cylindrical, $\frac{3}{4}$ to 1 in. long, resinous. Leaves in pairs, $1\frac{1}{2}$ to $2\frac{1}{4}$ in. long, $\frac{1}{12}$ in. or less wide, dark green, persisting three, four, or more years; leaf-sheath $\frac{3}{16}$ in. long, persistent. Cones obliquely conical, up to 2 in. long, $\frac{3}{4}$ in. wide at the base before expanding; scales terminated by a slender spine which wears away in time.

Native of the coast region of western N. America, from Alaska to S. California; discovered by Douglas in 1825; introduced shortly before 1855. It belongs to the group of two-leaved pines with persistent leaf-sheaths, and cylindrical, resinous winter-buds. In the absence of cones it might be confused with the mountain pine of Europe, P. uncinata, but in that species the leaves persist for five to ten years and the leaf-sheath is longer—up to $\frac{5}{8}$ in. long.

In recent years P. contorta has become an important forestry tree in Britain, especially as a pioneer tree on poor peaty soils. Among the largest specimens in collections are: Grayswood Hill, Haslemere, Surrey, pl. 1886, 66 × 8$\frac{3}{4}$ ft (1971); Warnham Court, Sussex, 73 × 9$\frac{1}{4}$ ft (1971); Westonbirt, Glos., in Broad Drive, 61 × 9 ft (1970); Bodnant, Denb., pl. 1876, 105 × 9$\frac{3}{4}$ ft (1974); Ashford Castle, Co. Mayo, Eire, 88 × 12$\frac{1}{4}$ ft (1966).

P. contorta, in the wide sense, is a very variable species and there is no unanimity as to how it should be subdivided. The two varieties treated below are not clearly demarcated and are themselves variable. The complex is discussed by W. B. Critchfield in Geographic Variation in Pinus contorta (Maria Moors Cabot Foundation Publ. Vol. 3, 1–118 (1957)).

var. LATIFOLIA S. Wats. P. murrayana and P. contorta var. murrayana of most authors, in part; P. contorta subsp. latifolia (S. Wats.) Critchfield LODGEPOLE PINE.—From typical P. contorta this variety can be distinguished by the thin bark of its trunk (rarely more than $\frac{1}{4}$ in. thick) of a pale grey or brown, covered with thin scales, but comparatively smooth; also by its longer, yellowish green leaves; the leaves also tend to be rather wider, but the difference is not marked or consistent enough to be of much value in identification. The tree itself attains to a considerably greater height than typical P. contorta and, compared with var. murrayana, the trunk is slender, rarely more than 1 ft in diameter in trees a century old. It is a closed-cone pine, shedding only a small proportion of its seed each year. The bulk of the cones remain closed on the tree for a considerable period, but release their seed in vast quantities after a forest fire. In this way it quickly colonises the devastated area and dense, even-aged stands grow up.

Whereas typical P. contorta inhabits the coastal region, the var. latifolia is a native of the Rocky Mountains, ranging from W. Alaska to Colorado, and ascending to 11,000 ft at the southern end of its range (to 6,000 ft in British Columbia). It was introduced shortly before 1855.

var. MURRAYANA (Balf.) Engelm. P. murrayana Balf.; P. contorta subsp. murrayana (Balf.) Critchfield; P. tamrac A. Murr.—This variety is tall-growing, like var. latifolia, but is much stouter, with a trunk 3 ft or more in diameter. It also differs in its pinkish bark, in bearing cones that usually shed their seed when ripe and soon fall from the tree, and in its rather broader leaves, up to $\frac{1}{10}$ in. wide. It is confined to the Cascade range and inner California and was discovered and introduced by Jeffrey, who collected cones for the Oregon Association in autumn 1852. No mature specimen has been traced but there are young trees in the trial plots of the Forestry Commission, which grow very slowly.

P. COULTERI D. Don   BIGCONE PINE

A tree 50 to 80 ft high, with a stout, erect trunk, 3 to 4 ft in thickness, whose bark is divided into deep broad ridges. Young shoots very thick, often glaucous, not downy; the terminal part carrying a cluster of crowded leaves, the lower part furnished with fringed, slender-pointed scales, 1 in. long. The older portions of the branchlet are rough with the remains of these scales, and the prominences on which the leaf-bundles were seated. Buds conical, resinous, slender-pointed, 1½ in. long, ¾ in. wide. Leaves in threes, falling the fourth year; 10 to 14 in. long, minutely toothed, grey-green, with lines of stomata on all three faces; leaf-sheaths persistent, 1 in. long. Cones 10 to 12 in. long, 5 to 7 in. thick; the scales terminated by a stout triangular spine.

Native of California; discovered by Dr Coulter in 1832; introduced by Douglas the same year. The cones of this remarkable pine are the heaviest and most formidably armed among three-leaved pines, but are not often borne in this country. It resembles *P. ponderosa* in leaf and shoot, but is a shorter tree with more spreading branches. The cones are very different, and more like those of *P. sabiniana* which, however, has smoother, more slender shoots, and greyer leaves. Coulter's pine is not common in cultivation, but is very striking in its somewhat gaunt branching, its terminal bunches of leaves, spreading like a sweep's brush, and its immense cones.

The following are some of the specimens recorded in recent years: Wakehurst Place, Sussex (Valley), 58 × 5 ft (1968); National Pinetum, Bedgebury, Kent, in Forest Plots, *pl.* 1935, 45 × 4¼ ft (1967), in pine collection, *pl.* 1926, 47 × 3¾ ft (1969); Royal Horticultural Society Garden, in Pinetum, 45 × 3¾ ft (1969); Dropmore, Bucks, *pl.* 1915, 56 × 7¼ ft (1970); Titley Court, Heref. (from Douglas introduction?), 98 × 12½ ft (1963); Edinburgh Botanic Garden, 59 × 4¾ ft (1970).

P. DENSIFLORA Sieb. & Zucc.   JAPANESE RED PINE

A tree 100 to 120 ft high in Japan, with a trunk 3 to 4 ft through; bark of trunk reddish, scaling; young shoots blue-white, glabrous; buds cylindrical, brown, resinous. Leaves in pairs, falling the third year, 2½ to 4 in. long, slender, dark green on both surfaces, margins very minutely toothed; leaf-sheath ¼ to ⅜ in. long, persistent, terminated often by one or two slender threads. Cones 1½ to 2 in. long, ¾ to 1 in. wide before expansion, conical, pointed; seed ¼ in. long, with a wing about thrice as long.

Native of Japan, Korea, and parts of China; introduced by Siebold from Japan in 1854. In that country it is a useful timber tree, filling much the same place in the flora there that the Scots pine does in Europe. It is one of the favourite plants upon which the Japanese gardeners exercise their dwarfing arts. The species is not likely to have any timber value with us. It resembles *P. sylvestris* in the resinous buds and reddish trunk, but is very different in general appearance, the leaves being green (not grey) and the young shoots glaucous (not green).

All the existing trees in Britain were planted this century and are mostly 35 to 50 ft in height and 2½ to 3¾ ft in girth. There are trees in this range of size in the National Pinetum, Bedgebury; at Wakehurst Place, Sussex; Westonbirt, Glos.; and in the Edinburgh Botanic Garden. A tree at Bicton in Devon is 48 × 5¾ ft (1968).

cv. 'AUREA'.—This behaves like *P. sylvestris* 'Aurea' in the leaves turning yellow in autumn and winter, changing to green again in spring and summer. Originally distributed as "*P. massoniana aurea*".

cv. 'UMBRACULIFERA'.—A very attractive Japanese garden variety, making a small, dense tabular shrub at first, but eventually a miniature, many-stemmed tree with a flat or mushroom-like crown and 10 ft or slightly more high. The cones are much smaller than in the wild trees. It is known in Japan as 'Tanyosho'.

P. ECHINATA Mill.   SHORTLEAF PINE

A tree 30 to 50 ft high in this country, over 100 ft high in the wild; young shoots quite glabrous, covered with blue-white bloom, slender, very brittle after they are one year old, the bark peeling the third year; terminal bud cylindrical, ¼ to ⅓ in. long, not resinous, scales fringed. Leaves in pairs or in threes, mostly falling the second year, 1½ to 4 in. long, slender, dull green; leaf-sheath ¼ to ½ in. long, persistent. Cones 1½ to 2½ in. long, ¾ to 1 in. wide at the base before expanding; conical, with a short, distinct stalk.

Native of the eastern United States from New York State southwards; cultivated in this country since early in the 18th century. It is but little known, and has, indeed, no conspicuous qualities to recommend it for garden or park. It is distinct in its blue-white young shoots, occasionally three-leaved clusters, and brittle shoots covered with peeling bark after the second year. In N. America it is a very valuable timber tree.

P. FLEXILIS James   LIMBER PINE   [PLATE 33

A tree 40 to 60, sometimes 80 ft high; branches long, slender; the young parts so flexible that they can be bent double without breaking; young shoots shining green, perfectly glabrous or with minute brownish down. Leaves in fives, persisting for about seven years, often pointing forwards, or the youngest ones even appressed to the branchlet, 2½ to 3½ in. long, triangular in section, all three sides marked with three or four white lines of stomata; margins quite entire, apex finely pointed; leaf-sheaths ½ to ⅝ in. long, soon falling away. Cones 3 to 5 in. long, 1½ in. thick before the scales open. *Bot. Mag.*, t. 8467.

Native of the Rocky Mountains from Alberta and British Columbia southward to S. California, Arizona, and New Mexico; it was introduced to the Harvard Botanic Garden, Boston, by Dr Parry in 1861, from Colorado, and must have reached Britain soon after, since the trees at Kew came from Dickson and Turnbull of Edinburgh in 1871–2. The reputed introduction by Jeffrey in 1851 was really of *P. albicaulis*.

P. flexilis is easily distinguished from all the other five-needled pines, except *P. albicaulis*, by the absence of teeth on the leaf-edges in combination with the deciduous leaf-sheaths and the glabrous or very finely downy young shoots. From *P. albicaulis* it is most reliably distinguished by its cones, which are longer (sometimes 10 in. long on wild trees), shed their seeds as soon as they are ripe, and soon fall from the tree.

A tree at Kew, by the Isleworth Gate, *pl.* 1872, measures 54 × 4¾ ft (1970). There are smaller examples in the Edinburgh and Cambridge Botanic Gardens and in the National Pinetum at Bedgebury.

P. GERARDIANA Wall.   CHILGOZA PINE

A tree up to 80 ft high in the wild, but usually much smaller, with a bark closely resembling that of *P. bungeana* (q.v.); young shoots glabrous. Leaves three in a bundle, dark green, 2 to 4 in. long, sharply pointed, persisting three or four years; sheath about ½ in. long, deciduous in the second year. Cones described by Brandis as 6 to 9 in. long, 4 to 5 in. wide at the base, the scales thick and woody, recurved and spine-tipped at the apex; seeds up to 1 in. long, with a rudimentary wing.

Native of the dry inner valleys of the N.W. Himalaya, and of N. Afghanistan; discovered by Captain Gerard of the Bengal Native Infantry and introduced in 1839 by Lord Auckland, the Governor-General of India, 'his Lordship being aware before he left England that the plants in nurseries or private collections were nothing more than P. longifolia [*P. roxburghii*]' (Gordon, in *Gard. Chron.* (1842), p. 52). But the species seems to have almost died out in cultivation, and has probably never been much planted. The only large specimen in the country grows in the University Botanic Garden, Cambridge. This was 17¾ ft high in 1915, at which time it was still branched to the ground (*Journ. R.H.S.*, Vol. 41, p. 2 and fig. 1). This tree now measures 39 × 2¾ ft (1969) and shows very well the characteristic plane-like bark. *P. gerardiana* is closely allied to *P. bungeana* of N. China, differing in the longer, more slender leaves, and in the larger cones.

The seeds of *P. gerardiana* are an important source of food in the region where it grows wild, and the tree is rarely felled.

P. HALEPENSIS Mill.   ALEPPO PINE

A tree rarely more than 30 to 50 ft high in this country, but 70 to 80 ft in favourable conditions; here it usually forms a rounded head of branches, but is more pyramidal in the south of Europe; young shoots pale grey, glabrous; buds slenderly conical, pointed, non-resinous, about ½ in. long, with the points of the scales slender, fringed, and recurved. Leaves in pairs (rarely in threes), falling the second and third years, $2\frac{1}{2}$ to $4\frac{1}{2}$ in. long, very slender; leaf-sheath $\frac{1}{4}$ to $\frac{1}{3}$ in. long. Cones pointing backwards, $2\frac{1}{2}$ to $3\frac{1}{2}$ in. long, 1 to $1\frac{1}{2}$ in. wide at the base, tapering to a slender point; scales unarmed; stalk $\frac{1}{4}$ to $\frac{1}{2}$ in. long; they are produced in pairs, threes, or singly and remain several years on the branches.

Native of S. Europe as far west as Spain and east to Asia Minor; introduced in the 17th century. Although tender in a young state it is hardy enough when once established; several examples at Kew have withstood $31°$ of frost, and are quite healthy. This species and *P. brutia* are distinguished among two-leaved pines by the non-resinous buds having recurved scales. The newly cut or bruised young wood has a most pleasant aromatic odour. It is the commonest pine along the south coast of Europe, and reaches perhaps its finest development along the Dalmatian coast, where I have seen it 70 to 80 ft high, remarkably handsome in its heavy plumose masses of foliage. It covers bleak rocky promontories near Dubrovnik. (See *P. brutia* for differences between it and the present species.)

There are still two trees in the collection at Kew, the measurements of which are 32 × 10 ft at ground level (1969) and 45 × $4\frac{3}{4}$ ft (1970). The species is very rare in Britain and no larger specimen than these has been recorded, except one at Tresco Abbey in the Isles of Scilly, which is 50 × $4\frac{1}{4}$ ft (1970).

P. HELDREICHII Christ
P. laricio var. *heldreichii* (Christ) Mast.

P. heldreichii is mainly represented in cultivation by the following variety, which is also commoner than typical *P. heldreichii* in the wild:

var. LEUCODERMIS (Ant.) Markgraf ex Fitschen *P. leucodermis* Ant.; *P. laricio* var. *leucodermis* (Ant.) Christ; *P. nigra* var. *leucodermis* (Ant.) Rehd.—A tree up to 90 ft high in the wild, but usually much smaller and sometimes shrubby; bark ash-grey, smooth, on old trees divided by narrow fissures into more or less rectangular plates; buds $\frac{5}{8}$ in. long, sharply pointed, not resinous, with brown, fimbriate scales; stems pale brown at first with a glaucous bloom, whitish the second year, grey the third. Leaves in pairs, very rigid and erect, persisting five years, dark green, 2 to 3 in. long; leaf-sheaths $\frac{3}{8}$ to $\frac{3}{4}$ in. long. Cones at first deep blue, dull dark brown and evenly coloured when ripe, ovoid-conic, 2 to 3 in. long; lower scales pyramidal at the apex, umbo with an erect or backward-pointing mucro. *Bot. Mag.*, n.s., t. 190.

Native of the Dinaric Alps of Yugoslavia, extending into Albania (see further on distribution below); described in 1863 from a specimen collected by Maly in the mountains north of the Gulf of Kotor, in S. Dalmatia. It is a tree of high altitudes, recalling *P. cembra* in its ability to withstand harsh conditions, but nearly always found growing on limestone (rarely on serpentine rock). It was introduced to Kew in 1890 and has since become a fairly common tree in collections. There was a reintroduction in 1902, by Mrs Nicholl, who collected seed on Prenj Planina in Hercegovina (Elwes and Henry, *Tr. Gt. Brit. & Irel.*, Vol. 2, p. 426).

Although often gnarled and stunted in the wild, the var. *leucodermis* makes

in cultivation a very handsome specimen of dense, narrow habit. Among the
largest examples are: Kew, from original introduction, 41 × 3 ft (1968);
Wakehurst Place, Sussex, *pl. c.* 1915, 54 × 6 ft (1971), and several others;
Pinetum of Royal Horticultural Society, Wisley, 54 × 3¼ ft (1969); Stratfield
Saye, Hants, 62 × 6 ft (1968); Tyninghame, East Lothian, 47 × 6¾ ft (1967).

Typical *P. heldreichii* was described a year earlier than *P. leucodermis*, from a
specimen collected by Heldreich on Mt Olympus in N. Greece. The distinguishing characters appear to be that in typical *P. heldreichii* the lower cone-
scales are not pyramidal at the apex as in var. *leucodermis*, that the branchlets
are brown in their second year, and that the leaves are more spreading, but the
differences are scarcely of specific value. The geographical distribution of
typical *P. heldreichii* is apparently not known for certain, but the type-locality
is at the southern end of the area of the species. It also extends into S. Italy,
where it occurs on some of the high mountains of Calabria and Lucania, e.g.,
on Mt Pollino, north of Castrovillari, but whether these trees would be referable
to typical *P. heldreichii* or to the var. *leucodermis* it is impossible to say.

P. heldreichii is related to *P. nigra*, differing markedly in its bark, in the grey
or glaucous young shoots, and in the uniform brown colouring of the cones.
There are also differences in leaf-structure and in the chemical composition of
the resin.

P. × HOLFORDIANA A. B. Jacks.

A hybrid between *P. ayacahuite* and *P. wallichiana*, described in 1933 from
trees growing at Westonbirt, Glos., and named after Sir George Holford, the
owner from 1892 until his death in 1926. They had been raised in 1904 from
the famous specimen of *P. ayacahuite* var. *veitchii* in the arboretum, pollinated
by a tree of *P. wallichiana* growing nearby. The shoots differ from those of
P. wallichiana in usually being hairy, and the cones are broader than in that
species. From *P. ayacahuite* it differs, at least in the type, by the apices of the
cone-scales not being reflexed, but A. F. Mitchell has found that second-
generation hybrids, of which many have been raised and distributed, often
incline strongly to *P. ayacahuite*, but can usually be identified by the orange-
brown bark, the greater vigour and the more open crown.

There are several specimens at Westonbirt of the original first-generation
hybrids, planted in 1906, ranging from 70 to 92 ft in height and 5½ to 7 ft in
girth (1974). Some others, of the first or second generation, are: Wakehurst
Place, Sussex, in West Wood, 79 × 7 ft (1970); Borde Hill, Sussex, *pl.* 1931,
62 × 9¼ ft (1974); R.H.S. Pinetum, Wisley, 60 × 9¼ ft (1969); Lythe Hill,
Haslemere, Surrey, 60 × 8 ft (1969).

P. × SCHWERINII Fitschen—Another hybrid from the pollen of *P.
wallichiana*, the seed-parent in this case being *P. strobus*, the Weymouth pine.
It was described in 1930 from a tree found growing on the estate of Fritz Graf
von Schwerin near Berlin, which had been planted in 1905 as *P. strobus*. It
resembles *P. wallichiana* in habit and in some foliage characters, but the cones
recall those of *P. strobus*. The same cross was made artificially at the Forest

Research Station, Alice Holt. One tree from the cross has grown 10 ft in three years (Mitchell, *Conifers in the British Isles*, p. 242).

P. JEFFREYI Balf.   JEFFREY PINE
P. ponderosa var. *jeffreyi* (Balf.) Vasey

A lofty tree said to attain 200 ft in the wild, but more commonly 100 to 130 ft, with a narrow crown and a dark, fissured bark; young shoots stout, greyish, with a pruinose bloom; buds only slightly resinous, with scales free at the tip. Leaves in bundles of three, 5 to 10 in. long, bluish green, persisting five to eight years, giving off a fruity scent when bruised; sheath persistent. Cones 3 to 8 in. long (sometimes to 10 in.), oblong-ovoid; scales each with a slender decurved prickle. Seeds about ½ in. long, wing up to 1¾ in. long. *Bot. Mag.*, t. 8257.

Native mainly of California in the Sierra Nevada and Siskiyous, but also occurring in S. Oregon, W. Nevada, and in the Mexican state of Baja California; discovered by Jeffrey in 1852 when collecting for the Oregon Association and introduced by him at the same time. *P. jeffreyi* is closely allied to *P. ponderosa* and at one time it was usual to regard it as a variety of that species. But recent investigations have shown that it is a distinct and stable species, differing from *P. ponderosa* in the chemical composition of the resin, the darker bark, less resinous buds with scales free at the tip, the colour of the young shoots and the leaves, in the usually larger cones with recurved prickles, and the heavier seeds. But the two species are very similar in their wood. In areas where both are present, *P. jeffreyi*, being more frost-resistant when young, tends to predominate in frost hollows and exposed ridges, while *P. ponderosa* prefers the slopes.

The most notable tree of *P. jeffreyi* grows at Scone Palace, Perth; planted in 1860 it measures 118 × 12½ ft (1970). Others are: Peper Harrow, Elstead, Surrey, 95 × 11 ft (1971); Hampton Park, Puttenham, Surrey, 90 × 10 ft and 75 × 10½ ft (1969); Warnham Court, Sussex, 92 × 7¼ ft (1963); Eastnor Castle, Heref., 82 × 9½ ft (1970); Gordon Castle, Moray, 89 × 7¾ ft (1970). In Eire, there is a splendid tree at Powerscourt, Co. Wicklow, *pl.* 1866, measuring 116 × 10¾ ft (1966).

P. jeffreyi makes a very ornamental specimen when young, densely leafy and of narrow habit, as is well shown by a tree growing in a front garden in Holdfast Lane near Haslemere. It was planted in 1935 and measures 55 × 4¾ ft (1964).

P. KORAIENSIS Sieb. & Zucc.   KOREAN PINE
P. mandshurica Rupr.

A tree reaching at its best 100 to 150 ft in height; young shoots thickly clothed with short, reddish-brown wool; winter-buds ½ in. long, cylindrical, with a tapered point, resinous. Leaves in fives, persisting to the third year; 3½ to 4½ in. long, dark glossy green, with white stomatal lines on two faces;

margins toothed the whole length, the apex bluntish; leaf-sheaths about ½ in. long, soon falling. Cones about 5 in. long, 2½ to 3 in. wide at the base, tapering thence towards the apex. Scales 1¼ in. wide, thick and woody. Seeds ⅝ in. long, not winged, edible.

Native of Korea, Japan, Manchuria, and the Russian Far East; introduced by J. G. Veitch in 1861. It is, perhaps, most closely allied to *P. cembra*, but the growth is more open, the leaves are much more spreading, blunter, and toothed quite to the apex. The cones, too, are twice as long. *P. koraiensis* is not a first-class pine in this country, growing slowly. A tree at Westonbirt, Glos., *pl.* 1880, measures 56 × 2¾ ft (1967). At Dawyck, Peeblesshire, there is a tree raised from seeds sent by Wilson from Korea in 1919. This measures 60 × 4¼ ft (1970).

cv. 'VARIEGATA'.—This has some of the leaves yellow, others striped longitudinally in yellow and green, others wholly green—all sometimes in the same bundle.

P. LAMBERTIANA Dougl.   SUGAR PINE

A tree 70 to sometimes well over 200 ft high, and with a trunk 3 to 8 ft in diameter; young shoots minutely downy; winter-buds ¼ in. long, usually round or blunt at the apex, the scales closely flattened. Leaves in fives, falling the third year, 3 to 4½ in. long, minutely toothed at the margins, bluish green, often spirally twisted; leaf-sheaths ½ to ⅝ in. long, soon falling completely away. Cones borne at the ends of the uppermost branches, 12 to 20 in. long, about 3 in. thick before expanding, the woody scales 2 to 2½ in. long, with a broadly pointed apex. Seeds ½ to ¾ in. long, nutty in flavour, the wing nearly twice as long.

Native of western N. America, in Oregon and California; introduced in 1827 by Douglas, who had also discovered it. It is probably the noblest of all pines. The popular name refers to a sugary exudation from the trunk. In this country it has rarely borne its remarkable cones. It is allied to, as well as a neighbour of, *P. monticola*, but besides the differences in cones, the buds are more rounded and the leaf is more sharply pointed in *P. lambertiana*. From *P. strobus* its uniformly downy shoots distinguish it. It likes a sheltered situation and a good loamy soil. Even then it grows but slowly, yet is handsome nevertheless. Unfortunately, *P. lambertiana* is susceptible to the white pine blister-rust (see *P. strobus*), and all the old specimens in Britain are dead. A tree at Dropmore, Bucks, planted in 1843, measured 95 × 11 ft when it died in 1950.

P. MONTEZUMAE Lamb.   [PLATE 35

P. devoniana Lindl.; *P. russelliana* Lindl.; *P. macrophylla* Lindl.; *P. filifolia* Lindl.; *P. grenvilleae* Gord.; *P. gordoniana* Hartweg

A tree up to 100 ft high in the wild, with a thick bark, furrowed even on quite young trees; stems rough from the persistent bracts; buds ovoid, with narrow, fringed scales. Leaves usually in fives (occasionally in sixes or sevens),

5½ to 10 in. long, occasionally longer, variable in thickness, flexible, spreading or pendulous, finely toothed, triangular in cross-section, with stomata on all three surfaces; sheaths ⅜ to ¾ in. long, sometimes longer. Young cones purple or dark blue, prickly. Mature cones ovoid to narrowly so or cylindrical, 3½ to 6 in. long, sometimes longer, dull or slightly lustrous brown, thick and tough, the exposed part more or less raised, transversely keeled, with a short, usually deciduous prickle.

Native of southern and central Mexico at subtropical and cool temperate latitudes, with its best development at 7,000 to 8,000 ft; also of Guatemala; introduced by Hartweg in 1839. All the trees grown as *P. montezumae* in Britain are of later date, and their identity is uncertain. They have grey-green leaves which stand out stiffly all round the shoots as in a chimney-sweeper's brush, whereas in typical *P. montezumae* the leaves do not have a grey tinge and they are usually more or less drooping; on the other hand they are quite as long as in *P. montezumae*. The cones should decide the matter, but they do not reach maturity in these cultivated trees. The fact that the leaves are borne in fives is of no significance, since the number of leaves per bundle is not a wholly reliable character for separating *P. montezumae* from *P. hartwegii* and *P. rudis*.

The tree at Grayswood Hill, Haslemere, Surrey, is the oldest of which the planting date is known; accepted as typical *P. montezumae* by Elwes and Henry, it was planted in 1881 and measures 55 × 9¼ ft (1968). A tree at Endsleigh, Devon, must be older than the Grayswood Hill tree; it measured 50 × 9½ ft in 1906 and is now 65 × 14 ft (1970). Others are: Sheffield Park, Sussex, 50 × 7 ft (1968); Bicton, Devon, 69 × 6 ft (1968); Sidbury Manor, Devon, *pl.* 1902, 48 × 10¼ ft (1959); Mount Usher, Co. Wicklow, Eire, *pl.* 1909, 54 × 9¾ ft (1966) and a smaller tree *pl.* 1925 [Plate 35]. In the National Botanic Garden, Glasnevin, there is an example of 36 × 6¾ ft (1974).

Apart from their remarkable foliage, these trees are also very distinct in their broad, dome-shaped crowns.

var. LINDLEYI Loud. *P. lindleyana* Gord.—Leaves very slender, drooping, 10 to 14 in. long, vivid green or sometimes glaucous. Apex of cone-scales flattened or slightly pyramidal. Probably tender. In foliage it bears a strong resemblance to *P. pseudostrobus* (see below).

P. HARTWEGII Lindl. *P. montezumae* var. *hartwegii* (Lindl.) Engelm.—This is a very near relative of *P. montezumae*, but is found in Mexico at higher levels and under colder conditions. The leaves are sometimes consistently in fives, sometimes in threes or in fours; they are stiff, 4 to 6 in. long, light green or grey-green. The cones are darker in colour than in *P. montezumae*, almost black; they are shorter, up to 4 in. long at the most, with thin scales.

It is hardy enough to have been grown at one time as far east as Pampisford in Cambridgeshire, but the existing large specimens are confined to more western parts. Two trees mentioned by Elwes and Henry early this century still exist: Eastnor Castle, Heref., 82 × 6½ ft (1970) and Strete Ralegh, Devon, 75 × 7 ft (1970).

P. RUDIS Endl. *P. montezumae* var. *rudis* (Endl.) Shaw—Leaves commonly in fives, as in *P. montezumae*, usually 4 to 6 in. long but occasionally up to 8 in., rigid and usually radiating all round the shoot, light green, glaucous or sometimes yellowish green. Cones resembling those of *P. hartwegii* but dull brown. According to Martinez it often occurs with *P. montezumae*. But it ascends in places quite as high up the mountains as *P. hartwegii*. It is conceivable that the trees grown in Britain as *P. montezumae* are intermediates between that species and *P. rudis*. Elwes and Henry, who followed Shaw in treating *P. rudis* as a variety of *P. montezumae*, considered that a tree growing in their time at Fota in Co. Cork, Eire, belonged here. Judging from its portrait, it closely resembled in habit what is now grown as typical *P. montezumae* (*Tr. Gr. Brit. & Irel.*, Plate 278).

Another ally of *P. montezumae*, and more distinct from it than are *P. hartwegii* and *P. rudis*, is P. PSEUDOSTROBUS Lindl., which was introduced by Hartweg in 1839 and described from the specimens he collected in Mexico. It is easily distinguished from those species by its very glaucous, more slender shoots. The bark of young trees is much smoother than in *P. montezumae*, but becomes rough eventually. The leaves are slender and drooping, as in *P. montezumae* var. *lindleyi*. A tree at Pencarrow in Cornwall, planted in 1849, attained a height of 65 ft but died recently. At Blackmoor, Hants, one planted in 1913 is 60 × 5¼ ft (1974).

P. MONTICOLA D. Don   WESTERN WHITE PINE

A tree up to 175 ft high, with a trunk 4 ft or more in diameter; young shoots downy; winter-buds ovoid, with flattened scales. Leaves in fives, 3 to 4½ in. long, rough at the margins (minutely toothed under the lens), glaucous green, with several lines of stomata on the inner sides; leaf-sheath about ⅝ in. long, soon falling. Cones 5 to 10 in. long, 1¼ in. wide before expanding, cylindrical, tapered, and curved towards the end; scales thin, smooth, rounded at the apex, terminated by a dark resinous scar (umbo).

Native of western N. America from British Columbia and Vancouver Island to California and bordering parts of Nevada, east to Idaho and Montana; introduced by Douglas in 1831. Although not so well known in this country as its eastern ally—*P. strobus*, it is a handsome tree for gardens, assuming a shapely, slender, pyramidal shape. It is liable to be confused with *P. strobus*, but the short down all over the shoot usually distinguishes it. Its leaves also are stiffer and stouter. It yields a useful timber in its native home, but in Europe is planted for ornament only.

Like *P. strobus* and *P. lambertiana*, this pine is very susceptible to white pine blister-rust, to which all the old specimens in the country have fallen victim. The largest survivors in Britain are 70 to 80 ft high, 5 to 9¾ ft in girth.

P. MUGO Turra   DWARF MOUNTAIN PINE
P. montana Mill.; *P. mughus* Scop.   [PLATE 32

A shrubby pine of variable habit (see below). Winter-buds cylindric, resinous, with numerous scales. Leaves two in a bundle, 1 to 3 in. long, vivid green, rigid, blunt, persisting at least five years and sometimes ten years or even more; leaf-sheath ⅜ to ⅝ in. long. Cones solitary or in clusters of two or three near the tips of the shoots, very shortly stalked or sessile, brown and glossy when ripe, 1 to 2 in. long, ovoid, symmetrical, the apex of the scales flat with a central boss, or more or less raised and then convex on the upper side, concave on the lower, with the boss displaced to the lower edge. Seeds small, winged.

Native of the mountains of Central Europe, the Carpathians, the Balkans, and of the Italian Apennines; introduced to Britain in the second half of the 18th century. In its best-known and most characteristic form, *P. mugo* is a low, spreading shrub forming dense entanglements of snake-like stems known in German as 'krummholz' or 'knieholz'. But it may be erect-branched. In the Alps *P. mugo* has its main distribution in the eastern limestone ranges, and is rare in Switzerland in its characteristic form (see further below).

The above description includes var. *pumilio* (Haenke) Zenari, which has cones with displaced bosses, in contrast to the typical variety with a central boss. There is no difference in habit between the two.

The dwarf mountain pine is extremely useful as an evergreen covering for dry slopes and mounds, and thrives in the poorest soil. Making no tap-root, it transplants well. There are numerous garden selections, propagated by grafting, of which the best known is 'GNOM'. This makes a dense bush up to about 6 ft in height and as much in width.

P. UNCINATA Mirb. *P. mugo* var. *rostrata* (Ant.) Hoopes; *P. montana* var. *rostrata* Ant. MOUNTAIN PINE.—This resembles *P. mugo* in foliage, but makes a tree up to 80 ft high and differs markedly in its cones, which are up to 2¾ in. long, very oblique at the base, the scales on the outer side with a protuberant pyramidal apex ending in a backward-pointing hook. But at the eastern end of the area of the species, the hook is absent or not so pronounced (var. ROTUNDATA (Link) Antoine).

P. uncinata, in contrast to *P. mugo*, has a predominantly western distribution. It is best developed in the eastern Pyrenees, where it yields an excellent timber, and extends thence into the Alps. In Switzerland there is a well-known stand in the Swiss National Park below the Ofen pass, where it forms secondary forest, usurping the place of the original forest of Arolla pine and larch, which was destroyed long ago to provide fuel for local iron-works. The mountain pine is capable of growing in poor soils both wet and dry, but is little used in this country as a plantation tree. In France its main use is for reafforestation in places where more productive species cannot thrive. There is a specimen in the University Botanic Garden, Cambridge, measuring 50 × 4½ ft (1969).

In their typical states *P. mugo* and *P. uncinata* are distinct enough in habit and in their cones, but in the Alps, and especially in Switzerland, a bewildering array of intermediate forms occur, which are probably the result of past hybridisation between the two species. In habit they vary from true trees through various shrubby but erect forms to the typical decumbent form of *P. mugo*, and the cones show a continuous variation from the asymmetrical, hook-scaled cones of *P. uncinata* to the symmetrical, flat-surfaced cones of *P. mugo*. But there is no correlation between habit and cone characters.

In forestry, the shrubby erect-growing intermediates are useful as a pioneer crop on poor soils, and for shelter in exposed places.

P. MURICATA D. Don   BISHOP PINE

P. edgariana Hartw.

A tree 50 to 90 ft high, with a rough brown bark, often flat-topped and with wide-spreading branches; young shoots densely leafy, glabrous, brown; terminal buds cylindrical, pointed, ½ to 1 in. long, coated with resin. Leaves in pairs, falling the third or fourth year, rigid, 3 to 5 (sometimes 7) in. long, semi-terete, dark green; leaf-sheath persistent, ½ to ⅝ in. long. Cones obliquely egg-shaped, 2½ to 3½ in. long, the boss on the scales terminated by a stiff, slightly hooked spine.

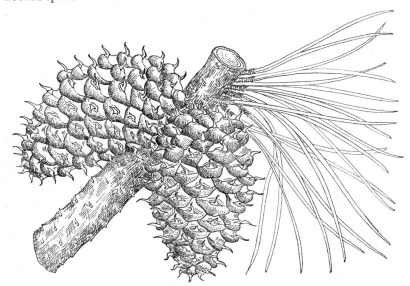

PINUS MURICATA

Native of California; originally discovered in 1832 at San Luis Obispo, from which it gets its popular name; introduced by Hartweg in 1846. This remarkable pine bears its cones in whorls of three to seven; they are deflexed, and the inner or less exposed side being less developed gives them their unsymmetrical shape. They remain on the tree and retain their seed for an indefinite period, at least twenty-five to thirty years, and often until the branch bearing them is 5 or 6 in. in diameter. This enables the species to survive forest fires, which, although they destroy the old trees, only affect the cones sufficiently to expand the scales and allow the uninjured seed to escape. The tree grows on exposed bluffs and headlands in Monterey and other places along the coast of California, where it is at times drenched with ocean spray. I have a letter from a correspondent in Guernsey, who says that it withstands the salt winds of that island even better than *P. radiata*. In such places it will be chiefly valuable as a shelter tree, its timber being inferior; but it is also handsome, and worth growing for its interest. Among two-leaved pines with persistent leaf-sheaths this is distinguished by its cylindrical, resin-covered buds and long, deep green leaves.

The tree at Claremont near Esher, mentioned in previous editions, still exists and remains healthy, though it has stopped growing. It measures 77 × 10 ft (1965). Some other notable specimens are: Sandling Park, Kent, 80 × 10 ft (1965); West Dean Arboretum, Sussex, 85 × 9½ ft (1971); Borde Hill, Sussex, in Warren Wood, 80 × 8¼ ft (1968); Albury Park, Surrey, 84 × 7¾ ft (1960); Ebernoe, Sussex, 87 × 13 ft (1971).

In addition to the common broad-crowned type with dark yellowish-green needles, there is another form, deriving from the northernmost wild stands, with a narrower crown and needles of a bluish shade of green. This type is represented by two trees at Wakehurst Place in Sussex, the larger 71 × 8½ ft (1964). It was planted in 1917 (Mitchell, *Conif. Brit. Isles* (1972) p. 221).

P. NIGRA Arnold   AUSTRIAN PINE

P. austriaca Hoess; *P. nigricans* Host; *P. laricio* var. *austriaca* (Hoess) Loud.; *P. laricio* var. *nigricans* (Host) Parl.

A tree sometimes over 100 ft high in the wild, with a broad crown and a dark, plated bark, young shoots brown when ripe, glabrous; buds brown, slightly resinous, broadly ovoid at the base, narrowed abruptly at the apex to a slender point. Leaves in pairs, 3 to 6 in. long, up to $\frac{1}{12}$ in. wide, falling in their fourth year, semi-terete, very minutely toothed, dark green, rather rigid; sheath about ½ in. long. Cones solitary, in pairs or in threes, ripe in their second year and then glossy brown, ovoid-conic or elongate-ovoid, 2 to 3 in. long, scales transversely ridged and sometimes terminated by a short prickle; seeds small, winged.

P. nigra (in the narrow sense as described above) has its northern limit south-west of Vienna, but its main distribution is from Istria and the Julian Alps southward through Yugoslavia to Greece; it has also been reported from a few localities in central and southern Italy. In Dalmatia it reaches to near sea-level on the Pelješac peninsula and on the island of Brač. The nurseryman Lawson of Edinburgh started to import seed of *P. nigra* in 1835 and two years later was offering one-year seedlings at 10 shillings a thousand.

The Austrian pine is very distinct in general appearance from, and decidedly inferior to, the Corsican pine (see var. *maritima* below). It has a rougher, shorter trunk, with more numerous branches, and heavier masses of darker green leaves, which on the whole are shorter, stiffer, and straighter than those of the var. *maritima*. The whole tree has a coarser, heavier aspect. It is very useful for growing on poor chalky soil, and as a shelter tree in bleak situations, especially near the sea. Its value as a timber tree is much less than that of var. *maritima*.

It appears to be a short-lived tree in cultivation, though the fact that it is so often planted in exposed positions may be the explanation for this. Some noteworthy specimens are: Keir House, Perths., *pl.* 1851, 75 × 13 ft (1970); Petworth House, Sussex, 112 × 11½ ft (1961); Bicton, Devon, 88 × 13¼ ft (1968); Bolderwood, New Forest, Hants, 115 × 12¾ ft (1970).

P. *nigra* in the broad sense is a variable and wide-ranging species, and the typical variety or subspecies, discussed above, is only a segment of it. It is now necessary to turn to the other subdivisions of the species, which are here given in geographical order, from east to west:

var. CARAMANICA (Loud.) Rehd. *P. laricio* var. *caramanica* Loud.; *P. caramanica* Delamarre; *P. pallasiana* D. Don; *P. nigra* subsp. *pallasiana* (D. Don) Holmboe; *P. nigra* var. *pallasiana* (D. Don) Aschers. & Graebn.; *P. tatarica* Hort.; *P. taurica* Hort. CRIMEAN PINE.—This variety or subspecies is not very clearly distinguished from typical *P. nigra*, but the cones are usually larger—up to 4 in. long. It occurs in Asia Minor, the Caucasus (where it is rare), in the Crimea, in the Balkans, and in the S. Carpathians. It was introduced to Britain around 1790 by Lee and Kennedy, who distributed plants raised from seeds sent from the Crimea by Pallas, a botanist of German origin famous for his explorations of Siberia. A. B. Lambert (who knew Pallas and bought his private herbarium) had two of the original trees in his collection at Boyton, which were heavily branched, 'the lower branches almost equalling the trunk itself in size' (Lambert, *Descr. Gen. Pinus*, 2nd Ed. (1828), Vol. 1, p. 14). This character is shown by old trees in British collections, which may be of Crimean provenance, but it is not a character of the var. *caramanica* as a whole (Mitchell, p. 224).

Some of the oldest specimens of the var. *caramanica* are: Dropmore, Bucks, *pl.* 1821, 90 × 14 ft at 3 ft (1970); Bury Hill, Surrey, *pl.* 1840, 102 × 14¾ ft (1971); Cuffnells, Hants, 124 × 12¼ ft (1970); Bicton, Devon, 105 × 12 ft (1968).

var. MARITIMA (Ait.) Melville *P. sylvestris* var. *maritima* Ait.; *P. laricio* Poir.; *P. nigra* subsp. *laricio* (Poir.) Maire; *P. nigra* var. *calabrica* (Loud.) Schneid.; *P. laricio* var. *calabrica* Loud.; *P. laricio* var. *corsicana* Loud.; *P. nigra* var. *poiretiana* (Ant.) Schneid.; *P. laricio* var. *poiretiana* Ant. CORSICAN PINE.— Crown slender, with short horizontal branches. Leaves more slender than in the Austrian pine and less rigid. At least in cultivated trees, there is also a difference in length, those of the Corsican being up to 6 or 7 in. long, while in the Austrian they do not much exceed 4 in. Cones 2 to 3 in. long, 1 to 1¼ in. wide, ovoid-conic, yellowish brown; scales transversely keeled.

A native of Calabria in the southern part of the Italian peninsula, of Sicily, and of Corsica; probably also of Algeria, though the trees there are sometimes separated as a distinct variety. The date of introduction is usually given as 1759, though this is simply the date of publication of the seventh edition of Miller's *Dictionary*, in which he mentions a cultivated pine which is thought to have been the Corsican. But it was not planted in any quantity until some years after the Napoleonic wars, when seed was distributed by the firm of Vilmorin. Even in France seed was scarce in the 1820s, and many thousands of seedlings of *P. sylvestris* growing in the Forest of Fontainebleau were worked over to Corsican by grafting in the years 1826–30 (Loudon, *Arb. et Frut. Brit.*, Vol. IV, p. 2130 and p. 2204); some of these trees still exist.

In Britain the Corsican pine now ranks as the fourth most important forest tree. Being a native of the Mediterranean region and needing more than average summer warmth, it is not suitable for the cooler and rainier parts of the country. But in south-eastern England it grows excellently on sandy soils, where it is displacing Scots pine. The annual rate of planting is about 4,000 acres. It is also useful for afforesting sand-dunes, being resistant to salt winds. It does not transplant well if allowed to remain more than two years in one spot, and should be put in when less than 1 ft high.

Some of the most notable specimens of the Corsican pine are: Dropmore, Bucks, *pl.* 1829, 120 × 14 ft (1970); Warnham Court, Sussex, *pl.* 1834, 100 × 11 ft (1971); Albury Park, Surrey, 110 × 12¼ ft (1966); Cuffnells, Hants, *pl.* 1856, 130 × 10 ft (1970); Stanage Park, Glos., *pl.* 1828, 144 × 11 ft (1970); Arley Castle, Worcs., *pl.* 1820, 125 × 14¼ ft (1961); Mells Park, Som., 125 × 13¼ ft (1962); near Llanfachreth, Merion., 70 × 15½ ft (1968).

The following measurements indicate rate of growth in the south-east: National Pinetum, Bedgebury, *pl.* 1926, 61 × 6 ft (1969); Dropmore, Bucks, *pl.* 1929, 61 × 5 ft (1970).

var. CEBENNENSIS (Godr.) Rehd. *P. laricio* var. *cebennensis* Godr.; *P. nigra* subsp. *salzmannii* (Dun.) Franco; *P. salzmannii* Dun.; *P. pyrenaica* Lapeyr., in part; *P. laricio* var. *pyrenaica* (Lapeyr.) Loud., in part; *P. monspeliensis* Salzm. ex Dun.; *P. laricio monspeliensis* Hort.; *P. laricio* var. *tenuifolia* Parl.—This, the westernmost race of *P. nigra*, is of little importance. It makes a small or medium-sized tree and is best distinguished by its orange shoots and its very slender leaves, only $\frac{1}{16}$ in. wide, not pungent at the apex. There is a specimen measuring 72 × 8¼ ft (1969) in the University Botanic Garden, Cambridge. A tree in the forest plot at Bedgebury (National Pinetum), *pl.* 1932, measures 47 × 3¼ ft (1965).

P. nigra has given rise to only one cultivar of any importance, namely:

cv. 'PYGMAEA'.—A slow growing, dense small bush or miniature tree. A plant at Kew attained 8 ft in height in forty years. Described by Carrière in 1855 as *P. laricio* var. *pygmaea*. This is not the same as *P. laricio* var. *pygmaea* Rauch ex Gordon, discovered on 'the highest region of Mount Amaro' and described as completely prostrate with spherical cones 'smaller than those of *Pinus pumilio*'. Gordon identified this plant with *P. magellensis* Schouw, which is a synonym of *P. mugo*.

P. PARVIFLORA Sieb. & Zucc.   JAPANESE WHITE PINE
P. pentaphylla Mayr; *P. parviflora* var. *pentaphylla* (Mayr) Henry; *P. himekomatsu* Miyabe & Kudo

A tree usually 50 to 70 ft in the wild, occasionally attaining 100 ft; young shoots minutely downy; winter-buds ovoid, $\frac{3}{16}$ in. long, some of their scales free at the tips. Leaves in fives, falling the third year, 1½ to 2½ in. long, very slightly toothed on the margin, twisted, with silvery lines of stomata on the inner surface; leaf-sheath ¾ in. long, deciduous. Cones egg-shaped, 1¼ to 4 in. long, oblong-ovoid, usually produced in whorls of three or four, borne in extraordinary profusion even by quite young trees.

A native of Japan; introduced by J. G. Veitch in 1861. As usually seen in this country it is a slow-growing, bushy tree with rather dark needles. As it bears heavy crops of cones, which turn back after opening and persist on the branches for six or seven years, it is not very ornamental. This form has the appearance of a Japanese garden variety and the plants may have been imported from one of the

Japanese nurseries early this century or in the last decades of the 19th century. Or it may derive from the original introduction by Veitch. The normal wild form is rare in Britain, the most notable example being a tree at Stourhead, Wilts, measuring 69 × 6½ ft (1970).

cv. 'GLAUCA'.—The plants in commerce under this name have conspicuously glaucous leaves and are said to be of comparatively dwarf habit, and to cone very freely.

P. PATULA Schlecht. & Cham.   [PLATE 34

A tree ordinarily 40 to 50 ft, sometimes 80 ft high, often branching low and acquiring a spreading round-topped shape when old; old bark rough, with a distinct reddish tinge. Young shoots glabrous, rather glaucous at first, becoming scaly and reddish brown. Winter-buds not resinous, ½ to ¾ in. long, cylindrical, covered with awl-shaped, pointed, fringed, brown scales which are free except at the base and slightly spreading. Leaves pendulous, normally in threes (occasionally in four or fives), 6 to 9 in. long, very slender, and very minutely toothed on the margins, persisting two to four years; basal sheath persistent, about 1 in. long. Cones shortly stalked, often in clusters of two to five, 2½ to 4 in. long, 1¼ to 1½ in. wide at the base; tapering upwards, curved, unequally sided at the base, pale shining brown.

Native of Mexico; discovered in 1828 and introduced then or soon after, as a plant 6 ft high is recorded by Loudon to have been growing in the garden of A. B. Lambert in 1837. It must be accounted one of the rather tender pines, and it is found at its best in Cornwall and similar places. This pine is unmistakable in its very slender, drooping leaves in bundles of threes with a persistent leaf-sheath. Very attractive and distinct for mild districts, it may also be tried in cooler places.

P. *patula* is uncommon in southern England, but there is a specimen in the Pinetum at Wakehurst Place, Sussex, planted around 1918, which measures 46 × 3½ + 3 ft (1971). A small tree, about twenty years planted, is growing well in the nursery of Messrs Hillier at Jermyns House, Romsey. But most of the recorded trees are in the south-west and in Ireland. The most notable of these are: Tregothnan, Cornwall, 57 × 7½ ft (1971); Tregrehan, Cornwall, 52 × 5½ ft (1971); Fota, Co. Cork, Eire, 54 × 6½ ft (1966); Powerscourt, Co. Wicklow, Eire, 54 × 5¼ ft (1966); Shelton Abbey, in the same county, 52 × 5¼ ft (1966).

P. GREGGII Engelm. P. *patula* var. *macrocarpa* Mast.—This pine from N.E. Mexico is closely akin to P. *patula* but less ornamental. Leaves in threes, bright green, shorter and not so pendulous. Cones like those of P. *patula*, but tawny yellow. The bark is very different, smooth and grey on young trees, grey and fissured on older trees. The tree at Leonardslee in Sussex mentioned in previous editions still exists and measures 47 × 6 ft (1962). In the National Pinetum at Bedgebury in Kent was a tree measuring 53 × 5½ ft (1970) which grew originally in the Temperate House at Kew and was moved to Bedgebury in 1926. It died in 1973.

P. PEUCE Griseb.   MACEDONIAN PINE

A tree up to 120 ft high in the wild; densely branched, and slenderly pyramidal; young shoots glossy green, quite glabrous. Leaves in fives, mostly falling in their third year, 3 to 4 in. long, very densely borne on the shoots, pointed forwards, three-sided; two of the sides have three or four lines of white stomata, the other one is bright green; margins roughened with tiny teeth; leaf-sheaths soon falling. Cones on stalks about $\frac{1}{4}$ in. long, themselves 4 or 5 in. long, $1\frac{1}{4}$ to $1\frac{1}{2}$ in. wide before expanding; scales in the middle about $1\frac{1}{2}$ in. long, half as wide, thin at the margins.

Native of Yugoslav Macedonia, where it was discovered by Grisebach near Bitolj in 1839; from there it ranges northward through Albania to north-east Montenegro (Crna Gora), and is also found in Bulgaria. It was introduced in 1864. One of the smaller and slower-growing pines, this is suitable for small gardens. It grows about 1 ft in height yearly. It is considered to be very closely allied to P. *wallichiana*, but the two are extremely distinct in general appearance. P. *peuce* is much denser in leaf and branch; its leaves are shorter, greener, and never have the kink near the base seen in P. *wallichiana*. The cones also are shorter and thicker. It resembles P. *cembra* more as a young tree, but that species has very shaggy young shoots.

P. *peuce* is an undemanding species, growing well on most soils. A tree at Stourhead, Wilts, measuring 93 × 12 ft (1970) is the largest in the country and probably from the original introduction. Two trees mentioned by Elwes and Henry early this century are: Kew, 42 × $3\frac{3}{4}$ ft (1909), now 59 × 6 ft (1969); and Bicton, Devon, 42 × $3\frac{3}{4}$ ft (1906), now 94 × 8 ft (1968). Some other examples are: Westonbirt, Glos., *pl.* 1876, 75 × $7\frac{3}{4}$ ft (1971); Wakehurst Place, Sussex, *pl.* 1915, 65 × $6\frac{1}{4}$ ft (1970); National Pinetum, Bedgebury, Kent, *pl.* 1926, 45 × 5 ft (1969).

P. PINASTER Ait.   MARITIME PINE, CLUSTER PINE
P. *maritima* Poir.; P. *sylvestris* Mill., not L.

A tree reaching 100 to 120 ft in height, forming a tall, rugged, dark trunk. Young shoots not downy, pale brown; terminal winter-buds, 1 to $1\frac{1}{4}$ in. long, $\frac{1}{8}$ to $\frac{1}{2}$ in. wide, cylindrical with a conical apex, clothed with awl-shaped, outwardly curving scales conspicuously fringed with silvery threads. Leaves in pairs, 4 to 8 in. long, $\frac{1}{12}$ in. wide, stiff and stout, dark green, falling the third and fourth years; slightly roughened at the margins; leaf-sheath $\frac{5}{8}$ to $\frac{3}{4}$ in. long, persistent. Cones usually borne in whorls, deflexed, 4 or 5 (sometimes 7) in. long, 2 to $2\frac{1}{2}$ in. wide at the base before opening, tapering to a point, bright brown, often persisting for many years.

Native of S.W. Europe and N. Africa; planted and naturalised in the Atlantic zone from S.W. France to Portugal; cultivated in Britain since the 16th century. As an old tree it is singularly picturesque, its dark, deeply fissured trunk being naked for two-thirds of its height. As a young tree it grows with great rapidity—2 ft per annum—and has a coarse, gaunt aspect. The leaves of this pine are the largest and stoutest of all hardy Old World pines and of all two-leaved pines, although they are of course exceeded in size by those of Californian and Mexican species. It is, as its common name implies, admirably adapted for maritime localities. The famous pine plantations of Bournemouth are largely composed of this tree. It is also one of the very best for light sandy soils. It yields a valuable product in its resin, but its timber is poor. Nowhere has its economic value been so efficiently demonstrated as in the Landes of France, south of Bordeaux. Here in 1904, mostly planted by man, it covered an area of about 1¾ million acres, yielding an annual revenue of £560,000, and this from land which previously was mainly desert. Among two-leaved pines it is distinguished by the size and length of leaf, and by the curly, fringed bud-scales.

The trees of the Atlantic zone differ from the wild trees in their shorter leaves and smaller cones and probably represent a cultivated race adapted to an oceanic climate. They are sometimes distinguished as subsp. ATLANTICA H. del Villar. The description given above is really of this subspecies, to which all the trees cultivated in Britain probably belong. In what is regarded as typical *P. pinaster* the leaves are 7 to 10 in. long and the cones 5½ to almost 9 in. long.

The maritime pine is short-lived in cultivation, though a few old trees survive, notably the following: Curraghmore, Co. Waterford, Eire, probably *pl.* 1770, 102 × 9¾ ft (1968); Sheffield Park, Sussex, *pl. c.* 1800, 85 × 15 ft (1968); Holme Lacy, Heref., 95 × 11 ft, with a superb bole of 80 ft (1974). Younger trees of which the planting date is known are: Wakehurst Place, Sussex, *pl.* 1913, 76 × 7¼ ft (1970); National Pinetum, Bedgebury, Kent, *pl.* 1926, 62 × 5¾ ft (1966).

P. PINEA L.   STONE PINE   [PLATE 37

A tree varying in height according to the position in which it grows, from 40 to 100 ft; forming in the open a comparatively low tree with a short, deeply fissured trunk, supporting a broad spreading head of branches more in diameter than it is high. When the tree has been drawn up by others it becomes much taller, but develops the characteristically shaped head as soon as the opportunity comes. Young shoots not downy, pale yellowish brown, more or less devoid of leaves at the base. Buds very characteristic on account of the curly pointed scales edged with long silvery threads by which they are matted together; ¼ to ⅝ in. long. Leaves in pairs, occasionally in threes, 3 to 5 in. long. Cones 4 in. wide, roundish egg-shaped, rounded at the top; glossy, pale brown. Seeds kidney-bean shaped, ¾ in. long.

Native of S. Europe from Spain and Portugal eastwards to Greece and Asia Minor; cultivated in England for probably four centuries at least. Its flat spreading head of branches is one of the most picturesque and characteristic objects of Italian scenery. A famous forest of this pine is that of Ravenna, near the coast of the Adriatic, about 16 miles long, and 1 mile wide, which, though man-made, has existed for at least 1,500 years and was called by Dante 'la divina foresta spessa e viva' (*Purgatorio*, XXVIII, line 2). The tree has always been valued in Italy for its edible seeds, and as their husks have been found in the refuse heaps of Roman encampments in Britain, they would appear to have been sent over for the use of the army in occupation. Young plants are apt to be cut by severe frosts, and transplant badly if allowed to remain more than two or three years in one place. The solitary, very glaucous needles about 1 in. long, characteristic of seedling one- or two-year-old plants, are frequently to be observed on scattered shoots over much older plants. Amongst two-leaved pines this is well distinguished by its habit, its large rounded cones, and by the fringed scales of the winter-bud.

The well-known tree at Kew near the Succulent House must have been planted in the first half of the last century; its measurements are 42 × 8¾ ft (1958). A tree at Embley Park, Hants, measuring 72 × 11¼ ft (1971), is the largest in the British Isles, both in height and girth. Some other specimens are: Leonardslee, Sussex, 51 × 8½ ft (1961); Pylewell Park, Hants, 46 × 8¼ ft (1968); North Manor, Crickhowell, Brecon, 60 × 10¾ ft (1971); Dartington Hall, Devon, 55 × 9½ ft (1968); Fota, Co. Cork, Eire, *pl.* 1847, 54 × 8 ft (1966).

P. PONDEROSA Laws.   WESTERN YELLOW PINE

A tree occasionally over 200 ft in the wild, with a perfectly erect, columnar trunk sometimes 8 ft thick, and comparatively short, often deflexed branches, forming a columnar or slenderly tapered head; bark of mature trees cinnamon or pinkish brown, divided into very large scaly plates; young shoots shining, reddish brown, glabrous, smelling of turpentine when cut. Buds cylindrical with a tapered apex, resinous, ¾ to 1 in. long, ½ in. thick, with appressed scales. Leaves in threes, falling the third or fourth year, 5 to 10 in. long; margins minutely toothed; leaf-sheath persistent, ⅝ to ⅞ in. long. Cones elongated oval, 3 to 6 in. long, 1½ to 2½ in. thick before opening; scales with a raised, short-prickly umbo. Seeds about ¼ in. long, with wing 1 in. long.

P. ponderosa has a very wide range in western N. America, from British Columbia to the Mexican border and eastward to the Rocky Mountains and even beyond them; it occurs, for example, in the Black Hills of Dakota. Introduced in 1827 by David Douglas. As a timber tree it is the most important of the N. American pines. Although thinly furnished with branches, it is, nevertheless, one of the most imposing and stately of the genus. It is variable in the length of its leaves and in the size of its cones. Some Rocky Mountain trees have the cones usually not more than 3 in. long and the leaves in pairs as well as in threes; these are sometimes distinguished as var. SCOPULORUM Engelm.

Some trees from the original introduction by Douglas still survive. They are: Dropmore, Bucks, *pl.* 1829, 98 × 9¾ ft (1970); Arley Castle, Worcs., *pl.* 1829, 114 × 7½ ft (1961); Bowood, Wilts, 120 × 13½ ft (1968); also, probably, Powis Castle, Montgom., 128 × 14 ft (1970). Some other notable specimens are: Highnam Court, Glos., *pl.* 1844, 85 × 13 ft (1970); Bicton, Devon, 104 × 11½ ft (1968); Scotney Castle, Kent, 120 × 10¾ ft (1971); Silia, Radnor, a superb tree, 121 × 10¾ ft (1970).

The var. *scopulorum* (see above) is represented at Kew by a tree planted in 1889, measuring 49 × 3 ft (1970).

P. PUNGENS Michx. f.   TABLE-MOUNTAIN PINE

A tree usually 20 to 40 ft high; young shoots reddish brown, shining, not downy, very stiff and sturdy, with the crowded leaves of the lateral branches more or less erect; bark scaly on young trees; buds cylindrical, ¾ to 1 in. long, very resinous. Leaves in twos, falling the third year; very rigid and sharply pointed, deep green, 2 to 3 in. long, somewhat spirally curved; leaf-sheath ¼ in. long, persistent. Cones usually in clusters of three or more, each cone 3 or 3½ in. long, 2 to 2½ in. wide at the base; the boss of each scale terminated by a broad, hooked spine.

Native of eastern N. America in the Appalachians; introduced in 1804. This pine retains the cones on its branches frequently fifteen or twenty years. It is one of the least ornamental of pines in cultivation and its timber is of little value. In the group of two-leaved pines with persistent leaf-sheaths and cylindrical resinous buds, it is distinguished by the stiff, spine-tipped leaves and bright red brown branchlets.

This rare pine is represented at Leonardslee, Sussex, by two trees, the larger measuring 57 × 3¾ ft (1969).

P. RADIATA D. Don   MONTEREY PINE
P. insignis Dougl. ex Loud.

A tree up to 115 ft high, with a trunk occasionally 6 ft thick; bark very rugged, dark brown; young shoots glabrous, yellowish brown; buds resinous, cylindrical. Leaves in threes, falling the third year, 2 to 5 in. long, soft and flexible, very dense on the branchlets, of a rich grassy green, convex on the outer face, faintly lined with stomata; margins minutely toothed; leaf-sheath persistent, ¼ to ½ in. long. Cones obliquely conical, rich bright brown, 3 to 5 in. long, 2 to 3 in. wide near the base; shortly stalked and more or less deflexed, so that the inner side is close to the branch and is imperfectly developed; the boss of the scale is diamond-shaped, with a minute prickle in the centre. The cones are usually borne in whorls of two or three, and remain closed for years upon the branches.

Native of Monterey, California, where it is confined to a few hills near the sea; introduced in 1833 by Douglas. In maritime situations in the south and west of Britain this pine thrives splendidly, growing at the rate of 4 or 5 ft annually, and average rates of 3 ft a year have been attained by some trees in southern England and well inland. As an example, Elwes and Henry mentioned a tree at Whiteknights, Reading, which measured 52 × 4 ft when eighteen years old from seed. A more recent example, cited by A. F. Mitchell, is a tree at Albury Park, Surrey, which, twenty-eight years planted, is 79 ft high. Such rapid growth is perhaps exceptional, but the many thriving trees in Surrey, Sussex, and even farther east show that the Monterey pine is able to survive hard winters and grow vigorously well outside the Atlantic zone.

On the other hand, P. radiata is tender when young and, according to Loudon, most of the seedlings from the original introduction by Douglas were killed in the winter of 1837–8. And being a warmth-loving species, it is not suitable for areas where the summer is cooler than average. But the browning of the foliage in winter, mentioned in previous editions, is not really damaging and may occur even in fairly mild winters if there are prolonged periods of dry, cold winds. But it renders the tree very unsightly for a time. Salt-laden winds from the Atlantic it withstands very well, and it is much used as a windbreak in the milder parts.

There are many notable specimens of *P. radiata* in the British Isles; measurements of over sixty of these will be found in A. F. Mitchell's *Conifers in the British Isles*. Of the trees listed by Elwes and Henry early this century nearly all survive. Among them are: Cuffnells, Lyndhurst, Hants, 140 × 12¼ ft (1961); Northerwood House, Hants, 116 × 18 ft (1963); Knowle Hotel, Sidmouth, Devon, 75 × 19 ft (1965); Haldon House, Devon, 94 × 19¼ ft (1967); Bodorgan, Anglesey, 70 × 24 ft at ground-level (1966). Some others, selected for size, or because they grow outside the optimum area, are: Sandling Park, Hythe, Kent, *pl.* 1848, 95 × 17½ ft at 6 ft (1965); Dropmore, Bucks, *pl.* 1839, 90 × 17¼ ft (1970); Albury Park, Surrey, *pl.* 1926, 95 × 8¼ ft (1970); Bicton, Devon, 85 × 21¾ ft (1967).

Although of no importance as a forestry tree in Britain, *P. radiata* is an important source of timber in the southern hemisphere, where the plantations now vastly exceed in acreage the original wild stands. It is now being tried as a plantation tree in Britain, and a great increase in its use is likely.

P. RESINOSA Ait.   RED PINE

A tree 50 to 70 ft high in this country, rarely twice as high in nature, with somewhat pendulous branches; young shoots deep yellowish brown, not downy; winter-buds resinous, conical, ⅝ in. long. Leaves in pairs, semi-terete, 5 to 6¼ in. long, falling the fourth year, and leaving the branchlets rough with the remains of the prominences on which each bundle was seated, dark lustrous green, minutely toothed on the margin; densely crowded on the branchlets, so that each year's crop is continuous with the preceding one; leaf-sheaths ⅝ to ¾ in. long, persistent. Cones egg-shaped, 2 to 2¼ in. long, 1 to 1¼ in. wide before opening; pale shining brown, scarcely stalked; scales unarmed.

Native of eastern N. America from Newfoundland and Nova Scotia south to Pennsylvania, west (in both the USA and Canada) to the region of the Great Lakes and slightly beyond; introduced in 1756 by the Duke of Northumberland. It is a handsome pine as seen in its native country and yields a useful timber. It belongs to the same group as *P. sylvestris*, *P. thunbergii*, and *P. nigra*, but is only likely to be confused with the last-named, which has a denser, more horizontal branching. The distinction given by Rehder is that the leaves of *P. resinosa* snap when bent, while those of *P. nigra* do not.

P. RIGIDA Mill.   NORTHERN PITCH PINE

A tree reaching about 80 ft in height, with a trunk 2 to 3 ft thick, often sending out adventitious shoots from the trunk and older branches; young shoots glabrous, pale brown; buds cylindrical, resinous. Leaves in threes, falling the third year, 3 to 4½ in. long, rigid, twisted, dark green, margins minutely toothed; leaf-sheath ¼ to ½ in. long. Cones very variable, ranging from conical to almost globose, and from 1 to 3½ in. long; occasionally small and numerous in clusters, long persisting; scales terminated by a short prickle.

Native of eastern N. America from S. Quebec to Georgia and Tennessee; introduced in the early 18th century. As a rule it is rather a scrubby tree of little ornament, but in some collections it has attained a height of 60 to slightly over 70 ft in height and up to 8 ft in girth. The example at Kew measures 56 × 5 ft (1970) and there is one in the Pinetum of the Royal Horticultural Society at Wisley of 66 × 8 ft (1970). It is very well distinguished by the small branches springing directly from the trunk. Some trees produce these twigs so freely that the trunks are almost covered with foliage, but the twigs never get very large, and mostly die after a few years.

P. SEROTINA Michx. POND PINE.—This is closely allied to P. *rigida*, and seems to differ chiefly in its greater length of leaf (twice as long). It is tender, and very rare. Native of the south-eastern United States from N. Carolina to Florida.

P. SABINIANA Dougl.   DIGGER PINE

A tree 40 to 50, occasionally 90 ft high, of curiously thin habit; young shoots blue-white, not downy, with the leaves clustered at the apex only, the major part naked except for the awl-shaped scale-leaves, ½ in. long. Leaves in threes, mostly falling the third year, 8 to 12 in. long, of a pale greyish green, with two narrow flat faces, and one rounded broad one, all lined closely with stomata, extremely minutely toothed at the margin, slenderly and sharply pointed; leaf-sheath ¾ to 1 in. long, persistent. Cones produced on stout stalks about 2 in. long, ovoid, 6 to 10 in. long, 4 to 6 in. thick, often remaining on the branch long after the seeds have fallen; scales terminated by a large, triangular, hooked spine.

Native of California, whence it was introduced by Douglas in 1832. Most nearly allied to P. *coulteri*, and with similar large, heavy, spiny cones, it is very readily distinguished by its thin foliage, smoother and more slender young shoots, and narrow cylindrical winter-buds. The young shoots when cut have the same orange-like odour as in P. *coulteri*, P. *ponderosa*, and P. *jeffreyi*. The seeds are large like those of P. *coulteri* (but with much shorter wings), and were formerly much eaten by the Digger tribe of Indians. It is not a particularly ornamental tree, being thinly furnished with foliage, but is interesting in the curious contrast between the heavy trunk and the thin, light, shadeless head of branches. It is a light-demanding tree, growing in the wild on hot, dry slopes, where it forms open stands on its own or mixed with oak.

There is an example in the Pinetum of the Royal Horticultural Society at Wisley, measuring 62 × 5 ft (1968), and a slightly larger one at Wakehurst Place, Sussex.

P. STROBUS L.   WEYMOUTH PINE

A tree usually 60 to 80, rarely above 100 ft high in this country, but known occasionally to have exceeded twice that height in the United States; bark of trunk shallowly fissured. Young shoots with a tuft of down extending downwards from each leaf-bundle, much of which soon falls away; winter-buds ovoid, with closely flattened scales. Leaves in fives, mostly falling the third year, 3 to 5 in. long, roughened on the margins, soft bluish green, with lines of white stomata on the inner sides; leaf-sheath about ½ in. long, soon falling completely away. Cones 5 to 8 in. long, about 1 in. in diameter before opening, cylindrical, tapering at the apex, curved; scales of cones thin, smooth, rounded, 1 to 1¼ in. long, half as wide.

Native of eastern N. America, with a very wide range, from Newfoundland west to Ontario and the Lake states, south to the N.E. states of the USA and the Appalachians; introduced before 1705. The common name of 'Weymouth' pine does not refer to the town, but to a Lord Weymouth, who is recorded to have planted it largely at Longleat about two hundred years ago. In France, the name has been contracted to 'Pin du Lord'. This pine has at various times been largely planted both in England and on the Continent, and is, no doubt, a valuable timber tree, especially in sunnier climates than ours, producing a white, easily worked, light timber, very useful for many purposes, but not remarkable for strength. One hundred years ago this tree covered enormous areas in eastern N. America, and was one of the richest assets of the country. Now fine specimens are comparatively scarce there.

It is an ornamental tree for gardens where the soil is not a heavy clay, especially up to its middle age. Unfortunately it is subject to the five-leaf pine blister-rust (*Cronartium ribicola*), a fungus which has currant as its secondary host. During the eighty years or so since it first appeared most of the finest specimens in the country have succumbed, though it remains a fairly common tree. Until a resistant strain is developed it cannot be recommended for general planting as an ornamental, which is a pity, as it thrives in this country and often produces self-sown seedlings.

Among the larger surviving specimens of Weymouth pine are: Bury Hill, Surrey, *pl.* 1850, 105 × 9¾ ft (1954); Puck Pits, New Forest, 128 × 8½ ft (1969); Nuneham, Oxon, 83 × 10 ft (1966); Fonthill, Wilts, 112 × 11 ft (1965); Ombersley Court, Worcs., 90 × 18 ft at 2 ft (1964); Chatsworth, Derb., 120 × 8½ ft (1971).

var. CHIAPENSIS Martinez—Although not in cultivation, and unlikely to thrive in this country, this Mexican variety is mentioned because of its phyto-geographical interest. The late Prof. Martinez, who described it in 1940, at first believed that the herbarium specimens he examined must have come from cultivated trees of *P. strobus*, but further investigation showed that the tree was genuinely wild in a few localities in Chiapas and Oaxaca, and it was later found in other regions, though it is nowhere frequent. From the southernmost stands of *P. strobus* in the USA it is separated by about 1,500 miles in a direct line. Other tree species of the eastern United States have a similar disjunct distribution, reappearing in similar or identical form in the rain-forests of Mexico, e.g., *Liquidambar styraciflua*.

f. NANA Hort.—The epithet *nana* has been used over the past 150 years for various dwarf or slow-growing forms of *P. strobus*. According to Krüssmann, some of the plants offered as 'Nana' at the present time are really 'Radiata' (*Handb. Nadelgeh.* (1970–1), p. 263).

cv. 'PROSTRATA'.—Of creeping habit. The original plant arose at the Arnold Arboretum and a propagation was sent to Kew around 1893, where it still grows in the Rock Garden, hanging vertically down the face of a rock. The botanical

name *P. strobus* f. *prostrata* Fern. & Weatherby is founded on a plant found growing wild in Newfoundland, of similar habit.

cv. 'RADIATA'.—A dwarf shrub wider than high, dense at first but later of
open habit; leaves pointing upward or radially spreading, not drooping. A plant
in the Arnold Arboretum was 4 ft high, 5 ft wide in 1930 (Hornibrook, *Dw. and
Sl. Gr. Conif.*, 2nd Ed., p. 208 and plate).

cv. 'UMBRACULIFERA'.—A very striking dwarf, short-stemmed variety
attaining about 6 ft, with an umbrella-shaped crown and drooping needles
(cf. 'Radiata').

P. SYLVESTRIS L.   SCOTS PINE   [PLATE 36
P. rubra Mill.

A tree rarely more than 100 to 120 ft in height, with a trunk 3 ft, sometimes
5 ft in thickness. Its crown varies in shape according to the density of the stand,
the age of the trees, and the race to which they belong. The bark usually has a
reddish tinge, especially in the crown, where it is thin and flaky; on the trunk
it may be cracked into large, fairly smooth plates; or ridged, with anastomosing
furrows; or with small, loose, concave plates. Young stems glabrous, green;
buds short-pointed, brown, usually more or less resinous. Leaves in pairs,
grey-green, varying in length from 1½ to 4 in. according to the vigour of the
tree and the race to which it belongs; leaf-sheath ¼ to ⅜ in. long, persistent. Cones
conical to ovoid, usually in some shade of brown, 1 to 2½ in. long; scales
rhomboidal at the apex, transversely keeled, flattish or sometimes raised, especially on the outward-facing side. Seeds winged, shed in spring.

P. sylvestris has its main distribution in northern Eurasia, from Scotland
through Scandinavia and the Baltic region to the Russian Far East, and in its
north–south range from beyond the Arctic Circle to the borders of the steppe.
In Central and Western Europe it was widespread in some phases of the post-
glacial epoch, but it is now confined to areas and habitats where for one reason
or another it can withstand the competition of deciduous forests or of the
common spruce. It is not now a native of the British Isles outside Scotland,
though it was still to be found in northern England a few centuries ago, and
some authorites hold that the Scots pine of the heathlands of southern England
may descend partly from trees which have persisted there since earlier post-
glacial times. North of the Mediterranean and in the Near East it ranges from
Spain and the Pyrenees to the Caucasus, but its distribution is patchy and it is
quite absent from peninsular Italy.

For gardens there is scarcely any tree more picturesque than an old Scots
pine, or with greater beauty of trunk, especially when lit by the low rays of the
winter sun. The poet Wordsworth preferred the Highland pine of Scotland 'to
all other trees except the Oak, taking into consideration its beauty in winter,
and by moonlight, and in the evening' (Letter to the nurseryman James Grigor
written from Rydall Mount, December 7, 1844).

Some notable specimens of Scots pine are: Kilkerran, Ayrs., *pl.* 1757, 102
× 13¼ ft (1970); Keir House, Perths., *pl.* 1827, 93 × 11¾ ft (1970); Kidbrooke
Park, Sussex, 105 × 7½ ft, with clear bole of 65 ft (1968); Compton Chamber-

layne, Wilts, 88 × 14¼ ft (1960); Forde Abbey, Dorset, 60 × 13¾ ft (1959); Oakley Park, Shrops., 113 × 10½ ft (1971); Hewell Grange, Worcs., 105 × 10¼ ft (1963); Tetton House, Som., 82 × 11¼ ft (1959).

The Scots pine provides one of the most important and widely used of timbers. Much of it is imported from N. Europe as yellow deal or redwood, and in earlier times as Riga fir, Danzig fir, etc., according to the port from which it was shipped. In this country the Scots pine is still an important plantation tree, despite the competition from faster-growing species such as Corsican pine and *P. contorta*. It is particularly suited to poor soils in the eastern parts of the country, where the climate is drier and the summers warmer than average. Planting by the Forestry Commission is at the rate of 2,000 acres annually, and the total area devoted to it in 1965 was 623,000 acres.

P. sylvestris is a very variable species, as might be expected, considering the diversity of the climates, soils, and altitudes in which it occurs. Many local varieties have been distinguished, but the characters of the wild trees may be to a large extent determined by the local environment, and are lost or modified when the variety is grown away from its native habitat. A few of the local races are mentioned below, together with the more important garden varieties:

var. ARGENTEA Steven—Foliage of a distinctly more glaucous or silvery hue. Described from the Caucasus. The f. *argentea* of Beissner is of general application to trees of this character, which are not confined to the Caucasus and may appear among seedlings.

cv. 'AUREA'.—Leaves yellowish green at first, becoming golden in winter, eventually green. In commerce in Britain by 1875. Examples are: Westonbirt, Glos., 39 × 3½ ft (1970); Hergest Croft, Heref., 25 × 3½ ft (1963); Smeaton, East Lothian, 43 × 3¼ ft (1966); Castlewellan, Co. Down, 47 × 5¼ ft (1970). Award of Merit 1964, when shown by Robert Strauss, Stonehurst, Sussex, where there is an example about 32 ft high (1964).

cv. 'BEUVRONENSIS'.—A dense, very slow-growing bush with blue-green leaves about 1½ in. long. It is believed to have originated as a witch's broom and was put into commerce by Transon Frères of Orleans, before 1891. According to Hornibrook an old specimen at Wakehurst Place in Sussex was slightly over 3 ft high and about 5 ft wide in 1932.

var. ENGADINENSIS Heer—A small tree up to about 30 ft; bark thin, reddish; buds resinous. Leaves about 1½ in. long, stiff, persisting five years. Cones brown, glossy; scales hooked at the apex with a thickened umbo surrounded at the base by a dark ring, said to be caused by a fungus. It was described from the Engadine but occurs elsewhere in the central valleys of the Alps and in the Dolomites. It ascends to 6,000 ft. It is thought by some to be a hybrid between *P. sylvestris* and either *P. mugo* or *P. uncinata*. But the var. LAPPONICA Fries, from northern Scandinavia, is very similar and cannot be a hybrid. Coming from a region where the summer days are very long it is said to grow poorly when introduced to more southern latitudes.

f. FASTIGIATA (Carr.) Beissn.—Of narrow habit, with ascending branches. It occurs occasionally in the wild. There is an example 21 ft high in the Royal Horticultural Society Garden, Wisley, Surrey (1968).

var. HAGUENENSIS Loud. HAGUENAU PINE.—This race, which occurs in Alsace near the Rhine, has no distinctive botanical characters, but is one of the best known provenances of the Scots pine. In France it was widely used in the last century for reafforestation and was also sold in quantity by some nurserymen in this country. In 1838, Lawson and Son of Edinburgh were offering one-year seedlings from Haguenau seed at 2 shillings a thousand.

var. RIGENSIS Loud. RIGA PINE.—A native of the Baltic region, distinguished by its narrow crown and its tall straight stems, which provided the masts for many warships in the days of sail. It proved to be the finest form of P. sylvestris in the trial plots planted by Ph.-A. de Vilmorin at Les Barres early in the 19th century, but is not generally considered to be of any value outside its native habitat. It is interesting that some of the seed used by de Vilmorin came not from the Baltic but from Brittany, where the Riga pine had been planted in the 18th century, presumably to supply the naval shipyards with timber.

var. SCOTICA Beissn. P. scotica Willd. ex Endl. HIGHLAND PINE.—The native pine of Scotland once formed extensive forests, now reduced to a few remnants. The best known of the surviving natural stands are on Loch Maree; around Loch Morlich in the Glenmore forest; and the Black Wood on the south side of Loch Rannoch. The distinctive characters of the Highland pine are said to be the grey-green to glaucous, shorter-than-average leaves and the tendency of the cone-scales to become pyramidal in the upper part of the cone, but it is doubtful whether it would be possible to identify a Highland pine with any certainty when it is grown outside its native habitat. It is sometimes erroneously stated that Philip Miller gave the Highland pine botanical status as P. rubra. This name, as is clear from his account, was given to the species as a whole.

The standard work on the Highland pine is: H. M. Steven and A. Carlisle, The Native Pinewoods of Scotland (1959).

cv. 'WATERERI' ('Pumila').—A slow-growing, but not dwarf, variety of dense habit, with glaucous leaves about 1½ in. long. It was put into commerce by the Knap Hill Nursery, near Woking, Surrey, under the name P. sylvestris pumila or the Dwarf Scotch, and first appeared in their advertisements in 1855. The original plant is believed to have been found on Horsell Common, some two miles from the nursery, by Anthony Waterer, who was joint owner of the firm at that time. Later in the century it was propagated by the Dutch nurseries and, until recently, was more appreciated in Holland and Germany than in the land of its origin. It was known on the Continent by the epithet watereri or waterana, and the former is now accepted as the correct cultivar name, despite the fact that 'Pumila' has priority. The original plant, beautifully situated and in perfect health, still grows in the Knap Hill Nursery, and is about 25 ft high and as much in width.

P. TABULIFORMIS Carr.   CHINESE PINE

P. sinensis sens. Mayr, not Lamb.; P. leucosperma Maxim.; P. wilsonii Shaw

A tree up to 80 ft high in the wild; young shoots glaucous at first, afterwards dull yellow or brownish, not downy; bark fissured, grey tinged with pink or orange; winter-buds oblong-ovoid, pointed, $\frac{1}{2}$ to $\frac{3}{4}$ in. long, the scales closely appressed. Leaves densely set on the shoots, mostly in pairs, sometimes in threes, 3 to 6 in. long; basal sheath persistent, $\frac{1}{4}$ in. long. Cones solitary, ovoid, up to $2\frac{1}{2}$ in. long, persisting on the branches several years.

P. *tabuliformis* is widespread in the mountains of China and descends to near sea-level in the plains of the north. It was introduced by Fortune from the neighbourhood of Peking in 1862, but the trees now in cultivation are from later reintroductions and mostly from seed sent from W. China by Wilson when collecting for the Arnold Arboretum. It is very rare in this country and of no ornamental value. An example at Borde Hill, Sussex, in Gores Wood, measures 52 × 2$\frac{1}{4}$ ft (1974). It was identified as P. *tabuliformis* by A. B. Jackson, and was raised from seeds collected by Wilson in Korea, distributed as P. *densiflora* (W.8815). Others are: Bayford, Herts, in Bells Wood, 45 × 3$\frac{1}{2}$ ft (1962); Edinburgh Botanic Garden, from Wilson 1369, 36 × 2 ft (1967).

P. *tabuliformis* was at one time known by the name P. *sinensis*, but the pine thus named by Lambert is P. *massoniana*, a species very rare in cultivation, and not treated here.

P. YUNNANENSIS Franch. P. *tabuliformis* var. *yunnanensis* (Franch.) Shaw— This species is allied to P. *tabuliformis* of which it was made a variety by Shaw. It differs in its stout, pinkish shoots, longer leaves 4 to 9 in. long, and larger cones up to 4 in. long. Native of W. China, introduced by Wilson in 1909. There are two trees at Kew from this introduction, the larger 36 × 4$\frac{1}{4}$ ft (1969). A tree at Borde Hill in Sussex, also almost certainly from the seeds sent by Wilson, measured 50 × 4 ft in 1957.

P. TEOCOTE Schlecht. & Cham.   TEOCOTE PINE

A large tree up to 90 ft high in the wild; young shoots brown, glabrous; winter-buds cylindrical, tapered at the top, clothed with fringed, awl-shaped, pointed resinous scales. Leaves normally in threes (sometimes in fours or fives), 5 to 8 in. long, exceedingly finely toothed, sharply pointed, falling away in their third year; basal sheath $\frac{1}{2}$ in. or less long, persistent. Cones produced singly or in pairs, elongated-ovoid, 1$\frac{1}{2}$ to 2$\frac{1}{2}$ in. long, $\frac{3}{4}$ to 1$\frac{3}{8}$ in. wide, brown.

Native of Mexico, where it is widespread. Hartweg sent home seeds in 1839 which were distributed by the Horticultural Society. Most of the plants raised from them died, but there were two trees at Bicton in Devon, one of which measured something over 60 ft in height and 7 ft in girth in 1920; both must have died before 1931, since there is no mention of them in the Conference Returns of that year. It is now very rare.

P. THUNBERGII Parl.   JAPANESE BLACK PINE, KURO-MATSU

P. *massoniana* Sieb. & Zucc., not Lamb.

A tree 80 to 100 ft (sometimes more) high, with a trunk 3 to 5 ft through; bark deeply fissured and darkly coloured; young shoots light brown, not downy;

buds egg-shaped to almost globose, narrowing at the top to a short, slender point, not resinous, but with pale brown scales edged with conspicuous whitish threads. Leaves in pairs, $2\frac{1}{2}$ to $4\frac{1}{2}$ in. long, persisting three to five years; straight, stiff, sharply but abruptly pointed; the margins are so minutely toothed as to be only just perceptible to the touch; leaf-sheath $\frac{1}{3}$ to $\frac{5}{8}$ in. long, persistent, with two grey curly threads at the top. The lower part of each year's shoot is furnished with scale leaves only. Cones narrowly egg-shaped, $1\frac{1}{2}$ to $2\frac{1}{2}$ in. long, about 1 in. wide; scales unarmed; although usually solitary or in pairs, the cones are sometimes clustered as many as fifty or sixty together, and then much smaller. *Bot. Mag.*, n.s., t. 558.

Native of Japan; introduced by John Gould Veitch in 1861. It is a very picturesque tree, with stiff, horizontal branches of often very unequal length, and although not likely ever to reach its natural dimensions in this country, well worth growing as an interesting and characteristic pine. The Japanese train it into many grotesque shapes. It is allied to *P. nigra*, but besides the marked difference in habit is easily distinguished by its broad, grey-white buds and shorter, stiffer leaves. In the wild it is a tree of maritime localities, and is used in Japan for fixing sand-dunes. Wilson saw some large trees growing by the shore in Shikoku whose trunks were washed by the waves in periods of flood tides or high seas.

Among the notable specimens of *P. thunbergii* are: Nymans, Sussex, *pl.* 1896, 62 × 6 ft (1970); Borde Hill, Sussex, seed sown 1890, 75 × $5\frac{3}{4}$ ft (1968); Lytchett Heath, Dorset, seed sown 1887, 65 × $7\frac{1}{4}$ ft (1966); Westonbirt, Glos., *pl.* 1880, 61 × $5\frac{1}{4}$ ft (1971).

P. VIRGINIANA Mill.   VIRGINIA PINE, SCRUB PINE
P. inops Soland.

A tree 30 to 50 ft high, but often of scrubby habit; bark scaly, young shoots covered with a vivid, pale, purplish bloom, smooth; winter-buds very resinous. Leaves in pairs, falling the third year, $1\frac{1}{2}$ to 3 in. long, twisted and curved; leaf-sheath persistent, $\frac{3}{16}$ in. long. Cones $1\frac{1}{2}$ to $2\frac{1}{2}$ in. long, 1 to $1\frac{1}{4}$ in. wide at the base, conical, prickly.

Native of eastern N. America; introduced early in the 18th century or perhaps before. The brightly coloured, slender young shoots of this species distinguish it among pines with short leaves in pairs. *P. echinata*, with slender, glaucous shoots, has its leaves often in threes.

P. WALLICHIANA A. B. Jacks.   HIMALAYAN PINE, BHUTAN PINE, BLUE PINE
P. excelsa Wall. ex D. Don, not Lamb.; *P. griffithii* McClelland, not Parl.

A tree reaching 150 ft in height in the wild, and already over 100 ft high in cultivation; young shoots stout, blue-green, perfectly free from down, slightly ridged below each bundle of leaves towards the apex. Leaves in fives, falling the second and third years, 5 to 7 in. long, triangular in section, two faces white with stomatic lines, the third bright green, margins minutely toothed, sharply pointed;

leaf-sheath ⅝ to ¾ in. long, soon falling wholly away. The leaves are often bent abruptly near the base, so that the greater part of the leaf is pendulous. Cones at first cylindrical, 6 to 10 in. long, 1½ to 1¾ in. wide, before opening, each on a stalk 1 to 2 in. long; scales 1½ in. long, 1 in. wide, with a small, pointed, thickened apex.

Native of the Himalaya; introduced by A. B. Lambert in 1823. It is a handsome tree especially when of middle age, and grows with great rapidity when young, the leading shoot increasing by 2 to 3 ft. annually. It thrives best in a good sandy loam, and in a position sheltered from fierce gales, which give it a bedraggled appearance. Very hardy, and bearing cones early. It is only likely to be confused in gardens with P. *armandii*, and P. *ayachahuite*, both of which have more or less downy shoots and different cones. Its glabrous shoots, its five-clustered leaves and quickly falling leaf-sheath, distinguish it from all other pines except P. *peuce* (q.v.). The shoots of P. *strobus* may be almost without down, but they are slender and do not have the bluish tinge of P. *wallichiana*; also its leaves are shorter and do not droop.

P. *wallichiana* is a short-lived tree in cultivation; many of the oldest trees are decrepit, although planted only a century or slightly more ago. Its rapid growth when young is shown by a tree at Albury Park, Surrey, *pl.* 1921, 72 × 4¼ ft (1954), 93 × 5½ ft (1968).

PIPTANTHUS   LEGUMINOSAE

A genus of about half a dozen species of deciduous or partially evergreen, soft-wooded shrubs with trifoliolate leaves and entire, stalkless leaflets. Flowers always yellow, borne in erect terminal racemes. Provided they have a suitable climate—and they are not completely hardy—they are easily grown if put in a sunny spot and given a reasonably good loamy soil.

P. CONCOLOR Craib

A deciduous or partially evergreen bush up to 6 or 8 ft high; young shoots clothed with white hairs, becoming glabrous and ultimately chestnut-brown. Leaves trifoliolate, the three leaflets on a common stalk 1 in. long. Leaflets narrowly oval to oblanceolate, tapered about equally towards both ends, entire, mostly 2¼ to 4 in. long, ¾ to 1¼ in. wide, rather glossy green above and but slightly paler green below, both sides very hairy when quite young, the upper one soon becoming glabrous, the lower one sparsely hairy. Racemes several inches long, with often three flowers at a joint, opening in May. Flowers pea-shaped, about 1 in. long, yellow, the standard petal stained with maroon. Calyx ½ in. long, glabrous inside, very hairy outside and on the margins; lobes slenderly pointed. Flower-stalk ¾ in. long, very hairy; ovary silky. Pods covered with appressed down, 2½ to 3½ in. long, ⅜ in. wide.

Native of W. Szechwan, China; introduced in 1908 by Wilson. It was at first thought to be a form of P. *laburnifolius*, but in that species the leaves are glaucous beneath, in this they are green. P. *concolor* can be grown away from a wall at Kew, which is more than can be said of P. *laburnifolius*. But possibly a really hard winter would kill it.

subsp. YUNNANENSIS Stapf P. *bicolor* Craib; P. *forrestii* Hort., not Craib—Shoots glabrous or only slightly hairy when young; leaves glaucous beneath (though this may not be a constant character). Introduced by Forrest from N.W. Yunnan. *Bot. Mag.*, t. 9234.

P. LABURNIFOLIUS (D. Don) Stapf [PLATE 38
Thermopsis laburnifolia D. Don; P. *nepalensis* Sweet

A shrub or low tree with very pithy young shoots; naturally 8 to 12 ft high, but growing taller against walls, where it is generally placed in England. When grown at Kew it is deciduous, but in milder climates it retains more or less foliage during the winter. Leaves alternate, consisting of three lanceolate, stalkless leaflets, 3 to 6 in. long, about one-third as wide, with a marginal nerve, glabrous except when quite young, dark green above, glaucous beneath; the common leaf-stalk 1½ to 2 in. long. Racemes stiff, erect, 2 to 3 in. long, and as much broad, hairy, and set with hairy bracts. Flowers pea-shaped, 1½ in. long, the stalk up to 1 in. long and, like the bell-shaped, deeply lobed calyx, very hairy; petals bright yellow. Pods 3 to 5 in. long, ¾ in. wide.

Native of the Himalaya; introduced to England in 1821. It thrives well against a wall, flowering in May, but is not permanently hardy in the open air at Kew. A shrub of exceptionally vigorous appearance, it is, nevertheless, not long-lived. It is easily propagated by seeds, which it ripens in quantity, and owing to its dislike of root disturbance should be grown in pots until planted in permanence.

P. FORRESTII Craib—In this species the leaflets are green, furnished with short, appressed hairs on both sides, and the young shoots are hairy. Flowers bright golden yellow. I saw a plant 6 ft high fully in bloom in the Edinburgh Botanic Garden during early June 1931. So the species is evidently perfectly hardy.

P. TOMENTOSUS Franch.—As in P. *forrestii*, the leaflets are hairy or even velvety on both sides, but more conspicuously so on the underside where the hairs are very dense; pod woolly, 2 to 3¼ in. long.

PISTACIA Mastic Trees ANACARDIACEAE

A genus of deciduous or evergreen trees of considerable economic importance in their native countries, but as a rule too tender to be of much garden value in this. Two species may be grown without protection in the open, viz., *P. terebinthus* and *P. chinensis*; the latter, although still rare, appears to be especially well adapted for our climate. The leaves of *Pistacia* are either simple, trifoliolate or pinnate, and the pinnate leaves are either equally or unequally so. Flowers inconspicuous, and without petals; male and female flowers usually occur on separate trees. The fruit is a drupe, with a one-seeded stone. The nearest ally in gardens to this genus is *Rhus*, from which *Pistacia* differs in the absence of petals.

The two species mentioned above may be grown in the open ground, but for the rest it will be necessary to provide wall space. Any ordinary garden soil suffices for them.

P. chinensis Bunge

A large deciduous tree up to 80 ft high in Central China. Leaves evenly pinnate, about 9 in. long, composed of usually ten or twelve leaflets, generally but not invariably without the terminal odd one. Leaflets ovate-lanceolate, long-pointed, unequally divided by the midrib, 2½ to 3½ in. long, ¾ in. wide, glabrous except when quite young. Flowers in a cluster of panicles near the end of the shoot, the male flowers crowded on an inflorescence 3 in. long, the female ones on a much more open, lax panicle 7 to 9 in. long. Fruit the size of large peppercorns, first red, then blue.

Native of Central and W. China, where the young shoots and leaves are eaten cooked as a vegetable by the Chinese. This is undoubtedly the best of the pistacias to cultivate in England. It was originally introduced to Kew by means of seed in 1897, and is apparently perfectly hardy, never having suffered in the least from cold up to now, although quite unprotected. It has no beauty of flower, but the foliage is of a glossy, cheerful green, and Mr Wilson (who sent home seeds during his 1908 and 1910 journeys in China) told me that it turns a gorgeous crimson before falling in autumn, rendering a large tree one of the most glorious pictures conceivable.

P. lentiscus L. Mastic

An evergreen bush or small tree, occasionally 15 or 20 ft high; young shoots warted, not downy. The leaves are evenly pinnate, consisting of four to ten leaflets without a terminal odd one; the common stalk is winged. Leaflets ¾ to 1½ in. long, ¼ to ½ in. wide; narrowly oblong to obovate, glabrous, with a very short, abrupt point. Flowers very densely packed in short axillary panicles 1 to 2 in. long. Fruits first red, then black, about the size of large peppercorns.

P. lentiscus is one of the most characteristic members of the Mediterranean macchie (maquis), and is found wherever this occurs, both within the Mediterreanean basin and in Portugal and Atlantic Morocco; also in the Canaries. It was in cultivation by the second half of the 17th century as a pot- or tub-plant, placed outside in summer and overwintered under glass with the oranges and myrtles (Evelyn's *Calendar*, under March). It is tender and needs the protection of a wall.

In the islands of the Greek Archipelago it produces by incision of the bark a resinous substance known as 'mastic', which is used locally for flavouring raki and is chewed to sweeten the breath. It is also used medicinally and as an ingredient in tooth-powder. The gum mastic tree of Chios is a cultivated race, sometimes distinguished as var. CHIA Duham.

P. TEREBINTHUS L.

A deciduous tree up to 30 ft or more high, sometimes a bush, with pinnate leaves up to 8 in. long; rachis is not winged. Leaflets usually seven or nine, ovate-lanceolate to oblong, 1½ to 2½ in. long, mucronate at the apex, entire, dark green, above, paler beneath, glabrous. Flowers in panicles 2 to 6 in. long, small, greenish. Fruits roundish oval, about ⅜ in. long, turning first red, finally purplish brown.

Native of the Canary Islands, N. Africa, and S. Europe eastward to N.W. Anatolia; in France it extends as far north as Chambery in the Savoy, and in Italy to the South Tyrol, but its main distribution is near the shores of the Mediterranean; in cultivation 1656. It is hardy at Kew, where there is a specimen measuring 45 × 2½ ft (1967). The flowers have no beauty, but the leaves have a pleasant resinous odour.

The bark of this species yields a resinous liquid known originally as terebinthine—a word which became corrupted to 'turpentine' and was then extended in meaning to denote the oil obtained from the resins of various conifers, notably pines.

subsp. PALAESTINA (Boiss.) Engl. *P. palaestina* Boiss.—Leaves even-pinnate, or the terminal leaflet much smaller than the lateral ones, or reduced to a bristle; lateral leaflets acuminate. This has a more eastern distribution than the typical state of the species.

P. ATLANTICA Desf.

—This species, which is probably of no interest for gardens, is allied to *P. terebinthus*, differing in its winged leaf-rachis and in its lanceolate leaflets, which are not mucronate as in *P. terebinthus*. It was originally described from Algeria, and is said by some authorities to be confined to N. Africa. But as now understood, it has a wide distribution in the Near East as far as W. Pakistan. In Europe it occurs only in parts of the E. Balkans and in the Crimea.

P. VERA L. PISTACHIO
P. reticulata Willd.; *P. trifolia* L.; *P. narbonensis* L.

A small deciduous tree 20 ft high, with long-stalked, pinnate leaves consisting usually of three or five leaflets, which are 1½ to 2½ in. long, ovate or obovate, stalkless, entire, downy on both sides. Flowers in erect panicles 3 or 4 in. long, small and of no beauty; the male panicles much denser than the female. Fruits reddish, oval, ¾ in. long.

Native of Central Asia, N. Afghanistan, and N.E. Persia, long cultivated and naturalised over the Mediterranean region and more recently grown commercially in other parts of the world, e.g., California; said to have been in cultivation in Britain in 1570, and certainly introduced before 1770, the erroneous date given in 'Don's Miller'. This is the tree that produces the well-known pistachio-nuts, the kernels of which are eaten raw, or cooked, or made into confectionery. It has not much beyond its economic interest to recommend it, for it needs the protection of a warm wall, and even then is occasionally injured by cold; with us its fruits are never developed. In warm climates the leaflets are as much as 3½ in. long by 2½ in. wide.

The natural stands in Soviet Central Asia occur in semi-desert areas at 2,000 to 6,500 ft. Their productivity is low, partly because male trees make up more than half the total and partly because they have been much damaged by overgrazing (Tseplyaev, *Forests of the USSR*, Eng. ed. (1965), p. 470). The best commercial stands consist of selected female varieties grafted on *P. atlantica* or *P. terebinthus*, intermixed with males (or with male branches grafted on them).

PITTOSPORUM   PITTOSPORACEAE

An interesting genus of evergreen shrubs and small trees whose headquarters are in Australia and New Zealand, whence come most of the species cultivated in the open air in the British Isles. The others described here are from Japan and China, but the genus is also represented in the Himalaya, the Malaysian and Pacific regions, and in Africa. Remarkably there is one species—*P. coriaceum* Ait.—on the island of Madeira, which has become exceedingly rare in the wild state, and one in the Canary Islands. The leading characters of the genus are: Leaves alternate. Flowers with five sepals, five petals, and five stamens alternating with the petals. Ovary superior, developing into a capsule with two to five leathery or woody valves. The generic name refers to the resinous or viscid substance by which the seeds are surrounded.

The pittosporums are essentially shrubs for the milder parts of the British Isles. At Kew they can only be grown against a wall. Several of the species are very handsome evergreens, and all here mentioned are charmingly fragrant when in flower. They are easily cultivated and thrive in a light loamy soil. Cuttings taken from the half-ripened wood will root in gentle heat. Seeds ripen in favourable localities, and may also be used.

The flowers in general must be regarded as more notable for their fragrance than their beauty.

P. ADAPHNIPHYLLOIDES Hu & Wang
P. daphniphylloides sens. Rehd. & Wils., not Hayata

An evergreen shrub or sometimes a tree up to 30 ft high, slightly downy on the young shoots and beneath the young leaves. Leaves narrowly oblong to narrowly obovate, tapered towards both ends, but more gradually towards the base, dark green, 2½ to 8 in. long, 1¼ to 3½ in. wide; stalk ⅝ to 1¼ in. long. Flowers ¼ in. long and wide, greenish yellow, crowded in several globose, umbellate clusters ¾ to 1½ in. wide that form a terminal panicle; main and secondary flower-stalks harshly hairy; petals oblong, ¼ in. long, blunt; anthers yellow. Fruits globose, ¼ to ⅜ in. wide, wrinkled, red.

Native of W. Szechwan, China, whence it was introduced by Wilson in 1904. He describes it as a handsome species found in woods, thickets, and rocky places, and as having leaves sometimes 10 in. long and 4 in. wide without the stalk. As it occurs at low altitudes (3,000 to 5,000 ft), it is probably best adapted for our milder localities. There is a healthy tree at Caerhays, in Cornwall, very noticeable for the size of its leaves, which must be about the largest found on any pittosporum that can be grown in this country; it is 11 ft high and 24 ft in spread (1966). Another was bearing fine crops of berries at Warley, Essex, in November 1934.

This species has been known by the erroneous name P. daphniphylloides Hayata, which properly belongs to a species native to Formosa. Hayata himself was really responsible for the original confusion, since he noted that Wilson's Veitch expedition specimen no. 3233 in the Kew Herbarium was 'exactly like' the Formosan plant; and Rehder and Wilson, having seen no Formosan specimens, followed him and accepted Wilson's Szechwan specimens as P. daphniphylloides (Pl. Wilsonianae, Vol. 3, p. 326).

P. BICOLOR Hook.

An evergreen shrub or even a small tree 30 to 40 ft high, the younger shoots clothed with a pale brown, close felt. Leaves entire, linear, leathery, tapered at each end, pointed, 1 to 2½ in. long, ⅛ to ¼ in. wide but made to look narrower by the rolling under of the margins; upper surface dark green and glabrous, lower one felted, at first white then brown, like the young shoots; stalk ⅛ in. or less long. Flowers solitary or in small clusters, axillary, ⅜ in. long, fragrant, each on a downy stalk as long as itself; petals oblong, deep maroon crimson; sepals narrower and one-third the length of the petals; stamens yellow. Fruits nearly globose, ¼ to ⅓ in. wide.

Native of Tasmania, Victoria, and New South Wales; in cultivation 1854. It requires winter protection at Kew but is hardy in the southern and western maritime counties, and has reached 28 ft at Exbury on the Solent, and 33 ft at Mount Usher, Co. Wicklow, Eire. Its flowering period extends from November to April, but the main crop is borne in the spring.

P. BUCHANANII Hook. f.

An evergreen shrub or small tree 10 to 20 ft high; young shoots and leaves silky downy, becoming glabrous by late summer. Leaves alternate, of thinnish firm texture, oblong-lanceolate to oval, quite entire, tapered at both ends, pointed or rounded at the apex, 2 to 5 in. long, ¾ to 2 in. wide, dark glossy green above, pale and indistinctly net-veined beneath; margins not wavy; stalk ¼ to ⅜ in. long. Flowers ⅜ in. wide, produced singly or in pairs from the leaf-axils each on a stalk ⅓ to ½ in. long; petals dark purple, narrow oblong; sepals ¼ in. long, ⅛ in. wide, pointed; ovary covered with silky white hairs. Seed-vessels globose, ½ in. wide, downy at first.

Native of the North Island, New Zealand, where it is said to be rare and local. It bears a certain superficial resemblance to *P. ralphii*, but that species is amply distinguished by its permanently downy leaves and terminal inflorescence. But its closest kinship is with *P. tenuifolium* and *P. colensoi*, from both of which differs in its larger leaves.

P. COLENSOI Hook. f.

An evergreen shrub or small tree ultimately 20 to 30 ft high; young shoots stout, loosely silky when young. Leaves rather leathery, oval, oblong, or slightly obovate, pointed or bluntish, mostly tapered at the base, 1½ to 4 in. long, ½ to 1¼ in. wide; downy only when quite young, dark glossy green above with a yellowish midrib, pale and net-veined beneath; stalk ⅓ in. or less long. Flowers ⅝ in. wide, solitary or in threes, produced at and near the end of the shoots in the leaf-axils. Petals dark red, ⅔ in. long, oblong, much recurved; sepals broadly ovate, downy. *Bot. Mag.*, t. 8305.

Native of the North and South Islands, New Zealand, up to 3,500 ft altitude. It is very closely akin to *P. tenuifolium*, which differs chiefly in its wavy-margined leaves, more slender shoots and, on the whole, smaller, paler green leaves. The two appear to be united by intermediate forms but are quite distinct in the typical states. It is cultivated and prized in many gardens in the south-west, Ireland, etc., but is not very hardy in our average climate. It flowers with great freedom in the gardens of Tresco Abbey, Scilly. At Wakehurst Place, Sussex, it grows well in the open ground and flowers in late spring and early summer.

P. CORNIFOLIUM A. Cunn.

An evergreen shrub 2 to 5 ft high, of neat habit, with the slender young shoots glabrous (or downy only when quite young). Leaves leathery, clustered at the end of the twig only, oval-lanceolate or narrowly obovate, pointed, tapered at the base to a very short stalk, 1½ to 3¼ in. long, ½ to 1¼ in. wide, entire, quite glabrous. Flowers mostly unisexual, dull red, produced in February and March two to five together at the end of the young twigs; each flower is ⅓ in. wide, the males borne on very slender, thread-like, downy stalks ½ to ¾ in. long, the females on shorter, stouter ones. Sepals and petals awl-shaped, the former much the shorter; anthers yellow. Seed-vessels egg-shaped, ½ in. wide. *Bot. Mag.*, t. 3161.

Native of the North Island of New Zealand up to 2,000 ft altitude; introduced by Allan Cunningham early in the 19th century. It is often found wild growing as an epiphyte on large forest trees or on rocks, rarely in pure earth. It is not hardy at Kew but can be grown in the open air in the south-west. In spite of its epiphytal character it succeeds well in ordinary soil. The flowers have a charming musk-like odour.

P. CRASSIFOLIUM A. Cunn.   KARO

An evergreen shrub or small tree 15 ft or more high, of dense habit. Leaves 1½ to 4 in. long, obovate to oblong, always narrowed at the base to a stalk ⅓ to 1 in. long, leathery, covered beneath with a pale brown or whitish felt, the margins revolute. Flowers unisexual in terminal clusters; males up to ten in each cluster, females up to five; petals strap-shaped, recurved, dark purple. Fruit roundish, dry, ⅔ in. across, containing numerous black seeds. *Bot. Mag.*, t. 5978.

Native of the North Island of New Zealand; not hardy at Kew except on a wall, where it makes an interesting evergreen, but does not flower freely.

P. RALPHII Kirk—Another New Zealand species, closely related to the above. It differs in its larger, oblong leaves more abruptly narrowed towards the stalk, in their margins not being revolute but flat, and in the smaller fruits.

Both *P. ralphii* and *P. crassifolium* are resistant to salt-laden winds and are used as shelter-hedges in the mildest parts.

P. DALLII Cheesem.

A small evergreen tree 12 to 18 ft high in the wild, of rounded shape, with a trunk up to 8 in. in diameter; older bark pale grey; young shoots glabrous, reddish. Leaves dark dull green, crowded towards the end of the shoot; oval-lanceolate, pointed, tapered about equally towards both ends, either coarsely or slightly toothed, or entire, 2½ to 4½ in. long, ½ to 1¾ in. wide, of stiff leathery texture, soon quite glabrous, midrib raised above and beneath; stalk reddish, ⅓ to ¾ in. long. Flowers white, fragrant, crowded numerously in a terminal cluster 1 to 2 in. across; individually ¼ to ⅔ in. long and ½ in. wide when expanded; petals narrowly obovate; sepals awl-shaped; anthers bright yellow; flower-stalks downy. Seed-vessels woody, egg-shaped, ½ in. long, with a short spine-like tip.

Native of the South Island, New Zealand. According to Cheeseman, 'it appears to be rare in its only known habitat in the mountains near Collingwood, Nelson, and only a limited number of adult plants have been seen'. More plants were found later, but all in the same restricted area in the mountains of N.W. Nelson. J. Dall, who discovered the species in 1905, obtained only imperfect fruiting specimens. He died in 1912, but it was found again by his friend F. G. Gibbs, in 1913, this time in bloom. Mr Gibbs, to whom Kew was indebted for seeds, described the tree as 'far more handsome than any of the other pittosporums I have seen'. The seeds he sent to Kew lay dormant for a year. Cuttings appear difficult to root, but can be easily grafted on *P. tenuifolium*.

P. dallii is the only species in New Zealand with regularly coarsely toothed leaves and white flowers. On the young plants at Kew, raised from the seeds sent by Mr Gibbs, the leaves varied from being coarsely toothed to entire, and some of the leaves on adult plants may also be entire or only slightly toothed. The flowers are very rarely borne on cultivated plants, even in New Zealand. It is, however, one of the hardiest of the pittosporums.

P. dallii has attained a height of about 25 ft at Tregothnan in Cornwall and at Ilnacullin in Co. Cork, Eire.

P. DIVARICATUM Ckn.

A usually low, densely branched, evergreen shrub rarely more than a few feet high in Britain, but said to be up to 12 ft high in the wild, with the stiff, downy young twigs much divided, tortuous, and interlaced. Leaves glabrous and variously shaped; on young plants linear to obovate, $\frac{1}{2}$ to $\frac{3}{4}$ in. long, $\frac{1}{8}$ in. wide, pinnately lobed or merely toothed, on mature plants $\frac{1}{4}$ to $\frac{3}{4}$ in. long, linear-obovate, oblong or ovate, variously toothed or not at all; dark green and of leathery texture. Flowers small, $\frac{1}{6}$ in. long, solitary, produced at the top of the twig; petals deep maroon, almost black, narrowly spoon-shaped. Seed-vessels nearly globose, $\frac{1}{4}$ in. wide.

Native of the North and South Islands of New Zealand. This is a curious shrub of little beauty, with a growth suggesting that of *Corokia cotoneaster*. It flowers in December in New Zealand and I have seen it blossoming in the Vicarage garden at Bitton, Gloucestershire, in May. It was grown there as "*P. rigidum*", a species under which it was included by Hooker in his *Flora of New Zealand*. The true *P. rigidum* (q.v.) differs from the present species in the branches not interlacing and in the flowers being nearly always axillary.

P. EUGENIOIDES A. Cunn.   TARATA

An evergreen tree 20 to 40 ft high, densely branched; young shoots glabrous, darkly coloured. Leaves clustered towards the end of each season's growth, narrowly oval or oblong, tapered at each end, 2 to 5 in. long, $\frac{1}{2}$ to $1\frac{1}{4}$ in. wide, perfectly glabrous on both surfaces, dark glossy green above, paler beneath; margins often wavy, stalk $\frac{1}{4}$ to $\frac{3}{4}$ in. long. Flowers very fragrant, $\frac{1}{16}$ in. wide, yellowish, densely and numerously packed in a cluster of short corymbs terminating the branch, each corymb 1 in. or less long; flower-stalks downy; petals strap-shaped, $\frac{1}{8}$ in. long; sepals much smaller. Fruits $\frac{1}{4}$ in. long, egg-shaped.

Native of New Zealand, where it occurs on both islands up to 2,500 ft altitude. Requiring winter protection at Kew, it is perfectly hardy in the milder parts more to the south and west and makes a handsome evergreen tree there, up to 30 ft or more high. The honey-like scent of the flowers is very charming and widely diffused. The leaves are also fragrant when crushed, and from them and the flowers, mixed with fat, the Maoris made an unguent with which they anointed their bodies.

cv. 'VARIEGATUM'.—In this form the leaf has a creamy-white margin of irregular width. Seen in Cornish gardens, usually as a small tree of columnar shape, with its peculiarly clean, clear leaf-colouring, it strikes one as about the most attractive of all variegated shrubs grown in the open air. It flowers just as freely as the normal green form, and is said to be hardier. It was introduced to cultivation in the early 1880s. There is an example 34 ft high at Bosahan, Cornwall, and two almost as tall at Castlewellan, Co. Down.

P. GLABRATUM Lindl.

An evergreen shrub 4 to 6 ft high, with quite glabrous young shoots, bearing the leaves in a cluster at the end. Leaves obovate to oblanceolate, tapered at both ends, but more gradually towards the base, 3 to 5 in. long, ¾ to 1½ in. wide, with entire, membranous margins, quite glabrous on both surfaces, dark green above, pale beneath; stalk ½ in. or less long. Flowers fragrant, dull yellow, produced singly or in few-flowered racemes in the leaf-axils of the young shoots in May; corolla ⅓ to ½ in. long, cylindrical at the base, dividing at the mouth in five oblong, recurved lobes, ⅙ in. long; flower-stalks usually ½ to ¾ in. long, glabrous. Fruit a glabrous, woody capsule, ⅝ in. long.

Native of the warmer parts of China; introduced by Fortune from Hong Kong in 1845, and reintroduced by Wilson from near Ichang in 1908. It has never become established in cultivation.

P. PATULUM Hook. f.

An evergreen shrub or small tree from 6 to 15 ft high; young shoots and flower-stalks downy, glabrous elsewhere. Leaves always narrow in proportion to their

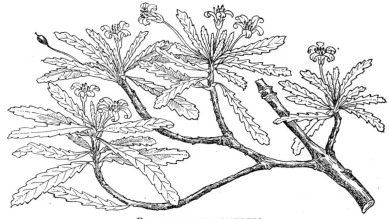

PITTOSPORUM PATULUM

length but otherwise variable; on young plants they are 1 to 2 in. long, as little as ⅛ in. wide, and conspicuously lobed their whole length; as the plants reach maturity the leaves become wider (⅜ to ½ in.), more or less shallowly toothed, often almost or quite entire, and of lanceolate shape; they are of leathery texture. Flowers rather bell-shaped, borne in May, four to eight together in a terminal cluster, each borne on a slender, downy stalk ½ in. long, very fragrant; petals nearly ½ in. long, oblong, blunt-ended, blackish crimson; sepals ovate-lanceolate, pointed, ciliate. Seed-vessels globose, ⅓ in. wide, woody.

Native of the South Island, New Zealand, at from 2,000 to 4,000 ft altitude; very local in its distribution. Its flowers are said to be the most fragrant of all New Zealand pittosporums. It is also one of the hardiest, and succeeds well at Wakehurst Place in Sussex, where there is a narrow bush in the open ground 28 ft high (1975).

P. REVOLUTUM Ait. f.

P. fulvum Rudge

An evergreen shrub up to 10 or 12 ft high, the young shoots felted with pale brown wool. Leaves lanceolate or narrowly ovate, much tapered at both ends, 1½ to 4½ in. long, ⅓ to 1¼ in. wide, glabrous above, covered beneath with brown wool, especially on the midrib; stalk ¼ to ½ in. long, woolly. Flowers ⅓ to ½ in. long, produced in spring on a terminal, few-flowered umbel, sometimes solitary. Petals yellow, recurved; sepals awl-shaped, ¼ in. long; flower-stalks woolly.

Native of New South Wales; introduced according to Aiton in 1795. It is rather distinct on account of the dense covering of brown wool on the young shoots and leaves. It is not hardy near London and is adapted only for the south-western counties and places with a similar climate.

P. RIGIDUM Hook. f.

An evergreen shrub up to 10 ft or more high (generally smaller), much branched but not interlacing; young shoots of juvenile plants densely clothed with reddish-brown down. Leaves obovate or oval, round-ended, tapered at the base to a short stalk; entire and glabrous on old plants, often coarsely toothed and downy on young ones, ¼ to 1 in. long, ⅛ to ⅜ in. wide. Flowers small, dull purple, produced singly from the leaf-axils, very shortly stalked. Seed-vessels roundish ovoid, ¼ in. wide, ending in a spine-like tip.

Native of the North and South Islands, New Zealand, up to 4,000 ft altitude. It is of no great ornament, but is a curious, often dwarfish, small-leaved shrub which one might easily pass when in flower without noticing the blossom. A shrub sometimes grown under this name in British gardens is really *P. divaricatum*, a very nearly related and perhaps more interesting shrub on account of its dense interlacing habit of branching; its leaves are much less frequently entire on adult plants than in *P. rigidum* and its flowers are terminal. Of *P. rigidum* there is a healthy bush in the Edinburgh Botanic Garden.

P. TENUIFOLIUM Gaertn.   KOHUHU   [PLATE 40
P. *mayi* Hort.

An evergreen tree up to 30 ft in height, with a slender trunk and dark coloured, almost black, young wood, and forming a dense mass of twiggy shoots. Leaves 1 to 2½ in. long, oblong, obovate or elliptic, glabrous, of a pale shining green; the margins entire but wavy. The flowers come in the axils of the leaves, usually singly, but occasionally two or more together, and have dark chocolate-purple petals ¼ to ½ in. long. The fruit is a capsule ½ in. in diameter, wrinkled when old, the valves thin.

Native of both the North and South Islands of New Zealand, reaching up to 3,000 ft altitude. Although it may be damaged or killed in severe winters, and be less hardy than such species as P. *patulum* and P. *dallii*, it seems to thrive better in our average climate than any other species so far introduced, as well as being the commonest. Even in eastern England it has attained 30 ft in sheltered places, and has produced self-sown seedlings in gardens as far east as Sussex. The flowers are borne very abundantly where it thrives, but are not conspicuous; their chief attraction is an exquisite honey-like fragrance, strongest in the evening, and then apparent yards away from the tree. The black young shoots and pale green leaves make a strong contrast. The cut foliage lasts long in water and is much used in floristry.

The following specimens have been recorded: Lanarth, Cornwall, 50 × 6 ft at 1 ft (1966); Tregrehan, Cornwall, 50 × 3¾ ft + 3 ft (1957); Newton Abbot, Devon, *pl.* 1885–90, 45 × 4½ ft (E. Hyams, *Journ. R.H.S.*, Vol. 91 (1966), p. 130); Lytchett Heath, Poole, Dorset, *pl.* 1889, 17½ ft high and 30 ft in circumference of spread (*Journ R.H.S.*, Vol. 56 (1931), p. 58); Abbotsbury, Dorset, 35 × 3 ft (1957); Powerscourt, Co. Wicklow, Eire, 35 × 6¼ ft (1966); Ashbourne House, Co. Cork, 33 × 4¾ ft at 3 ft (1966).

cv. 'GARNETTII'.—See below.

cv. 'JAMES STIRLING'.—Leaves roundish, smaller than average, being about ⅜ in. long, ½ in. wide. The original plant was found by Mr Stirling in the East Cape District (*Gard. Chron.*, May 10, 1967, p. 15).

cv. 'PURPUREUM'.—Leaves purple and holding their colour through the winter.

cv. 'SILVER QUEEN'.—Leaves pale green with an irregular whitish margin. Raised by the Slieve Donard Nursery, Co. Down. A.M. 1914. There is an example at Caerhays, Cornwall, *pl.* 1915, measuring 43 × 3¾ ft at 3½ ft (1966).

cv. 'WARNHAM GOLD'.—Leaves golden yellow. Raised in the nursery of the Greater London Council at Warnham Court, Horsham, Sussex.

P. 'GARNETTII'.—Leaves with a margin of white which becomes tinted with pink in winter. They are elliptic, oblong-elliptic or rather broad oblong-elliptic, up to 2¼ in. long and 1⅛ in. wide, slightly hairy beneath. Raised in New Zealand. It is usually treated as a cultivar of P. *tenuifolium* but may be a hybrid with P. *ralphii* as the other parent (*Gard. Chron.*, June 15, 1966, p. 607).

P. TOBIRA Ait.   TOBIRA   [PLATE 39

An evergreen, bushy shrub of stiff habit, sometimes 20 or more ft high. Leaves obovate, blunt or rounded at the apex, tapering at the base to a short stalk, 1½ to 4 in. long, ¾ to 1½ in. wide, leathery and glabrous, dark lustrous green, witn a pale midrib. Flowers about 1 in. across, fragrant, produced at the end of the shoot in clusters 2 or 3 in. across, the petals broadly oblong, creamy white, becoming yellowish with age. Fruit a pear-shaped capsule. *Bot. Mag.*, t. 1396.

Native of Japan, the Ryukyus, Formosa, Korea, and China; first introduced to Kew in 1804. This shrub is not strictly hardy, and at Kew requires wall protection. In the south-western counties and at Castlewellan in Co. Down it succeeds admirably unprotected, being there a densely furnished, healthy-looking evergreen. In the gardens of the south of France, Italy, Dalmatia, etc., it is one of the commonest of evergreens, producing its flowers from April onwards. There are some fine examples on the isle of Lokrum, near Dubrovnik, in Dalmatia, picturesque spreading bushes 20 to 25 ft high. The flowers of *P. tobira* have a scent like orange blossom.

cv. 'VARIEGATUM'.—Leaves margined with white.

P. UNDULATUM Vent.

An evergreen tree 30 to 40 ft high in this country; leaves large, laurel-like, 3 to 6 in. long, 1 to 2 in. wide, tapering towards both ends; glabrous, dark lustrous green above, pale beneath, quite entire, but wavy at the margins. Flowers in a terminal cluster of umbels 2 to 3 in. in diameter; each blossom creamy white, ½ to ¾ in. across. *Bot. Mag.*, n.s., t. 234.

Native of E. Australia, whence it was introduced in 1789. It is only hardy in the mildest counties; probably the finest specimen in the British Isles is at Rossdohan, Co. Kerry, in the garden made by S. T. Heard, now the property of Mr P. and Mr R. J. Walker. It is about 30 ft high. It flowers from May to July and the blossoms are pleasantly fragrant. The leaves are bright and handsome, the undulations of the margin not more marked than in some species, despite the specific epithet. It is also grown for its showy orange-coloured fruits, which ornament the tree in winter.

P. undulatum is a common ornamental tree in the warmer parts of Europe, also in Madeira, California, etc. It is naturalised in the Azores, to which it was introduced early in the 19th century, originally to shelter the orange groves from the Atlantic gales.

PLAGIANTHUS   MALVACEAE

A genus of a few species of trees, shrubs and herbs, natives of Australasia. It is allied to *Hoheria*, differing in the smaller flowers with linear stigmas and solitary carpels. With the removal to *Hoheria* of *H. glabrata* and *H. lyallii*, the genus *Plagianthus* becomes one of scant horticultural importance, though *P. betulinus* is occasionally met with in gardens.

P. BETULINUS A. Cunn.

A deciduous tree from 30 to 40 ft high in New Zealand, with a trunk sometimes 3 ft in diameter. In a young state its growth is remarkably elegant, consisting of a mass of slender, tortuous, interlacing branches, thinly furnished with foliage. At this stage the leaves are $\frac{1}{2}$ to $1\frac{1}{2}$ in. long, narrowly or broadly ovate, deeply and irregularly toothed and lobed; they are borne on slender, downy stalks, nearly or quite as long as the blade. As the trees approach the adult state, the growth becomes less straggling, the leaves increase in size until they are 3 in. long, and become less deeply lobed. Flowers produced very numerously on racemes at the end of the shoot and in the leaf-axils near, the whole forming a panicle as much as 9 in. long; individually the flowers are unisexual; the male flowers yellowish white, the females greenish.

Native of New Zealand and the Chatham Islands; introduced about 1870. Having a wide range in the wild it probably varies in hardiness. At Kew it has been damaged in winter even when grown against a wall, yet one of the finest specimens in the country grows in the nursery of Messrs Kaye at Silverdale, Carnforth, Lancs. This measures 40 × 3$\frac{3}{4}$ ft (1976). Others recorded recently are: Caerhays Castle, Cornwall, 50 × 4$\frac{1}{2}$ ft (1971); Bicton, Devon, 41 × 3 ft (1972).

P. DIVARICATUS Forst.

A much-branched shrub up to 8 ft high, with long, slender, flexible, tough, dark coloured, pendulous branchlets bearing alternate leaves either singly or two to five clustered at each joint; both stem and leaves are glabrous. On young plants the leaves are linear, $\frac{1}{2}$ to 1 in. long, $\frac{1}{12}$ in. or less wide, entire, bluntish; on adult plants they are smaller and often only $\frac{1}{4}$ in. or even less long. Flowers mostly unisexual, inconspicuous and of no beauty, yellowish white, $\frac{3}{16}$ in. wide, borne singly or a few together at the joints, very shortly stalked. Fruit globose, the size of a peppercorn, covered with very close pale down.

Native of New Zealand and the Chatham Islands; it was cultivated by the Vilmorins at Verrières, near Paris, and flowered there as long ago as May 1851. At Kew it was grown on a wall, for which it made a graceful and distinct covering, developing into a thick tangle of dark slender stems, many of them pendulous and unbranching for more than a foot of their length. They give the shrub an evergreen character. It is a characteristic member of the coastal vegetation of New Zealand.

P. PULCHELLUS (Willd.) A. Gray
Sida pulchella Willd.; *Gynatrix pulchella* (Willd.) Alef.

An evergreen shrub or tree. Leaves ovate, with a heart-shaped base, 2$\frac{1}{2}$ to 4$\frac{1}{2}$ in. long, green both sides, coarsely and irregularly toothed, often with two lateral lobes near the base; leaf-stalk slender, half as long as the blade. When young, the leaves and young wood are dotted with stellate hairs. Flowers produced on short racemes or singly, white, each $\frac{1}{4}$ in. across.

Native of S.E. Australia and Tasmania. It is a quick grower and flowers in July, but its blossoms have little beauty, nor has it shown the graceful and distinct growth of P. *betulinus*. It is also tender, and only hardy in mild districts.

PLANERA   ULMACEAE

A genus of one deciduous species in the south-eastern United States. From its allies *Ulmus*, *Celtis* and *Zelkova*, the first of which it resembles in foliage, it differs in the nut-like tubercled fruit. The genus is named after J. J. Planer, a German physician (1743–1789).

P. AQUATICA (Walt.) Gmel.   WATER ELM
Anonymus aquatica Walt.

A deciduous tree 30 to 45 ft high, with a trunk 15 to 20 in. in diameter; young shoots thin, downy. Leaves alternately arranged in opposite ranks, ovate or oval, 1 to 3 in. long, about half as wide, toothed (sometimes doubly so), scurfy downy beneath when young, ultimately harsh to the touch on both surfaces; veins about ten each side the midrib, forked near the margin; stalk $\frac{1}{8}$ to $\frac{1}{4}$ in. long. Flowers greenish, very small and inconspicuous, usually unisexual, sometimes bisexual, both sorts being found on the same tree. Males borne in few-flowered clusters, each one composed of a four-, sometimes five-lobed calyx with a corresponding number of stamens; females longer-stalked, borne one to three together in the leaf-axils of small lateral twigs. Fruits nut-like, $\frac{1}{2}$ in. in diameter, covered with elongated, wart-like excrescences, and containing one seed.

Native of the south-eastern United States, where it is frequently found in swamps. The tree is extremely rare in cultivation. What was once grown under its name usually proved to be *Zelkova carpinifolia*. The only known example grows in the Home Park at Windsor, and measures 72 × 8$\frac{1}{4}$ ft (1972).

PLANTAGO   PLANTAGINACEAE

A genus of over 250 species, nearly all of them herbs. Flowers small and inconspicuous, borne in heads or spikes. Calyx and corolla four-lobed. Fruit a many-seeded capsule.

P. CYNOPS L.   SHRUBBY PLANTAIN

An evergreen shrub 1 to 1½ ft high, with erect branches that are downy when young. Leaves opposite, narrowly linear, 1 to 2½ in. long, $\frac{1}{20}$ in. wide, grooved on the upper side, rough or bristly at the edges, rather triangular in cross-section. The tiny flowers are produced from June onwards crowded in an ovoid head scarcely ½ in. long, which is borne at the end of an erect, slender, downy stalk 1½ to 3½ in. long. Corolla ⅛ in. wide, four-lobed, yellowish white, the lobes lanceolate, just standing clear of a mass of broadly ovate bracts, which are green, pointed, and have a membranous, rather transparent margin.

Native of Central and S. Europe; cultivated by Gerard at Holborn in 1596, under the name *Psyllium sempervirens*. It is of interest as a shrubby member of the same genus as the common lawn pests, but has no beauty. It was found by Charles Baker flowering on Foxendown, Meopham, Kent, in August 1920, and H. N. Ridley has a note on its existence there in the *Journal of Botany* for 1920, p. 271. It was growing on a dry bank of chalk where there is very little soil, and, as there are no houses near the spot, Ridley considered it quite unlikely that a plant of so little attraction and so very rarely cultivated as this could have gained its footing there as an escape from gardens. He is, therefore, inclined to include it in the indigenous flora of England. But C. E. Britton, at p. 294 of the same journal, suggested it had most probably been introduced with imported seeds. He had found it in 1902 on the slopes of a Kentish hill between Cobham and Luddesdown.

PLATANUS   PLANE   PLATANACEAE

The planes are very distinct from any other group of trees and constitute in themselves the family Platanaceae, which is allied to the Hamamelid-aceae. There are about eight species, all natives of N. America and Mexico except *P. orientalis* of S.E. Europe and S.W. Asia and the anomalous *P. kerrii* from Indo-China. The leaves are alternate and palmately lobed, except in *P. kerrii*, which has entire, pinnately veined leaves. The arrangement of the main veins in some species is complex; it is often not truly palmate, since the ribs running out to the lobes do not spring from the same point, except in three-lobed leaves, and even in these the point of origin may be well above the base of the blade. The axillary buds in *Platanus* are concealed in summer by the swollen, hollow base of the petiole, which is furnished with a pair of stipules united at the base into a tube and often leafy at the apex.

The flowers are arranged in dense clusters and are unisexual; the male and female clusters are borne on the same tree but on separate peduncles. The female flowers develop into achenes, each with a large tuft of erect hairs at the base. The ripe fruit-balls are a characteristic feature of the planes; sometimes they are solitary, but more often they are strung two to six together on the pendulous, fibrous peduncle, which is sometimes branched. The fruit-balls persist more or less throughout the winter and, when they break up, release vast numbers of achenes, which are carried over long distances by the wind.

The bark of most species peels off in flakes, and after a stormy spring day the ground beneath a large plane will sometimes be seen strewn with pieces of bark torn off by the wind. This feature is most evident on strongly growing trees. The trunks of old trees become scaly or even fissured, though the branches continue to flake.

Some of the noblest trees of the northern hemisphere belong to this genus. Specimens of the European *P. orientalis* are known to have trunks 40 ft in circumference, and the American *P. occidentalis* growing in the Mississippi Valley has trunks about as large, and it occasionally reaches 170 ft in height. They like a deep, moist, loamy soil, and thrive better in the south of England than in the north. They are essentially sun-lovers. Seeds ripen on the London plane and *P. orientalis*, and germinate readily, but the former does not breed true and is best raised from cuttings, which should be made at the fall of the leaf, of shoots 8 to 12 in. long, with a 'heel' of old wood at the base, and placed under a handlight in a sheltered spot. In nurseries they are usually propagated from stools by layers. Young plants are rather subject to being cut back by frost.

The plane trees of town streets and promenades are under suspicion of causing serious bronchial irritation by shedding the hairs from their leaves, and especially fruits. These break up into minute particles which, floating in the air, are inhaled. Although the alleged evil influences of these particles on the throat and lungs (and even on the eyes and ears as well) were suspected and written about by the ancients—among others by Galen and Dioscorides—they never appear to have deterred either them or later generations from planting the tree freely. There seems to be little doubt that on the Continent it produces, or helps to produce, a catarrhal affection analogous to hay fever. In Britain the crops of fruit are not so large, and probably our damper climate prevents the hairs travelling far from the tree; at any rate, nothing has been proved against the tree to justify its wholesale condemnation.

The planes are susceptible to the fungus disease *Gnomonia veneta(platani)*, once known by the name *Gloeosporium nervisequum*, given to one of its two asexual (conidial) stages, and usually referred to as the plane-tree wilt disease or plane-tree anthracnose. The first sign of attack is the discoloration of the leaf-tissue between the principal veins; later all the young foliage may be killed, and cankers often develop on the stems if the attack has been severe. This disease is sporadic in its attacks. It is said to be favoured by cold, damp weather in spring and early summer, and to be more prevalent in country districts than in towns. It is not lethal, and the dead foliage is usually replaced later in the summer. But it weakens the tree and renders it unsightly. *P. occidentalis* is very susceptible, while *P. orientalis* is said to be immune. *P. acerifolia* is sometimes attacked, but the clones and seedlings probably vary in their susceptibility to the disease.

Reports that *P. orientalis* is attacked probably refer to *P. acerifolia* misnamed.

P. ACERIFOLIA (Ait.) Willd.   INTERMEDIATE PLANE,
LONDON PLANE   [PLATE 41

P. orientalis var. *acerifolia* of many authors and probably of Aiton; *P. occidentalis* Hort.,
in part, not L.; *P. orientalis* Hort., in part, not L.; *P. intermedia* Hort.; *P. vulgaris* var.
acerifolia Spach; for the names *P.* × *hispanica* and *P.* × *hybrida*, see pp. 269–70

A deciduous tree of the largest size, frequently over 100 ft high, with a
smooth, erect trunk, whose bark peels off in flakes, and a huge rounded head of
somewhat contorted branches, the terminal parts of which in large trees are
pendulous; young shoots and leaves covered at first with a dense, pale brown
wool much of which falls away by autumn. The leaves of mature trees are very
variable in shape, even on the same individual. The commonest type of leaf is
truncate to shallowly cordate at the base, three- or five-lobed, entire except for a
few teeth at the base or sparsely toothed throughout, mostly 6 to 7 in. long and
8 to 9 in. wide (measured between the tips of the two lateral lobes), the central
lobe broadest at its base, somewhat longer than wide, separated from the lateral
lobes by approximately right-angled sinuses (but by a lesser angle in some small,
three-lobed leaves); petiole 2 to 3 in. long. Towards the end of the summer
leaves are produced which are deeply cordate at the base, strongly toothed
(though sometimes almost entire on old trees) mostly five-lobed, sometimes
even seven-lobed; the sinuses are deeper than on the lower leaves, and the central
lobe is commonly constricted at the base; these leaves are mostly 6 to 7½ in.
long, 8 to 10 in. wide, and have a disproportionately short petiole, which is
1¾ to 2 in. long (usually shorter than the depth of the basal sinus). On some
shoots a peculiar type of leaf is produced which is smaller than in the previous
two types and wide for its length, mostly three-lobed, the lateral lobes spreading
almost horizontally; the base is cordate, and at its centre is a triangular wedge
devoid of tissue on the outside, its margins being formed by the bases of the
two lateral ribs; the petiole in this type of leaf is long in proportion to the size
of the blade, e.g. 2¾ in. long on a leaf 4 in. long. On the leaves of mature trees
the two main lateral ribs meet the central rib at the base of the blade, i.e., there
is no tissue between the apex of the petiole and the junction of the main ribs.
But this is not always the case on the leaves of the lowermost branches, which
are sometimes uncharacteristic both in this respect and in having an unusually
broad central lobe. There is also evidence that anomalous leaves are produced
after a tree has been heavily lopped, and on second growths, made after damage
by frost or the plane-tree wilt disease. The fruit-balls are mostly two to four on
each peduncle, about 1¼ in. wide, bristly at first, becoming smoother during the
winter owing to the breaking off of the styles near their point of insertion;
achene with hairs on the body as well as at the base, its head conical, glabrous
when mature.

Under the name *P. acerifolia* have been grouped various intermediates
between *P. orientalis* and *P. occidentalis*, of whose origin nothing is known for

certain, and whose taxonomic status is still undecided. Of these, at least in Britain, is the form, possibly a clone, that came in the last century to be known as the 'London plane', and was for a long time confused with *P. occidentalis*. The description given above is of this plane only; other forms of *P. acerifolia* are discussed below, and for two very distinct planes usually placed under *P. acerifolia*, see *P.* 'Augustine Henry' and *P.* 'Pyramidalis'.

In its fruits, the London plane is nearer to the oriental plane than it is to the western, but the fruit-balls are fewer on each peduncle and are less bristly when mature. The foliage of a single individual of the London plane is so variable that herbarium specimens rarely show its full repertoire, and can be very misleading. For the most part the leaves are not unlike those of *P. occidentalis*, especially of its var. *glabrata*, but the sinuses are somewhat deeper and the central lobe is usually longer than wide. The only leaves that indicate any affinity with *P. orientalis* are those borne at the ends of strong shoots, which often have the rhombic central lobe seen in most forms of the oriental plane, but their deeply cordate base is not a regular feature of that species. The young leaves are not so densely woolly as in *P. occidentalis*, and in this respect are more like those of *P. orientalis*.

Most modern authorities accept that *P. acerifolia* is a hybrid between *P. orientalis* and *P. occidentalis*. The belief finds support not only in the botanical characters of the London plane but also in its great vigour—a common feature of first-generation hybrids between related species—and in the variability of its seedlings. But the theory is still unproven, however likely it may be. It could be tested by making an artificial cross between the putative parents, and this has now been carried out. The cross was made in 1968 at the National Arboretum, Washington, USA, by F. S. Santamour, Jr, and the seedlings will throw much-needed light on this problem once they reach maturity (*Amer. Hort. Mag.*, Vol. 49 (1970), pp. 23–5).

Having at first taken the view that the London plane was a seedling variant of *P. orientalis* that became fixed by cultivation, Dr Henry later came to accept that it was of hybrid origin, and in his paper 'The History of the London Plane' he attempted to show that it had originated in the Botanic Garden at Oxford around 1670. This paper, written in collaboration with Margaret Flood, was published in 1919 in *Proceedings of the Royal Irish Academy*, Vol. 35 (B), pp. 9–28, and its main conclusions are summarised in *Gard. Chron.*, Vol. 66 (1919), p. 47. The Oxford tree, catalogued by the younger Bobart as *Platanus inter orientalem et occidentalem media*, is represented by two herbarium specimens dating from the latter part of the 17th century, which Henry identified with the London plane. One of the weaknesses of his argument is the absence of any proof that the tree originated at Oxford. If *P. acerifolia* is a hybrid between the oriental and western planes it is likely that the cross occurred—very probably more than once—somewhere in southern Europe, and that the Oxford tree, or the seed from which it was raised, came from a botanic garden in that region. But it should be remarked that, judging from one of the two herbarium specimens cited by Henry, it is questionable whether the Oxford tree was *P. acerifolia* and not some form of *P. occidentalis*.

Despite the mists that veil the early history of *P. acerifolia*, it must have been in cultivation in Britain by the middle of the 18th century, since the largest of the existing trees can hardly be less than 200 years old.* Being both hardy and vigorous, and easily increased by cuttings, it usurped the place of *P. occidentalis* and, to a large extent, that of *P. orientalis* also. With the coming of the industrial revolution and the growth of cities another virtue of *P. acerifolia* became manifest. It 'thrives better in and about London than any other park tree; consequently, it has been planted extensively there during the present century, and has succeeded so well that it has become known as the London Plane. In the numerous London squares and gardens it is certainly surprising to see how healthy, clean and fresh looking this Plane appears, particularly in Berkeley, Bedford and Mecklenburg Squares. Although surrounded by myriads of chimneys, its leaves for size and freshness can vie almost with the foliage in the country far removed from smoke and town atmosphere' (G. Berry, *The Garden*, Vol. 20 (1881), p. 372). Like so many of his contemporaries, Berry believed that the London plane was *P. occidentalis*, and referred to it as the "western" plane. There seems to be little doubt that this false western plane, or London plane, is a clone, or a group of very similar clones, distinguished not by any single leaf picked at random, but by a set of leaves, comprising many different shapes but constant from tree to tree. The London plane also has a characteristic crown: the branches are somewhat tortuous, and the perimeter is intricately branched, giving a winter silhouette which is surprisingly delicate for such a robust tree, and very different from that of the coarser and inferior 'Pyramidalis', with which the true London plane has been so lamentably confused.

Most of the older trees of *P. acerifolia* are probably of the London form, and similar planes are cultivated on the continent. For example, F. Jaennicke, in his admirable study of the planes (1892–7), illustrates his account of *P. acerifolia* with more than sixty drawings of leaves and leaf-sprays from German trees, mostly from old trees in the Stadtpark at Mainz planted early in th ecentury (*Abh. Leop.-Carol. Akad. Naturf.*, Vol. 77 (1901), plates VIII and IX). A match for every one of these leaves could be picked up in St James's Park or Green Park in late autumn. The Toulouse tree mentioned below is also very similar to the London plane, but it is likely that most trees of *P. acerifolia* growing in southern Europe differ in one way or another from the London form.

Among the old trees, one that appears to be distinct from the common London plane is the tree at the north end of the Rhododendron Dell, which, as mentioned in the footnote below, was probably planted in the 1770s. It bears an unusually

* The famous specimen of *P. acerifolia* in the palace gardens at Ely is supposed to have been planted by Gunning, who was Bishop of Ely from 1674/5 until his death in 1684. He had previously spent some years at Oxford, and Henry surmised that the Ely plane was one of the first propagations from the tree in the Botanic Garden there. But he offered no evidence that this plane dates from Bishop Gunning's time. Being short-trunked and heavily branched, it may be younger than its large girth suggests. The Barn Elms tree, which is of about the same girth as the Ely tree, may have been planted by Sir Richard Hoare, the banker, who bought the property in 1750 and improved it. The tree at Kew, at the head of the Rhododendron Dell, is believed to have been planted in the 1770s, when this part of the garden was laid out by Capability Brown. The dell, once known as the Hollow Walk, was excavated in 1773. In the 19th century the London plane was commonly known as *P. occidentalis*, so it is likely, but not certain, that the trees listed by Loudon under that name were really *P. acerifolia*; the oldest of those for which an age is given date from the 1730s or early 1740s.

high proportion of leaves in which the blade is deeply divided into entire lobes and deeply indented at the base; the central lobe is often inordinately long, and its base may reach to within 1 in. or less of the apex of the petiole. Up to six fruit-balls have been found on one peduncle in this plane, and the styles appear to be unusually long. The fruiting specimen depicted in Dr Henry's paper on the London plane appears to have been taken from this tree (op. cit., plate VI, fig. 3). Of the other specimens listed below, the tree at Witley Rectory is of the same character. See also *P. acerifolia* 'Palmata'. Such trees could represent different forms of the first-generation cross (assuming, of course, that *P. acerifolia* is a hybrid, which is not so far proven).

Especially in the streets of London, planes can be seen which are clearly not the true London plane and are yet quite different from 'Pyramidalis', the common street-plane. These nondescripts are younger than the planes of the parks and older squares of central London, and of no obvious merit. Considering that the true London plane and 'Pyramidalis' are so easily propagated by cuttings or layers the existence of these oddments is puzzling. The probable explanation is provided by Thomas Rivers, who remarked that British nurserymen, finding *P. orientalis* hard to propagate, imported seed from France which was in fact *P. acerifolia*—often grown on the continent as *P. orientalis*. According to him, the seedlings from these importations resembled the London plane but had more deeply cut leaves (*Gard. Chron.* (1866), p. 316). It is possible that the use of prunings as propagating material may have resulted in some of these inferior forms being perpetuated. Nondescript planes are to be found in the streets near Kew Gardens and specimens from some of them are preserved in the herbarium. The planes on the Thames Embankment, planted after the foreshore was built up in the late 1860s and early 1870s, seem to be a varied lot and different from the London plane. According to Berry they came from France, which, if true, would bear out Rivers's statement.

The following are some of the largest specimens of *P. acerifolia* measured in recent years: Kew, in Rhododendron Dell, 98 × 17¼ ft, bole 30 ft (1965); Osterley Park, Hounslow, London, 98 × 17¼ ft, bole 30 ft (1965); Barn Elms, London (grounds of the former Ranelagh Club), 103 × 20¼ ft (1903), 110 × 25 ft (1971); Riverside Gardens, Richmond, London, 123 × 17 ft and 99 × 18½ ft (1952); Montpelier Row, Twickenham, London, 120 × 18½ ft, bole 40 ft (1968); Ravensbury Park, Morden, London, 110 × 19½ ft and 96 × 20¼ ft (1968); Carshalton, Surrey, in Festival Walk, 123 × 21 ft (1967); Witley Rectory, Surrey, 115 × 20 ft (1965); Albury Park, Surrey, 110 × 15½ ft (1968); Woodcote House, Dorking, Surrey, 90 × 20½ ft (1956); Kelsey Park, Beckenham, Kent, 96 × 21 ft (1957); Woolbeding Rectory, Sussex, 102 × 16½ ft (1957); Blenheim Palace, Oxon, by the Cascades, 120 × 18¼ ft (1965); Pusey House, Oxon, 85 × 24 ft, bole 12 ft (1968); Mottisfont Abbey, Hants, 105 × 21¼ ft and a double tree 115 × 36 ft (1968); Cirencester Abbey, Glos., 108 × 18¾ ft (1972); Woolverstone Hall, Suffolk, 70 × 21 ft (1968); Kings College Meadow, Cambridge, 100 × 18½ ft (1969); Ely Cathedral, Cambs., 104 × 20½ ft (1903), 115 × 27¾ ft (1969).

var. HISPANICA (Muenchh.) Bean—See *P. hispanica* below, and *P.* 'Augustine Henry'.

var. MINOR Ten. *P. hispanica* Graeffer ex Ten.; *P. acerifolia* var. *hispanica*

Ten.—The name *P. acerifolia* var. *minor* was given by the Italian botanist Tenore to a plane cultivated in the gardens of the royal palace at Caserta near Naples under the name *P. hispanica*. It had very small leaves, cordate at the base, with triangular, almost entire lobes. Similar forms of independent origin have occurred elsewhere, and may be seedlings of the London plane or similar forms. Here may be mentioned a curious tree at Kew in Syon Vista that came from Van Houtte's nursery in the 1870s, but under what name is not certain. The leaves are mostly 4 in. or less long, ovate in general outline, broadly cuneate at the base, scarcely lobed, or with a pair of short lateral lobes; leaves at the ends of the shoots are more like those of the London plane, but much smaller.

cv. 'PALMATA'.—According to Thomas Rivers, who imported it from France, this plane makes a vigorous, erect tree; the leaves are more deeply lobed than in the London plane, and persist longer on the tree in the autumn; the bark flakes less (*Gard. Chron.* (1860), p. 47 and (1866), p. 316). A plane under the same name was sold by Barron's nursery, Elvaston, near Derby, in the last century. Rivers also mentions 'PALMATA SUPERBA', which may be the same as the plane sold by Späth's nursery, Berlin, as "*P. superba*". Young plants under both names were growing at Kew in the 1830s, but it is uncertain whether either still exists. There are, however, two fine trees in the collection which may well have come under distinguishing names, since both are very distinct from the ordinary London plane and are certainly worthy of distinction. One grows by the south-east corner of the Herbarium; the other stands north of the planting around King William's Temple, behind the collection of Japanese cherries.

cv. 'PYRAMIDALIS'.—See *P.* 'Pyramidalis'.

cv. 'SUTTNERI'.—A handsome variegated tree, its leaves being conspicuously blotched, spotted, or patched with creamy white, and sometimes almost wholly of that colour. It was introduced shortly after the middle of the last century, and almost certainly originated as a seedling. It is weaker-growing than the London plane, and rather susceptible to plane-tree wilt. Examples are: Holland Park, London, 54 × 4½ ft (1964); Heath Cottage, Puttenham, Surrey, 73 × 7 ft (1963); National Botanic Garden, Dublin, 60 × 3½ ft (1966). 'ARGENTEA VARIE-GATA', raised by Messrs Russell, then of Richmond, is similar to 'Suttneri', and the two may have become confused; it received an Award of Merit in 1897. In 'KELSEYANA' ('Aureo-variegata'), raised in the USA, the leaves are variegated with yellow. This clone (and 'Suttneri') were both wrongly placed under *P. occidentalis* by Jaennicke.

P. HISPANICA Muenchh. SPANISH PLANE (of Miller).—In 1770, Muenchhausen gave the name *P. hispanica* to the plane that Miller had first described in the 1759 edition of his *Dictionary*. Miller's description is as follows: 'The Spanish Plane-tree has larger leaves than either of the other sorts, which are more divided than those of the Occidental plane-tree, but not so much as those of the Eastern. Some of the leaves are cut into five and others but three lobes; these are sharply indented on the edges, and are of a light green; the foot-stalks are short, and covered with a short down. This is by some called the middle Plane-tree, from its leaves being shaped between those of the two other sorts. It grows rather faster than either of the other sorts, but I have not seen any very large trees of this kind.'
Muenchhausen added nothing of significance to Miller's description, but made the

suggestion that *P. hispan ca* might be a hybrid (*Vermischung*) between the oriental and western planes.

Unfortunately no specimen of Miller's Spanish plane can be traced, and its identity is uncertain. It is very probable—but perhaps unprovable—that it was the London plane or at least some very similar form. Miller's description agrees quite well with the London plane, and it is surely significant that Aiton gave 'Spanish plane-tree' as the vernacular name for *P. orientalis* var. *acerifolia* Ait., which is usually supposed to be the London plane. But Miller himself considered the maple-leaved plane (*acerifolia*) to be distinct from the Spanish plane, and there is some evidence that the London plane was grown by Miller at Chelsea under the name *P. occidentalis*. Since the evidence is so contradictory, the name *P. hispanica* Muenchh. must be regarded as of uncertain application. For the plane that Henry considered to be Miller's Spanish plane, see *P*. 'Augustine Henry'.

Later uses of the name *P. hispanica* should be mentioned, though they do not necessarily have any bearing on the typification of Miller's Spanish plane. The identity of the plane distributed by Loddiges' nursery under the name *P. hispanica* is uncertain; according to Loudon it resembled *P. orientalis* but had 'longer' leaves. *P. hispanica* Hort. ex Gord. (*Garden*, Vol. 1 (1872), p. 588) is a form of *P. occidentalis* and is probably the plane distributed commercially as *P. hispanica integrifolia* or *P. integrifolia*, which was placed under *P. occidentalis* by Wesmael as var. *hispan ca*. The leaves of this plane, which are matched by those of some wild trees, are very shallowly lobed and some are almost circular in outline, but with a deeply cordate base. Finally, a tree cultivated as *P. hispanica* at Caserta was referred by Tenore to *P. acerifolia* as var. *minor* (q.v.).

P. HYBRIDA Brot.—The name *P. hybridus* [sic] was given by the Portuguese botanist Brotero in 1804 to a plane described by him as fast-growing, with subpalmate, five-lobed leaves, the lobes acute and dentate. He suggested it might be a hybrid between *P. occidentalis* and *P. orientalis*, or a variety of the latter. The name *P. hybrida* has priority over *P. acerifolia* Willd., and is used by some authorities. But the identity of Brotero's plane is uncertain, and it therefore seems preferable to retain the more familiar and better established name *P. acerifolia* for this group. In the *Prodromus* Alphonse de Candolle gives *P. hybrida* Brot. as a synonym of *P. occidentalis*.

The specimens of *P. acerifolia* in Willdenow's herbarium have not been seen. But the French authority Dr P. Rivals, who examined them, has presented to Kew a set of specimens taken from a single tree of *P. acerifolia* growing at Toulouse and has annotated two of these as matching the specimens of *P. acerifolia* in Willdenow's herbarium. The Toulouse tree is evidently very similar to our London plane.

P. 'AUGUSTINE HENRY'

P. californica Hort., not Benth.; *P. racemosa* Hort., not Nutt.; *P. hispanica sensu* Henry (excluding synonyms *P. orientalis hispanica* Loud., *P. occidentalis hispanica* Wesmael and *P. macrophylla* Hort., not Muenchh.)

A tall tree with laxly pendulous lower branches, upper branches not contorted as in the London plane. Leaves rather thin, light green, mostly 10 to 12 in. wide, sometimes as much as 16 in. wide, commonly five-lobed, sinuses variable, from broad and shallow to deep and narrow, lobes finely tapered and edged with fairly regular slenderly tipped teeth, base mostly truncate and never deeply cordate, with or without a central wedge, and sometimes distinctly tapered at the base, especially on young trees; the secondary veins running out to the tips of the fourth and fifth lobes are usually directed forward, instead of spreading more or less horizontally as in the London plane; the two main veins, i.e., those running to the tips of the two upper lobes, meet the midrib at the base of the blade or slightly above it. The undersurface of the leaf is at first often as woolly as in *P. occidentalis* and the hairs on the veins persist rather longer than in the London plane. The petiole is 2¼ to 3½ in. long. The fruit-balls, not freely produced, are solitary, in pairs or threes; achene with an almost glabrous body.

This striking plane was received at Kew in 1878 from the Belgian nurseryman Van Houtte under the name "*P. californica*" and was sold under that name by other continental nurseries, and also by Lee's nursery, Hammersmith. It was also known as "*P. racemosa*", and this seems to have been the name under which it has been generally known in this country, at least in commerce. But *P. racemosa* Nutt. is the California plane, to which 'Augustine Henry' bears no resemblance at all, and *P. californica* Benth. is a synonymous name of this species. Dr Henry considered that "*P. californica*" was none other than the Spanish plane of Miller, and in his paper on the London plane he describes and figures it under the name *P. hispanica* Muenchh. But it is impossible to accept this conclusion, for which Henry offered no evidence beyond the general agreement between the Kew trees and Miller's scanty description of the Spanish plane. However, it was he who first gave a full account of this plane and first called attention to its merits. It is therefore appropriate that it should bear his name. *P.* 'Augustine Henry' is discussed and figured by Henry (as *P. hispanica* Muenchh.) in *Proc. Roy. Ir. Acad.*, Vol. 35 (B), pp. 18–19; pl. VII, fig. 5; pl. IV, pl. IX, fig. 9, no. 4. The reference-tree of this clone grows at Kew by the Azalea Garden, near the Iron Drinking Fountain (No. 10, Gardens Accession No. 0073.10001). It measures 98 × 10¼ ft (1973).

Even without a close examination of the leaves, 'Augustine Henry' can be distinguished from the London plane by the laxer lower branches, the smoother, more freely flaking trunk, the usually better developed central stem, and the different colour of the foliage, which verges on sea-green. The leaves are much more numerously and more elegantly toothed, and there is a tendency for the blades to droop at the edges and thus appear more attenuated at the base than in fact they are when flattened into the horizontal plane. The leaves are also on the average much larger than in the London plane. In addition to the reference-tree at Kew mentioned above, there is another of the same age nearby, in Syon Vista, which is very similar, allowing for its sunnier position, and is probably of the same clone. Some have been noticed in central London, the finest being one in St James's Park, on the slope north of the bridge, to the right of the path leading from The Mall to Queen Anne's Gate.

P. OCCIDENTALIS L.   WESTERN PLANE, BUTTONWOOD

P. vulgaris var. *angulosa* Spach; *P. macrophylla* Hort., at least in part; *P. hispanica* Hort., in part; *P. occidentalis* var. *hispanica* Wesm.

A tree up to 140 ft high in N. America, with a bark similar to that of the London plane. Leaves shallowly lobed, sometimes very indistinctly so (but occasionally they are quite as deeply lobed as on some leaves of the London plane), lobes acuminate at the apex, usually sinuately toothed, 4 to 7 in. long and about as wide, cordate or truncate at the base or sometimes with a decurrent wedge each side of the junction with the petiole (as so often in the oriental and London planes), densely stellate-tomentose when young, at length glabrous except for some down remaining on the midrib and veins beneath (but the original coating persists longer than in the oriental and London planes); petioles 3 to 5 in. long; stipules 1 to 1½ in. long, entire or toothed. Fruit clusters solitary (rarely in twos), on glabrous peduncles 3 to 6 in. long; achenes truncate to rounded at the apex, crowned by the short persistent base of the style and ringed only at the base with a tuft of hairs (in the oriental plane the achenes are rather more conical at the apex and sometimes the body of the achene is hairy; a more reliable difference is that in the oriental plane, and most of the hybrids, the peristent style is longer and the fruit-balls hence more bristly than in the American species).

Native of eastern and southern N. America from New England to Florida and west to the Mississippi basin and Ontario, south-west to Texas; introduced to Britain before 1634, probably from Virginia. This species has no value in British gardens. It has many times been raised from seed at Kew, and the young plants grow freely for a time, but owing to injury by spring frost and the attacks of a parasitic fungus (for which see p. 264) they rarely get beyond 6 ft in height. Early this century a tree at Kew raised from Michigan seed reached a height of 12 ft but became so diseased that it had to be cut down. Since *P. occidentalis* ranges over many climatically diverse regions, and ascends to 2,500 ft in the Appalachians, it seems to be not beyond the bounds of possibility that there might still be found a form of the western plane capable of growing well in our climate. But even then the attacks of the plane-tree disease *Gnomonia veneta*, to which this species is very susceptible, would probably make it worthless. Even in the United States it has been supplanted as an ornamental by the oriental and London planes. But before the disease reached this country, probably early in the 19th century, the American plane may have fared rather better than now. At any rate, there is a specimen in the British Museum of the true *P. occidentalis* taken from a tree growing at Kew in 1781; and in Bishop Goodenough's Herbarium there is a specimen bearing a mature fruit-ball which almost certainly came from a tree at Kew around that time.

During the 19th century *P. occidentalis* seems to have become rare in Europe, but some of the trees from the early introductions continued to exist, e.g., in France at Angers and near Montpelier. It also remained in commerce, but often under such incorrect names as "*P. macrophylla*" and "*P. hispanica*". At the present time (1974) there is a promising young tree at Kew raised in 1969 from seeds received from the National Arboretum, Washington, USA. At Borde Hill in Sussex a shrubby specimen has existed in a damp, shady place for about sixty years.

Although the true species has always been rare in this country, its name was once generally used in gardens for *P. acerifolia*. The first to question the correctness of this identification was the nurseryman Thomas Rivers, who expressed his doubts both to Loudon and Professor Lindley at some time during the 1830s, but apparently neither agreed with him. However, Rivers was vindicated in 1856, when Sir William Hooker, the Director of Kew, wrote to *The Gardeners' Chronicle* remarking that a tree in the collection planted as *P. occidentalis* was not the true species (the tree in question is almost certainly the fine specimen of London plane growing at the end of the Rhododendron Dell). After Hooker's intervention, and the correspondence that followed, it came to be accepted among the better informed that the plane so common in the parks and squares of London was not *P. occidentalis*, and discussion shifted to the problem of its identity and origin. But most nurserymen and a surprising number of botanists continued to confuse the two until well into this century.

var. GLABRATA (Fern.) Sarg. *P. glabrata* Fern.; *P. lindeniana sens.* S. Wats., not Mart. & Gal.; *P. racemosa sens.* Hemsl., not Nutt.; *P. densicoma* Dode, in part, *teste* Sarg.—Leaves mostly truncate to shallowly cordate at the base, more deeply lobed than in the typical state, with acute or rounded sinuses, the lobes slenderly acuminate, more or less entire except for small secondary lobes at the base of the blade and sometimes on the central lobe (but the leaves on strong shoots more numerously toothed). Fruit-balls and achenes as in typical *P. occidentalis*.

Native of N. Mexico (Coahuila, Nuevo Leon, and San Luis Potosi), extending into the USA, where it is common in W. Texas but occurs occasionally farther north and east. It was described from an herbarium specimen originally identified as *P. lindeniana*, a Mexican species with a more southern distribution. The epithet *glabrata* refers to the fact that the undersides of the leaves become nearly glabrous, whereas in *P. lindeniana* they are permanently hairy. Sargent retained the epithet when placing *P. glabrata* under *P. occidentalis*, though there does not seem to be any marked difference in leaf-indumentum between the variety and the typical state, unless it be that the young leaves in var. *glabrata* are less woolly.

It is tempting to suppose that the var. *glabrata* was introduced to Europe from Mexico at an early date, and that some cultivated planes considered by the early botanists to be intermediate between *P. occidentalis* and *P. orientalis* were really this variety and not *P. acerifolia*.

P. ORIENTALIS L.   ORIENTAL PLANE   [PLATE 42

A deciduous tree of the largest size, in this country occasionally 80 to 100 ft high, and 14 to 20 ft in girth of trunk; in open situations it usually branches a few feet from the ground into several large spreading limbs; young shoots at first covered with pale brown hair-tufts, becoming glabrous later. Leaves palmate, 6 to 10 in. wide, somewhat less in length, with five large lobes, and usually a smaller one on each side at the base; the lobes, which are half to two-thirds the depth of the blade, and lance-shaped, have each one to three large teeth or minor lobes at the sides. When they first unfold, the leaves are covered with a thick whitish-brown felt composed of stellate hairs which later falls away, leaving the leaf glabrous except near the veins beneath, and glossy above; stalk 1½ to 3 in. long. Fruit-balls two to six on each stalk, 1 in. wide, bristly. Achenes usually with hairs on the body as well as at the base, and conical and downy at the apex, which is tapered into the persistent style.

Native of Greece (including Crete) and of bordering parts of Bulgaria,

T A S—K

Yugoslavia, and Albania, found along mountain watercourses; planted as a shade tree since ancient times, from Italy to Persia, and later to Kashmir. A great age is attributed to some large and decrepit trees. Hippocrates, the 'Father of Medicine', who lived in the 5th century before Christ, is supposed to have taught under the great plane that still exists on the island of Cos. On the Bosporus near Buyukdere there is the plane of Godfrey de Bouillon, so called from the popular tradition that he and his knights camped near it in 1096 during the first crusade. This tree, estimated by de Candolle to be 2,000 years old, owes its huge girth to the fusion of several stems and is probably of no great age. It is not mentioned by the French botanist Tournefort, who visited the Levant in 1700-2. But compared to most deciduous trees, P. *orientalis* is certainly long-lived and, planted where its roots can reach underground water, attains majestic dimensions, both in the size of its crown and the girth of its trunk, which often exceeds 30 ft. Probably the two finest trees in Europe grow in the village of Trsteno on the Dalmatian coast a few miles north of Dubrovnik. In Kashmir, where the oriental plane is known by its Persian name—chenar—there are many fine trees around the Dal Lake, the oldest of which were probably planted in the time of Akbar the Great or his successor at the end of the 16th or early in the 17th century.

The date of the introduction of the oriental plane to Britain is usually given as 'before 1548' on the authority of William Turner, whose *The Names of Herbes* was published in that year. He mentions two 'planes', one at Morpeth in Northumberland, where he was born (*c.* 1510), the other at Barnwell Priory, which he visited while at Cambridge (1526-40). He no doubt saw a true oriental plane during his first exile (1540-7), part of which he spent in Italy. But in stating that the Morpeth and Barnwell trees were true planes he was relying on memory, for it is exceedingly doubtful whether he ever looked at either tree again, and certainly not before the publication of *The Names of Herbes*, which appeared only a short time after his return from his first exile. Later, in his *Herball*, he suggested that the oriental plane had been introduced by the monks, but he still knew of no examples save the two 'planes' he had seen in his youth. It is probable that the trees were really sycamore (called plane tree in Scotland) or Norway maple ('plane' in French). It seems more likely that the oriental plane was introduced towards the end of the 16th century, through the newly formed Levant Company.

The oriental plane is comparatively rare in gardens, having been ousted by the more rapidly growing London plane, which is not so picturesque nor so pleasing as an isolated lawn tree. From the common form of the London plane it is easily distinguished by its shorter, more rugged trunk, and its deeper, often doubly lobed leaves. Some forms of P. *acerifolia* have rather deeply cut leaves, but they are still very unlike those of the oriental plane, being relatively wider and with a broader central lobe.

A fine specimen of P. *orientalis* at Kew, near the Orangery and on the site of the famous 17th-century gardens of Sir Henry Capel of Kew House, measures 68 × 16 ft (1967). Other noteworthy specimens are: Woodstock Park, Kent, 89 × 25½ ft at the base (1959); Woolbeding Rectory, Sussex, 40 × 12½ ft (1972); Rycote Park, Oxon, 70 × 27¼ ft (1968); Exbury, Hants, 60 × 15¾ ft (1968); Corsham Court, Wilts, *pl. c.* 1760, 75 × 22 ft (1965); Melbury Park, Dorset,

50 × 19¾ ft (1971); Westonbirt, Glos., 82 × 10¼ ft (1972); Foxley, Heref., 85 × 14½ ft (1967); Trelowarren, Cornwall, 75 × 13½ ft (1966); Jesus College, Cambridge, *pl.* 1802, 90 × 17 ft (1972); Ely Cathedral, Cambs., Bishop's Palace, 90 × 15 ft and 80 × 15¼ ft (1969).

Although several varieties of *P. orientalis* have been distinguished, it is doubtful if any merits recognition. The var. *insularis* A.DC., founded on specimens from Cyprus and Crete, is described as having the leaves divided to below the middle into narrowly lanceolate lobes. It is often regarded as representing the normal wild state of the species, and perhaps correctly so, though it seems to be the case that trees in Cyprus (which may not be genuinely wild) have their leaf-lobes rather narrower than is usual in Grecian trees. The var. *liquidambarifolia* (Spach) Jaennicke represents a minor variation in which the lobes of the leaves are entire or only sparsely toothed. Trees planted in Kashmir, at least those by the Dal Lake, have larger, less deeply divided leaves than is normal in wild *P. orientalis*.

A name that occurs frequently in the literature of the planes is *P. cuneata* Willd. (*P. orientalis* var. *cuneata* (Willd.) Loud., *nom. illegit.*). This was given by Willdenow in 1805 to a small shrubby tree growing in the Berlin Botanic Garden. He cited *P. orientalis* var. *undulata* Aiton as a synonym, which suggests that *P. cuneata* was the plane sold by some English nurseries as the 'wave-leaved' plane. Loudon describes it under the name *P. orientalis* var. *cuneata*, which, though widely used, is clearly illegitimate, since he cited the earlier *P. orientalis* var. *undulata* Ait. as a synonym (*Arb. et. Frut Brit.* (1838), Vol. IV, p. 2034). Loudon's portrait of the tree growing in the garden of the Horticultural Society shows that the lobes of the leaves were irregularly reflexed—whence perhaps the popular name and Aiton's botanical epithet.

Shrubby plants found apparently wild on the south-eastern slopes of the Caucasus were identified by Koch as *P. cuneata* Willd., which he considered to be a good species, though it seems more likely that they were naturalised plants stunted by dry conditions. It has also been stated, certainly in error, that *P. cuneata* is a native of N.W. India. This conclusion was apparently based on the behaviour of young plants at Kew, raised from Kashmir seed, which were stunted and bore cuneate leaves. The fact that the leaves of *P. orientalis* are always cuneate in the seedling stage suggests, however, that these plants had simply failed to develop beyond the juvenile stage. Professor Henry, in his paper on the planes referred to under *P. acerifolia*, took a different view, arguing that *P. cuneata* Willd. was a seedling of the London plane. It is true that some cultivated trees agreeing with Willdenow's species in foliage and habit bear abnormal fruit-balls, with relatively few, often abortive achenes, and could well be of the origin suggested by Henry, but he offered no proof that the type of *P. cuneata* was abnormal in its fruits. Finally, it should be added that mature wild trees of *P. orientalis* may bear a juvenile type of leaf; on weak shoots there is a gradation from leaves with an attenuate base to those in which the base is truncate with a central wedge.

A few variants have arisen in Western Europe, some of which have been distributed commercially, though probably none is common. A tree at Kew, on the north side of Syon Vista, was received in the 1870s or 1880s as *P.* "nepalensis" and may be the same as the clone (?) that was known in the trade either by that name or as *P. laciniata,* and is said by Wesmael to have been put into commerce by the Belgian nurseryman L. de Bavay in 1847. The leaves on the Kew tree are up to 8 in. long, with elegantly tapered, deeply toothed lobes and a more or less cuneate base, but they really differ very little from those of wild trees. How this variant acquired the epithet *nepalensis* it is impossible to say; it certainly did not come from Nepal.

The status of 'DIGITATA' is uncertain. The fruit-balls are abnormally small, barely ½ in. wide, and according to Henry the achenes are infertile, as in the trees he considered to be *P. cuneata.* It may therefore be a seedling of the London plane and not a variant of *P. orientalis,* as is usually supposed. The leaves are about 6 in. long and wide, five-lobed, truncate with a central wedge or truly cuneate, the lobes separated by wide sinuses and edged with large, lobulate teeth. According to Gordon, who described it in 1872, it had been put into commerce by Loddiges' nurseries some thirty years earlier. No authentic example has so far been traced, but Henry considered that a tree in the University Botanic Garden, Cambridge, was the plane described by Gordon. Its foliage is shown in *Gard. Chron.,* Vol. 76 (1924), fig. 90. Another plane of uncertain status, growing in the same garden, was given botanical status by Henry as *P. cantabrigensis (Gard. Chron.,* loc. cit., fig. 92 and 93). This too is quite possibly a seedling of the London plane

P. 'PYRAMIDALIS'

P. pyramidalis Rivers ex Henry; *P. vulgaris* var. *pyramidalis* Kirchn.; *P. occidentalis* var. *pyramidalis* Jaennicke; ? *P. densicoma* Dode, in part; *P. acerifolia* Hort., in part.

A medium-sized tree, its lower branches horizontal, the upper usually ascending, but sometimes spreading on old specimen trees, forming a rounded or broadly oblong crown; bark on young trees brown, whitish or yellowish when first exposed, but not flaking freely and ceasing to do so earlier than in the London plane, and soon becoming rugged. Leaves rich green and glossy, mostly 6 to 7 in. wide, with usually three, more rarely five, rather short and broad, sparsely toothed lobes, truncate or shallowly cordate at the base, with or without a central wedge, main veins arising at or not much above the junction of the blade with the petiole. Although three female inflorescences may be produced on each peduncle, only one or two develop; solitary fruit-heads are perhaps the commoner, and are unusually large—about 1¾ in. across.

This plane was apparently raised (or first distributed) in France or Belgium, and was introduced to Britain about 1850. The epithet *pyramidalis* must have been attached to it when only young plants were known, since mature, untreated trees are broad-crowned. But if the lower, horizontal branches are removed the tree becomes vase-shaped. The trees in Vincent Square, London, opposite the Old Hall of the Royal Horticultural Society, are 'Pyramidalis', and show the characteristic habit very well. The one immediately opposite the main entrance appears in a photograph taken in 1904; it was then bushy and perhaps twenty years old (*Gard. Chron.*, Vol. 36, fig. 30). The docility with which 'Pyramidalis' accepts the removal of its lower branches, and its excellent response even to the crudest lopping, no doubt explains why it has become so common in streets and other line-plantings. But often it can be found planted in mixture with the London plane, with which it has been confused. A notable example is the Broad Walk in Green Park, London, between Piccadilly and the Queen Victoria Memorial, where the double lines on each side are made up of the two clones in mixture, 'Pyramidalis' being easily picked out even in winter, owing to its darker, more rugged bark and straighter branches. The specimen in Green Park planted by King George V and Queen Mary in 1911 is 'Pyramidalis'. It measures 75 × 9¾ ft (1968).

'Pyramidalis' is quite near to *P. occidentalis*, under which it was placed by Jaennicke. The fruit-balls are more bristly than in that species, and the achenes have hairs on the body as well as at the base, but in other respects it shows no sign of the influence of *P. orientalis*. From the London plane, of which Henry supposed it to be a seedling, it is distinct in its glossy leaves rarely more than shallowly cordate at the base and with a broader central lobe; also by the often solitary, very large fruit-balls and the quite different habit and bark. It is easily propagated by cuttings.

The *P. densicoma* of Dode appears to be based partly on 'Pyramidalis', partly on *P. occidentalis* var. *glabrata*.

P. RACEMOSA Nutt.
P. californica Benth.

A tree 40 to 100 ft high in California, with a trunk 2 to 6 ft in diameter; young shoots clothed with a thick wool which falls away during the summer. Leaves usually five- sometimes three-lobed, the lobes reaching half-way or more than half-way to the midrib, pointed and shallowly, often distantly, toothed, tapered to slightly heart-shaped at the base, thickly clothed below with pale, persistent down, especially along the midrib and veins, 6 to 12 in. wide, rather more in length; stalks stout, downy, 1 to 3 in. long. Flowers in ball-like clusters, two to seven of which occur on the pendulous stalk; by the time the fruits have developed the balls are ¾ in. across.

Native of California. Although introduced on several occasions it has proved to be tender. For the plane grown under the erroneous names "*P. racemosa*" or "*P. californica*", see P. 'Augustine Henry'.

P. WRIGHTII S. Wats. *P. racemosa* var. *wrightii* (S. Wats.) Benson—Near to *P. racemosa* but with the leaves more deeply divided, often cordate at the base, with five or seven elongate, almost entire lobes. Fruit-balls up to four on each peduncle. Native mainly of the USA in S. Arizona and S.W. New Mexico, but extending into Mexico. It has so far proved a failure at Kew.

PLATYCARYA   JUGLANDACEAE

A genus of a single species in E. Asia. As in *Pterocarya* the fruit is a winged nutlet, but the catkins of both sexes are erect, and the fruit-catkin is cone-like, with numerous imbricate bracts. The earliest name for the genus is *Petrophiloides*, the type of which is a fossil infrutescence found in London Clay deposits (Bowerbank, *Fossil Fruits of the London Clay* (1840), p. 43 and tt. 9, 10). The palaeobotanists Reid and Chandler accordingly transferred the living species to *Petrophiloides* in 1933. But under modern rules of nomenclature the name *Platycarya* must be used for this genus, although it was published later (1843).

P. STROBILACEA Sieb. & Zucc.

Fortunaea chinensis Lindl.; *Petrophiloides strobilacea* (Sieb. & Zucc.) Reid & Chandler

A small or medium-sized deciduous tree, with pinnate leaves, 6 to 12 in. long, branchlets with a solid pith. Leaflets five to fifteen, stalkless, ovate-lanceolate, obliquely wedge-shaped or rounded at the base, long and taper-pointed, sharply and often doubly toothed, $1\frac{1}{2}$ to $4\frac{1}{2}$ in. long, $\frac{1}{2}$ to $1\frac{1}{4}$ in. wide, with at first scattered hairs above and along the midrib and veins beneath, becoming glabrous later. Flowers unisexual, both sexes borne on the same tree, but on separate inflorescences; sepals and petals absent. Male catkins slender, cylindrical, drooping at the tip, 2 to $3\frac{1}{2}$ in. long, borne four to twelve together in a hairy panicle at the end of the young growths; female inflorescence terminal, surrounded by the male catkins, erect, usually solitary, $1\frac{1}{4}$ in. long, 1 in. wide, resembling a cone. In both sexes the flowers are produced in the axils of small, lanceolate scales, followed in the female by tiny winged nutlets which, with the wings, are only $\frac{1}{8}$ to $\frac{1}{6}$ in. across.

Native of Japan, Formosa, Korea, and China; introduced by Fortune from China in 1845 (a 'cone' had been sent to Britain some years earlier by Dr Cantor from Chusan, but this was seedless). Wilson found it in the Ichang area of Hupeh during his first and third expeditions to China and probably sent seeds in 1907. According to him it is usually a shrub or small tree in that area, only rarely seen up to 40 ft high. The Fortune introduction was not reliably hardy, but it is impossible to generalise about the hardiness of a species so widely distributed in the wild and so rare in gardens. In H. G. Hillier's collection at Jermyns House, Romsey, it grows well and bears fruit.

PLATYCRATER   HYDRANGEACEAE

A genus of a single species, confined to Japan. It is allied to *Hydrangea*, differing in having the sepals of the ray-flowers united and numerous stamens in the fertile flowers.

P. ARGUTA Sieb. & Zucc.

A low, deciduous, sometimes creeping shrub, with slender, glabrous stems. Leaves opposite, narrowly oval-lanceolate, the largest 5 to 8 in. long and 1 to 2 in. wide, tapering at both ends, the margins set with slender teeth, bristly hairy beneath; stalk ¼ in. long. Flowers of two kinds, viz. perfect and sterile, as in *Hydrangea*, produced in a lax terminal corymb. Perfect flowers 1 in. across, with four white, broadly ovate petals, two styles, very numerous yellow stamens, and a four-lobed calyx; the lobes ½ in. long, pointed, narrowly triangular. Fruits top-shaped, with the calyx-lobes persisting. Sterile flowers consist only of the united calyx-lobes, and form a white, flat, three- or four-sided disk, ¾ in. across, all the other parts of the flower being absent.

Native of Japan; introduced by way of St Petersburg about 1868. The plant is rather tender and apt to be cut to the ground in winter, or killed outright in severe frosts. I have never seen the sterile flowers above described on cultivated plants, usually there have been three perfect flowers produced in a corymb, the middle one opening first, each on a slender stalk 1 in. or less long. Both Siebold and Regel include sterile flowers in their figures (see *Flora Japonica*, t. 27, and *Gartenflora*, t. 516). The cultivated form without sterile flowers has been distinguished as var. HORTENSIS Maxim. Siebold says he found the plant growing on humid rocks with its branches flat on the ground. He mentions a curious use the Japanese made of the plant; this was to make an infusion of the leaves with which the images of Buddha were washed or baptised. But that was in 1835. The plant is easily increased by rather soft cuttings.

PODOCARPUS PODOCARPACEAE

A genus of about 100 evergreen trees and shrubs, with its main distribution in the warm-temperate and subtropical rain-forests of the southern hemisphere, but extending as far north as the Himalaya and Japan. Some species are important timber trees in their native countries. They are variable in their foliage, but all the main types are represented in the species described here. Male inflorescences cylindrical, catkin-like, usually in stalked or sessile axillary clusters, or solitary; or arranged in spikes (sect. *Stachycarpus*). The female inflorescence consists of a short axis, bearing a few scales of which only the upper one or two are fertile. The seed is much larger than the subtending scale, nut-like or drupe-like, coated by an excrescence of the carpel (epimatium). In the typical section (sect. *Podocarpus*) the inflorescences are borne in the leaf-axils, and the upper sterile scales become united with the stalk and develop into a fleshy, coloured receptacle on which the seed is borne; the seed is nut-like. To this group belong all the species treated, except those mentioned below. In the section *Stachycarpus* the female inflorescences are arranged in a spike;

there is no fleshy receptacle, but the seed itself develops a more or less fleshy layer on the outside. To this section belong *P. andinus*, *P. spicatus*, and *P. ferrugineus*, though the last is anomalous in having usually solitary fruits. The section *Nageia* is distinguished mainly by its broad leaves. The female inflorescence and fruit resembles that of the typical section, though, as in *P. nagi*, the receptacle sometimes remains dry.

Propagation is by seed if procurable, or by cuttings taken in late summer.

The generic name comes from the Greek *pous*, foot, and *karpos*, fruit, in allusion to the fleshy receptacle mentioned above.

P. ALPINUS Hook. f.

A low evergreen shrub, forming in cultivation a neat, dense, almost hemi-spherical mass of drooping branches; occasionally it makes a small tree in the wild, up to 10 ft high. Branchlets produced in whorls, very slender and inter-lacing, glabrous and green when young, later brown. Leaves $\frac{1}{4}$ to $\frac{1}{2}$ in. long, $\frac{1}{16}$ to $\frac{1}{12}$ in. wide, linear-oblanceolate, tapered at the base, rounded at the apex and often shortly apiculate, but not pungently pointed, dull green above, pale and greyish beneath from two bands of stomata, which are separated by a green, raised midrib. Fruit a small, bright red, plum-like body $\frac{1}{4}$ in. across, containing one seed.

Native of Tasmania and the mountains of New South Wales, quite hardy at Kew, where it has withstood 30° of frost without injury. It is a distinct shrub, and although quite healthy only attained 5 ft in height in fifty years or perhaps longer. Fruits have occasionally been borne at Kew.

A plant at Wakehurst Place, Sussex, probably half-a-century old, is about 5 ft high and 6 or 7 ft across, on a short, stout trunk. At Borde Hill in the same county there is a slightly smaller plant of about the same age.

P. ANDINUS Endl. PLUM-FRUITED YEW
Prumnopitys elegans Phil.

An evergreen tree 40 to 50 ft high in the wild state; very dense in habit; young shoots green, quite glabrous. Leaves linear, $\frac{1}{2}$ to $1\frac{1}{8}$ in. long, $\frac{1}{16}$ to $\frac{1}{8}$ in. wide, tapered to a short stalk bluntish or abruptly pointed at the apex; dark green above, with a dull glaucous strip each side the midrib beneath; they are densely and spirally set on the shoot (ten to fifteen to the inch), falling the third year. Male flowers in axillary and terminal panicles about 1 in. long. Fruits yellowish white, plum-like, $\frac{3}{4}$ in. long, consisting of a stone surrounded by a thin layer of

Podocarpus alpinus

flesh which is edible and tastes, according to Comber, like the Sweetwater grape. The seed has no resinous odour and was eaten by the Indians.

Native of the Chilean Andes, where it is now very rare; also of Argentina, where one stand near the Chilean frontier was discovered recently. It was introduced to Britain in 1860 by the Veitchian collector Richard Pearce from the Andes east of Chillan around 36° 40′ S., but whether it still occurs so far north it is impossible to say. Comber reintroduced it in 1926 from a remote valley on the frontier near Regolil, N.E. of Villarica (c. 39° S.), and the one known Argentine stand is in the same locality. Its southern limit is said to be around 40° S.

P. *andinus* needs a sheltered spot, especially one shielded from north and east winds, and in such a position will be found quite hardy in most gardens. It thrives in any good soil, including chalky ones. It is propagated by cuttings of late summer wood, taken with a heel.

Although rather slow-growing, P. *andinus* has attained in cultivation a size probably not equalled by any existing wild tree. A specimen at Bicton in Devon measures 71 × 4¼ ft (1968) and there is one of 62 × 4 ft at Tregrehan in Cornwall. But most of the largest trees measured by Alan Mitchell are in the size-range 35 to 50 ft in height and 2½ to 4½ ft in girth, and some are large shrubs rather than trees, being many-branched from near the base. The example at Kew measures 36 × 3¾ ft (1965).

P. andinus, like many podocarps, appears to be normally dioecious, so fruit cannot be expected unless trees of both sexes are grown. But some trees may bear both male and female flowers.

P. DACRYDIOIDES A. Rich.   NEW ZEALAND WHITE PINE, KAHIKATEA

Dacrydium excelsum D. Don; *P. excelsus* (D. Don) Druce

An evergreen tree up to 100 ft or more high, with a trunk 7 ft to 16 ft in girth, and drooping branches. Leaves of two kinds: (1) those of young trees which are arranged in two rows as in *Taxodium distichum* and are $\frac{1}{6}$ to $\frac{1}{3}$ in. long, $\frac{1}{24}$ in. wide, curved and pointed; (2) those of mature trees which are arranged all round the branch, are only $\frac{1}{16}$ to $\frac{1}{8}$ in. long, and, in their smallest state, scale-like, resembling the leaves of a juniper or cypress. There are intermediate types and often both forms of leaf occur on one branch. The trees are unisexual, the female bearing a black, egg-shaped fruit about $\frac{1}{6}$ in. long, the stalk of which is enlarged and becomes bright red and succulent.

Native of New Zealand, where it once formed extensive forests along the larger rivers and in swampy places; it was discovered during Cook's first voyage, and during his second visit he measured a tree 19 ft 8 in. in girth, with a clean bole of 89 ft. Unfortunately, this splendid species is tender, and even in the mildest parts remains a small but very elegant tree.

P. MACROPHYLLUS (Thunb.) D. Don

Taxus macrophylla Thunb.; *P. chinensis* Hort.

P. macrophyllus is mainly represented in cultivation by the following variety:

var. MAKI Sieb. *P. japonicus* Hort. Bogor. ex Sieb.; *P. chinensis* Sw.—An erect-branched shrub or small tree up to 20 ft high. Leaves arranged spirally round the shoot, crowded, erect to spreading, linear, tapering at both ends, 2$\frac{1}{2}$ to 3$\frac{1}{2}$ in. long, $\frac{1}{4}$ to $\frac{3}{8}$ in. wide, obtuse or slightly acute at the apex, of firm, rather leathery texture, the midrib prominently raised above and below, yellowish green when young, becoming dark green above.

Although long cultivated in Japan it is not native there, and even in China, whence it came originally, it is apparently known only as a garden plant. A similar podocarpus, found by Forrest in the Tali range of Yunnan, was at first identified as *P. macrophyllus* but later described as a new species—*P. forrestii* Craib & W. W. Sm. From *P. macrophyllus* var. *maki* it differs only in its dwarfer habit and rather broader leaves. It has apparently never been introduced to cultivation.

P. macrophyllus var. *maki* was introduced to Britain early in the 19th century but has never been common in gardens, being of slow growth and not perfectly hardy. Two variegated forms of it were introduced from Japan by Fortune in 1861, and again by J. H. Veitch in 1892. In 'AUREUS' the leaves are margined or striped with golden yellow, and 'ARGENTEUS' has a similar variegation in white.

Typical *P. macrophyllus* is a genuine native of Japan, where it ranges from the central part of the main island to Kyushu and the Ryukyu Islands; also of S. China. From the var. *maki* described above it differs in being a tree up to 50 ft high, with longer and sometimes broader leaves—up to 7 in. long and $\frac{1}{2}$ in. wide. A variant with long and relatively narrow leaves has been named var. ANGUSTIFOLIA Blume.

P. NAGI (Thunb.) Mak.
Myrica nagi Thunb.; *P. nageia* R. Br.

An evergreen tree up to 80 ft high in the wild state, with a trunk 8 ft in girth; bark of large trees smooth and brownish purple, ultimately scaling off in large flakes. Leaves opposite, thick and leathery, varying in shape from roundish ovate to lanceolate, pointed, tapered at the base, 1 to 3 in. long, $\frac{1}{2}$ to $1\frac{1}{4}$ in. wide, dark green, glabrous and glossy, with numerous veins running lengthwise. Male flowers in axillary, cylindrical, sometimes branched spikes $\frac{1}{2}$ to 1 in. long, $\frac{1}{6}$ in. wide. Females solitary or in pairs, developing a globose fruit about $\frac{1}{2}$ in. wide, covered with plum-like bloom.

Native of Southern Japan, Formosa, and China; introduced by Siebold to Ghent in 1830. Both Sargent and Wilson write enthusiastically of its beauty in Japan; the latter describes it as 'one of the most strikingly beautiful of all evergreen trees'. It has long been cultivated in the Temperate House at Kew, but is only likely to be hardy out-of-doors in the very mildest parts of our islands. It used to be grown in the open air at Pencarrow in Cornwall. This podocarpus is distinct from all those here mentioned in the wideness of its leaves as compared with their length. The Dutch traveller Kaempfer mistook it for a species of bay-laurel, and called it *Laurus juliflora* or the catkin-bearing laurel.

cv. 'ROTUNDIFOLIA'.—Leaves still more rounded than in the type (*Gartenfl.* (1864), pp. 37 and 562).

cv. 'VARIEGATA'.—A dwarf garden variety having leaves splashed with white. Introduced by Fortune in 1861 but perhaps no longer in cultivation.

P. NIVALIS Hook. f.   ALPINE TOTARA

A low evergreen shrub of dense, bushy habit (but said to be sometimes erect-branched and up to 10 ft high); stems coloured like the leaves when young, glabrous. Leaves densely set, rather irregular in posture, from more or less two-ranked to spreading radially all round the shoot, narrow-oblong, mostly $\frac{7}{16}$ to $\frac{3}{4}$ in. long, $\frac{1}{8}$ to $\frac{3}{16}$ in. wide, very rigid, with thickened margins, more or less abruptly narrowed at the apex to a short, hard point, tapered at the base to an indistinct petiole, dull medium green above, grooved along the line of the midrib, underside more glossy, with a prominent midrib. Fruit (perhaps not borne in this country) a small oblong-ovoid nut borne on a much enlarged, succulent, bright red receptacle.

Native of both islands of New Zealand, mostly between 2,000 and 5,000 ft. It was described in 1843, but probably not introduced until early this century, and then in several different forms, differing in habit and hardiness. The description of the foliage given above is from plants which are completely hardy and make wide bushes which, even when half-a-century old, are only 1 ft high and retain this habit even in shady woodland. But at Wakehurst Place, Sussex, a plant growing in full sun is about 6 ft high and as much in width.

It is said to hybridise in the wild with *P. hallii*, and the plant described by Cockayne as var. *erectus* is believed to be such a hybrid. Two forms of this cross are figured in *Conifers in Cultivation* (Report of Conifer Conference, 1931, fig. 51).

P. NUBIGENUS Lindl.

A medium-sized tree in the wild, usually under 50 ft but said to attain 75 ft. Leaves ¾ to 1¾ in. long, ⅛ to 3/16 in. wide, more or less radially arranged round the shoot, stiff, straight or sickle-shaped, mucronate, rich green above, lower surface with two broad pruinose bands. Male flowers in simple or compound spikes. Seeds about ⅜ in. wide, borne on a fleshy receptacle.

Native mainly of Chile; in the northern part of its range it occurs in the association dominated by *Fitzroya cupressoides* and in the moister form of *Nothofagus dombeyi* forest. In these latitudes it also occurs in Argentina (*c.* 41°–42° S.). In Chile it also occurs on the Pacific coast in Chiloe and in the archipelago at least as far south as the Messier Channel. This is a region of very high rainfall (up to 200 in. a year), which may help to explain the failure of *P. nubigenus* outside the moistest parts of the country, for it is not really tender. The four largest specimens in the British Isles are: Scorrier House, Cornwall, *pl.* 1878, 49 × 9¼ ft (1965); Pencarrow, Cornwall, *pl.* 1908, 36 × 3½ ft (1970); Kilmacurragh, Eire, 38 × 7½ ft and 47 × 4¼ ft (1966).

P. SALIGNUS D. Don

P. chilinus Rich.

A usually dioecious evergreen tree 40 to 60 ft high, but in this country a shrub except in the south and west; branchlets green, terete, quite glabrous. Leaves persisting two years, falling the third, linear, often sickle-shaped, tapered at the base, pointed at the apex, 2 to 4½ in. long, ⅛ to 3/16 in. wide, dark rather bluish green above, paler beneath, with numerous rows of minute stomata. Male flowers in a cluster of slender spikes 1 to 1½ in. long. Fruits egg-shaped, ¼ in. long, solitary or in pairs on a stalk ½ to ⅝ in. long and standing out at right angles from it.

Native of Chile, mainly in the region of *Nothofagus obliqua* forests, where it occurs here and there in open places but is nowhere a conspicuous feature of the vegetation. It was introduced around 1849, but all the present trees are of later date. It is by far the most elegant and distinct of all the podocarps that can be grown successfully in this country, and is hardy in a sheltered position as far east as western Kent, though it grows more luxuriantly in the Atlantic zone. The finest example in the British Isles grows at Ardnagashel in Co. Cork, Eire. It measures 64 × 9 ft (1966) and is rivalled by one at Bicton, Devon, measuring 62 × 3½ ft (1966). These are single-stemmed, in contrast to the splendid tree by the house at Penjerrick, Cornwall, which branches at about 6 ft and makes a pyramidal mass of foliage about 45 ft high.

P. SPICATUS Mirbel   MATAI

Dacrydium spicatum D. Don; *Prumnopitys spicata* (Mirbel) Mast.

An evergreen tree 40 to 80 ft high, with a rounded head of erect branches and a trunk 6 to 12 ft in girth; bark bluish black, scaling off in large flakes. On young plants the branches are very slender and pendulous, forming a dense tangle, the leaves thinly disposed on them or only towards the tips in two opposite rows. On mature plants they are set thickly on the twigs in two opposite rows. Each leaf is ⅛ to ½ in. long, $\frac{1}{16}$ in. wide, slightly curved, blunt or with a short point, of leathery texture, green above, rather glaucous with faint stomatic lines beneath. The twigs and leaves in this adult state are not unlike those of one of the short-leaved garden varieties of yew. The trees are unisexual; the males producing their cylindrical flowers, each ¼ to ⅓ in. long, in spikes 1 to 2 in. long to which they are attached at right angles; the females produce a black, globose, succulent fruit ¼ to ⅓ in. wide.

Native of both islands of New Zealand from sea level up to 2,000 ft altitude, originally discovered by Banks and Solander during Cook's first voyage. It is only suitable for the mildest parts of the British Isles and very rare.

P. spicatus and *P. ferrugineus* are the only New Zealand representatives of the section *Stachycarpus*, to which the S. American *P. andinus* also belongs. See further in introductory note, p. 280.

P. FERRUGINEUS D. Don MIRO.—A tree up to 80 ft in the wild, with a bark resembling that of *P. spicatus*. Leaves two-ranked, ½ to 1 in. long, about $\frac{1}{10}$ in. wide, recurved at the margin, slightly sickle-shaped, yew-green. Fruits fleshy, purplish red with a bluish bloom, about ¾ in. long. The specific epithet *ferrugineus* refers to the rusty-colour of the leaves of herbarium specimens. It is little known in Britain and almost certainly quite as tender as *P. spicatus*.

P. TOTARA D. Don   TOTARA

A fine evergreen tree in the wild, 40 to 80 ft, sometimes 100 ft high, with a trunk 6 to 18 ft in girth, clothed with thick, furrowed, stringy bark; young shoots glabrous, furrowed. Leaves leathery, stiff, linear with a sharp hard point, quite glabrous, dull green, often tinged with brown, ½ to 1¼ in. long, $\frac{1}{12}$ to ⅛ in.

wide; not stalked. Male and female flowers are borne on separate trees. Male flowers cylindrical, $\frac{1}{2}$ to $\frac{3}{4}$ in. long, axillary, solitary or two or three together at the top of a very short stalk. Female flowers axillary, solitary or in pairs. Fruit-stalk usually much enlarged, red, succulent, swelling out as large as a cherry and bearing one or two roundish seeds at the top.

Native of New Zealand, where it occurs throughout North Island; in South Island it is said to have its main distribution to the east of the divide, as far south as S.E. Otago; for altitudinal distribution see below. Owing to the confusion between this species and P. *hallii* the date of introduction is not known, but Lawson of Edinburgh was offering potted plants under the name P. *totara* in 1847. In New Zealand its timber is extremely valuable, being straight grained, reddish, and very durable.

Large specimens of P. *totara* are to be found only in the mildest parts of the British Isles, where the following examples have been measured in Cornwall: Trebah, Mawnan Smith, 53 × 8$\frac{1}{2}$ ft (1959); Enys, nr Falmouth, 59 × 5 ft (1962); Tregrehan, Par, 56 × 5$\frac{1}{4}$ ft (1971). In Eire there is an example measuring 30 × 4$\frac{3}{4}$ ft at the base at Ilnacullin, Garinish Island, Co. Cork.

cv. 'AUREUS'.—Leaves golden.

P. HALLII Kirk P. *totara* var. *hallii* (Kirk) Pilger; ? P. *cunninghamii* Col.— Very closely akin to P. *totara*, this tree is of smaller stature and only from 25 to 60 ft high; the bark, too, is thinner and papery and, according to Kirk, it is easily detached in large sheets. When young it is very distinct in its foliage, some of the largest leaves being 1$\frac{3}{4}$ in. long by $\frac{1}{4}$ in. wide, sharply pointed and linear-lanceolate in shape. On adult trees they become smaller, only $\frac{1}{2}$ to 1 in. long and $\frac{1}{8}$ in. wide, and more abruptly pointed. On young trees the leaves are mostly arranged distichously, i.e., in two opposite rows; on older ones all round the shoot. The branching of young trees is also looser and weaker. The flowers do not differ greatly from those of P. *totara*, and there seems to be no reliable difference between the two species in their adult leaves. But the seeds differ, those of P. *totara* being obtuse or rounded at the apex, while in P. *hallii* they are narrow-ovoid and acute at the apex. Intermediate forms are said to occur.

Native of North and South Islands and of Stewart Island. Between this species and P. *totara* there is considerable overlap in distribution and the two may occur together in the same forest. But, according to Cockayne, P. *hallii* occurs generally at higher altitudes than its relative and is sometimes found in stunted form in subalpine forest. Its timber is similar to that of P. *totara*, but not of such high quality.

P. ACUTIFOLIUS Kirk—A small erect shrub, slenderly branched, with linear leaves $\frac{5}{8}$ to 1 in. long, tapered at the apex to a slender, spine-tipped point, dull green, gold-green or brownish green above, the underside paler, with two fairly distinct bands of stomata; midrib not raised on either surface. Native of the South Island of New Zealand.

POLIOTHYRSIS FLACOURTIACEAE

A genus of a single species in China, allied to *Carriera*, which, however, has bisexual flowers, whereas in *Poliothyrsis* they are unisexual, though both sexes on the same plant. *Idesia* is another ally, but that has fleshy fruits.

P. SINENSIS Oliver

A deciduous tree up to 30 or 40 ft high, with ovate, slenderly pointed leaves 4¼ to 6 in. long and 2½ to 5 in. wide; rounded or sometimes heart-shaped at the base, very downy beneath, becoming glabrous as the season advances; stalk slender, downy, ¾ to 1¾ in. long. Flowers fragrant, borne in late summer in a terminal inflorescence, each flower ⅓ in. across, white, soon changing to yellow; they are unisexual, with both sexes on the same inflorescence; calyx-lobes ovate, pointed; styles three. Fruit an ellipsoid capsule ½ to ¾ in. long, many-seeded, seeds winged. *Bot. Mag.*, n.s., t. 480.

Native of China; discovered by Henry in the province of Hupeh about 1889. It did not reach English gardens until 1908, when Wilson sent seeds to the Arnold Arboretum, some of which were distributed in Europe. Some of the young seedlings raised at Kew perished in the severe winter of 1908-9, but others survived. These proved hardy and the species received an Award of Merit when shown from Kew on 30 August 1960. It deserves to be more widely grown for its fragrant flowers, which are borne late in the season—August and September. Wilson observes that the bark in adult trees is grey and deeply furrowed.

There is a specimen at Caerhays, Cornwall, measuring 49 × 3¾ (1971).

POLYGALA MILKWORT POLYGALACEAE

A large genus spread over both hemispheres and comprising herbaceous plants, shrubs and a few trees. Leaves alternate, simple, entire; flowers in racemes or spikes; sepals five, the three outer ones small, the two inner ones enlarged and petal-like, forming the 'wings' of the flower; petals usually three, united to one another to some extent and forming a keel; stamens commonly eight, united to form a tube. The name is derived from the Greek *polys-gala*, meaning much milk, some species being supposed to increase the flow of milk in cows.

P. CHAMAEBUXUS L.

A dwarf, creeping, evergreen shrub from 6 to 12 in. high, with glabrous, alternate, box-like, dull green leaves, ½ to 1 in. long, oval or narrow oblong, not toothed, but with a small pointed tip. Flowers ½ in. long, produced from the leaf-axils near the end of the shoot, singly or in pairs; they rather resemble the flowers of the pea family, and are creamy white, with the end of the keel bright yellow. The fruit is a flat, two-seeded capsule; seeds downy. *Bot. Mag.*, t. 316.

This charming little shrub is a native of the mountainous regions of Central Europe, also of the Apennines and of W. Yugoslavia, etc. It occurs most abundantly on calcareous formations. It succeeds in cool, moist positions,

POLYGALA CHAMAEBUXUS

forming neat tufts covered with the delightful flowers in April and May. Under cultivation it seems to thrive very well in a peaty soil or in a sandy loam. In positions where it thrives (and the Thames Valley with its dry, hot spells is not the most suitable) it is readily propagated by taking off the sucker growths with roots attached.

var. GRANDIFLORA Gaud. *P. chamaebuxus* var. *rhodoptera* Ball; *P. c.* var. *purpurea* Neilr.—Wings rose to crimson; keel often tinged with red (though it often is so even on plants with white wings). Plants of this character occur in the wild, often wholly taking the place of the normal form with white wings and a yellow keel.

P. VAYREDAE Costa

A dwarf, procumbent, evergreen shrub rarely more than 4 in. above the ground; twigs wiry, glabrous or slightly downy. Leaves alternate, linear, pointed, ½ to 1 in. long, $\frac{1}{12}$ in. wide, of rather leathery texture, glabrous except for the ciliate margins when young; very shortly stalked. Flowers produced during May from the leaf-axils of the previous season's shoots, singly or in twos or threes.

Outer sepals pale green or purplish, quite small; the two inner sepals ⅝ in. long, half as much wide, obovate, tapering to a narrow claw, bright rose-purple like the side petals; the keel is ½ in. long and terminates in a kind of hood which is yellow with a curious seven-lobed protuberance at the end. *Bot. Mag.*, t. 9009.

Native of Spain on the Eastern Pyrenees of Catalonia, confined to a small area. Discovered originally in the early part of last century, but apparently lost sight of until 1877, when it was re-discovered by Señor Vayreda. It is related to *P. chamaebuxus*, but is well distinguished by the narrow leaves and the seven-lobed crest terminating the keel. It is an equally charming tiny shrub, especially for the rock garden, where, given the same treatment as its ally, it will form good tufts.

POLYGONUM POLYGONACEAE

A widely distributed but mainly temperate genus, with about 300 species of annuals and perennials, the latter mainly herbaceous but a few with persistent, more or less woody stems. Leaves alternate, with sheathing stipules. Flowers usually in spikes, racemes or panicles. Perianth segments five (sometimes four or six), in two whorls, those of the outer whorl winged on the back in some species. Stamens five, sometimes more or fewer. Style with two or three stigmas. Fruit a three-sided or lens-shaped nutlet, enclosed by the persistent perianth.

P. BALDSCHUANICUM Reg.

Bilderdykia baldschuanicum (Reg.) D. A. Webb

A vigorous, deciduous twining climber, its shoots growing as much as 20 ft in one season, ultimately 40 ft or more high; stems slender, glabrous, grey. Leaves alternate, broadly ovate, heart-shaped or spear-shaped at the base, pointed or rounded at the apex, 1½ to 4 in. long, 1 to 2½ in. wide, glabrous, pale green. Panicles produced in summer and autumn in such abundance as to envelop the plant in a cloud of blossom; they are terminal on lateral shoots, much branched, 8 to 16 in. long. Flowers pale pink or almost white, each ⅓ in. across, with transparent ovate sepals in two whorls, the three in the outer whorl winged at the back, the wing passing downwards to the flower-stalk. As these wings persist on the pinkish young seed-vessel, they give it the characteristic three-angled shape. *Bot. Mag.*, t. 7544.

Native of Russia in S. Tadzhikstan; discovered by Dr A. Regel in what was then the Khanate of Baldzhuan, and described by his father in 1883. It has also been found in Afghanistan and W. Pakistan. It was introduced around 1894 by way of the St Petersburg Botanic Garden. It is a beautiful climber, and its value is enhanced by the late date of its blossoming and the beauty of its young fruits.

The best way to cultivate it is to give up to it some worn-out tree which it may be allowed to ramble over or envelop at will. Failing that, a stout spruce pole with the side branches left several feet long, or some such support, may be given it. Few climbers give so charming an effect in so short a time. It likes a rich loamy

POLYGONUM BALDSCHUANICUM

soil and a fully exposed position. Seeds rarely or never set with us, and the plant is best propagated by cuttings. These should be made in summer of pieces of the current year's growth, with a heel of older wood attached, and placed in gentle heat. Cuttings of leafless wood, made in February with a heel, will also take root.

P. AUBERTII L. Henry *Bilderdykia aubertii* (L. Henry) Moldenke—This species, which is closely allied to *P. baldschuanicum*, was described by Louis Henry in 1907 from a plant growing in the garden of the Paris Museum. This had been raised from seeds received from the French missionary Aubert in the spring of 1899, collected by him in the neighbourhood of Tatsien-lu (Kangting) in W. Szechwan, China. The species also occurs in Kansu and Shensi. The main botanical distinction would appear to be that in *P. aubertii* the inflorescence-axes are papillose, and that the panicles are narrow, erect and spike-like, borne laterally along leafy stems, while in *P. baldschuanicum* the inflorescence-axes are glabrous or almost so, and the inflorescences are crowded towards the ends of the shoots, so forming broad, compound panicles. The flowers in *P. aubertii* are rather smaller than in the Russian species, but there is no reliable difference in their colour. In his original description Henry gave as a further difference that the young growths of *P. aubertii* are tinged with red. He judged it to be inferior to *P. baldschuanicum* in its flowers, but the better of the two as a foliage plant, because of its luxuriant leafage.

It has been stated that many plants grown as *P. baldschuanicum* are really

P. aubertii, and that the latter is the commoner in cultivation. If so, a likely explanation is to be found in the fact that the plants raised from the seeds collected by Aubert were distributed without name. It was seven years before Henry published the name *P. aubertii*, and in the meantime plants may have been identified in other gardens as *P. baldschuanicum* and further distributed under that name. But the cultivated and naturalised material in the Kew Herbarium does not altogether bear out the statement that *P. aubertii* is the commoner species. Some specimens have the inflorescence-axes glabrous as in *P. baldschuanicum*; others have them more or less papillose—sometimes only slightly so—and presumably represent *P. aubertii*, though the type of inflorescence more often favours *P. baldschuanicum*.

P. aubertii grows as vigorously as the Russian species, and can be put to the same uses.

P. EQUISETIFORMIS Sibth. & Sm.—This species, a native of the Mediterranean region, is well worth growing for its distinct growth and abundant milky-white flowers produced in autumn. The plant consists of a dense mass of slender, mare's-tail-like stems about as thick as a knitting needle and 2 or 3 ft high. It needs a warm sunny corner, and even then is often cut back by winter cold.

P. VACCINIIFOLIUM Wall. ex Meissn.

Although usually classified in trade catalogues as an herbaceous plant, *P. vacciniifolium* is as much a shrub as many other borderline species included in this work and is usually classified as such by botanists. It forms a mat of slender, intertwining woody stems a few inches high, but is able to spread almost indefinitely by self-layering. Leaves deciduous, rich glossy green above, glaucous beneath, mostly elliptic, $\frac{1}{2}$ to $\frac{7}{8}$ in. long, acute at the apex, somewhat undulate; stipules deeply divided into narrow shreds. Flowers rosy pink, about $\frac{1}{8}$ in. long, subtended by glistening, golden-brown acuminate bracts, borne August to October in slender terminal and axillary spikes up to 3 in. long. Stamens six to eight, with pinkish purple anthers. Styles free, slender. *Bot. Mag.*, t. 4622.

Native of the Himalaya; introduced in 1845. It is perfectly hardy and flowers profusely in a sunny position, provided the soil is not too rich. An ideal carpeting plant for the large rock garden or the top of a dry wall, particularly lovely in autumn, when the older leaves turn bright red. Easily propagated by taking rooted pieces, or by cuttings. Award of Garden Merit 1955.

PONCIRUS   RUTACEAE

A genus of a single species, allied to *Citrus* and used in China as a stock on which to graft oranges. It differs in its deciduous, compound leaves and in other characters, such as its free stamens.

P. TRIFOLIATA (L.) Raf.

Citrus trifoliata L.; *Aegle sepiaria* DC.

A deciduous, very spiny shrub or small tree 8 to 20 ft high, often as much wide, with smooth, green, crooked, angular branchlets. The spines are from 1 to 2 in. long, very stiff, straight, and sharply pointed. Leaves of three, sometimes five leaflets, which are obovate, the middle one 1½ to 2 in. long, the side ones half as large; leaf-stalk winged. Flowers sweetly scented, produced from the axils of the spines before the leaves, pure white, 1½ to 2 in. across, with four or five concave obovate petals. Stamens pink, not united. Fruit like a small orange in colour and shape, about 1½ in. across, covered with down.

Native of Korea and N. China. This species is one of the most striking of hardy Chinese plants. It is hardy at Kew, having survived 30° of frost without injury; and although it does not often ripen fruit there, it flowers regularly during May every year. Its foliage is often scanty, but that enables its formidable armature to be the better seen. Were it common enough, it would make a good hedge plant: there is a hedge in the Public Garden of Milan 100 yds long, which, when I saw it, was only 3 ft high, too small for so vigorous a shrub as this, but which shows that it stands clipping well. In the western counties it fruits freely, and in the Vicarage garden at Bitton, near Bristol, there is a tree that has borne fruit for many years past. It is a plant every garden should contain for its beauty and distinction, its perfect hardiness, and its interest as a very close ally of the lemon and orange. The fruits are too bitter and acrid to be eaten raw, but they have been made into a conserve by boiling in sugar. It should be given a sunny position and a deep, moderately rich, soil. English ripened fruits produce good seed, from which I have raised young plants. It is also said that cuttings of half-ripened wood put in a close frame will take root.

PONCIRUS TRIFOLIATA × CITRUS SINENSIS. CITRANGE.—Hybrids between *P. trifoliata* and the orange were made by W. J. Swingle at Eustis, Florida, in 1897. Eleven were named in 1905, and a description of the more important clones will be found in Bailey's *Standard Cyclopaedia of Horticulture* under the heading 'Citrange'. The cross was also made in France in 1894 by Armand Bernard, and one of these hybrids, named after the raiser, was described and figured in *Revue Horticole*, also in 1905 (p. 244).

The citranges are hardy in southern England, but are most likely to flower and fruit if planted against a sunny wall. Although many of the Swingle hybrids were introduced to this country, they have never been much grown, possibly because they are no more ornamental, and less reliable in their flowering and fruiting, than *P. trifoliata*. An example of a citrange can be seen by the south entrance to the Temperate House at Kew.

POPULUS   Poplar   salicaceae

A group of large, usually quick-growing, deciduous trees, with alternate leaves pinnately veined or three-nerved at the base, those on vigorous shoots usually larger, and often different in shape and character from those on lateral twigs. Flowers produced in catkins on the naked shoots in spring, the sexes nearly always on separate trees. Male catkins more densely flowered than the female, the flowers composed of usually numerous stamens attached to a disk, and springing from the axil of a toothed or fringed scale, which soon falls away. Anthers red or purple. Female catkins lengthening until mature, the egg-shaped or rounded ovary seated in a cuplike disk, and crowned by two to four stigmas. The seed is surrounded by a conspicuous tuft of white, cottony hairs which enables it to be carried long distances by wind. Poplars occur in most parts of the northern hemisphere, from subarctic regions to subtropical ones, some inhabiting arid places, others always found in association with moisture.

There are four well-marked groups of poplars cultivated in Britain:

I Populus (Leuce)   White and Grey Poplars, Aspens

Younger trunks and main branches at first pale and smooth, then pitted with numerous diamond-shaped holes. Leaves toothed, often coarsely so, or lobed. Catkin-scales fringed with long hairs. This section can be subdivided as follows:

White and Grey Poplars.—Leaves on the long shoots woolly beneath, those of the short shoots less woolly or almost glabrous, and of different shape; petioles usually not much compressed laterally (except sometimes in *P. canescens*). Here belong *P. alba*, *P. canescens* and *P. tomentosa*, all species of the Old World. The first-named is propagated by hardwood cuttings, but *P. canescens* is not easy to root by this means.

Aspens.—Leaves glabrous or almost so beneath, more or less uniform in size and shape with laterally flattened stalks, and noted for their restless movement. This group includes *P. grandidentata*, *P. tremula*, and *P. tremuloides*, none of which roots readily from cuttings.

II Leucoides

This section, which lacks a popular name, comprises the American *P. heterophylla* and the E. Asiatic *P. lasiocarpa* and *P. wilsonii*. The leaves in this section are large and leathery, usually tomentose when young, and are of more or less the same size and shape on long and short shoots. The floral disk surrounding the lower part of the stamens or ovary is deeply lobed, and the ovary is hairy. The bark is rough and scaly.

III Tacamahaca   Balsam Poplars

These burst into leaf the first, and are distinguished by very gummy winter leaf-buds and leaves, which emit a pleasant balsamic odour, especially when just expanding in spring. Leaves usually whitish, but not woolly beneath; leaf-stalk not compressed. This group includes *P. angustifolia*, *P. balsamifera*, *P. candicans*, *P. laurifolia*, *P. maximowiczii*, *P. simonii*, *P. trichocarpa* to name only the better known. Most of these can be increased by hardwood cuttings in the open ground, or by suckers.

IV Aegiros Black Poplars

Leaves green on both sides and with compressed, slender stalks, nearly always in motion; margins translucent and cartilaginous. Trunks with a corrugated bark. This group, which is confined to N. America and western Eurasia, is mainly represented in cultivation by hybrids (see *P.* × *canadensis*). All the black poplars except some forms of *P. deltoides* are easily propagated by hardwood cuttings about 8 in. long, inserted in late winter in the open ground (February or March). If inserted in early winter they may rot. Many of the male black poplars in spring are handsome on account of their richly coloured catkins.

The section TURANGA, of which the best known species is *P. euphratica*, is not treated in this work, since neither this nor any other member of the group has ever become successfully established in this country.

Poplars do not produce good seed freely in cultivation, and when they do it will certainly produce hybrid plants unless male and female trees of the same species happen to grow near together, which is rarely the case. The polygamous clone of *P. lasiocarpa*, mentioned above, breeds true from seed, since male and female flowers are produced on the same plant and in the same catkin. The seed of poplars normally remains viable for a very short time after the capsules open, though it has recently been found that it will travel quite well in sealed packages, retaining its viability for a longer period than would have been thought possible a short while ago. The seed germinates rapidly in a moist soil—normally within two days. Hybrid poplars can be raised artificially by cutting branches from the two intended parents, placing them in water, and bringing them into flower under glass. Provided the flowering time can be made to coincide, cross-pollination is simple, and the seed will ripen on the female branch within a few weeks.

USES, CULTIVATION AND DISEASES*

On fertile and well-sheltered sites poplar grows faster than any other tree hardy in Britain. It reaches its greatest vigour in the milder parts of the country on deep, rich, and well-drained soils, and particularly in the southern half of England it can increase in length by more than 5 feet annually and attain a height of 100 feet in twenty years. In the northern and western parts of Britain, which are rather too cool and wet for most poplars, this rate of growth is only achieved in sheltered localities in warm summers. It is a mistaken belief that poplar thrives on wet soils,

* This section has been contributed by Mr J. Jobling, Forestry Commission, Forest Research Station, Alice Holt.

and vigorous growth cannot be expected where there is water-logging and poor drainage. Growth is also likely to be poor on very acid soils and on thin or dry soils, and in the most extreme conditions the trees may actually die. In exposed, upland localities planting should not be attempted at all.

Largely because of its rapid growth-rate poplar has been much used to shelter farmland, orchards, and playing fields, and to screen factories and other industrial development. It has also been planted extensively in gardens in urban areas to obscure eyesores, and to provide protection against wind, noise, and intruding neighbours. The Lombardy poplar has been used for screening and shelter much more than any other cultivar, although a few other narrow-crowned forms, notably *P. nigra* 'Plantierensis' and the hybrid black cultivars *P.* 'Eugenei' and *P.* 'Robusta' (q.v. under *P.* × *canadensis*), have sometimes been preferred and found local favour. Partly because black poplars are difficult to distinguish in the nursery, mixing of plants has occurred from time to time, and two or more cultivars are often found in the same planting. Usually the trees are planted in a single row and, in an effort to obtain early benefits, only a few feet apart.

In the last decade the fast-growing artificial balsam hybrid, *P. tacamahaca* × *trichocarpa* 32 has been increasingly used in line plantings as an alternative to Lombardy poplar, which it resembles in angle of branching and crown shape. This hybrid, like other balsam poplars, breaks into leaf much earlier than most black poplars, and on this account it has been much planted around orchards to protect early-flowering fruit varieties. It has also been planted around market gardens and arable farmland to protect tender crops against cold, drying spring winds, but since it is a female tree there is a risk that the cottony down surrounding the seed will adversely affect the appearance of certain types of market produce. Lettuces are probably the most likely crop to suffer in this way.

As poplars are regarded as comparatively short-lived trees they are seldom used in major landscaping. However, because many grow rapidly and reach large dimensions within a relatively short time they can be usefully planted to obtain an early effect whilst slower-growing species become established and attain a respectable stature, and then felled later. Some cultivars such as Lombardy poplar that always develop narrow, cylindrical crowns are useful in mixed plantings because of their contrasting shape.

Poplars are not trees to plant in confined spaces or close to roads, walls and buildings. They ordinarily have an extremely wide spreading root system, whose radius can easily exceed the height of the tree, and this can extract large quantities of water from the soil. As a result the soil shrinks and there is a consequent settlement of the foundations of walls and buildings. In the same way the foundations of roads may be affected. The risk of damage is very much greater in clay soils than in light soils, and in general it is advisable to plant not closer than 120 feet to any structure on a clay soil.

In parks and gardens female cultivars can be a nuisance because of the large quantity of cottony down that can be dropped from ripened catkins. Cultivars that sucker may also cause annoyance both for the damage they do and for the effort required to control them. Nevertheless, poplars are valuable trees for open spaces in towns and cities because of their tolerance of atmospheric smoke pollution. In the past, forms of the black poplar, masquerading under such names as the Manchester poplar, were planted in our smoky urban parks and squares to the almost total exclusion of other species and hybrids. In the past twenty years, as more and more cultivars have become available to the nursery trade, it has been demonstrated that many poplars other than the black poplar are able to thrive in a smoke-polluted environment. Poplars also grow tolerably well at the seaside, though only the white poplar, and to a lesser extent the grey poplar, can withstand blast from salt-laden winds. It is very doubtful if any poplar will succeed if its roots are subjected to saline conditions due to flooding by sea water.

Poplars are also planted on a commercial scale in this country to produce industrial wood. Prior to 1950 only a handful of landowners and foresters had undertaken any worthwhile planting for timber, but in the last two decades or so (partly due to the encouragement provided by planting grants) successful plantations, many already yielding merchantable produce, have been established throughout the country. Much of the planting has been undertaken by the private forestry sector, and by far the most productive stands are to be found in the southern half of England, where the best conditions prevail for sustaining high growth rates.

Poplars are notoriously intolerant of competition, both above and below ground, and attain their fastest rates of radial growth as single specimen trees, removed from other trees that might cast shade or compete for moisture and nutrients. The hybrid black poplars planted for timber are particularly bad in this respect and, in plantations, soon lose vigour at the onset of competition. Partly because of this problem, stands established primarily for the production of wood have the trees at wide spacings throughout the life of the crop. More often than not the trees are planted at a distance apart that will allow maximum growth rates until time of felling without the need to remove competing trees. Spacings at planting have increased from 18 feet to 24 feet during the past twenty years; at present, to attract planting grants, spacing may not be wider than 26 feet.

Poplar wood is soft, rather woolly in texture, and pale in colour. It has no smell or taste, and so is valuable for making into food containers, and has a low flammability. It is not durable in the open or in damp ground, and thus cannot be used for fence-posts unless previously treated with preservatives. The wood usually takes paints and glue well, and has a high resistance to abrasion, making it suitable for wagon bottoms, wheelbarrows and colliery tubs, and can be nailed without splitting, although some types of nails tend to pull through or pop out. The wood is ideally suited for the floors of oast houses and for brake-blocks because of its low flammability. The biggest use in this country is for matches, the best-known product from poplar wood, and the splints are dipped at one end in paraffin wax to give the required degree of flammability. Large poplar logs can be rotary peeled for veneers without special treatment. Uses for small-sized logs include fibreboard, wood chipboard, and certain types of pulp.

Cultivars planted for timber production have to be carefully chosen, as in addition to being fast growing they must be reasonably straight-stemmed, round and free from splits, insect damage and other serious defects. Trees grown for rotary peeling must also be easy to prune to obtain knot-free timber. The most commonly planted cultivars are: *P.* 'Eugenei', *P.* 'Gelrica', *P.* 'Robusta', and *P.* 'Serotina', all described under *P.* × *canadensis*. Others sometimes planted are *P.* 'Heidemij' and *P.* 'I–78', a cultivar of Italian origin recommended for the southern half of England. All of these are hybrid black poplars, which to produce timber of high quality must be cultivated on better sites. On wetter, more acid ground, notably in the cooler and wetter regions of the country, balsam poplars are better suited for growing for timber. The only cultivars available at the present time, however, are *P. trichocarpa* 'Fritzi Pauley' and the hybrid 'Tacatricho 32' (see under *P. balsamifera*).

Due to the interest abroad in poplar culture, a great deal of work is being conducted at research stations to breed and select new cultivars. Several new poplars have already been chosen for release to growers from the many thousands tested, and more are expected to be selected in the next few years for use for both amenity and timber production. Most of the tests are concerned with finding cultivars sufficiently resistant to the many diseases prevalent in western and central Europe to be grown to maturity free of infection. In practice all of the cultivars raised by the nursery trade in this country and its neighbouring states are susceptible to one poplar disease or another.

The most serious disease of poplar in Britain is called bacterial canker, caused by the bacterium *Aplanobacter populi*. This produces cankers on the branches and main stem, varying in size and appearance depending on the reaction of the cultivar to infection by the bacterium. Although trees are seldom killed outright by the disease, their growth rate may be seriously retarded and their amenity value greatly lessened due to die-back of the crown. Cankers on the stem markedly affect the value of the timber. All the cultivars raised by our nursery trade other than *P. trichocarpa* 'Fritzi Pauley' are susceptible to bacterial canker, but many can be grown with little or no risk of serious infection. The cultivars named above as suitable for planting for timber production can usually be cultivated free from damage if care is taken to ensure that there are no infected poplars in the locality. Infection can occur through exit-holes made by wood-boring insects or through leaf-scars after the leaves fall in the autumn. Pruning is unlikely to increase the risk of infection.

The most serious foliage disease is *Marssonina brunnea*, first observed in Britain as recently as 1967. It is causing great concern on the continent of Europe where infection has led to premature defoliation in several successive seasons in the last decade and the death of thousands of previously healthy trees. In this country attacks have so far been local and periodic, and most serious in East Anglia. *P.* 'Gelrica' and *P.* 'I–78' have proved to be the most susceptible cultivars. The related leaf-spot fungus *M. populi-nigrae* is the cause of death of branches of Lombardy poplar, defoliation and die-back most often occurring in the lower crown.

The only other fungi seriously attacking the leaves are the rusts (*Melampsora* species). These cover the undersurface of the leaves with small orange pustules and heavy infection can cause early defoliation. Severe damage occurs mainly in the nursery, where growth may be reduced, but the intensity of attack varies from year to year, and permanent damage is rare. There is no satisfactory remedy. A similar disorder, caused by the fungus *Taphrina aurea*, does much less harm although the orange blisters are very conspicuous and appear quite early in the growing season.

Die-back of poplar associated with the fungus *Dothichiza populea* is fairly common and often confused with bacterial canker, but is much less serious. The fungus attacks poplars weakened by overcrowding in the nursery or by poor planting and after-care. Infection can occur also through pruning wounds on young poplars, and pruning of nursery plants and of recently planted trees should be done in the early summer to allow the wounds to heal. Any measures that encourage the rapid establishment of newly planted trees will lessen the risk of *Dothichiza* damage.

Another fungus attacking the stem of poplar is *Cytospora chrysosperma*. This is found very commonly on dead wood but is not capable of invading a healthy tree. It should not be held responsible for the death of the wood on which it is found. It is conspicuous because it exudes long orange tendrils.

These diseases cannot usually be controlled other than by planting resistant cultivars and by ensuring that sources of infection are rigorously destroyed. There are very few resistant or slightly susceptible cultivars available at the moment but research workers are striving to select or breed new resistant clones.

P. ACUMINATA Rydb.

A deciduous tree up to 60 ft high in the wild; young shoots quite free from down, ordinarily round, but angled when very vigorous; buds slender-pointed, glutinous. Leaves ovate to somewhat diamond-shaped, wedge-shaped to rounded at the base, slenderly pointed, finely round-toothed, 2 to 4 in. long (larger on vigorous shoots), half as much wide, shining green on both sides and but little paler beneath; leaf-stalks 1 to 2½ in. long, slender. Catkins slender, not downy, up to 2¾ in long.

A native of western N. America from Montana and S. Dakota south to New Mexico and Arizona; discovered by Rydberg in Nebraska and described by him in 1893. It is probably not a good species but rather a hybrid complex resulting from the crossing of *P. angustifolia* with *P. sargentii* (or with *P. fremontii* in those areas where this species takes the place of *P. sargentii*). It differs from *P. angustifolia* and approaches the latter two species in its relatively broader leaves on longer, often slightly flattened, petioles and in other characters (Hitchcock et al., *Vascular Plants of the Pacific Northwest*, Pt 2, p. 34). Plants introduced to Kew in 1916 from the Arnold Arboretum made loose-habited trees with slender lax shoots, vividly green in leaf.

P. ADENOPODA Maxim.
P. silvestrii Pamp.

This is a Chinese ally of the aspen, differing from ordinary *P. tremula* in the long drawn-out apex of the leaves of mature trees and in the shallower undulations of the margin. There are also two conspicuously large glands where the blade joins the stalk which are distinctive (in *P. tremula* these are found only on the leaves of long shoots). The species is a native of Central and W. China and first appeared in cultivation about 1906 as "*P. Silvestrii*". These early plants were more persistently downy in leaf and young shoot than later ones. Wilson observed that wild trees varied in this character but that on old trees the leaves were always glabrous at maturity.

Another E. Asiatic aspen is P. SIEBOLDII Miq., a native of Japan and Sakhalin, which is well distinguished from *P. tremula* by the whitish down on the young shoots and the well-developed glands at the base of all the leaf-blades (as in *P. adenopoda*). In was in cultivation by 1887, when Messrs Simon-Louis offered it under the erroneous name "*P. rotundifolia*". Both these aspens are rare in cultivation.

P ALBA L. WHITE POPLAR, ABELE
P. alba var. nivea Ait.

A tree said to be 90 to 100 ft high, but I have seen none much more than half that size in this country; bark of trunk smooth; young shoots and lower surface of the leaves covered with a thick, vividly white wool, which on the lobed leaves persists and keeps white until the fall of the leaf. Leaves variable; rounded to slightly heart-shaped at the base, blunt-pointed; on short twigs they are broadly ovate or almost round, irregularly wavy at the margins, 1 to 2 in. long; on vigorous shoots and young trees they are much larger, usually of maple-like form, being deeply three- or five-lobed and from 1½ to 5 in. long, each lobe with a few large teeth. When the leaves first expand they are covered above with a loose white floss which falls away during the summer, leaving the upper surface very dark green and glabrous; stalk ½ to 1½ in. long, woolly. Male catkins about 3 in. long; females 2 in. long.

A native of western and central Eurasia and N. Africa, occurring in Europe mainly in the eastern and southern parts. It is not a native of Britain, where it has been much confused with *P. canescens*. Its eastern limit is in Central Asia and the N.W. Himalaya.

The true white poplar very rarely attains a large size in this country, being short-lived. Large trees identified as white poplar are almost invariably *P. canescens* (q.v. for the points of difference). The degree of lobing on the long shoots of *P. alba* is variable on wild trees, being most marked in those of south-eastern Europe and in Asia, and least in the var. SUBINTEGERRIMA Lange, from S. Spain and N. Africa, which has leathery leaves that are scarcely lobed even on the strong shoots. The poplar which Dode named *P. hickeliana* belongs to this variety.

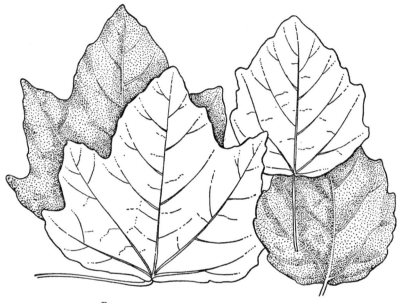

POPULUS ALBA: POPULUS CANESCENS

The foliage of *P. alba* sometimes turns a fiery red in the autumn, though yellow is the more usual colour. It is a useful tree in seaside localities, because of its tolerance of salt spray, and is also being increasingly used in roadside screens, etc.

Two trees in the University Parks, Oxford, appear to be true *P. alba*. Both are 8 ft in girth and just over 80 ft in height (1965). In Osterley Park, London, there is a specimen measuring 70 × 7½ ft (1965).

cv. 'GLOBOSA'.—A dwarf form making a rounded, bushy head. Leaves roundish, with slightly lobed or undulated margins. Very slow-growing. It was put into commerce by Späth towards the end of the last century but is little known in this country.

cv. 'PALETSKYANA'.—The poplar, described by Dode from a cultivated plant received from Russia, and named by him as a species, has the leaves on the long shoots very deeply lobed and probably represents the eastern race of *P. alba*.

cv. 'PYRAMIDALIS'. BOLLE'S POPLAR.—A slender pyramidal tree of great beauty, resembling the Lombardy poplar in habit, but wider in proportion to its height, and distinguishable in winter by its smooth, pale trunk. The leaves on the strong shoots are deep, glossy green above, densely white woolly beneath even in late summer, deeply lobed and lobulate; leaves on the spurs almost glabrous beneath by late summer, roundish in general outline, but coarsely lobulate.

This poplar is not known in the wild but is cultivated in Central Asia and the Near East. It was described by Bunge as *P. alba* var. *pyramidalis* from trees forming a little grove on the north side of the Karatau mountains, between Bokhara and Samarkand, and was introduced to Europe between 1875 and 1878. It has also been known as *P. bolleana* Carr., or *P. alba* var. *bolleana*. It is said to differ only in habit from the race of *P. alba* found in Central Asia, though some authorities consider it to belong to a distinct species.

The tree at Kew near the Fern House, mentioned in previous editions, was removed in 1953. The present specimen grows near Kew Road, close behind the General Museum, and measures 80 × 6¾ ft (1967); at Marble Hill, Twickenham, there is an example of almost exactly the same size (1968).

cv. 'RICHARDII'.—Upper surface of leaf golden yellow, the underside and the young shoots felted with white wool as in the type. First shown at the International Exhibition, Chelsea, 1921. There is an example at Syon House, London, measuring 50 × 5¼ ft (1968).

P. ANGULATA *see under* P. DELTOIDES

P. ANGUSTIFOLIA Torr.   WILLOW-LEAVED POPLAR
P. balsamifera var. *angustifolia* (Torr.) S. Wats.

A tree 50 to 60 ft high in the wild (Sargent), but, as seen in cultivation here, a low bushy-headed tree with short, much-forked, crooked branches; young shoots round, glabrous or minutely downy, especially towards the apex; winter-buds sticky, slender-pointed. Leaves lanceolate or ovate-lanceolate, 2 to 5 in. long, ½ to 1½ in. wide, wedge-shaped at the base, tapering gradually to a point at the apex, minutely and evenly round-toothed, green on both sides, although paler beneath, glabrous except sometimes for minute down beneath; stalk ordinarily about ½ in. long. Catkins not seen in this country, but the male ones described by Sargent as 1½ to 2½ in. long, densely flowered; the female catkins are 2 to 4 in. long when mature.

Native of western N. America, but not of the Pacific side of the Rocky Mountains. It is one of the balsam group with the characteristic odour, and is distinguished by its willow-like leaves, not white beneath. In foliage it most resembles *P. laurifolia*, but that species has angular, more downy young shoots, and leaves pale beneath.

P. BALSAMIFERA L.   BALSAM POPLAR
P. *tacamahacca* Mill.

A tree 100 ft high in the wild, but rarely more than half as high in this country, producing suckers freely; young shoots smooth, round; winter-buds thickly covered with a balsamic, very fragrant, viscid, yellowish resin, often 1 in. long, long-pointed. Leaves broadly ovate, rounded or slightly heart-shaped at the base, slender-pointed, very variable in size, round-toothed, ordinarily 2 to 5 in. long, 1¼ to 3 in. wide, dark shining green above, glabrous or slightly downy beneath, the pale or whitish ground conspicuously net-veined; stalk ⅔ to 2 in. long. Male catkins 3 in. long; female ones 4 or 5 in. long.

Native of N. America, where it is widely spread and abundant in the northern latitudes. It was introduced some time in the 17th century.

The balsam poplar was at one time represented in cultivation by a male clone, propagated by the suckers which it produced in great abundance. On vigorous suckers the leaves were occasionally of enormous size—up to 13 in. long and 10 in. wide. But this poplar was probably never very common; most of the plants grown under the name P. *balsamifera* were in fact P. *candicans*. The true P. *balsamifera* is a poor grower in this country—that is true both of the old clone and of subsequent importations. The great charm of P. *balsamifera* is the balsamic odour of the unfolding leaves in spring which fills the air around. But P. *trichocarpa*, its western ally, is just as fragrant and a more satisfactory tree in this country.

var. MICHAUXII (Dode) Henry   P. *michauxii* Dode; P. *balsamifera* var. *subcordata* Hylander—Leaves ovate, with a broad, rounded or subcordate base, slightly downy on the midrib and veins beneath; petioles and twigs also slightly hairy. This variety, which occurs wild in various localities in north-eastern N. America, has been confused with P. *candicans*, which is not known in the wild.

Dode, in describing this poplar (as a species), erroneously stated that it was the same as the poplar figured by the younger Michaux as P. *balsamifera* in *Hist. Arb. For. Amer. Sept.*, Vol. III, t. 13, fig. 1; the poplar there figured is in fact typical P. *balsamifera*. But this misidentification is insufficient reason for invalidating the name P. *michauxii*, and still less for rejecting Henry's var. *michauxii*, which is based on Dode's ample description, drawn probably from a cultivated plant, and on leaf specimens from wild trees sent to him by Prof. Sargent.

P. × JACKII Sarg.   P. *baileyana* Henry—A natural hybrid between P. *balsamifera* and P. *deltoides*. Leaves glabrous, broad-ovate, up to 6 in. long and 5 in. wide, cordate at the base, long-acuminate at the apex, whitish beneath, and with quadrangular petioles, but showing the influence of P. *deltoides* clearly in the presence of two glands at the junction of the petiole with the blade, and the translucent margin with scattered hairs; the acuminate leaf-apex and the relatively wide leaves, also derive from P. *deltoides*. This hybrid was described in 1913 from specimens collected by J. G. Jack in Canada (Nun's Island, at the mouth of the Chateauguay river and on the south bank of the St Lawrence at Beauharnois). The synonymous name P. *baileyana* is founded on the Jack specimens and also on one collected by L. H. Bailey near South Haven, Michigan, USA. The hybrid has since been found in numerous localities.

P. × jackii is of interest as a natural hybrid between a balsam and a black poplar, and could be regarded as the New World counterpart of *P. × berolinensis*, which has also been found in the wild.

P. BALSAMIFERA × P. TRICHOCARPA—This cross between the eastern and western American balsam poplars occurs spontaneously in the wild, but the cultivated trees are mostly the result of deliberate hybridisation. The best known of these is 'TACATRICHO 32' ('TT 32'). It is a fast-growing female tree of remarkably narrow habit, much used in plantation for timber production, and also for shelter and screening. See further on p. 295.

P. × BEROLINENSIS Dipp.

P. hybrida berolinensis K. Koch

A supposed hybrid between *P. laurifolia* (female) and the Lombardy poplar, which arose in the Botanic Garden of Berlin some time before 1865. It is a handsome tree of slender columnar shape, with downy, slightly angled young shoots. Buds viscid, pointed. Leaves broadly ovate and rounded at the base, or somewhat diamond-shaped and wedge-shaped at the base, slender-pointed, finely toothed like those of *P. laurifolia*, and with a thin translucent border, $1\frac{1}{2}$ to 4 in. long, upper surface bright green, lower side pale, scarcely whitish, both sides soon glabrous; leaf-stalk downy at first, $\frac{3}{4}$ to $1\frac{1}{2}$ in. long, not flattened.

The original tree was female. There is also a male form, originally distributed as *P. certinensis*, which is of unknown origin, but is believed to have originated in France.

P. × berolinensis is an uncommon tree in this country, but is widely planted in the prairie regions of N. America and the more continental parts of Europe, where it withstands the harsh winters and hot summers better than most poplars. In this country, the largest specimen grows in the poplar collection at Ryston in Norfolk; planted in 1914, it measures $85 × 8\frac{1}{2}$ ft (1969). A tree in the Forestry Commission collection at Alice Holt Lodge, nr Farnham, nineteen years planted, measures 52 ft × 2 ft 7 in. (1971).

P. × berolinensis is reported to occur occasionally in the wild where the two parent species are in contact.

The cross between *P. nigra* and *P. laurifolia* was made artificially by Schreiner and Stout, who raised 377 seedlings, of which three were named in 1934, namely, 'FRYE', 'RUMFORD', and 'STRATHGLASS'. The first is growing well in the Forestry Commission collection at Alice Holt, where there is an example, *pl.* 1953, which measures $62 × 4\frac{1}{4}$ ft (1973). The other two are also in the collection.

Two hybrids raised in Russia around 1880—'PETROWSKYANA' and 'RASUMOWSKYANA'—are closely allied to *P. × berolinensis*, and probably of the same parentage. The poplar that Dode named *P. OCTORABDOS* is also near to *P. × berolinensis*.

P. × berolinensis and its allies are susceptible to Marssonina, a fungus that causes premature leaf-fall and seriously reduces the growth rate of these hybrids.

P. × CANADENSIS Moench

P. × euramericana Guinier

An important group of hybrids deriving from the European black poplar P. *nigra* and its relative of eastern N. America P. *deltoides*, the earliest of which arose spontaneously in western Europe soon after the introduction of the American species. Being more vigorous than either parent, and easily propagated by cuttings, these hybrids were widely planted from the second half of the 18th century onwards. See further under 'Serotina', 'Marilandica', and 'Regenerata', which are the oldest existing clones in this group. It is probable that the poplar described by Moench as P. *canadensis* was 'Serotina', which was at one time often sold under that name.

These hybrids show the characters of the parental species in various combinations. In the American parent, P. *deltoides*, the leaves are always ciliate and there are two, sometimes more, glands at the junction of the petiole with the leaf-blade. In the European black poplar the leaf-margins are glabrous and the glands are absent. The hybrids usually have ciliate leaf-margins, at least on the youngest leaves, and glands are usually present on some leaves. Further, in P. *deltoides* the leaves on the strong shoots are truncate, rounded or slightly cordate at the base, in P. *nigra* cuneate. Some of the hybrids, notably 'Eugenei' and 'Marilandica', are nearer to P. *nigra* in this respect, while 'Serotina', 'Regenerata', and 'Gelrica' have the leaves on the strong shoots more or less truncate.

It was Augustine Henry who, among his many other achievements, first clearly distinguished the black poplar hybrids from the two parent species, and gave a comprehensive account of them in: Elwes and Henry, *Trees of Great Britain and Ireland*, Vol. 7 (1913), pp. 1841–51, and in *Gardeners' Chronicle*, Vol. 56 (1914), pp. 47 and 66–7. The most recent work in English is: G. S. Cansdale, *The Black Poplars* (1938).

'EUGENEI'.—A tree of columnar habit, producing short, comparatively weak, but spreading side branches; young shoots glabrous, somewhat angular. Leaves coppery when young, on ordinary branches 2 or 3 in. across (considerably larger on vigorous leading shoots), broadly triangular, widely tapered to nearly straight across at the base, slender-pointed, the margins set with rather coarse, incurved, gland-tipped teeth, and furnished more or less with minute hairs. It is a male tree; catkins 2½ to 3½ in. long; anthers red.

This fine tree originated in the nursery of Messrs Simon-Louis near Metz, around 1832, as a self-sown seedling found growing in a bed of young silver firs. Gabriel Simon, the founder of the nursery, named it 'le peuplier Eugène' after his infant son, born in 1829, who later carried out botanical explorations in China for the French government, during which he discovered and introduced P. *simonii*. The parentage of 'Eugenei' is uncertain, but is usually supposed to have sprung from 'Regenerata' pollinated by Lombardy poplar. If that is so, Gabriel Simon must have been among the first growers to plant 'Regenerata', which was first distributed only seventeen years before 'Eugenei' saw the light of day.

The original tree was 80 ft high and 9 ft in girth when twenty-five years planted; in 1904 it had reached 150 ft and girthed 23 ft at 4 ft; it died and was felled around 1945. A number of plants were procured for Kew in 1888, and one of these grew to be over 80 ft high and 5 ft in girth in a little over twenty years. Three trees of this batch still exist in the collection and the two largest measure 110 × 11½ ft and 120 × 11½ ft (1974). Other examples are: Edinburgh Botanic Garden, 105 × 11¼ ft and 98 × 11 ft (1970); Colesbourne, Glos., *pl.* 1903, 128 × 11½ ft (1970); Forestry Commission, Alice Holt, Hants, *pl.* 1954, 72 × 4¼ ft (1971).

In Cansdale's survey of the black poplars (1938), 'Eugenei' was stated to be 'perhaps the most liable to canker of all the Black Poplars'. It was later found that the poplar thus denounced was not the true 'Eugenei', which is in fact one of the most resistant to canker and is one of the poplars recommended by the Forestry Commission for use in plantation. It is often planted in screens on account of its comparatively narrow and symmetrical crown. In the USA, where it has been widely planted, it is known as "Carolina poplar".

'FLORENCE BIONDI'.—A hybrid black poplar of great promise raised by Schreiner and Stout, who gave the parentage as *P. deltoides* var. *virginiana* crossed with *P. nigra* var. *caudina*. Until named recently, it was known by its registration number—OP 226. A tree in the Forestry Commission collection at Alice Holt, seventeen years planted, measures 72 × 3½ ft (1973).

'GELRICA'.—A tall tree resembling 'Serotina' in habit; trunk remaining white for many years; young stems glabrous. Leaves unfolding at about the same time as those of 'Regenerata' and 'Marilandica', at first reddish brown, light green when mature, deltoid in outline, shallowly cordate at the base on long shoots, rounded to broad-cuneate on short shoots; petioles red-tinged. There are apparently at least two clones under the name 'Gelrica', one male, the other female.

This hybrid, selected in Holland at the end of the last century, was not introduced to Britain until much later and is still uncommon. Although not especially vigorous in its early years, its radial growth rate surpasses that of the older hybrids.

'MARILANDICA'.—A large tree with a rounded, almost spherical crown, and a corrugated, not burred, trunk; young shoots glabrous. Leaves light green, triangular-ovate, inclined to diamond-shaped, nearly always widely tapering at the base, and with a longer slender point, those on the long shoots 3 to 6 in. long, three-fourths as wide, margins ciliate on young leaves; glands at base none to two (usually none on those of the short shoots); stalks compressed, 1½ to 3 in. long. Catkins female, ultimately 4 to 6 in. long; stigmas two to four.

After 'Serotina' this is the oldest of the black poplar hybrids. It was described in 1816, and is believed to have arisen about 1800 from a cross between *P. nigra* and *P.* × *canadensis* 'Serotina'. It was at one time confused with the American black poplar, of which it was thought to be a female form; it is really nearer to *P. nigra*, differing in the burrless trunk and showing the influence of the American parent in the presence of stray cilia on the leaf-margins and, usually, of glands at the junction of the leaf-blade with the petiole.

Although common in some parts of the continent, 'Marilandica' has never been much planted in this country, owing to its poor stem shape and comparatively slow growth. The oldest and largest tree in the country grows at Kew on the lawn, near the Water Lily House. Planted around 1846, it measures 115 ×

17 ft (1974). Although handsome and imposing, it is not a perfect lawn tree, owing to the litter its cottony seeds make on the ground around midsummer.

'REGENERATA'. RAILWAY POPLAR.—The leaves of this clone resemble those of 'Serotina' in their shape, toothing, and other characters. But they are pure green, not sea-green, expand about a fortnight earlier and are scarcely coloured when young. 'Regenerata' also differs from 'Serotina' in being female, and the two trees are also very different in habit: in 'Regenerata' the branches arch outwards at the ends, vase-fashion, and are snagged, while the shoots are slender and pendulous; in 'Serotina' the bole and branches are clean, the branches curve inwards, forming a goblet-shaped crown, and the shoots spread upwards.

'Regenerata' arose in France, at Arcueil, in 1814, probably from a spontaneous cross between 'Serotina' and 'Marilandica'. It was bought by the nurseryman Romanent of Montirail, who named it 'le peuplier régénéré' and propagated it. But it was first put into commerce by Bujot of Chateau-Thierry and soon became common in the valley of the Ourcq, north of that town (Carrière, *Rev. Hort.* (1865), pp. 58, 276).

The date of introduction of 'Regenerata' to Britain is not known for certain, but it is almost beyond doubt that it is the poplar which the Knap Hill nursery introduced around 1870 and distributed as 'the new Canadian poplar' or '*P. canadensis nova*', recommending it for its very fast growth and its ability to grow well in a smoky atmosphere. It is still a very common tree in the London suburbs, especially near the railways, where it was used to screen goods-yards. It is no longer a recommended poplar in this country, being very susceptible to bacterial canker, and its planting in France north of the latitude of Paris has been banned for the same reason. Although female, it produces little cotton, as most of the flowers are sterile.

Some specimens of 'Regenerata' are: Kew, Queen's Cottage Grounds, 105 × 13 ft (1973); *pl.* 1887, 85 × 8 ft (1967); Hyde Park, London, by the Serpentine bridge, 90 × 11 ft (1967); Regents Park, London, four trees 70 to 85 ft high and 8¾ to 10¾ ft in girth (1967-8); Wildwood Road, Hampstead, London, 80 × 10¾ ft (1968).

Poplars similar to 'Regenerata', and probably of the same parentage, were also known as 'peupliers régénérés' and are cultivated in France. Two of these now have distinguishing names: 'Régénéré de l'Yonne' and 'Bâtard d'Hauterive'. The original clone is sometimes distinguished in France as 'Régénéré de l'Ourcq' (Pourtet, *La Culture du Peuplier* (1957), pp. 182-7).

'ROBUSTA'.—A very vigorous tree, with ascending branches; young shoots ribbed and minutely downy; winter-buds sticky, pointed, reddish brown. Leaves rich bronze when young, triangular-ovate, pointed, truncate or nearly so at the base, the margins set with even, rounded teeth which become wide apart towards the base; 2 to 5 in. long, 1½ to 4 in. wide; stalk 1 to 2 in. long, finely downy. The glands where the stalk joins the blade are either two, one, or absent altogether. This is a male tree and its catkins are 2½ in. long.

This hybrid arose in the nursery of Messrs Simon-Louis at Plantières, near Metz, in 1895, the seed-parent being *P. deltoides* 'Cordata' (*P. angulata cordata*) and the pollen-parent most probably *P. nigra* 'Plantierensis', which would have imparted to the hybrid its erect branching and downy young shoots. The pollen-parent was at first thought to be *P.* × *canadensis* 'Eugenei', but in that poplar the young shoots are glabrous, as they are in the seed-parent.

'Robusta' has been widely used in Britain since the second world war in commercial forestry and in screens and shelter-belts. It is perhaps the most ornamental of the hybrid black poplars, with its glossy, sea-green leaves, brilliantly coloured when they first unfold.

Being of comparatively recent origin, and fairly new to cultivation in this country, 'Robusta' is rarely seen as a large specimen. The most notable are: Bowood, Wilts, 105 × 9 ft (1964); Tortworth, Glos., 113 × 11½ ft (1974); Shinners Bridge, Totnes, Devon, 103 × 8¼ ft (1967); National Botanic Garden, Glasnevin, Eire, *pl.* 1900, 102 × 8 ft (1974). A tree in the Forestry Commission collection at Alice Holt, *pl.* 1951, is 66 × 4¾ ft (1971).

'SEROTINA'.—A large tree, always male, frequently over 100 ft high, with an open, rather gaunt habit, and extremely vigorous; young shoots glabrous, green, slightly angled. Leaves ovate-triangular, with a broad, straight base, and a short, abrupt, slender apex, 2 to 6 in. wide and long, regularly round-toothed, the margin translucent and at first minutely hairy; one or more glands occur at the base near the stalk, which is 1½ to 2½ in. long, glabrous, compressed. Catkins 3 to 4 in. long; flower-stalks glabrous; anthers rich red.

This hybrid, perhaps the oldest of the group, arose early in the 18th century, probably in France, though it became known there as the Swiss poplar (*peuplier suisse*). In this country, to which it was introduced late in the 18th century, it was known until recently as the "Canadian poplar" or the "black Italian poplar". It was once the most commonly planted of all poplars except the Lombardy, and is still a feature of the landscape both in the countryside and in suburbia, easily recognised by its goblet-shaped crown, bare of leaf until the first or second week of May, and its grey-green leaves. It responds well to pollarding and quickly regains its characteristic shape. Being of comparatively slow growth, it is no longer much grown in plantation, but is still of value in low-lying, frosty areas owing to its late flushing. It attains greater dimensions than any other exotic deciduous tree. Among the largest recorded specimens are: Fairlawne, Kent, 140 × 20¾ ft, with a clean bole of 45 ft (1965); Chelsworth, Suffolk, 118 × 21¾ ft, clean bole 30 ft (1968); Alresford, Hants, by the watercress beds, 112 × 20 ft (1965); Hyde Park, London, 105 × 16¾ ft (1967).

'SEROTINA AUREA' ('AUREA').—Leaves very yellow in spring and early summer, becoming yellowish green later. This variety originated in the nursery of van Geert at Kalmthout, Belgium, as a branch-sport, and was put into commerce in 1876.

'SEROTINA DE SELYS' ('SEROTINA ERECTA').—A tree of fastigiate habit, but in other respects resembling 'Serotina'. It arose in Belgium before 1818 and was first described by Baron de Selys-Longchamps in 1864. It would make an excellent substitute for the Lombardy poplar were it not that, like ordinary 'Serotina', it leafs late and therefore lacks the screening and shelter properties of the Lombardy.

P. CANDICANS Ait.   ONTARIO POPLAR, BALM OF GILEAD

P. gileadensis Rouleau; *P. ontariensis* Desf.; *P. balsamifera* var. *candicans* (Ait.) A. Gray

This poplar has the general character of *P. balsamifera*, the same sucker-producing habit, balsamic resin-covered buds, and odoriferous young foliage; also the whitish undersurface of the leaf conspicuously netted over with veins. But it differs in the following respects: its branches are more spreading than in *P. balsamifera*, and it thus forms a broader, more open crown; its leaves are broader and more generally heart-shaped, more downy beneath, and ciliate; and its leaf-stalks and young shoots are downy. It is a female clone the history of which is unknown, but most probably it arose in north-eastern N. America, where it has been cultivated since early colonial times as a shade tree, and was introduced from there to Europe in the 18th century. In Britain it has been known since 1773. Some authorities hold it to be no more than a clone of the north-eastern variety of *P. balsamifera* known as var. *michauxii* or var. *subcordata*, but according to another view it is a hybrid between *P. balsamifera* and *P. deltoides*.

At one time *P. candicans* was the commonest balsam poplar in Britain. In previous editions of this work it was said that it 'may often be seen in out of the way places in London suburbs, producing a swarm of suckers, and scenting the air around on moist spring days'. Unfortunately that is no longer true, for this poplar is very susceptible to bacterial canker and has become rare.

cv. 'AURORA'.—Leaves variously patterned with white flushed pink; some are marbled, other broadly margined with it, a few more white than green. But many leaves are wholly green, especially on the spurs, the variegation being best developed in summer on the long shoots. Hard pruning encourages the production of long shoots but perhaps also makes the tree more vulnerable to attacks of canker unless the cuts are sealed with a proprietary dressing. 'Aurora' was put into commerce in the 1920s by Messrs Treseder of Truro, who obtained their stock from a garden in north Devon. It was originally distributed as *P. candicans variegata* and received its present name in 1954; the Award of Merit was given to it in the same year.

There is also a yellow-variegated form of *P. candicans* in cultivation, which received an Award of Merit in 1898, as "*P. ontariensis variegata*". There are plants in the Forestry Commission collection at Alice Holt, heavily infected with canker.

P. CANESCENS (Ait.) Sm.   GREY POPLAR

P. alba var. *canescens* Ait.

A tree 100 ft high, with a trunk 12 ft or more in girth; bark of the young trunk and branches yellowish grey, with horizontal, angular scars, becoming furrowed like an oak or ash with age. Both the terminal part of the young shoots and the underside of the terminal leaves are covered with white or grey felt, and much of this is retained until the fall of the leaf, and it is never abundant on the short twigs or on the lower leaves of the strong shoots, which become usually green and glabrous by the end of the season. Leaves roundish on lateral twigs, much larger and ovate on strong leading shoots, the smaller ones 1 to 2 in. long, the larger ones 3 to 4 in. long; all with large, blunt, rounded teeth, and rounded or slightly heart-shaped at the base; stalk flattened, ½ to 3 in. long, carrying about the same amount of wool as that part of the shoot to which it is attached. Male catkins 2 to 4 in. long; stamens eight to fifteen. Female catkins ¾ to 4 in. long. Catkin-scales long-ciliate, laciniate, the divisions reaching less than half-way to the base; they are therefore intermediate in form between those of *P. alba* and *P. tremula*, since they are dentate in the former and divided more than half-way to the base in the latter.

P. canescens is of fairly wide distribution in Europe and occurs in southern and eastern England, where it is often confused with *P. alba*. It differs from that species in its leaves being grey rather than white beneath, except when quite young, and in those of the base of the shoot becoming glabrous or almost glabrous by autumn; the leaf-stalks are generally much longer and more naked, and the catkins are longer. The leaves are never maple-like in form, as they are on the strong shoots of *P. alba*. This is a very vigorous and handsome poplar, which produces suckers freely, and grows well on most soils, including chalky ones. It is used for shelter and, in some parts of the world, for checking soil-erosion.

Most modern authorities consider *P. canescens* to be a hybrid between *P. alba* and *P. tremula*. Its presence in Britain, where *P. alba* is not native, provides no argument against this hypothesis, since it is by no means certain that *P. canescens* itself is truly native. The great rarity of female trees suggests that it has been distributed by human agency. It should also be noted that the grey poplar often shows two aspen characters not mentioned in most descriptions: a thickened, cartilaginous margin to the leaf, and the presence on the leaves of strong shoots of two glands at the junction of the blade with the petiole; also that deliberate crosses between *P. alba* and *P. tremula* have produced trees indistinguishable from *P. canescens*.

The status of *P.* HYBRIDA Bieb., described from the Caucasus and often considered to be synonymous with *P. canescens*, is also a matter of dispute. In *Flora Europaea* it is stated to be *P. canescens* × *P. tremula*, a hybrid also reported from the British Isles.

Some large specimens of *P. canescens* are: Home Park, Windsor, Berks, 97 × 13¾ ft (1964); Tarrant Crawford, Dorset, 102 × 12¼ ft (1965); Conon House, Dingwall, Ross, 95 × 12¼ ft (1956). But the most notable specimen in the British Isles is a splendid tree at Birr Castle, Co. Offaly, Eire, which measures 105 × 15¾ ft (1966).

cv. 'AUREO-VARIEGATA'.—Leaves usually smaller than in the type, and marbled with yellow; poor, and apt to revert.

cv. 'MACROPHYLLA'. PICART'S POPLAR.—A large-leaved form of the grey poplar, the leaves being often 6 in. long on vigorous shoots.

cv. 'PENDULA'.—Branches slender and gracefully arching or pendulous.

P. TOMENTOSA Carr. *P. alba* var. *tomentosa* (Carr.) Wesm.; *P. pekinensis* L. Henry—Although usually compared with *P. alba*, this poplar is more closely allied to *P. canescens*. The main points of difference are: leaves of long shoots whiter beneath when young, edged with finer, often hook-like teeth; leaves on the short shoots mostly cordate at the base, with fairly regular broad teeth. It is widespread in China and especially common in the Peking region, but whether it is anywhere truly wild is uncertain. It is probably of hybrid origin, from a cross between the eastern race of *P. alba* and *P. tremula* var. *davidiana* (S. Bialobok, 'Studies on *P. tomentosa* Carr.' in *Arboretum Kornickie*, Yearbook 9 (1964), in English).

P. tomentosa was introduced to France in 1897. A tree in the Forestry Commission collection at Alice Holt, received from the USA as *P. tomentosa*, has not yet been verified botanically. It is of pendulous habit and most ornamental, worthy of cultivation whatever its identity.

P. DELTOIDES Marsh   EASTERN COTTONWOOD

P. monilifera Ait.; *P. nigra* var. *virginiana* Castigl.; *P. canadensis* Michx. f., not Moench; *P. deltoides* var. *monilifera* (Ait.) Henry; *P. deltoides* var. *virginiana* (Castigl.) Sudw.; *P. balsamifera* var. *virginiana* (Castigl.) Sarg.

A tree 100 ft or more high in the wild, with a short trunk and massive, spreading branches; bark pale greenish yellow on young trees, becoming grey and deeply furrowed; young stems glabrous, terete or slightly angled; buds brown, lustrous, resinous and balsam-scented, ovoid, acute, the lateral ones flattened. Leaves deltoid or broad-ovate, 3 to 5 in. long and about as wide, abruptly narrowed at the apex to a slender acute point, mostly truncate to shallowly cordate at the base, with two or three glands at the junction between the blade and petiole, medium green and glossy above, paler beneath, glabrous on both sides (or downy when young and more or less persistently downy on the veins beneath in f. PILOSA (Sarg.) Sudw.), margins with a translucent border, finely ciliate, crenate-serrate, or crenate-dentate, the teeth with callous, incurved tips; petioles much flattened laterally, 2½ to 4 in. long. Male catkins densely flowered, up to 2 in. long; female catkins 3 to 4 in. long, with distant flowers; scales divided into thread-like lobes. Stamens up to sixty or more, with red anthers. Stigmas three or four. Capsules three- or four-valved.

Native of eastern N. America; introduced, according to Aiton, in 1772. It is a rare tree in this country now, having long ago been displaced by its hybrids with the European *P. nigra*. From that species it differs in the shape of the leaf, which is very rarely broad-cuneate at the base, in its ciliate margins, and in the presence of petiolar glands. An example at Kew, *pl.* 1910, measures 75 × 6¼ ft (1967).

cv. 'CAROLIN'. CAROLINA POPLAR.—Stems of the long shoots strongly angled, almost winged. Leaves of strong shoots rather thick, triangular-ovate, longer than wide, usually cordate at the base. Petioles and lower veins tinged with red. Male. A large, heavily branched tree, retaining its foliage until late in the autumn. It attains a large size in the warmer parts of Europe, but is rare in this country and not entirely hardy. It is common in southern France, where it was once much planted for timber, but is giving way there to hybrids such as 'Robusta', which grow faster and are easier to propagate. It is an old clone of var. *missouriensis*, introduced to Europe early in the 18th century, and usually grown under the name *P. angulata* Ait. 'Carolin' is its modern clonal name.

cv. 'CORDATA'.—Resembling 'Carolin', but hardier, easier to propagate, with less angled branches and yellowish green petioles. It also differs in being female. It was described in 1861 from a tree growing in the nursery of Simon-Louis at Plantières near Metz, under the name *P. angulata cordata*, and was said to have come from the collection of a Monsieur David. It is a parent of *P.* × *canadensis* 'Robusta'. The French authority Pourtet mentions a poplar called 'ANGULATA DE CHAUTAGNE' which appears to be similar to 'Cordata'. This was selected around the middle of the last century in the *département* of L'Ain by the nurseryman Tallissieu, and cultivated locally.

var. MISSOURIENSIS (Henry) Henry *P. angulata* var. *missouriensis* Henry (July 1913); *P. deltoides* var. *angulata* (Ait.) Sarg. (August 1913); *P. angulata* Ait.—Branches of strong shoots usually strongly angled, bearing leaves up to 6 in. or even 7 in. long, and often longer than wide. Other differences sometimes given, but perhaps not shown constantly, are that the leaves tend to be acute or subacute rather than acuminate at the apex, more finely toothed, and with three or four glands at the junction between blade and petiole. This variety appears to be commonest in the south-east and in the Mississippi basin. Although distinct enough from the small- and short-leaved form of the north-east once known as *P. monilifera*, it is not clear how it is supposed to differ from typical *P. deltoides*, since the species was very scantily described by Marshall. It may even be that this variety really represents typical *P. deltoides*.

Of *P. angulata* Ait. it has been said that it resembles *P. deltoides* var. *missouriensis* in foliage, but differs in the abnormal inflorescence-bracts, which instead of being finely laciniate as in other black poplars, are merely dentate, i.e., the thread-like tips to the teeth are lacking. Henry, followed by later authorities, suggested that this character was the result of a mutation that occurred after the introduction of this poplar to Europe. Since, however, the Aiton specimens in the British Museum are without flowers it is impossible to say whether or not this character was shown by the trees from which *P. angulata* was described, and in the absence of evidence to the contrary it must be assumed that they resembled the wild trees in their inflorescence-bracts, as they do in foliage. It must be added that an examination of herbarium specimens suggests that the peculiar bracts are not a constant feature of the cultivated trees known as *P. angulata*. It is not unlikely that one and the same clone might vary in this respect according to season or the climate in which the tree is grown. For the clones usually placed under *P. angulata*, see 'Carolin' and 'Cordata'.

P. FREMONTII S. Wats.

This is the common cottonwood of California, and of other western states, which does not appear to have been introduced to Britain previous to 1904. It is one of the black poplars with the characteristic compressed leaf-stalk of that group. Leaves broadly diamond-shaped, triangular, or somewhat kidney-shaped, 1½ to 4 in. wide, usually less in length, the margin coarsely round-toothed, except at the short, abrupt point, and at the straight, broadly wedge-shaped or slightly heart-shaped base; stalk 1½ to 3 in. long, and, like the young shoots and leaves, soon quite glabrous. Catkins 2 to 4 in. long. From the black poplar of eastern N. America this appears to differ in its proportionately broader leaves without glands at the base. According to Jepson it is 40 to 90 ft high in California, having a round-topped, massive head of branches. It has no particular value for the garden, and is tender in some forms.

P. WISLIZENII Sarg.—This differs from *P. fremontii* in having the stalks of the female flowers conspicuously longer; they are ½ in. long, but only $\frac{1}{12}$ to ⅛ in. long in *P. fremontii*. Its habitat, in Texas, New Mexico, etc., is south and east of that of *P. fremontii*.

P. × GENEROSA Henry

This hybrid poplar was first raised at Kew in 1912 by crossing the female *P. deltoides* 'Cordata' with pollen from *P. trichocarpa*. The seed was ripe by the end of June and, being sown immediately, germinated the following October. The cross was repeated in 1914. The plants so raised made extraordinary growth and in seven years from sowing the seed were up to 37 ft high and 22 in. in girth of trunk.

The young shoots are glabrous, shining grey-green, and angled (but by no means so markedly as those of the seed-parent); winter-buds awl-shaped, about 1 in. long, freely supplied inside with yellowish, viscid, balsamic resin. Leaves deciduous, triangular-ovate, truncate or slightly heart-shaped at the base, pointed, the translucent margin set with regular, incurved, gland-tipped teeth; rather pale green above, greyish beneath but not so pale as in *P. trichocarpa*; they vary much in size, the largest 12 or 13 in. long, 9 or 10 in. wide, the smaller ones one-third those dimensions; leaf-stalk 3 to 4 in. long, more or less flattened, with two or three conspicuous glands where it joins the midrib. Many of the leaves turn a good yellow in autumn. Male catkins 4 to 5 in. long: stamens with reddish anthers and long white stalks; female catkins rather longer, ovary glabrous, stigmas usually three. The flowers open in April.

As a timber tree, *P. × generosa* has not fulfilled its early promise. The rapid growth of young trees is sustained provided they remain free from disease, but usually development is checked owing to infection by one disease or another, or by loss of height due to breakage. *P. × generosa* has no ornamental value. It is very susceptible to bacterial canker, and is usually the first to be attacked in a mixed planting. It is, however, of historic interest, as the first deliberate cross between a black poplar and a balsam poplar.

Two of the original trees at Kew, *pl.* 1914, measure 92 × 7½ ft (1970) and 75 × 6¼ ft (1967). A tree at Albury Park, Surrey, *pl.* 1928, is about 120 ft high and 8¾ ft in girth (1966).

P. GRANDIDENTATA Michx.   BIG-TOOTHED ASPEN

A tree up to 60 or 70 ft high in the wild; young shoots at first downy, becoming glabrous and glossy later; winter-buds coated with fine down. Leaves roundish ovate, the smallest sometimes oval, $1\frac{1}{2}$ to 5 in. long, mostly short-pointed, and with a broadly tapered or rounded base, the margin set with large broad teeth; at first they are covered with a loose grey wool which soon falls away, leaving them dark green above; stalk 1 to $2\frac{1}{2}$ in. long, slender, compressed towards the top. Catkins $1\frac{1}{2}$ to $2\frac{1}{2}$ in. long, the female ones becoming twice the length at maturity.

Native of eastern N. America; introduced in 1772, according to Loudon. The tree is exceedingly rare in Britain at the present time, and does not appear to thrive well. It appears to be most closely related to *P. tremula*, from which it differs in the downy young shoots and more downy winter-buds. Its deep toothing distinguishes it from *P. tremuloides*. It appears to be difficult to increase by cuttings, and was usually grafted on *P. canescens*, but softwood cuttings can be rooted by the mist technique.

There is a specimen at Birr Castle, Co. Offaly, Eire, measuring 42 × $1\frac{3}{4}$ ft (1966). It was planted in 1958.

P. 'PSEUDOGRANDIDENTATA'.—A weeping tree, propagated by grafting. Known since 1869, it was described by Dode in 1905 as a species—*P. pseudograndidentata*. The young shoots are covered with a whitish wool at first, and the leaves are similar in shape and toothing to those of *P. tremula*, but they are stouter in texture, 3 to $4\frac{1}{2}$ in. wide, not quite so long. It is of unknown origin and perhaps a hybrid between *P. grandidentata* and *P. tremula*. It is not the same as the *P. grandidentata* var. *pendula* of Loudon, which is based on reports of pendulous trees of *P. grandidentata* found in N. America. He added that a tree introduced to the garden of the Horticultural Society under this name was not in fact pendulous.

P. HETEROPHYLLA L.   SWAMP COTTONWOOD

A tree 40 to 100 ft high, young branches clothed at first with a thick felt as in *P. alba*, much of which falls away by late summer; winter-buds slightly gummy, bright red-brown. Leaves heart-shaped, up to 7 or 8 in. long and nearly as wide, rounded at the apex, shallowly and rather evenly toothed, covered on both surfaces when they unfold with a thick whitish down, which soon falls away from the upper surface, leaving it dark green, but remains longer on the lower surface, especially on the midrib and veins. The leaves hang laxly on their stalks, which are round, felted at first like the shoot, $1\frac{1}{2}$ to $3\frac{1}{2}$ in. long. Male catkins 2 to $2\frac{1}{2}$ in. long; female catkins longer.

Native of the eastern United States; introduced in 1765. Until the introduction of several new Chinese species this poplar had the largest leaves of any in cultivation, but unfortunately it does not thrive well with us. Loudon observes that he had not seen plants more than 5 or 6 ft high, and no tree any bigger has been recorded.

For the section *Leucoides*, to which *P. heterophylla* belongs, see the introductory note to *Populus*.

P. KOREANA Rehd.

A tree up to 100 ft high in the wild; young shoots shiny with viscid, fragrant gum, not angular nor downy. Leaves on the strong shoots ovate or oval, pointed, broadly wedge-shaped to slightly heart-shaped at the base, closely, evenly, and minutely toothed, 3 to 6 in. long, 1½ to 3 in. wide (sometimes up to 8 in. long and 6 in. wide), vivid green, glabrous, with the veins and veinlets impressed, midrib reddish, the underside whitish and glabrous; petiole stout, less than ½ in. long; leaves on short shoots similar, but narrower, more tapered

POPULUS KOREANA

at the base, sometimes minutely downy on the veins beneath and on the petioles, which may be up to ¾ in. long. Flowers and fruits similar to those of P. *maximowiczii*, but the male catkins shorter, up to 2 in. long, with fewer stamens (ten to thirty).

Native of Korea northward to the Ussuri region of Russia, and perhaps also of Japan. It is one of the balsam poplars, resembling and closely related to P. *maximowiczii*, which differs in its downy young shoots, and in its smoother leaves which are curiously folded and bent at the apex. It is one of the most ornamental of the genus but, like its ally, it is very susceptible to bacterial canker in this country, and is often damaged by spring frost.

P. LASIOCARPA Oliver

A tree 40 to 60 ft high; young shoots very stout, downy. Leaves on adult trees 6 to 10 in. long, 4 to 8 in. wide; heart-shaped, with a deep notch where the stalk joins the base, pointed, the margin regularly set with shallow, rounded, incurved, gland-tipped teeth; both surfaces are at first downy but the upper one soon becomes quite glabrous, the midrib and chief veins of a rich red; the lower surface remains downy until the fall, especially on the veins; stalk 2 to 4 in. long, round, red like the midrib. Male catkins about 4 in. long, ¾ in. thick, with numerous stamens; female catkins 6 or 8 in. long when mature; see further below. *Bot. Mag.*, t. 8625.

Native of Central China; discovered by Henry in 1888, and introduced for Messrs Veitch by Wilson in 1900. In regard to its foliage this is the most remarkable and striking of all cultivated poplars. I gathered a leaf on a small tree in the Coombe Wood nursery in October 1908, 14 in. long by 9 in. wide (without the stalk). The leaves do not decrease much in size as the tree grows older. The beauty of the leaf is also increased by the rich rhubarb-like red of the stalk and midrib. Wilson describes it as a shapely tree inhabiting moist woods. I doubt if the tree will succeed as well grafted as on its own roots; after a while there ought to be no difficulty in getting cuttings to take root. Mr Wilson told me that on one of his journeys he came to a little Chinese farm where the farmer had made an enclosure for his animals by driving stakes in the ground. These were of *P. lasiocarpa*, and they had taken root and grown freely.

To the above paragraph, taken unchanged from previous editions, it must be added that Wilson introduced *P. lasiocarpa* in the form of about a dozen small plants. Of these at least one was unusual in bearing polygamous catkins, the flowers in the basal part being staminate and those in the apical part of the catkin bisexual or pistillate. This form was among those distributed by Veitch, propagated by grafting, and seems to be the commonest in cultivation. In the nursery of Messrs Notcutt it bears fertile seed from which plants of the true species have been raised, and has even produced self-sown seedlings. But other plants are reported to be female.

What is perhaps the finest specimen of *P. lasiocarpa* grows in the Botanic Garden, Bath. It is 69 ft high and slightly over 6¼ ft in girth (1971). There are two trees at Westonbirt, Glos., measuring 50 × 3 ft and 56 × 2½ ft (1967).

P. LAURIFOLIA Ledeb.

A tree 40 to 70 ft high, of spreading, lax growth, branches ultimately pendulous, with conspicuously angular, grey young shoots, downy chiefly in the grooves; winter-buds covered with balsamic gum. Leaves lanceolate, narrowly oval or obovate, rounded or tapering at the base, taper-pointed, minutely and evenly toothed, the teeth gland-tipped, 1 to 5 in. long, ⅛ to 2 in. wide, dark green and glabrous above, slightly downy and conspicuously net-veined on a greyish ground beneath; stalk very variable in length even with leaves of the same size on the same shoot, ¼ to 1¼ in. long, downy. Male catkins 1½ to 2 in. long, at first erect, then drooping; stamens very numerous.

P. laurifolia was described from the Altai mountains and is reported to have its centre there and in the Dzungarski Alatau, but extends into E. Siberia and to parts of Mongolia and Chinese Central Asia. It was introduced to Britain about 1830, but has never become common, and has not much to recommend it for British gardens, although an example at Kew growing in damp clayey soil made a rather elegant pendulously branched tree and reached a height of 50 ft.

P. laurifolia belongs to the group of balsam poplars with narrow leaves and angular branches. It is a parent of *P. × berolinensis* (q.v.).

f. LINDLEYANA (Carr.) Aschers. & Graebn. *P. lindleyana* Carr.—Leaves on the strong shoots narrow-lanceolate, willow-like.

P. MAXIMOWICZII Henry

A tree up to 100 ft high in the wild, its bark smooth and yellowish on young trees, becoming grey and deeply fissured on the trunks of old trees; stems terete, downy, green tinged with brownish red on the exposed side; buds ⅝ to ¾ in. long, pointed, resinous. Leaves on the long shoots broad-elliptic, 3 to 5 in. long, 2¾ to 4¼ in. wide, rounded to slightly cordate at the base, apex very abruptly narrowed to a plicate cusp which points downward out of the plane of the leaf and often slightly to one side as well; those on the short shoots rather narrower, rounded-cuneate at the base. The leaves are slightly leathery, vivid green, dullish, reticulate above, whitish beneath, veins and veinlets finely downy on both surfaces, margins bluntly toothed, ciliate; petioles on the long shoots about ¾ in. long, on the short shoots 1 to 1½ in. long. Male catkins 2 to 4 in. long; stamens thirty to forty. Fruiting catkins up to 10 in. long; capsules shortly stalked, three- or four-valved, glabrous, ripening in September or October, much later than in most poplars.

A native of Japan, Manchuria, Korea, and the Russian Far East. It is a balsam poplar, closely allied to *P. suaveolens*, in which it was included until Augustine Henry separated it as a distinct species in 1913. At that time it was not in cultivation in Britain, but was introduced a few years later.

In the wild 'this poplar grows to a larger size than any other species of eastern Asia, and ranks with the largest trees that grow there' (E. H. Wilson, in *Pl. Wils.*, Vol. 3, p. 33). It is also one of the most ornamental and distinct of the genus. The leaves unfold early in the spring and turn yellow before falling late in the autumn. Unfortunately it is susceptible to bacterial canker, but there is a promising young female tree in the Alice Holt collection which has so far remained free of infection, though its neighbours of the same species are heavily infected. This tree, nineteen years planted, measures 38 × 2¾ ft. The only other recorded tree in the United Kingdom is one in the Edinburgh Botanic Garden, measuring 50 × 3½ ft (1967). All the other notable specimens are in Ireland: Rowallane, Co. Down, 55 × 5¼ ft, and, in Eire, Birr Castle, Co. Offaly, *pl.* 1927, 58 × 5¼ ft; Mount Usher, Co. Wicklow, 52 × 4¾ ft and 48 × 5½ ft; Headfort, Co. Meath, 78 × 5¾ ft (all measurements 1966).

P. maximowiczii has been used to produce hybrids for commercial planting. Of these the best known in Britain is 'ANDROSCOGGIN', one of the Schreiner and Stout hybrids, raised from *P. maximowiczii* pollinated by *P. trichocarpa*, and therefore wholly a balsam hybrid. It is very fast growing, and has some value as an ornamental, but is not resistant to bacterial canker. The leaves show the influence of the seed-parent in their broadly ovate to roundish, abruptly acuminate leaves. It is a male clone. A tree in the Alice Holt collection, nineteen years planted, measures 67 × 4¼ ft (1973).

Other named hybrids from *P. maximowiczii* raised by Schreiner and Stout are: 'GENEVA' and 'OXFORD', two sister seedlings from a cross with the male clone of P. × *berolinensis*; and 'ROCHESTER', from P. *maximowiczii* pollinated by P. *nigra* 'Plantierensis'. The last-named might have some value as an ornamental, judging by the tree at Kew, which has made a handsome, densely leafy specimen. Planted in 1934, it measures 62 × 4¾ ft (1967).

The Schreiner and Stout hybrids mentioned above were raised in the USA on behalf of the Oxford Paper Company, and are usually known as the 'OP hybrids'. Thirty-four different types of poplar were used in the breeding programme, and 13,000 seedlings were raised. After trial in the Company's nursery at Frye, Maine, sixty-nine first selections were made, of which ten that seemed to be outstanding were named and described in 1934 (E. J. Schreiner and A. B. Stout, *Bull. Torr. Bot. Club*, Vol. 61, pp. 449–60). The hybrids of P. *maximowiczii* mentioned above belong to this ten, and so also do those referred to under P. × *berolinensis*. A later selection from the OP hybrids is P. × *canadensis* 'Florence Biondi' (q.v.).

P. SUAVEOLENS Fisch.—P. *balsamifera sens.* Pallas in *Fl. Ross.*, pl. 41 (excl. fig. B)—A species closely allied to P. *maximowiczii*, differing in its almost glabrous, smaller leaves and in its glabrescent petioles and branchlets. Native of E. Siberia (Dahuria), Mongolia, and the Russian Far East.

The P. *suaveolens* of Fischer is a renaming (in 1841) of a poplar discovered by Pallas in Dahuria and figured in his *Flora Rossica* (1784), pl. 41, under the name P. *balsamifera* L. The plate, and the account accompanying it, also includes a poplar from the Altai mountains, of which a leaf is depicted as fig. B in plate 41. This Altai plant is P. *laurifolia*, but the type-specimen in the Fischer herbarium, which came from Pallas' herbarium, represents the Dahurian tree (Rehder, *Journ. Arn. Arb.*, Vol. 12, pp. 61–2).

Fischer seems to have interpreted his P. *suaveolens* in a wide sense, since he sent to Kew in 1843 a specimen under this name which had been collected by Schrenk in Central Asia in the Dzungarski Alatau; this is clearly not the same as Pallas' poplar from Dahuria, i.e., is not P. *suaveolens*, whatever Fischer may have thought. Also, oddly enough, the name P. *suaveolens* was in use in gardens and nurseries in western Europe some years before Fischer published it in 1841 (Loudon, *Arb. et Frut. Brit.* (1838), Vol. III, p. 1674; Vol. IV, pp. 2629, 2640, 2651). Presumably the plants so named derived from ones distributed by Fischer from the St Petersburg Botanic Garden, of which he was the first Director. But whether they were the true species it is impossible to say. P. *suaveolens* is the species typified by the Pallas specimen in Fischer's herbarium; it does not belong to any poplar that Fischer chose to call by that name.

The name P. *suaveolens* has been used for P. *cathayana*, P. *maximowiczii*, and even for P. *balsamifera*.

P. NIGRA L.   BLACK POPLAR

A tree 100 ft or more high, with a rugged trunk 5 or 6 ft in diameter, often forming large burrs on the surface; young shoots glabrous and round; buds glutinous. Leaves variable, broadly diamond-shaped, triangular or ovate, 2 to 4½ in. long; some are wider than they are long, others twice as long as they are wide, usually broadly tapered, sometimes straight across at the base, broad or slender-pointed, both surfaces green, quite glabrous, the translucent margins regularly and shallowly round-toothed; the teeth gland-tipped; stalk ¾ to 2¼ in. long, compressed to a knife-like form. Catkins 2 to 3 in. long; anthers deep red; stigmas two in female flowers.

P. *nigra* (including its varieties) is of wide distribution in western Eurasia. The true black poplar is not very frequently seen now, having been supplanted to a great extent by the hybrids that have sprung up between it and the American P. *deltoides*. From that species it can be distinguished by the absence of marginal hairs and basal glands on the leaves; both these characters are also present in the hybrids in a greater or less degree (see further under P. × *canadensis*). As a timber tree P. *nigra* is not equal to the hybrids but as a tree for parks and gardens it has advantages. It is more leafy, has a more compact and shapely habit, branches more freely and finely, and does not grow so rampantly.

The most recent study of P. *nigra*, by W. Bugala, was published in *Arboretum Kornickie*, Rocznik (Yearbook) 12 (1967), pp. 45–219, with an English summary.

cv. 'AFGHANICA' ('THEVESTINA').—A tree resembling the Lombardy poplar in habit, but with a strikingly white bark which becomes dark and slightly furrowed on old trees; trunk rounded (not buttressed as in 'Italica'). It also differs from 'Italica' in its foliage: the leaves on the short shoots are ovate, rounded at the base, acuminately tapered at the apex (deltoid, broadly cuneate at the base in 'Italica'); those on the long shoots are longer than wide, rounded at the base (wider than long and truncate or slightly cordate at the base in 'Italica'). It is a female clone and this is, of course, its chief distinction from 'Italica', which is male (P. *nigra* var. *afghanica* Aitch. & Hemsl.; P. *thevestina* Dode; P. *afghanica* (Aitch. & Hemsl.) Schneid.; P. *nigra* var. *thevestina* (Dode) Bean; P. *usbekistanica* Komar.

P. *nigra* 'Afghanica' arose by mutation from a race of the black poplar native to Central Asia, and is commonly cultivated there and over a wide area stretching from Kashmir to N. Africa, Turkey, and parts of south-eastern Europe (notably Bulgaria and S. Yugoslavia). Reports that the Lombardy poplar is to be found in Central Asia and the Middle East, etc., really refer to 'Afghanica', and the theory that the Lombardy poplar originated somewhere in this region stems from the same confusion. Whether the wild trees from which 'Afghanica' sprang should be regarded as a separate species or included in P. *nigra* is disputable. It is recognised as a distinct species by Bugala, who accepts for it the name P. *usbekistanica* Komar. But Dode's name P. *thevestina* has priority and would be the valid name for the species even though it is founded on the cultivated clone 'Afghanica' and not on a wild plant.

This account is based largely on the work by Dr Bugala cited above, in which pages 164–82 are devoted to 'Afghanica', with numerous illustrations (English summary p. 213).

var. BETULIFOLIA (Pursh) Torr. P. *betulaefolia* Pursh; P. *hudsoniana* Michx. f. DOWNY BLACK POPLAR.—A variety differing from the type in the young shoots, leaf-stalks, midrib, and main flower-stalk being downy (*Bot. Mag.*, t. 2898).

This poplar, or rather its naming, has a curious history. It was first recognised by the younger Michaux early in the 19th century growing on the banks of the Hudson River, near Albany, New York State; he named it P. *hudsonica*. There is no doubt, however, that it was of European origin and is now considered to be the western race of *P. nigra*. It occurs wild in north-west France but whether it is truly a native of Britain is a question that has been much debated. It was certainly much planted in Britain in earlier centuries, before the coming of the hybrid black poplars, and specimens collected in England are common in the older herbaria. The survey now being conducted by the Botanical Society of Britain may allow a definitive conclusion to be reached.

The downy black poplar, like the type, produces great burrs on the trunk, and up to its middle age at least it is a neat, densely branched leafy tree, very much superior to the gaunt, rampant hybrids now almost exclusively planted. It grows well in a smoky atmosphere and was for that reason once commonly planted in the industrial midlands—whence the name 'Manchester poplar' used for *P. nigra* var. *betulifolia* in previous editions of this work. Recently, C. A. Stace examined 100 specimens from the Manchester area and found that all were male (*Watsonia*, Vol. 8, pp. 391–3), which suggests that the trees comprise a single clone. At least one and probably all, the downy black poplars on Barnes Common, London, are also male.

cv. 'CHARKOWIENSIS'.—A tree with ascending branches, forming an oblong or broadly pyramidal crown; bark lighter coloured than is usual in *P. nigra*. Young branchlets faintly downy. Female.

This poplar arose as a self-sown seedling in a nursery near Kharkov in Russia at the end of the last century and was put into commerce in western Europe by Späth in 1907. The Polish authority Bugala suggests that *P. nigra* 'Afghanica' enters into its parentage.

'Charkowiensis' was once much planted in Germany, especially in the Rhine valley. In this country it has not attracted much attention and has no special quality to commend it. The largest recorded specimen grows in the National Botanic Garden, Glasnevin, Dublin, and measures 80 × 6¾ ft (1966). There is a tree of 56 × 3¼ ft (1973) in the Forestry Commission collection at Alice Holt, planted in 1953.

cv. 'ELEGANS'.—This poplar was apparently first distributed by the American firm of Ellwanger and Barry towards the end of the last century as *P. elegans* and is thought to be of the same parentage as 'Plantierensis'. It was described as of pyramidal habit, broader than the Lombardy, with downy and red-tinted petioles and young stems. Whether it was one of the Simon-Louis clones renamed or of independent origin it is impossible to say. There is a poor example at Kew, very slender, with orange twigs.

cv. 'GIGANTEA'. GIANT LOMBARDY POPLAR.—Resembling the common Lombardy, but of much broader habit and female. The origin of this poplar is unknown. According to Pourtet, a female fastigiate poplar was named *P. gigantea* by Dode and is cultivated to some extent in central France. But a poplar was received by Kew around 1880 as 'the Giant Lombardy' and it is almost certain that this is the tree listed as *P. nigra* var. *pyramidalis gigantea* in the early editions of the Kew *Hand-list* and mentioned as an example of a female Lombardy poplar in previous editions of the present work. The Kew tree, which grew near the Palace, was removed many years ago, but female trees of fastigiate but broad habit are still to be found in this country.

cv. 'ITALICA'. LOMBARDY POPLAR.—This well-known tree, the commonest of all fastigiate trees, differs from the type only in its slender tapering form and quite erect branches, and in its buttressed trunk (*P. nigra* var. *italica* Muenchh.; *P. nigra* var. *pyramidalis* Spach; *P. fastigiata* Desf.; *P. dilatata* Ait.).

The true Lombardy poplar is a male tree, propagated by cuttings, which began to spread from Lombardy into other parts of Europe early in the 18th century. It has been suggested that it is a distinct species native to Central Asia, but the Polish authority W. Bugala has pointed out that the fastigiate poplar of that region is not the Lombardy poplar but the very distinct 'Afghanica' (q.v.).

According to Aiton's *Hortus Kewensis*, the Lombardy poplar was introduced to Britain from Turin by Lord Rochford, around 1758, but the Duke of Argyll may have planted it earlier in his collection at Whitton near Hounslow. It was in commerce by 1775.

The Lombardy poplar grows fairly fast when young and should attain 50 ft in height in twenty-five years, but it is not a long-lived tree. The largest recorded specimens are mostly 100 to 115 ft in height and rarely more than 11 ft in girth. The true Lombardy poplar is held in less regard than formerly, and the reason for its fall from grace is obvious enough, especially in country districts, where repeated attacks by the Marssonina fungus often kill the lower part of the crown, and also weaken the tree by causing premature leaf-fall. It is almost a century ago since the ill-health of the Lombardy was first remarked on, and it was then suggested that the clone was beginning to die of old age, but in fact it is disease that is the primary cause. To some extent the true Lombardy has been displaced by the healthier and more vigorous 'Plantierensis'. This is all to the good, but 'Plantierensis' has no title to the name Lombardy poplar or 'Italica', and only confusion can result if it is sold as such.

As noted above, the true Lombardy poplar is a male clone. The so-called 'female Lombardy poplars' are almost certainly seedlings of typical *P. nigra* pollinated by 'Italica', and are generally less columnar than the male parent. Such trees have arisen in many places and on many occasions; see further under 'Gigantea' and 'Vert de Garonne'. The same cross could, of course, also produce male trees but these, being less obviously distinct from 'Italica', have attracted less attention. For the cross between *P. nigra* 'Italica' and *P. nigra* var. *betulifolia*, see 'Plantierensis'.

Fastigiate forms of black poplar have also arisen from *P. nigra* var. *pubescens* crossed with *P. nigra* 'Italica'. According to Bugala, trees of this parentage occur in Tuscany in both sexes; they are of dense, slender habit and are easily distinguished from 'Plantierensis' by the very dense and persistent down on the short shoots and inflorescences. The same authority states that crosses between 'Italica' and 'Afghanica' occur in those parts of Europe where both these fastigiate clones are cultivated.

cv. 'PLANTIERENSIS'.—Resembling the Lombardy poplar in habit though sometimes broader and with downy young leaves and stems (*P. nigra* var. *plantierensis* Schneid.; *P. plantierensis* Dode; *P. fastigiata plantierensis* Simon-Louis).

This poplar originated in the nursery of Messrs Simon-Louis, Plantières, near Metz, and is thought to have sprung from *P. nigra* var. *betulifolia*, pollinated by 'Italica'. Apparently some fifteen self-sown seedlings were found, of which at least two, one male, one female, were propagated and put into commerce in 1884–5. The name 'Plantierensis' is therefore not clonal.

Deriving as it does from the Atlantic race of P. *nigra*, 'Plantierensis' grows more vigorously in our climate than the true Lombardy poplar, which it has to some extent replaced in cultivation. In the course of his survey of the black poplar and its hybrids in Britain, G. S. Cansdale received eighteen specimens of true Lombardy to forty-five of 'Plantierensis' and remarked in his report: 'Both varieties commonly pass under the name "Lombardy Poplar" and are distinguished only by botanists, so that the superior numbers of the latter ("Plantierensis") may well be due to its representing a more vigorous stock.' (*The Black Poplars* (1938), p. 29.) In fact, the two are distinguishable without examination of the foliage, since 'Plantierensis' is a much leafier tree, with a denser crown.

More recently, Miles Hadfield and Alan Mitchell have found that a fastigiate black poplar common in the Severn valley from the Hereford area as far north as Leighton has downy twigs. The trees are leafier than the Lombardy, hold their foliage until later in the autumn, and are somewhat broader-topped. Examples are: Wellington Heath, Ledbury, 104 × 13½ ft (1966); Leighton Park, Montgom., 110 × 15¾ ft and 100 × 16¾ ft (1964); Croome Court, Worcs., 92 × 14 ft (1964). These trees exceed in girth any example of true Lombardy measured in recent years. Whether they represent the 'Plantierensis' of Simon-Louis or some other variety of similar origin it is impossible to say. Despite their large girth, the oldest are not necessarily more than eighty years old, but if they do derive from Plantières, they must have been planted very soon after Simon-Louis put their variety into commerce. Those trees on which catkins have been seen are male.

var. PUBESCENS Parl. *P. nigra* subsp. *caudina* (Ten.) Bugala; *P. caudina* Ten.; *P. hispida* Hausskn.—Stems and inflorescence axes densely hairy, also, to a varying degree, the petioles and the veins on the undersurface of the leaves. S. and S.E. Europe and N. Africa. The hairs on the stems are much denser and more persistent than in var. *betulifolia*.

cv. 'VEREEKEN'.—A fast-growing male clone with a columnar-conic crown, raised in Belgium and of recent introduction. An example in the Forestry Commission collection at Alice Holt, *pl*. 1954, measures 64 × 3¾ ft (1973).

cv. 'VERT DE GARONNE'.—In the valley of the Garonne and its tributaries, and in the Rhone valley, there is found a race of more or less fastigiate black poplars, the origin of which is uncertain; it may be spontaneous or, more probably, the result of pollination of native trees by 'Italica'. Some of these trees have been propagated vegetatively, notably 'Vert de Garonne', a female tree of good habit rather broader than 'Italica' and more leafy. Other clones that have been named are: 'BLANC DE GARONNE SEIHL' (male, fairly broad); and 'SARRAZIN DE SEIHL' (narrowly fastigiate, sex not ascertained). For this information we are indebted to Pourtet's work *La Culture du Peuplier* (1957).

var. VIADRI (Rüdiger) Aschers. & Graebn. *P. viadri* Rüdiger—An obscure variety, described in 1891 from trees growing on the Oder near Frankfurt (*Viadrus* is the Latin name for the Oder). It is said to occur in both sexes, and to be of fastigiate habit, though one tree received at Kew from Rüdiger proved to be ordinary *P. nigra*.

P. SARGENTII Dode   GREAT PLAINS COTTONWOOD
P. deltoides var. *occidentalis* Rydb.

This is one of the black poplars and is common on river banks in N. America, east of the Rocky Mountains from Saskatchewan to New Mexico. It is related to *P. deltoides*, the common black poplar or cottonwood of the E. United States, differing from it, according to Sargent, by its pale yellow branches, downy buds, much shorter stalk of the female flower, and by the larger, fewer teeth of the leaves. Judging by plants received from the Arnold Arboretum in 1919, it has nothing to recommend it for this country before the numerous black poplars already in cultivation.

P. SIMONII Carr.

A medium-sized tree with slender branches and elegant habit, bursting into leaf early; young shoots glabrous, prominently angled. Leaves diamond-shaped or obovate, tapering about equally to both ends, sometimes more abruptly towards the apex; minutely and regularly blunt-toothed, 2 to 5 in. long, 1¼ to 3½ in. wide, dark green above, very pale beneath, glabrous on both sides; stalks ½ to 1 in. long (shorter on the leaves of long shoots). Male catkins ¾ to 1¼ in. long; stamens eight.

Native of north and west-central China; discovered by Eugène Simon in 1862 N.E. of Peking and introduced by him at the same time by means of plants sent to the Paris Museum and to the Simon-Louis nursery at Plantières near Metz. It is one of the balsam group breaking into leaf early, and fragrant then. Its distinguishing characters are its angular young shoots devoid of down, and the variable but often very short leaf-stalk. The original tree at Plantières had a trunk white almost as a birch.

P. simonii is represented at Kew by a tree planted in 1899, measuring 48 × 2¾ ft (1967). It is, however, a very rare tree in this country, probably because of its susceptibility to bacterial canker.

cv. 'FASTIGIATA'.—A tree of narrow habit, with ascending branches. Introduced by F. N. Meyer from N. China in 1913. A fastigiate clone cultivated in Britain came from France under the name *P. simonii obtusata*. This may possibly represent a different clone from the one sent by Meyer.

P. CATHAYANA Rehd.—This species appears to be related to *P. simonii*, but with terete young stems and the leaves on the short shoots ovate or narrow-ovate, acuminate, rounded or broad-cuneate at the base, up to about 4 in. long. It was described by Rehder in 1931 and is said to be a native of China from W. Szechwan to Manchuria, possibly also of Korea, and to have been introduced by Wilson. A plant seen under the name *P. cathayana* agrees better with *P. trichocarpa*, but what is probably the true species grows in the Forestry Commission stool-beds at Alice Holt.

P. SZECHUANICA Schneid.

A tree up to 80 ft high in cultivation; young stems angled and hairy at first, becoming terete and glabrous, brownish green the first season, greyish the second; lateral buds slightly viscid, slender, loosely appressed. Leaves on strong shoots ovate or elongate-ovate, 7½ to 12 in. long, 5 to 8 in. wide, acute at the apex, mostly strongly cordate at the base, petioles stout, up to 3 in. long, reddish; leaves on young spurs 3 to 4¼ in. long, 1⅞ to 2½ in. wide, ovate to narrow-ovate, acuminate at the apex, rounded or slightly cordate at the base, petioles 1¼ to 2½ in. long, slender; leaves at the ends of old spurs resembling those of the long shoots but not quite so large; all leaves dark green above, undersides pale green, becoming whitish on dried specimens, midrib and main veins densely furnished with more or less persistent curled hairs which near the base of the blade extend onto the minor veins, margins crenate-serrate to serrate, petioles hairy at first like the midrib, becoming glabrous. Catkins not seen.

The above description is made from specimens taken from a tree at Weston-birt, Glos., grown as P. *szechuanica* var. *tibetica,* and from another at Stourhead, Wilts. The origin of these trees, which are very similar, is not known, but they agree well with material in the Kew Herbarium taken from young trees received from the Arnold Arboretum in 1916 under Wilson's number 4361; the corresponding herbarium specimen was collected by him in W. Szechwan near Mupin in 1910, and plants were sent under the same number. The description of P. *szechuanica* in previous editions of this work was based on the Kew plants, which no longer exist, and the hairiness of the shoots and leaves was remarked on. The Kew plants, and probably those at Westonbirt and Stourhead, came from the Arnold Arboretum under the name P. *szechuanica,* in which W.4361 had been included by Schneider. In 1933 Rehder described P. *cathayana* and transferred W.4361 to this new species. But the cultivated material under W.4361 in the Kew Herbarium agrees better with P. *szechuanica,* and that is certainly true of the Westonbirt and Stourhead trees. Probably all represent a pubescent form of that species. Wilson's 4257, collected during the Veitch expedition, appears to be the same; also a specimen collected by Forrest in Yunnan on the Mekong–Salween divide.

The measurements of the trees referred to above are: Westonbirt, 82 × 4¼ ft (1972); Stourhead, 82 × 5 ft (1965) and 80 × 7 ft (1970).

var. TIBETICA Schneid.—This variety is founded on specimens of uncertain attribution collected in the N.W. Himalaya by Thomson and by Schlagintweit. Schneider considered that they represented a pubescent form of P. *szechuanica* and under this variety he also placed Wilson's 4527, collected in Szechwan. If Schneider is right, the Westonbirt and Stourhead trees would be referable to var. *tibetica,* but further investigation may show that the balsam poplar of the N.W. Himalaya is specifically distinct from P. *szechuanica.*

P. VIOLASCENS Dode—This poplar was described by the French dendro-logist Dode in 1921 from a cultivated tree of Chinese origin, but he tells us nothing of its history. Plants cultivated in this country as P. *violascens* were received originally from France and bear a very strong resemblance to the pubescent form of P. *szechuanica* described above. Furthermore, the Polish authority W. Bugala has pointed out that plants in the Kornik collection, which came originally from Kew as *P. szechuanica*, are indistinguishable from *P. violascens* as represented at Kornik. There is therefore a strong probability that Dode described his species from a plant sent from the Arnold Arboretum as *P. szechuanica* Wilson 4361. His description agrees quite well with the pubescent form of *P. szechuanica*.

P. violascens is placed by Rehder in the section Leucoides, as a close relative of *P. lasiocarpa*, and Bugala holds that *P. szechuanica* also belongs to that section and has been wrongly considered to be a balsam poplar. But the Westonbirt and Stourhead trees described above appear to be balsam poplars, and it seems on the whole more likely that it is *P. violascens* which has been wrongly placed. But flowering material should decide the matter.

P. TREMULA L. ASPEN

A tree rarely more than 50 ft high in this country; winter-buds bright brown; young shoots glabrous. Leaves greyish green, roundish to broadly ovate; from ½ to 2 in. wide on the short lateral twigs, as much as 4 in. wide on vigorous long shoots, apex pointed, base rounded or straight, prominently toothed, the teeth being few, large (often ⅛ to ⅙ in. deep), blunt, and somewhat incurved, margin thickened, more or less woolly when young, becoming quite glabrous by autumn, or with remains of the down beneath towards the base near the leaf-stalk; stalk very slender, usually smooth, ½ to 2½ in. long, two-edged. On the leaves of vigorous shoots there is a pair of glands where it joins the blade. Male catkins grey, 2 to 4 in. long, produced in February.

The aspen is very widely distributed in the temperate zones of the Old World north of the deserts, from the Atlantic to the Pacific and the Bering Sea, but in N. Africa it occurs only in Algeria and it is absent from the Himalaya and Japan; in China it may not occur in its typical state, but is represented by a variety. In the British Isles it is commonest in the north and west.

The best known attribute to the aspen is the perpetual quiver of the leaf. 'To tremble like an aspen leaf' is a phrase whose use goes back to Spenser's time, perhaps long before. This movement is seen in other poplars with compressed leaf-stalks, but is never so marked as in this. A curious superstition prevailed in the Scottish Highlands (perhaps does so now) that the cross on which the Saviour was crucified was made of the wood of this tree, and it was, in consequence, held in abhorrence. In the north of England it is (or was, sixty years ago) regarded by peasant women and children with a feeling of dislike akin to fear, probably owing to some similar legend.

The aspen is only likely to be confounded with two other poplars—the one, *P. tremuloides*, an American species distinguished by the pale yellowish bark of young trunks and main branches, and by the smaller type of leaf, being very finely and evenly toothed, and furnished with hairs on the margin when young, but otherwise glabrous; the other, *P. canescens*, is easily distinguished by the whitish wool on the undersurface of the leaf, and also pale bark of the young trunk.

var. DAVIDIANA (Dode) Schneid. *P. davidiana* Dode—This Chinese aspen was described by Dode from a specimen collected by Père David in the mountains N.E. of Peking, and also occurs in W. China, whence Wilson introduced it to the Arnold Arboretum in 1907. It differs from the common aspen in the smaller, shallower teeth of the leaves, approaching the American *P. tremuloides*, also in its looser, more graceful habit. The full distribution of this variety is not known for certain, but it is said to range as far as Korea and the Amur region. For two other aspens of E. Asia see *P. adenopoda*.

cv. 'ERECTA'.—In the *Gardeners' Chronicle* of 12th June 1926, p. 414, there is mentioned as having been found in the woods of Svalov, Sweden, an aspen of fastigiate growth resembling the Lombardy poplar. It has been introduced to cultivation.

cv. 'PENDULA'. WEEPING ASPEN.—A male form with stiff, pendulous branches, propagated by grafting on *P. canescens*. It produces a great wealth of grey-purplish catkins in February and is one of the most conspicuous and beautiful of early-flowering trees, but is now uncommon.

cv. 'PURPUREA'.—Leaves with a purplish tinge, not very marked. A female tree.

var. VILLOSA (Lang) Wesmael *P. villosa* Lang—Shoots hairy until the second year. Leaves also more persistently downy than in the type. Trees of this character occur quite frequently in the wild.

P. TREMULA × P. TREMULOIDES.—Hybrids of this parentage are used in commercial plantations in Scandinavia, but have proved to be of no value in Britain, where they are subject to bacterial canker (Street, *Exotic Trees in the British Commonwealth*, p. 637).

'HILTINGBURY WEEPING', raised by Messrs Hillier in 1962, is the result of a deliberate cross between *P. tremula* 'Pendula' and *P. tremuloides* 'Pendula'.

P. TREMULOIDES Michx.   AMERICAN ASPEN

P. trepida Willd.; *P. graeca* Loud., not Ait.; *P. atheniensis* K. Koch, not Ludwig

A tree up to 100 ft high in the wild, but never even half that size in this country; trunk slender, paler than in *P. tremula* when young; young shoots reddish brown, glabrous. Leaves 1 to 2½ in. long and wide, very broadly ovate or roundish, with a short, abrupt apex, and a broad, rounded or nearly straight base, very finely toothed, and furnished with fine hairs on the margin, dark glossy green above, pale and dull beneath, glabrous on both sides; stalk slender, two-edged, 1 to 2½ in. long. Catkins 2 to 2½ in. long, more slender than in *P. tremula*.

P. tremuloides is perhaps the most widely distributed tree of N. America, occurring throughout Canada south of the tundra and in most parts of the USA with the exception of the south-east and some of the prairie states. In the west it ranges from N.W. Mexico to Alaska. It is often confused in gardens with the Old World *P. tremula*, from which it differs in characters pointed out under that species. According to Aiton, it was introduced in 1812, but there is some doubt as to this; a poplar grown under the name of *P. graeca*, but identical with

P. tremuloides, is said to have been cultivated in 1779. *P. tremuloides* has never succeeded very well in this country, where it is mainly represented by the following garden variety:

cv. 'PENDULA'. PARASOL DE ST JULIEN.—A pendulous variety. According to a note by M. Ferdinand Cayeux in the *Garden* for 21st January 1886, p. 65, it was found by a foreman in the employ of Messrs Baltet at St Julien, near Troyes, in 1865. It has more slender twigs than the weeping variety of *P. tremula*, but it is a female, and the catkins are not so striking as the male ones of the weeping aspen.

var. VANCOUVERIANA (Trel.) Sarg. *P. vancouveriana* Trel. ex Tidestr.— This variety, a native of British Columbia (including Vancouver Island) and also reported from Washington and Oregon, differs from the typical state in the young shoots being downy and in the leaves being woolly when young. Trelease, who describes it as a tree 15 to 35 ft high, says it is easily distinguished from *P. tremuloides* by the peculiar toothing of the leaves. 'The teeth are much larger than in any of its immediate allies and besides being crenulate are depressed so that each tooth viewed from the edge forms a double curve.'

P. TRICHOCARPA Hook.   BLACK COTTONWOOD

[PLATE 43

A tree often (according to Sargent) 200 ft high in certain parts of its habitat; young trees marked by a slender, pyramidal habit, and by the ultimately smooth, yellow-grey bark; winter-buds coated with fragrant balsamic gum, brown and slender; young shoots slightly angled, furnished at first with a slight down, soon nearly or quite glabrous. Leaves ovate, slightly heart-shaped at the base or broadly wedge-shaped, slender-pointed, finely and shallowly toothed, very variable in size, as much as 8 or 10 in. long, and half as wide on very vigorous leading shoots, down to 2 in. long, and 1 in. wide on lateral twigs, dark lustrous green above, very white and conspicuously net-veined beneath, soon quite smooth on both surfaces; stalk 1 to 2 in. long. Male catkins 2 to 2½ in. long; stamens numerous, mostly thirty to sixty. Female catkins up to 6 in. long; ovaries and capsules hairy, occasionally more or less glabrous; capsules three-valved.

Native of western N. America from S. Alaska to S. California, attaining its greatest size at low elevations in the valleys of British Columbia, Washington, and Oregon. It was first described as a species in 1852, from a specimen collected in Ventura Co., California, but was not introduced to Europe until the end of the century, probably from British Columbia. The type of the species had small, triangular-ovate leaves, somewhat broader than long, and hairy capsules. This variant is confined to California. The cultivated trees belong to the northern race, with larger leaves, longer than broad, and often nearly glabrous capsules. Strictly, this should be distinguished from the Californian type as var. HASTATA (Dode) Henry, though in practice it never is.

P. trichocarpa is undoubtedly the finest of the balsam poplars, if not of all poplars, and the quickest grower of the balsam species. The first tree to be planted at Kew, bought from Späth in 1896, became in thirteen years 55 ft high and about 4 ft in girth. Like so many species from the Pacific North-west, it is well adapted to our oceanic climate and grows well even where the summers are cooler than average and the soil more acid than is to the liking of most poplars. As the leaves unfold in spring they give off the same delicious fragrance as *P. balsamifera*, to which this species is closely allied. Unfortunately the clones of *P. trichocarpa* originally introduced to this country are very susceptible to bacterial canker, but resistant clones should be in commerce shortly (see below).

cv. 'FRITZI PAULEY'.—A fine clone of *P. trichocarpa* from Mt Baker, Washington, which has proved canker-resistant in the trials conducted by the Forestry Commission. Leaves dark green, very silvery beneath, up to 7 in. long, 3 in. or slightly more wide, evenly tapered to an acute point. The example at Alice Holt, *pl.* 1953, measures 80 × 5 ft (1973). Another good clone, which is slightly susceptible to canker, but hardly ever attacked, bears the provisional designation 'CF'. This too has made a fine tree at Alice Holt; the specimen there, also planted in 1953, measures 72 × 5¼ ft (1973).

P. TRISTIS Fisch.

A small tree of the balsam group, with downy, terete shoots. Leaves triangular-ovate, acute at the apex, rounded to slightly cordate at the base, about 4 in. long, 2 in. wide, dark green above, downy on the midrib and main veins and whitish beneath, margins ciliate, finely crenate; petioles downy. Flowers and fruits not seen.

P. tristis was described by Fischer in 1841 from a tree cultivated at St Petersburg (Leningrad) where it is said to be still grown as an ornamental, and to be so hardy that it is able to survive the winters of Murmansk and Verkhoyansk, north of the Arctic Circle (*Arb. Kornickie*, Ybk. IV (1959), pp. 132–3). It is not recognised as a species in the *Flora* of the Soviet Union, nor have matching plants been found in the wild (Elwes and Henry suggested that it might be the same as a poplar found wild at high elevations in the N.W. Himalaya, but Schneider disagreed). Except in the shape of its leaves and its small size, it bears some resemblance to *P. candicans*, another poplar of uncertain origin.

A tree considered to be the true *P. tristis* was introduced to Kew from Späth's nursery in 1896, but it did not thrive; although it made vigorous growths during the summer, they were frequently cut back during the winter, and it never got beyond a few feet high.

P. WILSONII Schneid.

A deciduous tree up to 80 ft high in the wild, of pyramidal shape, with a trunk 2 ft in diameter; young shoots soon glabrous, stout, not angled, olive-brown, becoming brown or purplish the second year; buds shining, slightly viscid. Leaves heart-shaped, bluntish at the apex, minutely toothed; from 3 to 9 in. long, 2½ to 7 in. wide, dull pale green above, pale greyish beneath and soon quite glabrous on both surfaces; stalk up to 6 in. long. Female catkins slender, downy, 3 to 6 in. long; ovary very woolly in the young state; male catkins not seen.

Native of Central and W. China; discovered and introduced by Wilson in 1907. This poplar is related to P. *lasiocarpa*, which is easily distinguished by its downy shoots and bright green leaves with red midrib and stalk. P. *wilsonii* is a fine poplar, with leaves of a notable size, but is rarer in cultivation than its ally P. *lasiocarpa*, partly because it is difficult to raise from cuttings and has to be propagated by grafting. So far as is known there is only one clone in cultivation, which is female.

The following specimens have been recorded: Borde Hill, Sussex, 50 × 3½ ft (est.) (1967); Edinburgh Botanic Garden, 36 × 2 ft (1967); Headfort, Co. Meath, Eire, 60 × 4 ft (1966); Annesgrove, Co. Cork, Eire, 60 × 5 ft (est.) (1968).

P. YUNNANENSIS Dode

A tree with strongly angled, glabrous, pale green (afterwards brown) young shoots; buds not downy, viscid. Leaves obovate-lanceolate to oval-lanceolate, much tapered to the base, more abruptly to the apex; marginal teeth rounded, glandular, bright vivid green above, pale and greyish beneath, glabrous on both surfaces, up to 6 in. long by 3 in. wide; stalk ¼ to ½ in. long. Leaves of this size, shape, etc., are as they occur on vigorous young trees; on older plants they are of ovate shape and often truncate at the base, or slightly cordate. Female catkins 4 to 6 in. long; seed-vessels glabrous.

Native of Yunnan, China. A living plant was sent to L. A. Dode, of Paris, by Père Ducloux some time previous to 1905, and from this the present stock of plants in cultivation was derived. It is one of the balsam poplars and perhaps most nearly allied to P. *simonii*. It never became common in cultivation and is now very rare in this country. It is, however, one of the most ornamental of poplars. There are two examples at Mount Usher, Co. Wicklow, Eire, the larger measuring 51 × 4¾ ft (1966).

POTENTILLA   CINQUEFOIL   ROSACEAE

Of this large genus the vast majority of the species are herbs, but a few are shrubs or subshrubs. Those treated here (with the exception of P. *salesoviana*) belong to the section *Fruticosae*, sometimes separated from *Potentilla* under the name *Dasiphora* or *Pentaphylloides*. These are true shrubs with a peeling bark and persistent stipules. Leaves alternate, pinnate or trifoliolate; leaflets entire. Flowers white, yellow or yellow flushed with red, in cymes or solitary. As in all members of the genus, an outer calyx (epicalyx) is present, consisting of five green bractlets alternating with the five yellowish sometimes red-stained sepals; the bractlets vary in size and shape according to the species and are sometimes divided almost or quite to the base into two or even three segments. Petals five, free. Stamens up to about twenty-five. Gynoecium consisting of numerous carpels inserted on the hemispherical, hairy receptacle; style inserted near the base of the carpel, narrow at the base, widening upward and terminated by a more or less expanded stigma. Each carpel develops into an achene which is hairy at the base and contains a single seed. For the differential characters of *P. salesoviana* see that species.

The section *Fruticosae* is a group of great complexity, difficult to treat taxonomically, and poorly represented in cultivation by plants of authentic wild origin. It has also been little studied. The group is at its most variable in the mountains of Soviet Central Asia, eastern Tibet and western China, where a bewildering array of forms is to be found, all essentially similar to *P. fruticosa*, yet differing from it, and from each other, in numerous minor characters. There is no work devoted to these Asiatic races as a whole. Apart from the treatment of the Russian plants in the *Flora* of the Soviet Union the most important contributions are: H. Handel-Mazzetti, *Act. Hort. Gotoburg.*, Vol. 13 (1939–40), pp. 289–301, and H. R. Fletcher, *Notes Roy. Bot. Gard. Edin.*, Vol. 20 (1950), pp. 207–8, 211–14, 216; H. L. J. Rhodes, *Baileya*, Vol. 2 (1954), pp. 89–96.

There are subshrubby species in other sections of the genus, some of which have been confused with *P. fruticosa* and its allies. *P. fruticosa* var. *inglisii* (Royle) Hook. f. belongs to P. BIFLORA Schlecht., and *P. fruticosa* var. *armerioides* Hook. f. is a variety of *P. biflora*—var. *armerioides* (Hook f.) Hand-Mazz. (syn. *P. articulata* Franch.). *P. biflora* is a prostrate or cushion-forming species of the Himalaya, W. China, Central Asia, etc., and is said to be very beautiful in some forms, but is not established in cultivation so far as is known. It is easily distinguished from *P. fruticosa* by the long, slender, almost terminal style. P. SERICOPHYLLA R. N. Parker, a native of the N.W. Himalaya and Afghanistan, is a dwarf, densely silky shrub with white flowers; style slender, acute at the apex. It is allied to P. LIGNOSA Schlecht., which has a more western distribution and extends into Asiatic Turkey.

P. TRIDENTATA Ait. is in cultivation, but is scarcely shrubby. It is a dwarf cushion plant with trifoliolate leaves, their leaflets toothed at the apex; flowers white. Native of N. America and Greenland.

For cultivation and propagation see the section on garden varieties.

P. ARBUSCULA D. Don

P. nepalensis D. Don, not Hook.; *P. rigida* Wall. ex. Lehm.; *P. rigida* Wall.; *P. fruticosa* var. *arbuscula* (D. Don) Maxim.; *P. fruticosa* var. *rigida* (Lehm.) Maxim.; *P. arbuscula* var. *rigida* (D. Don) Hand.-Mazz.; *P. fruticosa* of many authors, in part, not L.

P. arbuscula is allied to *P. fruticosa*, but both in cultivation and in the herbarium it is quite distinct. The stipules are a more prominent feature of the plant than they are in *P. fruticosa*, being darker in colour, opaque, conspicuously veined and not so closely wrapped round the stem. Although pinnate and with five leaflets in the type of *P. arbuscula*, the leaves are frequently trifoliolate and in some plants wholly so; there is even a form in which the leaves consist of a single leaflet (var. *unifoliolata* Ludlow). The leaflets are relatively broader than in *P. fruticosa*, especially on trifoliolate leaves, where they are broad-elliptic and scarcely more than twice as long as wide. In the typical state the leaflets are coated above with appressed, silky hairs but almost glabrous beneath. A character stressed by the Austrian botanist Handel-Mazzetti is that the venation of the leaflets is more closely meshed than in *P. fruticosa* and the lateral veins less prominent. In cultivated plants of *P. arbuscula* (and often in *P. davurica* also), the hairs are swollen at the base, so that the midribs of the leaflets and the young stems appear to the eye to be covered with 'goose-pimples'. The significance of this peculiarity is uncertain. It has been noted on herbarium specimens of *P. fruticosa* from Asiatic Turkey and Mongolia but does not seem to be a normal feature of that species. In his original description of *P. arbuscula*, Don said that his species differed from *P. fruticosa* in having an outer calyx composed of ten oval-rotund segments instead of five linear ones. This is perhaps not a wholly reliable difference, since the outer calyx segments in *P. fruticosa* are sometimes split, and in *P. arbuscula* they may be single and entire, but the difference would probably hold good for the majority of specimens. The flowers are usually larger than in *P. fruticosa*, sometimes remarkably large, and in cultivated plants the petals are more overlapping and often with crinkled edges. They appear to be hermaphrodite.

P. *arbuscula* is a native of the Himalaya, S.E. Tibet, W. and N. China. It was described by Don in 1825 from a specimen in Lambert's herbarium, sent by Wallich from Nepal. The synonymous name *P. rigida* was given to specimens in Wallich's main collection of Indian plants, catalogued under No. 1009, of which duplicates were distributed to several continental herbaria. Adopting the catalogue-name, Lehmann published a description in 1831, which happened to be based on a specimen which bore trifoliolate leaves only, which explains why the name *P. rigida* (or *P. fruticosa* var. *rigida* (Lehm.) Wolf) has come to be associated with this form, rather than with plants bearing leaves with five leaflets, or a mixture of the two kinds. In the following year Wallich himself published another description made from a plant with both sorts of leaf, but otherwise very similar (*Pl. Asiat. Rar.*, Vol. III, t. 228). The specimens named *P. rigida* represent the form of *P. arbuscula* commonest in Nepal and Kumaon, which makes a robust plant with rather stiff stems (whence, no doubt, the epithet *rigida*). Don's type looks as if it came from an intricately branched plant, and has rather smaller leaves. But only one species is involved.

P. *arbuscula* is mainly represented in gardens by plants from Kingdon Ward's 5774, which was found by him in 1924 on the Temo La and Nam La, making thickets about 2 ft high in the company of dwarf rhododendrons. It was accepted by the Austrian botanist Handel-Mazzetti as a pure *P. arbuscula*, though it disagrees with it in that the venation is not particularly dense and the lateral veins are raised on the underside. But it agrees well enough in other respects, especially the large, conspicuous brown stipules, which on the twigs conceal the internode on the side of their insertion. It is impossible to agree that it belongs to *P. parvifolia*, as has been suggested. It has also been placed under *P. fruticosa*, first as var. *grandiflora* Marquand (not Schlecht.) and later as f. *wardii* Rehd. It could, if thought necessary, be distinguished from typical *P. arbuscula* by transferring Rehder's name to that species. The Kingdon Ward form has been found many times since in S.E. Tibet and extends as far west as Nepal, where specimens with remarkably large flowers have been collected. A similar form occurs in Yunnan. Plants from KW 5774, which have been in commerce since the 1930s, are perfectly hardy and quite free flowering from midsummer, growing to about 3 ft high. The flowers are golden-yellow, about 1¾ in. wide. Award of Merit 1965, after trial at Wisley.

A trifoliolate form of *P. arbuscula* is in cultivation from Stainton, Sykes and Williams 8221, collected in Nepal in 1954. Plants from these seeds bear large, golden or pale yellow flowers rather late in the summer; the leaflets are of firm texture, ⅜ to ⅝ in. long, ¼ to ⅜ in. wide, bright green under the silky hairs. In the trifoliolate form distributed by Messrs Hillier, the leaflets are silvery green above from the dense coating of hairs and of less firm texture. Both forms are worth growing for their foliage alone.

var. ALBICANS (Rehd. & Wils.) Hand.-Mazz. *P. fruticosa* var. *albicans* Rehd. & Wils.—Described as having the leaves laxly appressed hairy above, white and silky-tomentose beneath. The type was a cultivated plant raised from seed sent by Wilson to the Arnold Arboretum from the Tatsien-lu (Kangting) area of W. Szechwan under W.1213a. The foliage was said to resemble that of 'Vilmoriniana' (q.v. in the section on garden varieties). The wild-collected specimen in the Kew Herbarium under W.1213a is typical *P. arbuscula*, but there are specimens from the same region collected by Père Soulié and by Pratt which have the leaves silky on both sides and probably represent var. *albicans*. It has also been collected in Bhutan. The garden clone 'Beesii' (q.v.) is near to var. *albicans*.

var. BULLEYANA Balf. f. ex Fletcher—Described as having leaves glabrous above and both white-tomentose and silky beneath. Found by Forrest in Yunnan and introduced by him, during his first expedition for A. K. Bulley. The plant in cultivation under this name has remarkable foliage: the leaves have five leaflets of firm texture, which are broad-elliptic and up to ¾ in. long, half as wide; they are densely silky and white beneath, but the upper surface is fairly densely appressed silky—sufficiently to give the foliage a silvery aspect in dry weather. It could just as well be referred to var. *albicans*. The flowers are deep yellow, about 1½ in. wide.

P. DAVURICA Nestl.

Dasiphora davurica (Nestl.) Komar. & Klob.-Alis.; *P. glabrata* Schlecht.; *Pentaphylloides glabrata* (Schlecht.) Schwarz; *P. glabra* Lodd.; *P. fruticosa* var. *davurica* (Nestl.) Ser.

A deciduous shrub up to 4 ft high, with a shreddy bark; young stems hairy; stipules brown, ovate or ovate-lanceolate, acute, more or less glabrous except for a tuft of hairs at the apex. Leaves with usually five leaflets, arranged as in *P. fruticosa*; leaflets of firm texture, oblong-elliptic or oblong-obovate, about ⅜ in. long, mucronate at the apex, glabrous on both sides except for scattered hairs on the margins, dark green and lustrous above, undersides with a dense venation as in *P. arbuscula*, the midrib and laterals not prominent. Flowers white (or sometimes pale yellow), ¾ to 1¼ in. wide, solitary, in few-flowered cymes, or occasionally in cymose panicles; pedicels hairy. Bractlets of outer calyx elliptic

or obovate, shorter than the sepals. Other floral characters as in *P. fruticosa*.
Bot. Mag., t. 3676.

Native of Russia from E. Siberia to the Pacific, N. and W. China, E. and S.E.
Tibet; introduced in 1822 by Loddiges, who received seeds from St Petersburg.
In its typical, glabrous state *P. davurica* is rare in cultivation, but there is a very
dwarf, compact form in commerce which agrees well with it but rarely flowers.
It is allied to *P. arbuscula*, both species typically having relatively broad leaflets
with a closely meshed venation. But both species have forms or varieties in
which this character is lacking. As in *P. arbuscula*, the hairs on the midrib
beneath, petiole and stem, when present, often have a swollen base.

The plants called 'Farrer's White', of which there are at least two clones, were
raised from seeds collected by Farrer in S.W. Kansu, probably under his field
number 460. These differ from typical *P. davurica* in having the leaflets sparsely
hairy, rather thin, with a lax venation. A form of *P. davurica* introduced by Purdom from Shensi is also not typical but approaches the var. *veitchii*—the name
under which it is figured in *Bot. Mag.*, t. 8637.

In Yunnan and in other parts of W. China and S.E. Tibet a form of *P. davurica*
occurs in which the calyx is brilliantly suffused with red. This variant was named
var. *rhodocalyx* (under *P. glabra*), but unfortunately this name is illegitimate for
technical reasons. In some Yunnan plants the red calyx is combined with a
nodding, bell-shaped flower—a character beautifully captured by Forrest's
specimen 23117 in the Kew Herbarium. Cultivated plants of this form, believed
to have been raised from Forrest 28574, show the red calyx quite well in some
seasons, but it is not a constant character. Some of these plants have the flowers
cream-coloured when they first expand and in (*P. glabra* var. *rhodocalyx*) 'RUTH'
they keep that colour even when open. Such plants could be referable to *P.* ×
sulphurascens (see below), but they do not show any other sign of hybridity.
We are not obliged to assume that *P. davurica* invariably has pure white flowers.

var. MANDSHURICA (Maxim.) Wolf *P. fruticosa* var. *mandshurica* Wolf;
P. glabra var. *mandshurica* (Maxim.) Hand.-Mazz.; *Dasiphora mandshurica* (Maxim.)
Juz.—A dwarf shrub with leaves resembling those of the type in texture and
venation but with somewhat wider leaflets, which are coated on both sides with
appressed silky hairs. It was described from Olga Bay, near Vladivostok, in
1873, but had been found by the Kew collector Charles Wilford in 1859 farther
up the coast. In the Wilford specimen the leaflets of the lower pair are ½ in.
long, ¼ in. wide. This variety is not confined to the coast. It was collected by
Komarov on the upper Yalu river in N.E. China, and according to Handel-
Mazzetti plants matching the Wilford specimen occur in Korea, and in China as
far south as the Muli region of S.W. Szechwan. In *Plantae Wilsonianae*, it is said to
be not uncommon in the dry valleys of N.W. Szechwan, but the specimen cited
—W.3172—is very different from typical var. *mandshurica*, judging from the
duplicate in the British Museum. See also 'Manchu', in the section on garden
varieties.

The status of Makino's *P. fruticosa* var. *leucantha* is uncertain. It occurs in
Japan in Shikoku, where it is the only shrubby cinquefoil, and also on the main
island. Rehder places it under var. *mandshurica*, to which it is near geographically.

var. SUBALBICANS (Hand.-Mazz.) *P. glabra* var. *subalbicans* (Hand.-Mazz.)
Hand-Mazz.; *P. fruticosa* var. *subalbicans* Hand.-Mazz.—A robust variety of

P. davurica with short-stalked flowers borne numerously in dense cymes; bractlets of outer calyx mostly oblong-lanceolate and longer than in typical *P. davurica*. In the type (Licent 4100 from Kansu), the leaves are silky above and coated beneath with a very dense silky tomentum. There are plants in cultivation which agree with this variety in flower and inflorescence, but not in their foliage, which is only sparsely hairy. One is grown as *P. fruticosa* var. *hersii* (an unpublished name) and the other actually as *P. fruticosa* var. *subalbicans*. Both have broad, dark green leaflets, with the close venation of typical *P. davurica*, and are free-flowering. The former was presumably raised from seeds collected by the Belgian engineer Joseph Hers.

f. TERNATA (Cardot) *P. fruticosa* var. *davurica* f. *ternata* Cardot; *P. glabra* f. *ternata* (Cardot) Hand.-Mazz.; *P. fruticosa* var. *tangutica* Wolf, *teste* Hand.-Mazz. —Leaves trifoliolate. Calyx sometimes flushed with red. Described from a specimen collected by the French missionary Soulié on the Mekong–Salween divide. Handel-Mazzetti gives *P. fruticosa* var. *tangutica* Wolf as a synonym—a variety described from specimens collected in Kansu and N.E. Tibet, with trifoliolate leaves and large flowers with a red-tinged calyx. Wolf supposed the flowers to be yellow, and it may be that he was right, since similar plants with yellow flowers have been collected in S.E. Tibet and could represent either a yellow-flowered form of *P. davurica* or a glabrous form of *P. arbuscula*. However, Handel-Mazzetti saw Wolf's type-specimens and concluded that at least one definitely had white flowers.

var. VEITCHII (Wils.) Jesson *P. veitchii* Wils.; *P. glabra* var. *veitchii* (Wils.) Hand.-Mazz.; *P. fruticosa* var. *veitchii* (Wils.) Bean—Leaflets hairy on both sides, as in var. *mandshurica*, but not so firm in texture and with the lateral veins prominent on the undersurface. The bractlets of the outer calyx are longer than in typical *P. davurica* and its Manchurian variety, about equalling the calyx in length. It is also more robust, growing to about 5 ft in height. The var. *veitchii* is a native of W. Hupeh, China, introduced by Wilson during his first expedition for Messrs Veitch, and was described by him, as a species, from a plant growing in Veitch's nursery, raised from his seed-number 1087 (corresponding to specimen W.2187). It also occurs in W. Szechwan, but some of Wilson's collections there, referred to the var. *veitchii* in *Plantae Wilsonianae*, seem to be less distinct from typical *P. davurica*.

Cultivated plants have flowers about ¼ in. wide, saucer-shaped when they first open; they are produced over a long period from later spring but never in great quantity, at least in the form available in commerce.

NOTE. *P. davurica* Nestl. (or *P. fruticosa* var. *davurica* (Nestl.) Ser.) is the name that was accepted by all botanists for the species treated here, until Handel-Mazzetti pointed out, in 1940, that Nestler had described the flowers (from an herbarium specimen) as yellow, while in *P. davurica* as generally understood they are white. He adopted for this species the name *P. glabra* Lodd. It is a frequent source of difficulty in this group that the petals, whether originally yellow or white, usually turn eventually in herbarium specimens to a dingy yellowish colour. Nestler's description, apart from the discrepancy over flower-colour, agrees perfectly well with the white-flowered species and his name is therefore retained here. It was published in the first half of 1816. The synony-

mous name *P. glabrata* Schlecht., also rejected by Handel-Mazzetti, was published some time in the same year, not in 1813 as stated in the *Index Kewensis*.
It may be added that Maximowicz accepted plants with pale yellow flowers as
part of the normal variation of the species.

P. × SULPHURASCENS Hand.-Mazz.—This putative hybrid was described
by Handel-Mazzetti from a specimen he himself collected in Yunnan S.E. of
Chungtien in 1914. It had flowers of a very pale sulphur colour, more campanulate than in *P. arbuscula* but less so than in the form of *P. davurica* growing
nearby. He took it to be a hybrid between the two.

P. × VILMORINIANA (Komar.) Konken *P. fruticosa* var. *vilmoriniana*
Komar.—A supposed hybrid between *P. arbuscula* and *P. davurica* raised by
Vilmorin from seeds received from Szechwan, China, in 1905. For a description,
see the section on garden varieties. The cultivated plant, which is almost certainly authentic, is hexaploid and, except in flower-colour, resembles *P. arbuscula*
var. *albicans*.

P. FRUTICOSA L.   SHRUBBY CINQUEFOIL
Dasiphora fruticosa (L.) Rydb.; *Pentaphylloides fruticosa* (L.) Schwarz

A deciduous shrub up to 3 or 4 ft high, sometimes prostrate or procumbent;
bark shreddy, brown or purplish brown when first exposed; young stems hairy;
stipules persistent, membranous, acute, sheathing part of the internode above
the leaf-insertion. Leaves odd-pinnate, with normally five leaflets, the upper
pair decurrent onto the rachis on the lower side; leaflets linear-oblong, oblong-
elliptic, or slightly lanceolate, acute, the terminal sometimes oblanceolate and
obtuse, mostly ⅜ to 1 in. long, average ratio of length to breadth about 4 : 1,
but sometimes 6 : 1 in forms with exceptionally narrow-elongate leaflets, margins entire, usually somewhat revolute, upper surface thinly coated, at least
when young, with a few long, spreading hairs, dull medium green, sea-green or
glaucous green, undersides paler, with spreading white hairs on the midrib and
main veins, in some forms more densely hairy, especially beneath; petiole sparsely
hairy, up to about ½ in. long. Flowers unisexual or hermaphrodite (see below),
up to 1 in. or slightly more wide, borne May to August in cymes, sometimes
solitary. Bractlets of outer calyx green, linear-elliptic, linear-oblong, or linear-
oblanceolate, but sometimes broader and bifurcate, about as long as the sepals
or slightly longer, tending to enlarge during flowering. Sepals yellowish or
greenish, triangular-ovate, acuminate. Petals bright yellow, more or less orbicular, with a short claw. Stamens about twenty-five, with yellow, ovate anthers.
Carpels numerous, buried at the base in the silky hairs of the receptacle; style
widening upward from a narrow base, with an expanded stigma. Achenes hairy.

 P. fruticosa is to be found throughout the colder parts of the northern hemisphere, but is absent from most of E. Asia (except the north-eastern part) and
has a patchy distribution in Europe. In the British Isles outside Ireland its main
stands are in upper Teesdale, but in the time of John Ray, who first recorded it
in 1670, it reached downstream to some miles below Egglestone Abbey and
also occurred on the River Greta near Brignall. It also inhabits crevices and rock-

ledges in two localities in the Lake District—The Pillar in Ennerdale and the Wastdale Screes. It has also been recorded from the Red Screes of Helvellyn. In Ireland its best-known occurrence is on the Burren in N.W. Clare, where it grows in damp hollows on the limestone pavement, but is found in a few other localities farther west and also around Lough Corrib in Galway and E. Mayo (Raven and Walters, *Mountain Flowers*, pp. 104–7; Elkington and Woodell, 'Biological Flora of the British Isles: Potentilla fruticosa L.' in *Journ. Ecol.*, Vol. 51 (1963), pp. 769–81).

Linnaeus knew of this species at first only as an English plant, but he suspected that it would prove to be a native of the island of Öland in his native Sweden (*Hort. Cliff.* (1738), p. 193). He found it there a few years later, on June 4 (o.s.), 1741. 'The "tok", as it is called in Öland, is a bush that is extremely rare in the world, for hitherto botanists have seen it only in York in England, and recently in Siberia, and now in south Öland. . . . It grew in tussocks in the *alvar*-land, beside low places where water stays the whole winter. It is as big as lavender or hyssop, has yellow flowers and sheds the outer bark layer every year.' (Öland and Gotland Journey, transl. M. Asberg and W. T. Stearn, in *Biol. Journ. Linn. Soc.*, Vol. 5 (1973), p. 56.) In the same work Linnaeus defines *alvar*-land: '. . . it is a low table-land, all dry, bare and sterile; the bedrock is a red limestone which is partly covered with earth a finger deep, partly bare' (loc. cit., p. 48). *P. fruticosa* also occurs on the island of Gotland and on the eastern side of the Baltic.

In Europe outside the British Isles and the Baltic region *P. fruticosa* is a curiously rare plant. It occurs here and there in the Pyrenees and in one locality in the Alpes Maritimes above St Martin-Vésubie. To find it again as a wild plant one must go east to the Rhodopi Mountains of Bulgaria. Farther east it is found in the Caucasus and bordering parts of Turkey, and in the Urals (where its area is fragmented). Beyond the Urals it extends to the Bering Straits, and on the American continent it ranges from Alaska to the Atlantic and southward through the Rockies and the mountains of California as far as New Mexico; in the east its southern limit is in New Jersey.

P. fruticosa has been divided into two subspecies (Elkington, in *New Phytologist*, Vol. 68, pp. 151–60). In the typical subspecies (subsp. *fruticosa*) the plants are dioecious, i.e., the flowers are effectively unisexual and the males and females are borne on separate plants. Usually the female flowers have well-developed anthers, but these are sterile. In males, carpels are usually not produced at all. A further characteristic of this subspecies is that the plants examined have all proved to be tetraploid, i.e., with twice the normal number of chromosomes in their body-cells. To this subspecies belong the plants of the British Isles and Baltic region. The other subspecies is:

subsp. FLORIBUNDA (Pursh) Elkington *P. floribunda* Pursh—It has long been known that *P. fruticosa* in North America bears hermaphrodite flowers, differing in that respect from the typical state of the species. Recently it has been shown that plants from as far apart as Nova Scotia and Alaska are diploid, i.e., with the normal complement of chromosomes (Bowden, *Journ. Arn. Arb.*, Vol. 38 (1957), p. 381). The interesting discovery has also been made that European plants from the Pyrenees and from the Rhodopi mountains of Bulgaria are also diploid and hermaphrodite (Elkington, *New Phytologist*, Vol. 68

(1969), pp. 151–60). Elkington has accordingly united these south European plants with those of North America under the above name, which is founded on one given provisionally by Pursh in 1814 to plants from Canada and New England which appeared to be distinct from *P. fruticosa* in various characters. Plants from Asiatic Turkey are referred to the subsp. *floribunda* in *Flora of Turkey*, Vol. 4, p. 45, on the grounds that the flowers are functionally hermaphrodite, though the chromosome status of these is not known. The status of plants from Siberia and N.E. Asia is undecided.

P. fruticosa also varies in habit, relative width of leaflets, density of indumentum, size of flower, and the number of flowers in each cyme. Whether any of the variations deserve taxonomic recognition can only be decided by detailed research. The following varieties are of no account, but details are given here since the names appear frequently in botanical and horticultural literature:

var. GRANDIFLORA Schlecht.—Flowers larger than normal; leaves broad-oblong, almost glabrous on both sides. Described from a specimen in Willdenow's herbarium, taken from a garden plant.

f. MICRANDRA (Koehne) Schneid. *P. micrandra* Koehne—Described by Koehne in 1896, apparently from a plant cultivated at St Petersburg as *Potentilla* 'new species', though the specimens he distributed came from plants in Späth's nursery, Berlin. It was said to differ from *P. fruticosa* in its dwarf habit and small anthers and was considered by Koehne to be matched by a specimen in the Royal Herbarium, Berlin, collected in Japan by Tschonoski. It was probably, as Schneider thought, nothing but a female plant of *P. fruticosa*. Plants cultivated on the continent as *P. fruticosa* 'Micrandra' have not been seen, but judging from the descriptions they are not the same as Koehne's plant. In this the flowers were of normal size, whereas in 'Micrandra' they are said to be very small.

var. PYRENAICA Schlecht. *P. prostrata* Lapeyr.; *P. fruticosa* var. *prostrata* (Lapeyr.) Gautier—Plants from high altitudes in the Pyrenees are sometimes of more or less prostrate habit and have been called var. *pyrenaica* or var. *prostrata*, but similar plants occur throughout the range of the species. The Pyrenean plants belong to the subsp. *floribunda* (see above). For the plants cultivated as *P. fruticosa* 'Pyrenaica', see 'Farreri Prostrata' in the section on garden varieties. These plants were also known in gardens as "var. *prostrata*" and acquired the erroneous cultivar name 'Pyrenaica' through confusion between var. *prostrata* Hort. and var. *prostrata* (Lapeyr.) Gautier (see synonyms above).

var. TENUILOBA Ser. *P. tenuifolia* Schlecht.; *P. fruticosa* var. *tenuifolia* (Ser.) Lehm. (the last-named variety has the same circumscription as var. *tenuiloba* Ser., but Lehman reverted to the epithet *tenuifolia* originally used by Schlechtendal).—This name (or var. *tenuifolia*) has been used for plants with narrower, more hairy leaflets than normal, some of them American, others probably belonging to the typical subspecies. According to Handel-Mazzetti, the type-sheet of *P. tenuifolia* also includes a specimen of *P. parvifolia*. Plants distributed commercially as *P. fruticosa* var. *tenuifolia* are typical *P. fruticosa*.

P. fruticosa has been in cultivation since the latter part of the 17th century but is little seen at the present time, having been displaced in gardens by allied species from China and the Himalaya and by various hybrids, with neater foliage and more striking flowers borne over a longer period. But it still deserves to be grown, as one of the most interesting of European shrubs. The best collection of *P. fruticosa* can be seen in the University Botanic Garden, Cambridge, where there are plants from North America (three localities), the British Isles (the Burren, the Pillar, Teesdale), and from Öland. The last is by far the most ornamental.

P. PARVIFOLIA Fisch. ex Lehm.
P. fruticosa var. *parvifolia* (Lehm.) Wolf; *Dasiphora parvifolia* (Lehm.) Juz.

A dwarf deciduous shrub allied to *P. fruticosa*. The leaves are small, usually not more than 1 in. long including the petiole, with commonly seven leaflets, the lowermost four inserted at the same point and forming a whorl (as sometimes, though not regularly, in *P. fruticosa*); they are linear or linear-lanceolate, acute, usually strongly revolute, grey-green above, hairy on both sides and often very densely so and white beneath. Flowers small, normally not much over $\frac{1}{2}$ in. wide, borne on long, slender pedicels; bractlets of outer calyx linear-lanceolate, equalling or shorter than the sepals.

P. parvifolia was described in 1831 from a cultivated plant, introduced to the St Petersburg Botanic Garden from the region of Central Asia known as Dzungaria. It also occurs in other parts of Central Asia, in Siberia, and probably in the inner ranges of Kashmir and Pakistan. It is not in cultivation in this country in its typical state, so far as is known, and is not represented in the Kew Herbarium by an authentic specimen. The above account is based on Lehmann's original diagnosis and figure, and on the description by Juzepchuk in the *Flora* of the Soviet Union. In the latter work it is acknowledged that *P. parvifolia* is a very variable species, and three 'races' are described, differing from the typical race in various characters.

The cultivated plants, which are from western China, may belong to *P. parvifolia* in the broad sense, but they are not typical, and may represent another race of the species. The leaves are bright green above, bluish or greyish beneath, only slightly hairy; the leaflets are obtuse or subacute, not or scarcely revolute, and often they are in fives. The flowers are $\frac{7}{8}$ to 1 in. wide, sometimes larger, solitary or in condensed cymes. They are certainly very distinct from *P. fruticosa*, more so perhaps than is typical *P. parvifolia*, with which, however, they agree in their small leaves and leaflets, the latter usually in sevens.

These cultivated plants mostly derive from seeds collected by Reginald Farrer in S.W. Kansu in 1914 (No. 188), but this sending also included seeds taken from what may have been a hybrid swarm between *P. parvifolia* and *P. davurica*. 'The deep golden type passes into the pure white by innumerable gradations of cream, amber, citron and butter-yellow—intermediate forms or hybrids; seed sent out embraces all these . . .' (Farrer, *The English Rock Garden*, Vol. II, p. 510). The plants raised from Farrer 188 showed a similar range of colour, except that no whites were produced, but those that have been perpetuated in commerce have bright yellow flowers and show no sign of hybridity. Their naming in gardens is confused. Some bear clonal names, others are called *P. fruticosa* var. *parvifolia* or *P. fruticosa* var. *farreri* (a name attributed to Besant but not supported by a description). See further in the section on garden varieties ('Farreri Prostrata', 'Klondike', and 'Gold Drop'). A fine form of *P. parvifolia* was introduced by Purdom from Shensi (see 'William Purdom' in the same section).

In Yunnan, and on the frontier between that province and Burma, Forrest found a form of *P. parvifolia* with flowers described by him as 'deep orange', 'deep chrome-orange', or 'deep ruddy orange'. Seeds were sent by him on at least three occasions, and possibly also by Farrer during his expedition to upper Burma. Whether all the plants in a stand had flowers of this colour or just the odd one here and there is not clear from Forrest's field-notes. There is no record of a plant raised from the wild seeds producing flowers of the colour described, but it did emerge in a later generation (see 'Tangerine' in the section on garden varieties). A plant in cultivation as Forrest's form of *P. fruticosa* is very like the forms of *P. parvifolia* from Kansu except that the foliage is darker, the leaflets are always in fives, and the flowers are larger. Some specimens collected by Forrest in Yunnan and identified as *P. parvifolia* appear to be nearer to *P. arbuscula*.

P. × REHDERIANA Hand.-Mazz. *P. fruticosa* var. *purdomii* Rehd. (not *P. purdomii* N. E. Brown)—The plant described by Rehder as *P. fruticosa* var. *purdomii* was raised from seeds collected by Purdom in Shensi in 1911 under his number 848. It was considered by Handel-Mazzetti to be a hybrid between *P. parvifolia* and *P. davurica* (*glabra*) var. *mandshurica*. In raising the taxonomic status of this plant, he had to alter the epithet, since the name *P. purdomii* had been published by N. E. Brown in 1914 for an herbaceous species. This putative hybrid is not in cultivation in Britain, so far as is known, or at least not in commerce. For *P. fruticosa* 'Purdomii' of gardens, see 'William Purdom' in the section on garden varieties.

P. SALESOVIANA Stephan
Comarum salesowianum (Stephan) Aschers. & Graebn.

A deciduous shrub of lax habit, 3 to 4 ft high, making coarse, erect, reddish growths, but little branched, silky, half covered with the large silvery stipules. Leaves pinnate, 2 to 4 in. long; leaflets five to nine, shortly stalked, oblong, ¾ to 1½ in. long, ¼ to ⅝ in. wide, increasing in size towards the end of the leaf, with broad angular teeth, dark green and glabrous above, grey-woolly beneath. Flowers rosy-tinted white, produced in June and July at the summit of a long-stalked corymb 4 to 6 in. high, each of the three to seven flowers 1½ in. across; petals obovate; calyx-lobes lanceolate, and as long as the petals, the five bracts smaller, linear, and about half as long, very downy.

Native of W. Siberia, Central Asia, Mongolia, N.W. China, Tibet, and the Himalaya; introduced in 1823. This species is very distinct from the other shrubby species in cultivation in its larger, more numerous, toothed leaflets, and in its coarser growths, which are hollow and die back considerably in winter. It belongs to the subgenus *Comarum*, which is treated as a separate genus by some botanists, on the ground that the receptacle becomes spongy in the fruiting stage, instead of remaining dry as is normally the case in *Potentilla*. The marsh cinquefoil (*P. palustris*), which is widespread in the northern hemisphere (including Britain), also belongs to this group.

With regard to its cultivation, Farrer wrote: '. . . it has been at Ingleborough these ten years, and has there in the fat, comfortable place assigned to it once produced (I think) one flower. But from what Purdom tells me I learn that P. Salesoviana requires quite other treatment, and requites it. For it is a plant confined to river shingles and suchlike barren, hungry places: there, as Purdom saw it, the bloom is free, and its effect of remarkable beauty. Let all those, then, who have P. Salesoviana immediately learn its true character by putting it on hunger-strike' (*Gard. Chron.*, Vol. 59 (1916), p. 100). Purdom saw it during his expedition to Kansu with Farrer, when he went off on his own to the Kokonor.

GARDEN VARIETIES AND HYBRIDS

The clones described below are those most widely available in commerce at the present time (1974). Some of these are of garden origin; others derive from seeds sent home by collectors from western China. In catalogues it is usual to list all the clones under *P. fruticosa* and this is not wholly incorrect, since the allied species recognised here—*P. arbuscula*, *P. davurica*, and *P. parvifolia*—have been treated as varieties of *P. fruticosa* by some botanists. But it should be remarked that none of the clones described below belongs to *P. fruticosa* in the narrow sense, with the possible exception of 'Jackman's Variety' and 'Goldfinger'.

The shrubby potentillas are among the most valuable of small shrubs, growing well in any moderately fertile soil and flowering over a period of many months. The start and duration of the display depends on the season and to some extent on the variety. Those that are of bushy habit—as most are, with the notable exception of 'Vilmoriniana'—make excellent weed-smotherers, and some of the larger sorts could be used to make a dwarf hedge.

Not so long ago it could have been said that the shrubby potentillas are free of serious pests and diseases, but in recent years some have suffered from a disorder that causes the petals to wither in the bud. 'Elizabeth' seems to be the worst sufferer. It is thought that Red Spider mite may be the cause of this trouble, and in view of this possibility it would be as well to cut affected plants heavily in early spring and later to spray them with some modern insecticide known to be effective against this pest, e.g., malathion. 'Elizabeth' is also subject to mildew.

Flowering as they do on the young shoots, the shrubby potentillas may be pruned quite hard in early spring, but such treatment delays the first flush of flowers and is certainly not necessary. It is more important to cut out old stems periodically to make room for new growth from the base.

The usual method of propagation is by soft-wooded cuttings, which are best taken in early summer. Cuttings of harder wood will also root, but the plants do not develop so quickly.

'BEESII' ('Nana Argentea').—Flowers buttercup-yellow, about $\frac{3}{4}$ in. wide, in few-flowered cymes, producing stamens only. Leaves with three or five leaflets, the lateral ones elliptic, about $\frac{7}{16}$ in. long, silvery above from the coating of appressed silky hairs, papillose beneath and with spreading hairs on the midrib and main veins; venation dense; hairs with swollen bases. Slow-growing but eventually 2 ft high and more in width. Put into commerce by Messrs Bees, who raised it from seed collected in China. It belongs to *P. arbuscula*, probably to var. *albicans*. A.M.T. 1966.

'ELIZABETH' ("*Arbuscula*").—Flowers rich, soft yellow, up to 1¾ in. in diameter, very pale on the back of the petals, borne in condensed cymes; segments of outer calyx mostly broad-spatulate and about as long as the sepals. Leaflets five, obtuse, shortly mucronate, the lateral ones more or less elliptic, ½ to ⅝ in. long, sparsely covered with appressed silky hairs above, densely coated beneath with erect or spreading hairs, which, like those on the petioles and stems, have a swollen base. Of bushy habit, to about 3 ft high, flowering at the end of every shoot for about five months, and one of the most delightful and useful of dwarf shrubs, though rather subject to mildew (and see the remarks in the introductory note). A.M.T. 1965.

The origin of 'Elizabeth' has not been ascertained. It was originally grown as "*P. arbuscula*" and has been in commerce under that name since the 1950s or perhaps earlier. It was named 'Elizabeth' by Messrs Hillier, but it is possible that this name is now used for two very similar clones. 'Elizabeth' is probably a hybrid between *P. arbuscula* and *P. davurica* var. *veitchii*. See also 'Longacre'.

'FARRERI PROSTRATA' ("*Pyrenaica*").—This name covers two clones descending from plants raised from Farrer's Kansu seed. One (not seen) is described as being completely prostrate, with rather small flowers, the other low and spreading, about 1½ ft high, 3 ft wide, with flowers about 1¼ in. wide, buttercup-yellow in both cases. Neither is common in cultivation. For the name "Pyrenaica" see *P. fruticosa* var. *pyrenaica*.

'FRIEDRICHSENII' ('Berlin Beauty').—A putative hybrid raised in Späth's nurseries from seeds of a plant of *P. davurica* (*glabra*) growing in the Copenhagen Botanic Garden, and described by Koehne in 1896. He considered the pollen-parent to have been *P. fruticosa*, which seems very likely. Several plants were raised, so the name is not clonal, but according to Koehne they were all very similar. 'Friedrichsenii' is little cultivated in this country and is inferior to 'Moonlight'. It makes a large shrub, with leaves resembling those of *P. fruticosa* but lighter green, plane, with the lateral veins scarcely raised beneath. Flowers light yellow. The plant examined by Bowden (op. cit.) was diploid, so the pollen parent must have belonged to the subsp. *floribunda*; typical *P. fruticosa* would produce a triploid.

'OCHROLEUCA' is a seedling of 'Friedrichsenii', raised by Späth, described as having creamy-white flowers and bright green leaves. Plants seen in cultivation under this name have flowers coloured as in typical 'Friedrichsenii'. Späth also raised and propagated a white-flowered seedling—'BEANII' (*P. fruticosa friedrichsenii leucantha* Späth; *P. fruticosa* var. *leucantha* Bean, not Mak.; *P. fruticosa* f. *beanii* Rehd.). It is doubtful whether the true clone is in commerce here.

'GOLD DROP'.—Flowers about ⅞ in. across in few-flowered cymes, the later crop borne on growths which overtop the first flush. Segments of outer calyx slender, Leaflets bright green, mostly in sevens, sparsely hairy, bluish green beneath, more or less elliptic, about ⅜ in. long. Stipules mostly shorter than the petioles, brown. Dwarf, bushy habit. It was originally grown as *P. fruticosa farreri* and was correctly given a distinguishing clonal name in the USA. See further under *P. parvifolia*.

'JACKMAN'S VARIETY'.—Flowers bright yellow, 1¼ to 1½ in. wide, borne numerously in cymes on shoots from the upper leaf axils, on pedicels ⅝ to ¾ in. long; segments of epicalyx narrow-elliptic or sometimes wider and bifurcate. Leaves bluish green above, rather coarse, leaflets often seven, the lower four whorled, up to almost 1 in. long and ¼ in. or slightly more wide. A vigorous large shrub to 4 ft high, more in width. The original plant was found in the nursery of Messrs. Jackman in a row of shrubby potentillas grown under the name *P. fruticosa grandiflora*, and was presumably a self-sown seedling. The parental stock was discarded, so no comparison can be made. F.C.C.T. 1965.

'GOLDFINGER', of recent introduction, is very similar to 'Jackman's Variety' but the flowers are larger, up to 1¾ in. or even slightly more wide. Both plants appear to be forms of *P. fruticosa*, not hybrids.

'KATHERINE DYKES'.—Flowers canary-yellow, 1 in. or slightly more wide, in small condensed cymes, very freely produced. Leaflets medium green with a slight glaucous tinge, with five or seven leaflets about ½ in. long, sparsely hairy on both sides. Habit dense, to about 4 ft high, 5 ft wide. Deservedly one of the most popular of the group, this shrub occurred as a self-sown seedling in the garden of W. R. Dykes, and is named after his wife. After the wife's death, Mrs Gwendolyn Anley was given the choice of one plant from the garden, and chose this. It received an Award of Merit when she showed it in 1944. It is possibly *P. parvifolia* (from N.W. China) crossed with *P.* × *friedrichsenii* (the latter entered into the parentage according to Mrs Anley's recollection (*Journ. R.H.S.*, Vol. 71 (1946), p. 101).

'KLONDIKE'.—Flowers 1½in. wide, deep bright yellow, in dense cymes, tending to become convex as they age; segments of outer calyx linear or oblong-elliptic. Leaflets mostly in fives, bright green above, blue-green beneath, up to ⅝ in. long. Raised by Kruyt of Boskoop, Holland, from *P. parvifolia* var. *farreri* and showing no signs of hybridity, though the flowers are unusually large. It is taller-growing than 'Gold Drop'. A.M.T. 1965.

'LONGACRE'.—Resembling 'Elizabeth', but of lower, more spreading habit, the stems more slender, the foliage a trifle darker, and the flowers not so cupped when they first open. It arose in Northern Ireland as a self-sown seedling in the garden after which it is named, and was put into commerce by the Slieve Donard nurseries. A.M.T. 1965.

'MANCHU' ("*Mandshurica*"). Flowers white, up to 1¼ in. wide, scantily borne over a long period; segments of outer calyx more or less elliptic, acute, or sometimes broader at the apex and bifurcate, Leaflets five, elliptic, ⅜ in. or slightly more long, silky-hairy above, more densely so beneath, lateral veins and cross-veins stout, prominent; hairs swollen at the base, giving to the midrib a decidedly warty appearance. A dense shrub of mounded habit, not much over 1 ft high. It appears to be a dwarf form of *P. davurica* var. *veitchii*, possibly introduced by Wilson. It does not belong to *P. davurica* var. *mandshurica* (*P. fruticosa* var. *mandshurica* Maxim.).

'MOONLIGHT' ('Maanelys').—Flowers about 1¼ in. wide, soft yellow, fading as they age but remaining darker at the centre; segments of the outer calyx oblanceolate, as long as the sepals, enlarging during flowering, often split. Leaflets mostly five, the laterals elliptic, ½ to ⅝ in. long, soft grey-green and silky above, underside whitish, hairy on the veins; hairs swollen at the base. A large, fairly dense shrub 4 to 5 ft high, 8 ft wide, well furnished to the base, flowering from May to July (to September in a good season). Raised in Denmark.

'PRIMROSE BEAUTY'.—Flowers about 1⅜ in. wide, pale primrose with a deeper centre, cup-shaped, flattening and paling as they age, few in each cyme. Leaflets five, those of the lower pair rather broadly elliptic or slightly obovate, up to ½ in. long and ¼ in. wide, grey-green and very silky above, undersides densely hairy, papillose; hairs with thickened bases. Of dense, picturesque habit, up to 4 or 5 ft high and 6 ft or so in width. Raised by Cannegieter of Hattem, Holland. It shows some affinity with 'Vilmoriniana', but is a far better garden plant and perhaps the finest of all the garden hybrids. A.M.T. 1965.

'SANDVED' ('Sandvedana').—Flowers ivory-white, about 1⅜ in. wide, short-stalked. Leaflets mostly in fives, sparsely hairy, pale grey-green beneath, about ¾ in. long, rather narrow. A bushy shrub to about 3 ft high, raised in Norway.

'TANGERINE'.—Flowers 1¼ in. wide, medium yellow more or less flushed with orange-red or sometimes evenly coloured tangerine red; segments of outer calyx oblanceolate-spatulate, as long as the sepals. Leaflets five, sometimes seven, oblong-elliptic or oblanceolate, obtuse, about ½ in. long, medium green above, grey-green beneath, sparsely hairy on both sides. A low, spreading shrub up to 2 ft high, 4 ft or more across. The flowers are striking but are never produced in quantity at any one time. The colouring is best developed in half-shade and in cool, cloudy weather; in hot, sunny weather the flowers are yellow.

'Tangerine' was raised at the Slieve Donard Nurseries, Newcastle, Co. Down. The history of this remarkable plant, given by the late Leslie Slinger, is as follows: In 1928 he found in the nursery an unnamed stock of a shrubby potentilla with golden-yellow flowers and was told by his father that it had been raised from a pinch of seed labelled 'Potentilla Red Flowered', which had been sent home by Farrer. Thinking that the parental plant was the result of a mutation which might recur, Mr Slinger raised generation after generation of seedlings and finally one was found which had a distinct tangerine blotch on some of the petals. This was named 'DONARD GOLD'; it had a poor constitution, and was hard to propagate. But a batch of seedlings from this plant produced 'Tangerine'.

As noted under *P. parvifolia*, Forrest found plants resembling 'Tangerine' on the Burma–Yunnan frontier. According to his field-notes under F.25010 and F.26944, Farrer had earlier sent seed from the same locality, though there is no reference to this in Farrer's published field-notes. 'Tangerine' is a fairly good match for Forrest's specimens under these two numbers.

'Tangerine' has given rise to two sports. 'SUNSET' has flowers of a deeper colour than in the parent. 'DAYDAWN' is a remarkable break, with flowers in which the ground-colour is cream, flushed or overlaid with peach-pink. For the new 'RED ACE', see *The Garden* (*Jn. R.H.S.*), Vol. 101 (1976), pp. 252–3.

'VILMORINIANA'.—Flowers creamy white with a yellow centre, up to 1½ in. wide; segments of outer calyx mostly elliptic, up to ¼ in. wide. Leaflets mostly ½ to ⅝ in. long (much larger on strong shoots), broad elliptic, silky and silvery above, densely white-silky beneath. A stiffly erect shrub to 4–5 ft; flowers borne sparsely over a long period. See also *P.* × *vilmoriniana*, under *P. arbuscula*.

'WILLIAM PURDOM' ("Purdomii").—Flowers canary-yellow with a deeper centre, 1⅛ in. wide, borne in dense cymes at the ends of the laterals from the previous year's wood, or on continuations of the previous season's laterals; anthers very small, apparently sterile, Leaflets five, those of the lower pair narrow-elliptic, acute, ½ to ¾ in. long, bright green above, pale beneath, with a few hairs above on the midrib beneath. A large shrub with erect main stems, about 4 ft high, 6 ft wide. F.C.C.T. 1966.

This potentilla was introduced by William Purdom from Shensi during his expedition in 1911 for the Arnold Arboretum and Messrs. Veitch. It is known as 'Purdomii', but is not the same as *P. fruticosa* var. *purdomii* Rehd., for which see *P.* × *rehderiana*. The present plant shows no obvious sign of hybridity, though it is certainly more robust than the plants from Kansu such as 'Gold Drop'. It is perhaps the finest of the yellow-flowered sorts. The flowers are of a very pleasing shade—one, too, that shows up better in the garden than the conventional buttercup-yellow.

'WOODBRIDGE GOLD'.—Flowers buttercup-yellow, about 1¼ in. wide, borne plentifully for several months; pedicels very short. Leaflets five, sometimes three, rich green and rather glossy, up to ⅝ in. long, ¼ in. wide, narrowly oblong-oblanceolate. Low-growing, to about 2 ft by 3 ft. A.M.T. 1965. Raised by Messrs Notcutt.

PRINSEPIA   ROSACEAE

A genus of three or four species of deciduous shrubs; the shoots have axillary spines and the pith is lamellate, i.e., reduced to thin transverse disks; leaves alternate; fruit a drupe. It is closely akin to *Prunus*, which is easily distinguished by its continuous pith. Named after James Prinsep (1800–1840), one-time Secretary to the Asiatic Society of Bengal, a meteorologist and a friend of Royle, the author of the name.

P. SINENSIS (Oliver) Oliver ex Bean
Plagiospermum sinense Oliver

A deciduous shrub of rather lax, spreading habit, about 6 ft high; stems armed with solitary, stiff, short spines, from beneath which spring the leaves; pith chambered (divided into thin plates). Leaves alternate on the shoots of the year, oblong-lanceolate, finely ciliate, 1½ to 3 in. long, about ½ in. wide; produced in clusters on the year-old shoots. Flowers borne singly in the leaf-axils on slender stalks ½ in. long; they are solitary, or clustered two to four together; each flower ½ to ¾ in. in diameter, petals five, bright yellow, roundish, tapered to a short claw. Fruits red and juicy, ⅗ in. long, ripening in August. *Bot. Mag.*, t. 8711.

Native of Manchuria; it was introduced from France in 1908 and is quite hardy.

P. UNIFLORA Batal.

A deciduous shrub of lax, spreading habit and free growth, 5 or 6 ft high; young shoots glabrous, pale shining grey, armed at each joint with a sharp slender spine ¼ to ½ in. long. Leaves linear, 1 to 2¼ in. long, ⅙ to ⅓ in. wide, pointed, the lower two-thirds toothed (sometimes sparsely), dark glossy green,

PRINSEPIA SINENSIS

glabrous. Flowers white, ⅗ in. wide, borne in early spring one to three together along with a cluster of leaves from the joints of the previous summer's growth, each flower on a glabrous stalk ⅙ in. long. Petals five, obovate, ⅕ in. wide; stamens ten; anthers yellow. Fruits globose, ⅓ in. wide, purple with a slight bloom when ripe.

Native of Shensi, China; introduced to the Arnold Arboretum by W. Purdom in 1911, thence to England a few years later. It is closely akin to *P. sinensis*, but that species has yellow flowers, longer flower-stalks, and mostly toothless leaves, *P. uniflora* grows very freely at Kew, making long, slender, very leafy shoots annually. But, flowering as it does early in the year, it is apt to suffer from inclement weather. For the same reason it rarely develops fruit. Farrer under his number 278 describes the fruits as 'glowing pendulous drops of crimson'; personally I have never seen living fruits but they appear in the dried state to be black-purple, and Batalin, the author of the name, describes them as 'schwarz, bereift'.

P. UTILIS Royle

A deciduous, very spiny shrub of exceedingly vigorous habit; young shoots slightly downy at first, soon glabrous. Spines stout, produced in every leaf-axil, eventually becoming 1 to 2 in. long and some bearing leaves. Leaves lanceolate, slender-pointed, tapered at the base, toothed, up to 4 in. long and 1¼ in. wide, dull green and quite glabrous. Flowers creamy white, fragrant, ¼ in. wide, produced from between the spine and the leaf in racemes 1 to 2 in. long, or sometimes few or even solitary. Fruits purple, cylindric, ½ to ¾ in. long. *Bot. Mag.*, n.s., t. 194.

Native of the Himalaya, where it is sometimes used for hedges, also of W. China. Although Hooker gives its height as 3 to 5 ft, a plant growing at Kew in a corner outside the Temperate House, facing north-east, is 9 ft high and 12 ft in diameter, a rampant grower. It is distinguished from the other two species by its usually racemose inflorescence, numerous stamens, and by flowering on the leafy shoots of the current season. Judging by dried specimens it often flowers in India with great freedom from the terminal leaf-axils in late autumn and winter, transforming the end of each shoot into a cylindrical wand of blossom, the fruits from such flowers being developed in April and May. To get it to flower well in this country it requires no doubt the sunniest spot obtainable and a lightish, not very fertile soil.

The material figured in the *Botanical Magazine* was supplied by Lt-Col. Mackenzie from his garden at Penmere near Falmouth—the flowers in mid-February and the fruits in the following June.

The Formosan plant described by Hayata under the name *P. scandens* is probably only a variant of *P. utilis*. It is of scrambling habit and reaches the tops of tall trees, but does not differ from the mainland species in any essential character.

PROSTANTHERA   LABIATAE

A genus of about fifty species of shrubs and subshrubs, confined to Australia and Tasmania, some very ornamental, but none reliably hardy in our average climate. Besides the two species treated here, there are others that could be grown outside in the mildest parts. P. LASIANTHOS Labill. (*Bot. Mag.*, t. 2434) has leaves 2 to 4 in. long and bears fine panicles of large, white or lilac, spotted flowers; it has flowered outdoors at Trewidden in Cornwall. P. CUNEATA Benth. (*Bot. Mag.*, n.s., t. 132) is similar to *P. lasianthos* in its flowers, but quite different in habit and foliage, being a dwarf shrub with roundish or obovate-cuneate leaves barely ¼ in. long. It is said to be hardier than *P. rotundifolia*, but is uncommon in gardens. Both species occur in Tasmania as well as on the mainland of S.E. Australia.

The mint bushes need a sunny position and do not thrive on shallow, chalky soils.

P. MELISSIFOLIA F. v. Muell.

This species is represented in cultivation by the following variety:

var. PARVIFOLIA Sealy *P. sieberi* Hort., not Benth.—An aromatic shrub or small tree up to 12 ft or so, minutely glandular in all its parts. Leaves of papery texture, ovate, broad-ovate, or broad-elliptic, mostly ⅜ to ⅝ in. long, $\frac{5}{16}$ to ½ in. wide, but occasionally up to 1 in. long, dark green above, undersurface bright green, conspicuously gland-dotted, downy on the midrib and main veins, margins with one or two teeth on each side, or entire, finely ciliate; petiole ⅛ to ¼ in. long. Inflorescence a short, terminal cluster of about eight flowers, or sometimes paniculate owing to the production of additional racemes from the uppermost leaf-axils; bracts soon deciduous. Calyx densely white-glandular on the outside. Corolla lilac-mauve, ½ in. or slightly more wide, almost as long, glandular on the outside and with finely ciliate margins; tube bell-shaped from a narrow base; upper lip rounded, its two lobes overlapping; median lobe of lower lip obovate-oblong, truncate, slightly longer than the ovate, obtuse lateral lobes. *Bot. Mag.*, t. 9687.

P. melissifolia is a native of S.E. Australia. The plant described here, though agreeing best with that species, differs from the typical state in its much smaller leaves, fewer-flowered racemes, and in having the corollas almost glabrous outside. It was obtained by Kew in 1929 from Messrs Duncan and Davies of New Zealand under the name "*P. sieberi*", but is quite distinct from the species so named by Bentham. It is not matched by any wild specimen in the Kew or British Museum herbaria, and its provenance is unknown. It was named *P. melissifolia* var. *parvifolia* Sealy in the article accompanying the plate in the *Botanical Magazine*.

P. melissifolia var. *parvifolia* is one of the finest of the mint bushes. Although certainly not hardy it is probably no more tender than *P. rotundifolia*, from which it differs in the larger, thinner, differently shaped leaves and the paler corolla, which is almost glabrous except for the ciliate margins. It grows quickly and is easily propagated by cuttings. It received an Award of Merit in 1940 as a shrub for the cool greenhouse when shown from Kew as "*P. sieberi*". It is possibly still grown under that name in some gardens.

P. ROTUNDIFOLIA R. Br.   MINT BUSH

An evergreen shrub of bushy habit, usually, as found wild, from 4 to 12 ft high; young branchlets very slender, clothed with a dense, short, greyish white down; both they and the leaves are aromatically scented when rubbed. Leaves opposite, either roundish, obovate, or oval; entire or with a few comparatively large teeth, from $\frac{1}{6}$ to $\frac{1}{3}$ in. long, usually about $\frac{1}{4}$ in. wide; dark, rather glossy green above, paler and dull beneath, both surfaces sprinkled thickly with tiny pitted glands; stalk $\frac{1}{12}$ to $\frac{1}{8}$ in. long. Flowers rich blue-purple or deep lilac, produced during April and May in short terminal racemes of five or more. Corolla $\frac{2}{3}$ in. wide, somewhat bell-shaped, but rather pouched on the lower side, with five rounded lobes, the lower lobes projecting more than the upper ones. Stamens four, purple, very short, attached to the base of the corolla. Calyx $\frac{1}{8}$ in. wide, helmet-shaped, with two unequal rounded lobes, scaly outside, purplish. Style purple, as long as the corolla. *Bot. Mag.*, t. 9061.

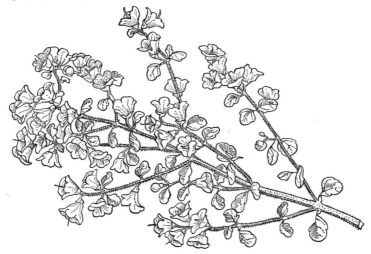

PROSTANTHERA ROTUNDIFOLIA

Native of Tasmania, whence it was introduced in 1824, and of S.E. Australia. This is one of the most beautiful of all cultivated Tasmanian shrubs, but is unfortunately too tender for all but the milder counties. Even there it is usually grown on a wall. In a climate like that of Kew it might, if given a sheltered place on some warm south wall, survive through a series of mild winters, but I am aware that even under most favourable conditions its tenure would be insecure. It is quite frequently seen in the gardens of Cornwall and S. Devon, always beautiful in the spring time. Nowhere have I seen it so fine as in the Rectory garden at Ludgvan, near Penzance. A plant on a wall there was, when I saw it, some 10 ft high, one gorgeous mass of blue-purple. I believe it is not a long-lived shrub, but it takes root very readily from soft cuttings in early summer.

PRUNUS   ROSACEAE

There is no genus of flowering trees which contributes so much to the beauty of English gardens in March, April, and early May as *Prunus*. Following the now generally accepted signification of the word, not only the plums (or *Prunus* proper) are dealt with under this heading, but the almonds and peaches (*Amygdalus*), apricots (*Armeniaca*), cherries (*Cerasus*), bird cherries (*Padus*), and the cherry laurels (*Laurocerasus*) also. With even this extended interpretation the genus is well distinguished by its fruit, which is always a one-celled, one-seeded drupe. The leaves are alternate, either deciduous or evergreen; the flowers white or rose-coloured, rarely yellowish; petals five, calyx five-lobed, stamens numerous.

In order to facilitate recognition of the species it will be necessary to denote the characters roughly distinguishing each subgenus and section. It should be said, however, that some species (perhaps hybrids) are of uncertain position.

subgen. PRUNUS   PLUMS AND APRICOTS

Axillary buds solitary. Terminal bud present. Flowers solitary or in clusters of two to four, sometimes more. Fruits grooved down one side. Stone usually flattened.

sect. 1 PRUNUS. PLUMS.—Leaves convolute in the bud (i.e., each half of the leaf is rolled inwards). Flowers stalked, solitary or in clusters of two or three. Fruits bloomy. Stones sculptured. Confined to the Old World.

P. cerasifera, P. cocomilia, P. consociiflora, P. domestica, P. salicina, P. simonii, P. spinosa.

sect. 2 PRUNOCERASUS. AMERICAN PLUMS.—Leaves usually conduplicate in bud as in the cherries (i.e., the two halves of the leaf are folded together lengthways like a sheet of notepaper). Flowers stalked, in clusters of three or more. Fruits as in sect. 1, but the stones usually smooth.

P. alleghaniensis, P. americana, P. angustifolia, P. hortulana, P. maritima, P. nigra, P. orthosepala, P. subcordata.

sect. 3 ARMENIACA. APRICOTS.—Leaves convolute in the bud. Flowers and fruits very short-stalked. Fruits velvety. This section is treated as a distinct subgenus by some authorities, or even as a separate genus—*Armeniaca*.

P. armeniaca, P. brigantina, P. mume, P. sibirica (*P. dasycarpa* is probably a hybrid between this group and sect. *Prunus*.)

subgen. AMYGDALUS   ALMONDS AND PEACHES

Axillary buds three, the centre one vegetative, the laterals producing flowers. Terminal bud present. Leaves conduplicate in the bud. Flowers and fruits very short-stalked or sessile. Fruits downy (except in the nectarine), stones grooved or pitted. This subgenus divides into two groups, each of which is treated as a separate genus by some authorities— *Persica*, the peaches, with a fleshy fruit; and *Amygdalus*, the almonds, with a dry fruit.

P. argentea, P. davidiana, P. dulcis, P. kansuensis, P. mira (stone smooth), *P. persica, P. tangutica, P. tenella, P. triloba.*

subgen. CERASUS   Cherries

Leaves conduplicate in the bud. Flowers in clusters, sometimes raceme-like, or in corymbs. Fruits not grooved, usually without bloom, and with a smooth and not flattened, usually more or less globose, stone. The cherries fall into two main groups:

(a) Dwarf shrubs, having the axillary buds in threes, as in the almonds and peaches. This is the section *Microcerasus*, which in Ingram's view should rank as a separate subgenus—*Lithocerasus* (*Orn. Cherries*, ¹p. 78).

P. besseyi, P. glandulosa, P. humilis, P. incana, P. jacquemontii, P. micro-carpa, P. prostrata, P. pumila.

(b) Trees or mostly large shrubs, with the buds solitary in each leaf-axil.

P. apetala, P. avium, P. campanulata, P. canescens, P. cerasus, P. concinna, P. conradinae, P. dielsiana, P. emarginata, P. fruticosa, P. incisa, P. litigiosa, P. mahaleb, P. maximowiczii, P. nipponica, P. pensylvanica, P. pilosiuscula, P. rufa, P. sargentii, P. serrula, P. serrulata, P. speciosa, P. subhirtella, P. tomentosa.

subgen. PADUS   Bird Cherries

Leaves conduplicate in bud. Flowers in racemes which are terminal on leafy branchlets.

P. cornuta, P. cuthbertii, P. grayana, P. padus, P. serotina, P. ssiori, P. virginiana. (*P. maackii* is anomalous in having short axillary racemes, borne on the previous season's wood, but is usually placed here.)

subgen. LAUROCERASUS   Cherry Laurels

Evergreen. Flowers in racemes like those of the bird cherries, but produced from the axils of the still persisting leaves of the previous year.

P. ilicifolia, P. laurocerasus, P. lusitanica.

The cultivation of *Prunus* generally is somewhat varied owing to the wide variety of the species composing it. Generally they are very hardy; where they are not, the fact is noted. All the deciduous species enjoy full exposure to sunlight; it is on this more than anything else that the flower crop depends. They all thrive on loamy soil, and most of them, the plums especially, are at home on limestone formations.

Many of the species, or most, can be increased by cuttings. This method of propagation is well worth trying for those that are found to be short-lived when grafted or budded. The cuttings should be made of young wood getting firm, with a heel attached, and put in gentle heat. Peaches and almonds are usually grafted or budded on plum stocks because of the greater hardiness of the plum. The various cherries may be worked on *P. avium*, and the bird cherries on *P. padus*. The cherry laurels may be increased by cuttings.

The species and cultivars of Prunus do not in general need annual pruning, the main exceptions being *P. glandulosa* and, when grown against a wall, *P. triloba*. But the ornamental peaches and apricots will flower better and be more healthy if the plant is kept open by cutting back old wood to a suitable young growth and removing growths that are badly placed. This should be done after flowering. Grown as a hedge, *P. cerasifera* and its hybrid *P.* × *cistena* should be trimmed after flowering, and the leaders should be shortened each year until the desired height is attained. See also *P. laurocerasus*.

The ornamental members of the genus are susceptible to many of the diseases that attack their orchard relatives, and works on fruit-growing or the R.H.S. *Dictionary of Gardening* should be consulted for an account of these. The only disease that calls for preventive spraying is the Leaf Curl disease of peaches and almonds, caused by the fungus *Taphrina deformans*, which over-winters on the bud-scales and attacks the young leaves, which become red, thickened and contorted, and eventually die. The plants should be sprayed in the autumn before leaf-fall with Bordeaux mixture at the rate of ½ pint to two gallons and again in late winter before the buds expand. It is pointless to spray in spring or summer after the disease has been noticed, but the affected leaves should be picked off and burned. The witches' broom disease—*Taphrina cerasi*—must be mentioned, as it is fairly common on some ornamental cherries, especially on *P. subhirtella* 'Autumnalis' and hybrids with *P. subhirtella* in their ancestry. The disease causes the tree to produce dense bunches of shoots, which are thicker than normal, come into leaf earlier, and bear no flowers. Once the disease has taken hold it is difficult to cure and the tree, apart from producing few flowers, becomes very unsightly. The witches' brooms should be removed as soon as noticed, and burned. Spraying with Bordeaux mixture as the leaves unfold is said to check the disease, but badly affected trees are best removed.

P. ALLEGHANIENSIS Porter   AMERICAN SLOE

A small deciduous tree, sometimes up to 20 ft high, but often a shrub a few feet high; branches erect, rigid, glabrous except when quite young, ultimately almost black, the spur-like growths sometimes terminating in a spine. Leaves ovate or oval-lanceolate, pointed, finely and sharply toothed, 2 to 3½ in. long, ¾ to 1¼ in. wide, downy on the midrib beneath; stalk ⅛ in. long, downy, without glands. Flowers ½ in. across, produced in April in stalkless umbel-like clusters of two to five, each flower on a slender stalk ¼ to ½ in. long; petals rather dull white, turning pink with age; calyx funnel-shaped at the base, with ovate-oblong, blunt lobes, downy. Fruits globose or slightly elongated, ½ to ⅔ in. in diameter, reddish purple, covered with blue bloom.

Native of the Allegheny Mts in Pennsylvania and W. Virginia, where its fruits are known as sloes, and used for preserving, etc. It does not appear to have been recognised in the United States as a distinct species until 1877, when it was named as above. First introduced in 1892 from the Arnold Arboretum to Kew, where for a time it grew and flowered very well, but did not fruit. This tree, however, has since died. It is allied to *P. americana*, but differs in its blue fruits.

P. AMERICANA Marsh.   AMERICAN RED PLUM

A deciduous tree up to 30 ft high, of graceful habit, with the trunk dividing low down, suckering freely and often forming thickets in the wild; bark dark brown, scaly; branches pendulous towards the ends; young shoots glabrous or slightly downy. Leaves oval or obovate, tapering abruptly to a drawn-out point and more gradually towards the base, 3 to 4 in. long, 1¼ to 1¾ in. wide, sharply and often doubly toothed, glabrous except for tufts of down along the midrib in the axils of the veins; stalk ⅓ to ¾ in. long, downy and usually without glands. Flowers 1 in. across, pure white, produced two to five together in stalkless umbels, each flower on a slender glabrous stalk ⅜ to 1 in. long; calyx reddish, lobes entire, hairy within. Fruits round or nearly so, 1 in. or less in diameter, first yellow, finally bright red; flesh yellow.

Native of the United States, where it is widely spread, reaching as far west as the eastern slopes of the Rocky Mountains. It and varieties derived from it are now largely grown in the eastern United States for the fruits. It has not yet borne fruit freely in Britain, although it flowers very well. The flowers have a faint and rather unpleasant odour. It is said to be extremely handsome when loaded with its red and yellow fruits. It may be distinguished from *P. hortulana* and *P. nigra* by the non-glandular leaf-stalks, and from *P. alleghaniensis* by the colour of its fruits and more graceful habit.

var. LANATA Sudw.   *P. lanata* (Sudw.) Mackenzie & Bush; *P. palmeri* Sarg.—Branchlets and undersides of leaves densely downy. Illinois to S. Missouri. This variety intergrades with the typical state.

P. MEXICANA S. Wats.—A tree up to 40 ft high closely allied to *P. americana* but forming a single trunk which becomes furrowed with age. Leaves more shortly acuminate and usually rounded at the base. Although described from N. Mexico, its main range is in the southern central USA.

P. × AMYGDALO-PERSICA (West.) Rehd.

Amygdalus Amygdalo-Persica West.; *A. hybrida* Poiteau & Turpin; *A. communis* var. *persicoides* Ser.; *P. amygdalus* var. *persicoides* (Ser.) Koehne

A group of hybrids between the almond and the peach, known since the sixteenth century and perhaps even earlier. The pioneer plant-breeder Thomas Knight raised the hybrid artificially early in the 19th century by pollinating the almond with the peach, and the cross has been repeated since, producing plants similar to 'Pollardii'. The almond-peach has leaves similar to those of the peach and is intermediate in its fruits, which usually have a thin, dry flesh and a flattened stone, which is bonier than in the almond; but various combinations of fruit and stone-characters can occur, even on the same tree. The hybrid is mainly represented in cultivation by:

'POLLARDII'.—Leaves like those of the common almond but more sharply toothed. Flowers bright pink, flushed deeper at the centre, about 2 in. across. Filaments of anthers deep pink. Shell of the stone both furrowed and pitted; kernels bitter. Rather earlier flowering than the common almond. It was raised around 1904 by Mr Pollard of Ballarat, Victoria, Australia, and was originally grown as P. *communis* or P. *amygdalus pollardii*. F.C.C. February 9, 1935. A.G.M. 1937.

P. AMYGDALUS *see* P. DULCIS

P. ANGUSTIFOLIA Marsh.   CHICKASAW PLUM
P. *chicasa* Michx.

A deciduous tree 15 to 20 ft high, with glabrous, lustrous, reddish young branchlets. Leaves 1 to 2 in. long, one-third as wide, oval-lanceolate, pointed, sharply toothed, tapering at the base to a reddish stalk ¼ to ½ in. long. Flowers white, ½ in. across, in clusters of two to four; calyx glabrous outside. Fruits bright red and shining, ½ in. across, round or nearly so.

A native of eastern North America from New Jersey to Florida and Texas, and west into the Mississippi basin. In the var. VARIANS Wight and Hedrick the leaves are somewhat larger, the flower-stalks longer and the stone pointed at the apex. This and the typical variety are the source of several varieties of plums cultivated in the southern States. Several times introduced to Kew, it never thrives, and it is probably only adapted for the warmest parts of the British Isles, and unless it bears fruits it is scarcely ornamental enough to be worthy of cultivation there. Its close ally, P. *watsonii*, is better worth growing. The P. *chicasa* of Michaux, usually regarded as synonymous with P. *angustifolia*, is said by Hedrick to be different.

P. WATSONII Sarg. P. *angustifolia* var. *watsonii* (Sarg.) Waugh SAND PLUM —A deciduous shrub or small tree 6 to 12 ft high, with glabrous, reddish branchlets. Leaves ovate, pointed, decurved, 1 to 1¾ in. long, ½ to ¾ in. wide, shallowly round-toothed, dark shining green above, paler below, quite glabrous on both surfaces; stalk ¼ to ⅓ in. long, grooved, with two glands near the base of the blade. Flowers white, ½ in. in diameter, produced in clusters of three or four, each on a slender stalk ¼ in. long. Fruits round, orange-red, ¾ in. in diameter, the stone deeply pitted.

Native of the central United States, where it is said to form thickets in low, sandy places near streams. It was first recognised as a distinct species by Sargent in 1894, having previously been confused with P. *angustifolia*, from which is differs in its 'thicker leaves, thicker skinned fruit, and smaller more deeply pitted stone'. It is very distinct from P. *angustifolia* in its behaviour under cultivation, thriving well where that species is a total failure. Introduced to Kew in 1897, but unfortunately it is no longer represented there. It flowers in late April and May, but is not one of the most effective plums in this country.

P. APETALA (Sieb. & Zucc.) Franch. & Sav.

Ceraseidos apetala Sieb. & Zucc.; *P. tschonoskii* Koehne

A small deciduous tree or (more often) a bush up to 16 ft high; young shoots hairy, slender. Leaves mostly obovate, with a slender, tail-like apex, tapering and often rounded at the base, conspicuously doubly-toothed, 2 to 4 in. long, 1 to 1½ in. wide, hairy on both sides, especially below; stalk ¼ to ½ in. long, very hairy. Flowers produced during May singly or in pairs, each on its slender hairy stalk ½ to ¾ in. long. The small white or pink petals very soon fall, and such little beauty as the flower possesses is in the calyx and stamens, which become purplish red. The calyx-tube is cylindrical, downy, ⅜ in. long, the lobes ovate, ⅛ in. long. Fruits roundish-oval, black, ⅜ in. long, the stalk elongated to 1 or 1⅜ in.

Native of Japan; introduced by Wilson in 1914. The leaves of this cherry are rather handsome and distinct in the long, tail-like point and in their hairiness. The most marked character of the species, however, is the persistent, coloured calyx and stamen filaments. In the style of the toothing of the leaves it has some resemblance to *P. incisa* and *P. nipponica*.

P. ARABICA (Oliv.) Meikle

Amygdalus arabica Oliv.; *A. spartioides* Spach; *Prunus spartioides* (Spach) Schneid.

An unarmed shrub of broom-like habit 3 to 6 ft high, with green, glabrous, angled branches, leafless in the hot season. Leaves linear-lanceolate, up to 1⅝ in. long, ⅛ to 3/16 in. wide, shortly stalked. Flowers solitary, sessile, borne in spring, each from a bud with numerous brown imbricating scales, ½ to ¾ in. wide, white or pinkish; receptacle partly concealed by the bud-scales, broad campanulate, glabrous or almost so. Ovary densely hairy. Fruits ovoid, slightly flattened, about 1 in. long; stone smooth.

P. arabica is an almond of unusual habit, occurring in dry steppe and open oak woodland from S. and E. Anatolia to Persia. As in many plants of arid regions, its stems have to a large extent taken over the function of photosynthesis.

P. SCOPARIA (Spach) Schneid. *Amygdalus scoparia* Spach—Closely allied to the preceding, but taller and sometimes a tree up to 20 ft high, with terete, not angled stems, and flowers up to 1 in. wide. It occupies similar habitats but is confined to Iran.

P. ARGENTEA (Lam.) Rehd.

Amygdalus argentea Lam.; *A. orientalis* Mill.; *P. orientalis* (Mill.) Koehne, not Walp.

A deciduous shrub or small tree with whitish, downy twigs. Leaves elliptical or ovate, short-stalked, ¾ to 1½ in. long, covered with a close silvery down. Flowers solitary or in pairs, ¾ in. across; petals rose-coloured, thin, and of short duration. Fruits egg-shaped, ⅝ in. long, pointed, rather compressed, covered with a close, white down.

Native of the Near East; in cultivation 1756. This almond is easily distinguished from all others of this genus in cultivation by the silvery leaves. It is not hardy in the open, and on a wall should be given a sunny place. In a shady position the leaves lose their whiteness, and suggest mildew rather than silveriness. It flowers very shyly in this country, and is only worth growing for the unusual aspect of its foliage.

P. ARMENIACA L. APRICOT
Armeniaca vulgaris Lam.

A round-headed, deciduous tree 20 to 30 ft high, with sturdy, tortuous branches; branchlets glabrous. Leaves broadly ovate to roundish, 2½ to 3½ in. long, 1½ to 2 in. wide, abruptly pointed, deep lustrous green, glabrous or with axil tufts beneath, evenly set with rounded teeth; stalk up to 1 in. long. Flowers white or pinkish, 1 in. across, produced singly on very short stalks from the previous year's wood, often crowded on short spur-like twigs. Fruits round, 1¼ in. wide in the wild state, larger under cultivation, yellow tinged with red, the stone having a thickened furrowed margin.

Native of N. China, where it was found genuinely wild by Dr Bretschneider and raised at Kew from seeds sent by him. It is also found wild in the Tian-Shan. It is, of course, best known as a fruit tree on walls, but is quite hardy in the open, where, however, it does not bear fruit satisfactorily. The fruiting apricot is believed to have been cultivated by the Chinese many centuries anterior to the Christian era, gradually spreading westwards to Europe. It existed in English gardens early in the 16th century, probably long before. Flowering in March and early April, the apricot has something to recommend it, but it must be regarded as an inferior flowering tree, not in the same class as the almond and peach. The specific name refers to its supposed Armenian origin.

var. ANSU Maxim. *P. ansu* (Maxim.) Komar.; *Armeniaca ansu* (Maxim.) Kostina —Leaves broad-ovate or orbicular-ovate, about 3 in. long, slightly less wide, broadly rounded to almost truncate at the base. Flowers usually twinned, very shortly stalked. Stone of fruit slightly roughened. A cultivated race of the more oceanic parts of E. Asia. In this country it is subject to brown rot and not very free-flowering.

In 1934, an Award of Merit was given to an apricot shown by Collingwood Ingram as *P. mume grandiflora*, the name under which the plant was received from an Italian nursery. However, he later pointed out that it really agreed better with *P. armeniaca* var. *ansu*. The flowers are of a bright rose, double (*Journ. R.H.S.*, Vol. 71, p. 36).

P. AVIUM L. GEAN, MAZZARD
Cerasus sylvestris Lund.; C. nigra Mill.

A deciduous tree up to 60 ft or more high, with a trunk occasionally 2 ft and upwards in diameter, the bark shining and peeling horizontally; young twigs glabrous. Leaves ovate to oval with a drawn-out point, 3 to 5 in. long, 1½ to 2 in. wide (sometimes considerably larger on vigorous young trees), rather coarsely and irregularly toothed, hairy along the veins and midrib beneath; leaf-stalk 1 to 1¾ in. long, with reddish glands near the blade. Flowers pure white, about 1 in. across, produced on stalks from 1 to 1¾ in. long, in stalkless clusters from the previous year's shoots, and from spur-like branches of earlier date. Fruits round, blackish red, ¾ in. in diameter, sweet or bitter but not acid.

Native of Europe, including Britain, and one of the parents of cultivated fruiting cherries, especially the black ones. In the woodland the gean is very desirable, and in suitable places makes a big tree; in plantations separated from the house by a valley it might be planted in numbers for its effect in April and early May, but in the garden itself it should give place to the improved varieties. There was a good deal of confusion in botanical works between this species and *P. cerasus*. But *P. avium* differs from *P. cerasus* in the following respects: it is a tree sometimes of full middle size (the other is more or less dwarf or shrubby); the leaves are more coarsely toothed and hairy beneath; the fruit is not acid.

Elwes and Henry record specimens of the gean nearly 100 ft in height and others with girths of up to 12 ft (more at the base). It is doubtful if any of these are still living. The following have been recorded recently and no doubt there are many others of comparable size: Borde Hill, Sussex, 70 × 10¼ ft (1968); Elvetham Park, Hants, 65 × 12½ ft (1963); Studley Royal, Yorks., 55 × 14¾ ft (1963); Smeaton, E. Lothian, 50 × 10¾ ft at 3 ft (1967). On deep, moist soil the gean and its double variety are fast growing, both in height and girth.

The gean is the usual stock for both the orchard cherries and many of the ornamentals (notably the Sato Zakura); mostly selected clones are used, propagated by layers or by root-cuttings.

None of the following garden varieties is of any importance, except 'Plena':

cv. 'ASPLENIFOLIA'.—Leaves deeply and irregularly toothed. 'LACINIATA' is the same or very similar.

cv. 'DECUMANA'.—A remarkable variety with large single flowers and enormous leaves, often 8 to 10 in. long, and broad in proportion. Raised in France before 1808. Also known as 'Nicotiniifolia'.

cv. 'NANA'.—A dwarf, stunted form with single flowers. It was described in the first edition of this work, but has never spread into gardens.

cv. 'PENDULA'.—Branches pendulous, but too stiffly so to be attractive.

cv. 'PLENA'.—This is the most beautiful of gean cherries, and one of the most beautiful of all flowering trees. Healthy trees never fail to flower in the utmost profusion, every branch and twig being wreathed from end to end with thick pendulous masses of the purest white blossom. Each flower is about 1½ in. across, and consists of thirty to forty petals lasting long in beauty; fruits are rarely or never formed. A.G.M. 1924.

The double gean in the form now commonly grown appears to have reached this country from France early in the 19th century. The fact that it was sometimes listed by continental nurserymen under the epithet *flore pleno majore* suggests that the form known earlier had smaller flowers.

cv. 'PREMORSA'.—Leaves of curious shape, with the appearance of having had the ends bitten off.

The orchard cherries deriving from *P. avium* have been classified as follows, but the names are only of historical interest:

var. DURACINA (L.) K. Koch *Prunus cerasus* var. *duracina* L.; *P. duracina* (L.) Sweet—Here belong the Bigarreau cherries, with firm-fleshed fruits.

var. JULIANA (L.) K. Koch *P. cerasus* var. *juliana* L.; *P. juliana* (L.) Gaudin— Under this name were placed the Heart cherries, with a soft flesh.

P. BESSEYI Bailey   ROCKY MOUNTAINS CHERRY
P. pumila var. *besseyi* (Bailey) Waugh

A dwarf deciduous shrub 2 to 4 ft high, with glabrous branchlets. Leaves grey-green, oval or oval-lanceolate, sometimes obovate, 1 to 2½ in. long, shallowly toothed on the upper two-thirds, glabrous. Flowers in stalkless clusters of two to four from the buds of the previous year's shoots; each flower pure white, ⅝ in. across, on a stalk ⅓ in. long; calyx green, with ovate, slightly toothed lobes. Fruits on more or less pendent stalks, oblong or nearly round, ¾ in. long, covered with a purplish bloom at first, finally black. *Bot. Mag.*, t. 8156.

Native of the hot, dry plains east of the Rocky Mountains in Colorado, Nebraska, Kansas, etc., where it promises to be a valuable fruit-bearing shrub. It is remarkably prolific there, and in Colorado sixteen quarts of fruit have been gathered from a bush three years old, and eighty fruits from a branch 1 ft long. It was introduced to Kew in 1900, and has proved to be an ornamental little shrub, flowering so freely in late April or early May as to make each twig a cylindrical mass of blossom. Its fruits are only sparingly borne in England.

P. UTAHENSIS Koehne—This is believed to be a hybrid between *P. besseyi* and *P. watsonii*; it originated as an accidental cross in the grounds of J. E. Johnson at Red River, Nebraska, but was first distributed after he moved to a new property in Utah. Fruits blue-black, bloomy.

P. × CISTENA (Hansen) Koehne *P. 'Cistena'* Hansen—A hybrid between *P. pumila* (or *P. besseyi*?) and *P. cerasifera* 'Pissardii', raised early this century by the well-known American plant-breeder Dr N. E. Hansen at the South Dakota State Experimental Station. It grows to about 6 ft high and as much wide and has oblanceolate pointed leaves 1½ to 2½ in. long, which are crimson when young, becoming bronzy red. Flowers white, borne usually in April just before the leaves expand; stalks and calyx purple. Fruits cherry-like, dark purple.

This shrub seems to have reached Britain in the mid-1950s and is now quite common in commerce as a hedging plant. 'Cistena' is the Sioux Indian name for baby and Koehne used the name as a scientific epithet.

P. BRIGANTINA Vill.   BRIANÇON APRICOT
P. brigantiaca Vill.; *P. armeniaca* subsp. *brigantiaca* (Vill.) Dipp.

A small, deciduous, bushy tree 10 to 20 ft high, with a short trunk. Leaves ovate or oval, often slightly heart-shaped at the base, shortly and abruptly pointed, the margins doubly and rather jaggedly toothed, 1½ to 3 in. long, 1 to 2½ in. wide, hairy beneath, especially on the veins and midrib; stalk ⅓ to ⅔ in. l ong. Flowers white or pinkish, ¾ in. or so across, two or more together. Fruit like a small apricot, of a rather clear yellow, smooth.

This tree grows spontaneously in the neighbourhood of Briançon, and occurs wild in the Maritime and Cottian Alps. From the seeds the Briançonnais express an inflammable, agreeably perfumed oil, known as *huile de Marmotte*. This apricot has little to recommend it for gardens.

P. CAMPANULATA Maxim.   BELL-FLOWERED CHERRY

A deciduous cherry tree up to 30 ft high, of graceful habit, free from down in all its parts; year-old shoots freely marked with warts. Leaves ovate, oval or slightly obovate, slender-pointed, broadly wedge-shaped to slightly heart-shaped at the base, margins regularly set with fine forward-pointing or in-curved teeth, 2½ to 4 in. long, 1 to 1¾ in. wide, nerves in six to eight pairs; stalks ½ to ¾ in. long. Flowers ¾ in. wide, produced in March and April, two to six together on main-stalks 1 to 1½ in. long that bear usually a couple of leaf-like bracts; individual flower-stalks ½ to ¾ in. long. Petals of a beautiful deep rose, roundish ovate, notched at the apex, ¼ in. wide. Calyx-tube rose-coloured except at the base, the reflexed, sparsely toothed lobes also rosy; stamens deep rose, anthers yellow. Fruits described as red, conical, ⅝ in. long, scarcely ½ in. wide. *Bot. Mag.*, t. 9575.

Native of Formosa and S. China and thought to be wild also in the Ryukyu

PRUNUS CAMPANULATA

Islands. The bell shape of the flowers to which the specific name refers seems to be characteristic of them in a young state only. It appears to have been introduced by Messrs Sander of St Albans in 1899, but owing to its tenderness was lost and not seen again until Wilson took plants from Japan to the Arnold Arboretum in 1915. Its flowers are, perhaps, the most highly coloured of all the genuinely wild types. Near London it needs the protection of a wall, but succeeds in the open ground in the mildest parts. At Kew it flowers freely in the Temperate House in March or even earlier. Award of Merit 1935.

P. CERASOIDES D. Don *P. puddum* Roxb.—This species, which belongs to the same group as *P. campanulata*, is represented in cultivation by var. RUBEA Ingram, which ranges from Kashmir along the Himalaya, through upper Burma to W. Yunnan. In the wild it makes a tall tree, bearing its rich carmine flowers well before the leaves in February or March. It was introduced to Britain by Kingdon Ward in 1931 (KW 9314) and flowered at Highdown in Sussex in 1938. Unfortunately in our climate the flowers are paler coloured than in the wild, and are borne with the unfolding leaves. Twigs reddish brown, glabrous. Leaves 2½ to 4½ in. long, oblong-elliptic acuminate or caudate, almost glabrous, bright green above, conspicuously veined, with simple, gland-tipped serrations. Flowers more or less bell-shaped, two to four in umbellate or shortly pedunculate clusters. Calyx-tube glabrous, bright crimson, its lobes ciliate and of the same colour. *Bot. Mag.*, n.s., t. 12. See also: Kingdon Ward, *Plant Hunter's Paradise*, pp. 149–50, and *Journ. R.H.S.* Vol. 71, pp. 321 and 74, p. 289.

P. CANESCENS Bois   GREYLEAF CHERRY

A deciduous shrub of dense, bushy habit, with ascending main branches, 6 to 10 ft high; bark smooth, mahogany-brown; branchlets more or less hairy. Leaves lanceolate or narrowly ovate, 1½ to 2½ in. long, ½ to 1 in. wide, coarsely and doubly toothed, the base rounded or tapering, the apex long-pointed, both surfaces, especially the lower one, furnished with persistent, soft, greyish hairs; stalk ¼ to ⅓ in. long, hairy, issuing from between two leaf-like, deeply toothed, hairy stipules ¼ in. long. Flowers rosy white, scarcely ½ in. wide, produced (each on a sparsely hairy stalk ⅓ in. long) in clusters of three to five; calyx tubular, with five triangular lobes half as long as the tube; petals soon falling. Fruits round to oblong, ½ in. in diameter, glabrous, red, with a pleasant cherry-like taste.

Native of China; obtained in 1898 from the province of Szechwan by Maurice de Vilmorin, and flowered at Les Barres in 1901. Introduced in 1905 to Kew, where it flowers about mid-April. It is a very distinct cherry because of the thick coat of soft hairs which covers the leaves and other younger parts of the plant, but is reduced in value as an ornamental plant by the fleeting nature of the petals. Bois, the author of the name, assumes a relationship between it and *P. maximowiczii*. The latter species, however, is very distinct in its stalked racemes several inches long furnished with leaf-like bracts. *P. canescens* is abundant in Wilson's later collectings.

P. × SCHMITTII Rehd.—A hybrid between *P. canescens* and *P. avium*, raised from a seedling of the former species at the Arnold Arboretum, in 1923. It makes a vigorous tree with an attractive mahogany-coloured bark and a narrow, vase-shaped crown. The bark and narrow habit come from *P. canescens*, the taller growth from *P. avium*, which *P.* × *schmittii* also resembles in the shape of its leaves and campanulate calyx-tube. The flowers are larger than in *P. canescens*, pale pink.

P. CANTABRIGIENSIS Stapf   CAMBRIDGE CHERRY

P. pseudocerasus sens. Koidz., not (?) Lindl.

In a previous edition under the heading of *P. pseudocerasus*, I gave a short description of a cherry, based on a specimen labelled by that name, which is preserved in the Lindley herbarium at Cambridge University. I there observed that the true *P. pseudocerasus* was probably not then in cultivation and that the trees grown under the name in gardens were mostly forms of *P. serrulata*. In February 1917 there flowered in the Cambridge Botanic Garden a cherry which, after being critically examined by the late Mr R. I. Lynch, the Curator, and compared with Lindley's specimen, was considered by him to be the true thing (see *Gardeners' Chronicle*, August 4, 1917, p. 47). I was afterwards furnished with flowering and leaf-bearing shoots and concurred with Mr Lynch's verdict. The flowers are pink, ¾ to 1 in. wide, produced on shortly stalked racemes three to six together; petals scoop-shaped, ⅜ in. long, scarcely as wide, notched at the apex; anthers yellow; style and ovary glabrous. Calyx-tube ³⁄₁₆ in. long and, like the flower-stalks, slightly hairy. The fruit is bright red, rather larger than the British wild cherry. The Cambridge tree is reputed to date back to Lindley's time and as the specimen in the herbarium is labelled "*P. pseudocerasus*" in Lindley's own handwriting, it was by most people concluded that the mystery of the cherry of that name was solved.

A flowering spray from the Cambridge tree has lately been figured in the *Botanical Magazine*, t. 9129, and Dr Stapf, the editor, whilst agreeing in the accompanying text that it matches Lindley's specimen, refused to agree that the latter is the true *P. pseudocerasus*, although it is labelled by Lindley himself. He pointed out that it does not match the *Botanical Register* plate (t. 800) which, in the absence of a co-related specimen, constitutes the only available evidence of what *P. pseudocerasus* really is. (It may be pointed out that although the *Botanical Register* picture is legended as "*Prunus paniculata, Thunberg*", the plant so called by Thunberg is really *Symplocos crataegoides* and not a prunus at all. It was to replace this erroneous name that Lindley substituted "*P. pseudocerasus*" for it. The figure, therefore, constitutes the standard on which the identity of the species is based.) Dr Stapf calls the Cambridge tree *P. cantabrigiensis*, and, if he is right, *P. pseudocerasus* remains as forlorn a mystery as ever, having appeared in the year 1819 as an introduction from China by a nurseryman called Samuel Brooks of Ball's Pond, Newington Green, London; flowered in the spring of 1824 in the Horticultural Society's Garden at Chiswick; been figured in the *Botanical Register* under a wrong name; and never been recognised since, either wild or cultivated.

P. cantabrigiensis is very hardy and flowers often in February. In the milder parts of the country where it had a chance to develop its flowers uninjured by frost it should be a handsome tree valuable for the exceptional earliness of its blossom.

To the above account, which is taken almost unchanged from previous editions, there is little that can usefully be added, except that two authorities on the oriental cherries, E. H. Wilson and C. Ingram, have both pointed out that the discrepancy between the Lindley specimen and the plate in the *Botanical Register* is of no account. The drawing in the plate was made from a plant which had flowered in the fruit-house of the Horticultural Society, and shows a shoot on which leaves and flowers appear together and the peduncle is much elongated, while in Lindley's specimen the peduncle is very short and the flowers precocious. But the length of the peduncle in this group of cherries is a fluctuating character, depending on the conditions under which the plant is grown and the season, becoming abnormally elongated if the flowers are produced when the leaves are almost fully expanded. But the name *P. pseudocerasus* has been so widely used in the past for other cherries that it is best discarded as of uncertain application.

The Cambridge cherry is very closely allied to P. INVOLUCRATA Koehne, a cherry cultivated in China for its fruits and described from a specimen collected by Wilson in W. Szechwan.

P. CERASIFERA Ehrh.   CHERRY PLUM, MYROBALAN
P. domestica var. *myrobalan* L.   [PLATE 45

A deciduous, round-headed tree up to 30 ft in height; young bark glabrous. Leaves ovate, oval or obovate, 1½ to 2½ in. long, 1 to 1¼ in. wide, toothed, downy along the midrib and veins beneath. Flowers ¾ to 1 in. across, pure white, produced usually singly, sometimes two or three together, at each bud of the previous year's shoots, but often crowded on short spur-like twigs so as to form dense clusters. Fruits smooth, red, 1 to 1¼ in. in diameter, round, indented at the junction with the stalk. *Bot. Mag.*, t. 5934.

The cherry plum is known only in cultivation, and certainly derives from the wild *P. divaricata* (see below). It is a well-known tree in gardens, and is sometimes used as a stock for grafting. As flowering trees it and *P. divaricata* are the most beautiful of the true plums, being almost covered with pure white blossom in March. The fruits are developed not infrequently at Kew, but never in great quantity. They are used for tarts, etc., like ordinary plums and are imported in small quantities from the Continent. *P. cerasifera* and the cultivars 'Nigra' and 'Pissardii' make good hedges.

cv. 'LINDSAYAE'.—Flowers pale pink, about ¾ in. wide. Collected in Persia by Nancy Lindsay in 1937 and given an Award of Merit when shown from Kew February 17, 1948.

cv. 'LOUIS ASSELIN'.—Leaves narrower than normal, edged with white. Raised by the French nurseryman Dauthenay and named after his foreman. Described 1895. Also known as 'Elegans'.

cv. 'PISSARDII'.—In spring this tree, like the type, is laden with blossom, which is of a delicate rose. Its foliage, however, is its most distinctive feature;

when it first expands it is of a tender ruby-red, changing later to claret colour, finally to a dull heavy purple. Its fruits, too, are purple. This variety was first noted in Persia by M. Pissard, gardener to the Shah, and by him was sent to France in 1880, whence it rapidly spread in cultivation, and is now a very common tree. A.G.M. 1928.

A number of selections from 'Pissardii' have been named, of which the best known in Britain is 'NIGRA', in which the flowers are of a slightly deeper pink and the purple of the leaves also deeper and more persistent. This is of American origin. The similar 'WOODII' was raised at Wood's nursery, Maresfield, E. Sussex, but apparently put into commerce by Späth's nurseries, Berlin, in 1910. Other named clones are in commerce.

In country gardens 'Pissardii' and its allies are often sparse flowering owing to the depredations of bullfinches.

P. DIVARICATA Ledeb. *P. cerasifera* subsp. *divaricata* (Ledeb.) Schneid.; *P. monticola* K. Koch—A deciduous tree or shrub with the same general aspect as *P. cerasifera*, neither does it appear to differ in the flowers or foliage. The fruits, however, are smaller (about ¾ in. across), yellow, and not indented at the junction with the stalk. Probably *P. divaricata* and *P. cerasifera* are only varieties of one species. They flower at the same time and are not distinguishable then. There was an old specimen near the Cactus House at Kew which was probably one of the largest in the country. It was 25 ft high, 27 ft through, and its trunk was 3 ft 8 in. in girth. The trees at Kew have rarely borne fruits, but these are quite distinct from cherry plums.

Unlike *P. cerasifera*, *P. divaricata* is a genuinely wild species ranging from the Balkans through Asia Minor to the Caucasus, Persia, and Central Asia. It is figured in *Bot. Mag.*, t. 6519.

P. × BLIREANA André *P. pissardii blireana fl. pl.* Lemoine; *P. cerasifera* var. *blireana* (André) Bean—A shrub or small tree of rounded habit to about 15 ft high and wide. Young leaves bronzy red, becoming more or less green by late summer. Flowers bright rose, double, and equal in beauty to a double-pink peach, about 1¼ in. across. They are borne on the bare stems in March or April.

This plum is believed to be a hybrid between *P. cerasifera* 'Pissardii' and a double form of *P. mume*. It was put into commerce by Lemoine in 1906 and received an Award of Merit when shown by Messrs Notcutt in 1914. A.G.M. 1928.

In *P.* × *blireana* 'MOSERI' the flowers are smaller and the leaves of a deeper shade. A.M. 1912.

P. 'TRAILBLAZER'.—Leaves narrowly to broadly oblong-obovate, acuminate, cuneate at the base, bronzy or purplish green above when mature, undersides purplish red. Flowers pure white, in sessile umbels, about ½ in. wide, cup-shaped, borne very profusely in early spring. Fruits not seen, said to be red and edible. A very attractive hybrid between *P. cerasifera* 'Nigra' and some form of *P. salicina*. According to Dr Boom, it is the same as 'Hollywood'.

P. CERASUS L.　　SOUR CHERRY

Cerasus vulgaris Mill.; *C. communis* Poiteau & Turpin

A deciduous bush or small rounded tree, suckering at the root and often making thickets in its wild state, but 10 to 20 ft high under cultivation. Leaves oval or ovate, abruptly short-pointed, 1½ to 3 in. long, half to two-thirds as wide, glabrous on both surfaces, rather lustrous above, the margins set with double gland-tipped teeth; stalk ½ to ¾ in. long, usually glanded. Flowers pure white, ¾ to 1 in. across, produced in clusters, each flower on a stalk ¾ in. long. Fruits red to blackish, roundish and depressed, with soft, juicy, acid flesh.

P. cerasus is a cultivated species to which belong many orchard varieties (see further below). It is naturalised over much of Europe (including Britain), and the Near East, but is not known anywhere as a truly wild plant. It is certainly related to *P. avium*, but distinct enough to rank as a separate species. In its naturalised state it produces suckers from the roots and never makes a tall tree as *P. avium* does. The leaves of *P. cerasus* are nearly or entirely without down; and the fruit is not sweet nor bitter, but acid. A further distinction is that the calyx-tube is campanulate, whereas in *P. avium* it is urn-shaped, i.e., constricted at the mouth.

The orchard varieties of *P. cerasus* have been grouped as follows:

var. AUSTERA L.—Fruits dark coloured and with a dark juice. Trees usually of rather pendulous habit. These are the Morello cherries.

var. CAPRONIANA L. *P. acida* Ehrh.; *P. caproniana* (L.) Gaudin—Fruits lighter red than in the Morellos, with a colourless juice. Trees usually erect branched, round-headed. Here belong the Amarelle cherries, of which the Kentish Red cherries are a local race.

var. FRUTESCENS Neilr. *P. acida sens.* K. Koch, not Ehrh.; *Cerasus collina* Lejeune & Cortois; *Prunus cerasus* var. *humilis* Bean (?)—Of shrubby, suckering habit. Fruits dark red. Various orchard varieties cultivated in the Soviet Union belong here; also the old variety known as 'OSTHEIM'. It is said to be naturalised in parts of Central Europe.

var. MARASCA (Host) Viv. *Cerasus marasca* Host—A vigorous tree whose fruits are employed in the manufacture of the famous Maraschino liqueur in Dalmatia, especially around the town of Zadar (Zara).

The cherries deriving from *P. cerasus* are self-fertile and will therefore fruit even if only a single specimen is grown. The Morello cherry fruits well on a north wall.

The following varieties are distinguished by their flowers, habit, or foliage

cv. 'DUMOSA'.—When budded or grafted on low standards, this makes a dwarf, round-headed tree, profuse in flower, and of very slow growth. A charming tree for a small lawn, where it may stand for many years and cause no inconvenience by overgowing. It is figured in *Garden*, Vol. 78, p. 201.

It is possible that this variety is really the same as 'GLOBOSA' ('Umbra-culifera'), which was put into commerce by Späth in the 1880s.

cv. 'PERSICIFLORA'.—Flowers double, pink. Known since the 17th century.

cv. 'RHEXII'.—Flowers pure white, 1½ in. across, very double, with stalks almost twice as long as in the type, but not so pendulous as in *P. avium* 'Plena'. It is scarcely so fine as that variety, and is subject to brown rot.

cv. 'SALICIFOLIA'.—Leaves long and narrow, 4 to 6 in. long, about one-fourth as wide, coarsely and doubly toothed. A distinct variety with single flowers.

cv. 'SEMIPLENA'.—Flowers semi-double, with normal carpels and occasionally producing fruit. The *P. cerasus* var. *plena* of Linnaeus is probably this variety and not 'Rhexii'.

cv. 'SEMPERFLORENS'. ALL SAINTS' CHERRY.—This remarkable variety has been cultivated in gardens since the 18th century, but its origin is not known. It is usually grafted on standards of cherry, and thus makes a small, very elegant round-headed tree, with pendent, slender branches and curiously clustered twigs, which in the leafless state render it easily distinguishable. The most interesting and attractive thing about it is its method of flowering. It bears a small crop of blossom in April when in ordinary leafless condition, and in ordinary clusters; it then goes out of flower until the new shoots are a few inches long (early June), when it commences to blossom again, and continues to do so until September. These second flowers, however, are produced singly from the leaf-axils, and from the ends of the young leaf-bearing shoots. This variety in reality produces during the growing season the flowers which ought normally to be (and are in other cherries) produced simultaneously the following spring. By the time the later flowers are open the earlier ones have developed fruit, which is acid, but pleasantly flavoured. An interesting and attractive lawn tree.

P. × GONDOUINII (Poiteau & Turpin) Rehd. *Cerasus gondouinii* Poiteau & Turpin; *P. × effusa* (Host) Schneid.—*P. × gondouinii* appears to be the correct name for hybrids between *P. cerasus* and *P. avium*. Here belong the Duke cherries. An ornamental cherry known as 'SCHNEE', cultivated in Germany and Holland, is considered by Dr Boom to be a hybrid of this parentage (*Dendroflora*, No. 3 (1966), p. 14; figured in op. cit., No. 1, p. 18).

P. COCOMILIA Ten.   NAPLES PLUM

A deciduous thorny bush or small tree, with glabrous shoots and oval or obovate leaves 1½ to 2 in. long, ½ to ¾ in. wide, finely toothed, nearly or quite glabrous. Flowers white, scarcely ½ in. wide, appearing towards the end of April on short stalks, mostly in pairs. Fruits yellow, well flavoured, of an oval or oblong form, 1½ in. long, scarcely 1 in. wide, tapered at the apex. But little is known of this plum in this country. It was first described early in the 19th century by Tenore, an Italian botanist who made a special study of the flora about Naples, where the species grows wild in hedges, etc. It also grows wild in Sicily and the S. Balkans. The specific name has been variously spelled. The tree has little to recommend it for gardens; it rarely bears fruit in this country.

P. CONCINNA Koehne

A deciduous shrubby cherry up to 6 or 8 ft high; young shoots soon glabrous. Leaves purplish when young, narrowly oval to obovate, sharply and finely toothed, long-pointed, rounded to tapered at the base, 1½ to 3 in. long, dull green above, greyish beneath, and slightly hairy on both surfaces especially when young; stalk ¼ in. long. Flowers white or pale pink, about 1 in. wide, produced either singly or up to four in a cluster; flower-stalk ½ in. long. Petals obovate, mostly notched; calyx-tube glabrous, tubular, tapered to the base; the lobes ovate-triangular, not toothed. Fruits roundish, ⅓ in. long, black.

Native of W. Hupeh, China; introduced by Wilson in 1907. This shrubby cherry is very rare in cultivation. It produces its flowers during March or April in great profusion in advance of the leaves and is then a very pretty shrub.

P. CONRADINAE Koehne

A deciduous tree of graceful habit up to 35 ft high; young shoots glabrous. Leaves oval to oval-lanceolate, or inclined to obovate; slender-pointed, mostly rounded at the base, toothed, often doubly so, 2 to 4½ in. long, 1 to 2¼ in. wide, glabrous or with sprinkled hairs above, more or less hairy on the veins beneath; stalk ½ in. long. Flowers produced on the leafless shoots during early spring in very shortly stalked clusters of two to five, each on a glabrous stalk ¼ to ⅝ in. long; white or pale pink, 1 in. wide. Calyx quite glabrous, the tube bell-shaped, the lobes triangular. Fruits red, ovoid, ⅖ in. long.

Native of W. Hupeh, China; introduced in 1907 by means of seeds sent to Kew from the Arnold Arboretum, Mass., which had been collected that season by Wilson, who first discovered the species. It is the best of the early-flowering wild cherries and is usually in bloom during normal seasons in February or early March. In the warmest counties it will flower in January. The petals are always notched at the end, occasionally lobed in addition, and the flowers frequently show a tendency to 'double'. Collingwood Ingram of Benenden, Kent, found in his collection a tree with this doubleness unusually developed. This is named 'SEMI-PLENA' (Bot. Mag., n.s., t. 551). It lasts longer in bloom than the single type. The flowers are pleasantly fragrant. If possible, it should be planted where it has an evergreen background to the north and east; this will give shelter to the early blossoms and bring out their beauty more definitely.

P. conradinae is allied to P. HIRTIPES Hemsl., described in 1887 from a specimen collected by Maries in Kiangsi, and is included in it by C. Jeffrey (Bot. Mag., loc. cit.). The view taken here is that P. conradinae is sufficiently distinct to justify retaining it as a separate species until more wild material is available for study.

P. CONSOCIIFLORA Schneid.

A small deciduous tree; young shoots glabrous, brown. Leaves oblanceolate to obovate, narrowed at the apex to a longish point, tapered at the base, minutely toothed, the teeth glandular, 1½ to 3 in. long, ¾ to 1¼ in. wide, undersurface with tufts of down in the vein-axils. Flowers ½ in. wide, white, fragrant, produced in April before the leaves, usually in twos or threes and often crowded on short twigs to make a cluster 1 in. across; calyx and flower-stalk quite glabrous, the former funnel-shaped with narrowly triangular lobes, the latter slender, about ¼ in. long; ovary glabrous.

Native of China; introduced by Wilson in 1900 when collecting for Messrs Veitch. Although it is a plum, its leaves are conduplicate in the bud state; that is, the two halves are folded together lengthwise like a sheet of notepaper, whereas in most plums they are convolute in bud, which means that each half of the leaf is rolled inwards. Judging by the trees at Kew, this plum is very similar to *P. salicina* with the same immense quantities of small white flowers which are quite pleasantly scented. *P. salicina* has always convolute leaves.

P. CORNUTA (Royle) Steud.   HIMALAYAN BIRD CHERRY
Cerasus cornuta Royle; *Padus cornuta* (Royle) Carr.

A deciduous tree 50 to 60 ft high in the wild; young shoots either finely downy or quite glabrous. Leaves ovate-oblong, or somewhat obovate, 3 to 6 in. long, 1½ to 2 in. wide, the base varying from heart-shaped to tapering, the apex slender-pointed, the margins finely toothed, downy along the midrib and veins beneath when young, deep dull green above, paler beneath; stalk ½ to 1¼ in. long, mostly with glands at the top. Flowers white, densely set on cylindrical, quite glabrous, or finely downy racemes, 3 to 6 in. long, ¾ to 1 in. wide; each flower is ¼ to ⅓ in. across. Fruits round, ⅓ in. in diameter, red, changing to dark brown purple. Flowers in May. *Bot. Mag.*, t. 9423.

Native of the Himalaya as far east as Sikkim, and the representative in that region of *P. padus*. So nearly are they allied that many botanists regard them as forms of one species. According to travellers in the Himalaya, *P. cornuta* grows to considerably larger size than does *P. padus* as we know it in England. The name cornuta (horned) refers to the shape of the fruits as often seen in the Himalaya. An insect deposits its eggs in the young fruit, and as the larvae develop they set up irritation and cause a curious growth, which is from 1 to 2 in. long and curled like a horn. It is analogous to the many galls that occur on our own trees—notably oaks.

P. NAPAULENSIS (Ser.) Steud. *Cerasus napaulensis* Ser.—This species is
closely allied to *P. cornuta* and most reliably distinguished from it by its fruits, which have thickened and markedly lenticellate pedicels. It differs, too, in its leaves, which are notably narrower than in *P. cornuta*, the blades being usually 2¾ to 4¾ in. long, ¾ to 1 in. wide, rarely up to 5¾ in. long and 1⅞ in. wide. Seringe aptly compared the foliage to that of *Salix fragilis*.

P. CUTHBERTII Small
Padus cuthbertii (Small) Small

A deciduous tree up to 20 ft high, with a trunk sometimes 6 in. in diameter in the wild state, but shrubby in cultivation here; young shoots downy. Leaves almost glabrous except for greyish hairs along the midrib beneath, obovate or oval, $1\frac{1}{2}$ to $3\frac{1}{2}$ in. long, more than half as wide, usually rounded or even notched at the apex, tapering at the base to a downy stalk $\frac{1}{4}$ in. long, margins very shallowly toothed, lower teeth glandular. Flowers very small, white, produced on leafy racemes 2 to 3 in. long, flower-stalks downy. Fruits red, roundish, $\frac{1}{4}$ in. in diameter.

Native of Central Georgia, USA, where it inhabits woods. It was introduced to this country in 1901, and, although slow-growing, has proved hardy so far. Allied to P. *serotina*, it differs very markedly in its round-ended leaves and downy shoots and flower-stalks. It is never likely, I think, to become so handsome a tree. Its flowers, which come in June, are not showy, but its foliage is handsome and distinct among bird cherries, and falls late.

P. DASYCARPA Ehrh.   BLACK APRICOT
Armeniaca dasycarpa (Ehrh.) Pers.

A deciduous tree 12 to 20 ft high, with purplish, glabrous twigs. Leaves oval to ovate, with a rather abrupt tapering point finely toothed, $1\frac{1}{2}$ to $2\frac{1}{2}$ in. long, two-thirds as wide, downy beneath on the midrib and main veins; leaf-stalk $\frac{3}{4}$ to 1 in. long, often glanded. Flower $\frac{3}{4}$ in. across, pure white, produced on the naked wood in March, each on a downy stalk. Fruits round, $1\frac{1}{2}$ in. across, black, with purple bloom, minutely downy.

P. *dasycarpa* is almost certainly a hybrid between the apricot and the cherry plum (P. *cerasifera*). According to Kostina in *Fl. SSSR* (Vol. 10, p. 599) many sorts of the plum-apricot are cultivated in Central Asia, Kashmir, Baluchistan, and Iran, regions in which the apricot and cherry plum are grown together and usually raised from seeds, so that the likelihood of spontaneous hybridisation between them is very great. P. *dasycarpa* bears fruit only sparsely in this country, but has been offered in German catalogues of fruit trees as 'plum-apricot'. The fruit is described as ripening in August, purple-black, covered with fine down, the flesh red, juicy, sweet, and of an apricot flavour. It would probably need wall treatment in this country to develop its fruit properly. It is worth cultivation as an early free-flowering tree.

P. DAVIDIANA (Carr.) Franch.   DAVID'S PEACH
Persica davidiana Carr.

A deciduous tree 20 to 30 ft high, with glabrous branchlets. Leaves 3 to 5 in. long, 1 to $1\frac{1}{2}$ in. wide, tapering to a long fine point like the almond, finely and sharply toothed, stalk $\frac{1}{2}$ to $\frac{3}{4}$ in. long, with one or two glands. Flowers white or pale pink, 1 in. across, produced singly on very short stalks from the buds of the previous year's shoots. Calyx glabrous, with five rounded, oblong lobes. Fruits spherical, $1\frac{1}{4}$ in. across, yellowish, downy; flesh thin; nut pitted. The twigs become grey by autumn.

Native of China; introduced to Paris in 1865, by means of seeds sent by the Abbé David, who stated that the tree made a beautiful and conspicuous feature in the vicinity of Peking. In English gardens this species is chiefly valuable for the earliness of its blossoms, which expand at any time between January and March, according to the weather, the normal time, perhaps, being about mid-February. Owing to their earliness, they are liable to injury (I have frequently seen snow resting on trees in bloom), and should be given a sheltered spot—the south-western side of a plantation of evergreens for preference. In such a position, given favourable weather the slender twigs, 1 to 2 ft long, wreathed with white (f. ALBA Hort.) or, in f. RUBRA (Bean) Rehd., rosy blossom, have a charming effect. Propagated by budding on almond or plum stocks. The white-flowered form received the Award of Garden Merit in 1927.

P. × DAWYCKENSIS Sealy   DAWYCK CHERRY

A deciduous cherry up to about 16 ft high; young shoots hairy, grey to purplish, becoming shining, glabrous and warty later. Leaves broadly oval to obovate, 2 to 5 in. long, 1½ to 2½ in. wide (those of the flowering shoots smaller), more or less slenderly pointed, coarsely round-toothed, slightly hairy above, glaucous-green and more or less hairy beneath. Flowers in shortly stalked downy umbels of two or three blossoms, each ⅝ in. across, petals roundish, overlapping, pale pink; style glabrous. Fruit a globose, scarlet-crimson cherry, ½ in. wide, stalk about 1 in. long. *Bot. Mag., t.* 9519.

Origin not definitely known, but most probably introduced from W. China early in the present century by E. H. Wilson. It is near enough to *P. dielsiana* and *P. canescens* to have suggested its being a hybrid between them. The original plant is at Dawyck in Peeblesshire.

P. DIELSIANA Schneid.

A deciduous cherry up to 30 ft high; young shoots glabrous. Leaves oval, obovate, or inclined to oblong, abruptly narrowed at the apex to a short slender point, rounded or slightly heart-shaped at the base, sharply and often doubly toothed, 3 to 7 in. long, 1¼ to 3 in. wide, glabrous above, distinctly downy beneath, especially on the midrib and veins; stalk ¼ to ⅝ in. long, usually downy and furnished with one to three large glands. Flowers 1 in. wide, pink or white, produced before the leaves, three to six in a cluster, each on a hairy stalk ½ to 1¼ in. long. Calyx-tube bell-shaped, hairy, its reflexed awl-shaped lobes longer than the tube; petals narrowly oval, deeply notched at the end. Fruits globose, ⅓ in. wide, red. The flowers spring from the axis of an involucre of conspicuously glandular-fringed bracts. *Bot. Mag., n.s., t.* 174.

Native of W. Hupeh, China; introduced in 1907 by Wilson. It has about the same degree of beauty as the other wild cherries introduced by Wilson at the same time, but is rather distinct on account of the downy undersurface of its large leaves, the hairy flower-stalks, and the very glandular-edged bracts. Nearly related to it is:

P. CYCLAMINA Koehne—This was introduced by Wilson from the same region in 1907 and also in 1904 from W. Szechwan, when collecting for Messrs

Veitch, in whose nursery it first flowered. It differs from *P. dielsiana* in the leaves being nearly or quite glabrous below, and in the glabrous leaf-stalk and calyx-tube. The flowers are a charming pink and a little over 1 in. wide, the oblong petals deeply notched at the end. The lobes of the calyx are longer than the tube and are much reflexed as in *P. dielsiana;* their resemblance to the recurved petals of a cyclamen suggested the specific name. Both species have very linear stipules about ½ in. long, conspicuously fringed with stalked glands.

At The Grange, Benenden, Kent, *P. cyclamina* has made a small, spreading tree which attained a height of 18 ft in thirty years. It is quite hardy there and produces self-sown seedlings, but Capt. Ingram suggests it might be more vigorous if grafted on gean. *Bot. Mag.*, n.s., t. 338.

P. DOMESTICA L.   PLUM

P. communis Huds.

A deciduous tree up to 15 or 20 ft high, or (under wild conditions) a shrub, of suckering habit, with brown, usually glabrous or almost so, unarmed branches. Leaves elliptical or obovate, downy beneath on the midrib and veins, 1½ to 3 in. long, of a dull greyish green, margins set with rounded even teeth; stalk usually downy, glandular, about ½ in. long. Flowers produced in April singly or in pairs, from the buds of the previous year's shoots, white, ¾ to 1 in. across; stalks ¼ in. long, glabrous. Fruits variable in shape, size, and colour. Stones flattened, sharp-angled, slightly pitted, usually free from the flesh.

For the origin of the plums and related fruits see below. It is occasionally met with in hedgerows, etc., as an escape from cultivation or semi-naturalised, but is not so common as the bullace, from which it is well distinguished by its unarmed branches and more or less glabrous twigs.

The plum is largely used as a stock for almonds, peaches, etc., being very hardy. It is not worth growing for ornament in gardens, at least in its typical form. An old tree in blossom is pretty, but not more so than the fruit-bearing plums commonly grown, of which it is one of the parents. The double-flowered 'PLANTIERENSIS' is sometimes grown as an ornamental.

subsp. INSITITIA (L.) Poir. *P. insititia* L. BULLACE.—Twigs downy and remaining so for a year or so; branches often thorny, brown. Leaves as in typical *P. domestica.* Fruits usually rounded or broadly ellipsoid, usually dark purple in naturalised trees. Stone not so flattened as in the plum, with blunt edges and clinging to the flesh.

The bullace is not a native of Britain but has become thoroughly naturalised. It is now little cultivated, but three orchard varieties are described in the latest supplement to the *Dictionary of Gardening.* The Mirabelle group of plums, with round, yellow fruits, belong to this subspecies. The damsons, too, are said to derive from it. They take their name from Damascus, where they have been cultivated since before the Christian era.

The Green Gage or Reine Claude is by some authorities given the rank of subspecies—subsp. ITALICA (Borkh.) Hegi; by others it is placed under subsp. *insititia.*

Modern research has shown that that *P. domestica* and its subspecies are hexaploid and of hybrid origin. The sloe, *P. spinosa*, is a tetraploid species and the cherry plum, *P. cerasifera* or *P. divaricata* diploid. In the Caucasus hybrids between them, which are triploid and sterile, are said to occur quite frequently. But doubling of the chromosome number gives rise to fertile, more or less true-breeding hexaploids and it is from these that the plums and their allies are derived (Crane and Lawrence, *The Genetics of Garden Plants*, ed. 4, pp. 237–8; Rybin, *Planta*, Vol. 25, pp. 22–58).

P. DULCIS (Mill.) D. A. Webb   ALMOND

Amygdalus dulcis Mill.; *A. communis* L.; *A. sativus* Mill.; *Prunus amygdalus* Batsch; *P. communis* (L.) Arcangeli (1882), not Huds. (1762)

A deciduous tree 20 to 30 ft high, erect branching when young, of bushy habit when old; branchlets quite glabrous. Leaves glabrous, lanceolate, 3 to 5 in. long, $\frac{3}{4}$ to $1\frac{1}{2}$ in. wide; long-pointed, margins finely toothed; stalk glandular, up to 1 in. long. Flowers 1 to 2 in. across, borne in March and April, singly or in pairs from the buds of the previous summer's twigs, each on a short stalk scarcely longer than the bud-scales. Calyx bell-shaped at the base, the five lobes $\frac{1}{6}$ in. long, oblong, rounded, downy towards the edges; petals rosy or nearly white. Fruit $1\frac{1}{2}$ to $2\frac{1}{2}$ in. long, not quite so much wide, covered with a velvety down; flesh rather dry, enclosing a smooth nut with a pitted shell.

The common almond of gardens described above, which is grown for its flowers rather than for its fruits, is one of many cultivated varieties that have arisen since the dawn of civilisation from the wild ancestral stock, usually considered to be native in S.W. Asia, the Balkans, and perhaps N. Africa. It was cultivated in Britain early in the 16th century, perhaps long before. Of the earliest blossoming trees it is the most beautiful, flowering in early spring when almost all other deciduous trees and shrubs are merely showing signs of reawakening growth, and providing then a delightful feast of softest colouring, which gives, perhaps, a deeper pleasure than any of the great genus *Prunus*. To see the almond at its best it should be given some sunny bay with evergreens like holly or holm oak as a background. With no other backing than the cold March sky, almond flowers lose half their charm. In Britain it is propagated chiefly by budding on the plum stock, and thrives very well. Seeds or seedlings can be obtained at very cheap rates from continental nurseries, but on its own roots it is said to be less hardy and more fastidious as to soil than it is when worked on the plum. The soil need not be particularly rich, but it should be warm and well drained. Although the almond occasionally produces good eatable nuts in England, it is never likely to be valued in gardens on that account. It is for its beauty of flower alone that it is cultivated. We can therefore ignore the numerous varieties that are grown in the south of Europe for their nuts.

For nomenclatural reasons, the name *P. amygdalus* has to give way to *P. dulcis* (Mill.) D. A. Webb, a combination first published in 1967. The earliest name for the almond was *Amygdalus communis*, given by Linnaeus in 1753. When Batsch transferred it to *Prunus* in 1801, he could not make the combination *P. communis* (L.), since that name had already been used by Hudson in 1762 for the plum, *P. domestica*. Batsch therefore published the name *P. amygdalus*, but under modern rules he ought to have used the earliest epithet available and there were in fact two to choose from, both published by Philip Miller in his *Dictionary* (1768). Miller restricted the name *Amygdalus communis* L. to the common almond, which 'is cultivated more for the beauty of its flowers, than for its fruit', and gave specific rank to two forms of sweet almond—*A. dulcis*, the common sweet almond or Jordan almond, and *A. sativus*, an early-flowering, small-kernelled sort. This was overlooked or ignored until 1967, when Professor Webb rectified the matter by making the combination *P. dulcis* (Mill.) D. A. Webb. This is the name used in *Flora Europaea*, Vol. 2 (1968), p. 78.

The sweet almond, i.e., *P. dulcis* in the narrow sense, is not cultivated in Britain, at least not frequently. But the common or ornamental almond of gardens is, in its fruits, nearer to the sweet than to the bitter almonds (see var. *amara*). Its kernels are perfectly edible and have a negligible content of prussic acid, the lethal intake for an adult being about 900 kernels, eaten at one sitting. But it is recommended that children should not be allowed to eat more than twenty to fifty at a time, according to age (*Journ. R.H.S.*, Vol. 68 (1943), p. 65).

cv. 'Alba'.—Flowers white.

var. AMARA (DC.) *Amygdalus communis* var. *amara* DC.; *P. amygdalus* var. *amara* (DC.) Focke BITTER ALMOND.—Flowers larger than ordinary, darkest in the centre, almost white towards the tips of the petals. Leaves broadest about the middle. The kernels, in ground form, or an essence or oil extracted from them, are used in confectionery, for macaroons, marzipan, etc.

cv. 'Macrocarpa'.—The name *Amygdalus communis* var. *macrocarpa* was given by Seringe to two varieties of sweet almond cultivated in France, the 'Amandier Sultane' and the 'Amandier Pistache', both with large fruits about 3 in. in length and flowers up to 2 in. across. The habit is rather more fastigiate than in the common almond. Award of Merit 1931.

cv. 'Pendula'.—Branches pendulous.

cv. 'Praecox'.—Flowers produced a fortnight earlier than in the type, frequently in February. In previous editions it was stated that this variety was also grown as var. *persicoides*, properly a synonym of *P.* × *amygdalo-persica*. But 'Praecox' has a sweet kernel, whereas in the almond-peach it is bitter. F.C.C. 1925.

cv. 'Roseoplena'.—Flowers pink, double.

P. WEBBII (Spach) Vierh. *Amygdalus webbii* Spach—A relative of the common almond found wild from Sicily through the S. Balkans to S. Asia Minor and in Crete. It is a much-branched spiny shrub or small tree with narrow-oblong leaves 1¼ to 1¾ in. long and ¼ to ⅜ in. wide. Flowers white, about ¾ in. across. *Bot. Mag.*, n.s., t. 118. It is quite hardy and has set fruit at The Grange, Benenden, Kent.

P. FENZLIANA Fritsch *Amygdalus fenzliana* (Fritsch) Lipsky—A relative of the common almond found in the Caucasus. It is a small bushy shrub with a dark purplish-red bark and greyish green rather glossy leaves, which are elliptic-lanceolate, 2¼ to 3¼ in. long, ⅝ to ¾ in. wide. Flowers rose-coloured; calyx-tube bell-shaped. Fruits globose.

P. EMARGINATA (Hook.) Eaton   BITTER CHERRY
Cerasus emarginata Dougl. ex Hook.

This species seems to be represented in cultivation by the following variety:

var. MOLLIS (Hook.) Brewer & Watson *Cerasus mollis* Dougl. ex Hook.; *C. pattoniana* Carr.—A deciduous tree, sometimes 30 to 40 ft high, with a trunk 1 ft or more in diameter; branches downy when young, becoming glabrous with age; bark exceedingly bitter. Leaves obovate-oblong, usually rounded or blunt at the apex, tapering towards the base, 1½ to 2½ in. long, scarcely half as wide, finely and bluntly toothed, downy beneath; stalk about ¼ in. long. Flowers dullish white, not ½ in. across, produced six to twelve together in May on corymbose clusters 1½ in. long, each flower on a downy stalk ¼ to ½ in. long; petals notched at the apex; calyx downy, lobes rounded. Fruits ¼ to ½ in. diameter, red, finally almost black.

A native of British Columbia and Oregon; discovered by David Douglas; introduced to Britain in 1861–2 and at first known in gardens as *Cerasus pattoniana*—the name under which the seeds were distributed. It is a handsome tree of healthy aspect and of neat habit, but its flowers are not sufficiently pure white to be really effective. The bark, leaves, and fruit are permeated by an intensely bitter principle.

Typical *P. emarginata* is less downy or almost completely glabrous, and is usually of smaller stature. It has a wider range in western North America than the var. *mollis*. It, too, was discovered by David Douglas.

P. × FONTANESIANA (Spach) Schneid.
Cerasus fontanesiana Spach; P. graeca Steud.

A deciduous, quick-growing tree 40 ft or more high; young shoots covered with shaggy down. Leaves ovate to oval, sometimes heart-shaped, 3 to 5 in. long, 1½ to 2½ in. wide, doubly round-toothed, somewhat hairy on the midrib and veins; leaf-stalk ¾ to 1¼ in. long, very downy, glandular. Flowers 1 in. across, white, produced during May on short, broad racemes of about five to seven, sometimes ten, flowers from the buds of the previous year's wood, each flower on a stalk ½ to ¾ in. long, the common stalk ¾ to 1 in. long, downy. Fruits globular, the size of a small cherry, somewhat bitter, nearly black, very sparingly borne.

This tree was originally introduced to Paris from Greece and is believed to be a natural hybrid between *P. avium* and *P. mahaleb*. The form of the inflorescence is certainly intermediate, and the very downy shoots show *P. mahaleb*. The tree has much the habit of *P. avium*, and when in flower it is quite as beautiful as the typical form of that species, or even more so.

P. FRUTICOSA Pall.   GROUND CHERRY
P. chamaecerasus Jacq.

A deciduous shrub 1 to 3 ft high, of low, spreading habit, with glabrous round twigs. Leaves obovate to narrowly oval, tapering to both ends, from

¾ to 2 in. long, ¼ to ¾ in. wide, with shallow, rounded teeth, dark glossy green, and quite glabrous; stalk ⅛ to ¼ in. long. Flowers white, ¾ in. across, produced in usually stalkless umbels of about four from buds on the previous year's shoots, each flower on a slender stalk ½ to 1 in. long. Fruits about the size of a large pea, very deep reddish purple.

Native of continental Europe and parts of Siberia; cultivated in England for more than three centuries. It is a shrub of neat and pleasing habit, forming naturally a low, mound-like mass of slender branches, and wearing a very healthy aspect because of the deep shining green of its foliage. In gardens it is rarely seen except grafted standard high on a cherry stock. In this way its branches form a mop-headed mass with the lower branches pendent of their own weight. The fruits have a cherry flavour, but are too harsh and acid to be palatable. It blossoms in early May.

cv. 'VARIEGATA'.—Leaves stained more or less with yellowish white, sometimes half the leaf being of this colour, the other half green.

P. × EMINENS Beck *Cerasus intermedia* Host; *P. reflexa* Hort., not Walp.— The cherry that has been grown in gardens under the name *P. reflexa* is thought to be a hybrid between *P. fruticosa* and *P. cerasus*. It differs from *P. fruticosa* in its more robust habit and sturdier branches, its more deeply and irregularly toothed leaves (of the same shining dark green), and its shorter-stalked flowers. A very pretty small tree with pendulous branches. Hybrids between the two species are fairly common in the wild.

P. GLANDULOSA Thunb.

P. japonica Sieb. & Zucc., in part, not Thunb.; *P. japonica* var. *β* Maxim.; *P. glandulosa* var. *glabra* Koehne; *Cerasus glandulosa* (Thunb.) Loisel.; *C. japonica* var. *glandulosa* (Thunb.) Komarov & Klobukova-Alisova

A dwarf bush of neat, rounded habit, up to 4 or 5 ft high, with glabrous branches. Leaves ovate-lanceolate, 1 to 2½ in. long, ¾ to 1 in. wide; more or less drawn out at the apex, finely toothed, almost or quite glabrous; stalk ¼ in. or less long; stipules linear, with gland-tipped teeth. Flowers white or rosy, scarcely ½ in. across, on stalks ¼ in. long, produced in April. Fruits scarcely ½ in. in diameter, red, making a bright display when freely borne. *Bot. Mag.*, t. 8260.

Native of N. China, Korea, and the southern part of the Ussuri region; described from Japan, but not native there. It is best known in its two double-flowered garden varieties (see below).

The single-flowered type appears to have been cultivated in Britain in Loudon's time as "*Cerasus japonica*", but it disappeared from gardens and was not introduced until late in the 19th century. It is allied to *P. humilis* (q.v.).

Of the double-flowered varieties of *P. glandulosa* there are two: 'ALBA PLENA', with white flowers, and 'ROSEA PLENA' (syn. 'SINENSIS'), with pink flowers. They provide a remarkable illustration of how much the flowers of a plant can be improved by cultivation. The typical plant in flower is a pretty but by no means striking shrub, whereas the double varieties are amongst the very élite of their class. The flowers carry numerous petals, and are 1 to 1¼ in. in diameter, and their stalks become ¾ in. or more long. The foliage too, is finer, the leaves measuring 3 to 4 in. in length by 1 in. in width. They flower in early May, later than the type. The double varieties have been cultivated, and brought to their present perfection, in China and Japan. The rosy-coloured one was introduced in the second half of the 17th century.

The double-flowered varieties were at one time used for forcing early into bloom under glass. Out-of-doors they are seen to best advantage planted against a south wall, where the flowering shoots should be pruned back almost to the older wood as soon as ever the flowers are faded. But they are also very delightful in the open ground but are more subject to die-back grown in this way. They can be propagated by cuttings, but layers prove more satisfactory as a rule. Both have received an Award of Merit.

P. JAPONICA Thunb.—This shrub is allied to *P. glandulosa* but differs in its ovate, acuminate, sharply double-toothed leaves. It is a native of China but named from a Japanese garden plant. A form with pink, semi-double flowers was in cultivation early in the 19th century and is figured in *Bot. Mag.*, t. 2176, and *Bot. Reg.*, t. 27. It was found more difficult to cultivate than *P. glandulosa* 'Rosea Plena' ('Sinensis') and probably soon dropped out of cultivation. The species is more subject to die-back than *P. glandulosa* in the British climate and no more ornamental (Ingram, *Orn. Cherries*, p. 175).

In *P. japonica* var. NAKAII (Lévl.) Rehd., the leaves are downy beneath. This was introduced by Wilson from Korea in 1918 (W.10596).

P. GRAYANA Maxim.   GRAY'S BIRD CHERRY
Padus grayana (Maxim.) Schneid.

A native of Japan, where it is a small tree 20 to 30 ft high, with a slender trunk. This species is very closely allied to our common bird cherry (*P. padus*), differing chiefly in the leaves, which have no glands on the very short stalks (almost invariably present in *P. padus*), and in the teeth being finer and more hair-like. The white flowers are borne in erect racemes up to 4 in. long. Fruits black, about the size of peas, narrowing towards the apex. The species inhabits the mountain forests of the main island of Japan, and the southern parts of Hokkaido. The true plant is very uncommon in cultivation.

P. HORTULANA Bailey

A deciduous tree 20 to 30 ft high, sometimes a shrub. Leaves ovate-lanceolate, 4 to 6 in. long, one-quarter as much wide, hairy below along the midrib and in the axils of the veins; margins set with glandular teeth. Flowers white, ¾ to 1 in. across, produced on the year-old wood in April and May in stalkless clusters of two to six; calyx-lobes glandular, toothed. Fruits roundish, ¾ to 1 in. in diameter, with a thick red or yellow skin.

Native of the southern and central United States; founded as a species in 1892, but known long before. It has been regarded as a hybrid between *P. americana* and *P. angustifolia*, but is now accepted as a good species. Many varieties of it are cultivated for fruits in the United States, which are especially well adapted for the Mississippi Valley and the southern States. They are known collectively as the Wayland or Hortulana plums. The Miner group probably also derives from *P. hortulana*. None of these varieties is of any economic value in Britain.

P. MUNSONIANA Wight & Hedrick—Allied to the above and first described as a separate species in 1911. Leaves narrower than in *P. hortulana*, being mostly lanceolate or oblong-lanceolate, and finely saw-toothed, the teeth tipped with reddish glands. Native of the southern USA, west of the Appalachians. Parent of the Wild Goose group of orchard plums.

P. HUMILIS Bunge
P. bungei Walp.

A low-growing, deciduous shrub 4 to 5 ft high, with downy young branchlets. Leaves oval or obovate with a tapering base, 1 to 2 in. long, half as wide, almost glabrous except when quite young, finely and doubly toothed; stalk ⅛ in. long; stipules ¼ in. long, linear, very glandular. Flowers pale pink, ½ in. across, produced singly, in pairs, or in threes from the buds of the previous year's wood, each on a stalk ⅓ in. long. Fruits bright red, very acid in this country, but not unpalatable, about ½ in. in diameter. *Bot. Mag.*, t. 7335.

Native of N. China; introduced to Kew in 1881 by Dr Bretschneider. This pretty dwarf cherry, which is cultivated in N. China for its fruits, is perfectly hardy. Nearly allied to *P. glandulosa*, it may be roughly distinguished by its downy shoots and its leaves being widest above the middle. From *P. jacquemontii*, with which it has been confused, its downy shoots also distinguish it. *P. jacquemontii*, besides, has laciniated stipules.

P. ILICIFOLIA (Hook. & Arn.) Walp.
Cerasus ilicifolia Hook. & Arn.; *Laurocerasus ilicifolia* (Hook. & Arn.) Roem.

An evergreen shrub of compact habit; branchlets glabrous. Leaves ovate, 1 to 2 in. long, ¾ to 1¼ in wide; rounded or slightly heart-shaped at the base, sharply toothed, the hollows between the teeth wide and rounded, dark glossy green, glabrous on both surfaces. Flowers in racemes 1½ to 3 in. long, produced in summer; each flower ⅓ in. across, white, on a stalk ⅙ in. long. Fruits roundish, but slightly pointed at the end, ½ in. in diameter, changing to red, then black-purple.

Native of California, and too tender to be of much value in any but the mildest parts of the British Isles as a shrub for the open ground. But on a sunny wall it should survive all but the hardest winters once it is established and flower well, at least in warm summers. Closely related to this species is:

P. LYONII (Eastw.) Sarg. *Cerasus lyonii* Eastw.; *P. integrifolia* Sarg., not Walp.; *P. ilicifolia* var. *occidentalis* (Nutt.) Brandegee—This grows taller than *P. ilicifolia* and has almost entire leaves, racemes up to 5 in. long and dark fruits. Native of several islands off the coast of California, including Sta Catalina.

PRUNUS ILICIFOLIA

P. CAROLINIANA (Mill.) Ait. *Padus caroliniana* Mill.—Another N. American cherry laurel and equally tender. Loudon states that in 1833 there was a bush 10 ft high at Swallowfield in Hampshire, but this is very doubtful. It was probably some form of common cherry laurel, wrongly named. *P. caroliniana* has entire leaves 3 to 4½ in. long, oblong-lanceolate; flowers creamy white, in short racemes; and black, shining, oblong fruit, ½ in. long. A native of S.E. United States, where it is used, much as the common laurel is here, to make hedges. Originally introduced in 1759, and many times since, it has never long survived, unless it be in some of the south-western counties.

P. INCANA (Pall.) Batsch   WILLOW CHERRY
Amygdalus incana Pall.; *Cerasus incana* (Pall.) Spach

A deciduous shrub 4 to 8 ft high, of rather open, loose habit; shoots minutely downy. Leaves oval-lanceolate or obovate, pointed, 1½ to 3 in. long, ⅓ to ⅔ in. wide; regularly, finely, and sharply toothed, tapering towards both ends, dark green and glabrous above, covered with a close white wool beneath. Flowers ¼ in. across, borne singly from the buds of the previous year's shoots; petals deep rosy red; calyx ¼ in. long, tubular, with five short, rounded, downy lobes. Fruits glabrous, red, ⅓ in. across.

Native of the Caucasus and Asia Minor; introduced in 1815. Its flowers appear in April along with the young leaves, and it is then very pretty. Sometimes confused with *P. tenella*, it is easily distinguished from that and most other species by the close white felt on the undersurface of the willow-like leaves. The fruit is quite different from that of *P. tenella*, being cherry-like. It is allied to *P. prostrata* (q.v.).

P. INCISA Thunb.   FUJI CHERRY   [PLATE 46
Cerasus incisa (Thunb.) Loisel.

A small, elegant, deciduous tree 20 to 30 ft high, more often a bush 6 to 18 ft high; young shoots slender, glabrous, and finally grey. Leaves reddish at first, obovate to ovate, slenderly pointed, sharply and doubly or trebly toothed, 1 to 2½ in. long, ⅔ to 1¼ in. wide, downy above and on the veins beneath; stalk ¼ to ½ in. long, hairy, slender, with two purple glands near the blade. Flowers ½ to ¾ in. wide, two to four borne on a main-stalk ⅛ to 1 in. long, each flower slenderly stalked and springing from the axil of a leaf-like deeply toothed bract; petals notched or jagged at the end, white or pale pink. Calyx-tube glabrous, tubular, wine-red, the lobes minutely ciliate; stamens thirty, their stalks reddish and the anthers yellow; style slightly hairy; ovary glabrous. Fruits roundish egg-shaped, ¼ in. long, purplish black.

Native of Japan; discovered by Thunberg as long ago as 1776. It was sent to Kew in 1916 from the Arnold Arboretum, and flowered annually there in early April, but has since been lost. It had, however, been introduced to Ireland in 1913. It is now well established in cultivation. Wilson describes it in Japan as very ornamental, and although the petals do not remain on the flower for any great length of time, the calyx and stamens persist and heighten in colour. According to the same authority the main flower-stalk is very variable in length, although in our cultivated plants it is usually very short. He observes that it is the only Japanese cherry that can be fashioned into dwarf trees which will live and flower freely in small pots. It may, therefore, have come over from Japan with the large shipments of dwarfed trees sent previous to 1914. It is undoubtedly one of the most beautiful of the wild cherries, profuse in blossom, and very distinct on account of the deep double toothing and long, drawn-out point of the leaf. A.G.M. 1930.

cv. 'PRAECOX'.—A winter-flowering variety, raised by Messrs Hillier. Award of Merit January 22, 1957.

var. SERRATA (Koidz.) Wils.—This is distinguished from the type by the leaves not being so markedly double-toothed, often simply toothed, each tooth ending a bristle-like point. According to Wilson it grows intermingled with the typical state of the species in parts of Central Japan. It has no other distinguishing character, but some plants distributed under the name P. incisa serrata are of dwarf, more spreading habit and are probably a garden clone.

P. (incisa × campanulata) 'OKAME'.—Flowers carmine-pink; calyx and flower-stalks reddish. March. This beautiful hybrid was raised by Collingwood Ingram, P. campanulata being the pollen-parent. Despite the tenderness of this species, 'Okame' is completely hardy and makes a bush or small tree of neat habit. Propagated by cuttings. Award of Garden Merit 1952.

Later, Capt. Ingram made the cross (P. incisa × P. campanulata) × P. sargentii. One of the resulting seedlings, named 'SHOSAR', has flowers similar to those of P. sargentii but produced some weeks earlier. It makes a narrow-crowned tree and colours well in the autumn.

P. JACQUEMONTII Hook. f.   AFGHAN CHERRY

Amygdalus humilis Edgew.; *Cerasus jacquemontii* (Hook. f.) Buser

A deciduous bush up to 12 ft high, with glabrous, slender, grey branchlets. Leaves ovate to obovate, pointed at both ends, up to 2½ in. long, by 1 in. wide, glabrous, sharply and regularly toothed; stalk ¼ in. long. The leaves on the flowering spurs are shorter and narrower than on the extension growths. Flowers one to three at each joint, very short-stalked, bright rosy pink, ⅓ to ½ in. in diameter; calyx funnel-shaped, ⅕ in. long, with short, pointed lobes. Fruits roundish, ⅝ in. long, red, juicy, containing a roundish stone ¼ in. or rather more long. *Bot. Mag.*, t. 6976.

Native of the N.W. Himalaya, W. Pakistan, and Afghanistan; introduced in 1879 by Dr Aitchison from the Kurram Valley, where it occurs at altitudes of about 6,000 ft. It has been confused with *P. humilis*, under the notice of which the distinctions have been pointed out. *P. jacquemontii* is a pretty cherry, perfectly hardy, and makes shoots over 1 ft long during a season, which are well furnished with flowers towards the end of the following April. Propagated by layers. There used to be bushes at Kew 12 ft high and 12 ft through. It needs a dry sunny position.

P. BIFRONS Fritsch   *P. jacquemontii* var. *bifrons* (Fritsch) Ingram; *P. prostrata*
var. *bifrons* (Fritsch) Schneid.; *P. afghana* Cardot; *P. erythrocarpa* (Nevski) Gilli; *Cerasus erythrocarpa* Nevski; *C. bifrons* (Fritsch) Poyark.—A shrub up to 6 ft high, sometimes prostrate, allied to *P. jacquemontii* but with the young growths downy and the leaves clad beneath with a white tomentum. The style is hairy at the base (usually glabrous in *P. jacquemontii*). Native of Afghanistan, the N.W. Himalaya, and Central Asia; introduced by the late George Sherriff from Kashmir in 1940. The specific epithet refers to the dimorphic leaves, those on the short, flowering shoots being shorter and narrower than on the long shoots, though the same characteristic is shown by *P. jacquemontii*. It needs the same conditions as that species.

P. KANSUENSIS Rehd.

Amygdalus kansuensis (Rehd.) Skeels

A tall, deciduous shrub or a small tree up to 20 ft high with a smooth, brown trunk. Leaves lanceolate, slender-pointed, 2 to 4 in. long, ⅜ to 1¼ in. wide, finely toothed, hairy along the midrib; stalk ⅛ to 3/16 in. long. Flowers crowded on the naked glabrous shoots, mostly in pairs and making cylindrical spikes 1 to 1½ ft long; they are white, ¾ in. wide, pink in bud; petals roundish ovate, ⅜ in. long; calyx grey, hairy outside, ciliate, the lobes oblong-ovate, ⅛ in. long; stamens white, anthers and style yellow.

Native of N.W. China, introduced to California by Meyer in 1914. It will be welcomed in gardens for its early blossoms which (regulated by the weather) may appear any time in late January or February. It is closely related to the common peach, the stone being widely, shallowly grooved but not pitted. Award of Merit when shown from Kew February 5, 1957.

P. LANNESIANA *see under* P. SPECIOSA

P. LAUROCERASUS L.   CHERRY LAUREL
Laurocerasus officinalis Roem.; *Padus laurocerasus* Mill.

An evergreen shrub of quick growth and wide-spreading habit, attaining a height of over 20 ft, twice as much in width; young shoots pale green and, like all other parts of the plant, devoid of hairs or down. Leaves of leathery texture, dark shining green, of various shapes and sizes, usually oblong, but sometimes oblanceolate, averaging from 4 to 6 in. in length by rather less than one-third as much wide, margin obscurely toothed; stalk about ½ in. long. The blade always bears on its lower surface near the base two or more glands. Flowers in axillary and terminal racemes, 3 to 5 in. long, ¾ in. through; each flower on a stalk ⅙ in. long, itself dull white, ⅓ in. across. Fruits black-purple, about ½ in. long, conical, and containing a similarly shaped stone.

A native mainly of the forest region that stretches from south of the Caspian through the western parts of the Caucasus and Transcaucasia and the mountains of Anatolia, south of the Black Sea; in Europe it occurs in the Belgrade forest near Istanbul, and in some of the mountain forests of Bulgaria; a relict stand occurs in Serbia, where it does not fruit but maintains itself by layering. Throughout most of its range it is associated with the oriental beech, and often with *Rhododendron ponticum*. It reached western Europe at the end of the 16th century and was in cultivation in Britain early in the next century.

P. laurocerasus flowers in April, nearly two months in advance of the Portugal laurel, but is not so ornamental. For some strange reason the cherry laurel is rarely seen at its best, which is when it is grown as an isolated specimen unmolested by the pruner. It then makes a vigorous evergreen of exceptional size and elegance. It bears pruning well, however, and is, in consequence, often used to form a low covering for banks and slopes by keeping it severely cropped. This may have been necessary in earlier times when dwarf evergreens were scarcer, but there are several now that may be made to serve such a purpose without having to undergo the periodical mutilation to which laurels are subjected. Still less is it adapted for planting in ordinary shrubberies, where its vigorous self-assertion and hungry roots give little chance for things near it.

The cherry laurel does not appear to be quite so hardy as the Portugal laurel, although on dry soil it is not much injured by any temperature above 5° F. It is admirably adapted for planting as undergrowth in thin woodland, where there is room for its full development. All the forms are easily increased by late summer cuttings placed in gentle heat. A considerable number of varieties are now offered by nurserymen, some of garden origin, some natural. Only the most distinct of these can be mentioned, and of these very few have been authoritatively described. A study of the cultivated varieties by H. J. van de Laar was published in *Dendroflora* No. 7 (1970), pp. 42–61 (in Dutch, with English summary and numerous illustrations).

cv. 'ANGUSTIFOLIA'.—Described by Loudon as a more dwarf-growing plant, which seldom flowers; leaves about one-third as wide as in the normal form, i.e., scarcely 1 in. wide (*Arb. et Frut. Brit.*, Vol. II, p. 716 (1838)). See also 'Parvifolia'.

cv. 'CAMELLIIFOLIA'.—Leaves of ordinary size, but curled and twisted. Curious, but not ornamental. There is an example at Wakehurst Place, Sussex, and another in the R.H.S. Garden at Wisley, in Seven Acres.

cv. 'CAUCASICA'.—A vigorous, erect shrub with more or less elliptic leaves up to 7 in. long, about 3 in. wide, deep green. One of the finest.

cv. 'COLCHICA'.—Leaves up to 7 in. long, 2 in. wide, tapering to the stalk.

cv. 'COMPACTA'.—Leaves about the ordinary size, but the habit dwarf and close. Introduced to Kew from Transon's nurseries, Orleans.

cv. 'HERBERGII'.—A dense erect shrub with narrow elliptic leaves up to 6 in. long, 1¼ in. wide, tapered at the apex, glossy. Very hardy and a good hedging plant. Raised in Germany.

cv. 'MAGNOLIIFOLIA'.—The finest of all the varieties in foliage, the largest leaves 10 to 12 in. long, 3 to 4½ in. wide. A strong grower, it may, if desired, be trained into tree form by tying up a lead and gradually removing the lower branches. It came to Kew under its present name from the Hon. Charles Ellis in 1897, but according to him was also known as *latifolia*. The variety 'MACROPHYLLA' (?'Bertinii'), raised at Versailles, seems to be similar, judging from the original descriptions (*Rev.Hort.* (1869), p. 180 and (1885), p. 18).

cv. 'MISCHEANA'.—Of spreading, more or less horizontal habit, with dark green leaves up to 5½ in. long, 2 in. or slightly more wide. Introduced by Späth's nurseries from the Balkans and put into commerce around 1900.

cv. 'OTINII'.—Leaves large and broad, but not remarkable for size so much as for their dark, almost black, lustrous green; the plant is of more compact habit than most varieties. Raised by Otin, head gardener at the Jardin des Plantes, St Etienne, France, before 1873, from seed of 'Caucasica'.

cv. 'OTTO LUYKEN'. Of compact, horizontal habit, 3 to 4 ft high eventually. Leaves dark green, about 4 in. long, slightly under 1 in. wide, tapered at both ends, tips slightly acuminate. Very free flowering. A variety of recent origin raised by Messrs Hesse of Weener, Hanover. A.M. 1968.

cv. 'PARVIFOLIA' ('Microphylla').—A dwarf, narrow-leaved form, the smallest leaves 1 in. long by ¼ in. wide only, and the plant 1½ to 2 ft high. It may occasionally be seen reverting back to the typical form.

This variety has apparently also been called *angustifolia* in gardens, though it is different from the 'Angustifolia' of Loudon. Both varieties were sometimes sold in the last century as "*Hartogia capensis*", properly an evergreen species from S. Africa, belonging to the Celastraceae.

cv. 'REYNVANII'.—Of dense, erect habit to about 5 ft high, with more or less elliptic, acute, dark green leaves up to 5 or 6 in. long and to 1¾ in. wide. raised in Holland. In cultivation in the University Botanic Garden, Cambridge.

cv. 'ROTUNDIFOLIA'.—Leaves about half as broad as long, yellowish green. Tall growing.

cv. 'SCHIPKAENSIS'.—Originally found wild near the Shipka Pass in Bulgaria, north of Kazanlik, and introduced to cultivation by Späth about

1886. It has narrow, entire leaves, 2 to $4\frac{1}{2}$ in. long, $\frac{3}{4}$ to $1\frac{1}{2}$ in. wide, and a certain elegance of habit, but is not so ornamental as some of the larger-leaved varieties. Racemes $2\frac{1}{2}$ to 3 in. high. Its great value is its extreme hardiness. It will withstand winters where no cherry laurel has been known to do so before, such as N. Germany and parts of N. America.

Although the plants originally distributed by Späth were probably all of one clone, the epithet *schipkaensis* seems to have been used for other introductions from the Bulgarian mountains, and for seedlings of the original variety. According to H. van de Laar, the true 'Schipkaensis' has relatively broader leaves than the plant described above.

cv. 'ZABELIANA'.—Of the same type as 'Schipkaensis' and equally hardy. Leaves also entire, narrow, and almost willow-like, the branches growing rather stiffly and obliquely upwards. Put into commerce by Späth in 1898. It is very free flowering and valuable as a specimen or for ground-cover, retaining its low habit even in shade. It attains a width of 12 ft or even more, but is usually under 3 ft in height. At Aldenham it reached 5 ft in height and 25 ft in spread.

P. LITIGIOSA Schneid.

P. pilosiuscula var. *media* Koehne, in part; *P. rehderiana* Koehne

A deciduous cherry up to 20 ft or more high; young shoots glabrous. Leaves ovate to oblong with a rounded base and a slender drawn-out apex, finely toothed, often doubly so, $1\frac{1}{2}$ to 3 in. long, half as much wide, downy on the midrib above and in the vein-axils beneath; stalk $\frac{1}{4}$ to $\frac{1}{2}$ in. long. Flowers opening in April with the young leaves in pendulous clusters of two or three on a main-stalk $\frac{1}{4}$ in. or less long; each flower on a glabrous stalk $\frac{3}{4}$ to 1 in. long, white, $\frac{3}{4}$ in. wide. Calyx-tube shortly cylindrical or funnel-shaped, the lobes triangular and ultimately reflexed; both reddish and quite glabrous. Stamens numerous, very conspicuous, $\frac{1}{3}$ in. long, white or pinkish; anthers yellow; style furnished with long hairs towards the base; ovary glabrous.

Native of Hupeh, China; first discovered by Henry; introduced by Wilson in 1907 and distributed as "*P. pilosiuscula media*". *P. litigiosa* is a very attractive tree when in bloom, with its profusely borne flowers hanging down more or less in a stiff row along the branches; they are, however, soon over. Its most closely related species is *P. pilosiuscula*, which has coarsely toothed leaves rough to the touch, with small stiff hairs on both sides but especially beneath; the main-stalk of the inflorescence is longer (up to 1 in.), both it and the individual stalks usually more hairy, sometimes very much more so.

P. LUSITANICA L.　　PORTUGAL LAUREL

Laurocerasus lusitanica (L.) Roem.; *Padus lusitanica* (L.) Mill.

An evergreen shrub of wide, bushy form, usually 10 to 20 ft, but occasionally 40 to 50 ft high, more in diameter; young branches quite glabrous and very dark. Leaves ovate or oval, $2\frac{1}{2}$ to 5 in. long, $1\frac{1}{4}$ to 2 in. wide, quite glabrous on both surfaces, very dark, glossy green above, paler below, shallowly roundish toothed. Racemes produced in June from the ends of the previous summer's shoots, and from the axils of their leaves, 6 to 10 in. long, 1 to 1¼ in. through, more or less erect. Flowers white, ⅓ to ½ in. across, calyx cup-shaped, with shallow, rounded lobes; stalk ⅛ in. long. Fruits dark purple, ⅓ in. long, cone-shaped, pointed.

Native of Spain and Portugal; in cultivation 1648. In all but the coldest parts of Great Britain the Portugal laurel is one of the handsomest and most effective of evergreens. It should be grown as isolated specimens, especially in thinly wooded parts of the grounds. Although it is chiefly valued for the luxuriance of its rich green lustrous foliage, it has some merit as a flowering shrub, for in June it produces an extraordinary profusion of long, slender racemes, whose only defect is that the flowers are rather dull. It is hardier than the cherry laurel, and on warm, well-drained soil withstands thirty-two degrees of frost without being in the least affected. A serious defect of the Portugal laurel is that it is susceptible to Silver Leaf disease (*Stereum purpureum*), for which see *Dictionary of Gardening*, Vol. 4, p. 1957.

subsp. AZORICA (Mouillef.) Franco—Leaves relatively wider than in the mainland plants, sometimes up to 5 in. long and 2½ in. wide. According to J. A. Franco, it also differs in its shorter, fewer-flowered racemes and in its fruits being longer than the pedicels (against more or less equal to them in typical *P. lusitanica*). Native of the Azores.

The Azores cherry laurel was introduced around 1860 by Osborne's once famous nursery at Fulham. F.C.C. 1866. It is hardy at Kew.

cv. 'MYRTIFOLIA'.—A shrub of neat, rounded habit, and of stiffer, closer growth than the type. Leaves much smaller, usually 1½ to 2 in. long.

cv. 'ORMISTONENSIS'.—Leaves dark green and leathery, of the ordinary size; habit compact.

cv. 'VARIEGATA'.—Leaves margined with white; more tender than the green forms.

All the forms of Portugal laurel are easily increased by late summer cuttings; the type also by seeds.

P. MAACKII Rupr.

Laurocerasus maackii (Rupr.) Schneid.

A deciduous tree up to 40 or more ft high in the wild state, very distinct through the bark of the trunk being smooth and of a striking brownish yellow colour, and peeling like that of a birch; young wood downy. The leaves are ovate, rounded at the base, pointed, very finely toothed, 3 or 4 in. long, by about half as wide, hairy on the midrib and veins, and are rendered very distinct by being covered with glandular dots on the lower surface. Racemes 2 to 3 in. long, springing from the previous season's wood, downy; calyx-tube cylindrical, bell-shaped, the lobes glandular-toothed; petals white, not so long as the stamens.

Native of Manchuria, Korea, and bordering parts of Russia; introduced to cultivation by way of St Petersburg (Leningrad) in 1910. It is of uncertain taxonomic status, differing from the ordinary bird cherries (*P. padus* and its allies) in that the racemes are borne on the year-old wood, and from the cherry laurels in being deciduous. It has a very distinctive yellowish brown, lustrous bark, but has no other claim to a place in gardens.

The following specimens have been recorded: R.H.S. Garden, Wisley, 30 × 4 ft (1968); Borde Hill, Sussex, 50 × 5 ft (1958); Westonbirt, Glos., *pl.* 1935, 35 × 5½ ft (1966). A tree at Wakehurst Place, although not more than sixty years old, is already in decline; it measures 35 × 7¾ ft (1968).

P. MAHALEB L.   SAINT LUCIE CHERRY
Cerasus mahaleb (L.) Mill.

A free-growing, deciduous tree up to 30 or 40 ft high in gardens, with a loose, spreading head of branches; young twigs downy. Leaves broadly ovate or roundish, with a short, abrupt, often blunt apex, the base rounded or slightly heart-shaped, shallowly toothed, 1 to 2½ in. long, ¾ to 2 in. wide, almost or quite glabrous above, more or less hairy on each side of the midrib beneath, glossy green; stalk ½ in. long, with a pair of glands. Racemes 1¼ to 2 in. long, carrying six to ten flowers, which are pure white, ½ to ¾ in. across, very fragrant, each on a stalk about ½ in. long. The racemes spring from the wood of the previous year, and are furnished towards the base with small leaf-like bracts. Fruits about ¼ in. long, somewhat egg-shaped, black.

Native of Central and S. Europe; in cultivation 1714. It flowers in the last week of April and early May, and is then one of the most beautiful of flowering trees, filling the air with fragrance for yards around. It is fast-growing, and if planted in very rich soil is apt to become rank and ungainly. In the sandy soil of Kew it thrives and blossoms remarkably well. Both the species and its varieties may be increased by cuttings made of moderately firm young wood, and placed in gentle bottom heat, also by layers. The type, raised from seed, has been used as a stock for grafting cherries on.

cv. 'BOMMII'.—A variety of pendulous habit, much more marked than in 'Pendula' itself.

cv. 'GLOBOSA'.—A dwarf, bushy variety of rounded habit and slow growth, distributed by Dieck's nursery. The *P. mahaleb compacta* of Späth's nursery was the same. Both these were placed by Rehder under *P. mahaleb* f. *monstrosa* (Kirchn.) Schneid., but the plant Kirchner described as *Cerasus mahaleb monstrosa* had very short and thick branches and branchlets. It is doubtful if it was clonally the same as 'Globosa'.

cv. 'PENDULA'.—A very beautiful tree, more graceful than the type, yet not strikingly pendulous. Raised by Lesuer's nursery, Rouen, in 1847 (*Rev. Hort.*, 1853, pp. 479–80). It received an F.C.C. when shown by Paul's nursery in 1874.

f. XANTHOCARPA (Roem.) Rehd. *P. m.* var. *chrysocarpa* Nichols.—Fruits yellow.

Coloured forms have been in cultivation, notably 'ALBOMARGINATA', which is a better tree of its class than most variegated forms of this genus, the leaves having a broad, unequal margin of yellowish white. There was also one with leaves more or less yellow ('AUREA').

P. MARITIMA Marsh.   SAND PLUM, BEACH PLUM

A deciduous shrub of low, compact habit 4 to 8 ft high and more in diameter, with grey, downy young branchlets, becoming dark with age. Leaves oval or obovate, $1\frac{1}{2}$ to 3 in. long, $\frac{3}{4}$ to $1\frac{1}{4}$ in. wide, saw-toothed, covered beneath when young with down, which becomes reduced to the midrib and veins towards the end of the season; leaf-stalk $\frac{1}{8}$ in. long, downy. Flowers white, $\frac{1}{2}$ in. across, produced in May usually in pairs or in threes at each bud on last year's shoots; on the short side spurs the flowers appear to be in clusters, owing to the crowded buds; flower-stalks $\frac{1}{3}$ in. long, downy. Calyx downy, funnel-shaped, with five rounded, oblong lobes. Fruits red or purple, round or oblong, $\frac{1}{2}$ to 1 in. in diameter. A yellow-fruited variety is also cultivated. *Bot. Mag.*, t. 8289.

Native of the eastern United States, frequently inhabiting sandy or gravelly places near the coast. Its fruits are gathered for preserving there, but they appear to vary in quality and sweetness. The flowers are borne profusely in this country, and the species is one of the most attractive of dwarf plums. Judging by its hardy, robust constitution, and by its natural habitats, it ought to succeed in exposed maritime localities in Britain.

Some orchard varieties of this species are cultivated in the USA.

P. MAXIMOWICZII Rupr.

A deciduous tree up to 20 or 50 ft high, with a slender trunk; branchlets downy, the down persisting through the first winter. Leaves ovate or oval, pointed, rounded to cuneate at the base, $1\frac{1}{2}$ to 3 in. long, $\frac{3}{4}$ to $1\frac{1}{4}$ in. wide, doubly toothed, downy on the midrib and veins beneath, and with scattered hairs above; stalk $\frac{1}{3}$ to $\frac{1}{2}$ in. long, downy. Flowers rather dull yellowish white, about $\frac{3}{8}$ in. across, produced in mid-May on stalked racemes 2 to $3\frac{1}{2}$ in. long, remarkable for the large leaf-like bracts with which they are furnished; from six to ten flowers occur on a raceme, each flower on a downy stalk $\frac{1}{2}$ to $\frac{3}{4}$ in. long calyx hairy, with pointed, toothed lobes. Fruits globose, $\frac{1}{6}$ in. wide, shining, at first red, then black; ripe in August.

Native of Korea, Manchuria, and Japan; introduced by Sargent to the United States in 1892, and by him sent to Kew in 1895. The tree is interesting and very distinct among cherries because of the conspicuous bracts on the inflorescence, which remain until the fruit is ripe; but neither in flower nor fruit is it particularly attractive as cherries go. It is very hardy. In autumn it turns a brilliant scarlet both in Japan and N. America, but in this country the colouring is not so striking.

P. MICROCARPA C. A. Mey.

Cerasus microcarpa (C. A. Mey.) Boiss.

A deciduous bush 3 or 4 ft high, of sturdy habit, with stiff, short-jointed branches and downy branchlets. Leaves broadly ovate, with a rounded base and acute apex, $\frac{1}{2}$ to 1 in. long, nearly as much wide, coarsely and sharply toothed, with a few scattered hairs when young beneath; stalk $\frac{1}{6}$ to $\frac{1}{4}$ in. long. Flowers produced in spring in clusters of two or three, from buds and spurs of older branches, each on a downy stalk $\frac{1}{3}$ in. long; the petals are rosy pink, the calyx cylindrical and glabrous. Fruits ovoid, nearly $\frac{1}{2}$ in. long, red or yellow. *Bot. Mag.*, t. 8360.

P. *microcarpa* (in the wide sense) has a wide range from S. and E. Anatolia eastward to N.W. Afghanistan, north to E. Transcaucasia and Transcaspia. It is an exceedingly variable species in habit, leaf-shape, colour and shape of fruit, and also in the amount of down on the leaves and twigs. The most downy forms can be distinguished as var. PUBESCENS (Bornm.) Meikle. The plant described above was introduced to Kew in 1890, apparently from Asia Minor. The shape of leaf shown by this plant is usually correlated with downiness, though the leaves are in fact fairly glabrous.

Coming from a dry region with hot summers, P. *microcarpa* needs the sunniest position available. It is hardly worth garden room, except perhaps in the driest parts of the country.

The variations of this species are discussed by the Polish botanist K. Browicz in *Rocz. Arb. Kornickie*, No. 13 (1968), pp. 5–23 (in English).

P. MIRA Koehne

A deciduous almond up to 30 to 35 ft high; shoots glabrous, smooth at first, becoming warty with age. Leaves lanceolate, 2 to 5 in. long, $\frac{3}{4}$ to $1\frac{1}{2}$ in. wide, dark green and glabrous above, rather glaucous and more or less grey-hairy along the midrib beneath. Flowers solitary or in pairs, axillary on the leafless shoots, opening in March and April, 1 to $1\frac{1}{4}$ in. wide; petals roundish-obovate, white, prettily tinged with pink, margins wavy; stamens with red stalks and yellow anthers. Fruits nearly globose, $1\frac{1}{4}$ in. long, velvety, the flesh edible but bitter, the stone smooth. *Bot. Mag.*, t. 9548.

Native of W. Szechwan, China, up to 8,000 ft altitude, discovered and introduced by E. H. Wilson in 1910. It is of great botanical interest in being the only almond known to have a smooth stone. It is evidently quite hardy and flowers and bears fruit freely. It succeeded particularly well at Kemsing in Kent growing on one foot of loam on chalk.

P. MUGUS Hand.-Mazz.

A deciduous thicket-forming shrub usually under 4 ft high in the wild, but occasionally reaching 10 ft; branchlets stout, downy; spurs short, covered with the persistent blackish bud-scales. Leaves thin, broadly oval, blunt or shortly acuminate at the apex, broadly wedge-shaped to rounded at the base, $\frac{3}{4}$ to $1\frac{3}{4}$ in. long, $\frac{1}{2}$ to 1 in. wide, rich green above, paler glaucous green beneath, glabrous except for scattered short bristles on the upper surface and usually some sparse down on the midrib beneath, margins doubly serrate; leaf-stalks $\frac{1}{8}$ to $\frac{3}{16}$ in. long, slightly downy. Flowers in clusters of two to five on stalks about 1 in. long on cultivated plants (shorter on wild specimens). Calyx-tube $\frac{5}{16}$ to $\frac{3}{8}$ in. long, between bell-shaped and cylindrical, puckered, green tinged with red; sepals oblong or oblong-ovate, obtuse, edged with stalked glands. Petals about $\frac{1}{4}$ in.

long, $\frac{3}{16}$ in. wide, rosy pink. Fruits roundish, red, about $\frac{3}{8}$ in. wide. *Bot. Mag.,* n.s., t. 494.

Native of the high mountains of N.W. Yunnan and bordering parts of Burma and S.E. Tibet (Tsarong), where it forms dense thickets in the subalpine and alpine zone up to 13,000 ft; introduced by George Forrest in 1922 from the Salween–Kiu Chiang divide. His F.22874 was from plants 3 ft high, but F.22875 came from a stand 3 to 9 ft high, which helps to explain why some cultivated plants grow taller than the 3 to 4 ft given by Handel-Mazzetti. *P. mugus* is an interesting cherry, and would be one of the most ornamental if it flowered more freely.

P. mugus is quite closely related to the Himalayan *P. rufa,* which is a tree and has larger leaves, covered when young with a rusty down. Another ally is *P.* LATIDENTATA Koehne, varieties of which are in cultivation. They are, however, of no ornamental value and are not further treated here. See Ingram, *Ornamental Cherries,* pp. 139–42.

P. MUME Sieb. & Zucc.   JAPANESE APRICOT, MEI
Armeniaca mume Sieb.

A deciduous tree of rounded habit 20 to 30 ft high, with glabrous, lustrous, green twigs. Leaves $2\frac{1}{2}$ to 4 in. long, roundish or broadly ovate, contracted at the end into a long tapering point, sharply and often doubly toothed, with scattered hairs on both sides, becoming glabrous except about the midrib beneath; leaf-stalk $\frac{1}{2}$ to $\frac{3}{4}$ in. long. Flowers pale rose, 1 to $1\frac{1}{4}$ in. across, fragrant, produced singly or in pairs (each on a very short stalk) from the joints of the previous year's wood; petals broadly obovate; calyx $\frac{1}{2}$ in. across, with oblong rounded lobes. Fruits described as yellowish, globose, 1 to $1\frac{1}{4}$ in. wide, scarcely edible; shell of nut perforated.

In China, *P. mume* has been cultivated as an ornamental for some 1,500 years, and is believed to be native in the northern parts of the country, also of Quelpaert Island, Korea. According to Handel-Mazzetti, it also grows wild in S.W. China. It was introduced to Japan at an early date and became one of the most popular of garden trees; according to Miyoshi, some three hundred varieties of it have been named there. It is also grown for its fruits, which are preserved by drying or salting and eaten as a vegetable.

P. mume was introduced to Britain in 1841, but it did not become established in cultivation here until the end of the last century, when various double forms began to be imported from Japan. Messrs Baltet of Troyes imported a pink-flowered double from Japan in 1878, which was first distributed as "*P. myrobalana fl. pleno*" or was placed under *P. cerasifera,* and this confusion seems to have lasted well into the present century. *P. mume* is, of course, an apricot, and not a plum.

The Japanese apricot is valuable in gardens, especially the double-flowered forms, for its early, profuse flowering, being generally in bloom about the same time as the almond, and at its best almost as beautiful. The flowers are delicately perfumed. For all that, it is not at all common, and few nurserymen list it. It should be given a sheltered place.

cv. 'ALBA'.—Flowers white.

cv. 'ALBA PLENA'.—Flowers white, double.

cv. 'ALPHANDII'.—Flowers semi-double, pink. The plants now under this name may not be all of one clone.

cv. 'BENI-SHIDON'.—Flowers ruby-crimson, single, about ¾ in. wide, very fragrant. Award of Merit February 14, 1961, when shown by the Sunningdale Nurseries. There is a fine specimen there on the office wall.

cv. 'GRANDIFLORA'.—See under *P. armeniaca* var. *ansu.*

cv. 'O-MOI-NO-WAC'.—Flowers white, semi-double.

cv. 'ROSEMARY CLARKE'.—Raised by the famous nurseryman and plant-breeder W. B. Clarke of California and said to have large, semi-double white flowers with a red calyx. It possibly belongs to *P. armeniaca* var. *ansu.*

cv. 'PENDULA'. Branches pendulous, flowers single, pale pink.

P. NIGRA Ait.   CANADA PLUM

A deciduous tree 20 to 30 ft high, branches erect, forming a narrow head. Leaves broadly elliptical or obovate with a long, abrupt apex, the base rounded or often slightly heart-shaped, 3 or 4 in. long, more than half as wide, doubly round-toothed, downy all over or only on the midrib and veins beneath; leaf-stalk ½ in. to 1 in. long, with two dark glands near the top. Flowers pure white, 1¼ in. across, produced three or four together in stalkless clusters, each flower on a reddish, glabrous stalk ½ in. or more long; calyx usually glabrous, reddish, with narrow-pointed glandular lobes. Fruits oval, 1 to 1¼ in. long, red or yellowish red, with a compressed stone ¾ in. long.

Native of Canada and the north-eastern United States; introduced in 1773. Flowers fragrant, produced towards the end of April, turning reddish with age. This plum has been much confused with *P. americana*, from which it differs in the broader, round-toothed, more downy leaves, in the glandular leaf-stalks, larger and more fragrant flowers, and stiffer habit. It was cultivated at Kew in the 18th century, but has never been common.

P. NIPPONICA Matsum.   JAPANESE ALPINE CHERRY
P. iwagiensis Koehne; *P. nikkoensis* Koehne; *P. ceraseidos Maxim.*, in part

A deciduous bush 8 to 16 ft high, or occasionally a bushy-headed tree up to 20 ft high; young shoots glabrous, grey by autumn, ultimately chestnut brown. Leaves ovate, sometimes obovate, with a long, tail-like point, and a usually rounded base, sharply and doubly toothed; thinly hairy when young, chiefly on the veins, 1½ to 3½ in. long, 1 to 1¼ in. wide; stalk ½ to ¾ in. long, glabrous. Flowers opening in May, solitary or in twos or threes, each on a glabrous or thinly hairy stalk ½ to 1¼ in. long; they are ¾ to 1 in. wide, white or pale pink. Calyx-tube glabrous, funnel-shaped to bell-shaped; petals rounded and entire or notched at the end. Fruits black, globose, ⅓ in. wide.

Native of Japan; introduced to the Arnold Arboretum in 1915. There has been considerable confusion between this species, *P. incisa*, and *P. apetala*, all three distinguished by having black fruits and a leaf with a long tail-like apex and a conspicuous double toothing. It is distinct enough in other respects from *P. apetala* (q.v.), a cherry very downy or hairy in many of its parts. *P. incisa* is also more or less downy on the young shoots, leaf-stalk and calyx, the leaves are smaller, the branchlets never become bright brown as in *P. nipponica*, and the flowers are normally smaller.

var. KURILENSIS (Miyabe) Wils. *P. ceraseidos* var. *kurilensis* Miyabe; *P. kurilensis* (Miyabe) Miyabe—This differs in having larger flowers and a downy leaf-stalk, calyx-tube, and flower-stalk. Native of N. Japan, the Kuriles, and Sakhalin; introduced to the Arnold Arboretum in 1905 and soon after to Britain. It is of dwarf habit and slow-growing in cultivation. The plant at Kew differs from the one grown as typical *P. nipponica* in its stiff, erect habit, larger calyx-tube, and more exserted stamens.

P. 'KURSAR'.—A hybrid raised by Collingwood Ingram from seed of *P. nipponica* var. *kurilensis*. It is one of the finest of the early cherries, bearing flowers of a remarkably vivid shade of pink in March, before the leaves; calyx and filaments of stamens dark red; pedicels hairy. It makes a vigorous fairly erect tree and colours orange in the autumn. A.M. 1952.

The name 'Kursar' was given by Capt. Ingram in the belief that the pollen-parent was *P. sargentii*. He now thinks there must have been an accidental exchange of labels, and that the pollen really came from *P. campanulata*, which he had crossed with *P. nipponica* var. *kurilensis* at the same time. He points out that *P. sargentii* is unlikely to have yielded a hybrid with flowers of such a deep pink (*A Garden of Memories*, pp. 181–2).

P. ORTHOSEPALA Koehne

A deciduous shrub or small tree, with glabrous, slightly zigzag, ultimately dark brown branchlets. Leaves oval or ovate, long-pointed, sharply saw-toothed, 2½ to 3 in. long, about 1 to 1½ in. wide, glabrous and glossy green at maturity; leaf-stalk ½ to ¾ in. long with a pair of glands towards the top, remaining downy longer than the blade. Flowers white, ⅝ in. across, produced during the second week of May in clusters of three or four; petals narrowly obovate; calyx-lobes downy on the inner surface and margins, not toothed; flower-stalk ⅓ in. long, glabrous. Fruits round, 1 in. across, nearly black covered with a blue bloom; flesh juicy, palatable.

This plum was described by Koehne in 1893 from a plant growing in Späth's nursery, Berlin, to which it had been introduced from the Arnold Arboretum. The original seeds were received by that institution in 1880 and according to the records were collected by Dr Engelmann in Texas. It has not been found wild there, and there is some evidence that the seeds really came from Kansas, where similar plants are found wild. These, and the typical *P. orthosepala*, may be hybrids between *P. americana* and *P. watsoniana*. The orchard variety 'Laire', cultivated in Kansas, is near to *P. orthosepala*.

This plum was at one time represented at Kew by a small tree obtained from Späth's nurseries in 1896.

P. PADUS L.   BIRD CHERRY

Padus racemosa Lam.

A deciduous tree, with strong, rather acrid-smelling bark, from 30 to over 50 ft high, of open, rather gaunt habit when young; the branchlets usually covered at first with a fine down, sometimes quite glabrous. Leaves oval or obovate, 3 to 5 in. long, 1½ to 2½ in. wide, pointed at the end, mostly rounded or slightly heart-shaped at the base, finely toothed, dull dark green above, glabrous beneath or with tufts of down in the vein-axils beneath; stalk glabrous, with two or more glands, ½ to ¾ in. long. Flowers fragrant, white, ⅓ to ½ in. wide, borne on drooping or spreading racemes 3 to 6 in. long, and from ¾ to 1¼ in. through, which terminate short leafy shoots; calyx with five shallow, rounded, often glandular lobes. Fruits round, ¼ to ⅓ in. in diameter, black, harsh and bitter to the taste.

The bird cherry is widely spread over the northern part of the Old World, extending in one or other of its forms from the British Isles to Japan. It is a very hardy tree, and not particular as to soil. Whilst the typical form may give place in gardens to such varieties as 'Plena' and 'Watereri', it is itself very charming when planted in thin woodland. The named varieties are best propagated by budding on seedlings of the type in July. The tree has little economic value, although the timber, when available, is valued by cabinet-makers, and the fruit (according to Loudon) has been used to flavour brandy and home-made wines. It flowers in May.

cv. 'ALBERTII'.—A very free-flowering variety, with short, crowded racemes. Received by Kew in 1902 from the Vilmorin collection; the name suggests that it was originally introduced to the St Petersburg Botanic Garden by Albert Regel.

cv. 'AUCUBIFOLIA'.—Leaves spotted after the manner of *Aucuba japonica;* of little value.

cv. 'AUREA'.—Young leaves yellowish. This form is of no particular value in regard to its leaves, which soon turn green, but it has good robust foliage and its flowers are of larger size than normal.

cv. 'COLORATA'.—Stems dark purple; young leaves coppery purple, later dark green, purplish beneath. Flowers pale pink.

var. COMMUTATA Dipp. *P. grayana* Hort., not Maxim.—A wild variety from Manchuria, remarkable for flowering about three weeks in advance of any other bird cherry, being usually in bloom by the middle of April. Its flowers are fully ½ in. across. Sometimes cut by late frosts.

cv. 'PENDULA'.—Branches pendulous.

cv. 'PLENA'.—Flowers large and double, longer-lasting than in the normal form.

cv. 'STRICTA'.—Racemes quite erect.

cv. 'WATERERI' ('Grandiflora').—Racemes up to 8 in. long; leaves with conspicuous tufts of down in the axils of the veins. Raised by the Knap Hill Nursery, before 1914. A.G.M. 1930.

P. × LAUCHEANA Bolle ex Lauche   *P. padus* var. *rotundifolia* Hort. ex

Koehne—Leaves almost as wide as long. Almost certainly a hybrid between
P. *padus* and P. *virginiana*.

P. PENSYLVANICA L. f. PIN CHERRY
Cerasus pensylvanica (L. f.) Loisel.

A deciduous tree reaching 30 to 40 ft in height, with a trunk 1½ ft in diameter;
bark bitter, aromatic, reddish and shining on the young shoots. Leaves ovate,
long-pointed, 3 to 4½ in. long, ¾ to 1¼ in. wide, glabrous, bright green, finely
toothed, the teeth much incurved and gland-tipped; stalk glabrous, ½ in. long,
with one or two glands at the top. Flowers ½ in. across, white, produced four to
ten together in umbellate clusters or short racemes, each flower on a slender
glabrous stalk ¾ in. long; petals round, downy outside at the base; calyx glabrous,
with rounded lobes. Fruits round, ¼ in. in diameter, red.

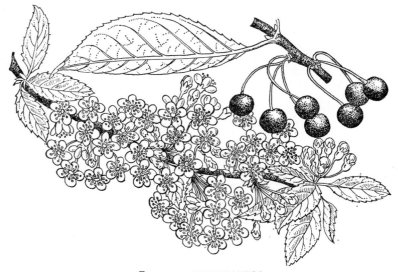

PRUNUS PENSYLVANICA

Native of N. America, where it is very widely spread; introduced to England
in 1773. It flowers very freely in this country at the end of April and in May when
the leaves are half-grown, and is very beautiful then. According to Sargent it is
a short-lived tree, but plays an important part in the preservation and reproduc-
tion of N. American forests. Its abundant seed is freely distributed by birds, and
the rapidly growing young trees give valuable shelter to the other trees longer-
lived than they are, which ultimately suppress them. It might be planted in thin
woodland, in places where our native P. *avium* thrives.

var. SAXIMONTANA Rehd.—Of shrubby habit. Leaves more shortly pointed.
Flowers fewer in each cluster. Rocky Mountains.

P. PERSICA (L.) Batsch   PEACH

Persica vulgaris Mill.; *Amygdalus persica* L.

A deciduous tree 20 ft high, of bushy habit; branchlets glabrous. Leaves lanceolate, 3 to 6 in. long, ¾ to 1½ in. wide; long-pointed, finely toothed, glabrous, stalk glandular, ½ in. long. Flowers usually solitary, sometimes in pairs, produced in early April from the buds of the previous season's growth, pale rose, 1 to 1½ in. across, with stalks scarcely longer than the bud-scales. Fruits fleshy, globose, clothed with velvety down, 2 to 3 in. across, yellowish suffused with red on the sunny side, enclosing a grooved stone.

The peach is one of those fruits which have been cultivated for so long, and over so wide an area, that its place of origin is doubtful. It is generally believed to be a native of China; it was certainly cultivated there hundreds, doubtless thousands, of years before it was known in W. Europe.

Closely allied to the almond, but less robust, it differs chiefly in its fleshy, juicy fruit with a wrinkled stone; also in the thinner, shorter-stalked leaves, smaller flowers, and in flowering two or three weeks later. The flowering peaches are some of the loveliest of all trees, especially the double red varieties. They are usually propagated by budding on plum stocks, but trees so raised rarely attain to great age. Quite possibly the peach is not in any case a long-lived tree, but worked on the plum it is very subject to canker and premature decay, owing to an imperfect adaptation of stock to scion. Yet it is difficult to suggest a better. On its own roots the peach succeeds in the south, but is too tender for the colder localities, and the fine double and richly coloured varieties now so popular can only be conveniently propagated by budding or grafting. Of varieties grown for fruit there are many, but with them we are not here concerned. The following, with the exception of f. *compressa* and var. *nectarina*, are 'flowering' peaches; the double-flowered ones often bear fruit:

cv. 'ALBA'.—Flowers white.

cv. 'ALBA PLENA'.—Flowers white, double. F.C.C. 1899, when shown by William Paul.

cv. 'AURORA'.—Flowers semi-double, Fuchsine Pink, petals frilled. Figured in *Journ. R.H.S.*, Vol. 76, fig. 74. A.M. April 4, 1950. Said to be more vigorous than 'Klara Mayer', with flowers of a clearer pink.

cv. 'CLARA MEYER'. See 'KLARA MAYER'.

f. COMPRESSA (Loud.) Rehd.—Remarkable for the flattened or compressed fruits. This was known in gardens early in the last century, and after being lost to cultivation was reintroduced from China in 1906. It is figured in Loudon, *Arb. et Frut. Brit.*, Vol. 2, p. 680. It is known as the flat peach.

cv. 'FOLIIS RUBRIS'.—Leaves reddish purple when young, becoming bronzy green. Fruits purplish. A.M. 1939.

cv. 'HELEN BORCHERS'.—Flowers Rose Bengal, semi-double. Raised by W. B. Clarke of San José, California. A.M. 1949.

cv. 'ICEBERG'.—Flowers white, semi-double. Raised by Clarke, see above. A.M. April 4, 1950.

cv. 'KLARA MAYER'.—Flowers clear pink, fully double. Put into commerce by Späth's nurseries at the end of the last century, and still one of the best varieties. A.G.M. 1939. Gerd Krüssmann, the German authority, has pointed out that the common spelling 'Clara Meyer' is incorrect.

cv. 'MAGNIFICA'.—Flowers crimson, double, up to 1¾ in. across; habit rather spreading and lax. F.C.C. to Messrs J. Veitch 1894.

var. NECTARINA (Ait.) Maxim. *Amygdalus persica* var. *nectarina* Ait.; *Persica laevis* DC.—This is the botanical name for the nectarine, which differs from the peach in its glabrous fruits.

cv. 'PALACE PEACH'.—Flowers dark crimson, semi-double, about 1 in. wide. A.M. March 26, 1946.

cv. 'RUSSELL'S RED'.—Flowers large, semi-double, bright Carmine Red. Raised by Messrs L. R. Russell. A.M. February 21, 1933.

cv. 'WINDLE WEEPING'.—Habit pendulous. Flowers semi-double, Solferino Purple. A.M. April 12, 1949.

P. PILOSIUSCULA (Schneid.) Koehne

P. tatsienensis var. *pilosiuscula* Schneid.; *P. pilosiuscula* var. *media*, Koehne, in part; *P. venusta* Koehne

A deciduous shrub or a small tree sometimes 40 ft high, with a trunk over 1 ft in diameter; young shoots sparingly hairy or glabrous. Leaves oval or obovate, the base wedge-shaped to rounded or slightly heart-shaped, the apex contracted to a slender point, conspicuously (often doubly) toothed, 1½ to 4 in. long, about half as much wide; sprinkled with, and roughened by, short bristles above, more thickly on the midrib and veins beneath; stalk about ½ in. long. Flowers produced with the young leaves in April two to four on a main-stalk ¼ to 1 in. long, the individual stalks up to 1⅛ in. long or sometimes solitary; they are white, ¾ in. wide; calyx-tube cylindrical to funnel-shaped with narrowly triangular more or less glandular lobes; style hairy towards the base; ovary glabrous. Fruits narrowly ovoid, ⅓ in. long, red, ripe in June. *Bot. Mag.*, t. 9192.

Native of W. Hupeh, China; originally discovered by Henry about 1888; introduced by Wilson in 1907. It belongs to the same group of cherries as *P. litigiosa*, which has only axil-tufts of hairs beneath the leaves and a much shorter main flower-stalk. *P. pilosiuscula* varies a good deal in regard to pubescence and in the var. SUBVESTITA Koehne (Wilson No. 41), the flower-stalks, young shoots, and both sides of the leaves are downy or hairy. P. POLYTRICHA Koehne appears to be merely a still more downy or even shaggy variety of this species, the downiness extending to the calyx. All these are pretty but their blossom is somewhat evanescent.

P. PROSTRATA Labill.   MOUNTAIN CHERRY
Cerasus prostrata (Labill.) Ser.

A deciduous shrub 2 to 3 ft high, of low, spreading habit, and measuring much more in width than it does in height. Branches slender, arching outwards and downwards, the young ones covered with a minute dark-coloured down. Leaves narrow-oblong to ovate or obovate, pointed, from 1 to 1½ in. long, sharply toothed, and downy or glabrous beneath. Flowers ½ to ¾ in. across, produced singly or in pairs with the young leaf-clusters from the previous season's shoots in April, very short-stalked; petals of a lively rose colour; calyx tubular. Fruits almost stalkless, red, ⅓ in. long, tapering towards the end.

This species was described in 1791 from Syria and has its main distribution in the mountains of the Near East, Crete, mainland Greece, Albania, W. Yugoslavia (as far north as Mt Velebit), and of N. Africa. It is absent from Central Europe and peninsular Italy, but occurs as a great rarity in Sardinia, Corsica, and S. Spain. In its native habitat it usually makes a close, stunted bush, very unlike the rather free-growing plant seen in this country. It needs a sunny position, and is admirably suited on some roomy shelf in the rock garden fully exposed to the sun. In such a position, following a hot summer, it flowers profusely enough almost to hide its branches. It is perfectly hardy at Kew, and it is rather remarkable that it remains so rare and little known, seeing that it was introduced (from Mt Lebanon) in 1802.

P. PUMILA L.   DWARF AMERICAN CHERRY

A deciduous shrub of variable stature, often a low bush about 2 ft high, but sometimes a slender shrub 6 to 8 ft high, with erect, dark secondary branches and prostrate main branches; branchlets glabrous. Leaves narrowly obovate, 1½ to 2 in. long, about one-third as wide, slightly toothed towards the apex, entire at the narrowed base, greyish green. Flowers white (sometimes rather dull) about ½ in. across, produced in stalkless umbels of two to four, each flower on a stalk ⅓ to ½ in. long. Fruits black or purplish, ⅓ to ½ in. diameter, without bloom, bitter.

Native of the north-eastern United States; cultivated in England in 1756. Its flowers appear in mid-May, and although small, so profusely are they borne that it is very pretty then, especially if grown in a mass, and if the whitest flowered forms are obtained, for some are much purer than others. Propagated by cuttings and layers. This species may be regarded as the type of a small, but very distinct group of dwarf American cherries. Of these the western sand cherry, P. besseyi, is here treated as a species (q.v.). The others, also regarded by some authorities as meriting specific rank, are:

var. DEPRESSA (Pursh) Bean P. depressa Pursh—A prostrate variety growing flat on the ground and scarcely rising 12 in. above it. Leaves broadest above the middle, tapered to the base, mostly rounded or obtuse at the apex. Native of north-eastern N. America.

var. SUSQUEHANAE (Willd.) Jaeg. P. susquehanae Willd.; P. cuneata Raf.; P. pumila var. cuneata (Raf.) Bailey—Resembling typical P. pumila in habit but usually under 3 ft high. Leaves obovate, bluntly toothed above the middle, whitish green beneath. Fruits astringent. Native of eastern N. America as far south as N. Carolina.

P. RUFA Hook f.

Cerasus rufa Wall., *nom. nud.*

A deciduous tree 15 to 20 ft high; young branches thickly covered with reddish-brown down. Leaves from 2 to 4 in. long, narrowly oval or oblong-lanceolate, with a long drawn-out apex, toothed, each tooth tipped with an egg-shaped gland, downy on the midrib and veins only when young; stalk ½ in. long. Flowers pink, ½ in. across, produced singly or a few together in clusters from the buds of the previous year's growth; calyx ⅓ in. long, funnel-shaped, with triangular, toothed lobes, hairy or glabrous; flower-stalk ⅓ to 1 in. long, slightly downy. Fruits longer than wide, red, fleshy.

Native of the central and eastern Himalaya, reaching to elevations of 12,000 ft. it was introduced to Kew about 1897, and proved quite hardy there, flowering in early May. This tree, however, died in 1950. It is distinct on account of the rusty-coloured down and the very glandular teeth of the leaves, but it is not one of the most ornamental of cherries. There are two distinct forms in cultivation, one of which has a close bark on the trunk, a glabrous or nearly glabrous calyx, and short flower-stalk; the other has a peeling bark, shaggy calyx, and flower-stalk occasionally over 1 in. long.

f. TRICANTHA (Koehne) Hara *P. tricantha* Koehne—Flower-stalks and calyx clad with long hairs. The second of the two cultivated trees mentioned above probably belongs here, but whether this character is always combined with a peeling bark it is impossible to say.

P. SALICINA Lindl.   JAPANESE PLUM

P. triflora Roxb.

A deciduous tree 20 to 30 ft high, with glabrous, dark young wood. Leaves obovate or oval, 3 to 4½ in. long, nearly half as wide, downy in the axils of the veins beneath, doubly round-toothed. Flowers white, ¾ in. across, produced in early April, each on a slender glabrous stalk ½ in. long, normally in threes from each bud of the previous year's shoots, but sometimes in pairs or singly; calyx with five rounded oblong lobes, glabrous, often slightly toothed. Fruits heart-shaped, 2 to 2¾ in. deep, nearly as wide, or globular with a deep depression where the stalk is attached; the colour in cultivated varieties varies considerably, being of different shades or combinations of red, orange, and yellow.

This tree is presumably a native of China, but does not appear to be known in a wild state. The name *P. triflora* was given by Roxburgh to a plant growing in Calcutta Botanic Garden early last century. It has long been cultivated by the Japanese, and in 1870 was introduced to California, where its cultivation has developed into an important industry. In this country its ornamental value is about equal to that of *P. cerasifera*, from which it differs in the shape of the fruits, the more numerous flowers at each node, and in the longer leaves. Whether it will prove worthy of cultivation for its fruit is very doubtful. Probably it requires a hotter summer than ours to develop its best qualities. A.M. 1926 (for its flowers).

PRUNUS SALICINA

P. SARGENTII Rehd.   SARGENT CHERRY

P. serrulata var. *sachalinensis* (F. Schmidt) Wils.; *P. sachalinensis* (F. Schmidt) Koidz.; *P. pseudocerasus* var. *sachalinensis* F. Schmidt

A deciduous tree 40 to 80 ft high in the wild, with a trunk sometimes 3 ft in diameter; young shoots glabrous. Leaves obovate to oval, drawn out at the apex into a long, slender point; rounded, sometimes slightly heart-shaped at the base, sharply toothed, 2 to 4 in. long, about half as wide; quite glabrous on both surfaces, often reddish when young; stalk glabrous, ½ to 1 in. long, with a pair of glands near the blade. Bracts red, oblong, ½ in. long, edged with small glandular teeth. Flowers 1¼ to 1½ in. across, of a lovely deep blush colour, produced two to six together in short-stalked umbels, each flower with a stalk 1 to 1¼ in. long; petals obovate, notched at the broad apex; calyx tubular, with five ovate, pointed lobes ¼ in. long, glabrous and entire; stamens deep rose. Fruit a small black cherry, ⅓ in. wide.

Native of northern Japan and Sakhalin. It was introduced to the USA in 1890, when Dr William Bigelow sent seeds to the Arnold Arboretum. Two years later, Prof. Sargent obtained a further supply of seeds from the Agricultural Institute at Sapporo in the North Island of Japan, and a share of these was sent to Kew in 1893, from which plants were raised and distributed to other collections.

P. sargentii is very closely allied to the hill cherry, *P. serrulata* var. *spontanea*, but has a more northern distribution and makes a larger tree; its leaves are rather broader, more coarsely toothed, and the inflorescence is a sessile umbel (a corymb in the hill cherry).

PRUNUS SARGENTII

This splendid cherry, probably the finest of the true cherries as a timber tree, is also one of the most beautiful in its autumnal colour and blossom. It flowers in April and the leaves turn orange and scarlet in late September and early October. It is propagated by grafting on gean, and on this stock will grow well in any average soil. On its own roots it might be more demanding. In good soil a top-grafted tree should reach 25 ft in height and 30 ft in spread in twenty years. There are numerous clones in cultivation, perhaps not distinct enough to warrant separate naming, but varying in the colour of the petals and in flowering-time. Those that open their flowers together with the unfolding richly tinted leaves make the finest display. A.G.M. 1928.

cv. 'RANCHO'.—Of narrow habit, with larger and deeper coloured flowers than normal. Raised in the USA and recently introduced to Britain.

P. 'ACCOLADE'.—Flowers deep rosy pink in the bud, opening blush-pink, semi-double, about 1½ in. wide, with twelve to fifteen petals, solitary or in umbels of three on slightly hairy pedicels ¾ to 1 in. long. Calyx bronze-coloured, the tube campanulate, about ¼ in. long; lobes serrated at the apex. Leaves dark green, deeply serrated. A very beautiful cherry raised at the Knap Hill Nursery from seeds received from the Arnold Arboretum, USA, shortly before the second world war. It is a hybrid of uncertain parentage but most probably *P. sargentii* × *P. subhirtella*. It is of spreading, open habit and flowers at about the same time as *P. sargentii*. Award of Garden Merit 1961.

P. 'HILLIERI'.—Flowers blush-pink, single, about 1¼ in. wide, borne on long, slender, slightly hairy pedicels; common-stalk short. Calyx-tube narrowly cylindric-funnel-shaped, bronzy red, glabrous; calyx-lobes narrowly ovate-lanceolate, irregularly toothed, hairy at the edge. Leaves bronze-coloured when young, double-toothed, hairy beneath on the midrib and main veins.

This cherry, raised by Messrs Hillier around 1928, flowers very freely about the middle of April. It makes a broad-crowned tree 25 to 30 ft high and about as wide and usually gives good autumn colour. A.M. 1959. It is a hybrid with *P. sargentii* as one parent, and was raised from seeds received from the Arnold Arboretum. It is difficult to accept that the other parent was *P. incisa*, as has been suggested. In its botanical characters it is near to *P.* × *yedoensis* and could be a form of *P.* × *juddii* (see below).

P. 'SPIRE'.—A fastigiate tree eventually attaining a width of 8 to 10 ft, or slightly more, giving fine autumn colour. Flowers soft pink, borne at the same time as those of 'Hillieri', of which it is a sister seedling (not a branch-sport as sometimes stated). The original plant, one of many raised from the seeds received from the Arnold Arboretum, was bought by the late Mr John Spedan Lewis and later propagated by Messrs Hillier. It still grows in the garden at Longstock House, Hants, now the property of the John Lewis Partnership.

P. × JUDDII E. Anderson—The typical form of this cross was raised in the Arnold Arboretum in 1914 from *P. sargentii*, pollinated by a tree of *P.* × *yedoensis* growing nearby. The unfolding leaves are not so deeply coloured as in Sargent's cherry, but are glabrous as in that species. Flowers borne in clusters of two to six on a short common-stalk, white flushed with deep pink. The influence of *P.* × *yedoensis* shows in the glandular-serrate calyx-lobes, and in the hairs at the base of the style (in *P. sargentii* the calyx-lobes are entire, the style glabrous).

P. SEROTINA Ehrh.   RUM CHERRY
Padus serotina (Ehrh.) Borkh.

A large deciduous tree, reaching in its most favoured situations a height of 80 to 100 ft, and occasionally found with trunks 16 ft in circumference. In England it is usually 30 to 50 ft high, the young bark glabrous, bitter, aromatic, not unpleasant to the taste. Leaves oval-lanceolate, sometimes narrowly obovate, tapering towards both ends, 2 to 5½ in. long, and from 1 to 1¾ in. wide, glabrous and shining above, paler beneath, and usually hairy along the midrib, margins set with shallow incurved teeth; stalk ¼ to 1 in. long. Flowers white, ⅓ in. in diameter, produced during late May and June in cylindrical racemes 4 to 6 in. long, ¾ in. diameter. Fruits black, ⅓ in. across, round, but rather flattened like an orange.

Native of N. America, where it is widely spread, reaching from Nova Scotia to Florida, and westwards to Dakota, Texas, Arizona, etc. At its finest, which is in the Allegheny Mountains of Virginia, it is probably the largest of the genus. In Great Britain it thrives very well, and makes a handsome middle-sized tree of graceful habit, whose dark glittering foliage in summer very much resembles that of a Portugal laurel, but it is of course deciduous, and dies off a pleasing yellow. The flowers are borne profusely, and some trees ripen abundant fruits; in the United States the latter are used for flavouring rum and brandy, and for that purpose are said to be equal to the Morello cherry. I am not aware that this tree has been tried under forest conditions here, but its timber is much valued by cabinet-makers, and judging by its behaviour at Kew it will thrive better than many trees on sandy ground. The largest specimen there is 65 ft high, with a trunk 6¼ ft in girth (1967).

Other specimens recorded recently are: Tubney Wood, Oxon., two specimens *pl.* 1906, 70 × 4 ft and 60 × 4¼ ft (1906); Westonbirt, Glos., 60 × 5½ ft (1968); Hewell Grange, Worcs., 68 × 7 ft (1963); Arley Castle, Worcs., 70 × 4½ ft (1966).

cv. 'ASPLENIFOLIA'.—Leaves deeply and irregularly cut at the margins.

cv. 'PENDULA'.—A pretty tree with weeping branches, usually budded on tall stems of *P. padus.*

f. PHELLOIDES Schwer. *P. serotina* var. *salicifolia* Nichols. ex Henry, not (Kunth) Koehne—Leaves lanceolate. Schwerin's description was made from a tree distributed early this century by Hesse's nurseries under the name "*Cerasus virginiana pyramidalis salicifolia*". A tree at Kew, planted around 1880, had similar foliage but was probably of different origin. The leaves hung loose and pendent, like those of a willow, and the branches were also pendulous.

P. SALICIFOLIA Kunth *P. serotina* var. *salicifolia* (Kunth) Koehne; *P. capuli* Cav.; *P. capollin* Zucc.—Closely allied to *P. serotina*, differing in its more leathery, almost glabrous, lanceolate leaves, and its larger, edible fruits. It has a wide distribution, from Mexico to Ecuador and Peru. The specific epithets *capuli* and *capollin* (see synonyms) are two forms of the vernacular name for it.

P. SERRULA Franch. [PLATE 47

P. serrula var. *tibetica* (Batal.) Koehne; *P. puddum* var. *tibetica* Batal.

A deciduous tree 30 to 50 ft high; bark of trunk shining brown, ultimately peeling; shoots finely downy when quite young. Leaves lance-shaped, rounded or wedge-shaped at the base, long and slenderly pointed, finely and regularly toothed, 2 to 4 in. long, ½ to 1¼ in. wide, downy along the midrib beneath and in the chief vein-axils, sometimes glabrous or soon becoming so; there are several large glands at the base near the stalk, which is ¼ to ½ in. long. Flowers white, ⅔ in. wide, produced usually in twos or threes (sometimes solitary or in fours) during April, each on its stalk ½ in. long. Calyx-lobes ovate-triangular, toothed; style finely downy towards the base. Fruits oval, ½ in. long, red.

Native of W. China; described from specimens collected by the Abbé Delavay in Yunnan; introduced by Wilson in 1908 from the region of Tatsien-lu (Kangting) in W. Szechwan and again by Forrest in 1913 from Yunnan. Wilson's introduction (W. 988) was referred by Koehne to var. *tibetica* (Batal.) Koehne but there is no reliable character by which this variety can be distinguished from the Yunnan trees.

Two characters make this cherry distinct; one is the narrowness and fine toothing of the leaves which are rather willow-like; the other is the beautiful bright brown peeling bark, at least of young trees. This feature alone makes the tree worth cultivating, for it is not more striking in any tree of similar character. So far as I have seen its flower beauty is not great. A.M. 1944 (for its bark). The following specimens have been recorded: Highdown, Sussex, *pl.* 1939, 20 × 3 ft (1965); Westonbirt, Glos., *pl.* 1937, 25 × 4¼ ft (Clay Island) and 30 × 3 ft (Morley Drive) (1965/6); Endsleigh, Devon, 55 × 4 ft (1963); Bodnant, Denb., 25 × 3¾ ft and 30 × 3½ ft (1966).

P. SERRULATA Lindl.

A deciduous tree sparsely branched; shoots quite glabrous. Leaves ovate to ovate-lanceolate, 3 to 5 in. long, 1¼ to 2½ in. wide, long and taper-pointed, toothed (sometimes doubly), quite glabrous on both surfaces, rather glaucous beneath. Flowers in short-stalked racemose clusters of two to five, white or tinged with rose, 1 to 1¾ in. across, double, not scented, individual stalks up to 1½ in. long; they open in April and early May along with the young leaves. Fruit a small black cherry.

P. *serrulata*, in the typical form described above, is a garden plant of China, introduced to Britain in 1822 from Canton. It is no longer very common in gardens, having been replaced by double-flowered varieties of Japanese origin (see Sato Zakura, p. 399). From any of these with similar flowers it is easily distinguished by its gaunt, flat-topped habit, and its rather small, scentless flowers.

Many species of plants native to E. Asia first became known in Europe in the form of garden varieties differing from the wild prototype in doubleness of flower or in some other character. Later, when the wild plants were discovered and needed a name, they had to become varieties of the garden plant first described. And so in this instance. For P. *serrulata* is considered to be no more than a garden derivative of the hill cherry of China and Japan, which has to be distinguished as a variety of P. *serrulata*, namely:

var. SPONTANEA (Maxim.) Wils. P. *pseudocerasus* var. *spontanea* Maxim.; P. *jamasakura* Sieb. ex Koidz.; P. *mutabilis* Miyoshi HILL CHERRY.—A tree 40 to 60 ft high, more or less glabrous in all its parts; bark brownish or greyish, marked with prominent and persistent lenticels. Leaves usually reddish brown when unfolding, elliptic-ovate to obovate-oblong, 3 to 4½ in. long, 1¼ to 1⅞ in. wide, acuminate at the apex, cuneate at the base, deep green above, dull and slightly glaucous beneath, simply or slightly double-serrate, the teeth ending in short bristles. Inflorescence a few-flowered corymb. Flowers white or pink, mostly ¾ to 1 in. wide; calyx lobes entire. Fruits dark purplish red when ripe, about ¼ in. wide.

The hill cherry or Yamazakura is best known from Japan, of which it is the national tree. 'It has been venerated, one might almost say worshipped, for so many centuries that it has now become inextricably associated with the lore and legend of the land. . . . There is hardly a shrine or temple or park in the whole country that is not adorned with a Cherry of some sort, while in many country districts they have been planted in such vast numbers that in spring and again in autumn, they literally dominate the scene' (C. Ingram, *Journ. R.H.S.*, Vol. 69 (1944), p. 126). In this article, Collingwood Ingram argues that the hill cherry was introduced to Japan from China, like so many other of its favourite garden plants, and remarks that during his many plant-hunting excursions in Japan he never met with the hill cherry growing at any distance from human habitations.

In China, the var. *spontanea* is truly wild in the mountains of the western provinces, whence it was introduced by Wilson in 1900 when collecting for Messrs Veitch. Trees from this seed have a greyish bark and the young leaves are not brightly tinted as is usual in the Japanese trees. They have been distinguished by Ingram as var. *hupehensis*, but the difference is scarcely of botanical significance.

The Japanese hill cherry is variable in the colouring of the unfolding leaves, in size and colour of flower, and in autumn colouring. The finest forms, and the most admired in Japan, are those with white flowers borne simultaneously with the copper-coloured young leaves. But in no form is it really common in Britain, where the more highly bred and larger-flowered garden cherries are much more widely planted. But at its best the hill cherry is one of the most beautiful of April-flowering trees. A.M. 1936.

var. PUBESCENS (Nakai) Wils. *P. jamasakura* var. *pubescens* Nakai; ? *P. jamasakura* var. *verecunda* Koidz.; ? *P. verecunda* (Koidz.) Koehne—Leaves, at least beneath, petioles and sometimes the inflorescence-axes downy; leaves green beneath, with coarser teeth than in the var. *spontanea*. Native of China, Korea, and Japan. It is represented in this country mainly by plants deriving from Collingwood Ingram's introduction from Seoul, Korea. The common clone of commerce is a fast-growing, fairly broad-crowned tree with pink flowers; the leaves are rather dull brown as they unfold, but colour splendidly in October.

JAPANESE GARDEN CHERRIES   SATO ZAKURA

An important group of ornamental cherries evolved in the gardens of Japan over the past two or three centuries. Although their origin is obscure, there is no doubt that many of them derive from the Oshima cherry, *P. speciosa* (*P. lannesiana* f. *albida*). In these the unfolding leaves are green or only slightly tinged with yellow or bronze, and their teeth end in long, slender bristles; the flowers are white or pale pink and usually fragrant; the bark is smooth and grey. Wilson, in *The Cherries of Japan*, placed these varieties under *P. lannesiana*. In others the young leaves are more richly tinted in shades of bronze or copper, the leaf-teeth are not so finely tipped, the flowers are not fragrant, and the bark is dark chestnut brown. These, e.g., 'Kanzan' and 'Fugenzo', were considered by Wilson to be forms of *P. serrulata* var. *sachalinensis*, i.e., *P. sargentii*. Collingwood Ingram doubts whether *P. sargentii* played any part in the development of the Sato Zakura, but considers that the hill cherry (*P. serrulata* var. *spontanea*) enters into their parentage.

However, under modern conventions of garden nomenclature, there is no need to be bothered with the taxonomic position of these cherries. It is perfectly correct to place the cultivar name immediately after the generic name, e.g., *Prunus* 'Kanzan'. In the present work they are placed under the heading *P. serrulata* only because it has been usual in this country, as a matter of convenience, to treat them all as varieties of that species. In Japan they are known collectively as the Sato Zakura, literally 'domestic cherries'.

The most important work on this group is Manabu Miyoshi's 'Die Japanische Bergkirschen', in *Journ. Coll. Sci. Imp. Univ. Tokyo*, Vol. 34 (1916). This contains a detailed description and coloured illustration of every variety of Sato Zakura growing in the then famous cherry collection at Kohoku on the river Arakawa, west of Tokyo, which was planted in 1886 by Kengo Shimidsu. In Miyoshi's time the collection had been half-destroyed by the reconstruction of the river embankment, but a complete duplicate collection was established in the Botanic Garden of Tokyo University. The original collection came from Magoemon's nursery and therefore represented varieties then available in commerce, but it was certainly not comprehensive. For example, there is no mention in Miyoshi's work of the cherry later named 'Hokusai', though this had been introduced to Europe before 1886. Other notable omissions are 'Tai Haku' and various cherries later introduced to Britain by Collingwood Ingram from Japanese temple gardens.

The standard British work on the Sato Zakura is contained in Part III of Collingwood Ingram's classic *Ornamental Cherries* (1948). Various problems of identification and naming are dealt with by Dr Mary Mountain in a valuable unpublished thesis, of which a copy is preserved in the Lindley Library of the Royal Horticultural Society. Other works dealing in part with the Sato Zakura are: E. H. Wilson, *The Cherries of Japan* (1916); Paul Russell, *Oriental Flowering Cherries* (US Dept. Agric. Circ. 313 (1934)); Geoffrey Chadbund, *Flowering Cherries* (1972).

Grafted on gean, as they now always are, the Sato Zakura will grow well in any average soil. They do not take kindly to regular pruning, nor do they need it. Any cutting needed to restrict size or to improve the shape of the tree should be done in early summer and the wound sealed at once with some proprietary compound such as 'Arbrex'.

'AMANOGAWA'   [PLATE 44

P. serrulata f. *erecta* Miyoshi; *P. lannesiana* f. *erecta* (Miyoshi) Wils.

A variety of strictly fastigiate growth, more so even than a Lombardy poplar. Young foliage yellowish. Flowers pink, fragrant, semi-double (about nine petals), sometimes developing the small, black fruits. Early to mid-May. A.G.M. 1931.

'ARIAKE'

P. serrulata f. *candida* Miyoshi; *P. lannesiana* f. *ariake* (Koidz.) Wils.

Young leaves bronze-coloured. Flowers single or occasionally with a few extra petals, pink in the bud, opening white slightly flushed with pink (as in 'Ojochin'), about $2\frac{1}{4}$ in. wide. It makes a sparsely branched tree up to 15 or 20 ft high and as much wide. Although not in the front rank of ornamental cherries, it has a good constitution and is recommended by Chadbund for cold and exposed localities.

'BOTAN' (*P. serrulata* f. *moutan* Miyoshi) is similar, but of poor constitution.

'ASANO'

P. serrulata f. *geraldinae* Ingram

This cherry closely resembles 'Kiku Shidare' but is of upright habit. Introduced from Japan by Collingwood Ingram, and named by him (*Journ. R.H.S.*, Vol. 54, pp. 168–9). The flowers are mauvish pink.

'CHEAL'S WEEPING'

P. (Cerasus) Chealii pendula Hort. ex *Journ. R.H.S.*, Vol. 41 (1915), p. lxiii

A weeping tree with steeply pendulous branches. Leaves lanceolate. Flowers pink, very double, 1 to 1¼ in. wide. Late April. A.M. 1915.

This cherry is often wrongly known by the Japanese name 'Kiku Shidare Zakura' (Weeping Chysanthemum Cherry), a later name which properly belongs to another cherry with similar flowers, but with branches which ascend from the trunk before arching downwards.

'DAIKOKU'

Unfolding leaves yellowish green. Flower-buds dark purplish red, very thick, with a broad, truncated end, opening towards the end of April. Inflorescence a loose, drooping corymb with a long, stout peduncle. Flowers over 2 in. across, purplish pink, with fifty or more petals and a cluster of leafy carpels at the centre. Calyx-lobes long and narrow. This cherry was named and described by Collingwood Ingram in 1925 (*Journ. R.H.S.*, Vol. 50, p. 85). Previously it had been called 'Beni-fugen', which is properly an alternative name for 'Fugenzo'. It appears to be very rare in Japan and is not described in Miyoshi's work. Daikoku is the name of the Japanese God of Prosperity.

A cherry grown in the R.H.S. Garden at Wisley as 'Fugenzo' and at Kew as 'Beni-fugen' is near to 'Daikoku' but differs, according to Miss Mountain, in its wide calyx-lobes and in the presence of a tuft of petals in the centre of the flower. She considers this cherry to be 'KURAMA-YAMA', cultivated under that name in the USA and described by Paul Russell (op. cit.).

'FUDAN ZAKURA'

P. serrulata f. *semperflorens* Miyoshi; *P. lannesiana* f. *fudanzakura* (Koidz.) Wils.

This cherry is notable for bearing its flowers sporadically throughout the winter and early spring. They are white, single, the precocious ones small, in sessile clusters, but those borne at the normal time are larger, and the clusters stalked. 'It is chiefly for indoor decoration that this cherry is valuable. If the boughs are cut and brought into the house at any time between the New Year and mid-March, the flowers will open in a few days' (Ingram, *Orn. Cherries*, p. 211). There are two old trees of this variety in the R.H.S. Garden at Wisley, on Weather Hill. A.M. 1930.

'FUGENZO'

P. pseudocerasus 'James H. Veitch'; *P. serrulata* f. *classica* Miyoshi, in part; *P. serrulata* f. *fugenzo* Makino, in part; *P.* 'Kofugen'; *P.* 'Benifugen'

Of spreading habit, with a rounded crown and intercrossing branches. Leaves finely toothed, richly copper-coloured when young. Flowers two or three in pendent clusters, rose-pink, very double (thirty-five or so petals), with two leafy carpels at the centre. It is one of the last of the Sato Zakura to bloom, usually in the second week of May. F.C.C. 1899.

Strictly, the name 'Fugenzo' is applicable both to the pink-flowered tree described above, and to 'Shirofugen', but in western gardens it is always used for the former, the correct name for which is really 'Kofugen' or 'Benifugen'.

'HISAKURA'

Under this name Collingwood Ingram describes a cherry with coppery-red young foliage and rosy-pink flowers, which are single or with a few extra petals, borne in loose corymbs of two to four in the second half of April. The Choshiu-Hisakura, described by Koidzumi and Miyoshi, appears to be similar but with flowers of a deep pink. Both writers evidently considered this to be one of the most beautiful of cherries, the former praising its flowers as 'valde pulcherrimi', but whether it is in cultivation it is impossible to say.

The name 'Hisakura' was at one time commonly but wrongly used for 'Kanzan'.

'BENDEN' (*P. serrulata rubida* Miyoshi) is similar to 'Hisakura' but the flowers are paler pink and borne earlier, about mid-April. It makes a vigorous tree and colours orange in the autumn (C. Ingram, *Orn. Cherries*, p. 221).

'HOKUSAI'

Young leaves bronzy, becoming dark green and rather leathery when mature. Flowers about 2 in. wide, semi-double (up to twelve petals), borne late April in loose corymbs. This cherry was in commerce originally under such names as *Cerasus flore roseo pleno* and was renamed 'Hokusai' by Collingwood Ingram in 1925, after Prof. Miyoshi had confirmed that it was not among the cherries described in his work, and lacked a Japanese name. It is probably the cherry figured in *Flore des Serres* in 1874 (t. 2238), in which case it is the oldest in gardens of the Sato Zakura. Capt. Ingram's original tree, planted in 1892, attained a height of 25 ft and twice that in spread; it broke in two in 1953 and had to be removed. The avenue of 'Hokusai' at Minterne Abbey, Dorset, mentioned in previous editions, has been decimated by honey-fungus.

It has been stated that 'Hokusai' is the same as the cherry named 'Udsu Zakura' (*P. serrulata* f. *spiralis* Miyoshi). But according to Miyoshi's figure and description that is an entirely different cherry, with very double flowers (about thirty petals), borne in umbels. 'Hokusai' has also been grown as *P. serrulata amabilis*, a name properly belonging to 'Higurashi', which is probably not in cultivation.

'Hokusai' is one of the best cherries for British gardens. It has a long flowering season, often extending into May, and the leaves colour well in the autumn.

'HORINJI'
P. serrulata f. *decora* Miyoshi; *P. serrulata* var. *sachalinensis* f. *horinji* Wils.

A small, sparsely branched erect tree. Leaves lanceolate, yellowish brown when young. Flowers semi-double (about fifteen petals), about 1¾ in. wide, pale pink; calyx purplish brown. Late April to early May. Collingwood Ingram considers this to be among the most beautiful of the cherries, despite its rather ungainly habit. A.M. 1935.

'ICHIYO'
P. serrulata f. *unifolia* Miyoshi

Leaves pale brown when young, soon becoming green. Flowers pale pink, double (about twenty-five petals), 1⅞ in. across, in a drooping cluster, each flower with one or two leafy carpels in the centre. 'There is a refined quality about its flowers that is lacking in many of the cultivated varieties. This is due, not only to the purity of their soft pink colour, but also to the open, somewhat disc-like form of the individual bloom. Owing to the petals being arranged in two rather tightly packed tiers, the flowers have a compact and evenly circular shape, with a slightly frilled edge' (Ingram, *Orn. Cherries*, p. 219). It flowers at mid-season (late April to early May) and attains about 25 ft in height and width. A.M. 1959.

'IMOSÉ'

'This is a fairly distinct cherry, characterised in mid-season by its dense, glistening grass-green foliage. Compared with other varieties, the immature leaves are also of a brighter and paler copper-red colour. . . . The soft mauvy-pink flowers, about 4·5 cm across, are completely double, having from twenty-five to thirty petals' (Ingram, *Orn. Cherries*, p. 242). It is a vigorous cherry, ultimately attaining, according to Chadbund, a height of 30 ft and a width of 25 ft. The leaves turn yellow before falling in November. 'Imosé', which is not described in Miyoshi's work, was introduced by Collingwood Ingram in 1927 from the Hirano Shrine, Kyoto.

'JO-NIOI'
P. serrulata f. *affinis* Miyoshi; *P. lannesiana* f. *jonioi* Wils.

Leaves with fairly large, finely tapered teeth, pale golden brown when young. Flowers white, single, about 1½ in. across, gorse-scented, borne late April and early May. Miss Mountain has questioned whether the tree grown as 'Jo-nioi' is really the true variety, which according to Miyoshi has steeply ascending branches, whereas the cultivated tree is of normal spreading habit; also, the true 'Jo-nioi' has an upright inflorescence owing to the thick flower-stalks, which is not really true of the tree cultivated here.

In 'TAKI-NIOI' the habit is spreading and the young leaves are reddish bronze. The flowers are similar to those of the cultivated 'Jo-nioi' but borne very late in the cherry season (about mid-May).

'KANZAN'
P. serrulata f. *purpurascens* Miyoshi; *P. serrulata* var. *sachalinensis* f. *sekiyama* (Koidz.) Wils.; *P.* 'Sekiyama'; *P.* 'Kwanzan'; *P.* "Hisakura"

A vigorous cherry, ultimately 40 ft high and as much wide. Leaves bronzy when young and remaining so for a time after they are fully expanded; toothing simple short. Flowers crimson in the bud, opening purplish rose, 2¼ in. across, with about thirty petals; carpels mostly leafy. Flowering season end April or early May. Autumn colour bronzy orange. The most widely planted of the Sato Zakura and understandably so, for it is of excellent constitution, very free-flowering and of the right habit for street-planting. Its only fault, apart from the impure pink of its flowers, is that in gardens it usurps the place of other cherries of more charm and character, and that it is too often planted in country districts, where it is grossly out of place in the spring landscape. A.G.M. 1930.

'Kanzan' (usually spelt 'Kwanzan' in the USA) and 'Sekiyama' are two renderings of the ideogram for a Chinese mountain sacred to Buddhists, the first being the Chinese name as pronounced in Japan, the second its name in the Japanese language. 'Hisakura' is an old and erroneous trade-name for it.

The cherry 'KIRIN' (*P. serrulata* f. *atrorubra* Miyoshi) is similar to 'Kanzan' but is of more spreading habit, with denser inflorescences.

'MIKURAMA-GAESHI'

P. serrulata f. *diversiflora* Miyoshi; *P. lannesiana* f. *mikuramakaisi* (Koidz.) Wils.;
P. serrulata 'Temari' of Ingram in *Journ. R.H.S.*, Vol. 50 (1925), p. 87

A small tree with ascending main stems, on which most of the flower-spurs are directly borne. Leaves short-toothed, pale brown when unfolding, soon green. Flowers single or semi-double, pale pink, about 2 in. wide, borne in compact almost sessile clusters. End April. A.M. 1946.

This cherry, as cultivated in Britain, descends from a plant at Kew which was identified by Wilson as 'Temari' on the basis of a specimen sent to him in America. But Collingwood Ingram, who at first used that name in his writings, later established that this cherry agrees better with Miyoshi's 'Mikurama-Gaeshi'.

'OJOCHIN'   [PLATE 50

A vigorous cherry of rather stiff habit, with broadly ovoid winter growth-buds and roundish inflorescence-buds. Leaves bronzy green when young, rather leathery when mature, many of the leaves rounded at the apex, i.e., lacking the usual acuminate tip. Flowers single or with a few extra petals, about 1¾ in. wide, pink in the bud, white flushed with pink when expanded; petals roundish. Flowering time end April and early May. A.G.M. 1926.

This cherry, for which 'Ojochin' is now the established name, really agrees better with the cherry described by Miyoshi under the Japanese name 'Senriko' (*P. serrulata* f. *picta*), but as the two are so similar it is perhaps best to ignore the discrepancy. The matter is discussed by Mary Mountain in her thesis.

'OSHOKUN'

P. serrulata f. *conspicua* Miyoshi

'In the colour of its blossom Oshokun is perhaps the most lovely of all the Japanese Cherries, for none have flowers of a purer or deeper blush-pink; but in the habit of growth it is perhaps the ugliest. . . . In twenty years my plants are scarcely more than 6 or 8 ft high, with gaunt, twisted boughs. . . . Carmine-red in the bud stage, the single flowers fade to a lovely malmaison pink when fully expanded. They are of medium size, and are borne in multiple and rather short-stalked clusters, usually towards the ends of the branches' (C. Ingram, *Orn. Cherries*, pp. 221–2).

'PINK PERFECTION'

This cherry was raised by Messrs Waterer, Son and Crisp in 1935 from a seed of 'Shimidsu' ('Okumiyako'). The pollen-parent is presumed to have been 'Kanzan'. It resembles the latter more than it does the seed-parent and flowers at about the same time, but the flowers are a clearer pink, and the young leaves a paler shade of bronze. It is of vase-shaped habit, and attains 25 ft in height and as much in width. A.M. 1945.

'SHIMIDSU'   [PLATE 48

P. 'Okumiyako' and *P. serrulata* f. *longipes* sens. Ingram in *Journ. R.H.S.*, Vol. 50 (1925), p. 89, not Miyoshi; *P.* 'Miyako' of some authors, not *P. lannesiana* f. *miyako* Wils.

Leaves pale brown when young, their teeth ending in long thread-like points. Flowers pink in the bud, opening pure white, semi-double, about 2 in. wide, borne in unusually long, pendulous corymbs of three to six, each with two leafy carpels in the centre; petals frilled. This lovely cherry is one of the last to bloom, usually around the middle of May, at the same time as 'Shirofugen' and 'Fugenzo'. There is a fine coloured illustration of it in Geoffrey Chadbund's *Flowering Cherries* (Plate 5), which shows the rounded crown characteristic of this variety. It is not a strong grower. A.G.M. 1933.

'Shimidsu' was introduced to cultivation early this century and was originally identified as being the cherry that Miyoshi described under the name *P. serrulata longipes*, with the vernacular name 'Okumiyako'. Later, however, Collingwood Ingram ascertained that it was not that variety and coined a new name for it— 'Shimidsu Zakura'—in honour of the Japanese founder of the famous collection of Sato Zakura on the Arakawa river. Recently, Mary Mountain, in her unpublished thesis, has suggested that this cherry should correctly be known as 'Shogetsu', and certainly it agrees quite well with Miyoshi's description under that name, and is probably the same as the 'Shogetsu' of American gardens.

'SHIROFUGEN'

P. serrulata f. *classica* Miyoshi, in part; *P. s.* var. *sachalinensis* f. *albo-rosea* (Mak.) Wils.; *P. serrulata* f. *fugenzo* subf. *alborosea* Mak.

A vigorous cherry of spreading habit. Leaves deep crimson-bronze when young, almost fully expanded at flowering-time but still richly coloured then. Flowers very double (about thirty petals,) pink in the bud, white when first open but ageing to pale mauvish pink with a deeper coloured centre; carpels two, leafy. This is one of the last of the Sato Zakura to flower (mid-May or even later) and one of the most beautiful. Because of its flat-topped, wide spreading crown it needs more room than most of this group—the fine specimen at Kew is almost 40 ft wide. A.G.M. 1959. It is closely related to 'Fugenzo' (q.v.).

'SHIROTAE'

P. serrulata f. *albida* Miyoshi; *P. lannesiana* f. *sirotae* (Koidz.) Wils.; *P. pseudocerasus* 'Mount Fuji' of Yokohama Nurseries; *P. serrulata* 'Kojima' Ingram (*Journ. R.H.S.*, Vol. 50 (1925), p. 90)

Leaves pale green when young, their teeth, and those of the bracts, ending in unusually long thread-like tips; stipules narrow, much dissected. Flowers white, fragrant, about 2 in. wide, semi-double, in pendent corymbs, produced early in the cherry season—early to mid-April. It is, with 'Tai Haku', the loveliest of the white-flowered Sato Zakura. It is of spreading habit, ultimately 30 ft wide, and best grown as a standard.

The nomenclature of this cherry is confused. It was originally imported from the Yokohama Nurseries as 'Mount Fuji' but was renamed 'Kojima' in 1925. Subsequently it was identified with the 'Shirotae' of Miyoshi and more recently it has been suggested that its correct name is 'Hosokawa'. This variety has long-peduncled inflorescences, as in the 'Shirotae' of our gardens, whereas the true 'Shirotae', as described and figured by Miyoshi, has a short-peduncled inflorescence. In other respects the two are very similar.

'SHUJAKU'

P. serrulata f. *campanuloides* Miyoshi; *P. serrulata* var. *sachalinensis* f. *shujaku* Wils.

Leaves yellowish bronze when unfolding, with rather small, short-aristate teeth. Flowers slightly bell-shaped, about $1\frac{5}{8}$ in. wide, semi-double (up to fifteen petals), pale pink, produced in corymbs of four to six at the end of April or early in May. This little-known cherry is recommended by Geoffrey Chadbund in his *Flowering Cherries;* he gives the ultimate size as 15 by 15 ft.

'YAE-AKEBONO' (*P. serrulata versicolor* Miyoshi) is similar to 'Shujaku' but the flowers are larger (up to 1¾ in. wide) and fewer in each corymb (three to five). It is subject to brown rot (Ingram, *Orn. Cherries*, p. 228). Another cherry in this group is 'OKIKU', but this, like 'Yae-akebono', is disease-prone and of poor habit. For a description see: C. Ingram, op. cit, p. 224.

'SUMIZOME'

The cherry cultivated under this name in Britain was introduced originally by Collingwood Ingram from the Arnold Arboretum. As he has pointed out, it differs from the 'Sumizome' of Wilson, which was described as having large, single flowers, white flushed with pink, and also with the 'Sumizome' of Miyoshi, which has decidedly small, white single flowers. In the present plant the flowers are double, with twelve to fourteen petals, soft pink, and almost 2 in. wide. Young leaves bronzy green.

'TAI HAKU'   GREAT WHITE CHERRY   [PLATE 51

A very vigorous tetraploid cherry, closely related to the wild hill cherry. Leaves reddish bronze when unfolding, very large when mature (up to 8 in. long), with pronounced 'drip-tips'. Flowers pure white, up to 2½ in. wide, saucer-shaped, single, on short pedicels, produced in mid- or late April. This is a lovely cherry whose pure white flowers contrast with the richly coloured young leaves. The foliage is healthy and handsome, and turns yellow or orange before falling. The bark, too, attracts attention with its very prominent brown lenticels. It grows 20 to 25 ft high and somewhat more in width. F.C.C. 1944.

'Tai Haku' is an old Japanese variety, once grown in the neighbourhood of Kyoto, which for some unknown reason became extinct there. All the existing plants descend from one half-dead bush found by Collingwood Ingram in 1923 in a Sussex garden, whose owner had received it in 1900 in a consignment of cherries from Japan. For the full story see his *Ornamental Cherries*, pp. 207–9.

'WASHI-NO-O' resembles 'Tai Haku' but has smaller flowers (about 1⅝ in. wide), which occasionally have a few extra petals. It is a vigorous cherry, but judging from the example at Kew it is inferior to 'Tai Haku'.

'TAKASAGO' *see* P. × SIEBOLDII

'TAO-YOMA'

Young leaves deep bronze-coloured, unfolding at the same time as the flowers, which are shell-pink at first fading to very pale pink, semi-double (up to twenty petals). Calyx and pedicels purple-brown. It is of wide-spreading habit. A very beautiful cherry, flowering in the second half of April or early in May. Collingwood Ingram, who introduced it from the Hirano Shrine, Kyoto, at first thought little of it but now ranks it second only to 'Tai Haku' (*A Garden of Memories* (1970), p. 183).

'UKON'

P. serrulata f. *grandiflora* Wagner; *P. s.* f. *luteovirens* Miyoshi; *P. lannesiana* f. *grandiflora* (Wagner) Wils.; *P. serrulata flore luteo pleno* Hort.

'Ukon' is the best known of a sub-group of the Sato Zakura in which the petals are tinted with yellow or greenish yellow. It is a vigorous, sparsely branched tree with semi-double flowers, and their colour is best described as pale buff-yellow. They are borne in late April and harmonise with the bronzy young leaves. A.M. 1923.

Another member of this group is 'GYOIKO', with yellowish flowers streaked with green and tinged with pink (*P. serrulata* f. *tricolor* Miyoshi) A.M. 1930. In 'ASAGI' the flowers are paler than in 'Ukon', single and borne earlier (*P. serrulata* f. *luteoides* Miyoshi).

'YAE-MURASAKI'

P. serrulata f. *purpurea* Miyoshi

Leaves copper-coloured when young. Flowers purplish pink, semi-double (eight to ten petals), borne in the second half of April. A very free-flowering variety of moderate growth, suitable for small gardens. The Japanese name means 'double purple'.

'YEDO ZAKURA'

P. serrulata f. *nobilis* Miyoshi; *P. lannesiana* f. *yedozakura* Wils.

Leaves broadly oblong or obovate, short-acuminate, golden brown when unfolding. Buds deep carmine red, truncate at the apex, flowers rich shell-pink, 2 in. wide, with eight to twelve petals; calyx-lobes short. It usually flowers in the first half of April. Not a strong grower.

'BENI-TORA-NO-O' (*P. serrulata formosissima* Miyoshi) is very similar.

'YOSHINO' *see* P. × YEDOENSIS

P. SIBIRICA L.   SIBERIAN APRICOT

Armeniaca sibirica (L.) Lam.

A deciduous bush or small tree; leaves ovate, the apex long drawn-out; 2 to 3½ in. long, half as wide, reddish at first, then bright green and glabrous above, with axil tufts of down beneath, margins finely toothed; stalk ½ to 1 in. long. Flowers mostly solitary, white or pink. Fruits scarcely stalked, about 1 in. long, yellow except on the sunny side, covered with a velvety skin; the flesh scanty, dry, harsh and scarcely edible; stone sharply edged; kernel of nut with an almond-like, bitter taste.

Native of the mountains of E. Siberia (Dahuria), where, according to Pallas the Russian botanist, some mountain-sides are covered with its pink blossoms in May, when the northern sides are purple with *Rhododendron dauricum*. It is also found in the Ussuri region, Mongolia, etc. Although an old tree in gardens (it was cultivated at Kew one hundred years ago), and still offered for sale by continental dealers, it is scarcely known in England nowadays. So far as I have seen, it has very little to recommend it for gardens, being of about the same value as the wild apricot, to which it is very closely akin. Its leaves have usually much more elongated points.

According to the *Flora SSSR* (Vol. 10, p. 595) this species withstands temperatures of −50° C. (90° F. of frost) in some parts of its range.

P. MANDSHURICA (Maxim.) Koehne *P. armeniaca* var. *mandshurica* Maxim.; *Armeniaca mandshurica* (Maxim.) Skvortz.—Allied to the preceding, but differing in the following characters: leaves doubly serrate, the teeth longer and narrower; fruits distinctly though shortly stalked; stones with blunt angles. Native of the Russian Far East, Manchuria, and Korea. It is said to attain a height of 50 ft in the wild.

P. × SIEBOLDII (Carr.) Wittmack   NADEN

Cerasus sieboldii Carr.; *Cerasus pseudocerasus rosea plena* Sieb. ex Verlot

A small deciduous tree attaining a height of 25 ft or so in Japan, with a vase-shaped crown and rather stout branches; branchlets glabrous (sometimes downy when young), greyish, darkening to iron-grey or purple. Leaves bronzy when unfolding, abruptly narrowed at the apex to an acuminate tip, rounded at the base, downy on both sides but more so beneath than above, margins shortly and mostly double-serrate. Flowers usually double or semi-double, white or pink; flower-stalks and peduncle downy, the latter variable in length from ⅜ to 1 in. or slightly more long. Calyx downy with entire lobes. Style hairy at the base.

P. × *sieboldii* is a somewhat variable hybrid, which arose in Japan. One parent is probably the Oshima cherry (*P. speciosa*); according to Ohwi, the other parent may be *P. apetala* (*Fl. Japan* (1965), p. 543). In Japan it is known as Naden or Musha-zakura. The name Takasago, generally used for it in Britain, was originally given by Miyoshi to a tree in the Kohoku Avenue (see p. 400), for which he could not find a name in the classical literature.

P. × *sieboldii* was introduced to Europe from Japan shortly before 1864. As represented in cultivation in this country it makes a small, rather slow-growing tree, bearing a profusion of semi-double, pale pink flowers rather early in the cherry season (around mid-April).

The cherry once grown as *Cerasus watereri* or *P. pseudocerasus watereri* belongs to P. × *sieboldii*, but judging from specimens in the Kew Herbarium it had considerably larger flowers than in other specimens, which may represent the original introduction by Siebold. In the form now cultivated as 'Takasago' the flowers have about twelve petals and are 1½ to 1¾ in. wide.

P. SIMONII Carr.   APRICOT PLUM

A small deciduous tree of slender, pyramidal habit, the branches erect, young shoots glabrous. Leaves oval-lanceolate, finely toothed, 3 to 4 in. long, 1 to 1¼ in. wide, resembling those of the peach; stalk short, glanded. Flowers white, solitary or in pairs, up to 1 in. across, opening in March and April; petals obovate. Fruits 2 in. wide, 1½ in. deep, tomato-shaped, very shortly stalked, uniform brick-red, smooth like a nectarine, the flesh apricot-yellow and pleasantly fragrant, aromatic, and very palatable.

There seems to be some doubt as to the origin of this tree, and although it is believed to be a native of north China, its wild habitat is unknown. It is cultivated about Peking, and was introduced originally to the Jardin des Plantes at Paris in 1867 by Eugene Simon, after whom it is named, and was put in commerce by Messrs Thibaut & Keteleer of Sceaux, near Paris, in 1872. It has borne fruits in the gardens of Aldenham House, Elstree, but this happens rarely, owing to flowers being so liable to damage by frost. Although called "Apricot" plum, its affinities are doubtful. Some authors regard it as a plum, but it appears rather to be intermediate between that and the nectarine. It is a useful fruit tree in California, and has been hybridised with *P. salicina*—the Japanese plum. Very distinct in its almost fastigiate habit.

P. SPECIOSA (Koidz.) Ingram   OSHIMA CHERRY

P. jamasakura var. *speciosa* Koidz.; *P. serrulata* var. *serrulata* f. *albida* Makino; *P. lannesiana* f. *albida* (Mak.) Wils.; *P. mutabilis* f. *speciosa* Miyoshi

A small deciduous tree with stout branches and a pale, smooth bark; young shoots glabrous, becoming pale shining grey by the autumn. Leaves usually tinged with brown as they unfold, glabrous, ovate or obovate, 3 to 5 in. long, slenderly acuminate at the apex, the margins set with single or double bristle-tipped teeth. Flowers single, fragrant, white, 1 to 1½ in. wide, produced during May in corymbose racemes whose main stalk is 1 to 3 in. long. The individual flowers are on stalks about 1 in. long, springing from the axils of conspicuous, obovate, fringed bracts about ½ in. long. Fruits egg-shaped, black, shining, about the size of a pea.

A native of Japan, where it is commonly planted, and occurs wild on Oshima (de Vries Island) and other islands of the Izu Archipelago, and on the adjacent mainland. It is little known in this country in its normal wild form, but many of the Japanese ornamental cherries (Sato Zakura) derive from it.

A double form of *P. speciosa* is known as 'Yae-oshima' (*P. lannesiana* f. *donarium* (Koidz.) Wils.)

P. LANNESIANA (Carr.) Wils.   *Cerasus lannesiana* Carr.—The cherry which Carrière named *Cerasus lannesiana* in 1873 had been sent to the Jardin d' Acclimatation, Paris, in 1870 by a M. Lannes of Montebello. The description was made from a potted plant about 1¼ ft high—not a very satisfactory type for a name that has been so much used. Despite the reasonably good colour plate, the identity of *P. lannesiana* is far from certain. Wilson considered it to be simply a pink-flowered form of the Oshima cherry, described above. If that were indeed the case, the name *P. speciosa* would have to give way to *P. lannesiana*, which has long priority, and the wild Oshima cherry would have to be treated as the white-flowered form of *P. lannesiana*, taking the name *P. lannesiana* f. *albida* (Koidz.) Wils.

However, it is by no means certain that Wilson's identification is correct. Collingwood Ingram has suggested that *P. lannesiana* is really the same as *P. sargentii* with which it agrees in having an umbellate inflorescence (in *P. speciosa* it is corymbose). It accordingly seems best to leave the name

P. lannesiana in abeyance. For the Japanese ornamental cherries which Wilson placed under *P. lannesiana* see Index.

P. 'UMINEKO'.—Flowers white, about 1¼ in. wide, single, in stalked umbels, borne in April together with the green unfolding leaves; filaments of stamens becoming pink as the flower ages. Of fastigiate habit when young, later more spreading. A hybrid between *P. speciosa* and *P. incisa* raised by Collingwood Ingram. A.M. 1928. *Umineko* is the Japanese name for the white-tailed sea-eagle.

The same cross was made in Holland by Mr Doorenbos and has yielded an almost identical tree, recently named 'SNOW GOOSE'.

P. SPINOSA L.   SLOE, BLACKTHORN

A deciduous, suckering shrub 10 or 15 ft high, or in gardens a small tree; bark of young shoots downy, many short branches terminated by a spine. Leaves varying from obovate to oval and ovate, ¾ to 1¾ in. long, ½ to ¾ in. wide; sharp-toothed, downy beneath on the midrib and veins, becoming sometimes quite glabrous with age. Flowers produced in March or early April usually on the naked wood, singly, sometimes in pairs, from the previous year's buds, each ½ to ¾ in. across, pure white, and borne on a glabrous stalk ⅕ in. long. Fruits round, ½ in. in diameter, at first blue, then shining black, very harsh to the taste.

The sloe is found wild in Britain and other parts of Europe as well as in N. Asia. It occurs in hedgerows and in woods, where it is occasionally a tree over 20 ft high. It is oftenest seen in wild places on poor soils as a scrubby bush. If introduced to the garden or park for ornament, it should be trained up into tree form. The wood of this species is very hard, and prized in rural districts for making hay-rake teeth.

cv. 'PLENA'.—Flowers not so wide as the single-flowered type, but pure white and very double, crowded on short, spiny branches whose blackness enhances their purity. Its slow growth makes it suitable for small gardens. It seems first to have appeared spontaneously at Tarascon. It is propagated by budding on the wild plum, whose suckers, if produced, are more easily detected than those of the wild sloe. A.M. 1950.

cv. 'PURPUREA'.—Leaves a beautiful red when young, becoming purple; flowers pink. Sent out by Barbier & Co., of Orleans, in 1903.

In the *Manual* of Messrs Hillier it is pointed out that the plant sometimes listed as *P. spinosa* 'Rosea' is probably a hybrid between *P. spinosa* and *P. cerasifera* 'Nigra'.

P. CURDICA Fenzl & Fritsch—This is intermediate between *P. spinosa* and *P. domestica* subsp. *insititia*. It is of spreading habit, less thorny; leaves downy on both sides when young; flowers white, ¾ in. across; flower-stalks downy; fruits blue-black. A very rare native of eastern Anatolia.

P. SSIORI F. Schmidt

Padus ssiori (F. Schmidt) Schneid.

Although, according to Sargent, this bird cherry is a common tree in Hokkaido (Yezo), and in the mountain forests of the main island of Japan, it was not brought into cultivation until 1915. The same author (*Forest Flora of Japan*, p. 38) observes that it is always easily distinguished by its pale, nearly white bark. Young shoots glabrous. Leaves 3 to 6 in. long, oblong, often inclined to obovate, the apex drawn out into a long slender point, the base more or less heart-shaped, the margins closely set with fine almost bristle-like teeth, thin, membranous, glabrous above and the same beneath except for the tufts of brownish down in the vein-axils; stalk slender, 1 to 1½ in. long, with one or two glands near the blade. Flowers small, white, produced in slender, glabrous cylindrical racemes 4 to 6 in. long, about 1 in. wide. The species has been found in Manchuria and Sakhalin. 'The wood is very hard and close-grained, and is used by the Ainos for numerous domestic purposes' (Sargent).

P. SUBCORDATA Benth.   OREGON PLUM

A deciduous tree up to 20 or 25 ft high in the wild, but often shrubby and forming thickets; branchlets reddish. Leaves broadly ovate or broadly oval, usually rounded or sometimes slightly heart-shaped at the base, 2 to 3 in. long, 1 to 2 in. wide, sharply sometimes doubly toothed, downy at first, becoming nearly or quite glabrous; leaf-stalk ½ to ¾ in. long, glandular. Flowers white, ⅔ in. across, produced in stalkless umbels of two to four blossoms, each on a stalk ¼ to ½ in. long. Fruits oblong, dark red or sometimes yellow, ½ to 1¼ in. long.

Native of Oregon and California, and although discovered by Hartweg in 1847, not introduced to Europe until about forty years later. In its native country its leaves turn a brilliant red before falling. It differs from most other American plums in having the young leaves rolled up from the sides (convolute in bud), as are the Old World species, whereas the N.E. American species are conduplicate in bud, i.e., the halves of the leaf fold up in bud like a sheet of note-paper. It succeeds at Kew, where there used to be a tree nearly 20 ft high.

P. SUBHIRTELLA Miq.

A small deciduous tree, with twiggy, erect branches, 20 to 30 ft high; branchlets hairy, especially when young. Leaves 1½ to 3 in. long, scarcely half as wide; ovate, taper-pointed, sharply, unequally, often doubly toothed; downy on the midrib and veins beneath; leaf-stalk ¼ in. long, hairy. Flowers in short-stalked clusters of two to five, each flower ¾ in. across, soft rose-coloured, becoming paler with age, and borne on a sparsely hairy stalk ⅓ in. long; calyx cylindrical, with short lobes; petals notched at the end. Fruits not seen by me, but described as round, shining black when ripe, ⅓ in. across.

Native of Japan; introduced to Kew in 1895, and since proved to be one of the most beautiful of the cherries. It flowers from the end of March until mid-April, before the leaves appear. It is easily propagated by cuttings put in about the middle of June, when the shoots are half woody.

var. ASCENDENS (Mak.) Wils. *P. pendula* var. *ascendens* Mak.; *P. aequinoctialis* Miyoshi—This is the normal state of the species as it occurs wild in the mountains of Japan, Korea, and W. China. The leaves are larger than in typical *P. sub-hirtella*, with ten to fourteen pairs of veins and up to 5 in. long; they are also relatively narrower, and the margins are less markedly double-toothed. The epithet *ascendens* is misleading, implying as it does that *P. subhirtella* is typically pendulous, which is not the case. It was originally used by Makino to distinguish the normal erect-branched form of the wild species from the pendulous form, which Maximowicz took as the type of the species and named *P. pendula* (see further under var. *pendula*).

The var. *ascendens* is little cultivated and really only of interest as the progenitor of the cultivated varieties.

cv. 'AUTUMNALIS'.—A small, spreading tree up to about 25 ft high and as much or more in width. Flowers semi-double, pink in the bud, opening almost white, about ¾ in. wide, the stamens pinkish darkening to crimson as the flowers fade, giving a bicolour effect. They usually start to appear in November, and the main display is usually before the hard weather sets in, and sometimes again in the early spring.   [PLATE 49
'Autumnalis' was apparently first distributed commercially in this country by the Daisy Hill Nursery around 1910, but a tree imported direct from Japan was planted at Borde Hill in Sussex some ten years earlier and must have been the largest in the country until it was smashed by a falling tree in the early 1960s; in 1933 it was 25 ft high and 42 ft in spread. It was at first grown under the name *P. miqueliana*.

'Autumnalis' received an Award of Merit when shown from Borde Hill in 1912 as "*P. miqueliana*", and an Award of Garden Merit in 1924.

cv. 'AUTUMNALIS ROSEA'.—Resembling the preceding, but with pale pink flowers. A.M. 1960.

cv. 'FUKUBANA'.—Flowers with twelve to fourteen notched petals, crimson in bud, opening deep pink. Introduced from California by Collingwood Ingram in 1927. It flowers over a period of some weeks from early April. It is perhaps not the same as *P. subhirtella* var. *fukubana*, shortly described by the Japanese botanist Makino in 1908; Wilson gives Makino's name as a synonym of *P. subhir-tella* var. *autumnalis*. A.M. 1938.

var. PENDULA (Maxim.) Tanaka *P. pendula* Maxim. SHIDARE-ZAKURA. —A cultivated race of Japan, differing from the wild prototype (var. *ascendens*) only in its habit; the main branches are arching and spreading, the branchlets pendulous. In its homeland, where it is planted in gardens and temple-grounds, it builds up into a tall, rather tortuously branched tree. But in Britain, it makes a weeping tree of umbrella-like form and does not rise much above the point of grafting. The usual form—'PENDULA ROSEA', often called 'Pendula' simply, the flowers are flesh-pink (indeed the epithet *carnea* would be more appropriate and was once in use at Kew). It was introduced to Britain around 1870 and originally known as *Cerasus japonica pendula* or *Cerasus pendula rosea*. A.M. 1930. In 'PENDULA RUBRA' the flowers are a deeper pink and the leaves lanceolate;

there is a double row of this variety at Kew leading up to the door of the Temperate House.

Another weeping variety is 'PENDULA PLENA ROSEA', introduced by Collingwood Ingram in 1928 from the Heian-Jingu temple, Kyoto. It resembles 'Pendula Rubra', but the flowers are double.

cv. 'ROSEA'.—A selection of *P. subhirtella* with rose-pink flowers.

cv. 'STELLATA' ('PINK STAR').—Flowers single, larger than in the type, with narrow-oblong petals. The flower clusters are set so close together at the ends of the branchlets that they seem to form a single panicle. This variety was raised by the American nurseryman W. B. Clarke and originally named 'Pink Star', but Collingwood Ingram gave it botanical status in *Ornamental Cherries* as var. *stellata*. It is depicted in that work in Fig. 26.

The following hybrids have *P. subhirtella* as one parent:

P. 'ACCOLADE'.—*See* under *P. sargentii*.

P. 'HALLY JOLIVETTE'.—A small tree of dense, rounded habit with narrow-ovate, tapered, sharply toothed leaves, hairy above and more densely so beneath; leaf-stalk reddish. Flowers double, pink in the bud, opening white, about $1\frac{1}{4}$ in. wide, borne over a period of two weeks or more in late April or early May. It is unlikely to exceed 15 ft in height. It was raised at the Arnold Arboretum, USA, by Prof. Sax, the parentage being *P. subhirtella* back-crossed onto a hybrid between *P. subhirtella* and *P. × yedoensis*.

P. 'PANDORA'.—Flowers single, about $1\frac{1}{4}$ in. wide, petals pale pink with a deeper edge. Flowering-time early April. A beautiful, very floriferous cherry with ascending branches, making a narrowly vase-shaped crown. It was raised by Messrs Waterer of Bagshot and received an Award of Merit in 1939, and the Award of Garden Merit in 1959. The parentage is *P. subhirtella* crossed with *P. × yedoensis*, and the second parent seems to predominate.

P. TANGUTICA (Batal.) Koehne

Amygdalus communis var. *tangutica* Batal.; *A. tangutica* (Batal.) Korshinsky;
P. dehiscens Koehne

A large deciduous bush up to 15 ft or more high, of dense habit; young shoots very minutely downy or glabrous, grey, becoming brown later, often spine-tipped. Leaves, except on the young shoots, mostly clustered on short spurs or at the nodes, oblanceolate or oblong, pointed or bluntish, tapered at the base, shallowly round-toothed, 1 to 2 in. long, $\frac{1}{4}$ to $\frac{1}{2}$ in. wide; stalk slender, $\frac{1}{2}$ in. or less long. Flowers solitary, stalkless, 1 in. wide, of a beautiful rosy pink, opening in March. Petals roundish-obovate; calyx-lobes fringed with pale hairs, otherwise glabrous; stamens white, with yellow anthers. Fruits described as $\frac{4}{5}$ in. wide, covered with velvety down, the fleshy part merely a thin layer; according to Wilson it dehisces (splits), on which character one of its specific names is based. *Bot. Mag.*, t. 9239

A native of W. China: discovered in W. Kansu by the Russian explorer

Potanin; introduced by Wilson in 1910 from the Sungpan valley, W. Szechwan, during his second expedition for the Arnold Arboretum and originally distributed under the name *P. dehiscens*. It is a beautiful species, very distinct in its bushy, twiggy mode of growth, but it has never spread into gardens. There are specimens at Highdown in Sussex and at Bodnant in North Wales, both raised from the seeds sent by Wilson.

Although classified as an almond, *P. tangutica* is one of the species linking the almonds with the peaches.

P. TENELLA Batsch   DWARF RUSSIAN ALMOND
P. nana (L.) Stokes, not Du Roi; *Amygdalus nanus* L.

A low, deciduous shrub of bushy form 2 to 5 ft high; twigs glabrous. Leaves obovate or oblong, 1½ to 3½ in. long, ½ to 1 in. wide, saw-toothed, dark glossy green above, pale beneath, glabrous on both surfaces. Flowers one to three on each bud of the previous year's shoots, rosy red, ½ in. long, ½ in. or more in diameter. Fruit like a small almond, 1 in. long, covered with velvety down, not often produced in England. *Bot. Mag.*, t. 161.

Native of S.W. Russia and parts of Central and S.E. Europe; long cultivated in this country (Aiton says since 1683). It is very pretty shrub, flowering abundantly in April, growing well on its own roots, and easily increased by layering. In spite of this it is frequently grafted on plum, and is short-lived in consequence.

P. tenella is a variable species in size, leaf-shape, relative length of sepals to calyx-tube, flower colour, etc. Plants with relatively broad leaves are sometimes distinguished as var. CAMPESTRIS (Bess.) Rehd. and plants with dark pink flowers, of which several clones have been introduced to cultivation, are known collectively as f. GESSLERIANA (Kirchn.) Rehd. Of these the best known in Britain is 'FIRE HILL', introduced by Lady Martineau from the Balkans; it received an Award of Merit in 1959. In 'ALBA' the flowers are white.

The plant described by Desfontaines in 1809 as *Amygdalus georgica* is considered by Rehder to be synonymous with *P. tenella*. Some Russian botanists recognise it as a distinct species, though the differences adduced are not very convincing.

P. TOMENTOSA Thunb.   DOWNY CHERRY

A deciduous shrub of spreading habit 4 to 8 ft high and twice as wide; branchlets covered densely with a close, pale down. Leaves obovate or oblong, with an abrupt point, 2 to 3 in. long, ¾ to 1½ in. wide, toothed, dark dull green, and furnished with scattered hairs above, paler and densely woolly beneath. Flowers ¾ in. across, white, tinted with rose, produced singly or in pairs at the joints of the previous year's growth, each on a stalk ⅙ in. long. Fruit bright red, about the size of a small cherry, slightly hairy, ripe in July. *Bot. Mag.*, t. 8196.

Native of N. and W. China, but introduced from Japan around 1870. It usually flowers about the fourth week in March, and is then an object of great beauty and charm. Shoots from 1 to 2 ft long are made in one season, and these the following spring are furnished from end to end with the delicately tinted flowers. It must be said, however, that its beauty is short-lived. The petals are fragile and easily fall, so that if sharp rain-storms or harsh winds are prevalent (as often happens when they are expanding), their full beauty is never displayed. Some sheltered nook should be chosen for it, a consideration to which its early blossoms entitle it. The fruits are not freely produced with us, although about Peking the shrub is cultivated for their sake. Propagated by layers and cuttings of half-ripened wood.

P. *tomentosa* has been collected in the Valley of Kashmir and in Ladakh, but these specimens may have come from cultivated plants. At any rate, it is not a native of the Himalaya as a whole, as is sometimes stated in reference books.

P. TRILOBA Lindl.
Amygdalopsis lindleyi Carr.

A deciduous shrub or small tree 12 to 15 ft high, young shoots usually glabrous. Leaves ovate or obovate, 1 to 2½ in. long, ¾ to 1¼ in. wide; tapering at both ends, irregularly, doubly, and rather coarsely toothed; slightly hairy beneath. Flowers pinkish white, ¾ to 1 in. across, produced singly or in pairs (sometimes more) from each bud of the previous year's shoots; calyx glabrous, ⅕ in. long, with shallow, rounded lobes. Fruits covered with pale down when quite young; not seen mature by me, but said to be red, ½ in. wide, globose and downy. *Bot. Mag.*, t. 8061.

cv. 'MULTIPLEX'.—Flowers 1½ in. across, of a delicate rose, very double. Leaves more obovate than in the type, often more or less three-lobed towards the apex. A.G.M. 1935.

Prunus triloba is a native of China, and the double-flowered variety was introduced by Fortune in 1855; it was upon this that Lindley founded the name.

It is the most popular and beautiful form of the species, flowering in the greatest profusion about the end of March or early in April. It is seen at its best against a south wall, where it should be pruned once a year as soon as ever the flowers are faded, cutting the blossoming twigs close back. Shoots 1 to 2½ ft long are then made, which flower the following year. It may be grown in the open ground, but does not flower so profusely there; it is also very extensively used for forcing early into bloom for greenhouse decoration. The single-flowered wild plant was of later introduction, but is by no means so exquisite a shrub as the other, neither do the flowers last as long. The form known in gardens as 'PETZOLDII' has ovate, not trilobed leaves.

Propagated by cuttings of firm wood or by layers. Plants worked on the plum stock are often troublesome because of suckers.

P. × ARNOLDIANA Rehd.—A hybrid raised at the Arnold Arboretum from the wild form of P. *triloba* pollinated by P. *cerasifera*. It is of interest as a plum–almond cross.

P. VIRGINIANA L.　　　VIRGINIAN BIRD CHERRY

Padus rubra Mill.; *Prunus nana* Du Roi

Usually a shrub in the wild state, 2 to 15 ft high, occasionally a tree, deciduous, with grey, glabrous branchlets. Leaves varying from broadly oval to broadly obovate, with a short abrupt point, finely toothed, 1½ to 5 in. long, two-thirds as wide, glabrous, shining, and dark green above, paler beneath, with tufts of down in the vein-axils beneath; stalk ½ to ¾ in. long, with two or more glands. Flowers white, ⅓ in. or rather more across, produced in racemes 3 to 6 in. long, 1 in. wide, terminating short leafy shoots. Fruits dark red, round, ⅓ in. across, very harsh to the taste.

Native of the eastern and central United States and Canada; introduced to England in 1724, but not often seen now. It is much rarer in gardens than its near ally, *P. serotina*, which has a black rather than a red fruit and proportionately narrower leaves. Also, in *P. serotina* the leaves have blunt, appressed teeth and the calyx is persistent in fruit; in the present species the teeth are spreading and pointed, and the calyx deciduous. *P. virginiana* flowers well during May in England, and is pretty then, but does not bear fruit so freely as our native bird cherry.

var. DEMISSA (Torr. & Gr.) Torr. *Cerasus demissa* Nutt. ex Torr. & Gr.; *P. demissa* Nutt. ex Dietr.—An erect shrub or small tree. Leaves usually slightly cordate at the base and downy beneath. Fruits dark red. Native of western N. America.

f. LEUCOCARPA (S. Wats.) Haynie—Fruits white.

var. MELANOCARPA (A. Nels.) Sarg. *Cerasus demissa* var. *melanocarpa* A. Nels.—Leaves glabrous beneath, rather thick. Fruits black. Native mainly of the Rocky Mountains.

cv. 'NANA'.—Of dwarf habit.

cv. 'SHUBERT'.—Leaves at first green, but becoming purple by June. An American variety of recent introduction to Britain.

P. × YEDOENSIS Matsum.　　　YOSHINO CHERRY

P. paracerasus Koehne; *P. yoshino* Hort.

A deciduous tree up to 40 or 50 ft high, of rounded, spreading habit, shortly trunked, usually wider than high; young shoots thinly clothed with soft hairs. Leaves oval, broadly ovate or obovate, rounded or broadly wedge-shaped at the base, rather abruptly narrowed to a slender point, doubly toothed, 2½ to 4½ in. long, 1½ to 2½ in. wide, dark green and glabrous above, downy on the midrib and veins beneath. Flowers borne in late March or early April, slightly fragrant, white or pink, produced in racemes of four or more, usually before (but sometimes with) the leaves; flower-stalks and calyx dull red, usually densely downy, but less so on young trees; calyx-tube cylindrical, lobes sharply toothed. Style either very downy or nearly glabrous. Fruits shining black, globose, ⅖ in. wide, bitter. *Bot. Mag.*, t. 9062.

According to Wilson, the origin of this cherry is doubtful. It is planted abundantly in Tokyo and Yokohama, where it is known as the 'Yoshino Cherry', but has not yet been found wild. It may be a hybrid between *P. speciosa* and *P. subhirtella*. Wilson describes it as 'remarkably distinct from all other Japanese or Chinese cherries and one of the most floriferous and beautiful of them'. It is perfectly hardy and grows vigorously, attaining a spread of about 40 ft. A.G.M. 1930.

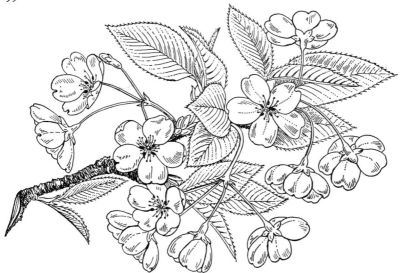

PRUNUS × YEDOENSIS

About 1910 it was obtained from Germany and was grown as "*P. para-cerasus*" at Kew, but was rare until the late 1920s, when large numbers were imported or raised in this country. It varies in the amount of pubescence on the undersurface of the leaf; sometimes the midrib and veins are densely covered with tawny down. In regard to habit, too, some trees are more erect and less spreading than others. If the tree is truly of hybrid origin, the fact that some of the stock now in nurseries has been raised from seed might account for this diversity.

cv. 'Ivensii'.—Main branches arching horizontally, branchlets slender and weeping. Flowers white. A seedling of *P. × yedoensis* raised by Messrs Hillier.

f. perpendens. Wils. Shidare Yoshino, Weeping Yoshino Cherry.—Branches pendulous.

P. 'Moerheimii'.—Of pendulous habit, usually seen as a shrub, but probably making a small weeping tree if top-grafted. Although put into commerce as *P. incisa moerheimii* it is not a cultivar of that species, but is very near to *P. × yedoensis*. Flowers pale pink fading to white, about ⅞ in. across. Pedicels and calyx with a few spreading hairs; sepals irregularly toothed; bracts oblanceolate, jaggedly toothed; style glabrous.

P. 'PINK SHELL'.—Petals shell-pink at first, fading to a lighter shade, spreading-erect, the corolla hence cup-shaped, about ¾ in. wide at the mouth. The flowers are borne in mid-April, three to five in a corymbose inflorescence, on slender hairy pedicels; calyx-tube narrow-campanulate, glabrous. A charming cherry, probably a seedling of *P.* × *yedoensis*, named by Messrs Hillier. A.M. 1969.

Other seedlings of *P.* × *yedoensis* are 'YOSHINO PINK FORM', raised by Messrs Waterer, Sons and Crisp, which also has flowers of a charming shade of pink, but borne later than in 'Pink Shell'; and 'AKEBONO', raised in the USA by W. B. Clarke of California. The latter has apparently never been introduced to Britain, though the raiser thought highly of it.

PSEUDOCYDONIA   ROSACEAE

A genus of a single species, often placed in *Cydonia* or *Chaenomeles*, but rather out of place in either genus. It differs from the former in its free styles and deciduous sepals, and from the latter (to which it is more closely related) in bearing its flowers singly on short leafy shoots.

P. SINENSIS (Dum.-Cours.) Schneid.

Malus sinensis Dum.-Cours.; *Cydonia sinensis* (Dum.-Cours.) Thouin; *Chaenomeles sinensis* (Dum.-Cours.) Koehne ("chinensis", sphalm.)

A small deciduous or semi-evergreen, unarmed tree, up to 30 to 40 ft high, with the bark of the trunk and main branches peeling off in flakes like that of a plane. Branchlets extremely hairy when quite young, afterwards glabrous and glossy. Leaves obovate, ovate, or oval, 2½ to 4½ in. long, 1½ to 2½ in wide; tapering to a stalk ½ in. long, which is furnished with hairs and gland-tipped teeth; upper surface glabrous, lower one covered with pale brown hairs, becoming nearly glabrous by autumn; margin regularly and minutely saw-toothed, teeth gland-tipped. Flowers solitary from the buds of the year-old shoots, or on short spurs, stalkless, soft carmine, 1 to 1½ in. across, petals oblong. Fruits egg-shaped, pale citron-yellow when ripe, 5 to 7 in. long.

Native of China; introduced to England in the last decade of the 18th century, but afterwards quite lost to cultivation. Reintroduced from Italy in 1898. It succeeds very well on a south wall, and bears fruits which, however, do not ripen or become so large as one sees them on the Italian Riviera, where the tree is much cultivated. In the open it is not quite satisfactory, and suffers in severe winters. This is due no doubt to lack of summer sun, for I saw it some years ago in the Vienna Botanic Garden 15 ft or more high in perfect vigour, and the winter cold there is greater than ours. It flowers in April and May. It should be raised from seeds, obtainable from S. Europe.

PSEUDOLARIX PINACEAE

The species described here, which is probably the only one of its genus, bears a marked resemblance to the larches in foliage and branching, but is remarkably distinct in its clustered male catkins (solitary in *Larix*), and in the large woody scales of the cone, which falls to pieces when ripe (remaining intact in *Larix*).

P. AMABILIS (Nelson) Rehd. GOLDEN LARCH

Larix amabilis Nelson; *Pseudolarix fortunei* Mayr; *Pseudolarix kaempferi* of some authors, not (Lindl.) Gord.; *Abies kaempferi* Lindl. (1854), not Lindl. (1833); *Chrysolarix amabilis* (Nelson) H. E. Moore

A deciduous tree, occasionally 100 to 130 ft high, with a trunk 2 to 3 ft thick; branches spreading horizontally; young shoots glabrous. Leaves linear, $1\frac{1}{2}$ to $2\frac{1}{2}$ in. long, $\frac{1}{12}$ to $\frac{1}{8}$ in. wide; produced in a radiating cluster from the end of short, spur-like branches, or on terminal shoots singly and spirally arranged.

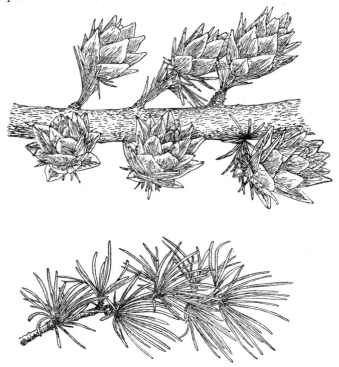

PSEUDOLARIX AMABILIS

Their arrangement and general aspect are similar to those of larch, but the leaves are stouter and larger than those of any true larch. In spring they are of a tender yellowish shade of green, and in autumn they turn a rich golden yellow before falling. Male flowers yellow, produced in densely clustered catkins about 1 in. across at the end of the short, spur-like branchlets. Cones about 2 in. long, nearly as wide; the scales thick, woody, triangular, blunt, often notched at the tip, ¾ to 1¼ in. long, ultimately spreading and falling away with the seeds.

Native of China, where it was discovered in the Chekiang province and introduced by Fortune in 1854. Slow-growing, but perfectly hardy, it is one of the most beautiful as well as one of the most interesting of trees. The finest tree I have seen was in Messrs Rovelli's nursery at Pallanza, on Lake Maggiore. This was nearly 70 ft high, and very fertile; when I saw it in 1912 there were beneath its boughs hundreds of young trees that had sprouted from its fallen seeds, varying from a few inches to 2 or 3 ft high. It dislikes limy soil.

Among the notable specimens of the golden larch are: Kew, 56 × 5¾ ft (1970); Leonardslee, Sussex, 45 × 6 ft (1969); Sheffield Park, Sussex, 46 × 5 ft (1968) and 48 × 4¾ ft (1960); Wakehurst Place, Sussex, 20 × 4½ ft (1970), at the junction of the entrance path with the Drive, and two others of about the same size, one on the Lawn and another in the Valley; Carclew, Cornwall, 64 × 7¾ ft (1962); Scorrier House, Cornwall, *pl.* 1872, 60 × 7¾ ft (1965).

PSEUDOPANAX   ARALIACEAE

A small genus of evergreen trees and shrubs, natives of New Zealand, Tasmania, New Caledonia, China, and Chile. Leaves digitately compound, trifoliolate or reduced to a single leaflet. Some New Zealand species go through a juvenile phase in which the leaves are markedly different from those of adult plants; the most notable instance—*P. crassifolius*—is treated below. Flowers in compound umbels, or in umbels arranged in the form of a panicle or raceme; pedicels jointed. Calyx entire or toothed. Petals five, valvate. Stamens five. Ovary with two to five locules. Styles two to five, more or less connate. Fruit fleshy, subglobose or compressed.

Pseudopanax, as here understood, includes species previously included in *Nothopanax* and *Neopanax* (see: W. R. Philipson, *N.Z. Journ. Bot.*, Vol. III (1965), pp. 333–8; H. H. Allan, *Fl. N.Z.*, Vol. I (1961), p. 433).

P. ARBOREUS (L. f.) W. R. Philipson
Panax arboreum L. f.; *Nothopanax arboreum* (L. f.) Seem.;
Neopanax arboreum (L. f.) Allan

A small, unisexual, evergreen tree of rounded shape, freely branched and 12 to 25 ft high, all its parts free from down; young shoots stout. Leaves digitate, the three, five, or seven leaflets arranged at the end of a main-stalk as in the horse chestnut. Leaflets elliptic-oblong to narrowly obovate, coarsely and bluntly toothed, tapered to both ends, often more abruptly at the apex; 3 to 8 in. long, 1 to 3 in. wide, dark glossy green above, paler beneath; stalks of leaflets ½ to 1 in. long; main-stalk up to 8 in. long, the base dilated and clasping the stem. Flowers in compound umbels terminating the shoot, their main-stalks short and thick or almost non-existent; from the end of each radiate eight to twelve primary divisions each on a stalk 2 to 4 in. long, and from the end of each of these radiate divisions of a third dimension to the number of ten or twenty, each ½ to 1½ in. long and bearing at the end a rounded umbel of some ten or fifteen flowers. These flowers are ¼ in. wide, greenish brown and of no beauty; petals five, obovate; stamens five, spreading. Fruits purplish black, rather compressed-globose, ¼ in. wide, crowned by the recurved styles. *Bot. Mag.*, t. 9280.

Native of New Zealand, mostly of the lowlands, but ascending to 2,500 ft; long introduced. It is not hardy at Kew, but there used to be a good tree in the Temperate House, where it grew for many years and became eventually as large apparently as it is found at home. In New Zealand the tree often begins life as an epiphyte on the stems of tree-ferns, down which it extends its roots until they reach the ground. It is a handsome foliage tree of a type unusual in the open air, but common enough in glass houses.

The following specimens were recorded in Eire in 1966: Ashbourne House, Co. Wicklow, 22 × 2¾ + 1¾ ft; Mount Usher, Co. Wicklow, 15 ft; Fota, Co. Cork, 24 ft.

P. LAETUS (Kirk) W. R. Philipson *Panax arboreum* var. *laetum* Kirk; *Nothopanax laetum* (Kirk) Cheesem.; *Neopanax laetum* (Kirk) Allan—This species is closely allied to the preceding, differing in its somewhat larger and relatively broader leaflets, which are up to 10 in. long and 4 in. wide; and in the reddish-purple petioles. A native of the North Island of New Zealand. Tender. The finest specimen in the British Isles grows at Castlewellan in Co. Down.

P. CRASSIFOLIUS (A. Cunn.) K. Koch
Aralia crassifolia A. Cunn.; *Panax longissimum* Hook. f.

This remarkable New Zealand tree is only hardy in the maritime counties of the south and west. It is evergreen and in the wild grows 20 to 50 ft high. The leaves are extraordinarily variable according to the age and development of the tree, and Cheeseman describes them in four distinct stages. At the first or seedling stage they are 1 to 2 in. long, diamond-shaped or ovate-lanceolate, tapered at the base, coarsely toothed or lobed. At the second and most remarkable stage the plant is a straight, erect, unbranched, slender stem, bearing the leaves on the upper part; they are then sword-shaped, very stiff, deflexed, often 1½ to 3 ft long but only 1 to 2 in. wide, of very leathery texture, the margins armed with large sharp teeth. At the third stage, when the tree begins to branch, the leaves are erect or spreading, some of them divided into three or five stalkless leaflets, whilst others retain the No. 2 shape but are only one-third as long. At the fourth or mature stage they become simple leaves again, 3 to 8 in. long, 1 to 1½ in. wide, linear to linear-obovate, either without teeth or toothed towards the apex and tapered at the base to a stout stalk ½ to 1 in. long. Sometimes the third stage is omitted and the tree never bears compound leaves. It is at that stage trees commence to flower, the sexes on different ones. The blossoms are small, of no beauty, produced in terminal compound umbels 3 or 4 in. across. Fruits globose, black, ⅕ in. wide.

There is a specimen of this araliad approaching the third stage at Wakehurst Place, Sussex, 27 ft high and 1½ ft in girth (1969). This is in the Valley. Two examples by the Heath Garden are at the second stage. Trees with two or more distinct types of leaves are very characteristic of the New Zealand flora, but in none is the diversity more remarkably developed than in this. The species was originally discovered during Cook's first voyage (1769–70).

P. FEROX (Kirk) Kirk *Panax ferox* Kirk—In this related species the leaves of the second stage (see above) are deflexed as in *P. crassifolius* and of similar shape, but are edged with broad-based lobules, roundish at the apex and usually equipped each with a sharp hook. The adult leaves are rather shorter than in *P. crassifolius*—up to about 6 in. long. A further distinction in wild plants is that the fruits are larger—about ⅜ in. wide (little more than half that in *P. crassifolius*). It is a native of both islands of New Zealand, but is found at lower elevations than *P. crassifolius*.

P. DAVIDII (Franch.) W. R. Philipson

Panax davidii Franch.; *Nothopanax davidii* (Franch.) Harms; *Acanthopanax diversifolium* Hemsl.

A small evergreen tree 10 to 20 ft. high; young shoots and leaves quite glabrous. Leaves leathery, very variable in shape, and either simple, bifoliolate (rarely), or trifoliolate; the simple leaf and the individual leaflets of the compound leaves are similar in size and shape, being narrowly lanceolate, tapered towards both ends, especially towards the apex which is very long and slender-pointed; margins remotely toothed, 3 to 6 in. long, ¾ to 1½ in. wide; dark glossy green; leaf-stalk 2 to 8 in. long, grooved on the upper side. The simple leaves have normally three longitudinal veins starting from the base; where the leaf consists of two leaflets one has a single vein, the other (usually larger) one has two; where there are three leaflets each has a single vein. Thus every leaf, whatever its shape, has three veins. Flowers small, greenish yellow, opening in July and August, and produced in pyramidal or rounded panicles 3 to 6 in. long composed of small umbels. Fruits black, roundish, compressed, ⅙ in. wide.

Native of W. and Central China; discovered by the French missionary David near Mupin in 1869 and introduced by Wilson in 1907 when collecting for the Arnold Arboretum. It makes a neat evergreen, quite distinct from any other hardy one in the diversity of its leaves. In this country (and sometimes in the wild) it makes a large shrub and is slow-growing. It is moderately hardy near London in a sheltered place but thrives better in the Atlantic zone.

It is easily increased by summer cuttings.

PSEUDOTSUGA PINACEAE

A genus of five or six species of large evergreen trees in western N. America, Mexico, China, Formosa, and Japan. Buds slender, acute, not resinous. Leaves set spirally, but spreading and crowded into two opposite rows, linear, grooved above, with two bands of stomata beneath. Cones pendulous, with persistent scales (as in *Picea*); bracts much longer than the scales and always a conspicuous feature of the cone (in *Picea* the bracts are very small and never exposed; the cones of *Abies* often have exserted bracts, but they are erect, and the scales are deciduous). The generic name *Pseudotsuga* implies a resemblance to *Tsuga*, but in that genus the cones resemble those of *Picea* (except in being smaller) and, as in *Picea*, the branchlets are roughened by the persistent leaf-bases, whereas in *Pseudotsuga* they are more or less smooth (as in *Abies*).

P. FORRESTII Craib

An evergreen tree 60 to 80 ft high, with more or less downy young shoots. Leaves 1 to nearly 2 in. long, $\frac{1}{12}$ in. wide, notched at the tips, grooved on the upper surface, marked with a whitish band of stomata at each side of the prominent midrib beneath. Cones 2 to 2½ in. long, 1¼ to 1½ in. wide, egg-shaped, distinctly stalked. The exposed, three-lobed part of the bracts is bent sharply back over the scales, the central lobe awl-shaped, the side ones triangular.

Native of Yunnan, China; discovered in 1914 by Forrest in mixed forests in the Mekong Valley at 10,000 ft, and introduced by him at the same time under F.13003. Plants were raised in the Edinburgh Botanic Garden, at Leonardslee and at Caerhays, but it has always been very rare in collections, being susceptible to damage by spring frosts. According to the Austrian botanist Handel-Mazzetti, who saw this tree during his travels in Yunnan, it is of a cedar-like habit in the wild, with horizontally spreading branches, and has a smooth bark.

In describing *P. forrestii*, Craib compared it to *P. sinensis*, giving as the difference that in *P. forrestii* the leaves are longer, the cones larger, and the bracts much longer. It is even more closely allied to *P. wilsoniana* (see below).

P. WILSONIANA Hayata—This species, a native of Formosa, has not been introduced to cultivation, so far as is known. It was at first identified by Hayata with *P. japonica*, but Wilson, who was shown a herbarium specimen during his visit to Japan in 1914, expressed the view that it represented a distinct species, and in the following year Hayata described it as such, naming it after Wilson. It seems to be very closely allied to *P. forrestii*, and in many recent works the two have been united under the name *P. wilsoniana*, which has priority. But so little is known about either that it seems better to keep them separate for the time being. It should be added that, if the two are really one and the same species, we have an example of disjunct distribution very similar to that shown by *Taiwania cryptomerioides* (q.v. in Vol. IV).

P. JAPONICA (Shiras.) Beissn.

Tsuga japonica Shiras.; *Abies japonica* Rovelli

A tree up to 100 ft in Japan, with a dull brown bark divided vertically into thin, narrow plates; shoots glabrous, yellowish or reddish at first, later pale grey; buds narrow-ovate, with chestnut-brown, non-resinous scales. Leaves of soft texture, linear, ¾ to 1 in. long, rounded and notched at the apex, upper side light green, rather deeply grooved along the midrib, lower side with a band of stomata on each side of the prominent midrib. Cones ovoid, 1½ to 1¾ in. long, with fifteen to twenty broad scales, which are rounded at the apex; bracts exserted, recurved, the middle lobe narrow and tapered to an acute point, the lateral lobes blunt-ended and laciniate.

A native of southern Japan, where it is confined to a few stands in Kii, Yamata, and Tosa provinces; it was discovered by Shirasawa in 1893 and introduced to Britain by Clinton-Baker in 1910 (but a few years earlier to Germany). It is of no ornamental value, but is of interest as the only pseudotsuga from E. Asia that has become established in cultivation in Britain, though even it is rare. There are examples 30 ft or slightly higher in the National Pinetum at Bedgebury, Kent; and at Wakehurst Place, Leonardslee, and Borde Hill, Sussex. The largest specimen recorded in the British Isles grows at Powerscourt in Eire; this measures 60 × 6 ft (1966).

The other Asiatic species resemble *P. japonica* in having the leaves bifid at the apex, but their shoots are downy and the cones larger.

P. MACROCARPA (Torr.) Mayr

Abies douglasii var. *macrocarpa* Torr.; *Pseudotsuga douglasii* var. *macrocarpa* (Torr.) Engelm.; *Abies macrocarpa* (Torr.) Vasey

This is a close ally of the Douglas fir, but according to Jepson is only from 30 to 90 ft high. It differs from *P. menziesii* in its leaves being incurved instead of straight, and taper-pointed instead of usually rounded at the apex. Cones larger, occasionally 6½ to 7½ in. long, with the bracts not protruded so much beyond the scales. Native of S. California and Lower California.

Although very distinct because of its large cones, it has not much value either as a timber producer or as an ornamental tree. It was introduced to cultivation in 1910 by H. Clinton Baker, who found it susceptible to injury by spring frost. One of the trees he planted at Bayfordbury, Herts, survives and measures 38 × 2¼ ft (1962). There are two grafted trees in the National Pinetum, Bedgebury, Kent, *pl.* 1925, the larger 60 × 5½ ft (1974).

P. MENZIESII (Mirbel) Franco   DOUGLAS FIR

Abies menziesii Mirbel; *P. douglasii* (Lindl.) Carr.; *P. taxifolia* (Lamb.) Sudw.; *Abies douglasii* Lindl.; *Pinus taxifolia* Lamb.   [PLATE 53

A tree 200 to 300 ft high, with a trunk 8 to 12 ft in diameter; main branches horizontal, secondary ones pendulous; young shoots usually more or less downy, with terminal buds that are ovate, pointed, $\frac{1}{4}$ to $\frac{1}{2}$ in. long, brown, shining; also occasional axillary buds along the shoot. Leaves disposed either all round the shoot or (especially on weak shoots) in two opposite ranks crowded, linear, $\frac{3}{4}$ to $1\frac{1}{2}$ in. long, $\frac{1}{16}$ to $\frac{1}{12}$ in. wide; rounded or blunt (never notched) at the apex, of various shades of green (from grass green to glaucous green), and with several lines of stomata each side the midrib beneath. Cones pendulous, shortly stalked, averaging $2\frac{1}{2}$ to 4 in. long and 1 to $1\frac{1}{2}$ in. wide at the base, slenderly egg-shaped, pointed, very distinct on account of the conspicuously obtruded bracts. Male flowers axillary, composed of a cylindrical cluster of orange-red stamens.

Native of western N. America from British Columbia to California; discovered by Menzies in 1793, and introduced by Douglas in 1827.

In favourable situations the Douglas fir grows with extreme rapidity, and has already reached in many places a stature of over 150 ft. To get it at its best it requires a climate where the rainfall is abundant, and at least a moderately good soil. On dry, hungry soil, and in bleak spots, it is a failure. To see this tree in its finest condition and in its greatest numbers one must visit the Perthshire properties. Solitary trees are magnificent, the enormous trunks supporting a mass of large plume-like branches.

PSEUDOTSUGA MENZIESII

The vernacular name Douglas fir is used for this species as a whole (and sometimes for the whole genus *Pseudotsuga*). But the typical state is often referred to as Oregon, Green, or Coastal Douglas fir, to distinguish it from the inland race (see var. *glauca* below).

It is impossible in a short list to do justice to the many notable specimens of Douglas fir growing in the British Isles. In *Conifers in the British Isles*, A. F. Mitchell gives statistics of 101 trees, the majority in Scotland, of which thirty-three are 150 ft high and over, and forty-two are more than 15 ft in girth. The following are from the original introduction by Douglas, or were planted before 1850: Eggesford Forest, Crediton, Devon, *pl.* 1837, 124 × 20¼ ft at 6 ft, dying back at top (1970); Walcot Hall, Shrops., *pl.* 1842, fine bole, 125 × 18¾ ft (1962); Powis Castle, Montgom., *pl.* 1842, 180 × 13½ ft (1970); Drumlanrig Castle, Dumfries, *pl.* 1832 (original introduction), 117 × 15½ ft (1970); Durris House, Kincard., *pl.* 1841, 154 × 17 ft (1970); Dawyck, Peebl., *pl.* 1835, 141 × 17 ft (1970); Dunkeld Cathedral, *pl.* 1846, 120 × 20¾ ft (1970).

As might be expected from its extended habitat, it shows much variation. In any large group of trees more or less distinct shades are discernible. The most distinct of the varieties are:

var. CAESIA (Schwer.) Franco *P. douglasii* f. *caesia* Schwer.—Leaves stiffer and grey-green, young shoots smooth or slightly downy, cones smaller, 2½ in. long, intermediate between those of the type and var. *glauca* and native of the N. Rocky Mountain region.

var. GLAUCA (Mayr) Franco *P. douglasii* var. *glauca* Mayr; *P. glauca* (Mayr) Mayr BLUE or COLORADO DOUGLAS FIR.—This differs in general appearance, and has its own habitat. The common and finest type of Douglas fir occurs near the Pacific coast, in British Columbia and Washington. The var. *glauca* is of inland and mountain distribution, and is hardy in places where the other will not live. It differs in being a smaller tree, in the leaves being stouter and often very glaucous, and in their having a turpentine-like odour. A more significant difference is that the cones are smaller, usually under 3 in. long, with reflexed bracts. But these distinguishing characters do not always appear in combination, and various intergrades occur which blur the boundary between the two races.

As an ornamental tree, the var. *glauca* is worth growing, especially the bluest forms (it varies much in that respect), but for timber it is valueless in this country. Some specimens of the Blue Douglas fir are: Warnham Court, Sussex, 94 × 4½ ft (1971); Wakehurst Place, Sussex, 64 × 3¼ ft (1964); Dropmore, Bucks, *pl.* 1906, 74 × 5¼ ft (1970); St Clere, Kent, 69 × 5 ft (1973).

The following are garden varieties:

cv. 'BREVIFOLIA'.—A bushy small tree with light green leaves more or less radially arranged, some backward pointing, ¼ to ½ in. long, blunt at the apex. Raised by William Barron and Son, Elvaston Nurseries, nr Derby, before 1875.

cv. 'FLETCHERI'.—A dwarf, usually flat-topped shrub, attaining 6 ft or even more in height, more in width. Leaves radially arranged, exposing their glaucous undersides, ½ to ¾ in. long. It was raised from imported seeds of the var. *glauca* at the end of the last century and put into commerce by Fletcher's Ottershaw nursery, Chertsey, Surrey. For the full history see Hornibrook's *Dwarf and Slow Growing Conifers*, Ed. 2, 225–6.   [PLATE 52

cv. 'FRETSII'.—A dwarf, pyramidal tree with dark green leaves, radially arranged and ⅜ to ½ in. long, rather wider than in 'Brevifolia'. Raised by Messrs Frets and Son of Boskoop, Holland, who thought at first that it might be a hybrid with *Tsuga sieboldii*. The largest recorded specimen in Britain grows in the Pinetum at the Royal Horticultural Society's Garden, Wisley, Surrey. It measures 41 × 3¼ ft (1969).

cv. 'Stairii'.—Foliage of a pale greenish yellow. It originated at Castle Kennedy, Wigtonshire, before 1871.

P. sinensis Dode

An evergreen tree described by its discoverer as 'grand et superbe' in the wild state; young shoots brown, minutely downy; winter buds brown, non-resinous. Leaves mostly in two opposite rows, notched at the end, $\frac{3}{4}$ to $1\frac{1}{4}$ in. long, $\frac{1}{16}$ to $\frac{1}{12}$ wide, furrowed above, with two whitish bands of stomata beneath. Cones $1\frac{3}{4}$ to $2\frac{1}{4}$ in. long, 1 to $1\frac{1}{4}$ in. wide; the bracts reflexed, three-lobed, the middle lobe $\frac{1}{8}$ to $\frac{1}{4}$ in. long, the side ones shorter.

Native of south-west and eastern-central China; discovered by the French missionary Maire in N.E. Yunnan, growing on limestone at 8,500 ft elevation; introduced by him in 1912 to Chenault's nursery, Orleans. More recently it has been found farther to the north-east, in Anwhei and Chekiang, and also in Szechwan. Plants were imported into Britain from Chenault in the 1920s, but they proved to be very sensitive to spring frosts and most of them were killed while still young.

PSEUDOWINTERA winteraceae

A genus of three species endemic to New Zealand, which were included in *Drimys* until 1933. From that genus they are distinct in their flowers; for in *Drimys* the calyx completely encloses the petals in the bud and fall as the flowers expand, while in *Pseudowintera* the calyx is small, cup-shaped, and persistent.

P. colorata (Raoul) Dandy

Drimys colorata Raoul; *D. axillaris* var. *colorata* (Raoul) Kirk

An evergreen glabrous shrub usually not more than 6 ft high in the wild and so far much smaller in cultivation, with an almost black bark. Leaves leathery, $\frac{3}{4}$ to $2\frac{1}{2}$ in. long, $\frac{3}{8}$ to $1\frac{1}{8}$ in. wide, elliptic to broadly so, or sometimes broadest above the middle, dull yellowish green above, blotched or margined with red or reddish purple, glaucous beneath. Flowers small, axillary, in clusters of two to four (sometimes more), each on a stalk about $\frac{3}{8}$ in. long. Calyx cup-shaped, entire or shallowly lobed. Petals yellowish green, about $\frac{3}{16}$ in. long. Carpels up to five in number, but only one or two maturing. Fruits black or dark red, about $\frac{3}{16}$ in. across, with two or three seeds.

Native of New Zealand, mainly in the South Island and Stewart Island. It is sometimes cultivated in the milder parts of the country for the curious variegation of its foliage, which gives it the appearance of a garden variety, though it is in fact a feature of all the wild plants. It is closely related to the following and sometimes treated as a variety of it:

P. AXILLARIS (J. R. & G. Forst.) Dandy *Drimys axillaris* J. R. & G. Forst. —This differs from *P. colorata* in its taller, often tree-like habit, and its larger leaves, dark green above and without the markings characteristic of *D. colorata*. It occurs on both the main islands of New Zealand.

PSORALEA   LEGUMINOSAE

A genus of over 100 species, mostly shrubs and subshrubs, natives mainly of the tropics and subtropics of both hemispheres, but a few temperate. Of the shrubby species, the one described here is almost hardy. The type of the genus—P. PINNATA L., from S. Africa—is tender, but could probably be grown outside in the mildest parts.

P. GLANDULOSA L.

A bushy shrub up to 10 ft high, all the vegetative parts and the peduncles and calyces warty with small black glands; young shoots slender, white-downy, longitudinally ribbed. Leaves alternate, trifoliolate, on stalks $\frac{3}{4}$ to $1\frac{1}{2}$ in. long; leaflets lanceolate, tapered to a long acute apex, rounded or wide-cuneate at the base, entire, deep green above, paler beneath, the terminal leaflet $1\frac{3}{8}$ to 3 in. long, $\frac{1}{2}$ to 1 in. wide, on a stalk $\frac{3}{8}$ to $\frac{5}{8}$ in. long, the lateral pair rather smaller and more shortly stalked. Inflorescences axillary, more or less downy, the flowers densely crowded into a spike-like raceme 1 to 2 in. long (but up to almost 5 in. long on wild plants), borne on a peduncle $1\frac{1}{2}$ to $3\frac{1}{2}$ in. long (up to 6 in. long on wild plants); calyx deeply cup-shaped about $\frac{3}{16}$ in. long, unequally divided to nearly half-way into five narrowly triangular, acute, erect lobes; corolla of the usual pea-flower form, petals white, the standard blotched with blue and the keel with a blue blotch on the lower surface; stamens and style included. Legume about $\frac{1}{4}$ in. long and half as wide, oblong-ellipsoid, hairy, indehiscent, enclosed in the hard dry calyx and containing a single seed. *Bot. Mag.*, t. 990.

Native of Peru, where it was originally discovered, and of Chile; introduced, according to Aiton, around 1770. It is variable in the degree of hairiness, some Chilean specimens being more hairy than the cultivated plants and others almost glabrous, while a Peruvian specimen has the stems, petioles, inflorescence axes, and calyces densely white villose.

Probably all the plants now cultivated in Britain derive from Harold Comber's introduction from Chile in 1926 (C.572). In his field-note he adds: 'much grown in Chile for the preparation of a refreshing drink made by whisking water with the young shoots and adding sugar. This is very good.' It is known there by the Indian name 'culén'. This form should be almost hardy in a sunny sheltered place. At Kew a plant has grown for many years outside the southern end of the Temperate House and flowers freely in summer.

PTELEA RUTACEAE

A genus of a few species of deciduous small trees or shrubs most fully represented in North America, but occurring also in Mexico. The leaves are usually trifoliolate but are sometimes made up of four or five leaflets, aromatic and (with a lens) seen to be covered with pellucid dots. Flowers small. The most distinctive feature of this genus is provided by the fruits, which are thin, flat and broadly winged, rather like hops or elm seed.

P. BALDWINII Torr. & Gr.

This species, described from Florida, is represented in cultivation by the following Californian variety:

var. CRENULATA (Greene) Jeps. *P. crenulata* Greene WESTERN HOP TREE.—A deciduous shrub or small tree up to 15 ft high, with trifoliolate leaves much smaller than those of *P. trifoliata*. Leaflets 1¼ to 2½ in. long, narrowly ovate to narrowly obovate, the terminal one the longest, downy beneath, entire or more or less crenately toothed. Flowers in small terminal corymbs. Fruits about ½ in. across. It differs from *P. trifoliata* in its narrower leaves, larger flowers, and narrow fruit-wing. Introduced to Kew in 1893. Not so notable a plant as its eastern ally.

P. LUTESCENS Greene

A deciduous small tree with slender young shoots of a pale yellowish grey at first, becoming shining pale grey with age, thickly covered with small warts, not downy. Leaves trifoliolate, the leaflets of lanceolate shape, faintly round-toothed, stalkless, slenderly pointed or bluntish, the side ones oblique at the base, 1¾ to 3½ in. long, ⅜ to ⅞ in. wide; shining green above, dull beneath, quite glabrous on both surfaces; main-stalk 1 to 2 in. long. Fruits elm-like, but occasionally two- or even three-winged, ¾ to 1 in. wide, wrinkled, notched at the top, glandular in the centre; seed flattish, oval.

Native of the Grand Canyon, Arizona. There was a small tree at Kew about 10 ft high which was raised from seed received from the Arnold Arboretum in 1914 as "*P. angustifolia*", which I believe to be *P. lutescens*. Dr Rehder collected this species on the Bright Angel Trail of the Grand Canyon in 1914 and it is probably from the seed he gathered then that this tree was raised. Another site for the species in the Grand Canyon is the Red Canyon Trail, where it was collected by Lester F. Ward in 1901 and distributed as "*P. angustifolia*". *P. lutescens* has the same odour as the well-known *P. trifoliata* and the leaves are thickly sprinkled with oil glands that show transparently when the leaf is held up to the light and examined through a lens. It is very distinct from the older species in its narrow lanceolate leaves.

P. TRIFOLIATA L.   HOP TREE

A low deciduous tree, usually under 25 ft high, often of greater breadth than height, with a short, comparatively thick trunk, often inclined. Leaves trifoliolate, the leaflets lanceolate, ovate or oblong, finely toothed or entire, downy beneath when young, the middle one the largest, and from 2 to 6 in. long, with a short stalk, the lateral leaflets unequal-sided, stalkless; the common leaf-stalk is 2 to 4 in. long. Held against the light and seen through a lens the blade is found to be dotted with oil-glands. Flowers borne on slender, downy stalks in corymbs 2 or 3 in. across during June and July, dull greenish white, ⅓ to ½ in. across. They are unisexual, the males soon falling away. Fruit in dense clusters, each a flat, thin disk from ⅔ to 1 in. across, consisting of an almost circular wing, with prominent netted veins surrounding one seed in the centre. Occasionally the fruit has more than one wing.

Native of S. Canada and the eastern United States; introduced to England in 1704. *Ptelea trifoliata* is one of the most distinct of hardy trees, and it is interesting for its large crops of curious elm-like fruits which often strew the ground in its neighbourhood throughout the winter, the fleshy part of the wing having decayed and left the netted veins. Very little of the seed is fertile in this country, but the tree is easily increased by cuttings. The bark, leaves, and young fruits emit a strong and aromatic scent when bruised, and the last have been suggested as a substitute for hops because of their intense bitterness. The tree is of picturesque habit, perfectly hardy, and appears to thrive in any well-drained soil. The leaves die off yellow in autumn.

cv. 'AUREA'.—Leaves yellow at first, later lime-green. Uncommon but very handsome. Raised in Germany at the end of the last century.

cv. 'FASTIGIATA'.—Branches erect.

cv. 'GLAUCA'.—Leaves blue-green instead of the ordinary rich dark green.

cv. 'HETEROPHYLLA'.—Leaves mostly trifoliolate as in the type, but others have four and some five leaflets; they are also narrower in proportion to their length. Distributed by Messrs Booth of Hamburg, before 1864. The same or a similar plant is named 'Pentaphylla'.

var. MOLLIS Torr. & Gr.—Leaflets broader than in the type, but its chief distinguishing characteristic is the dense permanent covering of greyish down on the lower surface.

PTEROCARYA   WING-NUT   JUGLANDACEAE

At present six of the seven species of *Pterocarya* known are in cultivation. They are deciduous trees with large, alternate, pinnate leaves and pithy young wood, the pith lamellate; leaflets varying from five to twenty-seven, toothed, more or less oblong. Flowers unisexual, both sexes borne on the same tree but on different catkins; male catkins about one-third the length of the female ones, pendulous in both sexes. The fruit is a small nut, large numbers of which are strung on slender spikes 8 to 20 in. long. From its allies in the same family—the walnuts and hickories—*Ptericarya* differs in the curiously winged nuts, and from the latter in the chambered pith.

In gardens the only species well known is the Caucasian one (of the rest five come from China, one from Japan), and no handsomer pinnate-leaved tree can be grown in our climate. The others also are handsome, but they have not yet shown their qualities as ornamental trees in Britain. All of them are moisture-lovers, and for their best development should be planted in deep loam. Young plants making vigorous succulent shoots are sometimes cut by winter cold, and even old trees are liable to injury by late spring frosts. Seeds afford the best means of propagation; some species produce suckers, and cuttings of the shoots may also be employed.

P. FRAXINIFOLIA (Lam.) Spach   CAUCASIAN WING-NUT
Juglans fraxinifolia Lam.; *P. caucasica* C. A. Mey.   [PLATE 54

A large deciduous tree, ultimately 80 to 100 ft high, usually much less in this country, and branching low down, forming a wide-spreading head; trunk of large trees 10 to 12 ft in girth, with deeply furrowed bark; ends of young shoots minutely scurfy. Leaves 8 to 18 in. (sometimes over 2 ft) long, composed of from three and a half to thirteen and a half pairs of leaflets; these are stalkless, oblong, obliquely rounded at the base, pointed, toothed, normally 2 to 4½ in. long by ¾ to 1¼ in. wide (occasionally, on vigorous shoots, 8 or 9 in. long); dark green, glabrous and glossy above, tufted with stellate hairs along the midrib beneath; common stalk round. Male catkins 3 to 5 in. long, cylindrical, the flowers closely packed. Female catkins 12 to 20 in. long, with the flowers scattered, afterwards developing nuts which, with the wings, are ¾ in. in diameter, roundish, oblique, horned at the top.

Native of the Caucasus and N. Persia, inhabiting moist places. It was introduced to France by the elder Michaux, who took back seeds from Persia in 1782. This tree likes a rich soil and abundant moisture, and whilst the fine specimens mentioned below show that it will thrive very well in the south of England, it loves more sunshine than our climate affords. The lover of trees will find nothing more interesting in and around Vienna than the magnificent examples of *Pterocarya fraxinifolia*. There, of course, the summers are much hotter, and the winters colder than ours; the tree bears fruit freely even in this country, and is very attractive in late summer when hung with the long slender catkins.

In previous editions a tree at Melbury Park, Dorset, was mentioned, which early this century measured 90 × 12 ft. It is now 105 × 17½ ft (1972) and there are three others there 75–88 ft high, 13½–15 ft in girth. Other examples are: Hyde Park, London, 58 × 10¾ ft (1967); Syon House, London, 67 × 11¼ ft (1967); Frensham Hall, Haslemere, *pl.* 1905, 70 × 7¾ ft (1968); Abbotsbury, Dorset, 115 × 12 ft (1972); University Botanic Garden, Cambridge, a huge many-stemmed bush 85 ft high, the largest stem 10 ft in girth (1969); Clare College, Cambridge, 70 × 16¾ ft at 2 ft (1969).

var. DUMOSA Schneid. *P. dumosa* Lav., *nom.*—A shrubby variety of dwarf habit, with small leaflets 2 or 3 in. long. Although first noticed in the Arboretum at Segrez, in France, this is apparently a truly wild form, judging by the following statement of Jean Van Volxem:

'The country around Lagodechi (in the Caucasus) is very interesting. Near the river are extensive swamps, where I saw P. caucasica growing sometimes as an enormous tree, sometimes as a large shrubby bush. The two forms are intermixed with each other, so that no condition of soil or exposure can explain the fact, and there is, as far as I saw, no intermediate form, and I could detect no difference between the two forms except as to habit and size.' (*Gardeners' Chronicle*, Vol. 7 (1877), p. 72.)

P. HUPEHENSIS Skan

A tree 70 ft or more high, with glabrous, minutely glandular young shoots. Leaves 7 to 12 in. long, composed of five, seven, or nine leaflets, which are oval-lanceolate, oblong, or slightly obovate, pointed, obliquely rounded at the base, toothed, 1½ to 5 in. long, ¾ to 2 in. wide; glabrous except for tufts of brownish down in the vein-axils beneath; common stalk glabrous, roundish, not winged. The fruiting catkin is 12 to 18 in. long, each nut with a pair of roundish wings, the whole rather more than 1 in. across.

Native of the mountains of Hupeh, China; discovered by Henry in 1888, and introduced by Wilson for Messrs Veitch in 1901. The young trees appear to be quite hardy. The species is closely allied to *P. fraxinifolia;* so far as we know at present it has not so many leaflets on each leaf, and they are slightly stalked. The base of the blade of the leaflet does not overlap the main-stalk as it usually does in *P. fraxinifolia.*

P. PALIURUS Batal.

Cyclocarya paliurus (Batal.) Iljinskaya

A tree 50 or more ft high, the young shoots downy, glandular. Leaves 8 to 12 in. long composed usually of seven or nine leaflets, which are oblong or oval, very obliquely tapered or rounded at the base, pointed or blunt at the apex, finely toothed, 2½ to 5 in. long, 1 to 2½ in. wide, dark glossy green, and glabrous except for fine down on the midrib on both surfaces; common stalk not winged, downy. Male catkins slender, 2½ to 4 in. long, frequently in pairs. Fruiting catkin 8 to 10 in. long, each nut surrounded by a wing, the whole forming a circular disk 1½ to 2½ in. across.

Native of the mountains of Central China; discovered by Henry in 1888, and introduced by Wilson for Messrs Veitch in 1901. The fruits of this species are very remarkable, suggesting miniature cymbals; in having the wing continuous all round the nut, they distinguish it from all other species. Seeds were again sent by Wilson during his later journeys.

P. × REHDERIANA Schneid.

A hybrid between P. *fraxinifolia* and P. *stenoptera*, raised in the Arnold Arboretum, near Boston, Mass., from seeds received in 1879 from Lavallée's collection of Segrez, where the cross had no doubt been effected by wind on trees growing together. As the seeds were received as P. *stenoptera*, that species was no doubt the mother plant. I saw the original hybrid in the Arnold Arboretum in June 1910, which was then 40 ft high and, owing to the faculty of producing sucker-growths from the root, forming by itself quite a grove. At least one of the parent species has the same faculty—rarely developed, however, unless the main stem is cut down. P. × *rehderiana* is intermediate between the parents. The common-stalk of the leaf has wings, but they are not so much developed as in P. *stenoptera*, and never toothed as they often are in that species. The wings of the fruit are shorter and rounder. In the Arnold Arboretum this hybrid has proved hardier and a better grower than either of its parents. Living plants were introduced to Kew in 1908 and have grown extremely well. One of them measures 72 × 9½ ft (1972).

Other examples are: Westonbirt, Glos., 66 × 11 ft (1972); Wakehurst Place, Sussex, 48 × 7¼ ft (1968); Borde Hill, Sussex, 62 × 7¾ ft (1971). A young tree at Kew, seventeen years planted, measures 52 × 5¾ ft (1970).

At Borde Hill there are also some spontaneous forms of P. × *rehderiana*, raised in the 1920s from seed of P. *fraxinifolia*. The presumed seed-parent grows a few yards from two specimens of P. *stenoptera*, both of which flower in most years.

P. RHOIFOLIA Sieb. & Zucc.   JAPANESE WING-NUT

A tree 80 to 100 ft high, trunk 8 to 10 ft in girth; young shoots nearly glabrous. Leaves 8 to over 12 in. long, composed of eleven to twenty-one leaflets, which are rounded at the base, pointed at the apex, oblong, finely and evenly toothed, 2½ to 4 in. long, 1 to 1½ in. wide; common-stalk not winged. The stalk and leaves vary in regard to pubescence, but the plants which grew at Kew were glabrous except for tufts of stellate down about the midrib and axils of the veins beneath; but in Japan a form is commonly much more downy on the leaves and leaf-stalks. Male catkins 3 in. long; females 8 to 10 in. long; wings of the nut horizontal, broadly crescent-shaped, the whole fruit ¾ to 1 in. across.

Native of Japan; introduced in 1888. It is quite hardy, and in a moist loam would apparently grow well. Professor Sargent found it abundant on Mt Hakkoda at 2,500 to 4,000 ft above sea-level, and almost the largest deciduous tree in that part of Japan.

The only recorded example of this species is one at Borde Hill, Sussex, measuring 50 × 3½ ft (1969).

P. STENOPTERA C. DC.

A tree 50 to 80 ft high, with a fissured trunk 6 to 8 ft in girth; young shoots and common-stalk of the leaf of some plants furnished with pale hairs persisting through the first winter, but in others both are quite glabrous. Leaves 8 to 15 in. long, composed of eleven to twenty-one (sometimes twenty-five) leaflets, which are oblong or narrowly oval, tapered at both ends, finely and regularly toothed, 2 to 5 in. long, $\frac{1}{3}$ to 2 in. wide; the common stalk winged in the spaces between each pair of leaflets, the wings sparsely toothed. Male catkins 2$\frac{1}{2}$ in. long; female ones 8 in. long. Nut roundish oval with a short beak, the two wings forward-pointing, narrow, tapering, $\frac{3}{4}$ in. long, $\frac{1}{5}$ in. wide at the base, forming a V.

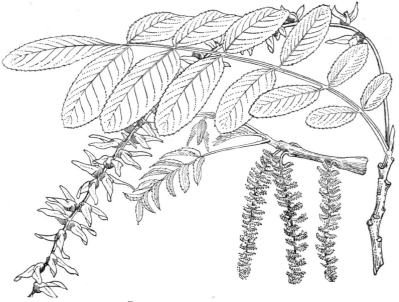

PTEROCARYA STENOPTERA

Native of China, whence specimens were sent to France by the missionary Joseph Callery in 1844, on which Casimir de Candolle founded the species. It appears to have been introduced to Europe about 1860. Its winged leaf-stalks and the forward-pointing narrow wings of the nuts distinguish it from P. fraxini-folia.

The largest of the few recorded specimens of P. stenoptera are: Kew, 65 × 8$\frac{3}{4}$ ft (1965); Chiltley Place, Liphook, 50 × 7$\frac{3}{4}$ + 7$\frac{3}{4}$ ft (1961); Wakehurst Place, Sussex, 60 × 7$\frac{1}{4}$ ft (1961); Tortworth, Glos., pl. c. 1885, 58 × 7 ft (1964).

PTEROCELTIS   ULMACEAE

Closely allied to Celtis, it is very distinct in its winged fruits, which more resemble those of Ulmus, but their arrangement singly in the leaf-axils of the shoots of the year make the tree very distinct from the elms. This is the only species of the genus known.

P. TATARINOWII Maxim.

A deciduous tree with the habit and general aspect of a celtis; young shoots slender and, like the leaves, at first clothed with small appressed hairs which mostly soon fall away. Leaves alternate, toothed, ovate lance-shaped, 2 to 4 in. long, ¾ to 2 in. wide, the apex with a long tapered point, the base three-nerved and broadly wedge-shaped, upper surface harsh to the touch, with innumerable minute warts, lower surface with tufts of down in the vein-axils; stalks ¼ to ⅓ in. long. Flowers unisexual, the males in stalkless clusters, the females solitary in the leaf-axils; neither of any beauty. Fruit a globose nut about ⅓ in. wide, surrounded by a circular wing notched at the top, the whole ½ to ¾ in. wide, borne on a slender stalk about ½ in. long.

Native of Central China; introduced to France in 1894 by Maurice de Vilmorin, who raised the first plants at Les Barres from seed. One of these I saw bearing fruit in July 1904, but none of its seeds had up to then proved fertile. It was introduced to Kew in 1897. Interesting botanically, it will probably only appeal to connoisseurs and lovers of curiosities, for the flowers are quite inconspicuous.

PTEROSTYRAX   STYRACACEAE

Bentham and Hooker united this genus to *Halesia*, apparently on insufficient grounds, for most botanists now concur in keeping the two separate. They are really very distinct. *Pterostyrax* is exclusively Chinese and Japanese (*Halesia* is eastern N. American); the inflorescence is paniculate and many-flowered; the parts of the flowers are in fives (fours in *Halesia*); the stamens are protruded in *Pterostyrax* (enclosed in *Halesia*); the pith is continuous (chambered in *Halesia*).

P. HISPIDA Sieb. & Zucc.
Halesia hispida (Sieb. & Zucc.) Mast.

A deciduous shrub 15 to 20 ft high, or a tree up to 30 or 40 ft high, of coarse, vigorous growth and spreading habit; young shoots glabrous. Leaves alternate, 3 to 8 in. long, 1½ to 4 in. wide; oval or obovate, wedge-shaped at the base, pointed, toothed, covered beneath with fine whitish down or nearly glabrous; stalk ½ to 1 in. long. Flowers white, fragrant, produced during June and July on axillary, downy, pendulous panicles, 4 to 9 in. long, 2 to 3 in. wide, with often two or three leaves at the base. Corolla of five oval lobes, divided almost to the base, finely downy on both sides, ⅓ in. long. Stamens, flower-stalks, and calyx downy. Fruits spindle-shaped, $\frac{1}{2}$ in. long, terminated by the persistent calyx-lobes and style, the whole densely clothed with pale brown hairs $\frac{1}{12}$ in. long. *Bot. Mag.*, t. 8329.

Native of Japan and China; introduced in 1875. This beautiful and distinct tree is very hardy and flowers almost every year, but most profusely when the preceding summer and autumn have been hot. It needs a good loamy soil and a sunny position. Seed is ripened occasionally, and this affords the simplest and best means of propagation.

P. CORYMBOSA Sieb. & Zucc. *Halesia corymbosa* (Sieb. & Zucc.) Nichols.— The true species of this name is very clearly distinguished from *P. hispida* by its fruits, which are $\frac{1}{2}$ in. long, $\frac{3}{8}$ in. wide, five-winged (not merely ribbed as in *P. hispida*), and covered with a very close down (not hairy). The panicles are broader, and there is some difference in the foliage, the leaves of *P. corymbosa* being smaller, up to 5 in. long. Native of Japan. It has been so little cultivated that nothing useful can be said about it as a garden plant. Most of the plants that have been grown under its name are really *P. hispida*.

PUNICA   PUNICACEAE

A genus of two species, the one not treated here—*P. protopunica*—a native of the island of Sokotra in the Gulf of Aden; for the remaining distribution see below. *Punica* was once placed in the Lythraceae (Loosestrife family), which is mainly herbaceous and temperate, but contains a few woody genera of the tropics and subtropics, such as *Lagerstroemia*. It is certainly allied to this family and also to the tropical Sonneratiaceae, but it now usually placed in a separate family, of which it is the only member.

The generic name derives from the Roman *Pomum* (or *Malum*) *punicum*, the Carthage apple, probably from the fact that the finest fruits came from there, while the specific epithet for the common pomegranate—*granatum* —derives from another name used by the Romans; this was *Malum* (or *Pomum*) *granatum*—the apple with the grain-like seeds.

P. GRANATUM L.   POMEGRANATE

A small deciduous tree up to 15 or 25 ft high, free from down in every part, often spiny. Leaves mostly opposite, narrow oblong, entire; 1 to 3 in. long, $\frac{1}{3}$ to 1 in. wide; stalks very short. Flower scarlet-red, 1 to $1\frac{1}{2}$ in. across, scarcely stalked, terminal on short side twigs, and often in pairs. Petals crumpled, normally five but often more; calyx with five or more lobes, and a funnel-shaped base to which the very numerous stamens are attached. Fruits rarely ripened in this country, deep yellow, roundish, $2\frac{1}{2}$ to 3 in. across, with the calyx-lobes adhering at the top, filled with a reddish, very juicy pulp and numerous seeds.

The pomegranate has been grown for its fruits in the south of Europe and N. Africa eastwards to Persia, Palestine, and India from remote antiquity. But it is probably only native of Persia and Afghanistan. Its praises are recorded in the earliest songs and writings that have been preserved to us. In the British Isles, where the tree has been grown for perhaps four centuries, ripe fruit is denied us. In the open ground the plant is killed back to ground-level in any but the mildest winters, and even on walls, where it thrives well, lack of sunshine precludes the development of palatable fruits. At the same time fruits are occasionally borne: in 1874, according to a letter preserved at Kew from Lady Rolle of Bicton, a magnificent tree that covered the whole front of a house in Bath was laden with fruit; and in 1911 fruits were produced, if not ripened, in various parts of the south. Grown on a sunny south wall, it bears its showy flowers quite freely from June to September, and is worth growing for their sake.

In the gardens of Versailles, visitors will have noticed growing in tubs many remarkable, very old pomegranate trees, with gnarled, crooked trunks which to all appearances are as old as the château itself.

The pomegranate can be raised from seeds, cuttings, or by grafting; the varieties by either of the two last methods; if grafted, seedling stocks of the type should be used.

cv. 'LEGRELLIAE'.—Flowers double; petals (according to the original description) salmon-pink variegated with white (but sometimes described as red variegated with yellow). It was introduced to Belgium shortly before 1858 by Mme Legrelle d'Hanis, who obtained it from her friend Mme Parmentier, a Belgian lady resident in Illinois, USA. It appears to be an unstable mutant from the double red, to which it reverts, but has also produced a branch-sport with white double flowers.

var. NANA (L.) Pers. *P. nana* L. DWARF POMEGRANATE.—Of dwarfer stature than the normal form, and smaller in its leaves (which are often relatively narrower than usual), and also in its flowers and fruits. *Bot. Mag.*, t. 634.

The first description of the dwarf pomegranate under the Linnaean system of nomenclature was published by Linnaeus himself in 1762 (*Sp. Pl.*, ed. 2, p. 676). This original form had been introduced to France at the end of the 17th century from the West Indies, where it was used as an ornamental hedging plant. Presumably it arose there as a mutation from the original stock brought from the Old World by the early colonists. This New World form had reached Dr Sherard's garden at Eltham in Kent by 1723 and was known to Philip Miller. He called it the dwarf American pomegranate and said that, unlike the normal European kind, it was too tender to survive our winters, but would bear flowers and fruits if kept under glass in moderate heat, and would grow to about 3 ft in a pot. 'The Fruit of this Kind', he wrote, 'is rarely much larger than a Walnut, and not very pleasant to the Taste.'

The dwarf pomegranate in commerce at the present time is probably of independent origin, since it is only slightly tender and survived the winters of 1961–3 in many gardens. It comes true when raised from seeds, which are available from seedsmen, and received an Award of Merit when shown by Messrs Sutton in 1936 as a coolhouse plant. It is advisable to grow it to flowering size in a greenhouse (three or four years) before planting it outside at the foot of a sunny wall.

cv. 'PLENA'.—Flowers double; the showiest form. Philip Miller remarked that the double-flowered pomegranate is less vigorous, but more floriferous, if grafted on the common sort, than on its own roots.

PURSHIA   ROSACEAE

A genus of two species in western N. America, belonging to the same tribe of the Rose family as *Dryas*, *Fallugia*, and *Cowania*. Flowers solitary, almost sessile. Carpels one, rarely two, with a short curved, persistent style. Fruit an achene, crowned by the persistent style. The genus is named after F. Pursh, a botanist of German birth who is the author of *Flora americae septentrionalis* (1814), one of the first works on the flora of N. America.

P. TRIDENTATA (Pursh) DC.

Tigasea tridentata Pursh

A deciduous grey shrub 3 to 6 ft high in cultivation, but occasionally 10 ft in the wild; young branchlets downy. Leaves wedge-shaped or obovate, ¼ to ⅝ in. long, ⅛ to ¼ in. wide towards the apex, where it is cut into three large, rounded teeth, tapering gradually towards the base, covered with white down beneath, grey-green and downy above. Flowers yellow, almost stalkless, produced in May, usually singly from buds on twigs of the previous year's wood; calyx covered with grey down, intermixed with gland-tipped hairs, funnel-shaped, five-lobed; stamens numerous, arranged in a ring. Each flower is about ⅓ in. wide. Fruits ½ in. long, downy, crowned with the persistent style.

Native of western N. America, from British Columbia to California; introduced by Douglas in 1826, first flowered in the Horticultural Society's Garden in 1830. According to Loudon, all the plants about London were killed during the winter of 1837–8, but plants grew unsheltered in a border at Kew for over twenty years. Unfortunately these have now been lost. It is not a very attractive shrub, although curious and interesting. It prefers a rather light soil, and can be propagated by layers.

PYRACANTHA ROSACEAE

The species whose descriptions are given below have been by various authors placed in *Cotoneaster*, *Mespilus*, and *Crataegus*. They are, no doubt, most closely allied to the last, differing chiefly in having leafy thorns, in being evergreen, and in the leaves being either entire or merely toothed, never lobed. There are also differences in the ovules. From *Cotoneaster* they are equally distinct in having thorny branches and toothed leaves. For the rest they may be described as evergreen shrubs with alternate leaves and white flowers; stamens about twenty; styles five. Fruits globose or orange-shaped, yellow, or scarlet. They are easily satisfied as regards soil, thriving in any that is warm and not very heavy. All the pyracanths are hardy in the open ground (except perhaps the uncommon *P. angusti-folia*, *P. crenulata*, and *P. koidzumii*) and will flower and bear fruits freely there. But few evergreen shrubs are better for furnishing a house-wall, and their fruits are safer there from the depredations of birds, especially in quiet country gardens. *P. coccinea* is one of the commonest of wall-shrubs but there are other species and hybrids which are just as fine and probably more resistant to scab. Open-ground plants need no regular pruning and should not be cut more than is absolutely necessary to restrict size. For plants grown close against a wall, careful training and tying-in of the branches is more important than pruning, but the season's growths may be shortened after flowering.

Many of the pyracanths are subject to attack by scab, which forms a sooty coating of spores on the foliage and fruits and causes the foliage to wither and fall prematurely; die-back may also occur. The recommended treatment is to spray with captan three times in March and April and twice in June. It is claimed for some of the modern hybrids that they are scab-resistant, but only trial could confirm this. The pyracanths are also susceptible to Fireblight (see Vol. I, p. 730, and *Dictionary of Gardening*, Supplement (1969), p. 307).

P. ANGUSTIFOLIA (Franch.) Schneid.
Cotoneaster angustifolia Franch.

An evergreen shrub probably 10 or 12 ft high, of dense, spreading, bushy habit; branches rather rigid, horizontal, often spine-tipped, covered the first year with a thick, grey down. Leaves narrow oblong or slightly obovate, rounded or tapered at the base, rounded at the apex with a minute tip or slight notch there; the larger leaves have a few minute dark stiff teeth near the apex, the smaller ones mostly entire; they are ½ to 2¼ in. long, ⅛ to ½ in. wide, glabrous, dark green above, covered beneath with a grey felt; stalk $\frac{1}{12}$ to ¼ in. long. Flowers white, ¼ in. across, in corymbs 2 in. wide, of little beauty; calyx and flower-stalk felted. Fruits brilliant orange-yellow when ripe, covered with grey down when young, ¼ to ⅜ in. in diameter, much flattened at the top; seeds five. *Bot. Mag.*, t. 8345.

Native of W. China; introduced to Kew by Lieut. Jones in 1899, and again a few years later through M. de Vilmorin. I saw it in great beauty at Les Barres in 1908, loaded with fruit, and the whole plant much more woolly than it is in Great Britain. After the hot summer of 1911, a plant on a wall at Kew bore fruit very freely. A later introduction of this species by Forrest has proved hardier than the first ones and they can be grown in the open. Its round-ended, nearly or quite entire leaves, and dense woolliness readily distinguish it from the other species. It is valuable in retaining its berries in full beauty until March, long after those of of *P. coccinea* have fallen.

P. ATALANTIOIDES (Hance) Stapf

Sportella atalantioides Hance; *P. gibbsii* A. B. Jacks.

An evergreen shrub 15 to 20 ft high, of erect habit, frequently destitute of spines; young shoots at first clothed with down but becoming glabrous and bright olive-brown by autumn. Leaves oblong, oval, or inclined to obovate, tapered either equally towards both ends or (more usually) abruptly tapered to a point; sometimes rounded at the apex, sometimes entire, sometimes finely toothed except towards the stalk, 1 to 3 in. long, ½ to 1⅓ in. wide, dark glossy green above, pale and dull beneath, glabrous except when quite young; stalk ⅛ to ⅓ in. long. Flowers ⅓ to ½ in. wide, white, produced in May or early June in corymbs 1½ to 2 in. wide which terminate short, leafy twigs that spring from the previous season's growths. Fruits rather flattened-globose, $\frac{3}{16}$ to ¼ in. wide, scarlet, topped by the shrivelled calyx-lobes, and persisting until March. *Bot. Mag.*, t. 9099 (flowering branch).

Native of Central China (Kweichow, S.E. Szechwan, W. Hunan, and W. Hupeh); introduced by Wilson in 1907. It was at first grown as *P. crenulata*, but in 1916 it was separated from that species by A. B. Jackson and named *P. gibbsii*, after the Hon. Vicary Gibbs, in whose garden at Aldenham there was a magnificent pyramidal specimen 20 ft high. But ten years later it was found that Hance had described the species in 1877, as *Sportella atalantioides*, from a specimen collected by the American missionary Nevin, amplifying the description in 1880 from a specimen collected by General Mesny.

This fine pyracanth is the strongest grower in the genus. Although the fruits are smaller than those of *P. coccinea*, they ripen later and remain for several months longer on the bushes. In all really essential botanical characters it does not differ much from the Himalayan *P. crenulata*, but is very distinct as a garden shrub. It is perfectly hardy, its leaves and flowers are larger, its growth much stronger, and it is often quite spineless. By training up a leading shoot and gradually removing the lower branches it can be made into a small tree, as was done at Aldenham.

P. atalantioides received the Award of Garden Merit in 1922. This was given to the normal red-fruited form. Yellow-fruited plants have also been raised, and an Award of Merit was given to one of these when shown from Wisley in 1936 (f. AUREA Hort.).

P. 'WATERERI'.—

A vigorous, dense shrub up to 8 ft high and as much across. Young stems densely hairy. Leaves mostly ¾ to 1¼ in. long, ¼ to ½ in.

wide (but occasionally up to 2½ in. long, ¾ in. wide), elliptic to elliptic-lanceolate, acute or subacute at the apex, faintly crenate in the upper third, sparsely hairy beneath on the midrib and main veins. A probable hybrid between *P. atalantioides* and *P. rogersiana*, raised by Messrs Waterer, Son, and Crisp. A.M. 1955. It is excellent as an open-ground specimen or even as a hedging plant.

P. COCCINEA Roem.   PYRACANTH, BUISSON ARDENT

Mespilus pyracantha L.; *Crataegus pyracantha* (L.) Med.;
Cotoneaster pyracantha (L.) Spach

An evergreen shrub or small tree up to 15 ft high, of very dense, leafy habit; young shoots covered with grey down, the slender thorns ½ to ¾ in. long; branches often thorn-tipped. Leaves narrowly obovate or oval, tapered at both ends, blunt-toothed; 1 to 2½ in. long on the barren shoots, ½ to 1½ in. long on the flowering ones, varying from ¼ to ¾ in. wide; dark glossy green above, paler beneath, glabrous except at the margins near the base; stalk ⅓ in. or less long, downy. Flowers white, ⅓ in. across, very numerously borne in early June in corymbs terminating short twigs which, springing from the shoots of the previous year, form one large panicle; flower-stalks and calyx slightly downy; calyx-lobes broadly triangular. Fruits brilliant coral-red, orange-shaped, about ¼ in. across.

Native of S. Europe and the Near East (including the Crimea and Caucasus); its western limit as a truly wild plant is uncertain; in cultivation in Britain 1629.

This well-known evergreen is more often seen growing against a wall than in the open, and no doubt bears fruit more abundantly there. It is, in fact, one of the most desirable of evergreen wall shrubs. But when once established it is quite hardy in the open; at Kew there are specimens 15 ft high that bear fruit profusely. The shrubs have to be netted, as birds (blackbirds especially) are very greedy for the fruits. The pyracanth should be used more than it is as an evergreen shrub. It bears pruning well, and its only defect is that it transplants badly except when young.

cv. 'KASAN'.—This variety, raised in Russia, is valued in the coldest parts of the Continent because of its great hardiness. In this country it is unlikely to be a success.

cv. 'LALANDEI'.—This was raised from seed by M. Lalande of Angers about 1874. It is of more vigorous, upright growth than the type, and has leaves of proportionately greater width on the average, as well as larger fruits of a more yellowish red, or orange. Award of Garden Merit 1925.   [PLATE 55

P. CRENATO-SERRATA (Hance) Rehd.

Photinia crenato-serrata Hance; *Pyracantha yunnanensis* Chittenden;
P. gibbsii var. *yunnanensis* Osborn; *P. fortuneana* (Maxim.) Li

An evergreen shrub 12 to 18 ft high, related to *P. atalantioides* and *P. rogersiana*. It differs from both in its leaves, which are obovate-oblong, broadest in the upper third or upper quarter of the blade, rounded at the apex, long-tapered to the base, 1 to almost 3 in. long, ⅜ to 1 in. wide, usually coarsely toothed. In *P. atalantioides* the leaves are broadest at or near the middle. In *P. rogersiana* they are smaller, not more than 1½ in. long except on vigorous shoots, and oblanceolate or oblong-oblanceolate. The inflorescence is downy, as in *P. atalantioides* (glabrous in *P. rogersiana*). *Bot. Mag.*, t. 9099, figs 5–10.

P. *crenato-serrata* is a native of China from N.E. Yunnan and W. Hupeh northward to Kansu and Shensi. It was discovered by J. Watters of the British Consular Service near Ichang in Hupeh and described in 1880. The French missionary Ducloux introduced it to Maurice de Vilmorin's garden at Les Barres, and from there it was distributed. But some at least of the plants grown in this country derive from seeds collected by Reginald Farrer in Kansu in 1914. It is useful in retaining its fruits until spring, if birds permit, but has never attracted as much attention as its two relatives *P. atalantioides* and *P. rogersiana*.

The name *Pyracantha fortuneana* (Maxim.) Li has been proposed for this species (*Journ. Arn. Arb.*, Vol. 25, p. 420). It is based on *Photinia fortuneana* Maxim., a name given to the species represented by material collected by Fortune in 1845 (no. A 69). However, as pointed out in *Bot. Mag.*, n.s., t. 74, the material of Fortune's A 69 at Kew seems better placed in *Photinia*, and does not belong to *Pyracantha crenato-serrata*.

P. 'TALIENSIS'.—This pyracanth was at one time in cultivation under the name "*P. crenulata taliensis*". It appears to be intermediate between *P. crenato-serrata* and *P. rogersiana* but nearer to the former. The leaves are similar in shape but smaller and finely toothed almost to the base. The young shoots are slightly downy, the leaves quite glabrous. It is very handsome in fruit, the berries being shining yellow, orange-shaped, ¼ in. wide, but falling much sooner than those of *P. crenato-serrata* and in colour by October. It was obtained by Kew from Messrs Chenault of Orleans in 1924, and from its name should have come from the Tali Range in Yunnan.

P. 'ORANGE GLOW'.—Fruits orange-red, oblate, about ⅜ in. wide when mature, but colouring around mid-September before they reach full size. Leaves mostly oblong-obovate, obtuse and mucronate at the apex, scarcely tapered at the base. A probable hybrid between *P. crenato-serrata* and *P. coccinea*, raised in Holland, very vigorous and free-fruiting, and making an excellent specimen in the open ground. Said to be scab-resistant.

P. CRENULATA (D. Don) Roem.   NEPALESE WHITE THORN
Mespilus crenulata D. Don; *Crataegus crenulata* (D. Don) Lindl.

Nearly allied to the common pyracanth (*P. coccinea*), this differs chiefly in the leaves being rounded instead of tapered and pointed at the apex, and in the smaller flowers and fruit. The leaves are ultimately quite glabrous, narrow-oblong or obovate, up to 2½ in long, ⅝ in. wide, rounded, but with a short bristle-tip. The styles differ from those of *P. coccinea* in being more separated at the base. Fruits orange-yellow. It is a large, more or less thorny bush, and can scarcely be regarded as more than a variety of *P. coccinea*. It is, however, much slower in growth and more tender. Being quite inferior to the European pyracanth, it is rarely seen in cultivation. It needs a south wall. Native of Temperate Himalaya.

P. ROGERSIANA (A. B. Jacks.) Chittenden

P. crenulata var. *rogersiana* A. B. Jacks.

A spiny evergreen shrub of erect habit probably 8 to 10 ft high, of dense rather pyramidal habit when young. Branchlets clothed with a short pale down, becoming glabrous and pale brown the second season. Leaves glabrous, set ¼ to ½ in. apart on the shoots, oblanceolate or narrowly obovate, slenderly tapered to the base, rounded or abruptly tapered at the apex, shallowly toothed except towards the base, each tooth tipped by a blackish gland, ½ to 1½ in. long, ⅛ to ½ in. wide, bright green above, paler dull green beneath; stalk slender, up to ⅓ in. long. Flowers white, ¼ to ⁵⁄₁₆ in. wide, produced in June on small corymbose racemes, each flower on a slender glabrous stalk ½ to ¾ in. long. Calyx-tube top-shaped, the lobes triangular, glabrous; petals round; stamens about twenty with smooth white stalks; styles five. Fruits ¼ in. wide, globose, golden yellow to reddish orange.

Native of Yunnan, China; discovered by Delavay in 1889; introduced by Forrest in 1911. A charming pyracanth named in honour of G. L. Coltman-Rogers of Stanage Park, Radnorshire, and the author of *Conifers and their Characteristics*, who first showed young plants at one of the Royal Horticultural Society's Shows at Westminster in March 1913. The most distinctive feature of this shrub in its group is the smallness of its leaves, which gives it a rather dainty appearance, especially in a small state. It is very hardy, bears fruit very abundantly and is the most attractive of the genus in its flowers. It received the Award of Garden Merit in 1937. Awards have also been given separately to the yellow-berried form (f. FLAVA Hort.) and to the orange-berried form (f. AURANTIACA Hort.).

P. 'ORANGE CHARMER'.—Fruits orange-red, about ⅜ in. wide and almost as long, colouring mid-September. Leaves oblong-lanceolate to oblong-elliptic, tapered at the base, or almost elliptic, obtuse to acute at the apex. A selection from a deliberate cross between *P. rogersiana* and *P. coccinea* made in Germany. 'GOLDEN CHARMER', perhaps not yet introduced to Britain, is another selection from the same cross, with orange-yellow fruits. Both said to be scab-resistant.

P. KOIDZUMII (Hayata) Rehd. *Cotoneaster koidzumii* Hayata—This species, endemic to Formosa, is allied to *P. rogersiana*, which it resembles in its oblanceolate leaves, long tapered at the base. But the leaves are entire (except on strong shoots) and the inflorescence and calyx-tube are downy. The date of its introduction to gardens is uncertain, but the plant at Kew, of which flowers and fruits are figured in *Botanical Magazine*, n.s., t. 205, was obtained from an American nursery in 1937. It is hardy at Kew, and fruits freely, despite the fact that in Formosa it is confined to low elevations. According to Dr Wyman, it is the commonest pyracantha in the gardens of the south-eastern United States, but in this country it is rare. 'MOHAVE', a hybrid between *P. koidzumii* and

P. coccinea raised in the USA, received an Award of Merit in 1973. It bears its large orange-red fruits from mid-August onwards and is said to be disease-resistant (*Gard. Chron.*, August 15, 1975, p. 26).

× PYRACOMELES   ROSACEAE

A genus of hybrids between *Pyracantha* and *Osteomeles*, containing, so far as is known, only the one cross described below.

× P. VILMORINII Rehd.

An evergreen shrub up to 6 ft high; young shoots slender, at first greyish-downy, soon glabrous. Leaves pinnate at the base, pinnately lobed towards the apex, 1 to 1½ in. long; leaflets or lobes five to nine, oval, rounded and toothed at the apex, glabrous or nearly so. Flowers white, $\frac{2}{5}$ in. wide, numerous in terminal corymbs; stamens twelve to fifteen. Fruits $\frac{1}{6}$ in. wide, globose, coral-red.

A natural hybrid between *Pyracantha atalantioides* and *Osteomeles subrotunda*, which appeared in Chenault's nursery at Orleans some time previous to 1922, when it had been obtained for, and was in cultivation in, the de Vilmorins' garden at Verrières. It develops numerous fruits and is very handsome when they are ripe in autumn. Said to come true from seed.

+ PYROCYDONIA   ROSACEAE

A genus of graft-hybrids between *Pyrus* and *Cydonia*. It was included in × *Pyronia* by Rehder, but under modern rules of nomenclature this name must be restricted to sexual hybrids between the two genera. For other examples of graft-hybrids see + *Crataegomespilus* and + *Laburnocytisus*.

+ P. DANIELII Winkl. ex Daniel
Pyronia danielii (Daniel) Rehd.

This graft-hybrid was raised in 1902 in the garden of St Vincent College, Rennes, by beheading a plant of the pear 'William's Bon Chrêtien' just above the graft-union, the stock being the common quince. It resembles the quince, having leaves on very short stalks, ovate, 1½ to 3 in. long, toothed, rounded at the base. It was named by Prof. Winkler of Hamburg after the Director of the garden. In 1913 Daniel raised another graft-hybrid of the same parentage, naming it after Winkler. This sprang, not from the graft-union, but from a root of the stock, which must have arisen from the graft-union many years previously (the plant was an old one). This hybrid—'WINKLERI'—has elliptic-ovate leaves, acuminate at the apex, more persistently downy than in the original form.

× PYRONIA   ROSACEAE

A genus of hybrids between the pears (*Pyrus*) and the quince (*Cydonia oblonga*). For graft-hybrids between pear and quince see + PYROCYDONIA

× P. VEITCHII (Trabut) Guillaum.
Cydonia veitchii Trabut

A hybrid between the pear 'Bergamotte Esperen' (seed-parent) and the Portugal quince (pollinator), raised by John Seden, hybridiser on the staff of Messrs Veitch. The cross was made in 1895 and two plants resulted. One had pear-like fruits and for this Messrs Veitch proposed the name *Pyronia* 'John Seden' in 1907. It was first described under the name *Cydonia veitchii* in 1916 from a plant cultivated at the botanical station in Algeria. In this form of the cross, which appears to be the only one grown in this country, the leaves are elliptic, 2 in. or slightly more long, tapered at both ends, downy when young. Flowers in threes, short-stalked, about 2 in. wide. The fruit is rounded, with a pear-like flesh of good flavour, and ripens in October, earlier than the seed-parent.

PYRUS   PEARS   ROSACEAE

Deciduous trees, rarely shrubs, with simple, toothed, but seldom lobed leaves and top-shaped or globose fruits rarely indented at the junction with the stalk, grit-cells abundant; styles two to five, free; stamens twenty to thirty.

The true pears include some of the tallest and bulkiest trees in its group of genera, but the species as a whole have not such striking attributes for the garden as some of the other sections. Their flowers are often beautiful, but they have little attractive colouring in fruit, and the leaves frequently die off black. Some, like *P. salicifolia* and *P. nivalis*, are particularly effective in their young expanding foliage, being covered with a snowy-white, thick down. The pears, although represented in N.E. Asia, are more particularly identified with Europe—especially S. and E. Europe—Asia Minor, and N. Africa. No species is a genuine native of the New World. Seeds ripen freely, but owing to the hybrid origin of some it is safer to graft the various sorts on their own or nearly allied seedlings—especially as many cultivated trees are of selected forms that could not be relied on to come true from seed.

P. AMYGDALIFORMIS Vill.

A small tree occasionally 20 ft or more high, or a large rounded shrub; branches sometimes terminated by a spine; young shoots slightly woolly at first. Leaves very variable in shape and size; oval, ovate, or obovate, 1½ to

PYRUS AMYGDALIFORMIS

2½ in. long, ½ to ¾ in. wide, wedge-shaped or rounded at the base, the margins very slightly round-toothed; covered with silky hairs when young, but becoming glabrous and lustrous above, and almost or quite glabrous beneath; stalks slender, ½ to 1½ in. long. Flowers white, 1 in. across, produced in April in corymbs 1½ to 2 in. across, carrying eight to twelve flowers; calyx white, woolly. Fruits rather orange-shaped, ¾ in. long, 1 in. wide, yellowish brown, produced on a short, thick stalk.

Native of S. Europe, especially in the countries bordering the northern shores of the Mediterranean. It has no particular merit in the garden except that in age it makes a quaint and picturesque tree; from its ally, P. *salicifolia*, it differs in its nearly glabrous leaves.

There is an example at The Grange, Benenden, Kent, measuring 41 × 6 ft at 3 ft (1972).

var. CUNEIFOLIA [Guss.] Bean   P. *cuneifolia* Guss.—Leaves smaller and narrower, with a slender, tapered base. Occasional in the wild. The plant described by Gussone came from Calabria.

var. OBLONGIFOLIA (Spach) Bean   P. *oblongifolia* Spach—This represents another extreme, with oblong or oval leaves, rounded at the base, the stalk 1 to 1½ in. long. Fruits yellowish, tinged with red on the sunny side, considerably larger than in P. *amygdaliformis*. It is common in Provence, and known there as the "Gros Perrussier". Perhaps a hybrid between P. *amygdaliformis* and P. *nivalis*.

var. LOBATA (Decne.) Koehne   P. *lobata* Koehne—Leaves on the strong shoots lobed.

P. PERSICA Pers.   P. *sinaica* Dum.-Cours.; P. *amygdaliformis* var. *persica* (Pers.) Bornm.—This is allied to P. *amygdaliformis* but has larger leaves and longer-stalked fruits, which are round and rather flattened. It was described early in the last century from a plant cultivated in France. It is not a native of Persia in spite of its name, nor of Sinai, and its native habitat, if indeed it ever had one, is not known. It is either a form of P. *amygdaliformis* or, as Schneider thought, a hybrid.

P. BETULIFOLIA Bunge

A slender, quick-growing, graceful tree 20 to 30 ft high; young shoots covered thickly with a grey felt which persists the whole of the year. Leaves ovate or roundish ovate, 2 to 3 in. long, 1¼ to 1½ in. wide, long-pointed, tapered or rounded at the base, regularly and sometimes rather coarsely serrated, downy on both surfaces at first, remaining so on the veins beneath throughout the season; dark green, glabrous and lustrous above; stalk 1 to 1¼ in. long, grey-felted like the shoot. Flowers eight to ten together in a corymb, white, each about ¾ in. across, on a downy stalk ¾ to 1 in. long; styles two or three; calyx downy, its short triangular teeth falling away from the small roundish fruit, which is about the size of a large pea, greyish brown with white dots.

Native of N. China; introduced to Kew in 1882 through seeds sent by Dr Bretschneider. The chief characteristics of the tree are its quick graceful growth, and small fruits not crowned by calyx teeth. Its fruit would appear to be of no value, but the tree is used by the Chinese as a stock on which they graft fruiting pears.

P. CALLERYANA Decne.

A small deciduous tree or large shrub; winter-buds up to ¾ in. long, scales tomentose on the back; young branchlets tomentose at first, glabrous the second year, or glabrous from the start. Leaves broad-ovate, acuminate to caudate at the apex, or sometimes roundish with a cuspidate or short-acuminate apex, base rounded or rounded-truncate, mostly 1¾ to 3¼ in. long, 1¼ to 2 in. wide, finely crenated at the margin, thinly leathery, dark green above, light green below, more or less hairy on the midrib and main veins beneath, glabrous at maturity; petioles slender, ¾ to 1⅜ in. long, tomentose at first, becoming glabrous. Inflorescence of six to twelve flowers, borne on a short densely hairy or glabrous peduncle. Flowers ⅝ to ¾ in. across; pedicels glabrous to tomentose, ⅜ to 1¹³⁄₁₆ in. long, rarely slightly longer. Calyx-tube widely and shallowly cup-shaped, glabrous; sepals narrowly triangular, finely woolly on the inside. Petals broadly obovate or suborbicular with a short claw. Stamens twenty. Ovary glabrous, or tomentose like the pedicels. Styles two or three. Fruits globose or obovoid, ⅝ to ¾ in. wide, brownish, densely white-dotted, borne on stiff stalks ⅝ to 2 in. long; calyx deciduous.

Native of Central and S. China; described in 1872 from a specimen collected by the French missionary J. Callery, among whose achievements was the compilation of a Chinese–Latin dictionary. It was introduced by Wilson from Hupeh in 1908 but, apart from colouring well in the autumn in some years, it really has nothing to commend it as an ornamental. Recently two cultivars have been introduced from the USA, namely; 'BRADFORD', selected at the Plant Introduction Station, Glenn Dale, Maryland, from trees raised from seed collected by F. Meyer in China in 1918; and 'CHANTICLEER', raised by Edward Scanlon. The former makes a dense, vigorous tree up to at least 50 ft high and 30 ft wide; 'Chanticleer' is described as having a narrowly conical crown. Both give good autumn colour in the USA.

The above description includes f. *tomentella* Rehd., an extreme form with the branchlets, young leaves, pedicels and ovaries notably tomentose.

Two species related to *P. calleryana* are P. FAURIEI Schneid. from Korea and P. DIMORPHOPHYLLA Makino, from Japan.

P. COMMUNIS L.   COMMON PEAR
incl. *P. communis* var. *pyraster* L., *P. pyraster* (L.) Burgsd.

A deciduous tree, usually 30 to 40, occasionally as much as 60 ft high, with a trunk 3 ft through; branches forming short stiff spurs, sometimes spiny. Leaves variable, from ovate, heart-shaped and oval, to almost round; from 1 in. to 4 in. long, up to 2 in. wide, very finely round-toothed or entire; stalk slender, 1 to 2 in. long; the leaves are variable in their downiness, but are either glabrous from the beginning or become nearly or quite so later, and glossy green. Flowers white, 1 to 1½ in. across, produced in corymbs 2 to 3 in. across, each flower on a more or less woolly stalk ½ to 1½ in. long. Fruits top-shaped or rounded, with a tapering or rounded base.

P. communis, in the broad sense, is a complex species and partly of hybrid origin. It comprises the wild pear, which by selection and by crossing with other species (probably *P. nivalis* and *P. cordata*) gave rise to the orchard pears (*P. communis* var. *culta* DC.). These in turn have frequently escaped back into the wild and become so intermingled and interbred with the ancestral wild pear that it is no longer possible to distinguish it from its naturalised offspring. All that can be said is that wild or seemingly wild pears as described above occur over much of Europe, including the British Isles.

In gardens the wild pear has not much claim to notice. Its graceful, often pendulous branches and large crops of flowers are beautiful, but the garden varieties are just as much so, and give useful fruits as well. The common pear (both wild and cultivated) is long-lived and yields an excellent timber, heavy, tough, and durable, which, however, is not plentiful enough to be of much importance in commerce.

cv. 'BEECH HILL'.—A tree of spire-like habit.

P. CORDATA Desv. *P. communis* var. *cordata* (Desv.) Briggs; *P. communis* var. *briggsii* Syme—Although sometimes regarded as a variety of *P. communis*, this is really a very distinct species. It is smaller in all its parts than *P. communis*. The leaves, sometimes heart-shaped, but often rounded or broadly wedge-shaped at the base, are usually less than $1\frac{1}{2}$ in. long, finely and evenly round-toothed. Flowers smaller, in distinct racemes. Fruits globular, $\frac{3}{8}$ to $\frac{1}{2}$ in. in diameter, brown spotted with white, smooth. These small rounded fruits afford the best distinction between this pear and *P. communis*. Long known as a native of France, Spain, and Portugal, it was, in 1865, also discovered wild in the south-west of England by T. R. Archer-Briggs.

P. COSSONII Rehd. *P. longipes* Coss. & Durieu, not Poit. & Turp.; *P. communis* var. *longipes* (Coss. & Durieu) Henry—Also of the *P. communis* group and very nearly allied to *P. cordata*, this pear is a native of Algeria, especially in the mountain gorges above Batna. It is a small tree or shrub, with glabrous branchlets. Leaves roundish oval or broadly ovate, 1 to 2 in. long, $\frac{1}{4}$ to $1\frac{1}{2}$ in. wide, the base sometimes slightly heart-shaped, more especially tapering, very finely and evenly round-toothed, quite glabrous on both sides, lustrous above; stalk slender, 1 to 2 in. long. Flowers white, 1 to $1\frac{1}{4}$ in. across, produced in corymbs 2 to 3 in. in diameter. Fruit about the size and shape of a small cherry, produced on a slender stalk 1 to $1\frac{1}{2}$ in. long, turning from green to brown as it ripens, the calyx-lobes falling away. Introduced to Kew from France in 1875.

The following specimens have been recorded: Edinburgh Botanic Garden, *pl.* 1903, 46 × $4\frac{1}{4}$ ft (1967); Borde Hill, Sussex, 55 × 4 ft (1968).

P. SYRIACA Boiss.—This species is related to the wild pear of Europe, from which it differs in its relatively narrower leaves, which are ovate or ovate-lanceolate, up to 2 in. long and 1 in. or slightly more wide. The fruits are smaller, about $\frac{3}{4}$ in. wide. It occurs wild from Turkey and Cyprus to the Caucasus, Iraq, and Persia.

P. GLABRA Boiss.

P. *syriaca* var. *glabra* (Boiss.) Wenzig

A tree 15 to 20 ft high, with often spine-tipped branches; young shoots at first covered with grey wool, becoming glabrous by summer. Leaves 1½ to 4 in. long, ⅓ to ¾ in. wide, linear-lanceolate, long-pointed, slightly round-toothed or quite entire, green on both sides and quite glabrous almost from the very first on both sides; stalk ⅓ to 1½ in. long. Flowers 1 in. across, white, produced in a cluster of five to eight; flower-stalks and the inner face of sepals more or less woolly. Fruits roundish.

Native of Persia. In Decaisne's observations on this species (*Jardin Fruitier*, vol. i, t. 11), it is stated that the pips of this pear are pickled in brine by the Persians and eaten. The tree is rare in gardens, where, indeed, it has little to recommend it.

P. × MICHAUXII Poir.

A small tree with unarmed branches forming a rounded head. Leaves entire, ovate or oval-oblong, blunt at the apex, or with a short, abrupt point, up to 3 in. long, 1 to 1½ in. wide, covered when young with white, cottony down, which afterwards falls away and leaves them shining and glabrous above. Flowers white, in very short corymbs. Fruits globose or top-shaped, greenish yellow when ripe, spotted with brown. By some curious error this tree was long regarded as a native of N. America; but no true pear is indigenous to the New World. It is probably from the Levant, and no doubt a hybrid between *P. amygdaliformis* and *P. nivalis*. It differs from the former in its entire leaves.

P. NIVALIS Jacq.   SNOW PEAR

A small tree, sturdy in habit; young shoots thickly covered with a white wool. Leaves oval or obovate, 2 to 3 in. long, ¾ to 1¼ in. wide, entire, covered when young on both sides, but especially beneath, with a white wool much of which falls away later. Flowers pure white, 1½ in. across, produced in April in conspicuous clusters. Fruit roundish, 1½ in. or more wide, yellowish green, borne on a stalk as long or longer than itself.

Native of Central and S.E. Europe from Austria and Hungary to Rumania and Greece; introduced early in the 19th century. It is a very beautiful tree early in the season, owing to its pure white leaves and abundant flowers. There is an example at Kew measuring 39 × 4½ ft (1970).

P. × CANESCENS Spach—Probably a hybrid between *P. nivalis* and *P. salicifolia*. Its leaves are of the same size as those of *P. nivalis*, lanceolate or narrowly oval, finely round-toothed, very white when young, shining dark green when mature. Fruits pale green, much shorter stalked than in *P. nivalis*. There is an example in the Edinburgh Botanic Garden.

P. ELAEAGRIFOLIA Pall.—A small, spiny tree closely allied to *P. nivalis*. Leaves more or less of the same shape, but covered on both sides with a whitish

or greyish wool, and with smaller fruits. Native of the Crimea, Asia Minor, and
S.E. Europe. In var. KOTSCHYANA (Boiss.) Boiss. the branches are not spiny
and the leaves are lanceolate. Native of Asia Minor.

P. SALVIFOLIA DC. POIRIER SAUGER.—A close ally of *P. nivalis*, but
with longer-stalked leaves broad-cuneate to rounded at the base. It was described by de Candolle from the Orleans neighbourhood, where, and in other
places, it is grown to make perry. It occurs wild or naturalised in various parts
of Europe and is considered by some authorities to be a hybrid between *P. nivalis*
and the common pear.

P. PASHIA D. Don

P. variolosa G. Don; *P. kumaoni* Decne.; *P. pashia* var. *kumaoni* (Decne.) Stapf

A small unarmed or spiny tree; branchlets glabrous when mature, usually
more or less woolly when young. Leaves ovate or oblong-ovate, 2 to 4 in. long,
1¼ to 2 in. wide, usually rounded at the base, apex varying from long-tapered to
blunt, glabrous when mature but often woolly when young, especially beneath,
margins set with fine, rounded teeth; stalk 1 to 1½ in. long. Flowers white (rose-
tinted at first in some cultivated trees), about ¾ in. across, closely packed in
rounded corymbs 2 in. across, each flower on a stalk ½ to ¾ in. long; calyx-lobes
ovate to triangular, obtuse or acute; typically the inflorescence-parts are woolly
but they may be glabrous or almost so; styles three to five; stamens twenty-five
to thirty. Fruits nearly globular, but narrowed towards the stalk, brown with
pale specks, ¾ to 1 in. across. *Bot. Mag.*, t. 8256.

P. *pashia* is of wide distribution in temperate Asia, from Afghanistan throughout the Himalaya and then through Burma and Assam to W. China; introduced
1825. This is one of the most distinct and ornamental of pears, with its compact
flower clusters, the rounded, overlapping petals and the cluster of deep red
stamens in the centre of the flower. The leaves on sucker shoots or on vigorous
shoots of cut-back trees are frequently deeply three-lobed. In the Himalaya the
fruit is eaten after having been bletted, like a medlar.

The species varies greatly in indumentum from plants with the young leaves
and inflorescence densely tomentose to plants with these parts glabrous. The
latter have been distinguished as var. *kumaoni* (Decne.) Stapf but only represent
an extreme state of the normal variation of the species.

P. *pashia* was reintroduced by Forrest from Yunnan.

P. PYRIFOLIA (Burm. f.) Nakai   SAND PEAR

Ficus pyrifolia Burm. f.; *P. serotina* Rehd.; *P. sinensis* of some authors, not Lindl.,
nor Poir.

A tree up to 40 ft or so high; branchlets glabrous or almost so when mature,
reddish or purplish brown; buds glabrous. Leaves oblong-ovate or ovate, 2¾ to
4 in. long, about half as wide, acuminately tapered at the apex, usually rounded
at the base, more rarely cordate or broad-cuneate, hairy beneath when young,
becoming glabrous, margins conspicuously bristle-toothed as in *P. ussuriensis;*
stalk 1¼ to 1¾ in. long. Inflorescence glabrous or slightly hairy, composed of a
loose corymb of six to nine flowers on stalks 1¼ to 2 in. long. Calyx-lobes ovate,

acute, hairy on the inside, margins finely toothed. Petals obovate, about ¾ in. long. Styles usually five, glabrous. Fruits globular, brown spotted with white, about 1¼ in. long and wide, of hard and gritty texture.

Native of W. and Central China. In its primitive, wild state it is little known in cultivation, but was introduced by Wilson in 1909 when collecting for the Arnold Arboretum.

var. CULTA (Mak.) Nakai P. sinensis var. culta Mak.—Numerous orchard varieties of P. pyrifolia are cultivated in China and Japan, with larger, softer fruits and usually with larger, relatively broader leaves. For these var. culta is the collective name. Some of these varieties were introduced to the United States in the first half of the last century, and, crossed with European sorts, gave rise to a race of hybrids for which the botanical name is P. × LECONTEI Rehd., of the type is the variety 'Leconte'. These hybrids are better adapted to the of the southern states than the European orchard varieties.

cv. 'STAPFIANA'.—Fruits obovoid, larger than in the type. Figured in Bot. Mag., t. 8226, as "P. sinensis" and named P. pyrifolia f. stapfiana by Rehder. It was propagated at Kew from graft-wood received from Prof. Decaisne of Paris in 1875.

P. REGELII Rehd.

P. heterophylla Reg. & Schmalhausen, not Steud.

A small tree ultimately 20 to 30 ft high, whose young branches are covered with a close grey down which persists over the first winter. Leaves exceedingly

PYRUS REGELII

variable in shape, the two extreme types of which are: (1) ovate with a rounded base and pointed apex, 2 to 3½ in. long, ¾ to 1½ in. wide; bluntly, unequally, and rather coarsely toothed; (2) cut back to the midrib into three to seven narrow, linear lobes, which are ¾ to 2 in. long, ⅛ to ¼ in. wide, finely toothed (see figure). Between these two forms of leaf, which may occur on the same plant, there are many intermediate ones. For the rest, the leaves are of firm, rather leathery texture, and very downy when young, remaining more or less so until they fall; the pinnatifid form, however, appears to be less downy than the undivided one. Flowers white, ¾ to 1 in. across, produced a few together in small clusters. Fruit like a small ordinary pear.

This extraordinary pear was originally discovered in E. Turkestan by Albert Regel, and was raised and distributed (about 1891) by Dr Dieck of Zoeschen, Germany. The two forms of leaf described above would never be regarded as belonging to the same species, but I have seen both, as well as intermediate ones, on the same plant.

P. SALICIFOLIA Pall.   WILLOW-LEAVED PEAR

A tree 15 to 25 ft high with a spreading crown, the main branches more or less horizontal, the young branchlets elongated and more or less pendulous; branchlets and buds covered when young with a white, silky down. Leaves 1½ to 3½ in. long, ⅛ to ⅔ in. wide, narrowly lanceolate, tapering gradually towards both ends, covered when young on both sides with a beautiful silvery-grey down; later in the year this falls away from the upper surface, leaving it shining green; margins quite entire; stalk ½ in. long or less, sometimes scarcely noticeable. Flowers pure white, about ¾ in. across, produced in April, closely packed in small rounded corymbs, the calyx and flower-stalk covered with white wool. Fruits of the typical pear shape, 1 to 1¼ in. long and wide.

Native of Russia in the region of the Caucasus, from the steppes north-east of the main range south to Armenia; it extends some way into N.E. Anatolia (Turkey) and also occurs in N.W. Persia. It was discovered by the German botanist and explorer P. S. Pallas and introduced by him to Britain in 1780.

P. salicifolia is the most ornamental of all the pears. Its leaves and flowers often open simultaneously, and it then presents a very charming picture, the willow-like leaves being of a conspicuous silky white. After the flowers fade, the leaves remain silvery for some weeks, gradually, however, becoming greener on the upper surface. The fruit is harsh to the palate, and of no value.

P. salicifolia is mainly represented in cultivation by 'PENDULA', a very elegant tree with the branches more drooping than ordinary; but in the type they are more or less pendulous.

P. USSURIENSIS Maxim.
P. sinensis Decne., not Lindl.

A deciduous tree 40 to 50 ft high; young shoots warted, nearly or quite glabrous, turning purplish brown the second year, often long and unbranched especially in var. *ovoidea*. Leaves roundish ovate to obovate-oblong, 2 to 4 in. long, rounded or slightly cordate at the base, abruptly narrowed to a short, slender point, margin beautifully, finely and regularly bristle-toothed; glabrous or nearly so; stalk slender, 1 to 2¼ in. long. Fruit globose on a very stout stalk, greenish yellow, 1 to 1½ in. across, hard and inedible; calyx persistent.

Native of N.E. China, Korea, and the Ussuri region of the Russian Far East; introduced about 1865. This pear flowers very freely at Kew in late April and is then a very distinct and handsome tree.

var. HONDOENSIS (Nakai & Kitachi) Rehd. *P. hondoensis* Nakai & Kitachi— This occurs wild in Japan. Its leaves are more strictly ovate, with fine, more appressed toothing; very handsome in blossom.

var. OVOIDEA (Rehd.) Rehd. *P. ovoidea* Rehd.—Remarkable for its curiously gaunt habit, the branches few and scarcely forked. Fruits conical, juicy, pale yellow, 1½ in. long and wide.

QUERCUS   OAKS   FAGACEAE

A large genus of evergreen and deciduous trees and shrubs, of which about 450 species are known. Sixty to seventy are in cultivation. Leaves alternate, a spiral of five making one circuit of the branchlet, frequently lobed somewhat deeply, but occasionally merely toothed or even entire. The down on the leaves, etc., is mostly stellate. Male and female flowers occur on the same trees, but on separate inflorescences. The males are numerous on pendulous catkins, small, green or greenish, forming sometimes tassel-like clusters; females few and quite inconspicuous. The most distinctive feature of the oak is its fruit, which consists of a usually egg-shaped or rounded nut (acorn), the lower part of which is more or less enclosed by a cup covered with woody, sometimes fringe-like scales. The acorn frequently takes two seasons to mature. The cup of the acorn develops from the involucre of the flower and is the counterpart of the husk of *Fagus* and *Castanea*, but normally it encloses only a part of the nut (acorn) and does not split into valves nor show any sign of vertical subdivision. Another distinction, of course, is that in *Quercus* a single nut is produced (the female flowers being solitary in each involucre), while in *Fagus* the fruit contains two nuts, each developed from a separate flower; in *Castanea* there are one to three and normally three in *Nothofagus*. Here it should be pointed out that the term 'fruit' in the descriptions of the individual species is used for the nut together with its cup, in accordance with botanical usage, and the word 'acorn' is used for the nut only.

CLASSIFICATION.—Various classifications of the genus have been proposed. The major groupings are based mainly on characters of flower and fruit, such as the length and form of the style, the presence or absence of a tomentum on the inner side of the wall of the acorn (endocarp), and the position of the aborted ovules on the seed (the ovary in *Quercus* contains six ovules, only one of which develops into a seed). The foliage does not always serve to place a species, since leaves of similar type occur in two or more sections, and may vary greatly in each. For example, *Q. suber*, the cork oak, belongs to the same section as *Q. cerris*, and has produced with it a hybrid of great vigour—the Lucombe oak—though the two species are superficially very unlike. On the other hand *Q. ilex* closely resembles *Q. suber* in its foliage yet is distant from it taxonomically and nearer to the common oak, with which it has hybridised (*Q.* × *turneri*).

The following synopsis is taken from Mme. A. Camus' work *Les Chênes*, which is the only comprehensive work on the genus. Below the rank of section each letter indicates a subsection, but the botanical names of the subsections are not given, since they are not in common use.

subgen. CYCLOBALANOPSIS

Leaves persistent, toothed in a few species but commonly entire and never lobed. Acorn-cups (cupules) with concrescent scales arranged in concentric rings. This group is confined to E. Asia and Malaysia, and is almost wholly tropical to warm-temperate in distribution. The cultivated species are from W. China, Japan, and the Himalaya. The group shows far less variation than the subgenus *Quercus*, and its subdivisions are really equivalent to the subsections of that subgenus.

- A. *Q. lineata*, *Q. oxyodon*
- B. *Q. myrsinifolia*
- C. *Q. glauca*
- D. *Q. acuta*

subgen. QUERCUS

Leaves deciduous or persistent, entire, toothed or lobed. Acorn-cups covered with imbricated scales, which are free or concrescent, and appressed, erect or recurved.

sect. CERRIS.—Styles elongated, scarcely or not expanded at the apex. Scales of acorn-cup elongated and sometimes reflexed. As defined by Camus, this group includes species in which the interior of the acorn-shell (endocarp) is densely tomentose (e.g., *Q. coccifera*), but in the majority it appears to be glabrous or slightly hairy. With a few exceptions the acorn takes two years to ripen. In the first five subsections the leaves are persistent, in the last three deciduous, though sometimes late in falling. This section is confined to the Old World and the majority of the species are natives of Europe and W. Asia.

- A. *Q. gilliana*, *Q. phillyreoides*, *Q. semecarpifolia*
- B. *Q. baronii*
- C. *Q. alnifolia*
- D. *Q. calliprinos*, *Q. coccifera*
- E. *Q. suber*

F. *Q. afares, Q. castaneifolia, Q. ithaburensis, Q. libani, Q. macrolepis, Q. trojana*

G. *Q. acutissima, Q. variabilis*

H. *Q. cerris*

sect. MESOBALANUS.—A small group of species, considered to be intermediate between sect. *Cerris* and sect. *Quercus*, on the grounds that the styles are elongated as in the former, but swollen at the apex as in the latter. But biologically they seem to be nearer to sect. *Quercus*, hybridising readily with *Q. robur*. All are species of Europe and W. Asia, except *Q. dentata*.

A. *Q. dentata*

B. *Q. pontica*

C. *Q. frainetto, Q. macranthera, Q. pyrenaica*

sect. QUERCUS (Lepidobalanus).—Leaves commonly lobed and deciduous, at least in the cultivated species, but sometimes coriaceous and persistent, as in, e.g., *Q. ilex*. Styles very short or wanting, abruptly widened into the stigma. Acorn-cup with short, usually appressed scales; inner wall of acorn usually glabrous, but tomentose in a few sections. Aborted ovules basal. This large group is the only one that occurs in both the Old and New World. It has many representatives in Mexico, but few of these have ever been introduced and not many are likely to be hardy with us. It is convenient to classify the subsections geographically:

OLD WORLD SPECIES

A. *Q. lanata, Q. leucotrichophora (incana), Q. lodicosa*

B. *Q. engleriana*

C. *Q. ilex*

D. *Q. aliena, Q. glandulifera, Q. mongolica*

E. *Q. boissieri, Q. canariensis (mirbeckii), Q. faginea, Q. fruticosa, Q. infectoria, Q. tlemcenensis*

F. *Q. hartwissiana*

G. *Q. petraea, Q. pubescens.* Minor species: *Q. brachyphylla, Q. congesta, Q. dalechampii, Q. iberica, Q. mas, Q. virgiliana*

H. *Q. robur.* Minor species: *Q. brutia, Q. haas, Q. pedunculiflora, Q. thomasii*

EAST AMERICAN SPECIES

A. *Q. bicolor, Q. michauxii, Q. muehlenbergii, Q. prinoides, Q. prinus*

B. *Q. stellata*

C. *Q. lyrata*

D. *Q. alba*

E. *Q. macrocarpa*

WEST AMERICAN SPECIES

A. *Q. sadleriana*

B. *Q. douglasii*

C. *Q. garryana, Q. lobata*

D. *Q. gambelii, Q. utahensis*

MEXICAN SPECIES
A. *Q. glabrescens*
B. *Q. reticulata*; also *Q. warburgii* (of Mexican affinity, but not known in the wild and possibly a hybrid)

sect. PROTOBALANUS.—A small group called by Trelease 'the intermediate oaks'. They resemble the section *Quercus* in several respects, e.g., the short styles and the position of the abortive ovules, but the fruits take two years to ripen and the inside of the shell of the acorn is tomentose, as in the section *Erythrobalanus*. It is represented in cultivation by *Q. chrysolepis* and the closely allied *Q. vacciniifolia*. Another member, *Q. tomentella*, grows at Exbury but does not thrive.

sect. ERYTHROBALANUS.—This New World section is mainly represented in cultivation by the red oaks and willow oaks of N. America. In the former the leaves are lobed, and the lobes are awn-tipped and never rounded (except sometimes in *Q. arkansana*, *Q. marilandica*, and *Q. velutina*); in the willow oaks the leaves are entire but usually have an awn at the apex; in *Q. nigra* and to a lesser degree in *Q. laurifolia* they are obscurely lobed. With the exception of *Q. kelloggii*, all these species are natives of eastern and central N. America. In the live oaks of the west, the leaves are coriaceous and entire or spinose.

The styles in this section are elongated and capitate. The fruit usually takes two years to ripen; the wall of the acorn is tomentose on the inside; and the abortive ovules are apical.

Central America, and especially Mexico, is very rich in species of the section *Erythrobalanus*. No fewer than thirty-five of the subsections recognised by Trelease in *The American Oaks* are native to this region, and there is one in South America, in the Andes of Colombia. But only two Mexican species are known to have reached maturity in Britain.

RED OAKS
A. *Q. arkansana*, *Q. marilandica*
B. *Q. laevis*
C. *Q. falcata*
D. *Q. ilicifolia*
E. *Q. palustris*
F. *Q. velutina*
G. *Q. rubra*, *Q. coccinea*, *Q. shumardii*, *Q. ellipsoidalis* (mentioned under *Q. palustris*)
H. *Q. kelloggii*

WILLOW OAKS
A. *Q. imbricaria*, *Q. laurifolia*, *Q. phellos*
B. *Q. nigra*

WESTERN AND SOUTH-WESTERN LIVE OAKS
A. *Q. agrifolia*, *Q. wislizenii*
B. *Q. hypoleucoides*

MEXICAN SPECIES
A. *Q. crassifolia*
B. *Q. crassipes*

The oaks are amongst the finest of the large trees of temperate regions. The two native of Britain, *Q. robur* and *Q. petraea*, are the largest and longest lived of our deciduous trees, and produce the most valuable timber. Nor are they surpassed in rugged beauty and strength. Their maximum duration of life is probably not less than one thousand years. For some reason the planting of oaks in parks and gardens has fallen into desuetude in recent times. Beyond a few of the commoner sorts, they are now stocked by very few nurserymen, who cannot, of course, be expected to keep up supplies for which there is no demand. With one exception, no firm now grows oaks in such number and variety as did Lee of Isleworth, Smith of Worcester, or Booth of Hamburg, a century ago.

Some deciduous species are amongst the handsomest and most striking in foliage of all our big trees, and would impart distinction to any demesne, whilst *Q. coccinea* and *Q. palustris* give the richest touches of crimson to our autumn landscape. *Q. ilex* forms a class by itself among evergreen trees hardy with us. Oaks, as a whole, thrive best on good deep loams. The old conception that the value of a soil for agriculture was indicated by the size and quality of the oaks upon it has many times been verified, not only in this country but in others, especially by the early settlers in both the east and west coast regions of N. America.

Oaks should always if possible be raised from acorns, which should be kept from getting dry after gathering until sown. Grafting has, perforce, to be resorted to for special varieties and rare species; but although one may see occasionally fine grafted specimens, the practice should only be adopted where absolutely necessary, for it tends to shorten the life of the tree, and in the end retard its growth. Unless 'wild-source' seed can be obtained, grafting must also be used to increase those species which cross readily with the common oak. A notorious example is *Q. canariensis*, which rarely comes true when raised from domestic seed, and the same seems to be true of *Q. pyrenaica* and *Q. frainetto*.

I strongly advocate getting all oaks into their permanent places as soon as possible. If I could, I would sow all acorns *in situ*, for thereby the tap-root is preserved and the plant never checked, but for many reasons that is not often possible except in pure forestry. Few trees in nurseries need transplanting with greater regularity every two or three years than oaks do if their final removal is to be accomplished safely, and few suffer more through shifting if their roots have been allowed to wander at will for a longer term. Evergreen species especially are liable to die. They should never be transplanted until after they show signs of growth in late May or early June, or else in September.

Some of the deciduous oaks are infested with an extraordinary variety of gall-producing insects, the best known of which are those that produce oak-apples and flat, circular, disk-like galls, sometimes so dense on the leaf as to partially overlay each other. Although frequently a disfigurement, and inducing a premature yellowing of the leaf, the production of galls does not seem to have noticeable effects on the health of trees. There is no generally practicable means of preventing them.

Q. ACUTA Thunb.

Q. laevigata Bl.

An evergreen tree up to 30 or 40 ft high in Japan, often shrubby in this country; young shoots and leaves covered at first with a brown floss, then quite glabrous. Leaves stout and leathery, oval, sometimes inclined to ovate; tapering or (especially in young plants) rounded at the base and with slenderly tapered, often bluntish points, 2½ to 5½ in. long, ⅞ to 2¼ in. wide; the margins entire and undulated; stalk up to 1 in. long, at first downy like the young wood. The upper surface is dark glossy green; lower one dull, yellowish; veins eight to ten each side the midrib. Fruits crowded on a spike; cup downy.

Introduced from Japan by Maries about 1878 to the Coombe Wood nursery, where one of his original plants became a bushy tree over 20 ft high. It has proved to be perfectly hardy and is a useful evergreen of slow growth. It is only likely to be confused with *Lithocarpus edulis* (q.v. in Vol. II).

A tree at Kew, although planted in 1888, measures only 15 × 1¼ ft (1965). Growth is better south of London and in the western counties: Grayswood Hill, Surrey, 34 × 3 ft + 2¾ ft (1968); Wakehurst Place, Sussex, and Borde Hill, Sussex, shrubby trees about 20 ft high (1967–8); Warnham Court, Sussex, 30 × 1½ ft (1969); Westonbirt, Glos., Loop, 33 × 2¼ ft at 3 ft (1971); Killerton, Devon, 41 × 3 ft at 6 ft and, by Chapel, 45 × 3 ft + 2½ ft (1970); Caerhays, Cornwall, 42 × 5½ ft (1971), and several others 33 to 39 ft high; Trewithen, Cornwall, 30 × 2¾ ft at 2 ft (1971).

Q. ACUTISSIMA Carruthers

Q. serrata Sieb. & Zucc., not Thunb.

A deciduous tree up to 50 ft high, with a slender trunk; young shoots at first downy, soon becoming glabrous. Leaves oblong or narrowly oval, rounded or broadly tapered at the base, terminated by a slender bristle-tipped point; each of the twelve to sixteen parallel veins at either side the midrib running out into a bristle-like tooth ⅙ in. long; the leaves are 3 to 7 in. long, 1 to 2¼ in. wide, upper surface glabrous and shining, lower surface not so bright and of a paler green, with tufts of down in the vein-axils; the stalk slender, ⅝ to 1¼ in. long. Acorns (not seen in this country) small, and half embedded in cups which are covered with long, slender, pointed, downy scales.

Native of China, Japan, and the Himalaya; introduced from Japan to Kew by Richard Oldham about 1862. It is a neat and cheerful-looking tree suitable for a limited space. Sargent says that in Japan it springs up on waste land in great numbers, but is only valued as fuel. Silkworms feed on its leaves. Nearly allied to it is *Q. variabilis*, with a corky bark, the leaves grey-felted beneath, and with shorter teeth. The only other oak with which it is likely to be confused is

Q. castaneifolia, but that may be easily distinguished by its shoots being downy throughout the first season or longer, by the thicker, shorter, quite downy leaf-stalk, and by the absence of the bristly termination to its coarser teeth.

The largest recorded specimen grows at Highnam Court, Glos.; this measures 77 × 7 ft (1971). The best at Kew, in the Ash collection, is 59 × 5½ ft (1971).

subsp. CHENII (Nakai) Camus *Q. chenii* Nakai—According to Camus, this subspecies differs from typical *Q. acutissima* in its quite glabrous leaves, smaller fruits, and cups with shorter more slender scales. It was discovered by the Chinese botanist Y. Chen in Anwhei province and also occurs in other parts of southern central China. There are small examples at Kew by the Victoria Gate and at Borde Hill in Sussex.

Q. AGRIFOLIA Née   ENCINA

An evergreen tree up to 80 ft or more high in California; young shoots densely covered with starry down. Leaves hard in texture, oval or roundish, heart-shaped to tapered at the base, margined with slender, spiny teeth; 1 to 2 in. long, ¾ to 1½ in. wide, dark shining green and glabrous above, paler, not so glossy beneath, and glabrous except for tufts of down in the vein-axils; stalk ¼ to ½ in. long, stellately downy. Acorns cone-shaped, solitary or in pairs, stalkless, about 1 in. long, ⅝ in. wide near the base, tapered gradually to a point, the lower third enclosed in a cup which is silvery within, and covered with close, flattened scales without. They ripen the first year.

Native of California and of Mexico (in Baja California); introduced for the Horticultural Society by Hartweg, in 1849; now very rare. Among cultivated evergreen oaks with spiny toothed leaves it is distinct by reason of the tufts of down in the vein-axils and the tapered, conical acorns. It is an interesting oak, but of no particular merit.

There are several examples of this oak at Kew, which are quite hardy and occasionally bear acorns. The largest is 52 × 5¾ ft (1971).

Q. ALBA L.   WHITE OAK

This is one of the most magnificent trees of its native country, reaching in places 100 to 150 ft, with a trunk 3 to 6 ft in diameter, producing a splendid timber with much the same qualities of durability, etc., as our native species. The bark is divided into narrow, flat ridges which tend to spread outward at the base, giving to the trunk a rather shaggy appearance. Young shoots soon glabrous. Leaves obovate, five- to nine-lobed, 5 to 9 in. long, scarcely half as wide, narrowed at the base, the upper surface dark, glossy green, the lower one pale or glaucous, and at first downy; petiole ½ to 1 in. long, yellowish green. Fruits sessile, solitary or in twos; acorn about ¾ in. long, about one-fourth enclosed in the cup, which is covered with warty scales.

Native of eastern N. America from S.E. Canada to Florida, west in the USA to E. Texas and E. Iowa, attaining its greatest size in the valleys between the Appalachians and the Mississippi. Although introduced to Britain early in the

18th century, it has, after many trials, proved a failure in this country, though perhaps not so complete a failure as was suggested in previous editions of this work. The field-characters by which it can best be distinguished from our common oak are the larger, longer-stalked leaves and the very different, loosely ridged bark. Unlike our common oak, the leaves of *Q. alba* usually colour before falling, and this is true of trees at Kew, which, though of no ornamental value in themselves, sometimes turn a rich, brilliant red in autumn.

The following specimens have been recorded: Kew, *pl.* 1897 (?), 53 × 3¼ ft (1972); *pl.* 1904, 44 × 4 ft and 39 × 3½ ft (1967); Windsor Great Park, 52 × 5¼ ft (1967); Westonbirt, Glos., in Willesley Drive, *pl.* 1877, 50 × 3½ ft (1972); University Botanic Garden, Cambridge, 53 × 4¾ ft (1969); Edinburgh Botanic Garden, three trees, the largest 40 × 3¼ ft (1967).

Q. ALIENA Blume

A deciduous tree 60 ft or more high; young shoots bright yellowish green, not downy, but slightly warted. Leaves obovate to oblong-lanceolate, pointed or rounded at the apex, always tapered at the base, very coarsely wavily toothed with ten to fifteen often bluntish teeth on each margin, veins conspicuous, parallel, running from the midrib to the point of each tooth, 4 to 8 in. long, 2 to 4½ in. wide, dark lustrous green and glabrous above, pale or even semi-glaucous and covered with a fine close felt beneath; stalk ½ to 1¼ in. long. Fruits stalkless or nearly so, mostly solitary but occasionally developing in twos or threes, ½ to 1 in. long, downy at the top, the cup enclosing one-third to one-half of the acorn, the scales appressed, downy.

Native of Japan, Korea, and China; introduced in 1908 to Kew. They are notable for the fine dark green leaves which strongly resemble those of the American chestnut oak, *Q. prinus* in their large size, obovate shape and prominent parallel ribs. That species is, however, well distinguished, in the adult state at any rate, by the distinctly stalked acorns and somewhat smaller leaves.

Q. aliena is very rare in cultivation, the only recorded specimens being two in the Oak collection at Kew from the introduction of 1908. They measure 58 × 3¼ ft and 48 × 3¼ ft (1972), the latter being the var. *acuteserrata*.

var. ACUTESERRATA Maxim., has the teeth of the leaf more pointed; and often terminated by a distinct mucro. It is part of the normal variation of the species.

Q. ALNIFOLIA Poech   GOLDEN OAK OF CYPRUS

An evergreen small tree or shrub; young shoots clothed with grey down. Leaves stiff and hard in texture, roundish or broadly obovate, the terminal part toothed, the margins of the older leaves deflexed so that the inverted leaf has very much the shape of a shallow scoop, 1 to 2¼ in. long, and about the same or rather less wide; upper surface dark glossy green, lower one yellow or greyish yellow, covered with a dense close felt; stalk downy like the young wood, ¼ to ⅜ in. long. There are five to eight prominent veins each side the midrib. Acorns

1 to 1½ in. long, ⅓ to ½ in. wide, broadening from the base upwards, and thus somewhat truncheon-shaped, but ending in a short point; cup about ½ in. deep, with downy scales, the upper ones spreading or reflexed.

Native of Cyprus; introduced to Kew in 1885, where it has proved perfectly hardy, but slow-growing. The peculiar attraction of this oak is the yellow undersurface of its leaves, but out-of-doors in England this colour is only slightly developed, and the undersurface is really greyish. But on the young leaves of a plant grown in a cool greenhouse at Kew the yellow was as markedly developed as in *Chrysolepis chrysophylla*.

The rarity of this oak in gardens may in part be due to the difficulty of obtaining acorns from Cyprus in viable condition. At the present time the only example at Kew grows against the Temperate House. The largest specimen of the very few recorded grows at East Bergholt Place, Suffolk; this measures 27 × 1¾ ft (1972). There is a smaller one at Borde Hill, Sussex, grafted on *Q. cerris*.

Q. ARKANSANA Sarg.

A deciduous tree 20 to 30 ft high; young shoots clothed with short, clustered hairs, which mostly fall away by autumn. Leaves obovate or broadly wedge-shaped, often lobed towards the apex, the midrib always, and the lobes often, terminated by a short bristle (mucro), base mostly tapered, sometimes rounded, 2 to 3½ in. long, 1½ to 2½ in. wide, on first expanding they are covered with clustered hairs which soon fall away, leaving the upper surface glabrous and of a clear pleasant green, the lower surface glabrous also, except for tufts of down in the vein-axils; midrib and veins pale coloured and prominent beneath; leaf-stalk ½ in. or rather more long. Fruits described as solitary or in pairs borne on a short stalk; acorn roundish egg-shaped, ½ in. wide; cup shallow.

Native of Arkansas and Alabama, where it is rare and local; introduced from the Arnold Arboretum to Kew, where it has succeeded well and is now a bushy-headed tree measuring 46 × 3½ ft (1972). It is related to *Q. marilandica*, but the leaves are not so firm and leathery nor ordinarily so deeply lobed. It is intermediate between that species and *Q. nigra*, and is possibly the result of past crossing between them.

Q. BARONII Skan

Q. dielsiana Seemen

An evergreen (or it may be, in cold climates, sub-evergreen) shrub 6 ft or more high; young shoots very slender, furnished with starry down at first, becoming nearly or quite glabrous by late autumn. Leaves ovate-lanceolate to oblong, pointed at the apex, rounded to wedge-shaped at the base, the margins set with triangular spine-tipped teeth, ¾ to 2½ in. long, ⅜ to 1½ in. wide, dark green and at first starry downy on both surfaces, becoming nearly glabrous by autumn except on the midrib and especially at the base beneath; stalk 1/12 to ¼ in. long. Fruits short-stalked, solitary; acorns roundish egg-shaped, ⅓ to ½ in. wide, silky at the top; cup ½ to ¾ in. wide, with reflexed, awl-shaped downy scales.

Native of W. China; originally discovered by the Italian missionary Giraldi, in Shensi, in 1895; introduced in 1914, probably by F. N. Meyer. Wilson found it common in warm, semi-arid regions of the Min River in W. Szechwan.

There is an example 9 ft high in the National Botanic Garden, Glasnevin, near Dublin (1966).

Q. BICOLOR Willd.   SWAMP WHITE OAK
Q. platanoides Sudw.

A deciduous tree 60 to 70 ft (occasionally more) high, with loose, scaly bark, young shoots slightly downy at first, becoming glabrous. Leaves obovate, 3 to 7 in. long, 1½ to 4 in. wide, tapered at the base, the six to eight shallow, rounded lobes at each side often reduced to mere undulations towards the top, upper surface dark polished green, soon becoming glabrous; lower surface pale grey, clothed with a close, soft felt; midrib and stalk yellowish, the latter ½ to ¾ in. long, more or less downy. Fruits borne usually in pairs on a more or less downy stalk 2 to 3 in. long; acorn about one-third enclosed in the cup.

Native of eastern N. America; introduced in 1800. Although the best of the white oaks for this country it is not a first-rate tree. At Kew it is quite healthy, the trunk very shaggy through the bark being attached in loose scales. The undersurface of the leaf on the trees at Kew is not so silvery white as it usually is in N. America, but even here the soft felt beneath renders it distinct. Its acorns are occasionally formed with us, but rarely ripen, although in nature they mature in one season.

Q. bicolor is well represented at Kew, where the largest examples in the Oak collection are 62 × 5¾ ft and 62 × 6¾ ft (1972); the former is known to have been planted in 1873. There is another of about the same size near the Japanese Gateway. Other specimens are: Syon House, London, 70 × 9¼ ft (1967), and Pampisford, Cambs., 75 × 6¼ ft (1969).

Q. CALLIPRINOS Webb   SINDIAN OR PALESTINE OAK
Q. pseudococcifera Labill., not Desf.; *Q. coccifera* var. *calliprinos* (Webb) Boiss.

Brief mention is made of this oak in previous editions, where, following Boissier, Hooker, and other botanists, I regarded it as a variety of the Kermes oak, *Q. coccifera*. Since then Dr Stapf has studied the Palestine oaks (*Kew Bulletin*, 1920, p. 258) and has come to the conclusion that they represent one type which may be regarded as a good species distinct from *Q. coccifera*, and to which the name *Q. calliprinos* belongs. This name was given by Webb in 1838. Other authors have made several species and several varieties.

Q. calliprinos differs from *Q. coccifera* in the large size it attains; it is occasionally a large tree with a trunk 3 ft and upwards in diameter; its leaves are larger and more oblong in outline; the acorns have larger cups (sometimes over 1 in. deep) the scales of which are linear or lanceolate-oblong, free from the middle upwards and covered with close grey down. It is a native of the eastern Mediterranean, including Algeria, and of the Near East.

During the campaign against the Turks in the first Great War, acorns of this oak were occasionally gathered by soldiers and sent home. Some were sent to Kew by Major M. Portal, D.S.O., from which plants were raised.

A sentimental and historic interest is attached to *Q. calliprinos* because it is the species to which belongs the famous tree known as 'Abraham's Oak', or the 'Oak of Mamre'. This tree grows at Hebron, just below the Russian convent which overlooks the Plain of Mamre, and it is the largest and oldest specimen of its kind known. It is popularly regarded as marking the spot where grew the tree under which Abraham pitched his tent, and on this account is held sacred by Christian, Jew, and Mahommedan alike. In its prime the trunk was 23 ft in girth. Dr Stapf, basing his calculations on the annual rings of a branch preserved at Kew, considered Abraham's oak to have started its career about A.D. 1150, the time of the Second Crusade. Four hundred years later, when Belon the naturalist visited Hebron, he made no mention of this tree, although it must by then have been of goodly size. But apart from the circumstance that fine trees of *Q. calliprinos* were no doubt much commoner then than now in Palestine, the explanation of the omission of Belon to mention this oak is due rather to the fact that, at that time, the legend of Abraham was attached not to an oak but to a species of pistacia or terebinth.

Abraham's oak was much damaged during the winter of 1856–7 when a great snowstorm occurred. In the streets of Jerusalem the snow lay deep for many days. The accumulation on this oak was so great that it broke down one of its finest branches, and it was from this that the piece now preserved at Kew was cut. Sir Joseph Hooker records that owing to the superstition that anyone who should cut or maim the tree would lose his first-born son, it was difficult to get anyone to cut up this branch for transportation.

Q. CANARIENSIS Willd.   ALGERIAN OAK

Q. mirbeckii Durieu; *Q. lusitanica* var. *baetica* Webb; *Q. lusitanica* subsp. *baetica* (Webb) A. DC.

A deciduous tree of stately habit, 60 to 90 ft high in Britain, up to 120 ft high in Algeria, with a thick, rugged bark; young shoots ribbed, covered when young with a loose flock, soon glabrous, brown the second year. Leaves oval or obovate, coarsely toothed or lobed, rounded to heart-shaped or auricled at the base, variable in size but usually $3\frac{1}{2}$ to 6 in. long, 2 to $3\frac{1}{4}$ in. wide (often larger on young trees), densely coated on both sides when unfolding with a reddish, floccose tomentum, becoming dark green and quite glabrous above, the underside rather glaucous, also glabrous except for traces of brownish flock on the midrib, especially towards the base and on the stalk, which is $\frac{1}{2}$ to 1 in. long; ribs in eight to fourteen pairs, fairly straight and regularly spaced. Fruits ripening the first season, scarcely stalked, clustered; acorns about 1 in. long; cup with flattened, downy scales, enclosing the lowest third of the acorn.

Native mainly of N. Africa but also found in the Iberian peninsula, mostly in its southern part. It does not occur wild in the Canary Islands. The date of introduction to Britain is not known, but the oak discussed by Loudon under the queried name *Q. australis* may well have been *Q. canariensis;* if so, it was introduced to the garden of the Horticultural Society from the neighbourhood of Gibraltar in 1835. There was an introduction to France by General Pelissier around 1845 by means of acorns, some of which were sent by Louis Philippe to Queen Victoria, who distributed them among the ladies of the court.

Q. canariensis is perfectly hardy, and one of the handsomest of all oaks. It is a vigorous grower and notable for the rich green and large size of its leaves, which remain on the branches until Christmas, sometimes a month or two later. It produces fertile acorns but hybridises so readily with the common oak that its seedlings are rarely true. Fortunately it grows well when grafted on the common or the durmast oak and this is the best way of increasing it if wild-source seed cannot be obtained.

The oldest specimen of the Algerian oak at Kew grows near the Isleworth Gate; it came from Booth of Hamburg in 1869 and measures 74 × 10¾ ft (1968). The following are in the main Oak collection: *pl.* 1882, from the Joad Bequest, 68 × 7 ft (1968); *pl.* 1895, 66 × 6¼ ft (1965) (this tree was bought from Lee's nursery for half-a-crown and measured 49 × 4½ ft in 1938); *pl.* 1904, 64 × 5¾ ft (1965).

Some of the notable trees in other collections are: Ham Manor, Sussex, two trees mentioned by Elwes and Henry, the larger 70 × 8¼ ft (1907), now 76 × 13¾ ft (1965); Melbury Park, Dorset, 80 × 10¼ ft (1970); Tortworth, Glos., 75 × 10 ft (1965); Osborne, Isle of Wight, 90 × 8¼ ft (1964); Howick, Northumb., *pl.* 1851, 60 × 7 ft (1958); Holkar, Lancs, 75 × 12 ft (1971).

Q. CASTANEIFOLIA C. A. Mey.   [PLATE 57

Q. castaneifolia subsp. *aitchisonii* Camus

A wide-spreading, deciduous tree reaching 100 ft in height in the wild; buds with linear stipules; young branches downy. Leaves narrowly oval or oblong, tapered at both ends, margined with coarse, triangular teeth, each terminated by a small, slender, abrupt mucro, 3 to 7½ in. long, 1¼ to 3 in. wide, dark glossy green above and glabrous except when quite young, underside dull greyish and clothed with minute down, occasionally almost glabrous; stalk ½ to 1 in. long, downy. The larger leaves have ten to twelve pairs of parallel veins, prominent beneath, which run out and furnish the short mucronate tip of the tooth. Fruits solitary or in pairs (occasionally up to five) on a short, stout, downy peduncle, ripening the second year. Acorns ¾ to 1¼ in. long, flattened at the top, and half enclosed in a cup with reflexed downy scales.

Native of the forest region south and south-west of the Caspian Sea (N. Persia and bordering parts of Russia). It is a very striking and handsome tree, with a leaf resembling that of a Spanish chestnut in form; but it has always been rare in this country. The splendid tree at Kew, planted around 1846, is by far the largest and oldest in Britain. In 1909 it measured 60 × 9½ ft and is now 90 × 19½ ft (1972). Also in the collection are two trees raised from seeds brought home from Persia by Dr James Aitchison in 1885. The herbarium specimen collected by him came from near Gorgan (Asterabad), and no doubt the seeds were of the same provenance. These trees measure 44 × 5¾ ft and 55 × 7 ft (1964–5). Some other specimens are: Batsford Park, Glos., 70 × 9¾ ft (1971); Longleat, Wilts,

QUERCUS CASTANEIFOLIA

92 × 11½ ft (1971); Abbotsbury, Dorset, 66 × 6 ft (1972); East Bergholt Place, Suffolk, 60 × 5½ ft (1972).

Q. AFARES Pomel *Q. castaneifolia* of some authors, in part, not C. A. Meyer; *Q. castaneaefolia* var. *incana* Batt. & Trabut; *Q. castaneaefolia* var. *algeriensis* Bean —This species is so closely allied to *Q. castaneifolia* that some botanists have not recognised it even as a variety. Chiefly it differs in its flowers and fruits, notably in the female flowers having four or five slender spreading styles (only three, shorter and more erect, in *Q. castaneifolia*); in the shallower acorn-cup with longer, more slender scales; and in the more clustered and often more numerous fruits. There seems to be no reliable difference in the leaves, but the young stems are more densely downy and the bark is more deeply furrowed.

Q. *afares* is a native of Algeria, where it forms forests in the coastal mountains from Algiers eastward and is also found in bordering parts of Tunisia. In its native habitat it attains a height of 75 ft. It is rare in cultivation and less vigorous than *Q. castaneifolia*, judging from the trees at Kew. Of these there are two, raised from seeds sent from Algeria in 1869, of which the larger measures 71 × 8¼ ft (1972). The leaves of these trees are smaller than in *Q. castaneifolia*, the largest being 4 to 5 in. by 1¾ in.

Q. CERRIS L.   TURKEY OAK
Q. lanuginosa Lam.

A noble deciduous tree over 120 ft high, with a trunk occasionally more than 6 ft in diameter; winter-buds all furnished with long, linear, downy stipules; young shoots covered with a close, greyish down. Leaves thin and hard in texture, oval or oblong, tapered at both ends, very coarsely toothed or lobed, the lobes penetrating one-third to two-thirds towards the midrib; normally 2½ to 5 in. long, 1 to 3 in. wide, but very diverse in shape, size and lobing, dark lustrous green and harsh, with starry down above, dull greyish green and closely covered with similar down beneath, with seven to ten pairs of veins; stalk ½ to ¾ in. long. Fruits usually solitary, ripening in their second season, very shortly stalked; acorns 1 to 1¼ in. long, depressed at the apex; cup clothed with long, linear, downy scales.

Native of southern Europe and parts of central Europe, from S.E. France through the southern Alps and the Apennines, the Balkans, E. Austria, Czechoslovakia, and the Carpathians of Rumania; represented by a subspecies in Asiatic Turkey; in cultivation by 1735. It is a very hardy tree attaining to dimensions under cultivation nobler than those of most introduced trees. As a timber tree it has very little value, being much inferior to the common oak. As a purely ornamental tree, however, for avenues, etc., it has some points in its favour, being quicker-growing and more elegant in growth.

Perhaps the finest example of the Turkey oak in Britain grows at Knightshayes, Devon; its measurements are 128 × 23½ ft (1970). At Mamhead in the same county the Turkey oak has been cultivated since before 1749 and there were several specimens there in 1835 80 to 100 ft high and 12 to 15 ft in girth (at ground-level). The largest there now measures 82 × 23¼ ft (1963). Other notable specimens are: St Anne's Court, Chertsey, Surrey, 65 × 26½ ft (1965); Beauport, Sussex, 102 × 15¾ ft, with a 40 ft bole (1965); Ombersley Court, Worcs., 110 × 17¼ ft (1964); Bulstrode Park, Bucks, 110 × 20½ ft (1967); Nettlecombe, Som., 100 × 19½ ft (1959); Powderham Castle, Devon, 111 × 19¾ ft and 105 × 20½ ft at 4 ft (1970); Strete Ralegh, Devon, 117 × 11½ ft (1970).

The old Turkey oak at Kew near the Orangery, planted around 1762, was damaged by bombing during the second world war and had to be felled in the winter of 1972–3. It measured 82 × 15 ft in 1967.

var. AMBROZYANA (Simonkai) Rehd.—See under *Q.* × *hispanica*.

var. AUSTRIACA (Willd.) Loud. *Q. austriaca* Willd.—In this variety, said to be prevalent in south-eastern Europe, the leaves are edged with regular, entire, triangular lobes, and are greyer beneath than in the typical state.

f. LACINIATA (Loud.) Schneid. *Q. cerris* var. *laciniata* Loud.—Leaves lobed almost to the midrib, often much narrower than in the type, between which and this variety are several intermediate forms.

subsp. TOURNEFORTII (Willd.) O. Schwarz *Q. tournefortii* Willd.—According to Dr Schwarz the distinguishing characters of this subspecies, found in Asiatic Turkey, are: leaves permanently grey tomentose beneath, with nine to fifteen pairs of veins and leaf-stalk ¾ to 1¾ in. long; cup larger than in the European race, ⅝ to 1¼ in. wide.

cv. 'VARIEGATA'.—Leaves bordered by a white band of varying width, which penetrates here and there to the midrib. A rather effective variegated tree.

Q. × LIBANERRIS Boom—A hybrid between *Q. cerris* and *Q. libani* described from a tree growing in the Trompenburg Arboretum, Rotterdam. It differs from *Q. cerris* in having the lateral buds without stipules; young shoots glabrous; leaves very glossy above, glabrous beneath, with ten to sixteen pairs of shallow lobes terminated by long bristle-tips.

Q. CHRYSOLEPIS Liebm.   MAUL OAK

An evergreen tree up to 40 to 60 ft high in the wild, with a short, thick trunk, but scarcely more than a shrub as yet in cultivation; young shoots covered with starry down. Leaves 1 to 3½ in. long, half to almost as wide, ovate or oval, the smaller ones often roundish, heart-shaped at the base, terminated by a spiny tooth, also furnished on young plants with four to ten large spiny teeth at each side, terminating as many parallel veins. On old trees the leaves are described as entire. The upper surface is at first furnished with stellate down, but soon becomes nearly or quite glabrous, and of a dark shining green; lower surface dull and at first yellowish downy, but often glabrous the second year; stalks 1/12 to 1/6 in. long, clothed with starry down. Fruits solitary or in pairs, scarcely stalked; acorns egg-shaped, ¾ to 1 in. long, the downy cup enclosing less than half its length.

Native of California; introduced by Sargent in 1877, but the trees now in cultivation are of later date. It is distinguished among evergreen oaks with foliage of the same character, by the yellowish appressed down beneath the leaves, which, however, is not so thick on plants cultivated in this country as it is in W. America. Of this tree Sargent observes that, in its native state, it is surpassed in majestic dignity and massive strength by no other American species except *Q. virginiana* of the southern Atlantic states. Trees exist with heads of branches fifty yards across.

At Kew there are two examples of this oak planted in 1904, the larger 33 × 3¾ ft (1972). The tree in the National Botanic Garden, Glasnevin, Dublin, may be older: it measures 40 × 5 ft (1966).

Q. VACCINIIFOLIA Kell. *Q. chrysolepis* var. *vaccinifolia* (Kell). Engelm.—This is sometimes associated with the above as a variety, but is probably a quite distinct species. It is a prostrate shrub up to 4 ft high, with small, oval, mostly entire leaves, covered beneath with a pale grey scurf. Introduced in 1900. Wild on rocky hillsides in Oregon and California. It is quite hardy at Jermyns House, near Romsey, Hants.

Q. COCCIFERA L.   KERMES OAK, GRAIN TREE

Q. pseudococcifera Desf.; *Q. coccifera* var. *pseudococcifera* (Desf.) A. DC.

An evergreen shrub up to 10 or 12 ft high, of sturdy, dense, neat habit, some-times a small tree up to 15 or 20 ft high; buds glabrous or soon becoming so; young shoots at first clad with starry down, soon glabrous. Leaves stiff and hard, broadly oval, oblong, or ovate, rounded or heart-shaped at the base, ending in a stiff, sharp spine similar to the three to five with which each margin is armed, ½ to 1½ in. long, half to three-quarters as wide, dark green above, slightly paler below, shining and glabrous on both sides; stalk about ⅛ in. long, slightly downy at first, soon glabrous. Fruits ripening the second year, usually solitary on a short stalk about ½ in. long; acorn ½ to 1 in. or slightly more long, one-half to two-thirds enclosed in the cup, which is covered with spreading, spiny scales.

QUERCUS COCCIFERA

Native of the western Mediterranean (including N. Africa), giving way east-ward to *Q. calliprinos;* also of Portugal and Atlantic Morocco; cultivated in Britain since the 17th century. Of the dwarf evergreen oaks, this is perhaps the most pleasing in the glitter of its foliage and neat bushy habit. It is as prickly-leaved and well armed as a small-leaved holly. It is variable in foliage.

Q. coccifera has reached 20 ft in height in the Heath Garden at Wakehurst Place in Sussex. At the other extreme Mr Hillier has a very dwarf and compact plant at Jermyns House, Ampfield.

Q. coccifera obtains its popular name of 'Kermes oak' from being the host plant on which the kermes insect (*Chermes ilicis*) breeds. This insect, after certain treatment, produces a beautiful scarlet dye remarkable for its richness and lasting quality, once much employed and known in commerce as 'grain' or 'scarlet grain', but now, owing to cheaper substitutes, fallen into disuse. Three sprigs of *Q. coccifera* or 'grain tree' still form the crest of the Dyers' Company, whose arms were granted to them between 1420 and 1450. From this one may gather how high was the estimation in which 'Kermes' was held in the Middle Ages; but so much has this dye disappeared from modern use that until the matter was investigated at Kew, the Company itself did not know to what tree the sprigs were supposed to belong. For an interesting account of this oak in regard to its connection with the dye, and various allusions to the latter quoted from Chaucer and Shakespeare, see *Kew Bulletin* (1910), p. 167.

Q. × AUZENDI Gren. & Godr. ("*auzendri*").—A hybrid between *Q. coccifera* and *Q. ilex*, found wild in S. France, etc. Its leaves resemble those of *Q. coccifera* but are more or less felted beneath; the fruits are more like those of the other parent in having appressed scales; they are borne two or three together on a stalk up to 1 in. long. It used to be cultivated in the Heatherside Nursery near Bagshot.

Q. COCCINEA Muenchh.   SCARLET OAK

A deciduous tree up to 70 or 80 ft high; young shoots warted, not downy; winter-buds downy towards the points, up to ¼ in. long. Leaves 3 to 6 in. long, 2½ to 4½ in. wide (in young trees as much as 6 in. wide), obovate or oval, tapered at the base, deeply seven- sometimes nine-lobed, the lobes oblong or triangular, coarsely and unequally toothed at the apex, dark green above, paler beneath, both sides lustrous and glabrous, except that there are sometimes tufts of brownish down in the vein-axils beneath; stalk 1½ to 2½ in. long, glabrous, yellow. Acorns ½ to 1 in. long, two-thirds as wide, one-third to one-half enclosed in a deep, thin-edged cup.

Native of eastern N. America; introduced about the end of the 17th century. The true scarlet oak retains its leaves until November or December, and for the last six or eight weeks they are of a brilliant red, and make one of the richest of autumnal effects. But early frost may cause the leaves to wither before they have coloured, and trees raised from seed cannot be relied on always to give the autumn colouring expected of this species.

In its native country the scarlet oak does not attain such a large ultimate size as the red oak (*Q. rubra*) and reaches maturity at an earlier age. It is less demanding in its soil requirements, and is commonly found on dry, rather acid soils. Early this century, Elwes and Henry remarked on the scarcity of the scarlet oak in Britain and knew of no better tree than one at Arley Castle, measuring 78 × 6¼ ft (1904). The following specimens, recorded in recent years, probably all less than a century old: Kew, by Main Gate, 56 × 6¼ ft (1967), near Oak collection, 60 × 6¼ ft (1965); Syon House, London, 70 × 8¼ ft (1968); Osterley Park, London, four trees 65 to 70 ft high, 5¾ to 6¾ ft in girth (1965); Windsor Great Park, China Island, 75 × 9 ft (1964); Frensham Hall, nr Haslemere, Surrey, *pl.* 1905, 80 × 6¼ ft (1968); Nymans, Sussex, *pl.* 1902, 80 × 7¼ ft (1968); Sheffield Park, Sussex, four trees 70 to 75 ft high, 7 to 8¼ ft in girth (1968); Grayswood Hill, Surrey, 80 × 8¼ ft (1971); Westonbirt, Glos., opposite Wigmore Bottom, 80 × 5¾ ft (1967), Circular Drive, 78 × 8¼ ft (1969), three in The Downs *pl.* 1926, 57 to 65 ft high, 5 to 6 ft in girth; Saltram House, Devon, 77 × 7¼ ft (1970); Killerton, Devon, in Park 55 × 7 ft (1970); Sandon Park, Staffs., 74 × 9¾ ft (1969).

cv. 'SPLENDENS' ('Knap Hill')—A selection with unusually brilliant autumn colouring, introduced by the Knap Hill Nursery at the end of the last century. Award of Garden Merit 1927. A specimen at Kew, grafted at 1 ft, is 65 × 7¼ ft (1969).

Q. CRASSIFOLIA Humb. & Bonpl.

A deciduous tree up to 100 ft high in the wild; stems and leaves densely coated when young with a rust-coloured tomentum. Mature leaves very thick and leathery, obovate or broadly oblong-elliptic or roundish, broadly obtuse or sometimes almost truncate at the apex, cordate, truncate or occasionally rounded at the base, up to 4¼ in. long and 3¼ in. wide, upper surface glabrous or almost so, with all the veins impressed, lower surface densely tomentose, with mostly four to seven prominent lateral veins each side the midrib, many of them branched, margins of the young leaves slightly serrated, those of the mature leaves irregularly sinuated but otherwise entire except for the bristles terminating the lateral veins and their branches; petioles very short. Fruits ripening the first season; acorns about ¾ in. long, one-third to one-half enclosed in a shallow cup with brown, appressed scales.

Native of central Mexico. There may have been early introductions of this species, but the only specimen known to exist in the British Isles grows at Caerhays Castle, Cornwall, This was raised from seeds collected by the American botanist G. B. Hinton in 1939 under field-number 6402, and measures 41 × 2¼ ft (1971). The above description of the foliage is made from this tree. A younger, very vigorous example at Kew has leaves as much as 7½ in. long and 4½ in. wide, on stalks up to ¾ in. long.

Q. CRASSIPES Humb. & Bonpl.

A medium-sized evergreen tree; branchlets densely downy; buds very small. Leaves leathery, oblong-elliptic, broadest slightly below the middle, obtuse to subacute and usually mucronate at the apex, rounded to slightly cordate at the base, 2 to 3½ in. long, rarely over 1 in. wide, glabrous above when mature, clad beneath with a close tomentum which only gradually wears away, margins entire or slightly undulated; petiole up to ¼ in. long. Fruits ripening in the second year, solitary or in pairs, on short stalks; acorn ovoid, enclosed in its lower half by a top-shaped cup ½ to ¾ in. wide, with appressed, ovate, slightly downy scales.

Native of Mexico; introduced by Hartweg in 1839 for the Horticultural Society. Although now scarcely known in cultivation, this seems to be one of the hardier of the Mexican oaks. A tree at Carclew in Cornwall, possibly from the original introduction, measured 64 × 5¼ ft in 1908 and was still alive in 1933. Trelease, the American authority on the oaks, thought that the Carclew tree was Q. mexicana Humb. & Bonpl., but this species and Q. crassipes are very closely allied and distinguishable only by their fruits, which were not borne by the Carclew tree.

Q. DENTATA Thunb.   DAIMIO OAK
Q. daimio K. Koch

A deciduous round-headed tree 60 or more ft high, described as being of ungainly, unpicturesque habit when old; young shoots stout, densely covered with greyish soft hairs. Leaves amongst the largest of all hardy oaks, occasionally over 1 ft long and 6 or 7 in. wide, the smallest one-third those dimensions, obovate, tapered at the base, blunt or rounded at the apex, the margin with five to nine rounded lobes or deep undulations at each side. When quite young the upper surface is covered with minute down, the undersurface with a whitish felt; but, as the season advances, the down falls away from the upper surface, the lower one remaining sparsely downy. Acorns ½ to ¾ in. long, rounded; the cup covered with long, narrow, downy scales.

Native of Japan and of the mainland of N.E. Asia; introduced to Europe in 1830. It is a remarkable oak on account of its enormous leaves, but has never been really a success in this country, and is usually short-lived. Its habit is thin and gaunt. The undersurface of its leaves sometimes presents an extraordinary appearance because of an infestation of disk-like galls, so thickly placed as to overlap each other.

At the present time there are two examples of this oak in the collection at Kew, neither of much beauty: one, *pl.* 1893, is 30 × 2½ ft, the other, *pl.* 1907, 17 × 1¼ ft (1965). It has thrived better at Osterley Park on the other side of the Thames where there is a fine tree measuring 37 × 4¼ ft (1965) and another of about the same size. Others recorded recently are: Westonbirt, a crowded tree in Willesley Drive, 50 × 3¾ ft (1967); The Grange, Benenden, Kent, 36 × 2¼ ft (1972); Trewidden, Cornwall, 40 × 4¾ ft (1959); Caerhays, Cornwall, 47 × 4¼ ft (1971); Edinburgh Botanic Garden, *pl.* 1931, 38 × 3 ft (1970).

cv. 'PINNATIFIDA'.—A Japanese garden variety with the leaves deeply dissected into narrow, crisped lobes; described in 1879. It is in cultivation in Britain.

Q. DOUGLASII Hook. & Arn.   BLUE OAK

A deciduous tree usually under 40 ft high, but occasionally taller in sheltered places, with a smooth, ashy bark; buds ovoid, with deciduous stipules; young stems densely downy, slowly becoming glabrous. Leaves bluish green, rigid, falling late in the autumn, oblong or elliptic, obtuse at the apex, broadly cuneate to almost truncate at the base, 2 to 3 in. long, 1 to 1¾ in. wide, margins varying from sinuately toothed to almost entire, glabrous above except for scattered stellate hairs, finely hairy beneath; petiole less than ½ in. long. Fruits solitary or paired, almost sessile. Acorn ovoid or elongate-ovoid, 1 in. or slightly more long; cup enclosing only the base of the acorn, with appressed, downy scales.

Native of California up to 4,000 ft, often associated with evergreen oaks and *Pinus sabiniana*. Although apparently quite hardy, and with strikingly sea-green leaves, it is uncommon in cultivation. Some authorities place it in the section *Erythrobalanus*, though in most of its characters it agrees better with the section *Quercus*, in which it is retained by Camus (*Les Chênes*, Vol. III, p. 1252).

Q. ENGLERIANA Seemen

Q. obscura Seemen; *Q. sutchuenensis* Franch.

A small evergreen tree 20 to 30 ft high, the young shoots clothed at first with a close, dense, grey down. Leaves leathery, narrowly ovate to oblong, mostly rounded at the base, slenderly pointed, ribs in nine to thirteen pairs, very prominent beneath, each one running out at the margin to a sharp tooth up to $\frac{1}{12}$ in. long, 3 to 7 in. long, 1 to 2 in. wide, dark shining green and glabrous above, paler and covered with a brown wool beneath; stalk $\frac{1}{4}$ to $\frac{3}{8}$ in. long, clothed with brown wool. Stipules awl-shaped, up to $\frac{1}{2}$ in. long, silky-hairy. The fruits, which ripen the first year, are solitary or two or three together, acorns egg-shaped, about $\frac{1}{2}$ in. long, the cup $\frac{3}{8}$ in. wide, $\frac{1}{4}$ in. deep, the scales grey-downy, appressed.

Native of Hupeh and Szechwan, China; introduced to the Coombe Wood Nursery by Wilson in 1900. He observes that this is always a small tree and is common in rocky places at from 3,000 to 6,000 ft altitude. The old leaves fall in spring as the new ones unfold. Wilson observes that the leaves are sometimes quite untoothed. As regards foliage this is undoubtedly one of the finest of hardy evergreen oaks and in the milder counties should make a very handsome tree. Named after Prof. A. Engler (1844–1930), for long Director of the Dahlem Botanic Garden, Berlin.

The only recorded specimens of *Q. engleriana* are: Werrington Park, Cornwall, 38 × 2¼ ft (1966), and Caerhays, Cornwall, 17 × 2 ft (1971).

Q. FAGINEA Lam.

Q. lusitanica Webb, not Lam.; *Q. lusitanica* var. *baetica* Coutinho, not Webb

A tree up to 70 ft high, with a thick brownish or greyish bark divided into more or less rectangular blocks, or occasionally a shrub; winter-buds ovoid, more or less downy; young stems covered at first with greyish or whitish hairs. Leaves rather leathery, usually persisting on the tree through the winter, variable in shape, oblong or elliptic, sometimes ovate-elliptic or oblong-obovate, mostly 1 to 3 in. long, $\frac{1}{2}$ to 1¾ in. wide, but sometimes larger, obtuse to rounded at the apex, cordate, rounded or truncate at the base, the upper surface sparsely stellate-hairy at first, becoming glabrous and grey-green, undersurface more or less densely grey-felted beneath, sometimes almost glabrous when mature, margins fairly regularly set with acute, mucronate teeth; lateral veins usually four to twelve in number, more or less parallel and mostly running out to the teeth; leaf-stalk about $\frac{3}{8}$ in. long, tomentose. Fruits ripening the first year, borne singly or in pairs on a peduncle about $\frac{1}{2}$ in. long; cup hemispherical or urn-shaped, with appressed tomentose scales; acorn oblong-ovoid, about one-third to one-fifth enclosed in the cup, about 1 in. long.

A native of Spain and Portugal, and possibly also of N. Africa (see below); introduced in 1835. It is an exceedingly variable species in the size, shape, and toothing of the leaves. The above description includes the subsp. *broteri* (Coutinho) Camus, with leaves permanently felted beneath, as well as the more glabrous typical subspecies. *Q. faginea* is closely allied to *Q. canariensis*, which is included in it by some botanists. But in *Q. canariensis* the young leaves and stems are covered with a brownish flock, traces of which remain throughout the growing season, and are never felted, and the teeth are more like lobes and obtuse to rounded.

The following specimens of *Q. faginea* have been recorded: Kew, in Oak collection, *pl.* 1931, 46 × 3 ft (1972) and another of 49 × 5¼ ft (1972); Osborne House, Isle of Wight, *pl.* 1847, 49 × 5¼ ft (1972); Edinburgh Botanic Garden, *pl.* 1919, 49 × 4¾ ft (1967) and another of 47 × 4¾ ft (1970).

Q. TLEMCENENSIS (A. DC.) H. del Villar *Q. faginea* var. *tlemcenensis* (A. DC.) Maire; *Q. faginea* subsp. *tlemcenensis* (A. DC.) Maire & Weiller; *Q. pseudosuber* var. *tlemcenensis* A. DC.; *Q. pseudosuber* Desf., not Santi—In N. Africa oaks are found which are intermediate between *Q. faginea* and *Q. canariensis*, and for this reason some botanists have united the two species, distinct though they are in their typical states. These intermediates are probably the result of past hybridisation and are best treated as a distinct species. The alternative, if *Q. faginea* and *Q. canariensis* are kept separate, is to treat these intermediates as varieties of one or the other species.

A fine example of *Q. tlemcenensis* grows in the garden of Capt. Collingwood Ingram at Benenden, Kent, raised from seed collected by him in Morocco. It is a handsome, vigorous tree with leaves up to 4¾ in. long and almost 2 in. wide, elliptic or elliptic-oblong, still in mid-August coated beneath with a film of white hairs and edged with blunt, shallow, lobe-like teeth; veins in seven to eight pairs, all running out to teeth.

Q. FALCATA Michx. SPANISH OAK

Q. cuneata of some authors, not Wangenh.; *Q. rubra sens.* Sarg., not L.; *Q. triloba* Michx., *Q. falcata* var. *triloba* (Michx.) Nutt.; *Q. nobilis* Hort. ex K. Koch.

A deciduous tree up to 70 or 80 ft high in the wild; young shoots and leaves covered with stellate scurf. Leaves obovate, three-lobed with a wedge-shaped base, or more ovate and five- or seven-lobed, 4 to 7 in. long, 3½ to 5 in. wide, the terminal lobe mostly oblong, 2 to 3½ in. long, the side ones shorter, triangular, or scythe-shaped—often furnished with a few bristle-teeth. The upper surface is dark glossy green, the lower one dull grey and more persistently downy; stalk ¾ to 1½ in. long, slender. Fruits very shortly stalked, acorns about ½ in. wide and long, the cup shallow or saucer-shaped.

Native of the eastern and south central United States; introduced in 1763, but extremely rare. According to Sargent, the two forms of leaves occur sometimes on the same tree, sometimes on separate trees.

var. PAGODIFOLIA Elliott *Q. pagoda* Raf.; *Q. rubra* var. *pagodifolia* (Elliott) Ashe—This is a very well marked variety, treated as a species by Camus and perhaps deserving subspecific rank. The lobing is more regular than in the typical variety, the lobes being in three to five pairs, spreading more or less horizontally. It is most plentiful in the lower Mississippi basin but also occurs in the Atlantic states, usually in bottomlands.

Q. FRAINETTO Ten.   HUNGARIAN OAK, FARNETTO

Q. farnetto Ten.; *Q. conferta* Kit.; *Q. esculus* L., in part, *nom. ambig.*;
Q. pannonica Booth ex Gord.

A deciduous tree of stately habit, up to 100 ft high in the wild; young shoots slightly downy, glabrous and grey the second year. Leaves obovate, but deeply cut into six to ten oblong lobes at each side, the largest of which are 2 in. deep, and penetrate from half to three quarters of the distance towards the midrib; they frequently have two to five rounded teeth on one or both sides. The largest leaves are 6 to 8 in. long, and 3 to 4½ in. wide; the smallest about half those dimensions, all tapering at the base to a short stalk ⅓ in. or less long, the blade usually prolonged at each side into a pair of short auricles. The upper surface is dark green and soon becomes glabrous, the lower one downy, and greyish green. Fruits ½ to ¾ in. long, scarcely stalked, produced two to four together, the lower half of the acorn enclosed by the cup, which is clothed outside with flattened downy scales.

Native of S. Italy, the Balkans, Rumania, and parts of Hungary; introduced about 1837. It is one of the handsomest of all oaks of the sessile-flowered group, and thrives well in cultivation. It is only likely to be confused with *Q. macranthera*, a species very distinct, nevertheless, in its woolly shoots and in its buds with long, persistent stipules. Occasional crops of acorns are produced on cultivated trees.

At Kew the oldest specimen of the Hungarian oak is a grafted one, planted about 1840 and measuring 70 × 11¼ ft (1971); in the Pagoda Vista there is a pair of trees received from the Knap Hill Nursery in 1893, also grafted, the larger of which measures 67 × 10 ft (1965). Other notable specimens are: Osterley Park, London, 75 × 10¼ ft with a bole of 40 ft, and another 77 × 10¾ ft (1965); Syon Park, London, 75 × 11¼ ft (1967); Grayswood Hill, Surrey, 70 × 10¾ ft (1971); Brook House, Ardingly, Sussex, 60 × 11 ft (1973); Woburn, Beds., 60 × 11¼ ft (1962); Stratfield Saye, Hants, 85 × 10½ ft (1968); Westonbirt, Glos., in the Park 70 × 11¼ ft (1966), in Main Drive, 85 × 9½ ft (1970); Tortworth, Glos., 90 × 10½ ft (1964); Munden, Herts, *pl.* 1885, 85 × 9¼ ft (1968); Edinburgh Botanic Garden, *pl. c.* 1856, moved 1865, 67 × 8 ft (1967).

Q. FRUTICOSA Brot.

Q. humilis Lam.

A semi-evergreen shrub often forming matted scrub about 1 ft high, but in good soil and other conditions it is to be found 3 to 6 ft (rarely 12 ft) high. Leaves almost sessile, 1 to 2 in. long, oval, rounded or subcordate at the base, spiny-toothed, more or less matted at first with grey, stellate down beneath; veins and marginal teeth in four to seven pairs, the latter triangular and spiny-pointed. Acorns about 1 in. long, ovoid, about two-thirds enclosed by the cup which is on a stalk ½ in. long.

Native of the south-western part of the Iberian peninsula, and of N.W. Morocco. Near Lisbon it is, or used to be, abundant as matted scrub about 1 ft high. It was cultivated in the Milford Nurseries, near Godalming, as long ago as

1827, and an acorn-bearing shoot was figured in the *Gardeners' Chronicle*, June 24, 1874, p. 113. The late Sir Oscar Warburg of Boidier, near Epsom, and Capt. Collingwood Ingram of Benenden, Kent, reintroduced this oak. It is hardy.

Q. GAMBELII Nutt.   SHIN OAK

A deciduous suckering shrub up to 10 or 15 ft high, or a small tree, with a thick, fissured bark; buds ovoid, with persistent stipules; young shoots covered at first with a pale, rusty down. Leaves of firm texture, obovate or oblong-obovate, $2\frac{3}{4}$ to $4\frac{3}{4}$ in. long, $1\frac{1}{4}$ to $2\frac{1}{4}$ in. wide, obtuse at the apex, narrowed to a roundish base, dark, dull green and almost glabrous above, paler and downy beneath, with three to six pairs of deepish, obtuse, entire lobes on each side; petiole $\frac{1}{2}$ to $\frac{3}{4}$ in. long. Fruits ripening the first season, borne on a slender peduncle less than 1 in. long. Acorn ovoid, acute, up to $\frac{7}{8}$ in. long; cup hemispherical, enclosing about half the acorn; scales thickish, downy, appressed except at the tip.

Native of the Rocky Mountains, USA, at high altitudes; introduced towards the end of the last century. It is perfectly hardy, but of no ornamental value.

var. GUNNISONII (Torr.) Wenzig *Q. alba* var. *gunnisonii* Torr.; *Q. gunnisonii* (Torr.) Rydb.—Dwarfer than the type, the leaves scarcely paler below than above, narrow-obovate or elliptic, acorn shorter, obtuse. Native of the Rocky Mountains from Colorado and Utah southwards. There is a small example at Kew.

Q. GARRYANA Hook.   OREGON OAK

A deciduous tree often 60 to 80 ft high, with a broad compact head of tortuous branches; buds $\frac{3}{8}$ in. long and, like the young shoots, densely clothed with reddish-brown down. Leaves obovate in main outline but with two or three deep, rounded or blunt lobes at each side, the base usually wedge-shaped, 2 to 5 in. long, not so wide, dark shining green and glabrous above, more or less downy and conspicuously veined beneath; stalk downy, $\frac{1}{2}$ to 1 in. long. Fruits stalkless, usually solitary; acorns oval or obovoid, about 1 in. long, the base enclosed in a shallow, downy cup.

Native of western N. America, from British Columbia to N. California. This tree bears considerable resemblance to our native oak in shape of leaf and acorn, but is very distinct in the hairy shoots and large downy winter-buds. It has many times been introduced to this country, but I have never seen other than quite small trees, and it is evidently not well adapted to our climate. Douglas named it after his friend, Nicholas Garry of the Hudson's Bay Company, who greatly assisted him in his early journeys.

There is a specimen in the Edinburgh Botanic Garden, *pl.* 1924, measuring 26 × 3 ft.

Q. GILLIANA Rehd. & Wils.

A small evergreen tree up to 25 ft high, or a bushy shrub; young shoots brown, clothed at first with loose starry down. Leaves leathery, oval, or slightly obovate, rounded or slightly heart-shaped at the base, rounded at the apex, margins stiffly toothed on young plants, becoming largely entire on adult ones, 1 to 2½ in. long, ½ to 1⅓ in. wide, dark glossy green, sprinkled beneath when young with starry down; stalk ⅛ in. or less long. Fruits (which ripen the first year) borne two to four together on a short, stiff stalk, acorn-cup hemispherical, enclosing about half the acorn, downy inside scales appressed, triangular, clothed with yellowish-grey down.

Native of W. Szechwan and Yunnan, China; introduced by Wilson in 1910. This oak requires rather warmer conditions than exist in places like Kew.

Q. GLABRESCENS Benth.

An evergreen small tree or large shrub; branchlets stellate-hairy when young. Leaves thick and leathery, oblong-elliptic to oblanceolate, up to 4 in. long and 1¼ in. wide, coarsely toothed or undulately lobulate in the upper third to one-half of their length, apex obtuse to acute, base cuneate to obliquely truncate, upper surface dark green, glossy, rugulose, downy on the midrib, lower surface paler, with scattered hairs or almost glabrous, midrib, veins and veinlets prominent, the laterals mostly running out to the mucronately tipped teeth or lobules; petiole about ¼ in. long. Fruits ripening the first year, two or three on a downy peduncle. Acorn ovoid, about ⅝ in. long; cup with appressed, downy scales, enclosing one half to one third of the acorn.

Native of Mexico; discovered by Hartweg and introduced by him, or by Fox-Strangways, about 1839. There was a specimen in the old Botanic Garden of Trinity College, Dublin, which in 1909 measured 25 × 2½ ft. At the present time there is an example in the National Botanic Garden, Glasnevin, Dublin, *pl.* 1937, measuring 20 × 1 ft, and a smaller one at Kew, of shrubby habit.

Q. glabrescens is a handsome oak, apparently quite hardy, easily recognised by its thick, dark green, narrow, rugose leaves, waved or sharply toothed in the upper part, both types of leaf occurring on the same spray. On wild plants the leaves are sometimes entire.

Q. GLANDULIFERA Blume

Q. serrata Thunb., *nom. ambig. propos.*

A deciduous tree up to 30 or 45 ft high, of elegant habit; young shoots with silky, appressed, and forward-pointing hairs. Leaves obovate or narrowly oval, 2 to 7 in. long, 1 to 2½ in. wide, tapered at both ends, with six to twelve incurved, gland-tipped teeth at each side, and eight to fourteen pairs of parallel veins running out to the apex of the teeth; dark green above, greyish beneath, both surfaces white with appressed silvery hairs when quite young, much of which falls away from the upper one; stalk ¼ to ½ in. long. Fruits small, solitary, or several on a short stalk; cup shallow.

Native of Japan, Korea, and China. It was introduced from Japan in 1893 by Prof. Sargent of the Arnold Arboretum, USA, and there are three fine specimens at Kew in the Oak collection by the Thames, raised from the seeds he sent. They measure 64 × 6 ft, 62 × 5½ ft, and 54 × 4½ ft (1972). It was reintroduced from

China by Wilson in 1909, under W.1294, collected in woodland near Mupin in W. Szechwan. A tree at Kew from this sending is 54 × 4¼ ft (1972). Judging from these trees, *Q. glandulifera* is one of the most ornamental of hardy oaks. The elegantly shaped leaves are often very narrow in proportion to their length; on one tree at Kew they are not much over 1½ in. wide. No other specimen has been recorded in the British Isles apart from one in the National Botanic Garden, Glasnevin, Eire, measuring 36 × 3 ft (1966).

Q. GLAUCA Thunb.

Q. annulata Sm.; *Cyclobalanopsis glauca* (Thunb.) Oerst.

An evergreen tree up to 50 ft high, or a large shrub; young stems brown or purplish brown, downy at first, soon glabrous. Leaves elliptic, oblong, or narrow-ovate, sometimes broadest slightly above the middle, acuminate at the apex, usually tapered, sometimes rounded, at the base, glabrous above, the underside glaucous and more or less permanently coated with appressed silky hairs, main veins in eight to twelve pairs, prominent beneath, margins of leaf sharply toothed in the upper part; petiole up to about ½ in. long. Fruits one to three in each cluster, ripening the first season; acorns about ¾ in. long, about one-third enclosed in a downy cup with six or seven raised rings.

Interpreted in a broad sense, this species has a very wide distribution in E. Asia, from Japan and Formosa through China to the Himalaya, where it occurs in the outer ranges and does not ascend above 5,000 ft; it is also found in the Khasi Hills. It is variable and should perhaps be divided into subspecies. Although first described from Japan, the earliest introduction was from Nepal in 1804. Later the Kew collector Richard Oldham sent it from Japan (*c.* 1861), and it is also in cultivation from seeds collected by Wilson in W. China. According to him it is the commonest evergreen oak in W. Hupeh and E. Szechwan, where it grows from river-level to 5,000 ft. He described it as a 'handsome tree with a bushy, flattened-round head of widespreading branches'.

Q. glauca is very rare in gardens and only suitable for the mildest parts of the country. There is an example at Caerhays in Cornwall of 20 × 1½ ft (1971) and a slightly smaller one at Exbury, Hants.

Q. HARTWISSIANA Stev.

Q. armeniaca Kotschy; *Q. stranjensis* Turrill

A small deciduous tree with dark brown or purplish-brown glabrous young stems. Leaves mostly obovate or oblong-obovate, usually rounded or obtuse at the apex and obliquely cordate at the base, 3 to 5 in. long, 1½ to 2½ in. wide, dark green, glabrous and somewhat lustrous above, underside paler with a few hairs along the midrib, margins with five to nine pairs of short fairly equal lobes; veins in seven to ten pairs, more or less parallel, running out to the apices of the lobes; intercalary veins absent or almost so; petiole yellowish, ¾ to 1 in. long. Fruiting peduncles 1¼ to 3¼ in. long, bearing two to five fruits; cup similar to that of *Q. robur* but thicker; acorn ovoid, about 1 in. long, ½ in. wide.

Native of the western Transcaucasus, Turkey (including the European part), and E. Bulgaria. The main interest of this species is that, according to Mme Camus, it bears a marked resemblance to the fossil species *Q. roburoides*, which was widespread in Europe at the end of the Tertiary period and may have been the ancestor of the present-day *Q. robur*, *Q. petraea*, and allied species. Dr Schwarz places it in section *Robur*, as the only species of the series *Primitivae*. The primitive feature of this oak is the venation of the leaves: in *Q. robur*, which *Q. hartwissiana* resembles in its pedunculate fruits, the leaves have intercalary veins, i.e., veins running out to sinuses or fading away before they reach the margin of the leaf. In *Q. hartwissiana* all the laterals run out to the apices of the lobes and are more or less parallel—an unusual feature among European oaks, though it is shown by *Q. petraea* and its allies, which, in this respect, are nearer to the putative ancestral species.

Q. × HISPANICA Lam.

A group of hybrids between *Q. cerris*, the Turkey oak, and *Q. suber*, the cork oak, mainly represented in cultivation by the original Lucombe oak ('Lucombeana') and its derivatives. The name *Q. hispanica* was published by Lamarck in 1783; under it he described three oaks growing in the Trianon Garden, of which one was the Fulham oak (see 'Fulhamensis' below); he thought this came from Gibraltar, whence the epithet *hispanica*. The one he called the aegilops-leaved oak is thought to have been 'Lucombeana'. Until recently this was known as *Q. lucombeana* Sweet and the various named seedlings and related forms were placed under this name as varieties. Now all must be treated as cultivars of *Q. × hispanica*. In the following account 'Lucombeana' is treated first and the others follow in alphabetical order.

'LUCOMBEANA'. LUCOMBE OAK.—A semi-deciduous tree up to 100 ft high, forming a large, rounded head of branches as much in diameter; the trunk has a corrugated bark like that of the Turkey oak, and is buttressed in the same way at the base; terminal bud furnished with linear scales; young shoots covered with grey down. Leaves oval or ovate, broadly tapered and unequal-sided at the base, with seven to nine parallel veins running out, and forming the tips of, triangular sharp teeth on the margin, 2 to 5 in. long, 1 to 2 in. wide; upper surface glossy green, lower one covered with a close grey felt; stalk ¼ to ½ in. long. Fruits solitary or in pairs on a short, stout stalk, ripening the second year, ¾ to 1 in. long, the acorn more than half enclosed in a cup covered with narrow, downy scales that are reflexed at the base, but erect towards the rim of the cup.
[PLATE 56

A hybrid between the cork oak and the Turkey oak raised about 1763 from seed of the latter by Lucombe, a nurseryman of Exeter, who propagated it in large quantities by grafting on Turkey oak. It is a handsome and stately tree of a distinct habit when mature, with spreading branches upswept at the ends and swollen at the base. This is well shown in the drawing of the original tree in its winter state reproduced by Loudon (*Arb. et Frut. Brit.*, Vol. III, fig. 1712). The bark is scarcely corky and the leaves persist throughout much of the winter on the outer part of the crown. The original clone, i.e., the true 'Lucombeana', is comparatively rare outside the south-west, but there is a fine specimen at Kew measuring 67 × 14¾ ft (1965). Others outside Devon and Cornwall are: Scotney Castle, Kent, 108 × 13½ ft (1971); Wilton House, Wilts, *pl.* 1817, 80 × 17 ft (1971); Wooton House, Dorset, *pl.* 1765, 76 × 16 ft (1959).

Notable specimens in Devon are: Killerton, in the Park, 88 × 16¼ ft (1970); Powderham Castle, 90 × 17¼ ft and 97 × 17¼ ft (1970); Castle Hill, *pl.* 1770, 88 × 21 ft at 4 ft (1970); Bicton, in the American Garden, 102 × 13 ft (1967); Cowley Place, Exeter, 83 × 19¼ ft (1967); Dartington Hall, 88 × 14¾ ft (1968); Saltram House, 80 × 17¼ ft (1970); Knightshayes, 100 × 14¼ ft (1959); Sharpham, Totnes, 78 × 15 ft at 3 ft (1965).

In Cornwall, the tree at Carclew mentioned by Elwes and Henry still exists. Some measurements of it are: 74½ × 7 ft (1823); 100 × 13 ft (1903); 105 × 15½ ft (1965). It is one of an original group of ten trees, estimated to have been planted a few years before 1775.

'Lucombeana' produces fertile acorns, and from these many trees have been raised which show considerable variation within the limits set by the two parent species. It is not necessary, nor indeed easy, satisfactorily to define all these variations on paper, although they are palpable enough when the trees grow together. When seedlings of 'Lucombeana' deviate towards the Turkey oak the bark shows little or no corkiness and the foliage is strictly deciduous. When, on the other hand, the influence of the cork oak predominates, it is evident in the corky bark and in the nearly or quite evergreen leaves. Five seedlings of the Old Lucombe oak, as it came to be known, were raised and selected in the nursery of Lucombe and Pince—three in 1762 and two around 1830. These are mentioned below. Home-raised seedlings must have been planted in many collections; and there is also the possibility that the same cross may have occurred elsewhere and been propagated (see 'Cana Major' and 'Fulhamensis').

'CANA MAJOR'.—This was described by Loudon, who said it was named by the Hammersmith Nursery but knew nothing of its origin. According to Elwes and Henry, it resembles two of the second-generation seedlings raised by Lucombe and Pince—'Dentata' and 'Incisa'.

'CRISPA'. NEW LUCOMBE OAK.—A corky-barked nearly evergreen form; leaves brilliant dark green above, white beneath, rather smaller than in 'Lucombeana' and wrinkled at the edge; habit more compact. Raised in the Exeter Nursery by Mr Lucombe junior in 1792, from seed of the original tree. According to Loudon, 'Crispa' had a bark about 1 in. thick. In 'SUBEROSA', another of the seedlings of 1792, the bark is twice as thick; the leaves are smaller than in 'Lucombeana', ovate, with rounded or sinuated mucronate teeth. The original grew by the entrance to the Exeter Nursery until 1903, when it was cut down. Elwes, who saw it shortly before its demise, considered that the tree by the Chapel at Killerton in Devon was 'Suberosa'. The tree he had in mind still grows there and measures 87 × 15 ft (1970); it is grafted at ground-level.

'DENTATA'.—Resembling 'Lucombeana' in foliage, but with a corkier bark. Raised by Lucombe and Pince at the same time as 'Diversifolia'. Not to be confused with 'Fulhamensis', which is also, though incorrectly, known as 'Dentata'.

'DIVERSIFOLIA'.—Leaves of extraordinary shapes; usually the middle part of the blade is reduced to a narrow strip about ⅛ in. wide each side the midrib, widening at the apex like the bowl of a spoon, sometimes entire, sometimes three- or five-lobed; the base with from one to five shallow or deep, rounded or pointed, lobes. The leading types of leaves may be described as fiddle-shaped and spoon-shaped. Bark corky; habit very erect; evergreen.

This oak, although certainly of the same parentage as the Lucombe oak, is of uncertain origin. It was distributed by Smith's Nursery, Worcester, before 1877.

An oak with similar but larger and thinner leaves is 'HETEROPHYLLA', which is a seedling of 'Lucombeana' raised by Lucombe and Pince around 1830. The leaves are 3 to 4 in. long and there is the further difference that the acorn-cups are narrowed at the base, whereas in 'Diversifolia' they are hemispherical.

'FULHAMENSIS' ('Dentata') FULHAM OAK—This is a tall oak with a round head of branches more slender and graceful than those of 'Lucombeana' or the other varieties (see Loudon, *Arb. et Frut. Brit.* (1838), Vol. VII, plates 278b and c). Leaves somewhat shorter and relatively broader than in 'Lucombeana', ovate, about 3 in. long and 1½ in. wide. Scales of acorn-cup all reflexed, except for a few near the rim.

This clone descends from a tree of unknown origin that grew in the nursery of Whitley and Osborne at Fulham—now built over. Elwes and Henry suggest that it may have been propagated from an unrecorded seedling of the original Lucombe oak. But if the Fulham oak grew in the Trianon Garden, Paris, as early as 1783 (see above), this theory is scarcely plausible. The tradition in the Fulham nursery was that it was raised there from seed but, if so, the tree growing there in Loudon's time cannot have been the original plant, since it was grafted on common oak.

The Fulham oak was originally described by Watson under the name *Q. cerris* var. *dentata*, but the same name had been given earlier to a seedling of the Lucombe oak (see above). 'Fulhamensis' is in any case the established name.

'FULHAMENSIS LATIFOLIA'.—A seedling of the Fulham oak, raised and put into commerce by Osborne's nursery shortly before 1838. Leaves elliptic, rounded at the apex, shallowly toothed, about 3½ in. long, 2½ in. wide.

In parts of south-west Europe an oak is found here and there which closely resembles the Lucombe hybrids and is most probably a spontaneous hybrid of the same parentage—*Q. cerris* × *Q. suber*. In Provence it is known as *drouis* or *druino* and in Italy as *falso-sughero* (false cork oak). In the former region it has been found in the absence of *Q. cerris*, but Mme Camus has pointed out in her monograph that this species was once commoner in S. France than it is at the present time. She was in no doubt that this oak is a hybrid between the Turkey and cork oaks, and treats it under *Q.* × *hispanica*. Indeed, her account of this hybrid is largely devoted to the wild trees, the Lucombe and Fulham oaks being relegated to a separate section as 'formes de culture'.

If Mme Camus is right, the following names would fall under *Q.* × *hispanica* as synonyms: *Q. pseudosuber* Santi (1795) (not *Q. pseudosuber* Desf., 1799); *Q. fontanesii* Guss.; and, probably, *Q. crenata* Lam.

Q. 'AMBROZYANA'.—A small, almost evergreen tree raised by Count

Ambrozy in his arboretum at what is now Mlynany in Czechoslovakia, before 1909. It is near to *Q. cerris*, but with shorter leaves 3 to 3¾ in. long, ovate or oblong-ovate, with entire long-mucronate teeth, of stiff, leathery texture, persisting until spring in most years. Rehder and other authorities place it under *Q. cerris*, but it is more likely to be a hybrid of that species, possibly, as Schneider thought, with *Q. suber*, in which case it would rank as a cultivar of *Q. × hispanica*. There is a fine specimen in Mr Hillier's arboretum at Jermyns House, Ampfield, Hants, probably the only one of any size in this country.

Q. HYPOLEUCOIDES Camus
Q. hypoleuca Engelm., not Miq.

An almost evergreen tree usually 20 to 30 ft high, occasionally taller; young stems grey tomentose, slowly becoming glabrous and reddish brown. Leaves persisting for a year or slightly more, lanceolate to elliptic, tapered at the apex to an acute point, 2 to 4 in. long, up to 1 in. wide, upper surface at first covered with whitish or greyish stellate hairs, becoming glabrous, dark green and lustrous, lower surface with a persistent dense white or grey tomentum, margins usually entire, sometimes undulately toothed or even faintly spine-toothed; petiole about ½ in. long. Fruits usually solitary, sessile or shortly stalked; acorns ovoid–conic, ½ to ⅝ in. long, one-third enclosed in a thick hemispherical cup downy on the inside, covered with appressed, obtuse, downy scales.

Native of the south-western USA, where, according to Sargent, it occurs on slopes of cañons and on high ridges at 6,000 to 7,000 ft. Of recent introduction.

Q. ILEX L.   HOLM OAK   [PLATE 61

An evergreen tree of large size, attaining in favourable places a height of 70 to 90 ft, and developing in open situations a huge head of densely leafy branches as much across, the terminal portions of the branches, usually pendulous in old trees; trunk sometimes over 20 ft in girth; young shoots clothed with a close grey felt. Leaves very variable in shape, most frequently narrowly oval or ovate-lanceolate, 1½ to 3 in. long, ½ to 1 in. broad, rounded or broadly tapered at the base, pointed, sometimes entire, sometimes (especially on young trees) more or less remotely toothed. When quite young both surfaces are clothed with whitish down, which soon falls away entirely from the upper surface leaving it a dark glossy green; on the lower surface it turns grey or tawny, and persists until the fall of the leaf; stalk ⅛ to ⅝ in. long. Fruits produced one to three together on a short downy stalk, ripening the first season; acorns usually ½ to ¾ in. long in this country; cups with appressed, downy scales.

Native of the Mediterranean region; cultivated in England since the 16th century. The holm oak is in many respects the finest of all evergreen trees, apart from conifers, cultivated in the British Isles. Its foliage is most abundant, and the branches form heavy dark masses on the tree. The habit of young trees is curiously diverse, some being of distinctly pendulous habit, others rigidly pyramidal. The leaves, too, vary very much in size, shape, and toothing. On strong sucker shoots I have gathered them 5 in. long and 2¼ in. wide, but that is very unusual. This oak likes a warm, rather light soil, and is perfectly hardy in the south and west of England, and near the coast. In very severe winters it is occasionally denuded of foliage. It thrives well near the sea, and is much planted on the sea-front of some of the southern watering-places, where it is seen as a dense, flat-headed bush, stunted, but otherwise quite healthy. It has one defect as a tree in trim gardens, due to shedding the leaves of the previous year during May and June, and making an unsightly litter day after day. One way of avoiding this nuisance is to plant the ground underneath the branches with ivy, amongst which the leaves fall and automatically disappear. Grown in wood under semi-forest conditions, the holm oak makes a tall slender trunk of rather picturesque appearance, due to the corrugation of the bark. It may also, if so desired, be clipped into rounded or pyramidal shapes and kept permanently dwarf. It should only be propagated by acorns, which it produces in quantity in dry hot seasons. The seedlings should be grown on in pots and planted out when small in spring or summer, after the first or second flush of growth is completed.

Although there are no notable specimens of *Q. ilex* at Kew, the species thrives well there. The plantings on either side of the Syon Vista are largely composed of this species, intermixed with forms of *Q.* × *hispanica* and *Q.* × *turneri*. The largest in the collection, by the North Gallery, measures 70 × 13 ft (1952). Other old specimens in or near London are: Chiswick House, London, 70 × 21 ft (1952); Frogmore, Berks, 55 × 19¼ ft (1967). Farther to the south-west the following have been recorded: Melbury, Dorset, 70 × 13¼ ft (1971); Knightshayes, Devon, 82 × 20¾ ft at 3 ft (1959); Dartington Hall, Devon, 75 × 13¼ ft, with a 15-ft bole (1968); Killerton, Devon, 79 × 17¼ ft at 4 ft, and 92 × 14 ft, with a 10-ft bole (1970). But the most remarkable specimen in the British Isles grows at Westbury Court, Glos.; although only 45 ft high it is 24½ ft in girth at 3½ ft and has a spread of 96 ft from west to east and 77 ft from north to south (1973).

var. BALLOTA (Desf.) A.DC. *Q. ballota* Desf.; *Q. rotundifolia* Lam.—A variety from the southern part of the Iberian peninsula and N. Africa, sometimes treated as a distinct species. It has large, sweet acorns which are roasted as sweet chestnuts are. It is, or was, even grown in orchards in S. Spain and propagated by grafting. It is to its acorns that it owes such distinctness as it possesses. The leaves are mostly oblong, rounded at both ends, with a mucronate tip, ½ to 2 in. long, grey beneath as in the holm oak. Sometimes they are roundish. It is neither so hardy nor so handsome as the common holm oak, and does not fruit freely in this country. It has been confused with round-leaved forms of *Q. ilex*. See also *Q. gramuntia* below.

cv. 'CRISPA'.—A curious form with small orbicular leaves, averaging about ½ in. in length, the margins decurved. Very slow-growing, and a curiosity merely; known in gardens since the early 19th century.

cv. 'FORDII'.—Leaves of a peculiarly dark glossy green, narrow, 1 to 2½ in. long, ⅜ to ⅝ in. wide, the margins wavy and more or less toothed. Of narrow habit. Raised in Lucombe and Pince's Nursery at Exeter. Described in 1843.

cv. 'GENABII'.—Leaves very large and leathery, as much as 5 in. long by 2½ in. wide, coarsely toothed towards the apex. Distributed by Smith's Nursery, Worcester, before 1870.

var. GRAMUNTIA.—See note on *Q. gramuntia* below.

cv. 'LATIFOLIA'.—A large-leaved form like 'Genabii', the leaves of about the same size, but not so thick and rigid, toothed towards the apex.

cv. 'ROTUNDIFOLIA'.—Leaves broad-elliptic to almost orbicular. There is an example at Kew at the eastern end of the Syon Vista. Not to be confused with *Q. ilex* var. *ballota*, which is treated in some works under the name *Q. ilex* var. *rotundifolia*.

Q. GRAMUNTIA L., *emend.* Sm. *Q. ilex* var. *gramuntia* (L.) Loud.—The name *Q. gramuntia*, published by Linnaeus in the first edition of his *Species Plantarum* (1753) is taken from Magnol's diagnosis of an oak discovered in the woods of the Gramont estate near Montpelier, in the 17th century: 'Ilex fol. rotundioribus et spinosis e luco gramuntio' (Magnol, *Botanicum Monspeliense* (1676), p. 140). Sir James Smith, who purchased the Linnaean herbarium, in which Magnol's specimen is still preserved, noted that Linnaeus' own description was evidently drawn from another Magnol specimen which does not differ from *Q. ilex*. To remedy the confusion he provided an amended description made from a tree, apparently a cultivated one, which in his view agreed with the specimen from the Gramont woods (Rees' *Cyclopaedia*, Vol. 29 (1819), *Qu.* 30). As described by Smith, *Q. gramuntia* is a small, straggly tree with very short-stalked, almost orbicular, leaves barely 1 in. wide, edged with strong, divaricating spinous teeth, dark green above, densely woolly beneath. Fruits not described.

At one time a tree was in cultivation at Kew which resembled *Q. gramuntia* *sensu* Sir James Smith, and was certainly very distinct from normal *Q. ilex*. But that species is a polymorphic one, of which countless minor fluctuations have been described and named, and there can be little doubt that the Gramont tree was one of these. Later botanists searched for it in the woods there and found nothing but common *Q. ilex*. Of the many variants enumerated by Mme Camus the one that comes nearest to the Gramont tree was found in the *département* of Var in S.E. France, and was named var. *spinifolia* Albert. Some oaks that have been grown as *Q. gramuntia* or *Q. ilex* var. *gramuntia* are *Q. ilex* var. *ballota*.

Q. ILICIFOLIA Wangenh.　　BEAR OAK, SCRUB OAK
Q. nana (Marsh.) Sarg.; *Q. rubra* var. *nana* Marsh.; *Q. banisteri* Michx.

A small deciduous tree up to 20 or 30 ft high, more frequently a rounded shrub; young shoots hoary with short down. Leaves 2 to 4 in. long, 1 to 2½ in. wide, obovate or oval in the main, but deeply three-, five-, or seven-lobed, the apex and the lobes narrowly triangular, pointed, and terminated by a bristle-like tip, the base wedge-shaped, dark glossy green and glabrous (or soon becoming so) above, clothed beneath with a close whitish felt; stalk ¼ to ⅝ in. long, slender. Fruits solitary or in pairs; acorns ½ in. long, roundish, ripening the second season, the lower half enclosed in a short-stalked cup with thin, flattened, downy scales.

Native of the eastern United States; introduced in 1800. A neat-habited and interesting oak, distinguished among the species with similar leaf shape by its small stature and the felted undersurface of its leaves. The freedom with which it bears acorns has led to the suggestion that it may make good pheasant covert.

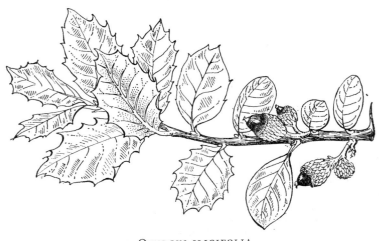

QUERCUS ILICIFOLIA

In Messrs Barbier's nursery at Orleans and at Les Barres I have seen it bearing great crops, but it does not produce them so freely in Britain. Its leaves die off scarlet and yellow in America, but are rarely highly coloured with us.

Q. IMBRICARIA Michx.   SHINGLE OAK

A deciduous tree, 50 to 60 ft high; young shoots soon glabrous, angled. Leaves narrowly oval or oblong-ovate, 4 to 7 in. long, 1 to 3 in. wide; tapered at both ends, often blunt at the apex, nearly always entire (rarely three-lobed near the apex); dark polished green and glabrous above, covered all the season beneath with a short grey starry down; stalk $\frac{1}{4}$ to $\frac{5}{8}$ in. long. Fruits solitary, seldom in pairs; acorns $\frac{1}{2}$ to $\frac{2}{3}$ in. long, nearly as broad, the shortly-stalked, shallow cup about half covered with thin flattened scales.

Native of the south-eastern and central United States; introduced by John Fraser in 1786. This handsome and striking oak is uncommon in cultivation in spite of its early introduction. It is quite distinct from all other cultivated deciduous oaks in the long, narrow, entire leaves, downy beneath.

At Kew there is a fine broad-leaved specimen of *Q. imbricaria* in the Oak collection, measuring 66 × 5½ ft (1972) and one of 70 × 4¾ ft at Syon House, London (1967). Apart from these the only large specimens recorded are two at Tortworth, Glos.; their measurements are 84 × 6½ ft and 61 × 6½ ft (1964).

In Q. INCANA Bartr. (*Q. cinerea* Michx.), which is probably not in cultivation in Britain, the leaves are entire and downy beneath as they are in *Q. imbricaria*, but are shaped like those of *Q. phellos*, and the young stems are downy, not glabrous as in *Q. imbricaria*.

Q. INFECTORIA Oliv.

A deciduous or almost evergreen shrub or small tree up to about 20 ft high; buds ovoid, slightly downy; young stems soon glabrous. Leaves leathery, oblong to oblong-elliptic, 1¾ to 2⅜ in. long, ⅝ to 2 in. wide, obtuse at the apex, glabrous on both sides except for a few scattered hairs beneath, main lateral veins in mostly five to seven pairs, intercalary veins present, margins dentate, crenate, or sinuate, the teeth usually mucronate; petiole ¼ to ½ in. long. Fruits more or less as in *Q. faginea* but scales of acorn-cups usually swollen.

Native of the N. Aegean and N.W. Anatolia, rare in cultivation. The galls produced by this oak are used in dyeing, whence the specific epithet, and also in medicine.

Q. BOISSIERI Reut. ex Boiss. *Q. infectoria* subsp. *boissieri* (Boiss.) Gurke—Allied to *Q. infectoria*, but branchlets tomentose, at least when young; leaves larger, up to almost 5 in. long in some varieties, 1¼ to sometimes almost 3 in. wide, adult leaves rarely quite glabrous beneath and often persistently tomentose; lateral veins in seven to eleven pairs, fairly straight and parallel; intercalary veins rare except on leaves of the second flush; margins of leaves dentate, sometimes merely undulate, or occasionally quite entire; petiole up to almost 1 in. long.

Q. boissieri is of wider distribution than *Q. infectoria*, from Cyprus and Anatolia to western Iran and the Caucasus, south to Palestine, and is often a quite tall, forest-forming tree. It is subdivided into varieties with a lengthy synonymy, but the species is so rare in cultivation that a detailed treatment is beyond the scope of this work. There is an example at Kew obtained from James Booth of Hamburg, planted in 1870, which measures 58 × 6¼ ft (1967).

Some very striking variants of *Q. boissieri* occur in Cyprus, judging from the specimens in the Kew Herbarium.

Q. KELLOGGII Newberry   CALIFORNIAN BLACK OAK
Q. tinctoria var. *californica* Torr.; *Q. californica* Cooper; *Q. sonomensis* A. DC.

A deciduous tree up to 80 ft or more high in the wild, the bark very dark coloured in age, smooth and grey on young trees; winter-buds downy at the tips, otherwise glabrous; young shoots downy at first. Leaves oval in the main, but cut into deep lobes after the fashion of *Q. coccinea*, the lobes (usually seven or nine) being oblong and furnished with two to four bristle-tipped teeth, the space between the lobes rounded at the base. The leaves are 3 to 6 in. long, two-thirds as wide; dark shining green and glabrous above, paler beneath, and either downy or becoming almost or quite glabrous; stalk yellowish like the midrib, at first slightly downy, 1 to 1½ in. long. Fruits solitary or a few on a stalk; acorns 1 to 1¼ in. long, downy at the top, one-third to two-thirds enclosed in a cup which has ovate-lanceolate scales, and is borne on a short, thick stalk.

Native of California and Oregon; very rare in cultivation, but a handsome tree with the red oak type of foliage. It is quite hardy, and occasionally produces fertile acorns at Kew; they take two seasons to mature, and at the end of the first are almost entirely enclosed in the cup. It is the only oak west of the Rocky

Mountains which possesses the red or black oak character of leaf. It may be said to represent there the *Q. velutina* of the eastern states, but the leaves are not covered with a flock when young as they are in that species, and the winter-buds are glabrous except for the downy tips; in *Q. velutina* they are tomentose. Both species differ from the other N. American red oaks in having the upper scales of the cups only loosely appressed.

The following specimens have been recorded: Kew, *pl.* 1873, 55 × 4¾ ft (1967); Tortworth, Glos., *pl.* 1878, 80 × 8½ ft and 67 × 5¾ ft (1964).

Q. × KEWENSIS Osborn

This remarkable evergreen hybrid oak was raised at Kew in 1914 from acorns gathered from *Q. wislizenii*, an evergreen species from California. Three plants were raised and it was soon evident from their foliage and rate of growth they were not of pure parentage. The leaves are 1½ to 3½ in. long, ¾ to 1¾ in. wide, oblong-ovate in main outline, but with the margins cut into five or six tri-angular lobes ⅛ to ½ in. deep, each lobe and the apex having a mucronate tip, the base subcordate or truncate, dull green and glabrous above, shining green with loose stellate hairs on the midrib and stalk beneath, the latter ¼ to ½ in. long. Young shoots slightly furnished at first with stellate hairs, bright brown. The tree is evergreen, its branching slender, dense and erect; the largest example in 1932 was about 28 ft high and growing vigorously. Acorns ¾ to 1 in. long, ½ in. wide, taking two years to reach maturity like those of *Q. wislizenii*.

The mother tree is standing in the Oak collection at Kew and it is fairly certain that its female flowers were fertilised by wind-blown pollen from a large Turkey oak (*Q. cerris*) growing some forty yards away. The angular lobing of the leaves of *Q. × kewensis* is very suggestive of the Turkey oak and so is its fine network of veins on the undersurface. But the dull grey-green beneath the leaves of the Turkey oak and the very characteristic thread-like stipules that surround its buds disappear in the hybrid, which is also quite evergreen.

The original tree at Kew now measures 30 × 5 ft (1972).

Q. LAEVIS Walt.

Q. catesbaei Michx.

A deciduous tree usually 20 to 30 ft, but occasionally twice as much high, with a narrow, round-topped head of more or less contorted branches; winter-buds coated towards the point with rust-coloured down; young shoots reddish, soon becoming nearly glabrous. Leaves of the typical 'red' oak shape, being obovate to triangular in main outline, wedge-shaped at the base, but very deeply cut into three, five, or seven lobes which reach to within ½ in. of the midrib; the lobes vary from roughly rectangular to roughly triangular and are themselves toothed, each having a long bristly tip, 4 to 8 in. long, rather less wide; both surfaces are shining green at maturity and quite glabrous except for tufts of reddish down in the axils of the veins; stalk ¼ to ¾ in. long. Fruits usually solitary on a very short stalk; acorns egg-shaped to roundish oval, ¾ in. long, with a ring of white scurf surrounding the conspicuous mucro at the summit; cup thin, enclosing one-third of the acorn, its scales extending down one-third of the inner surface as well as over the entire outer one.

Native of the S.E. United States; introduced in 1823, but now, and perhaps always, very rare in cultivation. Loudon, writing of the tree in 1837, did not know of any tree near London. Certainly it is far from thriving as well as most of the 'red' oaks. Plants at Kew only reached about 8 ft in height in fifteen years. According to Sargent the leaves are sometimes 12 in. long by 10 in. wide. It is distinct among the 'red' oaks by reason of its very short leaf-stalks. The leaves turn reddish brown before falling.

Q. LAMELLOSA Sm.

An evergreen tree of large size (up to 120 ft high with a trunk girthing 15 ft); scales of buds round and downy; young shoots furnished at first with tawny down. Leaves variable in size and shape, mostly narrowly oval or oblong, rounded or broadly tapered at the base, pointed, the margins usually conspicuously and sharply toothed except towards the stalk, dark glossy green above, glaucous and at first downy beneath, ordinarily 6 to 10 in. long, 2½ to 4 in. wide; stalk 1 to 1¾ in. long; ribs sunken above, very prominent beneath, in usually twenty to twenty-five pairs. Fruits stalkless, solitary to as many as four on a short stout spike, the flattish acorn 1 in. or more across, almost enclosed by the cup which is twice as wide and made up of about ten thin, concentric downy rings set one above the other.

Native of the Himalaya from Nepal to Assam, S.E. Tibet, Upper Burma, and Yunnan; discovered in Nepal by Buchanan-Hamilton in 1802. Of all the Asiatic oaks that are likely to grow outside in any part of this country this is the finest alike in the size of the leaves and that of the acorn-cups. Sir Joseph Hooker described it as the noblest of all oaks. A leaf collected by him in Sikkim about 1850 and preserved at Kew is 15 in. long and 9 in. wide; another is 18 in. long by 6 in. wide, and has thirty-five pairs of veins. It is found up to 9,000 ft altitude in Sikkim, at about the same elevation as *Rhododendron grande*, and they ought to be of similar hardiness.

The only example of any size recorded in the British Isles is one at Caerhays, Cornwall, raised from seeds collected by Forrest in 1924 on the border between Burma and Yunnan (F.24183). It measures 32 × 3½ ft at 3 ft (1966).

Q. × LEANA Nutt.

A natural hybrid between *Q. imbricaria* and *Q. velutina*, of which there are several fine trees in this country. The leaves in shape approach those of *Q. imbricaria*, being oblong and tapered at both ends; they are, however, rarely entire as in that species, but are more or less irregularly, and either deeply or shallowly lobed, 3 to 7 in. long, 1 to 2½ in. wide; dark green and glossy above, furnished with a scurfy down beneath, but not so thickly as in *Q. imbricaria*. Young shoots more or less scurfy with starry down. This oak is named in honour of T. G. Lea, who discovered it about 1830, near Cincinnati, Ohio. According to Sargent, it is scattered widely as solitary individuals over the south-eastern

United States. From the variable character of trees given this name, especially in shape and pubescence of leaf, it is probable that it represents trees of different origin, although *Q. imbricaria* is undoubtedly one parent. In 1910 I saw trees in the Arnold Arboretum with leaves 3 to 5 in. wide. It is always a vigorous, handsome oak.

The example at Kew in the Oak collection, *pl.* 1877, measures 64 × 6 ft (1964). Others on record are: Leonardslee, Sussex, 60 × 2¾ ft (1969); Highclere, Hants, 55 × 6 ft (1968); Westonbirt, Glos., 63 × 5¼ ft (1967).

Some other hybrids between a willow oak and a red oak may be mentioned here (see also *Q.* × *ludoviciana*):

Q. × HETEROPHYLLA Michx. f.—A natural hybrid between *Q. phellos* and *Q. rubra (borealis)*. It is a vigorous tree which has attained in cultivation a height of over 80 ft and a girth of around 11 ft; buds glabrous or shortly downy. Leaves mostly 3 to 6 in. long, varying, even on the same tree, from entire to lobulate or lobed, the venation irregular, soon glabrous above, glabrous also beneath except for axillary tufts; petioles ½ to 1 in. long. Fruits, probably rarely produced in this country, intermediate between those of the parents.

This oak was described in 1812 from a tree growing on John Bartram's property near Philadelphia, USA. The younger Michaux is believed to have collected acorns from it and sent them to France, so some of the cultivated trees may descend from the original type-tree. But the hybrid occurs elsewhere in the USA and may have arisen independently in cultivation also.

There is an example at Borde Hill, Sussex, which came from Rovelli's nurseries as "*Q. viridis*" and was at first identified by an American botanist as *Q* × *morehus* and later as *Q* × *heterophylla*, which seems to be correct. It measures 56 × 6 ft (1967) and has more than doubled its girth in 22 years.

Q. × RUNCINATA (A.DC.) Engelm. *Q. rubra* var. *runcinata* A.DC.—A hybrid between *Q. rubra* and *Q. imbricaria*. Leaves obovate-oblong in general outline, 4 to 6 in. long, 2 to 3 in. wide, some as deeply lobed as in *Q. rubra*, others less so, the lobes in three or four pairs, entire or sparsely toothed; undersurface with scattered rust-coloured hairs and with a few long hairs in the vein-axils; petiole up to 1 in. long. Fruits intermediate between those of the parents.

Q. × SCHOCHIANA Dieck.—A hybrid between *Q. phellos* and *Q. palustris*. It occurs occasionally in the wild, but the original form arose at Wörlitz in Germany and was distributed by Dieck at the end of the last century. Probably all the plants cultivated in Europe descend from this. Leaves in their general shape resembling those of *Q. phellos*, but with the margins undulated, or with a few small, irregularly spaced lobes. There is an example in the Winkworth Arboretum measuring 30 × 2½ ft (1969).

Q. LEUCOTRICHOPHORA Camus
Q. incana Roxb. (1814), not Bartr. (1791)

An evergreen tree up to 80 ft high, whose bark peels off the trunk in large flakes; young shoots clothed with close grey felt. Leaves oblong-lanceolate or narrowly oval, wedge-shaped at the base, tapered to a fine slender point; margins conspicuously toothed except towards the base, 2½ to 6 in. long, 1 to 2 in. wide, upper surface dark green soon becoming glabrous, lower one clothed with a pure white close felt which persists until the leaf falls; the veins are prominent beneath and number eight to twelve each side the midrib; stalk ⅓ to ⅝ in. long. Fruits solitary, or sometimes two or three together on a very short, felted stalk; acorns egg-shaped to conical, 1 in. long; acorn-cups ½ in. wide, enclosing about half the acorn, with appressed, whitish scales. The fruits ripen in their second season.

Native of the Himalaya, up to elevations of 8,000 ft. The oak is interesting as the almost inseparable companion in the wild of *Rhododendron arboreum*, and it was no doubt introduced to this country about the same time—1815. It just misses being hardy at Kew. During a series of mild winters it will grow 7 or 8 ft high, but a fairly hard winter will cut it back to ground-level and a really hard one kill it outright. It is remarkable that so distinct and beautiful a tree—for the felt beneath the leaves is perhaps the whitest seen in cultivated oaks—should have been so long neglected in the gardens of the south and west. The whiteness of the leaves as seen from the ground and the flaking bark are very noticeable.

There is a small plant of this species at Kew on the Temperate House Terrace. The only open-ground specimen recorded is one of 46 × 3¼ ft at Trewithen in Cornwall (1971).

Q. LANATA Sm. *Q. lanuginosa* D. Don, not Lam.—This species is closely allied to *Q. leucotrichophora*, but the felt on the undersides of the leaves is rusty or fawn-coloured and, according to Camus, the fruits ripen in the first year. Native of the Himalaya, S. China, and Indonesia; introduced about 1818 but probably not now in cultivation.

Q. LODICOSA Warb.—An evergreen tree attaining a height of 70 ft in the wild, belonging to the same group as *Q. leucotrichophora* and, as in that species, the leaves are covered beneath with a dense white felt. The main distinction from *Q. leucotrichophora* lies in the fruits; the cup is very thick and ¾ to almost 1 in. wide and the correspondingly large acorns, indented at the apex. This species was described in 1933 from a specimen collected by Kingdon Ward in the Tsangpo Gorge, S.E. Tibet. It was introduced from N.E. Upper Burma in 1924 by Forrest under F.25405; a tree at Caerhays, Cornwall, raised from these seeds, measures 28 × 1½ ft (1966).

Q. LIBANI Olivier   LEBANON OAK

A deciduous tree of elegant growth not apparently attaining to a great size; young shoots clothed at first with minute down. Leaves oblong-lanceolate, rounded at the base, tapered to a fine point, 2 to 4 in. long, ½ to 1 in. wide, dark glossy green above, paler green beneath; stalk about ½ to ¾ in. long. On our cultivated trees the leaves soon become glabrous on both surfaces except for a few hairs on the midrib and veins, but on wild specimens the undersurface is frequently thickly covered with down. Springing from each side the midrib at an angle of 45°, and running out to the margin, where each forms the bristle-like point to a triangular tooth, are nine to twelve parallel veins. Fruits solitary or in pairs on a thick woody stalk ½ in. or more long, on which they ripen the second year; acorns about 1 in. long on cultivated trees and more than half enclosed in a large cup; lower scales ovate, the upper ones smaller and narrower.

Native of the mountains of Syria, including Mt Lebanon, and of Asia Minor and Kurdistan; introduced to Paris about 1855. Although the branches are slender and elegant they are scarcely pendulous on young trees. Acorns are frequently produced, but they do not become so large as those of some native trees. Among cultivated oaks this is most nearly allied to *Q. trojana* (*macedonica*), but in that species the crown is denser; the leaves thicker, with mucronate but not bristle-tipped teeth, and scarcely stalked; and the female flowers and the fruits are sessile (in *Q. libani* the female flowers are borne on a stout peduncle which becomes woody as the fruits ripen). In *Q. acutissima* the leaves are much larger and bright green.

QUERCUS LIBANI

Q. libani is not as common in gardens as it deserves to be. At Kew there are two specimens in the Oak collection: *pl.* 1883, 41 × 2¾ ft (1965), and *pl.* 1899, 48 × 5¼ ft (1967). Others recorded recently are: Wakehurst Place, Sussex, 45 × 4 ft (1965); National Pinetum, Bedgebury, *pl.* 1930, 50 × 3¼ ft (1971);

Tortworth, Glos., *pl.* 1906, 68 × 6½ ft (1964); Ryston, Norfolk, *pl.* 1909, 32 × 3¼ ft (1969); Edinburgh Botanic Garden, *pl.* 1903, 36 × 2½ ft (1970).

Q. LOBATA Née   VALLEY OAK
Q. hindsii Benth.

A deciduous tree of the largest size, often over 100 ft high in the wild, the trunk occasionally as much as 10 ft in diameter, and forming a broad head of branches; young shoots downy. Leaves oval or obovate, tapered at the base, rounded or blunt at the apex, with four or five rounded lobes at each side, 1½ to 3 in. long, ⅝ to 1¾ in. wide, dark green and glabrous or nearly so above; pale, dull and downy beneath, especially on the midrib; margin edged with fine hairs; stalk ⅛ to ½ in long, downy. Fruits scarcely stalked; acorns slenderly conical, pointed, 1¼ to 2 in. long, mostly solitary, about one-fourth enclosed in the cup.

Native of W. California; introduced to Kew by Bolander in 1874, but possibly in cultivation before. A stately tree in its own country, it has little to recommend it in this, being of exceedingly slow growth and not striking in foliage. It reaches its greatest size on deep moist loam, and in some of the Californian valleys not infrequently 100 to 150 ft high, with trunks 8 to 10 ft through. Its timber is of poor quality, but many fine trees are preserved in the fields of the West for the sake of the shade their wide-spreading branches afford. A tree at Kew near the Ash collection, *pl.* 1874, measures 67 × 7¾ ft (1967) with a deeply furrowed bark.

Q. × LUDOVICIANA Sarg.
Q. × *subfalcata* Trelease; *Q.* × *ludoviciana* var. *subfalcata* (Trelease) Rehd.

A medium-sized tree; young shoots scurfy at first; buds light brown, the scales slightly ciliate. Leaves copper-tinted when young, in general outline obovate to elliptic, mostly with a well-developed lobe on either side in the upper half, other leaves with more numerous, unequal lobes; terminal lobe entire or obscurely lobulate, usually acute and sometimes falcate, lateral lobes acute or obtuse, mostly bristle-tipped, base of blade cuneate, usually asymmetric, overall size of lobed leaves 4½ to 7 in. long, 2 to 3¾ in. wide; terminal leaf on some shoots narrow-elliptic, almost entire and, e.g., 3½ in. long, ⅝ in. wide; blade dark glossy green, glabrous above, underside paler, dull green, slightly scurfy and with abundant loose tawny down on each side the midrib and main laterals; petioles ¼ to ⅜ in. long. Flowers and fruits not seen.

A hybrid between *Q. falcata* var. *pagodifolia* and *Q. phellos*, described by Professor Sargent in 1913 from a tree found in St Landry parish, Louisiana. The description given above is made from a tree at Borde Hill in Sussex, identified as being this hybrid by Dr Rehder of the Arnold Arboretum in 1932. It came from Rovelli's nursery, Pallanza, Italy, but under what name is not recorded. It agrees moderately well with the dried specimen from the type-tree sent by Prof. Sargent to Kew, except that in this specimen there are numerous 'phellos-type' leaves at the end of the shoot, which are up to 7 in. long and only ¾ to 1¼ in. wide, lobed, undulate or entire. On the Borde Hill tree such leaves are sparsely produced and on the tree at Kew in the Oak collection, which is otherwise similar, they have not been noticed.

_Q._ × _ludoviciana_, as seen in cultivation, is one of the most ornamental of the oaks, with healthy, glossy foliage richly tinted when it unfolds and remaining on the tree without withering until late in the autumn. The example at Kew in the Oak collection by the Thames, _pl._ 1936, measures 42 × 2¾ ft (1967).

In _Q._ × _ludoviciana_ 'MICROCARPA' all the leaves are elongate, up to 4½ in. long and 1 in. wide, some entire and others with up to five rather sharp lobulate teeth on each side, underside scurfy, with denser hair on the midrib. It was sold by Booth of Hamburg, before 1880, apparently as "_Q. rubra_" or "_Q. phellos microcarpa_". It is not known to be in cultivation in this country.

The hybrid named _Q._ × _subfalcata_ by Trelease is thought to be _Q. phellos_ crossed with typical _Q. falcata_. It appears to be very similar to typical _Q._ × _ludoviciana_.

Q. MACRANTHERA Fisch. & Mey.

A deciduous tree up to 60 ft high, with very stout young shoots and leaf-stalks covered with a thick, soft, greyish down that becomes dark, and persists through the second season; buds clothed with slender, hairy stipules ¾ in. long. Leaves broadly obovate, tapered at the base, the margin conspicuously cut into seven to eleven rounded lobes down either side, each lobe ½ to 1 in. deep, sometimes with one to three teeth on its lower side. The largest leaves are 6 in. long and 4 in. wide, the smallest half as large, green, with minute hairs above, pale beneath, and clothed with soft down; stalk ½ to ⅝ in. long. Fruits scarcely stalked; acorns about 1 in. long, the lower half enclosed by a cup which is covered outside with erect, lanceolate, downy scales.

Native of the Caucasus and Transcaucasus, and of N. Iran (in the forest region south of the Caspian). It is one of the most distinct of the oaks of western Eurasia, with large leaves equalling _Q. frainetto_ and _Q. canariensis_ in that respect, but distinct from them in the densely downy shoots and undersurface of the leaves. A further distinction is that in neither of those species do the buds bear persistent stipules. _Q. macranthera_ is quite hardy and occasionally produces fertile acorns in this country.

The date of introduction was given in previous editions as 1895, this being the year in which a plant was received at Kew from Späth's nursery, Berlin. But William Barron and Son listed it in their catalogue for 1874, with no mention of its being a novelty, and the trees at Westonbirt are certainly older than any at Kew, and are believed to have been planted around 1878. The measurements of these are: in Mitchell Drive 80 × 6¾ ft (1972), in Broad Drive 60 × 7 ft (1967). Some others recorded recently are: Kew, _pl._ 1895, 47 × 3¼ ft (1965) and _pl._ 1908, 62 × 4¼ ft (1972), both in the Oak collection; Caerhays, Cornwall, 52 × 4¾ ft (1971); East Bergholt Place, Suffolk, 50 × 3¾ ft (1972); Jephson Park, Leamington, 46 × 4 ft (1971); Edinburgh Botanic Garden, three specimens of almost equal size, the largest 52 × 6 ft (1970).

Q. MACROCARPA Michx. BURR OAK

A deciduous tree 80 to 170 ft high in the wild; bark with prominent, fairly firm ridges; young shoots and buds downy. Leaves obovate, 4 to 10 in. (sometimes 1 ft) long, about half as wide, wedge-shaped at the base, five- or seven-lobed, the terminal lobe often large (consisting of about half the leaf), ovate and itself wavy-lobed, the lower lobes often reach almost to the midrib, dark green, glabrous and glossy above, covered beneath with a pale, dull, minute felt; stalk up to 1¼ in. long, downy. Acorn ¾ to 1½ in. long, usually solitary, about half enclosed in a cup distinguished by having the scales near the rim almost thread-like and forming a fringe, on account of which this tree is often known as the 'mossy-cup oak'.

Native of eastern N. America; introduced in 1811. It is very similar to *Q. bicolor*, but is distinguished by the more deeply lobed leaves, and especially by the acorn cup. Like all the white oaks of America, it is not very happy in our climate, but there are a few healthy trees at Kew, the largest of which, near the Ash collection, measures 67 × 6¾ ft (1967). In the Oak collection there are two specimens: *pl.* 1871, 52 × 5¾ ft; *pl.* 1874, 56 × 4½ ft (1972).

Q. LYRATA Walt.—This is sometimes though rarely seen in gardens, and is not suited to our climate. It is allied to *Q. macrocarpa*, but its acorn is distinguished by being almost or entirely enclosed in the cup. The leaves are obovate, deeply five- to nine-lobed, the largest 7 to 9 in. long, nearly half as wide, dark green and glabrous above, pale and downy beneath; stalk up to ¾ in. long. Native of the southern United States, where it is occasionally 100 ft high; introduced in 1786.

It is known as the 'overcup oak'.

Q. MACROLEPIS Kotschy

Q. aegilops subsp. *macrolepis* (Kotschy) Camus; *Q. aegilops* var. *macrolepis* (Kotschy) Boiss.; *Q. graeca* Kotschy

A small semi-deciduous tree usually less than 50 ft high in the wild, but taller in damp, sheltered localities, with a dark, fissured bark; buds ovoid, with long, linear stipules; young stems velvety. Leaves shed in late autumn or early spring, oval to oblong, acute at the apex, rounded, truncate or slightly cordate at the base, 2½ to 3 in. long, 1¼ to 1¾ in. wide (but sometimes almost 5 in. long and up to 4 in. wide), hairy on both sides when young, upper surface eventually glabrous to the eye, lower surface covered with a persistent indumentum of short hairs, margins edged with mostly five to seven pairs of large, triangular, acute, bristle-tipped teeth, but sometimes almost entire (in which case the main veins still run out to bristles); petiole ¼ to 1 in. long. Fruits almost solitary, ripening the second year; cup hemispheric, up to 2 in. wide including the scales, which are flexible, hairy on both sides, fairly thin, the lower ones short, appressed, those of the middle ranks strap-shaped or lanceolate, up to ⅝ in. long and ¼ in. wide, spreading and often slightly reflexed, the uppermost scales longer and narrower, those at the rim usually erect and pressed against the acorn, which is ellipsoid to ovoid, up to 1¾ in. long, half or more enclosed in the cup.

Native of Greece, Albania, and Turkey, where it occurs both in the European part and in western, central, and southern Anatolia; cultivated in Italy and perhaps native in the south-east, where there is, or was, a fine stand at Tricase, south of Otranto; introduced to Britain in the 18th century. The remarkable feature of this oak is the size of the acorn-cups and the length of the scales. Because of their high content of tannin they were at one time an important article of commerce.

var. VALLONEA (Kotschy) Zohary *Q. vallonea* Kotschy; *Q. aegilops* subsp. *vallonea* (Kotschy) Camus—This variety, which occurs with the type in W. Anatolia, differs in the thicker, woody, angular and more spreading scales of the cup, and in this respect resembles some forms of *Q. ithaburensis*. The cups are as rich in tannin as those of typical *Q. macrolepis*.

Q. macrolepis is uncommon in cultivation and rarely develops mature fruits. The following examples have been recorded (probably belonging to the typical variety): Kew, 40 × 4¼ ft (1972); Syon, London, 47 × 5 ft (1966); Westonbirt, Glos., 40 × 2¾ ft (1967); Tortworth, Glos., *pl.* 1846, 50 × 5 ft (1964).

Q. ITHABURENSIS Decne. *Q. aegilops* subsp. *ithaburensis* (Decne.) Eig; *Q. aegilops* var. *ithaburensis* (Decne.) Boiss.; *Q. pyrami* Kotschy; *Q. aegilops* subsp. *pyrami* (Kotschy) Camus; *Q. aegilops* var. *pyrami* (Kotschy) Boiss.—This ally of *Q. macrolepis* is a native of S.E. Anatolia, Syria, and Palestine, and was described in 1835 from a specimen collected on Mt Tabor. It is very variable in the size and shape of the cups and acorns, and in the cup-scales, which are thick and woody (hence differing from those of typical *Q. macrolepis*), but vary much in shape and posture. In one specimen in the Kew Herbarium they are thread-like —this probably represents var. DOLICHOLEPIS Zohary. The leaves are mostly 2 to 3 in. long, ovate to lanceolate, rather more shallowly toothed than in *Q. macrolepis*.

Q. pyrami, here included in *Q. ithaburensis*, was described by Kotschy from the plain of the river Ceyhan (*anc.* Pyramus) in Cilicia (S.E. Anatolia). One of its differential characters was said to be that the leaves are often fiddle-shaped from a deep indentation below the middle. But according to Zohary, this peculiarity is met with occasionally in other oaks of the Aegilops group. It is apparently commonest on shoots of the second flush and perhaps also on young, vigorous plants. At any rate, two trees at Kew under the label *Q. aegilops* var. *pyrami* have not been observed to produce such leaves recently, except on branch-sprouts. They measure 59 × 5¼ ft and 47 × 4½ ft (1971).

Q. AEGILOPS L.—Linnaeus' account of this species is so confused that most botanists have rejected the name as of uncertain application, though there can be little doubt that it was intended for *Q. macrolepis* or one of its allies. Mme Camus adopts the name and under it distinguishes seven subspecies, but she did not venture to suggest which of these was *Q. aegilops sens. strict.*

Q. MARILANDICA Muenchh.   BLACK JACK OAK

Q. nigra Wangenh., not L.; *Q. cuneata* Wangenh.

A deciduous tree 20 to 40 ft high, forming a low, spreading head of rugged branches; bark divided into small, squarish blocks; young shoots covered with scurfy stellate down, becoming shining grey the second year. Leaves broadly obovate, tapered to a narrow, rounded or wedge-shaped base, broad and three-lobed at the apex, the lobes sometimes shallow and little more than undulations, sometimes broad, deep oblong, each with subsidiary lobes or teeth terminated by a bristle. The leaves vary from 2 to 7 in. long, and are nearly or quite as much wide, upper surface dark polished green, at first covered with stellate scurf; lower surface paler, with conspicuous lines and tufts of down along the midrib and veins; stalk ¼ to ½ in. long. Fruits solitary or in pairs on a short, thick, downy stalk; cup one-third to two-thirds the length of the acorn, which is about ¾ in. long.

Native of the eastern United States; introduced early in the 18th century. Occasionally its leaves turn rich red in autumn, but more often brown. It is a slow-growing and comparatively dwarf oak, but its foliage is striking. The three-lobed form of leaf in *Q. falcata* is rather like the above, but has a slender stalk twice or more than twice as long.

Q. MONGOLICA Fisch.

This species is mainly represented in cultivation by the following variety:

var. GROSSESERRATA (Bl.) Rehd. & Wils. *Q. grosseserrata* Bl.; *Q. crispula* Bl.—A large deciduous tree 80 to 100 ft high; young shoots irregularly furnished with pale warts, but not downy. Leaves obovate, 4 to 9 in. long, 2½ to 5½ in. wide, tapered to a pair of auricles at the base, pointed at the apex, ten to fifteen teeth on each margin, the largest from ½ to ¾ in. deep, triangular, and again toothed, dark, rather glossy green above, pale beneath, glabrous except on the midrib and veins, which are more or less downy on both surfaces; stalk ⅛ to ⅓ in. long, glabrous. Fruits one to three on a short stalk; acorn about one-third enclosed in the hemispherical cup.

Native of Japan, Sakhalin, and the southern Kuriles; introduced to Kew in 1893 by means of seeds collected by Prof. Sargent during his visit to Japan in the autumn of that year. Although it appears to be quite hardy in this country, this oak does not thrive so well with us as it does in the eastern United States. In the suburbs of Boston, Mass., and in the Arnold Arboretum trees of the same generation as those at Kew are already remarkably striking for their size, rude vigour, and splendid foliage. Even on young trees in this country I have measured leaves 12 in. by 7 in., but on adult trees no doubt they are much smaller.

One of the trees at Kew raised from the seeds collected by Prof. Sargent has developed into a splendid specimen measuring 61 × 6¾ ft (1972).

Q. mongolica, in its typical state, may not be in cultivation in Britain. It occurs in Japan, Sakhalin, and the S. Kuriles but has its main distribution on the mainland of N.E. Asia; despite the specific epithet it scarcely extends into Mongolia, however. From the above variety it differs in its leaves, with more rounded, entire lobes, and in the very thick, woody scales of the fruit-cups.

Q. MYRSINIFOLIA Blume

Q. vibrayeana Franch. & Sav.; *Q. bambusifolia* Fort., not Hance;
Cyclobalanopsis myrsinifolia (Bl.) Oerst.

An evergreen tree 30 to 50 ft in the wild, or even higher, but a bush or
shrubby tree in cultivation; young shoots glabrous, warted the second year.
Leaves lanceolate, broadly tapered or rounded at the base, and with long,
slender points, the upper half toothed, 2½ to 4 in. long, ⅝ to 1¼ in. wide, pale
shining green above, somewhat glaucous beneath, glabrous on both surfaces;
stalk ½ in. long. When young the leaves are of a rich purplish red, very striking
against the green of the older foliage. The female flowers are produced on long
slender peduncles, the upper part of which falls away, the persistent lower part
up to 2 in. long, bearing two to four fruits ripening the first season; acorn
narrow-ovoid, ¾ to 1 in. long, set in shallow hemispherical cup, the scale of
which are arranged in seven to nine concentric rings.

Native of S. China, Laos, and Japan; introduced from China by Fortune in
1854. As a garden oak, it is chiefly notable for the colour of its young foliage
and graceful, narrow leaves. With *Q. acuta* it is the hardiest member of the
subgenus *Cyclobalanopsis*. There are examples 35 to almost 40 ft in height and
1¾ to 2¼ ft in girth at Syon House, London; Tittenhurst, Berks; Leonardslee,
Sussex; and Caerhays, Cornwall (1967–72).

Q. NIGRA L.   WATER OAK

Q. aquatica Walt.

A deciduous tree up to 80 ft high in the wild; young shoots glabrous. Leaves
often crowded at the end of short twigs, extremely variable in shape, mostly
obovate, tapered at the base and rounded or bluntish at the apex; some, however, are narrow-oblong, like those of *Q. phellos*, and entire; others have several
shallow or deep lobes towards the apex; they vary from 1½ to 4 in. long, and
from ½ to 2 in. wide, and are of a pale green and glabrous on both surfaces
except for tufts of down in the vein-axils beneath; stalk $\frac{1}{10}$ to ¼ in. long. Fruits
usually solitary; acorn ½ in. broad and long, one-third enclosed in a broad,
shallow, short-stalked cup with appressed scales.

Native of the southern United States; in cultivation 1723. It retains its leaves
quite fresh until about the New Year. Its affinities are with *Q. phellos*, which,
however, never has the broad, obovate or lobed leaves. In the southern United
States it is popular as a shade tree for streets, etc. This oak must not be confounded with the 'Black Jack oak'—the *Q. nigra* of Wangenheim—a very
different tree. (See *Q. marilandica*.)

There is a fine specimen of *Q. nigra* at Kew by the Isleworth Gate measuring
58 × 6¼ ft (1968). A tree in the Oak collection, *pl.* 1874, is 50 × 5¾ ft (1972).
The only other large specimen recorded grows at Pylewell Park, Hants; it
measures 52 × 8¾ ft at 5½ ft (1968).

Q. OXYODON Miq.

Q. lineata var. *oxyodon* (Miq.) Wenzig; *Cyclobalanopsis oxyodon* (Miq.) Oerst.

A low-growing evergreen tree up to 30 ft high, with wide-spreading branches forming a flattened crown; young shoots soon becoming glabrous. Leaves hard and leathery, narrowly oblong, long and slenderly pointed, rounded to tapered at the base, conspicuously toothed, teeth incurved, 3 to 8 in. long, 1 to 3 in. wide, dark glossy green and glabrous above; glaucous and covered with close felt beneath; midrib yellowish beneath and, like the twelve to twenty pairs of veins, conspicuously raised on the undersurface. Fruits (which ripen in one year) not stalked but clustered on a spike 1 to 1½ in. long near the end of the shoot; acorns are about ½ in. wide, the cup basin-shaped, concentrically ringed.

Q. oxyodon was described from a specimen collected in the Khasia Hills of Assam (N.E. India). It occurs also in the E. Himalaya, Upper Burma, and W. China and was introduced by Wilson in 1900 from W. Hupeh while collecting for Messrs Veitch. Coming from low altitudes it is unlikely to be hardy outside the milder counties, and the only example on record is at Caerhays, Cornwall. This measures 30 × 1¾ ft (1965).

Q. PALUSTRIS Muenchh.   PIN OAK

A deciduous tree 70 to 100 ft high, forming a dense head of slender branches pendulous at the ends; bark broken into flat, scaly ridges; young shoots not downy, warted; winter-buds about ⅛ in. long. Leaves 3 to 6 in. long, nearly as wide, obovate, tapered or cut nearly straight across at the base, five- or seven-lobed, the lobes reaching three-quarters of the way to the midrib, oblong or triangular, unequally toothed near the apex, both surfaces are glossy green and glabrous, except that, in the vein-axils beneath, there are large conspicuous tufts of greyish down; stalk very slender, up to 2 in. long. Acorn about ½ in. long and broad, flattish at the base, where it is enclosed by a shallow saucer-shaped cup.

Native of the eastern United States from New England to northern N. Carolina, westward to western Kansas and Oklahoma; introduced to England in 1800. It occasionally bears crops of acorns, which require two seasons to mature. It is one of the very best growers among American oaks cultivated in this country, and is very elegant in its slender branches, especially whilst young or of the middle size. The leaves often turn deep scarlet in autumn, but I do not think it is so effective and reliable in this respect as *Q. coccinea*; on the dry soil at Kew it is, at any rate, much inferior. It is frequently confused with *Q. coccinea*, but *Q. palustris* is distinguished by its more densely branched graceful head, by the invariable and conspicuous tufts of down beneath the leaf, by the shallower acorn-cup, and by the glabrous winter-buds. From *Q. rubra* it differs in the more deeply divided leaves, polished green on both sides.

The largest of the following specimens are well up to the average size of mature wild trees: Kew, near the Victoria Gate, 84 × 8½ ft (1963), Oak collection, 72 × 7¾ ft (1972); Syon Park, London, 78 × 8 ft (1967); Marble Hill, Twickenham, London, 80 × 8½ ft (1968); Mill Hill School, London, 75 × 9½ ft

QUERCUS PALUSTRIS

(1964); Godinton Park, Kent, two very fine trees measuring 62 × 7¾ ft and 64 × 9 ft (1965); Canford, Dorset, a tree dead at the top, 80 × 8 ft in 1906, now 68 × 12½ ft (1965).

Q. palustris is a quick-growing tree in a deep, moist, light soil, but not long-lived.

Q. × RICHTERI Baenitz—A hybrid between *Q. palustris* and *Q. rubra*, described from cultivated trees but also reported from the wild. Mme Camus, who saw only foliage specimens, considered it to be indistinguishable from *Q. coccinea* in its leaves. But the acorn-cup is shallower than in that species.

Q. ELLIPSOIDALIS E. J. Hill *Q. coccinea* var. *microcarpa* Vasey NORTHERN PIN OAK.—Although classified by botanists with *Q. coccinea* this species resembles *Q. palustris* in habit and, as in both these species, the leaves are glabrous beneath except for axillary tufts. From *Q. coccinea* it differs in the smaller buds (only ⅛ in. long) and in having almost sessile fruits with the cups gradually tapered at the base. From *Q. palustris* it differs in the deeper cup of the fruit, which encloses one-third to one-half of the acorn. It occurs west and south of the Great Lakes, in dry soil. There is a specimen in the Edinburgh Botanic Garden, measuring 40 × 2¾ ft (1967).

Q. PETRAEA (Mattuschka) Lieblein   DURMAST OAK, SESSILE OAK

Q. robur Spielart *Q. petraea* Mattuschka; *Q. sessiliflora* Salisb.; *Q. sessilis* Ehrh.

A deciduous tree attaining the same size as the common oak, *Q. robur*, and not differing in its bark; it differs in its habit, having straighter branches and a trunk that usually penetrates further into the crown than is the case with the common oak; buds usually rather more elongated and acute at the apex. Leaves broadest at or only slightly above the middle, hence not so markedly obovate or oblanceolate as in *Q. robur* and less tapered to the base, which is cuneate or cordate and lacks the auricles characteristic of the common oak; the texture is usually somewhat firmer, the upper surface rather more glossy, and the underside has persistent hairs on the midrib and main veins and sometimes scattered stellate hairs on the surface of the blade; intercalary veins, i.e., veins running out to the sinuses between the lobes, are much less frequent than in *Q. robur*, and the lobing is more regular; the stalk, very short in the common oak, is $\frac{3}{8}$ to $1\frac{1}{4}$ in. long in the durmast oak. Female flowers with almost sessile stigmas (styles usually well developed in *Q. robur*). The common name 'sessile oak' refers to the fruits, which are borne directly on the twig and not on a long slender peduncle as in *Q. robur*. The scales of the acorn-cup are rather more numerous and more closely imbricated than in *Q. robur*. [PLATE 60

The general distribution of *Q. petraea* is similar to that of *Q. robur*, with the notable difference that it does not extend so far to the east on the Continent. In the British Isles the durmast oak avoids the heavy clay soils of the Weald and the Midland Plain but is the commoner species on siliceous soils in the north and west, and is also to be found on light, non-calcareous soils in southern England, often in association with the common oak.

The fine tree at Whitfield, Herefordshire, mentioned in previous editions, still exists and measures 135 × 14¼ ft (1963). Others measured recently are: Oakley Park, Shrops., 111 × 22¼ ft and 85 × 23¼ ft (1971); Nettlecombe, Som., 112 × 21¾ ft and 95 × 23 ft (1959); Shobdon, Heref., about 90 × 30 ft (1973); Croft Castle, Heref., 50 × 26½ ft (1960); Knowle Park, Kent, 130 × 17½ ft (1969).

On the Continent, the durmast oak comes into leaf and flowers up to two weeks later than the common oak and hybrids between them are therefore by no means common. It is said, however, that in the British Isles there is less difference in flowering time and that hybrids are commoner in consequence. However, both species are variable and minor deviations from the norm are sometimes wrongly taken to be the result of hybridity. For example, the fruits in the durmast oak are sometimes borne on peduncles, but in such cases the peduncle is thick at the base, where it resembles a normal twig. True hybrids, for which the correct name is Q. × ROSACEA Bechstein, would show such combinations as auricled leaves, downy beneath, on stalks of intermediate length; or pedunculate acorns, leaves almost glabrous beneath but not auriculate, etc.

The durmast oak has not been so prolific of varieties as *Q. robur*, but most of the following are or have been in cultivation at Kew:

cv. 'AFGHANISTANENSIS'.—Leaves oval or obovate, with shallower lobes than the type. Fruits with a distinct stalk as much as ½ in. long. It was distributed by Booth's Flottbeck Nurseries, Hamburg, around the middle of the last century. It is unlikely to have come from Afghanistan, as they claimed. There are three examples at Kew, the largest 85 × 7¾ ft (1971).

cv. 'COCHLEATA'.—Leaves decurved at the margin, so that the centre is humped or hooded. The tree at Kew, planted in 1871, has mostly reverted.

cv. 'COLUMNA'.—Of columnar habit, with rather narrow and elongated, sparsely and irregularly lobed leaves. Put into commerce by Messrs Hesse of Weener, Hanover, shortly before the second world war.

cv. 'FALKENBERGENSIS'.—According to the original description this had short, serrated leaves resembling those of *Q. cerris*. They are very downy beneath. It was discovered near Falkenberg near Hamburg and was put into commerce by Booth's Flottbeck Nurseries in 1837.

cv. 'GIESLERI'.—Leaves long and narrow, entire or unequally lobed. Put into commerce by Späth towards the end of the last century.

cv. 'INSECATA'.—Leaves very long and narrow, with irregular, slender, forward-pointing lobes, some leaves reduced almost to threads. Leaves on the Lammas growths more or less normal. It was originally named *Q. sessiliflora laciniata*, a name used much earlier by Lamarck and de Candolle for a wild form with deeply lobed leaves.

f. MESPILIFOLIA (Wallr.) Rehd.—Leaves lanceolate to narrowly oblong, up to 5 in. long, 1 in. wide, tapered at both ends, sinuately lobed to almost entire. It occurs occasionally in the wild, and was described by Wallroth, as *Q. robur* var. *mespilifolia* from a tree found in the Harzgebirge. The garden variety 'LOUETTEI' is of this nature, but is of rather pendulous habit. In the very similar f. SUBLOBATA (Kit.) Schneid., the leaves are more lobed, but still unusually long and narrow. Here belongs the garden variety 'GELTOWIENSIS', distributed by the Royal Nurseries at Geltow near Potsdam.

There are two specimens of f. *mespilifolia* at Kew, the larger, on Palace Lawn, measuring 72 × 7 ft (1970).

cv. 'MUSCAVIENSIS'.—Leaves of first growth often nearly or quite entire, those of the second or July growth nearer the type and lobed.

cv. 'PENDULA'.—Branches very pendulous, forming an umbrella-shaped crown. Raised in France around 1867 in the garden of the Military Hospital, Vincennes, and propagated by grafting.

cv. 'RUBICUNDA'.—Young leaves reddish purple. The same or a similar variety is known as 'Purpurea'.

Q. DALECHAMPII Ten. *Q. lanuginosa* subsp. *dalechampii* (Ten.) Camus; *Q. robur* subsp. *sessiliflora* var. *tenorei* A. DC.—A poorly defined species which has been very variously interpreted by botanists. It appears to be intermediate between *Q. petraea* and *Q. pubescens*, and is possibly the result of past hybridisation between them. According to Mme Camus it is confined to Italy (mainly the south). Dr Schwarz, who gives a description greatly at variance with hers, attributes to it a wider range.

Q. IBERICA Bieb.—Very closely allied to *Q. petraea*. Leaves with up to eight or even ten pairs of lobes, usually with rather large axillary tufts of hairs beneath. Fruits on a short peduncle. Native of Transcaucasia, said to be common around Batum.

Q. MAS Thore—This is recognised as a distinct species by Dr Schwarz, but Mme Camus doubted whether it was really any more than a local variant possibly meriting the rank of subspecies. The leaves are rather larger than in

Q. petraea, with up to ten pairs of narrowish, forward-pointing lobes; the fruit peduncles are silky hairy. Pyrenees and N. Spain.

Q. PHELLOS L. WILLOW OAK

A deciduous tree from 70 to 100 ft high, forming a rounded or columnar head of branches; bark glabrous, grey; young shoots and leaves at first downy, then glabrous. Leaves pale green, thin, oblong-lanceolate, tapered at the base, mostly pointed at the apex, entire, or slightly wavy on each margin; 2 to 5½ in. long, ⅓ to 1 in. wide; stalk ⅛ to ¼ in. long, minutely downy or glabrous. Acorns (rarely seen on introduced trees) scarcely bigger than a large red currant, and produced in a shallow, saucer-shaped cup.

Native of the Atlantic states of the USA to northern Florida, thence westward through the lower Mississippi valley to eastern Texas; introduced early in the 18th century. It is quite distinct from all the other cultivated deciduous oaks in its glabrous, narrow, normally untoothed leaves. In the young state it is a very elegant tree. Although not common in Britain, it thrives here and reaches a large size, as the following measurements show: Kew, near the Pagoda, a forked tree 70 × 12 ft at 3 ft (1967); in the Oak collection, 64 × 7¼ ft (1972) and *pl.* 1901, 77 × 7 ft, grafted at ground-level (1972); Knap Hill Nursery, Surrey, 60 × 11½ ft (1961); Cobham Hall, Kent, 82 × 12¼ ft (1965); Highnam Court, Glos., 52 × 8 ft at 4 ft (1970); Bicton, Devon, 57 × 6¾ ft at 4 ft (1968); Glendurgan, Cornwall, 40 × 5¾ ft (1965).

Q. LAURIFOLIA Michx. *Q. rhombica* Sarg.; *Q. obtusa* (Willd.) Ashe; *Q. hybrida* Ashe; *Q. hemisphaerica* Bartr. ex Willd.—Leaves glabrous beneath except for axillary tufts, as in *Q. phellos*, some of them shaped more or less as in that species, others asymmetrically widened on one side in the upper half, or obovate with a rounded apex, or rhombic-elliptic, or even asymmetrically lobed. It is possibly the result of hybridisation between *Q. phellos* and *Q. nigra* (Burk, *Journ. El. Mitch. Sc. Soc.*, Vol. 79 (1963), pp. 159–63).

Q. PHILLYREOIDES A. Gray

A large evergreen shrub of rounded, bushy habit, or a small tree 20 to 30 ft high; young shoots clothed with starry scurf. Leaves leathery, obovate or oval, heart-shaped or rounded at the base, tapering at the apex to a blunt or rounded tip, shallowly and usually bluntly toothed at the upper half, 1¼ to 2½ in. long, ¾ to 1¼ in. wide, bright dark green above and glabrous except on the midrib; paler and also glossy beneath; stalk ¼ in. or less long, clothed with stellate scurfy down, which extends along the lower part of the midrib. Acorns ½ to ¾ in. long, formed but rarely developed in this country.

Native of China and Japan; introduced in 1861 by Richard Oldham when collecting for Kew. The largest specimen at Kew is about 26 ft high and through —a handsome cheerful bush, well clothed to the ground with shining foliage. It is remarkable that this oak is not better known in gardens. From the rest of the evergreen oaks it can be distinguished by the bright green, nearly glabrous surfaces of its leaves, combined with an absence of spine-tipped teeth.

The specimen at Kew mentioned above measures 26 × 2¼ ft (1971) and is from the original introduction by Oldham. Another, in the Oak collection, was planted in 1908 and was probably raised from seeds collected by Wilson in China; it measures 23 × 2¼ ft (1972). There are smaller plants at Wakehurst Place and Westonbirt. On the Oldham tree at Kew, and on two of the Wakehurst specimens, the young foliage is bronze-tinted.

Q. PONTICA K. Koch   ARMENIAN OAK

A low deciduous tree or shrub, usually under 20 ft high; young shoots glabrous, stout, strongly ribbed. Leaves oval or obovate, broadly tapered at the base, rather abruptly pointed; sharply, coarsely, and unequally toothed; 4 to 6½ in. long, 1¾ to 3½ in. wide, slightly glossy, glabrous, green with a yellow midrib above; glaucous beneath and hairy along the midrib and chief veins. When young there are also appressed hairs over the whole lower surface. The leaf is strongly marked by (usually) sixteen or seventeen ribs running out from the midrib to the points of the teeth at an angle of about 45°; stalk ¼ to ½ in. long, at first slightly hairy, yellow.

Native of N.E. Anatolia, the Caucasus, and Transcaucasus; introduced to Germany by Dr Dieck of Zoeschen, about 1885, but not to England until considerably later; the specimen at Kew, which is the largest and oldest in the country, came from Späth's nursery, Berlin, in 1909. Acorns were collected in the wild by Lord Kesteven a few years earlier but there is no record of any plant from this introduction.

Q. pontica is a very striking oak, its strongly ribbed leaves sometimes as much as 8 in. long by 4 in. wide. The shoots bear conspicuously large terminal buds, whose slender scales are clothed with silky hairs. It is slow-growing, but bears fertile acorns when quite young.

The specimen at Kew referred to above measures 25 × 2¾ ft (1972) and there are bushes about as high at Leonardslee, Sussex, and Mount Usher, Co. Wicklow, Eire. A specimen at Castle Milk, Dumfr., measures 18 × 2¾ ft (1966).

Q. × HICKELII Camus—A hybrid between *Q. pontica* and *Q. robur*, likely to occur when the former species is raised from seed in gardens. It grows taller and faster than *Q. pontica*, and has smaller buds. Leaves variable in size and shape, up to 7½ by 4 in., mostly obovate, evenly tapered to a narrow, slightly auriculate base, but some leaves obovate-elliptic, and a few cuneate at the base; veins fairly spaced, up to sixteen pairs on the largest leaves, down to twelve on the smallest, prominent beneath; margins set with lobulate teeth, mostly obtuse at the apex and mucronate, some themselves toothed; deep glossy green above, paler and duller beneath, quite glabrous on both sides; petiole very short. Fruits not seen.

Q. × hickelii was described from a plant raised in France from seeds of *Q. pontica* collected in 1922. The above description is drawn up from a plant at Borde Hill in Sussex which came from the Aldenham collection as *Q. pontica*. It is a handsome oak, but no substitute for the seed-parent.

Q. PRINOIDES Willd.   CHINQUAPIN OAK

A deciduous shrub, spreading by means of root-suckers, and forming dense thickets; young shoots ribbed, not downy. Leaves obovate, tapered at the base, pointed, with four to seven coarse, triangular teeth at each side, 3 to 6 in. long, about two-thirds as wide, dark glossy green and glabrous above, grey and minutely downy beneath; stalk ¼ to ½ in. long. Fruits scarcely stalked; acorn up to ¾ in. long, nearly half enclosed by the cup.

Native of the eastern and central United States; introduced in 1828. It is interesting and curious as a suckering oak, but has little to recommend it for ornament. It is said not to exceed 15 ft in height in the wild, but I have only seen it one-third that height in cultivation, and never bearing acorns.

Q. PRINUS L.   CHESTNUT OAK

Q. montana Willd.; *Q. prinus* var. *monticola* Michx.

A deciduous tree usually not more than 70 ft high in the wild, but occasionally taller specimens are met with; on mountain slopes and rocky places a small scrubby tree; bark very dark, thick, with broad, close ridges; young shoots glabrous. Leaves obovate to oblong-obovate, 3 to 7 in. long, 1½ to 3½ in. wide, tapered at the base, more abruptly so to the apex; from each side the midrib there spring ten to fifteen prominent parallel veins, each of which, except one or two at the base, runs out to the apex of an oblique, rounded tooth. The upper surface is dark, glossy green and glabrous, midrib bright yellow, lower surface green or greyish, coated with fine, appressed stellate down or almost glabrous; stalk yellow, ½ to 1 in. long, glabrous. Fruits solitary or in pairs, sessile or on a short stout common-stalk; acorns oval, 1¼ in. long; cup enclosing one-third to one-half of the acorn, about ¾ in. wide, its scales downy, swollen, fused together except at the tips.

Native of the eastern USA, mainly in the Appalachians and their foothills, where it attains its largest size, but extending north to parts of New England and west to Ohio, Indiana, and N.E. Mississippi; introduced 1800 (perhaps earlier) but never a common tree. It bears a certain resemblance to *Q. canariensis*, but that species has very distinctive loose floccose hairs on the midrib beneath.

Q. MICHAUXII Nutt.   *Q. prinus* var. *palustris* Michx.; *Q. prinus* of many authors (and of Linnaeus in part) SWAMP CHESTNUT OAK.—A close ally of *Q. prinus*, the most reliable difference being that the scales of the acorn-cup are free to the base, with the upper ones often forming an erect fringe round its rim; the cup is also larger, to 1¼ in. wide, and the fruits are almost sessile. The leaves are rather more deeply and sharply toothed. The bark is thinner, less furrowed, with looser ridges. Native mainly of the Atlantic coastal plain and the Mississippi basin, in moist soils and growing taller than *Q. prinus*, which is a species of drier, upland habitats.

Q. michauxii is rare in cultivation, though introduced in the 17th century. It is mentioned because the present edition of Rehder's *Manual* (1940) and of many other older works use the name *Q. prinus* for this species, and *Q. montana* for the species which, at the present time, is usually considered to be the one better entitled to be called *Q. prinus*. The use of the name *Q. prinus* is discussed by Fernald in *Journ. Arn. Arb.*, Vol. 27 (1946), p. 391.

Q. MUEHLENBERGII Engelm. *Q. acuminata* (Michx.) Sarg., not Roxb.; *Q. prinus* var. *acuminata* Roxb.—This is another close ally of *Q. prinus*. The leaves are usually narrower than in that species or *Q. michauxii*, the teeth are sharper, often incurved, and are tipped by a glandular mucro. The scales of the cup are concrescent as in *Q. prinus*.

Q. PUBESCENS Willd.
Q. lanuginosa Lam., *nom. illegit.*

A medium-sized deciduous tree, rarely exceeding 70 ft in the wild state, with a rather open crown, sometimes a shrub; bark more deeply furrowed than in the common oak, the ridges on old trees broken into segments by transverse furrowing; winter-buds and first-year stems covered with soft, grey hairs. Leaves mostly 2 to 3½ in. long, about half as wide, obovate or narrowly so, obtuse at the apex, cuneate or slightly heart-shaped at the base, with usually four to eight rounded or pointed lobes on either side, upper surface at first covered with grey down, most or all of which falls away by the end of the summer, lower surface permanently and usually very thickly covered with down; stalk ¼ to ¾ in. long. Fruits either very shortly stalked or stalkless, solitary or as many as four together, each acorn about half enclosed in the cup, which is covered with very numerous closely appressed downy scales.

This species has a wide range from W. France and N. Spain through Central Europe and the Balkans to the Caucasus. It is a warmth- and light-loving species, found, in favourable climatic conditions, on both siliceous and limestone soils, but usually only on limestone at the northern extremities of its range. The true species is very rare in cultivation and of no importance as an ornamental. Its chief claim to attention is that in south-eastern Europe and parts of southern Central Europe it is the dominant tree in associations that contain so many of the most interesting of European small trees and shrubs, e.g., *Ostrya carpinifolia*, *Carpinus orientalis*, *Prunus mahaleb*, *Fraxinus ornus*, *Cornus mas*, etc. Owing to the felling of the oak canopy this association now mostly takes the form of deciduous brushwood (shiblyak).

There are three examples of *Q. pubescens* at Kew, the largest measuring 68 × 9 ft (1965).

subsp. PALENSIS (Pallasou) Schwarz *Q. palensis* Pallasou.—Leaves less than 2¾ in. long, less lobed than in typical *Q. pubescens*. Scales at the base of the cup convex, united, those at the top longer, free, with cuspidate tips. Pyrenees and N. Spain.

Q. BRACHYPHYLLA Kotschy *Q. lanuginosa* subsp. *brachyphylla* (Kotschy) Camus—A small tree or shrub. Leaves elliptic to broadly so, with usually three or four broad, blunt lobes on each side, mostly 2 to 2½ in. long, 1½ to 2 in. wide, rounded or truncate at the apex; lateral veins springing from the midrib at a rather wide angle. Scales of acorn cup appressed, the lower ones ovate, swollen, the upper ones lanceolate, thinner. A very distinct species, common in Crete and also found on the mainland of Greece, in the archipelago, and on the mainland of Anatolia around Izmir (Smyrna).

Q. CONGESTA Presl *Q. pubescens* var. *congesta* (Presl) Gurke—Leaves up to 5½ in. long, with six to eight pairs of lobes, undersides grey-green, more or less downy. Scales of acorn-cup linear-lanceolate, not appressed. Said to be common in Sicily and according to Dr Schwarz is also found in Sardinia and southern France.

Q. VIRGILIANA (Ten.) Ten. *Q. robur* var. *virgiliana* Ten.; *Q. lanuginosa* var. *virgiliana* (Ten.) Camus—Some authorities consider this to be no more than a race of *Q. pubescens*, distinguished by its sweet, edible acorns, which are often over 1 in. wide and roundish in shape. So interpreted it is confined to Italy. But Dr Schwarz defines it as a distinct species whose identity has been obscured by hybridisation with *Q. pubescens*, from which it differs in its larger leaves (up to 6 in. or slightly more long) on petioles up to 1 in. long (twice as long as in *Q. pubescens*) and the loosely appressed scales of the acorn-cup. He gives as its distribution: Corsica and Sardinia east through Italy and the Balkans to the Black Sea.

Q. PYRENAICA Willd.
Q. toza DC.; *Q. tauzin* Pers.

A deciduous tree up to 70 ft high, with slender, often pendulous branches; young shoots densely clothed with grey down. Leaves very variable in size, from 3 to 9 in. long, 1½ to 4½ in. wide, conspicuously and deeply lobed; the lobes four to seven on each side, oblong, rounded or pointed, the larger ones often coarsely round-toothed; dark glossy green, and with sparse, minute, starry down above; grey and felted beneath; stalk downy, ¼ to ¾ in. long. Fruits produced two to four together on a downy, erect stalk ½ to 1½ in. long; acorn about half enclosed by a cup with appressed downy scales.

Native of S.W. Europe and Morocco; introduced, according to Loudon, in 1822. It is a very distinct and elegant oak, well marked by the deeply and pinnately lobed leaves, and by their dense, close felt beneath; when young, the leaves are covered above also with a whitish or yellowish scurf of stellate hairs and render the tree very conspicuous in early summer. The leaves show, however, much variation in size and character of lobing. In its velvety downiness it much resembles *Q. macranthera*, which has more but shallower lobes and very prominent and persistent bud-stipules. A closer ally is *Q. frainetto*, but in that species the leaves have more numerous lobes (up to ten or twelve on each side) and are larger.

Elwes and Henry recorded a tree at Clonmannon, Co. Wicklow, Eire, 66 ft high with a trunk 9 ft in girth. This tree still exists and, though the trunk is hollow, it is still a fine specimen, measuring 63 × 14 ft (1968). Other examples recorded recently are: Kew, 58 × 4¾ ft (1965); The Grange, Benenden, Kent, *pl.* 1925, 45 × 3½ ft (1967); Tittenhurst, Berks, 47 × 4½ ft (1963); Highclere,

Hants, 53 × 6 ft (1968); Borde Hill, Sussex, 50 × 4¾ ft (1971); Westonbirt, Glos., 68 × 6¼ ft (1967); Edinburgh Botanic Garden, 48 × 3¼ ft (1967).

There are no distinctive cultivars of *Q. pyrenaica*, but the branches are sometimes rather pendulous and the garden epithet *pendula* is sometimes applied to these. The Westonbirt specimen mentioned above is of this nature, and there is another pendulously branched tree in Holland Park, London.

Q. PYRENAICA × Q. ROBUR.—Hybrids of this parentage occur in the wild and are said to be quite common in France around Angers. They have also been noted in cultivation, e.g., at Tortworth, Glos.

Q. RETICULATA Humb. & Bonpl.
Q. diversicolor Trelease

A small tree or shrub in the northern part of its range, but said to grow tall in the mountains of Mexico; branchlets at first covered with a fawn or brownish tomentum, later glabrous. Leaves oblong-obovate, 2¾ to 4 in. long, 1¼ to 3 in. wide, usually obtuse or rounded at the apex, rounded or slightly cordate at the base, of stiff, leathery texture, upper surface conspicuously net-veined, dark green and glabrous except for scattered stellate hairs, undersurface coated with a yellowish, stellate tomentum, the midrib and reticulations prominent, margins undulately toothed, the teeth mostly ending in short rigid mucros, the basal part sometimes almost entire; veins in about eight pairs, each running out to a tooth or sometimes branching near the margin; petiole about ¼ in. long. Fruits ripening the first season, borne two to six together at the end of a slender peduncle up to 3 in. or even more long; acorn about ½ in. long, its lower quarter enclosed in a cup-shaped or hemispherical cup, with tomentose, ovate, appressed scales.

Native of N. Mexico, extending into the south-western USA (S.E. New Mexico and S.E. Arizona); introduced to Britain from Mexico in 1839. It may not have been in cultivation continuously since then, but was growing at Kew in 1883 and is now in commerce.

Q. ROBUR L.   COMMON OAK, PEDUNCULATE OAK
Q. pedunculata Ehrh.   [PLATE 58

A deciduous tree which develops in the open ground a broad, spreading head of rugged branches wider than the tree is high. In such positions, fully grown trees are 60 to 80 ft high, but where they are growing close together they reach 100 ft or more in height; young shoots glabrous. Leaves stalkless or shortly stalked, obovate or oblong, ordinarily 2 to 4 in. long, ¾ to 2½ in. wide, the margins cut into three to six rounded lobes, tapered towards the base, where are two small lobes; upper surface dark green, lower one greyish, glabrous. Fruits one to several on a slender stalk 2 to 5 in. long; acorn variable in size and shape; cup hemispherical, with appressed, triangular, obtuse, imbricated scales, which are glabrous or slightly downy.

The common oak of Britain is well known as one of the longest-lived and most valuable timber trees of the world. It is spread pretty generally over Europe and the Caucasus. Although its timber is in less demand now that it was before iron and steel came into use for ship-building, it is still the best that can be used in house-building—floors, panelling, and the like. None other lasts so well, has so much beauty, or satisfies one's sentiment so completely in an English house.

It is only likely to be confused with *Q. petraea*, the durmast oak, which differs in having comparatively long-stalked leaves, but stalkless or nearly stalkless acorns; its leaves, too, are always more or less downy beneath, and have not the little lobes or auricles at the base common to *Q. robur*. Intermediate or hybrid forms occur (see further under *Q. petraea*).

The following are some of the most notable specimens of common oak in Britain:

Fredville Park, Kent, 37½ ft girth (1967); Bidborough, Kent, 'Bounds Oak', 40 × 25½ ft (1959); Panshanger, Herts, 70 × 23½ ft, fine bole (1969); Witley, Surrey, 'Forrard Oak', 80 × 13¾ ft (1961), a tree often in full leaf by March; Sheffield Park, Sussex, 90 × 20 ft, bole 20 ft (1968); Easebourne, Sussex, 70 × 27½ ft (1961); Kidbrooke Park, Sussex, 110 × 18¼ ft, bole 20 ft (1968); Cowdray Park, Sussex, 85 × 23½ ft, bole 16 ft (1967); Bramshill, Hants, 'Keeper's Oak', 55 × 22½ ft (1965); Corsham Court, Wilts, bole 30 ft to fork, 70 × 25½ ft (1964); Holme Lacey, Heref., 75 × 34 ft, superb tree (1962); Powderham Castle, Devon, 97 × 20 ft, bole 50 ft (1963); Hazelgrove, Bruton, Som., 70 × 32¼ ft (1961); Walcot Hall, Lydbury, Shrops., 70 × 26 ft (1959); Sherwood Forest, Notts, 'Major Oak', 55 × 33½ ft (1965); Althorp, Northants, 'Crimea Oak', 60 × 21½ ft, fine bole (1964); Studley Royal, Fountains Abbey, Yorks, 120 × 11½ ft (1966); Drumlanrig Castle, Dumfr., 103 × 18½ ft, bole 40 ft (1970); and in Perthshire: Blair Drummond, 115 × 20¾ ft (1954); Dunkeld Cathedral, 100 × 16½ ft, fine tree (1971); Gash House, 102 × 15½ ft (1962); Doune House, 113 × 17½ ft, bole 20 ft (1970); Rossie Priory, 113 × 12¾ ft (1970).

The following trees are pollards, i.e., trees which when younger were heavily cut to provide firewood or browse for deer: Cowdray Park, Sussex, 25 × 39 ft (1967); Mottisfont Abbey, Hants, 45 × 34¼ ft (1968); Lyndhurst, Hants, 'Knightwood Oak', 105 × 23¼ ft (1965); Melbury Park, Dorset, 'Billy Wilkins', 30 × 37½ ft (1957); Radley College, Herts, 75 × 28¼ ft (1968); Bowthorp, Lincs, 40 × 39¾ ft (1965).

The common oak has produced many varieties of horticultural interest, of which the following is a selection. On the whole, they are of less ornamental value than the corresponding varieties of the common beech, and certainly much rarer in cultivation.

cv. 'ATROPURPUREA'.—See under f. *purpurascens*.

cv. 'CONCORDIA' GOLDEN OAK.—Leaves of a bright yellow lasting through the summer, but liable to scorch; not of a strong constitution. It appeared in Van Geert's nursery at Ghent about 1843, and had reached this country by 1868, in which year it received a First Class Certificate when shown by the nurseryman Lee of Hammersmith. The variety 'Aurea Leucocarpa' is similar, but is probably no longer in cultivation. There is a fine specimen of 'Concordia' at Wilton House, Wilts, measuring 41 × 4½ ft (1971).

cv. 'CRISPA'.—Leaves small, very wrinkled.

cv. 'CRISTATA'.—Leaves densely clustered, small, contorted, oblique, the midrib dividing the blade into two unequal halves. Described by Dr Henry from a tree growing wild in Savernake Forest, where it was known as the Cluster oak (*Gard. Chron.*, Vol. 61 (1917), pp. 34–5). A plant raised from its acorns was true to type and more were sown in 1917, from which the present garden stock is almost certainly descended. Messrs. Hillier received plants from Dr Henry around 1919. The example at Kew, *pl.* 1925, measures 30 × 3 ft (1972).

cv. 'DOUMETII'.—Leaves cut almost to the midrib into rather narrow, undulated and twisted lobes. Raised in the famous Arboretum de Balaine towards the end of the last century and put into commerce by the nurseryman Treyve of Moulins.

f. FASTIGIATA (Lam.) Schwarz *Q. fastigiata* Lam.—Of narrow, fastigiate habit. The most famous oak of this kind was one of dense, cypress-like habit which grew wild in a forest at Haareshausen, two miles from Babenhausen (south-east of Frankfurt-am-Main). This appears to have first come to notice during the Seven Years War and was propagated by grafting around 1783. One of the original trees raised from it grew at Wilhelmshöhe near Cassel and from it, or from the parent tree at Haareshausen, most of the fastigiate oaks cultivated in Germany, and perhaps in other countries, are believed to be descended. The tree at Wilhelmshöhe measured 100 × 8½ ft at 3 ft in 1883. But there is also a race of oaks in the western Pyrenees which, according to Mme Camus, differs from the common oak not only in being often of fastigiate habit but also in botanical characters, notably the more closely arranged scales of the acorn-cup and the more regularly lobed leaves, glaucous beneath. According to her, fastigiate oaks cultivated in France belong to this race.

A tree at Whiteknights, Reading, now dying back, measures 60 × 10½ ft (1962). This may be the one planted by the Marquis of Blandford around 1800, and a younger, healthy tree of 77 × 7¾ ft could be a seedling from it (several were raised in 1867, see *Gard. Chron.*, Vol. 19 (1883), p. 252). Other notable specimens are: Bagshot Park, Surrey, from Potsdam, *pl.* 1908, 80 × 8 ft and 62 × 6½ ft, the latter with the shape of a Lombardy poplar, the former less narrow (1969); Wakehurst Place, Sussex, 66 × 6¼ ft (1966); Melbury Park, Dorset, 73 × 8 ft (1967); Woburn Abbey, Beds., *pl.* 1875, 67 × 7¾ ft at 3½ ft, with a broad crown (1961); Dawyck, Peebl., 65 × 4½ ft (1961), with a narrow crown, and 76 × 5 ft (1966) with a wider crown.

The fastigiate oak comes partly true from seed and has no doubt often been propagated that way, whence the variability of cultivated specimens. A very slender form, perhaps a clone, is known as 'CUPRESSOIDES'. Loudon described 'HODGINSII', perhaps of independent origin, said to be of more fastigiate habit, and with smaller leaves, than in the common oak. 'GRANBYANA' is of broadly pyramidal rather than columnar habit. In 'FASTIGIATA PURPUREA' the leaves are purple at first, later dark green. According to Krüssmann, this was raised by the nurseryman Kleinert of Graz, around 1895. Nothing is known of 'FASTIGIATA RUBRA', offered by the Lawson Company of Edinburgh earlier in the last century, but presumably it was similar.

cv. 'FENNESSII'.—Leaves very variously shaped, some long and narrow, scarcely or not at all lobed, often hooded; others deeply and raggedly cut, never so regularly as in 'Filicifolia'. They usually hang loosely from the branches, and are 3 to 9 in. long, ½ to 2 in. wide. Raised in Ireland by Fennessey and Son of Waterford around 1820. It was put into commerce as *Q. pedunculata fennessi*, but the varietal epithet became corrupted to "Trinessii". Loudon included it in his var. *heterophylla* and it has in consequence acquired the cultivar name 'Heterophylla' (*Arb. et Frut. Brit.*, Vol. 3, p. 1735 and fig. 1571).

cv. 'FILICIFOLIA'.—Leaves cut almost or quite to the midrib into narrow, slender, pointed lobes about ¼ in. wide. They are hairy along the midrib beneath, whence the suggestion that this cultivar belongs to *Q* × *rosacea* (*Q. robur* × *Q. petraea*). But Dr Schwarz, the German authority on the oaks, places it under *Q. robur*. The fruits are pedunculate, as in *Q. robur*, and the leaves are short-stalked as in that species, though, owing to the reduction in the surface of the leaf-blade they appear to be long-stalked.

'Filicifolia' is one of the most elegant of cut-leaved trees, but slow-growing. An example at Kew, near the Restaurant, measures 40 × 4¼ ft (1973) and there are two others in the Oak collection by the Thames. It is said to have been found wild in southern Germany, and was put into commerce shortly before 1854.

cv. 'HETEROPHYLLA'.—See under 'Fennessii'.

cv. 'HOLOPHYLLA'.—Leaves stalked, oval or slightly obovate, perfectly entire, blunt at the apex, and with the ordinary pair of auricles at the base, 1 to 3½ in. long, ½ to 1½ in. wide; stalk ¼ to ½ in. long. Acorn-stalk 3 in. or more long. This remarkable oak was distributed at the beginning of this century by Jacob Jurissen and Son of Naarden, Holland, under the name *Q. sessiliflora longifolia*. In transferring it to *Q. robur*, Rehder altered the varietal epithet to *holophylla* to avoid confusion with another oak (not treated here).

cv. 'PECTINATA'.—Resembling 'Filicifolia', with which it has been confused, differing from it in the more regularly arranged lobes, not reaching so far to the midrib.

f. PENDULA (Loud.) Schwarz *Q. pedunculata* var. *pendula* Loud.—Branches in some degree pendulous. This variant occurs in the wild, and the cultivated trees are no doubt of many independent origins. The finest example known to Loudon grew at Moccas Court, Herefordshire (*Arb. et Frut. Brit.* (1838), Vol. III, p. 1732); it still existed seventy years later but by then had ceased to weep. The finest weeping oak known at the present time also grows in Herefordshire, but whether it was propagated from the Moccas Court tree is not known. It grows at Whitfield and measures 95 × 14½ ft (1963).

f. PURPURASCENS (DC.) K. Koch—Young leaves and shoots purple. This form was originally described by de Candolle in 1808 from a tree growing in the Maule Forest near Le Mans. 'PURPUREA', distributed by Loddiges' nursery before 1838, was of this character. Later in the century other purple oaks came into commerce, of which the most striking is 'NIGRA', with very deep purple foliage which keeps its colour late and has a slight pruinose bloom. 'ATROPURPUREA' has the young foliage deep purple, becoming brownish later; it is very slow-growing, reaching 30 or 40 ft in height.

f. VARIEGATA (West.) Rehd.—There are several forms of variegated common oak, but very few are of much value in the garden and virtually none is in commerce. The leaves are variously marked with white or yellow, either on the margins or over the blade generally. A curious form once grown at Kew is green on the first growth of the season, variegated on the second.

Q. BRUTIA Ten. *Q. robur* var. *brutia* (Ten.) Ten.; *Q. robur* subsp. *brutia* (Ten.) Schwarz—Allied to *Q. robur*, differing in the, on the average, larger leaves, their undersides (and the twigs) downy, at least when young, lobing deeper. Fruit-peduncles tomentose (*fide* Camus); scales of acorn-cup with spreading tips. Native of S. Italy.

Q. HAAS Kotschy *Q. robur* var. *haas* (Kotschy) Boiss.—A tall tree in the wild, with a deeply furrowed bark; young stems velvety in their first season. Leaves much larger than in the common oak, 4 to 8 in. long, $1\frac{3}{4}$ to $2\frac{3}{4}$ in. wide, glabrous and dark green above, underside bluish green and permanently covered with a thin coating of stellate hairs; lobes in three to five pairs, broad, rounded at the apex; petiole up to $\frac{1}{4}$ in. long. Fruiting peduncle $1\frac{1}{2}$ to 3 in. long, slender, tomentose. Acorn $1\frac{3}{4}$ to 2 in. long; cup with downy appressed scales. Native of Anatolia. An interesting species, allied to *Q. pedunculiflora* and *Q. brutia*, and through them to *Q. robur*. It has been introduced to Britain, but no large specimen has been recorded.

Q. PEDUNCULIFLORA K. Koch *Q. pedunculata* subsp. *pedunculiflora* (K. Koch) Maire & Petitmengin; *Q. haas* var. *atrichoclados* Borbas & Bornm.; *Q. brutia* subsp. *pedunculiflora* (K. Koch) Schwarz—This species is near to *Q. haas* and intermediate, both in its characters and in geographical distribution, between it and *Q. brutia*. The leaves are smaller than in *Q. haas* and the fruits shorter, but the main point of distinction is that the fruit-peduncles are glabrous. Native of the Caucasus, Transcaucasia, Asia Minor, and S.E. Europe (Greece, Bulgaria, Rumania, and European Turkey).

Q. THOMASII Ten. *Q. robur* var. *thomasii* (Ten.) Wenzig; *Q. brutia* var. *thomasii* (Ten.) Simonkai—The taxonomic position of this oak is uncertain. Mme Camus treats it as a variety of *Q. robur*, remarking, however, that it is intermediate between it and *Q. brutia* (see above) and possibly to be regarded as a minor species. It differs from *Q. brutia*, and approaches *Q. robur*, in having the leaf-undersides and fruit-peduncles glabrous, but the leaves are deeply lobed as in *Q. brutia* and the scales of the cup are rather spreading at the tips. A distinctive feature of *Q. thomasii* is that the cup is very shallow, enclosing only the base of the acorn. Native of S. Italy (Calabria and Campania).

There are two examples at Kew. One came from Lee in 1881; the other was bought from Sprenger of Naples in 1904 by H. J. Elwes and presented by him to Kew.

Q. RUBRA L. RED OAK [PLATE 59

Q. borealis var. *maxima* (Marsh.) Ashe; *Q. rubra* var. *maxima* Marsh.; *Q. maxima* (Marsh.)
Ashe; *Q. borealis* Michx.; *Q. rubra* var. *borealis* (Michx.) Farwell; *Q. ambigua* Michx. f.;
Q. rubra var. *ambigua* (Michx. f.) Fern.

A deciduous tree from 60 to 80 ft high, with a trunk 3 to 6 ft in diameter;
young shoots warted, not downy; winter-buds brown, about ¼ in. long, almost
glabrous. Leaves oval or obovate, usually tapered, sometimes rounded at the
base, with three to five lobes at each side, the lobes obliquely triangular or ovate,
pointed, and with a few unequal teeth; the blade is 4 to 9 in. long, 4 to 6 in.
broad, dark green and glabrous above, pale dull green or greyish beneath,
usually with tufts of brownish hairs in the vein-axils; stalks yellowish, glabrous,
1 to 2 in. long. Acorns ¾ to 1¼ in. long, nearly as wide, flat at the bottom, which
is set in a shallow, almost saucer-shaped cup covered with closely appressed,
short broad scales; they take two seasons to mature. Some trees (especially in
the northern part of the area) bear fruits with narrower, more ovoid acorns and
deeper cups.

Native of eastern N. America; introduced early in the 18th century. The red
oak is undoubtedly the best grower among the American species introduced to
Britain. In a young state it grows vigorously, and its fine, boldly cut foliage
makes it one of the handsomest of deciduous trees. It frequently ripens acorns at
Kew, from which young trees are raised. Its leaves change in autumn to a dull
reddish or yellowish brown. The red oak is much confused with *Q. coccinea*
and *Q. palustris*, but it has larger leaves than either, usually not so deeply lobed,
dull beneath, and not so bright above.

The following are the most notable of the red oaks recorded in Britain in
recent years. For comparison, it should be noted that the largest girth so far
measured in the United States is 22¾ ft at 3 ft. Kew, Specimen Avenue, 70 × 10¾
ft (1963); N.E. of Pagoda, 65 × 10¾ ft (1963); near Japanese Gateway, 80 × 10¾
ft (1965); Oak collection, *pl.* 1874, 47 × 10 ft (1972); Cassiobury Park, Herts,
90 × 14½ ft (1904), 100 × 19¾ ft (1965); Sindlesham, Berks, in Bear Wood,
80 × 16¾ ft (1970); Fairlawne, Kent, 72 × 14¾ ft (1965); Leonardslee, Sussex,
80 × 11¼ ft (1968); West Dean Arboretum, Sussex, 95 × 14 ft (1970) and
110 × 11¼ ft (1967); Pains Hill, Cobham, Surrey, 80 × 18 ft (1961); Westonbirt,
Glos., in Main Drive, 90 × 11 ft (1967); Melbury Park, Dorset, 80 × 15¼ ft
(1971) and 88 × 16 ft at 4 ft (1971); Patshull House, Staffs, 66 × 12¼ ft (1970);
Killerton, Devon, 82 × 14 ft (1970); Gordon Castle, Moray, 85 × 11 ft (1956);
Drumlanrig Castle, Dumfries, 85 × 13¼ ft (1970).

cv. 'AUREA'.—In spring the leaves of this form of red oak are of a beautiful
clear yellow, giving as bright an effect from a distance as flowers. To those who
admire trees of this character it may be recommended as one of the best. It
needs a sheltered spot with an evergreen background, and is nothing like so
vigorous as the green-leaved type. According to Dr Boom, this oak arose in the
Netherlands about 1878. There is an example at Kew measuring 50 × 5¾ ft
and smaller ones in other collections. Award of Merit 1971.

Some botanists recognise var. *borealis* (Michx. f.) Farwell, with a more northern distribution, and differing not only in the deeper acorn-cup but also in the

smoother, paler bark on the upper part of the trunk and the branches (Fernald, *Gray's Manual of Botany* (1950), p. 546).

It has been suggested that the oak described by the younger Michaux as *Q. ambigua* is a hybrid between *Q. rubra* and *Q. coccinea*, and Elwes and Henry considered that some trees growing at Arley Castle, Worcs., were of this origin. The leaves were held late and coloured brilliant scarlet before falling, and the fruits resembled those described for *Q. ambigua*. Here it might be added that seed once distributed by the firm of Vilmorin under the name *Q. ambigua* had the reputation for producing trees that coloured well in the autumn. But *Q. rubra* is a variable species and Michaux's *Q. ambigua* is now considered to be one of the many forms it assumes. Certainly there are no grounds for supposing that a tree of *Q. rubra* that gives good autumn colour is *ipso facto* a hybrid with *Q. coccinea*. Both species vary in that respect.

Q. SADLERIANA R. Br. Campst. DEER OAK

A semi-evergreen thicket-forming shrub usually under 6 ft high; young stems more or less glabrous. Leaves ovate, elliptic, or slightly obovate, bluntish at the apex, rounded to cuneate at the base, mostly 2½ to 4 in. long, 1¾ to 2 in. wide, the mature leaves almost glabrous, glossy rich green above, paler beneath, the lateral veins in twelve to fourteen pairs, very prominent beneath, parallel, running out to short, acute teeth, petioles ¼ to 1 in. long, glabrous; stipules silky, ½ to 1 in. long. Fruits sessile, ripening the first year, usually borne singly; acorn ovoid, 1 in. or slightly more long, the cup enclosing about one-third of it; scales of cup acute, appressed, downy.

Native of the mountains of S.W. Oregon and N. California up to 9,000 ft; discovered by Jeffrey in 1851 or 1852 when collecting for the Oregon Association, and described in 1871. In Dr Schwarz's classification of the genus *Quercus*, this species is more closely allied to Old World species such as *Q. pontica* and *Q. glandulifera* than it is to any other American oak, which makes it of considerable botanical interest.

Q. SEMECARPIFOLIA Sm.

Q. aquifolioides Rehd. & Wils.

An evergreen or sub-evergreen tree attaining a height of 100 ft in favourable situations and a girth of 18 ft, but sometimes a shrub; young shoots furnished with soft, rust-coloured down. Leaves leathery, oval or oblong, usually rounded at the apex and more or less heart-shaped at the base; on young trees they are spiny-toothed at the margins but on old ones become entire, 2 to 4 in. long, two-thirds as much wide; dark green above and soon glabrous except on the midrib, paler and covered with fawn-coloured down beneath; veins eight to twelve each side the midrib, forking before they reach the margin; stalk $\frac{1}{12}$ to ⅛ in. long. Leaves on water-shoots quite glabrous beneath. Fruits solitary or in pairs on a short downy stalk; acorn globose to egg-shaped, ½ to 1 in. wide, the base enclosed in a thin, shallow cup with triangular, erect, ciliate scales. The fruits take fifteen months to reach maturity.

QUERCUS SEMECARPIFOLIA

Q. semecarpifolia has a wide distribution, ranging from eastern Afghanistan through the Himalaya to W. China. Although described by Sir James Smith in 1819, it was probably not introduced until 1900. In that year J. S. Gamble of East Liss, Hants, received acorns from Chakatra in the N.W. Himalaya, from which two seedlings were raised which by 1909 were 10 and 15 ft high respectively (*Journ. R.H.S.*, Vol. 40 (1914), p. 78). Of these one still exists in a garden on the Highfield Estate and measures 47 × 5½ ft (1972). At Tregrehan in Cornwall there are two trees which are possibly older than the East Liss specimen; their measurements are 52 × 5 ft and 56 × 6¾ ft (1971).

In the Himalaya *Q. semecarpifolia* is a gregarious tree, often dominating on north-facing slopes, and ascending to 12,000 ft. In W. Szechwan, on the uplands near Kangting (Tatsien-lu), it is a thicket-forming shrub, ascending to the upper limits of woody vegetation and often associated with *Juniperus squamata* and certain small-leaved species of rhododendron (*Pl. Wils.*, Vol. III, p. 221).

Q. SHUMARDII Buckl.

Q. schneckii Britt.; *Q. shumardii* var. *schneckii* (Britt.) Sarg.; *Q. texana* of some authors not Buckl.

A deciduous tree up to 120 ft high with a long clear bole and a spreading crown; bark on old trees thick, with pale ridges divided by darker coloured furrows; buds ovoid, acute, greyish or pale dull yellow, glabrous. Leaves obovate to broad-elliptic in general outline, up to 8 in. long, 4 to 5 in. wide, seven- to nine-lobed, the lobes separated by deep sinuses (shallower on leaves of lower branches), furnished with numerous bristle-tipped teeth, rather glossy green above, glabrous on both sides when mature except for large axillary tufts beneath; petioles slender, 2 in. or slightly more long. Fruits usually solitary; acorn ovoid, about 1 in. long; cup of varying depth, from saucer-shaped and enclosing only the base of the acorn to deeply cup-shaped.

Native of the eastern USA from Texas to the Atlantic, north in the Mississippi valley almost to the Great Lakes and in the east to N. Carolina. It is allied to *Q. rubra* and *Q. coccinea* but distinguished from both in the absence of fruits by the pale buds and the large axillary tufts on the leaf-undersides.

There are two examples at Kew, the larger *pl.* 1901, 57 × 5 ft (1965).

Q. STELLATA Wangenh. POST OAK

Q. obtusiloba Michx.; *Q. minor* (Marsh.) Sarg.; *Q. alba* var. *minor* Marsh.

A deciduous tree 50 to 60 ft high in the wild; young shoots covered with short, close, brownish down which persists until the fall of the leaf. Leaves obovate or almost obversely triangular in main outline, but with usually three large lobes towards the end and often two to four smaller ones lower down, lobes rounded, base tapered, 4 to 8 in. long, 3 to 5 in. wide, upper surface dark, brightish green, rough to the touch; lower surface pale, dull, and sprinkled thickly with stellate hairs; stalk ⅛ to ¾ in. long. Fruits solitary or in pairs; acorn ¾ to 1 in. long, broadly egg-shaped, downy at the top; the cup, which encloses about one-third, is covered with pointed, downy, appressed scales.

Native of the United States, where it is widely spread, extending from Massachusetts southwards to Florida and westwards to Nebraska and Texas. Although, according to Aiton, it was introduced in 1800, it has always been uncommon. Sargent remarks that its rounded head of foliage is so dark as to appear nearly black in the landscape and that it is always a beautiful tree. It is akin to *Q. alba* and *Q. utahensis*, but the rough upper surface of the leaf distinguishes it.

Q. SUBER L. CORK OAK [PLATE 62

An evergreen tree up to 60 ft high, with a trunk 5 ft in diameter, whose bark is remarkably thick and corky; young shoots covered with a close, grey down. Leaves oval, ovate or oblong, 1 to 2½ in. long, ⅝ to 1½ in. wide, rounded or abruptly tapered at both ends, toothed except near the base, upper surface dark glossy green, glabrous except when quite young; lower surface clothed with a minute grey felt; stalk ¼ to ½ in. long, minutely downy. Fruits ripening the first year, borne singly or in pairs on a short, downy stalk.

Native of the west Mediterranean region; said to have been cultivated by the Duchess of Beaufort in 1699. The bark of this tree (which affords the best distinction between it and other evergreen oaks) produces the common cork of everyday use. It is stripped from the trunk and chief branches every eight or ten years. Portugal is the great centre of the cork industry.

var. OCCIDENTALIS (Gay) Arcangeli *Q. occidentalis* Gay—In her work on the oaks, Mme Camus remarks that this is a physiological race of the cork oak rather than a distinct botanical variety or subspecies. It is found on the Atlantic side of Europe, from S.W. France through N.W. Spain and Portugal to W. Morocco, and differs chiefly in flowering more or less continuously. Fruits from the spring flowers ripen in autumn in the normal way, but ripening of the fruits from the later flowers is retarded by the winter and is not completed until the following summer or autumn. Another distinction is said to be that the old leaves usually drop as soon as the spring flush occurs, whereas in the normal form they persist for two or three years. The bark is only slightly thinner than in the normal form and is put to the same uses. This Atlantic race has proved to be much hardier than the Mediterranean cork oak and it is probable that the large trees growing in Britain belong to it.

The cork oak seems to thrive best in the south-western corner of Britain, and almost all the large specimens are to be found there: Mamhead, Devon, *pl.* 1765, 45 × 15 ft at 1 ft (1963); Haldon Grange, Devon, 60 × 10¾ ft (1967); Powderham Castle, Devon, 46 × 14 ft at 4 ft, and two others of somewhat smaller girth (1970); Poltimore, Devon, 45 × 13½ ft at 3 ft (1964); Sharpham, Totnes, Devon, 56 × 14½ ft at 4 ft (1965); Sidbury Manor, Devon, *pl. c.* 1830, 55 × 10½ ft (1959); Tregrehan, Cornwall, 70 × 9¼ ft at 4 ft (1957) and 60 × 10¼ ft (1965); Anthony House, Cornwall, 60 × 14¾ ft (1971); Ince Castle, Cornwall, 50 ft high, on three stems, the largest 11 ft in girth (1969); Sherborne Castle, Dorset, 67 × 10¾ ft (1963); Linton Park, Maidstone, Kent, *pl.* 1778, 49 × 10¼ ft (1970); Puttenham, Surrey, 49 × 10¾ ft at 3½ ft (1966); Osborne House, Isle of Wight, 50 × 10¼ ft (1972).

Q. TROJANA Webb
Q. macedonica A. DC.

A small semi-evergreen tree of slender, pyramidal habit when young; branchlets dull and grey, furnished at first with stellate scurf. Leaves ovate-oblong, slightly heart-shaped at the base, taper-pointed, with nine to twelve parallel veins either side the midrib, each terminating at the apex of a comparatively large, incurved, triangular mucronate tooth, 1¼ to 2¾ in. long, ½ to 1¼ in. wide, shining with a rather metallic lustre above, duller beneath; both surfaces quite glabrous by the time the leaf is fully grown; stalk ⅛ in. or less long. Fruits usually solitary, scarcely stalked, ¾ to 1¼ in. long; acorn truncate; middle scales of cup recurved, the upper ones upright or incurved.

Native of S.E. Italy (Apulia), the western Balkans, and also found in one restricted area in W. Anatolia; introduced to Kew in 1890. A very distinct oak, rather stiff in habit and retaining its leaves until December or later. It is very hardy, and I have never seen it injured by frost. As described, this oak resembles *Q. libani*, but it is really a much stiffer tree, the leaves are shorter and greyer green, and both they and the fruits are much shorter stalked.

There are several examples of this species at Kew, the largest, *pl.* 1904, measuring 62 × 5¾ ft (1972). Others are: Edinburgh Botanic Garden, *pl.* 1905, 38 × 4¼ ft (1967); Batsford Park, Glos., 66 × 18 ft (1971); Hergest Croft, Heref., *pl.* 1911, 45 × 3¾ ft (1961); Wakehurst Place, Sussex, 45 × 4 ft (1965).

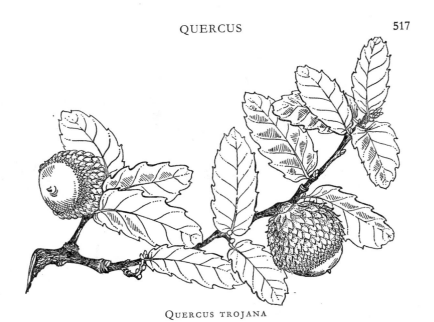

QUERCUS TROJANA

Q. × TURNERI Willd.

A supposed hybrid between *Q. ilex* and *Q. robur*, raised before 1780 in the nursery of Mr Spencer Turner, Holloway Down, Essex, in the latter half of the 18th century. It is a tree of spreading habit, growing sometimes over 50 ft in height, with foliage which persists through the winter until February or March, according to the mildness or otherwise of the season. But even after the mildest winters the tree, so far as I have seen, is always destitute of foliage for some weeks. The young shoots are clothed with a dense pale down. Leaves leathery, oblong-obovate to almost elliptic, mostly rounded but unequal at the base, bluntish at the apex, and with four to six rounded lobes on each margin, 2½ to 4½ in. long, ¾ to 1¾ in. wide; dark green and glabrous above, paler beneath and downy at the base, also on the midrib and veins. Female inflorescences up to 6 in. long, with numerous flowers, all save the basal one or two abortive. Fruits on a stalk 1 to 2 in. long; acorns about ¾ in. long, the lower half enclosed in a cup with downy, erect, appressed scales.

The above is a description of Turner's oak as usually represented in gardens and grown under the name *Q. turneri* both in this country and the Continent since early in the 19th century. However, it is not quite the same as the oak originally described by Willdenow (see below), and has to be known as *Q. × turneri* 'PSEUDOTURNERI'. According to Schneider, who first distinguished it from typical *Q. × turneri*, it was also known as *Q. austriaca sempervirens*.

Q. × turneri was described by Willdenow in 1809 from a plant growing in a conservatory in the Berlin Botanic Garden, which had been bought from Loddiges' nursery in England. Judging from his description and figure, and from the leaves from the type specimen preserved at Kew, typical *Q. × turneri* had shorter, relatively broader leaves, with smaller teeth, each terminating in a minute mucronate tip. However, there is a later specimen at Kew collected in 1863 from what was almost certainly the same tree, which by then was growing in the open ground. The leaves had become larger and for the most part relatively narrower, in fact not so very unlike those of 'Pseudoturneri'. It is possible that Turner raised two plants, both of which were propagated. Or it might be that the original tree bore both types of foliage and that its offspring by grafting varied according to the shoot from which the scions were taken. The possibility that seedlings had been raised from the original tree by the early 19th century can be ruled out as an explanation, since no tree had even flowered by 1838, according to Loudon, and the Berlin tree had still not flowered up to 1863. But acorns had been borne by 1880 on a tree of 'Pseudoturneri' at Kew. A seedling raised from it produces both the short, broad 'typical' leaves and the longer, narrower ones characteristic of 'Pseudoturneri'.

A tree at Whiteknights near Reading, considered by Elwes and Henry to represent typical _Q._ × _turneri_, measures 57 × 10½ ft (1971). A specimen of 'Pseudoturneri' grows at Kew not far from the old Ginkgo. It is probably the one received around 1865 under the name _Q. austriaca hybrida_ (_Gard. Chron._, Vol. 14 (1880), p. 714, as _Q. glandulifera_, with which it was at first erroneously identified). It is a dense tree with a bark resembling that of the holm oak parent, grafted at ground-level and measuring 50 × 13½ ft at 1 ft (1965).

Q. UTAHENSIS (A. DC.) Rydb.

Q. stellata var. _utahensis_ A. DC.; _Q. submollis_ Rydb.

A deciduous tree 30 to 50 ft high; young shoots densely covered with yellowish-grey down, which on young plants persists until the end of the season. Leaves obovate in main outline, but deeply three- to five-lobed on each side, the lobes penetrating from half-way almost up to the midrib, and the larger middle lobes again lobed; the apex of the lobes may be either rounded or pointed; 3 to 5 in. long, 1¼ to 3 in. wide (in young vigorous plants larger), dark shining green and almost glabrous above, dull, pale, and persistently downy beneath; stalk ¼ to ⅝ in. long. Fruits solitary or in pairs; acorn ½ to ¾ in. long, broadly egg-shaped; the cup, which encloses the lower one-third, is covered with short, appressed, downy scales.

Native of the S.W. United States; introduced to Kew in 1912. Among other places it is wild in the Grand Canyon, Arizona. The dense soft down, especially of the shoots and undersurface of the leaves, is a marked character and the lustrous dark green of its leaves gives it a handsome appearance. It is one of the 'white' oaks of N. America.

Q. VARIABILIS Blume

Q. bungeana Forbes; _Q. chinensis_ Bunge, not Abel

A deciduous tree up to 80 ft high, with a thick, corky bark; young shoots slightly hairy. Leaves oblong or narrowly oval, 3 to 7 in. long, 1 to 2 in. wide, broadly tapered or somewhat rounded at the base, pointed, the margins set with bristle-like teeth $\frac{1}{10}$ in. long, which terminate the nine to sixteen pairs of parallel veins; upper surface dark dullish green, glabrous; lower one pale grey and covered with a minute close felt.

Native of China, Japan, and Korea; introduced by Fortune in 1861, and in 1882 by Dr Bretschneider; in both instances from the neighbourhood of Peking, where it is a common tree. Although a finer tree than its near ally, *Q. acutissima*, its foliage is not so bright. It differs from that species most noticeably in the whitish undersurface and smaller teeth of the leaves. The acorn also is smaller and almost hidden in the cup, which has long curly scales. The bark has some economic value as a source of cork. On young trees it is blackish at first, and is not long before it shows its corky nature.

Q. variabilis is represented at Kew by several trees of which the oldest is from the Bretschneider introduction of 1882. This measures 48 × 3¾ ft (1973). Two others were raised from seeds collected by Wilson in W. Szechwan in 1908 during his Arnold Arboretum expedition, the larger 39 × 3¼ ft (1972). Others are: Borde Hill, Sussex, in Stonepit Wood, 30 × 3 ft (1967); Caerhays, Cornwall, 30 × 3½ ft (1966) and a smaller tree, *pl.* 1923, raised from seed collected by Forrest in Yunnan (F.22256).

Q. VELUTINA Lam.   BLACK OAK
Q. tinctoria Michx.

A deciduous tree 70, 80, or more ft high; young shoots at first covered with brownish starry down; buds very downy, ¼ to ½ in. long. Leaves oval or obovate, 5 to 12 in. long, half to two-thirds as wide; more or less deeply five- or seven-lobed; the lobes ovate or triangular, toothed or nearly entire; upper surface dark green and shining, glabrous or becoming so, lower surface paler, covered with a thin, scattered scurf, and with tufts of down in the vein-axils; stalk 1 to 2½ in. long. Fruits solitary or paired, scarcely stalked; acorns ovoid to hemispherical; cup bowl-shaped, about half-enclosing the acorn, the middle and upper scales loosely imbricated.

Native of eastern N. America, extending well beyond the Mississippi; introduced in 1800 but not common. The bark and acorns of this species are permeated by a yellow principle, and from the former a yellow dye, quercitron, is obtained. Despite its common name (which refers to its dark bark) *Q. velutina* is one of the red oak group, and among these it is distinguished by its yellow inner bark, large downy buds, and the stellate down on young leaf and shoot. The leaves vary in the depth of the sinuses, which may be quite shallow or reach up to two-thirds of the way to the midrib.

There is a fine specimen of *Q. velutina* at Kew by the Isleworth Gate, measuring 54 × 7¾ ft (1972) (see also 'Rubrifolia'). Others are: Westonbirt, Glos., in Broad Drive, 70 × 7¾ ft (1969); Batsford Park, Glos., *pl.* 1900, 77 × 8¾ ft (1971); Bicton, Devon, 65 × 7½ ft (1968); Curraghmore, Co. Waterford, Eire, 62 × 7 ft (1968).

cv. 'ALBERTSII'.—Leaves, at least on young plants, up to 14 in. long, 8 in. wide. Raised in Holland and in commerce in Britain by 1875.

cv. 'RUBRIFOLIA'.—'About 1893, during a visit to Lee's old nursery at Isleworth, I found growing there a remarkably large-leaved form of this Oak [*Q. velutina*]. They called it Champion (or Champion's) Oak and the leaves measured as much as 15 in. in length. It figures in the Kew Hand-list and in catalogues as "var. *rubrifolia*", but I know of no authority for the name' (W. J. Bean in *New Flora and Sylva*, Vol. 11 (1939), p. 152). The oak in question was probably known as Champion oak, which is really an old name for the red oak, meaning 'field oak'. By the end of the last century this use of the word 'champion' had fallen into disuse, and it was probably thought that it meant the oak with the largest leaves. The history of Lee's oak is not known. The tree at Kew, which came from Lee in 1893, measures 72 × 7¾ ft (1972). It is grafted on common oak.

Q. WARBURGII Camus   CAMBRIDGE OAK

Q. obtusata sens. Henry, not Humb. & Bonpl.; *Q. genuensis* Hort.;
Q. rugosa genuensis Hort.; *Q. hartwegii* var. *glabrata* Trelease

A semi-evergreen tree so far only known in cultivation, where it has attained a height of almost 60 ft (see below); young stems glabrous, greenish brown in late summer, ageing to greyish brown. Leaves persisting on the tree until spring, rather leathery, obovate to oblanceolate, mostly rounded at the apex, tapering from about the middle to a narrow truncate, sometimes slightly auricled base, 2½ to 5 in. long, 1½ to 3 in. wide, dull green and slightly rugose above, palish grey-green and rather veiny beneath, glabrous on both sides, margins shallowly and irregularly lobulate, the main lateral veins ending in short mucros; petiole glabrous, ¼ to ½ in. long. Fruits borne singly or in pairs on fairly slender peduncles about 1½ in. long; acorns glabrous, ovoid, about 1 in. long; cup hemispherical, enclosing about one-third of the acorn, with numerous appressed scales which are grey-hairy at the base, glabrous and brown at the tips, and decrease in size from the base of the cup upwards.

Most and probably all the trees of *Q. warburgii* in this country were distributed by the nurseryman Smith of Worcester in the 1870s, or derive from these. He had received the seeds from the Genoa Botanic Garden in 1869 under the name *Q. rugosa*, and sent out grafted plants under the name *Q. rugosa genuensis* (i.e., 'of Genoa'). In 'Elwes and Henry' (Vol. 5, p. 1312), this oak was referred to *Q. obtusata*, which, like the true *Q. rugosa*, is a Mexican species. In 1933, E. F. Warburg pointed out that this identification was incorrect and proposed for it the provisional name *Q. genuensis* Hort. (*Journ. R.H.S.*, Vol. 58, pp. 186–7). Finally, it was given botanical status by Mme Camus in 1939 as *Q. warburgii* (*Les Chênes*, Vol. 2, pp. 621–3 and 793). She groups it with *Q. obtusata* but remarks that it differs in its smaller, more glabrous leaves, longer female catkins, and in the thinner, more appressed scales of the cups.

The status of *Q. warburgii* is uncertain. Warburg and Camus both suggested that it might be a hybrid, though neither mentioned the possibility that it might have *Q. robur* as one parent. In fact, its resemblance to the common oak is slight and anyway superficial.

The planting date and origin of the famous tree in the University Botanic

Garden, Cambridge, is not certain, but, like the Kew tree, it is grafted on common oak and could be one of the set sent out by Smith of Worcester. It measures 58 × 7½ ft (1969); in 1910 it was 39 ft high (*Journ. R.H.S.*, Vol. 41, p. 8 and fig. 5). The tree at Kew, which came from Smith in 1873, measures 39 × 4 ft (1967). Both trees bear fertile acorns quite frequently.

Q. WISLIZENII A. DC.

An evergreen oak, varying in the wild from a mere shrub to a tree 70 or more ft high; young shoots furnished with a loose, scattered, starry down. Leaves oblong to ovate, rounded or slightly heart-shaped at the base, terminated and edged with slender, spiny teeth, 1 to 2¾ in. long, ½ to 1¾ in. wide, often entire on adult native trees, both sides shining green and quite glabrous; stalk ⅛ to ¼ in. long, downy, the stellate down often continued down the midrib. Acorn ¾ to over 1 in. long, about ⅓ in. wide, two-thirds enclosed in a cup with thin, downy, flattened scales, ripening the second year.

Native of California; introduced to Kew in 1874, where it has proved hardy but slow-growing. It has also borne acorns there. In its glossy green leaves, glabrous on both surfaces, it resembles only *Q. coccifera*, but the tree is of much more open habit, and the leaves are larger. Henry has also pointed out differences in the shape of the buds; in *Q. wislizenii* they are conical, pointed, and longer than the rounded blunt ones of *Q. coccifera*. In the allied *Q. agrifolia* the leaves are convex above, with conspicuous tufts of hairs in the vein-axils beneath, and the fruits ripen in one season.

The example at Kew, *pl.* 1874, measures 40 × 2½ ft (1973). It has spiny leaves, but on a tree in the Sunningdale Nurseries, about 35 ft high, they are almost entire.

RAPHIOLEPIS *see* RHAPHIOLEPIS

REEVESIA STERCULIACEAE

A genus of three or four evergreen shrubs or trees in the Himalaya, the Khasi Hills, Burma, China, and parts of Malaysia. Leaves alternate, entire. Flowers white in terminal corymbose panicles. Calyx funnel-shaped or campanulate, unequally toothed. Petals five, clawed. Ovary borne on a long-exserted gynophore. Staminal column adnate to the gynophore, terminated by a globose cluster of sessile anthers, which enclose the ovary. Fruit a woody, five-valved capsule.

The genus is revised by J. Anthony in *Notes Roy. Bot. Gard. Edin.*, Vol. 15 (1926), pp. 121–9. It is named after John Reeves senior (1774–1856), who introduced many Chinese plants to Britain during his service with the East India Company at Macao and Canton.

R. PUBESCENS Mast.

R. *sinica* Wils.; *Eriolaena yunnanensis* W. W. Sm.

An evergreen tree up to 60 ft high, or a shrub sometimes no more than 6 ft high; stems and leaves densely coated when young with a bronzy pink indumentum. Leaves leathery, dark green, very variable in shape and size, oblong, ovate, or elliptic, usually acuminate at the apex, rounded to cordate at the base, 3 to 6 in. long, 1½ to 2¾ in. wide, occasionally longer and more slender, glabrous above when mature, coated beneath with a buff-coloured tomentum of stellate hairs; petioles stellate-downy, up to 1⅜ in. long. Inflorescence a terminal many-flowered panicle, borne in summer. Flowers creamy white (sometimes rose-coloured, yellow, or dull crimson on plants seen by Forrest in Yunnan). Calyx about $\frac{3}{16}$ in. long. Corolla about ½ in. wide; petals spreading-erect, ½ in. long, including the claw, which is contained in the calyx. Staminal column ¾ to 1⅜ in. long. Capsules pear-shaped, 1⅜ in. long, 1 in. wide. *Bot. Mag.*, t. 9258.

Native of the E. Himalaya, upper Burma, S.W. and W. China, and Siam; described from the Sikkim Himalaya in 1874, but probably not introduced until Wilson sent seeds from W. Szechwan, where the species is at the northern extremity of its range. The seeds were collected in 1910 from a tree—the only one seen—growing by a stream on the descent from the Panlan-shan, and were distributed by the Arnold Arboretum. Among the gardeners who received seeds was J. C. Williams of Caerhays, and it was he who provided the flowering and fruiting material depicted in the *Botanical Magazine* in 1929; the species had first flowered at Caerhays five years previously. R. *pubescens* was collected by Forrest on many occasions in Yunnan.

So far as is known, only one mature plant of R. *pubescens* grows in the open in the British Isles and that is the remarkable specimen at Trewithen in Cornwall, which measures 38 × 4¾ + 3¾ ft (1971). The large tree at Caerhays was killed in the winter of 1962–3. R. *pubescens* received an Award of Merit when shown by Sir Henry Price, Wakehurst Place, Sussex, on July 27, 1954. The original plant there no longer exists, but there is still a small example in the Heath garden there.

R. *pubescens* should survive most winters in a sunny, sheltered place in southern England, but is unlikely to really thrive except in the mildest parts. It deserves to be grown more frequently for the vivid colouring of its young foliage and for its interesting flowers.

REHDERODENDRON   STYRACACEAE

A genus of nine or ten species of deciduous trees, one in Indochina, the others in S. and W. China. Flowers in short, leafless, axillary racemes or panicles. Corolla with five petals free from one another except at the very base. Ovary inferior. Fruits very large, ribbed, not winged, containing one to three cylindrical seeds.

The genus *Rehderodendron* was established by Dr H. H. Hu in 1932, and named by him in honour of Dr Alfred Rehder of the Arnold Arboretum. The species described here, R. *macrocarpum*, is the type-species of the genus and the only one so far introduced to cultivation. By 1935 seven other species had been described, and two others were added later. The fact that all these were entirely new discoveries, not transfers from other genera, is further proof of the vast wealth of the temperate flora of China. The history of this genus also shows that even so diligent and observant a plant collector as Wilson may sometimes be caught napping. For, as Dr Hu pointed out, he most probably passed near the type-tree of *Rehderodendron* during his visit to Mount Omei.

R. MACROCARPUM Hu

A small deciduous tree 20 to 30 ft high in the wild; young twigs red, sparsely hairy. Leaves alternate, oblong-ovate or oblong-lanceolate, 2¾ to 6 in. long, 1⅜ to 2 in. wide, acuminate at the apex, cuneate at the base, glossy green and glabrous above, lower surface grey-green, downy on the veins, margins red-tinged and finely toothed; petioles red, about ½ in. long. Flowers borne in May in short, leafless, cymose racemes or panicles from the twigs of the previous year; pedicels ⅜ to ½ in. long. Calyx grey-hairy, with five triangular teeth about ¼ in. long. Petals five, white, united at the base, obovate to elliptic-oblong, ½ to ⅝ in. long, ¼ in. wide, rounded at the apex. Stamens ten, unequal, five being slightly longer than the petals, the other five, alternating with them, much longer and prominently exserted; anthers yellow. Style one, slender, glabrous. Fruits oblong or ellipsoid, 2 to 2¾ in. long, seven- to ten-ribbed, the outer coat at first green, becoming red on the exposed side, finally brown and woody, the inner wall thick and fibrous. Seeds one to three, cylindrical, about 2 in. long, brown when ripe.

R. *macrocarpum* was described in 1932 from a fruiting specimen collected on Mount Omei in W. Szechwan, at the south-west corner of the Red Basin. Here it occurs at around 6,000 ft and, so far as is known, is endemic to this one mountain, though a closely related species has been described from the Mapien area, sixty miles to the south. Professor Hu, who described R. *macrocarpum*, sent seeds to the Arnold Arboretum in 1934 from which plants were raised. A number of these were given to gardens in Britain, but only two survived. Of these one grows at Maidwell Hall in Northamptonshire, and the other at Trewithen in Cornwall (further details concerning the introduction of R. *macrocarpum* will be found in the article by Oliver Wyatt in *Gard. Chron.*, October 15, 1960, p. 399).

The tree at Trewithen produces fertile seeds, and is the parent of the plants now available in commerce in Britain. It measures 36 × 3 ft (1971).

RHAMNUS   BUCKTHORN   RHAMNACEAE

There are few groups of trees and shrubs comprising so many hardy species as *Rhamnus* that possess so little garden value. They have scarcely any beauty of flower, the blossoms being small, and either green, yellowish green, or brownish. The fruits are more attractive, being often very abundant and reddish when approaching ripeness. When fully ripe they are usually black or very dark purple.

The genus contains about 160 species of evergreen or deciduous trees and shrubs, the hardy ones widely spread over northern temperate latitudes. The leaves are normally alternate, but occasionally opposite; the flowers perfect or unisexual, with the sexes on the same or separate trees. Flowers with a four- or five-lobed calyx and the same number of petals and stamens; petals sometimes absent. Fruit a drupe, roundish or top-shaped, usually from $\frac{1}{6}$ to $\frac{1}{3}$ in. in diameter, enclosing two to four seeds.

The genus is divided as follows:

subgenus RHAMNUS.—Winter-buds protected by scales. Flowers usually tetramerous, unisexual, with three or four styles.

subgenus FRANGULA.—Winter-buds naked. Flowers usually pentamerous, hermaphrodite, with a single style. Here belong (of the species treated below): R. *californica*, R. *caroliniana*, R. *frangula*, R. *latifolia*, R. *purshiana*, and R. *rupestris*. This subgenus is sometimes separated from Rhamnus as the genus *Frangula*.

Useful characters for identifying the species are: the number of veins of the leaf, and whether they are parallel or converging; the absence or presence of marginal teeth; the arrangement of the flowers—whether in stalked or stalkless clusters; and the presence or absence of spines at the tips of the side twigs. Various members of the genus yield yellow or green dyes, and most of them have laxative or purgative properties in bark and fruit.

They are easily cultivated in any ordinary soil. Some do not strike root readily from cuttings, but can be layered; seeds afford the best means of propagation when obtainable. The best species for gardens are: R. *alaternus*, as a dense evergreen; R. *fallax* and R. *imeretina*, for fine foliage; R. *pumila* and R. *rupestris*, as dwarf shrubs; and R. *purshiana*, for its medicinal interest and as a handsome tree.

The gender of *Rhamnus* is a matter for dispute. The name derives from the Greek *rhamnos*, which is feminine and was taken unchanged into Latin. But the early botanists latinised the name to *Rhamnus* and treated it as masculine.

R. ALATERNUS L.

Alaternus phylica Mill.; *A. glabra* Mill.; *A. latifolia* Mill.; *Rhamnus alaternus* var. *latifolia* Ait.; *R. alaternus* var. *integrifolia* Boiss.

An evergreen, sometimes unisexual shrub of rounded, bushy habit reaching 10 to 12 ft in height, occasionally twice as high; young branchlets covered with a close, minute down. Leaves oval or oblong, sometimes inclined to obovate. ¾ to 2 in. long, ½ to 1 in. wide, tapered at both ends and with a short abrupt apex, margins thickened and more or less toothed, especially when young, sometimes entire, often conspicuously three-nerved at the base, dark glossy green and glabrous except for some down on the lower part of the midrib above, and for tufts in the lowermost vein-axils beneath; chief veins two to five each side the midrib; stalks ⅙ to ¼ in. long, downy. Flowers yellowish green, very small (⅛ in. diameter), crowded on short, axillary, umbel-like racemes, scarcely ½ in. long, expanding in April. Fruits black, ¼ in. long.

Native of the Mediterranean region, also of Portugal, Atlantic Morocco, and the Crimea; introduced early in the 17th century if not before. The specific epithet *alaternus* is an old generic name, not an adjective, and therefore retains the masculine ending even though *Rhamnus* is feminine.

The alaternus is a useful, cheerful-looking evergreen of much the same character as phillyrea, but with alternate leaves. It has no beauty of flower, and little of fruit, although the latter are occasionally produced in such abundance as to be noticeable; but it makes a dense mass of pleasant greenery. Easily propagated by cuttings, and perfectly hardy.

var. ANGUSTIFOLIA (Mill.) Ait. *Alaternus angustifolia* Mill.; R. *perrieri* Hort.—A very distinct variety with lanceolate or linear-oval, conspicuously toothed leaves, as long as those of the type, but only from ⅙ to ⅜ in. wide. There is a form of it with slightly variegated leaves. This variety is so distinct that the older authors considered it specifically distinct from the ordinary R. *alaternus*. In my experience it is not so hardy.

cv. 'ARGENTEOVARIEGATA'.—A form with leaves intermediate in shape between those of the type and var. *angustifolia*, often somewhat deformed. They are conspicuously margined with creamy white. This is a really well-variegated shrub, but is more tender than the type.

cv. 'MACULATA'.—A poor form with leaves irregularly and sparsely blotched with yellow.

R. ALNIFOLIA L'Hérit.

A low deciduous shrub of spreading but compact habit, rarely more than 3 ft high; young shoots minutely downy. Leaves oval, tapered about equally at both ends, rather prominently and unevenly round-toothed, 1½ to 4 in. long, ⅝ to 2 in. wide, glabrous above, slightly downy on the veins beneath; veins in about six to eight pairs; stalk ¼ to ½ in. long, downy on the upper side. Flowers yellow-green, produced usually in twos or threes; petals absent; calyx-lobes and stamens five. Fruits black, ¼ in. across, roundish or top-shaped, containing three seeds.

Native of N. America, on both the eastern and western sides; introduced in 1778. A neat bush.

R. ARGUTA Maxim.

A deciduous shrub 6 ft or more high; young shoots glabrous, sometimes spine-tipped. Leaves mostly alternate, sometimes opposite, ovate, oval, or roundish, mostly pointed, sometimes bluntish at the apex, tapered, rounded, or slightly heart-shaped at the base; margins finely and regularly set with sharp, almost bristle-pointed teeth, veins in four to six pairs, 1 to 2½ in. long, half to three-quarters as wide, bright green and glabrous; stalk ¼ to 1 in. long. Flowers greenish, produced in axillary clusters or on short leafy spurs, each on a slender, glabrous stalk ½ to 1 in. long. Fruits roundish pear-shaped, ¼ in. long, black.

Native of N. China and originally described in 1866 from specimens collected by Dr Tatarinov in 1851. W. Purdom found it in the province of Chili in 1909, and it is probably from his seed that the plants now in cultivation were raised. The species is distinct amongst the Chinese species by the bristle-tipped teeth of its leaves and its long-stalked flowers and fruit.

R. CALIFORNICA Eschs. COFFEEBERRY
Frangula californica (Eschs.) A. Gray

An evergreen bush, ultimately 10 or 15 ft high; young shoots downy the first season. Leaves oblong or oval, mostly rounded at the base, rounded or broadly pointed at the apex, minutely or not at all toothed, 1 to 4 in. long, about half as wide, glabrous above, downy on the veins beneath, veins parallel, usually in eight to twelve pairs; stalk ⅙ to ⅜ in. long, downy at first, glabrous the second season. Flowers in downy, short-stalked umbels. Fruits ¼ in. across, dark purple, globose.

Native of western N. America, from Oregon southwards. With some affinity to R. *purshiana* in the stalked flower-clusters, this is easily distinguished by its dwarfer, purely shrubby habit, its evergreen foliage, and more globose fruits.

var. OLEIFOLIA Hook.—This has smaller, narrower leaves, oblong-ovate, 1¼ to 2½ in. long, ½ to 1 in. wide, uniformly toothed. There are, no doubt, forms intermediate between this and the type.

subsp. TOMENTELLA (Benth.) C. B. Wolf R. *tomentella* Benth.; R. *californica* var. *tomentella* (Benth.) Brewer & Watson—A very distinct form, the under-surface of the leaves being covered with a close, velvety, yellowish or greyish felt; young shoots and leaf-stalks the same.

Other subspecies are described by C. B. Wolf in R*ancho Santa Ana Bot. Gard. Mon.*, Vol. 1 (1938), pp. 64–70.

All these buckthorns are interesting evergreens, and have in their bark aperient properties identical with those alluded to under R. *purshiana*; they help to meet the demand for the Cascara Sagrada drug (see R. *purshiana*).

R. CATHARTICA L.   COMMON BUCKTHORN

A deciduous shrub 10 to 20 ft high, ultimately of tree-like habit; young shoots slender, glabrous; lateral branchlets often terminated by a thorn. Leaves bright green, sometimes alternate, often opposite or sub-opposite, oval or ovate, tapered or rounded and often unequal at the base, pointed at the apex, finely toothed, 1 to 2½ in. long, half as wide; mostly glabrous, but in one uncommon form (var. PUBESCENS Bean) downy, especially beneath; veins three or four each side the midrib, converging towards the apex; stalk slender, ¼ to 1 in. long. Flowers small, green, produced in the lower leaf-axils, and forming a dense cluster at the base of the young shoot. Fruits black, about ¼ in. across.

Native of Europe, W. and N. Asia, found in Britain, where it is fairly common. A vigorous shrub, which by pruning away the lower branches may easily be made to assume a tree form. It has no particular merit, although the leaves die off sometimes a pleasing yellow, and a tree laden with the black fruits is striking. Allied to R. *davurica* (q.v.).

The berries are purgative, whence the specific epithet.

R. COSTATA Maxim.

A deciduous shrub, ultimately 15 ft high, of spreading habit; young shoots glabrous, stout. Leaves opposite, ovate-oblong, pointed, tapering below to a narrowly heart-shaped or cuneate base; unevenly and shallowly toothed, 3 to 5 in. long, 1¼ to 2½ in. wide, pale green on both sides, strongly ribbed, ribs about twenty, upper surface wrinkled, and furnished with a few hairs, when quite young; undersurface downy, especially on the ribs; stalk about ⅛ in. long, downy on the upper side. Flowers green, few or solitary on slender, glabrous stalks, ¾ to 1¼ in. long, produced at the base of the young shoots. Fruits top-shaped, black, ⅓ in. across, two-seeded.

Native of Japan; introduced in 1900. One of the handsomest of buckthorns in foliage, and belonging to the many-veined group, which includes R. *fallax* and R. *imeritina*. From R. *fallax* it is distinguished by its downy leaves, and from both by the long flower-stalk and strongly wrinkled upper surface of the leaf. It has also a very short leaf-stalk.

R. DAVURICA Pall.

A deciduous shrub or small tree, ultimately 30 ft high; young branchlets glabrous; lateral twigs sometimes thorn-tipped. Leaves alternate or often nearly opposite, oblong or oval, tapering at the base, slender-pointed, finely toothed, 1½ to 4 in. long, ¾ to 1½ in. wide, glabrous or somewhat downy beneath; veins in four to six pairs, converging towards the apex; stalk slender, ¼ to 1 in. long. Flowers produced from the lower joints of the young shoots in June, forming dense clusters. Fruits black, about ¼ in. in diameter.

Native of W. Siberia, the Russian Far East, N. China, and Mongolia, and with a variety in Japan (not treated here). It is very closely allied to R. *carthartica* and does not differ from that species in flower or fruit, but its leaves are longer, uniformly wedge-shaped at the base and with one or two more pairs of veins. Of little garden value except in rough shrubberies.

R. FALLAX Boiss.

R. *alpina* subsp. *fallax* (Boiss.) Maire & Petitmengin; R. *alpinus* var. *grandifolius* Loud.; R. *carniolicus* Kern.

A deciduous shrub 4 to 10 ft high, of stiff habit; young shoots glabrous. Leaves oval or somewhat ovate, heart-shaped or rounded at the base, shortly tapered at the apex, finely and regularly toothed, $1\frac{1}{2}$ to $5\frac{1}{2}$ in. long, 1 to $3\frac{2}{3}$ in. wide, dark green and glabrous except for minute tufts of hairs in the vein-axils beneath; veins parallel, in from twelve to over twenty pairs; stalks $\frac{1}{4}$ to $\frac{5}{8}$ in. long, downy when young on the upper side. Flowers yellowish green, produced in clusters of three to seven from the leaf-axils and joints near the base of the current year's shoots; petals and stamens four; stalk $\frac{1}{4}$ in. or less long. Fruits black, $\frac{1}{4}$ in. across.

Native of S.E. Europe from the Styrian alps south to Greece. It is closely allied to R. *alpina* (see below) and perhaps not specifically distinct from it. It is also allied to R. *imeretina* (q.v.), which differs in the leaves being very downy beneath but equally many-veined. R. *fallax* and R. *imeretina* are the most handsome-foliaged of the deciduous buckthorns.

R. ALPINA L.—This species is closely allied to R. *fallax*, differing in its smaller leaves (up to $2\frac{3}{4}$ in. long) with fewer pairs of veins (up to twelve); also the twigs and bud-scales are downy. It has a more western distribution, from N.W. Italy and Switzerland through S. and Central France to N. Spain.

R. FRANGULA L.   ALDER BUCKTHORN
Frangula alnus Mill.

A deciduous shrub or a small tree up to 15 or 18 ft high; young shoots downy. Leaves oval or obovate, 1 to 3 in. long, scarcely half as wide; wedge-shaped or rounded at the base, often with a short abrupt point, not toothed; dark glossy green and glabrous above, paler and often somewhat downy beneath; veins parallel, usually in eight or nine pairs; stalk $\frac{1}{4}$ to $\frac{1}{2}$ in. long. Flowers clustered two to ten together in the leaf-axils of the young shoots, bisexual, the parts in fives; calyx and flower-stalk glabrous. Fruits at first changing from green to red, then to dark purple, $\frac{1}{4}$ in. across, roundish, two-seeded.

R. *frangula* is widely distributed in western Eurasia and is a native of Britain, though absent from Scotland and the north-west. It is a rather handsome small fruiting tree with foliage of a cheerful green. Under the name of "dogwood" its wood is used (as charcoal) in the manufacture of the finest gunpowders. The bark has purgative properties.

f. ANGUSTIFOLIA (Loud.) Schelle—This has narrowly oblong or oblanceolate leaves, from $\frac{1}{4}$ to 1 in. wide, the margins uneven or jagged.

cv. 'ASPLENIFOLIA'.—A remarkable form with leaves as long as in the type, but only from $\frac{1}{12}$ to $\frac{1}{6}$ in. wide as a rule.

var. LATIFOLIA Dipp.—Found in the Caucasian region, this has larger, broader leaves than the type, up to 3½ in. long and 2 in. wide.

R. LATIFOLIA L'Hérit. *Frangula azorica* Tutin—This species, a native of Madeira and the Azores, has leaves up to 5 in. long, 3 in. wide, with ten to sixteen pairs of parallel veins and a stalk 1¼ in. long. Akin to R. *frangula*, it differs not only in its larger, more numerously veined leaves, but also in having a downy flower-stalk and calyx, the former up to ⅝ in. long. Fruits nearly ½ in. across, red, then black. Introduced in 1778; now very rare, but worth growing for its handsome foliage. *Bot. Mag.*, t. 2663.

R. × HYBRIDA L'Hérit.

An evergreen or partially evergreen shrub up to 12 ft high, of spreading habit, more in diameter than it is high; shoots glabrous. Leaves ovate to oblong, rounded or widely tapered at the base, pointed, 1½ to 4 in. long, ¾ to 1¾ in. wide, shallowly and finely toothed, glabrous on both surfaces, rather pale green; about seven veins each side the midrib; leaf-stalk ⅛ to ⅓ in. long.

The original plant of R. × *hybrida* was raised by L'Héritier shortly before 1778 from seed of a female plant of R. *alpina* and was described by him in 1788. The pollen-parent, according to him, was certainly R. *alaternus*.

cv. 'BILLARDII'.—This form, with small, narrow, more lanceolate leaves, is considered to be a form of R. × *hybrida*, but is very dissimilar, especially in the conspicuous jagged toothing. Its form of leaf suggests that it might have originated from R. *alaternus* var. *angustifolia*.

R. IMERETINA Kirchn.

A deciduous shrub up to 10 ft high, with very sturdy shoots sparsely downy when young. Leaves oblong or oval, rounded or slightly heart-shaped at the base, taper-pointed, finely toothed, 4 to 10 in. long, 2 to 4 in. wide, veins parallel in fifteen to twenty-nine pairs, upper surface dark green and soon glabrous, except in the sunken midrib and veins; lower surface downy, especially on the veins; stalk ½ to ¾ in. long, downy. Flowers green, in small, axillary clusters. Fruits ⅖ in. long. *Bot. Mag.*, t. 6721.

Native of the western Caucasus up to 8,500 ft, and of N.E. Anatolia; introduced to western Europe in the 1850s by the nurseryman James Booth of Flottbeck near Hamburg. He apparently listed it as R. *imeretina* in his catalogue but the name was first validated by Kirchner in *Arboretum Muscaviense* (1864), a descriptive catalogue of the trees and shrubs growing in the Muskau Arboretum, Germany. It was introduced to Britain in 1879 and at first confused with R. *libanotica* (see below).

R. *imeretina* is a very handsome, large-leaved, quite hardy shrub—the finest of all the buckthorns. The leaves may occasionally be as much as 14 in. long and 6 in. wide. The leaves die off a deep bronzy purple in the autumn.

R. LIBANOTICA Boiss.—This closely allied species is distinguished from

R. imeretina by its smaller leaves with only fifteen or fewer pairs of veins. Native of Lebanon, the Latakia area of Syria, and S. Anatolia.

R. INFECTORIA L.   AVIGNON BERRY

A deciduous shrub of spreading habit up to 7 ft high, the side twigs spine-tipped; young shoots downy. Leaves very variable, mostly oval, but also ovate or obovate; tapered at both ends, finely toothed, $\frac{1}{2}$ to $1\frac{1}{2}$ in. long, $\frac{1}{4}$ to $\frac{3}{4}$ in. wide, upper surface dark green, mostly glabrous, or with down on the midrib, lower one smooth or slightly downy; veins in three or four pairs converging upwards; stalk $\frac{1}{8}$ to $\frac{1}{3}$ in. long, usually downy. Fruits two-seeded, black.

Native of S.W. Europe. It has longer, firmer-textured leaves than *R. saxatilis*, but the two are perhaps only varieties of the one species. The fruit is (or was once) used by dyers under the name of *Graine d'Avignon*. There is a rather handsome bush at Kew, 7 ft high, and 15 ft in diameter, distinguished by its dense, gnarled branches.

R. JAPONICA Maxim.

A deciduous shrub up to 8 or 9 ft high; lateral branchlets occasionally spine-tipped or reduced to short spurs with the leaves crowded at the end; young shoots glabrous. Leaves glossy pale green on both sides, obovate, always tapered at the base, broadly pointed or rounded at the apex, finely toothed except sometimes near the base, 1 to 3 in. long, $\frac{1}{2}$ to 1 in. wide; with three to five pairs of veins converging towards the apex; stalk $\frac{1}{8}$ to $\frac{3}{4}$ in. long. more or less downy. Flowers greenish brown, produced in May in dense hemispherical clusters at the end of the short, spur-like branches; stalks glabrous, $\frac{1}{3}$ in. long; calyx-lobes four, triangular; stamens four. Fruits globose, $\frac{1}{4}$ in. across.

Native of Japan; introduced in 1888. It flowers with great freedom, and the blossoms have a faint pleasant fragrance. It is distinct in its bright green, uniformly obovate leaves produced on spurs.

R. LANCEOLATA Pursh

An erect shrub up to 6 or 7 ft high, the young shoots glabrous or slightly downy. Leaves ovate-lanceolate, oblong-lanceolate, or oval, broadly wedge-shaped or rounded at the base, with short, slender or bluntish points, finely toothed, 1 to $3\frac{1}{2}$ in. long, $\frac{1}{2}$ to $1\frac{1}{4}$ in. wide, glabrous or slightly downy; veins parallel in six to nine pairs; stalk up to $\frac{1}{3}$ in. long, mostly downy. Flowers produced in twos or threes in the axils of the young leaves, yellowish green; the parts in fours; stalks about $\frac{1}{3}$ in. long. Fruits black, roundish, $\frac{1}{4}$ in. across, two-seeded.

Native of the eastern and central United States. This buckthorn flowers with extreme freedom, the short-stalked blossoms being crowded along the young shoots and forming cylindrical clusters.

R. PUMILA Turra   DWARF BUCKTHORN

A low, sometimes procumbent shrub usually only a few inches high, of stunted habit; young shoots downy. Leaves variable in outline, sometimes roundish, sometimes narrowly oval, ¾ to 2 in. long, more or less tapered at the base, mostly finely toothed; glabrous, or with down along the midrib and veins; veins parallel in from five to eight pairs; stalk downy, ⅛ to ⅓ in. long. Flowers pale green, the parts in fours. Fruits globose, blue-black.

RHAMNUS PUMILA

Native of the mountains of Central and S. Europe, mainly on limestone; in cultivation 1752. It inhabits crevices of rocks, and is of the curious gnarled type common in such places. It has some beauty in fruit, and is best adapted for the rock garden, where it makes a neat and pleasing tuft, although less close and compact than in the wild.

R. PURSHIANA DC.   CASCARA SAGRADA
Frangula purshiana (DC.) Cooper

A deciduous tree up to 40 or 50 ft high in the wild; young shoots conspicuously downy. Leaves oblong or oval, rounded at the base, with a short, bluntish apex, either minutely toothed or entire, 2 to 5 in. long, 1 to 3 in. wide, downy beneath and on the veins above, veins parallel, in ten to fifteen pairs; stalk ½ to ¾ in. long, downy. Flowers in stalked umbels, opening in July; sepals and petals five, flower-stalks downy. Fruits top-shaped, ⅓ in. long, black, usually three-seeded.

Native of western N. America; introduced in 1891. A handsome small tree, although without any beauty of blossom, forming a broad leafy head of erect or spreading branches. It is allied to R. *frangula*, but has more numerous parallel veins in each leaf that are downy above, and differs in the distinctly stalked flower-clusters, the common-stalk being often ½ in. or more long. R. *purshiana* is the source of the well-known drug, cascara sagrada, one of the most popular of aperient medicines. It is obtained from the bark, and so great was the demand that £20,000 worth was sent from the states of Oregon and Washington in 1907. The consequence is that natural supplies are being rapidly used up, and it has been suggested that the cultivation of this tree in the southern and western parts of the British Isles might prove profitable. The bark of trees raised and grown at Kew has been proved to possess the aperient quality as fully as that of wild trees.

R. CAROLINIANA Walt. *Frangula caroliniana* (Walt.) A. Gray—This is nearly related to R. *purshiana*, and may be regarded as its E. American representative. It differs from the above in having narrower, more pointed leaves, with fewer (eight to ten) pairs of parallel veins. It resembles it in having stalked umbels, but the stalks are much shorter. Introduced in 1819, according to Loudon, but now rarely seen, and perhaps not very hardy. It varies from a shrub to a tree 30 to 40 ft high. Fruits red, becoming black, ⅓ in. wide, sweet.

R. RUPESTRIS Scop.

Frangula rupestris (Scop.) Schur

A deciduous shrub of low, spreading habit, from 8 to 30 in. high; young shoots covered with fine hairs. Leaves oval, or inclined to oblong, or sometimes orbicular, rounded at the base, pointed or rounded at the apex, ¾ to 2 in. long, about half as wide, minutely or not toothed; dull green and glabrous (or with the veins downy) above, greyish beneath, and finely hairy on the midrib, veins, and stalk; veins parallel, in five to eight pairs. Flowers in downy, stalked umbels of three to eight. Fruits at first red, then black, roundish top-shaped, ¼ in. wide, three-seeded.

Native of the limestone ranges from N.E. Italy through W. Yugoslavia to Greece, and a characteristic member of the karst vegetation; in cultivation 1752. In habit and leaf it resembles R. *pumila*, but is distinguished by the more hairy shoots and stalked inflorescences. The latter are sometimes borne on short, lateral, leafy twigs springing from the leaf-axils. It belongs to the sub-genus *Frangula*.

R. SAXATILIS Jacquin   ROCK BUCKTHORN

A low, spreading, deciduous shrub, rarely more than 2 ft high; young shoots minutely downy, lateral branchlets often ending in a spine. Leaves glabrous or nearly so, narrowly oval, ovate or obovate, tapered at the base, often bluntish at the apex, finely toothed, ½ to 1 in. long, ¼ to ½ in. wide; veins two to four each side the midrib, converging towards the apex; stalk ⅙ in. or less long. Flowers very small, greenish yellow. Fruits black, top-shaped, three-seeded.

Native of the mountains of Central and S.E. Europe; in cultivation 1752.

A curious dwarf or stunted shrub inhabiting rocky places, belonging to the same group as R. *tinctoria* and R. *infectoria*, but distinguished by its dwarf habit and smaller, glabrous leaves.

R. TINCTORIA Waldst. & Kit.   DYER'S BUCKTHORN
R. *saxatilis* subsp. *tinctoria* (Waldst. & Kit.) Nyman

This species belongs to the same group as R. *infectoria* and R. *saxatilis*, and is a deciduous shrub up to 4 or 6 ft high, the side branchlets spine-tipped. It is distinguished from both its allies by the very hairy leaf-stalk. The largest leaves are 2 in. long by 1 in. wide, the smallest ½ in. long; oval, more or less downy beneath, and with usually three, sometimes four pairs of veins converging towards the apex. Fruits black, top-shaped.

Native of S.E. Europe; introduced in 1820, but of little garden value.

R. UTILIS Decne.

A deciduous shrub 6 to 9 ft high; young shoots slender, glabrous, occasionally becoming spine-tipped. Leaves oblong to narrowly obovate, mostly tapered at the base, contracted at the apex to a short, slender point, shallowly and bluntly toothed, 1½ to 5 in. long, ¾ to 2 in. wide, veins in five to eight pairs, yellowish, glabrous except for yellowish down beneath in the vein-axils and on the veins when young; stalk ¼ to ½ in. long. Flowers yellowish, ¼ in. wide; petals lanceolate. Fruits black, ¼ in. wide, globose-ovoid, each on a stalk ¼ in. long.

Native of Central and Eastern China; long in cultivation, but sometimes confused with R. *davurica*, which differs in its longer leaf-stalks—often 1 in. long—whilst the leaf-blades are, on the average, shorter. Both species provide the raw material for the production of the dye known as China Green.

RHAPHIOLEPIS   ROSACEAE

A genus of about fifteen species of evergreen shrubs, natives of E. Asia, belonging to the same group of the Rose family as the apples, pears, hawthorns, and quinces, etc. Leaves stout and leathery, alternate, shortly stalked. Flowers in terminal racemes or panicles; petals five; stamens fifteen to twenty; ovary two-celled. The following kinds succeed in a good, well-drained soil.

R. × DELACOURII André

An evergreen shrub of free, bushy growth, of rounded well-furnished habit probably 6 to 8 ft high ultimately; young shoots at first downy, soon becoming glabrous. Leaves obovate, toothed at the terminal half, wedge-shaped at the base, tapered more abruptly to the blunt or rounded apex, 1½ to 3½ in. long, ¾ to 1½ in. wide, of leathery texture, quite glabrous; stalk ¼ to ⅜ in. long. Flowers borne in erect terminal panicles 3 or 4 in. high, of pyramidal shape; each flower is ½ to ¾ in. wide, the five obovate petals of a lovely rosy pink; flower-stalks downy; calyx with five awl-shaped downy lobes.

A hybrid between *R. umbellata* and *R. indica*, raised by Delacour, gardener at the Villa Allerton, Cannes, towards the end of last century. It was named and figured in the *Revue Horticole*, 1900, p. 698. A number of forms varying in leaf and colour of flower were raised, the one selected having 'corolles entièrement rosées, du ton le plus frais et le plus charmant, rappelant le rose de Chine'. I first saw it in flower in Mr Chenault's garden at Orleans in 1913 and obtained it for the Kew collection. It is a very charming evergreen and judging by its behaviour during the trying winter of 1928–9 it is hardy enough for most parts of the country. Spring would appear to be its normal flowering season, but it is curiously variable in that respect. Lady Moore records it as being 'covered with fully open flowers' at Glasnevin on January 14, 1922, and blossom may usually be seen some time in late summer and autumn. It transplants badly and it is advisable for it to be pot-grown until given a permanent place. *R. umbellata* differs from it in its stiffer leaves, sturdier growths, and white flowers; *R. indica* by its narrowly lanceolate leaves.

R. INDICA (L.) Lindl.

Crataegus indica L.

This species is not very hardy, but can be grown successfully on a warm sunny wall. It has narrow, toothed, lanceolate leaves, 2 or 3 in. long, and short terminal, very pretty racemes of white flowers ⅝ in. wide, tinged, especially towards the centre, with pink. The numerous pink, erect stamens are a notable feature of the inflorescence, which is 2 to 3 in. long.

Native of China; introduced about the beginning of the 19th century. It was figured in the *Bot. Mag.*, t. 1726 as *Crataegus indica*. An admirable shrub for the south-western counties. Its habit is quite free and graceful when satisfactorily placed.

R. UMBELLATA (Thunb.) Makino　　　　　[PLATE 64

Laurus umbellata Thunb.; *R. japonica* Sieb. & Zucc.; *R. ovata* Briot; *R. umbellata* f. *ovata* (Briot) Schneid.; *R. umbellata* var. *integerrima* Hook.

An evergreen shrub of sturdy, rounded form, up to 10 ft in height, with downy young wood. Leaves very stout and leathery, broadly oval or obovate, tapering at the base to a stout stalk ½ in. long, round or blunt-pointed, the terminal part usually shallow-toothed, the lower entire, 1½ to 3½ in. long, about two-thirds as much wide. When young, the leaf is covered on both sides with a loose felt of grey down which rapidly falls away, leaving the surfaces quite glabrous, or with a few pieces of down about the midrib. Flowers fragrant, white, ¾ in. across, produced in a stiff terminal panicle or raceme 3 or 4 in. high, in June. Calyx very woolly, funnel-shaped, with five narrow, pointed lobes. Fruits pear-shaped, blue-black, erect, ½ in. long, one-seeded. *Bot. Mag.*, t. 5510.

Native of Japan and Korea; introduced about 1862. This striking shrub would appear to be hardier than is generally supposed; it is quite healthy in the open at Kew, but no doubt likes a sheltered spot. It is a handsome shrub, well worth growing for the sake of its pure white scented blossoms. Propagated by seeds, or cuttings made of half-ripened shoots.

RHAPHITHAMNUS VERBENACEAE

A genus of two evergreen species, natives of Chile and Argentina. Leaves opposite, entire. Corolla tubular, with four or five lobes. Stamens four. Fruit a fleshy drupe.

R. SPINOSUS (A. L. Juss.) Moldenke

Volkameria spinosa A. L. Juss.; *R. cyanocarpus* (Hook. & Arn.) Miers;
Citharexylon cyanocarpum Hook. & Arn.

An evergreen shrub or small tree, ultimately 20 or 25 ft high, with a dense growth and very leafy branches; young shoots covered with erect, bristly down and armed with axillary spines, which on the year-old branches become ½ to 1 in. long, slender and needle-like. Leaves opposite, often in threes, set about ¼ in. apart, ¼ to ¾ in. long, ⅙ to ½ in. wide, broadly ovate, pointed, rounded at the base, dark green and glabrous above, pale beneath, with at first minute bristles especially on the midrib, also on the very short stalk. Flowers pale blue, produced in April singly or in pairs in the leaf-axils of the previous summer's growth, each on a very short, bristly stalk. Corolla slender, tubular, ½ in. long; calyx bell-shaped, 1/12 in. long, toothed; stamens four, included within the corolla. Fruits ⅛ to ½ in. across, globose, bright blue.

Native of Chile and Argentina; introduced by W. Lobb about 1843. It is only hardy at Kew against a wall, and one must go to Ireland or the south-west to see it at its best. Its blue fruits are even more ornamental than its flowers.

RHODODENDRON

ERICACEAE

CONTENTS

INTRODUCTION

GENERIC INTRODUCTION

Introducing the first part of his son's work *The Rhododendrons of the Sikkim Himalaya* (1849), Sir William Hooker remarked: 'Perhaps, with the exception of the Rose, the Queen of Flowers, no plants have excited a more lively interest throughout Europe than the several species of the genus *Rhododendron*, whether the fine evergreen foliage be considered, or the beauty and profusion of the blossoms. . . .' At the time the elder Hooker wrote those words the number of species known (including azaleas) was around 50, to which his son, in the three parts of his famous work, added a further 19, all of which he had himself discovered in one small segment of the Himalaya. The number of species at present recognised is in the region of 800, of which over 500 are cultivated in Britain in the open ground. The size of the genus is impossible to estimate with any precision, since many species at present recognised will certainly be relegated to synonymy in the near future. No doubt others will be described, but it is probable that the trend will be downwards. Further botanical exploration, while it may result in new discoveries, is just as likely to bring to light links between species at present considered to be distinct.

The name Rhododendron, used originally by Greek authors for the oleander, derives from *rhodon*, rose, and *dendron*, tree.

The majority of the species are erect shrubs 3 to 30 ft high, a few are intricately branched shrublets or prostrate, very few are trees with a definite trunk; some are epiphytes. Leaves persistent, more rarely deciduous, alternate, with a few exceptions, entire. A character separating *Rhododendron* from all but a few other ericaceous genera is that the early development of the inflorescence (and mostly of the shoots also) takes place within a bud made up of numerous scales (perulae) the innermost of which subtend the flowers and usually fall away as the inflorescence expands; but the inflorescence-bud in the subgenus *Tsutsia* (q.v.) is exceptional. In most species the inflorescence-buds are terminal only, but a few species bear supplementary inflorescences in the uppermost leaf-axils and in others all the inflorescences are axillary and the terminal bud is then either vegetative or is not formed. The inflorescence varies from umbellate to corymbose or racemose, depending on the length of the rachis and the length and posture of the pedicels, which have a pair of deciduous bracteoles at the base. Calyx varying from well developed and leafy or fleshy to a mere rim. Corolla deciduous, five- to eight-lobed, funnel-shaped to campanulate, sometimes tubular or with a slender basal part more or less abruptly widening into a spreading limb, which is sometimes zygomorphic; the corolla is never urn-shaped (urceolate) as in many

539

ericaceous genera. Stamens usually twice as many as the corolla-lobes (sometimes more numerous, occasionally fewer); filaments and anthers without appendages; anthers dehiscing by apical pores. Ovary superior, with five or often more chambers; style terminal, with a capitate or (more rarely) discoid stigma. Fruit a septicidal capsule, containing numerous small often winged or tailed seeds.

The genus is distributed through the more humid and cooler parts of the northern hemisphere, and extends across the Equator to New Guinea and north-east Queensland. Yet over much of this area it is poorly represented. The genus is at its most abundant and most varied in the Sino-Himalayan region—the great ranges that border the Tibetan plateau on the east and south, from western Szechwan southward to N.W. Yunnan and then westward across the upper Irrawaddy and the eastern feeders of the Brahmaputra to the Himalaya. Yet even in this region, though rhododendrons are almost everywhere abundant above 8,000 ft, they are still unequally distributed in terms of variety. The heartland of the genus is a region of small extent, which cannot be precisely defined, but could be said to have its eastern limit along a line that stretches from the Tali range in Yunnan north-west to the great gorges of the Mekong and Salween, and its western limit in Sikkim and bordering Nepal. In India its southern limit is of course the plains of Assam; in Burma and Yunnan the southern border is less definite, since mountains high enough to support a temperate flora extend far to the south, and many harbour rhododendrons, but the boundary of 'Rhodoland', as Kingdon Ward nick-named it, could be taken as a line drawn from Tali in Yunnan to Myitkyina in Burma, near the confluence between the two upper branches of the Irrawaddy. This in fact corresponds well with the southern limit of the Sino-Himalayan floristic region in these longitudes. The boundary on the inner, Tibetan side, is determined by the limit of penetration of the Indian monsoon. In Sikkim the transition from the rhododendron world to the arid wastes of Tibet is very abrupt, but in the Himalaya east of 92° E. the range is comparatively low and allows the monsoon, and with it both forest and rhododendrons, to penetrate to the ranges beyond the Tsangpo. Farther east the boundaries of Rhodoland are the great peaks that stand above the feeders of the Irrawaddy and the gorges of the Salween and Mekong around 28° N. (See map pp. 544–5.)

The climate of this area is as favourable to plants as it is abominable for humans, wrapped in mist and rain-cloud during the period of the monsoon, when the rhododendrons flower and make their growth, and with heavy winter snow, which may fall as early as October and blocks the higher passes from midwinter until April or even June. But the snow, though it makes human traffic difficult or impossible, is as beneficial to plants as the summer rain, protecting or mulching them in winter and supplying them with water as it melts. Fortunately, rhododendrons do not need in cultivation the precise conditions that they enjoy in the wild, for if they did it would be impossible to grow them. But all who have grown the monsoonal rhododendrons will have witnessed the almost ceremonial lifting of the leaves that takes place sometimes in spring, or early summer on warm muggy days, as if in exile they were remembering their homeland.

To enumerate the types of rhododendron found in the heartland region would be pointless, since the majority of the series and subseries into which the genus is divided are either endemic to it or at least have the majority of their species within it. Yet the absences are significant. Apart from a few species of the Obtusum subseries (subgen. *Tsutsia*) the azaleas are not native to this region, and the large section *Vireya*, which has its main development in Indonesia, New Guinea, etc., is very poorly represented in Sino-Himalaya. It is also of interest, for the possible light it throws on the history of the genus, that groups widely distributed in China, such as the Argyrophyllum and Fortunei subseries, are either absent from the heartland region or poorly represented there, and that the Ponticum series, which extends to North America and Western Europe, is also absent. So the heartland of the genus may not have been its original homeland. Certainly the genus cannot have originated in the Himalaya, as was once thought even by some botanists, for these mountains are young and had probably not even emerged from the sea when the first rhododendrons appeared on the earth. There is in fact a marked falling off in variety westward along the Himalaya, so much so that Sikkim, despite its wealth of species, lacks many of the types characteristic of the heartland area, a notable absentee being the Neriiflorum series. On the other hand, the Himalaya have a few specialities of their own, notably *R. griffithianum* and the Cinnabarinum group.

No other woody genus has produced such a diversity of species and life-forms in such a small area as *Rhododendron* in the Sino-Himalaya west of the Mekong. It is almost beyond belief how many perfectly distinct species are to be found in a single square mile, and within a *cubic* mile the variety is even greater, for the deep valleys and gorges cut by the rivers allow the more warmth-loving species to penetrate to within sight of the eternal snow. It is appropriate to take Sikkim as an example, even though, as already mentioned, it is relatively poor in species. In this tiny segment of the Himalaya, barely 50 miles long from north to south and 40 miles wide, there are about thirty species, representing twenty-three series or subseries. The genus here is just as abundant as it is farther east. 'It is the traveller's constant companion throughout every day's march; on the right hand and on the left of the devious paths, the old bushes are seen breast high or branching over head, whilst the seedlings cover every mossy bank' (Hooker). But on the Doshong La, a pass at the eastern end of the Himalaya, there are, by Kingdon Ward's reckoning, twenty-five species. Below, in the vicinity of the Pemakochung monastery at the head of the Tsangpo Gorges, Frank Ludlow and his companions collected twenty species during their expedition of 1946–7. 'It seemed as though Pemakochung was the birth-place of the genus, the very epicentre from which it had sprung' (*Gard. Chron.*, Vol. 143 (1958), p. 103).

It is the diminished variety of the rhododendron populations rather than any falling off in abundance that characterises the northern and more eastern parts of Sino-Himalaya. East of the Mekong the climate becomes less humid as the influence of the Indian monsoon weakens, though the Tali range is still very rainy on its western side and represents an eastern outpost of the rhododendron heartland. North-eastward from Tali the types of rhododendron so characteristic of the Irrawaddy–Salween divide gradually disappear and we enter the region of the rhododendron moorlands in and around the double bend of the Yangtse, where the Lapponicums and Anthopogons come into their own and the elepidote (Hymenanthes) rhododendrons are of the tougher sort. The climate here is more agreeable and it is no wonder that Forrest preferred the Lichiang range to the richer areas farther west. It reminded him of his native Scotland.

Farther north again we enter the Wilson territory of western Szechwan, which so far as its rhododendron flora is concerned has very little in common with the heartland region. The Hymenanthes (elepidote) rhododendrons here are predominantly of the Maculiferum, Argyrophyllum, and Fortunei type, and red-flowered rhododendrons, already on the wane east of the Mekong, are represented by a single, anomalous species— R. strigillosum. The Triflorum type of rhododendron is much better represented here than it is in the heartland region. The distinctness of the rhododendrons of northern Sino-Himalaya is emphasised by the absence of any heartland types from Mount Omei, and neighbouring mountains, which are exceptionally humid; the epiphytic rhododendrons here belong to the endemic Moupinense series. The Grande and Falconeri series, both so characteristic of the heartland area, are both represented in W. Szechwan, but by very anomalous members.

In central and eastern China the rhododendrons, in the narrow sense, are represented almost wholly by members of the Fortunei, Argyrophyllum, and Maculiferum subseries and the lepidote Triflorum series, but Hupeh has one notable endemic, R. auriculatum. The azaleas and azaleastrums now become an important feature of the rhododendron flora; Hong Kong alone has five of these (and one member of the Argyrophyllum subseries). In S.E. China and mainland S.E. Asia generally, south of the Rhododendron heartland, the genus is comparatively poorly represented, mainly by members of the Ciliicalyx subseries and Azaleastrums of the Stamineum series. The Hymenanthes (elepidote) rhododendrons, so richly represented in the heartland region, are scarce here, but one member of the Irroratum series occurs in Malaya and two in Sumatra. These are the only Hymenanthes rhododendrons in the Malesian region, which is the home of an extraordinary development of the lepidote rhododendrons—the section or subgenus Vireya—which represents in terms of species perhaps a quarter of the whole genus (see further on page 575).

The rhododendron flora of Japan has virtually nothing in common with the Sino-Himalayan region—an interesting fact, considering that so many Japanese trees and shrubs have close relatives in the Himalaya. No other country is so rich in azaleas, which here meet rhododendrons whose main home lies in continental north-east Asia (s. Dauricum, R. parvifolium and R. aureum).

North America and western Eurasia are the main home of the Ponticum

series and the Luteum azaleas, two groups which are poorly represented
in eastern Asia, and three small endemic series (*s.* Carolinianum and *s.*
Albiflorum in North America and *s.* Ferrugineum in Europe). *R. lapponicum* is common to Europe (Scandinavia) and North America.

When the first two volumes of this work were published in 1914 the
species of *Rhododendron* introduced in the 18th and early 19th centuries had
mostly been displaced by their hybrids, but Hooker's Sikkim rhododendrons and other Himalayan species were grown in some western gardens
and were beginning to move eastward to the gardens of Sussex. The latest
novelties in 1914 were the Wilson rhododendrons from Szechwan and
Hupeh, none then more than about twelve years old and some still to
flower. Among these were some of the finest species in the genus—
R. auriculatum, R. calophytum, R. discolor, R. sutchuenense, and *R. augustinii.*
Yet Wilson's work was no more than a prologue to the great rhododendron epic. It is mainly due to the wonderful work and amazing industry of
George Forrest, also to his organisation and training of native collectors,
that rhododendrons are so prominent in horticulture today. He worked
chiefly in N.W. Yunnan and bordering parts of Tibet and Burma, in
latitudes considerably to the south of Wilson's area and with a more humid
climate, and his introductions on the whole are not so easy to cultivate
successfully in our average climate. Forrest died at Tengyueh on 5
January 1932, just as he was on the point of returning home from what he
had intended should be his last collecting expedition.

Frank Kingdon Ward started his career as a plant collector in China.
But his efforts there largely duplicated those of Forrest and it is fortunate
for us that from 1924 onwards he devoted his energies to parts of Burma
that were beyond the reach of Forrest's collectors, and to the easternmost
Himalaya, which is quite as rich in species as the Forrestian territory farther east, as was proved by Kingdon Ward's pioneer journey of 1924 and
the later explorations by Ludlow and Sherriff and their companions.
Unlike Forrest, who wrote well but reluctantly, Kingdon Ward was a
prolific writer and it is to him that we owe much of our knowledge of the
landscapes, peoples, and plant associations of the rhododendron heartland.

The American Collector J. F. Rock sent large quantities of rhododendron seed from N.W. Yunnan, among which were fine forms of species
already introduced by Forrest; his 1923–4 collections, the so-called
'Rock 59s', are particularly well represented in gardens, Reginald Farrer
discovered and introduced several species during his expedition to the
Burma–Yunnan border and we are indebted to his companion Euan Cox
for a fine account of this area (*Farrer's Last Journey*). But Forrest's achievement must still be considered the greatest, and the discovery and first
introduction of the newer Asiatic rhododendrons now in gardens are
directly due to him and to those who organised and financed his expeditions. He was the pioneer and was working for enthusiasts with the land
and means to raise and cultivate his rhododendrons in quantity. By the
time of his death appetites were becoming jaded and species were beginning to be thrust aside by the new hybrids. Rhododendrons from seed

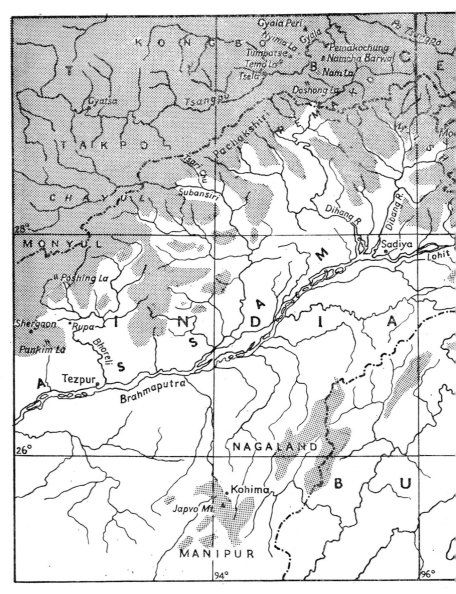

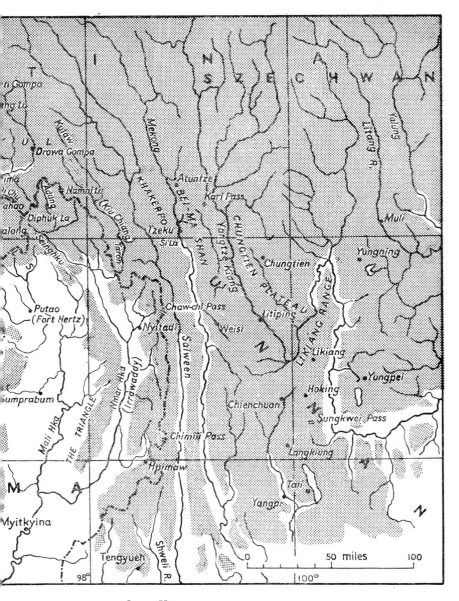

sent by other collectors after his death and since the second world war are consequently not so well represented in gardens as those introduced in Forrest's lifetime. This is true even of Kingdon Ward's rhododendrons, most of those grown being from his expeditions in the 1920s.

CULTIVATION

SOIL.—For all practical purposes it is true to say that rhododendrons and azaleas, like most ericaceous plants, are lime-hating and need a soil well on the acid side of neutral if they are to thrive. The acidity or alkalinity of a soil is expressed by the logarithmic pH scale. A neutral soil has a pH value of 7 (10^{-7} being the concentration of hydrogen ions in neutral water). A pH value below 7 indicates that the soil is acid, a reduction by one integer signifying a tenfold increase in the concentration of free hydrogen ions. A 'limy' soil may have a pH value of 8 or slightly more. Rhododendrons prefer a soil with a pH value of around 5. All plants need a certain quantity of calcium in their tissues, and rhododendrons, like many other ericaceous plants, have the ability to extract it even from soils where it is present in very small quantities—hence their ability to thrive on acid soils. But they lack the ability to control the amount absorbed by their roots, and on calcareous soils will take up excessive calcium at the expense of other nutrients such as iron and magnesium. It appears to be this factor, rather than alkalinity *per se*, that is important. Dr Henry Tod has shown that rhododendrons can be grown in quite strongly alkaline soils provided the base is magnesium and not calcium (*R.C.Y.B. 1959*, pp. 19–24). In California, *R. occidentale* has been found growing in a soil with a pH value at the roots of 7·6 to 8·6, but here the rock was serpentine and the source of alkalinity magnesium (*R.C.Y.B. 1957*, pp. 47–51).

In parts of N.W. Yunnan and bordering Szechwan there are limestone ranges that carry an abundance of rhododendrons and here too the limestone is said to be of the magnesian type, but nothing seems to be known about the chemical and physical qualities of the soil in which the rhododendrons actually grow. A few species are said to be moderately lime-tolerant in cultivation and of course it is possible with ingenuity to cultivate rhododendrons in chalky districts by growing them in raised beds, and to acidify slightly alkaline soils by the use of various chemicals, but such matters are beyond the scope of a general work such as this. Rhododendrons look most in place on the soils that are naturally suited to them and elsewhere they are an incongruous intrusion.

Most naturally acid soils can be made to suit rhododendrons. The easiest to convert are the 'heath-soils' that develop on sandstone formations such as the Lower Greensand or Bagshot Sands or on the older non-calcareous rocks of the north and west. But light fibrous loams are just as good or even better, though rarer. The most difficult soil to adapt to rhododendron culture is one of a heavy clayey nature—one that gets cold and wet in winter, hard and liable to crack in summer droughts. The method of improving such heavy soils is really the same whatever is to be grown in them, except, of course, that lime cannot be used when rhododendrons are the object. The addition of well-decayed leaves is always an advantage, whatever the soil. Peat is also invaluable, for although it contains little in the way of nutrients it increases the acidity of the soil, makes it more retentive of moisture and improves the texture of heavy soils. Well-decayed manure is useful, and so too is garden compost, provided the activator used to make it does not contain lime. But raw or half-decayed leaves and other vegetable matter such as sawdust should never be used. Roots cannot assimilate material in that state and its gradual decay and consequent shrinkage produces a looseness or 'puffiness' of the soil, besides having a denitrifying effect.

It is often said that rhododendrons are shallow rooting, and this is true in the sense that they produce feeding roots near the surface and that they can exist if need be in thin, humous soils, even on mossy rocks. But, provided the soil beneath them has been well prepared or is naturally porous and well aerated, their roots will go deep and it is obviously to the plant's advantage that part of its root system should lie where the soil is permanently moist or at least slow to dry out, and below the level to which frost normally penetrates in a hard winter. So cultivation to a depth of 2 ft or so is always advisable, especially in dry districts.

A mature garden soil is not so suitable for rhododendrons as a virgin one. The plants, especially if they are small, seem reluctant to push their roots into it, perhaps because the sort of soil that the gardener normally aims to produce for his herbaceous plants or kitchen garden crops is rather too crumby for rhododendrons. But in time they will adapt to it, especially if a peaty mixture is put round their roots as a starter. Old garden soils should, incidentally, always be regarded with suspicion, as they may have been heavily limed in the past.

SITING AND PLANTING.—All the rhododendrons and azaleas are light-loving plants, but none is averse to protection from the hottest sun and some need it, especially when making their new growth. The most tolerant of full exposure to sun are the Hardy Hybrids, the azaleas and the smaller-leaved lepidotes. The species most in need of cool, half-shaded positions are those that have their homeland in the rainiest parts of Sino-Himalaya and in general all those with large leaves (most of which come from this region anyway). The provision of shade presumes as a rule the existence of at least moderately sized trees, and to plant rhododendrons near enough to benefit from their shade involves, or may involve, competition at the root. Rhododendrons are all moisture lovers, both at the root and in the atmosphere, and although in places where the rainfall is fifty or more inches per annum the soil may keep moist enough for both trees and rhododendrons in association, in the drier and especially in the eastern counties, the close proximity of such greedy trees as elms, beeches, limes, birches, or sycamores makes the cultivation of rhododendrons very unsatisfactory unless artificial watering can be done, and trenches periodically dug deep enough to keep the tree roots at bay. There is the further consideration that if rhododendrons are planted under the spread of trees they will be deprived of the benefit of all but the heaviest summer rain. For these reasons, no doubt, rhododendrons situated fully in the open may suffer less in a droughty summer than those grown under a dense canopy. Also, rhododendrons planted under low branches, but with abundant side-light, are inclined to grow outwards towards the light, almost horizontally if need be, and so quickly lose their shape.

The best of all places that can be provided for rhododendrons is oak woodland, in which the stand has been thinned to admit abundant light, but is still dense enough to cover the ground with light shadows. In the wild, rhododendrons are often associated with conifers and in this country are often grown successfully in woodland of Scots pine. Birch woodland is less suitable; in mountainous districts it may be that the silver birch is able to send its roots deep into fissures, but on shallow soils it is a greedy tree, and the downy birch even more so. However, few planters nowadays have woodland at their disposal or the means to prepare it. By exploiting the shade cast by ornamental garden trees or buildings it is possible to grow even those species and hybrids that need cooler conditions, and the higher the average rainfall the less need there is for shade. On the whole, the necessity for shade has been too much stressed, and as a result rhododendrons have been condemned to live in dark woodland where they flower sparsely and become ugly, gangling objects and often suffer from permanent drought and starvation near the trunks of greedy trees. It should also be borne in mind that the sun tolerance of rhododendrons increases dramatically once the plant has grown wide enough to shade its own roots, though this applies, of course, only to those that are of naturally bushy habit.

In choosing rhododendrons the garden climate must be borne in mind. The flowers of most rhododendrons will be killed by a few degrees of frost, so it is hopeless for the owner of a frosty garden to expect much from plants whose flowering time is before mid-April. The incidence of fine-weather frost is governed to a large extent by local topography. In one garden, situated towards the top of a slope, the early-flowering hybrid Praecox will give its wonderful display four years out of five, while in another, less than a mile away but in a cold-air sump, the owner will be lucky if he sees it in flower one year in three. A tree canopy may help to ward off fine-weather frost but it cannot be relied on. The best policy in the less favoured gardens is to avoid the earliest flowerers altogether or to choose those that take up little room but pay for their keep by their good foliage and habit, e.g., Elizabeth, Cilpinense, or *R. leucaspis*. The Lapponicums mostly have flowers that will withstand a few degrees of frost and very rarely cause disappointment. Some early flowerers, such as *R. mucronulatum* and *R.* Nobleanum, open their trusses over a period of several weeks in most seasons, so some at least of the flower-buds may escape damage. There is always one comfort to be taken when a promising display has been ruined by frost: the plants have been prematurely deadheaded and will grow all the better in the following summer. Loss of young growths through frost is a different matter, but is less frequent, since the majority of species and hybrids do not flush until May or later.

If it is the growths from terminal buds that are killed, no great harm is done, since there is a reserve of axillary buds to produce a second growth later, though next season's flower may be lost if the plant is one that normally produces its flower-buds on growths from terminal buds. The loss of axillary growths by frost can be damaging, especially if it is repeated year after year, but very few rhododendrons produce axillary growths early enough to be killed by frost.

Most of the rhododendrons treated in this work are hardy in the sense that they will withstand low winter temperatures in still air. But continuous biting, dry winds can be very damaging, and the more so if the ground is deeply frozen, since the plant is then unable to replace the moisture lost by the leaves. So protection from the north and east is very important if the more demanding rhododendrons are grown. Mulching, always beneficial, also helps here, by keeping frost out of the ground.

The planting of rhododendrons and other evergreens has been dealt with in the introductory chapters (see Vol. I, p. 63) and there is little that need be added here. The plant should always be placed in the ground with the top of its root ball level with the surrounding soil or at the centre of a shallow depression, which can be filled with a light mulch. The advantage of planting in a saucer is that it makes watering easier in the early stages and helps to keep the mulch in place. It is important to achieve as perfect a union as possible between the root ball and the planting soil by filling in every nook and cranny and carefully firming the mixture with a rammer. It is not enough merely to spade back the soil and tread it in. It is always advisable to add extra peat to the planting soil, and perhaps sand also, especially if it is heavier than the soil in the ball, as is often the case when the plant has come from one of the specialist nurseries, most of which are situated on light sandy soils.

At what spacing to plant rhododendrons is a question difficult to answer. Obviously it is quite impracticable to give each plant from the start the space it will need a quarter-century on and, rhododendrons being sociable plants, it is neither necessary nor desirable to do so. The dwarfer species and hybrids are so easily shifted around when young, or even middle-aged, that they can be planted closely to begin with and respaced after a few years, by which time their relative vigour and habit will be evident and the final arrangement can be made with confidence. Eventually they will grow into each other, but there is no harm in that provided each has adequate living-space. The larger rhododendrons cannot easily be moved around like so much furniture and should be well spaced from the start. Provided the plants are of similar vigour and habit a spacing of around 8 ft should be sufficient, for most of the larger elepidote rhododendrons, less if they are all of the same clone or species, and 5 to 6 ft for plantings of azaleas and Triflorum rhododendrons.

TRANSPLANTING.—The moving of large rhododendrons has already been dealt with in the Introductory Chapters (see Vol. I, pp. 60–6). Rhododendrons that have been growing in well-prepared soil can be moved at any age; the limit is set entirely by the labour and tackle available. But rhododendrons that were planted when young in inadequately prepared positions are a different matter. If the soil is suitable for them, and if they are mulched deliberately or by natural leaf-fall, they may thrive. But when they come to be lifted it may be found that they have subsisted off the leafy top layer of the soil and developed a root system like a door mat. Such plants do not transplant well. Young plants, when shifted from one part of the garden to another, should be lifted with a fork, not chopped out with a spade. Evergreen sorts, when young, can safely be moved at any time, except when making their growths or in hot, dry weather. But deciduous azaleas should always be moved at the normal time, the earlier the better.

MULCHING, FEEDING, AND WATERING.—Rhododendrons are all moisture-loving, and delight in a continuously cool damp condition at the root. For plants whose roots are not shaded by their own lower branches, a surface mulching of 4 to 6 in. of leaves is very beneficial. If the soil is poor, a proportion of one-third well-rotted manure may be added to the mulch. Bracken is useful as a mulch, and has considerable nutritional value if cut when the fronds are just fully expanded. Peat is perhaps for most gardeners the most readily available material and is invaluable for protecting the roots of young plants.

Contrary to what was once supposed, rhododendrons respond well to artificial fertilisers, but they should be used in moderation and there is no need to use them at all if the plant is healthy and vigorous. Obviously the fertiliser should be a balanced one formulated for general garden use. It has been suggested that fertilisers that supply phosphorus in the form of calcium superphosphate leave an alkaline residue, but research has shown that is has no such effect.

Except in the driest parts, or where rhododendrons are growing in a rooty soil, artificial watering is not absolutely essential and many large collections in this country have grown up without it. But there is no doubt that rhododendrons benefit greatly from the generous use of the hose or sprinklers, especially when they are making their young growths. Once their growths have hardened, the drought tolerance of rhododendrons increases remarkably.

DEAD-HEADING.—Whenever time and opportunity allow, the flowers of all rhododendrons and azaleas should be removed as soon as they have faded, at least from young plants. The truss will usually break off in one piece between thumb and forefinger, but care should be taken not to remove the upper buds or young growths at the same time, as can easily happen. Curiously enough it has not, so far as is known, even been scientifically proved that this practice benefits the plant or causes it to flower more freely, but if it does not do so much money and labour has been expended in vain over the years, both by nurserymen and garden owners. Generally azaleas and the dwarfer lepidotes flower freely every year even if they set seed; these are not as a rule dead-headed, though they might well live longer if they were. At the other extreme, some rhododendrons with heavy trusses, or which flower late, are inclined to make weak shoots from below the inflorescence whether or not this is removed. These shoots terminate in a growth-bud which in the following year produces a stronger growth ending in a flower-bud, so that what appears to be a single shoot is really the product of two seasons' growth. The individual branch is therefore biennial in its flowering, but so long as all the branches are not in step some flowers are produced every year, but always on shoots that have sprung from a terminal bud. In some rhododendrons the flower-buds terminate a growth of three or more segments, or no growth at all may be made from below an inflorescence until the following season.

PRUNING AND DISBUDDING.—Rhododendrons require no regular pruning and, provided they are grown in adequate light, will never need pruning of any sort. Most will respond to hard cutting if for any reason (usually overcrowding or too much shade) they have grown out of shape or become drawn up. Rhododendrons with a smooth, peeling bark are an exception, since they owe this attractive feature to the sloughing off of the outer bark, which takes the dormant growth-buds with it when it is shed. Hard pruning of grafted plants is also unlikely to be a success, for the removal of the top growth will almost certainly result in a forest of suckers from the stock.

Plants that flower when young will develop a bushy habit naturally, since the flowers automatically 'stop' the shoot on which they are borne. However, in the absence of flower-bud the same effect can be achieved simply by cutting off the terminal growth-bud as it expands; the axillary buds will then grow out just as they would have done if the shoot had ended in flowers. If this disbudding is not done, or if the plant is already leggy when received, the longer branches should be shortened in spring to just above a cluster of dormant side-buds. However, many large-leaved, tall-growing rhododendrons are best not treated in this way, since they are not by nature bushy and anyway will normally produce growths both from terminal and axillary buds even before they reach the flowering stage.

Some large-flowered rhododendrons flower too freely for their health when they are young, and should be relieved of some of their flower-buds, especially if more than one is produced at the end of each shoot, as may happen on young and vigorous plants.

Here it should be mentioned that Hardy Hybrids and some other elepidote hybrids are often propagated by grafting onto Ponticum stocks, which may give trouble by sending up suckers. These should be watched for and chopped off with a spade as soon as noticed, but often they are not noticed if the scion has leaves resembling those of *R. ponticum* or if, as is sometimes the case, the seedling used as the stock is itself a hybrid. Deciduous azaleas are now rarely propagated by grafting and plants raised this way should be avoided, as they always sucker abominably.

PROPAGATION*

Rhododendrons are normally propagated from seeds, layers, cuttings and grafting scions on to suitable root-stocks.

* Contributed by F. P. Knight

The following account is mainly for the amateur gardener concerned with raising a few plants. The professional propagator will know how to cope with producing the quantities he requires.

The introduction of species from the wild has hitherto been almost entirely from collected seed, but the day may come when outstanding superior forms found by botanical collectors can be quickly established in cultivation by making use of modern methods of packaging and transport to send back cuttings and scions by air. Expeditions could be served by helicopters to carry the vegetative material to the nearest airport from which it could be quickly brought home and handled by skilled propagators. This method would short-circuit by many years the distribution to gardens by the present practice of waiting for plants to flower from seed and then to select the good forms and propagate these from cuttings or grafts.

SEEDS.—Seeds from plant collectors in the field do not always arrive at what is generally taken as the optimum time for sowing, and the recipient has to adapt the basic principles to suit the particular circumstances. The successful raising of rhododendrons from seeds saved from cultivated plants really begins with the careful harvesting of the seeds, and the correct storage of these until sowing-time, which will depend on the facilities available.

The flowering period of different rhododendrons extends over several months and seeds are rather slow in developing and ripening. First of all it is important to remember that the species do not come true from seeds where these are collected from plants growing in a mixed collection, where the flowers have become 'open-pollinated'. If it is intended to collect seeds from individual species it is necessary to prevent cross pollination by covering the flowers by 'bagging' the truss with some suitable artificial device.

According to the kinds, seeds will ripen from late summer to the depth of winter, and a watchful eye must be kept so that they are not lost through the seed vessels splitting and the seeds escaping. It will be noticed that gradually the colour of the capsules will change from green to brown and that they will become hard to the touch. The time to collect is when these changes are completed, and the capsules should then be placed in transparent seed packets so that the final ripening and splitting open can be observed. The packets are best stored in vermin- and insect-proof tin boxes and placed in a cool dry place. Cleaning the seeds from the capsules requires meticulous care, particularly when different kinds are being handled in rotation. The straying of a few seeds of one into those of another can in due course cause a lot of trouble.

It will be found in practice that most of the seeds will have become dispersed from the capsules and will be found loose in the packets. Any which remain can be ejected by the blade of a knife. It is most important to separate the broken-up capsules from the seeds, as the debris from these, if sown with the seeds, can be responsible for promoting 'damping-off'. The storage period will depend on the time for sowing. If a warm greenhouse or frame is available a most successful time for sowing is from late January to the end of February. If only cold conditions can be provided sowing must wait until mid-April.

The ideal is to sow earlier in warm conditions so that the maximum growing season lies ahead to allow for the development of sturdy young plants which have become hardened to withstand the first winter. To raise small quantities of plants a good method to follow is to sow in a clean flower pot about 3½ in. in diameter. This should be drained in the accepted fashion by placing broken crocks in the bottom and covering these with coarse peat to prevent the fine sowing mixture from filtering through. A suitable soil mixture is made up from seven parts by bulk of fine moss peat and three parts of silver sand which must not be alkaline.

The pots should be filled practically level with the rim but the mixture should neither be rendered hard nor soft and spongy. The pots are then placed in a shallow container of rain-water so that this percolates to the surface, and then left to drain. The seeds are then sown thinly on the surface and sprinkled over with a very light 'sugaring' of fine dry silver sand. The pots are then placed on a moisture-conserving base of clean weathered ashes from which the dust has been sifted, or on a bed of peat on a suitable warm greenhouse stage or in a frame where the temperature is maintained at from 55° to 60° F.

A sheet of newspaper should be laid over the pots but prevented from touching the soil surface by some artificial means.

From this point the daily care consists of changing the paper each morning, germination normally takes place in about two to four weeks from the date of sowing and it is necessary to watch out for any pot which shows signs of becoming dry, and immersing this in rain-water, which should be of the same temperature as the house or frame. It is during the early days of the life of the tender new seedlings that 'damping-off' can occur and a close daily scrutiny of each pot should be made so that at the very beginning any tiny areas affected can be removed by simply taking these out with a pair of tweezers. The little depressions thus caused on the surface should be filled with dry, clean silver sand.

Germination will not occur in every pot at the same time, and before the seedlings have time to become white and drawn the pots must be placed on an open stage or shelf near the glass and carefully shaded. It is now simply a question of balancing the daily treatment required against the weather conditions, for example shading should not be continuous during a succession of very dull days.

By the end of April the most forward seedlings will be ready for pricking off into boxes, using the same basic mixture as that in which the seeds were sown, except that it need not be of such fine texture, while some propagators at this stage like to mix in a small proportion of fine acidic sandy loam, which helps the young plants over the intermediate stage between the seed pots and eventually planting out in prepared nursery beds.

The boxes at first are kept in the warm greenhouse or frame, kept shaded and watered as necessary and then transferred to a cold frame during the summer months and the plants gradually hardened off. Some will make sufficient growth to enable them to be planted out in late September or October, whereas the more backward ones will have to be over-wintered in the frame until the spring. It could be said that at this stage the very specialised work of the propagator gives way to established methods of cultivation.

Where no heated facilities can be provided sowing must be delayed until April, when the actual technique of sowing will be the same, but results of course will be slower. The light intensity will be greater and shading must be provided. Damping-off is a greater risk, and growth by the autumn will generally not be sufficient to allow for planting into nursery beds.

LAYERING.—This method of propagation comes naturally next to seeds, and many examples can be seen where branches at ground level have rooted into the surface soil or mulch. Layering provides the amateur gardener with an ideal trouble-free method of raising a few plants from the specimens he cultivates without detriment to these. A good time to 'put-down' the layers is in October but this can be extended into the early winter, and early spring.

It is usual to select the tips of branches of the larger-leaved plants, including deciduous azaleas, which are nearest to the ground. The length required is ideally about 12–15 in., which means going back from the growing point to two- or even three-year-old wood. The objective should be to produce young new plants of good shape, and this is accomplished by removing any leaves which are growing on the portion of stem to be buried and simply causing a wound on the underside of the stems by scraping away the bark or skin with a knife. It is not necessary to make any incision in the wood. The branch should then be buried firmly in the soil which should of course have been prepared by digging and improved if necessary by the addition of peat or leaf-mould with a little sand mixed in. Suitable wooden pegs can be driven into the ground to keep the branches firm; the growing tip should be bent abruptly upwards so that the layered portion resembles a fully bent elbow-joint. The tip can be kept upright by tying this to a small stake. It is better to complete the work with the disturbed soil matching the level of that which surrounds the parent plant rather than build up an artificial mound which will become very dry.

Sufficient roots will normally have developed to enable the layers to be cut away in about eighteen months to form independent new young plants.

Maintenance throughout this period consists of making certain that the layered branches are not dislodged in any way, such as being loosened by sharp frost, or by the tunnelling action of moles.

For small rhododendrons such as those in the Lapponicum series small rooted portions can be obtained by either pegging down suitable twigs, or by planting the parent plant deeper than usual and working in among the branches a generous quantity of peat and sand; this must be made as firm as possible and 'topped up' when necessary.

CUTTINGS.—In recent years because of improvements in propagating equipment there has been more progress in raising a wide range of rhododendrons from cuttings than by any other method. The propagating house in an up-to-date establishment is akin to the production line in a factory. The main change is that of raising from cuttings large quantities of hardy hybrids and deciduous azaleas which were previously increased by grafting. The amateur concerned only with raising small quantities has not been overlooked by the designers of equipment for he can purchase well-designed portable electrically heated propagating units.

It is convenient to broadly classify rhododendrons into groups according to the leaf-sizes in order to prescribe the treatment now being given.

The very small-leaved kinds such as those in the Lapponicum series with their hybrids respond well to cold treatment and there is no valid reason to change the established method of taking cuttings, about $1\frac{1}{2}$ in. long in the late summer months as soon as the current season's growth has become firm. The cuttings are made at a leaf joint and dibbled into a mixture of equal parts of fine peat and silver sand, either in boxes or pots which are placed in a draught-proof cold frame and kept shaded and moist. Here they will root slowly and be ready to prick out into a prepared nursery bed in the following spring. There is much to be said for using bell-glasses where these are still to be had and inserting the cuttings in September or October. For the larger-leaved kinds, particularly the hardy hybrids, the amateur can watch with interest the specialist nurserymen turning out large quantities of plants by using mist units, soil-heating cables and specialised lighting. He will not generally be able to emulate these but can raise plants from cuttings by taking these from late August to October. These should be made from the current year's growths, selecting the side shoots about 3 in. long, avoiding the strong central terminal shoots. The cutting is made at a leaf joint, and any leaves growing on the portion to be inserted should be cut off. It is usual to reduce the leaves which remain on the cutting, by cutting these in half. The terminal buds, whether flowering or growth buds, are removed. Some propagators wound the cutting at the base by removing with a sharp knife a thin shaving of the green skin without cutting deeply into the wood, and then dipping the exposed surface into a proprietary rooting powder according to the manufacturer's instructions. The wounded area provides a larger rooting surface than that available from the small basal cut surface.

The cuttings are then inserted in the sand and peat mixture in pots or boxes and these placed in the electrically heated propagating unit. The time taken for rooting varies with the kinds being increased, but the new young plants should be ready after hardening off for planting into prepared beds the following summer. In the absence of special propagating units the containers should be placed in a frame with a temperature of 65° F. and shaded when necessary.

GRAFTING.—Grafting is still undertaken by nurserymen, and despite existing prejudice about grafted plants and their attendant suckering nuisance, it must be clear to all that when a single rhododendron has received the R.H.S. Award of Merit or First Class Certificate the quickest way to increase and distribute this is by grafting every available scion on to a root-stock. Once this initial propagation is over then future stocks can be raised from cuttings or layers.

A simple method is to select young root-stocks of *Rhododendron ponticum* with a single clean stem of about 'pencil' thickness and on to this in January or February graft a scion, making the union just above the point where the stem and root join. It is now usual to use a side-graft made simply by taking a shoot of the previous summer's growth, about 3in. long and cutting away a longitudinal section of this into the wood, and making a corresponding matching cut on the stem of the root-stock. The two cut surfaces are fitted together and tied with raffia or grafting string. The root-stock with its scion is then buried in a bed of peat in a heated frame which is covered by a glass light or well-fitting polythene sheeting. The scion and stock will knit together and be ready for removing into cold frames by April or May.

Propagators differ about leaving the top growth on the root-stock until the union is completed, or cutting this off at the time of grafting. But then, professional propagators differ about many methods and this comes out very clearly at a plant propagators' conference.

There is still much to learn, and experimental work should be continuous.

PESTS, DISEASES, AND DISORDERS

Rhododendrons and azaleas are remarkably free from pests and diseases when grown in the open ground and rarely is any so serious as to call for regular spraying. The most lethal enemy of rhododendrons, as of many other trees and shrubs, is honey fungus (*Armillaria mellea*), on which a note will be included at the end of Volume IV. The more important pests and diseases specific to *Rhododendron* are mentioned here; for further details see the *Dictionary of Gardening* published by the Royal Horticultural Society, and the papers listed in the Bibliography.

PESTS

RHODODENDRON BUG or RHODODENDRON FLY (*Stephanitis rhododendri*).—This pest, believed to be a native of north-eastern North America, made its appearance in Britain at the beginning of this century. It is a sucking insect, whose presence can be detected in May and June by a mottling of the upper leaf surface and the presence of rusty or chocolate spots beneath. Eventually the leaf turns brown, and if the attack is severe and the summer dry, the plant may be severely weakened. The adult bug has a black body, almost transparent, lacy wings, and long antennae. It is about $\frac{1}{8}$ in. long. The eggs are laid in late summer and autumn beneath the new leaves under the epidermis alongside the midrib, and the young start to hatch out towards the end of May. The young bug is wingless, with antennae about as long as the body. It gradually develops into the adult state and in late summer the adults move to the young leaves, where the eggs are deposited. Despite their large wings the bugs do not fly, though when conditions are right they may be carried passively by the wind to infect new plants. Mild attacks can be checked by picking off the affected leaves and burning them. In the case of severe attack the undersides of the leaves should be sprayed two or three times with BHC or malathion at three-week intervals. The rhododendron bug seems to have a particular liking for hybrids deriving from *R. catawbiense* and *R. maximum* and thrives best on plants growing in full sun. So it is the older hybrids, which are normally planted in sunny positions, that are most prone to attack, but the most susceptible, such as 'Boule de Neige' and 'Francis B. Hayes' are no longer in commerce.

RHODODENDRON LEAFHOPPER (*Graphocephala coccinea*).—This is not in itself a serious pest, but is now thought to be an indirect cause of attacks by the fungal disease known as bud blast (q.v.). The young emerge in spring and feed on the leaf-sap, without causing any noticeable harm. The adult, which is about ½ in. long, with green and yellow wings, appears in July and the eggs are laid in the bud-scales during late summer and autumn. The recommended treatment is to spray with malathion two or three times during August and September, but this is only necessary in the event of severe attacks of bud blast.

RHODODENDRON WHITE FLY (*Dialeurodes chittendeni*).—This member of the white fly family was first noticed in Britain in 1926 and is named after a former Director of the R.H.S. Garden at Wisley, where the pest was first studied. The scale-like larvae feed on the undersides of the leaves from the time they hatch in August until the following April, when they pupate; the winged adults emerge in June. They fly up in swarms when an infected bush is shaken, but do not travel far. The sucking of the sap by the larvae weakens the plant, and the honeydew they secrete may cause the development of sooty moulds on the leaves beneath them. But the pest has proved to be less damaging than was at first thought. Curiously enough, this white fly, although thought to be a native of the Himalaya, shares with the pests already mentioned a preference for the Hardy Hybrids and their parents in the Ponticum subseries.

Various weevils scallop the edges of rhododendron leaves, but the damage they do in this country scarcely justifies the use of chemicals against them.

DISEASES

BUD BLAST (*Pycnostysanus azaleae*).—This disease attacks hybrids with members of the Ponticum series in their ancestry and is indigenous to eastern North America. It was first recorded in Britain in the 1940s and has since become fairly widespread. The first sign of the disease is the appearance in late autumn or early winter of brown patches on the outer scales of the flower-buds. Eventually the bud is killed and becomes covered with pin-headed bristles; these are the spore-bearing organs that give rise to the next year's infection. There is good evidence that the fungus invades the bud through punctures made by the female rhododendron leafhopper when depositing eggs, though it has never been suggested that the fungus is solely dependent on this means of entry. In some gardens only a few buds are killed by the disease and it suffices to pick these off and burn them. Spraying against fungus itself is not effective and the best means of control, in the event of serious infestations, is to spray against the rhododendron leafhopper, as recommended above. Before the appearance of the characteristic bristles it is not at once obvious whether the bud has been killed by bud blast or by frost. But bud-tender rhododendrons are for the most part not subject to bud blast, and frost-damaged buds break off easily, while those killed by bud blast remain firmly attached to the stem.

AZALEA GALL (*Exobasidium vaccinii*).—In Britain this disease seems to be commonest on evergreen azaleas. On plants grown out-of-doors it appears in May on the new leaves, which become blistered and thickened and eventually turn white when the fungus reaches the spore-bearing stage, by which time the leaf itself has become almost wholly replaced by the fungus. The disease is much less serious than it looks and it usually suffices to pick off the affected leaves and burn them.

PETAL BLIGHT (*Ovulinia azaleae*).—This disease attacks and destroys the flowers of evergreen azaleas, without harming the plant itself, and is most likely to occur in warm, damp weather. It has been found on deciduous azaleas and on some hardy hybrid rhododendrons. Of Asiatic origin, it reached the USA in the 1920s and often ruins the display in the south-eastern states, where the evergreen azaleas are much grown. The first sign of attack is the appearance of small specks on the corollas, white on coloured flowers, light brown on white flowers. Within a matter of three days or so the flowers dissolve into a slimy mass and remain for a long time on the bush in a withered state. If only a few plants are attacked the dead flowers should be picked off at once and burned, to prevent the release of spores, which spread the disease and also give rise to resting bodies (sclerotia) which drop to the ground and in the following season give off spores to start a new cycle of infection. The most promising means of control is to spray with the systemic fungicide benomyl when the buds show colour and then at seven-day intervals until just before they open.

SILVER LEAF (*Stereum purpureum*).—It is not generally known that this disease, often called 'plum silver leaf', attacks many woody plants, including rhododendrons, causing die-back of the branches but not betraying its presence by a silvering of the leaves, as it does on plums and damsons. There is nothing that can be done about it, except to cut out all dead branches (which the wise grower does as a matter of routine). The cherry and Portugal laurels are both subject to the disease and could be a source of infection in some gardens.

DISORDERS

Most rhododendron troubles are due not to pests or diseases, but to unsuitable conditions at the root, wrong siting or damage by frost. If, in a normal season, the foliage becomes yellow between the veins but these remain the normal green, the plants may be suffering from lime-induced chlorosis, either because the natural soil is too alkaline for them or because it has been heavily limed in the past. It is reported that the use of leaf-mould from trees growing in chalky soils may also contain enough lime to cause chlorosis. A more uniform yellowing of the foliage could indicate nitrogen deficiency (likely to occur if undecayed or half-rotted vegetable matter is added to the soil); or the plant may have been given a too sunny position.

Distortion of the foliage is the result either of dryness at the root at the time the young growths are unfolding, or of damage by spring frost, which often deforms or burns the leaves while leaving the new shoot unharmed. Spring frost may also cause bark-split. If this is noticed early enough the affected branch may survive if the split is bound with tape or treated with a proprietary sealing compound. Rhododendrons that flower before early May are most subject to bark-split, especially if their stems are exposed.

SELECT BIBLIOGRAPHY

Abbreviations

R.Y.B.   *Rhododendron Year Book*

R.C.Y.B.   *Rhododendron and Camellia Year Book*

Journ. R.H.S.   *Journal of Royal Horticultural Society*

Periodicals, etc.

AMERICAN RHODODENDRON SOCIETY.—*Quarterly Bulletin*, 1947–

RHODODENDRON SOCIETY.—This small and exclusive society published privately three volumes of notes by its members over the period 1916–31. Among the members were leading botanists, and the garden owners who financed the Forrest expeditions.

ROYAL HORTICULTURAL SOCIETY.—*Rhododendron [and Camellia] Year Book*, Nos 1–25 (1946–70). This valuable publication came to a close in 1970 with the Year Book for 1971. Camellias were first included in No. 8 (Year book for 1954).

—— *Rhododendrons 1972, Rhododendrons 1973, Rhododendrons 1974 with Camellias and Magnolias*. A continuation of the *Year Book* in more modest form.

RHODODENDRON ASSOCIATION.—This association, the forerunner of the present Rhododendron Group of the R.H.S., published a Year Book between 1929 and 1939.

GENERAL

ABERCONWAY, LORD.—'Rhododendrons in the Garden', *R.Y.B.* *1949*, pp. 20–5.

ANDRÉ, E.—*Plantes de Terre de Bruyères*. Paris, 1864.

BASFORD, J. S.—'Some Rhododendrons in the West of Scotland', *R.C.Y.B. 1966*, pp. 21–30.

BOND, JOHN.—'Shade Trees for Rhododendrons', *R.C.Y.B. 1971*, pp. 48–55.

BOWERS, C. G.—*Rhododendrons and Azaleas*. Ed. 2, New York, 1960.

CAMPBELL, ILAY.—'Giants of the West', *R.C.Y.B. 1964*, pp. 9–16.

COWAN, J. M.—'Rhododendrons in the Royal Botanic Garden, Edinburgh', *R.Y.B. 1953*, pp. 33–57.

COX, E. H. M. and P. A.—*Modern Rhododendrons*. London, 1956.

COX, P. A.—*Dwarf Rhododendrons*. London, 1973.

—— *Rhododendrons* (Wisley Handbook 2). R.H.S., London, 1972.

DAVIDIAN, H. H.—'Rhododendrons in the Royal Botanic Garden, Edinburgh', *R.C.Y.B. 1959*, pp. 9–18; Part II, *R.C.Y.B. 1960*, pp. 42–53.

FINDLAY, T. H.—'The Preparation and Planting of a Virgin Woodland for Rhododendrons', *R.C.Y.B. 1955*, pp. 45–7.

FLETCHER, H. R.—*The International Rhododendron Register*. R.H.S., London, 1958. (Additions have been published annually in *R.C.Y.B.*, starting in No. 16, and latterly in *Rhododendrons*.)

—— 'The Rating of Merit of Rhododendron Species', *R.C.Y.B. 1962*, pp. 30–47.

GORER, G.—'Some Notes on Rhododendrons of the Maddenii Series and their Hybrids', *R.C.Y.B. 1968*, pp. 17–26.

GROOTENDORST, H. J.—*Rhododendrons en Azalea's*. Vereniging voor Boskoopse Culturen, 1954.

HANGER, FRANCIS.—'The Cultivation of Rhododendrons', *Journ. R.H.S.*, Vol. 70, pp. 355–62 (1945).

KINGDON-WARD, F.—*Rhododendrons*. London, 1949.

HARDY, A.—'An Adventure with Rhododendrons', Part II, *R.C.Y.B. 1971*, pp. 34–41.

LEACH, DAVID G.—*Rhododendrons of the World*. London, 1962.

LEE, F. P.—*The Azalea Book*. Princeton, 1958.

LUCAS PHILLIPS, C. E. and BARBER, PETER N.—*The Rothschild Rhododendrons*. London, 1967.

MANGLES, J. H.—The numerous articles and notes contributed by Mangles to the *Gardeners' Chronicle* and other periodicals between 1879 and 1884 were republished by *The Rhododendron Society* in 1917 (*Notes*, Vol. I, pp. 41–116).

MILLAIS, J. G.—*Rhododendrons and the Various Hybrids*. London, 1917.

—— *Rhododendrons and the Various Hybrids*. Second Series. London, 1924.

ROTHSCHILD, LIONEL DE.—'Some Notes on Rhododendrons', *R.Y.B. 1953*, pp. 7–31; *R.C.Y.B. 1954*, pp. 33–56.

—— 'Notes on the Series of Rhododendrons', *Year Book of the Rhododendron Association, 1933–39*.

—— 'Notes on Rhododendron Hybrids', ibid., 1933–9.

ROYAL HORTICULTURAL SOCIETY.—*The Rhododendron Handbook*; Part I,

Rhododendron Species, 1967; Part II, *Rhododendron Hybrids*, 1969. This Handbook is periodically revised. The dates given are those of the editions current in 1975.

RUSSELL, J. P. C.—'Rhododendrons as Foliage Plants', *R.Y.B. 1951–2*, pp. 52–9.

RUSSELL, JAMES.—*Rhododendrons at Sunningdale*. Windlesham, 1960.

STREET, F.—*Rhododendrons*. 1965.

URQUHART, BERYL L.—*The Rhododendron*. Vol. I, 1958; Vol. II, 1962. Sharpthorne, Sussex.

WALLACE, R. & CO. LTD.—*Rhododendron Species*. n.d.

WATSON, WILLIAM.—*Rhododendrons and Azaleas*. London, 1911.

WRIGHT, DAVID.—'The Grouping of Rhododendrons', *R.C.Y.B. 1964*, pp. 47–62; *R.C.Y.B. 1965*, pp. 105–18; *R.C.Y.B. 1971*, pp. 73–7.

BOTANICAL

AMMAL, E. K. JANAKI, *et al.*—'Polyploidy in the Genus Rhododendron', *R.Y.B. 1950*, pp. 92–8.

COWAN, J. M.—*The Rhododendron Leaf*. Edinburgh, 1950.

—— 'A survey of the Genus Rhododendron', *R.Y.B. 1949*, pp. 29–56.

HEDEGAARD, J.—'Beiträge zur Kenntnis der Morphologie von Rhododendron-Samen' (in the Year Book for 1968 of the German Rhododendron Society).

HOOKER, J. D.—*Rhododendrons of the Sikkim Himalaya*. London, 1849–51.

HUTCHINSON, J.—'Evolution and Classification of Rhododendrons', *R.Y.B. 1946*, pp. 42–7.

KINGDON WARD, F.—'Observations on the Genus Rhododendron', *R.Y.B. 1947*, pp. 99–114.

MAXIMOWICZ, C. J.—*Rhododendreae Asiae Orientalis*. St Petersburg, 1870.

PHILIPSON, MELVA N. and W. R.—'The Classification of Rhododendron' *R.C.Y.B. 1971*, pp. 1–8.

—— 'The History of Rhododendron Classification', *Notes Roy. Bot. Gard. Edin.*, Vol. 32 (1973), pp. 223–38.

REHDER, A. and WILSON, E. H.—*A Monograph of Azaleas*. Cambridge, Mass., 1921.

SEITHE, A.—'Die Haarformen der Gattung Rhododendron L.', *Bot. Jahrb.*, Vol. 79(3) (1960).

SLEUMER, H.—Ericaceae—*Rhododendron*, in *Flora Malesiana*, Ser. 1, Vol. 64 (1966), pp. 474–668.

—— 'The Genus Rhododendron L. in Indo-China and Siam', *Blumea*, Supplement IV (1958), pp. 39–59.

—— 'Ein System der Gattung Rhododendron L.', *Bot. Jahrb.*, Vol. 74(4) (1949), pp. 511–53.

STEVENS, P. P.—'A Classification of the Ericaceae: Subfamilies and Tribes', *Bot. Journ. Linn. Soc.*, Vol. 64 (1971), pp. 1–53.

STEVENSON, J. B. (ed.).—*The Species of Rhododendron*. London, 1930. Ed. 2, 1947. The second edition is essentially the same as the first, but descriptions of an additional 31 species were bound in.

RHODODENDRONS IN THE WILD

COWAN, J. M. (ed.).—*The Journeys and Plant Introductions of George Forrest.* London, 1952.

COX, E. H. M.—'Are there more Rhododendron Species to be Found and Introduced?', *R.C.Y.B. 1967*, pp. 21–4.

—— *Farrer's Last Journey.* London, 1926.

—— *Plant-hunting in China.* London, 1945.

COX, P. and P., and HUTCHISON, P.—'An Expedition to North East India', *R.C.Y.B. 1966*, pp. 61–77.

COX, P. and HUTCHISON, P.—'Rhododendrons in North-Eastern Turkey', *R.C.Y.B. 1963*, pp. 64–7.

FANG, W. P.—'Rhododendrons of Mount Omei', *R.Y.B. 1947*, pp. 115–23.

FORREST, G.—'The Flora of North-Western Yunnan', *Journ. R.H.S.*, Vol. 41 (1915), pp. 200–8.

—— 'Notes on the Flora of North-Western Yunnan', *Journ. R.H.S.*, Vol. 42 (1916), pp. 39–46.

—— 'Exploration of N.W. Yunnan and Tibet 1921–1922', *Journ. R.H.S.*, Vol. 49 (1924), pp. 25–36.

—— Lectures to Rhododendron Society, *Rhod. Soc. Notes*, Vol. II, pp. 3–23 (1920), 147–58 (1923).

FLETCHER, H. R.—*A Quest of Flowers; The Plant Explorations of Frank Ludlow and George Sherriff.* Edinburgh, 1975.

HARA, H.—'Occurrence and Distribution of Rhododendrons in Japan', *R.Y.B. 1948*, pp. 112–27.

HERKLOTS, G. A. C.—'The Rhododendrons of Hong Kong', *R.Y.B. 1949*, pp. 183–6.

HOOKER, J. D.—*Himalayan Journals.* London, 1854.

—— 'On the Climate and Vegetation . . . of East Nepal and the Sikkim Himalaya Mountains', *Journ. Hort. Soc.*, Vol. 7 (1852), pp. 69–131.

INGWERSEN, W. E. Th.—'The Rhododendrons of Europe', *R.Y.B. 1947*, pp. 21–8.

KEENAN, J.—'George Forrest, 1873–1932', *Journ. R.H.S.*, Vol. 98 (1973), pp. 112–18.

KINGDON WARD, F.—*The Land of the Blue Poppy.* Cambridge, 1913. 2nd Expedition (1911). N.W. Yunnan and bordering S.E. Tibet. No collections of rhododendron seed recorded.

—— *In Farthest Burma.* London, 1921. 5th Expedition (1914). Upper Burma, including Imaw Bum and Hpimaw, on the Irrawaddy–Salween divide. No rhododendron seed collected.

—— *The Mystery Rivers of Tibet.* London, 1923. 3rd Expedition (1913). N.W. Yunnan and bordering Tibet. Rhododendron seed-numbers, four only (406, 529, 768, 793).

—— *The Romance of Plant Hunting.* London, 1924. A confusing book. The early chapters are based on several of the author's expeditions before and immediately after the first world war. But Chapters VIII to XIII describe his visit to the Yungning–Muli area north of the Yangtse bend in 1921 (6th Expedition) and the first half of 1922 (7th Expedition, first part). Rhododendron seed-numbers for the 6th Expedition are 3776–5005, mostly collected in this area.

—— *From China to Hkamti Long*. London, 1924. Chapters I & II describe the route followed from Burma to Yungning in China in 1921 (6th Expedition). The main part of the book, however, is devoted to the Tibetan Marches and a journey thence across the Salween and Upper Irrawaddy to Hkamti Long in Burma (7th Expedition). Rhododendron seed-numbers 5384–5602.

—— *The Riddle of the Tsangpo Gorges*. London, 1926. 8th Expedition (1924). Describes what was, perhaps, the author's most fruitful journey, during which the extraordinary wealth of rhododendrons within and north of the region of the great Tsangpo bend was revealed for the first time.

—— *Plant Hunting on the Edge of the World*. London, 1930. Part I covers the author's 9th Expedition (1926) to the Seinghku and Di Chu valleys, on the borders between N.W. upper Burma, Tibet and Assam. Rhododendron seed-numbers 6735–7642. Part II is devoted to the 10th Expedition (1927–8), to the Mishmi Hills of Assam (Delei Valley). Rhododendron seed-numbers 7701–8592.

—— *Plant Hunter in Tibet*. London, 1934. 12th Expedition (1933). The area visited reaches from Assam northward through Rima across the snow-range to the Upper Salween. Rhododendron seed-numbers 10351–11060.

—— *Plant Hunter's Paradise*. London, 1937. 11th Expedition (1930–1). Upper Burma, mainly the Adung Valley, with a short incursion into Tibet. Rhododendron seed-numbers 9130–10231.

—— *Assam Adventure*. London, 1941. 13th Expedition (1935). Himalaya East of Bhutan (Balipara Frontier Tract and Mönyül and Tsari); mountains north of Tsangpo. Seed-numbers 11378–12414.

—— *Burma's Icy Mountains*. London, 1949. 14th Expedition (1937). After an unsuccessful attempt to resume plant exploration in China, the author paid a second visit to the Adung valley in the far north-west of Burma. Rhododendron seed-numbers 13006–13550. Chapters 17–24 describe the American Vernay-Cutting expedition to the Burma–China frontier (1938–9). Rhododendron seed-numbers 00005–00460.

—— *Plant Hunter in Manipur*. London, 1952. An expedition to Eastern Manipur for the New York Botanical Garden. Rhododendron seed-numbers 17044–17818.

—— *Return to the Irrawaddy*. London, 1956. Kingdon Ward's last expedition (1953), which took him to the Triangle, a mountainous region between the two main branches of the Upper Irrawaddy. Rhododendron seed-numbers 20601–22036.

—— *Pilgrimage for Plants*, with a Biographical Introduction and Bibliography by W. T. Stearn. London, 1960. A collection of essays, of which Chapter 7 is devoted to rhododendrons. It was Kingdon Ward's last work, and is particularly valuable for the summary of his plant-hunting expeditions and voluminous writings, contributed by Dr W. T. Stearn of the British Museum (Natural History).

—— 'Plant-hunting in the Triangle, North Burma', *Journ. R.H.S.*, Vol. 80 (1955), pp. 174–90.

—— 'Botanical Explorations in North Burma', *Journ. R.H.S.*, Vol. 71 (1946), pp. 318–25.

—— 'Six Months in Mönyul', *Journ. R.H.S.*, Vol. 69 (1944), pp. 267–72, 305–7.

—— 'Rhododendrons in the Wild', *R.Y.B. 1949*, pp. 9–19.

—— 'Collectors' Numbers. Reasons for their Retention', *R.C.Y.B. 1956*, pp. 48–51.

—— 'Rhododendrons in Burma, Assam and Tibet', *R.Y.B. 1947*, pp. 13–20.

LANCASTER, R.—'An Account of the Species found by the University College Bangor Nepal Expedition 1971', *Rhododendrons 1972*, pp. 24–32.

—— 'Rhododendron Species encountered on the Hilliers Plant Trek to East Nepal 1973', *Rhododendrons 1973*, pp. 39–45.

ROCK, JOSEPH F.—*The Ancient Na-Khi Kingdom of Southwest China*. Cambridge, Mass. (1947). 2 vols. Although primarily an historical and ethnographic work, it contains superb collotype plates illustrating the landscapes of N.W. Yunnan and S.E. Szechwan, and four useful maps.

SCHWEINFURTH, ULRICH.—*Die horizontale und verticale Verbreitung der Vegetation im Himalaya* (Bonner Geographische Abhandlungen Heft 20). Bonn, 1954.

SKINNER, HENRY T.—'In Search of Native Azaleas', *R.C.Y.B. 1957*, pp. 9–28 (abridged from *Morris Arboretum Bulletin*, Vol. 6 (1955), Nos 1 and 2).

STAINTON, J. D. A.—*Forests of Nepal*. London, 1972.

SYKES, W. R.—'Rhododendrons in Western Nepal', *R.C.Y.B. 1954*, pp. 62–7.

SYNGE, P. M.—'Sir Joseph Hooker and the Rhododendrons of the Sikkim Himalaya', *R.Y.B. 1955*, pp. 38–51.

TAYLOR, GEORGE.—'Plant Collecting in South-eastern Tibet', *Journ. R.H.S.*, Vol. 72 (1947), pp. 130–44, 166–77.

WARD, F. KINGDON.—See Kingdon Ward, F. Most of the author's works are signed F. Kingdon Ward and usually indexed under Ward, F. K. But from the late 1940s he hyphenated his name, and his later books and articles are therefore indexed under Kingdon-Ward, F. For convenience, all references to his writings in this Bibliography are listed under Kingdon Ward, F.

WILSON, E. H.—'Rhododendrons of Hupeh Province', *Rhod. Soc. Notes* Vol. II (1923), pp. 160–74.

—— 'Rhododendrons of North-Eastern Asia', ibid. (1922), pp. 93–106.

—— 'Rhododendrons of the Bonin and Liukiu Islands and of Formosa', ibid. (1924), pp. 228–40.

—— 'Rhododendrons of Eastern China', op. cit., Vol. III (1925), pp. 18–28.

—— *A Naturalist in Western China*. London, 1913. 2 vols.

HYBRIDS

ABERCONWAY, LORD, *et al.*—'Aims in Breeding Rhododendrons . . .', *R.C.Y.B. 1960*, pp. 19–41.

ABERCONWAY, LORD.—'Rhododendron Hybrids', *Journ. R.H.S.*, Vol. 76 (1951), pp. 257–64.

BARBER, P. N.—'Rhododendrons at Exbury', *Journ. R.H.S.*, Vol. 94 (1969), pp. 379–86; *R.C.Y.B. 1970*, pp. 25–35.

FINDLAY, T. H.—'Notes on Rhododendron Hybrids at the Great Park, Windsor', *R.C.Y.B. 1967*, pp. 73–4.

—— 'Some Dwarf Rhododendron Hybrids raised at Windsor', *R.C.Y.B. 1971*, pp. 58–9.

GEORGE, ARTHUR.—'Modern Compact Rhododendron Hybrids', *Journ. R.H.S.*, Vol. 96 (1971), pp. 449–55.

—— 'Choosing Rhododendrons for a Small Garden', *Journ. R.H.S.*, Vol. 98 (1973), pp. 541–5.

HILLIER, H. G., *et al.*—'Symposium on the Most Popular Rhododendron Hybrids', *R.C.Y.B. 1963*, pp. 68–82.

HOBBIE, DIETRICH.—'Rhododendrons at Linswege, Oldenburg, Germany', *R.C.Y.B. 1959*, pp. 43–8.

PUDDLE, C. E.—'Dwarf Rhododendrons for the Small Garden', *R.Y.B. 1950*, pp. 27–37.

PUDDLE, F. C.—'The Breeding of Pedigree Rhododendrons', *R.Y.B. 1948*, pp. 35–41.

ROSE, F. J.—'Hybrid Rhododendrons', *R.Y.B. 1949*, pp. 88–97.

RUSSELL, J. P. C.—'New Types of Hybrid Rhododendrons for the Small Garden, *Journ. R.H.S.*, Vol. 70 (1945), pp. 225–32.

SLOCOCK, O. C. A.—'Garden Hybrid Rhododendrons', *R.Y.B. 1949*, pp. 101–13.

STREET, F.—*Hardy Rhododendrons*. London, 1954.

PESTS, DISEASES, AND DISORDERS

ANON.—'Bud Blast on Rhododendrons and Azaleas', *Journ. R.H.S.*, Vol. 75 (1950), pp. 230–2.

BAILLIE, A. F. H. and JEPSON, W. F.—'Bud Blast Disease of Rhododendron . . .', *Journ. R.H.S.*, Vol. 76 (1951), pp. 355–65.

—— —— 'Rhododendron Bud Blast', *R.Y.B. 1951–52*, pp. 72–8.

BROOKS, AUDREY V.—'Disorders of Rhododendrons and Camellias', *Rhododendrons 1974*, pp. 57–62.

—— 'Diseases of Rhododendrons and Camellias', *Rhododendrons 1975* (seen in manuscript by courtesy of Miss Brooks and the Royal Horticultural Society).

HARRIS, K. M.—'Pests of Rhododendrons', *R.C.Y.B. 1968*, pp. 146–55.

HOARE, R. H.—'The Rhododendron Bug', *Journ. R.H.S.*, Vol. 48 (1923), p. 16–21.

SLOCOCK, O. C. A.—'The Lacewing Fly', *Y.B. Rhod. Ass. 1934*, pp. 89–92.

STREET, F.—'Some Observations and Notes on Bud Blast on Rhododendrons', *R.Y.B. 1950*, pp. 72–7.

WILSON, G. F.—'Insect Pests of Rhododendrons', *Journ. R.H.S.*, Vol. 50 (1925), pp. 46–54.

—— 'A Leaf-hopper (Jassid) on Rhododendron', *Journ. R.H.S.*, Vol. 62 (1937), pp. 210–13.

—— 'The Rhododendron White Fly', *Journ. R.H.S.*, Vol. 54 (1929), pp. 214–17 and (same title) *Journ. R.H.S.*, Vol. 60 (1935), pp. 264–71.

THE SPECIES

CLASSIFICATION

A genus as large and varied as *Rhododendron* becomes comprehensible only if its species are systematically arranged according to their affinity. The classification currently used in Britain was devised by Sir Isaac Bayley Balfour of the Royal Botanic Garden, Edinburgh, and further developed by other botanists there after his death in 1922. When work on the genus began there early this century the most authoritative classification was the one that Maximowicz had provided in his *Rhododendreae Asiae Orientalis* (1870), in which the genus had been divided into seven sections. But, as Balfour pointed out in discussing Maximowicz's section Osmothamnus, 'In the years that have passed since Maximowicz wrote upon the East Asiatic Rhododendrons, China has supplied us with more Rhododendrons than were then known from the whole world.' Taxonomic units below the rank of Maximowicz's sections were needed if the new material was to be rendered intelligible, and so the practice grew up in the herbarium of grouping together species according to their apparent affinity, each group being termed a 'series' and given the name of the oldest or best-known member of the group. This was usually either a Himalayan species, e.g., the Thomsonii series, or a Yunnan species discovered earlier by one of the French missionaries and described late in the 19th century by Franchet, e.g., the Taliense series. It was essentially an informal and tentative scheme, which can be seen evolving in Balfour's discussions of the new species (more than three hundred of them) that he described between 1916 and 1922 in *Notes from the Royal Botanic Garden, Edinburgh*.

The Balfourian method was never given formal expression in Sir Isaac's lifetime, and might have retained its empirical character were it not that gardeners growing the new rhododendrons from China and bordering parts were in urgent need for some guide through the hundreds of names they had to contend with. For the benefit of members of the Rhododendron Society a tentative classified list of species was compiled by Edinburgh botanists and circulated in 1924 (*Rhod. Soc. Notes*, Vol. II, pp. 215-27). It was, presumably for the sake of completeness, extended to cover the whole genus (with the exception of the Malayan, Indonesian, and New Guinea species). The fourth edition of the list, much amended, appeared in 1928 and is the basis of the arrangement adopted in *Species of Rhododendron*, published in 1930. This book is a remarkable monument to the collaboration that then existed between botanists and amateur growers. Published by the exclusive Rhododendron Society under the editorship of J. B. Stevenson of Tower Court, it was the work of three leading botanists: Dr Rehder of the Arnold Arboretum, who described the azaleas;

H. F. Tagg of the Royal Botanic Garden, Edinburgh, who treated the elepidote rhododendrons; and Dr J. Hutchinson of Kew, who was responsible for the lepidote rhododendrons and most of the azaleastrums. Single-page descriptions were given of each species and for the first time all the series were provided with diagnoses and with keys to their constituent species. The book was a fine achievement and has probably been as much used by botanists as by gardeners. In the forty-five years since it was published many new species have been described and brought into cultivation, and various amendments have been made to the classification originally adopted. An abbreviated edition is published by the Royal Horticultural Society as Part I of *The Rhododendron Handbook*, revised every five years or so.

It is an obvious defect of the British system of classification that the series are of unequal taxonomic status. Those originally constituted by Balfour were for the most part equivalent to subdivisions of Maximowicz's sections, and the term 'series' was not inappropriate for them. But some series are certainly entitled to rank as sections, e.g., *s.* Anthopogon, *s.* Ovatum, and *s.* Stamineum, while the azaleas, which in *Species of Rhododendron* are grouped in a single series, represent two whole sections of Maximowicz's classification, each of which should probably rank as a subgenus. However, the botanists who instituted the series classification, and those who have since sought to improve it, have not had as their aim to provide a systematic arrangement of the whole genus, much of which lies outside their sphere of interest. A classification of conventional form was published in 1949 by Dr H. Sleumer (see Bibliography), in which the genus is divided into subgenera, sections, and subsections. It is, to a large extent, based on *Species of Rhododendron* and the earliest of the revisions by Cowan and Davidian (further mentioned below). Where appropriate, the British series (or, in some instances, subseries) are given the rank of subsections, and are given names according to the rules of botanical nomenclature; thus the Thomsonii series and the Heliolepis series become respectively the subsections *Thomsonia* and *Heliolepida*. Some series, such as those mentioned at the beginning of this paragraph, receive higher rank. Sleumer's system has the merit of providing botanists with subgeneric taxa of the usual form, but the author himself claimed no finality for it and indeed anticipated that it would need modification in the light of later research.

In the following synopsis no attempt has been made to present a botanical classification of the genus, but the series, instead of being treated in alphabetical order, have been grouped under four headings: Lepidote Rhododendrons; Elepidote or Hymenanthes Rhododendrons; Azaleas; and Azaleastrums. This arrangement, it is hoped, will make for a better understanding of the genus.

Since 1946, revisions of some of the series of *Rhododendron* have appeared in the *Rhododendron and [Camellia] Year Book*, published by the Royal Horticultural Society. The work was begun by Dr J. M. Cowan and H. H. Davidian of the Royal Botanic Garden, Edinburgh, and continued by the latter after Dr Cowan's death in 1960. References to these important revisions, which have been of great assistance in preparing this new edition, are given below in the appropriate place.

Lepidote Rhododendrons

The lepidote species are characterised by the presence of scales on various parts of the plant, most obviously on the undersides of the leaves. These scales, really glandular hairs of complex structure, consist of a very short stalk surmounted by a multicellular head, which is usually surrounded by a rim made up of radially arranged cells, the whole scale, seen from above under low magnification, having the appearance of a shield with a central boss or umbo. The edge of the shield may be entire, crenated, or sometimes (as in *s*. Anthopogon) deeply incised. Rarely, as in *s*. Trichocladum, the rim is absent. These elaborate glandular hairs take the place of the simple glandular hairs found in other types of rhododendron, but never among the lepidote species. In addition to scales, the lepidote species also frequently bear eglandular hairs, but these are always simple; the branched hairs so frequent among the Hymenanthes rhododendrons are unknown among the lepidotes. The Edgeworthii series, which is unusual among the lepidotes in having a dense indumentum, is no exception to this rule, since the covering is made up of simple hairs.

It has been found that the presence of scales is, at least in the species examined, almost perfectly correlated with another character, namely, that the leaves are convolute in the bud, i.e., folded forward, whereas in all other groups of *Rhododendron* they are revolute, the margins being folded back so as to conceal most of the undersurface (J. Sinclair, *Notes Roy. Bot. Gard. Edin.*, Vol. 19 (1937), pp. 267–71).

As in most rhododendrons (except the Azaleastrums) the flowers are produced from terminal buds, but three series have axillary inflorescences, i.e., the flower clusters are borne in the axils of the uppermost leaves and truly terminal buds are not formed (or at least not as a general rule). Some other lepidote species (e.g., *R. yunnanense* and *R. lutescens*) also have axillary inflorescences, but in these a terminal bud is formed and usually produces flowers, so the axillary clusters are really supplementary (but in *R. lutescens*, on some shoots, all the inflorescences are axillary and the terminal bud vegetative).

In the species treated here, the corolla is mostly narrowly to widely funnel-shaped (verging on rotate in some species), tubular or campanulate, and the limb is occasionally zygomorphic (especially in the Triflorum series). Other shapes are found among the Malesian lepidotes and when these are taken into account the corolla-shape is more diverse among the scaly-leaved rhododendrons than in any other group.

In most of the hardier species the seeds are plain, i.e., without appendages. In the section Vireya (the Malesian lepidotes and their few Sino-Himalayan allies) the seeds are tailed at each end, and similar but shorter appendages occur among epiphytic species, e.g., in *R. edgeworthii* and some members of the Maddenii series.

Polyploidy, rare elsewhere in the genus, is common among the lepidotes. In two series, *s.* Cinnabarinum and *s.* Heliolepis, no diploids have been recorded; and in two others, *s.* Lapponicum and *s.* Triflorum, polyploids outnumbered diploids among the plants examined (Janaki Ammal *et al., R.Y.B. 1950*, pp. 94–6).

The lepidote rhododendrons are the most numerous group in the genus, with over 500 species at present recognised (though over half of these belong to the mainly Malesian section Vireya). They also have the widest ecological and geographical range. All epiphytic species are lepidote, but so too are virtually all the alpines; the northernmost rhododendron, *R. lapponicum,* and the southernmost, the Australian *R. lochae* (not treated here), are both lepidote. They are sparingly represented in North America and western Eurasia, but in Sino-Himalaya they are very numerous and are the only type of rhododendron found in the Malesian region, apart from the exceptions mentioned on page 542.

In Sleumer's classification the lepidote rhododendrons are split into four subgenera. The series with (?) constantly axillary inflorescences are grouped in two subgenera—*Rhodorastrum* (Maxim.) C. B. Clarke and *Pseudorhodorastrum* Sleumer—the former comprising the Dauricum series, the latter the Scabrifolium and Virgatum series. It is debatable, however, whether this character should be given such taxonomic weight. All the other lepidotes are grouped in a single subgenus with the exception of the Trichocladum series, which is given subgeneric rank as subgen. *Pseudazalea* Sleumer, another controversial decision.

There is much to be said for keeping all the lepidote rhododendrons in a single subgenus, at least for the time being. The subgenus would take the name subgen. RHODODENDRON, of which the principal synonyms are: *Rhod.* sect. *Lepipherum* G. Don; *Osmothamnus* DC.; *Rhod.* sect. *Osmothamnus* (DC.) Maxim.; *Rhod.* sect. *Eurhododendron* Maxim., in part; *Rhod.* subgen. *Eurhododendron* Series B C. B. Clarke; *Rhod.* subgen. *Lepidorhodium* Koehne.

s. ANTHOPOGON

Revision: *R.Y.B. 1947* (2), pp. 55–86.

Dwarf evergreen shrubs with small aromatic leaves; scales lacerate (with a jagged edge). Flowers in terminal clusters, very shortly stalked. Corolla tubular with a spreading limb, less than 1 in. long, white, rose, or pale yellow. Stamens commonly five, occasionally up to ten, included in the tube. Ovary five-celled; style very short. Its distribution is: borders between Pakistan and Afghanistan (*R. collettianum*); Himalaya; thence east and north to Kansu; Siberia. A very distinct group of 14 species, easily recognised in flower by the concealed stamens and style. Its position in Sleumer's classification is: subgenus *Rhododendron* section *Pogonanthum*.

s. BOOTHII

Revision: *R.Y.B. 1948* (3), pp. 60–79.

Evergreen shrubs, often epiphytic, varying in habit and size of leaf. Scales on underside of leaf uniform in colour. Inflorescence terminal, with up to ten flowers. Corolla usually campanulate or tubular-campanulate, white, rose, pink or yellow, five-lobed, up to 1¾ in. long. Stamens ten. Style stout and bent downwards (except in *ss*. Tephropeplum). The whole series is confined to the wetter parts of the Sino-Himalayan region, from Bhutan through the Assam Himalaya and S.E. Tibet to upper Burma and N.W. Yunnan.

ss. Boothii.—Dwarf or medium-sized shrubs, often epiphytic. Leaves 1 to 5 in. long, glaucous beneath. Inflorescence with three to ten flowers. Corolla campanulate, yellow. Five species, the four in cultivation all uncommon and rather tender.

ss. Megeratum.—Dwarf shrubs. Leaves up to 2 in. long, hairy at the margin and often on the upper surface; undersurface glaucous. Inflorescence one- or two-flowered. Corolla campanulate to rotate, yellow or white. Two species, both fairly hardy but early flowering. See R. *leucaspis*.

ss. Tephropeplum.—Shrubs up to 10 ft high. Leaves up to 5 in. long, the undersides glaucous and usually densely scaly. Corolla tubular-campanulate, white, pink, purplish, yellow, or cream. Style slender, straight. Four species, the commonest being the variable R. *tephropeplum*.

s. Camelliiflorum

Represented in cultivation only by the type-species (q.v.).

s. Campylogynum

Revision: *R.C.Y.B. 1954* (8), pp. 78–84.

This series has now been reduced to a single species, R. *campylogynum* (q.v.), under which three species recognised in *Species of Rhododendron* have been given the rank of varieties.

s. Camtschaticum *see* Therorhodion, Vol. IV.

s. Carolinianum

Small or medium-sized evergreen shrubs with leaves mostly 2 to 3¾ in. long. Inflorescence terminal. Corolla funnel-shaped or funnel-campanulate, about 1½ in. wide, light rosy purple or pink, sometimes white, scaly outside. Stamens ten. A group of three closely related species, allied to the Heliolepis series, natives of the eastern USA.

s. Cinnabarinum

Tall or medium-sized evergreen shrubs. Leaves mostly 1½ to 3 in. long, often glaucous when young, densely scaly beneath. Inflorescence terminal (also axillary in R. *keysii* and the closely related R. *igneum*). Corolla usually tubular or tubular-campanulate, but campanulate in R. *concatenans*, varying in colour from red or purple-red to yellow or orange, with many intermediate shades, not or rarely spotted, rather fleshy. This is essentially a Himalayan series, extending as far east as the Mishmi Hills. Of the five species, two—R. *concatenans* and R. *xanthocodon*—are closely related to R. *cinnabarinum* and will probably be sunk in it before long. The only other cultivated member is R. *keysii*. All these are hexaploid, i.e., have three times the normal number of chromosomes in their body cells. The interesting R. *tamaense*, at present unplaced, shows some kinship with the Cinnabarinum series but is also near to R. *oreotrephes* of the Triflorum series.

s. Dauricum

This group of two or three species has been given the rank of section (sect. *Rhodorastrum*) because of its rather distinct inflorescence. The flowers are produced singly (rarely in twos) from clustered axillary buds and the young growths spring from below the flower-bearing part of the shoot. For further details see R. *dauricum* and R. *mucronulatum*. The series is confined to N.E. Asia (including Japan). In Sleumer's classification it ranks as a subgenus.

s. Edgeworthii

Revision: *R.C.Y.B. 1964* (18), pp. 111–18.

This series, with three species, is represented in cultivation mainly by R. *edgeworthii* (*bullatum*), which is easily recognised among lepidote rhododendrons by its rugose leaves densely tomentose beneath and its fragrant, white or rose-tinted, funnel-shaped flowers. Although many lepidote rhododendrons are bristly or downy, it is very uncommon for them to have such a dense indumentum. Indeed only two other species show this character, and both are on that account grouped with R. *edgeworthii*, namely, R. *seinghkuense* and R. *pendulum* (qq.v.), neither of which bears much resemblance to it in floral characters. The series is confined to the eastern Himalaya, upper Burma, and N.W. Yunnan.

s. Ferrugineum

Dwarf evergreen shrubs, Leaves up to 1½ in. long, densely scaly beneath, crenulate in two species; scales entire. Inflorescence shortly racemose or umbellate. Corolla tubular with a spreading limb, pink. Style short, included. This series, with three species, is the only one endemic to Europe (Pyrenees to Balkans) and not closely related to any other series.

R. *ferrugineum* is now taken as the type-species of the genus *Rhododendron*.

s. Glaucophyllum

Revision: *R.Y.B. 1948* (3), pp. 79–93 (as Glaucum series).

This group is mainly represented in cultivation by the typical subseries, of which the leading characters are as follows: Small evergreen shrubs. Leaves up to 3¾ in. long, their undersides usually glaucous, with scales of two kinds, the smaller scales pale yellow, variously spaced, the larger dark brown, scattered. Inflorescence terminal with up to ten flowers. Calyx well developed, up to almost ½ in. long. Corolla campanulate, up to 1 in. long, pink, rose, slaty purple, or yellow. Style usually short, stout and bent (but often straight in R. *glaucophyllum*). Five species in the rainier part of Sino-Himalaya, from E. Nepal to N.W. Yunnan.

The other subseries of Glaucophyllum comprises R. *genestierianum* (q.v.) and R. *micromeres* (not treated).

s. Heliolepis

Closely allied to the Triflorum series and, according to Hutchinson, scarcely separable from it by any definite characters. At present nine species are recognised, some precariously based and likely to be sunk when the series comes to be revised. The series ranges from upper Burma through W. China as far north as Kansu. All the cultivated plants examined have proved to be polyploid.

s. LAPPONICUM

Revision: Melva N. and W. R. Philipson, 'A Revision of *Rhododendron* section *Lapponicum*', *Notes Roy. Bot. Gard. Edin.*, Vol. 34 (1975), pp. 1–71.

Dwarf evergreen shrubs. Leaves usually less than 1 in. long, aromatic in most species, scaly on both sides, the scales of the underside of varying density and either uniform in colouring or bicolorous. Inflorescence terminal, few-flowered. Corolla usually less than 1 in. wide, funnel-shaped with a short tube, in various shades of lavender, pink, purple, or violet, rarely yellow, white only in albino forms. Stamens five to ten, usually hairy at the base, exserted (rarely included in the tube). Style variable in length, often even in the same species.

The main concentration of species is in the drier and bleaker parts of the Sino-Himalayan region, where they dominate over vast tracts in some areas, especially on the borders between Yunnan and Szechwan, in the mountains around the two great bends of the Yangtse river. In the rainier parts of Sino-Himalaya they are less common. Outside Sino-Himalaya there are two closely related species—R. *lapponicum* and R. *parvifolium*—which between them girdle the globe in high latitudes.

The Lapponicum series is taxonomically a difficult one, in which polyploidy is common and natural hybrids occur. The revision referred to above, in which the series is given the rank of a section of the subgenus *Rhododendron*, appeared in August 1975, when most of the present volume was in proof and shortly before it finally went to press. However, an effort has been made to incorporate or mention the authors' main conclusions. They have stressed, and would certainly like the warning to be repeated, that the botanical key provided is based on herbarium specimens, in which the colouring of the scales—a character so useful for identification—is darker than on living plants. Leaves of the previous season's growth should always be used when a living specimen is taken through the key.

s. LEPIDOTUM

Revision: *R.Y.B. 1948* (3), pp. 93–101.

A horticulturally unimportant group of three species, recognisable by the relatively long pedicels, the small, rotate corolla and sharply bent style. R. *lepidotum* is one of the most widely distributed of Sino-Himalayan species. The other two are confined to the Himalaya.

s. MADDENII

There has been no revision of this group since Dr J. Hutchinson constituted and discussed it in 'The Maddenii Series of Rhododendron', *Notes Roy. Bot. Gard. Edin.*, Vol. 12 (1919), pp. 1–84. This is the basis of his treatment of the series in *Species of Rhododendron* (1930).

The species in this group are on the average much larger than other lepidotes, both in the size of the plant and in the dimensions of leaf and flower. The leaves are persistent, mostly over 3 in. long and up to 8 in. long in some species. Inflorescence terminal with up to seven flowers. Corolla funnel-shaped, tubular-funnel-shaped, or funnel-campanulate, rarely less than 2 in. long, white, pink, or yellow, often fragrant. Style nearly always scaly, at least in its lower part.

There are three subseries, all three reaching as far west as Sikkim or E. Nepal and as far east as Yunnan. The Ciliicalyx subseries, which is the most widely distributed of the three, is also represented in S.E. China, Thailand (where the *ss.* Maddenii also occurs), and in the former Indochina. Mostly the species occur at low altitudes, as epiphytes or on rock-ledges or by torrents. Very few of these beautiful shrubs can be grown outdoors near London, except most of the Maddenii subseries and a few members of the Ciliicalyx subseries such as *R. fletcherianum*, *R. valentinianum*, *R. ciliatum*, and *R. johnstoneanum*.

ss. MADDENII.—Medium-sized or large shrubs (*R. manipurense* sometimes a tree). Calyx variable. Corolla narrowly funnel-shaped, white or light pink. Stamens fifteen to twenty-five. Ovary-cells ten to twelve. Eight species are at present recognised but this is likely to be reduced when the group comes to be revised. The characters used to separate the species are poorly correlated, and too much weight has been given to size of calyx and the precise number of stamens. The hairs on the stamen-filaments, the presence or absence of which is made a leading character in *Species of Rhododendron*, are sparsely and irregularly developed, and sometimes reduced to a few watery excrescences. Polyploidy is rife in this group. Some plants have even been found to be dodecaploid, i.e., with six times the normal number of chromosomes. On the average the species in this subseries are hardier than in the other two, and all those in cultivation are late-flowering.

ss. CILIICALYX.—Calyx mostly small, frequently ciliate. Most species have ten stamens and a six-celled ovary. Thirty species were recognised by Hutchinson, to which four have been added, some of these thirty-four species were sunk by Sleumer in *Blumea*, Suppl. IV (1958), pp. 40–7. The number is certainly excessively large, considering the limited range of variation in this group. Some species are founded on minor characters that probably fluctuate even in a local population.

ss. MEGACALYX.—Calyx well developed, often large and leafy, not ciliate, except in *R. lindleyi*. Stamens normally ten. Ovary-cells five. Another character given by Hutchinson is that the midrib of the leaf is prominent above and the upper side of the petiole convex (slightly grooved in *R. megacalyx*). In the other two subseries the midrib is sunken and the petiole concave. The group is a small one, with about nine species.

s. MICRANTHUM

This series consists of a single species (q.v.), not closely related to any other rhododendron. The flowers resemble those of *Ledum*, except that the segments are united at the base, and are borne in racemes. The seeds have a short appendage at each end. N. and N.W. China.

s. MOUPINENSE

Of the three closely related species in this series, only *R. moupinense* (q.v.) is in cultivation. All three are frequently epiphytic and are confined to a small area of S.W. Szechwan.

s. SALUENENSE

Revision: *R.C.Y.B. 1954*, pp. 84–98.

Small, mainly dwarf shrubs, sometimes more or less prostrate. Leaves up to 1½ in. long, densely coated beneath with crenulate scales. Inflorescence few-flowered, terminal. Calyx well developed. Corolla funnel-shaped or rotate, downy outside, purple or crimson. *R. fragariiflorum*, provisionally placed in this series, is anomalous, and near to the Lapponicum series. The other seven species, all very closely allied, differ from the Lapponicum series in the larger calyx, usually enclosing the capsule, and the crenulate scales. The series is distributed in the E. Himalaya, upper Burma, N.W. Yunnan and bordering parts of Tibet, in the alpine and subalpine zones. In this region the Lapponicum series is poorly represented.

s. SCABRIFOLIUM

Revision: *R.C.Y.B. 1964* (18), pp. 118–33.

Small or medium-sized shrubs; branchlets downy or bristly (except in *R. racemosum*). Leaves persistent, up to 4 in. long, mostly downy or bristly above, green and downy beneath (but the undersides glaucous and glabrous in *R. racemosum*, glaucous and slightly downy in *R. hemitrichotum*). Inflorescences axillary on the upper part of the previous season's growths, each cluster with one to four flowers but sometimes terminal only in *R. spinuliferum*. Corolla funnel-shaped to tubular (saccate in *R. spinuliferum*), white or pink, up to 1 in. long. Six species in S.W. China, mostly in rather dry habitats and apparently absent from the rainier parts of Sino-Himalaya.

In Sleumer's classification, this series, with *s.* Virgatum, constitutes the subgenus *Pseudorhodorastrum*, characterised by: inflorescences axillary; new growths from pseudoterminal buds or from buds below the flower-bearing part of the shoot.

s. TRICHOCLADUM

The eleven species at present recognised in this group are for the greater part distinct from most other lepidotes in their deciduous leaves and precocious flowers, and have on that account been given by Sleumer the rank of a subgenus—*Pseudazalea*. But some species are evergreen, e.g., *R. viridescens* (which is also late-flowering), and a completely deciduous habit is found in some other lepidote species. Furthermore the number of deciduous species in this series is greatly inflated and could be reduced to but one, *R. trichocladum* itself (q.v.). A more distinctive feature of the group is the rimless, bun-shaped scales on the undersides of the leaves.

s. TRIFLORUM

Revision: *R.C.Y.B. 1963* (17), pp. 156–222.

Lightly branched shrubs mostly of moderate size, rarely small trees. Leaves persistent, rarely semi-deciduous or deciduous, up to 6 in. or so long, usually of rather thin texture, scales on undersurface of variable density. Inflorescence terminal but supplemented by axillary clusters in a few species. Calyx small. Corolla (except in the Hanceanum subseries and the anomalous *R. concinnoides*) funnel-shaped, zygomorphic ('butterfly-shaped'), usually speckled in the upper part, white, yellow, greenish yellow, pink, lavender, purple, or deep magenta. Style long, slender (except in *R. afghanicum*). The largest subseries is the YUNNANENSE, with seventeen species; the AUGUSTINII subseries (four species) is similar, but differs in having the leaf-midrib hairy beneath. The TRIFLORUM subseries (eight species) differs in its constantly yellow or greenish-yellow flowers. *R. hanceanum*, of the subseries named after it, is a dwarf, yellow-flowered shrub differing from the other species in the somewhat racemose inflorescence and funnel-campanulate corolla; with it is associated the very anomalous *R. afghanicum*.

The typical, yellow-flowered subseries is widely distributed, from E. Nepal to W. Szechwan, and has one species in Japan. The Augustinii and Yunnanense subseries are essentially Chinese in distribution, being absent from the Himalaya and rare west of the Salween; mainly they are thicket-forming shrubs of open places or light woodland at moderate elevations.

s. UNIFLORUM

Revision: R.Y.B. *1948* (3), pp. 51–60, 101–9.

Dwarf shrubs. Leaves not much more than 1 in. long, their undersides glaucous, with small uniform scales. Inflorescence terminal, with one or two flowers. Calyx very small, except in R. *ludlowii*. Corolla campanulate or funnel-shaped, purple, pink, or rosy pink (yellow in R. *ludlowii*), hairy outside. Style slender and straight. This description excludes the anomalous R. *monanthum*, a taller shrub with leaves up to 2 in. long, their scales not uniform, and with the corolla not hairy outside. Apart from this there are six species in the eastern Himalaya and upper Burma.

s. VACCINIOIDES

This series, as defined in *Species of Rhododendron*, comprises the few northern outliers of a large group of lepidote species native mainly to the Malayan peninsula, Java, Borneo, Sumatra, the Celebes, the Philippines, and New Guinea (one species, R. *lochae*, in Australia). Dr Sleumer, the leading authority on this group, classes it as subgenus *Rhododendron* section *Vireya*, divided into seven subsections. The species treated in *Species of Rhododendron*, and listed under *s.* Vaccinioides in the present *Rhododendron Handbook* (1967), belong, with one exception, to the subsection *Pseudovireya* (C. B. Cl.) Sleumer, of which R. *vaccinioides* is the type. This is in cultivation, and so too is the newly discovered R. *santapaui*.

The bulk of the section *Vireya*, which contains almost 300 species, occurs within the region covered by the great *Flora Malesiana*, and it has become usual to refer to them as the 'Malesian rhododendrons' (the English word 'Malaysian' has a narrower circumscription, and is not appropriate). The Malesian species are not hardy in Britain and not treated in this work. A detailed and well-illustrated account of the group by Dr H. Sleumer has been published in *Flora Malesiana* and is available separately (Series I, Vol. 6, part 4 (1966)). The Malesian Vireyas have been represented in cultivation since the 1840s. In that and the next decade several species from the western part of the region were introduced to the nurseries of Messrs Veitch by Thomas Lobb, including R. *javanicum* (*Bot. Mag.*, t. 4336); others were sent in the late 1870s by the Veitchian collector Charles Curtis. Between 1874 and the early years of this century Messrs Veitch raised and put into commerce about 200 hybrids from these introductions, some of great complexity, which were familiar glasshouse plants before the first world war. In recent years there has been a revival of interest in the Malesian Vireyas, thanks to the introduction of species that tolerate cooler conditions than the old Veitchian species and hybrids, which came mostly from low altitudes. Many of the recent introductions are from New Guinea, which is the richest of all the islands in rhododendrons, having some 155 species, forty of which were introduced to Europe and America in the 1950s through the Rijksherbarium, Leyden,

Holland. For further information see the section on Malesian rhododendrons in *The Rhododendron Handbook* and the articles by Michael Black in the *Rhododendron and Camellia Year Book* for 1966, 1967, and 1970. Also, for figures of recently introduced species, see *Botanical Magazine*, new series, tt. 552, 575, 600, 610, 653.

s. VIRGATUM

Revision: *R.C.Y.B. 1964* (18), pp. 106–7, 130–3.

This series contains only *R. virgatum* (*oleifolium*), characterised by the one-flowered, axillary inflorescences, and seeds with a fairly well-developed appendage at each end. It is part of Sleumer's subgenus *Pseudorhodorastrum* (see *s.* Scabrifolium).

ELEPIDOTE (HYMENANTHES) RHODODENDRONS

The species grouped here are what most gardeners would think of as 'typical' or 'true' rhododendrons, for they far outnumber the lepidote rhododendrons in cultivation and, because of their greater bulk, they are more conspicuous. But, as already pointed out, it is the lepidote species *R. ferrugineum*, the alpine rose, that is the type of the genus *Rhododendron*. The elepidote rhododendrons are very uniform in their essential botanical characters and in the estimation of most botanists constitute a single subgenus, for which the correct name is subgen. HYMENANTHES (Bl,) K. Koch. The principal synonyms are: *Hymenanthes* Bl. (the type of which, and hence of the subgenus, is *R. degronianum* f. *heptamerum*); *Rhod.* sect. *Eurhododendron* Maxim., in part; *Rhod.* subgen. *Eurhododendron* Series A C. B. Clarke (excl. *R. edgeworthii* and *R. pendulum*); *Rhod.* sect. *Leiorhodium* Rehd.; *Rhod.* subgen. *Leiorhodium* (Rehd.) Pojarkova.

The term 'elepidote' applied to these rhododendrons refers, of course, to the fact that the modified glands, or scales, characteristic of the subgenus *Rhododendron*, do not occur in this group; glands, when present (as they often are on one part or another of the plant), are of simple structure. A further distinction, which marks the group off from all other subdivisions of the genus, is that the non-glandular hairs on the leaves and stems are, with few exceptions, branched and often of elaborate structure. In many species these hairs form a dense coating on the underside of the leaf, the nature of which depends on the structure of the hairs and their density. The Hymenanthes rhododendrons are mostly medium-sized to large shrubs or trees, very rarely dwarf. The leaves are always persistent, and usually last for two years. The inflorescence is terminal (though in some young and vigorous garden hybrids the uppermost axillary buds may also produce flowers). The corollas usually have the normal five lobes, but seven-lobed corollas are common in *s.* Fortunei, mostly eight-lobed in *s.* Falconeri and *s.* Grande, and there are exceptions in other series also. The number of stamens is usually double that of the corolla-lobes, though often only approximately so when the latter are in excess of five. The number of chambers in the ovary is commonly more than five in this group, though rarely more than twice the number of corolla lobes. The seeds are very uniform, all being of what Kingdon Ward termed the 'forest type', i.e., more or less winged and with a frilly protrusion at one end.

Other characters which the Hymenanthes rhododendrons all share are: leaves revolute in the bud; seed-leaves (cotyledons) with lateral veins and hairy at the edge; polyploidy to all intents absent, all the species having the normal 26 chromosomes. The Philipsons have shown that the Hymenanthes rhododendrons are unique in this genus in their nodal anatomy.

The Hymenanthes rhododendrons have more or less the same distribution as the genus as a whole, except that they are scarcely represented in the Malesian region and do not extend so far north as the lepidotes. The group as a whole has a narrower ecological range than the lepidotes. No species has developed an epiphytic habit and the group is consequently rare in the warm-temperate rain-forests of Sino-Himalaya. Also they have failed to evolve more than a very few dwarf species, whence their rarity in the alpine zones and moorland regions of Sino-Himalaya, which the lepidotes, with less baggage to carry, have colonised with such remarkable success. On the other hand, where conditions are suitable for their growth, they may form dwarf forests or thickets of vast extent.

In Sleumer's classification, the subgenus *Hymenanthes* contains but a single section, divided into numerous subsections. For the most part these subsections correspond to the series of the Edinburgh classification; thus the Ponticum series becomes subsect. *Pontica*. But in some instances he has, usually with good reason, partly or wholly broken up those series that are divided into subseries, giving to the latter the rank of subsection. His more important conclusions are mentioned in the appropriate place.

s. ARBOREUM

The species of the typical subseries, of which about eight are at present recognised, are mostly trees with a distinct bole, or large shrubs. Leaves up to 10 in. long, leathery; indumentum of the undersurface bistrate, with an upper layer of dendroid hairs and a lower layer of rosulate hairs (but one or the other sometimes lacking in R. *arboreum*). Inflorescence a dense, many-flowered truss. Calyx small. Corolla campanulate or tubular-campanulate, with nectar-pouches at the base, usually deep red but sometimes rose or white (forms of R. *arboreum*), or in shades of purplish blue to purple-lilac (R. *niveum*). Apart from R. *niveum* and R. *lanigerum* (qq.v.) the subseries is made up of R. *arboreum* and its allies, a taxonomically difficult complex with a wide range from the W. Himalaya to Yunnan, south to S.W. Peninsular India, Ceylon, middle Burma, Thailand, and the former Indochina.

ss. ARGYROPHYLLUM.—This subseries was originally set up as an independent series, and its reinstatement was proposed by Cowan (*Rhodo. Leaf*, p. 78). The inflorescence is laxer than in *ss.* Arboreum and usually fewer-flowered; the corolla is narrowed at the base and nectar-pouches are absent. In most of the species the leaves are covered beneath with a thin but continuous covering of rosulate hairs (the so-called 'plastered' indumentum), but in R. *insigne* the indumentum is silvery and burnished. In a few species, however, notably R. *floribundum* and R. *hunnewellianum*, the covering is woolly; these (group AA. in the key in *Species of Rhododendron*) are separated by Sleumer as subsect. *Floribunda*. The subseries Argyrophyllum (including the R. *floribundum* group) is Chinese in distribution, from Kansu to Yunnan, east and south to Hupeh, Chekiang, Kwangtung, and Fukien (but a rhododendron akin to R. *coryanum* occurs at the eastern end of the Himalaya). The cultivated species are from Szechwan and Hupeh.

s. Auriculatum

This series now contains one species—R. *auriculatum* (q.v.). At one time
R. *griersonianum* was incongruously associated with it, but is now placed in a
separate series, also monotypic.

s. Barbatum

Medium-sized shrubs or small trees, mostly characterised by the presence
of bristly glandular or eglandular hairs on the petiole, extending in some
species to the midrib and even to the underside of the blade; other types of hair
occur in this series, but only in a few species do the leaves have a close, continuous indumentum. The leaves are 3 to 8 in. long. In all the subseries except
ss. Maculiferum the calyx is well developed and, in some species, coloured.
The corolla is five-lobed, tubular to more or less campanulate, never truly
funnel-shaped.

ss. Barbatum.—Young shoots and petioles coarsely bristly (except in R. *imberbe*).
Blade glabrous to loosely woolly beneath. Truss dense. Corolla tubular-campanulate or
campanulate, red, with conspicuous nectar-pouches. Four species in the Himalaya.

ss. Crinigerum.—The two closely related species placed here are related to the
Glischrum subseries, but the leaves have a continuous brown felt-like indumentum
beneath.

ss. Glischrum.—Young stems and petioles clad with bristles which in some species
extend to the midrib beneath, in others cover the whole undersurface of the blade.
Compound hairs may also be present, and two species, R. *hirtipes* and R. *vesiculiferum*,
have peculiar bladder-like hairs on the veins. Corolla white, rose, more rarely crimson.
Ten species in the Assam Himalaya, upper Burma, N.W. Yunnan and bordering parts of
Tibet.

ss. Maculiferum.—Small or medium-sized shrubs for the most part. Leaves
rarely more than 6 in. long, glabrous beneath except for hairs or glands on the midrib.
Inflorescence lax, with up to fifteen flowers. Calyx small. Corolla white or rose (except
in the red-flowered R. *strigillosum*, which, according to Cowan, is out of place here and
should be transferred to the Glischrum subseries). The distribution is similar to that of
s. Arboreum *ss*. Argyrophyllum—Szechwan, Hupeh, Anwhei, and Formosa. In Sleumer's classification this group is detached from the other subseries (subsect. *Barbata*)
as subsection *Maculifera*.

s. Campanulatum

Revision: R.Y.B. *1949* (4), pp. 159–82.

As Cowan and Davidian point out in their revision, this group is a heterogeneous assemblage of Himalayan species, having little of significance in common and 'no more closely allied to each other than are some of them to certain
other species now in other series'. However, they retained it in its original form
until all the groups with which its members have some kinship have been
revised. Apart from the Himalayan habitat, the species have in common a more
or less elliptic leaf, obtuse at both ends (though R. *wallichii* frequently has
oblanceolate leaves, tapered at the base). In all the species the leaf is more or less
coated with hairs beneath, though glabrous in some forms of indumented species,
and also in R. *succothii*. The hairs are of diverse structure, four different types
being represented in the series. The corolla is campanulate or funnel-campanu-

late (tubular-campanulate in R. *fulgens*), yellow and spotted in R. *lanatum*, lilac, rosy purple, pink or white in R. *campanulatum*, R. *wallichii* and R. *tsariense*, deep red in R. *fulgens*, R. *sherriffii*, and R. *succothii*. Except in R. *lanatum* and R. *tsariense* the ovary is glabrous or almost so. R. *tsariense* is dwarf in some forms and R. *fulgens* is usually a fairly small shrub; the others are of larger size. R. *campanulatum* ranges farther to the north-west than any other elepidote species; the others are confined to the region east of E. Nepal and most do not extend west of Bhutan.

s. FALCONERI and *s.* GRANDE

These two series, although well distinguished by a character mentioned below, have so much in common that it is preferable to treat them together.

Large shrubs or trees, with stout, tomentose young stems. Leaves leathery, large to very large, indumented beneath. In both series there are species in which the petiole is very short and is winged on the upper side owing to the decurrence of the leaf-blade (R. *basilicum* in *s.* Falconeri and R. *praestans*, R. *coryphaeum*, and R. *semnoides* in *s.* Grande). The two series differ in the nature of the hairs that compose their indumentum. In *s.* Falconeri the upper stratum is made up of peculiar funnel- or cup-shaped hairs, which produce a thick indumentum; in a few species these hairs are sparse and there is a thinner indumentum composed mainly of the lower stratum of rosulate hairs. In the Grande series a thin, skin-like or plastered unistrate indumentum is the rule rather than the exception, and where an upper layer is present, giving a woollier indumentum, the hairs are of a more conventional kind. In both series the inflorescence is a many-flowered terminal truss with a well-developed rachis sometimes over 2 in. long. The calyx is always very small. The corolla is predominantly campanulate with a broad, rounded base, and is often oblique. Its colour is white (though rarely), creamy white, yellow, or in various impure shades between red and purple. The lobes are commonly eight (rarely the standard five) and are unusually short for the genus. The number of stamens is around double that of the lobes. The ovary is nearly always tomentose, with between eight and sixteen chambers (occasionally up to twenty). It is interesting that in both series there are anomalous species in W. Szechwan with glabrous ovaries (see R. *galactinum* and R. *watsonii*).

The two series have much the same distribution. Mostly they are confined to the rainiest parts of Sino-Himalaya, from N.W. Yunnan through upper Burma to N.E. India, where they extend through the Himalaya to E. Nepal and are represented in the Naga Hills by R. *macabeanum* in *s.* Grande. But R. *fictolacteum* ranges as far as S.W. Szechwan (where its relative R. *rex* is also found); and there are two (perhaps three) species in W. Szechwan (see above). The maximum development of the two series in the monsoonal region is between 8,000 and 10,000 ft, where they often form forests of their own on steep slopes where the soil is too thin to support forest trees; R. *arizelum* extends into the subalpine zone.

s. FORTUNEI

Large shrubs or trees. Leaves 4 to 10 in. long (except in *ss.* Orbiculare and *ss.* Oreodoxa), glabrous when mature, usually rounded or obtuse at the apex.

Inflorescence terminal, often with a well-developed rachis. Corolla funnel-shaped to campanulate, 2 in. or more wide, white, pink, or rose, commonly six- or seven-lobed. Stamens twelve to twenty-five, rarely ten. Style slender (except in *ss*. Calophytum). The series has its main distribution in China and is rare west of the Mekong (but see *ss*. Griffithianum).

ss. FORTUNEI.—Calyx small, usually edged with glands. Style glandular to the tip. Eight species in China, two extending into bordering parts of Burma and one into Siam.

ss. GRIFFITHIANUM.—*R. griffithianum* (q.v.) is the sole member of this subseries. It is exceptional in its mainly Himalayan distribution and in its large calyx.

ss. CALOPHYTUM.—Of the two closely allied species in this subseries only *R. calophytum* is cultivated. It is anomalous in having a stout style with a large discoid stigma.

ss. DAVIDII.—The main species in this subseries is *R. sutchuenense* (q.v.) which differs from ss. Fortunei in the glabrous style and differently shaped leaves and from *ss*. Calophytum in the funnel-campanulate corolla and capitate stigma. The type-species is probably not in cultivation and is little known botanically. *R. planetum*, the only other species, is not known in the wild. All the species are Chinese (Hupeh and Szechwan).

ss. ORBICULARE.—The two species in this subseries are characterised by broad-elliptic to roundish leaves, cordate or auriculate at the base, a shape not met with in the other subseries. Both are Chinese.

ss. OREODOXA.—The two main species in this subseries, R. *oreodoxa* and R. *fargesii*, are unique in the series by reason of their rather small elliptic leaves and perhaps represent two races of a single species, ranging from Hupeh to Szechwan and Kansu. The other two species were described from cultivated plants.

s. FULVUM

Revision: R.Y.B. *1949* (4): pp. 159–64, 176–82.

A small group, in which five species were recognised in *Species of Rhododendron*, reduced to two by Cowan and Davidian in their revision. It is closely allied to *s*. Campanulatum, differing in the oblanceolate to obovate leaves and the narrow, cylindrical seed-capsule. In both species the ovary is glabrous. It has a wide range, from S.W. Szechwan to the eastern end of the Himalaya.

s. GRIERSONIANUM

R. *griersonianum* (q.v.), the only member of this series, was grouped with R. *auriculatum* until removed to a series of its own by H. H. Davidian in 1963 (R.C.Y.B. *1964*, pp. 109–11).

s. IRRORATUM

The typical subseries consists for the most part of species with the following characters: Medium-sized shrubs or small trees. Leaves of hard texture, glabrous at maturity, with a cartilaginous edge, usually acute at the apex, mostly 3 to 5 in. long. Inflorescence terminal with seven to fifteen flowers. Corolla tubular-campanulate and up to 2 in. long, more rarely saucer-shaped, white, pink, magenta, or red, often spotted or with basal markings. Ovary glandular, or tomentose or both glandular and tomentose, or glabrous. Style glandular to the tip in some species, in others glabrous, in one hairy. R. *agastum* and two allied species are out of place in this series, having leaves with a persistent indumentum beneath, and in Cowan's view are more akin to *s*. Arboreum *ss*. Argyrophyllum. At present about twenty-five species are recognised, ranging from Bhutan to Yunnan and Kweichow, south to Siam and the former Indochina. Remarkably there is also a species in the Malayan peninsula (but belonging to the R. *agastum* group, see above) and two in N. Sumatra.

The Parishii subseries, which should probably be given independent status, comprises a few species in which (excluding R. *venator*) the young stems and leaf-undersides are clad with a floccose tomentum of stellate hairs which gradually wears away. The leaves are obtuse or rounded at the apex, of softer texture than in *ss.* Irroratum. All have deep red, tubular-campanulate, fleshy corollas and are confined to Burma and bordering parts of Yunnan and N.E. India.

s. LACTEUM

Revision: *R.C.Y.B. 1956* (10), pp. 122–55.

Large or medium-sized shrubs (rarely dwarf). Leaves 3 to 7 in. long (longer in R. *beesianum*, shorter in the dwarfer species), indumentum of the undersides commonly suede-like or felted or powdery, sometimes reduced to a thin veil of hairs or almost wanting. Inflorescence rather dense, with rarely fewer than eight flowers on pedicels mostly less than 1 in. long (but laxer in the anomalous R. *wightii*). Calyx very small (except in one species not in cultivation). Corolla campanulate to funnel-shaped, 1 to 2 in. long usually blotched or spotted, white, pink or yellow. Style usually glabrous. A series of some fourteen species, none common in cultivation, ranging from S. Szechwan through N.W. Yunnan and S.E. Tibet to the Tibetan side of the E. Himalaya and Bhutan; R. *beesianum* extends into northernmost Burma. R. *wightii*, provisionally included in this series, is Himalayan.

s. NERIIFLORUM

Of this series H. F. Tagg wrote: 'At first sight this assemblage under one series has a heterogeneous appearance, but analysis shows that it represents an unmistakable phyletic grouping. Three characters are of special importance: the inflorescence is never congested; the corolla is almost invariably unspotted; the ovary is usually densely hairy or hairy and glandular or very rarely entirely glandular' (*Species of Rhododendron*, p. 507).

ss. NERIIFLORUM.—Small or medium-sized shrubs. Leaves rarely more than 4 in. long, papillose beneath in most species and either glabrous or with a more or less detersile indumentum. Corolla tubular-campanulate, 1¼ to 1¾ in. long, fleshy, scarlet or crimson, with darker nectar-pouches. Ovary narrow, tapered into the style. About seven species from N.W. Yunnan and bordering part of Tibet through upper Burma to the E. Himalaya as far west as Bhutan.

ss. FORRESTII.—Dwarf or prostrate shrubs. Leaves up to 2 in. long, those of the cultivated species glabrous, broad-elliptic to obovate, rounded at the apex (but narrower and thinly hairy beneath in others). Corolla red or pink, fleshy, tubular. Ovary tomentose or glandular or both. The distribution is similar to that of the typical subseries except that it does not extend so far into the Himalaya.

ss. HAEMATODES.—Small or medium-sized shrubs to about 10 ft (R. *mallotum* sometimes a small tree). Leaves on the average larger than in the other subseries, up to 6 in. long, obtuse to rounded at the apex, clad beneath with a brown to fawn woolly indumentum (but becoming rather thin in some forms of R. *chaetomallum*). Corolla tubular-campanulate, 1¼ to 2 in. long, fleshy, nearly always red or scarlet (white in the anomalous R. *chionanthum*), with conspicuous nectar-pouches. Calyx cup-shaped, coloured and fleshy in some species. Ovary relatively broad, hairy or glandular. Nine species (at present) in the rainiest part of Sino-Himalaya, from N.W. Yunnan (mostly west of the Mekong) through upper Burma to the Mishmi Hills of Assam. A taxonomically difficult subseries, much in need of revision. Cultivated plants are sometimes difficult to place even though they are known to have been raised from wild seed.

ss. SANGUINEUM.—'This subseries is one of the most distinctive of the genus, but, at the same time, one of the most complex; the species intergrade and overlap in bewildering confusion; among elepidote Rhododendrons no other assemblage of plants is so difficult to arrange in phyletic sequence.' (J. M. Cowan, 'Rhododendrons of the *Rh. sanguineum* Alliance', *Notes Roy. Bot. Gard. Edin.*, Vol. 20 (1940), pp. 55–91.) The species grouped in this subseries are closely allied, but the plants show different combinations of characters usually considered to be of taxonomic importance, e.g., to take some of Dr Cowan's examples: flower-colour; corolla thin or fleshy; ovary glandular or eglandular; indumentum thin, woolly or none. Altogether, there are some 200 possible character-combinations, of which 120 are known from herbarium specimens to actually exist. Some thirty of these combinations had been given specific status before a halt was called; the rest, which logically should have been given the same status, were placed under this or that "species" according to which of its characters was thought to be of most importance (Cowan, op. cit., pp. 56–7, 60). In his revision Cowan recognised eight species based mainly on leaf-shape and leaf-indumentum, relegating the other described species to the rank of subspecies and giving the same rank to some other combinations not previously named. The treatment was rather elaborate and not wholly consistent, since the numerous combinations existing in R. *aperantum* were left unnamed.

The species are mostly small shrubs. Leaves mostly between obovate and oblong, up to about 4 in. long, with a covering beneath of rosulate hairs giving a plastered, mealy or cobwebby indumentum according to their density; but in R. *citriniflorum* the indumentum is woolly and bistrate, and in some species the undersides are glabrous and usually papillose. Calyx variable, from small to large, fleshy in R. *dichroanthum* and R. *parmulatum*. Corolla variable in colour even in the same species, and sometimes darker red than in any other elepidote rhododendron; except in R. *parmulatum* it is unspotted.

s. PONTICUM

Medium-sized to large shrubs, rarely dwarf. Leaves up to 10 in. long and rarely as short as 3 in., mostly with an indumentum beneath, but glabrous at maturity in a few species. Inflorescence terminal with rarely fewer than eight flowers; rachis usually well developed; pedicels rarely less than 1 in. long, elongating after flowering, the uppermost more or less erect or sometimes all the pedicels erect and fastigiate; the posture of the pedicels, helped by the longish rachis, gives to the inflorescence a shape usually termed 'candelabroid'. Corolla funnel-shaped to campanulate, rather more deeply divided than in most Hymenanthes rhododendrons, though this character tends to be obscured in some species by the overlapping of the lobes at the base; except sometimes in the Japanese species the corolla is five-lobed and somewhat zygomorphic. Stamens commonly ten and ovary chambers five (except in flowers with extra lobes).

The geographical distribution of the series is unique among the Hymenanthes rhododendrons, but is parallelled by that of the Luteum azaleas. There are no species in the Sino-Himalayan region proper, the only Chinese species—R. *adenopodum*—being a native of Hupeh and bordering parts of E. Szechwan. The other species range from Japan (and Formosa if R. *hyperythrum* is included) through N. Asia to western Eurasia and N. America. Two subseries are recognised. In the typical subseries (R. *ponticum* and the three American species) the leaves are stated to be glabrous, though in some forms of R. *maximum* they have a persistent thin indumentum beneath. In *ss*. Caucasicum, with about seven species, the leaves are indumented beneath except in R. *aureum*. It seems to be generally agreed that R. *brachycarpum* should be excluded from this series, and the Formosan R. *hyperythrum* is only provisionally included in it. The nearest ally of *ss*. Caucasicum would seem to be *s*. Arboreum *ss*. Argyrophyllum.

s. TALIENSE

Although poorly represented in cultivation, the species of the Taliense group are an important constituent of the rhodoreta of Sino-Himalaya, where they have their maximum development in the bleaker parts and are virtually absent from areas that receive the full weight of monsoonal rain. The leaves are mostly rather thick, clad beneath with a thick, woolly or felted indumentum which is usually brown or reddish (or, if paler, then spongy), and in most species is composed of ramiform hairs with an undercoating of rosulate hairs (but see *ss*. Wasonii). Inflorescence terminal with a very short rachis. Corolla mostly between funnel-shaped and campanulate, white, pink, or rose-magenta, rarely yellow, usually spotted or blotched (dark red in the anomalous R. *gymnocarpum*).

ss. TALIENSE.—The ten species in this subseries have flowers with a very small calyx, and the ovary is glabrous. Except in the little-known R. *purdomii* the leaf-indumentum is woolly or felted, and the hairs are often bound together by a sticky secretion. This subseries extends farther west than the others, occurring in the eastern Himalaya on both sides of the range; if R. *purdomii* (a native of Shensi) is excluded, the north-eastern limit is in S.W. Szechwan.

ss. ADENOGYNUM.—Calyx well developed, mostly ¼ to ⅜ in. long, deeply lobed, glandular (but very small in R. *alutaceum*, included because in other respects it resembles the type). Ovary always glandular, sometimes tomentose also. R. *prattii* is anomalous, for although the calyx is large, the leaves are uncharacteristic in their greater than average width and thin indumentum. Eighteen species are at present recognised, ranging from N.W. Yunnan (mostly east of the Mekong) through Szechwan to Kansu.

ss. ROXIEANUM.—The species grouped in this subseries are for the most part of dwarf stature and confined to high elevations in N.W. Yunnan and bordering Szechwan. But R. *roxieanum* itself sometimes attains 10 ft in the wild, and there is one species (R. *recurvoides*) in Burma. Apart from R. *forrestii*, R. *pronum* (not treated here) is the dwarfest of the Hymenanthes rhododendrons and attains perhaps the highest elevation (15,000 ft). The majority are slow-growing shrubs with narrow, often strongly recurved, heavily indumented leaves and small, dense inflorescences. The calyx is small. For two anomalous species at present placed in this series, see R. *gymnocarpum*.

ss. WASONII.—The seven species in this subseries, all natives of Szechwan or Kansu, have flowers with a small, eglandular calyx (against usually large and glandular in *ss*. Adenogynum) and a tomentose ovary (glabrous or almost so in *ss*. Taliense). The leaves are always flat and comparatively broad, so confusion with *ss*. Roxieanum is unlikely. Although the indumentum is usually woolly, there is great diversity in hair-structure in this series (Cowan, op. cit., pp. 66, 82).

s. THOMSONII

Revision: R.Y.B. *1951–2* (6), pp. 116–83.

The Thomsonii series is the most difficult of all to comprehend, for the species grouped in it seem to have so little in common that it is impossible to define the group except in the vaguest terms. However, there is no need to belabour this difficulty, which is fully discussed by Cowan and Davidian in their valuable revision of the series. The group is more easily understood if it is realised that the type, R. *thomsonii*, is not the central species but rather an extreme. The middle position is occupied by the Campylocarpum subseries, which has obvious affinity with *ss*. Thomsonii in one set of characters (leaf- and corolla-shape) and with *ss*. Selense in another (notably the partly glandular style and the slender, often curved seed-capsule). In Cowan and Davidian's words: 'The Thomsonii series represents an alliance which cannot be strictly defined, a loosely linked yet recognisable natural association.'

Nearly all the species are medium-sized shrubs. Leaves thinly leathery, obtuse to rounded at the apex, obtuse or cordate at the base, undersides glabrous or with an inconspicuous veil of hairs (see also R. *hookeri*). Inflorescence terminal, loose, with rarely more than twelve flowers. Corolla-shape variable (see subseries). Ovary commonly glandular (though not in some species of *ss*. Thomsonii). Style glandular at least at the base (except in *ss*. Thomsonii). Capsule variable (see subseries).

ss. THOMSONII.—Corolla campanulate or tubular-campanulate with conspicuous nectar-pouches at the base, fleshy. Calyx variable, often very large. Style without glands. Capsule short and stout, or oblong. Ten species from N.W. Yunnan to E. Nepal.

ss. CAMPYLOCARPUM.—Leaves 1 to 4 in. long, mostly relatively broad. Calyx small. Corolla campanulate, yellow, pink, or white. Ovary glandular; style glandular in the lower part. Capsule slender, cylindric or oblong, sometimes curved. Six species, perhaps reducible to four, from N.W. Yunnan to E. Nepal.

ss. CERASINUM.—R. *cerasinum* (q.v.) resembles R. *thomsonii* in shape of corolla but differs markedly in foliage and in having the style glandular to the tip. The only other species in the subseries is known only from a single collection and is not cultivated; it is geographically far removed from R. *cerasinum* (W. Szechwan).

ss. SELENSE.—A polymorphic group, uncommon in cultivation. Leaves mostly oblong or elliptic. Branchlets slender, bristly-glandular or sometimes glabrous. Corolla usually near to funnel-shaped (but campanulate in R. *eurysiphon* and in some forms of R. *esetulosum*), pink, rose, or white, often spotted or blotched. Ovary and lower part of style glandular. Capsule slender, usually curved. Eleven species in N.W. Yunnan, bordering Tibet and upper Burma.

ss. SOULIEI.—Very near to *ss*. Campylocarpum, in which it was included by Balfour, but with a cup-shaped corolla and the style glandular throughout. Four species from W. Szechwan to the eastern end of the Himalaya.

ss. WILLIAMSIANUM.—The one species in this subseries (q.v.) resembles R. *souliei* and its allies in having the style glandular to the tip, and R. *callimorphum* (in *ss*. Campylocarpum) in its pink, campanulate corolla and short broad leaves. It differs from nearly all species in the Thomsonii series in its dwarf habit and few-flowered inflorescence.

AZALEAS

In *Species Plantarum* (1753) Linnaeus distributed the species of *Rhododendron* known to him between two genera, according to the number of stamens (a character of great importance in his system of classification).

In his genus *Rhododendron* he placed the species with ten stamens (*R. ferrugineum, R. hirsutum, R. dauricum*, and *R. maximum*). His genus *Azalea* comprised species with five stamens, of which four are members of the Azalea series of *Rhododendron*: *R. indicum* (*A. indica* L.), *R. luteum* (*A. pontica* L.), *R. viscosum* (*A. viscosa* L.), and *R. periclymenoides*, better known as *R. nudiflorum* (*A. lutea* L., altered to *A. nudiflora* in the second edition of the *Species Plantarum*). The two remaining founder-members of Linnaeus' *Azalea* were *R. lapponicum*, a lepidote rhododendron that happens to have five stamens instead of the normal ten (*A. lapponica* L.); and a distant relative of *Rhododendron*, named by Linnaeus *A. procumbens*, now known as *Loiseleuria procumbens* (L.) Desvaux.

In splitting *Rhododendron* (as now understood), Linnaeus showed less taxonomic insight than his predecessor the French botanist Tournefort, whose genus *Chamaerhododendros* contained originally both the azalea *R. indicum* and the two lepidote rhododendrons *R. ferrugineum* and *R. hirsutum* (*Institutiones Rei Herbariae* (1700), p. 604), to which he added, after seeing them in the wild in Turkey, *R. ponticum* and the common yellow azalea *R. luteum* (*Corollarium* (1703), p. 42). As soon came to be realised, Tournefort and not Linnaeus had the rights of it. The number of stamens in the genus *Rhododendron* is not generally a character of much significance, and may fluctuate even among closely allied species. It happens that the azaleas of the Luteum subseries, of which Linnaeus knew three, have consistently five stamens; but *R. indicum*, also with five stamens, belongs to a group—the Obtusum subseries—in which the number is mostly between six and ten. In the century or so after the publication of *Species Plantarum* botanists either gave the genus *Azalea* half-hearted acceptance or transferred the known azaleas to *Rhododendron*. The *coup de grâce* to *Azalea* as a separate genus was given by Maximowicz in his authoritative work *Rhododendreae Asiae Orientalis* (1870), which laid the foundation for all later classifications of the genus. In gardens the genus *Azalea* was kept distinct from *Rhododendron* long after it had become botanically disreputable to do so. At the present time the word 'azalea' is still used in an informal sense for the species and hybrids of the Azalea series, and quite properly so, and still has standing as a subgeneric name (see below).

A leading character of the azaleas is that not only are scales absent from all parts of the plant (the species are 'elepidote') but, as Almuth Seithe has pointed out, their hairs are always unbranched. Also, the majority of the species are deciduous or (as in many species of the Obtusum subseries) drop the leaves formed in spring while retaining through the winter a cluster of thicker and smaller leaves at the apex of the shoot (the so-called summer-leaves). A deciduous habit is elsewhere found in *Rhododendron* only among the lepidote species—commonly in *s.* Dauricum and *s.* Trichocladum, rarely in *s.* Triflorum and *s.* Lepidotum. The azaleas are slenderly branched shrubs. The inflorescence is always terminal and umbellate (even when it is many-flowered the rachis is very short). The corolla is usually funnel-shaped or rotate, with a fairly deeply divided, more or less zygomorphic limb; the markings, when present, are on the upper-central or three upper lobes, as is usually the case with zygomorphic corollas. The number of stamens is often below the standard ten, and very rarely more than that. The ovary is consistently five-celled. The seeds are winged or unwinged, never tailed.

In *Species of Rhododendron* the Azalea series is divided into six subseries, which in a strictly botanical classification should probably be regarded as representing two subgenera (only the principal synonyms are given):

subgen. AZALEA (L. *emend.* Desv.) Planch. *Azalea* L., in part; *Rhodora* L.; *Anthodendron* Reichb.; *Rhod.* sect. *Pentanthera* G. Don; *Rhod.* a. *Anthodendron* Reichb. ex Endl.; *Rhod.* sect. *Azalea* (L.) Maxim., in part; *Azalea* subgen. *Pentanthera* (G. Don) Koch; *Rhod.* subgen. *Anthodendron* Endl. ex Rehd. & Wils., in part; *Rhod.* subgen. *Pseudanthodendron* Sleumer; *Rhod.* subgen. *Pentanthera* (G. Don) Pojarkova—The subseries or sections of this subgenus have terminal buds of the usual form characteristic of most members of the genus, i.e., they are composed of numerous perulae and are sharply demarcated from the surrounding leaves; the upper axillary buds are subtended by fully developed leaves, as again is normal in the genus (cf. subgen. *Tsutsia*).

ss. LUTEUM.—Erect deciduous shrubs. Inflorescences with up to about fifteen often fragrant flowers. Calyx mostly rather small. Corolla funnel-shaped, the tube as long as the limb or longer, the outside downy or glandular, rarely glabrous, white, pink, yellow, orange, or red, Stamens five, exserted. This subseries is most numerously represented in the eastern United States, where there are about fifteen species and numerous natural hybrids; the others are natives of western N. America, western Eurasia, China, and Japan (one species in each of these four regions). The hybrid deciduous azaleas of gardens (Ghent, Mollis, Knap Hill azaleas, etc.) all derive from crossings within this group. The botanical name for this group (as a section) is sect. *Azalea* (sect. *Pentanthera* G. Don).

ss. CANADENSE.—Deciduous erect shrubs. Inflorescence with two to eight flowers. Corolla widely campanulate, white, pink, purple, or purplish red, two-lipped in R. *canadense* and to a lesser degree in R. *vaseyi*. Stamens ten (fewer in R. *vaseyi*). The two species mentioned are natives of eastern N. America. The other two members of the subseries, R. *albrechtii* and R. *pentaphyllum*, are natives of Japan and differ in some respects from the American species. The botanical name for this subseries is sect. *Rhodora* (L.) G. Don, and the type is R. *canadense*, for which Linnaeus created the genus *Rhodora* in 1762.

ss. NIPPONICUM.—This subseries, which consists of a single species (q.v.), is of uncertain taxonomic status and perhaps wrongly placed in the subgenus *Azalea*. Its sectional name is sect. *Viscidula* Matsum. & Nakai.

subgen. TSUTSIA Planch. *Rhod.* sect. *Tsutsutsi* G. Don, in part; *Rhod.* sect. *Tsusia* Planch. ex Maxim.; *Rhod.* subgen. *Tsutsutsi* (G. Don) Pojarkova; *Rhod.* subgen. *Anthodendron* Endl. ex Rehd. & Wils., in part—Here are placed two subseries, *ss.* Obtusum and *ss.* Schlippenbachii, in both of which the buds show unusual features, usually stated, for both groups, to be that the flowers and young shoots are produced from the same bud. So far as the Schlippenbachii subseries is concerned, judging from the living plants examined, this is a crude over-simplification. The flower-buds and growth-buds are distinct, as is usual in the genus, but the uppermost axillary buds are subtended by leaves which have become partly modified into bud-scales (perulae). The bases of these persist through the winter, forming an outer covering to the true bud, but fall off as the flowers expand in spring. The statement 'flowers and young growths from the same bud' is true only if this compound structure is regarded as a single bud.

The first to note that the buds of the Obtusum subseries are unusual was Maximowicz, who, in the work mentioned above, gives 'Young growths from the same bud as the flowers' as the diagnostic character of his section *Tsusia* [so spelt by him], which comprised the then known species of the Obtusum subseries. However, in the supplement to his monograph, published in 1871, he withdrew this diagnosis,* confessing that it had been based on inadequate study. The peculiarity of this group, as he pointed out in the supplement, is that the flower-buds are surrounded by very few fully developed scales, and these are concealed by the bases of the uppermost leaves, which form a tuft at the apex of the shoot and persist through the winter. The innermost of these leaves are partly converted into bud-scales, as can be seen from their flattened, etiolated bases. According to Maximowicz, whose observations were based on plants grown under glass at St Petersburg, the young growths spring from these intermediate leaves, but on plants grown out-of-doors, judging from those examined, the growth-subtending leaves are more or less normal. Another character remarked on by Maximowicz in his supplementary note is that the axillary growth-buds are not formed, or at least do not become visible, until the flowers are over, so that the processes of bud-formation and shoot-expansion are more or less simultaneous; also, these buds consist of very few scales.

ss. OBTUSUM.—Shrubs mostly of small size, sometimes prostrate; young stems and (more or less densely) the leaves, clad with erect or appressed hairs. Leaves partly deciduous, but at least the uppermost persistent. For buds see above. Inflorescence few-flowered. Corolla funnel-shaped or funnel-campanulate, mostly 1½ to 2 in. wide, white, in various shades of purple, pink, or bright red (never yellow). Stamens five to ten (very rarely more or fewer). Ovary hairy and sometimes glandular. Seeds plain. This group has its greatest development in the maritime parts of E. Asia; in the Sino-Himalayan region it occurs only as an intrusion at comparatively low altitudes. About thirty species are recognised, mostly little known. Only a few are cultivated, these mostly Japanese. The numerous garden hybrids are also mainly derived from Japanese species (and the mainland R. *simsii*).

The botanical name for the Obtusum subseries, regarded as a section, would be sect. *Tsutsia*.

ss. SCHLIPPENBACHII.—Erect shrubs or sometimes small trees. Leaves deciduous (except sometimes in R. *farrerae*), usually forming whorls at the ends of the branchlets (but scattered on long shoots). For buds, see introductory note to the subgenus. Inflorescence terminal, one- to six-flowered. Corolla campanulate to funnel-shaped with a spreading limb, white (rarely), pink, purple, or red, usually spotted. Stamens six to ten. Seeds plain. Seven or eight species in Japan and continental E. Asia, where the subseries ranges from S. China through Hupeh to Manchuria and Korea.

The botanical name for this subseries, as a section, is sect. *Brachycalyx* Sweet (sect. *Sciadorhodion* Rehd. & Wils.).

ss. TASHIROI.—This subseries consists of a single species, R. *tashiroi*, not treated here. It is discussed by Rehder in *Species of Rhododendron*, p. 121.

* The revised diagnosis appears in *Bull. Acad. Imp. Sc. St Petersb.*, Vol. 16, pp. 412–13 (*Mel. Biol.*, Vol. 8, pp. 166–7).

Azaleastrums

The azaleastrums, or 'false azaleas', are a rather heterogeneous assemblage of species, grouped together in the subgenus Azaleastrum Planch. ex Koch (*Rhod.* sect. *Azaleastrum* Planch. ex Maxim.), the type of which is R. *ovatum*. The group is elepidote (without scales) and the hairs when present, are always unbranched—a combination they share with the azaleas. Apart from that, the leading character of the azaleastrums is that the inflorescences are always axillary and few-flowered (solitary in some species). The young growths spring from terminal or pseudoterminal buds, or from buds below the inflorescences. There are four series, each of which ranks as a section in Sleumer's classification.

s. Albiflorum.—The only member of this series is R. *albiflorum* (q.v.), a native of western N. America (sect. *Candidastrum* Sleumer).

s. Ovatum.—Evergreen small shrubs. Leaves glabrous, with a pronounced mucro. Flowers solitary from many-scaled axillary buds. Calyx-lobes large and broad. Corolla in most species deeply lobed, with a short tube and spreading limb (but tubular-funnel-shaped in R. *vialii*), white, pink, or crimson. Stamens five, exserted. Capsule very short. Five species, perhaps reducible to two, natives mainly of central and south China, rare in Sino-Himalaya. Since this group contains the type of the subgenus it takes the botanical name sect. *Azaleastrum* (*syn.* sect. *Euazaleastrum* Sleumer).

s. Semibarbatum.—The one species in this subseries, a native of Japan, differs from all other members of the genus in its dimorphic stamens (see description). It was given generic rank by a Japanese botanist as *Mumeazalea semibarbatum* whence the sectional name sect. *Mumeazalea* (Makino) Sleumer.

s. Stamineum.—This, the largest and finest group of azaleastrums, takes the botanical name sect. *Choniastrum* Franch., the type of which is R. *stamineum*, though the first species to become known to science was R. *moulmainense* Hook., not treated here. They are shrubs or small trees up to 40 ft high, with evergreen glabrous or more rarely hairy leaves, which often form 'pseudo-whorls' at the ends of the shoots. Inflorescences with up to about five flowers, which are fragrant in some species; bud-scales numerous, often persistent. Calyx mostly small or obsolete. Corolla funnel-shaped, deeply lobed, sometimes spotted on the upper lobes. Stamens ten, usually exserted. Capsule long and narrow, the valves sometimes adhering at the apex. About fifteen species in S.E. Asia, occurring in Sino-Himalaya only at low elevations; the southern limit is in the Malayan peninsula, the northern in Hupeh, and the western in the Assam Himalaya. Unfortunately the finest species are very tender.

DESCRIPTIONS

R. ABERCONWAYI Cowan

An evergreen shrub up to 8 ft high; young stems floccose and sparsely glandular. Leaves very brittle, rather convex above, $1\frac{1}{2}$ to 3 in. long, $\frac{1}{2}$ to $1\frac{3}{8}$ in. wide, oblong, oblong-elliptic, or narrow-ovate, acute to obtuse at the apex, rounded to broad-cuneate at the base, glabrous on both sides when mature, midrib deeply impressed above, prominent beneath; stalk up to $\frac{1}{3}$ in. long, glandular, and minutely downy. Flowers borne May or June in a more or less racemose truss of six to twelve; rachis minutely downy and glandular, varying much in length and up to 2 in. long; stalks $\frac{5}{8}$ to $1\frac{7}{8}$ in. long, glandular and downy. Calyx small, glandular at the margin. Corolla five-lobed, saucer-shaped, 2 to 3 in. wide, white or white tinged with pink, usually more or less spotted with crimson. Stamens ten, glabrous. Ovary densely glandular; style glandular to the tip.

Native of E. Yunnan; discovered and introduced by Chinese collectors trained by George Forrest, who after his death in 1932 were employed for several seasons by the first Lord Aberconway to continue his work. The seed was sent in 1937, and from it plants were raised in several gardens. It was described in 1948.

R. *aberconwayi* is unlike any other known rhododendron but probably best placed in the Irroratum series. It is variable in the size and colouring of its flowers but a very fine rhododendron at its best, and perfectly hardy. It needs a fairly sunny position. Shown by the Crown Estate Commissioners, Windsor Great Park, it received an Award of Merit in 1945, as an unnamed species of the Irroratum series.

R. ADENOGYNUM Diels

An evergreen shrub said to grow 9 ft high in the wild, with the stout young shoots woolly at first, becoming glabrous. Leaves with decurved margins, oblong inclined to ovate, pointed, tapered, or rounded at the base, 2 to 6 in. long, $\frac{3}{4}$ to $1\frac{3}{4}$ in. wide, dark green, finely wrinkled, and at maturity glabrous above, covered beneath with a tawny, suède-like felt; stalk without glands, $\frac{1}{2}$ to $1\frac{1}{4}$ in. long. Flowers opening in April and May in trusses of six to twelve, fragrant. Calyx-lobes five, oval, $\frac{3}{16}$ to $\frac{3}{8}$ in. long, very glandular; flower-stalk up to $1\frac{1}{4}$ in. long, glandular. Corolla white, tinged with pink or rose-magenta, spotted with crimson, bell-shaped, $1\frac{1}{2}$ to $2\frac{1}{2}$ in. long, 2 to 3 in. wide, the five lobes rounded. Stamens ten, $\frac{1}{2}$ to $1\frac{1}{4}$ in. long, stalks white, downy at the base. Ovary glandular but not downy; style $1\frac{1}{8}$ in. long, very glandular towards the base. *Bot. Mag.*, t. 9253. (s. Taliense ss. Adenogynum)

R. *adenogynum* was discovered by Forrest in 1906 in N. W. Yunnan, on the eastern flank of the Lichiang range, at altitudes of 11,000 to 12,000 ft and introduced by him four years later. As he originally found it, it was scattered in small clumps over grassy mountain slopes, and occurs in similar situations on the neighbouring Chungtien plateau and in bordering parts of S.W. Szechwan. Although one of the more decorative of the Taliense series, and flowering when quite young, it is rarely seen outside specialist collections. It is quite hardy.

R. ADENOPHORUM Balf. f. & W. W. Sm.—Closely allied to the preceding, but with the leaves slightly glandular above when young, and with small glands beneath concealed by the indumentum. The petiole, too, is glandular as well as tomentose. Introduced by Forrest in 1913 from N.W. Yunnan. Flowers similar to those of R. *adenogynum*, borne in April.

R. ADENOPODUM Franch.

An evergreen shrub 4 to 10 ft high; young shoots thinly felted and glandular. Leaves leathery, 3 to 8 in. long, 1 to 2 in. wide, oblong-oblanceolate with an acute point, tapered to a cuneate base, glabrous above, but covered beneath with a close, greyish felt; stalk ½ to 1 in. long, felted. Flowers pale rose, usually speckled within, 2½ to 3 in. across, produced in April in rather loose terminal racemose clusters, the rachis up to 2 in. long. Calyx-lobes oblong, ciliate, ⅛ to ¼ in. long. Corolla broadly funnel-campanulate, with five rounded lobes. Stamens ten, as long as the corolla, hairy at the base. Ovary densely clad with long-stalked glands. Style glabrous.

Native of Central China; discovered by the French missionary Farges in N.E. Szechwan; introduced by Wilson in 1900 from W. Hupeh when collecting for Messrs Veitch. A year later Farges sent seeds to M. Vilmorin, and it first flowered in a greenhouse at Les Barres in 1909. According to Wilson it is rare in western Hupeh, known to him from only two or three localities in the Hsing-shan district, where it grows in thin woods at 5,000 to 7,000 ft. Because of its racemose inflorescence, it is placed in the Caucasicum subseries of the Ponticum series, and certainly it appears to be more closely allied to R. *smirnowii* of N.E. Asiatic Turkey than to any Chinese rhododendron. It is rather a dull rhododendron, but it was admired by Gerald Loder and received an Award of Merit on April 7, 1926, when shown by him from his garden at Wakehurst Place, Sussex.

R. AGANNIPHUM Balf. f. & Ward
R. *vellereum* Tagg

An evergreen shrub 2 to 8 ft high in the wild, sometimes a small tree up to 15 ft high; young stems stout, glabrous or almost so. Leaves thick and leathery, elliptic, oblong-elliptic, oblong-lanceolate, or oblong-ovate, 2 to 4½ in. long, ¾ to 2 in. wide, acute or obtuse at the apex, base rounded, obtuse or slightly cordate, dark green and glabrous above, lower surface coated with a close, continuous, often rather spongy felt with a glossy skin, varying in colour from silvery white to fawn or pale yellow; petiole ⅜ to ¾ in. long, glabrous. Flowers twelve to twenty in a fairly dense truss, opening in April; rachis up to ⅝ in. long; pedicels ⅜ to 1½ in. long, glabrous or slightly floccose. Calyx very small. Corolla varying from white to rose, spotted with crimson, five-lobed, funnel-campanulate to cup-shaped, up to 2 in. across. Stamens ten, downy at the base. Ovary glabrous, conoid; style glabrous, with a discoid stigma. *Bot. Mag.*, n.s., t. 147. (s. and ss. Taliense)

R. *aganniphum* has a wide distribution, from the Muli region of S.W. Szechwan through N.W. Yunnan to the Tibetan side of the Assam Himalaya; discovered by

Kingdon Ward in 1913 on the Doker La (Mekong–Salween divide) and introduced by him in the same year. The type of R. *vellereum*, here included in R. *aganniphum*, was collected, also by Ward, in Tibet above the Tsangpo river, near Nang Dzong, in the transition zone where forest and alpine scrub gives way to xerophytic vegetation. The flower truss figured in the Botanical Magazine is from a plant raised from KW 5656, the original introduction, collected in the same area, where 40° F. of frost is not uncommon in winter. Seeds sent later by Ludlow and Sherriff are also from this part of Tibet. R. *aganniphum* is quite a pretty rhododendron but flowers too early for most gardens. In some forms the leaf-indumentum is remarkably thick and spongy.

R. AGASTUM Balf. f. & W. W. Sm.

An evergreen shrub or small tree up to 20 ft high; young shoots thinly floccose and sticky with small glands. Leaves oblong or oblong-elliptic, rounded to obtuse or subacute and mucronate at the apex, up to 6 in. long and 2 in. wide, glabrous above, clad beneath with a more or less persistent film-like coating of hairs; petiole about 1 in. long. Flowers up to twenty or so in a terminal truss on pedicels about $\frac{7}{8}$ in. long, opening in early spring, sometimes as early as February. Calyx minute. Corolla tubular-campanulate, about $1\frac{3}{4}$ in. long, 2 in. across, five- to seven-lobed, rose-coloured or white tinged with pink, speckled and blotched with crimson (sometimes unspotted). Stamens ten to fourteen, downy at the base. Ovary glandular; style stout, partly or wholly glandular, with a large discoid stigma. *Bot. Mag.*, t. 9577. (*s.* and *ss.* Irroratum)

Native of mid-Yunnan at comparatively low altitudes; discovered by Forrest in 1913 and 1914 near the border between Yunnan and Burma, north-west of Tengyueh, and above the Yangpi valley, south-west of the Tali range. The date of introduction is uncertain, but the truss depicted in the *Botanical Magazine* is from a plant that flowered in E. J. P. Magor's garden at Lamellen, Cornwall, in April 1929. The true species appears to be very rare in cultivation.

R. ALABAMENSE Rehd.

Azalea nudiflora var. *alba* Mohr

A deciduous shrub up to 5 ft high, sometimes dwarf and stoloniferous; young stems clad with pale appressed hairs, sometimes only sparsely so. Leaves obovate to elliptic or oblong-elliptic, $1\frac{1}{4}$ to $2\frac{1}{4}$ in. long, about half as wide, acute to slightly acute at the apex, cuneate at the base, slightly hairy above, densely so and usually glaucous beneath, margins ciliate. Flowers fragrant, borne with the unfolding leaves in May, in a terminal cluster of six to ten, on glabrous or sometimes hairy pedicels up to $\frac{3}{8}$ in. long. Calyx very small, clad with bristly eglandular hairs. Corolla tubular-funnel-shaped, about $1\frac{1}{2}$ in. wide at the mouth, white, with or without a yellow blotch, tube slender, about 1 in. long, hairy and sometimes glandular outside, expanding gradually into the limb, lobes ovate or oblong-ovate. Stamens ten, about twice as long as the tube. Ovary densely appressed-hairy, glandular or eglandular. (*s.* Azalea *ss.* Luteum)

Native of the south-eastern USA; introduced to Britain in 1922. Mrs Norman

Henry considered this to be one of the most enchanting of the American azaleas. 'With its supremely beautiful velvety white flowers that appear, so abundantly, before the leaves that sometimes the stems are invisible, it is a fair sight indeed, and as for fragrance, it is utterly unlike any other Azalea with which I am familiar, the odour being full and mellow with much of the rich sweetness of some of the oriental Lilies' (*R.Y.B. 1946*, p. 36).

R. *alabamense* was first described as late as 1901, and then as a variety of *R. nudiflorum* (now *R. periclymenoides*). But, among other characters, the pure white flowers distinguish it from that species and from *R. prinophyllum* and *R. canescens*. Despite its southern habitat, *R. alabamense* is perfectly hardy in Britain.

For natural hybrids between *R. alabamense* and *R. canescens* see: H. T. Skinner, 'In Search of Native Azaleas' (*R.C.Y.B. 1957*, pp. 11 and 15).

R. ALBIFLORUM Hook. [PLATE 65

R. warrenii Macbride

A deciduous shrub 5 or 6 ft high in the wild, the young shoots furnished with short, dark hairs. Leaves narrowly oval, 1 to 2½ in. long, ½ to ¾ in. wide, tapering towards both ends, thin and glabrous except that, like the very short stalk, they are furnished when young on the midrib with hairs similar to those on the stems. Flowers creamy white, ¾ in. wide, drooping, produced singly or in pairs from lateral buds on the growth of the previous year during June and July, when the young shoots are in full leaf. Corolla open bell-shaped, with five short, rounded lobes. Calyx ⅓ in. long, green, the lobes ovate and edged with glands. Stamens ten, shorter than the corolla, hairy at the base; flower-stalk ⅓ in. long, glandular-downy. *Bot. Mag.*, t. 3670. (*s.* Albiflorum)

Native of western N. America from Oregon to British Columbia, forming impenetrable thickets just above the tree-line and along streams. It is a pretty species, very distinct because of the large calyx, the axillary flowers, and the dark hairs on the young wood like those of an azalea of the Obtusum subseries, only not so numerous and persistent. It is not an easy plant to satisfy, but Andrew Harley succeeded with it in his garden in Perthshire, where it was planted in a fairly sunny position and a rather poor, stony soil (*New Fl. and Sylv.*, Vol. 9 (1937), p. 128).

R. ALBRECHTII Maxim.

Azalea albrechtii (Maxim.) O. Kuntze

A deciduous azalea described as of thin, loose habit and 3 to 5 ft high in the wild, but taller in cultivation; young shoots furnished with partly sticky hairs at first. Leaves often arranged in clusters of five at the end of the twig, dark green, obovate to oblanceolate, tapered to the base, finely bristle-toothed on the margin, 2 to 4 in. long, about half as much wide, being broadest above the middle, upper surface thinly set with appressed hairs, undersurface grey-downy, especially about the midrib and chief veins; stalk short, hairy. Flowers opening in late April or early May in clusters of three to five. Calyx very small and like the flower-stalk (which is ⅓ to ¾ in. long) clothed with curled glandular hairs. Corolla 1½ to 2 in. wide, bright purplish rose, spotted with green on the upper lobes; lobes five, roundish obovate; tube downy at the base. Stamens ten, of unequal length, the longest equalling the corolla, mostly hairy at the base. Ovary covered with pale, glandular, erect hairs; style glabrous, curved, longer than the stamens. *Bot. Mag.*, t. 9207. (*s.* Azalea *ss.* Canadense)

Native of central and northern Japan; described from specimens collected in 1860–2 by Dr Albrecht of the Russian Consulate at Hakodate. For a long time it remained unknown to cultivation, although seeds under the name were several times obtained for Kew, which invariably proved to be R. *reticulatum*. It was not introduced to this country until 1914, when the Arnold Arboretum distributed seeds collected by E. H. Wilson during his visit to Japan, but it remained scarce and much sought after for another quarter-century. Writing in 1934, Lionel de Rothschild said he had seen no plant over 3 ft high and called it 'rare and fastidious' (*Rhod. Ass. Handb. 1934*, p. 94). The material figured in the *Botanical Magazine* came from a plant presented to Kew in 1925 by George Johnstone of Trewithen, Cornwall, who had raised it from the Wilson seeds.

R. *albrechtii* is one of the most beautiful of the azaleas. The colour of its flowers is always strikingly vivid, but varies from a fairly pure intense pink to a less pleasant magenta-pink. Unlike most deciduous azaleas, it seems to prefer woodland conditions and a moist, leafy soil. Rightly placed, it grows vigorously to 6 ft or even taller, and flowers unfailingly. It received an Award of Merit on April 13, 1943, when shown from Bodnant. The clone 'Michael McLaren' was awarded a First Class Certificate when shown from the same garden on May 1, 1962. In this the flowers are coloured Solferino Purple.

R. AMBIGUUM Hemsl.

An evergreen shrub up to 15 ft high in the wild, with a rough bark; young shoots covered with pale yellow, glistening scales. Leaves aromatic, oval, sometimes slightly obovate or ovate, 1½ to 3 in. long, ⅝ to 1¼ in. wide, scattered along the shoot, pointed, rounded or slightly heart-shaped at the base, dark green and somewhat scaly above, downy along the midrib, paler and much more scaly beneath, the scales large, some yellowish brown, others dark brown or black; stalk ¼ to ⅜ in. long. Flowers produced in April or May in terminal trusses of five to six. Calyx minute, scaly. Corolla pale yellow with yellow-green spots on the upper lobes, about 2 in. wide, broadly funnel-shaped, slightly scaly outside. Stamens ten, whitish, hairy near the base. Ovary scaly; style glabrous. *Bot. Mag.*, t. 8400. (*s.* and *ss.* Triflorum)

R. *ambiguum* is abundant in W. Szechwan, China, whence it was introduced by Wilson in 1904. It is a species of little ornamental value, allied to the Himalayan R. *triflorum*, but in that species the leaves are glabrous on the midrib above, and the scales on the underside are very small, widely spaced (more than their own diameter apart) and equally coloured (Davidian, *R.C.Y.B. 1963*, pp. 172, 174).

R. ANTHOPOGON D. Don

incl. R. *haemonium* Balf. f. & Cooper; R. *anthopogon* var. *haemonium* (Balf. f. & Cooper) Cowan & Davidian

An evergreen shrub 2 ft or less high, of compact habit; young branchlets hairy and covered with brown scurf; leaf-bud scales deciduous. Leaves oval or ovate, 1 to 1½ in. long, ½ to ¾ in. wide, dark, rather glossy green above, covered with brown scales beneath; stalk ¼ in. long. Flowers white, pink, or sulphur-coloured, ½ to ¾ in. across, produced in a small terminal cluster, 1 to 1½ in. wide. Corolla thin, almost transparent, tube hairy inside expanding at the mouth into five wavy lobes; calyx-lobes oblong, pale green, ⅛ in. long, fringed at the margin; stamens five to eight, very short, and included within the tube; flower-stalk scaly, ⅙ in. or less in length; style short and thick. Flowers in April. *Bot. Mag.*, t. 3947. (*s.* Anthopogon)

Native of the high Himalaya from Kashmir eastwards, up to 16,000 ft altitude, where it covers large areas; introduced in 1820. The whole plant has a strong, aromatic, slightly acrid odour, especially when crushed. It is an interesting little plant, and one of the hardiest of Himalayan species, but not in any way showy.

The Award of Merit was given on April 29, 1969 to the clone 'Betty Graham', with deep pink flowers, raised from Ludlow and Sherriff 1091 and shown by E. H. M. and P. A. Cox.

R. HYPENANTHUM Balf. f.—This rhododendron is very closely related to R. *anthopogon* and was not distinguished from it until 1916. In the true R. *anthopogon* the scales that surround the base of the winter-buds fall away as soon as, or soon after, the leaves open; but in R. *hypenanthum* these scales—triangular, overlapping, and ciliate—remain clasping the twigs for several years. So far as is known, the flowers in R. *hypenanthum* are always yellow. It is a native of the Himalaya, but has not yet been found east of Nepal.

R. ANTHOSPHAERUM Diels

R. *eritimum* Balf. f. & W. W. Sm.; R. *chawchiense* Balf. f. & Farrer; R. *gymnogynum* Balf. f. & Forr.; R. *heptamerum* Balf. f.; R. *persicinum* Hand.-Mazz.

An evergreen shrub or a small tree up to 30 ft high. Leaves oblong, oblong-lanceolate, or oblong-oblanceolate, 4 to 6 in. long, ⅞ to 1⅞ in. wide, acute to obtuse at the apex, glabrous. Flowers in terminal trusses of ten to fifteen, borne early in spring, sometimes in February; pedicels ⅜ to ⅝ in. long, floccose and sometimes glandular also. Calyx minute, usually glabrous, but sometimes with the same covering as the pedicels. Corolla five- to seven-lobed, tubular-campanulate, 1½ to 3 in. long, commonly crimson, rose-magenta or blue-magenta, with darker nectar-pouches at the base and sometimes spotted inside, occasionally white or, in the type of R. *persicinum*, peach-coloured. Stamens ten to fourteen, downy near the base or glabrous. Ovary glabrous or slightly hairy; style glabrous. *Bot. Mag.*, t. 9083. (*s.* and *ss.* Irroratum)

Native of N.W. Yunnan and bordering parts of upper Burma; discovered by Forrest below the Sungkwei pass in 1906 and introduced by him. Although hardy in a sheltered position south of London, its flowers are of little beauty and both they and the young growths are often destroyed by frost.

R. APERANTUM Balf. f. & Ward

A dwarf evergreen shrub, forming in the wild broad spreading mats 6 to 20 in. high, more rarely erect and up to 5 ft high; younger branches thickly set with roundish-ovate, membranous scales (perulae) up to ¼ in. long, which persist for several years. Leaves oval-obovate, more tapered to the base than the apex, ¾ to 1½ in. long, ½ to ⅝ in. wide, dark green above, glaucous-white and nearly glabrous beneath; very shortly stalked. Flowers produced in clusters of three to six. Corolla between funnel- and bell-shaped, 1½ to 1¾ in. long, scarcely as much wide, varying in colour from white to different shades of rose, orange-red, and yellow. Stamens ten, ¾ in. long, glabrous. Ovary covered with branched hairs and usually with glandular bristles also. Calyx with small glands on the margins of the shallow lobes; flower stalks ½ to ⅝ in. long, downy. *Bot. Mag.*, t. 9507. (*s.* Neriiflorum *ss.* Sanguineum)

R. *aperantum* was discovered by Kingdon Ward in 1919 on the western spur of Imaw Bum, a mountain in N.E. Burma on the divide between the eastern Irrawaddy (Nmai Hka) and the Salween, and was introduced by him in the same year. But the type of the species was collected by Farrer in the following year on the Chawchi pass, farther to the north on the same divide, a few months before his death. He wrote of it: 'it is simply one of the most radiantly lovely things you ever saw, and when you do see it, your mouth just opens and shuts feebly. It is common, in drifts and sheets; and, for the altitude, and for its stature, rather large in all its parts. In stature it ranges from half an inch, or less, to about six inches, spreading widely, and often plastered flat against a rock, where starved. The flowers ... are very large, and in a sequence of the most glorious warm pink tones—absolutely clean of mauve or blue shades—through hot flesh-pinks, rose-pinks, salmon-pinks, to flushed snow and pure white' (*Gard. Chron.*, Vol. 70 (1921), p. 209).

Most of the plants in cultivation are from seeds sent by Forrest between 1925 and 1931 from the same part of Burma and from bordering parts of China. Unfortunately, R. *aperantum* has proved a sad disappointment in cultivation, as it flowers poorly. Probably a moist position with abundant sky-light but protected from the strongest sun would suit it best. A crimson-flowered form received an Award of Merit in 1931, when shown by Lord Headfort from his garden in Ireland.

R. ARAIOPHYLLUM Balf. f. & W. W. Sm.

An evergreen shrub up to 16 ft high; young shoots glabrous or soon becoming so. Leaves red when young, lanceolate, slenderly pointed, broadly tapered at the base, 3 to 5 in. long, ⅝ to 1¼ in. wide, glabrous and green on both surfaces except for traces of wool on the midrib beneath; stalk ¼ to ½ in. long. Flowers in a racemose cluster of about eight. Calyx little more than a wavy rim, glabrous; flower-stalk glabrous, slender, up to 1 in. long. Corolla open bell-shaped, 1½ in.

long, rather more wide, white often flushed with rose-lavender, with a crimson blotch at the base and similarly coloured spots on the upper lobes, the five lobes are notched in the middle and their margins are uneven. Stamens ten, downy at the base; ovary minutely downy, style glabrous, red, only as long as the corolla. (*s.* and *ss.* Irroratum)

R. *araiophyllum* was found by Forrest in 1913 on the Shweli–Salween divide at 9,000 to 10,000 ft and introduced from that region of Yunnan; Farrer later sent seeds from farther north on the Burma side of the frontier. It is one of the most attractive members of the Irroratum series and has brightly coloured young growths, though these, like the flowers, may be cut by frost. The flowering time is April or early May. Award of Merit May 4, 1971, when shown by Kew from Wakehurst Place (clone 'George Taylor').

R. ARBORESCENS (Pursh) Torr.

Azalea arborescens Pursh

A deciduous shrub up to 20 ft high in the wild; young shoots glabrous. Leaves obovate or oval, pointed at both ends, 1½ to 3½ in. long, one-third to half as wide, glossy green and glabrous above except on the midrib, pale, glaucous, and glabrous beneath; margins edged with minute bristles. Flowers fragrant, 1½ in. long, 2 to 2½ in. wide, white tinged with pink; corolla-tube hairy-glandular, the lobes spreading; stamens five, bright red, much protruded; style still longer; flower-stalk ¼ in. long, glabrous, or sometimes bristly. Calyx-lobes linear, ⅛ to ¼ in. long, very bristly. (*s.* Azalea *ss.* Luteum)

Native of eastern N. America in mountainous regions; discovered by John Bartram, and introduced in 1818. This azalea, although now but little known, is one of the most beautiful of its kind, and is valuable in flowering late (June and July) when the plants have become leafy. It is allied to R. *viscosum* (whose flowers also expand after the young leaves), differing in its larger size, in the shining foliage, in the only slightly sticky corolla-tube and in its longer style and stamens. In drying, the foliage acquires a perfume like that of mown grass.

Award of Merit June 10, 1952, to a fine form with ten flowers to the truss, shown by Murray Adams-Acton (clone 'Ailsa').

var. RICHARDSONII Rehd.—A variety of the higher mountains at 3,800 to 5,200 ft, usually not much over 4 ft tall, and with somewhat smaller and more glaucous leaves.

R. ARBOREUM Sm.

R. *windsorii* Nutt.; R. *arboreum* subsp. *windsorii* (Nutt.) Tagg

R. *arboreum* attains in the wild a height of 40 ft or more and may be narrow and erect with a single stem or many-branched from the base and more spreading girths up to 15 ft at the base have been recorded. Leaves stiffly leathery, oblong-lanceolate to oblong-oblanceolate, 4 to 8 in. long, 1¼ to 2¼ in. wide. obtuse to subacute at the apex narrowed gradually or more abruptly to the base, dark green and, when mature, glabrous above, clad beneath with, in the typical state, close indumentum composed of rosulate hairs, but in other forms, where an upper layer of dendroid hairs is present, it may be thicker and more woolly or spongy; typically it is silvery white, but more commonly brown; lateral veins about twenty on each side, they and the minor reticulations prominent, but often obscured by the indumentum; petiole $\frac{1}{2}$ to $\frac{3}{4}$ in. long (rarely longer). Inflorescence dense corymb of about twenty flowers on a rachis up to about 1 in. long, borne normally in March or April; pedicels very short, about $\frac{3}{8}$ in. long, downy or glandular or both. Calyx very small, with the same covering as the pedicels; lobes broadly triangular. Corolla tubular-campanulate, $1\frac{3}{4}$ to 2 in. long and wide, blood-red in the typical form, with darker markings on the usually indented lobes and nectar-pouches at the base. Stamens ten, glabrous. Ovary conoid, downy and often glandular also, ten-chambered. (s. and ss. Arboreum)

R. *arboreum*, in its typical state, appears to be confined to the Himalaya, though in slightly different forms it extends farther to the east and south. The first account of it was published in 1799 by Capt. Thomas Hardwicke, who had seen it flowering three years earlier in Kumaon, south-east of Dehra Dun. It was first formally described and named in 1804 by James Smith, using Hardwicke's notes and drawings, and introduced to cultivation some ten years later (see further below). In the Himalaya it ranges as far west as Kashmir, where it is found only on the outer and rainier side of the mountains that border the Vale of Kashmir on the south, but is best known from Kumaon and the Himalaya of Nepal and Sikkim. The typical state of the species is, at least for the most part, confined to low elevations, from 5,000 to 8,500 ft. The natural vegetation at these altitudes is temperate forest, much of which has been destroyed by fire, but R. *arboreum* survives, even on hot, sunny, grass-clad slopes, or in secondary forest of oak or pine; whether it is capable of regenerating in such habitats is not clear. At higher elevations, at least in the Nepal and Sikkim Himalaya, it gives way to the following variants, usually treated as subspecies:

subsp. CAMPBELLIAE (Hook. f.) Tagg R. *arboreum* var. *roseum* Lindl.; R. *album* Sw.; R. *campbelliae* Hook. f.; R. *arboreum* var. *campbelliae* (Hook. f.) Hook. f.—In typical R. *arboreum* the indumentum is a thin silvery felt that covers the lateral veins and minor reticulations but, these being prominent, does not actually obscure them; also the flowers are blood-red, or at least commonly so. But at altitudes above 8,000 ft the prevailing form has a thicker, usually brown indumentum and the flowers are crimson, pink, or white, sometimes pink at the edge and white at the centre. There appears to be no constant difference in shape of leaf. The altitudinal overlap between typical R. *arboreum* and this subspecies is considerable and the correlation between flower-colour and indumentum is far from perfect, but it remains true that the richest coloured forms do not occur much above 8,000 ft and that there is a tendency for the indumentum to become thicker and darker with altitude.

subsp. CINNAMOMEUM (Wall. Cat.) Tagg R. *cinnamomeum* Wall. ex Lindl.— This resembles the subsp. *campbelliae* but the leaf-indumentum is cinnamon-coloured or rusty and sometimes rather loosely woolly. The flowers are typically white, with coarse spotting, but can be pink or crimson. It is apparently confined to high altitudes and its distribution outside Nepal, whence it first became known, is uncertain.

Outside the Himalaya, R. *arboreum* extends across the Brahmaputra into Burma and south through the Khasi Hills and other hills of Assam, Nagaland and Manipur to Mount Victoria in eastern Burma (Arakan). But the plants in these areas are mostly untypical: the indumentum is often composed of rather long, interwoven hairs and is honeycombed with holes (alveolar); the leaves are relatively short and broad in some forms from Manipur and the Khasi Hills and in some respects recall R. *nilagiricum* and R. *zeylanicum*. It is also interesting that in these eastern and southern forms the richly coloured flowers of typical R. *arboreum* are sometimes combined with an indumentum of the type characteristic of subsp. *campbelliae*. However, these variations are of no importance horticulturally. A very distinct form was introduced by Bailey and Morshead in 1914 from the Nyamjang Chu on the border between Bhutan and Assam and was named R. *morsheadianum* by Millais; it was reintroduced by Kingdon Ward from the same area ten years later (KW 6403). The leaves have a very close, burnished indumentum resembling that of R. *insigne* and straight, deeply impressed lateral veins.

The first recorded flowering of R. *arboreum* in cultivation was of the typical form and took place at The Grange, Alresford, Hants, in 1826. When the seed was introduced and by whom is not known, but a possible source is Francis Buchanan Hamilton, who made important botanical collections in India and is known to have sent seeds of R. *arboreum* to the Calcutta Botanic Garden in 1810 from near the borders of Nepal (where he had discovered the white-flowered form of the species during a visit in 1802–3). It is also recorded that he sent seeds of a red- and a white-flowered form to the Edinburgh Botanic Garden in 1820. Neither date agrees well with a first flowering in 1826, the first being too early and the latter too late. Another possibility is that the seeds were collected during the military expedition to Nepal in 1814–16, and is borne out by the date of introduction given by Loudon—1817 (Prain and Bean, R*hod. Soc. Notes* Vol. I, pp. 175–9; Cowan, *R.Y.B. 1953,* pp. 38–9). Three years after the conclusion of peace with Nepal, Dr Nathaniel Wallich arrived in Katmandu and sent seeds to Britain in 1820 of the subsp. *campbelliae* and *cinnamomeum*, which were widely distributed. The rose-coloured form, sown in 1821, flowered at Knight's nursery, Chelsea, in 1828 and was named R. *arboreum* var. *roseum* by Lindley; the first recorded flowering of the white form of subsp. *campbelliae* was in a garden at Chester, and of the subsp. *cinnamomeum* at Rollisson's nursery, Tooting, in 1836.

Both typical R. *arboreum* and the subsp. *campbelliae* were reintroduced by Hooker in 1849–50 from the interior of Sikkim, the former from near Chungthang (Hooker's 'Choongtam'), at the confluence of the Lachen and Lachung rivers, and both it and the subsp. *campbelliae* from the Laghep valley, an eastern feeder of the Tista (*Himalayan Journals,* Vol. II, pp. 186, 197). The oldest extant specimens in the British Isles are probably from these seed-collections. Those at Stonefield in Argyll are remnants of the plantings made by John Campbell, a friend of the elder Hooker and a relative of Dr Campbell, the Political Resident at Darjeeling, who did more than anyone to make the younger Hooker's Sikkim expedition a success (the subsp. *campbelliae*, originally described as a species, is named after his wife). The famous colony of R. *arboreum* at Lochinch in Wigtownshire, in which pink and white forms predominate, was planted by the 10th Earl of Stair in the early 1860s, and is also from the Hooker seed.

The typical state of the species, usually distinguished in gardens as 'blood-red arboreum', is not reliably hardy outside the milder parts, and is by no means common even there. South of London the best-coloured forms, though they may survive quite severe winters once established, are often cut by spring frost and rarely attain a good size. The Tregothnan form, raised from seeds collected in the Himalaya by a former Viscount Falmouth, was tried at Exbury by Lionel de Rothschild and found to be hardier there than other blood-red forms.

The subsp. *campbelliae* is much hardier, but, like all forms of R. *arboreum* it flowers dangerously early and does not reveal its full beauty until twenty or so years old. Typically the flowers are pink, but both in the wild and in cultivation they may be white at the centre and pink at the edge, or wholly white except for the spotting. Many seedlings were raised by the Cornish nurseryman Gill, either from plants at Tremough (the oldest of which were from the Hooker seed) or from seed collected in the Himalaya, and some of these he propagated and named, such as 'Blushing Beauty', with white, pink-tinted flowers, and 'Mrs Henry Shilson', a fine pink with larger flowers, fewer in the truss, than normal, and almost certainly a hybrid.

The subsp. *cinnamomeum* is also hardy, but slow-growing and usually more bushy than the subsp. *campbelliae*.

The following clones of R. *arboreum* have received awards: 'Goat Fell', from Brodick Castle Gardens, Isle of Arran, A.M. May 5, 1964; 'Rubaiyat', from Exbury, A.M. April 2, 1968 (both these of the blood-red type); R. *arboreum* 'Tony Schilling', from Wakehurst Place, Sussex, F.C.C. April 2, 1974 (a form of subsp. *campbelliae*).

R. DELAVAYI Franch. R. *pilovittatum* Balf. f. & Forr.—This species was described from specimens collected in Yunnan, China, by the French missionary Delavay, and as usually understood it is a native of that province and parts of Burma, Thailand, and the former Indo-china. How it differs from R. *arboreum* has never been made clear. H. F. Tagg, in *The Species of Rhododendron*, p. 17, says: 'The best distinguishing feature is in the indumentum; in R. *arboreum* it is usually thin and more or less plastered, whereas in R. *delavayi* it is of a somewhat spongy texture, the surface more or less fissured.' This is not much to base a species upon and is not even reliable. Some specimens in the Kew Herbarium, collected by Delavay and others in Yunnan, have an indumentum differing in no way from that of R. *arboreum*, though the leaves tend to be shorter than in that species. Other specimens from Yunnan have the 'spongy' type of indumentum, but this is also to be seen on some specimens from the eastern Himalaya and the Khasi Hills (and in R. *nilagiricum* and R. *zeylanicum*).

Delavay discovered this rhododendron in 1884; it was introduced to France at about the same time and thence to Kew in 1889. The first flowers seen in the British Isles were borne on a plant at Kilmacurragh, Co. Wicklow, in 1904. It was later reintroduced by Forrest from various parts of Yunnan, where it extends as far to the north-east as the Lichiang range and into the southern parts of the province. Like R. *arboreum*, it occurs in drier habitats than most rhododendrons, and according to Forrest is at its best on the margins of pine forests.

R. *delavayi* is uncommon in cultivation and tender in its best forms, which are mostly to be found in Scottish collections (Lochinch, Brodick, and Crarae). It has reached 10 ft in height at Wakehurst Place in Sussex. *Bot. Mag.*, t. 8137.

R. PERAMOENUM Balf. f. & Forr.—Closely allied to R. *delavayi*, differing in the longer, relatively narrower leaves 3 to 6 in. long, up to scarcely 1 in. wide, less rugose above, and with a closer indumentum beneath. It was discovered by Forrest on the Shweli–Salween divide, Yunnan, near the frontier with Burma and was introduced by him.

R. ARGYROPHYLLUM Franch.

An evergreen shrub up to 20 ft high in the wild, the quite young shoots clothed with a loose, white scurf, or sometimes glabrous. Leaves oblong-lanceolate, tapered at the base, pointed, 2½ to 5 in. long, ½ to 1¼ in. wide, glabrous and bright green above, the lower surface covered with a close white scurf; stalk ½ in. or less long. Flowers borne in May in a lax truss of as many as twelve; flower-stalks slender, up to 1½ in. long. Calyx small, with glabrous triangular lobes. Corolla white blush or pink, more or less spotted with pink on the upper lobes, broadly funnel-shaped, about 1½ in. wide. Stamens twelve or fourteen, shorter than the corolla, white with down at the base (but glabrous in var. LEIANDRUM Hutch.). Ovary downy; style glabrous. *Bot. Mag.*, t. 8767. (*s.* Arboreum *ss.* Argyrophyllum)

Native of W. Szechwan; discovered by the Abbé David in 1869 near Mupin; introduced by Wilson in 1904. It is a fine species at its best, with flowers of a delicate pink very freely borne, and makes a well-shaped narrow bush. It is also very distinct in the pure white undersurface of the young leaves. It is a variable species. Typically, the flowers are narrowed to the base, but in var. CUPULARE Rehd. they are nearer to cup-shaped. The leaves may be rounded at the base, not tapered as described above for the more typical form. Award of Merit May 1, 1934, when shown by Gerald Loder, Wakehurst Place, Sussex (this may have been var. *cupulare*).

var. NANKINGENSE Cowan—Leaves larger, very silvery white beneath, and with large trusses of pink flowers, which are more than 2 in. across. Found by A. N. Steward on the Lao Shan, Kweichow province, in 1931, and introduced by him to the Edinburgh Botanic Garden in the following year. Award of Merit April 30, 1957, when shown by the Crown Estate Commissioners, Windsor Great Park (clone 'Chinese Silver').

R. HYPOGLAUCUM Hemsl.—A close ally of R. *argyrophyllum*, perhaps a geographical subspecies. It is found to the east of R. *argyrophyllum*, in N.E. Szechwan and Hupeh, and according to Wilson, who introduced it in 1900, it is locally abundant in thin woods or, at its altitudinal limit, growing in open country among rocks, and attaining a height of 20 ft and as much in width. The flowers are white or pink, more or less spotted, sometimes densely so, rather like those of R. *argyrophyllum* var. *cupulare* in shape, borne in May. The main distinction from its ally seems to be that the leaves are relatively broader, 2 to 4 in. long, 1 to 1½ in. wide, and the ovary is usually glandular as well as hairy. *Bot. Mag.*, t. 8649.

R. ARIZELUM Balf. f. & Forr.

An evergreen shrub or a small tree up to 20 ft high; young shoots, leaf-stalks, and undersurface of leaves covered with a velvety, cinnamon-brown felt, which is especially richly coloured beneath the leaves; these are obovate, tapered at the base, rounded at the apex, and with a short mucro there, 5 to 9 in. long by 1½ to 3½ in. wide; stalk ½ to 1 in. long. Flowers borne in April, crowded, fifteen to twenty-five together, in a truss 5 or 6 in. across, each on a downy stalk 1 to 1½ in. long. Calyx very small. Corolla bell-shaped, 1½ to 2 in. wide, eight-lobed, in colour either white, creamy yellow, or yellow tinged with rose, with a dark crimson blotch or streaks of crimson at the base. Ovary densely downy but not glandular; style glabrous. (s. Falconeri)

. In the wild, R. arizelum often occurs with R. sinogrande though at higher altitudes, and the range of the two species is very similar—from the Salween westward through upper Burma to the eastern end of the Himalaya. Forrest's sendings are from various localities along the divide between the Salween and the eastern Irrawaddy, from the Shweli–Salween divide in the south, where he first found it in 1917, to as far north as 28° 50′ N. Near the north-western end of its range it was found by Kingdon Ward in 1924 on the far (southern) side of the Doshong La. The most recent collections in the Himalaya are Ludlow and Sherriff's 2753 from the upper Subansiri, not far east of the Bhutan frontier, and Cox and Hutchison 427, collected in 1965 in the same region but nearer to the plains of Assam.

In the wild R. arizelum is a gregarious species: 'One cliff, which faced the cold east, was painted pink and yellow for 2000 ft with flowers of R. arizelum. Looking squarely at this cliff from the river, one saw about 250 acres of rhododendron blossom. . . . The trees stood touching one another, and there must have been fifty thousand of them in bloom together' (Kingdon Ward, Plant Hunter's Paradise, p. 206, referring to the Adung valley, a feeder of the Irrawaddy). The variation in flower-colour was also remarked on by Farrer: 'Typically, its blossom is of a creamy white. . . . But I have seen it vary to citron and once even to apricot-yellow, while there is no end to its developments into the loveliest rosy shades' (Gard. Chron., Vol. 69 (1921), p. 274, referring to plants on the Burma–Yunnan frontier). There is also variation in the size and form of the truss, some plants in cultivation having very poor, flat-topped trusses. However, even when its flowers disappoint, R. arizelum makes a fine specimen, striking both in leaf and bark. Of the young foliage of R. arizelum in the Mishmi Hills Kingdon Ward wrote: 'In August the young leaves project like silver spears powdered with bronze-dust from amongst the tawny red and bottle green of the old leaves' (Plant Hunting on the Edge of the World, p. 278).

R. arizelum is hardy in a sheltered place near London but, like all the big-leaved rhododendrons, it attains its greatest size in the Atlantic zone. An Award of Merit was given to a form with a globular truss of about twenty flowers, coloured Solferino Purple with a dark crimson blotch in the throat, shown from the National Trust Gardens, Brodick, Isle of Arran, April 9, 1963.

var. RUBICOSUM Cowan & Davidian—Under this name is distinguished a form with bright crimson flowers, raised by Lord Stair at Castle Kennedy, Wigtownshire, from Rock 59550. The seed was collected in 1923 on the slopes of

Kenichunpu, Irrawaddy–Salween divide, just north of 28° N., at 12,000 ft. Award of Merit April 9, 1963.

R. ATLANTICUM (Ashe) Rehd.

Azalea atlantica Ashe

A deciduous, stoloniferous shrub up to 3 ft high; young shoots glabrous apart from scattered appressed hairs and occasional glandular hairs. Leaves obovate to oblong-obovate, rounded to subacute at the apex, cuneate at the base, light green or bluish green above, green or slightly glaucous beneath, usually glabrous on both surfaces apart from the slightly hairy midrib. Flowers fragrant, borne in May with or slightly before the leaves in clusters of four to ten, very fragrant, on hairy pedicels up to ½ in. long. Calyx up to ⅛ in. long, glandular-ciliate. Corolla white, flushed with pink outside, tubular-funnel-shaped, the tube glandular, 1 to 1½ in. long, rather gradually widening to the limb, which is 1¼ to 1½ in. across; lobes acute, each with a line of stalked glands along the midrib outside. Stamens about twice as long as the tube. Ovary clad with bristly, sometimes gland-tipped, hairs; style longer than the stamens.   (*s. Azalea ss.* Luteum)

Native of the eastern USA in the coastal plain from Delaware to South Carolina; introduced to Britain in 1922. 'In late April and early May the Coast azalea makes a truly splendid sight as a multi-hued understory to the open pine woods of the coastal Carolinas. Since it is highly stoloniferous it recovers promptly in the wake of a brush fire or roadside trimming or grazing, so that the year following will again see hundreds of upright flower clusters on wiry, knee-high stems borne by one plant an acre or more in extent' (H. T. Skinner, *R.C.Y.B. 1957*, p. 13). In this article, Dr Skinner suggests that typical *R. atlanticum*, described mainly from plants growing in Virginia and the Carolinas, may be the result of introgression of genes from *R. canescens* and *R. nudiflorum*, and that the original form of the species, uncontaminated by hybridisation, is represented by plants found in Delaware, which are white-flowered and far more glandular than typical *R. atlanticum*.

R. atlanticum is an azalea of great charm, very hardy and growing vigorously in moist soil. But flowering as it does at the peak of the rhododendron season it will go unnoticed unless planted well away from its more flamboyant rivals. It associates well with low-growing herbaceous plants.

The Award of Merit was given on May 25, 1964 to the clone 'Seaboard', exhibited by the Crown Estate Commissioners, Windsor Great Park.

R. AUGUSTINII Hemsl.   [PLATE 66

R. chasmanthum Diels; *R. chasmanthoides* Balf. f. & Forr.

An evergreen shrub from 4 to 10 ft high, of bushy habit, but sometimes up to 25 ft high in the wild; shoots hairy the first and second years, scaly the first. Leaves oblong-lanceolate, 1½ to 4 in. long, ½ to 1 in. wide, tapering to a fine point, tapered or rounded at the base, upper surface dark green, minutely wrinkled, and covered with fine down, undersurface scaly, and with pale bristle-like hairs on the midrib; stalk up to $\frac{1}{4}$ in. long, hairy like the midrib. Flowers in May in clusters of three or four. Calyx usually very small. Corolla $2\frac{1}{2}$ in. across, broadly funnel-shaped, wavy at the margins, varying in colour from white to pink, purplish pink, and bluish, with yellow, olive-green, or brownish spots on the uppermost lobes. Stamens ten, reddish brown, hairy near but not at the base. Ovary scaly; style downy at the base or glabrous. *Bot. Mag.*, t. 8497 and n.s., t. 79. (*s.* Triflorum *ss.* Augustinii)

Native of Central and W. China; discovered by Augustine Henry near Patung, Hupeh, in 1886. It first flowered in Europe in Maurice de Vilmorin's collection at Les Barres, raised from seed sent by the missionary Farges; the plants had pale purple to white flowers. To Britain it was introduced by Wilson, who in 1900 collected a large quantity of seed near Changyang, Hupeh. More was sent by him from other parts of the province and from Szechwan during his expeditions for the Arnold Arboretum. For the Forrest introduction see below under var. *chasmanthum*.

According to Wilson, R. *augustinii* is a very common species in Hupeh and ranges far into Szechwan. 'It is', he wrote, 'partial to the margins of woods but is happiest in open rocky situations where it is fully exposed to the sun.' It is exceedingly variable in the colouring of the flowers. According to Wilson, the most common shades in the wild are pale purple to rose-purple. But near-blue forms also occur and by selection, and by crossing the best-coloured plants, these forms have come to predominate in the great rhododendron gardens, of which they are now one of the chief glories. But these near-blue plants are really a race of cultivars and are not representative of the species as a whole. It has been said that the bluer the flower the more tender the plant, but this may not be true of garden-raised seedlings. Some of the paler shades are just as beautiful, though they may not look so impressive on the show-bench. R. *augustinii* is not a species for gardens subject to spring frosts and is inclined to be shy-flowering in cool gardens.

Plants originally grown under the name R. *chasmanthum*, now included in R. *augustinii*, were raised from seeds collected by Forrest and by Rock in various parts of N.W. Yunnan. There is really no significant botanical difference between these southern forms and the type, but Davidian has pointed out that they usually have more flowers per truss (up to six), and the lobes of the corollas tend to be reflexed. These can still be distinguished as var. CHASMANTHUM (Diels) Davidian. Some at least of the Forrest introductions flower somewhat later than the Wilson forms. This is true, for example, of the batch raised at Exbury from F.21470. A selection from these received an Award of Merit when shown by Lionel de Rothschild on June 3, 1930, and a First Class Certificate on June 7, 1932, so the flowering time of this form is about three weeks later than is normal for R. *augustinii*.

There is a form of R. *augustinii* with red flowers, raised from Forrest 25914, collected near Wei-hsi, which has been named var. RUBRUM Davidian. It flowers earlier than normal, in late March or early April.

cv. 'ELECTRA'.—Flowers $2\frac{1}{2}$ in. wide, violet-blue, with a yellow-green flare, in trusses of up to seven. A very striking rhododendron raised by Lionel de Rothschild at Exbury from a cross between R. *augustinii* and its var. *chasmanthum*. A.M. April 30, 1940.

R. AURICULATUM Hemsl.

An evergreen shrub or small tree 10 to 30 ft high in the wild; branchlets very thick and sturdy. Leaves very large, 6 to 13 in. long, 2 to 5 in. wide, oblong, the apex rounded except for a short abrupt point, the base with two well-marked lobes (or auricles) to which the specific name refers, upper surface dull dark green, hairy on the midrib when young, becoming glabrous, lower surface clothed with rust-coloured hairs, ultimately whitish brown; stalk up to 1¾ in. long, stout, bristly. The leaf-blade is of very leathery texture. Flowers 3 to 4 in. deep, scarcely as wide at the mouth, funnel-shaped; white or pink, six to eight in a truss; flower-stalk stout, 1 to 1½ in. long, glandular-hairy. Calyx small. Corolla seven- or eight-lobed, downy outside; stamens fourteen or sixteen, glabrous. Seed-pod 1½ in. long, ½ in. wide. *Bot. Mag.*, t. 8786. (*s.* Auriculatum)

R. *auriculatum* was discovered by Augustine Henry in the neighbourhood of Ichang, W. Hupeh, China in 1885, and was described four years later. It also occurs in Szechwan and Kweichow, but is nowhere common. It was introduced by Wilson in 1901 when collecting for Messrs Veitch, and flowered at Caerhays, Cornwall, in 1912, at Kew five years later.

R. *auriculatum* is remarkable for flowering and starting into growth well after midsummer has passed, July and August being the usual months, though a few buds may open even later. The flowers are fragrant, and the lower part of the young shoots is furnished with lurid crimson scales. But the flowers are apt to brown very quickly if the weather is hot and dry. It is perfectly hardy, but in gardens with a shorter than average growing season the new growths may not ripen sufficiently to withstand an early frost. In the milder parts it has attained a height of 30 ft, but in southern England it is unlikely to exceed 15 ft, though its width is often greater than this. Shade from the hottest sun is essential.

Among the best-known of its hybrids are Polar Bear and 'Argosy Snow White'.

R. AUSTRINUM (Small) Rehd.

Azalea austrina Small; R. *nudiflorum* var. *luteum* Curtiss ex Rehd.

A deciduous azalea up to 9 ft high; young shoots and leaf-stalks furnished with soft down mixed with which are numerous gland-tipped hairs. Leaves oval to obovate, 1½ to 3½ in. long, both surfaces downy, especially the lower one; margins bristly. Flowers slightly fragrant, borne in April or May eight to fifteen in a cluster; flower-stalks about ¼ in. long, hairy and glandular. Lobes of calyx downy outside, margined with gland-tipped hairs. Corolla pale to deep yellow or orange, with a cylindrical tube ¾ in. long, downy, glandular and more or less stained with purple or red outside. Stamens five, 2 in. long, downy below the middle; anthers yellowish. Ovary covered with whitish hairs, some of them glandular. Style slightly longer than the stamens, downy near the base. (*s.* Azalea *ss.* Luteum)

Native of the south-eastern USA, from Georgia and N. Florida to S.E. Mississippi; discovered before 1865 by Dr Chapman; introduced to Britain by Sargent in 1916. In general aspect it resembles R. *canescens* but differs in flower-colour and is more glandular. It has proved quite hardy at Kew despite its southern provenance.

R. BAILEYI Balf. f. [PLATE 67

R. thyodocum Balf. f. & Cooper

An evergreen bush of rounded shape 3 to 5 ft high; young shoots covered with reddish-brown scales. Leaves often clustered at the end of the shoot, oval, ovate or obovate, broadly wedge-shaped at the base, bluntish at the apex but with a distinct mucro there, 1 to 2½ in. long, ½ to 1⅓ in. wide, dark glossy green and scurfy above; pale yellowish brown (at first glaucous) beneath, completely covered with crenulate scales; stalk ⅓ to ⅗ in. long. Flowers produced during May in one or more racemes at and near the end of the shoot, the main-stalk up to 1 in. long; individual flower-stalks up to 1½ in. long. A raceme will carry sometimes twelve or more flowers, usually fewer. Calyx small with five scaly unequal lobes. Corolla flattish, deep red-purple with dark spots on the upper three lobes, 1⅛ in wide, five-lobed, the lobes rounded, scaly outside. Stamens ten, with rosy purple stalks, glabrous at the base, more or less downy above; anthers brown. Ovary covered with whitish scales; style red-purple, much bent over. *Bot. Mag.*, t. 8942. (*s.* Lepidotum *ss.* Baileyi)

Native of the E. Himalaya, not found west of Sikkim and rare even there; introduced by Lt-Col. F. M. Bailey in 1913 from near the border between Tibet and E. Bhutan and reintroduced by Roland Cooper from Bhutan in the following year. It differs from R. *lepidotum* in the more numerous flowers in each raceme, the brown undersides of the leaves and the crenulate scales.

Award of Merit April 26, 1960 when shown by A. C. and J. F. Gibson, Glenarn, Dunbartonshire.

R. BALFOURIANUM Diels

An evergreen shrub up to 8 ft high in the wild; young shoots and midrib at first scurfy. Leaves oblong or narrowly ovate, sharply pointed, rounded at the base, 2½ to 4½ in. long, ¾ to 1½ in. wide, dark dullish green above, silvery grey with scurfy down beneath; stalk ½ to ¾ in. long. Flowers in trusses of six to nine. Calyx deeply lobed, the five lobes ovate, blunt, ¼ in. long, and, like the flower-stalks (which are about 1 in. long), very glandular. Corolla bell-shaped, 1¾ in. deep, rather more wide, five-lobed, pale rose with crimson spottings. Stamens downy at the base, shorter than the corolla; ovary and lower part of style densely glandular. (*s.* Taliense *ss.* Adenogynum)

Native of W. Yunnan, where it was found by Forrest on the Tali Range in 1906. It is perfectly hardy at Kew. Closely related to R. *adenogynum*, it is still very distinct in the pale metallic-looking under surface of the leaf.

var. AGANNIPHOIDES Tagg & Forr.—Leaves longer, more lanceolate, up to 4¼ in. long, 1¾ in. wide, with a thicker indumentum. Style not glandular. Found by Forrest in the Muli region of S.W. Szechwan, and introduced by him. The truss figured in *Bot. Mag.*, n.s., t. 531, is from a plant raised from Kingdon

Ward's seed-number 4177, collected in the same region and originally distributed as R. *clementinae*, a quite different species. He greatly admired the wild plants and refers to them under this erroneous name in *Romance of Plant Hunting*, p. 159.

R. BARBATUM G. Don

R. *lancifolium* Hook. f., not Moench

An evergreen shrub or small tree, the bark peeling from the branches and leaving them blue-grey and smooth; winter-buds viscid; branches yellowish, sometimes glabrous, sometimes bristly. Leaves in a terminal cluster, oblong, heart-shaped at the base, terminated by a short, fine point, 4 to 9 in. long, 1 to 3 in. wide, dark dull green and ultimately glabrous above, pale and usually woolly at first beneath; stalk ½ to 1 in. long, conspicuously bristly on the upper side and at the base of the midrib. Flowers densely packed in a hemispherical truss about 4 in. wide, rich scarlet. Calyx with five glabrous ovate lobes, ¼ in. long. Corolla bell-shaped, 1½ in. across, five-lobed. Stamens ten. Ovary clad with long-stalked glands; style glabrous. (*s.* and *ss.* Barbatum)

Native of the Himalaya as far west as Kumaon, at 8,000 to 12,000 ft; introduced probably in 1829 (it was flowering in at least three gardens in 1848). This rhododendron is hardy in a sheltered spot at Kew, where it flowers in April. It is somewhat gaunt of habit, but worth growing for its marvellous richness of colour. It is, of course, much finer in Cornwall and similar places. There is some variation in the bristliness of the stems and leaves.

R. ARGIPEPLUM Balf. f. & Cooper—This differs from R. *smithii* (see below) only in having a whiter and more persistent leaf-indumentum. It was described from specimens collected by Roland Cooper in Bhutan in 1915, and has also been found in Sikkim and in the Assam Himalaya. Cooper's specimens were in fruit only, but in the Ludlow and Sherriff collections from Bhutan the flowers are described as bright rose or deep pink. For R. *argipeplum* at Glenarn see *R.C.Y.B. 1968*, p. 197.

R. IMBERBE Hutch.—This was described in 1928 from a plant at Kew of unknown origin, raised at the end of the last century. The differences from R. *barbatum* were given as: petioles and stems entirely without bristles, leaves relatively broader and shorter, calyx-lobes ciliate. It is matched by wild specimens from Kumaon, but is probably no more than a form of R. *barbatum*.

R. SMITHII Hook. R. *barbatum* var. *smithii* (Hook.) C.B. Cl.—Related to R. *barbatum*, but with the leaves clad beneath with a loose, greyish-white indumentum which becomes patchy by late summer. Native of the E. Himalaya. As seen in cultivation it is of more compact habit than R. *barbatum*, the leaves darker, with more impressed veins. *Bot. Mag.*, t. 5120. It was introduced by Booth from just east of Bhutan and first flowered in 1859.

It has been overlooked by botanists that the name R. *smithii* Hook. (1859) is illegitimate, being antedated by R. *smithii* Sweet (1831).

R. basilicum Balf. f. & W. W. Sm.

R. *megaphyllum* Balf. f. & Forr.; R. *regale* Balf. f. & Ward

An evergreen shrub or small tree up to 30 ft high; young shoots clothed with red-brown, soft felt. Leaves oval or obovate, rounded at the apex, less so or broadly tapered at the base, 6 to 13 in. long, about half as much wide, dark green and ultimately glabrous above, covered beneath with a rich red-brown down; stalk very stout, flattened above, up to 1¼ in. long. Flowers opening in April, numerously and closely packed in a truss 5 in. or more wide. Calyx a mere wavy rim; flower-stalks 1 to 1⅓ in. long, downy. Corolla broadly and obliquely bell-shaped, eight-lobed, 1½ in. wide, pale yellow flushed with rose and blotched with crimson at the base. Stamens sixteen, nearly or quite glabrous. Ovary densely clothed with down; style glabrous.   (s. Falconeri)

Native of N.W. Yunnan and bordering parts of upper Burma, but of limited distribution; discovered by Forrest in 1910 on the Shweli–Salween divide and introduced by him in 1912. His F.24139 is also from this area and a plant raised from it received an Award of Merit when shown by Col. The Lord Digby, Minterne Abbey, Dorset, in 1956. It is also in cultivation from Farrer 873 (Hpimaw pass, Nmai–Salween divide) and Rock 03904. It occurs at altitudes of up to 11,000 ft.

R. *basilicum* is perfectly hardy south of London in light woodland.

R. batemanii Hook.

An evergreen shrub up to 20 ft high; young shoots at first covered with pale rust-coloured wool. Leaves lanceolate-oblong, pointed, rounded or broadly tapered at the base, 4 to 9 in. long, 1½ to 2½ in. wide, dull dark green, ultimately glabrous above, clothed beneath with a soft, pale brown felt; stalk ¾ to 1 in. long, felted. Flowers produced in spring, twelve to twenty crowded in a terminal hemispherical truss 5 or 6 in. wide. Corolla bell-shaped, 2 in. wide, soft rosy crimson spotted on the upper side. Stamens ten, downy at the base; anthers brown. Ovary brown-felted; style 1½ in. long, glabrous. Calyx small with unequal pointed lobes; flower-stalk 1 in. long, downy. *Bot. Mag.*, t. 5387.

R. *batemanii* was discovered and introduced by Booth in 1850; flowered by James Bateman at Knypersley Hall, Staffordshire, in February 1863. Lost sight of in most gardens for many years, it has survived in the Earl of Stair's garden at Loch Inch in Wigtownshire. It is considered to have some affinity with R. *campanulatum* but is very distinct in the narrow, pointed leaves, in the rich red of the flowers, and in the very downy ovary and flower-stalk. J. G. Millais suggested that it is a hybrid between that species and R. *arboreum*, an origin which would explain the differences from R. *campanulatum* just enumerated. It is hardy at Kew.

There is another rhododendron which has been preserved in cultivation in the gardens at Loch Inch in a somewhat similar way. This is called there "R. *nobile*" and is a very handsome plant with bright carmine flowers in trusses about 4 in. across, opening in April and May. The leaves are covered with felt beneath. The name "R. *nobile*", however, really has no standing because Wallich, the botanist who first used it in his Indian herbarium (now preserved at Kew), gummed on to one sheet (No. 1521) flowering specimens of two distinct species, one of which is R. *nilagiricum*, and labelled them "R. *nobile*". He never published a description. The Loch Inch plant therefore has no right to this name and it is something of a mystery how it acquired it. It was quite hardy when grown at Kew.

R. BEANIANUM Cowan

An evergreen shrub up to 10 ft high, with ascending branches and of lax habit; young shoots clad with brown flock and usually gland-tipped bristles. Leaves mostly oblong or elliptic-oblong, sometimes broadest just above the middle, up to 3¾ in. long and 1¾ in. wide, rounded and mucronate at the apex, rounded or slightly cordate at the base, upper surface at first coated with brown flock, later glabrous, rich green, the main veins and reticulations impressed, lower surface densely covered with a rich-brown felt; petiole about ¾ in. long. Inflorescence a terminal truss of six to ten flowers, opening in late March or April; pedicels about ¾ in. long, bristly and floccose. Calyx fleshy, cup-shaped, irregularly lobed. Corolla five-lobed, tubular-campanulate, crimson or occasionally pink, about 1½ in. long, with five dark nectar-pouches at the base. Ovary conoid, densely hairy; style hairy at the base. *Bot. Mag.*, n.s., t. 219. (*s.* Neriiflorum *ss.* Haematodes)

R. *beanianum* was discovered by Kingdon Ward in June 1926 in the upper Seinghku valley, N.W. Burma (KW 6805). He wrote of it: 'One of the most splendid sights was the "Haematodes" rhododendron. . . . Some specimens fairly spouted flowers, for besides being entirely smothered, scarlet pools of fallen corollas lay beneath. The species grows between 9,000 and 11,000 ft, but not higher, and the flower colour varies, being sometimes much paler—carmine or almost pink in extremes, but then the glands stand out as hectic, blood-red spots. It varies in size, too, from a good-sized bush eight or ten feet high to a scrubby plant' (*Gard. Chron.*, Vol. 81 (1927), p. 303).

The flowering specimen collected by Kingdon Ward was apparently lost, but he sent home seeds and the species was described in 1938 from plants growing at Exbury. KW 6289, from the same valley, is also R. *beanianum*. In his account of this species, Dr Cowan also cited a flowering specimen collected by Kingdon Ward two years later in the Delei valley (KW 8254), but see below.

R. *beanianum* is striking both in flower and foliage. But it is of ungainly habit and too early-flowering for most gardens. Also, whole stems are apt to be killed to the ground by late frosts.

Award of Merit March 31, 1953, when shown by Col. The Lord Digby, Cerne Abbey, Dorset (raised from KW 6805).

var. COMPACTUM Cowan—Leaves glossy; stems and petioles without bristles. Habit more compact. Found by Kingdon Ward in 1933 in the Tibetan province of Zayul, near the source of the Delei river, not far from where he had collected his KW 8254 five years previously (see above). He introduced it under KW 11040. This variety is very distinct from typical R. *beanianum* in general appearance and flowers later. Plants under KW 8254 seem near to var. *compactum*.

R. BEESIANUM Diels

R. colletum Balf. f. & Forr.; *R. emaculatum* Balf. f. & Forr.

An evergreen shrub or small tree up to 20 ft high; young shoots stout, nearly ½ in. in diameter, soon glabrous. Leaves elliptic-oblong, inclined to oblanceolate, rather abruptly narrowed to a short point, rounded or slightly heart-shaped at the base, 6 in. to over 1 ft long, 1½ to 3½ in. wide, dark green and glabrous above, covered beneath with a thin, close, red-brown, felt-like down; stalk up to 1¼ in. long, slightly flattened or winged. Flowers in a racemose truss of twenty or more and 5 or 6 in. across, each flower on a downy stalk 1 to 1½ in. long. Calyx merely a wavy rim. Corolla openly bell-shaped, 2 in. long and wide, white to deep rich rose with a few crimson markings or a basal blotch, five-lobed. Stamens ten, downy at the base, about 1 in. long; ovary cylindrical, covered with brown down; style glabrous, 1 in. long. *Bot. Mag.*, n.s., t. 125 (s. Lacteum)

R. beesianum was discovered by Forrest in 1906 on the eastern flank of the Lichiang range in N.W. Yunnan and was subsequently found to have a wide range, from S.W. Szechwan to the eastern end of the Himalaya. It occurs at 11,000 to 14,000 ft and often forms miniature forests above the coniferous belt. Forrest sent seed of this species many times from 1906 onwards, and so later did Kingdon Ward and Rock. It is one of the large-leaved species of the Lacteum series and, like *R. lacteum* itself, is difficult to cultivate and uncommon, though quite hardy. It needs shelter from wind and some shade. There are fine specimens in the Edinburgh collection, and at Blackhills, Morayshire.

R. BOOTHII Nutt.

An evergreen shrub 6 to 8 ft, sometimes 10 ft high, of loose habit; young shoots at first very hairy. Leaves leathery, oval-ovate, slenderly pointed; 3½ to 5 in. long, 1¼ to 2½ in. wide, dark green and ultimately glabrous above, but sprinkled with long hairs when young and hairy on the margins; scaly beneath; stalk about ¼ in. long and clothed with shaggy hairs like the young shoot. Flowers rich yellow, seven to ten of them closely packed in a terminal cluster, opening in April and May. Calyx membranous, deeply five-lobed, the lobes broadly ovate, rounded, ¼ in. long, sparsely hairy on the margins. Corolla 1 to 1½ in. wide, bell-shaped at the base, separating into five broad, rounded lobes; scaly outside. Stamens ten, their stout stalks very hairy at the lower half; anthers standing just clear of the corolla-tube. Ovary ¼ in. long, conical, closely covered with scales, surmounted by a glabrous, thick, much decurved style. *Bot. Mag.*, t. 7149. (s. and ss. Boothii)

A little-known species, discovered by Thomas Booth on December 16, 1849, in an outer range of the Assam Himalaya, north-west of Tezpur, growing epiphytically on oaks at about 5,000 ft, and introduced by him. *R. camelliiflorum* and *R. edgeworthii* also grew as epiphytes in the same locality. He wrote in his journal: 'found many on old decayed and blown down trees on the ground, destitute of seeds or flower buds. With great difficulty and delay I obtained seed of these species by climbing such trees as were practicable, and cutting off the boughs on which they were located' (*Gard. Chron.*, 1862, p. 406). It was found again in the same area but farther north by Kingdon Ward in 1935 (fruit) and 1938 (flower), between Tembang and Lagam (*Assam Adventure*, p. 266; *Gard. Chron.*, Vol. 102 (1937), p. 143).

R. *boothii* is not hardy near London, but has been successfully grown in the open air in the south-west. It is however very rare in cultivation. Its flowers and trusses are small, but attractive in the uncommon colour.

R. MISHMIENSE Hutch. & Ward—It is doubtful whether this rhododendron is really specifically distinct from R. *boothii*, though it differs in having the pedicels villous, instead of bristly as in that species. It was introduced by Kingdon Ward from the Mishmi Hills, Assam, in 1928. An Award of Merit was given in 1940 to a plant under this name but Kingdon Ward, who saw it, appears to have doubted whether it was his R. *mishmiense*. He described it (the plant exhibited) as having flowers 'of a muddy or pasty margarine-yellow, with a dull crimson rash of measles' (*Gard. Chron.*, Vol. 107 (1940), p. 323). The plants he saw in the wild had lemon-yellow flowers.

R. BRACHYANTHUM Franch.

An evergreen shrub probably 4 to 5 ft high, of rather stiff habit; young shoots reddish, scaly, becoming bright brown and smooth the second season. Leaves oblong to narrowly oval, usually tapered at the apex (sometimes rounded) to a mucro, tapered at the base, $1\frac{1}{2}$ to $2\frac{1}{2}$ in. long, $\frac{1}{2}$ to 1 in. wide, dark glossy green above, slightly scaly and very glaucous beneath; stalk $\frac{1}{8}$ to $\frac{1}{4}$ in. long. Flowers from three or four to as many as eight or ten in a cluster, each on a slender scaly stalk $\frac{3}{4}$ to $1\frac{1}{2}$ in. long. Calyx green, scaly outside, very large for the size of the flower, $\frac{5}{8}$ to $\frac{3}{4}$ in. wide with five leaf-like rounded lobes spreading out away from the corolla. Corolla clear pale yellow or tinged with green, bell-shaped with five broadly ovate, pointed, recurved lobes; $\frac{5}{8}$ in. long, $\frac{3}{4}$ to 1 in. wide. Stamens ten, shorter than the corolla, clothed with pale hairs to the middle and upwards; ovary scaly; style about as long as the stamens, quite smooth, swelling to a broad stigma at the top. *Bot. Mag.*, t. 8750.   (s. and ss. Glauco-phyllum)

R. *brachyanthum* was discovered by the Abbé Delavay in the mountains above Tali about 1884; it was found again by Forrest in 1906 in the same range at 10,000 to 11,000 ft and was introduced by him. It seems to be more local in the wild, and rarer in cultivation than the var. *hypolepidotum*. In its best form this is a charming and distinct species with flowers shaped like those of a campanula and of a pleasing yellow, with a large foliaceous calyx. But in other forms the green-tinted flowers are dull. It seems to be quite hardy and flowers about midsummer. Although so different in colour, the flowers in shape of corolla and size of calyx strongly resemble those of R. *glaucophyllum*. The seed-vessel in both is hidden by the persistent calyx, and the leaves of both have a strong odour.

Award of Merit May 23, 1966, when shown by Collingwood Ingram, Benenden, Kent (clone 'Jaune').

var. HYPOLEPIDOTUM Franch. *R. hypolepidotum* (Franch.) Balf. f. & Forr.; *R. charitostreptum* Balf. f. & Ward—This differs from the type only in having the underside of the leaves much more densely scaly and glaucous green rather than whitish. *Bot. Mag.*, t. 9259. It has a fairly wide distribution in N. Burma and bordering parts of Yunnan. Forrest, who introduced it, sent seeds from the Salween–upper Irrawaddy and Mekong–Salween divides; Kingdon Ward from the Imaw Bum, where it grows near the summit with *R. aperantum* and also from the Seinghku valley (both in upper Burma); and Rock from Tsechung (Mekong watershed). Award of Merit June 26, 1951, when shown by the Crown Estate Commissioners, Windsor Great Park (clone 'Blue Light').

R. SHWELIENSE Balf. f. & Forr.—Very near to *R. brachyanthum* var. *hypolepidotum*, differing in the corolla being pink, tinged with yellow and densely scaly outside. Introduced by Forrest from the Shweli–Salween divide, Yunnan, in 1924. It is uncommon in cultivation.

R. BRACHYCARPUM G. Don

R. fauriei Franch.

A robust evergreen shrub 6 to 10 ft high; young shoots downy. Leaves narrowly oblong, 4 or 5 in. long, $1\frac{1}{2}$ to $1\frac{3}{4}$ in. wide; with a short, abrupt tip and a rounded base; upper surface glabrous, the lower one more or less felted; stalk $\frac{1}{2}$ to $\frac{3}{4}$ in. long, very stout. Flowers creamy white, flushed with pink, or yellowish, up to twenty in a rounded cluster 4 to 6 in. across; rachis up to $1\frac{1}{4}$ in. long,

RHODODENDRON BRACHYCARPUM

lengthening in fruit; pedicels up to $1\frac{1}{4}$ in. long, downy. Calyx-lobes five, shallow. Corolla 2 in. across, broadly funnel-shaped, five-lobed, the lobes broad and rounded, emarginate, the three upper ones spotted with brownish or greenish yellow. Stamens ten, hairy at the base. Ovary covered with brown down; style glabrous. *Bot. Mag.*, t. 7881.

Native of Japan at subalpine elevations, descending to near sea-level in Hokkaido; also of the Kuriles and, in the broad sense, of Korea; introduced to Britain towards the end of the last century. It is a very hardy shrub and for that reason valued in regions too cold for most of the species whose hardiness in the British Isles is taken for granted. It is at present placed in the Ponticum series, subseries Caucasicum—a very artificial grouping. Dr Cowan pointed out that the hairs composing its leaf-indumentum closely resemble those of the Lacteum series.

subsp. TIGERSTEDTII Nitzelius—This Korean race is more robust than the Japanese, with stouter stems, larger leaves 6 to 10 in. long, 2 to $3\frac{3}{4}$ in. wide. The flowers are white, with greenish spotting, up to nearly 3 in. wide, the calyx is more developed and the fruit-stalks are longer ($1\frac{1}{4}$ to 2 in. long, against $\frac{3}{4}$ to $1\frac{1}{4}$ in. long in the Japanese plants). This subspecies was named by T. Nitzelius in honour of Mr Tigerstedt, who introduced it to his famous Mustila Arboretum in southern Finland from the Kongosan in central Korea (*Deutsche Baumschule*, July 1970, pp. 207–12). Plants in Britain raised from seeds collected by Wilson in Korea may belong here.

R. BRACTEATUM Rehd. & Wils.

An evergreen shrub 3 to 6 ft high; young shoots not downy, bearing below the leaves proper linear 'bracts' (really depauperate leaves) $\frac{1}{4}$ to $\frac{5}{8}$ in. long, some of which persist to the second or even third year. Leaves oval with a tendency to ovate or oblong, rounded at the base, terminated by a short mucro, $\frac{3}{4}$ to 2 in. long by about half as much wide; dark green and thinly-scaly above, paler and more scaly beneath; stalk $\frac{1}{8}$ to $\frac{1}{4}$ in. long. Flowers borne three to six in a cluster, the corolla about 1 in. wide, white, strongly blotched and dotted with deep wine red, bell-shaped at the base, the five lobes spread out widely; stamens ten, the lower half hairy; ovary very scaly; style almost or quite glabrous; calyx small, unequally lobed; flower-stalks $\frac{1}{2}$ to 1 in. long. *Bot. Mag.*, t. 9031. (*s.* Heliolepis)

Native of W. Szechwan, China; introduced in 1908 by Wilson. He and Rehder considered it to be most closely related to *R. yanthinum* (*concinnum*), while later authorities in classification associate it with *R. oreotrephes*, but to neither of them does it bear much resemblance in general appearance when in bloom. It is now placed in the Heliolepis series. The figure in the *Botanical Magazine* was made from a plant growing at Caerhays in Cornwall, where it flowers about mid-June. The crushed leaves have a curious odour resembling that of black currants; this, with the persistent 'bracts' mentioned above, make the species easily recognised. The flowers are not large but they are daintily pretty.

R. BREVISTYLUM Franch.
R. *porrosquameum* Balf. f. & Forr.

An evergreen shrub up to 10 ft high; young shoots densely scaly. Leaves oblong-lanceolate, slenderly pointed, more or less tapered at the base; 2 to 4 in. long, 1 to 1¾ in. wide; dark green above, tawny green beneath, rather thinly scaly on both sides; stalk ¼ to ½ in. long. Flowers in clusters of four to eight, opening in June and July. Corolla widely funnel-shaped, 1½ in. wide and nearly as long, conspicuously scaly outside, downy at the base inside, pale to deep rose with crimson markings on the upper lobes. Stamens ten, very downy on the lower half; ovary thickly scaly; style pubescent towards the base. Calyx small, wavy-lobed, scaly, sometimes slightly ciliate; flower-stalk up to 1 in. long, scaly. (s. Heliolepis)

Native mainly of N.W. Yunnan but also found farther west, on the Irrawaddy–Lohit divide; discovered by Père Soulié on the Se La, Mekong–Salween divide in 1875 and introduced by Forrest in 1912. It was reintroduced by Kingdon Ward in 1926 from the valley of the Di Chu, a tributary of the Lohit rising at the Diphuk La, at the meeting point of Assam, Burma, and Tibet. He saw it in flower on July 13 and remarked in his field note: 'Now almost in full bloom, still a fine sight a fortnight later. Very free-flowering, a beautiful late species' (KW 7108).

R. *brevistylum* is allied to R. *heliolepis*, also a late-flowering species, but differs in the short style and in having the leaves tapered and not rounded at the base.

R. PHOLIDOTUM Balf. f. & W. W. Sm.—This is very closely allied to R. *brevistylum* and is placed under it in synonymy in the article accompanying *Bot. Mag.*, t. 8898. It was introduced by Forrest in 1910 and the plate in the Botanical Magazine is from a plant at Edinburgh raised from the original seeds (F.6762).

R. BUREAVII Franch.

An evergreen shrub or small tree, as much as 20 ft high in the wild; branchlets stout, with the same coating as on the undersides of the leaves, which are leathery, broad-elliptic to ovate, 3 to 5 in. long, 1 to 2 in. wide, dark green, slightly rugose, soon glabrous above, the undersides (and also the shoots and petioles) coated with a bright rusty red wool intermixed with glands; petiole stout, about ¾ in. long. Flowers in trusses of ten to fifteen, borne in April or May; pedicels about ¾ in. long, densely woolly; rachis very short. Calyx deeply divided into five obtuse, ciliate lobes. Corolla funnel-campanulate, about 1¾ in. long, white or rose, usually with crimson markings. Ovary densely clad with bright brown hairs intermixed with glands; style hairy and glandular at the base. (s. Taliense ss. Adenogynum)

Native of N.W. Yunnan, where it forms thickets above the coniferous forests; discovered by Père Delavay in 1896 near Lankiung, north of Tali. Forrest sent seeds in 1904. His next sending was in 1918, from the Sungkwei pass (F.15609).

Although the flowers are unremarkable R. *bureavii* is worth growing for its handsome foliage, if the true species can be obtained. It is perfectly hardy, but is slow-growing and usually seen as a dense shrub 6 to 8 ft high. It received an Award of Merit when shown from Exbury in 1939.

R. BUREAVIOIDES Balf. f., described from specimens collected by Wilson in W. Szechwan, is probably not specifically distinct from R. *bureavii*. He sent seeds to Messrs Veitch in 1904.

R. BURMANICUM Hutch.

An evergreen shrub usually under 6 ft high and often dwarf in the wild; young stems scaly and slightly bristly. Leaves oblanceolate to obovate, abruptly narrowed to a mucronate tip, tapered at the base, densely scaly on both sides, the scales less than their own diameter apart or even overlapping, undersurface green between the scales; petioles up to ⅜ in. long, scaly and edged with erect hairs. Flowers fragrant, borne in terminal trusses of five or six on scaly stalks up to ⅞ in. long. Calyx minute, fringed with bristles. Corolla five-lobed, narrowly funnel-campanulate, 1½ to 2 in. long, yellow, greenish yellow or greenish white, scaly on the outside. Stamens ten, hairy in the lower part. Ovary densely scaly; style scaly.   (*s.* Maddenii *ss.* Ciliicalyx)

Native of Mt Victoria, a mountain just over 10,000 ft high in the Southern Chin Hills, south-west Burma. It was discovered there by Lady Wheeler Cuffe and introduced by her to the Glasnevin Botanic Garden, where it first flowered in May 1914. Although not hardy enough for cultivation outdoors near London, it succeeds in several gardens on the west coast of Scotland.

R. PACHYPODUM Balf. f. & Forr.—Closely allied to R. *burmanicum*, but with the leaves glaucous beneath between the scales, less scaly above, and with fewer flowers in each cluster (usually in twos or threes). The corollas are white or yellow, or white streaked with yellow. Introduced by Forrest in 1913 from the Tali range, Yunnan, where it grows at 7,000 to 10,000 ft. It is less hardy than R. *burmanicum*, but has been grown in the open air in the mildest parts.

R. *pachypodum* received an Award of Merit as a greenhouse plant when shown from Exbury in 1936. This form, with white flowers bearing a streak of yellow on the upper lobe, was raised from Kingdon Ward's 3776, collected in 1921 in S.W. Yunnan at 8,000 ft at the head of the Nam Ting valley, south of Shunning-fu.

R. CALENDULACEUM (Michx.) Torr.

Azalea calendulacea Michx.

A deciduous shrub up to 10 or more feet high; young shoots bristly-hairy. Leaves obovate or oval, 2 to 4 in. long, ¾ to 1¼ in. wide, with a few scattered hairs above, downy beneath, especially on the midrib and veins; leaf-stalk hairy, very short. Flowers of various shades of red, orange, and yellow, scarcely fragrant, produced in showy terminal clusters of five or more. Corolla-tube about ½ in. long, glandular-hairy; lobes often 1 in. long, often considerably longer than the tube; calyx-lobes edged with long, erect hairs; flower-stalk ¼ in. long, glandular-hairy. Flowers in May or early June.   (*s.* Azalea *ss.* Luteum)

Native of eastern N. America in the Alleghenies. This is the most brilliantly coloured of all wild azaleas, and is the source of the scarlet and orange-coloured garden hybrids. Bartram gives this description of his first sight of this azalea in the Carolina mountains: 'I saw the blossoms covering plants on the hill-sides in such incredible profusion that, suddenly opening to view from deep shade, I was alarmed by the apprehension of the hill being on fire.'

R. *calendulaceum* was brought to England by John Lyon in 1806, but there may have been an earlier introduction, since the azalea named *A. aurantiaca* by Dietrich in 1803 came from England and was probably a form of this species.

A.M. 1965 to clone 'Burning Light', shown by the Crown Estate Commissioners.

R. BAKERI (Lemmon & McKay) Hume *Azalea bakeri* Lemmon & McKay; R. *cumberlandense* E. L. Braun—Allied to R. *calendulaceum*, but flowering about three weeks later and generally of dwarfer, more compact habit, rarely up to 9 ft high; said to be superior as an ornamental. Native mainly of the Cumberland plateau. See further in R.C.Y.B. *1957*, pp. 20–1, 23.

R. CALLIMORPHUM Balf. f. & W. W. Sm.

R. *hedythamnum* Balf. f. & Forr.; R. *cyclium* Balf. f. & Forr.

An evergreen shrub up to 9 ft high in the wild, forming a rounded bush in cultivation as wide as it is high; young shoots usually clothed at first with stalked glands. Leaves round to roundish ovate, the base truncate, rounded or heart-shaped, the apex with a short mucro, 1 to 3 in. long, usually not quite so wide, dark glossy green and with scattered hairs above, glaucous beneath with glands on the midrib and margin; stalk ⅜ to 1 in. long, usually very glandular. Flowers opening during April and May in a terminal truss of five to eight flowers. Calyx very small with shallow triangular lobes, glandular like the flower-stalk which is ¾ in. long. Corolla openly bell-shaped, five-lobed, 1½ in. long and wide, pale or deep rose with a blotch of intense crimson at the base, lobes notched. Stamens ten, their white stalks from ½ to 1 in. long, glabrous except for (occasionally) a few minute hairs at the base; anthers brown. Ovary covered with red glands, of which a few extend a short way up the style. *Bot. Mag.*, t. 8789. (*s.* Thomsonii *ss.* Campylocarpum)

Native of W. Yunnan and N.E. upper Burma; found by Forrest on the Shweli-Salween divide and introduced by him in 1912; later sendings are from farther north on the E. Irrawaddy–Salween divide and the Tali range. R. *callimorphum* is a very pretty species of neat habit. It is variable in flowering-time, which is mid- to late May or even early June in some forms. It is hardy at Kew when given a sheltered place and some shade.

R. MYIAGRUM Balf. f. & Forr.—This differs from R. *callimorphum* in its flowers being white; they are bell-shaped and 1¼ to 1½ in. wide. Leaves nearly orbicular, 1 to 2 in. long. The specific name, meaning 'fly-catcher', applies to the flower-stalks, which are furnished with such viscid glands that small flies are caught thereon in great numbers. Forrest's specimens, collected wild in W. Yunnan, are covered with them. Introduced in 1919. Flowers in May and June.

It has a restricted distribution near the borders between N.W. Yunnan and
Burma and is really no more than a white-flowered form of R. *callimorphum*.

R. CALOPHYTUM Franch.   [PLATE 68

An evergreen tree up to 45 ft high. Leaves obovate to oblanceolate, abruptly
pointed, wedge-shaped at the base, 8 to 12 in. long, 2 to 3½ in. wide, glabrous
except for some floss on the midrib beneath when young. Flowers up to thirty
in trusses 6 to 8 in. across. Flower-stalk 1½ to 3 in. long, glabrous. Calyx very
small. Corolla five- to eight-lobed, 2½ in. wide, not so deep, bell-shaped, white
or rosy with a large, conspicuous, dark crimson blotch at the base. Stamens
sixteen to twenty-two, of very unequal length but shorter than the corolla,
slightly downy at the base; ovary and style glabrous; stigma very large, ¼ in.
wide, yellow; seed-pod 1 in. long, ⅓ in. wide. Flowers in April. *Bot. Mag.*, t.
9173.   (*s.* Fortunei *ss.* Calophytum)

Native of W. Szechwan; discovered by the Abbé David near Mupin in 1869.
Wilson introduced it in 1904 when collecting for Messrs Veitch and again in
larger quantity four years later, during his first expedition for the Arnold
Arboretum. According to him it is common in the forests of W. Szechwan,
and grows to a larger size than any other rhododendron found in that region.

It is one of the noblest of Chinese rhododendrons and is perfectly hardy,
needing only shelter from wind and some shade. In its very large, almost
glabrous leaves it resembles R. *sutchuenense* but they are of a richer green, the
flowers are smaller, on longer, red stalks. The knob-like stigma is very conspicuous.

A form with white flowers flushed with pink received an Award of Merit on
March 9, 1920, when shown by Messrs Reuthe, who had flowered the species
for the first time in 1916. The beautiful pale pink form grown at South Lodge,
Lower Beeding, Sussex, was awarded a First Class Certificate when Dame Alice
Godman showed it on April 4, 1933.

R. CALOSTROTUM Balf. f. & Ward
R. *rivulare* Ward, not Hand.–Mazz.; R. *riparium* Ward

An evergreen shrub up to 4 ft or perhaps more high, of rounded compact
shape; young shoots densely scaly. Leaves oval or obovate, rounded or bluntish
at the apex, tapered at the base to a very short stalk, ¾ to 1⅛ in. long, ⅓ to ½ in.
wide, dull grey green or glossy glaucous green above, brownish with a dense
layer of overlapping scales beneath, edged when young with bristles. Flowers
terminal, usually in pairs, opening in May, each on a scaly stalk 1 in. or so long.
Calyx ¼ in. long, with five broadly ovate, purplish lobes, scaly, sometimes densely
so. Corolla open and flattish, 1½ in. wide, pale pink to magenta purple with
deeper spots on the upper side, five-lobed, the lobes overlapping, downy outside. Stamens ten, ½ in. long, purple with a dense tuft of hairs at the base. Ovary
covered with pale scales; style purple with a few hairs at the bottom. *Bot. Mag.*,
t. 9001.   (*s.* Saluenense)

R. *calostrotum* was discovered by Kingdon Ward in 1914 on the eastern spur of the Imaw Bum, an isolated peak in upper Burma on the Nmai (eastern Irrawaddy)–Salween divide. When he reached the summit in 1919 from the western side he found, and collected seed of, what he thought was the same species (KW 3390), but it appears that what he found on that occasion was really R. *keleticum*. So the credit for its introduction belongs to Farrer and Cox, who collected seeds in the same year on the top of the Hpawshi Bum, about twenty miles to the south-east of the type-locality. Here it 'covers the barest braes and tops of moorland in a close, flat carpet of dark foliage, from which on pedicels (in pairs) of an inch or so, rise large, round blossoms of a rich, warm magenta-rose' (Farrer 1045; *Gard. Chron.*, Vol. 66 (1919), p. 289). Forrest later sent seeds from other localities on the same divide, whence it ranges westward as far as the eastern end of the Himalaya. In the wild it is usually an erect shrublet up to 2 ft high, but mat-forming in exposed positions.

R. *calostrotum* flowered at Kew in April 1923 when only two or three inches high. No more delightful rhododendron for the rock garden has been introduced. So large are the flowers and so freely are they borne that a small plant may be literally hidden beneath them. It produces fertile seed in plenty and is easily raised from cuttings. Provided the soil is moist it can be grown in full sun.

Award of Merit May 8, 1935, to a form raised at Nymans from Forrest 27065.

cv. 'GIGHA'.—Flowers described as deep claret-red (International Rhododendron Register, Additions 1968–9). A plant under this name received a First Class Certificate May 4, 1971; flowers described as light rosy-red.

var. CALCIPHILUM (Hutch. & Ward) Davidian R. *calciphilum* Hutch. & Ward—Leaves smaller than in the type, up to ½ in. long. Described from Kingdon Ward's 6984, collected in the Seinghku valley, N.W. upper Burma and introduced under that number. He found it forming tight tufts on limestone screes (whence the epithet *calciphilum* and the nickname "Limestone Rose" which he gave to it). In the wild it flowers later than the normal form (which occurs in the same valley) and has kept this character in cultivation, where it flowers late May. The leaves are somewhat glaucous.

R. CALOXANTHUM Balf. f. & Farrer

An evergreen shrub 3 to 5 ft high; young shoots glandular. Leaves broadly oval to roundish, 1½ to 2½ in. long, not quite so wide, pale glaucous green beneath, glabrous or nearly so at maturity; stalk about ⅓ in. long, glandular. Flowers in trusses of four to nine opening in April and May. Corolla bell-shaped, 1¾ in. wide, scarcely so long, five-lobed, scarlet in bud, sulphur- to orange-yellow when fully open; stamens ten, up to 1 in. long, not downy; ovary densely furnished with stalked glands which extend to the lower third of the pistil. Calyx small and like the flower-stalk (which is about ½ in. long) thickly clad with glands. (*s.* Thomsonii *ss.* Campylocarpum)

R. *caloxanthum* was discovered by Farrer and Cox on the Hpimaw and Chimili passes, upper Burma, near the border with China, in 1919 and was introduced from there (Farrer 937). Farrer described the flowers as vermilion in bud, flushed with apricot and tipped with orange-scarlet as they open, finally clear citron yellow. In the following year Farrer found it farther north, on the Chaw-chi pass, where it is even more abundant, covering the open slopes and precipice ledges in dense masses of 2–3 ft jungle (Cox, *Farrer's Last Journey*, pp. 225 and 239).

Plants raised from Farrer 937 agreed well with the wild parents in their flowers and this form received an Award of Merit when shown from Exbury on May 1, 1934. Farrer described the young shoots as 'almost cobalt blue', a character which did not show on the plants raised from his seeds, though there are forms of the species in cultivation which have the mature leaves distinctly glaucous. R. *caloxanthum* is perfectly hardy south of London, in light woodland. It is very closely allied to R. *campylocarpum*, and according to Cowan and Davidian the two species merge into one another.

R. TELOPEUM Balf. f. & Forr.—This species really only differs from R. *caloxanthum* in having on the average rather smaller leaves, up to 2 in. long, $1\frac{5}{8}$ in. wide, and the two should really be united, under the name R. *telopeum*, which has priority. It was described from a specimen collected by Forrest in Tsarong, S.E. Tibet, at the northern end of the Irrawaddy–Salween divide.

R. CAMELLIIFLORUM Hook. f.
R. *sparsiflorum* Nutt.; R. *cooperi* Balf. f.

An evergreen shrub up to 6 ft high, of sparse straggling habit, often growing wild on the trunks and forks of trees; young shoots very scaly. Leaves oblong-lanceolate, pointed, $2\frac{1}{2}$ to 4 in. long, $\frac{3}{4}$ to $1\frac{1}{2}$ in. wide, dark green above; almost covered with brown glistening scales beneath, between which, however, the glaucous surface of the leaf is visible; stalk $\frac{1}{4}$ to $\frac{3}{8}$ in. long. Flowers produced in July, usually in pairs. Corolla $1\frac{1}{2}$ in. wide, white tinged with rose, the base broadly bell-shaped; lobes five, rounded, overlapping, scaly outside. Stamens twelve to sixteen, downy towards but not at the broadened base. Ovary scaly; style $\frac{5}{8}$ in. long, with a broad thick stigma; glabrous except for a few scales near the ovary. Calyx $\frac{1}{4}$ in. long, scaly at the base, the lobes deep, oval, rounded at the end. Flower-stalk $\frac{1}{4}$ in. long. *Bot. Mag.*, t. 4932.   (*s.* Camelliiflorum)

Native of the Himalaya from E. Nepal to Bhutan, to 10,000 ft altitude. It was discovered in Sikkim by J. D. Hooker and introduced in 1851 to Kew. It is quite uncommon, which is no matter for great regret, for it is one of the least ornamental and most difficult of rhododendrons.

R. CAMPANULATUM D. Don   [PLATE 69
R. *edgarii* Gamble; R. *mutabile* Royle

An evergreen shrub usually not more than 10 ft high in the wild; bark peeling; young shoots glabrous. Leaves oval, 3 to $5\frac{1}{2}$ in. long, $1\frac{1}{4}$ to $2\frac{1}{2}$ in. wide; abruptly tapering at the apex, tapering, rounded, or slightly heart-shaped at the base, glabrous above, densely covered beneath with a red-brown felt; stalk $\frac{1}{2}$ to 1 in. long, often reddish. Flowers rosy purple of numerous shades, or almost white, 2 in. across, produced during April in rather loose clusters about 4 in. wide.

Calyx downy, small and scarcely lobed. Corolla broadly bell-shaped, with five notched lobes, the upper ones dark purple-spotted. Stamens ten, glabrous or sometimes downy towards the base; flower-stalk about 1 in. long. *Bot. Mag.*, t. 3759. (s. Campanulatum)

Native of the Himalaya from Kashmir to some way east of Bhutan, from 10,000 to 14,000 ft. According to Loudon, Loddiges' nursery received seeds from Wallich in 1825, but there may have been earlier introductions to private gardens. In 1844 it was referred to as 'one of the best hardy evergreens we have' (*Gard. Chron.* (1844), p. 379). It is very variable in the colour of the flowers, which are sometimes quite pale, sometimes of a bright bluish purple, sometimes lilac or even white; in the amount of felt at the back of the leaf; and in the colour of the leaf-scales that accompany the young bursting shoots, which are sometimes rich crimson, sometimes green. At its best it is a beautiful rhododendron, though not held in much regard at the present time. In Scotland it has attained a remarkable size, e.g., 30 ft in height and 4½ ft in girth at breast height at Benmore, Argyll (*R.C.Y.B. 1964*, p. 13; op. cit., *1968*, fig. 17).

cv. 'KNAP HILL'.—Flowers large, of a beautiful shade of blue-mauve. Raised at the Knap Hill Nursery. Award of Merit when shown from Exbury, May 5, 1925.

Two other forms that have received the same award are: 'Roland Cooper' and 'Waxen Bell', both exhibited by the Royal Botanic Garden, Edinburgh (see *R.C.Y.B. 1965*, p. 166, and op. cit., *1966*, p. 163).

var. AERUGINOSUM (Hook. f.) Hook. f. R. *aeruginosum* Hook. f.—Young leaves glabrous above, described by J. D. Hooker as 'of a verdigris hue'. He found it in Sikkim growing with R. *fulgens* at 13,000 to 15,000 ft, and at first considered it to be a distinct species. It is cultivated only for the beauty of its young foliage.

R. WALLICHII Hook. f. R. *campanulatum* var. *wallichii* (Hook. f.) Hook. f.— In *Species of Rhododendron* this is distinguished from R. *campanulatum* by the undersides of the leaves being sparsely dotted with tufts of hair, in contrast to the continuous felt of the other species. However, Cowan and Davidian have pointed out that the indumentum in R. *campanulatum* is sometimes quite as sparse as in R. *wallichii*. The difference between them lies in the nature of the hairs themselves: in R. *campanulatum* they are slender-stemmed, with numerous long thread-like branches, in R. *wallichii* they are stout-stemmed, with short, broad branches (*R.Y.B. 1949*, p. 176). Since microscopic hair-structure is an important taxonomic character in *Rhododendron*, R. *wallichii* is recognised as a distinct species, though it does not otherwise differ from R. *campanulatum*. It is figured in *Bot. Mag.*, t. 4928, and its known range is from Nepal to the Assam Himalaya.

R. CAMPYLOCARPUM Hook. f.

R. *campylocarpum* var. *pallidum* Millais; R. *campylocarpum* var. *elatum* Hort.

An evergreen shrub 4 to 10 ft high, occasionally taller; branchlets slender, glandular. Leaves 1½ to 4 in. long, about half as wide, mostly elliptic or oblong-elliptic, obtuse or rounded at the apex, usually truncate or slightly cordate at the base, upper surface dark glossy green, lower surface paler glaucous green or even whitish, glabrous on both sides; petiole up to 1 in. long, sometimes reddish, often glandular. Flowers four to nine in a loose terminal cluster, each on a stalk up to 1 in. long, which is usually glandular. Calyx small, glandular-ciliate and usually glandular on the back also. Corolla five-lobed campanulate, 2½ to 3 in. across, varying in colour from creamy white through pale primrose to sulphur yellow, often with a crimson mark in the throat and usually more or less tinged with pinkish buff or apricot in the bud. Stamens ten, glabrous or slightly downy at the base. Ovary densely glandular; style usually glandular in the lower part, never throughout. The specific epithet refers to the curving of the seed-capsule in the fruiting plants seen by Hooker, but often it is straight. *Bot. Mag.*, t. 4968.　　(s. Thomsonii ss. Campylocarpum)

Native of the Himalaya from Nepal eastward, and of the Mishmi Hills, Assam; discovered by J. D. Hooker in east Nepal late in 1848 and introduced by him. Of all the rhododendrons he saw during his famous expedition, R. *campylocarpum* was the one he most admired, with its flowers 'of surpassing delicacy and grace'. It is perfectly hardy in a sheltered place near London but, flowering in April or early May, the display is sometimes spoilt by frost.

R. *campylocarpum* varies in the colour of its flowers, and in habit. In his Latin diagnosis Hooker described the flowers as white or deep straw-coloured ('*saturate straminea*'); in the English text he said: 'tinged of a sulphur hue and always spotless'. In the beautiful plate accompanying the description, based on his specimens and field-sketches, the flowers are depicted as pale creamy yellow, without blotch (*Rhododendrons of the Sikkim Himalaya*, t. 30). His account must be based on plants growing near the border between Sikkim and Nepal, north-west of Kangchenjunga, since he was in that area throughout June 1849, the month in which he found the species in flower. But the seeds he sent home were collected in November 1849 and were from a different locality, between Tumloong and the Cho La, on the frontier between Sikkim and Tibet. Some of the plants raised in Britain from these seeds proved to be remarkably compact, with flowers of a clear yellow and this form was taken by Millais to represent typical R. *campylocarpum*. To a laxer form commoner in gardens, with pale primrose-yellow flowers, he gave the distinguishing epithet *pallidum* (*Rhododendrons*, 2nd series, p. 100; *Rhodo. Soc. Notes*, Vol. II, p. 73). It should be obvious, however, that what came up from the seeds that Hooker collected 'blind' in the early winter of 1849 is really of no botanical relevance, as the species was not described from them, but from wild plants that Hooker had seen in another area.

The name R. *campylocarpum* "var. *elatum*" is used in gardens for the form commonest in cultivation, which is tall-growing and has corollas with a red blotch at the base. It is said that in breeding the so-called Hooker form gives mainly yellows, while the "var. *elatum*" throws pinks and ivory-whites as well as yellows.

R. PANTEUMORPHUM Balf. f. & W. W. Sm. R. *telopeum* f. *telopeoides* Tagg—
This species differs from R. *campylocarpum* only in having the leaves commonly oblong rather than elliptic, and in its somewhat dwarfer habit. It was discovered

by Forrest north-west of Tseku, Yunnan, on the Mekong–Salween divide and was later collected by him and by Rock in other parts of Yunnan. The gap between the easternmost stations of R. *campylocarpum* and the type-locality of R. *panteumorphum* is not great, and is bridged by the related R. *wardii*, which was found originally not far from Tseku and also occurs in the eastern Himalaya.

R. CAMPYLOGYNUM Franch.

R. *damascenum* Balf. f. & Farr.; R. *glauco-aureum* Balf. f. & Forr.

A usually dwarf, evergreen shrub of densely branched, close growth; young shoots thinly scaly. Leaves obovate, tapered at the base, rounded but with a short mucro at the apex; margins recurved and crinkled, $\frac{1}{3}$ to 1 in. long, $\frac{1}{8}$ to $\frac{1}{2}$ in. wide, dark bright green and glabrous above, pale green or slightly glaucous beneath and slightly scaly at first; stalk $\frac{1}{10}$ in. long. Flowers solitary or in twos or threes at the end of the shoot, nodding, each produced on a slender, slightly scaly stalk 1 to 1$\frac{1}{2}$ in. long. Calyx five-lobed; the lobes $\frac{1}{6}$ in. long, glabrous. Corolla of various shades of purple from rosy to plum-coloured or almost black purple, widely bell-shaped, $\frac{2}{3}$ in. long, five-lobed, the lobes rounded and scarcely recurved. Stamens ten (sometimes eight or twelve), downy and widened towards the base; anthers yellowish brown. Ovary glandular-scaly; style glabrous, purple, decurved so as to protrude between the lower lobes of the corolla. *Bot. Mag.*, t. 9407A.   (*s.* Campylogynum)

R. *campylogynum* ranges throughout the rainiest part of the Sino-Himalayan region, from the Tali range and the Mekong–Salween divide in the east through upper Burma to the eastern Himalaya, at altitudes of 11,000 to 15,000 ft (rarely lower). It is therefore one of the most alpine of rhododendrons. It was discovered by the Abbé Delavay in 1884 in the Tali range, whence it was introduced by Forrest in 1912. In the following year Kingdon Ward collected seeds near one of the glaciers of the Ka-kar-po group, on the borders between Yunnan and Tibet. The plants there 'appeared to have black or deep plum-coloured flowers. When, however, the sun shone through them, the flowers were seen to be blood-red, which is how they would appear to their bee-visitors, since the flowers stand horizontally' (*Mystery Rivers of Tibet*, p. 75).

This pleasing species flowers in May and is admirable for the rock garden by reason of its neat habit and rich purple flowers. In some forms, however, the flowers are purplish pink or flesh-pink. In the clone named 'Thimble', they are salmon-pink (Award of Merit, May 23, 1966, when shown by Capt. Collingwood Ingram, The Grange, Benenden, Kent).

A white-flowered form of R. *campylogynum*, grown by Capt. Collingwood Ingram at Benenden, Kent, received an Award of Merit when he exhibited it on June 12, 1973. He has given it botanical status as var. *leucanthum* (*R.C.Y.B. 1969*, p. 49) and it received the award under that name.

var. MYRTILLOIDES (Balf. f. & Ward) Davidian R. *myrtilloides* Balf. f. & Ward—Of dwarfer habit, with smaller flowers up to $\frac{1}{2}$ in. or so long. This variety was discovered by Kingdon Ward in 1914 in upper Burma, on a spur of Imaw Bum at about 13,000 ft (not 15,000 ft as is sometimes stated). Most of the plants originally grown as R. *myrtilloides* were raised from three batches of seed collected in the same area in 1919. KW 3172 was from plants growing in a river-bed under Imaw Bum at 8,000 ft, growing in 'heath-like masses on slaty rocks' and with plum-coloured flowers. Apparently all the seed came from one plant; twenty years later he found it again during the Vernay-Cutting expedition and again took seed from it. He also collected seed on Imaw Bum itself at 12,000–13,000 ft, from plants with port-wine-coloured or flesh-pink flowers (KW 3303). The third collection was by Farrer and Cox from the Hpimaw ridge a short way south of Kingdon Ward's hunting-ground, at around 12,000 ft (Farrer 1046). 'Imagine yard upon yard of turf cushioned with masses of small, shining, dark-green leaves, out of which rise delicate glandular flower-stalks. From each hangs a single little bell-shaped trumpet of sculptured wax, a deep mahogany inside and a claret exterior that is covered with the bloom of a purple plum. There is another form, a uniform claret-mahogany inside and out' (Cox, *Farrer's Last Journey*, p. 98). Kingdon Ward later collected seed at the eastern end of the Himalaya (KW 5842, nicknamed by him "Plum Warner"), but the plants under this number were originally grown as typical R. *campylogynum*. [PLATE 70

As a rock-garden plant the var. *myrtilloides* has all the virtues of the type, except that it has the reputation of being rather more difficult to cultivate well, at least in the Burmese forms originally introduced. It received an Award of Merit on June 6, 1925 (a pink-flowered form raised at Exbury from KW 3172) and a First Class Certificate on June 8, 1945 (a form with rose-magenta flowers, also from Exbury).

Other varieties recognised by Davidian are:

var. CELSUM Davidian—Of erect habit. Found by Forrest in the Tali range, Yunnan, growing 4 to 6 ft high.

var. CHAROPOEUM (Balf. f. & Farrer) Davidian R. *charopoeum* Balf. f. & Farrer; R. *caeruleo-glaucum* Balf. f. & Forr.—Flowers larger, up to 1 in. long. Introduced by Forrest.

var. CREMASTUM (Balf. f. & Forr.) Davidian R. *cremastum* Balf. f. & Forr.— Of erect habit, up to 4 ft high in the wild, with larger leaves up to 1½ in. long, pale green on both surfaces. Discovered and introduced by Forrest. Award of Merit May 24 1971, to clone 'Bodnant Red'.

R. CANADENSE (L.) Torr.   RHODORA
Rhodora canadensis L.; R. rhodora Gmel.

A deciduous shrub rarely more than 3 to 4 ft high; branches erect-growing; branchlets glabrous except when quite young. Leaves narrowly oval, tapering about equally to either end; mostly 2 to 2½ in. long, ½ to ¾ in. wide, with scattered bristles on the upper surface and margins, lower surface downy, becoming, in some plants at least, nearly or quite glabrous before falling. Flowers bright rosy purple, 1 to 1½ in. wide, produced in April in a cluster of about six at the end of naked twigs. The corolla has its three upper lobes united almost to the end, and erect; the two lower ones narrow-oblong, divided to the base, and spreading. Calyx green, the lobes shallow, rounded, glandular at the margins; flower-stalks ¼ in. long, glandular: stamens ten, downy quite at the base; anthers purple. *Bot. Mag.*, t. 474. (s. Azalea ss. Canadense)

Native of eastern N. America; introduced in 1767. This is one of the brightest and most pleasing of early-flowering shrubs, and one of the hardiest. Once considered distinct enough to constitute a separate genus (*Rhodora*), it was later united with *Rhododendron*. But from all the deciduous species, the curious two-lipped corolla consisting of one broad, erect segment and two spreading narrow ones, and (from most) the ten stamens distinguish it. The twigs of the year are remarkable also in thickening gradually towards the end. Increased by seed. Often growing in swamps in the wild, it loves a moist position under cultivation.

R. CANESCENS (Michx.) Sweet

Azalea canescens Michx.; R. *bicolor* Pursh

A deciduous shrub up to 10 or 15 ft high, closely allied to R. *periclymenoides* and joined to it by intermediates. It differs chiefly in the densely downy winter-buds and young branchlets, the corollas glandular as well as hairy outside, and the soft, appressed hairs on the ovary (in R. *periclymenoides* they tend to be bristly). The leaves are usually grey-downy beneath, especially on the midrib and veins, and it is then distinguishable from R. *periclymenoides* by that character alone; f. SUBGLABRUM Rehd., however, has the leaves almost glabrous beneath, but does not otherwise differ from typical R. *canescens* and should not be confused with R. *periclymenoides*.

Native of the eastern USA, mainly in the coastal plains of the south-east but reaching as far north as N. Carolina and west to Tennessee. According to Loudon it was introduced in 1810, but has been much confused with R. *periclymenoides*.

R. CAROLINIANUM Rehd.

R. *punctatum* var. β Ker; R. *punctatum* Small, not Andrews

This species is closely related to R. *minus* (*punctatum*) and was identified with it as a variety until 1912, when Dr Rehder gave it its present name. It was orginally introduced to England by John Fraser in 1811, but, according to Rehder, was subsequently lost to cultivation, not being seen again in this country until re-introduced from H. P. Kelsey's nursery, Carolina, in 1895. It is an evergreen shrub of more compact habit than the true R. *minus*, young shoots scaly. Leaves elliptic to elliptic-obovate, broadly wedge-shaped at the base, tapered at the apex to an often bluntish point, 1 to 3½ in. long, ½ to 1¼ in. wide, glossy green and soon glabrous above; densely covered with ultimately dark scales beneath; midrib yellowish; stalk stout, ⅛ to ⅓ in. long. Flowers four to ten in a terminal truss, opening in May. Corolla five-lobed, about 1½ in. wide, pale rosy purple, faintly or not at all spotted, the lobes rather longer than the tube. Stamens ten, with a band of down near the base; ovary scaly; style glabrous; flower-stalk ½ in. long. (*s.* Carolinianum)

Native of the mountains of N. and S. Carolina and Tennessee. The true R. *minus* (*punctatum*) differs from R. *carolinianum* in the following particulars: its leaves are more pointed; its habit straggling and taller; the corolla-lobes are shorter than the tube and much more scaly outside (in *R. carolinianum* the corolla is only slightly or not at all scaly); corolla conspicuously spotted.

R. carolinianum is by far the best species in the series to which it gives its name, especially in the form with very pale rosy-pink flowers and deep red young stems. According to the American authority D. G. Leach 'the less rusty the leaf undersurface, the lighter will usually be the color of the flowers and the later the plant will bloom' (*Rhododendrons of the World*, p. 139). The leaves of the previous year usually colour brilliant red before falling in the autumn. A.M. May 20, 1968.

var. ALBUM Rehd.—Flowers white. There are two forms of this in cultivation. One is tall-growing with leaves more acuminately pointed than usual and with a yellowish blotch in the flowers. This is very vigorous and produced thickets of self-sown seedlings in peaty woodland. This may represent the wild form, said to be common in North Carolina along the Blue Ridge. The other cultivated form is much dwarfer and more compact and has flowers heavily spotted with green.

R. CHAPMANII A. Gray—This species, confined to the pinelands of the coast region of N. Florida, is closely allied to *R. carolinianum*. The leaves are distinct in their oval shape and rounded apex, 1 to 2½ in. long, more than half as much wide. Flowers with a longer tube—¾ in. or slightly more long, the lobes sometimes crisped. Although hardy, it is in no way superior to *R. carolinianum* as a garden plant.

R. CATAWBIENSE Michx.

An evergreen shrub 6 to 10 ft high, forming eventually a large spreading bush wider than high—a dense thicket of branches and leaves. Leaves oval or oblong, 3 to 6 in. long, 1¼ to 2 in. wide, broadest above the middle, dark glossy green above, pale beneath, glabrous on both sides; stalk ½ to 1¼ in. long. Flowers lilac-purple, produced in a large cluster 5 or 6 in. across; corolla 1½ in. long, 2½ in. broad, with five short, rounded spreading lobes; calyx with five shallow, triangular pointed lobes; stamens white, downy at the base; flower-stalks 1 to 1½ in. long, glandular-downy; ovary brown-felted; style red. *Bot. Mag.*, t. 1671. (*s.* and *ss.* Ponticum)

Native of the slopes and mountain summits of the south-eastern United States, where it is described as forming dense thickets 'through which the traveller can only make his way by following old bear tracks'. In the gardens of Britain, to which it was introduced in 1809 by John Fraser, it has proved one of the most valuable evergreen shrubs for ornament ever introduced. In the hands of nurserymen, but chiefly of the Waterers, it has given birth by selection and hybridisation to a most valuable group of evergreen garden rhododendrons— hardy and easily grown—the group which flowers in May and June. The characteristics of this group, as compared with the companion group derived from *R. ponticum*, are their broad foliage and greater hardiness.

R. CAUCASICUM Pall.

An evergreen, low shrub, usually under 3 ft in height, with slightly downy young shoots. Leaves sometimes rather leathery, glabrous and dark green above, more or less clothed with brownish-red felt beneath; narrowly oval or slightly obovate, 2 to 4 in. long, ¾ to 1½ in. wide; stalk stout, ¼ in. long. Flowers yellowish white or pink-tinged, spotted in the upper part of the throat, borne in May in candelabroid trusses; bud-scales slow to fall. Corolla 2 in. wide, funnel-campanulate, wavy-edged; stamens ten; calyx very small; flower-stalk slightly downy, about 1½ in. long; seed-pods erect. *Bot. Mag.*, tt. 1145 and 3422. (*s.* Ponticum *ss.* Caucasicum)

Native of the Caucasus, Russian Armenia, and north-eastern Asiatic Turkey, forming a dense scrub at or above the timber-line; introduced in 1803. Although its hybrid progeny is numerous in gardens, the true species is itself now scarcely ever seen. It is an interesting dwarf bush, remarkable for its dense habit and slow growth. Since it approaches 9,000 ft in the wild it is perfectly hardy in this country and flowers when quite young. It was reintroduced by Apold, Cox, and Hutchison from Turkey in 1962 (*R.C.Y.B. 1963*, pp. 66–7).

R. *caucasicum* is the parent of many hardy, early-flowering hybrids, of which the best-known are the crosses with R. *arboreum* and their offspring (grex Nobleanum). Others are of more complex origin. Some of these hybrids show the influence of R. *caucasicum* in their erect, clustered peduncles and persistent bud-scales. In some the finely impressed venation of the leaf of R. *caucasicum* is also evident.

R. AUREUM Georgi R. *chrysanthum* Pall.—This species is related to R. *caucasicum*, differing in the always yellow flowers and the smaller, glabrous, strongly net-veined leaves. It is a dwarf, slow-growing shrub with a wide distribution in the mountains of northern Asia, from the Altai to the Russian Far East and Korea; it also ranges south through Sakhalin to central Japan. Probably the present garden stock is of Japanese provenance, though the species was introduced from Russia in 1796. It is not an easy species and scarcely worth growing in Britain.

R. NIKOMONTANUM Nakai, found wild in Japan, is supposed to be a natural hybrid between R. *aureum* and R. *brachycarpum*.

R. CEPHALANTHUM Franch. [PLATE 71
R. *chamaetortum* Balf. f. & Ward

An evergreen shrub of bushy habit up to 3 or 4 ft high; young shoots thickly covered with scurf-like scales and bristly. Leaves oval to oblong, rounded or tapered, and with a short mucro at the apex, ½ to 1¼ in. long, ¼ to ½ in. wide, the margins decurved; dark glossy green above, clothed beneath with a dense scurfy coating of scales at first whitish, ultimately pale brown; stalk ⅛ to ¼ in. long. Flowers densely clustered in a terminal head of eight or more blossoms which is 1½ to 2 in. wide. Each flower is about ⅔ in. long and wide, the corolla white, narrowly tubular at the base, spreading at the mouth into five rounded lobes with crinkled margins, the throat filled with white down. Stamens five, ¼ in. long, enclosed within the corolla-tube, slightly downy towards the base; ovary very scaly; style short, glabrous; calyx deeply five-lobed, scarcely half as long as the corolla, the lobes narrowly ovate, scaly outside, fringed with hairs; flower-stalk ⅛ in. long, scaly. (s. Anthopogon)

Native of W. Szechwan, N. W. Yunnan, and bordering parts of Tibet and upper Burma at 9,000 to 15,000 ft; discovered by the French missionary Delavay in 1884 and probably introduced by him. Seeds were later sent by Wilson, Forrest, Kingdon Ward and Rock from various parts of its range. It is a very charming dwarf species, very hardy, and flowers in April. In the form first grown in gardens the flowers were white, but more commonly they are pink or flushed with pink. In Kingdon Ward's 6914 they are deep pink; this is a robust form, introduced from the Seinghku valley, upper Burma.

var. CREBREFLORUM (Hutch. & Ward) Cowan & Davidian R. *crebreflorum* Hutch. & Ward—A very dwarf variety with pink flowers. Stamens six, with glabrous filaments. It was described from a specimen collected by Kingdon Ward in the Delei valley, Assam Himalaya, in 1928. (KW 8337, 'A very lovely alpine from rock ledges at 13,000 ft'), but he had introduced it two years earlier from the Seinghku valley, upper Burma (KW 6967, a dwarf shrub only 6 or 8 in. high, growing on precipitous slopes, with rather large flowers, few in each truss, white flushed with pink; collected at 13,000 ft). A plant raised from KW 6967 received an Award of Merit when exhibited by Lt-Col. Messel, Nymans, Sussex, on May 1, 1934.

R. CERASINUM Tagg

An evergreen shrub up to 10 ft high, sometimes a small tree twice that height in forests; branchlets glandular or eglandular. Leaves leathery, oblong-elliptic, elliptic, or oblanceolate, 2 to 4 in. long, ⅞ to 1¾ in. wide, obtuse or rounded at the apex, glabrous on both sides, midrib and main veins impressed above. Flowers borne in May or early June in trusses of five to seven on glandular stalks up to ¾ in. long. Calyx very small, glandular on the rim. Corolla five-lobed, campanulate, 1½ to 1⅞ in. long, scarlet, crimson, or creamy white with a cherry-red band at the mouth; nectaries dark purple or almost black. Stamens ten, with glabrous filaments. Ovary conoid, glandular; style glandular throughout. *Bot. Mag.*, t. 9538. (s. Thomsonii ss. Cerasinum)

R. *cerasinum* was discovered by Kingdon Ward in 1924 on the Doshong La, a pass in Tibet at the eastern end of the Himalaya. 'It grew in dense drenched thickets by the torrent, as a bush 8 to 10 ft high; later we found it in the forest, a bigger bush, or small tree, 15 to 20 ft high. The flowers are large, fleshy, in loose drooping trusses of five, and of an intense burning scarlet; at the base of the corolla are five circular jet-black honey-glands, each about the size of a shirt-button.' This is the form that he nicknamed "Coals of Fire" (KW 5830).

Two years later Kingdon Ward found the same species in upper Burma overhanging a torrent that flows into the Seinghku river, one of the feeders of the Irrawaddy. In this form, which he nicknamed "Cherry Brandy", the flowers are cherry-red throughout, or creamy white at the base with a cherry-red rim (KW 6923). As it happened, Tagg chose this form as the type of the species, whence the epithet *cerasinum*. The nickname is not very apt for either subform but on the collector's recommendation it has continued to be used for the plants raised from KW 6923 to distinguish them from the Doshong La form, i.e., "Coals of Fire" (*Gard. Chron.*, Vol. 87 (1930), p. 330).

An Award of Merit was given in 1938 to the self-coloured subform of "Cherry Brandy", when shown from Nymans, Sussex, on June 8 (*Gard. Chron.*, Vol. 103 (1938), p. 442 and fig. 179). The picotee form with the white, red-rimmed flowers has never received an award, though it is very charming. Unfortunately, *R. cerasinum* is rather shy-flowering in many gardens, though it grows well and is perfectly hardy.

R. CHAETOMALLUM Balf. f. & Forr.

An evergreen shrub up to 4 or 5 ft high; young shoots thickly clothed with twisted, bristly hairs. Leaves obovate, rounded at the end, tapered at the base, dark green and glabrous above except when quite young, velvety with a coat of tawny down beneath, 2 to 4 in. long, 1 to $1\frac{1}{4}$ in wide; stalk $\frac{1}{5}$ in. long, stout, hairy like the shoot. Flowers in clusters of six to ten opening in March and April, on bristly stalks. Calyx red, up to $\frac{3}{8}$ in. long, with five lobes unequal in shape and size. Corolla bell-shaped, $1\frac{3}{4}$ in. long and $2\frac{1}{2}$ in. wide, deep crimson, five-lobed. Stamens ten, up to 1 in. long, glabrous; anthers chocolate brown. Ovary densely woolly; style glabrous. *Bot. Mag.*, n.s., t. 25 (*s.* Neriiflorum *ss.* Haematodes)

R. *chaetomallum* was discovered by Forrest in 1917–18 on the Mekong–Salween divide, N.W. Yunnan, growing in open thickets and on boulder-strewn slopes at 11,000 to 13,000 ft and was introduced by him at the same time under F. 14987, collected under the sacred mountain Ka-kar-po. From the Mekong it ranges westward across upper Burma and a variety has been discovered in the eastern Himalaya.

It is a variable species, distinguished from other members of the Haematodes subseries by the more or less bristly but not glandular young shoots and petioles, the lax, few-flowered truss, and the tomentose but not glandular ovary. Although a handsome species, it flowers too early for most gardens. The Award of Merit was given on April 7, 1959, to a form with Turkey Red flowers, raised at Exbury from Forrest 25601, collected on the Nmai (E. Irrawaddy)–Salween divide. The wild plants were said to have almost black-crimson flowers.

var. CHAMAEPHYTUM Cowan—Near var. *hemigymnum* but prostrate and almost glabrous. Described from Ludlow, Sherriff, and Taylor 3786, collected in the eastern Himalaya above Molo, near the border between Tibet and Assam.

var. GLAUCESCENS Tagg & Forr.—Leaves rather glaucous above.

var. HEMIGYMNUM Tagg & Forr.—Indumentum of leaf-undersurface thinner than normal, tending to wear off as the season advances. Forrest's 25605 is referred to this variety, but a plant raised from the corresponding seed-number at Tower Court, which received an Award of Merit in 1957, has the leaves densely brown-tomentose beneath.

var. XANTHANTHUM Tagg & Forr.—Flowers creamy yellow flushed or striped with rose or rosy crimson; or striped and margined bright rose-pink on a yellowish base.

R. CHAMPIONIAE Hook.

An evergreen shrub probably some 6 or 8 ft high; young shoots clothed with stiff outstanding hairs, some of which are gland-tipped. Leaves elliptic-lanceolate, pointed, mostly wedge-shaped at the base, 3 to 5 in. long, 1 to 1¾ in. wide; dark green, sprinkled on both surfaces with pale bristles that are especially abundant on the midrib beneath and on the margins; stalk ½ to ¾ in. long, very bristly. Flowers as many as six in a terminal cluster, usually fewer, opening in May. Corolla pink, 3½ in. wide, the base narrowly tubular and ¾ in. long, separating into five oblong, bluntish lobes 1½ to 2 in. long. Stamens ten, 2 in. long, downy at the lower half. Calyx-lobes five, linear, very unequal, ⅛ to ½ in. long, very bristly on the margins; flower-stalk very bristly, ¾ to 1 in. long. *Bot. Mag.*, t. 4609. (*s.* Stamineum)

Native of Hong Kong on Mt Victoria, where it is rare; found also in the province of Fukien, China, by Dunn in 1905. It was discovered in 1849 by Lt-Col. Champion, after whose wife it was named by the elder Hooker. Although no longer there it was introduced to Kew in 1881 and flowered in the Temperate House in 1894, but was a shy bloomer. It is a quite tender shrub and I have only seen it in the open air at Caerhays.

R. CHARITOPES Balf. f. & Forr.   [PLATE 72

A dwarf evergreen shrub up to 2 ft high in the wild; young shoots scaly. Leaves obovate, the apex mucronulate, the base wedge-shaped, 1 to 2¾ in. long, ½ to 1⅛ in. wide, glossy dark green above, pale green and fairly thickly sprinkled over with yellowish shining scales beneath; stalk ⅙ in. long. Flowers opening in May, usually three (sometimes two to four) in a terminal cluster, each on its slender scaly stalk which is ¾ to 1 in. long. Calyx large for the size of the flower, ⅓ in. long, cut to the base into five ovate lobes, scaly outside. Corolla bell-shaped, five-lobed, about 1 in. wide, clear pink, speckled with crimson. Stamens ten, hairy on the lower two-thirds; ovary densely scaly; style ⅓ in. long, thick and glabrous. *Bot. Mag.*, t. 9358. (*s.* and *ss.* Glaucophyllum)

Native of N.E. upper Burma, found in the Shing Hong pass by Farrer in June 1920. It was then in flower and he describes it as a 'particularly charming plant with three- (rarely four-) bloomed inflorescences. Flowers of a clear apple-blossom pink flushed more warmly in the upper lobes, and speckled with crimson; and with a deep rose tube.' Farrer died before he could harvest the seeds of his 1920 discoveries, but four years later Forrest met with this species near the type-locality and introduced it (F.25570 and 25581).

It is a very attractive little shrub, quite hardy, though its expanding flower-buds may be killed by late frost. Often it produces a quite heavy crop of flowers in the autumn, though at the cost of next spring's display.

R. TSANGPOENSE Hutch. & Ward—This species is very near to R. *charitopes*. The differential characters given by Cowan and Davidian are the narrow-obovate to oblong-elliptic leaves, against broad-obovate in R. *charitopes*, and the smaller calyx, up to ¼ in. long. It was discovered by Kingdon Ward in 1924 on the Doshong La, S.E. Tibet, in the mountains enclosed by the Tsangpo bend.

It is uncommon in cultivation. Award of Merit May 2, 1972, when shown by Major A. E. Hardy, Sandling Park, Kent (clone 'Cowtye').

var. PRUNIFLORUM (Hutch.) Cowan & Davidian R. *pruniflorum* Hutch.; *R. sordidum* Hutch.—Leaves more densely scaly beneath, slightly overlapping to their own diameter apart (against mostly three to six times their own diameter apart in the typical state). This variety was found by Kingdon Ward in 1926 on both sides of the Irrawaddy–Lohit divide, on the frontier between Burma and Assam and was introduced by him. According to the field notes, the colour of the flowers in KW 6924 (Seinghku valley) was plum-purple and in KW 7188 (Di Chu valley) 'plum-purple or inclining to crimson on the one hand, or to violet on the other'. He later found the same variety on Kaso peak in the Mishmi Hills, Assam (KW 8415), flowers described in field note as claret-coloured; the specimen under this number is the type of R. *sordidum*, a synonym of var. *pruniflorum*. As met with in cultivation this variety usually has flowers of a slaty purple.

Cowan and Davidian also describe R. *tsangpoense* var. CURVISTYLUM, with smaller, tubular-campanulate flowers. This was found by Kingdon Ward on the Doshong La (KW 5843) and was considered by him to be a natural hybrid between R. *campylogynum* var. *myrtilloides* (KW 5842) and typical R. *tsangpoense* (KW 5844). In this connection it is interesting to note that Farrer found in Burma some plants which he considered to be hybrids between R. *campylogynum* var. *charopoeum* and R. *charitopes*, to which R. *tsangpoense* is closely related (see above).

R. CHRYSEUM Balf. f. & Ward
R. *muliense* Balf. f. & Forr.

A dwarf, evergreen, much-branched shrub 1 to 2½ ft high; young shoots densely covered with a rather loose scurf of reddish scales, which become darker and fewer the second year, the bark of the branchlets becoming finally grey and peeling. Leaves stout, aromatic, oval, or inclined to obovate, mostly bluntish at both ends, ½ to ¾ in. long, $\frac{3}{16}$ to $\frac{5}{16}$ in. wide, dark green, covered with shining scales above, paler and rather glaucous beneath with the scales less dense; stalk $\frac{1}{12}$ in. long, scaly. Flowers deep sulphur yellow to pale yellow, four to six in a terminal cluster, opening in May. Corolla ¾ to 1 in. wide, with a funnel-shaped base and five ovate lobes ⅜ in. long, slightly scaly outside, covered with white down in the tube. Stamens five to ten, ½ in. long, each with a tuft of white down at the base; ovary very scaly; style glabrous or slightly downy at the base. Calyx very scaly, five-lobed, the lobes oblong, ⅙ in. or less long. *Bot. Mag.*, t. 9246. (*s*. Lapponicum)

R. *chryseum* is a species of alpine and subalpine scrub at 12,000 to 14,000 ft, from S.W. Szechwan through N.W. Yunnan to upper Burma. It was discovered by Kingdon Ward in 1913 below the glaciers of Ka-kar-po, on the Mekong–Salween divide; introduced by Forrest five years later from the Beima-shan, a short way to the east of the type-locality, on the Mekong–Yangtse divide. The type of R. *muliense*, now included in R. *chryseum*, was collected in the Muli region of S.W. Szechwan.

In the original description the corolla of R. *chryseum* is described as golden, but in the plants from the first introduction, and from some later ones, they are too pale to deserve that term. It is very hardy and suitable for the rock garden but in many gardens it is not at all free-flowering and cannot be relied on as a foil for the purple- or lavender-flowered species of the Lapponicum series, and in any case blooms later than most of these.

In their revision of the Lapponicum group, M. N. and W. R. Philipson reduce R. *chryseum* to the status of a variety of the purple-flowered R. *rupicola* (q.v.), and give the same rank independently to R. *muliense* (here treated as synonymous with R. *chryseum*). Now that they have pointed it out, it becomes obvious that except in flower-colour there is really no difference between the two species. It is interesting that Kingdon Ward found R. *chryseum* growing in the upper Adung valley, Burma, in the company of purple-flowered plants that were in other respects indistinguishable from it (*Gard. Chron.*, Vol. 93 (1933), pp. 170–1).

R. CHRYSODORON Hutch.

An evergreen small shrub; young shoots sparingly bristly. Leaves oval, rounded at the base, also somewhat rounded at the apex but furnished with a conspicuous mucro there; mostly 2 to 3 in. long, 1 to 1½ in. wide, bright green and glabrous above, glaucous green and scaly beneath, more or less ciliate; stalk ⅛ to ½ in. long, bristly. Flowers in terminal clusters of about five. Calyx rimlike. Corolla bell-shaped, 1½ in. long and wide, with five lobes each 1 in. wide, notched about the middle, of a beautiful unspotted canary-yellow; stamens downy on the lower half. Ovary and flower-stalk very scaly; style bent. *Bot. Mag.*, t. 9442. (*s.* and *ss.* Boothii)

This species first came to notice in 1931, when Lord Stair sent it to Edinburgh for naming. It had been raised from seeds received under the number Forrest 25446 and probably collected in N.W. Yunnan, but the corresponding herbarium specimen is R. *ciliicalyx* and the field note refers to this. It proved to be a hitherto unknown species and was given the name R. *chrysodoron* but this was first published in 1934 by Hutchinson, who drew up his description from a flowering spray shown by Lord Aberconway at the R.H.S. Show on February 20. It received an Award of Merit on that occasion as a hardy shrub, but it is generally reckoned to be tender and is, besides, too early-flowering to be of much use as an outdoor plant, March or early April being its usual season. It is, however, a beautiful species, not too large for the cool greenhouse.

R. *chrysodoron* is also in cultivation from seeds collected by Kingdon Ward in the Adung valley, upper Burma, where it grows perched high on trees or on rocks in the river-bed (Field Notes for 1931, under KW 9221; *Plant Hunter's Paradise*, p. 132).

R. CILIATUM Hook. f. [PLATE 73
R. *modestum* Hook. f.

An evergreen shrub of stiff, wide-spreading habit, rarely more than 3 to 4 ft high out-of-doors near London; young branchlets covered with bristly hairs.

Leaves oval or obovate, tapering sometimes equally to both ends, sometimes more gradually towards the base, 2 to 4 in. long, ¾ to 1½ in. wide, bristly on the upper surface and on the margins, scaly beneath; stalk bristly, ¼ to ⅓ in. long. Flowers beautiful rosy red in bud, pale pink on opening, becoming almost white with age, 2½ in. across, produced three to five in a cluster during March and April. Calyx-lobes rounded ovate, bristly on the margins. Corolla widely bell-shaped, with broad notched lobes. Stamens ten, hairy at the base. Ovary scaly; style glabrous. *Bot. Mag.*, tt. 4648, 7686. (s. Maddenii *ss.* Ciliicalyx)

RHODODENDRON CILIATUM

Native of the Himalaya from E. Nepal eastward; discovered by J. D. Hooker in Sikkim and introduced by him in 1850. Hooker found it in valleys of the interior at 9,000 to 10,000 ft, 'growing in clumps 2 ft high, generally in moist rocky places'. It flowered at Kew in 1852, and was figured in the *Botanical Magazine* the same year with the varietal epithet *roseo-album*. The explanation for this quite superfluous addition is that Hooker never saw the species in full flower and sent home to his father at Kew a colour sketch made apparently from a truss in which the flowers had aged to a deep purplish pink, as shown in the plate in *Rhododendrons of the Sikkim Himalaya*, which was drawn and coloured from his sketch and herbarium specimens.

R. *ciliatum* is a perfectly hardy species and is best suited in a lightly shaded position protected from the east and north. It frequently gives a very charming display in April if the weather be kind, but a few degrees of frost will ruin it.

Crossed with other hardy species, R. *ciliatum* has given rise to several attractive hybrids, of which the best known are the Praecox and Cilpinense grexes.

It is also the parent of such half-hardy hybrids as 'Princess Alice' and 'Countess of Haddington'.

R. CILIICALYX Franch.
R. atentsiense Hand.-Mazz.

An evergreen shrub of rather diffuse habit, 8 to 10 ft high; young shoots bristly and slightly scaly. Leaves narrowly oval, or oblanceolate, tapered at both ends, pointed, 2½ to 4½ in. long, 1 to 2 in. wide, dark glossy green above, glaucous-green beneath and thickly sprinkled with golden-brown scales; stalk ⅓ to ½ in. long, bristly and slightly scaly. Flowers produced in March and April in a terminal truss of usually three blossoms. Flower-stalks ½ in. long, stout, scaly. Calyx five-lobed, the lobes ⅛ in. long, conspicuously fringed with white bristles ⅛ in. long. Corolla pure white except for a yellow stain on the upper side of the tube; the base is funnel-shaped, the five rounded wavy lobes spreading and giving the flower a diameter of 4 in. Stamens ten, about 2 in. long, white, very hairy at the base. Ovary scaly; style 2½ in. long, scaly at the base. *Bot. Mag.*, t. 7782.   (s. Maddenii ss. Ciliicalyx)

R. *ciliicalyx* was discovered by the Abbé Delavay in 1884 in W. Yunnan, in the mountains east of Lankiung (north of Lake Tali), and was introduced from Paris to Kew in 1892, first flowering there in 1900. It was later reintroduced by Forrest from the borders between Yunnan and Burma and more recently by Kingdon Ward from the Triangle, during his last expedition to Burma (1953). According to him R. *ciliicalyx* is not usually an epiphyte. 'On the contrary, it is more often a slim shrub ten to twelve feet high . . . though it needs strong support from the surrounding thicket to keep it upright. Out of bloom, its shining plum-purple bark betrays it. . . . Very occasionally it is an epiphytic shrub, appearing as a pale summer cloud in a big tree' (*Return to the Irrawaddy*, p. 161).

This beautiful species, one of the very finest of white rhododendrons, grows well in the Temperate House at Kew, where it has protection from more than one or two degrees of frost. Here it is covered with blossom every spring. It is only likely to succeed out-of-doors in the milder parts of Cornwall and similar places. The flowers are sometimes pink and they have a faint sweet fragrance. It is closely related to the much hardier Himalayan R. *ciliatum*, whose style has no scales and whose habit is dwarfer, more spreading and bushy. The bristly calyx is distinctive.

Although not the oldest species in its group, R. *ciliicalyx* has been taken as the 'type' of a large and taxonomically difficult subseries of the Maddenii series. In this some thirty-five species have been placed, many of them distinguished by unreliable characters. In a cursory study of the subseries, Dr Sleumer has reduced the number to twenty and remarks that still more drastic reduction may be necessary ('The Genus Rhododendron in Indochina and Siam', *Blumea*, Suppl. IV (1958), pp. 40–7). There can be no doubt that most of his judgements will be upheld when the group is subjected to a detailed revision, but in the meantime it seems best to maintain those of the reduced species which are familiar in cultivation. See also R. *johnstoneanum* and R. *veitchianum*.

R. CARNEUM Hutch.—In describing this species (*Bot. Mag.*, t. 8634) Dr Hutchinson remarked that it is very near to R. *veitchianum* (q.v.), differing in its smaller, flesh-pink, unblotched flowers, and smaller, more ciliate calyx lobes. However, Dr Sleumer places it under R. *ciliicalyx* in synonymy, and certainly it strongly resembles that species also. It was described from a cultivated plant raised from seeds collected in the Northern Shan States, Burma, in 1912 and is therefore intermediate geographically between the two species. It is tender. Award of Merit April 5, 1925, when shown by Lionel de Rothschild from Exbury.

R. DENDRICOLA Hutch.—A very tender species from upper Burma at low elevations, discovered by Kingdon Ward in the valley of the Nmai Hka (upper Irrawaddy) in 1914, growing as an epiphyte on tall trees, and was later found by him as far west as the Mishmi Hills, Assam. The truss figured in *Bot. Mag.*, t. 9682, was from a plant raised from Forrest 26459, collected on the Nmai Hka–Salween divide at 9,000 ft. R. *dendricola* resembles R. *ciliicalyx* in general aspect, and is included in it by Sleumer, but it differs in the very small rim-like calyx and in having the corolla scaly outside. The flowers are white or white tinged with pink, sometimes barred with pink on the outside, with a yellow flare in the throat, fragrant, up to 4 in. long, in trusses of three or four.

R. SCOTTIANUM Hutch.—In *Bot. Mag.*, t. 9238, where this species is figured, Dr Hutchinson remarks that it is really very near to R. *ciliicalyx*, but the bristle-like ciliations on the calyx are fewer or wanting, the scales on the undersurfaces of the leaf are denser, the corolla is scaly outside, and the style is scaly up to the mid-point or beyond. It was discovered by Forrest near Tengyueh in Yunnan, near the frontier with Burma, and introduced by him. It is a very tender but beautiful species, with fragrant white or rose-flushed flowers up to 4 in. long. It is difficult to agree with Dr Sleumer that this species is the same as R. *lyi* (q.v. under R. *johnstoneanum*), from which it differs in having branchlets without bristles, leaves generally broader, with the scales beneath much closer, and larger flowers.

R. SUPRANUBIUM Hutch.—A close ally of R. *ciliicalyx* and included in it by Sleumer, but perhaps distinct enough to rank as a separate species. The leaves are thinner and smaller, elliptic to oblanceolate-elliptic, $1\frac{1}{2}$ to $2\frac{5}{8}$ in. long, $\frac{1}{2}$ to just over 1 in. wide. The corolla is smaller, and though the young shoots, petioles, base of leaf-blades, and calyx-lobes may have a few weak hairs at first, these seem to be soon lost. It was described from specimens collected by Forrest on the eastern flank of the Tali range, W. Yunnan, in rocky situations at 11,000 to 12,000 ft, and was introduced by him in 1910. Farrer and Cox reintroduced it in 1919 from near Hpimaw on the Nmai Hka–Salween divide, upper Burma, growing as an epiphyte at 8,000 ft, 'with very large and lovely flowers, intensely fragrant, of pure rose-flushed white with a yellow base. . . . A most exquisite beauty' (Farrer 848). R. *supranubium* seems to be uncommon in cultivation and has never received an award.

R. CINNABARINUM Hook. f.

An evergreen shrub 6 to 10 ft high, sometimes taller, somewhat thin and sparse
of habit, the branches long and slender, scaly when young. Leaves 2 to 4 in
long, ¾ to 1¼ in. broad; oval, tapering about equally to each end, glabrous, and
of a greyish-green metallic lustre above, scaly beneath, and varying in colour

RHODODENDRON CINNABARINUM

from glaucous green to reddish brown; stalk ⅛ in. long. Flowers funnel-shaped,
and like those of *Lapageria*, 1¼ to 2 in. long, very variable in colour; ordinarily
of a dull cinnabar red, produced during May and June, from five to eight in
terminal heads. In other forms the corolla is orange-red outside, yellowish
within, sometimes greenish. Flower-stalk ⅛ in. long, scaly. Calyx with four short,
broadish lobes, and one longer narrow one, or sometimes with all five nearly
equal, scaly. Stamens ten, scarcely so long as the corolla, hairy at the base.
(*s*. Cinnabarinum)

Native of the Himalaya from E. Nepal to the region of the Tsangpo bend and
slightly beyond, but not reported from Burma or China; discovered by J. D.
Hooker in Sikkim and introduced by him in 1850. This distinct and interesting
species is remarkable for the variability of the colour of its flowers and of the
undersurface of its leaves. But the differences between some of the intermediate
forms are so unimportant that botanists regard them all of one species. The
following variants, mostly only of horticultural interest, have been named:

var. AESTIVALE Hutch.—This name was given by Dr Hutchinson to a plant
growing at Borde Hill, Sussex, which was unusually late-flowering (July) and
had narrower leaves than normal.

var. BLANDFORDIIFLORUM Hook.—Flowers red outside, yellowish or
greenish within. *Bot. Mag.*, t. 4930. Introduced by J. D. Hooker. A plant of this

character received an Award of Merit when shown from Bodnant on May 29, 1945.

var. PALLIDUM *Bot. Mag.*, t. 4788—Flowers pale pinkish purple, rather widely funnel-campanulate, slightly speckled. Like the preceding, this was raised from the seeds collected by Hooker.

var. PURPURELLUM Cowan—Flowers shorter than in the type and campanulate, rich plum-purple. Described from Ludlow and Sherriff 1354, collected in the Tibetan Himalaya in 1936. Award of Merit May 1, 1951, when shown by Capt. Collingwood Ingram, Benenden, Kent (raised from Ludlow, Sherriff, and Taylor 6349).

var. ROYLEI (Hook. f.) Hort. R. *roylei* Hook. f.—Flowers intense rosy red or plum crimson. It was originally described by J. D. Hooker as a species. A few years later he sunk it in R. *cinnabarinum* but in gardens the name R. *roylei* continued to be used by gardeners, 'who, quite reasonably, refuse to call the dusky beauty by the same name as the smaller-flowered orange or madder-coloured one' (W. Watson, *Gard. Chron.*, Vol. 64 (1918), p. 38). A selection from the var. *roylei*, named 'MAGNIFICUM', received an Award of Merit when shown by Messrs Reuthe on May 7, 1918. This was described as having flowers dark crimson on the outside, orange-red inside. The same award was given on May 19, 1953, to a clone named 'Vin Rosé', with flowers described as Currant Red outside, Blood Red inside, shown by the Crown Estate Commissioners, Windsor Great Park.

R. *cinnabarinum* is a perfectly hardy species in a sheltered position, and needs only light shade. 'This is one of those rhododendrons which looks its best when viewed with the sun behind a bush in flower. The effect is then dazzling, for there is a certain quality and brilliance added to the shining flowers, which is not noticeable when seen only against a dark background' (Millais).

R. *cinnabarinum* is a parent of many fine hybrids, the best known of which are the Lady Rosebery and Lady Chamberlain grexes. Details of these and others will be found in the section on hybrids.

R. CITRINIFLORUM Balf. f. & Forr.
R. *chlanidotum* Balf. f. & Forr.

A dwarf evergreen shrub 2 to 4 ft high, with obovate or oblong leaves tapering to the base, 1½ to 3½ in. long, ½ to 1½ in. wide, densely clothed beneath with loose tawny wool. Flowers opening in April or early May in clusters of six to eight; stalks clad with tawny bristles. Calyx variable in size. Corolla typically clear, unspotted, lemon-yellow, but sometimes rose-coloured, or in intermediate shades, bell-shaped, 1¾ in. long, five-lobed. Stamens ten, downy at the base or glabrous. Ovary matted with tawny hairs and glandular bristly; style glabrous. (s. Neriiflorum ss. Sanguineum)

This variable species resembles R. *sanguineum* in the shape and texture of its leaves, but they differ markedly in their thick indumentum of matted hairs. It was described from specimens collected by Forrest on the Mekong–Salween divide, N.W. Yunnan, and introduced by him. Although the flowers were said in the original description to be lemon-yellow, the authors cite Forrest's 14271, in which the flowers were described in the field note as 'soft rose without markings'. The species also occurs in S.E. Tibet (Tsarong) on the Salween–Irrawaddy divide.

The following subspecies are placed under R. *citriniflorum* by Cowan (*Notes R.B.G. Edin.*, Vol. 20, p. 75).

subsp. AUREOLUM Cowan—Ovary without glands. Otherwise not differing from the type.

subsp. HORAEUM (Balf. f. & Forr.) Cowan R. *horaeum* Balf. f. & Forr.—Resembling the type in foliage, but flowers deep crimson. Ovary tomentose, without glands. Introduced by Forrest from S.E. Tibet (Tsarong), later by Rock. The subsp. RUBENS Cowan is the same, but the ovary is glandular as well as tomentose.

R. CLEMENTINAE Forr.

An evergreen shrub 4 ft and upwards high in the wild, with stout, stiff young shoots, leaf-buds four-angled. Leaves oval, mostly heart-shaped at the base, rounded at the apex, $2\frac{1}{2}$ to 5 in. long, rather more than half as much wide, dull green and without down at maturity above, covered beneath with a soft, thick, pale brown felt; stalk $\frac{1}{2}$ to $\frac{3}{4}$ in. long. Flowers produced in a terminal truss of seven to fifteen flowers. Calyx minute. Corolla bell-shaped, creamy white flushed with rose or bright rose usually dotted with crimson, 2 in. wide, six- or seven-lobed; stamens double the number of the corolla lobes, scarcely half the length of the corolla, downy at the base; ovary and style glabrous. *Bot. Mag.*, t. 9392. (*s.* and *ss.* Taliense)

Native of S.W. Szechwan, N.W. Yunnan, and S.E. Tibet; discovered by Forrest in 1913 on the Chungtien plateau and introduced by him. He evidently thought highly of this species, which he dedicated to his wife, but in cultivation it is unremarkable in its flowers and worth growing only for its handsome foliage, which is steely blue when young. It is perfectly hardy.

R. COELICUM Balf. f. & Farrer

An evergreen shrub up to 6 ft high in the wild; young stems glabrous, not glandular. Leaves leathery, obovate, about 3 in. long, $1\frac{5}{8}$ in. wide, rounded and mucronate at the apex, obtuse at the base, glabrous above, clad beneath with a dense cinnamon-coloured indumentum which conceals the lateral veins but not the midrib. Petiole about $\frac{3}{8}$ in. long. Flowers borne March or early April, up to fifteen together in a compact truss on glandular stalks about $\frac{3}{8}$ in. long. Calyx cup-shaped, fleshy, about $\frac{1}{4}$ in. long, with five irregular lobes. Corolla tubular-campanulate, scarlet or crimson, about $1\frac{1}{2}$ in. long. Ovary glandular and tomentose; style glabrous. (*s.* Neriiflorum *ss.* Haematodes)

R. *coelicum* was discovered by Farrer on the Chawchi pass, upper Burma, between the Salween and the upper Irrawaddy (Nmai Hka). He described it as a thin, low little bush, flowering in the snow, and 'making blots of scarlet, visible for miles.' It is introduced by Forrest from the Tsarong region of S.E. Tibet, some way to the north of the type-locality, growing at 13,000 to 14,000 ft and making a shrub 4 to 5 ft high (F.21830). It belongs to the same subgroup as *R. haematodes*, *R. chaetomallum*, and *R. catacosmum*, but in those species the inflorescence is lax and few-flowered and the young stems and petioles are tomentose and without glands.

R. coelicum received an Award of Merit when shown by Col. The Lord Digby on April 19, 1955 (raised from F.21830).

R. POCOPHORUM Tagg—Closely allied to *R. coelicum*, differing in the glandular-bristly young shoots and petioles, and the glandular but not tomentose ovary. The leaves are also somewhat larger—up to 6 in. or slightly more long and 1½ to 2½ in. wide—and it attains about 10 ft in height, though usually less. According to the original description, there are fifteen to twenty flowers in the truss, but cultivated plants, even those raised from the wild seed, have far fewer. Most of the collections by Forrest and Rock are from the divide between the upper Irrawaddy and the Salween in S.E. Tibet, and the former introduced it from there in 1921. Tagg identified as *R. pocophorum* Kingdon Ward's no. 8289 from the Delei valley, Assam, but neither his specimen nor the plants raised from the seed under this number agree well with this species.

A plant at Nymans, raised from KW 8289, received an A.M. in 1971, on March 30, under the clonal name 'Cecil Nice'.

R. COLLETTIANUM Aitch. & Hemsl.

An evergreen shrub of dwarf habit in cultivation, but described as 8 to 10 ft high in the wild. Leaves 2 to 3 in. long, ⅓ to ⅝ in. wide; narrowly oval, pointed at both ends, dark dull green above, covered with brownish scales beneath; when crushed they have a strong, resinous, aromatic odour; stalk about ⅓ in. long. Flowers 1 in. across, white, produced during May in terminal clusters 2 to 2½ in. across. Corolla with a funnel-shaped tube, hairy within, the five rounded oblong lobes not fully spreading; calyx with five narrow, oblong lobes rounded at the end, scaly, and very hairy at the margins; stamens ten, almost hidden within the corolla-tube, hairy near the bases. *Bot. Mag.*, t. 7019.   (s. Anthopogon)

Native of the border region between Afghanistan and Pakistan; discovered in the Kurrum valley in 1879 by Sir Henry Collett and Dr Aitchison, and introduced the same year to Kew. It first flowered in the Kew rock garden in May 1888, and it is for such a position that it appears best adapted. It is allied to *R. anthopogon*, but the flowers have ten stamens and it is a more robust plant, with larger leaves.

For an account of this species and of *R. afghanicum* in their native habitat see *R.C.Y.B. 1970*, pp. 177–81.

R. CONCINNUM Hemsl.

R. coombense Hemsl.; *R. yanthinum* Bur. & Franch.; *R. concinnum* f. *laetevirens* Cowan; *R. concinnum* var. *lepidanthum* (Rehd. & Wils.) Rehd.; *R. yanthinum* var. *lepidanthum* Rehd. & Wils.

An evergreen shrub or small tree up to 15 ft high; young shoots scaly. Leaves scattered along the branches, aromatic, elliptic or oblong-elliptic or broadest slightly above or below the middle, apex varying from obtuse to acute or acuminate, base rounded or broadly tapered, 1 to 3½ in. long, ½ to 1⅜ in. wide, dark green or glaucous green and scaly above, pale brown to dark brown beneath from the densely arranged scales; stalk up to ⅜ in. long. Flowers in terminal trusses of two to eight, opening in May. Calyx very variable, reduced to a rim or with five rounded or pointed lobes, scaly at least on the margin, sometimes fringed with hairs. Corolla five-lobed, widely funnel-shaped, coloured in some shade of purple or reddish purple, occasionally white, usually spotted with brown or crimson, scaly on the outside, rarely without scales, glabrous or slightly hairy towards the base. Stamens ten, hairy at the base. Ovary densely scaly; style glabrous or slightly hairy at the base. *Bot. Mag.*, tt. 8280, 8912. (*s.* Triflorum *ss.* Yunnanense)

Native of W. Szechwan; discovered by the Rev. Ernst Faber on Mt Omei; introduced by Wilson in 1904. It is a variable species in leaf-shape, calyx, colour of flowers, etc. It is perfectly hardy but now little cultivated except for the variety previously known as R. *pseudoyanthinum* (see below). The following varieties are recognised by Davidian in his revision of the Triflorum series:

var. BENTHAMIANUM (Hemsl.) Davidian R. *benthamianum* Hemsl.—Flowers lavender-purple. Scales of leaf-undersides dissimilar, some dark brown, others yellowish brown. Described from a plant raised by Messrs Veitch from the seeds sent by Wilson.

var. PSEUDOYANTHINUM (Hutch.) Davidian R. *pseudoyanthinum* Hutch.—Flowers deep reddish magenta. Leaves larger than normal. This was raised by Messrs Veitch from Wilson's seeds and is figured in *Bot. Mag.*, t. 8620, as R. *concinnum*. The colour of the flowers is arresting but not beautiful.

R. AMESIAE Rehd. & Wils.—Very closely allied to R. *concinnum*, the distinguishing character being the bristly leaf-stalk and the often ciliate calyx. *Bot. Mag.*, t. 9221. It has about the same decorative value as R. *concinnum* but is rare in cultivation. Introduced by Wilson from W. Szechwan in 1910, during his second expedition for the Arnold Arboretum, under W.4233 (from woodlands near Mupin).

R. POLYLEPIS Franch. R. *harrovianum* Hemsl.—An inferior species allied to R. *concinnum*, differing in the relatively narrower leaves (up to 4 in. long and 1½ in. wide), more densely scaly beneath, the scales mostly contiguous or overlapping. *Bot. Mag.*, t. 8309.

R. CORIACEUM Franch.

R. *foveolatum* Rehd. & Wils.

An evergreen shrub or small tree from 10 to 25 ft high; young shoots pale grey with down. Leaves oblanceolate, 5 to 10½ in. long, 1½ to 3½ in. wide, dark green and glabrous above, grey white and downy beneath; stalk 1 in. or less long, cylindrical, pale yellowish green like the midrib. Flowers borne rather loosely in a truss fifteen to twenty together. Calyx a mere rim; flower-stalks downy, ¾ to 1 in. long. Corolla between funnel- and bell-shaped, up to 2½ in.

wide, five- to seven-lobed, white or rose-tinted, with a crimson blotch at the base and sometimes similarly coloured spots on the upper lobes. Stamens double the number of corolla-lobes, scurfy at the base; ovary downy; style glabrous. *Bot. Mag.*, n.s., t. 462.   (*s.* Falconeri)

Native of N.W. Yunnan, where it was found on the Mekong–Salween divide by the Abbé Soulié in 1898, flowering in March; afterwards in the same region by Père Monbeig and by Forrest who introduced it. It occurs up to 13,000 ft altitude, and is hardy in climates like that of the inland parts of Sussex and Hampshire. It is a handsome-leaved species of the Falconeri series, distinct therein by reason of the grey-white colouring of various parts. It has suffered from Lionel de Rothschild's condemnation of it as 'a long way the worst rhododendron in the series', with small white flowers and not worth growing. In fact, some plants raised from Forrest 25622 and 25872 have large, very beautiful flowers.

R. *coriaceum* received an Award of Merit when shown by the Crown Estate Commissioners, Windsor Great Park, on April 14, 1953 (clone 'Morocco').

R. CRASSUM Franch.

An evergreen shrub or small tree up to 20 ft high; young shoots stout, scaly. Leaves usually crowded at the end of the shoot, leathery, oval, narrowly obovate or oblanceolate, pointed, tapered at the base, $2\frac{1}{2}$ to 6 in. long, 1 to $2\frac{1}{2}$ in. wide, dark glossy green and wrinkled above, rather glaucous beneath but thickly sown with red-brown scales. Flowers delightfully fragrant, three to six in a terminal cluster, each on a thick scaly stalk, $\frac{1}{2}$ to $\frac{3}{4}$ in. long. Calyx scaly at the base, deeply five-lobed, the lobes $\frac{1}{4}$ to $\frac{1}{2}$ in. long, glabrous. Corolla funnel-shaped, $2\frac{1}{2}$ to $3\frac{1}{2}$ in. long, creamy white to rosy white, scaly outside, five-lobed, the lobes roundish ovate and 1 in. long. Stamens fifteen to twenty, downy at the lower part. Ovary and style scaly, the latter 2 to $2\frac{1}{2}$ in. long. Seed-vessel very stout, $\frac{3}{4}$ to $1\frac{1}{4}$ in. long, $\frac{1}{2}$ in. wide, ribbed. *Bot. Mag.*, t. 9673.   (*s.* and *ss.* Maddenii)

Native of N.W. Yunnan and upper Burma at 8,000 to 12,000 ft altitude; discovered by the Abbé Delavay about 1885 in the Tali range, Yunnan. It was introduced by Forrest in 1906 and first flowered with E. J. P. Magor at Lamellen, Cornwall, in 1914.

This beautiful rhododendron may be regarded as the Yunnan representative of R. *maddenii*, a well-known Himalayan species long cultivated in greenhouses. Being much the hardier, it is a valuable acquisition. It has lived in the open air at Kew through a few mild winters and occasionally flowered, but it needs a milder climate. It flowers in June and, starting late into growth, escapes late spring frosts, which may account for its comparative hardiness. R. *maddenii* differs in having glabrous stamens and the calyx-lobes are only $\frac{1}{6}$ in. long. Forrest has introduced a number of forms of R. *crassum* differing in the shape and size of the leaves, some of which have glabrous stamens. Award of Merit June 24, 1924, when shown by T. H. Lowinsky, Sunninghill, Berks.

R. CRINIGERUM Franch.

R. *ixeuticum* Balf. f. & W. W. Sm.

An evergreen shrub up to 20 ft high in the wild; young shoots and leaf-stalks very sticky with glandular bristles. Leaves oblong-lanceolate to oblanceolate, tapered to a narrow, often rounded base, slenderly pointed, 3 to 7 in. long, ¾ to 1¾ in. wide, dark glossy green and soon glabrous above; clothed beneath with a soft tawny felt, with many small, ultimately dark glands on the midrib; leaf-stalk ⅝ in. long. Flowers about twelve in a truss. Calyx deeply five-lobed, the lobes narrowly oblong, ¼ in. long, glandular-bristly and hairy like the flower-stalks which are up to 1 in. long. Corolla bell-shaped, 1½ in. long, five-lobed, white with a dark blotch at the base and sometimes flushed with rose. Stamens ten, downy at the base. Ovary thickly furnished with stalked glands; style glabrous except at the base. *Bot. Mag.*, t. 9464. (s. Barbatum ss. Crinigerum)

R. *crinigerum* was discovered by the French missionary Soulié in 1895 on the Mekong–Salween divide and introduced by Forrest in 1914. It seems to be a fairly common species in the Yunnan–Tibet borderland, from the Kari pass on the Mekong–Yangtse divide westward to the upper Irrawaddy, and all the sendings by Forrest and Dr Rock are from this region. But Kingdon Ward later found it as far west as the Delei river in the Mishmi Hills, Assam (KW 7123). It bears some resemblance to R. *glischrum* and R. *habrotrichum* in its flowers, but the dense, velvety covering beneath the leaf distinguishes it.

R. *crinigerum* is a very handsome species at its best, and is represented in the Windsor Great Park collection by a fine group of plants raised from KW 7123 and from various seed collections by Forrest and Rock. The material figured in the *Botanical Magazine* is from Rock 59186, collected on Mt Kenichunpu, Irrawaddy–Salween divide. R. *crinigerum* received an Award of Merit in 1935, when shown from Exbury on April 30.

var. EUADENIUM Tagg & Forr.—Indumentum thinner, not completely concealing the undersurface of the leaf. There is a very striking example of this variety in the Windsor collection, raised from Rock 03908, with leaves about 9 in. long.

R. BAINBRIDGEANUM Tagg & Forr.—Leaves on the average shorter and relatively wider, much less pointed at the apex, otherwise not differing much from R. *crinigerum*. Introduced by Forrest in 1922 from the Tsarong region of S.E. Tibet, where it occurs on the Salween–Irrawaddy divide. Seeds collected later by Rock are from the same area.

R. CUNEATUM W. W. Sm.

R. *ravum* Balf. f. & W. W. Sm.; R. *cheilanthum* Balf. f. & Forr.; R. *sclerocladum* Balf. f. & Forr.

An evergreen shrub of rather erect growth 4 to 6 ft high, scaly. Leaves oval, often inclined to obovate, tapered about equally to both ends; 1 to 2 in. long, ½ to 1 in. wide, dark glossy green and scaly above, dull and rusty beneath with brownish-yellow scales; stalk ⅙ in. long. Flowers produced in April in terminal clusters of three to six. Calyx reddish, $\frac{1}{4}$ to $\frac{1}{3}$ in. long, deeply five-lobed, the lobes scaly outside and fringed with bristles; flower-stalk $\frac{1}{2}$ to $\frac{3}{4}$ in. long. Corolla widely funnel-shaped, 1 to $1\frac{1}{2}$ in. long and wide, five-lobed, deep rose coloured, downy in the throat. Stamens ten, their white stalks with a tuft of down towards the base; anthers brown, well exposed. Ovary scaly; style slender, glabrous, 1 in. long. *Bot. Mag.*, t. 9561. (*s*. Lapponicum)

R. *cuneatum* was found by Forrest in 1910 in the Lichiang range, N.W. Yunnan, growing on the margins of pine forests at 12,000 ft. His later collections are all from the drier parts of N.W. Yunnan and S.W. Szechwan, where it is apparently always found on limestone. It is at present placed in the Lapponicum series, with which it disagrees in its habit, large leaves, and in the shape of the corolla, which is funnel-shaped and zygomorphic, whereas in the Lapponicum series it is near to rotate in shape, i.e., has a tubular base abruptly widening into the limb. It is a hardy, quite pretty species, flowering in April.

R. CYANOCARPUM (Franch.) W. W. Sm.

R. *thomsonii* var. *cyanocarpum* Franch.; R. *hedythamnum* var. *eglandulosum* Balf. f. & Forr.

An evergreen shrub 5 to 12 ft high, with glaucous green young shoots. Leaves oval to roundish, the base sometimes heart-shaped, $2\frac{1}{2}$ to 4 in. long, $1\frac{3}{4}$ to 3 in. wide; blue-green, ultimately dark green above, glaucous beneath, glabrous or nearly so; stalk stout, $\frac{1}{2}$ to $1\frac{1}{8}$ in. long. Flowers in trusses of as many as ten, fragrant. Calyx cup-shaped, up to $\frac{1}{2}$ in. long, with five broad lobes, glabrous, glaucous. Corolla between funnel-shaped and bell-shaped, about 2 in. long, varying from white or creamy white tinged with rose to rich rose, five-lobed, the lobes 1 in. wide and notched in the middle; stamens ten, their stalks smooth, anthers brown; ovary and style glabrous, eglandular (but ovary glandular in var. ERIPHYLLUM Tagg). *Bot. Mag.*, n.s., t. 155. (*s.* and *ss.* Thomsonii)

Native of W. Yunnan, China, at 10,000 to 12,000 ft altitude; originally discovered by the Abbé Delavay, who only saw the plant in its seed-bearing state. It remained a rather mysterious plant until Forrest, in 1906, collected it in flower on the Tali range, to which it seems to be confined. It was then seen, as Franchet had duly noted, to be closely related to the Himalayan R. *thomsonii*, but to differ in the colour of the flowers (those of R. *thomsonii* are blood-red) and in their being fragrant, also in the larger, more oval, and more conspicuously veined leaves. Both have a large, cup-shaped, characteristic calyx and the bluish or bluish-purple seed-vessel to which the specific name refers. The species is in cultivation in southern and western gardens, where it flowers in March and April.

R. DAURICUM L.

A deciduous or semi-evergreen shrub up to 6 ft in height; young shoots scaly and downy. Leaves oval, rounded at the apex, tapering or rounded at the base, $\frac{1}{2}$ to $1\frac{1}{2}$ in. long, $\frac{1}{4}$ to $\frac{5}{8}$ in. wide, dark glossy green and slightly scaly above, paler and scaly beneath. Flowers bright rosy purple, 1 to $1\frac{1}{2}$ in. across, produced during January and February singly from each one of a cluster of scaly buds at the end of the previous summer's growth, where there are usually but one or two flowers open at a time. Corolla flat, saucer-shaped; calyx-lobes five, short. *Bot. Mag.*, t. 636 (*s.* Dauricum)

Native of Russia from E. Siberia to the Pacific, and of N.E. Mongolia, N.E. China, Korea, and Japan; grown in English gardens since 1780. It is one of the earliest of rhododendrons to flower, showing its blossoms usually in January, sometimes even when snow is on the ground, but later in some seasons. For this reason, although its beauties are of a modest kind, it is well worth growing in a small group, preferably in some spot sufficiently sheltered to mitigate to some extent the harshness of wind and weather at the inclement season when its blossoms appear.

cv. 'MIDWINTER'.—A selection with Phlox Purple flowers. Award of Merit March 19, 1963; First Class Certificate February 4, 1969, on both occasions when exhibited by the Crown Estate Commissioners, Windsor Great Park.

var SEMPERVIRENS Sims R. *dauricum* var. *atrovirens* Hort.; R. *ledebourii* Poyark.—Leaves very dark green, persisting through the winter and still clothing the plant at flowering-time, which, in the plant figured in *Bot. Mag.*, t. 8930, is March or April. It has recently been given specific status as R. *ledebourii*, on the grounds that it occupies a distinct area in the Altai and E. Siberia, where it does not overlap with typical R. *dauricum* (*Fl. S.S.S.R.*, Vol. 18 (1952), pp. 54, 722). It was in cultivation by 1817, in which year it was figured in *Bot. Mag.*, t. 1888. There was a reintroduction in 1967, when M. Robert de Belder sent some plants to Britain raised from seeds received from Russia under the name R. *ledebourii*.

R. DAVIDII Franch.

An evergreen shrub 4 to 12 ft high, leaves and young shoots glabrous, the latter yellowish. Leaves oval-oblong, broadly wedge-shaped at the base, terminated by a short, abrupt tip; 3 to 6 in. long, ¾ to 2 in. broad; pale green, netveined beneath; stalk ½ to ¾ in. long. Flowers produced ten or more together in a raceme up to 6 in. long; corolla widely bell-shaped, 1¾ to 2 in. across, sevenlobed, lilac-purple spotted with a deeper shade on the upper side; calyx, flowerstalk, style and ovary glandular; stamens fourteen, not downy. (*s.* Fortunei *ss.* Davidii)

R. *davidii* is named after the French missionary David, who discovered it near Mupin in W. Szechwan in 1869. Wilson found it again in 1904, when collecting for Messrs Veitch, and sent home seeds, but the true species is very rare in cultivation. The plants originally distributed as R. *davidii* in this country are R. *oreodoxa*. It is related to that species and to R. *fargesii*, but differs from both in the much longer leaves and in the remarkably elongated inflorescence-rachis.

R. DAVIDSONIANUM Rehd. & Wils.

R. *charianthum* Hutch.

An evergreen shrub up to 10 ft high; young shoots at first purplish red, scaly. Leaves narrowly oblong-lanceolate, 1 to 2½ in. long, ⅓ to ⅞ in. wide, dark glossy green and slightly scaly above, dull brown and densely scaly beneath. Flowers opening in April in clusters of two to five at the end of the shoot and in the terminal leaf-axils, each on a scaly stalk ⅓ to ½ in. long. Corolla about 1¼ in. long, 1¾ in. wide, pale rose with a few red dots on the upper side. Stamens ten, paler than the corolla, downy at the base. Ovary covered with minute scales; style glabrous. *Bot. Mag.*, tt. 8605, 8665, 8759.   (s. Triflorum ss. Yunnanense)

Native of W. Szechwan and N.W. Yunnan; discovered and introduced by Wilson in 1904, but described from a specimen he collected four years later during his first expedition for the Arnold Arboretum, during which he again sent seeds. It grows up to 10,000 ft altitude and according to Wilson is very common near Kangting (Tatsien-lu), in sunny exposed places, where it flowers with great freedom. Seen at its best R. *davidsonianum* is a very pretty shrub, its flowers delicate in hue and abundant, varying in shade and spotting. A fine pink-flowered form grown at Bodnant received a First Class Certificate on May 3, 1955, when shown by Lord Aberconway and the National Trust. It had received an Award of Merit twenty years earlier.

R. DECORUM Franch.

R. *spooneri* Hemsl. & Wils.; R. *franchetianum* Lévl.; R. *giraudiesii* Lévl.; R. *hexandrum* Hand.-Mazz.

An evergreen shrub variable in habit, some forms being dense and bushy, others erect and attaining a height of 25 ft in cultivation; young stems glabrous. Leaves leathery, oblong to oblong-elliptic or broadest slightly above or below the middle, 2 to 6 in. long, 1⅛ to 2⅞ in. wide, obtuse to rounded at the apex, cuneate-rounded at the base, medium green and glabrous above, glaucous green beneath and glabrous there except for minute down not visible to the naked eye; petiole ¾ to 1⅛ in. long, glabrous. Flowers fragrant, usually eight to ten in a terminal cluster on a more or less glandular rachis 1 in. or slightly more long; pedicels glandular, up to 1⅝ in. long. Calyx very small, six- or seven-lobed, glandular. Corolla widely funnel-campanulate, 2 to 3 in. across at the mouth, white or rose-coloured, hairy inside at the base, six- to eight-lobed, the lobes rounded. Stamens twelve to eighteen, the filaments downy at the base. Ovary densely glandular; style covered throughout with white or yellowish glands. *Bot. Mag.*, t. 8659.   (s. and ss. Fortunei)

R. *decorum* is one of the most widely spread of Chinese rhododendrons. It was introduced by Wilson in 1901 from near Kangting (Tatsien-lu) in W. Szechwan; he later sent seeds from Mupin in the same province, where the Abbé David discovered the species in 1869. Later sendings by Forrest, Kingdon Ward, and Rock, are from various parts of Yunnan, where R. *decorum* seems to be very common in the less rainy parts, often growing on sunny, brackeny slopes or in open woodland of *Pinus armandii*. In Burma it seems to be uncommon, though

Farrer and Cox sent seeds of a large-leaved tender form from the borders between it and Yunnan. According to Kingdon Ward, the flowers of R. *decorum* were eaten in Tali, and called the 'white-flowered vegetable'.

R. *decorum* varies in hardiness, as might be expected from its wide range. The largest-flowered forms are tender, while some of the hardier forms are worthless, with papery, crumpled flowers. It also varies in habit, flowering-time, and the colour of the flowers.

R. DEGRONIANUM Carr.*

R. *metternichii*, nom. illegit., f. *pentamerum* Maxim.; R. *japonicum* (Bl.) Schneid. var. *pentamerum* Hutch.

An evergreen shrub of variable habit in the wild, usually not more than 6 ft high in this country, and of compact habit; young branches thinly white-tomentose at first, becoming glabrous. Leaves elliptic, oblong-elliptic, or lanceolate-elliptic, obtuse or bluntly acute at the apex, sometimes bluntly and broadly cuspidate, base cuneate, commonly 3 to 5 in. long and $\frac{7}{8}$ to $1\frac{3}{4}$ in. wide, sometimes up to 7 in. long and 2 in. wide, dark green or olive-green and glabrous above when mature, covered beneath with a suede-like tomentum which is whitish at first, becoming fawn to rusty or brownish at length; petioles stout, $\frac{1}{2}$ to $\frac{3}{4}$ in. long. Inflorescence terminal, with up to fifteen flowers (more in some cultivated plants); pedicels more or less tomentose, up to 1 in. or slightly more long. Calyx reduced to a mere rim, or very short and bluntly lobed. Corolla between funnel-shaped and campanulate, $1\frac{1}{2}$ to 2 in. wide, usually either five-lobed (in typical R. *degronianum*) or seven-lobed (in var. *heptamerum*), but sometimes six- or eight-lobed, pale rose-pink or sometimes white, unmarked or with reddish spots. Stamens ten (fourteen in var. *heptamerum*), filaments white, anthers yellow. Ovary densely rusty tomentose; style white, just overtopping the stamens.

* This species was first described in 1784 by Thunberg, who confused it with R. *maximum* L. and treated it under that name. This misidentification was noted by Blume but, being acquainted only with the form with seven-lobed corollas, hitherto unknown in *Rhododendron*, he considered that the species represented a new genus, and called it *Hymenanthes japonica* (1826). Nine years later Siebold and Zuccarini restored the species to *Rhododendron*, naming it R. *metternichii*, but they cited the earlier name *Hymenanthes japonica* Bl. as a synonym, thus rendering their own epithet illegitimate. The name for the species in *Rhododendron* should take Blume's earlier epithet, and the combination was in fact made by Schneider in 1909. It could be argued that it was made too late, for a Japanese azalea of the Luteum subseries had been named *Azalea japonica* by Asa Gray in 1859, and this name was transferred to *Rhododendron* by Suringar in 1908, i.e., one year before the publication of the combination R. *japonicum* (Bl.) Schneid. However, the name R. *japonicum* (A. Gr.) Suringar was expressly stated by Suringar to be provisional, and it therefore remained without standing until Rehder and Wilson took it up in their *Monograph of Azaleas* (1921). The correct name for the species generally known as R. *metternichii* is therefore R. *japonicum* (Bl.) Schneid. But the name R. *japonicum* (A. Gr.) Suringar has been so widely used for the azalea since 1921 that to restore the name R. *japonicum* to its proper use now would only invite confusion. It therefore seems best to take up the earliest name for the species after R. *metternichii*, and that is R. *degronianum* Carr. The two names bear a slightly different meaning, since the former is based on the heptamerous form, the latter on the pentamerous.

Fruits cylindric to ovoid, up to 1 in. long, dark brown, with remains of the tomentum persisting. *Bot. Mag.*, t. 8403 (the typical five-lobed form). (*s.* Ponticum *ss.* Caucasicum)

Native of central and southern Japan at altitudes of up to 6,000 ft. The typical, five-lobed variety was in cultivation in Britain by 1894; Nicholson gives 1870 for the introduction of "*R. metternichii*", i.e., the seven-lobed variety, but Fortune may have sent it from Japan in 1862 to Standish's nursery. *R. degronianum* is a perfectly hardy species, but not much grown in this country. It is a variable species, not only in the number of lobes and other parts of the flower, but also in colour, in the form of the truss, in density of indumentum and in habit. In the 1930s K. Wada distributed 'Wada's Form', described in his catalogue as having a dense, cinnamon-brown, woolly tomentum, as in *R. mallotum*; and 'Metternianum', said to be a dwarf grower with five- or six-lobed flowers. Dwarf, compact forms are found on some of the islands off the inner coast of the main island of Japan. Of these Wada listed 'Sadoense', from Sado Island (38° N.); a form from Oki Island, farther to the south-west, is now available in commerce.

The variations of this species in the wild have been studied by Frank Doleshy, who has published interesting reports in the *Quarterly Bulletin of the American Rhododendron Society* (Vol. 22 (1968), pp. 145–59; Vol. 24 (1970), pp. 68–79; Vol. 26 (1972), pp. 193–5).

f. ANGUSTIFOLIUM (Makino) Sealy, *comb. nov.* R. *metternichii* f. *angustifolium* Makino; R. *stenophyllum* Makino, not Hook. f.; R. *metternichii* var. *angustifolium* Bean; R. *makinoi* Tagg—Leaves strikingly narrow and sometimes sickle-shaped, up to 6 in. or slightly more long, but not more than ¾ in. wide; the midrib is often deeply impressed above, and the margins are usually revolute. The taxonomic status of this variant is controversial. It is said to be confined to a restricted area in central Japan and is usually regarded as a distinct species— R. *makinoi*. Its specific status was upheld by the Edinburgh botanist H. F. Tagg, who pointed out that plants at Edinburgh differed from *R. degronianum* not only in the narrowness of the leaves, but also in flowering later, and not making their new growth until September. But Nitzelius, in the paper already referred to, points out that some cultivated plants agreeing with R. *makinoi* make their growth at the normal season, while some plants of R. *degronianum* flush late. Also that a plant agreeing with R. *makinoi* was raised in the Göteborg Botanic Garden from seeds collected on Mt Hito, Kyushu, far to the south of the area to which R. *makinoi* is supposed to be confined.

var. HEPTAMERUM (Maxim.) Sealy, *comb. nov.* R. *metternichii* Sieb. & Zucc., *nom. illegit.*; *Hymenanthes japonica* Bl.; R. *metternichii* var. *heptamerum* Maxim.; R. *hymenanthes* Makino var. *heptamerum* (Maxim.) Makino; R. *japonicum* (Bl.) Schneid. (1912), not (A. Gr.) Suringar (1908)—Corolla seven-lobed; stamens fourteen; ovary seven- or eight-chambered. From the limited number of specimens available for study, it is impossible to decide whether the heptamerous flower of this variety is correlated with other characters. But T. Nitzelius, who examined a wide range of material and carried out field-studies in Japan, concluded that there was no other difference between the five-lobed and seven-lobed plants, and refused to recognise them as even varietally distinct, pointing out that several Chinese species vary in the number of corolla-lobes (*Act. Hort.*

Gotoburg., Vol. 24 (1961), pp. 159–67). It certainly seems doubtful whether the species can be usefully categorised into five- or seven-lobed varieties, since some plants are intermediate in this respect, and eight-lobed forms are known.

R. YAKUSHIMANUM Nakai R. *metternichii* var. *yakushimanum* (Nakai) Ohwi— Yakushima, where this rhododendron occurs, is a small island lying at the southern end of the Japanese archipelago, some 90 miles south of Kagoshima in Kyushu. The island, best known as the home of the conifer *Cryptomeria japonica*, has several peaks rising above the tree-line, the highest of which is Mt Miyanoura, some 6,500 ft above sea-level. On these mountains the R. *degronianum* complex occurs in several forms. Some are tall-growing (up to 25 ft high) and grow in the forests; at the other extreme are forms from exposed places, which are dense, low-growing or even prostrate, with narrow, strongly revolute leaves. Owing to the inadequacy of Nakai's original account of R. *yakushimanum* (1921), and the lack of a type specimen, it is impossible to know for certain what he regarded as the typical state of his species, nor the location of the plants on which his description is based. But from his diagnosis, and from a later account (in Nakai and Koidzumi, *Trees and Shrubs Indigenous in Japan*, rev. ed. (1927)), typical R. *yakushimanum* has short leaves (up to 2¾ in. long according to the original diagnosis), with revolute margins, and differs from R. *degronianum*, which too has dwarf forms, in being more densely hairy in all its parts. This is not much on which to found a species, but it is convenient to retain R. *yakushimanum* as such, at least in garden nomenclature.   PLATE 95

The following articles contain interesting information on R. *yakushimanum* in the wild: *R.C.Y.B. 1961*, pp. 52–8, by A. F. Serbin on plants growing on Mt Hanano-Ego, reprinted from *Qtly Bull. Amer. Rhod. Soc.*, where there is a later article by the same author in Vol. 19 (1965), pp. 75–82, and another by Frank Doleshy in Vol. 20 (1966), pp. 79–85; *Gard. Chron.*, Vol. 156 (1964), pp. 112, 115, by K. Wada; *Intern. Dendrol. Soc. Yr Bk 1972*, pp. 28–9, by R. de Belder, with a striking photograph of R. *yakushimanum* on Mt Miyanoura. For the taxonomy of this species see: J. M. Cowan, *Journ. R.H.S.*, Vol. 72 (1947), pp. 391–3, and T. Nitzelius, *Act. Hor:. Gotoburg.*, Vol. 24 (1961), pp. 158–9, 162, 166–7.

R. *yakushimanum* owes its fame in Britain to two plants received by Lionel de Rothschild at Exbury from K. Wada's Hakoneya Nurseries, Numazushi, Japan, in 1934 (1936?). One of these, moved to the Royal Horticultural Society Garden at Wisley, was exhibited at the Chelsea Show in 1947 and received a First Class Certificate. Ever since, the Wisley clone—now named 'KOICHIRO WADA'—has been one of the most admired of rhododendrons. It is of very dense habit, with dark green doubly convex leaves about 3 in. long, thickly tomentose beneath (the indumentum at first white, becoming brown) and felted with white above when young; flowers twelve in a dense truss; corolla campanulate, about 2¼ in. wide, of an exquisite apple-blossom pink in bud, ageing to pure white with faint speckling. In 1947 the original plant was 2½ ft high and 3½ ft across; its present dimensions (1975) are 4 ft 8 in. by 7 ft. The Exbury clone is very similar to 'Koichiro Wada' and scarcely less beautiful. It is a trifle more erect-growing, with rather smaller leaves, and there is less spotting in the flower. Both are perfectly hardy, flower towards the end of May, and will stand full sun. Other plants are in cultivation which were imported as seedlings collected in the wild.

During the past twenty years, R. *yakushimanum* (in particular the clone 'Koichiro Wada') has been more used in hybridising than any other species, except R. *griersonianum*. See further on p. 826.

R. DESQUAMATUM Balf. f. & Forr.

R. *catapastum* Balf. f. & Forr.; R. *stenoplastum* Balf. f. & Forr.; R. *squarrosum* Balf. f.

An evergreen shrub or small tree up to 25 ft high; young branchlets scaly, not hairy. Leaves 3¼ to 4 in. long, 1 to 1¾ in. wide, elliptic, oblong-elliptic, or occasionally lanceolate or oblanceolate, acuminate at the apex, cuneate to rounded at the base, upper surface dull green and varying from densely scaly (type of R. *catapastum*) to not scaly (type of R. *desquamatum*), underside densely scaly, the scales unequal in size and the larger ones darker than the others; petioles about ½ in. long, scaly. Inflorescence terminal, with four to eight flowers on pedicels ½ to ¾ in. long, scaly. Calyx rim-like, scaly. Corolla funnel-shaped, very often widely so or almost flat, up to about 1½ in. long and 2 in. wide, scaly on the outside, varying in colour from mauve or pinkish mauve to purple, spotted with crimson. Ovary densely scaly; style glabrous. Flowering-time March or April. *Bot. Mag.*, t. 9497. (*s.* Heliolepis)

Native of N.W. Yunnan and of bordering parts of Szechwan, Tibet, and Burma. Although found earlier by one of the French missionaries, R. *desquamatum* was described from a specimen collected by Forrest on the Shweli-Salween divide, near the border between Yunnan and Burma in 1917. The flowers were described as 'saturated purple' and the leaves as being devoid of scales on the upper surface (whence the specific epithet). The type of R. *catapastum* was a fruiting specimen collected by Forrest in the mountains north of Yungpeh, east of the Yangtse; in this the leaves are scaly above and the flowers (which Forrest saw on a later visit) rose or purplish rose. It is now included in R. *desquamatum*, though Hutchinson provisionally kept the two separate in his article accompanying the plate in the *Botanical Magazine*.

R. *desquamatum* is closely allied to R. *rubiginosum*, but the leaves and flowers are larger and, more significantly, the scales on the leaf underside are unequal in size and colour. The purple-flowered forms of this species are very fine. They were mainly raised from seeds collected on the Salween–Nmai Hka divide, not far north of the type locality, e.g., Farrer 875 and Forrest 26482 and 26488. But there is some variation even in plants from a single seed-collection. Sprays from five plants of F.24535, exhibited by Capt. Talbot Fletcher on April 5, 1938, had flowers ranging from clear pale mauve to reddish mauve. The species received an Award of Merit on the basis of this exhibit.

R. DETONSUM Balf. f. & Forr.

An evergreen shrub up to 12 ft high; branchlets stout, at first floccose and glandular, soon glabrous. Leaves oblong or oblong-elliptic, acuminate at the apex, rounded at the base, 3 to 5 in. long, 1½ to 1¾ in. wide, glabrous above, covered beneath with a thin brown indumentum which gradually falls away, leaving the underside almost glabrous by late summer; petiole ⅝ to 1½ in. long, glabrous. Flowers about ten together in a lax truss, opening in May; pedicels up to 2 in. or slightly more long, glandular and floccose. Calyx about ¼ in. long, with five oblong or roundish lobes. Corolla funnel-campanulate, pink with carmine speckling in the throat, five- to seven-lobed, about 3 in. wide. Stamens ten to fourteen, filaments downy in the lower third of their length. Ovary cone-shaped, glandular; style glandular except near the tip. *Bot. Mag.*, t. 9359.   (*s.* Taliense *ss.* Adenogynum)

R. *detonsum* was discovered by Forrest in N.W. Yunnan in 1917 on the eastern flank of the Sungkwei range, just west of the Yangtse, and was probably introduced by him from the same area in the same year. It first flowered at Edinburgh in 1917. At its best, as figured in the *Botanical Magazine*, this is one of the finest species for flower in the Taliense series. The truss figured there is from the Edinburgh plant.

R. DIAPREPES Balf. f. & W. W. Sm.
R. *rasile* Balf. f. & W. W. Sm.

An evergreen shrub 10 to 25 ft high; young shoots and leaves quite glabrous. Leaves elliptic-oblong, rounded or rather heart-shaped at the base, bluntish at the apex, as much as 12 in. long by 4 in. wide, usually smaller, lightish green above, rather glaucous beneath; stalk 1 to 1¾ in. long. Flowers rather fragrant, opening in late June or July in trusses of seven to ten. Corolla seven-lobed, 4 to 5 in. across, funnel-shaped at the base, white or faintly rose-tinted, greenish and downy inside the tube at the base. Stamens eighteen or twenty, downy at the base; ovary and style glandular from top to bottom. *Bot. Mag.*, t. 9524   (*s.* and *ss.* Fortunei)

R. *diaprepes* was found by Forrest in 1913 on the Shweli–Salween divide, Yunnan, near the border with Burma, at 9,000 ft. It was introduced by him from the same area in the same year (F.11958). Both in leaf and flower this is the finest of the Fortunei subseries, the latter exceeding even the flower of R. *discolor* in size. It scarcely differs from R. *decorum* in essential botanical detail, but grows in a warmer and moister region, and is better suited for the maritime parts of the south and west of Britain. But it seems to be little cultivated at the present time and is best known as a parent of the hybrid Polar Bear, which flowers at the same time and is much hardier. It received an Award of Merit when shown by Lionel de Rothschild from Exbury on June 29, 1926.

cv. 'GARGANTUA'.—A triploid plant with larger flowers and leaves than normal, raised from F.11958. Award of Merit June 23, 1953.

R. DICHROANTHUM Diels

An evergreen shrub 2 to 5 ft high, of stiff close growth; young shoots at first white with a close down, grey the second season. Leaves obovate to oblanceolate, tapered abruptly at the apex to a short mucro, always more or less wedge-shaped at the base, 2 to 4 in. long, ¾ to 1½ in. wide, dark green and glabrous above, covered beneath with a glaucous white, thin, scurfy down; stalk ¼ to ½ in. long. Flowers opening in May, six to eight in a terminal truss; flower-stalk ½ to 1 in. long, white with down. Calyx very variable in the size and shape of the lobes; ⅙ to 1 in. long and awl-shaped to roundish ovate, approximating the corolla in colour. Corolla fleshy, elongated-bell-shaped, 1¾ in. long, scarcely so wide; the colour is variable in different plants and may be of various shades of

RHODODENDRON DICHROANTHUM

orange, often more or less suffused with pink. Stamens ten, scarcely as long as the corolla, slightly downy at the base. Ovary clothed with white down and fascicled hairs; style glabrous. *Bot. Mag.*, t. 8815. (*s.* Neriiflorum *ss.* Sanguineum)

Native of the Tali range, Yunnan, China; discovered by Forrest in 1906 and introduced to cultivation by him. His F.11597, with deep orange flowers, is perhaps the most desirable form, but others are very attractive. Forrest describes some shades as 'creamy rose' or 'yellowish rose'. In its best forms this is one of the most attractive members of the series and quite hardy.

subsp. APODECTUM (Balf. f. & W. W. Sm.) Cowan R. *apodectum* Balf. f. & W. W. Sm.; R. *jangtzowense* Balf. f. & Forr.; R. *liratum* Balf. f. & Forr.—Distinguished from typical R. *dichroanthum* by its very leathery, round-based leaves. It appears to be confined to the Shweli–Salween divide, and was introduced by Forrest in 1913. *Bot. Mag.*, t. 9014.

subsp. HERPESTICUM (Balf. f. & Ward) Cowan R. *herpesticum* Balf. f. & Ward—This is easily distinguished from typical R. *dichroanthum* and subsp. *apodectum* by the flower-stalks, calyces, and ovaries being furnished with glands. Also the leaves are more like those of R. *sanguineum* in size and shape, being oblanceolate or oblong-elliptic, up to 3 in. long and 1½ in wide. The shoots are sometimes bristly. This subspecies was discovered by Kingdon Ward in July 1914 in upper Burma, on the northern slope of Imaw Bum, a mountain just over 13,000 ft high on the divide between the Salween and the upper

Irrawaddy (Nmai Hka), forming tanglements about 1 ft high. It is fairly widely distributed in the borderland between Yunnan and Burma, and was sent many times by Forrest, who introduced it.

subsp. SCYPHOCALYX (Balf. f. & Forr.) Cowan R. *scyphocalyx* Balf. f. & Forr.—This does not really differ from the subsp. *herpesticum* in any character of genuine taxonomic importance, but typically it is four or five times as tall and the leaves are larger and thinner. But intermediate forms occur. It was discovered by Forrest in 1919 about twenty miles to the west of the type-locality of subsp. *herpesticum* and has the same distribution. He sent seeds many times from 1919 onward and it is also in cultivation from Farrer 1024, this too collected in 1919. The flowering-time of both subspecies is mostly May. The colour range of wild plants is extraordinarily wide—rose-orange, yellowish crimson, coppery yellow, fiery bronze, flame, orange, cinnabar-scarlet, very dark yellowish crimson, etc. Unfortunately, cultivated plants often bear flowers the colour of marmalade or mustard-pickle.

subsp. SEPTENTRIONALE Cowan R. *scyphocalyx* var. *septentrionale* Tagg MS—Leaves as in subsp. *herpesticum*, but ovary without glands. Flowers yellow or yellow flushed rose. Introduced by Forrest. He found it originally about 50 miles to the north of the type-locality of subsp. *scyphocalyx*, whence the epithet *septentrionale*.

R. DIPHROCALYX Balf. f.
R. *burriflorum* Balf. f. & Forr.

An evergreen shrub 5 to 15 ft high; young shoots and leaf-stalks clothed with a mixture of glandular bristles and short down. Leaves 2½ to 6 in. long, 1 to 2¼ in. wide, elliptical to oblong, bright green above, pale and rather glaucous beneath, nearly or quite glabrous at maturity except on the midrib; stalk ½ to ¾ in. long. Flowers opening in April and said to have as many as twenty flowers in a truss. Calyx very large, ½ to ¾ in. long, unequally five-lobed, rather bell-shaped, bright red, but conspicuously spotted on one side. Corolla bell-shaped, 1¼ in. long, bright red to light rosy crimson with a crimson blotch at the base and crimson spots. Stamens ten, slightly downy at the base; ovary covered with tawny down as is also the base of the style. (s. Barbatum ss. Glischrum)

Native of W. Yunnan, China. It first appeared as a 'rogue' amongst R. *habrotrichum* in E. J. P. Magor's garden at Lamellen in Cornwall, where it flowered in 1918. Sir Isaac Balfour appears first to have regarded it as a hybrid. Tagg, however, united with it the R. *burriflorum* described as a species by Balfour from a specimen collected by Forrest in W. Yunnan in 1918. It is remarkable for the size and colouring of its corolla-like calyx. A handsome rhododendron scarcely hardy enough to succeed at Kew.

R. DISCOLOR Franch.
R. *mandarinorum* Diels; R. *kirkii* Hort.

A shrub 10 to 18 ft high, of robust habit, free from down in all its parts; young shoots stout, yellowish. Leaves oblong or narrowly oval, 3 to 8 in.

long, $\frac{3}{4}$ to $2\frac{1}{2}$ in. wide, tapered about equally at both ends, sometimes heart-shaped at the base, the apex with a short mucro, upper surface deep green, lower one pale, stalks $\frac{1}{2}$ to $1\frac{1}{4}$ in. long, stout, purple. Flowers white or faintly blush-tinted. Calyx small, glandular on the margins at first. Corolla funnel-shaped, $2\frac{1}{2}$ to 3 in. long and wide, six- or seven-lobed. Stamens twelve to sixteen, not downy, shorter than the corolla; ovary and style glandular. *Bot. Mag.*, t. 8696. (s. and ss. Fortunei)

Native of Central China (E. Szechwan, Hupeh, Hunan, and Kweichow); discovered by the French missionary Farges between 1891 and 1894; introduced by Wilson in 1900, when collecting for Messrs Veitch, and again in greater quantity in 1907, during his first expedition for the Arnold Arboretum. According to him it is a common species in the woodlands of Hupeh and E. Szechwan between 4,500 and 7,000 ft. It flowered in Veitch's Coombe Wood nursery in 1911.

R. *discolor* is a fine species and perfectly hardy. It does not flower until late June or early July and starts into growth late. For this reason it is less satisfactory in northern gardens, where the young wood may not ripen before winter sets in. Even in the south it should be given a moderately sunny position, but sheltered from wind. It was awarded a First Class Certificate when Kew exhibited it on June 27, 1922. A fortnight later a pale pink form, shown from Bodnant, received an Award of Merit.

Because of its late flowering and hardiness, R. *discolor* has been much used in hybridising. The Angelo, Argosy, Albatross, Antonio, Lady Bessborough and Azor grexes all have R. *discolor* as one parent.

R. DRYOPHYLLUM Balf. f. & Forr.

R. *helvolum* Balf. f. & Forr.; R. *intortum* Balf. f. & Forr.; R. *levistratum* Balf. f. & Forr.; R. *sigillatum* Balf. f. & Forr.; R. *theiophyllum* Balf. f. & Forr.; R. *vicinum* Balf. f. & Forr.

An evergreen shrub 4 to 12 ft high, or occasionally a small tree up to 25 ft high; branchlets clad with a brown to fawn-coloured or whitish tomentum. Leaves mostly oblong-elliptic or oblong-lanceolate, 2 to $3\frac{1}{2}$ in. long, $1\frac{1}{2}$ to 2 in. wide, acute to acuminate at the apex, loosely tomentose above at first, becoming more or less glabrous, underside coated with a thin brown suede-like indumentum made up of long-rayed hairs; petiole about $\frac{1}{2}$ in. long. Flowers up to about sixteen in an umbellate cluster, opening in April or May. Calyx minute. Corolla between funnel-shaped and campanulate, about $1\frac{3}{4}$ in. wide, white to pink or creamy white, spotted or unmarked. Ovary narrow-cylindric, usually glabrous or nearly so; style glabrous or slightly downy at the base. (s. Lacteum)

R. *dryophyllum* occurs, often at high altitudes, from S.W. Szechwan (Muli area) across N.W. Yunnan to the Tibetan Himalaya, where it has been collected not far from the eastern frontier of Bhutan; it has also been found in the Seinghku valley, N.W. upper Burma. It was introduced by Forrest.

R. DUMULOSUM Balf. f. & Forr.—Differing from R. *dryophyllum* only in its constantly dwarf habit and smaller leaves.

R. PHAEOCHRYSUM Balf. f. & W. W. Sm.—Similar to R. *dryophyllum* and with more or less the same distribution, but with the ovary always completely glabrous and the indumentum of the leaves beneath tending to be agglutinate, i.e., with the hairs more or less glued together by a resinous secretion. Wing-Cdr F. L. Ingall of Corsock, Stranraer, won the McClaren Cup for a truss from his fine form of R. *phaeochrysum* when he exhibited it at the Rhododendron Show in 1964 (*R.C.Y.B. 1965*, fig. 10). R. AGGLUTINATUM Balf. f. & Forr. is in turn closely allied to R. *phaeochrysum* and linked to it by intermediates, but typically has smaller leaves and flowers (Cowan and Davidian, *R.C.Y.B. 1956*, pp. 146–7).

R. EDGEWORTHII Hook. f.   [PLATE 75

R. *bullatum* Franch.; R. *sciaphilum* Balf. f. & Ward

An evergreen shrub of thin loose habit up to 8 ft high; young shoots $\frac{3}{16}$ in. thick, clad with a thick, tawny felt. Leaves thick and leathery, narrowly oval-ovate, rounded or broadly tapered at the base, pointed, $1\frac{1}{2}$ to $5\frac{1}{2}$ in. long, $\frac{3}{4}$ to 2 in. wide, glossy green and without down at maturity above but with a network of deeply sunken veins giving it a puckered (bullate) surface; lower surface thickly covered with tawny felt; stalk up to 1 in. long. Flowers produced during May in terminal clusters usually of two to four, but occasionally five or even six, richly fragrant; flower-stalk $\frac{1}{2}$ to $\frac{3}{4}$ in. long, shaggy. Calyx deeply five-lobed, the lobes rounded, $\frac{1}{2}$ in. long, usually scaly outside, shaggy on the margins and often on the surface also. Corolla fleshy, scaly outside, waxy-white with a yellow stain inside and tinged with pink outside; shallowly trumpet-shaped, five-lobed, $2\frac{1}{2}$ to $4\frac{1}{2}$ in. wide, the lobes $1\frac{1}{2}$ to 2 in. wide. Stamens ten, shorter than the corolla, shaggy with down at the base. Ovary very woolly; style scaly and slightly downy towards the base, rarely without scales. *Bot. Mag.*, t. 4936 (*s.* Edgeworthii)

R. *edgeworthii* is a species of wide range from E. Nepal to Yunnan and S.W. Szechwan. It was discovered by J. D. Hooker in Sikkim and described by him in 1851. 'The majority of my specimens were obtained from land-shoots, or -slips, in the rocky ravines, which bring down in their course those Pines on the limbs of which this species delights to dwell.' Hooker also introduced it. R. *bullatum*, now included in R. *edgeworthii*, was described from specimens collected by the French missionary Delavay in 1886. Forrest later found it on the eastern, drier, flank of the range growing on humus-covered ledges and along the base of cliffs at an altitude of 8,000 to 10,000 ft or even higher and published an account, illustrated by his own photographs, in the *Gardeners' Chronicle* for 1909 (Vol. 46, p. 378, fig. 166 and Supplementary Plate). He first sent seeds in 1910 and subsequently there were many further sendings by him and other collectors from various parts of the range of the species and from an 8,000 to 13,000 ft span of altitude. Where there is forest, and where the climate is very humid, R. *edgeworthii* is usually epiphytic; but in drier parts, or in scrub, it is ground-dwelling.

The old Himalayan form of R. *edgeworthii*, although tender, has been grown outdoors in the milder parts for over a century. The plants once known as R. *bullatum* are variable in hardiness. Tender forms are Farrer 842 from above Hpimaw on the Salween–Irrawaddy divide; and Forrest 26618 from the same area, both from epiphytic plants. The Award of Merit plant of 1923 was from the former number and the F.C.C. plant of 1937 from the latter (in both instances as shrubs for the cool greenhouse). The hardiest form is considered to be Dr Joseph Rock's 59202, with pink-tinged flowers, found as a low shrub 2 to 3 ft high among rocks on Mt Shenzi, at 13,000 ft; this form was introduced in 1923 and first exhibited by Lord Stair at the Rhododendron Show in 1930. Forrest's 21564 from the Chienchuan–Mekong divide has also proved to be moderately hardy. Both these forms are from near the eastern end of the range of R. *edgeworthii*. There is also a fine hardy form of the species at Bodnant, Denbighshire, known as the Kingdon Ward Pink Form. This received an Award of Merit on May 5, 1946.

R. SEINGHKUENSE Ward—This uncommon and tender species, at present placed in the Edgeworthii series, was discovered by Kingdon Ward in the Seinghku valley, north-west Burma, in 1926. The leaves are not unlike those of R. *edgeworthii* but in other respects it is very distinct, the corolla being sulphur-yellow, rotate-campanulate, with a short, bent style. The seed sent by Kingdon Ward under his no. 6793 was mixed with that of R. *edgeworthii*, which occurs in the same valley, and the true species is rare in cultivation. It has also been found in the neighbouring Adung valley, and in Yunnan. It received an Award of Merit when shown by the Crown Estate Commissioners in 1953.

R. ELLIOTTII W. W. Sm.

A small evergreen tree, much branched; young shoots furnished with short, branched hairs. Leaves narrowly oval-oblong, pointed, broad cuneate at the base 4 to 6 in. long, two-fifths as wide, dull green above, shining beneath, stalk about 1 in. long, downy when quite young. Flowers in a terminal truss of about twelve, 5 in. across, opening in late May and June. Corolla rich scarlet, funnel-shaped below, spreading at the top into five rounded, notched lobes which give it a diameter of 2½ in., freely crimson spotted; stamens ten, red, glabrous. Ovary stellate-tomentose; style clad with stellate hairs and stalked glands. *Bot. Mag.*, t. 9546. (*s* Irroratum *ss.* Parishii)

R. *elliottii* was discovered by Sir George Watt in 1882, on Mt Japvo in the Naga Hills, Assam, at 9,000 ft, where it grows with R. *macabeanum* and R. *manipurense*. It was first fully described from his specimens in 1914, by Sir William Wright-Smith, but Brandis had given a short description earlier. It was not introduced to gardens until 1927, when Kingdon Ward collected seed on Mt Japvo (KW 7725), and received an Award of Merit when two plants raised from this seed were exhibited at Chelsea on May 30, 1934, by J. J. Crosfield of Embley Park, Hants. It received a First Class Certificate three years later.

Two years after it had made its appearance at Chelsea, Lionel de Rothschild wrote: 'When we come to R. *elliottii* . . . we have one of the finest scarlet rhododendrons that has ever been sent back. Flowering as it does in June . . . it will undoubtedly leave its stamp on many of the hybrids of the future.' He himself began to use R. *elliottii* as a parent at about this time, the result being such well-known hybrids as Fusilier, Grenadier, Kiev, and Golden Horn. The hybrids 'Billy Budd', 'Beefeater', and 'Royal Blood', raised in the R.H.S. Garden, Wisley, by Francis Hanger, also have R. *elliottii* as one parent.

R. *elliottii* is not really satisfactory in the open except in the mildest parts, since it starts into growth so late that the young shoots are often cut by autumn frost before they are properly ripened. It is very closely allied to R. *facetum* (q.v. under R. *eriogynum*), differing in having the leaves abruptly narrowed at the base (tapered in R. *facetum*).

R. ERIOGYNUM Balf. f. & W. W. Sm.

An evergreen shrub up to 10 ft high; young shoots soon glabrous. Leaves oblong-elliptic or oblanceolate, the apex pointed or rounded; 4 to 8 in. long, 1¼ to 3 in. wide, ultimately glabrous on both surfaces, glittering beneath; with a thin transparent marginal line; stalk ½ to 1¼ in. long. Flowers in a truss of twelve to sixteen, opening in June. Calyx ⅕ in. long, fleshy, reddish, the lobes wavy. Corolla bell-shaped, 1¾ in. deep, 2 in. wide, clear bright red with five deep purple pouches at the base, five-lobed. Stamens ten, 1 in. or more long, downy at the lower third or half. Ovary densely covered with tawny, starry down, which extends more thinly up the style. *Bot. Mag.*, t. 9337.   (*s.* Irroratum *ss.* Parishii)

R. *eriogynum* was discovered by Forrest in the Tali range, Yunnan, in 1914, and was introduced by him in the same year. All the cultivated plants derive from this one sending (F.13508). This beautiful species has flowered in gardens south of London and has attained 15 ft at Wakehurst Place in Sussex. Like its allies (see R. *elliottii* and R. *kyawii*) it flowers and comes into growth late in the season and is the parent of many late-flowering hybrids, such as Romany Chal and the incomparable Tally Ho.

Award of Merit June 24, 1924, when shown by T. H. Lowinsky of Sunninghill, Berks.

R. FACETUM Balf. f. & Ward—This species is very closely akin to, and probably not specifically distinct from, R. *eriogynum*. Kingdon Ward discovered it below the Feng-shui-ling pass, on the border between Burma and Yunnan, in June 1914 (Kingdon Ward, *In Farthest Burma*, p. 60). Farrer and Cox found it five years later from Hpimaw Hill, a little to the north of the Feng-shui-ling pass, growing 20 to 30 ft high in deep woodland at 8,500 to 9,000 ft, with flowers 'of so dazzling a pure light rose-scarlet as to numb one's sight for some minutes after looking away from it' (Cox, *Farrer's Last Journey*, p. 226). They collected seeds in the autumn, but in the previous May Forrest or one of his Chinese collectors found a plant in fruit even nearer to the type-locality, so he was the first to introduce it.

R. *facetum* comes from a moister region than R. *eriogynum* and its leaves are somewhat thinner in texture. It is also more tender. The main and secondary flower-stalks are more or less glandular; they are not so in R. *eriogynum*. R. *facetum* received an Award of Merit on July 5, 1938, when shown by Admiral Heneage-Vivian, Clyne Castle, Swansea.

R. EROSUM Cowan

An evergreen shrub or small tree, up to 30 ft high; branchlets slender, clad with stalked glands; bud-scales deciduous. Leaves leathery, oval, oblong-oval, obovate, obtuse to broadly rounded at the apex, rounded to subcordate at the base, up to 6½ in. long and 3¾ in. wide, clad beneath with a woolly greyish or light brown indumentum which gradually wears away; petiole glandular-bristly, up to ¾ in. long. Inflorescence a terminal umbel of twelve to fifteen flowers, opening in March or April; pedicels about ⅜ in. long, glandular. Calyx cup-shaped, pink, with short, irregular, gland-fringed lobes. Corolla five-lobed, funnel-campanulate, deep crimson or deep rosy pink, about 1½ in. wide. Ovary densely covered with stalked glands; style glabrous. (*s.* Barbatum *ss.* Glischrum)

A native of the eastern Himalaya, found by Ludlow and Sherriff in 1936 on the Tibetan side of the range (Chayul and Tsari) at 10,000 to 12,000 ft, and introduced by them. Although not so fine in flower as R. *barbatum*, which it somewhat resembles, it has striking foliage.

R. EXASPERATUM Tagg—This species resembles R. *erosum* in its broad leaves, rounded at the apex, but their undersurface is glandular bristly (not woolly, later glabrous, as in R. *erosum*), and the foliage bud-scales are persistent. R. *exasperatum* was introduced by Kingdon Ward in 1926 from the Seinghku valley in north-west Burma, where it grows at 10,000 ft 'only in the tanglewood on precipitous broken rock faces, where water drips continuously and everything is moss bound'. From there it ranges west through the Delei valley to the eastern end of the Himalaya, where it was found on several occasions by Ludlow and Sherriff and their companions. It is rather more tender than R. *erosum* and less attractive in its flowers (which, at least in the Kingdon Ward forms, are brick-red with an orange flush). The young growths are richly tinted.

R. EUDOXUM Balf. f. & Forr.

An evergreen shrub up to 6 ft high in the wild. Leaves thinly leathery, oblong-elliptic to oblong-obovate, rounded at the apex, up to 2⅞ in. long and 1 in. wide, glabrous above when mature, underside clad with a 'very thin discontinuous mealy indumentum composed of branched or star-like hairs . . . scattered over the undersurface of the leaf. At the same time the undersurface of the leaf is very minutely papillate and has a greenish brown appearance' (Cowan, *Notes R.B.G. Edin.*, Vol. 20, p. 77). Inflorescence a terminal umbel of three to six flowers, opening in April or May (later in some forms). Calyx fleshy at the base, up to ¼ in. deep. Corolla tubular-campanulate, 1½ in. long, crimson or pink. Stamens downy at the base. Ovary tomentose and glandular; style glabrous. (*s.* Neriiflorum *ss.* Sanguineum)

R. *eudoxum* is a native of N.W. Yunnan and bordering parts of Tibet (Tsarong) on the Mekong–Salween and Salween–Irrawaddy divides and was introduced by Forrest. It received an Award of Merit when shown by E. H. M. and P. A. Cox on April 26, 1960 (a form with flowers of the shade of pink known as Solferino Purple, with a deeper crimson tinge at the base).

subsp. BRUNNEIFOLIUM (Balf. f. & Forr.) Cowan R. *brunneifolium* Balf. f. & Forr.—Differing from the typical state mainly in having the ovary eglandular.

R. FULVASTRUM Balf. f. & Forr.—Leaves with a thin indumentum beneath (not continuous and plastered as in R. *sanguineum*), but differing from R. *eudoxum* in that the indumentum is cobwebby, not mealy as in that species, and is made up of scattered, long-branched hairs (Cowan). Ovary tomentose, eglandular. Flowers typically pale yellow, but rose, pink, or yellowish red in subsp. MESO-POLIUM (Balf. f. & Forr.) Cowan.

R. FALCONERI Hook. f.

R. *venosum* Nutt.

A large shrub or a small tree, ultimately over 30 ft high, with stiff, very thick, somewhat sparse branches, woolly when young. Leaves oval or oblong, 6 to 12 in. long, 2½ to 6 in. wide (sometimes larger), very stout, thick, and strongly veined, the upper surface dark green, curiously wrinkled, but otherwise smooth; the lower surface covered with a dense, rust-coloured felt; stalk 1 to 2 in. long. Flowers about 2 in. across, creamy white or pale yellow, sometimes shaded with lilac, and marked with a conspicuous dark purple blotch at the base, fragrant, produced in spring in large terminal clusters 6 to 9 in. across; the twenty or more flowers tightly packed. Corolla bell-shaped, 2 in. long, its lobes varying in number from eight to ten; calyx scarcely observable; stamens twelve to sixteen, shorter than the corolla; style about as long as the corolla, stout, and surmounted by the large knob-like stigma; flower-stalk downy, 1 in. long. *Bot. Mag.*, t. 4924. (*s.* Falconeri)

Native of the Himalaya from Nepal to Bhutan. It was described by J. D. Hooker in 1849, and it was he who introduced it effectively, though at the time that he sent seeds (1850) it was already in cultivation in a few gardens, raised from seeds sent by Col. Sykes in 1830.

R. *falconeri* is one of the noblest of the genus. A moisture-loving species, it thrives best in the western and northern parts of the British Isles, where all the finest specimens are to be found. But it is really quite hardy and grows well near London in high-lying places with a rainfall of 30 in. or over. At Glenarn, Rhu, Dunbartonshire, there is a remarkable specimen probably raised from the seeds sent by Hooker. It is about 30 ft high and girthed 6¼ ft at ground-level in 1950 (*R.Y.B. 1950*, fig. 46; *R.C.Y.B. 1964*, fig. 1; *New Fl. & Sylv.*, Vol. 6 (1933), fig. xvi).

Other notable specimens are: Stonefield, Argyll, from the Hooker introduction, 28 ft high and as much in spread, trunk almost 4 ft in girth at 1 ft (*R.C.Y.B. 1956*, p. 18 and fig. 9); Muncaster Castle, Cumberland, *pl.* 1920 when 10 ft high, *c.* 35 ft high and as much wide (*R.C.Y.B. 1953*, p. 61); Minterne, Dorset, *pl.* 1893, over 30 ft high (ibid., p. 10 and fig. 1); Trengwainton, Cornwall, *pl.* 1897, 35 ft high, 50 ft across, on several trunks (*R.C.Y.B. 1953*, p. 61).

R. EXIMIUM Nutt. R. *falconeri* var. *eximium* (Nutt.) Hook. f.—Allied to R. *falconeri*, differing in the brown, mealy tomentum that covers the upper surface of the leaves during their first season or even for longer, and in the rose-coloured or pinkish flowers. It was introduced by Thomas Booth by means of seeds which he collected on an outer range of the Assam Himalaya, N.W. of Tezpur, on December 17, 1849. *Bot. Mag.*, t. 7317.

A plant at Stonefield, Argyll, believed to be from the original introduction, was 16 ft high and 33 ft in breadth in 1955 (*R.C.Y.B. 1956*, p. 18).

R. FARGESII Franch.

An evergreen shrub 10 ft high, of bushy habit; leaves oblong-ovate, rounded at the apex, slightly cordate at the base, 2 to 3½ in. long, 1½ to 2½ in. wide, dull grey-green above, pale and rather glaucous beneath, glabrous at maturity on both surfaces; stalk 1 to 1¼ in. long. Flowers in a terminal truss of six to eight. Calyx shallowly seven-lobed, glandular-downy like the flower-stalk. Corolla widely funnel-shaped, seven-lobed, 2 in. deep, 2½ in. wide, pale rose or purplish pink, often with deeper spots on the upper side. Stamens twelve or fourteen, glabrous, about half as long as the corolla, white with brown anthers. Style longer than stamens, glabrous; ovary glandular. *Bot. Mag.*, t. 8736. (*s.* Fortunei *ss.* Oreodoxa)

Native of W. Hupeh and E. Szechwan at 6,500 to 9,500 ft in mixed woods or with conifers and birches, or forming thickets on exposed slopes and mountain tops; discovered by the French missionary Farges between 1891 and 1894 and introduced by Wilson in 1901 from W. Hupeh. According to him, it is extremely floriferous in the wild, sometimes flowering so abundantly that the bushes exhaust themselves and die. This is also true of the cultivated plants. It is very closely allied to R. *oreodoxa* (q.v.) and has the same value in gardens; it differs in its glandular ovary and relatively broader leaves.

Award of Merit March 9, 1926, when exhibited by Gerald Loder, Wakehurst Place, Sussex (flowers pale rosy pink, spotted); also to clone 'Budget Farthing', April 15, 1969, shown by Lord Aberconway and the National Trust, Bodnant, Denbigh.

R. ERUBESCENS Hutch.—Near to R. *fargesii*, differing in the larger leaves with the midrib and lateral veins impressed above, and in the hairy filaments of the stamens. Described from a plant raised from seeds collected by Wilson in China. Uncommon in cultivation. *Bot. Mag.*, t. 8643.

R. FARRERAE Tate

Azalea farrerae (Tate) K. Koch; *A. squamata* Lindl.

A low, deciduous or semi-evergreen azalea; young shoots furnished with brown, appressed, bristly hairs; grey and glabrous the second year. Leaves usually two to four at the end of the twigs, ovate to oval or rarely obovate, pointed, ¾ to 1½ in. long, ¼ to 1 in. wide, bristly on the midrib beneath when young and on the margins, otherwise glabrous; distinctly net-veined beneath; stalk ¼ in. or less long, hairy like the young shoots. Flowers solitary or twin, opening in spring. Calyx small, covered like the very short flower-stalk with brown down. Corolla 1½ to 2 in. wide, rose-coloured, of varying depth of shade with purple spots on the upper lobes; the tube short, funnel-shaped, spreading into five oblong, round-ended lobes. Stamens eight or ten, ½ to ¾ in. long, glabrous. Ovary covered with erect brown bristles; style well protruded, glabrous. (*s.* Azalea *ss.* Schlippenbachii)

Native of Hong Kong and the adjacent mainland of China; introduced by Captain Farrer of the East India Company in 1829. It was again introduced to the Horticultural Society's garden at Chiswick by Fortune and flowered there about 1846. It is very rare in cultivation now. It is found in the same region as R. *championiae* and is only likely to succeed in the very mildest parts of Britain in the open air. It is most nearly related to R. *mariesii* which has a leaf-stalk up to ½ in. long; both these belong to the same group of azaleas as R. *schlippenbachii* and R. *reticulatum*.

R. MARIESII Hemsl. & Wils.—Allied to R. *farrerae*, differing in the larger leaves, 1½ to 3 in. long, about half as wide, on almost glabrous stalks up to ½ in. long (hence about twice as long as in R. *farrerae*). The flowers, borne in April on the bare wood, are pink or rose, spotted with reddish purple on the upper lobes. Native of eastern and central China, and of Formosa, at altitudes of up to 4,000 ft. It was introduced to Kew in 1886 by Augustine Henry and reintroduced by Wilson in 1900, in both cases from the neighbourhood of Ichang in W. Hupeh.

is uncommon in cultivation and not entirely hardy. *Bot. Mag.*, t. 8206.

R. FASTIGIATUM Franch.

R. *impeditum* Hort., in part, not Balf. f.

A moderately compact shrub up to 3 ft high. Leaves oblong-elliptic to oblong-lanceolate, about ⅜ in. long in the type, but up to ⅝ in. long in some cultivated plants, margins often recurved, upper surface glaucous green, sea-green or deep steely blue, conspicuously dotted with scales, undersides papillose and whitish between the scales, which are opaque, uniform, spaced less than their own diameter apart, sometimes contiguous or even overlapping; petiole very short. Inflorescence terminal, composed of three to five very short-stalked flowers, produced in April or May. Calyx well developed, about as long as the corolla-tube, deeply lobed, scaly outside and fringed with weak hairs. Corolla ¾ to 1 in. wide, in some shade of purple or blue-purple, widely funnel-shaped to almost rotate, with a short tube, hairy inside at the base. Filaments of stamens hairy. Style equalling the stamens or longer, glabrous.   (*s.* Lapponicum)

Native of Yunnan, China; discovered by Père Delavay in the Tali range and described in 1885; introduced by Forrest from the same area in 1906. According to him, it occurs there on cliff-ledges in pine forests on the eastern (drier) side of the range and is the dominant species on the Sungkwei pass some 50 miles north of Tali. It is variable in the colour of its flowers and also in the degree of glaucousness of its foliage, though the leaves are always glaucous when young. In some plants (usually grown as R. *impeditum*), the leaves remain sea-green or dark blue-green throughout the winter, and are then more decorative than most members of the series. The habit is also variable, some forms being dwarf and slow growing, others more robust and open. The specific epithet refers to the straightness and dense arrangement of the branchlets on the type-specimen, not to the habit of the plant as a whole.

R. *fastigiatum* received an Award of Merit when shown by Messrs Reuthe in 1914.

R. IMPEDITUM Balf. f. R. *fastigiatum* of the 1st edition of this work, not Franch.; R. *semanteum* Balf. f., *nom. inedit.*—This species was discovered by Forrest on the eastern and western flanks of the Lichiang range, Yunnan, in 1910, and was introduced by him in that year. It was at first considered to be R. *fastigiatum*, and went into cultivation under that name, but was described as a new species in 1916. Balfour wrote: 'Like that plant [R. *fastigiatum*] in its cushion habit its foliage is very different, and one can distinguish the two plants at a glance. R*h. fastigiatum* has a grey hoary appearance, R*h. impeditum* dark green. Both the plants have discontiguous under-leaf scales, but whilst in R*h. fastigiatum* the bare intervals of epidermis are greyish, often tinted slightly red, in R*h. impeditum* the epidermis is mat green.' This difference in leaf-colouring is especially noticeable in the young growths, and there is the further difference that in R. *fastigiatum* the scales on the blade beneath, seen under low magnification, are opaque, waxy and very solid in appearance, whilst those of R. *impeditum* are light brown and lustrous. But on year-old leaves of R. *fastigiatum* a few of the scales have lost their wax, and even on younger leaves the scales on the midrib beneath are like those of R. *impeditum*. Other distinctions are that the flowers are usually not more than three per truss and are mauve rather than purple. But the key-character relied on by Balfour—outside of corolla scaly in R. *fastigiatum*, not so in R. *impeditum*—does not hold good. There is no constant difference in size or shape of leaf.

R. *impeditum* is not common in commerce, but is available from specialist nurseries (this, of course, applies to the true species, not to R. *fastigiatum* masquerading as R. *impeditum*). It received an Award of Merit in 1944 when shown by the Sunningdale Nurseries, who raised it from Rock 59263, collected in the type-area. Earlier, the same award had been given to a plant from seed of F.20492, collected in the Muli area of S.W. Szechwan and distributed under the unpublished name R. *semanteum*. No example of this form has been seen, but the name R. *semanteum* is given as a synonym of R. *impeditum* by Hutchinson in *Species of Rhododendron*.

R. LITANGENSE Balf. f. ex Hutch.—This is near to R. *impeditum*, but cultivated plants under the name differ from the dwarf compact form of R. *impeditum* in their more erect habit and their darker leaves and flowers.

R. FERRUGINEUM L.

A dwarf, slow-growing evergreen shrub of close habit, ultimately 3 or 4 ft high and wide, forming a dense hemispherical mass; young shoots covered with rust-coloured scales. Leaves narrow-oblong or oval, tapering at both ends, 1 to $1\frac{3}{4}$ in. long, $\frac{1}{4}$ to $\frac{1}{2}$ in. wide; dark glossy green and slightly scaly above, but thickly covered beneath with golden-brown, ultimately rust-coloured scales. Flowers rosy scarlet or deep rose, $\frac{1}{2}$ to $\frac{3}{4}$ in. wide and long, produced in June in terminal clusters of six to twelve blossoms; corolla scaly outside, funnel-shaped at the base, with five spreading, oblong lobes; calyx-lobes very short; stamens ten, hairy at the base; flower-stalk $\frac{1}{3}$ in. long, scaly.

Native mainly of the European Alps and Pyrenees, but also found in the Jura and the mountains of W. Yugoslavia; farther to the south and east it is replaced by R. *kotschyi*. It avoids limestone, though it may occasionally be found on heavily leached limestone soils or where there is an accumulation of peat over the bedrock. It was in cultivation in Britain in 1740.

Visitors to the Alps well know this shrub as the 'Alpine rose', often covering miles of mountainside and making one of the most gorgeous of Alpine pictures in July. It finds the conditions of the Thames Valley too hot and dry for it, but in the cooler midland and northern counties is a charming bush of neat, healthy aspect, flowering freely every summer. It has produced several varieties, some, no doubt, of garden origin, which vary chiefly in the colour of the blossom, but even in a wild state one may notice in a day's walk many variations of colour between rosy pink and rosy scarlet, and on rare occasions a white-flowered plant.

f. ALBUM (D. Don) Zab. R. *ferrugineum* var. *album* D. Don—Flowers white. It is rare in the wild, and protected in most alpine countries. Award of Merit June 10, 1969.

f. ATROCOCCINEUM (Bean) Rehd. R. *ferrugineum* var. *atrococcineum* Bean— This is the form whose flowers most nearly approach scarlet.

cv. 'VARIEGATUM'.—Leaves with a thin border of creamy white; of no value.

R. FERRUGINEUM × R. HIRSUTUM.—Hybrids between these two species are quite common in the wild and back-cross with the parents, giving rise in places to a series of forms uniting the two. It is said that in some localities these intermediates are more common than either parent, and may even occur where one or the other is absent (Hegi, *Fl. Mitteleuropa*, Vol. V.3, p. 1644). The correct name for this group of hybrids would appear to be R. × HALENSE Gremblich, the type of which is near to R. *ferrugineum*, but with some hairs at the margin and with calyx-lobes very short. Gremblich also gave the name R. × *hirsutiforme* to forms near to R. *hirsutum*. The R. × *intermedium* of Tausch was defined as being half-way between the two species, but this name is illegitimate.

R. KOTSCHYI Simonkai R. *myrtifolium* Schott & Kotschy, not Lodd.; R. *ferrugineum* var. *myrtifolium* (Schott & Kotschy) Schroeter; R. *ferrugineum* subsp. *myrtifolium* (Schott & Kotschy) Hayek—This has the general aspect of R. *ferrugineum*, but is usually smaller in habit; its leaves average under 1 in. long, the corolla is downy outside, and it is especially distinguished by the much shorter style. In the typical form the flowers are of the same colour as in R. *ferrugineum*, but there is also one with white flowers. Native of the Carpathians and of the mountains of Bulgaria and Yugoslav Macedonia. *Bot. Mag.*, t. 9132.

R. FICTOLACTEUM Balf. f.

R. *lacteum* var. *macrophyllum* Franch.; R. *lacteum* sens. *Bot. Mag.*, t. 8372, not Franch.

An evergreen tree said to be as much as 45 ft high; young shoots clothed with brownish down. Leaves varying from narrowly elliptical to oblanceolate and from tapered to slightly heart-shaped at the base, the apex rounded and mucronate, 5 to 12 in. long, 2 to 4½ in. wide; dark green and glabrous above, covered beneath with a dense brown felt; stalk ¾ to 1½ in. long. Flowers opening in April or early May in a truss of twelve to fifteen, on stalks 1 to 1½ in. long. Calyx inconspicuous. Corolla bell-shaped, 1¾ to 2½ in. wide, white, creamy white, or rose-tinted, with a dark crimson blotch at the base, seven or eight-lobed. Stamens fourteen or sixteen, unequal in length but all shorter than the corolla, downy at the base; anthers red-brown. Ovary felted; style glabrous. *Bot. Mag.*, t. 8372. (*s.* Falconeri)

R. *fictolacteum* is widespread in Yunnan and S.W. Szechwan, occurring in areas drier, or at least much less rainy, than is usual for members of its series; it is also found in S.E. Tibet. It was discovered by the French missionary Delavay in Yunnan, north of Tali; he sent seeds to Paris, whence seedlings were sent to Kew in 1889. It was first flowered in Britain in 1910, by F. D. Godman of South Lodge, Sussex. A truss from this plant was figured in the *Botanical Magazine* (t. 8372) under the name R. *lacteum* Franch., with which it had been wrongly identified by Hemsley. Sir Isaac Bayley-Balfour established that it was in fact a species entirely distinct from R. *lacteum* and named it R. *fictolacteum* (*Gard. Chron.*, Vol. 59 (1916), p. 168).

R. *fictolacteum* was reintroduced by Forrest in 1910 from the Sungkwei pass and later from other parts of Yunnan, and is also in cultivation from seeds collected by Dr Rock. It is a very hardy species, occurring in the wild at altitudes mostly between 12,000 and 13,000 ft, and at its best it is very fine, though in recent years it has been overshadowed by its relative R. *rex* (see below). It received an Award of Merit when shown by Messrs Reuthe in 1923. The same award was given in 1953, on April 14, to a form raised by Lord Digby from Rock 59255. In this plant, named 'Cherry Tip', the flowers are white, flushed pink, bright cherry pink in bud. The seeds were collected by Rock in the Lichiang range.

A fine form was found by Forrest in 1922 on the Chienchuan–Mekong divide, with white flowers flushed with pink, in a large truss (F.22020).

R. REX Lévl.—Allied to R. *fictolacteum*, but differing in the longer, relatively broader leaves and the greyish or buff indumentum of the leaf-undersides and the much stouter branchlets. It was described by Léveillé in 1914 from specimens collected by Maire in N.E. Yunnan, and appears to be confined to the borders between Yunnan and S.W. Szechwan. Kingdon Ward's 4509, now usually referred to R. *rex*, was found in a shady limestone gorge in the Muli region in 1921. 'It grows 40 ft high, bearing leaves 18 inches in length and 6 inches wide, dark green above, and covered below with a thick flocculent chocolate coloured felt. It flowers in April, the corolla being milk-white, with a few purple specks peppered over the upper part, coalescing to form a deep blotch at the base' (Kingdon Ward, *Romance of Plant Hunting*, p. 176). Plants raised from the seed of KW 4509 have proved to be of varying worth, but the best are very fine. Also referred to R. *rex* are plants raised from Dr Rock's 03800. The following have received awards: KW 4509 from Embley Park, F.C.C. May 21, 1935; KW 4509 from Bodnant, A.M. April 16, 1946; Rock 03800, clone 'Quartz', from the Crown Estate Commissioners, Windsor Great Park, A.M. May 3, 1955 (*R.C.Y.B. 1956*, fig. 25).

R. FLAMMEUM (Michx.) Sarg.

Azalea calendulacea var. *flammea* Michx.; R. *speciosum* (Willd.) Sweet, not Salisb.; *Azalea nudiflora* var. *coccinea* Ait.

A deciduous azalea up to 6 ft high; young shoots finely downy and bristly. Leaves obovate, oval, or oblong, 1½ to 2½ in. long, half as much wide; upper surface bristly, lower one finely downy with bristles on the midrib; margins bristly; stalk $\frac{1}{6}$ in. long. Flowers opening in April and May, up to as many as fifteen in a truss. Corolla funnel-shaped, about 1¾ in. long, the tube slender, cylindric, and downy outside; scarlet or bright red with an orange-coloured blotch on the upper lobe. Stamens five, 2 in. long, downy below the middle. Ovary clothed with bristly, not glandular hairs; style 2 in. or more long, downy at the base. Calyx with five very small, ciliate, ovate, or oblong lobes. Flower-stalks bristly. (*s.* Azalea *ss.* Luteum)

Native of the S.E. United States from Georgia to S. Carolina. This, the most brilliantly coloured of all American azaleas, was in cultivation as long ago as 1789, and was figured in the *Botanical Magazine* in 1792 (t. 180). Old plants may still be in gardens, but the name appears to have been lost. It was in cultivation at Kew in 1881 as '*Azalea nudiflora coccinea*'. Plants were sent to England by Professor Sargent in 1916. It has been confused with R. *calendulaceum*, but differs in the slender corolla-tube which is not glandular as it is in that species. The flowers also are more numerous in the truss, and the colour 'is always scarlet or bright red and never varies to yellow' (Rehder). R. *calendulaceum* is a more northern shrub and hardier, but, as may be gathered from what is stated above, R. *flammeum* is quite hardy in this country. No doubt many of our richest-coloured deciduous azaleas owe much of their vivid red and scarlet hues to this species.

R. FLAVIDUM Franch.

R. *primulinum* Hemsl.; R. *psilostylum* Balf. f.

An evergreen shrub about 2 ft high, of rounded, bushy habit, branches densely scaly. Leaves leathery, ovate-oblong, ½ to 1 in. long, ¼ to ⅜ in. wide; rounded at the base, dark green above, paler beneath, scaly on both surfaces; stalk $\frac{1}{6}$ in. long. Flowers 1 to 1¼ in. across, primrose-yellow, becoming paler with age, produced during April in a terminal cluster of three to six. Corolla with a very short, rather downy tube, and flat, spreading, rounded lobes, wavy at the margins. Calyx pale green, the five lobes oblong, ¼ in. long, covered like the flower-stalk (which is ⅛ in. long) with transparent yellowish scales. *Bot. Mag.*, t. 8326. (*s.* Lapponicum)

Native of W. Szechwan, China; introduced to cultivation by Wilson for Messrs Veitch in 1905. This delightful little species is very distinct through the clear pale yellow of its flowers, and is a valuable acquisition for the rock garden or some place where dainty little plants can grow without danger of being overrun by stronger neighbours. The leaves when crushed have a pleasant, aromatic odour.

The plant known in gardens as R. *flavidum album* is very distinct in its taller growth, larger leaves and larger, white flowers. Probably a hybrid. In cultivation by 1925.

R. FLOCCIGERUM Franch.

An evergreen shrub 3 to 6 ft high; young shoots clothed at first with brownish-red wool. Leaves narrowly oblong-lanceolate, sharply pointed, tapered at the base, 2 to 4½ in. long, ⅓ to 1 in. wide; dull green and glabrous above, covered with loose brownish-red wool beneath; stalk ¼ to ½ in. long. Flowers opening during March and April in trusses of four to eight; stalks ⅜ to ½ in. long, loosely downy. Calyx shallowly five-lobed. Corolla bell-shaped, 1¼ in. long and wide, five-lobed; in colour it is very variable, ranging from blood-red to yellow tinged with rose. Stamens ten, about 1 in. long quite glabrous; anthers black-purple. Ovary clothed with whitish felt; style about as long as the stamens, downy only near the ovary (if at all). *Bot. Mag.*, t. 9290.   (*s.* and *ss.* Neriiflorum)

R. *floccigerum* was discovered by the French missionary Soulié on the Mekong–Salween divide near Tseku. Forrest, who sent home seeds for the first time in 1914, found it in various parts of N.W. Yunnan, from the Chungtien plateau to the Salween–Irrawaddy divide and south to the mountains between the Chien-chuan river and the Mekong. It is a hardy but early-flowering species of comparatively dwarf habit, with flowers which, in the best forms, are quite as fine a red as in R. *neriiflorum*. But the colour in this species varies a good deal and a plant at Kew bears flowers of rich salmon red. Some of an indeterminate mixture of rose and yellow shades are very poor and dull. One of the best is depicted in the *Botanical Magazine* (loc. cit. supra). The species is hardy enough for Kew. The narrow leaves, covered thickly beneath with loose rufous floss, constitute one of its most distinctive characters in the section to which it has been assigned.

var. APPROPINQUANS Tagg & Forr.—Differing in the more or less glandular branchlets and petioles and in having the mature leaves glabrous beneath except for traces of flock on the midrib. Introduced by Forrest. Award of Merit March 19, 1957, when shown by Lord Digby, Minterne, Dorset (a form with flowers of a pale cream colour, edged with pale cherry-pink).

R. FLORIBUNDUM Franch.

An evergreen shrub up to 5 ft high in the wild; of stiff erect habit when young; branchlets clothed with grey down. Leaves of stiff, hard leathery texture, elliptical-lanceolate, tapered at both ends, margins recurved, 3 to 6 in. long, 1 to 1¾ in. wide, dark dull green, much wrinkled above, clothed beneath with a dull white felt; stalk ½ to ¾ in. long. Flowers in a compact truss of eight to twelve flowers, opening in April. Calyx minutely triangularly lobed and, like the short flower-stalk, felted with white down. Corolla purplish lavender at first, turning paler, with a blackish crimson blotch at the base and spots on the upper side, bell-shaped, five-lobed, 2 to 3 in. wide. Stamens ten, anthers brown, ovary clothed with erect white bristles, style 1½ in. long, glabrous or slightly downy at the base like the stamens. *Bot. Mag.*, t. 9609.   (*s.* Arboreum *ss.* Argyrophyllum)

Native of W. Szechwan; discovered by the French missionary David near Mupin in 1869; introduced by Wilson from the same area in 1903. The flowers vary in colouring, and the better lavender-coloured forms are very pleasing. There is a particularly fine form at Borde Hill in Sussex, with lavender-purple flowers about 3 in. across and a deep maroon blotch at the base of the corolla. The species is moderately hardy at Kew but is seen to better advantage farther south.

The Award of Merit was given on April 30, 1963, to the clone 'Swinhoe', shown from Exbury. Flowers Roseine Purple with a dark crimson blotch; lobes frilled.

R. FORMOSUM Wall.
R. gibsonii Paxt.

An evergreen shrub of rather open thin habit, 8 or 10 ft high; young shoots, leaves, flower-stalks, calyx, and ovary scaly. Leaves oblanceolate to obovate, usually broadest above the middle, tapered at the base, pointed; 1½ to 3 in. long, ½ to 1½ in. wide; glossy green above, glaucous beneath; margins and leaf-stalks usually fringed with long hairs when young. Flowers sweetly scented, produced two to four together in May and June. Calyx very small; flower-stalks up to ½ in. long. Corolla funnel-shaped, 2 to 2½ in. long; white tinged with pink, yellow in the throat, with the five lobes roundish ovate and about 1 in. long. Stamens ten, shorter than the corolla, densely clothed with hairs on the lower half. Ovary six-celled; style well protruded, scaly at the base. *Bot. Mag.*, t. 4457. (s. Maddenii ss. Ciliicalyx)

Native of Assam in the Khasi, Jaintia, and Naga Hills, and of N.W. upper Burma; introduced about 1845 by Gibson (who collected plants for the then Duke of Devonshire) and named after him by Paxton. But it had been discovered in 1815 and previously named by Wallich in 1832. In the south and south-western counties it succeeds well out-of-doors, but in our average climate needs protection in winter. Being easily cultivated and bearing charmingly fragrant flowers, it has long been a favourite. Some beautiful hybrids have been raised from it crossed with R. *edgeworthii*, e.g., 'Fragrantissimum' and 'Sesterianum'. Crossed with R. *nuttallii* it is a parent of 'Tyermanii'.

A beautiful form of R. *formosum*, grown under glass at Edinburgh, received an Award of Merit in 1960. The flowers are flushed with pale orange in the throat and slightly tinged with pink on the outside. There is a similar plant in the Temperate House at Kew.

R. ITEOPHYLLUM Hutch. R. *formosum* var. *salicifolium* C. B. Cl.—This is closely allied to R. *formosum* but very distinct in appearance, owing to its willow-like leaves, which are linear or linear-oblanceolate and 2 to 3⅝ in. long and up to ⅜ in. wide. Usually they are not or only slightly ciliate at the margins. The corolla may be downy on the outside near the base (as in R. *formosum*) or glabrous. *Bot. Mag.*, n.s., t. 563.

This species was discovered by J. D. Hooker and T. Thomson during their visit to the Khasi Hills in 1850, and was introduced by Thomas Lobb, the Veitchian collector. It is cultivated outdoors in the mildest parts of the country.

R. FORRESTII Balf. f. ex Diels

R. *repens* Balf. f. & Forr.; R. *forrestii* var. *repens* (Balf. f. & Forr.) Cowan & Davidian

A slow-growing, creeping, evergreen shrub a few inches high on the level, but capable, according to Forrest, of climbing the faces of moist rocks 3 to 5 ft high, attaching itself, like ivy, by roots from the stems. Leaves broadly obovate to nearly orbicular, rounded at the apex, usually more or less tapered at the base, $\frac{1}{2}$ to $1\frac{1}{2}$ in. long, $\frac{1}{3}$ to $\frac{7}{8}$ in. wide, dark glossy green and with conspicuously grooved veins above, pale beneath or more or less stained with purple; stalk $\frac{1}{8}$ to $\frac{1}{2}$ in. long, reddish, slightly downy and glandular. Flowers usually solitary, but sometimes in pairs or threes borne in April or May; pedicels up to 1 in. long, glandular. Calyx small, shallow, fringed with glands. Corolla narrowly bell-shaped, $1\frac{3}{8}$ in. long and wide, deep crimson, with five rounded deeply notched lobes. Stamens ten, white, glabrous; anthers dark brown. Ovary conical, clad with pale glands; style glabrous, longer than the stamens. *Bot. Mag.*, t. 9186. (*s.* Neriiflorum *ss.* Forrestii)

Native of N.W. Yunnan, upper Burma, and also of S.E. Tibet, where it extends to the region of the Tsangpo bend and some way farther west; the altitudinal range is 10,000 to 14,000 ft. Forrest discovered this species in the mid-summer of 1905 in Yunnan on the Mekong–Salween divide, but a few weeks later he narrowly escaped death at the hands of the rebel lamas and all the material was lost, with the rest of his collections, except for one small fragment sent home earlier, from which Diels described the species in 1912. More material was collected by Forrest in 1914 and 1918 in the same area, but in most of these specimens the undersides of the leaves were green or glaucous-green beneath, whereas in the type they are purple beneath, as they are in seedlings. The green-back forms were given specific status as R. *repens*, and it is by this name that the species was known for many years. But Dr Stapf of Kew considered that the peculiar coloration of the foliage in typical R. *forrestii*, even if fixed and regular, was too slight a distinction, and reduced R. *repens* to a synonym of R. *forrestii*. This judgement was accepted in previous editions, as it is here, but it should be noted that Cowan and Davidian, in the article cited below, prefer to maintain R. *repens* as a variety of R. *forrestii*.

Later collections have shown that R. *forrestii*, in its typical small-leaved, red-flowered, creeping form, is only one constituent of a puzzling complex of plants, all essentially alike but differing in habit, size of leaf, in the colour of the flowers, and the number in each inflorescence. Great variation is found even in a single wild locality—so much so that some batches of wild seed have produced plants of diverse character, some or all of which differ from the corresponding herbarium specimen. Cowan and Davidian, in their taxonomic treatment of R. *forrestii* and its immediate allies, recognise two varieties of R. *forrestii* (one of them var. *repens*), and a second species—R. *chamaethomsonii*—which is, however, linked to R. *forrestii* by intermediates (*R.Y.B. 1951–2*, pp. 66–71). The diagnostic characters and synonyms are as follows:

var. TUMESCENS Cowan & Davidian R. *repens* var. *chamaedoxa*, *nom. inedit.*, in part—Plant dome-shaped in the centre with the outer branches creeping. Leaves somewhat larger than in the type. Described from a cultivated plant raised from KW 5846. This variety is difficult to distinguish from R. *chamae-thomsonii* var. *chamaethauma* (see below).

R. CHAMAETHOMSONII (Tagg & Forr.) Cowan & Davidian R. *repens* var. *chamaethomsonii* Tagg & Forr.—A dwarf but not creeping shrub, up to 3 ft high. Leaves oblong-obovate to obovate, up to 3 in. or even slightly more long, sometimes slightly hairy beneath. Flowers crimson up to four or even five in each truss. Calyx larger than in R. *forrestii*, fleshy. Described from specimens collected by Forrest and Rock in N.W. Yunnan and bordering parts of Tibet.

var. CHAMAETHAUMA (Tagg) Cowan & Davidian R. *repens* var. *chamae-thauma* Tagg; R. *repens* var. *chamaedoron* Tagg & Forr.; R. *repens* var. *chamaedoxa*, *nom. inedit.*, in part—Leaves smaller than in the type of R. *chamaethomsonii*. Described from KW 5847, collected on the Doshong La at the eastern end of the Himalaya; the synonymous name R. *repens* var. *chamaedoron* is founded on specimens collected by Forrest and by Rock in the area where typical R. *chamaethomsonii* was first found, and links this species with R. *forrestii* through the latter's var. *tumescens* (Cowan and Davidian, op. cit., p. 71).

The plants of R. *forrestii* and R. *chamaethomsonii* in the Tower Court collection (most of which are now in the Species Collection in Windsor Great Park) were discussed by Roza Stevenson in R.Y.B. *1951-2*, pp. 60–5. The following survey of the main introductions of R. *forrestii* and R. *chamaethomsonii* is based partly on this and on the note by Cowan and Davidian already referred to, partly on collectors' field notes, the writings of Kingdon Ward, and other sources.

F.13259 (1914)—The original introduction of R. *forrestii* (as R. *repens*). Plants were distributed by J. C. Williams from Caerhays.

F.19515 (1921)—Seed collected on the Londre La, Mekong–Salween divide. Some plants at Edinburgh have the leaves purple beneath as in typical R. *forrestii*, while in others they are green beneath (Cowan and Davidian, op. cit., p. 68).

F.21768 (1922)—From the divide between the Salween and the Kiuchiang (upper Irrawaddy). The herbarium specimen under this number is R. *chamae-thomsonii* var. *chamaethauma*, but some of the plants raised from the seeds agree better with R. *forrestii*.

KW 5845 (1924)—This is Kingdon Ward's "Scarlet Runner", from the Doshong La, at the eastern end of the Himalaya. The wild plants were prostrate, rising no more than 2 in. above the ground, and grew on bare gneissic rocks on the sunny side of the slope; flowers scarlet, solitary. The seed under this number and KW 5846 were distributed as R. *repens* var. *chamaedoxa*, an unpublished name. The plants at Tower Court raised from KW 5845 differed markedly from the wild plants described by Kingdon Ward in being bushy and up to 19 in. high, with carmine flowers borne three or four to each truss, and with large leaves. These plants, and others at Edinburgh from the same batch of seed, are referred by Cowan and Davidian to R. *chamaethomsonii* var. *chamaethauma*. The discrepancy between these cultivated plants and Kingdon Ward's description is so great as to suggest that at least part of the seed under KW 5845 did not come from the true "Scarlet Runner". The plants were buried in snow when he returned to the Doshong La for the seed-harvest and it was only with great difficulty that he managed to get any seed at all (*Gard. Chron.*, Vol. 78 (1925), p. 330).

KW 5846 (1924)—Also from the Doshong La. "Scarlet Pimpernel", as Kingdon Ward dubbed it, grew on sheltered ledges with "Plum Warner" (*R. campylogynum*). 'At first sight it looked like a darker edition of Scarlet Runner, but on closer inspection it was seen to be a bigger plant, with larger leaves and darker flowers, borne two or three in a truss instead of singly.' One plant at Tower Court from this number was identified as *R. chamaethomsonii* var. *chamaethauma*, while a plant at Edinburgh from the same batch is the type of *R. forrestii* var. *tumescens* (see above). A plant from KW 5846 received an Award of Merit when shown from Bodnant in 1932.

KW 5847 (1924)—This is Kingdon Ward's "Carmelita" and the third of the trio from the Doshong La. 'It is bigger again, with still larger leaves, and flowers of luminous carmine, in threes. It grows socially, in foot-deep tangles, and is not really a creeping plant at all. . . .' (*Riddle of Tsangpo Gorges*, p. 102). The specimen under this number is the type of *R. chamaethomsonii* var. *chamaethauma*, but it is not certain whether any plant from the seed of KW 5847 is in cultivation.

KW 6832 (1926)—From the Seinghku valley, in northernmost Burma, near the borders with Assam and Tibet, at 11,000 ft. It grew 'plastered on rocks and steep talus in very exposed situations', and was considered by Kingdon Ward to be the same as his "Scarlet Runner" (see above), but 'not such a brave sight'. Seed was distributed as *R. repens* and a plant raised from it at Tower Court received a First Class Certificate (as *R. repens*) in 1933. This plant has produced large crops of beautifully coloured flowers every year and is depicted in *R.Y.B. 1951–2*, fig. 56. It is, however, not a typical example of *R. repens* (*R. forrestii* as here understood), since, although low growing, it is not creeping, the leaves are larger, and the flowers are up to three in each truss. It is referred by Cowan and Davidian to *R. chamaethomsonii* var. *chamaethauma*.

Rock 59174 (1923)—From Kenichunpu on the divide between the Salween and the upper Irrawaddy (Kiuchiang) at 13,000 ft, making a shrub 1 to 2 ft high. Dr Rock's fruiting specimen was referred to *R. repens* var. *chamaethomsonii* (now treated as a separate species), but the plants raised from seed of Rock 59174 at Tower Court proved to be intermediate between *R. forrestii* var. *tumescens* and *R. chamaethomsonii* var. *chamaethauma*, and one of them received an Award of Merit under the former name in 1957. On the other hand, a plant at Nymans in Sussex, from the same seed-number, is bushy and about 2½ ft high. It is interesting to note that seed collected by Dr Rock in the same area during his expedition for the American Rhododendron Society in 1948 (Rock 92) has produced plants varying from upright to prostrate and differing, too, in size of leaf and in number of flowers per inflorescence(*Qtly Bull. Amer. Rhod. Soc.*, Vol. 11, p. 148).

R. forrestii and *R. chamaethomsonii* are both shy-flowering in some forms, but reliable clones are available in commerce. Both need a cool, moist soil and a position where they are exposed to the open sky but protected from the sun during the hottest part of the day. Their flowering time is April or May.

R. forrestii is the parent of several low-growing, mostly red-flowered hybrids, of which the most famous is the Elizabeth grex.

R. FORTUNEI Lindl.

An evergreen shrub, ultimately 10 to 12 ft high, usually less in this country and of wide-spreading habit; branches stout, soon glabrous. Leaves oblong, with a tapering, rounded, or heart-shaped base, abruptly pointed; 4 to 8 in. long, 2 to 3½ in. wide, quite glabrous on both surfaces, pale green above, slightly glaucous beneath; stalk stout, purplish, ½ to 1 in. long. Flowers fragrant, produced in May, somewhat loosely arranged in terminal clusters of eight to twelve; each blossom is 2½ to 3 in. across, of a lovely blush tint on opening, becoming paler afterwards. Calyx so small as to be scarcely discernible. Corolla seven- (or rarely eight-) lobed, flattish; stamens fourteen to sixteen, much shorter than the corolla, glabrous; ovary and base of style glandular. *Bot. Mag.*, t. 5596.   (*s.* and *ss.* Fortunei)

Native of eastern China; discovered by Fortune in Chekiang province in 1855 and introduced to Glendinning's nursery by means of seeds he collected the same autumn. Plants raised from these seeds were auctioned in 1859 and the species was named in that year by Lindley, but it was first properly described in 1866, in the *Botanical Magazine*, from a flowering specimen received from Mr Luscombe of Coombe Royal, Devon. The plate is a poor one and does not show the glands on the pedicels, style, and outer surface of the corolla characteristic of the species, though they are shown on the type specimen at Kew from which the original painting was made.

R. *fortunei* is a beautiful rhododendron, and is of interest as the first hardy species of 'true' rhododendron (as distinct from azalea) received from China.

Of the first-generation hybrids of R. *fortunei* the best known are those with R. *griffithianum* (the famous Loderi grex), R. *thomsonii* (Luscombei grex), and R. *campylocarpum* (grexes Gladys and Letty Edwards). These and others are described in the section on hybrids. In that section see also 'Lavender Girl' and 'Duke of York'.

R. FRAGARIIFLORUM Ward

A dwarf tufted shrub up to 8 or 9 in. high; branchlets scaly and downy. Leaves aromatic, obovate to elliptic, up to ½ in. long, half as wide, rounded at the apex, dark olive-green and glossy above, scaly on both sides, the scales on the undersurface widely spaced, dark brown or yellow; margins bristly. Inflorescence a terminal cluster of two to six flowers on pedicels about ¼ in. long. Calyx five-lobed to the base, about ⅙ in. deep. Corolla between funnel-shaped and rotate, coloured 'crushed strawberry', five-lobed, between ½ and ¾ in. long, glabrous outside. Stamens ten, exserted. Ovary densely scaly; style longer than the stamens, glabrous.

R. *fragariiflorum* was discovered by Kingdon Ward in 1924 on the Temo La and Nyima La, Tibet, in the mountains immediately to the north of the Tsangpo bend, at 14,000 to 15,000 ft, growing gregariously with other dwarf rhododendrons; it was subsequently found in the main Himalayan chain, where it extends almost as far west as the Bhutan frontier. It is at present placed in the Saluenense series, but, as Kingdon Ward remarked when describing the species, it is really intermediate between this group and the Lapponicum series. Although later reintroduced by Ludlow and Sherriff it seems to be rare in gardens. The specific epithet refers to the colour of the flowers.

R. FULGENS Hook. f.

An evergreen shrub 6 to almost 20 ft high, with stiff branches and peeling bark. Leaves oval, 3 to 4 in. long, 1½ to 2 in. wide; rounded at the end except for a short, abrupt tip, somewhat heart-shaped at the base; covered beneath with a thick reddish-brown felt. Flowers blood-red, 1 to 1¼ in. across, densely packed in hemispherical trusses 3½ in. wide. Calyx very small, shallowly lobed. Corolla bell-shaped, with five shallow, notched lobes; stamens ten, much shorter than the corolla, not downy; ovary glabrous, style crimson. *Bot. Mag.*, t. 5317. (s. Campanulatum)

Native of the Himalaya from Nepal eastward; introduced by J. D. Hooker in 1850. This species is very similar to R. *campanulatum* in foliage, but is not quite so hardy nor so free in growth. Its flowers are rich red and appear during March and April. A suitable spot for it is some sheltered outskirt of woodland, especially where the flowers may be protected from early morning sunlight. At Kew the various titmice are very fond of pecking a hole through the base of the corolla, presumably to get at the honey. An ornamental feature of the plant is the crimson bracts that accompany the young growth in spring.

Award of Merit March 21, 1933, when exhibited by Gerald Loder, Wakehurst Place, Sussex.

R. SUCCOTHII Davidian—A species apparently allied to R. *fulgens*, differing in having the leaves glabrous beneath, very shortly stalked (up to barely ¼ in. long), clustered in whorls on the branchlets. It resembles R. *fulgens* in its flowers and peeling bark. Discovered in 1915 by Roland Cooper in Bhutan, where seeds were collected by Ludlow and Sherriff in 1937 and again in 1949. It was also found by Kingdon Ward in 1938 on the Poshing La, Assam Himalaya. The species is named after Sir George Campbell of Succoth, Bt, and was described in 1965 (*R.C.Y.B. 1966*, p. 103).

R. FULVUM Balf. f. & W. W. Sm.
R. *fulvoides* Balf. f.

An evergreen shrub or small tree 9 to 20 ft high; young shoots covered with a brownish-yellow felt, some of which remains till the following year. Leaves stout and leathery, oblong to oval, abruptly narrowed to a mucro at the apex, tapered to slightly heart-shaped at the base, 4 to 8 in. long, 1½ to 3 in. wide, very dark green and glabrous above, clothed beneath with a richly cinnamon-coloured, red-brown, or fawn-coloured felt; midrib prominent, ultimately naked and pale. Flowers produced in March and April, up to twenty in a globose truss 4 in. wide. Calyx small, glabrous; flower-stalk ½ to ¾ in. long. Corolla white to pale or bright rose with a fine crimson blotch at the base, bell-shaped, 1½ in. long, five- or six-lobed, each lobe ⅗ in. long and nearly 1 in. wide. Stamens ten, very minutely downy at the base; anthers dark brown. Ovary and style glabrous. *Bot. Mag.*, t. 9587.   (*s.* Fulvum)

R. *fulvum* is a species of wide range, from the Muli area of S.W. Szechwan, through N.W. Yunnan, the Yunnan–Burma borderland, and S.E. Tibet as far as the eastern Himalaya, where Ludlow and Sherriff collected it in the Tibetan province of Chayul; it occurs mostly at 10,000 to 12,000 ft. Forrest discovered it in 1912 on the Shweli–Salween divide and sent home seeds many times from that year onwards. It is quite hardy. The flowers, without being more than ordinary, are attractive enough; the most striking character of the plant is the felt-like covering of the undersurface of the leaf. In Forrest's 8989, his original importation, this is a rich brown-red, but it is sometimes pale fawn or bright cinnamon. There is also variation in the upper surface of the leaf. In some forms, e.g., F.25076, it is smooth and the margins are slightly recurved. In others, less striking, the surface is flat and the lateral veins are impressed.

A pink-flowered form received an Award of Merit when shown from Bodnant on April 4, 1933.

R. GALACTINUM Balf. f.

An evergreen tree up to 25 ft high; young shoots grey-downy at first, glabrous later. Leaves 5 to 10 in. long, 2 to 4 in. wide, from oblong-ovate to oblanceolate; soon glabrous above, densely clothed beneath with pale yellowish grey or pale brown velvety down; stalk 1 to 1½ in. long. Flowers about fifteen in a rounded truss opening in April and May. Calyx a mere wavy rim. Corolla seven-lobed, bell-shaped, 1¼ in. long, white tinged with pink outside, with a blotch and spots of crimson inside. Stamens fourteen, white with down at the base; ovary and style glabrous. *Bot. Mag.*, n.s., t. 231.   (*s.* Falconeri)

Native of Szechwan, China; discovered and introduced by Wilson in 1908. The flowers were unknown until plants flowered in this country in 1923, or possibly before. Like most of the rhododendrons of Wilson's introduction, it is quite hardy at Kew and is well worth growing in similarly unfavourable spots.

R. GENESTIERIANUM Forr.

An evergreen shrub described by Forrest as being found by him from 4 to 12 ft high in the wild; young shoots glabrous, glaucous. Leaves aggregated about the end of the twig, of thin texture, lanceolate or oblanceolate, slenderly pointed, wedge-shaped at the base; 2 to 4 (sometimes 6) in. long, ¼ to 1½ in. wide, bright green above, very glaucous beneath, glabrous on both sides except for a few scales beneath; stalk ¼ to ¾ in. long. Flowers in a distinctly racemose cluster of twelve or more, opening in April. Calyx small, shallowly or not at all lobed, glabrous. Corolla narrowly bell-shaped, about ½ in. long, of fleshy texture and plum-purple covered with a bloom, the five lobes erect. Stamens ten, glabrous, both they and the anthers purple-red to bright crimson; ovary purplish, scaly; style glabrous, bent over. *Bot. Mag.*, t. 9310.   (*s.* Glaucophyllum *ss.* Genestierianum)

Native mainly of upper Burma and S.E. Tibet (Tsarong); discovered by Forrest on the Salween–Irrawaddy divide in 1919 and introduced by him. He called it 'altogether a distinct species much to be desired for our gardens'. But Farrer, who saw it near the type-locality in the following year, remarked: 'Most curious and almost ugly, hardly to be known at first glance for a Rhododendron.' Kingdon Ward wrote of it: 'This is a slim shrub ... with willow-like leaves snow-white beneath, as though powdered with talcum. The flowers, borne on long pedicels in loose heads of twenty, thirty or more, are tiny, plum-purple, and in bud look like large black currants. It is not a beautiful plant, having a solemn, rather funereal look; but like so many departures from the normal in this immense genus, is undeniably interesting' (*Return to the Irrawaddy*, p. 161).

Gardeners seem to have agreed with Farrer and Kingdon Ward, for the species is very rare in cultivation. Nor is it altogether hardy.

R. GLAUCOPHYLLUM Rehd. [PLATE 76

R. glaucum Hook. f., not (Lam.) Sweet

An evergreen shrub 3 to 6 ft high, of bushy habit, and usually wider than it is high; young branches, leaves, flower-stalks, and calyx covered with reddish-brown scurf or scales. Leaves oval or oblong, 1 to 3 in. long, ⅓ to ¾ in. wide; margins recurved; upper surface dark dull green, lower one glaucous white or sometimes pale brown when young; stalk ⅛ to ⅓ in. long. The leaf when crushed has a strong, rather resinous odour. Flowers ¾ to 1¼ in. wide, rosy red, produced during May in terminal clusters of usually five or six (sometimes eight to ten). Calyx large, with five ovate, pointed lobes, ⅓ in. long, scaly outside. Corolla bell-shaped, with five spreading, rounded lobes, slightly scaly outside; Stamens

RHODODENDRON GLAUCOPHYLLUM

ten, downy at the base. Style straight or bent. *Bot. Mag.*, t. 4721. (*s.* and *ss.* Glaucophyllum)

Native of the Himalaya from E. Nepal eastward at 10,000 to 12,000 ft; introduced by J. D. Hooker in 1850. It is quite hardy in a sheltered place, and pretty when well in bloom, though not showy. The hybrid 'Rosy Bell' derives from this species.

var. LUTEIFLORUM Davidian—Flowers clear yellow. This interesting and attractive variety was discovered by Kingdon Ward and his wife in 1953 during their expedition to the northern part of the Triangle, a region of upper Burma lying between the two main branches of the upper Irrawaddy, the Nmai Hka and the Mali Hka. When he first saw it the flowers were over and he took it to be ordinary *R. glaucophyllum*. 'My surprise, therefore, was great when the bright November sunshine so warmed the fat winter buds of this little plant that they blurted into brief flower, revealing golden corollas! It was a brighter and better *R. brachyanthum*' (*Return to the Irrawaddy*, p. 172). It was introduced by him the same year and was described in 1960.

A First Class Certificate was given in 1966 to a clone of the var. *luteiflorum* named 'Glen Coy', shown from the Brodick Castle Gardens, Isle of Arran (*R.C.Y.B. 1967*, Pl. 4).

var. TUBIFORME Cowan—Corolla tubular, style straight. Introduced by Ludlow and Sherriff from east Bhutan (L. & S. 2856).

R. GLISCHRUM Balf. f. & W. W. Sm.

An evergreen tree up to 25 ft high in nature, mostly seen in cultivation as a shrub of stiff, rather gaunt habit; young shoots, leaf-stalks, and flower-stalks all glandular-bristly. Leaves narrowly oblong, often inclined to oblanceolate, rather abruptly narrowed at the apex to a slender point; tapered, rounded, or slightly heart-shaped at the base, 6 to 12 in. long, 1½ to 3 in. wide, dark green or yellowish green and eventually glabrous above, pale green beneath and more or less furnished all over with bristly down, but especially on the midrib. Flowers borne during May in trusses 5 or 6 in. across, of up to fifteen or more, on stalks up to 1½ in. long. Calyx deeply five-lobed, the lobes ⅜ in. long, oblong, blunt, bristly. Corolla bell-shaped, five-lobed, 2 in. wide, varying in colour from a dull magenta-pink to a purplish rose with a dark blotch at the base. Stamens ten, 1 to 1¼ in. long, glandular-downy towards the base. Ovary and base of style clothed with white bristles. *Bot. Mag.*, t. 9035. (*s.* Barbatum *ss.* Glischrum)

R. glischrum was discovered by Forrest on the Kari pass, Mekong–Salween divide in 1914, and was introduced from there. Subsequently it was collected over a wide area from here westward to the eastern end of the Himalaya. The type specimens bore only withered flowers, but Forrest noted the colour of his later findings as 'plum-purple', 'clear rose', or 'white flushed rose'. In cultivation, many of the plants raised from the wild seeds had flowers of an unpleasant magenta shade, but in the best forms, which may be the minority, they are clear red in the bud, opening rosy pink or rosy lilac. *R. glischrum* is hardy in woodland near London, but is probably best suited in the rainier parts of the country. It is, in any case, rarely seen outside collections.

var. ADENOSUM Cowan & Davidian—Calyx shorter than in the type. Leaves somewhat smaller, with short bristly glands on the underside. Described from Dr Rock's 18228, collected in S.W. Szechwan and in cultivation at Edinburgh from his seed-number 03837.

R. GLISCHROIDES Tagg & Forr.—This species, perhaps no more than a local variety of R. *glischrum*, is known from a comparatively small area on the Irrawaddy–Salween divide, within the range of R. *glischrum* itself. The main botanical distinction is that the veins on the leaf-undersides are clothed with fine hairs as well as bristles. But as seen in cultivation it is a finer species, the leaves dark green with impressed veins and the flowers white more or less flushed with pink. It was found and introduced by Forrest.

Two other relatives of R. *glischrum*, neither of much importance, may be mentioned here:

R. RUDE Tagg & Forr.—This differs from R. *glischrum* in the relatively broader leaves, up to 7½ in. long, 3 in. wide, covered on the upper surface as well as beneath with gland-tipped bristly hairs. The flowers are smaller and are sometimes barred with pink on the outside. It was found in the same area as R. *glischroides* and was introduced by Forrest under F.25645.

R. VESICULIFERUM Tagg—Leaves thinner than in R. *glischrum*, more rugose, with bladder-like hairs along the midrib and main veins in addition to the normal simple hairs. It was discovered by Kingdon Ward in the Seinghku valley N.W. upper Burma and introduced by him (KW 6856; flowers 'in large trusses, pinkish purple, splashed with dusky purple at the base.'). He later reintroduced it from the Adung valley a short way to the east, where the flowers vary in colour from white to deep rose. The clone 'High Flier' received an Award of Merit on April 30, 1968, when shown by the Crown Estate Commissioners, Windsor Great Park.

R. GRANDE Wight

R. *argenteum* Hook. f.; R. *longifolium* Nutt.

An evergreen tree or large shrub up to 30 ft high; young shoots stout, clothed with silvery scurf. Leaves stiff and leathery, oblong to oblanceolate, tapered at both ends, 6 to 15 in. long, 3 to 6 in. wide, dark green and glabrous above, beautifully silvery or covered with dull tawny down beneath; stalk 1 to 2 in. long. Flowers sometimes twenty-five to thirty, opening during March and April in a rounded truss 5 to 7 in. wide. Calyx a mere rim; flower-stalk glandular, and it may be slightly downy, like the calyx. Corolla bell-shaped, 2 to 3 in. long and wide, ivory white, with conspicuous blotches at the base, eight-lobed. Stamens sixteen, downy at the base. Ovary downy and densely glandular; style glabrous or nearly so; stigma large, disk-like. *Bot. Mag.*, t. 5054. (*s.* Grande)

Native of the Himalaya from Nepal eastward; described in 1847 from a specimen collected in Bhutan. In 1850 it was introduced from the Sikkim Himalaya by J. D. Hooker, who found it on Tonglo (west of Darjeeling) and Sinchul (S.E. of Darjeeling), both of which at that time lay within the domains of the

Rajah of Sikkim. Hooker redescribed it under the name R. *argenteum*, which remained in use until well into this century and has not even now disappeared from garden nomenclature, though there is really no doubt that the Sikkim and Bhutan plants represent the same species. In this connection H. F. Tagg, the Edinburgh authority, wrote: 'In its typical condition [R. *grande*] is characterised by the oblong-oblanceolate leaves with their silvery undersurface. Forms occur in cultivation with a rougher and somewhat tawny indumentum. It was at one time thought that these might represent R. *grande* as opposed to R. *argenteum* with its more silvery under surface. There seems little doubt that R. *argenteum* is a synonym of R. *grande*' (*The Species of Rhododendron*, 2nd ed., p. 310). The synonymous name R. *longifolium* is founded on a narrow-leaved specimen collected by Booth in the Assam Himalaya.

One of the most magnificent of rhododendrons, this unfortunately can only be grown in the open air in the mildest counties. The finest examples are to be seen in Cornwall and western Scotland, where it has attained a height of over 30 ft.

R. SIDEREUM Balf. f.—This is closely related to R. *grande*, but the leaves are as a rule narrower, only $1\frac{1}{4}$ to $2\frac{3}{4}$ in. wide, and up to 10 or 12 in. long, Corolla eight-lobed, bell-shaped, creamy white to yellow, with a crimson blotch at the base, nearly 2 in. wide. It was discovered in N.E. upper Burma in 1912 by Capt. Abbay, during the expedition that brought the frontier area around Hpimaw under British administration. Seven years later it was collected almost simultaneously in the Hpimaw area by Farrer and Cox, by Kingdon Ward, and by Forrest's native collectors, who, as Mr Cox records, came over the Hpimaw pass from China, much to Farrer's indignation (*Farrer's Last Journey*, p. 45). It was introduced the same year (Farrer 872 and Forrest 18054). According to Farrer it is a prevailing rhododendron in the upper forest zone around Hpimaw at 9,000 to 10,500 ft. Kingdon Ward sent seeds from the Seinghku valley, N.W. upper Burma, in 1926 (KW 6792), and from the Assam Himalaya in 1938 (KW 13649).

R. *sidereum* is rather uncommon in cultivation and no more hardy than R. *grande*. It received an Award of Merit when shown from Brodick in the Isle of Arran on May 5, 1964 (clone 'Glen Rosa', with primrose-yellow flowers).

R. GRIERSONIANUM Balf. f. & Forr.

An evergreen shrub of lax, open growth up to 7 ft or more high; young shoots glandular-bristly and hairy. Winter-buds very distinct, being encased by bracts extending well beyond the bud and free at the ends. Leaves oblong-lanceolate, pointed, tapered at the base, 4 to 7 in. long, 1 to $1\frac{3}{4}$ in. wide; dull green above, covered with a pale buff wool beneath; stalk $\frac{3}{4}$ to $1\frac{1}{2}$ in. long, glandular and hairy like the young shoots. Flowers opening in June, loosely arranged in trusses of five to twelve flowers. Calyx small and like the flower stalk, which is $1\frac{1}{4}$ to $1\frac{1}{2}$ in. long, viscous and downy. Corolla rosy scarlet, trumpet-shaped, narrowed to a fluted cylindrical tube at the base, five-lobed, 3 in. wide, $2\frac{1}{2}$ in. long, the lobes roundish ovate, $1\frac{1}{4}$ in. wide, with darker crimson lines running into the throat, very downy outside especially towards the base. Stamens ten, crimson, $1\frac{1}{2}$ to 2 in. long, slightly downy on the lower half; anthers very dark

RHODODENDRON GRIERSONIANUM

brown. Ovary covered with pale tawny felt; style crimson, downy at the base. *Bot. Mag.*, t. 9195. (*s.* Griersonianum)

R. *griersonianum* was discovered by Forrest in June 1917 in W. Yunnan, near the Burma border, on the divide between the Salween and the Shweli, a tributary of the Irrawaddy, growing at 9,000 ft in open situations. He introduced it in the same year and sent seeds again in later years, all from this area, to which the species is apparently confined. In his field notes for 1924 he wrote: 'Extremely local; essentially a plant of the open, seldom, if ever, seen in the shade, though the glades where it is seen at its best are always more or less sheltered. In addition to the striking beauty of the flowers it is a most shapely shrub.' (F.24280)

R. *griersonianum* is one of the finest and most remarkable of Forrest's introductions. It was at first incongruously grouped with R. *auriculatum*, a species with which it really has nothing in common except the awl-shaped bud-scales. There it remained in the Auriculatum series, until 1964, when H. H. Davidian put matters right by placing R. *griersonianum* in a series of its own. It is taxonomically an isolated species, distinct from all others so far discovered in the combination of the awl-shaped bud-scales, the densely glandular inflorescence and ovary, and the uniquely coloured trumpet-shaped corolla. It is probably a relict species.

R. *griersonianum* is moderately hardy but needs the conditions suggested by Forrest's field note, i.e., a sheltered but fairly sunny position. It flowered at Caerhays, Cornwall, and Borde Hill, Sussex, in 1923, and received a First Class Certificate when shown jointly by Lionel de Rothschild and T. H. Lowinsky at Chelsea on May 27, 1924. No other species of *Rhododendron* has been so much used in hybridising—the R.H.S. Handbook lists about 150 hybrids with R. *griersonianum* as one parent, and of these almost one-third have received an Award of Merit or a First Class Certificate. Many of these are described in the section on hybrids.

R. GRIFFITHIANUM Wight   [PLATE 77

R. aucklandii Hook. f.; *R. oblongum* Griff.

An evergreen shrub, or occasionally a small tree, with erect branches and peeling bark. It is quite devoid of down or hairs in all its parts. Leaves narrowly oblong, 6 to 9 (sometimes 12) in. long, about one-third as much wide; rather pale green above, slightly glaucous beneath; stalk 1 to 1½ in. long. Flowers white with a pink tinge, slightly fragrant, 5 or 6 in. diameter, produced loosely in a cluster of about six. Calyx ¾ to 1 in. across, buckler-like, scarcely lobed. Corolla widely bell-shaped, with five large, rounded lobes notched in the middle; stamens up to sixteen, much shorter than the corolla; style 1½ in. long, with a large knob-like stigma; flower-stalk 1 to 1¾ in. long. *Bot. Mag.*, t. 5065. (*s.* Fortunei *ss.* Griffithianum)

Native of the Himalaya from E. Nepal eastward, and of the Mishmi Hills, Assam, apparently everywhere uncommon; described from a specimen collected by Griffith in Bhutan; introduced in 1850 by J. D. Hooker from Sikkim, where he found it growing at 7,000 to 9,000 ft in the inner ranges. In some respects this is the finest of all rhododendrons, especially in regard to the size and width of the individual flower, which resembles some fine lily and is occasionally 7 in. across. But it is variable in the size both of its flowers and of its leaves.

R. *griffithianum* is not hardy near London, but in the mildest parts it has a height and width of 20 ft or even more. There is a fine specimen growing under glass at Edinburgh, raised from seeds collected by Roland Cooper in Bhutan in 1914, and now 20 ft high.

Many of the finest first-generation hybrids have R. *griffithianum* as one parent, and details of the best-known of these will be found in the section on hybrids. See also p. 820 for a note on the hardy hybrids deriving from R. *griffithianum*, of which 'Pink Pearl' is the type.

R. GYMNOCARPUM Balf. f. & Tagg

An evergreen shrub up to 4 ft high; shoots slender, floccose when young and slightly glandular. Leaves leathery, oblong-elliptic, or broadest slightly above or below the middle, up to 4 in. long and 1½ in. wide, obtuse at the apex, cuneate to rounded at the base, dark green and glabrous above, lower surface glandular and coated with a fawn-coloured felt; petiole very short. Inflorescence a loose truss of three to ten flowers, opening in April; rachis very short; pedicels about ⅝ in. long. Calyx minute. Corolla broadly campanulate, about 1 in. deep and twice as wide, claret-red to deep vivid crimson, with darker markings on the upper side, five-lobed. Stamens ten, filaments downy at the base. Ovary conoid, glabrous, or almost so.

This species was found by Forrest in S.E. Tibet under Ka-kar-po on the Mekong–Salween divide in 1918, and introduced by him the same year. It is an anomalous species, originally placed in series Taliense, subseries Roxieanum, though Dr Cowan pointed out that the leaf-indumentum is uncharacteristic of that group and very like that of R. *citriniflorum* (*s.* Neriiflorum *ss.* Sanguineum). It received an Award of Merit when shown from Exbury on April 30, 1940. R. MICROGYNUM Balf. f. & Forr., also from Ka-kar-po, is very closely allied, and was described earlier.

R. HABROTRICHUM Balf. f. & W. W. Sm.

A bushy evergreen shrub up to 10 ft high, or a small tree up to 25 ft high; young shoots purplish, clothed with bristles up to ¼ in. long and gland-tipped. Leaves ovate-oblong, rounded or heart-shaped at the base, slenderly pointed, 3 to 6½ in. long, 1½ to 3 in. wide, dark green above, paler green and bristly on the midrib but not on the veins beneath, margins bristly; stalk up to 1 in. long, very glandular-bristly. Flowers produced in April in compact trusses about 4 in. across. Calyx five-lobed, the lobes ⅜ to ½ in. long, glandular-bristly like the flower-stalk, which is ½ to 1 in. long. Corolla bell-shaped, 1½ to 2 in. wide, white or pale rose with usually a blotch of purple at the base, five-lobed, the lobes rounded and notched in the middle. Stamens ten, varying from half to nearly as long as the corolla, downy towards the base. Ovary and base of style glandular-bristly.   (*s.* Barbatum *ss.* Glischrum)

R. *habrotrichum* was discovered by Forrest in 1912 on the Shweli–Salween divide, near the border between Yunnan and Burma, and appears to be mainly confined to that area (Kingdon Ward's 3042, collected in Burma about 50 miles farther north, is probably R. *habrotrichum*, however). It flowered at Kew in April 1920. Whether this species and R. *glischrum* are really specifically distinct is very much to be doubted. But the latter, at least in its typical form, is distinguished from R. *habrotrichum* by its longer, relatively narrower and more tapered leaves, with shorter bristles more or less all over the undersurface.

Its garden value is the same as that of R. *glischrum* and R. *glischroides*. A pink-flowered form received an Award of Merit on May 2, 1933, when shown by the Sunningdale Nurseries.

R. HAEMATODES Franch.

An evergreen shrub of close, dwarf habit as seen in cultivation but said by Forrest in a field note to be sometimes 6 to 10 ft high; young shoots clothed with a dense brown wool. Leaves leathery, obovate, abruptly contracted at the apex to a small mucro, tapered gradually to the base, 1½ to 3½ in. long, ¾ to 1½ in. wide, dark glossy green above, densely felted with reddish-brown wool beneath; stalk ¼ to ½ in. long, woolly. Flowers in a terminal cluster of six to ten, on slender, downy stalks up to 1½ in. long opening in mid-May. Calyx red, unequally five-lobed, up to ⅓ in. long. Corolla funnel-shaped with five broad, rounded, erect lobes; 1½ to 2 in. long, nearly as much wide, scarlet to deep, rich, almost blood red. Stamens ten, ½ to ¾ in. long, glabrous or nearly so; anthers brown. Ovary densely woolly; style glabrous. *Bot. Mag.*, t. 9165. (*s.* Neriiflorum *ss.* Haematodes)

R. *haematodes* was discovered by the Abbé Delavay in the Tali range, Yunnan, where it is associated with R. *neriiflorum* at 12,000 to 13,000 ft. The cultivated plants descend mainly from seed-collections by Forrest in the same area in 1910 (F.6773) and 1917 (F.15521), both from low-growing plants, which may explain why this species is usually seen in gardens as a shrub only a few feet high and more in width. It is certainly one of the best of his introductions so far as this country in general is concerned, for it is very hardy. Its dwarf habit and slow growth make it suitable for the rock garden. It is the type species of a section of the Neriiflorum series distinguished mainly by the thick woolly covering on the young shoots and underneath the leaf. The richly coloured flowers are very effective and as a rule come late enough to escape frost. In the var. CALYCINUM Franch., the coloured calyx is remarkably developed so that the lobes may be as much as ¾ in. long.

R. *haematodes* received a First Class Certificate when shown by A. M. Williams, Werrington Park, Cornwall, on April 27, 1926.

R. CATACOSMUM Tagg—Allied to R. *haematodes*, but with stouter shoots, larger obovate leaves up to 4½ in. long, rounded at the apex, a more widely campanulate corolla and a larger, cup-like calyx. The flowers are rosy crimson, deep crimson, or scarlet, in lax trusses of about nine, on pedicels 1 in. long, opening in March or April and often caught by frost. The shoots are woolly, not bristly as in R. *chaetomallum*, to which it bears some resemblance. It is a shrub up to 9 ft in the wild, found by Forrest in S.E. Tibet in side-valleys on the Salween–Kiuchiang divide at 13,000 to 14,000 ft and was introduced by him in 1921. Although highly praised it is uncommon in gardens and has never received an award.

R. HANCEANUM Hemsl.

An evergreen shrub 3 to 4 ft high; young shoots glabrous. Leaves lanceolate to narrowly obovate, usually tapered, sometimes rounded at the base, slenderly pointed, very unequal in size, and varying from ½ to 4 in. in length, by ¼ to 1¾ in. in width; dark green, rather scaly above, pale and freely sprinkled with small scales beneath; stalk up to ¼ in. long. Flowers numerous in one or two terminal clusters. Calyx-lobes ³⁄₁₆ in. long, oblong with a rounded end, scaly. Corolla about 1 in. long, funnel-shaped, deeply lobed, varying from white to clear yellow; stamens ten, protruded, downy at the lower half; seed-vessel about half as long again as the persistent, deeply lobed calyx; style glabrous; ovary scaly. It blossoms in March or April. *Bot. Mag.*, t. 8669. (*s.* Triflorum *ss.* Hanceanum).

A native of S.W. Szechwan, discovered by the Rev. E. Faber on Mt Omei about 1886. It was introduced by Wilson from the Mupin area during his first expedition for the Arnold Arboretum (W.882 'bush 1 m. tall, flowers clear yellow'). According to him it is locally very common, forming dense thickets at 8,000 to 10,000 ft. He collected seed again in October 1910, this time from plants 1 to 3 ft high (W.4255).

R. hanceanum is quite an attractive shrub, especially in its dwarfer forms, known in gardens as *R. hanceanum nanum* (possibly raised from W.4255, see above). One of these, subsequently given the clonal name 'Canton Consul', received an Award of Merit when shown by the Crown Estate Commissioners, Windsor Great Park, on April 16, 1957. The flowers in this plant are described as cream-coloured, but there is another dwarf form in cultivation with flowers of a clear yellow.

R. AFGHANICUM Aitch. & Hemsl.—This species is placed in the Hanceanum subseries by Davidian, but he remarks that it differs from it in many important characters and indeed does not fit well into any of the present series of *Rhododendron*. It is also geographically far removed from *R. hanceanum*, found only in a few localities in E. Afghanistan and bordering parts of Pakistan. It is figured in *Bot. Mag.*, t. 8669, but was later lost to cultivation until Hedge and Wendelbo collected seeds in 1969. An interesting account by them on this species in its native habitat will be found in the *R.C.Y.B. 1970*, pp. 177–81. Although of botanical interest, it is unlikely that *R. afghanicum* will be of any value as an ornamental.

R. HEADFORTIANUM Hutch.

An evergreen shrub at present 3 to 4 ft high in cultivation, but probably becoming taller; young shoots loosely scaly. Leaves narrowly oblong or oblong-lanceolate, 2½ to 5 in. long, less than half as wide, apex mucronate, soon glabrous above, glaucous and scaly beneath; stalk ½ to 1 in. long. Flowers solitary. Calyx with five deep oval lobes about ½ in. long; stamens ten, about the length of the corolla-tube, hairy towards the base. Corolla funnel-shaped, 4 in. long, nearly as wide across, the five rounded, spreading lobes, cream-coloured, faintly tinged with pink; at the base are five oblong pouches. *Bot. Mag.*, t. 9614.   (*s.* Maddenii *ss.* Megacalyx)

This species was described from a plant raised by Lord Headfort from seeds collected 'blind' by Kingdon Ward in November 1924 in the Tsangpo Gorge, S.E. Tibet (KW 6310). According to his field note it made a dwarf plant there, 1 to 1½ ft high, growing as an epiphyte or on cliffs and boulders, but in cultivation it has grown taller. Dr Hutchinson, in describing *R. headfortianum*, included in it a specimen without flowers or fruits collected by Kingdon Ward in the Delei valley, Assam, in 1928, under KW 8546. But that number is really *R. lindleyi* (q.v.).

R. headfortianum appears to be uncommon in cultivation.

R. HELIOLEPIS Franch.

R. plebeium Balf. f. & W. W. Sm.

An evergreen shrub up to 10 ft high; young shoots greyish, scaly. Leaves ovate-lanceolate, pointed, rounded at the base, 2 to 4 in. long, 1 to 1¾ in. wide, dark green above, rather tawny green beneath and sprinkled thickly with glistening scales; stalk ¼ to ¾ in. long. Flowers four to seven in a loose cluster, opening in late May or June. Calyx $\frac{1}{10}$ in. long, with rounded lobes, scaly like the flower-stalk, which is $\frac{1}{2}$ to $\frac{3}{4}$ in. long. Corolla widely funnel-shaped, 1 to 1$\frac{1}{3}$ in. long and wide, scaly outside, rosy red with crimson markings. Stamens ten, $\frac{1}{2}$ to $\frac{3}{4}$ in. long, densely downy at the base; ovary densely scaly; style as long as the stamens, downy at the base.   (*s.* Heliolepis)

Native of N.W. Yunnan and bordering parts of Burma; discovered by the French missionary Delavay in 1886 between Tali and Hoching; introduced by Forrest in 1912 from the Shweli–Salween divide. In its leaf it bears a strong resemblance to the well-known *R. rubiginosum* in the same series, but flowers much later and is valuable on that account. A form raised from Forrest 26961 received an Award of Merit when shown by Mrs Stevenson of Tower Court, Ascot, on May 29, 1954. The seeds under this number were collected by Forrest in 1925 near the Chimi-li pass on the Burma–Yunnan border, near to where Farrer and Cox had collected seeds six years earlier.

R. HEMITRICHOTUM Balf. f. & Forr.

An evergreen shrub 2 to 3 (sometimes 4 or 5) ft high, with slender, softly downy young shoots. Leaves oblong to narrowly ovate or oblanceolate, pointed, tapered at the base to a very short stalk; margins recurved; 1 to 1$\frac{1}{2}$ (sometimes 2) in. long, $\frac{1}{4}$ to $\frac{1}{2}$ (sometimes $\frac{3}{4}$) in. wide; dull green and downy above, glaucous and scaly but downy only on the midrib beneath. Flowers produced in April usually in pairs from several of the terminal leaf-axils, constituting altogether a crowded cluster 1$\frac{1}{2}$ to 2 in. wide. Calyx saucer-shaped, not lobed, scaly like the flower-stalk which is $\frac{1}{4}$ in. long. Corolla white to pale rose, $\frac{1}{2}$ to $\frac{3}{4}$ in. wide, funnel-shaped at the base with five broadly ovate lobes. Stamens ten, slightly downy towards the base; ovary scaly, style glabrous.   (*s.* Scabrifolium)

R. hemitrichotum was described from a specimen collected by Forrest in the Muli mountains of S.W. Szechwan at 12,000 ft in July 1918 and was introduced by him the following winter (F.16250). Kingdon Ward sent seeds from the same area three years later (KW 4050), and there have been later sendings from S.W. Szechwan and also from Yunnan. In describing this species, Balfour compared it with *R. mollicomum* (q.v.), from which it differs in the white underside of the leaves. This character it shares with *R. racemosum*, and Davidian has pointed out that the two are closely allied. The chief distinction is that *R. hemitrichotum* is a more downy species; typically, too, it has the leaves much narrower than in *R. racemosum*, but this is a less reliable character for distinguishing the two species. It flowers quite young when raised from seed, sometimes in three or four years. It is hardy at Kew, having grown there in the open air since 1922.

R. HEMSLEYANUM Wils.

An evergreen shrub or small tree 10 to 20 ft high; young stems stout, slightly downy; leaf-buds conical. Leaves thick and leathery, oblong or oblong-ovate, 6 to 8 in. long, 2$\frac{3}{4}$ to 3$\frac{1}{2}$ in. wide, rounded at the apex, deeply cordate-auriculate at the base, upper surface dark green, glabrous, lower surface paler, papillose, lateral veins parallel, in thirteen to fifteen pairs; petioles stout, up to 1¾ in. long, sparsely glandular. Flowers borne in May in a racemose corymb of up to twelve; pedicels up to 1⅜ in. long, glandular and slightly hairy. Calyx very small. Corolla white, funnel-campanulate, seven-lobed, 2 to 2⅝ in. long. Stamens fourteen, glabrous. Ovary glandular, conoid; style glandular throughout, with a discoid stigma. *Pl. Omeienses*, t. 30; *R.Y.B. 1947*, fig. 29. (*s.* and *ss.* Fortunei)

This interesting species was discovered by Wilson on Mt Omei in W. Szechwan in 1900 and is said to be endemic to that area. He did not collect seeds, and the species was quite unknown in Britain except from written accounts until Mr E. H. M. Cox obtained seeds from the Rhododendron Test Garden at Portland, Oregon, USA, from which plants were raised and distributed from 1969 onwards by Glendoick Gardens Ltd. He had seen the plants flowering there in May 1964 and published a short note on it in the *Rhododendron Year Book* for 1966 (p. 133 and fig. 53).

In describing this species Wilson compared it with R. *auriculatum*, which it resembles in the shape and general appearance of the leaves. But in other respects it seems to be nearer to the Fortunei series, in which it at present resides. Plants from Glendoick are growing well in several gardens, and one flowered in Cornwall in 1973. The wavy edge of the leaves shown by some of these plants seems to be a characteristic of the species.

R. HIPPOPHAEOIDES Balf. f. & W. W. Sm.

An evergreen shrub 4 to 5 ft high, of erect growth when young, making long slender shoots with half a dozen or more leaves to the inch, scurfy. Leaves mostly oblong or narrowly oval, apex often bluntish or rounded, more tapered at the base; ¾ to 1½ in. long, ⅓ to ½ in. wide; dark dullish green above, greyish beneath, both surfaces scaly but the lower one more copiously so; stalk ⅛ to ⅙ in. long. When crushed, the leaf emits a slightly acrid odour. Flowers four to eight together, crowded in a roundish umbel about 1½ in. wide, opening normally in March and April. Calyx $\frac{1}{10}$ in. long, five-lobed, with a few hairs at the rounded end of each lobe. Corolla flattish, saucer-shaped, ¾ to 1 in. wide, five-lobed (the lobes roundish), the short tube hairy. Forrest describes the flowers as deep purplish blue, blue-purple, pale bluish rose, and blue. One plant at Kew gave rosy-pink flowers. Stamens normally ten, purple, about ⅙ in. long, downy at the base; anthers dark reddish brown. Ovary very scaly, green; style red, glabrous; flower-stalk ⅙ to ¼ in. long, scaly. *Bot. Mag.*, t. 9156. (*s.* Lapponicum)

Native of N.W. Yunnan east of the Mekong and of S.W. Szechwan. It was first collected by Kingdon Ward (in flower) in May 1913 in the upper valley of the Chung river, a tributary of the Yangtse, at 10,500 ft. He described it as a dwarf shrub forming carpets or separate tufts 9 in. to 1 ft high in open pine forest. In July of the same year Forrest found it in flower on the mountains north-east of the Yangtse Bend at 11,000 to 12,000 ft, as a shrub 4 to 5 ft high with blue flowers, growing in alpine scrub, and introduced it by means of seeds collected the same autumn (F.10333, in flower, and F.11487, in fruit). Other Forrest collections cited in the original description are: F.12461, from the Lichiang range, a shrub of 2 ft with pale bluish-rose flowers, from open marshy meadows; F. 12562, mountains west of the Fengkow valley, at 12,000 ft, a shrub of 3 to 4 ft with lavender-blue flowers, growing in boggy, peaty meadows; and F.12633, from the Chungtien plateau, from open, moist, stony pasture. Forrest later sent seed from the Lichiang range under four numbers, one from plants with flowers of a 'bright rose' and Dr Rock's 59241 and 59615 were also from this area. Forrest's 15450 and 15459, collected in 1917, are from the Haba Shan, the continuation of the Lichiang range north of the Yangtse.

R. *hippophaeoides* is one of the best and most widely planted of the Lapponicum series. It first flowered in gardens in 1917 and received an Award of Garden Merit eight years later. It is perfectly hardy, and its flowers, produced in March and April, are rarely damaged by frost. As will be seen from Forrest's field notes, it often occurs in the wild in wet ground. In cultivation it does not need such conditions, but Lionel de Rothschild found that it would survive in ground lying wet in winter where other members of the series died out.

cv. 'SUNNINGDALE'.—Flowers deep lavender-blue, about ¾ in. wide, up to eleven or so in a dense truss, opening over a long period. This is a selection from a batch of plants raised at the Sunningdale Nurseries and known collectively as the Haba Shan form, so probably raised from Forrest's 15450 or 15459 (see above). In another clone from this batch the flowers are larger but fewer in each truss.

R. FIMBRIATUM Hutch.—Judging from the type-material at Kew, this seems to be very close to R. *hippophaeoides*. It was described from a plant raised at Headfort from Forrest's 22197, to which the corresponding field-specimen is R. *ravum*, quite a different species now included in R. *cuneatum*.

R. HIRSUTUM L.

An evergreen shrub of the same habit as R. *ferrugineum*, 2 to 3 ft high; young shoots bristly and scaly. Leaves narrowly oval, occasionally somewhat obovate or lanceolate, about 1 in. long, ¼ to ½ in. wide, bright green above, somewhat scaly beneath, the margins crenulate, fringed with bristles. Flowers rosy pink to rosy scarlet, ½ in. to ¾ in. across, produced in June in terminal clusters. Calyx and flower-stalk bristly and scaly, the latter ½ to 1 in. long. Corolla slightly scaly outside, funnel-shaped at the base, the lobes spreading. *Bot. Mag.*, t. 1853. (*s.* Ferrugineum)

Native of the central and eastern Alps and of N.W. Yugoslavia; cultivated by John Tradescant 1656. This species although palpably a close ally of R. *ferrugineum*, and having the same popular name, is in several respects very distinct. The bristly character of the leaves, shoots, and calyx to which the specific name refers is, of course, its most distinctive feature, but it differs also in being greener and less scaly underneath the leaf, and in the usually longer calyx-lobes and flower-stalk.

In the wild, R. *hirsutum* is usually found on a limestone formation, but its soil preferences are not so definite as those of R. *ferrugineum*, which is never found on limestone except where the soil is so leached as to be slightly acid or unless there is an accumulation of peat above the substrate, whereas R. *hirsutum*, despite its preference for calcareous soils, can and does grow on slightly acid oils. Where the two species are contiguous, R. *hirsutum* is confined to dry, open, stony soils and screes, while R. *ferrugineum* prefers damper and shadier locations, with a soil richer in humus. A further difference is that R. *hirsutum* is a less gregarious species, rarely forming extensive pure stands as its ally so often does (Hegi, *Fl. Mitteleuropa*, Vol. V.3, p. 1639).

f. ALBIFLORUM Goiran—Flowers white. According to Schroeter it is less common in the wild than the white-flowered R. *ferrugineum*. 'ALBIFLORUM LACINIATUM' is a curiosity which arose in cultivation on a white-flowered plant and was grown by Froebel of Zurich; the leaves at the base are quite deeply incised (Schroeter, *Pflanzenleben der Alpen*, p. 113).

f. LATIFOLIUM (Hoppe) Zab. R. *hirsutum* var. *latifolium* Hoppe—Leaves broad, almost rounded (see Schroeter, op. cit., fig. 36).

R. HIRTIPES Tagg

An evergreen shrub or small tree up to 20 ft high but 5 ft high or less in exposed situations; young shoots glandular-bristly. Leaves oblong-elliptic or broad-elliptic, rounded at both ends, 2¼ to 5 in. long, 1¾ to 3 in. wide, margins bristly at first, glabrous above when mature except for scattered hairs and glands on the midrib, undersurface at first covered with bladder-like (vesicular) hairs which later collapse and become dry, resinous dots; petiole glandular-hairy, ½ to ¾ in. long. Flowers three to five in a terminal umbellate inflorescence, opening in April; pedicels ¾ in. long, glandular-bristly. Calyx up to ½ in. long, usually tinged with red. Corolla broadly funnel-campanulate, five-lobed, red in the bud, opening rose-pink to almost white, banded with pink on the outside and speckled crimson inside, about 2 in. long, 2½ in. wide. Ovary conoid, glandular; style glandular at the base. (*s.* Barbatum *ss.* Glischrum)

R. *hirtipes* was discovered by Kingdon Ward in 1924 near Tsela Dzong, in S.E. Tibet, in the valley of the Tsangpo, and was introduced by him (KW 5659). It 'grew some 20 ft high and had large rounded leaves and loose trusses of three or four big bell-shaped flowers of the most delicate shell pink and ivory white, arranged in alternating broad bands. It was, I think, the most bewitching Rhododendron we saw' (*Riddle of Tsangpo Gorges*, p. 45; *Gard. Chron.*, Vol. 87 (1930), p. 330). It was later reintroduced by Ludlow, Sherriff, and Taylor from the same area. It is not common in cultivation but judging from the plant in the Valley Gardens, Windsor Great Park, raised from the original introduction, it is quite as beautiful as its discoverer had promised, though some plants are said to be of little worth. Another fine form was raised by A. C. and J. F. A. Gibson, Glenarn, Rhu, Dunbartonshire, from Ludlow, Sherriff, and Taylor 3624. This received an Award of Merit on April 13, 1965 (clone 'Ita').

R. HODGSONII Hook. f. [PLATE 74

An evergreen shrub or small tree up to 20 ft high; bark peeling. Leaves large, slightly obovate, rounded at the apex, tapering at the base, 6 to 12 in. long, 3 to 4 in. wide, very leathery, dark green and glossy above, with brownish-red down beneath; stalk very thick, 1 to 2 in. long. Flowers rosy lilac or magenta-purple, 1½ to 2 in. across, packed in a rounded truss about 6 in. wide. Calyx very small. Corolla bell-shaped, with eight to ten lobes; stamens about twice as many, shorter than the corolla. Ovary downy. *Bot. Mag.*, t. 5552. (*s.* Falconeri)

Native of the Himalaya from Nepal to some way east of Bhutan; introduced by J. D. Hooker in 1850 from Sikkim, where it is according to him one of the characteristic plants of the interior at 10,000 to 12,000 ft. 'It is found alike at the bottom of the valleys, on the rocky spurs or slopes of the hills, in open places, or in the gloomy pine-groves, often forming an impenetrable thicket, not merely of twigs and foliage, but of thickset limbs and stout trunks, only to be severed with difficulty, on account of the toughness of the wood. As it is easily worked, and not apt to be split. it is admirably adapted for use in the parched and arid climate of Tibet; and the Bhoteas make from it cups, spoons, and ladles, and the saddle, by means of which loads are slung upon the "yak". The leaves are employed as platters, and serve for lining the baskets which contain the mashed pulp of *Arisaema* root (a kind of Colocass); and the customary present of butter or curd is always enclosed in this glossy foliage.' (Hooker)

With its large rich green leaves and its beautiful bark, R. *hodgsonii* is one of the noblest of rhododendrons and a worthy companion to R. *falconeri*, which Hooker introduced at the same time. It is hardy enough, but does not succeed so well at Kew as it does at Edinburgh, where there are several fine plants 15 ft or slightly more high. In the Atlantic zone it has attained a height of 15 ft and a spread of 37 ft at Stonefield, Argyll, and 25 ft at Logan in Wigtownshire.

In *Rhododendrons 1973* (p. 43), Roy Lancaster remarks that in the part of eastern Nepal visited by him in 1973 two forms of R. *hodgsonii* occur, one with deep magenta or reddish-purple flowers in congested heads, the other with larger, pink flowers, in looser trusses.

R. HOOKERI Nutt.

An evergreen shrub 10 to 14 ft high; young shoots glabrous. Leaves oval-oblong, rounded at both ends with a short mucro at the apex, 3 to 5 in. long, about half as much wide, green and glabrous above, rather glaucous beneath and glabrous except along the veins upon which, at fairly regular intervals, occur little tufts of down; stalk up to 1⅛ in. long. Flowers produced in late March or April ten to fifteen in a truss, on stalks up to 1 in. long. Calyx cup-shaped, up to ⅞ in. long. Corolla blood-red sometimes pink, bell-shaped, 1½ to 2 in. wide, five-lobed, the lobes rounded and deeply notched in the middle; stamens ten, quite glabrous; ovary and style glabrous, the latter longer than the stamens but shorter than the corolla. *Bot. Mag.*, t. 4926. (*s.* and *ss.* Thomsonii)

Native of the Himalaya from Bhutan eastward, and of the Mishmi Hills; discovered by Booth in 1849 in an outer range just east of the Bhutan frontier, and introduced by him. For many years this handsome and richly coloured species was one of the rarest of rhododendrons; even now, although it is becoming more widely spread in gardens, it is still quite uncommon. It is related to R. *thomsonii*, but is well distinguished from that and all other known rhododendrons by the curious tufts of down scattered along the chief veins beneath the leaf, and nowhere else. It is grown out-of-doors, really successfully, in the southern and western maritime counties only, although 30 or 40 miles south of London it has survived pretty severe winters. In view of this tenderness it is interesting to note Booth's record that, when and where he first collected it, frost and snow were very severe and continuous; also that it is associated in the wild with *Pinus wallichiana*, a perfectly hardy pine.

A hardier form of *R. hookeri* was introduced by Kingdon Ward in 1938 from the Poshing La in the Assam Himalaya.

R. hookeri was awarded a First Class Certificate when shown from Bodnant on March 21, 1933.

R. HOULSTONII Hemsl. & Wils.

R. *fortunei* var. *houlstonii* (Hemsl. & Wils.) Rehd. & Wils.

An evergreen shrub up to 12 ft high, with stout, glabrous branchlets. Leaves oblong or slightly obovate, 3 to 6 in. long, $\frac{3}{4}$ to 2 in. wide, narrowed abruptly at the apex to a short point, tapered or rounded at the base, both surfaces perfectly smooth, the upper one dark green, the lower very pale; stalk purple, $\frac{1}{2}$ to $1\frac{1}{8}$ in. long. Flowers eight or more in a truss, flesh-pink, about 3 in. across. Corolla widely bell-shaped, seven-lobed; stamens twelve or fourteen, with glabrous stalks; summit of ovary and base of style hairy-glandular; flower-stalk covered with viscid stalked glands, 1 in. or more long.   (*s.* and *ss.* Fortunei)

Native of W. Hupeh and E. Szechwan; discovered by Augustine Henry in 1888 and introduced by Wilson in 1900 from the Hsing-shan region of Hupeh. It first flowered in Veitch's Coombe Wood nursery in 1913. According to Wilson it is a woodland species, but never seen by him more than 15 ft high and always compact. In the wild it flowers in late April or early May, about three weeks earlier than *R. fortunei*. It is allied to that species, but differs in the tapered base of the leaves, the glandular flower-stalks, the bell-shaped corolla and longer stamens.

R. HUNNEWELLIANUM Rehd. & Wils.

R. *leucoclasium* Diels

An evergreen shrub up to 15 ft high in the wild; young shoots covered with a short grey felt. Leaves oblanceolate, slenderly pointed but tapering more gradually towards the base, 2 to $4\frac{1}{2}$ in. long, $\frac{1}{4}$ to 1 in. wide, dark green, glabrous above at maturity, clothed beneath with a loose grey felt; stalk $\frac{1}{4}$ to $\frac{1}{2}$ in. long. Flowers produced in March or April in clusters of five to eight on downy stalks $\frac{3}{4}$ in. long. Calyx small, shallowly lobed, downy. Corolla bell-shaped, five-lobed, 2 to $2\frac{1}{4}$ in. wide, $1\frac{3}{4}$ to 2 in. deep, pink to pale rosy-lilac, spotted with maroon on the three upper lobes. Stamens ten, the longest about as long as the corolla, their stalks white, downy at the base; anthers dark brown. Ovary and base of style clad with white down, the latter nearly 2 in. long. Seed-vessel $\frac{3}{4}$ in. long, covered with tawny down.   (*s.* Arboreum *ss.* Argyrophyllum)

Native of W. Szechwan, China; discovered and introduced by Wilson in 1908. A distinct species on account of its stiff, very narrow leaves, grey-white beneath. It is perfectly hardy at Kew, but increases slowly in size because of its being so frequently cut back by late spring frosts, and for the same reason flowers there infrequently. It flowered with Lt-Col. Stephenson Clarke at Borde Hill, Sussex, in March 1918. Related to R. *floribundum*, it differs in its smaller, narrower leaves, more slenderly tapered at the base. It is named after the Hunnewell family, well known and ardent patrons of horticulture and botany in Massachusetts.

R. HYLAEUM Balf. f. & Farrer

An evergreen shrub or tree, up to 40 ft high, with a pinkish, flaking bark. Leaves leathery, oblanceolate to obovate, rounded to obtuse at the apex, narrowed to a roundish or slightly cordate base, 3 to 7 in. long, 1 to 2 in. wide, glabrous on both sides; petiole up to 1 in. long. Flowers in a terminal cluster of ten to twelve; pedicels ⅜ to ⅝ in. long, eglandular. Calyx cup-like, undulate, up to ⅜ in. long. Corolla tubular-campanulate, five-lobed, fleshy, up to 1¾ in. long, pink, spotted, with five nectar-pouches at the base. Ovary eglandular (but see below); style glabrous. (s. and ss. Thomsonii)

R. *hylaeum* was discovered by Farrer in 1920 on the Chawchi pass, on the border between Burma and Yunnan, and was introduced by Forrest and by Kingdon Ward in 1924. Forrest's seed was collected near the type-locality (F.24660), but the seed sent home by Kingdon Ward (KW 6401) was taken from a fruiting branch collected by one of his bearers near Pemakochung at the head of the Tsangpo gorge. It is also in cultivation from seeds collected in the Seinghku valley, north-west Burma (KW 6833).

R. *hylaeum* is an uncommon species, but is quite hardy south of London in a sheltered place. It is handsome in foliage and bark, but otherwise of no ornamental value. Although the ovary in R. *hylaeum* is said by Cowan and Davidian to be always eglandular, it is glandular in some cultivated plants, which would therefore come out in their key as R. *eclecteum*, some forms of which resemble R. *hylaeum* in flower, though the typical variety of R. *eclecteum* is very distinct from it in foliage.

R. HYPERYTHRUM Hayata
R. *rubropunctatum* Hayata, not Lévl. & Van.

A dense evergreen shrub usually not more than 6 ft high in cultivation, but twice that in width; branchlets stout, glabrous. Leaves leathery, oblong-elliptic or oblong-oblanceolate, acute and mucronate at the apex, margins strongly recurved (at least in the cultivated form), 3½ to 6 in. long, 1 to 1¾ in. wide, dark green and glabrous above, with an impressed midrib, undersurface dotted with minute punctulations, which are more evident on dried specimens than on live material, glabrous, but the prominent midrib at first covered with a floccose tomentum; petiole at first hairy like the midrib, up to 1 in. long. Inflorescence a racemose umbel of about ten flowers opening in April or May; pedicels up to

1¾ in. long, floccose. Calyx small, the lobes triangular, ciliate, about ⅛ in. long. Corolla five-lobed, funnel-campanulate, about 1¾ in. long and wide, pink or white and more or less speckled in wild plants, pure white and almost unspeckled in the cultivated form. Filaments of stamens downy at the base. Ovary coated with short, spreading or appressed hairs, scarcely glandular; style hairy at the base. *Bot. Mag.*, n.s., t. 109. (*s.* Ponticum *ss.* Caucasicum)

Native of Formosa, where it is said to be very local. It was described from a specimen collected on the central ranges, while the type of R. *rubropunctatum* was collected at the northern extremity of the island, where the species occurs north and east of Taipei. It was described by Hayata in 1913 and introduced by Lionel de Rothschild to Exbury in the 1930s. It is of uncertain taxonomic position, but seems to be very distinct from R. *morii*, in which it was included by Kanehira. It is at present placed in the Caucasicum subseries of *s.* Ponticum. R. *hyperythrum* is perfectly hardy, needs only light shade and a sheltered position, grows quickly and flowers when quite young. In the form usually seen in cultivation the flowers are pure white and almost unmarked, in this respect differing from most wild plants (see the note by K. Wada in *Rhododendrons 1972*, pp. 33–4). R. *hyperythrum* is one of the best species for a small garden, being of neat habit, with striking foliage and beautiful flowers.

R. IMPERATOR Hutch. & Ward

A dwarf evergreen shrub forming in the wild a flat, mat-like growth only a few inches high; young shoots slightly scaly; older bark peeling. Leaves aromatic, oblanceolate to narrowly elliptical, rounded to pointed at the mucronate apex,

RHODODENDRON IMPERATOR

always wedge-shaped at the base, 1 to 1½ in. long, ⅛ to ½ in. wide, glabrous and dark green above, glaucous and very thinly scaly beneath; midrib yellowish; margins decurved; stalk ¼ in. or less long. Flowers solitary or in pairs, opening in May, borne on red stalks up to 1 in. long. Calyx slightly but distinctly five-lobed. Corolla funnel-shaped with reflexed lobes, 1 to 1½ in. wide, scarcely so long, downy all over outside, pinkish purple in various shades, unspotted. Stamens ten, purple, downy quite at the base only; ovary scaly; style rather longer than the corolla, slender, glabrous, red. *Bot. Mag.*, n.s., t. 514. (s. Uniflorum)

R. *imperator* was discovered by Kingdon Ward in 1926 under the Diphuk La in upper Burma, near the source of the Seinghku river, a feeder of the Irrawaddy, between 10,000 and 11,000 ft, and was introduced by him (KW 6884). His field note reads: 'A flat thin mat plant, weaving itself over the surface of almost bare granite rocks in a well-shaded gully; thus it is out in the open, but hardly gets any sunshine. Flowers bright unblemished purple, with crimson style. . . . Leaves aromatic. Very showy.' Later he wrote: 'What was remarkable about it was that I found only one plant, which bore only a few flowers, most of which I left for seed, and that returning to the spot five months later I collected only five or six capsules of good seeds; moreover, I never found another plant and no other collector has either' (*Gard. Chron.*, Vol. 119 (1946), p. 230).

R. *imperator* first flowered in 1930 and received an Award of Merit four years later when exhibited by Lord Swaythling. It is a beautiful plant for the rock garden but not entirely hardy. Kingdon Ward gave it the nickname "Purple Emperor", whence the specific epithet *imperator*.

R. PATULUM Ward—Kingdon Ward's statement (see above) that R. *imperator* has never been rediscovered is doubtfully true. For two years later he himself found and described R. *patulum*, which is really so near to R. *imperator* botanically that Cowan and Davidian could find no significant difference except that the scales on the undersurface of the leaves are more closely spaced, being one to one-and-a-half their own diameter apart, against two to six times in R. *imperator*. A minor difference is that the flowers in R. *patulum* are often pink and sometimes spotted.

Kingdon Ward found this species in the Delei valley, Mishmi Hills, at 12,000 to 13,000 ft, 40 miles or so to the north-west of the type-locality of R. *imperator*. According to his field note (KW 8260) it makes a perfectly prostrate creeper forming extensive mats on steep rock or earth slopes, fully exposed. It is just as fine a species as its ally, but has the reputation of being more difficult to cultivate.

R. INDICUM (L.) Sweet

Azalea indica L.; *A. macrantha* Bunge; *R. macranthum* (Bunge) D. Don; *R. indicum* var. *macranthum* (Bunge) Maxim.; *R. breynii* Planch.; *R. decumbens* D. Don

An evergreen shrub, sometimes a dense bush from 3 to 6 ft high, sometimes low and more or less prostrate; young shoots slender, stiff, clothed with flattened, appressed, bristle-like hairs pointing towards the end of the branch. Leaves lanceolate to oblanceolate, tapered at the base, pointed, often sparsely toothed,

1 to 1½ in. long, ¼ to ¾ in. wide; dark green and rather glossy above, paler beneath, with appressed red-brown bristles on both sides; stalk $\frac{1}{12}$ to ⅛ in. long. Flowers opening in June, solitary or in pairs at the end of the shoot. Calyx and flower-stalk appressed-bristly. Corolla broadly funnel-shaped, about 1½ in. long, rather more wide, five-lobed, bright red to scarlet, sometimes rosy red. Stamens five, about the same length as the corolla, slightly downy towards the base. Ovary covered with erect bristles; style glabrous.

Native of S. Japan; introduced in 1833 by a Mr M'Killigan to Knight's nursery at Chelsea. It had long been cultivated by the Japanese, and Wilson, when in Japan, found that some two hundred sorts are recognised by them. Although it—or rather its varieties—held a place in European gardens for some years, it was rapidly displaced after the year 1850 by the Chinese species, R. *simsii* (q.v.), a species with many varieties also, somewhat more tender than R. *indicum* and better adapted for greenhouse cultivation, especially for forcing early into bloom. These two species and their varieties have been much confused by botanists and have usually been referred to collectively as "Indian Azaleas". R. *simsii* is distinguished by its usually ten (sometimes eight) stamens to a flower. The true R. *indicum* is rare in gardens. Although not robust in habit, it and the following varieties are hardy there, and this cannot be said of R. *simsii* and its forms:

cv. 'BALSAMINIFLORUM'.—A miniature shrub usually only one foot or so high. Leaves ½ to 1 in. long, ⅛ to ⅙ in. wide, glossy green above, grey beneath, bristly on both surfaces. Flowers very double, salmon red, in the bud state very much resembling small rosebuds. It has lived in the open air at Kew for many years but grows slowly and prefers a rather warmer climate. Suitable for the rock garden. Introduced from Japan about 1877. It is perfectly hardy, but needs slight shade and moist soil. It has also been known as *Azalea rosaeflora*.

cv. 'CRISPIFLORUM'.—This has thicker leaves than the type and, bright rose flowers with wavy margins. Introduced by Fortune about 1850. *Bot. Mag.*, t. 4726.

cv. 'LACINIATUM'.—Corolla rich red, split to the base into narrow, strap-shaped segments nearly 1 in. long, $\frac{1}{12}$ to ⅛ in. wide. Often the two or three upper segments are united half-way down. Calyx five-lobed, the lobes ⅛ in. long, bristly, pointed. Stamens five, red; style 1¼ in. long, red. It flowers in the open air at Kew in June, but can be regarded only as a curious monstrosity.

cv. 'VARIEGATUM'.—Flowers striped red and white. Introduced with the type in 1833 to Knight's nursery at Chelsea, and a favourite variety for breeding from in the early days. Rather tender. In England it disappeared from cultivation, but a similar plant was later introduced from Japan under the name 'Matushima'.

R. *indicum* is known in Japan as the 'Satsuki-tsutsuji', or Fifth-month Azalea 'from the fact that it blossoms in June, which is the fifth month of the year reckoning by the old Chinese calendar' (Wilson). But the Satsuki group of azaleas, of which several hundred varieties have been named in Japan, are probably for the most parts hybrids of R. *indicum* with various other evergreen species; see further in the section on evergreen azalea hybrids.

R. ERIOCARPUM (Hayata) Nakai R. *indicum* var. *eriocarpum* Hayata; R. *simsii*

T A S—Z

var. *eriocarpum* (Hayata) Wils.—Little seems to be known of this azalea, which is perhaps intermediate between R. *indicum* and R. *simsii*, and was described from a specimen collected on Kaganoshima, an island about 40 miles south-west of Yakushima at the northern end of the Ryukyus. No specimen has been seen, but according to Hayata the leaves are 1 in. long, obovate or obovate-oblong; inflorescences three- to four-flowered; stamens nine or ten. The colour of the flowers was not stated, but according to Wilson, who saw fresh specimens from . neighbouring islands, they are white, pink, or rose-coloured. The plants culti- vated as R. *simsii* var. *eriocarpum*—the so-called Gumpo azaleas—came from Japanese nurseries and therefore cannot be regarded as authentic; they are men- tioned in the section on evergreen azalea hybrids, their taxonomic position being uncertain.

R. *eriocarpum* appears to be in many respects similar to R. TAMURAE (Makino) Masamune, of Kyushu and Yakushima, for which see Ohwi's *Flora of Japan*. The author of this work evidently considers that the plants described by Nakai, when raising Hayata's variety to specific rank, are in fact R. *tamurae*, but that does not affect the validity of the combination R. *eriocarpum* (Hayata) Nakai, which is typified by Hayata's original specimen and description. If in fact only one species is involved it would take the name R. *eriocarpum*.

R. NAKAHARAI Hayata—A low or prostrate shrub. Leaves oblong-elliptic or oblong-ovate, sometimes obliquely so, acute and apiculate at the apex, $\frac{1}{2}$ to $\frac{3}{4}$ in. long, $\frac{3}{16}$ to $\frac{3}{8}$ in. wide, rich glossy green above, paler beneath, appressed- bristly on both sides, especially on the margins and the midrib beneath. Flowers one to three in the truss. Calyx-lobes ovate or narrow-ovate, strigose on the outside and at the edges. Corolla deeply lobed, scarlet with a darker flare on the upper lobe, about $1\frac{3}{8}$ in. wide. Stamens six to ten; anthers purple. Native of the Tatun range in northern Formosa. This description is made from the clone named 'MARIKO', which is of uncertain provenance. Owing to lack of herbarium material of the true R. *nakaharai* it is impossible to say whether it represents the true species, though it agrees quite well with published descrip- tions. It appears to be related to both R. *simsii* and R. *indicum*. 'Mariko' is a useful plant, as it is quite hardy and bears its showy flowers in late June or July. It is an ideal plant for the rock garden and stands full sun.

R. INSIGNE Hemsl. & Wils.

An evergreen shrub described by Wilson as from 12 to 18 ft high in the wild, but usually seen in cultivation as a rounded bush of stocky growth. Leaves very hard and firm in texture, narrowly elliptical to lanceolate, sharply pointed, tapered at the base, glossy dark green above, covered beneath with a close silvery down that ultimately turns brown, 2 to 5 in. long, $\frac{1}{2}$ to 2 in. wide; stalk thick and flattish, $\frac{1}{3}$ to $\frac{3}{4}$ in. long. Flowers opening in May in hemispherical trusses 4 to 5 in. wide, carrying fifteen or more flowers. Calyx small, shallowly five-lobed; slightly downy like the flower-stalk, which is up to 2 in. long. Corolla bell-shaped, five-lobed, 2 in. wide, $1\frac{1}{4}$ to $1\frac{1}{2}$ in. deep, soft pink, the upper lobes maroon-spotted; the outside is broadly striped with deep rosy pink. Stamens normally ten, $\frac{1}{3}$ to $\frac{5}{8}$ in. long, downy at the base; ovary thickly downy; style glabrous. *Bot. Mag.*, t. 8885.   (s. Arboreum *ss*. Argyrophyllum)

Native of W. Szechwan, China; introduced in 1908 by Wilson, who found it growing on the limestone bluffs of Mt Wu. It had, however, been seen by Henry and Pratt long before. It is an attractive and distinct species, considered to have some affinity with R. *arboreum*. The deep rosy bands of colour at the back of the corolla (they occur also in R. *thayerianum*) are very effective; the metallic lustre of the undersurface of the leaf is distinctive. It flowered when only 1 ft high and is very hardy at Kew.

R. *insigne* received an Award of Merit when shown from Bodnant on June 12, 1923.

R. INTRICATUM Franch.

A dwarf evergreen shrub usually 6 to 12 in. high, perhaps ultimately 18 in.; young shoots scurfy, with reddish scales. Leaves roundish ovate, $\frac{1}{4}$ to $\frac{1}{2}$ in. long, half or more than half as wide, dark green above, pale beneath, both surfaces covered with glistening scales; leaf-stalk distinctly formed, but only $\frac{1}{12}$ in. long. Flowers in terminal trusses of frequently five or six; each flower $\frac{5}{8}$ in. across, violet-purple in the bud state, becoming paler and lilac-coloured after opening. Calyx-lobes five, short, triangular. Corolla with a short tube and five rounded, spreading lobes. Stamens ten, almost entirely included within the corolla-tube, downy at the base. Style shorter than stamens. *Bot. Mag.*, t. 8163.   (s. Lapponicum)

R. *intricatum* was discovered by the Abbé Soulié in W. Szechwan in 1895, some way to the west of Kangting (Tatsien-lu), and was introduced by Wilson in 1904 when collecting for Messrs Veitch. Only three years later, in April 1907, that firm exhibited seedlings a few inches high but full of flower, and the species was straightway awarded a First Class Certificate (but under the erroneous name R. *nigropunctatum*). It was later reintroduced from the Muli area of S.W. Szechwan by Forrest and by Kingdon Ward.

This rhododendron makes a neat little bush of rounded form suggesting a pygmy tree, and it flowers when only a few inches high; this, together with the colour of the flowers and the profusion in which they are borne, render it a singularly attractive little plant for the rock garden or some such place, where tiny, slow-growing plants are not in danger of being smothered by stronger ones. Coming from high Alpine regions, it is quite hardy.

R. PERAMABILE Hutch.—In describing this species, Dr Hutchinson remarked that it could be no more than a 'luxurious state' of R. *intricatum*. The type is a cultivated plant, raised from Forrest 20463, the field-specimen corresponding to which is R. *yungningense*. It grows up to $2\frac{1}{2}$ ft high and has leaves $\frac{1}{2}$ to almost 1 in. long.

R. IRRORATUM Franch.

An evergreen shrub of rather stiff habit up to 12 ft high; occasionally a tree twice as high in the wild; young shoots minutely downy and glandular. Leaves of firm and rather leathery texture, narrowly elliptical, sharply pointed, tapered at the base; 2 to 5½ in. long, 1 to 1¾ in. wide; ultimately glabrous on both surfaces; veins in thirteen to sixteen pairs; stalk ⅓ to ⅗ in. long. Flowers in a terminal hemispherical truss, 4 in. wide, of about fifteen blooms opening in April. Calyx with five shallow triangular teeth, covered like the flower-stalk with minute glands; the latter is ½ to 1 in. long. Corolla bell-shaped, with the five rounded lobes notched and wavy at the margin; 1½ to 2 in. long and wide; the colouring varies, and although the ground is white, sometimes pure, sometimes yellowish, sometimes suffused with rose, it is always or nearly always more or less spotted, sometimes conspicuously so. Stamens ten, white or yellowish, about 1 in. long, minutely downy towards the base; anthers brown. Ovary densely glandular, as is also the style the whole of its length. *Bot. Mag.*, t. 7361.   (*s.* and *ss.* Irroratum)

Native of N.W. Yunnan at altitudes of 8,000 to 10,000 ft. It was discovered by Père Delavay near Lankiung in 1886 and introduced by him to France, thence to Kew, where it first flowered in 1893. However, the species is now mainly represented in cultivation by plants from the seeds collected by Forrest and by Dr Rock in the region from the Tali range northward to the Chungtien plateau and eastward beyond the Yangtse to Yungpeh. It seems to be a common species on the Sungkwei pass N.E. of Lankiung, in scrub and thickets.

R. *irroratum* is variable in the colour of its flowers. The form with white or blush-coloured flowers is represented in gardens by the lovely Rock 59220 and also by his 59212, 59620, and 59581, all represented in the Species Collection, Windsor Great Park. A form with pale creamy-yellow flowers was introduced by Forrest from the Sungkwei pass under his number F.5851. According to his field notes, F.21323 from south-west of Lichiang had orange-yellow flowers. Most remarkable are the forms with heavily spotted flowers, of which one was growing at Kew in 1911 and is figured in the *Gardeners' Chronicle* for that year (Vol. 49, facing page 350). This was presumably from the Delavay introduction. A similar form received an Award of Merit in 1957 when shown from Exbury on March 19 under the clonal name 'Polka Dot', but this plant has a very large number of flowers per truss for R. *irroratum* and could be a hybrid between it and R. *arboreum*. The normal white-flowered R. *irroratum* received an Award of Merit on the same occasion, exhibited from Minterne by Lord Digby.

R. JAPONICUM (A. Gray) Suringar ex Wils.

Azalea japonica A. Gray; R. *molle* Sieb. & Zucc., not G. Don; R. *molle* var. *glabrior* Miq.; *A. mollis* var. *glabrior* (Miq.) Reg.; R. *sinense* Maxim., not Sweet; *Azalea mollis* (Sieb. & Zucc.) André, not Blume

A deciduous bush, of rounded habit, 4 to 8 ft high, with stiff, erect branches; young shoots sparsely hairy. Leaves narrowly oval or obovate, 2 to 4 in. long, ¾ to 1¼ in. wide; dark green and sparsely hairy above, more or less glaucous and slightly hairy beneath when young, especially on the midrib and margins. Flowers six to ten in a cluster, produced during May on the end of leafless shoots, the corolla being of various shades of soft rose, salmon-red, and orange-red, 2½ to 3½ in. wide, the lobes oblong; calyx-lobes oblong to linear-oblong, as long as the ovary, conspicuously edged with long whitish hairs; flower-stalk ½ to 1 in. long, hairy. *Bot. Mag.*, t. 5905   (*s.* Azalea *ss.* Luteum)

Native of the main island of Japan and of Hokkaido, in open grassland and scrub, never in woods or dense thickets (Wilson); introduced to the Continent in 1830(?) and to Britain in the 1860s. It was taken up by the Ghent nurserymen, who used to raise it in large quantities from seed, mainly for forcing, and in that way many colour variants came to be selected, some of which come true from seed if self-pollinated. See further in the section on hybrids, under Mollis Azaleas, under which it is customary to group the named selections of R. japonicum as well as the hybrids between it and the closely allied R. *molle* (*sinense*), q.v.

R. JOHNSTONEANUM Watt ex Hutch.

An evergreen shrub occasionally up to 12 ft in the wild, but dwarf at high altitudes; young branchlets scaly and bristly. Leaves elliptic or slightly obovate, 2 to 4 in. long, ¾ to 1½ in. wide, rounded or obtuse at the apex, slightly narrowed at the base, densely scaly beneath, fringed with hairs when young; petioles up to ¾ in. long. Inflorescence a terminal truss of usually three or four flowers, opening in April or May; pedicels about ⅜ in. long, scaly. Calyx very short, oblique, fringed with long hairs. Corolla funnel-shaped, five-lobed, about 2¼ in. long, 3 in. wide, scaly on the outside, very fragrant, variable in colour, but typically white with a rose-purple flush along the midrib of the lobes on the outside, yellow on the upper side of the throat and with some crimson spotting on the upper lobe; sometimes pure white with a purple flush, or creamy white with a yellow tinge in the throat but with no hint of pink or purple. Stamens ten, downy in the lower half. Ovary scaly, style scaly except near the apex. Capsule six-celled. (*s.* Maddenii *ss.* Ciliicalyx)

Native of Assam, in the Naga Hills and Manipur; discovered by Sir George Watt early in 1882 in several localities at 6,000 to 11,000 ft; he named it after the wife of the Political Agent in Manipur and sent seeds and specimens to Kew, with detailed field notes, but the species was not described until 1919.

One of the summits on which Sir George Watt found this species was Mt Japvo in the Naga Hills, near the border with Manipur, near Kohima, and it was introduced from there by Kingdon Ward in 1927 (the seedlings from Watt's sending all eventually died off). Seven years later the species received an Award of Merit when exhibited by Lt-Col. L. C. R. Messel of Nymans, Sussex. In the plant shown, the flowers were creamy white with a yellow blotch inside on the upper part of the tube. In 1941 the same award was given to a plant under the distinguishing name 'Rubeotinctum', in which each lobe is striped with pink on the outside and there is a pink flush in the yellow patch in the throat. This was shown by Lt-Col. Bolitho of Trengwainton, Cornwall, and is actually the more typical form. But both plants were raised from the same batch of seed (KW 7732).

R. *johnstoneanum* is perhaps the hardiest member of the Ciliicalyx subseries after R. *ciliatum* and has lived out-of-doors in several gardens in southern England ever since it was first introduced almost half-a-century ago, though the finest plants are to be found in the milder parts.

R. *johnstoneanum* has produced plants with more or less double flowers. A clone with fully double flowers named 'Double Diamond' received an Award of Merit on April 17, 1956 (*R.C.Y.B. 1957*, fig. 29).

R. LYI Lévl.—Related to R. *johnstoneanum*, differing in its narrower leaves and less bristly shoots, but perhaps not specifically distinct. If the two species were to be united, as they have been by Dr Sleumer, then the combined species would have to take the name R. *lyi*, which has priority.

R. *lyi* was discovered in Kweichow, Central China, by a native collector Jean Ly, working for the French missionaries, and was introduced to Europe by seeds which they sent to M. Vilmorin. It is rather tender, and not common in cultivation. *Bot. Mag.*, t. 9051.

R. KAEMPFERI Planch.

R. *obtusum* var. *kaempferi* (Planch.) Wils.; *Azalea indica* var. *kaempferi* (Planch.) Rehd.; R. *indicum* var. *kaempferi* (Planch.) Maxim.

An evergreen or semi-evergreen shrub up to 10 ft high; young twigs covered with appressed, forward-pointing bristles. Leaves of two forms: spring leaves (i.e., those on the lower part of the fully developed shoot) lanceolate, ovate, or elliptic, up to 2 in. long, ⅜ to 1⅛ in. wide, mostly deciduous, at least in cold localities; summer leaves (i.e., those formed later in the season and situated nearer to the terminal bud) smaller and elliptic or obovate, mostly persisting through the winter; both types glossy green above, paler beneath, with scattered bristly hairs on both surfaces. Flowers produced about mid-May (later in some forms), two to four in terminal clusters on silky-hairy stalks about ¼ in. long. Calyx-lobes five, narrowly ovate or elliptic, hairy outside and at the margins. Corolla funnel-shaped, five-lobed, 1½ to 2 in. across, coloured some shade of red, with faint purplish or crimson spotting on the upper lobes. Stamens five, hairy in the lower part, anthers yellow or sometimes purple. Style glabrous. (*s.* Azalea *ss.* Obtusum)

Native of Japan, where it is widespread. According to Wilson it is a sun-loving plant, 'seen to best advantage in open thickets on mountain slopes'. It was introduced to the United States by Prof. Sargent in 1892, thence to Kew two years later, but there may have been an earlier introduction by Charles Maries to Messrs Veitch in 1878.

R. *kaempferi*, at least in the forms commonly cultivated, is a perfectly hardy species. It varies greatly in flower-colour; some plants have flowers in hard shades of orange-scarlet; others, with some pink in the colouring, are very beautiful. Always the colour tends to fade quickly in the sun, so light shade is desirable. Although the normal flowering-time is May, some clones flower later but appear nevertheless to be pure R. *kaempferi*, not hybrids of the naturally late-flowering R. *indicum*. Two such clones bear the names 'Daimio' and 'Mikado'.

A clone named 'Eastern Fire' was awarded a First Class Certificate on May 24, 1955, when exhibited by the Crown Estate Commissioners, Windsor Great Park, and had received an Award of Merit two years earlier. The flowers are described as Camellia Rose, darkening towards the tips of the lobes.

R. *kaempferi* is a parent of many of the hardiest evergreen azalea hybrids.
R. *kaempferi* f. *multicolor* Wils. and f. *mikawanum* (Makino) Wils. are con-
sidered by Hara to represent for the most part hybrids between R. *kaempferi* and
R. *macrosepalum* (H. Hara, *R.Y.B. 1948*, p. 120).

R. 'OBTUSUM'.—The plant named *Azalea obtusa* by Lindley was introduced
by Fortune from the Poushan nursery, Shanghai, China, in 1844, and is figured
in *Bot. Reg.*, Vol. 32 (1846), t. 37. There is no doubt that the original stock came
from Japan, where according to Wilson the same azalea is much cultivated
around Tokyo and Yokohama. There was a later introduction by Veitch from
Japan, which differed slightly from Fortune's plant, but curiously enough
neither seems to be in cultivation in Britain at the present time. From Lindley's
figure and description it is evident that 'Obtusum' is a hybrid of R. *kaempferi*.
The small flowers, described by Lindley as glowing red, have oval, acute, widely
spaced lobes, the upper one spotted; the summer (persistent) leaves are obovate,
obtuse, dark green, the spring leaves bright green, elliptic-lanceolate, acute.
The small flowers and dense habit suggest that the other parent was R. *kiusianum*,
and that, like 'Amoenum' and 'Ramentaceum' (qq.v. below), it came originally
from the mountains of Kyushu. 'Obtusum', then, is simply one of the many
garden clones deriving mainly or wholly from R. *kiusianum* or from natural
hybrids between it and R. *kaempferi*. Wilson's view, however, was that R.
kaempferi and R. *kiusianum* were states of one and the same variable species, and
that plants such as typical R. *obtusum* were linking forms, uniting the two extremes, which he admitted were very distinct (Rehder and Wilson, *Monograph of
Azaleas* (1921), p. 40). For this polymorphic "species" he therefore adopted the
name R. *obtusum* (Lindl.) Planch. and under it he placed R. *kaempferi* as a variety,
while R. *kiusianum* appears as a synonym of R. *obtusum* f. *japonicum* (Maxim.)
Wils. He failed to notice that the name R. *obtusum* (Lindl.) Planch. is illegitimate,
since it is long antedated by R. *obtusum* Wats., used in 1825 for some form or
hybrid of R. *ponticum*. However, the illegitimacy of the name is really a minor
consideration, of importance only to a botanist who considers that Wilson's
taxonomic treatment of the group is correct. If the type of R. *obtusum* (Lindl.)
Planch. is a hybrid between two distinct species, as is now generally accepted,
the name, even if legitimate, could be used only for other hybrids of the same
parentage.

The botanical synonymy of R. 'Obtusum' is: R. *obtusum* (Lindl.) Planch.
(1854), *nom. illegit.*, not Wats. (1825); *Azalea obtusa* Lindl.; R. *indicum* var.
obtusum (Lindl.) Maxim.

R. KIUSIANUM Makino R. *indicum* var. *amoenum* f. *japonicum* Maxim.;
R. *indicum* var. *japonicum* (Maxim.) Makino; R. *obtusum* f. *japonicum* (Maxim.)
Wils.; R. *kaempferi* var. *japonicum* (Maxim.) Rehd.; R. *amoenum* var. *japonicum*
(Maxim.) Bean—Although in its essential characters this species is quite near to
R. *kaempferi* it is very distinct in general aspect. It is a low, dense, sometimes
prostrate shrub, usually under 3 ft high in the wild. The spring leaves are variable in shape, mostly broad-elliptic to obovate, obtuse and up to about ¾ in. long,
glossier and darker than those of R. *kaempferi* (at least on most cultivated plants);
the summer leaves are obovate, oblanceolate, or elliptic, mostly obtuse, and at
least the uppermost ones are persistent through the winter; all the leaves are

covered with appressed hairs. Flowers in twos or threes. Calyx well developed, with ciliate lobes. Corolla about 1 in. wide, varying in colour from mauve to light or dark magenta-pink, sometimes white, usually unspeckled (at least in cultivated plants), with a short tube and spreading limb. Stamens five, as in R. *kaempferi*.

R. *kiusianum* is an endemic of Kyushu, the southernmost of the four main islands of Japan, where it occurs on the mountains and volcanoes in open places above 2,500 ft. It was first described in 1870 by the Russian botanist Maximowicz, as R. *indicum* var. *amoenum* f. *japonicum*, from specimens collected on Mt Unzen in central Kyushu. The Japanese botanist Makino raised the plants to the rank of variety—R. *indicum* var. *japonicum* (Maxim.) Makino—and in 1914 gave them specific rank, but had to find a new epithet, since the name R. *japonicum* had been applied to two other species. Thus R. *kiusianum* and R. *obtusum* f. *japonicum* (Maxim.) Wils. are both typified by the Unzen specimens and Maximowicz's description.

R. *kiusianum* was introduced from the wild by Wilson, who collected seed in 1918 on Nishi-Kirishima and sent it to the Arnold Arboretum. The seed was widely distributed, and the older plantings in Britain derive from it, but there have been other importations of seed and plants since then. The Kyushu azalea is not much planted in gardens but deserves to be more common, as it is hardy in most forms and the flowers, though small, are borne abundantly in May or early June. Owing to its dense habit it is an excellent weed-smotherer and would not be out-of-place in the heather garden.

R. 'AMOENUM'.—A shrub of dense habit, building up tiers of branches and eventually 5 or 6 ft high (occasionally even taller), more in width. Spring leaves rich green and rather thick, elliptic or elliptic-obovate, persistent on strong shoots, summer leaves smaller, obovate to spathulate, both sorts clad with appressed hairs on both surfaces, but especially above and on the margins. Flowers in twos or threes, borne in May. Corolla funnel-shaped, rosy purple, ¾ in. wide. Calyx-lobes narrow-oblong, ⅜ in. long, resembling the corolla in shape and colour, and giving the appearance of one flower growing out of another—a character known to gardeners as 'hose-in-hose'. *Bot. Mag.*, t. 4728.

R. 'Amoenum' was introduced by Fortune in 1850 from the Poushan nursery near Shanghai, China, for Standish, and Noble. Like 'Obtusum', which he had found in the same nursery six years earlier, it is of Japanese origin; and is not specifically distinct from R. *kiusianum*. The botanical synonymy is: R. *amoenum* (Lindl.) Planch.; *Azalea amoena* Lindl. (1852); R. *indicum* var. *amoenum* d. *genuinum* Maxim.; R. *obtusum* var. *amoenum* Wils. It will be seen that the name R. *amoenum* has long priority over R. *kiusianum*, which could take the name R. *amoenum* var. *japonicum* (Maxim.) Bean. The only reason for retaining the name R. *kiusianum* in the present revision is that there is a still earlier name to be considered (see 'Ramentaceum').

Although long treated as a greenhouse shrub, 'Amoenum' is quite hardy and a very pleasing evergreen, flowering most profusely and at all times a neat shrub. It grows slowly, and may be only 3 ft high after twenty years, though more than twice that in width. This is a valuable characteristic in many positions, especially where a permanently low evergreen mass is desired without the trouble and perhaps unsightliness of a periodical cropping. There is a pink-flowered branch-sport 'Amoenum Coccineum', which is apt to revert to the normal form.

R. 'RAMENTACEUM' ('Obtusum Album').—This azalea was introduced by Fortune from Hong Kong in 1846 and described by Lindley in 1849. It never became established in this country but, in common with many other azaleas grown in Britain in the 1840s and 1850s, it found its way to the USA, and was cultivated in the Holm Lea Collection at Brookline. It was reintroduced to Britain early this century but apparently again lost. From Lindley's original description and figure, and from herbarium specimens of cultivated plants, 'Ramentaceum' would seem to be an azalea similar to those members of the Kurume group that have white or pale pink flowers. The corolla is white, 1¼ in. long and wide, and the spring leaves are broad-elliptic to roundish, up to 1½ in. long. Lindley's epithet *ramentacea* refers to the chaffy, awl-shaped hairs to be seen on the stems of R. *kiusianum*, R. *kaempferi*, etc. The fact that the original introduction was from Hong Kong need not be a cause for surprise, since there is abundant evidence for the cultivation of Japanese azaleas in the coastal cities of China. Wilson considered 'Ramentaceum' to be no more than a white-flowered, large-leaved form of R. *obtusum* f. *japonicum*, i.e. of R. *kiusianum*, and if he is right then R. *ramentaceum* would be the correct name for R. *kiusianum*, over which it has long priority. But this is a matter best left until the Kyushu azaleas have received the thorough taxonomic study that they deserve. The botanical synonymy of R. 'Ramentaceum' is: R. *ramentaceum* (Lindl.) Planch. (1854); *Azalea ramentacea* Lindl. (1849); R. *obtusum* f. *album* Schneid.

It should be added that R. *sataense* Nakai, described in 1949, seems to be near to 'Ramentaceum', judging from an authentic specimen in the Kew Herbarium, collected on Mt Kaimon, near Kagoshima in Kyushu.

R. KEISKEI Miq.

An evergreen shrub 6 ft high in the wild; young branches slightly scaly. Leaves 1½ to 2½ in. long, ¾ to 1¼ in. wide, oval-oblong, pointed at the apex, rounded or tapered at the base, more or less scaly on both surfaces, but especially beneath; stalk about ¼ in. long. Flowers pale, rather dull yellow, 1¼ to 2 in. across, in clusters of about four or five; corolla broadly bell-shaped; calyx undulated into five very shallow lobes; stamens ten, slightly downy; flower-stalk scaly, ½ to ¾ in. long. Blossoms in April and May. *Bot. Mag.*, t. 8300. (*s.* and *ss.* Triflorum)

Native of Japan from the main island southward as far as Yakushima; introduced in 1908 and quite hardy. It is a rather variable species, both in habit and in the size and shape of its leaves. In his collection at The Grange, Benenden, Kent, Capt. Collingwood Ingram has a tall-growing plant which he considers to be a good match for typical R. *keiskei*, in which the leaves are lanceolate, acute, up to 3 in. long and ¾ in. wide, and the petioles bristly when young. The commonly cultivated form, by contrast, is of low-growing habit and has shorter and relatively broader leaves, which are obtuse or subacute at the apex, with a stout midrib and glabrous petioles. Ingram considers the latter to represent a distinct species, which he has named R. *laticostum* (*R.C.Y.B. 1971*, pp. 28–30).

These two cultivated forms are certainly very distinct, but the difference would probably be much less clear-cut if a wide range of wild specimens were examined. In the same article, Ingram published a second species, R. *trichocalyx*, described from a cultivated plant. He informs us that he is now satisfied that the plant in question is a hybrid of garden origin.

cv. 'YAKU FAIRY'.—A prostrate plant with flowers about 1¾ in. across in trusses of two to five. Leaves lanceolate, up to 1½ in. long. Award of Merit April 14, 1970, when shown by Barry N. Starling. It was collected on Mt Kuromi, Yakushima (see R.C.Y.B. *1971*, pp. 104–6).

R. KELETICUM Balf. f. & Forr. [PLATE 80

A dwarf evergreen shrub, forming a low dense mound (but sometimes prostrate and mat-forming); young shoots slender, densely scaly, not or scarcely bristly. Leaves elliptic, oblong-elliptic, or sometimes broadest slightly below the middle, rounded to acute and mucronate at the apex, ¼ to ⅞ in. long, about half as wide, upper surface glossy, usually more or less scaly, undersurface densely brown-scaly, margins bristly or glabrous; petiole about ⅙ in. long, scaly, usually without bristles. Flowers solitary, in pairs or in threes on glabrous or bristly reddish stalks up to 1¼ in. long. Calyx tinged with red, five-lobed to the base, up to ⅜ in. long, margins bristly. Corolla open funnel-shaped to almost rotate, about 1½ in. wide, in some shade of purplish crimson, spotted with reddish purple or red-magenta, downy and scaly on the outside. Ovary scaly; style red, glabrous. (*s.* Saluenense)

R. *keleticum* was discovered by Forrest in 1919 in Tsarong, S.E. Tibet, on the Salween–Kiuchiang divide, growing in 'open, peaty, stony pasture and on cliffs and screes'. He introduced it from this locality in the same year, and all his later sendings (and Kingdon Ward's 5430) are from the same region, though it is also found in bordering parts of Burma. It is perfectly hardy and one of the best of all rhododendrons for the rock garden, quickly forming a dense bush and flowering in late May or June when the danger of spring frosts is past. It received an Award of Merit in 1928, when shown by Messrs Gill and Son of Falmouth. A fine form was introduced by Rock in 1948, during his expedition for the American Rhododendron Society.

R. NITENS Hutch.—Scarcely differing from R. *keleticum* in its botanical characters but more erect and flowering even later (June–July). Described from a cultivated plant, raised from KW 5842. The seeds were collected by Kingdon Ward in November 1922 on the Taru Tra, west of the Taron (Kiuchiang), at 12,000 ft, during his journey from Yunnan to Fort Hertz (Putao) in Burma.

R. RADICANS Balf. f. & Forr.—This species too is closely allied to R. *keleticum*, and comes from the same area, but has relatively narrower leaves up to ⅜ in. long, one-third or less wide, and is of more prostrate habit. The most prostrate form is Forrest's original introduction (F.19919) of 1921, from open, stony moorland at 15,000 altitude, on the Salween–Kiuchiang divide, some twenty miles south of the type-locality of R. *keleticum*. It makes an interesting shrub for the rock garden, soon covering a wide area on a damp ledge, but does not flower freely in some gardens. Other forms are nearer to R. *keleticum* in habit and not so good.

R. KEYSII Nutt.

An evergreen shrub 6 ft or more high; the young shoots, the undersurface of the leaves, leaf-stalk, and flower-stalk densely covered with brownish-red, glistening scales. Leaves 2 to 4 in. long, ⅜ to 1¼ in. wide, oval-ovate, tapering at both ends; stalk ⅓ to ⅔ in. long. Flowers crowded in short clusters, several of which are borne during May and June from buds near the end of the previous year's shoot, and at the time of flowering surmounted by the young shoot of the current year. Each flower is ¾ to 1 in. long, ¼ in. wide—a brick-red, cylindrical tube with five small, blunt, yellow teeth at the mouth; calyx very small; flower-stalk ¼ in. long. *Bot. Mag.*, t. 4875.   (s. Cinnabarinum)

Native of the eastern Himalaya, from Bhutan to the region of the Tsangpo bend; introduced by Booth from Bhutan in 1851. But most of the plants now in collections derive from seed collected by Kingdon Ward in the early winter of 1924 in Pemako, S.E. Tibet, on the southern side of the Doshong La, where it grows in thickets on the southern slopes of the valley or as undergrowth in the forest at 9,000 to 10,000 ft. These plants (KW 6257) are hardier than the form originally introduced from Bhutan but the species, although of some value for its late flowering, is really little more than a botanical curiosity. It is allied to R. *cinnabarinum*, but the flowers are much smaller, correa-like, and produced from axillary as well as terminal buds.

Award of Merit June 27, 1933 to a form raised from KW 6257 in which the flowers are uniform red except for a slight yellow tinge at the tips, shown by Lionel de Rothschild, Exbury. It was named var. *unicolor* by Hutchinson.

R. KONGBOENSE Hutch.

An evergreen shrub usually 2 to 3 ft high, but found by Kingdon Ward up to 8 ft high in open forest. Leaves oblong or oblong-lanceolate, up to 1 in. long, about half as wide, with scattered scales above, undersides densely coated with light brown scales. Flowers in a dense terminal head, very shortly stalked, opening in April or May. Calyx up to 3/16 in. long, scaly. Corolla rosy pink, narrowly tubular, densely hairy inside and out, not scaly. Stamens five, glabrous, just reaching to the mouth of the tube. Ovary usually densely scaly; style about as long as ovary, glabrous. *Bot. Mag.*, t. 9492.   (s. Anthopogon)

R. *kongboense* was discovered by Kingdon Ward in 1924 on the Doshong La at the eastern end of the Himalaya, in the Tibetan province of Kongbo, and was introduced by him during the same expedition. It is of taller and laxer growth than most members of the Anthopogon series, and with flowers of an unusually deep shade of pink. It is perfectly hardy, but not common in gardens. The leaves are highly aromatic and were burnt as incense by rich householders in Kongbo (Kingdon Ward, *Assam Adventure*, p. 72).

R. KYAWII Lace & W. W. Sm.

R. *prophanthum* Balf. f. & Forr.

An evergreen shrub up to 15 or 20 ft high; young shoots at first furnished with starry down and glands, afterwards glabrous. Leaves between oblong and oval, 6 to 12 in. long, 2 to 4 in. wide, dark green and loosely downy above and finally glabrous there, the undersurface at first covered with starry down and glands like the young shoots, much or all of which wears away leaving it pale and shining green; stalk up to 2¼ in. long. Flowers opening during July and August in trusses of twelve to sixteen, the main flower-stalk downy and glandular. Calyx ⅜ in. wide, with five broad shallow lobes; flower-stalk ½ to 1 in. long, bristly glandular. Corolla fleshy, funnel-shaped, 3 in. wide by 2¼ in. deep, rich crimson, downy outside, five-lobed, the lobes 1 in. wide; there are five darkly coloured pouches at the base. Stamens ten, crimson, up to 1⅝ in. long, downy at the base. Ovary covered with tawny down; style 1¾ in. long, crimson, glandular over most of its length. *Bot. Mag.*, t. 9271.   (s. Irroratum ss. Parishii)

Native of eastern upper Burma; discovered in 1912 by Maung Kyaw, a collector in the Burmese Forest Service, after whom it is named. He found it near the Hpyepat bungalow, two stages short of Fort Htagaw, on the track from Myitkyina to Hpimaw on the Yunnan frontier. Seven years later Farrer and Cox collected seeds at the type-locality on their way back from the frontier area (Farrer 1444, Nov. 1919). But in the previous May Forrest had found a plant some 35 miles farther north at 9,000 ft, bearing last year's capsules, and collected seed, so the credit for introducing the species belongs to him (F.17928, originally distributed as R. *prophanthum*).

R. *kyawii* is a magnificent species, but is seen to best advantage in the mildest parts or in a cool greenhouse. There is a plant at Eckford, Argyll, planted about 1930, 13 ft high and 40 ft in circumference (*R.C.Y.B. 1968*, p. 47). It is closely related to R. *eriogynum*, having the same starry down on various parts, the same glittering undersurface of the adult leaf, and the same habit of growing late in the season; but the foliage, flowers and the plant itself are larger.

R. AGAPETUM Balf. f. & Ward—Very closely allied to R. *kyawii* and perhaps not specifically distinct. It was found by Kingdon Ward in 1914 growing on limestone cliffs below Hpimaw, on the Burma–Yunnan frontier, and was introduced by him in 1922 from the Taron Gorge, some 120 miles farther north. Forrest's 24680, of which the field specimen is identified as R. *agapetum*, was actually collected only a few miles from the type-locality of R. *kyawii*.

R. PARISHII C. B. Cl.—As the type of the Parishii subseries this species must be mentioned, though it is very tender and only suitable for cultivation in a large greenhouse. It was described in 1882 from a specimen collected by the Rev. C. Parrish at the southern end of the Dawna range, south-east of the Burmese port of Moulmein, at 6,500 ft. In 1912 it was rediscovered in the type-locality by J. H. Lace, Chief Conservator of Forests, Burma, who collected flower and fruit from which the species was more amply described in 1914 (*Notes Roy. Bot. Gard. Edin.*, Vol. 8, p. 213). It is interesting that the affinity between R. *parishii* and R. *kyawi*, described in the same issue of the *Notes*, was not remarked on, perhaps because R. *parishii* is very distinct from that species (and other members of the subseries) in its relatively short, broad leaves, only twice as long as wide. In leaf-indumentum and floral characters they are very similar.

R. LACTEUM Franch.

R. *mairei* Lévl.

An evergreen shrub or a tree up to 30 ft high; young shoots ½ in. thick, at first scurfy, becoming glabrous. Leaves oblong-ovate, shortly pointed, rounded or slightly heart-shaped at the base; 4 to 8 in. long, about half as much wide; dark green and glabrous above, clothed beneath with a fine, close tawny felt, much of which sometimes wears off before the leaf falls; stalk ¾ to 1½ in. long. Flowers opening in April, closely packed twenty or thirty together in a truss up to 8 in. across, on downy stalks up to 1 in. long. Calyx a mere wavy rim. Corolla bell-shaped, soft or canary yellow, 2 in. wide, five-lobed, not markedly blotched. Stamens ten, downy towards the base. Ovary covered with whitish down; style glabrous. *Bot. Mag.*, t. 8988.   (*s.* Lacteum)

R. *lacteum* was discovered by the French missionary Delavay near Hoking, Yunnan, in 1884, forming almost pure forests on Mt Koua La Po at 9,500 to 12,500 ft; it was introduced by Forrest from the Tali range, some seventy-five miles farther south, in 1910 (F.6778, with canary-yellow flowers). Subsequently he sent seeds from the Chienchuan–Mekong and Salween–Irrawaddy divides, but some of these were from plants with pale yellow or even white flowers.

Unfortunately, R. *lacteum* is not easy to grow and many once-famous plants are now dead. It is also a shy seeder and difficult to increase by layering, consequently very rare in gardens. It is said to grow best in a very acid soil.

R. *lacteum* was awarded a First Class Certificate on April 13, 1967, when shown by S. F. Christie from his garden at Blackhills, Morayshire (clone 'Blackhills'). The plant there, about 15 ft high, bears primrose-yellow flowers, without spot or blotch (*R.C.Y.B. 1968*, p. 25 and Frontispiece). There are some fine plants at Corsock, Galloway, raised from seeds collected by Forrest during his last expedition, one 20 ft high and wide (*R.C.Y.B. 1965*, pp. 50–1 and Plate 2).

R. LANATUM Hook. f.   [PLATE 78

An evergreen shrub rarely more than 6 or 7 ft high in cultivation, but said to be sometimes a small tree in the wild; young shoots, undersurface of leaves, and flower-stalks thickly covered with a pale brown felt. Leaves obovate to narrowly oval, rounded at the end, 2½ to 5 in. long, 1 to 2¼ in. wide, upper surface at first covered with whitish wool which ultimately falls away except at the base of the midrib, leaving it dark green; stalk ¼ to ½ in. long. Flowers in a terminal cluster of usually six or seven but sometimes ten, opening in April, on stalks ½ to ¾ in. long. Calyx very small. Corolla 2 to 2½ in. wide, bell-shaped, five-lobed, pale yellow dotted with red, the lobes rounded, ¾ in. wide. Stamens ten, downy at the base; anthers dark brown. Ovary woolly; style glabrous. (*s.* Campanulatum)

Native of the Himalaya from E. Nepal eastward; discovered by J. D. Hooker late in 1848 in E. Nepal, at 10,000 to 12,000 ft, and introduced by him. Lionel de Rothschild wrote of this species: 'R. *lanatum* . . . is the most difficult member of this series to cultivate in our climate. It has pretty yellow flowers, while its leaves have an attractive tawny, woolly tomentum underneath. It is hardy in most gardens, but cannot stand drought and, above all, requires more leaf soil than most rhododendrons, and unless it is given plenty of suitable woodland soil round the roots and beech haulm and oak leaves dug in and a good mulching of bracken or leaf soil on the top, is very ill-tempered and often looks a stubborn and seedy plant' (*Year Book Rhod. Ass. 1934*, p. 109).

var. LUCIFERUM Cowan—Leaves narrower, oblong, pointed at the apex. Described from specimens collected by Ludlow and Sherriff in S.E. Tibet in 1936, and introduced by them. The type is from the Bimbi La, in Tsari. In the field note they remark: 'Indumentum of dried leaf is skinned off and rolled up and sold as wicks for butter lamps'—whence the epithet *luciferum*.

R. TSARIENSE Cowan—Leaves smaller than in R. *lanatum*, 1 to 2½ in. long, ⅜ to 1¼ in. wide, rounded or slightly cordate at the base, very shortly stalked. Flowers pink, cream-coloured, or white, often spotted with pink. Discovered by Ludlow and Sherriff in the Tsari region of the Tibetan Himalaya in 1936 and introduced by them. According to the collectors' field notes the species varies in habit and may grow 12 ft high. Their seed-number 2766 was from plants 2 to 5 ft high, and an example at Edinburgh from this sending was only 2 ft high in 1960, when almost a quarter-century old. In 1964 an Award of Merit was given to clone 'Yum-Yum' with white flowers flushed with pink, exhibited by Maj.-Gen. and Mrs Harrison, Tremeer, Cornwall, on April 7. The original plant, then about 4 ft high and as much across, was raised from Ludlow and Sherriff 2858, collected 1936; according to the field note, the parent plants were 8 to 10 ft high.

R. *tsariense*, in its dwarf forms, would be worth planting even if it never flowered. It makes a rugged, compact specimen, and the leaves, powdered with brown above all through the summer, become glabrous and rich olive-green in winter.

R. LANIGERUM Tagg
R. *silvaticum* Cowan

An evergreen shrub or small tree, up to 40 ft high in the wild; young stems clad with whitish or grey wool. Leaves oblong, oblong-lanceolate, or oblong-oblanceolate, 6 to 10 in. long, 1½ to 3 in. wide, obtuse, rounded or sometimes cuspidate at the apex, cuneate to rounded at the base, lateral veins impressed, glabrous above when mature, clad beneath with a dense whitish or grey felt; petiole up to ⅞ in, long, woolly. Inflorescence a dense terminal truss of up to forty or so flowers, opening late February to April; pedicels ⅜ to ⅝ in. long. Calyx ⅛ in. or slightly less long. Corolla campanulate or tubular-campanulate, about 2 in. wide, carmine or rosy purple, five-lobed. Stamens ten. Ovary clad with grey or white wool; style glabrous.   (*s.* and *ss.* Arboreum)

R. *lanigerum* was described in 1931 from a specimen collected by Kingdon

Ward in 1928 in the Delei valley, Mishmi Hills, Assam (KW 8251), growing with other big-leaved rhododendrons at 10,000–11,000 ft. He collected seed, and all the plants known as R. *lanigerum* up to about 1960 are from this number. However, as it has later proved, Kingdon Ward had found R. *lanigerum* earlier, in 1924, growing in Pemako on the southern side of the Doshong La, at the eastern end of the Himalaya, at 9,000–10,000 ft. He collected seed but never saw the plants in flower, and his fruiting specimen was at first taken to be R. *niveum* (KW 6258). It was described as a new species in 1936, under the name R. *silvaticum*, the details of the flowers and inflorescence being taken from a plant at Muncaster Castle, raised from KW 6258. The two species were placed in different series—R. *lanigerum* in *s.* Falconeri, as an aberrant member, and R. *silvaticum* in *ss.* Arboreum. So it remained until about 1961, when exhibits at the early R.H.S. shows under the name R. *silvaticum* were pronounced to be R. *lanigerum*, of which R. *silvaticum* appears as a synonym in the R.H.S. *Handbook*, 1963 (and in later editions). R. *lanigerum* (*silvaticum*) was also found by Kingdon Ward in the Tsangpo Gorge, where seed was later collected by Ludlow, Sherriff, and Elliot (no. 13591, from Pemakochung).

R. *lanigerum*, at its best, is a splendid species, with beautifully coloured flowers in noble trusses, but the numerous awards given to it are a testimony more to its variability than to its worth as a garden plant, since it flowers too early in the spring to be reliable in its display. The type-introduction (KW 8251) seems to be uncommon, and is said to be rather tender. It received an Award of Merit on March 29, 1949, when shown by Col. E. Bolitho, Trengwainton, Cornwall (flowers carmine). The other awards have all been given to forms exhibited as R. *silvaticum* (or originally grown under that name). These are: 'ROUND WOOD', A.M. March 20, 1951, shown by Crown Estate Commissioners, Windsor, and Mrs Stevenson (flowers crimson, twenty in the truss); 'SILVIA', A.M. April 13, 1954, shown by R. Olaf Hambro, Logan House, Stranraer (flowers pale crimson suffused white, forty in the truss; R.C.Y.B. *1955*, frontispiece); 'STONEHURST', A.M. March 14, 1961, shown by Ralph Strauss, Stonehurst, Ardingly (flowers cherry-red; R.C.Y.B. *1962*, fig. 29); 'CHAPEL WOOD', F.C.C. February 21, 1967, and previously an A.M. February 28, 1961, shown by the Crown Estate Commissioners, Windsor (flowers Neyron Rose, forty to fifty in the truss; R.C.Y.B. *1962*, fig. 27).

R. LAPPONICUM (L.) Wahlenb.

Azalea lapponica L.

A dwarf evergreen shrub rarely more than 1 to $1\frac{1}{2}$ ft high, the lower branches often prostrate; young wood very scaly, becoming warted. Leaves oblong, rounded or abruptly tapered at the apex, $\frac{1}{4}$ to 1 in. long, $\frac{1}{8}$ to $\frac{1}{4}$ in. wide, rough and dark green above, covered beneath with brownish-yellow scales; stalk $\frac{1}{12}$ to $\frac{1}{8}$ in. long. Flowers bright purple, $\frac{3}{4}$ in. across, produced three to six together in a small cluster. Calyx and flower-stalk very scaly; calyx-lobes triangular, fringed; stamens five to eight, about as long as the corolla, quite devoid of down; flower-stalk $\frac{1}{4}$ to $\frac{1}{2}$ in. long. *Bot. Mag.*, t. 3106. (*s.* Lapponicum)

Native of northern Scandinavia, often on limestone, and of North America in high latitudes, also found on a few mountain tops in the north-eastern USA. It was introduced to Britain in 1825 but was soon lost to cultivation and although reintroduced many times since then it has never become established. It probably requires exceptionally cool, moist conditions and a long snow-cover. It is a very pretty plant, the colour of the flowers being very bright, and with more blue in them than almost any other species. See also R. *parvifolium*.

R. LEPIDOSTYLUM Balf. f. & Forr.

An evergreen dwarf shrub of mounded habit, up to 3 ft high, more across; branchlets bristly and scaly. Leaves thin, ovate to obovate, obtuse at the apex, about 1½ in. long and ⅝ in. wide, intensely glaucous above, especially when young and in the following winter, paler and scaly beneath, very bristly at the margin; petioles up to ⅜ in. long, bristly. Flowers solitary or in twos, terminal, borne in June on stalks ¾ to 1¼ in. long. Calyx about ⅜ in. deep, scaly and bristly. Corolla funnel-shaped, five-lobed, about 1½ in. wide, pale yellow or greenish yellow, with darker spotting, downy and scaly on the back. Stamens ten, hairy at the base. Ovary scaly and bristly; style slender, scaly at the base.   (s.Trichocladum)

R. *lepidostylum* was described from a specimen collected by Forrest in 1919 on the Jangtzow Shan, Shweli–Salween divide, near the border between Yunnan and Burma, and was introduced by him from the same area in 1924 (F.24633). According to his field note it makes there a compact shrub 1 to 1½ ft high, growing on humus-covered boulders and on ledges of cliffs at 11,000 to 12,000 ft. He made no mention of the striking colour of the foliage for which alone this species is valued in gardens, the flowers being negligible. This feature was apparently first remarked on in print by A. T. Johnson eleven years after the species was introduced: 'Not much over 1 ft in height, but extending laterally to two or three feet, this Rhododendron would be well worth a place for its foliage alone, for the leaves are almost luminously glaucous, especially in winter. The leaves, ovate or obovate, are covered with silvery bristles, which, fringing the margins and stalks, render the foliage still more attractive' (*Gard. Chron.*, Vol. 98 (1935), p. 224). The remarkable foliage and characteristic habit of R. *lepidostylum* is well shown in the colour photograph of a clump at Brodick in the Isle of Arran, reproduced in the *Year Book* for 1951-2, fig. 55.

R. *lepidostylum* is perfectly hardy and starts into growth so late that the young growths are unlikely ever to be damaged by frost. It received an Award of Merit on June 24, 1969, when shown by Capt. Collingwood Ingram, Benenden, Kent.

R. CAESIUM Hutch.—This unimportant species comes from the same region as R. *lepidostylum* and, like it, is evergreen or almost so. It is a shrub up to 4 ft high, with aromatic leaves oblong-lanceolate to elliptic, 1½ to 2 in. long and 1 in. wide, dull green above, glaucous beneath. Flowers about three in a terminal truss opening in May or early June. Calyx minute, with a few bristly hairs. Corolla funnel-campanulate, greenish yellow or pale yellow with green markings, about ¾ in. long. It was described from a plant at Exbury raised from Forrest 26798 collected in Yunnan near the border with Burma in latitude 25° 54′ at 10,000 ft.

R. LEPIDOTUM G. Don

R. *obovatum* Hook. f.; R. *lepidotum* var. *obovatum* (Hook. f.) Hook. f.; R. *salignum* Hook. f.; R. *lepidotum* var. *chloranthum* Bot. Mag., t. 4802; R. *elaeagnoides* Hook. f.; R. *lepidotum* var. *elaeagnoides* (Hook. f.) Franch.; R. *sinolepidotum* Balf. f.; R. *cremnastes* Balf. f. & Farr.

A low evergreen or sometimes almost deciduous shrub up to 4 ft high; young shoots slender, warted, and scaly, sometimes bristly. Leaves varying from obovate to lanceolate, up to 1 in. or slightly more long, and about half as wide, densely scaly on both sides; stalks up to ⅛ in. long. Flowers produced in late May, June, or July, singly or a few together in terminal trusses; pedicels ½ to 1½ in. long. Calyx five-lobed, scaly, sometimes fringed with hairs. Corolla flat and open (rotate), varying from yellow, greenish yellow, or white to crimson or shades of pink or purple. Stamens eight to ten, hairy in the lower part or for up to two-thirds of their length. Ovary scaly; style short, stout, bent. *Bot. Mag.*, tt. 4657, 4802, 6450.   (*s.* and *ss.* Lepidotum)

R. *lepidotum* is one of the most wide-ranging of rhododendrons, found from the N.W. Himalaya through S.E. Tibet, upper Burma, and N. Yunnan to S.W. Szechwan. It is mainly a subalpine species, occurring at up to 15,000 ft altitude. It was described in 1835 and introduced fifteen years later by J. D. Hooker from Sikkim, but probably most of the cultivated plants are from seeds collected in China. Both in the wild and in cultivation it is a variable species, especially in flower-colour, but no varieties were recognised by Cowan and Davidian in their revision of the Lepidotum series.

cv. 'REUTHE'S PURPLE'.—Flowers purplish red (R.H.S. Colour Chart 80A). Award of Merit May 22, 1967.

R. LOWNDESII Davidian—Near to R. *lepidotum*, but deciduous, with bristly leaf-margins and petioles and the scales on the leaf-undersides more widely spaced. It is a dwarf shrub, up to 1 ft high in the wild, with dull yellow flowers marked with crimson on the upper lobes. It was discovered by Col. Donald Lowndes in the Marsyandi valley, Nepal, behind the Annapurna massif, and was later collected in other inner valleys of central and western Nepal. These inner valleys north of the rain screen are rather arid, and the deciduous habit of this species is perhaps an adaptation to the local climate.

R. *lowndesii* flowered at Wisley and Edinburgh in 1956, raised from seeds collected in 1952 by Polunin, Sykes and Williams. A larger quantity was introduced in 1954 by Stainton, Sykes and Williams. The species is difficult to cultivate, especially in the southern parts of the country. Peter Cox recommends a perfectly drained soil and a position facing north but with plenty of light and no overhang (*Dwarf Rhododendrons*, p. 124).

R. LEPTOTHRIUM Balf. f. & Forr.

R. *australe* Balf. f. & Forr.

An evergreen, diffusely branched shrub up to 20 ft high in the wild, with slender downy twigs becoming grey, the down persisting at least two years. Leaves thin, oval-lanceolate, rounded at the base, tapering at the apex to a short mucro, $1\frac{1}{2}$ to 3 in. long, $\frac{5}{8}$ to 1 in. wide, at first a pleasing purplish red then dark green and glabrous except for the midrib, which is downy above and below; stalk $\frac{1}{4}$ to $\frac{3}{8}$ in. long, covered with grey down. Flowers solitary from the clustered terminal leaf-axils, opening in May; pedicels slender, $\frac{5}{8}$ in. long, downy, rosy purple. Calyx with five ovate or oblong lobes $\frac{3}{8}$ in. long, ciliate. Corolla deep magenta rose with crimson spots, about $1\frac{3}{4}$ in. wide, five-lobed, the lobes oblong and as long or longer than the tube, which is downy inside. Stamens five, the lower half downy. Ovary covered with sticky glands; style glabrous. *Bot. Mag.*, n.s., t. 502. (*s.* Ovatum)

Native of W. Yunnan, China; introduced by Forrest in 1914 from the border between Yunnan and Burma (western flank of the Shweli–Salween divide), but described from specimens collected by him in 1918 on the Mekong–Yangtse divide. A closely related species occurs in Burma. *R. leptothrium* is closely allied to R. *ovatum*, differing in having the leaves mainly elliptic, in its deeper coloured corollas with oblong (not orbicular) lobes, and in having the calyx-lobes edged with short, gland-tipped bristles. It is a tender species—much less hardy than the cultivated form of R. *ovatum*. It is botanically interesting, but not of much ornamental value, though the young growths are attractively tinted.

R. LEUCASPIS Tagg　　　　　　[PLATE 79

An evergreen shrub 1 to 2 ft high; young shoots and leaf-stalks bristly. Leaves elliptic to obovate, tapered at the base, rounded at the apex, the mucro at the end often curiously reflexed, $1\frac{1}{2}$ to $2\frac{3}{4}$ in. long, $\frac{1}{2}$ to $1\frac{1}{4}$ in. wide, dark glossy green and sparsely bristly above; glaucous and thickly set with shining yellowish scales beneath; stalk $\frac{1}{4}$ in. long. Flowers terminal, mostly in pairs, sometimes solitary or in threes, opening in February or March. Calyx $\frac{1}{3}$ in. long, with five deep, broadly ovate or obovate lobes, scaly only at the base, fringed with soft hairs; flower-stalk $\frac{1}{4}$ in. long, scaly but not bristly. Corolla flat and open, 2 in. wide, pure white, with five broadly rounded, overlapping lobes; slightly scaly outside, hairy in the throat. Stamens ten, their white stalks hairy except towards the top; anthers chocolate-brown. Ovary densely clad with whitish scales; style thick, curved, whitish, glabrous. *Bot. Mag.*, t. 9665. (*s.* Boothii *ss.* Megeratum)

R. *leucaspis* was discovered by Kingdon Ward in the Tsangpo gorge, at the extreme eastern end of the Himalaya, in November 1924 (KW 6273). It was 'growing among rocks and beneath Bamboos, at the foot of a lofty cliff called the Musi La, or the Sulphur Mountain—there was a sulphur spring here, and I think it watered the Rhododendron. The slope immediately below the cliff was almost precipitous, and there were regular thickets of R. leucaspis dotted about here. It was not in flower, but I collected seeds, and it first flowered in this country in 1928' (Kingdon Ward, *Gard. Chron.*, Vol. 94 (1933), p. 65). He reintroduced the species in 1926 from the Di Chu valley on the borders between Assam and Tibet (KW 7171), about 200 miles to the south-east of the original locality. This time too he never saw the species in flower. To complete the story of R. *leucaspis*, it was reintroduced by Ludlow, Sherriff, and Elliot in 1947 from the place where Kingdon Ward had originally found it (L.S. & E. 13549; *Gard. Chron.*, Vol. 143 (1958), p. 102).

RHODODENDRON LEUCASPIS

Few rhododendrons are held in greater affection than R. *leucaspis*, with its flowers so large in proportion to the size of the plant and the large chocolate anthers so oddly contrasting with their background of creamy white. It is perfectly hardy and has lived out-of-doors in many gardens for almost half a century, still retaining its dwarf habit. But the flowers, borne so early, are often destroyed by frost. It received an Award of Merit on February 12, 1929, when three plants were shown from Exbury by Lionel de Rothschild; they were less than 1 ft high and only four years old from seed, but bore flowers of the full size—about 2 in. across. At that time it was still known as *Rhododendron* KW 6273, but was named and described two months later. It was awarded a First Class Certificate in 1944.

R. MEGERATUM Balf. f. & Forr. R. *tapeinum* Balf. f. & Forr.—This species is closely allied to R. *leucaspis*, differing in its yellow or cream-coloured flowers, in its densely bristly flower-stalks, and in the more glaucous undersides of the leaves. It was discovered by Forrest in 1914 on the Kari La, Mekong–Yangtse divide, growing on ledges of cliffs at 12,000–13,000 ft, and was introduced by him. Here it seems to be at the eastern end of its area, which extends westward into the eastern Himalaya, as far as the headwaters of the Subansiri. Forrest seems to have met with it only as a ground-dwelling plant, but in upper Burma and farther west it is often an epiphyte on fir or larch. It is mostly found between 10,000 and 12,000 ft. *Bot. Mag.*, t. 9120.

R. *megeratum* is less easy to cultivate than R. *leucaspis* and less often met with as an outdoor plant. Also, some forms have flowers in rather uninteresting shades of yellow. The species received an Award of Merit when exhibited by Lord Swaythling on April 30, 1935 (plant raised from seeds collected by Kingdon

Ward in 1926 in the Seinghku valley, N.W. upper Burma), and again on April 28, 1970, when shown from Bodnant by Lord Aberconway and the National Trust.

R. LINDLEYI T. Moore   [PLATE 81

R. bhotanicum C. B. Clarke

An evergreen shrub of lax habit, often found in nature as an epiphyte on various species of trees; young shoots slightly scaly, otherwise glabrous. Leaves oblong to oval, rounded at both ends, 2½ to 6 in. long, ¾ to 2 in. wide; glaucous and scaly beneath; stalk ¾ in. long. Flowers in clusters of four to eight, fragrant. Calyx ⅝ in. long, deeply five-lobed, the lobes oblong-ovate fringed with whitish hairs; flower-stalk ½ in. long, scaly, not downy. Corolla white, funnel-shaped, 3 to 3½ in. long and wide, five-lobed. Stamens ten, very downy at the lower half. Ovary and base of style thickly covered with red-brown scales. *Bot. Mag.*, n.s., t. 363.   (s. Maddenii ss. Megacalyx)

Native of the eastern Himalaya as far west as E. Nepal and of the Mishmi Hills, the Naga Hills, and Manipur; described in 1864 from a plant growing in Standish's nursery, where it had been raised from seeds collected in the Himalaya. As it later turned out, J. D. Hooker had found it in 1848–9 in Sikkim and the Darjeeling region but confused it with *R. dalhousiae*. *R. lindleyi*, at least under its correct name, remained a rare species in gardens until Kingdon Ward reintroduced it in 1928 from the Delei valley in the Mishmi Hills, where he found it as a slim shrub sometimes 10 to 12 ft high growing in thickets on an exposed cliff with eleven other species of rhododendron, at 9,000 ft (KW 8546). It is also in cultivation from seed collected by Ludlow and Sherriff in the Tibetan Himalaya, in 1936, from plants up to 15 ft high, growing at 7,000 to 8,500 ft.

R. *lindleyi* is one of the most beautiful species of the genus, with flowers of an exquisite fragrance that Thomas Moore, in his original description, likened to a mixture of lemon and nutmeg. It has to be grown in a cool greenhouse over much of the country, but flourishes in the open in many gardens on the west coast of Scotland and in other parts of the Atlantic zone. It is by nature a straggly shrub and therefore best grown on a wall or mixed with other rhododendrons of almost the same height. But on the Isle of Gigha, off the coast of Argyll, there are plants grown fully in the open which are of compact habit (*R.C.Y.B. 1958*, fig. 5).

The Kingdon Ward introduction from the Mishmi Hills received an Award of Merit in 1935, when shown from Exbury on April 14, 1935, and a First Class Certificate two years later, on this occasion exhibited by Adm. Heneage-Vivian, on May 4. More recently the Award of Merit has been given to two clonal forms of R. *lindleyi*: to 'Dame Edith Sitwell', shown by Geoffrey Gorer, Sunte House, Haywards Heath; and to 'Geordie Sherriff', raised and shown by Mr A. C. and Mr J. F. A. Gibson, Glenarn, Rhu, Dunbartonshire.

R. DALHOUSIAE Hook. f.—This species, originally confused with R. *lindleyi*, differs from it in the young shoots being bristly as well as scaly, in the downy flower-stalks, in the calyx-lobes not being fringed with hairs, and in the style being scaly for about two-thirds of its length from the base. It is a native of the Himalaya from E. Nepal to Bhutan, and was discovered by Hooker in Sikkim in 1848. *Bot. Mag.*, t. 4718. It is rather less hardy than R. *lindleyi* and not superior to it in any respect, so less common in gardens. Award of Merit 1930, as a shrub for the cool greenhouse. It flowers in May or June. The flowers vary in colour from white to pale yellow or greenish yellow.

R. RHABDOTUM Balf. f. & Cooper—Very closely allied to R. *dalhousiae*, scarcely differing except in the colour of the corolla, which has strips of crimson running down the outside of each lobe along the median rib. *Bot. Mag.*, t. 9447. It was described in 1917 from a flowering specimen collected two years previously by Roland Cooper in Bhutan. Cooper found it in the Punakha valley, growing as a tree 12 ft high at 8,000 ft, on dry rock faces; his specimens of R. *dalhousiae*, collected in the same area, were from 6,500 ft. R. *rhabdotum* was introduced by Kingdon Ward in 1925, who collected seed 'blind' in February near the border between Bhutan and Assam, while on the way home from his famous exploration of the Tsangpo gorge and the mountains around it (KW 6415). The plants from which he took the seed were sprawling shrubs 2 to 3 ft high, growing by the Nyamjang river. Ludlow and Sherriff later reintroduced it from the same part of the Himalaya and also from Bhutan. It is a definitely tender species, but is grown in the open in a few gardens in the mildest parts.

[PLATE 88

R. LONGESQUAMATUM Schneid.

R. *brettii* Hemsl. & Wils.

An evergreen bush up to 12 ft or so high; young shoots stout, clothed thickly with brown, shaggy, branched hairs, and long, dark bud-scales, which persist for two or more seasons. Leaves oblong, inclined to obovate, pointed at the apex, rounded or slightly heart-shaped at the base, 2½ to 5 in. long, 1 to 1¾ in. wide, dark green and glabrous except for the midrib, which is shaggy beneath like the young shoots and leaf-stalks—the latter about ½ in. long; underside of blade dotted with pustule-like glands. Flowers opening in May, ten or more in a truss on stalks up to 1 in. or slightly more long. Calyx-lobes ½ in. long, glandular, and hairy. Corolla bell-shaped, about 2 in. across, white or pink, with a dark red blotch. Stamens ten, downy at the base. Ovary densely glandular; style glandular at the base. *Bot. Mag.*, t. 9430. (*s.* Barbatum *ss.* Maculiferum)

Native of W. Szechwan at 9,000 to 11,000 ft; discovered by Wilson and introduced by him in 1904. It is a very hardy and free-flowering species, remarkable for the stout, shaggy young shoots and the large, petaloid calyx. In a letter to Kew, F. R. S. Balfour of Dawyck remarked that garden warblers often build their nests among its hairy twigs and leaves.

R. LONGISTYLUM Rehd. & Wils.

An evergreen shrub up to 6 or 7 ft high, with only slightly scaly young shoots. Leaves narrowly oval or oblanceolate, much tapered towards the base, ¾ to 2 in. long, ¼ to ¾ in. wide, dark dullish green and with a fine network of sunken veins above, quite pale and sprinkled thinly with very small scales beneath;

stalk ⅛ to ⅙ in. long. Flowers produced in March and April, eight to twelve or more crowded in a terminal cluster. Calyx pale green, scaly, five-lobed, the lobes $\frac{1}{12}$ to ⅙ in. long, fringed with hairs. Corolla white or pink, ¾ in. long and wide, with five ovate, bluntish lobes. Stamens ten, unequal, the longest slightly exceeding the corolla, downy at the base; anthers yellow. Ovary scaly; style 1 to 1⅛ in. long, glabrous, often reddish.   (s. Triflorum ss. Yunnanense)

Native of W. Szechwan, China; introduced in 1908 by Wilson, who describes it as growing on cliffs and scrub-clad slopes fully exposed to the sun. Rehder and Wilson write of the great length of the style as 'most remarkable'; but, compared with some of its newer allies, it does not exceed the corolla to any very notable degree. They considered it to be related to R. *micranthum*, but that species has much smaller, more numerous flowers in a cluster, smooth stamens, and flowers much later.

R. LUTESCENS Franch.

R. *costulatum* Franch.; R. *lemeei* Lévl.

An evergreen shrub 3 to 7 ft high, of loose habit; young shoots reddish, slender, scaly. Leaves lanceolate, with a long slender point and a tapered base, 1½ to 3½ in. long, ½ to 1¼ in. wide; dark green above, paler and more scaly beneath; stalk ¼ to ⅓ in. long. Flowers pale yellow, produced singly or occasionally in pairs from several buds at the apex of the shoot, terminal and axillary. Calyx scarcely lobed. Corolla broadly funnel-shaped, 1 in. wide. Stamens ten, protruded, hairy near the base. Ovary, calyx, and flower-stalk scaly, the last ½ in. long. *Bot. Mag.*, t. 8851.   (s. and ss. Triflorum)

Native of W. Szechwan and N.E. Yunnan, mainly at altitudes of 6,500 to 9,500 ft; discovered by the Abbé David; introduced by Wilson in 1904 for Messrs Veitch and again during his two expeditions on behalf of the Arnold Arboretum. According to him it is very common in thickets and margins of woods fully exposed to the sun, and is one of the earliest rhododendrons in its area to open its flowers. It is the finest yellow-flowered species in the Triflorum series but unfortunately in cultivation too it is early-flowering, sometimes as early as February and never later than April, so its display is often spoilt by frost. Also, some plants are somewhat tender, though it is said that Wilson's later introductions are hardier than the first. The bronzy young growths are an attractive feature of this species.

The well-known Exbury variety of R. *lutescens*, with large lemon-yellow flowers, was the result of deliberate crossing between two selected plants. It was awarded a First Class Certificate when exhibited by Lionel de Rothschild on March 22, 1938. An Award of Merit was given on March 31, 1953, to the clone 'Bagshot Sands', raised at Tower Court and exhibited by Mrs Stevenson; in this the flowers are primrose-yellow and about 1½ in. wide.   [PLATE 83

R. LUTEUM Sweet

Azalea pontica L.; R. *flavum* G. Don

A deciduous shrub of vigorous, rather stiff habit, 8 to 10 ft high; young shoots viscous, glandular. Leaves linear-oblong, 2½ to 5 in. long, ¾ to 1½ in. wide;

with a short, abrupt tip, more tapering at the base; at maturity glaucous, hairy beneath along the midrib and at the margins; stalk hairy, $\frac{1}{3}$ in. or less long. Flowers fragrant, rich bright yellow, $1\frac{1}{2}$ to 2 in. across, crowded in several clusters at the end of the previous year's naked shoots, in May, on sticky, glandular stalks $\frac{1}{2}$ to $\frac{3}{4}$ in. long. Calyx-lobes small, ovate, edged with glanded hairs. Corolla-tube $\frac{1}{2}$ in. long, hairy. Stamens five, hairy at the base like the style. *Bot. Mag.*, t. 433. (*s.* Azalea *ss.* Luteum)

Native mainly of the western Caucasus, where it grows from sea-level to the subalpine zone, and of bordering parts of Turkey. In Russia it is also found in the N.W. Ukraine and bordering parts of White Russia, and there is an isolated stand under State protection in Poland (Wola Zarczycka, near Leżaysk). Outposts have also been reported from E. Austria and N.W. Yugoslavia. It was introduced to Britain from the Caucasus by Pallas in 1792 to Lee and Kennedy's nursery and again by Anthony Hove of Warsaw in 1796.

This beautiful perfectly hardy azalea, the only yellow one known until the advent of R. *molle* (*sinense*), and the parent or the predominant parent of all the older yellow garden varieties, is still one of the most useful and generally cultivated of all shrubs. It blossoms unfailingly, and with an exquisite fragrance. Added to this is its fine autumn colouring, in shades of red, orange and purple. Coming freely from seed, it is the chief stock used for grafting the choicer varieties on. This probably explains its abundance in gardens, for being a vigorous grower it will, unless watched, often send up strong sucker growths that in time smother out the more finely bred sorts grafted on it.

R. *luteum* produces thickets of self-sown seedlings when grown in grass-free undisturbed soils and has become semi-naturalised in some localities. It is of great phytogeographic interest as the only European azalea, belonging to a subseries which has its headquarters in N. America, but represented in E. Asia also.

R. LYSOLEPIS Hutch.

An evergreen shrub up to $1\frac{1}{2}$ ft high, occasionally taller, of dense, fastigiate habit; branchlets scaly. Leaves oblong-elliptic, $\frac{1}{2}$ to $\frac{3}{4}$ in. long, about $\frac{3}{16}$ in. wide, covered above with lustrous scales spaced about their own diameter apart, scales on the undersides rather more widely spaced than above. Flowers purple-violet or rosy purple, usually three in each truss, about 1 in. wide, very shortly stalked, borne in April or May. Calyx unequally five-lobed, about $\frac{1}{10}$ in. or slightly less deep, usually with a few straggly hairs on the margin, sparsely scaly. Corolla rotate, glabrous and not scaly outside. Stamens ten, hairy at the base. Ovary scaly; style glabrous, shorter than the shortest stamen. (*s.* Lapponicum)

R. *lysolepis* was described in 1930 from plants growing at Kew, of unstated origin, but is matched by Kingdon Ward's 4456, found by him in the Muli region of S.W. Szechwan, forming 'heath-like brooms' on slate rocks below limestone cliffs, at 11,000 ft. He sent home seeds in 1921, from which the Kew plants were presumably raised. In its best-coloured forms it is quite pretty, but some plants raised from the original seeds produced flowers of an unpleasant shade of bluish magenta.

According to the Philipsons, in their revision of the Lapponicum group (1975), R. *lysolepis* is a natural hybrid, but it is difficult to accept their conclusion that one parent is R. *flavidum*. It should have been remarked above that the description is based on a cultivated plant that has distinctly broader leaves than in the type, but in other respects agrees very well with it.

R. MACABEANUM Watt ex Balf. f.

A large evergreen shrubby tree in the wild, attaining a height of 40 to 50 ft; young stems coated with a woolly greyish tomentum. Leaves thick and leathery, clustered at the ends of the shoots, oblong-elliptic to broadly oval, up to 1 ft long, 6 to 9 in. wide, rounded and mucronate at the apex, narrowed or obtuse at the base, dark green above, undersurface whitish or greyish white, at first woolly from a coating of long-branched hairs which later fall away, leaving a suede-like indumentum of rosulate hairs; midrib and lateral veins prominent beneath; petiole stout, about 1 in. long, tomentose. Inflorescence a dense umbel of up to thirty flowers, opening in March or April; pedicels about $\frac{7}{8}$ in. long, tomentose. Calyx rim-like. Corolla pale sulphur yellow to deep yellow, sometimes ivory-white, tubular-campanulate, pouched at the base, the upper pouches purple inside, almost 3 in. long, 2 to $2\frac{1}{4}$ in. wide, eight-lobed. Stamens sixteen, included in the corolla, with glabrous filaments. Ovary sixteen-chambered, tomentose; style glabrous, with a large crimson or pink stigma. *Bot. Mag.*, n.s., t. 187. (s. Grande)

Native of Assam in the Naga Hills and Manipur. It was discovered by Sir George Watt on Mt Japvo at 8,000 to 9,500 ft on March 9, 1882; a few weeks later he collected it again on the summit at 9,800 ft, where, as in neighbouring mountains at about the same altitude, it forms dwarf forests. In addition to making field notes, Sir George Watt drew up a description of this rhododendron, and tentatively gave it the status of a variety of R. *falconeri*. He named it after Mr M'Cabe, Deputy Commissioner for the Naga Hills, who helped him during his visit. But Watt's account lay in manuscript until 1920, when Sir Isaac Bayley Balfour used it, and the specimens he collected, to make a formal description of this rhododendron, as a new species. Seven years later, Kingdon Ward collected seeds from the Japvo stand, and from these all the older plants in gardens are derived (KW 7724). He again gathered seeds in March 1935, this time from farther east, on a ridge at 9,000 ft below Mt Sarameti (KW 11175).

R. *macabeanum* is hardy in woodland near London and thrives and flowers beautifully in several gardens, notably at Nymans in Sussex. But it grows faster and attains its greatest size in the milder and rainier parts, where plants from the original introduction are now around 25 ft in height. At Kew, the climate is too dry for it, but it grows well at Edinburgh, where there is a fine specimen in the Rhododendron Walk. The yellow of its flowers varies much in depth, even in the plants from Kingdon Ward's original collection. At Trengwainton, where Sir Edward Bolitho raised many plants from KW 7724, some are deep yellow and among the finest in the country. But the trusses shown by him in 1937 and 1938 were of pale yellow flowers, though still fine enough for the species to receive the Award of Merit on the first occasion and a First Class Certificate on the second. The famous plant at Trewithen, Cornwall, was a gift from Sir Edward Bolitho to George Johnstone and is one of the original seedlings. This has flowers of a very deep yellow and measures 23 ft in height and 35 ft in width (1974). It is portrayed in *R.C.Y.B. 1962*, fig. 14.

R. MACROPHYLLUM G. Don

R. californicum Hook.

An evergreen shrub up to 12 ft or sometimes more high; branches stout and erect. Leaves elliptic to oblong, inclining to obovate, 3 to 6 in. long, 1¼ to 3 in. wide, tapering at the base, dark green above, paler beneath, quite glabrous on both surfaces; stalk ½ to 1 in. long. Flowers produced during May, twenty or more in a terminal truss; rachis about 1 in. long; pedicels 1½ to 2 in. long, glabrous or slightly downy. Calyx small, with five, short, broad lobes. Corolla bell-shaped, with five waxy lobes, 2 to 2½ in. across, rich rosy purple to pink or sometimes white, with brown spots on the upper lobes. Stamens ten, shorter than the corolla, downy at the base. Ovary covered with white, appressed hairs; style glabrous. *Bot. Mag.*, t. 4863.   (*s.* and *ss.* Ponticum)

Native of California northwards to British Columbia; introduced by W. Lobb in 1850, but now rare in gardens. It may be considered as the western form of *R. catawbiense*, differing in its more erect growth, in having the leaves tapered at the base, in the more rosy tinted flowers, and the often glabrous flower-stalks. The calyx-lobes in *R. catawbiense* are also longer, more pointed and triangular. It is quite hardy.

R. MACROSEPALUM Maxim.

R. linearifolium Sieb. & Zucc., *nom. illegit.*, var. *macrosepalum* (Maxim.) Makino; *Azalea macrosepala* (Maxim.) K. Koch

A semi-evergreen shrub usually under 3 ft high, of spreading habit; young shoots clad with short, erect, mostly gland-tipped hairs, intermixed with longer, spreading, flattened hairs. Lower leaves deciduous in autumn, mostly oblong or oblong-elliptic, sometimes broadest above or below the middle, up to 2½ in. long and 1 in. wide, acute or acuminate at the apex; persistent leaves smaller, obtuse at the apex; both sorts slightly rugose above, hairy on both sides and on the margins; petioles hairy, up to ¼ in. long. Flowers fragrant, opening in April or May in terminal clusters usually of four to six, but sometimes up to ten; pedicels up to ¾ in. long, glandular. Calyx green, with five narrow, pointed, strap-shaped, hairy lobes ¾ in. to more than 1 in. long. Corolla rose-pink to reddish purple, widely funnel-shaped, 1½ to 2 in. wide, five-lobed, the upper lobes spotted with purple. Stamens usually five, sometimes more numerous. Ovary clad with appressed, white, glandular hairs; style glabrous.   (*s.* Azalea *ss.* Obtusum)

Native of Japan in Shikoku and the southern half of the main island. It was introduced to Europe by Maximowicz, but apparently did not reach Britain until 1914, when seeds were received which Wilson had collected in Japan. According to him it is common in pine woods and open situations, on its own or with

R. *kaempferi*. It is a quite attractive azalea, easily recognised by the unusually long calyx-lobes, but is not common in gardens. It may be cut back in hard winters, and the flower-buds, which start to swell early in spring, are often damaged by frost; or the buds open prematurely, exposing the individual flowers before they are fully developed.

cv. 'Linearifolium'.—An abnormal garden clone with narrowly linear leaves 2 to 3 in. long, usually ⅛ to 3/16 in. wide, at the middle, tapering gradually to each end. Flowers in a terminal cluster of about three. Corolla with long, narrow lobes of about the same shape as the leaves and up to 1½ in. long, bright rosy lilac, hairy at the base. (R. *linearifolium* Sieb. & Zucc. (1846), *nom. illegit.*, not Poir. (1808); *Azalea linearifolia* (Sieb. & Zucc.) Hook., *Bot. Mag.*, t. 5769.)

This unusual and decorative azalea is evidently a sport from R. *macrosepalum*, and is very distinct in its long, narrow leaves and corolla-lobes. It was introduced from Japan by Standish and first flowered in his nursery at Ascot in 1867. It is hardy at Kew and worth growing for its remarkable aspect.

It has been usual to treat 'Linearifolium' as the nomenclatural type of the species, and to place the normal, wild form under it as a variety—R. *linearifolium* var. *macrosepalum*. As it happens, the name R. *linearifolium* Sieb. & Zucc., given to this garden variety, is illegitimate, and it is therefore correct to adopt the arrangement that accords with common sense, and put the garden variety under the name of the wild species.

R. ripense Makino R. *mucronatum* var. *ripense* (Makino) Wils.—Near to R. *macrosepalum*, but with constantly ten stamens and hairs of ovary eglandular. Native of S. Japan. It is uncertain if the true species is in cultivation. See further on p. 930.

R. maculiferum Franch.

An evergreen shrub 8 to 10 ft high in cultivation and of dense, bushy, very leafy habit; young shoots at first woolly. Leaves oblong, narrowly oval or obovate, rounded or slightly heart-shaped at the base, abruptly narrowed to a short point, 3 to 5½ in. long, 1 to 2½ in. wide, dark green and glabrous above, woolly beneath, but only on the midrib where the wool is dense at the base, fading away upwards until at the upper third it quite disappears; stalk ½ to 1½ in. long, downy like the base of the midrib. Flowers opening in March and April in loose trusses 4 in. wide composed of six to ten blossoms, on woolly stalks up to 1 in. long. Calyx small, with five triangular lobes. Corolla five-lobed, bell-shaped, 1½ in. wide, pale rose to white with a dark crimson, almost black spot at the base, to which the specific name refers. Stamens ten, shorter than the corolla, their stalks downy at the base; anthers black or nearly so. Ovary cylindrical, 3/16 in. long, covered with short, pale tawny hairs; style glabrous. (*s.* Barbatum *ss.* Maculiferum)

Native of W. Hupeh and bordering parts of Szechwan; discovered by Père Farges early in the 1890s and introduced by Wilson, who collected seeds in the Changyang district of W. Hupeh in December 1900 and sent them to Messrs Veitch. According to him, it is a woodland plant in the wild, found in W. Hupeh at higher altitudes than any other rhododendron except R. *fargesii* (up to 10,000 ft). Normally it is a bushy shrub in the wild, 8 to 15 ft high, but Wilson saw one plant which made a tree about 30 ft high.

R. *maculiferum* is a well-marked species with its bell-shaped flowers, marked at the base with a dark crimson blotch. In some forms the corolla is pure white and the blotch almost black—a remarkable contrast. It flowers in March and April, not always freely, and is inclined to hide its trusses in the luxuriant foliage. It is quite hardy, but very rare in gardens.

R. MADDENII Hook. f.

R. jenkinsii Nutt.

An evergreen shrub up to 9 ft high, of open habit; bark papery; young shoots grey, clad with red-brown scales. Leaves lanceolate to oblong-lanceolate, sharply pointed, tapered at both ends, 3 to 6 in. long, 1¼ to 2½ in. wide, dark green above, green or glaucous beneath but nearly covered with scales; stalk ½ to 1 in. long. Flowers very fragrant, produced from June to August in clusters of two to four. Calyx up to ⅝ in. long, but usually smaller. Corolla white, sometimes flushed with rose on the outside, funnel-shaped, 4 in. long and wide, five-lobed, the lobes rounded, over 1 in. wide; scaly outside. Stamens twenty, 2 in. long, glabrous; anthers orange-yellow. Ovary and style completely clad with scales. *Bot Mag.*, t. 4805. (s. and ss. Maddenii)

Native of the Himalaya from Sikkim eastward; discovered by J. D. Hooker in 1849 in Sikkim, near the village of Choongtam, and introduced by him. It occurs at 5,000 to 9,000 ft altitude, and is not hardy in our average climate, but is a delightful shrub in Cornwall and other mild places, one of its good qualities being that it flowers later in the season than most rhododendrons; another that it is easily grown. It is named after Major Madden, who belonged to the Bengal Civil Service in 1849.

R. BRACHYSIPHON Hutch. R. *brevitubum* Balf. f & Cooper (1917), not J. J. Smith (1914).—This species was described from a specimen collected by R. Cooper in Bhutan near Punakha, from bushes 8 ft high, growing on a steep, dry hillside. It is supposed to differ from R. *maddenii* in the much smaller corolla, with a tube only half the length of what it is in R. *maddenii*, and in the downy filaments of the stamens. However, the Japanese expedition to Bhutan in 1967 found plants in the Punakha region some of which agreed with R. *maddenii*, others with R. *brachysiphon*, while others again were intermediate between the two species. Dr Hara has accordingly placed R. *brachysiphon* under R. *maddenii* in synonymy.

The plants cultivated as R. *brachysiphon* derive mainly or wholly from Kingdon Ward's 6276, collected 'blind' in the Tsangpo gorge, Tibet, at Pemakochung, in 1924. Although the flowers are much smaller than in typical R. *maddenii*, they are quite pretty, borne just as late in the season, and just as fragrant. Also, the plants are perfectly hardy in a sheltered position south of London.

R. MANIPURENSE Balf. f. & Watt R. *maddenii* var. *obtusifolium* Hutch.— This species was discovered by Sir George Watt in 1882 in the Naga Hills, Assam, on Mt Japvo and neighbouring mountains, at 8,000 to 10,000 ft. A plant

in the Temperate House at Kew, raised from the seeds which he sent, was named
R. *maddenii* var. *obtusifolium* by Hutchinson in *Bot. Mag.*, t. 8212, but nine years
later this rhododendron was given specific rank by Sir Isaac Bayley Balfour,
who made his description from the specimens collected by Watt.

R. *manipurense* was reintroduced by Kingdon Ward, who visited Mt Japvo
in 1927 and collected seeds of this and three other rhododendrons originally
found by Sir George Watt (R. *macabeanum*, R. *elliottii*, and R. *johnstoneanum*).
According to his field note under KW 7723, it makes a stout bush on razorback
ridges, but becomes a fine tree in the forest, and also occurs as a tree 20 to 30 ft
high on the face of the mountain, in company with R. *macabeanum*. Kingdon
Ward also collected seeds in the Adung valley, N.W. upper Burma; in the Di
Chu valley, on the borders between Assam, Tibet, and Burma; and in the Mishmi
Hills, Assam.

The key-character used in *Species of Rhododendron* to distinguish R. *manipurense*
and R. *polyandrum* from R. *maddenii* is: stamen-filaments hairy in the lower part
against glabrous in R. *maddenii*. But these hairs are not a very positive feature,
being more in the nature of scattered, thick, watery excrescences, which can be
seen on specimens otherwise agreeing with typical R. *maddenii*. The leaves of
R. *manipurense* are commonly rounded at the apex, against acute in R. *maddenii*,
but there are plants in the Himalaya, agreeing with R. *maddenii* in most respects,
in which the leaves are obtuse. However, R. *manipurense*, at least in its type-
locality, is a more robust plant than R. *maddenii*. Also, plants from KW 7723
appear to be quite hardy.

R. POLYANDRUM Hutch.—In describing this species, from a specimen collected by Cooper in Bhutan, Hutchinson remarked that it is very near to R.
manipurense, differing in its oblong or oblong-lanceolate leaves, rounded to
obtuse at both ends, and in having flowers with twenty-five stamens. Cooper
sent seeds to Edinburgh, but the first introduction to private gardens was by
Kingdon Ward, who collected seed of what he took to be R. *maddenii*, growing
in the Nyamjang Chu, Mönyul, just south of the border between Tibet and India
where the two countries abut on north-west Bhutan (KW 6413, collected
February 1925). When plants flowered at Nymans, Sussex, eight years later they
were identified as R. *polyandrum* by Dr Hutchinson, and the species received an
Award of Merit when shown by Lt-Col. Messel on May 9, 1933. In this form the
flowers are creamy white, yellow in the throat, but three years later another
form from Nymans received the same award, with rose-pink flowers. Both
forms are hardy there.

Kingdon Ward collected R. *polyandrum* in flower in 1938, some way south of
the place where he collected the seeds thirteen years before, and reintroduced it.
It may also be in cultivation from Ludlow and Sherriff 3164, collected in Bhutan.

As noted above, R. *manipurense*, with which Dr Hutchinson compared R.
polyandrum, is very near to R. *maddenii*, and this is also true of R. *polyandrum*. In
this connection it is interesting to note that Ludlow and Sherriff's 3164, collected in the Maru Chu valley at 8,000 ft, has twenty-three stamens with hairy
filaments, and was therefore identified as R. *polyandrum*, while their 3147, from
the same valley at 7,000 ft, has only twenty stamens to the flower and their
filaments are glabrous, thus agreeing better with R. *maddenii*, though Dr

Cowan noted that the two specimens were otherwise very similar (*Notes R. B. G. Edin.*, Vol. 19, p. 321). Furthermore, the plants raised from Kingdon Ward 413 vary considerably in their foliage. In one specimen preserved at Kew they are acute at the apex, as in R. *maddenii*, not rounded-obtuse as in the type of R. *polyandrum*. Also, some of these plants have glabrous stamens, as in R. *maddenii*, not hairy as in the type of R. *polyandrum*.

R. MALLOTUM Balf. f. & Ward
R. *aemulorum* Balf. f.

An evergreen shrub or a small tree, in the wild up to 15 ft high; young shoots stout, downy. Leaves obovate, 3 to 7 in. long, half or rather more than half as much wide, dark dull green and wrinkled above; covered beneath with a rich, soft, brownish red wool; veins twelve to fifteen on each side of the midrib which is terminated by a yellowish, knob-like, shining mucro. Flowers in March or April in hemispherical trusses about 5 in. wide, carrying over a dozen blossoms; flower-stalk about ½ in. long, very woolly. Calyx very small. Corolla tubular-bell-shaped, rosy scarlet to deep crimson, 2 in. wide, 1½ in. long, with five notched lobes, each ⅞ in. wide. Stamens ten, ¾ to 1 in. long, glabrous; anthers dark brown. Ovary silky-hairy; style glabrous, 1½ in. long. *Bot. Mag.*, 9419. (*s.* Neriiflorum *ss.* Haematodes)

R. *mallotum* was discovered by Kingdon Ward in 1914 above the Hpimaw pass, N.E. upper Burma, on the Nmai–Salween divide. It was introduced by Farrer in 1919 from the same locality, and also simultaneously by Forrest, from the China side of the divide. E. H. M. Cox, who accompanied Farrer on his 1919 expedition, later wrote: 'The entire Burmese side north of the pass was studded with it, rising squat and sturdy out of a sea of Bamboo. It was particularly uniform in size, always about 16 ft in height, with a shiny bronzed trunk. . . The flowers were of the deepest and most luminous scarlet imaginable, giving out a glow of hidden light even on the darkest day. . . . Out on that hillside, with its top above the sea of green, it has to bear the brunt of every wind that blows' (*Farrer's Last Journey*, p. 54).

As Mr Cox anticipated, R. *mallotum* has proved quite hardy, though it needs light shade and shelter from cold winds. But flowering so early, its value for frosty gardens lies only in its beautiful leaves, etched above, and clad beneath and on the stalks with a vividly coloured indumentum. It is of erect rather narrow habit, usually much taller than wide. The Award of Merit was given to it on March 7, 1933, when shown from Borde Hill, Sussex, by Col. S. R. Clarke.

R. MARTINIANUM Balf. f. & Forr.

An evergreen shrub 3 to 6 ft high, with slender but stiff young shoots furnished with glands. Leaves clustered at the end of the shoot, oval inclined to oblong, abruptly tapered towards both ends, ending in a very distinct mucro; ¾ to 1¾ in. long, half as much wide; more or less glandular when young, eventually glabrous or nearly so, rather glaucous beneath; stalk ¼ in. long, glandular.

Flowers two or three together in a terminal cluster each on a glandular stalk up to 1¼ in. long. Calyx small, fringed with glands. Corolla widely funnel-shaped, five-lobed, 1 in. long, 2 in. wide, pale rose with a dark blotch at the base, often speckled with crimson, the lobes reflexed. Stamens ten, downy at the base. Ovary and base of style glandular.   (s. Thomsonii ss. Selense)

Native of N.W. Yunnan, bordering parts of S.E. Tibet, and of upper Burma, introduced by Forrest in 1914 and also in cultivation from seeds collected by Rock and by Kingdon Ward. It is named after John Martin, who had charge of the rhododendrons at Caerhays Castle, Cornwall. In its best forms, with clear pink flowers heavily freckled with crimson and borne on a low compact bush, this is one of the most charming of rhododendrons, but is rarely met with in gardens. Kingdon Ward's 6795 from the Seinghku valley, upper Burma, is unusual in having roundish leaves, recalling those of R. thomsonii.

R. EURYSIPHON Tagg & Forr.—This species is closely allied to R. *martinianum*, differing in its campanulate instead of funnel-campanulate corolla. It is possibly a natural hybrid between it and R. *stewartianum*.

R. MAXIMUM L.
R. *procerum* Salisb.

An evergreen shrub or, in the wild, sometimes a tree over 30 ft high, with a short trunk 1 ft in diameter; young wood reddish and scurfy; outer flower-bud scales leaf-like, the inner ones reflexed at the apex. Leaves narrowly obovate to oblong, 4 to 10 in. long, 1 to 2½ in. wide, cuneate at the base, dark green above, pale beneath, and covered there with a close, thin indumentum which usually disappears within a few months but sometimes persists for more than a year; stalk stout, ½ to 1 in. long. Flowers up to thirty in a compact terminal truss on viscid and downy stalks 1 to 1½ in. long. Calyx with ovate, rounded lobes, slightly downy, 3/16 in. long. Corolla wide campanulate, rose-coloured or purplish pink, spotted with greenish yellow or deep yellow-orange on the upper lobes, about 1½ in. across, with five rounded lobes. Stamens eight to twelve, the filaments downy. Ovary glandular-hairy; style glabrous. *Bot. Mag.*, t. 951.   (s. and ss. Ponticum)

Native of the eastern USA; introduced to Britain in 1736 by Peter Collinson, but now rarely seen in gardens. Its trusses are small and are produced late, at the end of June and in July, and make little display among the young growths, which by that time are almost fully expanded. It has, however, played its part in the development of the hardy hybrids (see further on pages 818–19).

f. ALBUM (Pursh) Fern.   R. *maximum* var. *album* Pursh; R. *purshii* G. Don—Flowers white; wild with the type.

R. MEDDIANUM Forr.

An evergreen, stoutly branched shrub up to 6 ft high, glabrous in all its parts; young shoots glaucous. Leaves oval or inclined to obovate, broadly tapered to rounded at the base, rounded and with a short mucro at the apex; 3 to 5 in. long,

. to 3 in. wide; dark dull green above, paler green beneath; stalk stout, $\frac{1}{2}$ to $1\frac{1}{4}$ n. long. Flowers in a terminal truss of five to ten, opening in March and April, on glandular, reddish stalks up to 1 in. long. Corolla deep crimson, tubular-campanulate, $2\frac{1}{2}$ in. long and wide, five-lobed, the lobes shallow, rounded and notched; stamens ten, with white stalks, shorter than the corolla. Ovary and style eglandular. *Bot. Mag.*, t. 9636. (*s.* and *ss.* Thomsonii)

R. *meddianum* appears to be a local species, known only from the mountains between the eastern Irrawaddy and the Salween, near the borders between Yunnan and Burma. It was discovered by Forrest in 1917 on the Shweli–Salween divide at 10,000 to 11,000 ft. It is an eastern representative of the Himalayan R. *thomsonii*, with a similar bark, but with larger, less rounded leaves and usually longer corollas. According to Forrest's field notes the colour of the flowers varies from deep crimson to almost black crimson, or even blue-black with a plumlike bloom on the outside. Many of the cultivated plants belong to the var. ATROKERMESINUM Tagg, which really differs from the typical state only in having a densely glandular ovary, though the varietal epithet refers to the colour of the flowers in the wild plants, which according to Forrest is 'deep purple crimson' or 'deep wine crimson'. Curiously enough, the usual flower-colour in cultivated plants, both of the typical state and of the variety, is a splendid crimson-scarlet.

R. *meddianum* is hardy in woodland south of London and makes a fine display in March or April, weather permitting. The var. *atrokermesinum* received an Award of Merit when shown by Olaf Hambro, Logan, Wigtownshire, on April 13, 1954. The clone 'Machrie', which received the same award on April 13, 1965, is now considered to be a hybrid of R. *meddianum*, not the true species.

R. MEGACALYX Balf. f. & Ward

An evergreen shrub up to 10 ft or 15 ft high in the wild, described by Ward as of 'tall, loosely knit' habit. Leaves oblong-oval, often inclined to obovate, mostly rounded at the apex, 4 to 6 in. long, 1 to 3 in. wide, strongly veined, dull light green and glabrous above, densely furnished with sunken, yellow-brown scales beneath; stalk $\frac{1}{2}$ to $\frac{3}{4}$ in. long, with a shallow groove on the upper side. Flowers drooping, opening April to early June in loose clusters of three to five, with a nutmeg-like fragrance. Pedicels stout, up to $1\frac{1}{4}$ in. long, glabrous. Calyx very large, bell-shaped, $\frac{3}{4}$ to $1\frac{1}{8}$ in. long, with five deep, rounded ovate lobes, glabrous and without scales. Corolla funnel-shaped, 4 in. long and as much wide, pure white or flushed with pinkish purple, stained with pale yellow at the base inside. Stamens ten, shorter than the corolla, downy at the lower part. Ovary and base of style scaly. Capsule very short, about $\frac{3}{4}$ in. long, surrounded by the persistent calyx. *Bot. Mag.*, t. 9326. (*s.* Maddenii *ss.* Megacalyx)

Native of the borderland between China and upper Burma westward across the upper Irrawaddy to the region of the Tsangpo bend, at the eastern end of the Himalaya; discovered by Kingdon Ward in 1914 in the valley of the Nmai Hka, Burma, at 7,000–8,000 ft; introduced by Forrest in 1917 from the Shweli–Salween divide, about 20 miles south of the type-locality. Two years later Farrer and Cox collected seeds a few miles north of the original locality and at the same altitude.

'It is a tall shrub, or small spindly tree, with large, loose heads of blossom, passing over by the middle of May. The long stout pedicels are clothed in a sort of blue bloom, the big conspicuous calyx is crimson and pink and green. The flowers are of enormous size, pure white, flushed with pink, orange-anthered, and limp in texture, so as to suggest some floppy, snow-white flowered Gloxinia. Add to all this an intense fragrance of clove, and you may imagine with what acclamations I gathered in this new recruit . . .' (Farrer, *Gard. Chron.*, Vol. 66 (1919), p. 161). The fragrance is usually likened to that of nutmeg, whence Kingdon Ward's nickname for the species—"Nutmegacalyx".

R. *megacalyx* is too tender to be grown outdoors in the London area, but succeeds in some gardens of the Atlantic zone. It received an Award of Merit when shown by Adm. Heneage-Vivian of Clyne Park, Swansea, on June 7, 1937.

R. MICRANTHUM Turcz.
R. *pritzelianum* Diels; R. *rosthornii* Diels

An evergreen shrub of bushy form, ultimately 4 to 6 ft high; branches slender, scaly, and slightly downy when young. Leaves narrowly oval or oblanceolate, tapering at both ends, $\frac{3}{4}$ to $1\frac{1}{2}$ in. long, $\frac{1}{4}$ to $\frac{1}{2}$ in. wide, glabrous above, very scaly beneath; stalk $\frac{1}{4}$ in. or less long. Flowers dull white, $\frac{1}{3}$ to $\frac{1}{2}$ in. across, numerous and densely packed in a short, terminal, rounded raceme $1\frac{1}{4}$ to $1\frac{1}{2}$ in. across, on slender, scaly stalks up to $\frac{3}{4}$ in. long. Calyx with linear lobes $\frac{1}{16}$ in. long. Corolla bell-shaped at the base, with five flatly spreading, oval lobes as long as the tube; stamens ten, longer than the corolla, not downy. Style shorter than the stamens, glabrous. *Bot. Mag.*, t. 8198. (s. Micranthum)

Native of North and Central China, and of Korea; first collected by the French missionary d'Incarville in the middle of the 18th century in the mountains north of Peking and described in 1837 from a later collecting in the same area; apparently not introduced to Britain until Wilson sent seeds to Messrs Veitch from W. Hupeh in 1901. According to him it is a rare plant in Hupeh, growing in cliffs at 5,000 to 6,000 ft and favouring 'fully exposed and windswept rocky places'. It is remarkably distinct in its racemes of small, numerous flowers, which open in May, and give the plant at that time a strong resemblance to *Ledum groenlandicum*. Still, it is not in the front rank of rhododendrons.

R. MICROPHYTON Franch.

An evergreen azalea 1 to 3 (or occasionally up to 6) ft high, of bushy, twiggy habit; young shoots densely clothed with pale, reddish-brown, appressed, flattened, forward-pointing bristles. Leaves oval, ovate, or lanceolate, $\frac{1}{2}$ to $1\frac{1}{2}$ in. long, $\frac{1}{3}$ to $\frac{3}{4}$ in. wide, pointed, of a bronzy tinge when young, bright green above when older and sprinkled with bristles; the lower surface paler and with appressed bristles, especially on the midrib, margins bristly; stalk $\frac{1}{12}$ to $\frac{1}{8}$ in. long. Flowers four to six together in terminal clusters opening in April and May. Calyx-lobes five, varying from $\frac{1}{16}$ to $\frac{1}{6}$ in. long, covered with bright brown bristles like the flower-stalks, which are $\frac{1}{6}$ in. long. Corolla pale rosy lilac with carmine or crimson spots on the three upper lobes, $\frac{3}{4}$ to $1\frac{1}{4}$ in. wide and long, five-lobed, the lobes ovate, spreading, contracted at the base to a cylindrical tube, faintly downy inside. Stamens $\frac{5}{8}$ to $\frac{7}{8}$ in. long, downy towards the base; anthers deep rose. Ovary covered with bright brown hairs; style glabrous. (s. Azalea ss. Obtusum)

Native of Yunnan, China; discovered by the Abbé Delavay about 1884, and a little later by Henry. Forrest found it on the eastern flank of the Tali range in 1906, but did not send seeds until 1913. It belongs to the Obtusum group of azaleas, characterised by the forward-pointing appressed bristles on the vegetative parts; the long cylindrical tube of the corolla is distinctive. It is a pretty, free-flowering plant, the flowers sometimes almost white. Only hardy in the south and west.

R. MINUS Michx.

R. punctatum Andrews; R. cuthbertii Small

An evergreen bush up to 20 ft high in the wild, sometimes taller; young shoots rough with scales. Leaves oval-lanceolate to narrowly obovate, tapering at both ends, the apex usually acuminate, $1\frac{1}{2}$ to 3 in. long, $\frac{1}{2}$ to $1\frac{1}{2}$ in. wide, dark green and nearly glabrous above, thickly dotted beneath with minute red-brown scales; stalk $\frac{1}{4}$ to $\frac{1}{2}$ in. long. Flowers in dense terminal trusses, opening in June; pedicels up to $\frac{3}{4}$ in. long. Calyx-lobes very short. Corolla 1 to $1\frac{1}{2}$ in. wide, funnel-shaped, pale pinkish purple, spotted on the upper side with brownish-red, densely scaly on the outside. Stamens ten, hairy at the base. Ovary scaly; style glabrous. Bot. Mag., t. 2285. (s. Carolinianum)

Native of the south-eastern USA from South Carolina to Georgia and Alabama; introduced in 1786. As seen in this country it is inferior to its ally R. carolinianum, from which it differs in its more pointed leaves, in the corollas being densely scaly on the outside, and in their longer tubes, $\frac{2}{3}$ in. or more long. It also flowers later, usually in June.

For the hybrids of R. minus, see p. 834.

R. MOLLE (Bl.) G. Don

Azalea mollis Bl.; Azalea sinensis Lodd.; R. sinense (Lodd.) Sw.

A deciduous azalea, closely allied to R. japonicum. The most obvious difference is that the leaves of R. sinense are coated beneath throughout the season with a dense felt of soft down and that the buds, too, are conspicuously downy. The calyx-lobes are shorter and not so bristly, and the flowers are always in some shade of yellow.

R. molle, once better known as Azalea sinensis, is common in Chekiang, China, and also occurs in other provinces of eastern China. According to Wilson it grows among coarse grasses and shrubs and in thin pinewoods, and makes a small, sturdy shrub 2 to 5 ft high. Fortune is very eloquent of its beauty as seen wild in China, especially on the hills about Ningpo, where, he wrote, 'the yellow

Azalea sinensis seemed to paint the hillsides, so large were the flowers, so vivid the colours'. Fortune sent seeds in 1845, but there had been an earlier introduction to Loddiges' nursery, in 1823. In this century, seeds have been collected by Wilson near Ichang, in W. Hupeh, where the species is near its western limit, and also by Forrest, who found it growing in a lamasery garden (F.25477). Another reintroduction was by Rock under his no. 59226, from the foot of the Litiping range in Yunnan, but it is not clear whether the plants were wild or cultivated. This sending is of interest, since plants raised from it were used by Lionel de Rothschild in the breeding of the Exbury strain of the Knap Hill azaleas.

R. *molle* is hardy, but lacks stamina and has always been rare in gardens. But, by crossing with the more vigorous R. *japonicum* and other azaleas it has given rise to some of the finest of the yellow-flowered hybrids. It is also a parent of the azaleodendrons 'Broughtonianum Aureum' and 'Smithii Aureum'. See further in the section on hybrids.

R. MOLLICOMUM Balf. f. & W. W. Sm.

An evergreen shrub up to 6 ft high; young shoots very downy. Leaves of stout leathery texture, narrowly oval or oblong, tapered at the base, rather blunt at the apex, $\frac{3}{4}$ to 2 in. long, $\frac{3}{16}$ to $\frac{1}{2}$ in. wide, dull green above, downy on both surfaces, especially on the midrib beneath and on the strongly decurved margins; somewhat scaly beneath; stalk $\frac{1}{8}$ in. or less long. Flowers opening in April and May usually in pairs from the terminal leaf-axils, each flower on a downy stalk about $\frac{1}{4}$ in. long, the whole forming a truss 2 or 3 in. wide. Calyx very small, scarcely lobed, very downy. Corolla pale pink to rosy red, $\frac{3}{4}$ in. long, 1 in. wide, slenderly funnel-shaped at the base, dividing at the top into five oblong lobes; slightly scaly outside, slightly downy inside the tube. Stamens ten, well protruded, their slender stalks downy on the lower half. Ovary scaly and downy; style downy at the base, slender, 1 in. or so long, standing along with the stamens half an inch beyond the corolla. (*s.* Scabrifolium)

Native of Yunnan and S.W. Szechwan, China, up to altitudes of 11,000 ft; discovered and introduced by Forrest in 1913; first flowered at Caerhays in 1917. Notable characteristics are the soft down which covers shoots, leaves, flower-stalks, and calyx, the protruded stamens and style, and the mixture of scales and down beneath the leaf. It is a pretty rhododendron, evidently hardier than is generally supposed, as it has lived and flowered annually in the open air at Kew since 1923. At the same time it is better suited with milder conditions. It received an Award of Merit when shown from Bodnant April 8, 1931.

R. *mollicomum* is akin to R. *scabrifolium* and R. *spiciferum*, but has narrower flowers and lacks the bristly hairs seen in those two species.

R. MOLLYANUM Cowan & Davidian

A small evergreen tree, so far around 20 ft high in cultivation; young stems stout, covered with a thin grey wool. Leaves very thick and rigid, up to 12 in. long and $2\frac{1}{4}$ to 4 in. wide in the type, rounded at the apex, tapered towards the base, glossy and dark green above, with impressed lateral veins, undersurface covered with a thin, shining, silvery-white indumentum; petiole up to 1⅝ in. long, thinly grey-woolly. Flowers in a terminal umbel of up to twenty, opening in April or May; pedicels up to 2 in. long, woolly. Calyx minute. Corolla pink or sometimes white edged with pink, with a crimson blotch at the base, obliquely campanulate, about 2½ in. long and wide. Stamens fifteen or sixteen. Ovary clad with matted hairs; style glabrous, about as long as the corolla, with a large discoid stigma.   (s. Grande)

R. *mollyanum* was described in 1953 from a plant at Brodick in the Isle of Arran, raised from Kingdon Ward's seed no. 6261, collected in the middle of December 1924 near Gompo Ne, S.E. Tibet, above the Tsangpo gorge. Two months earlier he had found trees on the southern side of the Doshong La, none of which had flowered or fruited that year and, judging from his field note, he considered these to represent the same species as those from which he later took seed, though they bore leaves much larger than in cultivated R. *mollyanum*— 2 ft long and 8 or 9 in. wide. Owing to some unexplained confusion the field specimen under KW 6261 is R. *exasperatum* and none corresponding to R. *mollyanum* has been traced. The type of the species is therefore a specimen taken from the Brodick plant.

R. *mollyanum* is allied to both R. *grande* and R. *sinogrande*, differing from the former in the larger more leathery leaves, rounded at the apex, from the latter in the narrower and smaller leaves and fewer stamens; and from both in the pink flowers.

R. *mollyanum* is perfectly hardy and grows well in woodland south of London. There is some variation in the colouring of the flowers and in the size of the leaves, but they are never quite as long, and certainly not as wide, as on the plants described by Kingdon Ward, but it was not from these that the seeds were taken. A First Class Certificate was given on April 9, 1957, to the clone 'Benmore', when a truss was exhibited at a meeting of the Rhododendron and Camellia Committee held in Scotland. It was raised from seed at the Younger Botanic Garden, Benmore, about fifteen years previously.

R. *mollyanum* is named after the late Duchess of Montrose, known as Molly to her family but, as Kingdon Ward pointed out, the name is of very doubtful validity, since the almost identical name R. *mollianum* had been published many years previously for a New Guinea rhododendron.

R. PUDOROSUM Cowan—Near to R. *grande*, but with pink or magenta-pink flowers and with the stems densely covered with bud-scales, which persist for two or three years. Discovered by Ludlow and Sherriff in 1936 on the Tibetan side of the Assam Himalaya, above the Chayul and Tsari rivers, tributaries of the Subansiri. It is in cultivation and flowered at Edinburgh in 1972.

R. MONOSEMATUM Hutch.

An evergreen shrub closely related to R. *pachytrichum*, of sturdy, bushy habit and probably capable of growing 10 ft or more high. It differs chiefly from R. *pachytrichum* in the young shoots and leaf-stalks being furnished with straight, unbranched, gland-tipped bristles; in R. *pachytrichum* the hairs are curly, branched and not gland-tipped. Leaves oblong, 3 to 6 in. long, 1 to 1½ in. wide, green on both surfaces and glabrous except for some hairs at the base of the midrib. Flowers produced in April, a dozen or so together, in hemispherical terminal trusses 4 in. wide. Calyx and flower-stalk glandular. Corolla bell-shaped, 1¼ in. wide, white tinged with rose, marked at the base with a black-purple blotch and a few spots. Stamens ten, white, downy at the base; anthers dark purple. Ovary covered with short glands, mixed with longer whitish hairs, style glabrous. *Bot. Mag.*, t. 8675. (*s.* Barbatum *ss.* Maculiferum)

R. *monosematum* was found by Wilson on the Wa Shan, W. Szechwan, in 1903, and was described from a cultivated plant, raised from the seeds which he sent to Messrs Veitch. It will be seen from the description given above that it differs from R. *pachytrichum* in the glandular character of the hairs on branchlet, leaf-stalk, flower-stalk, calyx, and ovary. It has about the same hardiness and the same garden value.

R. MORII Hayata
R. *pachysanthum* Hayata

An evergreen shrub or tree, occasionally 30 ft high in the wild; young shoots at first floccose-hairy and glandular, becoming glabrous. Leaves oblong-lanceolate, 2½ to 5 in. long, ¾ to 1½ in. wide, abruptly narrowed at the apex to a sharp, horny point, base truncate or rounded, dull green and glabrous above, paler and glossy beneath, with traces of flock and glands on the prominent midrib, otherwise glabrous; petiole ½ to 1 in. long, with the same covering as the midrib. Flowers ten to fifteen, borne in April or May in a loose terminal truss; rachis about ¾ in. long; pedicels 1 to 1½ in. long, slightly glandular-hairy. Calyx minute, fringed with glands. Corolla five-lobed, widely campanulate, up to 2 in. long and wide, white or pale pink, usually with rich red speckling merging into a blotch at the base, but in some forms the markings are less pronounced. Stamens finely downy at the base. Ovary clad with short, spreading, usually gland-tipped hairs, but sometimes the hairs are eglandular; style glandular at the base or eglandular. *Bot. Mag.*, n.s., t. 517. (*s.* Barbatum *ss.* Maculiferum)

Native of Formosa, where, according to Wilson, it is the common rhododendron of the forests above 6,500 ft; he introduced it in 1918, from Mt Arisan. It is perfectly hardy in a sheltered place, and very beautiful in its flowers, especially when these are speckled and blotched with clear red. It appears to be correctly placed in the Maculiferum subseries of Barbatum, where its nearest Chinese ally is R. *pachytrichum*. It received an Award of Merit when shown by Capt. Collingwood Ingram, Benenden, Kent, on May 1, 1956.

R. ANHWEIENSE Wils.—This species was discovered in 1923 in southern Anhwei, China, and described from fruiting specimens (as R. "*anwheiense*", an orthographic error); it was again collected in fruit two years later. It appears to be allied to R. *morii*, though the leaves are remarkably small, only 2 in. or so long on wild plants, 3 in. long on cultivated plants, which have white, sparsely or densely speckled flowers borne in April or May in trusses of about ten;

corolla campanulate, $1\frac{3}{8}$ to 2 in. wide. It is hardy, but only the forms with conspicuously speckled corollas are worth growing.

R. MOUPINENSE Franch.

A dwarf evergreen shrub 2 to 4 ft high; young shoots hairy, much of the hairiness disappearing by autumn. Leaves leathery, obovate, or oval, rather convex above, rounded or slightly heart-shaped at the base, usually rounded and with a short mucro at the apex, $\frac{3}{4}$ to $1\frac{1}{2}$ in. long, about half as wide, dark, slightly glossy green, and glabrous except for some minute down on the midrib above, pale and covered with minute scales beneath, margins ciliate at first towards the base; leaf-stalk $\frac{1}{8}$ to $\frac{1}{4}$ in. long, furnished with dark hairs. Flowers one to three in a terminal cluster, opening in February or March; flower-stalks short, scaly. Calyx about $\frac{1}{6}$ in. long, scaly and hairy on the outside, with broadly rounded lobes. Corolla white or pink, sometimes spotted with purple or crimson, five-lobed, funnel-shaped, up to 2 in. across. Stamens ten, downy in the lower part. Ovary scaly; style glabrous. *Bot. Mag.*, t. 8598.   (*s.* Moupinense)

RHODODENDRON MOUPINENSE

Native of W. Szechwan, where it grows as an epiphyte on evergreen oaks and other broad-leaved trees, but sometimes on rocks and cliffs; discovered by Père David in 1869; introduced by Wilson in 1909, during his first expedition for the Arnold Arboretum. It flowered with Miss Ellen Willmott of Great Warley, Essex, in 1913 and received an Award of Merit when she showed it the following year on February 10. The pink-flowered form received the same award when shown from Bodnant on February 23, 1937. It is a delightful rhododendron and perfectly hardy, but flowering so early it is rarely seen in perfection in frosty gardens. It is the parent of many early-flowering hybrids.

R. MUCRONULATUM Turcz. [PLATE 85

R. *taquettii* Lévl.; R. *dauricum* var. *mucronulatum* (Turcz.) Maxim.

A deciduous shrub of erect, thinnish habit, up to 6 or 8 ft high, the twigs slender and glabrous except for a few scales. Leaves lanceolate or inclined to oblanceolate, slenderly pointed, $1\frac{1}{4}$ to 4 in. long, $\frac{1}{2}$ to $1\frac{1}{4}$ in. wide; of thin texture; stalk $\frac{1}{8}$ to $\frac{1}{4}$ in. long. Flowers produced singly from each of a cluster of buds at the end of the naked shoots, sometimes as many as six at the tip of one shoot, often opening successively; flower-stalk $\frac{1}{4}$ in. long, hidden by the scales of the flower-bud. Calyx small, shallowly five-lobed. Corolla pale rose-purple, opening widely, $1\frac{1}{2}$ to 2 in. across, five-lobed, downy outside. Stamens ten, their stalks downy at the base; anthers dark purple. Ovary covered with close, minute scales; style glabrous. *Bot. Mag.*, t. 8304. (s. Dauricum)

Native of N. China, the Ussuri region of Russia, Korea, and Japan (where it is found only in the parts nearest to Korea—N. Kyushu and the Chugoku district of the main island). According to Wilson, it is abundant in Korea in thin woods and open country, and especially so in the north, where it forms the undergrowth of larch forest on volcanic soils. It was described in 1837 from specimens collected on the Pohuashan near Peking, and introduced from there to the Arnold Arboretum, USA, in 1882 by Dr Bretschneider. The first recorded introduction to Kew was in 1907, when plants were received from a Yokohama nursery, but Edinburgh had it nine years earlier from an unknown source.

Under cultivation the flowering season of this species varies according to the weather. At Kew, as a rule, it is at its best from Christmas to the beginning of February. I have seen it in splendid bloom on Christmas Day. The flowers are destroyed by about five degrees of frost, but are often succeeded by a fresh crop. After a hard winter and spring, flowers will open as late as April. This shrub must be included amongst the very best of winter flowerers, for few give so beautiful a display so early in the year. In botanical detail it scarcely differs from R. *dauricum*, but in its greater size and vigour, its larger more pointed leaves, and its larger flowers it is very different. It is also superior as a garden shrub.

R. *mucronulatum* has twice received an Award of Merit when shown from Kew: on February 12, 1924 (flowers purplish rose) and on January 8, 1935 (flowers light rose). It was given a First Class Certificate on January 22, 1957, when shown by the Crown Estate Commissioners, Windsor Great Park (clone later named 'Winter Sunset', flowers rich purplish rose).

cv. 'CORNELL PINK'.—Flowers Phlox Pink (a pure medium pink with no hint of purple). It is a selection from over one thousand plants, raised by Henry T. Skinner at Cornell University, USA, from seeds of R. *mucronulatum* bought from the Yokohama Nursery Company in 1931. It was named and put into commerce in 1952 (*R.C.Y.B. 1967*, p. 132). Award of Merit when shown from Kew, March 30, 1965.

R. NERIIFLORUM Franch.

R. *euchaites* Balf. f. & Forr.

An evergreen shrub or small tree up to 25 ft high; young shoots reddish, woolly at first. Leaves oblong to narrowly obovate, rounded to abruptly tapered at both ends, mucronate, 2 to 4 in. long, 1 to 1½ in. wide; dark green above, glaucous-white beneath, glabrous except on the midrib beneath; stalk ⅓ to ¾ in. long, reddish and downy when young. Flowers six to twelve in a truss 3 to 4 in. wide, opening in March or April; pedicels about ½ in. long, downy. Calyx membranous, varying in size and very irregular, with five unequal rounded lobes. Corolla rich crimson, tubular-bell-shaped, 1½ to 1¾ in. long, not so much wide, with five rounded, notched lobes. Stamens ten, white, glabrous, ¾ to 1¼ in. long; anthers very dark brown. Ovary felted; style slightly overtopping the stamens, glabrous except just above the ovary. *Bot. Mag.*, t. 8727. (*s.* and *ss.* Neriiflorum)

Native of mid-Yunnan westward through upper Burma to the eastern Himalaya, where it reaches almost as far as Bhutan. It was discovered by Père Delavay in the Tali range, Yunnan, and introduced from the same area by Forrest in 1910 (F.6780). Here, at least on the eastern flank of the range, where there is little forest, it makes a shrub 2 to 8 ft high, occurring in open pinewoods, shaded gullies, or rocky pastures, at 10,000 to 12,000 ft. The seeds of the original introduction were taken from low-growing plants and produced dense, very free-flowering bushes, but these eventually grew much taller than the parental wild plants, e.g., to 10 ft high at Werrington Park in Cornwall.

Plants of Tali provenance are rare in gardens. Mostly, the cultivated stock derives from seeds collected farther west, where R. *neriiflorum*, though often a dwarf shrub at subalpine elevations, is more commonly taller growing, and sometimes a small tree. These plants, once usually known by the synonymous name R. *euchaites*, make erect, rather lax shrubs up to 15 ft high. The flowers are usually of the purest crimson-scarlet and borne in great profusion in late March, April, or May. Out of flower, the species is easily recognisable by its neat, oblongish leaves, glaucous white beneath. It is perfectly hardy in light woodland south of London, and received an Award of Merit when shown from Bodnant on March 26, 1929.

A form of R. *neriiflorum* with leaves tapered at the apex, a fewer-flowered inflorescence, and smaller calyx, was introduced by Farrer and Cox in 1919 from the pass above Hpimaw, Burma, on the Salween–Nmai Hka (Irrawaddy) divide. It was given specific status as R. *phoenicodum* Balf. f. & Farrer, but should probably be regarded as part of the normal variation of the species. It is figured in *Bot. Mag.*, t. 9521.

R. PHAEDROPUM Balf. f. & Farrer—This differs from R. *neriiflorum* in having the ovary glandular as well as hairy. Also, at least in the type-plants, the colour of the flowers ranges from straw-yellow to salmon rose and light scarlet, but such aberrations in colour are common in the Neriiflorum series. This species, perhaps no more than a glandular state of R. *neriiflorum*, was discovered by Farrer on the Nmai Hka (Irrawaddy)–Salween divide above Nyitadi in 1920. Plants found by Ludlow and Sherriff in S. Tibet and Bhutan were referred to it by Dr Cowan.

R. NIPPONICUM Matsum.

A deciduous azalea described as of bushy habit and from 3 to 6 ft high; the stiff young shoots reddish brown and clothed with glandular bristles. Leaves scarcely stalked, obovate, rounded, and often notched at the apex, tapered to the base, 2 to 6 in. long, half as much wide, more or less appressed-bristly above and beneath. Flowers opening about midsummer, six to fifteen in a cluster, the pedicels ½ to ¾ in. long, sticky with glands. Calyx small, with five ovate, ciliate lobes. Corolla narrowly bell-shaped, scarcely 1 in. long, white with five short, slightly spreading lobes. Stamens ten, unequal in length but all shorter than the corolla, downy below the middle. Ovary glandular-hairy; style glabrous. *Bot. Mag.*, n.s., t. 491. (*s.* Azalea *ss.* Nipponicum)

Native of the mountains of Central Japan, where it occurs only in a few localities; discovered in 1883. Its existence in gardens is apparently due to E. H. Wilson, who found it on the hills around Toge in 1914 and sent seeds to the Arnold Arboretum. It first flowered at Kew in June 1921, but this species is no longer there. The blossom is very disappointing, being small and hidden away in the young growths. But in foliage it is one of the finest of azaleas and it takes on brilliant orange and crimson tints in autumn. The bright reddish-brown bark is also pleasing. Botanically it is distinct in having the stamens and style included within the somewhat tubular corolla, which resembles that of *Menziesia ciliicalyx* in shape.

R. NIVALE Hook. f.

R. *paludosum* Hutch. & Ward

A compact twiggy shrub with erect or interlacing stems, up to about 3 ft high, sometimes ground-hugging. Leaves less than ½ in. long, elliptic to roundish, obtuse or rounded at the apex, scaly on both sides, the scales beneath close or contiguous, brown, but intermixed with less numerous darker ones. Flowers solitary or in pairs. Calyx well developed, usually as long as the ovary, the lobes scaly on the back and at the margin. Corolla purple, lavender, or pink, about ¾ in. wide. Stamens usually ten, occasionally fewer, downy in the lower part. Style glabrous, or sometimes downy at the base, usually longer than the stamens. (*s.* Lapponicum)

A native of the Himalaya at high altitudes from Nepal eastward and of the trans-Himalayan ranges of S.E. Tibet where it reaches farther into the dry zone than any other rhododendron; its southern limit is the Diphuk La, near the common border of Burma, Assam, and Tibet (KW 7058). It is in cultivation but uncommon.

subsp. BOREALE Philipson & Philipson R. *nigropunctatum* Franch.; R. *ramosissimum* Franch.; R. *alpicola* Rehd. & Wils.; R. *violaceum* Rehd. & Wils.; R. *oresbium* Balf. f. & Ward; R. *stictophyllum* Balf. f.; R. *vicarium* Balf. f.; R. *batangense* Balf. f.; R. *oreinum* Balf. f.; R. *yaragongense* Balf. f.—Calyx shortly lobed or reduced to a shallow cup. Style usually shorter than the stamens. Colouring of the scales on the underside of the leaf sometimes more uniform than in typical R. *nivale.*

This subspecies, with the synonyms listed above, was constituted by M. N. and W. R. Philipson in the revision of the Lapponicum group, published in 1975 (see p. 572). It occurs in W. Szechwan, bordering parts of Tibet and N.W. Yunnan. The first introduction appears to have been by Wilson from W. Szechwan when collecting for Messrs Veitch (seed-number 1543) and was grown as R. *nigropunctatum* (*Bot. Mag.*, t. 8529). At the present time there are plants from Rock 24385 in the Edinburgh Botanic Garden, previously grown as R. *stictophyllum*, but the rhododendron in commerce under this name agrees none too well with R. *nivale* subsp. *boreale* and indeed bears some resemblance to R. *lysolepis*. It is, however, one of the prettiest of the Lapponicums.

The authors remark that the type of R. EDGARIANUM Rehd. & Wils., collected by Wilson in W. Szechwan in 1908, appears to be a hybrid of R. *nivale* subsp. *boreale* with some undetermined species. He sent seeds, but the plants now grown as R. *edgarianum*, at least those seen, are from Forrest 16450, collected on the Beima-shan. The seed was distributed as R. *oresbium*, which is included in R. *edgarianum* in *Species of Rhododendron*, whence its present name. However, in the Philipsons' revision R. *oresbium* is included in R. *nivale* subsp. *boreale*, while Forrest's original specimen under 16450 is referred to R. *tapetiforme* (a species not treated here). The plants themselves do not agree either with R. *nivale* subsp. *boreale* nor with R. *tapetiforme* (nor with R. *edgarianum*). This "R. *edgarianum*" is a quite useful Lapponicum, of dwarf, erect habit, bearing light purple flowers at the end of May.

R. NIVEUM Hook. f.

An evergreen shrub of sturdy habit, up to 15 ft high; young shoots clothed with a whitish felt. Leaves narrowly-oblong, 3 to 7 in. long, 1 to 2½ in. wide, tapering at the base, more rounded at the apex. When the young leaves unfold they are covered all over with a snow-white floss, which falls away from the upper surface, leaving it very deep green, but which persists beneath and turns a pale brown. Flowers up to twenty, sometimes more numerous, in a compact, rounded head 3 to 4 in. across, borne on short, felted stalks. Calyx minute. Corolla tubular-campanulate, five-lobed, 1¾ to 2 in. long, purplish lilac or dull plum-coloured, with darker nectar-pouches at the base. Stamens ten, shorter than the corolla. Ovary felted; style glabrous, with a small stigma. *Bot. Mag.*, t. 4730. (*s.* and *ss.* Arboreum)

R. *niveum* was discovered by J. D. Hooker in Sikkim in November 1849, growing around Lachen, Lachung, and Chola at 10,000 to 12,000 ft, and not uncommon there. But outside Sikkim it seems to be rare.

It is quite hardy at Kew in a sheltered position but enjoys a moister climate. The unusual colour of the flowers among rhododendrons, and the striking snowy-white covering of its young leaves, gives this species a certain distinction and makes it well worth growing, though not in the neighbourhood of pure reds, with which its flowers clash gratingly. Its flowering season is April to May.

Hooker noted that the indumentum of R. *niveum* is sometimes rusty-red in the wild. This form is figured in *Bot. Mag.*, t. 6827, as var. *fulvum*.

R. *niveum* is a variable species, and some forms are much inferior to others in colour and size of flower. The Award of Merit was given on April 17, 1951, to a form with Imperial Purple flowers in trusses of up to thirty, exhibited by Mrs Stevenson, Tower Court, Ascot.

Some garden seedlings are thought to be hybrids between R. *niveum* and R. *falconeri*, e.g. 'Colonel Rogers', raised at Riverhill, Sevenoaks, and 'Trevarrick', raised in Cornwall, where hybrids of this putative parentage are fairly common. Another is 'Mecca', which received an Award of Merit on May 4, 1965, when exhibited by Mrs Douglas Gordon, Littleworth Cross, Surrey. In this the flowers are white with a light purple flush, in rounded trusses of up to forty-two. These plants are not further dealt with in the section on hybrids.

R. NUTTALLII Booth
R. *sinonuttallii* Balf. f. & Forr.

An evergreen shrub or small tree from 12 to 30 ft high, of straggling, thinly branched habit, often growing in nature as an epiphyte on the branches and forks of large trees; young shoots very stout, scaly. Leaves stout and leathery, oval, tapered at both ends, shortly pointed, 5 to 12 in. long, 2½ to 4½ in. wide, greyish, strongly reddish veined and thickly sprinkled with scales beneath, at first reddish above, ultimately pale green, much puckered and wrinkled. Flowers fragrant, usually three to six in a terminal truss (as many as eleven have been known), opening in May horizontally or rather nodding. Calyx deeply five-lobed, the lobes oblong, rounded at the end, 1 in. long, ½ in. wide. Corolla funnel-shaped at the base, of wax-like texture, ivory-white suffused with yellow in the throat, 4 to 5 in. long and measuring about the same across the five spreading, rounded lobes. Stamens normally ten, 2½ in. long, downy towards the base; anthers ⅓ in. long, reddish brown. Ovary and base only of style scaly, the latter up to 3 in. long. *Bot. Mag.*, t. 5146.   (s. Maddenii ss. Megacalyx)

Native of the eastern Himalaya, S.E. Tibet, and upper Burma. It was discovered by Thomas Booth in 1849–50 in the Dafla Hills, Assam Himalaya, growing 'on the banks of the Papoo, swampy ground amongst Yews and Oaks at 4000–5000 ft'. It was introduced by him, and first flowered in 1858 with Otto Forster of Augsburg, who had bought a grafted plant from Standish and Noble three years previously. At Kew it flowered in the following year in the Rhododendron House, when 9 ft high.

In regard to the individual flower, which suggests a lily in size and texture, this is the most magnificent of rhododendrons. Flowers are frequently 6 in. wide. Unfortunately it is too tender to be grown in the open air even in Cornwall. It is not a strong-rooting shrub and likes a sandy, peaty, well-drained soil. Healthy plants make shoots one foot or more long in a season.

R. *nuttallii* received a First Class Certificate more than a century ago. The Award of Merit was given in 1955 to a form raised from Ludlow and Sherriff seeds, shown by the Sunningdale Nurseries.

The name var. *stellatum* was given by Hutchinson to a form with rather smaller flowers than normal and a spreading calyx, raised from seeds collected by Kingdon Ward in the Tsangpo gorge, S.E. Tibet, in 1924. Plants from these seeds (KW 6333) are said to be somewhat hardier than the common form. Award of Merit 1936.

R. OBLONGIFOLIUM (Small) Millais
Azalea oblongifolia Small

A deciduous azalea up to 6 ft high; young shoots more or less bristly. Leaves obovate to oblanceolate, $1\frac{1}{2}$ to 4 in. long, $\frac{1}{2}$ to $1\frac{1}{2}$ in. wide. Flowers slightly fragrant, produced after the leaves in seven- to twelve-flowered clusters. Calyx small, bristly. Corolla funnel-shaped, pure white, with a cylindrical tube $\frac{3}{4}$ to 1 in. long and more or less glandular and hairy outside. Stamens five, about 2 in. long, hairy below the middle; ovary covered with bristly hairs; style longer than the stamens. (*s*. Azalea *ss*. Luteum)

Native of Arkansas, Oklahoma, and Texas, growing, according to Rehder, in moist sandy woods or on the margins of sandy bogs or streams; introduced by means of seeds sent to Britain by Prof. Sargent in 1917. Numerous plants were raised which have proved quite hardy at Kew, where it flowers in July and even later. The leaves are glaucous beneath and bristly on the midrib and margins. It seems to be very close in botanical relationship to R. *viscosum*, but Rehder relies on its longer, more oblong calyx-lobes, its downy winter-buds and larger leaves. I do not consider it so good a garden azalea as R. *viscosum*, but it is worth noting that in Oklahoma it has been found growing on limestone.

R. OBTUSUM *see under* R. KAEMPFERI

R. OCCIDENTALE (Torr. & Gr.) A. Gray [PLATE 86
Azalea occidentalis Torr. & Gr.

A deciduous, rounded bush 8 ft or more high; young shoots slightly downy. Leaves oval or obovate, 2 to 4 in. long, $\frac{3}{4}$ to $1\frac{1}{2}$ in. wide, tapering at the base, often rounded at the apex; upper surface glossy green and furnished with scattered hairs, lower surface pale, rather glaucous, downy (at least when young); stalk downy, $\frac{1}{4}$ in. or less long. Flowers fragrant, white with a blotch of yellow on the upper side, $2\frac{1}{2}$ to 3 in. across, produced in terminal clusters of six to twelve after the leaves, during June and July. Calyx-lobes up to $\frac{3}{16}$ in. long, ciliate. Corolla-tube 1 in. or more long, downy; stamens and style protruded, 2 to $2\frac{1}{2}$ in. long. *Bot. Mag.*, t. 5005. (*s*. Azalea *ss*. Luteum)

Native of western N. America; introduced by Wm Lobb for Messrs Veitch about 1851. This beautiful azalea is the only species of its section found west of the Rocky Mountains. It has many points of resemblance to, and appears to be the Western representative of, R. *arborescens*, but has larger yellow-blotched flowers and its foliage is quite hairy beneath; the calyx also is shorter. It does not blossom until the great azalea season is over, or until it is itself in almost full leaf. It is one of the best summer-flowering shrubs, although it has taken horticulturists a long time to find that out. In 1857, Lindley, then the high priest of gardening, pronounced it to be 'of little value'. Anthony Waterer of Knap Hill and Koster of Boskoop, by crossing it with the bright-coloured azaleas that flower earlier, laid the foundation of a beautiful race of late-flowering varieties. See further in the section on hybrids, p. 914.

R. OLDHAMII Maxim.

An evergreen much-branched shrub 5 to 10 ft high; young shoots densely clothed with outstanding reddish hairs and some flattish bristles. Leaves elliptic to elliptic-ovate or oval, pointed, tapered at the base, 1 to 3½ in. long, ½ to 1½ in. wide, dull green and downy on both surfaces, especially beneath, wrinkled and rough to the touch above; stalk up to ⅓ in. long, bristly and hairy like the young shoots. Flowers in a terminal cluster of two to four. Calyx green, with rounded or ovate and pointed lobes up to ⅓ in. long, usually smaller; covered like the flower-stalk with glandular, sticky hairs. Corolla 2 in. wide, funnel-shaped at the base, spreading out into five rounded lobes ¾ in. long, orange-red except on the upper lobes which are stained with pink and dotted with dark purple. Stamens ten, ½ to 1 in. long, red, with purple anthers and a downy base. Ovary bristly; style smooth, red, 1½ in. long. *Bot. Mag.*, t. 9059. (*s.* Azalea *ss.* Obtusum)

Native of Formosa only; discovered by Richard Oldham, the Kew collector, in 1864. First introduced for Messrs Veitch by Chas. Maries in 1878. I do not think any of his generation of plants survived, and the species was, no doubt, lost to cultivation until Wilson reintroduced it in 1918. In the past it has flowered in a cool greenhouse at Kew at such diverse seasons as February and August, but its normal time is April. In the open air there it will not survive even mild winters, and is only hardy in the south and west. It is handsome in flower, but not more so than many of the so-called 'Indian' azaleas (R. *simsii*) to which it is related, but easily distinguished by its larger leaves and the soft, spreading, frequently glandular hairs (not appressed flattened bristles) on the young shoots. Wilson calls it the 'common red-flowered azalea of Formosa'; it is found on that island from sea-level up to 8,500 ft.

R. ORBICULARE Decne.
R. *rotundifolium* Franch.

An evergreen shrub up to 6 or 10 ft high; young shoots stout, purplish, glandular. Leaves almost orbicular, but usually somewhat longer than broad, 2 to 4 in. long, deeply auricled at the base, rounded at the apex, with a minute tip formed by a slight prolongation and thickening of the midrib; quite glabrous, dark green above, glaucous beneath; stalk 1½ to 2 in. long, very stout. Flowers borne in April or May, up to ten or so in a terminal truss 6 in. across; flower-stalks glabrous, up to 2¼ in. long. Calyx minute, glabrous. Corolla widely bell-shaped, 2 to 2½ in. across, seven-lobed, pale magenta-pink. Stamens about four-teen, shorter than the corolla. Ovary glandular, style glabrous. *Bot. Mag.*, t. 8775. (*s.* Fortunei *ss.* Orbiculare)

Native of W. Szechwan, China; discovered by Père David around 1870; introduced to Britain by Wilson in 1904. It is a very distinct rhododendron, making a dense bush of rounded habit if not crowded. But the flowers are usually of a cold shade of bluish pink which is far from attractive. It received an Award of Merit in 1922.

R. CARDIOBASIS Sleum.—Leaves similar in shape to those of R. *orbiculare*, but cordate (not auricled) at the base, and somewhat larger. It differs markedly from R. *orbiculare* in having the pedicels and rachis glabrous, and the style (as in *ss*. Fortunei) glandular to the tip. It was described from a specimen collected in Kwangsi province, S. China, a region remote from the homeland of R. *orbiculare*.

R. OREODOXA Franch.

R. *haematocheilum* Craib; R. *limprichtii* Diels; R. *reginaldii* Balf. f.

An evergreen shrub with stout twigs up to ¼ in. thick, sparsely set with glandular hairs when young, soon glabrous. Leaves oblong, rounded to heart-shaped at the base; rounded, with a short blunt tip at the apex; up to 3½ in. long by 1⅛ in. wide; glabrous and dark green above, paler beneath; veins in thirteen to fifteen pairs; stalk ⅓ to ⅔ in. long. Flowers eight to ten in a rounded truss 4 in. across. Calyx minute, usually glandular. Corolla broadly funnel-shaped, seven-lobed, 2 in. wide, the tube scarcely 1 in. long. In the bud state the flower is almost blood-red, changing when open to carmine, then to a lilac shade. Stamens fourteen, about as long as the corolla-tube, white and glabrous; anthers purplish brown. Ovary and style glabrous, the latter longer than the stamens. *Bot. Mag.*, t. 8518.   (*s*. Fortunei *ss*. Oreodoxa)

Native of W. Szechwan and Kansu; discovered by Père David near Mupin in 1869; introduced in 1904 by Wilson for Messrs Veitch, who appear to have distributed it at first as "R. *davidii*", a name properly belonging to a different species. It first flowered in their Coombe Wood nursery in 1913. Lionel de Rothschild wrote of this rhododendron: 'It is one of the first species to open its flowers, which it often does at the end of February or early March, and therefore only fitted for a sheltered garden and a sheltered situation, but the flowers in bud are more frost-resisting than any other rhododendron I know; the flowers open from the bud and show individual bells tightly folded and bright red, and in this shape it will often stand several degrees of frost without being injured, taking advantage of the first few days of mild weather to show its beauty.' Farrer, who re-introduced R. *oreodoxa* from Kansu, described it as 'a tidy, tall, steep-domed bush' or 'a no less tidy, well-furnished tree of some fourteen feet with a comely rounded head'. This is also the habit of the cultivated plants from the Wilson introduction.

R. *oreodoxa* received an Award of Merit when shown from Exbury on April 6, 1937.

R. OREOTREPHES W. W. Sm.

R. *artosquameum* Balf. f. & Forr.; R. *exquisitum* Hutch.; R. *timeteum* Balf. f. & Forr. R. *siderophylloides* Hutch.; R. *cardioeides* Balf. f. & Forr.; R. *depile* Balf. f. & Forr.; R. *hypotrichotum* Balf. f. & Forr.; R. *phaeochlorum* Balf. f. & Forr.; R. *pubigerum* Balf. f. & Forr.; R. *trichopodum* Balf. f. & Forr.

An evergreen shrub or small tree. Leaves elliptic, oblong-elliptic to roundish, 1 to 3½ in. long, ¾ to almost 2 in. wide, obtuse to rounded at the apex, broad-cuneate or rounded or slightly cordate at the base, green or grey-green above, sparsely to densely scaly and more or less glaucous beneath (brownish in densely scaly forms), both sides glabrous except for occasional down on the midrib above; stalk up to ⅝ in. long. Flowers three to eleven in a terminal truss (occasionally also produced from the upper leaf-axils), opening in April or May; flowerstalks up to 1⅛ in. long. Calyx small, shallowly lobed. Corolla funnel-shaped or sometimes inclining to bell-shaped, five-lobed, 2 to 2½ in. across, in some shade of rosy pink or purplish pink, unspotted or with markings of crimson or reddish brown. Stamens ten, hairy towards the base. Ovary densely scaly; style glabrous. *Bot. Mag.*, tt. 8784, 9597. (*s.* Triflorum *ss.* Yunnanense)

R. *oreotrephes* has a wide range in the Sino-Himalayan region, from S.W. Szechwan westward through N.W. Yunnan and upper Burma to S.E. Tibet, where it extends as far as the region of the Tsangpo bend, occurring at altitudes of mostly 9,000 to 13,000 ft, in open thickets and scrub, or as undergrowth in pine woodland. It was introduced by Forrest in 1910 from the Lichiang range, Yunnan, and described from a specimen he collected there; later he sent seeds on many occasions, as also did Kingdon Ward and Rock. It is a somewhat variable species, though less so than is suggested by the numerous synonymous names, which are founded on minor fluctuations. The plants originally grown as R. *oreotrephes*, i.e., the species in its old and narrower sense, are themselves far from uniform. The flower-colour ranges from pearly grey lavender to deep rosy lavender; the foliage is more or less glaucous, especially on the undersides, and on some plants it is very noticeable even on the upper surface of the young leaves—J. C. Williams compared the best forms in this respect to the sea-holly. Harry White raised a fine garden race at the Sunningdale Nurseries by crossing his two best forms of R. *oreotrephes* (*Y.B. Rhod. Ass. 1939*, p. 30).

Of the species now included in R. *oreotrephes*, Lionel de Rothschild most admired R. *exquisitum*, described from a plant growing at Exbury which had been raised at the Sunningdale Nurseries from F.20489, collected in S.W. Szechwan (see further below under awards).

R. *oreotrephes* is perfectly hardy, though in cold gardens it may lose most of its leaves in winter; usually it does not flower until May, so the display is not often spoilt by frost. Lionel de Rothschild found at Exbury that R. *oreotrephes* (at least in the old sense) resents being moved, and Mr Cox confirms this from his experience at Glendoick; so it is best put in when young.

The following forms of R. *oreotrephes* have received the Award of Merit: May 24, 1932, shown from Exbury as R. *timeteum*, raised from Rock 59593, flowers rosy purple; May 21, 1935, as R. *siderophylloides*, shown by J. J. Crosfield, Embley Park, Hants, bright pinkish mauve flowers, spotted within, leaves bright green above; May 25, 1937, as R. *exquisitum*, shown from Exbury, flowers light mauvish pink with some crimson speckling.

R. ORTHOCLADUM Balf. f. & Forr.

An evergreen shrub of densely twiggy, bushy, shape, 3 to 4 ft high; young shoots very slender, densely scurfy. Leaves narrowly oblong or lanceolate, tapered at both ends; ⅓ to ¾ in. long, 1/12 to ⅕ in. wide; dark slightly glaucous green and scaly above, furnished with glistening yellowish scales beneath, and sometimes with scattered larger brown ones; stalk to $\frac{3}{4}$ in. long. Flowers two to four closely packed in terminal clusters 1 in. wide. Calyx minute, with small lobes covered thickly with glistening scales like the flower-stalk, which is only $\frac{1}{12}$ in. long. Corolla pale mauve, $\frac{3}{4}$ in. wide, with a very short, downy tube, five-lobed, the lobes rounded, ovate, $\frac{1}{4}$ in. long. Stamens ten, purple, about $\frac{1}{4}$ in. long, with a tuft of down near the base; anthers red. Ovary scaly; style glabrous, reddish, shorter than, or equalling, the stamens. (s. Lapponicum)

Native of N.W. Yunnan and S.W. Szechwan at alpine elevations, in open pastures, on stony slopes, cliffs, etc., sometimes on limestone; discovered and introduced by Forrest in 1913. This is a pleasing dwarf shrub with some resemblance to R. scintillans, but paler in colour of blossom than is usual in that species, and with a shorter style, which varies in length, but does not usually extend to the level of the anthers. There is also some variation in the density of the scales beneath the leaves; in some forms they almost conceal the surface of the blade, in others they are more widely spaced. It is quite hardy at Kew, grows well, and flowers freely towards the end of April, and is noticeable for its neat habit and rounded shape when young. Eventually it will reach a height of 4 ft, but remains of fairly dense habit; wild plants appear to be mostly quite dwarf.

var. LONGISTYLUM Philipson & Philipson—Style longer than the stamens, as in R. scintillans, from which this variety can be distinguished by the much closer scales on the leaf-undersides. Introduced by Forrest (F.21988).

cv. 'MICROLEUCUM'.—Flowers pure white, about $\frac{3}{4}$ in. wide, very freely borne. A small, dense shrub to about 2 ft high (R. microleucum Hutch.; R. orthocladum var. microleucum (Hutch.) Philipson & Philipson) Bot. Mag., n.s., t. 171A. 'Microleucum' was described in 1933 from a plant growing in Lionel de Rothschild's collection at Exbury, which had almost certainly been raised from seeds gathered by Forrest in W. China. It is evidently an albino form, not a good species, and in the article accompanying the plate in the Botanical Magazine, Cowan and Davidian took the view that it is nearer to R. orthocladum than it is to R. scintillans, with which Hutchinson compared it. It is known only in cultivation, and no purple-flowered form has been found that matches it precisely in botanical characters. 'Microleucum' is one of the most attractive of the Lapponicums, and received a First Class Certificate when shown from Exbury in 1939.

R. OVATUM (Lindl.) Maxim.

Azalea ovata Lindl.; R. bachii Lévl.

A bushy evergreen shrub up to 8 ft or so high in Hupeh, possibly taller in other parts; young stems downy and slightly glandular bristly. Leaves dark green and glossy, tinged with purple when young, very variable in shape even on the same plant, ovate to broad-elliptic, obovate-elliptic, or rhombic-elliptic, the apex acute or obtuse, sometimes emarginate, always with a very pronounced mucro, base rounded to cuneate, $1\frac{1}{4}$ to $2\frac{1}{4}$ in. long, $\frac{3}{8}$ to $1\frac{1}{2}$ in. wide, glabrous except for the shortly downy midrib, margins often distinctly serrated with bristle-tipped teeth; petiole $\frac{1}{8}$ to $\frac{3}{4}$ in. long. Flowers solitary from axillary buds near the ends of the preceding year's shoots, produced towards the end of May or in June, on glandular-hairy stalks up to $1\frac{1}{2}$ in. long. Calyx-lobes oblong to broadly obovate, rounded at the apex, up to almost $\frac{1}{4}$ in. long, with or without a fringe of glandular hairs. Corolla pale purple, pink, white, or white suffused with pink, very widely funnel-shaped, almost flat, 1 to $1\frac{1}{4}$ in. wide, with five rounded lobes, the upper three speckled. Stamens five, unequal, the filaments hairy towards the base. Ovary downy; style glabrous. *Bot. Mag.*, tt. 5064, 9375. (*s.* Ovatum)

Native of Eastern and Central China. It was introduced in 1843–4 by Fortune, who found it growing in the Chusan Archipelago (south-east of Shanghai) and in the tea-district of Chekiang. But the present garden stock almost certainly derives entirely from the seeds sent home by Wilson in 1900 and 1907 from Hupeh, where the species is at its western limit. According to him it is not uncommon in that province at 4,000 to 7,000 ft, on cliffs and in rocky places where it is sheltered from strong winds, and makes there a twiggy bush seldom more than 8 ft high. Both his collections of seed were from the Changyang-hsien district at 5,000 to 7,000 ft. It is a plant from one of these sendings, raised at Caerhays and presented to Kew, that is figured in the *Botanical Magazine*, t. 9375 (as R. *bachii*). The earlier plate represents the Fortune introduction.

R. *ovatum* (the Wilson form) is not entirely hardy and is rather slow-growing and difficult; possibly inadequate summer-heat is the source of the trouble rather than outright tenderness. It is uncommon in gardens, but available in commerce and represented in the Species Collection, Windsor Great Park, by an example about 6 ft high.

R. *leptothrium* (q.v.) is closely allied to R. *ovatum*. So too is R. HONGKONG-ENSE Hutch. (*Azalea myrtifolia* Champion, *Bot. Mag.*, t. 4609), which was included in R. *ovatum* by Maximowicz, and is discussed and figured under that name by Dr Herklots in *R.Y.B. 1949*, p. 184 and fig. 56. It is a native of the New Territories of Hong Kong and of Kwangtung; is obviously too tender to be grown out-of-doors in the British Isles and may not be in cultivation. The flowers are pure white, spotted with crimson purple, about 2 in. wide, and the young growths are bright red and pink. Dr Herklots considers it to be the most beautiful of the Hong Kong rhododendrons.

R. PACHYTRICHUM Franch.

An evergreen shrub or small tree up to 20 ft high; young shoots conspicuously furnished with a dense coat of brown curly bristles $\frac{1}{8}$ in. long. Leaves 3 to 6 in. long, 1 to 2 in. wide, narrowly oblong or inclined to obovate, abruptly narrowed at the apex to a short fine point, rounded at the base, dark green and soon glabrous above, bristly on the margins at first, and on the midrib beneath; stalk $\frac{1}{3}$ to 1 in. long, with the same mossy character as the young shoot. Flowers opening in April, borne in compact trusses of up to ten on shaggy stalks about $\frac{5}{8}$ in. long. Calyx minute, glabrous or sparsely hairy. Corolla white or pale rose, with a dark blotch at the base, $1\frac{1}{2}$ in. wide, scarcely so deep, bell-shaped, five-lobed. Stamens ten, shorter than the corolla, downy at the base. Ovary densely hairy; style glabrous. (*s.* Barbatum *ss.* Maculiferum)

Native of W. Szechwan, where according to Wilson it is one of the commonest and most widely dispersed species and occurs up to an altitude of 11,000 ft. It was discovered by the Abbé Soulié and introduced by Wilson in 1903 for Messrs Veitch. It is a perfectly hardy species, but rather too early-flowering for most gardens and anyway only worth planting in selected colour-forms as the flowers often have a magenta tint. The Award of Merit was given in 1963 to the clone 'Sesame', with rosy-pink flowers, when exhibited by Lord Aberconway and the National Trust, Bodnant, on April 18.

R. PARADOXUM Balf. f.

A dense evergreen shrub up to 8 ft high; young branchlets densely white-scurfy; terminal leaf-buds elongate, their outer scales woolly, awl-shaped, with curved tips, much longer than the inner scales. Leaves oblong, 2 to 5 in. long, 1¼ to 2 in. wide, obtuse to rounded and abruptly mucronate at the apex, rounded to obtuse at the base, upper surface rugulose, glabrous, lower pale green with a patchy and scurfy grey or brown indumentum, midrib and lateral veins prominent; petiole about 1 in. long. Flowers about eight in a cluster, opening in April or May; pedicels about 1 in. long, hairy. Calyx minute, hairy. Corolla five-lobed, campanulate, about 1¾ in. long, white with lines of crimson speckles uniting at the base into a crimson blotch. Stamens ten, with dark anthers, filaments downy at the base. Ovary cylindric, densely hairy; style glabrous. (s. Taliense ss. Wasonii)

R. *paradoxum* was described in 1922 from a plant raised from Wilson's 1353, collected during his first expedition for the Arnold Arboretum. But the herbarium specimen under that number is R. *wiltonii*, and so too were many of the plants raised from this batch of seed. R. *paradoxum* is certainly distinct from R. *wiltonii*, which has a much thicker indumentum and differently shaped leaves, but might be a hybrid of it.

R. INOPINUM Balf. f.—Resembling R. *paradoxum*, but the terminal leaf-buds not as described above, and the leaves above only faintly rugulose. This too appeared as a rogue among plants raised from seeds collected by Wilson. The packet was labelled W.1866, but the corresponding herbarium specimen is a species of *Lonicera*. Some of the plants raised from this batch proved to be R. *wasonii*.

R. PARMULATUM Cowan

An evergreen shrub up to 3 or 4 ft high; young shoots glabrous; bark flaking, purplish brown. Leaves oval, rounded at the apex to a short mucro, almost similarly rounded at the base to the stalk, 1½ to 2¼ in. long, about half as wide, glabrous above, loosely papillose beneath (not downy), stalk ⅕ to ⅖ in. long. Flowers in trusses of about six, on glabrous stalks ½ to ¾ in. long. Calyx a flat, circular disk ⅓ in. or so wide. Corolla widely campanulate, 1¾ in. deep, 2¼ in. wide across the five bilobed, reflexed lobes which are 1 in. wide, white flushed pink, veined with crimson and with deeper-coloured pouches at the base.

Stamens ten, shorter than the tube, anthers dark brown. Ovary glabrous; style glabrous. *Bot. Mag.*, t. 9624.

R. *parmulatum* was discovered by Kingdon Ward in 1924 on the Doshong La, S.E. Tibet, at the eastern end of the Himalaya, and was introduced by him (KW 5875). Most of the cultivated plants are from this sending, perhaps all, but it was found again by Ludlow, Sherriff, and Elliot in 1946–7 (L.S. & E. 13612). It first flowered at Edinburgh and at Borde Hill in Sussex, in April 1936.

R. *parmulatum* is an interesting and very distinct species, at present placed in the subseries Sanguineum of the Neriiflorum series, though it is unique in that group in the colour and markings of its flowers. It is hardy in a sheltered place near London.

R. PARRYAE Hutch.

An evergreen shrub or small tree in the wild, sometimes epiphytic, with a pinkish-purple, peeling bark. Leaves narrowly oblong-elliptic, subacute to rounded and mucronate at the apex, 2¼ to 3¾ in. long, 1⅛ to 1¾ in. wide, dark green above, glaucous green beneath, scaly on both sides, but more densely so beneath; petiole ½ in. or slightly more long, scaly. Flowers fragrant, in terminal trusses of three or four on pedicels up to 1 in. long. Calyx very small, scaly and shortly ciliate. Corolla widely funnel-shaped, up to 4½ in. wide, white with a prominent orange-yellow blotch, lobes five, undulated, slightly scaly near the middle, the tube slightly scaly and downy near the base outside. Stamens ten, downy towards the base. Ovary densely scaly; style scaly in the lower half. (*s.* Maddenii *ss.* Ciliicalyx)

R. *parryae* was discovered by Mrs Parry, wife of an officer in the Indian Civil Service, growing on the Blue Mountain, Lushai Hills, in the south-eastern corner of Assam at 6,000 ft. She collected a fruiting specimen in February 1927, from which seeds were taken by Charles Raffill when it arrived at Kew. When a plant flowered in 1933 it proved to be a new species, which was described by Dr Hutchinson in that year (*Gard. Chron.*, Vol. 93, p. 386).

R. PARVIFOLIUM Adams
R. *palustre* DC.

An evergreen shrub of sparse habit and thin, wiry, erect or spreading branches, 2 to 3 ft high; young wood scurfy. Leaves slightly aromatic when crushed, ⅓ to ¾ in. long, ⅙ to ¼ in. wide, narrowly oblong-obovate, dark green above, pale beneath, scaly on both sides, the scales beneath pale at first, darkening as the leaf ages; petiole very short. Flowers borne in a small terminal cluster of mostly three to five; pedicels up to ¼ in. long, scaly. Calyx with five small, angular lobes, scaly, sometimes ciliate. Corolla rosy purple or rose, rotate-funnel-shaped, ½ to ¾ in. across, slightly hairy in the throat, lobes five, rounded. Stamens ten, hairy towards the base. Ovary densely scaly, style glabrous, longer than the stamens. *Bot. Mag.*, t. 9229. (*s.* Lapponicum)

Native of N.E. Asia from E. Siberia to the Russian Far East, south to N.E. China, N. Korea, Sakhalin, and the north island of Japan (Hokkaido); also of the Aleutians and Alaska; introduced to Britain soon after 1877. It is allied to *R. lapponicum* and has often been supplied for it, but is distinguished by the larger leaves, the ten stamens with filaments hairy towards the base (five to eight, filaments hairy only at the very base in *R. lapponicum*), and usually by the taller growth. It blossoms early, from January to March according to the mildness or otherwise of the weather.

f. ALBIFLORUM Herder—Flowers white.

f. ALPINUM Glehn *R. confertissimum* Nakai—A procumbent form from alpine elevations and exposed habitats.

R. PEMAKOENSE Ward

A dwarf evergreen shrub with scaly and sometimes shortly downy young stems. Leaves obovate or oblong-obovate, obtuse to rounded at the apex, $\frac{1}{2}$ to $1\frac{1}{8}$ in. long, $\frac{1}{4}$ to $\frac{1}{2}$ in. or slightly more wide, dark green and slightly scaly above, the undersides glaucous and dotted with brown scales spaced up to one-and-a-half times their own diameter apart; petioles up to $\frac{1}{8}$ in. or slightly more long. Flowers solitary or in pairs, terminal, on stalks up to $\frac{3}{4}$ in. long at flowering-time, lengthening in fruit. Calyx small, scaly. Corolla five-lobed, widely funnel-shaped, 2 to $2\frac{1}{4}$ in. wide, purplish pink, scaly and hairy outside. Stamens ten, hairy at the base. Style slender, straight, usually glabrous, sometimes with a few scales or hairs at the base. (*s.* Uniflorum)

R. *pemakoense* was found by Kingdon Ward in fruit in 1924 during his winter journey through the Tsangpo gorge in the Tibetan province of Pemako, and was described by him in 1930 from the plants raised from the seeds he collected (KW 6301). Most of the seeds came from plants which he found on November 30 'on cliffs up the glens above the Tsangpo gorge, on Namcha Barwa and Sanglung'. But a small proportion was collected some days earlier at Pemako-chung, and Kingdon Ward later came to doubt whether the specimens he collected in these two localities really represented the same species. There appears to be no record of any rogues having appeared from KW 6301, but it may be that the variation of R. *pemakoense* in cultivation, such as it is, is due to the fact that the seeds came from two localities.

R. *pemakoense* is one of the most delightful of dwarf rhododendrons, making a low, densely branched mound which, weather permitting, flowers so freely in March or April that almost every leaf is concealed by its large corollas. Unfortunately, the buds are liable to be killed by frost once they start to show colour. According to James Comber, a plant at Nymans, raised from the original seeds, bore 120 flowers in 1931, when six years old (*Gard. Chron.*, Vol. 89 (1931), p. 375). In a later article he remarked that some plants there spread by underground runners, an unusual feature in *Rhododendron*.

An Award of Merit was given to R. *pemakoense* on April 24, 1928, when Sir John Ramsden showed a pan of seedlings a few inches high, bearing flowers described as white with a lilac flush outside, which is not the characteristic colour of the species and suggests that the pan may have come from a greenhouse. The plants were shown under the field number, as the species had not then been named.

R. UNIFLORUM Hutch. & Ward—This species was described in 1930 from specimens collected by Kingdon Ward on the Doshong La, S.E. Tibet, at the end of June 1924 (KW 5876). He collected seeds in the following autumn. R. *uniflorum* is so like R. *pemakoense* that Cowan and Davidian were able to find only one difference that might be relied on, namely that in R. *uniflorum* the scales on the undersides of the leaves are more widely spaced, being three to six times their own diameter apart. If the two were united it would have to be under the name R. *uniflorum*, which has a few months' priority, but they decided to retain R. *pemakoense* as a separate species provisionally. It should be added that the type-localities of the two species are not much more than 10 miles apart as the crow flies.

R. PENDULUM Hook. f.

A small evergreen shrub up to 4 ft high, sometimes epiphytic in the wild; branchlets densely coated with a brown or fawn wool. Leaves mostly oblong to elliptic, obtuse or rounded at both ends, up to 2 in. long, and 1 in. wide, almost glabrous above when mature, coated beneath with brown or fawn wool and with scattered brown scales; petiole up to ½ in. long, woolly. Flowers in twos or threes, sometimes solitary, borne in April or May. Calyx five-lobed, up to ⅜ in. long, hairy. Corolla rotate-campanulate, about 1½ in. wide, white with a yellow throat and sometimes slightly tinged with pink, more or less scaly on the outside. Ovary woolly; style short, bent, woolly and scaly at the base.   (*s.* Edgeworthii)

Native of the Himalaya as far west as Sikkim, where it was discovered by J. D. Hooker in 1849. It is not of much beauty, but of interest as an almost hardy member of the Edgeworthii series.

R. PENTAPHYLLUM Maxim.

R. *pentaphyllum* var. *nikoense* Komatsu; R. *nikoense* (Komatsu) Nakai; R. *quinquefolium* var. *roseum* Rehd.

A deciduous, sometimes tree-like azalea up to 20 ft high; young shoots often in tiers, thinly hairy when young, red-brown, becoming grey the second season. Leaves produced in a whorl of five at the end of the shoot, oval to oval-lanceolate, pointed, wedge-shaped at the base, 1¼ to 2½ in. long, half as much wide, midrib downy on both surfaces, margins toothed and ciliate; stalk ⅛ to ⅓ in. long, thinly glandular-hairy. Flowers terminal, opening in April or May, solitary or in pairs; flower-stalk ½ in. long, varying from densely glandular to quite glabrous. Calyx with five triangular teeth ⅕ in. or less long. Corolla bright rose-pink, not spotted, 2 in. wide, with five spreading, rounded, often notched lobes. Stamens ten, of unequal length, downy at the base; anthers yellow; ovary and style glabrous.   (*s.* Azalea *ss.* Canadense)

Native of central and southern Japan, where it grows in woodland, and is fond of partial shade. Wilson, who saw it wild in the Nikko region, wrote highly of its beauty both in bloom and in autumn, when the leaves change to rich orange and crimson.

In its foliage it resembles R. *quinquefolium*, but that species has white flowers, and produces its flowers and leafy shoots from the same bud, whereas in R. *pentaphyllum* they come from separate buds. It is rather slow to flower and prefers a sheltered place in moist leafy soil.

R. *pentaphyllum* received an Award of Merit on April 14, 1942, when shown by Lord Aberconway, Bodnant.

R. PERICLYMENOIDES (Michx.) Shinners

Azalea nudiflora L., *nom. illegit.*; *A. periclymenoides* Michx.; R. *nudiflorum* (L.) Torr.

A deciduous azalea up to 9 ft high in its native state; young wood bristly Leaves mostly obovate, some oblong, tapering at both ends, 1½ to 3½ in. long, one-third to half as wide, green on both sides with a few scattered hairs above, bristly on the midrib beneath and on the margins. Flowers faintly scented, in clusters of six or more, the corolla-tube hairy, pink, ¾ in. long; the five lobes paler, expanding, and giving the flower a diameter of 1½ to 2 in.; stalk ⅛ to ½ in. long, bristly like the small calyx; stamens five, pinkish coloured, standing out well beyond the corolla; seed-vessels ¾ in. long, bristly. Blossoms in May. (*s. Azalea ss.* Luteum)

Native of eastern N. America; introduced by Peter Collinson in 1734. It is one of the chief parents of the great race of garden azaleas, but is itself very rarely seen now. The flowers appear to be variable in colour, even in a wild state, although of some shade of red or pink, or purplish. Of the N. American azaleas, whose flowers expand before the leaves, this differs from R. *calendulaceum* in the longer-tubed, differently coloured corolla, and in the bristly midrib of the leaf, and from R. *canescens* in the hairy, not glandular, corolla-tube.

R. PONTICUM L.

R. *lancifolium* Moench; R. *speciosum* Salisb.

An evergreen shrub or small tree, attaining a height of 25 ft in the wild; branchlets soon glabrous. Leaves oblanceolate or elliptic-oblanceolate, 4 to 8 in. long, 1 to 2½ in. wide (but sometimes larger in the Caucasian forests), dark green above, paler beneath, glabrous; petiole ½ to 1⅛ in. long. Inflorescence a terminal corymb with up to fifteen flowers, opening in late May or June; rachis 1 in. or slightly more long, glabrous or slightly glandular (tomentose in subsp. *baeticum*, and occasionally in the typical subspecies); pedicels ¾ to 1¾ in. long, lengthening in fruit, glabrous or slightly glandular. Calyx very small, with five blunt teeth about 1/10 in. long. Corolla funnel-shaped, about 2 in. wide, light purple or rosy purple, the upper lobe usually marked with greenish or brownish spots. Stamens ten, filaments hairy at the base. Ovary and style glabrous. *Bot. Mag.*, t. 650. (*s.* and *ss.* Ponticum)

R. *ponticum* has its main and most continuous distribution in the region of the Black Sea. East of the sea, it is an important ingredient of the rich forests of western Transcaucasia (Colchis), growing under beech, *Picea orientalis* or *Abies nordmanniana*, also ascending above the tree-line, where it occurs in dwarfed form at well over 6,000 ft altitude. It is, or was, also found at sea-level in the neighbourhood of Batum, forming thickets up to 20 ft high in association with the cherry laurel (*Prunus laurocerasus*). South of the Black Sea it extends through the Pontic ranges of N. Anatolia from Lazistan and N. Kurdistan in the east to Bithynia in the west. Only in this century was it established that R. *ponticum* is also a native of the Balkans, where it occupies a small area in the Strandja mountains of N.W. European Turkey and bordering parts of S.E. Bulgaria. Here it occurs with other elements of the Colchic forests, e.g., the cherry laurel, *Daphne pontica* and *Vaccinium arctostaphylos*. Well to the south-east of its main area, R. *ponticum* occurs in the mountains of the Lebanon, where it is scattered.

subsp. BAETICUM (Boiss. & Reuter) Hand.-Mazz. R. *baeticum* Boiss & Reuter; R. *ponticum* var. *myrtifolium* (Lodd.) G. Don, in part, *nom. confus.*, not R. *myrtifolium* Lodd.—It is a remarkable and surprising fact of plant geography that R. *ponticum* should also occur as a genuine native in parts of Portugal and southern Spain. But the fossil evidence shows that it is an ancient inhabitant of western Eurasia, which existed in Russia early in the Tertiary Period and even in comparatively recent geological times occurred in Central Europe and as far north as Ireland. Its existing stands, both in the east and the west, are the remnants of a once much wider area, which has become fragmented by climatic change. The precise distribution of R. *ponticum* in the Iberian peninsula at the present time is not known in detail. But in Portugal it is certainly to be found in Alta Beira province at the north-western end of the Serra do Caramulo; in the Serra de Monchique above Foia (Algarve) and near Odemira, also in S. Portugal (Alentejo). In Spain R. *ponticum* is confined to S. Andalucia, where it occurs (or did in the last century) in several localities in an area about 35 miles long from south to north and 6 or 7 miles wide, stretching from the hills near Tarifa on the Atlantic coast through the mountains behind Algeciras and then as far north as the Sierra de Galina. In Portugal, and probably in Spain also, it is near the limits of its climatic tolerance, and confined to streamsides and other wet or shaded places.

Whether R. *ponticum*, in what might be termed its Atlantic area, is really distinct enough from the eastern race to merit botanical distinction is a moot question. The most reliable difference is that the rachis of the inflorescence in specimens from Spain and Portugal appears to be invariably tomentose, especially near the apex and at the insertions of the pedicels, whereas in Caucasian and Anatolian specimens it is usually glabrous, but by no means invariably so. There is no constant difference in foliage nor, so far as can be ascertained, in any other character discernible in an herbarium specimen, though no doubt experimental cultivation would reveal many minor points of distinction.

In Aiton's *Hortus Kewensis* the date of introduction of R. *ponticum* is given as 1763. It may be that plants or seed were acquired by Kew in that year, but the first commercial introduction, according to Loudon, was by Conrad Loddiges, whose career as a nurseryman started in 1770. In Weston's compendium of the catalogues of the London nurseries, called *Flora Anglicana*, R. *ponticum* makes its appearance in the supplement (1780); in the main work (1775) there is no mention of it. Whether the early introductions were of typical R. *ponticum* from the Black Sea region, or of subsp. *baeticum* from Spain or Portugal, is not known for certain. We have it on the authority of the German botanist Pallas, writing in 1784, that the plants in English gardens originated from Gibraltar, which may be true at least of the Kew plants, for there is a specimen in Bishop Goodenough's herbarium collected, probably at Kew, in the 1780s, which has the tomentose rachis characteristic of subsp. *baeticum*. But there may well have been commercial importations of typical *R. ponticum* too.

No rhododendron has obtained so secure a footing in Britain as this. On light acid soils it is the commonest of exotic evergreens and, in the right place, as by lakesides, one of the most beautiful. Although no longer much planted as an ornamental, it is useful as a windbreak and draught-stopper and, where there is room, as a cheap, fast-growing informal hedge. It is commonly used as stock on which the garden hybrids are grafted, and to this practice, no doubt, the presence of great drifts of this shrub in many gardens is due. For when plants are left unwatched the stock frequently sends up sucker-growths, and it then becomes only a matter of time before the finer-bred and less assertive scion is overwhelmed.

R. ponticum is an invasive plant, establishing itself on acid soils where the natural vegetation has been disturbed by fire or by the planting of conifers. For this reason it is disliked by both conservationists and foresters. Its presence far from human habitation is, however, not always the result of self-seeding, for it was at one time much planted as game covert and many thriving woodland colonies are probably the result of this misguided practice. Once established, it is difficult to eradicate, cutting it to the ground being quite futile unless the regrowth is treated with a suitable brushwood killer.

It is questionable whether the cultivated and naturalised plants are entitled to the name *R. ponticum*, for there can be no doubt that the species has become contaminated by hybridisation. As early as 1806 it was stated that hybrids had sprung up between *R. ponticum* and *R. maximum*, and it seems so likely as to be almost certain that crossing between *R. ponticum* and the Hardy Hybrids has taken place continuously during the last 150 years. Some plants sent out by nurseries as *R. ponticum* are obvious hybrids and none the worse for that. Naturalised plants on the Surrey–Sussex border, examined recently, resembled *R. ponticum* in foliage and colour but showed signs of hybridity in the larger calyx and very glandular pedicels deriving from *R. maximum*, and in the presence of hairs on the ovary, which suggest the influence of *R. catawbiense*, another parent of the Hardy Hybrids. But another colony, a mile or so away, and probably seeded from a different property, agreed perfectly with *R. ponticum* subsp. *baeticum*.

The cultivated rhododendron named *R. obtusum* by Watson in 1825 is of uncertain identity. If it came from Armenia, as he stated, it must have been a form of *R. ponticum* or a hybrid between it and *R. smirnowii*. It has been treated as a variety of *R. ponticum*, but the Swiss botanist de Candolle, who was acquainted with the living plant, considered it to be near to *R. catawbiense* and possibly a hybrid. It was a low bushy plant with thick glabrous elliptic leaves obtuse at the apex, slightly cordate at the base, and rosy flowers (Watson, *Dendr. Brit.*, t. 162; de Candolle, *Prodromus*, Vol. 7, p. 722).

The following were treated as variants of *R. ponticum* in previous editions, but there is a possibility that some are really hybrids:

f. ALBUM (Sweet) Zab.—White-flowered forms of R. *ponticum* are rare, the 'white ponticum' sometimes seen among seedling plants being an obvious hybrid with R. *maximum* or, more likely, with some Hardy Hybrid with R. *maximum* in its parentage. But what appears to have been a white form of the true R. *ponticum* was in cultivation at Kew. See also the note by Cox and Hutchison in *R.C.Y.B. 1963*, p. 66.

cv. 'CHEIRANTHIFOLIUM'.—Flowers pale purple; the plant dwarf and compact; leaves 2 to 3 in. long, $\frac{3}{8}$ to $\frac{1}{2}$ in. wide, very wavy at the margins. It is very unlike R. *ponticum* in every respect, and almost certainly a hybrid.

cv. 'LANCIFOLIUM'.—A small edition of the type; leaves 2 to 4 in. long, $\frac{1}{2}$ to $\frac{3}{4}$ in. wide. Flowers in small trusses, almost white in the centre, suffused with purple towards the margin. The plant is dwarf and compact, rarely more than 6 to 8 ft high. It is distinguished from 'Cheiranthifolium' by the leaves being flat, not wavy.

cv. 'VARIEGATUM'.—Leaves smaller and narrower than in the type, edged with creamy white. Another variegated form was 'AUCUBIFOLIUM', with yellow-spotted leaves.

An interesting variant of R. *ponticum* still in cultivation has bronzy purple leaves which hold their colouring well in the winter. It is possibly the same as 'Foliis Purpureis', for which the nurseryman William Paul received a First Class Certificate in 1895.

R. PRAESTANS Balf. f. & W. W. Sm.

A large evergreen shrub or small tree up to 30 ft high. Leaves oblong-lanceolate, up to $1\frac{1}{2}$ ft long, 6 to 8 in. wide, broadest near the apex, tapered to a very short winged petiole (the wings really representing the decurrent base of the blade), blackish green, glossy and glabrous above, underside clad with a shining skin-like light grey or fawn indumentum. Flowers in a truss of twenty or sometimes more, opening in April or May; pedicels slightly over 1 in. long. Calyx minute. Corolla obliquely campanulate, eight-lobed, up to almost 2 in. long, pink or magenta-rose, with a crimson blotch in the throat. Stamens sixteen, glabrous. Ovary tomentose; style as long as the corolla or slightly shorter, glabrous. (*s.* Grande)

Native of N.W. Yunnan, upper Burma, and the Assam Himalaya; discovered by Forrest in 1914 on the Kari pass, Mekong–Yangtse divide, at 13,000 ft, and introduced by him. It is fairly near to R. *sinograde*, but occurs at higher altitudes, and even out of flower is easily distinguished by the leaves being broadest near the apex and tapering at the base, where the blade reaches to the leaf-insertion, forming two wings along the petiole.

Dr Rock later collected seeds on the Mekong–Salween divide, also from 13,000 ft (Rock 59085 and 59462). Kingdon Ward's no. 13653 is from his 1938 expedition to the Assam Himalaya, and was collected on the Poshing La, where R. *praestans* ascends higher than any other big-leaved rhododendron and varies in the colour of its flowers from crimson to cerise and purple (*Assam Adventure*, p. 262).

R. *praestans* is one of the hardiest of the big-leaved rhododendrons and has proved to be wind resistant at Brodick in the Isle of Arran (*R.C.Y.B. 1966*, p. 26).

R. CORYPHAEUM Balf. f. R. *semnum* Balf. f.—This is almost the same as R. *praestans* in its essential botanical characters, but the flowers are creamy white or pale creamy yellow. It was introduced by Forrest in 1918 from the Mekong–Salween divide in latitude 28° 12′. Rock's 59480 from the same area would seem to be intermediate between this species and R. *praestans*, judging from his field note, according to which the wild plants had flowers varying in colour from white to pink.

R. *coryphaeum* received an Award of Merit when shown by Edmund de Rothschild, Exbury, on April 18, 1963 (clone 'Exbury', with white flowers tinted with translucent yellow, blotched ruby-red in the throat).

R. SEMNOIDES Tagg & Forr.—This species resembles R. *praestans* in the short, winged petiole, but it is very distinct from it in the loose, woolly, brown indumentum of the leaf-undersides. It was discovered by Forrest on the Salween–Kiuchiang divide at 12,000 to 13,000 ft and was introduced by him from that locality in 1922. It seems to be rare in the wild and is not common in cultivation. *Bot. Mag.*, n.s., t. 18.

R. PRAETERITUM Hutch.

An evergreen shrub probably 10 ft or more high; young shoots downy. Leaves oblong, rounded, or slightly heart-shaped at the base, abruptly narrowed at the apex to a short mucro, 3 to 5½ in. long, 1¼ to 1¾ in. wide; dark dull green above, pale green, and ultimately glabrous beneath except on the midrib; stalk ⅓ to ⅝ in. long. Flowers opening in March about eight in a truss 4 in. wide. Calyx shallowly five-lobed, glabrous; flower-stalks ½ to ¾ in. long, loosely downy at first. Corolla bell-shaped, 1¼ to 1½ in. long and wide, pink or pinkish white, five-lobed, each lobe notched, ¾ to 1 in. wide. Stamens ten, ⅝ to 1¼ in. long, slightly downy towards the base; anthers chocolate-purple. Ovary and style quite glabrous. (*s.* Fortunei *ss.* Oreodoxa)

R. *praeteritum* was described in 1922 from a plant at Kew, raised from seeds collected by Wilson in China for Messrs Veitch, probably in W. Hupeh. From R. *oreodoxa* itself it differs in having a five-lobed corolla and only ten stamens; the flower-stalks of R. *oreodoxa* are also glandular. It was at first confused with R. *maculiferum*, from which it is clearly distinguished by having no blotch on the corolla and a quite smooth ovary. It is very hardy and has about the same garden value as R. *fargesii*; on account of its early opening the blossom is liable to damage by frost.

R. PRATTII Franch.

R. *faberi sens.* Hort. Veitch., not Hemsl.

A stiff evergreen shrub up to 12 ft high in the wild; young shoots clothed with loose brown down, becoming glabrous. Leaves stiff and hard in texture, oval or broadly ovate to ovate-oblong, abruptly narrowed at the apex to a short point, rounded or slightly heart-shaped at the base, 3 to 8 in. long, 1½ to 3½ in. wide; glossy dark green and soon nearly or quite glabrous above, thinly downy beneath in two layers, the upper one brown and wearing off in great part, the under one paler, close, and permanent; stalk ⅝ to 1⅛ in. long. Flowers produced in April and May a dozen to twenty together in a truss 3 to 6 in. wide; flower-stalks ¾ to 1 in. long, covered with tawny, glandular down. Calyx divided almost to the base into five ovate membranous lobes ⅓ to ⅝ in. long, downy outside, and glandular-ciliate. Corolla white, pink-tinged, with a crimson blotch and spots at the base, 1½ to 2 in. long and wide, bell-shaped, downy inside towards the base, five-lobed, the lobes ½ in. long. Stamens ten, ⅓ to 1 in. long, downy at the base; ovary felted; style glabrous or glanded at the base, longer than the stamens. *Bot. Mag.*, t. 9414.   (*s.* Taliense *ss.* Adenogynum)

Native of W. Szechwan, China; discovered by Pratt near Tatsien-lu (Kang-ting); introduced by Wilson in 1904. It is quite hardy at Kew and flowers regularly; the foliage is handsome, but the colouring is not particularly effective. The large membranous calyx is distinctive. Wilson describes it as a woodland species and it undoubtedly needs partial shade. It has been very much confused in gardens with *R. faberi*, owing to its having been wrongly identified with that species in the *Plantae Wilsonianae*, vol. i, p. 533, and distributed from the Coombe Wood Nursery under that name. The true *R. faberi* is distinct in the thicker woolly tomentum beneath the leaf and is rare in cultivation.

On April 18, 1967, the Award of Merit was given to a seedling of *R. prattii* exhibited by Major A. E. Hardy, Sandling Park, Kent, and named 'Perry Wood'.

R. PRIMULIFLORUM Bur. & Franch.

R. *fragrans* (Adams) Maxim., not Paxt.; *Azalea fragrans* Adams; R. *adamsii* Rehd.; R. *clivicola* Balf. f. & W. W. Sm.; R. *cremnophilum* Balf. f.; R. *gymnomiscum* Balf. f. & Ward; R. *praeclarum* Balf. f. & Farrer; R. *tsarongense* Balf. f. & Forr.

An evergreen strongly aromatic shrub 1 to 4 ft high; young shoots densely covered with scales; leaf-bud scales soon falling. Leaves oval or inclined to oblong, tapered about equally to both ends, but with a mucro at the tip, ½ to 1 in. long, ¼ to ½ in. wide, dark, rather bright green and somewhat scaly above, thickly covered beneath with reddish scurf; leaf-stalk ⅛ in. long. Flowers in a many-flowered, compact, hemispherical truss opening in spring. Calyx ¼ in. long, five-lobed, the lobes unequal in length, sometimes fringed with hairs, finely downy outside. Corolla white, pale yellow, or rose, ¾ in. long, tubular, spreading above into five rounded lobes, downy outside, hairy in the tube. Stamens five, enclosed in the tube, finely downy at the base or glabrous. Ovary scaly, dome-shaped; style very short, stout, glabrous, with a broad flat stigma. (*s.* Anthopogon)

R. *primuliflorum*, as interpreted by Cowan and Davidian, is one of the most wide-ranging of rhododendron species, with a disjunct distribution. Its northern area lies in Russia, from E. Siberia east to the Sea of Okhotsk, and in N. Mongolia. South of the Gobi desert its area stretches from the Chinese province of Kansu southward to N.W. Yunnan and westward to E. and S.E. Tibet. It is reported that fossilised peat soils lie beneath the sands of the Gobi desert so the separation of the species into two areas may be of comparatively recent date.

This species was described, as *Azalea fragrans*, from a specimen collected in Russia near the mouth of the river Lena, and later as *Azalea pallida*, also from Russia. But neither of these names is valid in *Rhododendron*, and it was not until 1921 that Rehder provided the name R. *adamsii* for the Russian plants. But in the meantime Franchet had given the name R. *primulaeflorum* to a specimen collected in Tibet between Lhasa and Batang and that is therefore the valid name for the species as a whole.

R. *primuliflorum* (the name is so spelt under modern rules) is represented in gardens by plants raised from seeds collected in W. China and bordering parts of Tibet, where it occurs at altitudes of up to 14,000 ft. It is closely allied to R. *cephalanthum* but in that species the stamens are sometimes up to eight in number and the bud-scales are persistent. It is rare in cultivation.

var. CEPHALANTHOIDES (Balf. f. & Forr.) Cowan & Davidian R. *cephalanthoides* Balf. f. & Forr.—Corolla-tube densely downy outside.

R. PRINOPHYLLUM (Small) Millais

Azalea rosea Loisel. *nom. illegit.*; R. *roseum* (Loisel.) Rehd.; *Azalea prinophylla* Small; *A. nudiflora* var. *rosea* Sweet

A deciduous azalea 3 to 9 ft high; young shoots downy and usually sparingly bristly. Leaves dull or bluish green, oval to obovate, 1½ to 2½ in. long, slightly downy above, densely grey-woolly beneath; margins ciliate. Flowers fragrant, produced during May in clusters of five to nine. Calyx and flower-stalk downy. Corolla bright pink, with a cylindrical tube ¾ in. long, covered outside with thin down and gland-tipped hairs, and with five ovate abruptly pointed lobes. Stamens five, 1½ in. long, downy below the middle; ovary covered with pale silky down; style overtopping the stamens, downy towards the base. (*s.* Azalea *ss.* Luteum)

Native of eastern N. America; probably introduced early in the 19th century or even earlier as it grows in the older settled States, but always much confused with R. *periclymenoides* and R. *canescens*. To the former it is closely related, but Rehder distinguishes it by its 'pubescent winter-buds and pubescent bluish green leaves, shorter stamens and more or less glandular corolla with larger broader lobes and wider tube'. Being found wild in the States of New York, Massachusetts, etc., this azalea is quite hardy and was once grown under Sweet's name given above. Seeds of this species were sent to England by Sargent in 1922. It is found on limestone in the New York State.

R. *prinophyllum* received an Award of Merit when shown by Mrs Stevenson, Tower Court, Ascot, on May 24, 1955.

R. PROTISTUM Balf. f. & Forr.

R. *giganteum* and R. *magnificum* are the best known of a group of three closely allied and doubtfully distinct species, which, if they were to be united, would have to take the name of the third member, R. *protistum*, which was the first of the trio to be described. It therefore seems best to bring all three together under the oldest name, but to describe R. *giganteum* rather than R. *protistum* in the narrow sense, which is little known in cultivation, but which is discussed below. The group is studied by Dr J. Cowan in *Notes Roy. Bot. Gard. Edin.*, Vol. 21 (1955), pp. 279–88.

R. GIGANTEUM Tagg—A tree up to 80 ft high and almost 8 ft in girth at 5 ft from the ground, or a large shrub; young stems stout, grey-felted. Leaves elliptic to oblanceolate, broadest just above the middle, 5 to 14 in. long, up to 5 in. wide, mostly about three times as long as wide, obtuse or subacute at the apex, narrowed to a slightly auricled base, with twenty to twenty-four pairs of impressed lateral veins, glabrous above when mature, clad beneath with a dense buff or brown woolly indumentum (but the undersides glabrous in young plants); petiole stout 1 to 2 in. long. Inflorescence a racemose umbel of up to almost thirty flowers, opening in early spring. Calyx very small, with eight wavy teeth. Corolla elongate-campanulate, fleshy, 2¼ to 2¾ in. long, 2 to 2¼ in. wide, eight-lobed, deep rose-purple shading to a paler tint, with eight darker-coloured nectar-pouches at the base. Stamens sixteen, glabrous. Ovary about ⅜ in. long, densely coated with a fawn tomentum partly persisting on the capsule; style stout with a large discoid stigma. *Bot. Mag.*, n.s., t. 253. (s. Grande)

R. *giganteum* was discovered by Forrest in the autumn of 1919 in S.W. Yunnan, near the border with Burma, some 50 miles north of Tengchung (Tengyueh), at between 9,000 and 10,000 ft. Only three trees were found, the largest (which was felled) 80 ft high, more than 40 ft in spread, with a girth of 7¾ ft at 5 ft. The trees were in fruit and a fair quantity of seed was gathered (F.18458). Two years later, when on his way east from Burma in March, Forrest made a special detour to get flowering specimens, and the species was described in 1926 from the material he collected during these two visits. Further specimens and seed were collected later in the same region and as far north as 27° on the Nmai Hka–Salween divide, but some of these later findings were of no great size.

R. *giganteum* first flowered in 1934 with Edgar Stead of New Zealand, and two or three times later at Arduaine in Argyll. The original plant at Arduaine is 20 ft high and 25 ft wide (1966) and the truss portrayed in the *Botanical Magazine* is from it. R. *giganteum* has proved to be a very tender species, suitable only for the mildest parts and rare even there. Another Scottish garden where it thrives is Brodick in the Isle of Arran, where it is represented by Forrest's number 27730, collected in 1926 on the Shweli–Salween divide, not far from the type-locality. This form received a First Class Certificate when exhibited on February 17, 1953 (the number F.19335 given for this plant in the present R.H.S. Handbook is erroneous, being in fact the number attached to the flowering type-specimen collected by Forrest in 1921). See further in the articles by the Duchess of Montrose and J. P. T. Boscawen in *R.Y.B. 1951–2*, pp. 9–10 and fig. 2; and by J. Basford in *R.C.Y.B. 1966*, p. 25.

R. MAGNIFICUM Ward—This species was discovered by Kingdon Ward in 1931 in the Adung valley, a western feeder of the Nmai Hka in the far north-western corner of Burma. He described it in his field-note as follows: 'A big tree, up to 50 ft high, and 6 ft in girth towards the base; may bear flowers as a shrub 10 ft high. Leaves with a coating of snow-white felted hairs beneath, which slough off later; on young plants, often 18 ins. long by 9 ins. wide, on maturer trees 12 ins. long by 6 ins. wide. Trusses hemispherical, about 30-flowered, corolla 3 ins. long, darker or lighter rose-purple, with 8 dusky purple honey pockets at the base, but no flash, the colour variable, but uniform for each tree; some have almost crimson flowers. Blooms from mid-February to the end of March, according to altitude. Never gregarious like R. sinogrande. . . . Common along the river bank in mixed forest between 6,000 and 7,000 ft, where the finest specimens were seen. A tree by the river, 50–60 ft high, carried over 500 trusses, and in mid-February was a gorgeous spectacle.'

Kingdon Ward collected seed under his number 9200 and in 1935 described this rhododendron as a new species. As it happens, he had found something similar five years earlier in the neighbouring Seinghku valley, growing with R. sinogrande, but the plants apparently made no impression on him at the time, probably because he arrived too late to see them in flower. He collected seed under KW 6782, which was distributed under the name 'R. giganteum var.', this being the identity given in his field-notes. But his herbarium specimens were identified as R. sinogrande, and consequently the plants raised from KW 6782 have been grown either as 'Ward's giganteum' or as R. sinogrande. However, Dr Cowan considered that these plants are R. magnificum. KW 6782 is represented at Brodick Castle, where it flowers regularly. For further details see the articles in the Year Book cited above.

As to the botanical characters of R. magnificum, the difference between it and R. protistum would seem to be the rather denser indumentum and the colour of the flowers (see below); from R. giganteum, in its mature state, it differs in the thinner, cobwebby indumentum, but we cannot be sure that the type trees in the Adung valley did not, out of reach, bear leaves with an indumentum similar to that of R. giganteum.

R. protistum (in the narrow sense) was discovered by Forrest in 1918 as a shrub 20 to 30 ft high, growing at 13,000 ft on the Mekong–Salween divide in latitude 28° N. Between 1919 and 1925 he sent at least six batches of seed, gathered on the Salween–Irrawaddy divide between 26° 20' and 28° 24' at altitudes of up to 14,000 ft, but no plant under its original field-number has been traced in Britain—at least none is mentioned by Cowan. Plants grown under the name R. protistum without collector's number could as well have been raised from Kingdon Ward seed (see below). Young grafted plants of R. protistum F.24775, received from the USA in 1968, are growing at Wakehurst Place, Sussex.

Essentially, R. protistum is the same as R. giganteum, differing in the undersides of the leaves being dull green and glabrous, or coated with at most a thin veil of hairs. It may simply be a state of the species in which the glabrous, juvenile foliage is slow to give way to the adult type seen in typical R. giganteum. In the type from the Mekong–Salween divide the flowers are more campanulate than in R. giganteum and creamy white flushed with rose, but all Forrest's later collections are of foliage and fruit only, so little is known about its flowers, and nothing at all about those borne by the plants from which Forrest collected seed.

Among other introductions of the R. *protistum* complex the most interesting are KW 21498 and 21602, collected by Kingdon Ward in The Triangle, N. Burma, during his last expedition (1953). These have not yet flowered. The wild specimen under 21498 appears to be near to R. *protistum*, while 21602, with rather broad leaves covered beneath with a fluffy, buff indumentum, suggests R. *giganteum*. Others are: KW 7427 from the Seinghku valley (where R. *magnificum* KW 6482 was collected); KW 7642 (from the Di Chu valley, Tibet, distributed as R. *sinogrande*, but R. *magnificum* according to Cowan); and KW 8069 (from the Delei valley, Assam, distributed as R. *protistum* aff.). KW 13681, from the Poshing La, Assam Himalaya, is cultivated at Nymans in Sussex as R. *magnificum*, but the identity of the plants is uncertain.

R. PRUNIFOLIUM (Small) Millais

Azalea prunifolia Small

A deciduous azalea up to 9 ft high in the wild; young shoots glabrous, purplish red, becoming greyish later. Leaves oval, or obovate to oblong; 1½ to 4 in. long, ½ to 1½ in. wide; green and glabrous on both surfaces except on the midrib which is slightly downy above and very sparingly bristly beneath, margins ciliate; stalk ⅛ to ¼ in. long. Flowers produced in July or August in clusters of four or five, on hairy stalks. Calyx very small. Corolla vermilion or orange or in an intermediate shade, or dark red, funnel-shaped, the tube ¾ to 1 in. long, glabrous or nearly so outside, downy inside. Stamens five, 2 to 2½ in. long, the lower half downy; ovary covered with pale bristly not glandular hairs. (*s.* Azalea *ss.* Luteum)

Native of Georgia and Alabama; found in shady ravines on the banks of streams; introduced to Britain by Prof. Sargent in 1918. Rehder describes it as the most glabrous of all American azaleas and very distinct in being entirely without glandular pubescence except occasionally on the outside of the corolla lobes.

R. *prunifolium* is said to make a magnificent display in its native habitat, but in this country it is less remarkable, perhaps because our summers are too cool for it. It is uncommon in gardens, though quite hardy. It received an Award of Merit when shown by the Crown Estate Commissioners, Windsor Great Park, on August 1, 1950 (clone 'Summer Sunset', with vermilion flowers).

R. PRZEWALSKII Maxim.

R. *kialense* Franch.

An evergreen shrub of very compact, slow growth, forming a close hemispherical bush; young shoots bright yellow, glabrous, stiff, and stout. Leaves oval or obovate, 2 to 4 in. long, 1 to 1½ in. wide, tapered or rounded at the base, pointed; dark green and glabrous above, more or less scurfy, and with netted veins beneath; stalk yellow. Flowers borne in April or May in compact trusses about 3 in. across; stalks up to 1 in. long, glabrous. Calyx inconspicuous. Corolla white or pink, spotted with rose-purple or unspotted, five-lobed, between funnel-shaped and bell-shaped, about 1¼ in. across. Stamens ten, glabrous or downy near the base. Ovary and style glabrous and without glands. (*s.* Lacteum)

Native of W. China; first collected in Kansu by the Russian traveller Przewalsky, in 1880; introduced to cultivation by way of St Petersburg. Wilson, who found it further south in 1904, observes that it reaches higher altitudes in W. China than any other broad-leaved rhododendron. He found it up to 14,500 ft. Its yellow buds, young shoots, and leaf-stalks combined with its dense close habit make cultivated plants very distinct, but it appears to be very shy-flowering. Some plants have the young shoots balsamic scented.

R. PSEUDOCHRYSANTHUM Hayata

An evergreen shrub of variable habit in the wild, sometimes up to 10 ft high, but a dwarf bush at high altitudes; young stems stout, clad with grey floccose hairs and stalked glands. Leaves thick and rigid, crowded, lanceolate, oblong-elliptic or oblong-oblanceolate, 1½ to 3 in. long, ¾ to 1¼ in. wide, apex rounded, abruptly narrowed to a short, stiff point, rounded at the base, dark green above, paler beneath, both surfaces at first clad with a loose, greyish flock which gradually wears away; petiole about ½ in. long. Flowers borne in April, ten to twenty in a fairly dense truss, on glandular pedicels up to 1 in. long. Calyx minute, fringed with glands. Corolla five-lobed, campanulate, 1¼ to 1¾ in. long and wide, pale pink or white, speckled within, and with deeper-coloured streaks outside along the ridges. Stamens ten, hairy at the base. Ovary glandular-hairy; style glabrous. *Bot. Mag.*, n.s., t. 284.   (*s.* Barbatum *ss.* Maculiferum)

Native of Formosa, where according to Wilson it grows gregariously on the higher peaks of the central range, covering large areas with impenetrable thickets, and preferring open, rocky, wind-swept situations. Wilson introduced it in 1918 from the summit of Mt Morrison, at over 13,000 ft, where it grows only 1 ft high. There was a second introduction around 1938, when seeds collected by Prof. Yashiroda were received in this country. It is related to R. *morii*, but that species has the leaves less hairy when young and also longer and relatively narrower.

R. *pseudochrysanthum* is a hardy but slow-growing species, best grown in full sun or only slight shade. It does not flower freely when young, but patience will be rewarded, for it is one of the most beautiful of the hardy kinds. It is rarely more than 4 ft high in cultivation, but grows much wider than high.

R. *pseudochrysanthum* received an Award of Merit when shown by Edmund de Rothschild from his garden at Exbury on May 1, 1956. The truss figured in the *Botanical Magazine* is also from a plant at Exbury.

R. PUMILUM Hook. f.   [PLATE 87]

An evergreen dwarf shrub with scaly minutely downy branchlets. Leaves elliptic to obovate-elliptic, rounded to obtuse at the apex, ½ to ¾ in. long, about half as wide, bright green or bluish green above, glaucous and scaly beneath (sometimes with a few scales on the upper surface also); leaf-stalks very short, scaly. Flowers solitary, in twos or threes, from terminal buds; pedicels up to 1 in. long, elongating in fruit. Calyx five-lobed, scaly, up to ⅓ in. long. Corolla campanulate, five-lobed, ½ to ¾ in. long, pink or rose-coloured, downy and slightly scaly outside. Stamens ten, included. Ovary densely scaly; style straight, included in the corolla, glabrous.   (s. Uniflorum)

R. *pumilum* was discovered by J. D. Hooker in 1849 in the Sikkim Himalaya. It was, he wrote, the smallest of all the rhododendrons he saw. 'Its slender woody stem roots among moss, *Andromeda fastigiata*, &c., ascends obliquely, and bears a few spreading branches, 3 to 4 inches in length. . . . An extremely elegant species, and apparently very rare; for I have only gathered it twice, and each time in the wildest district of Sikkim, where its elegant flowers appear soon after the snow has melted, when its pretty pink bells are seen peeping above the surrounding short heath-like vegetation, reminding the botanist of those of *Linnaea borealis*.'

R. *pumilum* also occurs in E. Nepal, and to the east of Sikkim ranges as far as N.W. upper Burma. It was apparently not introduced, or at least not successfully, until Kingdon Ward found it on the Dohong La at the eastern end of the Himalaya in 1924, forming hassocks and mats on steep alpine turf. In 1926 he collected seeds from the Seinghku valley in Burma (KW 6961). This form, which he nicknamed "Pink Baby", carried 'solitary or paired flowers of a delicate shell-pink, hoisted above the crowded leaves on long crimson stalks . . .'. More recently seeds have been sent by Ludlow and Sherriff and also by Stainton (from E. Nepal).

R. *pumilum* is very distinct from R. *uniflorum* and its immediate allies in its campanulate flowers and elliptic leaves. Indeed, it bears a certain resemblance to R. *campylogynum*. It is quite hardy and suitable for the rock garden. The Award of Merit was given on April 30, 1935, to a form raised from KW 6961, exhibited by Lord Swaythling, Townhill Park, Hants.

R. LUDLOWII Cowan—Allied to R. *pumilum* and of similar dwarf habit, but differing most markedly in its yellow flowers, spotted with reddish brown inside. The calyx is larger than in R. *pumilum* and leafy, and a further point of distinction is that the obovate leaves are faintly crenated at the edge. It was discovered by Ludlow and Sherriff in 1936 on the Lo La, a pass at 13,500 ft on the border between Tibet and Assam, near the source of the Siyom river, a tributary of the Brahmaputra. Two years later, they and George Taylor collected seeds a short way to the north, on Tsari Sama, Tibet, and from these the cultivated plants derive. *Bot. Mag.*, n.s., t. 412.   [PLATE 82

R. *ludlowii* is not an easy plant to cultivate successfully. But Mr R. B. Cooke, who supplied the flowering piece figured in the *Botanical Magazine*, grew it successfully in Northumberland in a raised bed on the north side of a hedge, where it is screened from the sun for about six hours in the middle of the day. It is slow-growing, but bears flowers when the plant is still not much larger than its own corolla. Perhaps this rhododendron's chief claim to distinction is that it is a parent of the lovely 'Chikor' and 'Curlew', described in the section on hybrids.

R. QUINQUEFOLIUM Bisset & Moore

A deciduous azalea of low, bushy habit, but sometimes a small tree in the wild; shoots glabrous, branches erect, forked. Leaves produced in whorls of five (with sometimes one or two very small ones in addition) at the end of the shoot only, broadly obovate or somewhat diamond-shaped, rounded at the apex, except for a short, abrupt tip, tapering at the base to a very short bristly stalk; they vary in size in each set of five, the largest being 1½ to 2 in. long by 1 in. wide, the smallest not half as large, upper surface sparsely hairy when young, the lower one hairy about the margin and along the midrib; both sides pale green, often with a purplish margin. Flowers solitary, in pairs or in threes, produced with the young leaves from the terminal bud. Corolla broadly funnel-shaped, 1½ in. across, white with green spots, the lobes ovate. Stamens ten, hairy at the base. (*s.* Azalea *ss.* Schlippenbachii)

RHODODENDRON QUINQUEFOLIUM

Native of Japan; discovered by Mr Bisset in 1876; introduced about twenty years later by Lord Redesdale. This azalea is most distinct and attractive in its foliage, especially in spring when the leaves are of a tender green bordered with purple, each whorl of five forming an umbrella-like group at the top of a slender twig; they usually colour well in the autumn. It is also very beautiful in April when covered with its white flowers, though these are not borne freely on young plants. It needs a sheltered position in light shade.

R. *quinquefolium* received an Award of Merit when shown by the Dowager Countess Cawdor, Haslemere, on April 28, 1931. A First Class Certificate was given to a fine form grown at Exbury, exhibited on April 18, 1967, by Edmund de Rothschild. It bears the clonal name 'Five Arrows'.

R. RACEMOSUM Franch.

An evergreen species varying in habit from a dwarf compact shrublet to a tall, straggly bush; young stems scaly, usually deep red, glabrous or slightly downy, never bristly. Leaves up to 2 in. long and 1 in. wide, oval, elliptic, oblong, or broadest slightly above or below the middle, usually rounded or obtuse at the apex, upper surface dull or glossy, with or without scales, underside glaucous and scaly, both sides glabrous or almost so; petiole very short. Flowers produced in April or May from axillary inflorescence-buds, which may be concentrated near the apex of the shoot or more widely spread along it; individual clusters with one to six flowers; pedicels up to ⅜ in. long. Calyx very small. Corolla widely funnel-shaped, pale to deep pink or rose-coloured, about 1 in. wide, the tube shorter than the lobes. Stamens ten, usually downy at the base. Ovary scaly; style usually longer than the stamens, glabrous, or downy at the base. *Bot. Mag.*, t. 7301.   (*s.* Scabrifolium)

Native of W. China, common in the drier parts of Yunnan, found at 9,000 to 14,000 ft in open places or as undergrowth in oak or pine woodland. It was first raised in the Jardin des Plantes, Paris, in 1889, and was introduced to Kew in November of that year. The seed had been gathered and sent to Paris by its discoverer, Père Delavay. R. *racemosum* soon spread into gardens and was awarded a First Class Certificate as early as 1892. But the present garden stock mainly derives from later sendings by Forrest, Kingdon Ward, and Rock.

R. *racemosum* is one of the most distinct and pretty of the dwarfer rhododendrons. Its most remarkable feature, which it shares with other members of the Scabrifolium series, is the production of flowers from the leaf-axils along the previous year's wood. Often from six to more than twelve inches of the shoot will be laden with blossom—very different from the single truss which in *Rhododendron* is usually seen terminating the shoot. On vigorous garden seedlings the season's growths are sometimes compound, consisting of the main shoot and several short laterals on which inflorescence-buds are developed. Another peculiarity of some garden plants is that a proportion of the inflorescence-buds abort and turn grey.

The flowers of R. *racemosum* vary much in depth of colour, but in a large group raised from seed—and few rhododendrons can be more easily or quickly raised by this means—the paler-coloured plants serve as a foil to those with flowers of a richer colour, and the total effect is delightful. But if there is room for only one or a few plants, a selection raised from cuttings is preferable.

A very dwarf and compact form of the species, with flowers of a deep cerise pink, was sent by Forrest in 1921 from the Sungkwei pass, Yunnan, under number F.19404—'the finest form I have yet seen' he added in his field notes. The true form is available in commerce, but some plants sent out as R. *racemosum* F.19404 are evidently seedlings taken from open-pollinated plants, and are quite worthless.

cv.'GLENDOICK'.—A tall-growing clone with deep pink flowers, distributed by Glendoick Gardens Ltd, Perth.

cv. 'ROCK ROSE'.—Flowers bright pink. Habit erect, to 4 or 5 ft. Award of Merit April 28, 1970, when shown by the Hydon Nurseries. The original plant was raised at Tower Court from Rock 59578.

There is also a white-flowered form in cultivation.

R. × PALLESCENS Hutch.—The name R. *pallescens* was given by Hutchinson in 1933 to a plant at Exbury which arose as a stray from seeds under Rock's number 59574. It is a small, erect-branched shrub with oblong-lanceolate or oblanceolate leaves up to 3 in. long, glaucous and sparsely scaly beneath. Flowers with the characteristic shape of the Triflorum series but smaller, about 1 in. or slightly more wide, white, flushed with pink at the edges, produced from axillary as well as terminal buds and forming a dense cluster. Hutchinson suggested that the plant might be a natural hybrid between R. *racemosum* and R. *davidsonianum*, and Davidian, in his revision of the Triflorum series, confirms this identification. The original plant received an Award of Merit on May 2, 1933.

The rhododendron named R. FITTIANUM by Balfour is without any doubt a natural hybrid of R. *racemosum*. It differs chiefly in its leaves, which are light green beneath and densely coated with pale yellowish uniform scales; and in the rosy-purple flowers more numerous in each truss and borne later. It is also stouter branched and the young stems are green. It was described in 1917 from a 'rogue' among seedlings of Forrest's 10278, sent home in 1913 and raised at Werrington Park, Cornwall, where Mr Fitt was head gardener. A peculiarity of this plant, according to Balfour, was that the flowers were borne at the ends of axillary shoots bearing a few leaves at the base. However, the plant was only four years old when described and as pointed out above it is quite usual in vigorous seedlings of R. *racemosum* for some of the axillary flower-buds to be replaced by short shoots ending in a flower-bud. These shoots may bear a few normal leaves at the base, but others, shorter, are furnished only with bract-like scales similar to those found at the base of any flower-bud of adult R. *racemosum* and are, in effect, stalked buds. Thus the fact that 'Fittianum', as it should be called, showed this peculiarity merely serves to emphasise its affinity with R. *racemosum*.

'Fittianum', in the herbarium, bears a superficial resemblance to R. *dauricum* var. *sempervirens*, which explains why R. *fittianum* Balf. f. appears as a synonym of R. *dauricum* in *Species of Rhododendron*.

A hybrid between R. *racemosum* and 'Fittianum', really a back-cross, has been named 'FITTRA'.

R. RETICULATUM G. Don

R. *rhombicum* Miq.

A deciduous azalea 5 to 8 ft high with stiff, erect, somewhat sparse branches, covered with a loose brownish wool when young. Leaves diamond-shaped, 1 to 2½ in. long, ¾ to 1½ in. wide; dark dull green and very hairy above when young, becoming almost or quite glabrous by autumn; paler and very finely net-veined beneath; stalk ⅙ to ⅓ in. long, brown-woolly. Flowers solitary or in pairs (rarely twice as many). Calyx small, five-toothed, very hairy like the flower-stalk, which is about ¼ in. long. Corolla purple, almost or quite unspotted, 1½ to 2 in. across, lobes oblong, ½ in. wide, the three upper ones erect, the two smaller ones more deeply divided and pointed downwards. Stamens ten. Ovary densely coated with long white hairs (brown when dry); style glandular in the lower half. *Bot. Mag.*, t. 6972. (*s.* Azalea *ss.* Schlippenbachii)

Native of Japan; described in 1834 from a young plant without flowers growing in Knight's nursery, Chelsea. The original description is so incomplete that Don's species was put on one side as incompletely known until Wilson resurrected it in the *Monograph of Azaleas* (1921). Until then it had been known by Miquel's name R. *rhombicum*. The Knight introduction was probably lost, but the species was reintroduced to Europe around 1865 and reached Britain soon after. It is quite a pretty species, bearing its showy flowers before the leaves unfold, but the colouring inclines to magenta-purple as a rule and clashes badly with reds and near-blues. It is perfectly hardy.

R. *reticulatum* is a somewhat variable species in the wild, and several of its forms have been given specific rank by Japanese botanists (see *R.Y.B. 1948*, pp. 114–16, and Ohwi's *Flora of Japan* (1965), pp. 700–2). The description given above is of the form commonly cultivated in this country; all the garden specimens in the Kew Herbarium belong to it, including the original of the plate in the *Botanical Magazine*. This form, easily recognised in the flowering stage by the ten stamens, densely hairy ovary and the style glandular in the lower half, agrees well with the form given specific rank by Makino as R. *wadanum*. It is comparatively low-growing, seldom more than 8 ft high.

R. DILATATUM Miq.   R. *reticulatum* f. *pentandrum* Wils.—Leaves soon glabrous on both surfaces, hence distinguishable from the common form of R. *reticulatum* even when out of flower. Stamens five only. Ovary glandular, not hairy; style glabrous. *Bot. Mag.*, t. 7681. Native of Japan; introduced by Messrs Veitch in 1883. Although it is very similar to R. *reticulatum* (*wadanum*) in general appearance, the distinctive characters given above appear to be well correlated and together make it more than just a five-stamened form of that species. It has the same garden value.

R. RIRIEI Hemsl. & Wils.

An evergreen shrub up to 25 ft high; branchlets furnished with a loose white scurf when quite young. Leaves narrowly oval or broadly oblanceolate, 3 to 6 in. long, 1 to 2 in. wide, tapered at both ends, usually more abruptly towards the apex; glabrous and green above, covered beneath with a very close scurf, at first white, turning grey; midrib yellow below. Flowers borne in February or March in trusses of five to ten; pedicels about $\frac{3}{8}$ in. long, covered with a thin, whitish wool. Calyx $\frac{1}{8}$ in. or slightly more long, with triangular or oblong lobes. Corolla deep to pale magenta-purple with darker nectar-pouches at the base, about 2 in. long, widely bell-shaped, five- or sometimes seven-lobed. Stamens ten, glabrous, included in the corolla, filaments purple. Ovary covered with pale greyish wool; style glabrous. Capsule very large, $1\frac{1}{4}$ in. long, $\frac{3}{8}$ in. wide.   (s. Arboreum ss. Argyrophyllum).

R. *ririei* was discovered by Wilson on Mt Omei, W. Szechwan, where it occurs at 4,000 to 6,000 ft in open places or woodland, and was introduced by him for Messrs Veitch in 1904. It bears some resemblance to R. *niveum*, but that species has many more flowers in a tighter truss. It is rare in gardens and flowers too early to be suitable for general planting, but is quite hardy and has reached a height of 20 ft at Wakehurst Place, Sussex. It received an Award of Merit on February 24, 1931, when shown from Bodnant.

R. ROXIEANUM Forr. [PLATE 89

R. *coccinopeplum* Balf. f. & Forr.; R. *cucullatum* Hand.-Mazz.; R. *poecilodermum* Balf. f. & Forr.; R. *recurvum* Balf. f. & Forr.; R. *aischropeplum* Balf. f. & Forr.

A small evergreen shrub, usually under 6 ft high in the wild, but occasionally tree-like and up to 15 ft high; young shoots clothed with reddish-brown wool; inner bud-scales persisting on the branchlets for several years. Leaves linear, linear-oblong, or narrow-oblanceolate, 1¾ to 4¾ in. long, rarely over 1 in. wide and usually much less, pointed (more rarely blunt) at the apex, narrowed at the base to a stout petiole, which is tomentose like the young stems, upper surface of blade dark green, dull or glossy, midrib grooved, underside thickly covered with a reddish-brown or sometimes paler-coloured tomentum, concealing the raised midrib, margins usually recurved. Flowers ten to twenty in a tight terminal truss, opening in May; pedicels tomentose, with or without glands. Calyx very small, glandular and usually downy also. Corolla funnel-shaped to campanulate, 1¼ to 1½ in. long, white or white flushed with pink or cream-coloured, with or without crimson spots. Stamens ten, hairy in the lower part. Ovary tomentose, with or without glands; style hairy at the base. *Bot. Mag.*, t. 9383. (s. Taliense ss. Roxieanum)

A native of alpine and subalpine moorland or tree-line coniferous forest, from S.W. Szechwan through the bleaker parts of N.W. Yunnan to S.E. Tibet; discovered by Forrest in 1912 and introduced by him. It is a variable species, especially in habit and relative width of leaf, but curiously enough the taller forms are not broader-leaved as might be expected. Rock's 59205 was described by him as a small tree 10 ft high but with linear, almost needle-shaped leaves. R. *roxieanum* is slow-growing, and also slow to reach the flowering state, but makes an interesting specimen.

var. OREONASTES (Balf. f. & Forr.) R. *recurvum* var. *oreonastes* Balf. f. & Forr.—Leaves linear, less than ¼ in. wide. Described from a plant only 2 ft high found by Forrest on the Kari La, Mekong–Yangtse divide, at 14,000 ft. It is not a very distinct variety, since taller forms may have very narrow leaves also (see above) and comparatively dwarf forms may have leaves of the normal width. Award of Merit May 1, 1973, when exhibited by the Crown Estate Commissioners, Windsor Great Park.

R. PROTEOIDES Balf. f. & W. W. Sm.—Near to R. *roxieanum*, but with the leaves about half as long as in that species and blunt or rounded at the end; mostly they are under 2 in. long and ¼ to ½ in. wide. The flowers in the type were yellow, but they may be creamy yellow or white. It is a dwarf shrub, usually under 2 ft high in the wild, and some plants found by Forrest were creeping and only 3 to 6 in. high. Most of his seed-collections were from the Mekong–Salween divide around Ka-kar-po at altitudes of 12,000 to 14,000 ft, but his F.16609 was from the Muli region, S.W. Szechwan.

R. RECURVOIDES Tagg & Ward—Although resembling R. *roxieanum* in habit and aspect, this species is nevertheless very distinct in the glandular-bristly young stems, petioles, and outer bud-scales, and in the presence of stalked glands in the leaf-indumentum. It was discovered by Kingdon Ward in 1926 in the valley of the Dichu, a river which rises on the border between Tibet and Assam and flows west into the Lohit some miles south of the Tibetan town of Rima. He described it in his field note as a compact bushy shrub usually 2 to ft high or less, flowering when quite small and growing on the sunniest side of steep granite screes among boulders. It is in cultivation from the seeds he collected in the type-locality and received an Award of Merit when shown by Col E. Bolitho, Trengwainton, Cornwall, in 1941 on March 25. But April or May is its usual flowering-time.

R. RUBIGINOSUM Franch.

A stiff-habited, erect-growing evergreen shrub 6 to 20 ft high, branchlets becoming warty. Leaves 1½ to 3½ in. long, ½ to 1 in. wide; narrowly oval, tapering gradually to each end, upper surface glabrous, dull green, lower one covered with reddish brown scales; stalk ¼ to ½ in. long. Flowers in terminal clusters of four to seven, produced in April and May; pedicels scaly, about ½ in. long. Calyx very small. Corolla 1½ to 2 in. wide, rosy lilac, spotted with maroon on the upper side, the tube funnel-shaped, lobes wavy-margined. Stamens ten, downy towards the base. Ovary densely scaly; style glabrous. *Bot. Mag.*, t. 7621. (s. Heliolepis)

Native of S.W. Szechwan (Muli region), N.W. Yunnan, and bordering parts of S.E. Tibet; introduced to Paris in 1889 by Père Delavay and thence to Britain. It is also cultivated from seeds sent later by Forrest and Rock. It is a somewhat stiff, dull-foliaged shrub but is very free-flowering. Its nearest ally is R. *desquamatum*, but that species has the leaves broadest below the middle and the scales on the undersides of the leaves are unequal, some being larger and darker than others, whereas in R. *rubiginosum* they are uniform.

R. *rubiginosum*, in the form originally introduced, was slightly tender at Kew, but the later introductions are usually reckoned to be perfectly hardy. The Award of Merit was given on May 3, 1960, to the clone 'Wakehurst', with Mallow Purple flowers, borne from axillary as well as terminal buds, forming clusters of up to twenty-five.

R. RUBROPILOSUM Hayata
R. *caryophyllum* Hayata; R. *randaiense* Hayata

An evergreen azalea up to 9 ft high in the wild; young shoots covered densely with flattened, appressed, grey to red-brown hairs. Leaves oblong-lanceolate to oval-lanceolate, ½ to 1¾ in. long, ½ to ¾ in. wide, slightly hairy above, thickly furnished beneath with forward-pointing bristly hairs, especially on the midrib. Flowers in clusters of three or four. Calyx and flower-stalks bristly. Corolla funnel-shaped, with five spreading lobes, pink spotted with dark rose, ¾ to 1 in. wide. Stamens seven to ten, shorter than the corolla, downy near the base as is also the longer style. (s. Azalea ss. Obtusum)

Native of Formosa, up to 10,000 ft altitude. Wilson, who visited its native habitat in 1918, found many plants flowering in October. During the same journey he introduced the species to cultivation by means of seeds. It is not likely to be hardy except in such climates as that of Cornwall. It differs from *R. indicum* in the more numerous stamens and in the downy style; the latter character distinguishes it also from *R. tosaense* and *R. simsii*. W. R. Price, who visited Formosa in 1912, also found it blooming in October. It is uncertain whether this species is still in cultivation.

R. RUPICOLA W. W. Sm.

An evergreen shrub 2 to 4 ft high, young shoots, leaves (on both sides), outside of calyx-lobes, ovary, and flower-stalks all very scaly. Leaves oval, often inclined to oblong, rounded but with a tiny mucro at the apex, $\frac{1}{2}$ to $\frac{3}{4}$ in. long, $\frac{1}{6}$ to $\frac{1}{3}$ in. wide, dark green above, yellowish grey between the scales beneath; stalk $\frac{1}{12}$ to $\frac{1}{8}$ in. long. Flowers opening in April and May in a terminal cluster of three to five, each on a very short stalk. Calyx $\frac{1}{6}$ in. long, deeply five-lobed, the lobes oblong, deep purple, fringed at the margin. Corolla $\frac{7}{8}$ in. wide, of a rich plum-purple, the tube very short and clothed inside with white hairs, five-lobed, the lobes ovate-oblong, rounded at the end, spreading, sprinkled more or less with scales outside, mostly up the middle. Stamens normally ten, but sometimes as few as seven, purple, $\frac{1}{2}$ in. long, tufted with white down near the base; anthers pale brown. Ovary scaly towards the top; style overtopping the stamens, purple, glabrous. (*s.* Lapponicum)

Native of N.W. Yunnan and S.W. Szechwan at 12,000 to 14,000 ft; discovered by Forrest in 1910 in the Lichiang range and introduced by him in the same year. Its flowers, although small, are of a wonderfully rich purple, this colour extending to the style and the filaments of the stamens. *R. russatum*, which often bears flowers of a similar colour, differs in having much larger leaves and a downy style. *R. rupicola* is perfectly hardy.

R. ACHROANTHUM Balf. f. & W. W. Sm. *R. propinquum* Balf. f. & Ward— This differs from *R. rupicola* in having five or six stamens only, and a more densely scaly ovary, but is probably not specifically distinct from it. It was introduced by Forrest in 1918 from the mountains north-east of Chungtien and is also in cultivation from seeds collected by Kingdon Ward in north-east upper Burma.

R. RUSSATUM Balf. f. & Forr.

R. osmerum Balf. f. & Forr.; *R. cantabile* Hutch.

A dwarf evergreen shrub, ultimately a yard or more high, of bushy, densely leafy habit; young shoots covered with red and yellow scales. Leaves borne along nearly the whole of the shoots, half a dozen to the inch, oval or ovate, round-ended, $\frac{3}{4}$ to $1\frac{3}{4}$ in. long, half as much wide, dark dull green above, rusty yellow beneath, both surfaces very scaly; stalk $\frac{1}{10}$ to $\frac{1}{6}$ in. long. Flowers opening in March and April in close clusters of five to ten; pedicels up to $\frac{1}{4}$ in. long. Calyx deeply cut into five ovate or oblong lobes about $\frac{1}{6}$ in. long, fringed with hairs. Corolla a vivid purple-blue, about 1 in. wide, with five spreading lobes and a funnel-shaped base that is hairy in the throat. Stamens ten, conspicuously exposed, hairy towards the base, the stalks reddish; anthers brown. Ovary scaly; style red, hairy at the base. *Bot. Mag.*, t. 8963.   (*s.* Lapponicum)

Native of N.W. Yunnan and S.W. Szechwan at 11,000 to 13,000 ft, in open places, boggy pastures, cliff-ledges, etc.; discovered by Forrest in 1917 on the Kari pass, Mekong–Yangtse divide, and cultivated from seeds he sent in that year and many times later. It is one of the most richly coloured and desirable of the series, and is perfectly hardy. The flowers vary in the intensity of the colouring and in the proportion of blue in the purple; they are almost indigo in some forms. The white centre to the corolla, usually a prominent feature of this species, comes from the hairs in the throat and at the base of the stamens.

It received an Award of Merit on May 3, 1927, when shown from Werrington Park, Cornwall, by A. M. Williams (flowers intense violet-blue) and a First Class Certificate when shown by Lionel de Rothschild, Exbury, on April 4, 1933 (flowers intense purple). It received an Award of Garden Merit in 1938.

R. SALUENENSE Franch.

R. amaurophyllum Balf. f. & Forr.; *R. humicola* Wilding

An evergreen shrub 1½ to 4 ft high; young shoots scaly and conspicuously bristly. Leaves oblong to oval, with a distinct mucro at the abruptly tapered or rounded apex and a bristly scaly stalk $\frac{1}{12}$ in. long, $\frac{3}{4}$ to 1 in. long, $\frac{1}{4}$ to $\frac{1}{2}$ in. wide, dark glossy green with minute scales above, more tawny, paler and scaly beneath. Flowers produced in April and May in pairs or threes from the end of the shoot; pedicels $\frac{1}{4}$ to $\frac{1}{2}$ in. long, bristly and scaly. Calyx $\frac{1}{3}$ in. wide, with five ovate, conspicuously fringed lobes. Corolla rosy-purple or purplish crimson with darker spots, widely open, 1½ to 1¾ in wide, with five broad, rounded, overlapping lobes, very scaly and softly downy outside; downy in the throat. Stamens ten, purplish, with a tuft of down at the base. Ovary densely scaly; style glabrous. *Bot. Mag.*, t. 9095.   (*s.* Saluenense)

R. saluenense was discovered by the Abbé Soulié in 1894 on the Salween–Mekong divide, near the French Mission station at Tseku, and was later found in other parts of N.W. Yunnan and bordering areas of S.E. Tibet; introduced by Forrest in 1914. It is the tallest-growing and largest-leaved of the series to which it gives its name, and useful to provide height in a planting of dwarf species. Some forms are low-growing and scarcely to be distinguished from *R. chameunum*. It is perfectly hardy. It received an Award of Merit when shown from Exbury by Lionel de Rothschild on April 17, 1945.

R. CHAMEUNUM Balf. f. & Forr.   *R. cosmetum* Balf. f. & Forr.; *R. charidotes*

Balf. f. & Farrer—As Davidian has pointed out in his revision of the Saluenense series, this species really differs from *R. saluenense* only in its smaller leaves up to $\frac{7}{8}$ in. long, sparsely scaly above, and its dwarfer habit, and is linked to it by intermediates.

R. PROSTRATUM W. W. Sm.—When Sir William Wright Smith described

this species he remarked it was very near indeed to *R. saluenense*—so near that he hesitated to separate it by anything more than a varietal name. It differs in the smaller leaves, less than 1 in. long, and in the prostrate or hummocked habit.

It occurs at high altitudes in S.W. Szechwan and N.W. Yunnan; the type was collected on the Litiping near the upper limit of vegetation at 15,000 to 16,000 ft. It is suitable for the rock garden and quite hardy, though inferior to R. *radicans* and R. *keleticum*. It is figured in *Bot. Mag.*, t. 8747.

R. SANGUINEUM Franch.

An evergreen shrub up to 6 ft high; young stems clad with greyish hairs; bud-scales deciduous. Leaves obovate, elliptic or oblong, obtuse or rounded at the apex, cuneate at the base, up to 2½ in. long and 1 in. wide, of leathery texture, dull medium green above, undersurface coated with a thin, continuous indumentum of branched hairs; petiole about ⅝ in. long. Flowers opening in May, in clusters of three to six. Calyx variable in size, up to ⅜ in. long but sometimes reduced to a mere rim. Corolla bell-shaped, about 1½ in. long, five-lobed, crimson, with nectar-pouches at the base. Stamens ten, with glabrous or downy filaments. Ovary densely tomentose, not glandular; style glabrous.   (s. Neriiflorum ss. Sanguineum)

Native of N.W. Yunnan and S.E. Tibet; discovered by the Abbé Soulié on the Se La, Mekong–Salween divide, in 1895; introduced by Forrest in about 1917. In its natural habitat it is a small shrub, usually under 4 ft high, occurring in open situations at 12,000 to 14,000 ft. It is hardy, but of little value in gardens, being very shy-flowering in most forms.

The above description is of R. *sanguineum* in the narrow sense. There are, however, many rhododendrons which resemble it closely in the size, shape, and indumentum of the leaves and in the general characters of inflorescence and flowers, but differing from R. *sanguineum*, or among themselves, in the colour of the flowers, in the presence or absence of glands on the ovary, and in having the foliage bud-scales either persistent or deciduous. Since these variations are not correlated, the group is very difficult to treat taxonomically. This problem, which concerns other species in the Sanguineum subseries also, is discussed by Dr J. M. Cowan in: 'Rhododendrons of the *Rh. sanguineum* Alliance', *Notes Roy. Bot. Gard. Edin.*, Vol. 20, pp. 55–91. Dr Cowan's treatment of the variations of R. *sanguineum* is followed here, though it is perhaps rather too elaborate for horticultural purposes.

subsp. ATRORUBRUM Cowan—Flowers black-crimson, differing from subsp. *haemaleum* in the eglandular ovary, from subsp. *didymum* in the deciduous bud-scales. Described from a specimen collected by Forrest on the Salween–Kiuchiang (upper Irrrawaddy) divide.

subsp. CLOIOPHORUM (Balf. f. & Forr.) Cowan R. *cloiophorum* Balf. f. & Forr.; R. *asmenistum* Balf. f. & Forr.; R. *cloiophorum* subsp. *asmenistum* (Balf. f. & Forr.) Tagg—Flowers rose-coloured, or rose more or less flushed with yellow. Foliage bud-scales deciduous. Ovary tomentose, not glandular. N.W. Yunnan and bordering parts of S.E. Tibet.

subsp. CONSANGUINEUM Cowan—Resembling typical R. *sanguineum* in flower colour, differing in having the ovary glandular as well as tomentose. In cultivation from seeds collected by Forrest and by Rock in N.W. Yunnan and bordering parts of Tibet; also from Kingdon Ward's 6831 from the Seinghku valley, upper Burma. The type is F.25507, collected on the Mekong–Yangtse divide. Some plants agreeing with this subspecies flower more freely than typical R. *sanguineum*.

subsp. DIDYMUM (Balf. f. & Forr.) Cowan　R. *didymum* Balf. f. & Forr.— Flowers black-crimson as in subsp. *haemaleum* but with the ovary glandular as well as tomentose. Foliage bud-scales persistent. Described from Forrest 20220, collected on the Salween–Kiuchiang divide at 14,000 to 15,000 ft and cultivated under this number and also from seeds collected later in the same area. The wild plants are of dwarf habit (up to 2 ft high) and this character has been retained in cultivated plants. *Bot. Mag.*, t. 9217.

This rhododendron, better known as R. *didymum*, is the most distinct of its group. The colour of the flowers is rather funereal unless lit up by a gleam of sunshine. It is hardy, and flowers very late, in June or even July. Among its hybrids are 'Carmen', 'Arthur Osborn', and the Red Cap grex. These and others are described in the section on hybrids.

subsp. HAEMALEUM (Balf. f. & Forr.) Cowan　R. *haemaleum* Balf. f. & Forr. —Flowers blackish crimson, otherwise not differing from typical R. *sanguineum*. *Bot. Mag.*, t. 9263. N.W. Yunnan.

subsp. HIMERTUM (Balf. f. & Forr.) Cowan　R. *himertum* Balf. f. & Forr.; R. *nebrites* Balf. f. & Forr.; R. *poliopeplum* Balf. f. & Forr.—Flowers in some shade of yellow. Ovary tomentose, not glandular. Foliage bud-scales deciduous. N.W. Yunnan. Differs from R. *citriniflorum* in having leaves with a thin, plastered indumentum, as in all the subspecies of R. *sanguineum*. In R. *citriniflorum* the indumentum is thick and woolly.

subsp. LEUCOPETALUM (Balf. f. & Forr.) Cowan　R. *leucopetalum* Balf. f. & Forr.; R. *cloiophorum* subsp. *leucopetalum* (Balf. f. & Forr.) Tagg—Flowers white. Found by Forrest on the Mekong–Salween divide and introduced by him (F.14270).

subsp. MELLEUM Cowan—Flowers yellow as in subsp. *himertum*, but ovary tomentose and glandular.

subsp. MESAEUM Cowan　R. *mesaeum* Balf. f. MS—Sir Isaac Bayley Balfour gave the unpublished name R. *mesaeum* to a rhododendron found by Forrest on the Salween–Kiuchiang divide, 2 ft high, with black-crimson flowers. According to Dr Cowan it has the ovary tomentose but not glandular, and represents an eglandular expression of subsp. *didymum*, but it is also very near to subsp. *haemaleum*, and the seeds that Forrest collected under the type-number and later numbers were in fact distributed as R. *haemaleum*, but this subspecies is typically taller-growing and has deciduous bud-scales (persistent in subsp. *mesaeum*).

subsp. ROSEOTINCTUM (Balf. f. & Forr.) Cowan　R. *roseotinctum* Balf. f. & Forr.; R. *mannophorum* Balf. f. & Forr.; R. *torquatum* Balf. f. & Farrer—Near to subsp. *cloiophorum*, but with the ovary both tomentose and glandular. N.W. Yunnan, bordering parts of S.E. Tibet and upper Burma. The colour of the flowers is typically creamy white edged with deep rose-crimson, but also in various combinations of pink and yellow.

R. SARGENTIANUM Rehd. & Wils.

A low evergreen shrub up to 2 ft high and 3 ft or more across, with numerous erect branches which, when young, are covered with down and dark scurf. Leaves aromatic when crushed, oval, $\frac{1}{3}$ to $\frac{2}{3}$ in. long, half as much wide; dark glossy green and soon glabrous above, very scurfy beneath; leaf-stalk about $\frac{1}{8}$ in. long. Flowers produced in May, six to twelve together in a loose terminal cluster, each bloom on a stalk $\frac{1}{5}$ to $\frac{3}{8}$ in. long, thickly covered with yellowish scurf. Calyx about $\frac{1}{8}$ in. long or shorter. Corolla pale yellow, $\frac{1}{2}$ in. long and wide, the base a cylindrical tube hairy inside, spreading at the mouth into five lobes, scaly outside. Stamens five, glabrous, hidden in the corolla-tube. Ovary scaly; style shorter than the stamens. *Bot. Mag.*, t. 8871 (*s.* Anthopogon)

Native of W. Szechwan in the Mupin area; discovered and introduced by Wilson in 1903–4 for Messrs Veitch, and again during his second expedition for the Arnold Arboretum. It grows at 11,000 to 13,000 ft, on rocks or cliffs, or forming heaths. It is a charming shrub of dwarf, compact habit, but does not flower very freely. It is very hardy. An Award of Merit was given to it in 1923 when shown from Bodnant on May 8 by Lady Aberconway and the Hon. H. D. McLaren.

cv. 'WHITEBAIT'.—Flowers nearly white, borne more freely than usual. Award of Merit May 6, 1960, when shown by E. H. M. and P. A. Cox, Glendoick, Perthshire.

R. SCABRIFOLIUM Franch.

An evergreen shrub of thin, lanky habit, 6 to 8 ft high, young shoots slender but rather rigid, clothed with pale wool and long hairs. Leaves distributed along the branchlets, narrowly oval to oblong-lanceolate, pointed, tapered at the base, $1\frac{1}{2}$ to $3\frac{1}{2}$ in. long, $\frac{3}{4}$ to 1 in. wide, dark green and with stiff short hairs above; paler, scaly, and hairy beneath especially on the prominent midrib and veins; stalk $\frac{1}{8}$ to $\frac{1}{4}$ in. long. Flowers produced in March or April from several of the axils of the terminal leaves in two- to four-flowered umbels, the whole forming a many-flowered cluster 3 or 4 in. wide. Calyx hairy and scaly, $\frac{1}{8}$ in. long, with five deep, pointed lobes. Corolla white or pale pink, $1\frac{1}{4}$ in. wide, with a short tube and five ovate, blunt, spreading lobes $\frac{1}{2}$ in. long. Stamens ten, with pink stalks $\frac{1}{2}$ in. long, downy at the base. Ovary scaly and clothed with short, whitish hairs; style $\frac{3}{4}$ in. long, hairy towards the base. *Bot. Mag.*, 7159. (*s.* Scabrifolium)

Native of Yunnan, China; discovered by Delavay in 1883, introduced to the Jardin des Plantes at Paris in 1885, whence plants were sent to Kew in 1888 that flowered two years later. It is an interesting and (in its clothing of stiff hairs and flatly open flowers) a distinct species, but not one of the more attractive ones. It was rediscovered and introduced in 1913 by Forrest, who found it in other parts of Yunnan in open situations up to 11,000 ft. It is, however rather tender. Its nearest ally is R. *spiciferum*, which has a similar indumentum on its stems and leaves, but much smaller leaves.

R. SCABRUM G. Don

R. sublanceolatum Miq.; *R. liukiuense* Komatsu; *R. sublateritium* Komatsu

An evergreen azalea, stiffly branched, bushy, probably up to 6 ft high, the branchlets having the dark forward-pointing bristles of this group. Leaves 1 to 3 in. long, $\frac{1}{2}$ to $1\frac{1}{2}$ in. wide; oblanceolate, or oval, tapered at the base, terminated by a short mucro; glabrous and dark green above, paler and with dark appressed hairs like those of the stem beneath and on the margins; stalk $\frac{1}{4}$ to $\frac{1}{2}$ in. long. Flowers up to six in a cluster, on hairy pedicels. Calyx with rounded or obtuse lobes, glandular-ciliate and appressed-hairy, up to $\frac{1}{4}$ in. long, occasionally longer and acute. Corolla rose-red to scarlet, with darker markings on the upper lobes, broadly funnel-shaped, up to almost 4 in. across, the lobes five, rounded at the apex. Stamens ten, nearly as long as the corolla, downy towards the base. Ovary clad with appressed bristly hairs and glands; style glabrous. *Bot. Mag.*, t. 8478. (*s.* and *ss.* Obtusum)

Native of the Ryukyu Archipelago, commonest, according to Wilson, in the Okinawa group of islands and on Takuno island. It is not a native of Japan proper, but is cultivated in the southern parts of the country. It was introduced by Messrs Notcutt about 1909 and received an Award of Merit when they exhibited it at the Temple Show in 1911. The seedlings raised by them varied much in colour. Its best forms are some of the richest coloured of all azaleas, but it is not very hardy, and needs a warmer climate than that of Kew.

R. SCHLIPPENBACHII Maxim. [PLATE 90

A deciduous shrub up to 10 or 15 ft high; twigs bristly when young. Leaves in a terminal cluster of about five, each $2\frac{1}{2}$ to 5 in. long, $1\frac{1}{2}$ to 3 in. wide, obovate or somewhat diamond-shaped, tapering at the base, blunt or slightly notched at the apex, glabrous on both surfaces except for a few scattered bristles above and loose down beneath when young. Flowers in clusters of three to six, on glandular-hairy stalks about 1 in. long, opening in April or May. Calyx about $\frac{3}{16}$ in. long, glandular-hairy, with ovate lobes. Corolla 3 to $3\frac{1}{2}$ in. across, widely funnel-shaped, with five rounded lobes, white or soft rose, spotted with reddish brown on the three upper lobes. Stamens ten, downy towards the base. Ovary and lower part of style glandular. *Bot. Mag.*, t. 7373. (*s.* Azalea *ss.* Schlippenbachii)

Native mainly of Korea, but also found in bordering parts of Russia and China; long cultivated in Japan, but not indigenous there. It was discovered by Baron Schlippenbach on the coast of east Korea in 1854 and collected again nine years later in the Korean archipelago by Richard Oldham. The first introduction was by J. G. Veitch in 1893, from a Japanese garden, but most of the cultivated plants in Britain derive from the seeds which Wilson collected in Korea in 1917 and 1918.

R. schlippenbachii is a plant of exquisite beauty, and its fine leaves, suffused with purplish red when young, are the largest and most striking among azaleas. Unfortunately it suffers from a defect very common in trees and shrubs from the mainland of north-east Asia: it is excited into growth by early warmth only to have its young growths destroyed by frost. So far as winter frost is concerned it is quite hardy, but is a hopeless subject except in warm or elevated districts where spring frosts are infrequent. Being an inhabitant of thin oakwoods in a region with hot and sunny summers it needs plenty of light and does not thrive in very acid soils. A light soil enriched with leaf-mould is better than a peaty one.

R. *schlippenbachii* received an Award of Merit when shown by Messrs Veitch in 1896. A form with Rhodamine Pink flowers from Bodnant was given a First Class Certificate in 1944, and the clone 'Prince Charming' from Leonardslee received the same award in 1965 when shown by Sir Giles Loder. In this too the colour of the flowers is Rhodamine Pink.

R. SCINTILLANS Balf. f. & W. W. Sm.

An evergreen shrub up to 3½ ft high, of twiggy habit; young shoots very slender, erect, densely scaly. Leaves oblong-lanceolate, abruptly pointed, tapered at the base, ¼ to ¾ in. long, ⅙ to ⅜ in. wide, dark green above, greyish beneath, scaly on both sides; stalk 1/16 to ⅛ in. long. Flowers three to six in a terminal cluster 1½ in. wide, opening in April. Calyx very small but distinctly lobed,

RHODODENDRON SCINTILLANS

scaly, fringed towards the end of the lobes; flower-stalk very short and scaly. Corolla lavender-blue to purplish blue, ¾ to 1 in. wide, the ovate lobes sometimes reaching to within ⅛ in. of the base; throat downy; stamens ten, downy at the base, ½ in. long. Ovary scaly; style purple, distinctly longer than the stamens, glabrous. (*s.* Lapponicum)

Native of N.W. Yunnan and S.W. Szechwan; discovered by Forrest on the pass between Lankiung and Hoching and introduced by him from the type-locality in 1913 (F.10014). It is a characteristic species of the rhododendron moorlands, found at altitudes up to 14,500 ft. The undersides of the leaves resemble those of R. *impeditum*, the scales being spaced at about their own diameter apart, with a green surface between, but the leaves are relatively narrower, and it is taller-growing. The flowers vary in colour from pale lavender-blue to a deep near-blue, and both extremes are attractive; they are frost-resistant and the plant itself is of course completely hardy. A lavender-blue form was awarded a First Class Certificate when shown from Exbury on May 1, 1934.

In their revision of the Lapponicum group (1975), M. N. and W. R. Philipson submerge R. *scintillans* in R. POLYCLADUM Franch.

R. SEARSIAE Rehd. & Wils.

An evergreen shrub 6 to 10 ft high; young shoots freely set with pale scales, prominently warted the following year. Leaves narrowly oblong or oblanceolate, slenderly pointed, much tapered at each end, 2 to 3½ in. long, ½ to ⅞ in. wide, dark green and at first scaly above, becoming glabrous; glaucous beneath, freely sprinkled with small yellowish scales, amongst which are scattered large brown ones; margins slightly decurved; stalk ¼ to ⅓ in. long, scaly. Flowers produced during late April and May in terminal clusters of four to eight, occasionally augmented by others from the uppermost leaf-axils; common flower-stalk ¼ to ½ in. long; individual stalks ⅓ to ⅝ in. long, scaly. Calyx very scaly, small, five-lobed. Corolla 1 to 1½ in. long, 1½ to 2 in. wide, the base funnel-shaped, the five lobes ovate-oblong, rounded at the end; pale lavender to almost white spotted with pale green, not scaly outside. Stamens ten, of varying length, downy towards but not at the base; anthers pale brown; style glabrous, slightly overtopping the stamens. *Bot. Mag.*, t. 8993. (*s.* Triflorum *ss.* Yunnanense)

Native of W. Szechwan; discovered by Wilson on the Wa-shan in 1908 and introduced by him. It is distinguished from its allies by the undersides of the leaves, which show a mixture of closely arranged yellow and brown scales on a glaucous ground. In R. *zaleucum* the leaves are also glaucous beneath—more intensely so than in R. *searsiae*—but the scales are more widely spaced, mostly twice to four times their own diameter apart, usually less than their own diameter apart in R. *searsiae*. A pretty and quite hardy species.

R. SELENSE Franch.

R. *metrium* Balf. f. & Forr.; R. *nanothamnum* Balf. f. & Forr.; R. *axium* Balf. f. & Forr.; R. *chalarocladum* Balf. f. & Forr.; R. *dolerum* Balf. f. & Forr.

An evergreen shrub up to 10 ft high; branchlets slender, usually glandular, hairy or glabrous. Leaves oblong to oval or obovate, 1 to 3½ in. long, ½ to 1½ in. wide, rounded or obtuse at both ends, or sometimes slightly cordate at the base, dark green and glabrous or almost so above, underside paler and sometimes slightly glaucous, glabrous, or sometimes with a thin coating of hairs which often wears off by late summer; petiole up to 1⅛ in. long. Flowers in terminal clusters of four to eight, opening in April or May; pedicels up to 1⅛ in. long, glandular and sometimes hairy. Calyx up to ¼ in. long, more or less glandular, sometimes hairy on the margin. Corolla between funnel-shaped and bell-shaped, 1½ to 1¾ in. long and wide, five-lobed, varying in colour from white to various shades of rose, usually unspotted, but often with a crimson blotch at the base. Ovary densely glandular, sometimes slightly hairy also; style glabrous, sometimes slightly glandular at the base. (*s.* Thomsonii *ss.* Selense)

Native of N.W. Yunnan, bordering parts of S.E. Tibet, and of S.W. Szechwan; discovered by the French missionary Soulié on the Se La, Mekong–Salween divide, in 1895; introduced by Forrest from the same area in 1917. It is a somewhat variable species in shape and size of leaf, degree of glandularity, flowercolour, etc., and numerous species, now included in R. *selense*, were made out of its fluctuations. It is one of those species that is rarely seen in cultivation outside the gardens where it was raised from the wild seed. Growing by the thousand on its native mountainsides it must be a lovely sight when in flower, but the individual plant makes little display and is very slow to reach flowering age.

The following varieties are retained by Cowan and Davidian in their revision of the Thomsonii series;

var. DUSEIMATUM (Balf. f. & Forr.) Cowan & Davidian R. *duseimatum* Balf. f. & Forr.—Ovary tomentose. Leaves oblong-lanceloate, 3 to 4 in. long.

var. PAGOPHILUM (Balf. f. & Ward) Cowan & Davidian R. *pagophilum* Balf. f. & Ward—This name is retained by Cowan and Davidian for plants with small elliptic leaves and small flowers (usually dark rose to crimson in colour). In the type, the leaves were about 2 in. long and 1⅛ in. wide.

var. PROBUM (Balf. f. & Forr.) Cowan & Davidian R. *probum* Balf. f. & Forr.—A form with white, unmarked flowers.

R. DASYCLADUM Balf. f. & W. W. Sm. R. *rhaibocarpum* Balf. f. & W. W. Sm.—This is nearly related to R. *selense*, but the young shoots and petioles are very bristly-glandular. The corolla is white, rose, or lilac-pink, with a crimson blotch at the base. It is usually a tall shrub in cultivation, and flowers quite freely. The deeper-coloured forms are attractive. It occurs wild within the area of R. *selense*.

R. SETIFERUM Balf. f. & Forr.—Near to R. *dasycladum*, and with the same bristly-glandular branchlets and petioles, but with thick, leathery leaves. It was introduced by Forrest under F.14006 from the Salween–Mekong divide. The flowers are white, with crimson markings at the base.

R. SEMIBARBATUM Maxim.

A deciduous shrub 2 to 8 ft high with downy and hairy, glandular young shoots. Leaves oval to ovate, very variable in size from ¾ to 2 in. long, ⅜ to 1 in. wide, bluntish at the apex, rounded or nearly so at the base, minutely toothed on the margins and slightly bristly on the midrib and veins beneath; stalk up to ⅜ in long, downy and bristly. Flowers solitary, produced from lateral buds near the ends of the branchlets (the terminal bud is a growth-bud); pedicels ⅛ in. or slightly more long, glandular and bristly, like the short calyx. Corolla rotate with a short tube and five rounded, spreading lobes, white or yellowish white, freely dotted with red at the base, about ¾ in. across. Stamens five, very unequal, the three lower ones glabrous or nearly so, the other two much shorter and nearly covered with bristles. Ovary globose, bristly in the upper part; style glabrous. *Bot. Mag.*, t. 9147. (*s.* Semibarbatum)

Native of central and southern Japan; described by Maximowicz from a specimen collected by Tschonoski; it was introduced by him to St Petersburg, but did not reach Britain until Wilson sent seeds in 1914, which were distributed by the Arnold Arboretum. As a garden plant it has little to recommend it, but it is of considerable botanical interest as a member of the Azaleastrum group (see p. 588).

R. SEROTINUM Hutch.

An evergreen shrub of loose straggling habit; young shoots and leaves glabrous. Leaves oval-oblong, rounded to shallowly cordate at the base, rounded and mucronate at the apex, 3 to 7 in. long, 1¼ to 2¾ in wide, dull green above, rather glaucous beneath; stalk ¾ to 1½ in. long. Truss composed of six to eight flowers which are fragrant. Calyx small, ⅓ in. wide, with shallow rounded lobes; flower-stalk slightly glandular, 1 to 1¾ in. long. Corolla 3 to 3½ in. wide, funnel-shaped at the base, seven-lobed, the lobes spreading, notched in the middle, white flushed with rose and glandular outside, blotched and stained with red inside the funnel. Stamens fourteen to sixteen, of unequal length, their stalks white and downy at the base; anthers pale brown. Ovary and style glandular. *Bot. Mag.*, t. 8841. (*s.* and *ss.* Fortunei)

This species was introduced to Kew in 1889 from the Jardin des Plantes, Paris, where it was raised by seeds collected by Delavay in Yunnan. It came as R. *decorum* and remained under that name until the true R. *decorum* of Wilson's introduction flowered and showed the differences. The real R. *decorum*, as is now well known, is a sturdy, compact bush; R. *serotinum* is so lanky and so loth to branch that a plant was trained up a pillar at Kew as a sort of climber. The blotch at the base of the corolla and the reddish stains are further distinctions. Lastly it flowers in September, a fact which explains its specific name. Otherwise the two are very much alike in their blossom. It is quite hardy and gives a noble truss of blossom as the figure above quoted shows.

R. SERPYLLIFOLIUM (A. Gray) Miq.
Azalea serpyllifolia A. Gray

A low evergreen azalea, perhaps 2 or 3 ft high, with the slender wiry stems covered thickly with appressed, linear, dark brown bristles, that point towards the end of the shoot. Leaves narrowly oval or obovate, ¼ to ¾ in. long, ⅛ to ¼ in. wide, dark green, and thinly furnished above and on the margins with bristly hairs, paler and with a few bristles beneath, base tapering to a very short stalk. Flowers mostly solitary at the end of short twigs, on pedicels ⅛ in. or less long, opening in May. Calyx small, with five rounded bristly lobes. Corolla pale rose or white, funnel-shaped, about ¾ in. across, with five oblong lobes. Stamens five. Ovary clad with appressed hairs; style glabrous. *Bot. Mag.*, t. 7503. (*s*. Azalea *ss*. Obtusum)

Native of central and southern Japan. This quaint and pretty little shrub is not often seen, though it is said to be quite hardy. It was introduced for Messrs Veitch by Charles Maries, and flowered with them in 1882. The white-flowered form has been distinguished as f. ALBIFLORUM Makino.

R. SETOSUM D. Don

A dwarf evergreen shrub 6 to 12 in. high, of close, bushy habit; young shoots densely clothed with pale bristles and minute down. Leaves oblong, tapered at the base, rounded at the apex, ⅜ to ⅝ in. long, bristly on the margins, very scaly above, rather glaucous and less scaly beneath. Flowers three to eight in a terminal cluster; pedicels scaly, slender, about ¼ in. long. Calyx comparatively large, scaly and downy, divided almost to the base into five ovate lobes about ¼ in. long. Corolla about 1 in. across, reddish purple, lobed to two-thirds of its depth. Stamens ten, hairy at the base. Ovary scaly; style glabrous. *Bot. Mag.*, t. 8523.

Native of the Himalaya as far west as Kumaon; introduced in 1825. It is an alpine rhododendron, found at altitudes of up to 16,000 ft. 'It is the *Tsallu* of the Sikkim Bhoteas and Tibetans, who attribute the oppression and headaches attending the crossing of the loftiest passes of Eastern Himalaya to the strongly resinous odour of this and of R. *anthopogon*, Wall. (*Palu* of the natives). The species certainly abounds near the summits of all the passes, and after hot sunshine fills the atmosphere with its powerful aroma, far too heavy to be agreeable, and greatly aggravating the discomforts of toiling in the rarefied medium of these elevations' (Hooker).

R. *setosum* is at present placed in the Lapponicum series, though its deeply lobed corolla, large calyx, and bristly stems are not in keeping with that series. It is an interesting species, with brightly coloured flowers, but is difficult to cultivate successfully in southern England, where it misses its winter covering of snow and is often excited into growth too early.

R. SHEPHERDII Nutt.

It seems doubtful if the real R. *shepherdii* be now in cultivation, but as plants under the name exist in gardens and as the name itself is familiar to rhododendron lovers, a few words may be given to it. The true plant was discovered in 1850 in the Assam Himalaya by Booth, on the notable journey during which he found R. *nuttallii*, R. *boothii*, and R. *hookeri*. Nuttall, when describing the various new species of the journey, was only able to put on record the characters of the leaves and leaf-buds of R. *shepherdii*. According to the *Botanical Magazine* of 1859, the figure which appeared there was made from a plant which Nuttall himself had flowered at Nutgrove in Cheshire. As no authentic specimen of the wild R. *shepherdii* appears to exist in the leading herbaria, this figure must be regarded as the base on which this rhododendron as a species stands (*Bot. Mag.*, t. 5125).

R. SHERRIFFII Cowan

An evergreen shrub or small tree up to 20 ft high in the wild; young stems green, with scattered short, black bristles. Leaves oblong or oblong-ovate, obtuse at the apex, slightly cordate at the base, 2 to 3 in. long, 1 to 1½ in. wide, deep dull green above, lateral veins slightly impressed, lower surface, except the midrib, covered with a thick brown indumentum made up of long-rayed hairs with ribbon-like arms; petioles bristly like the young branchlets. Flowers in a racemose cluster of three or four on pedicels about ½ in. long. Calyx crimson, cup-shaped, shallow, with rounded usually rather irregular lobes. Corolla tubular-campanulate, fleshy, deep crimson, up to 1⅞ in. long, ⅝ to ⅞ in. wide at the mouth, with five dark nectar-pouches at the base. Stamens ten, with glabrous filaments. Ovary oblong, glabrous; style exserted, glabrous. *Bot. Mag.*, n.s., t. 337.

R. *sherriffii* was discovered by Ludlow and Sherriff in 1936 in the Tibetan Himalaya near Lung, in the valley of the Chayul Chu, one of the feeders of the Subansiri, growing at 11,000 to 12,500 ft, and was introduced by them in the same year (L. & S. 2751). In describing this species Dr Cowan remarked 'This is a plant noteworthy not only for beauty of flower but also for unusual botanical characteristics. So distinctive is it that it does not fit well into any recognised series and should perhaps be placed alone in a new series. . . . If no thick in-dumentum were present on the leaf, the shape would suggest that *Rh. sherriffii* might well be placed in the Thomsonii series.' It is provisionally placed in the Campanulatum series, near R. *fulgens*.

The truss figured in the *Botanical Magazine* is from a plant in the Windsor collection, raised originally at Tower Court from L. & S. 2751. The species received an Award of Merit when shown by the Crown Estate Commissioners on March 8, 1966. As this date indicates, it is an early-flowering species.

R. SIDEROPHYLLUM Franch.

R. *ionandrum* Balf. f.; R. *jahandiezii* Lévl.; R. *leucandrum* Lévl.; R. *obscurum* Balf. f.; R. *rubropunctatum* Lévl. & Van.

An evergreen shrub 4 to 9 ft high; young wood slightly scaly. Leaves aromatic, oval-lanceolate, tapering about equally to each end, 1½ to 2½ in. long, ⅜ to ⅝ in. wide, bright green and slightly scaly above, densely scaly beneath, the scales yellowish; stalk ⅛ in. long. Flowers produced during May in terminal and axillary clusters of six to eight; pedicels about ¾ in. long, scaly. Calyx minute. Corolla of a pale blush tint with two groups of brown spots on the upper side, up to 1½ in. across, flat, open, short-tubed. Stamens ten, pinkish white, hairy at the base, anthers dark red. Ovary scaly; style glabrous. (*s.* Triflorum *ss.* Yunnanense)

Native of Yunnan, S.W. Szechwan, and Kweichow; probably first introduced by Forrest. It belongs to the same group as R. *yunnanense*, and its flowers are equally pretty. But the leaves are never bristly above, as they often are in R. *yunnanense*, they are more scaly beneath, the stamens are not so much pro-truded beyond the corolla as in that species; the flowers are smaller and earlier.

It frequently produces a considerable number of flower clusters densely packed at the end of the shoot.

R. *siderophyllum* received an Award of Merit when shown by Edmund de Rothschild, Exbury, on March 20, 1945.

R. SIMSII Planch.

Azalea indica sens. Sims in *Bot. Mag.*, t. 1480, not L.; R. *indicum* var. *simsii* (Planch.) Maxim.; R. *indicum* of many authors, in part, not (L.) Sweet

An evergreen or semi-evergreen shrub 3 to 8 ft high in the wild; young shoots clad with appressed, flattened, forward-pointing hairs. Spring leaves (those on the lower part of the shoot) elliptic, oblong-elliptic, or ovate, up to 2 in. long and 1 in. or slightly more wide, acute to acuminate at the apex, cuneate at the base, often deciduous; summer leaves (those near the apex of the shoot) leathery, more persistent than the spring leaves, obovate to oblanceolate, up to 1½ in. long and ½ in. wide; both kinds dull green above, paler beneath, clad on both sides, but more densely beneath, with appressed bristly hairs; the same type of hair covers the petiole, which is about ¼ in. long or slightly shorter. Flowers opening in May, in terminal clusters of two or three, sometimes up to five or six, on densely appressed-bristly stalks up to ⅜ in. long. Lobes of calyx ovate or triangular, sometimes as much as ¼ in. long but usually somewhat shorter, ciliate on the margin. Corolla five-lobed, broadly funnel-shaped, up to 2 in. wide on wild plants, coloured in some shade of red, with darker markings on the central or all three upper lobes. Stamens normally ten, rarely eight, never fewer. Ovary appressed-bristly; style glabrous. *Bot. Mag.*, t. 1480. (s. Azalea ss. Obtusum)

Native of southern and central China as far west as Yunnan and as far south and east as Hong Kong; also of Formosa, Burma, Thailand, and bordering territories. According to Wilson it is common in the area of the Yangtse valley from near Ningpo to Mount Omei, in rocky places, on cliffs, and in thin dry woods and thickets. In Burma it is found on both branches of the Irrawaddy above the confluence near Myitkyina, growing on cliffs and rocks along the mainstreams and their tributaries, even where the surrounding vegetation is Indo-Malayan hill jungle, and is often completely submerged during the rainy season. Farrer writes of it as 'smeared like an interminable bloodstain' along both banks of the Ngaw Chang, a tributary of the eastern branch, and Kingdon Ward likened it in flower to 'the glow from an active volcano at night'.

In China, R. *simsii* has long been valued as a garden plant and was introduced from there to Europe at an uncertain date, but before 1812, in which year Sims figured it in the *Botanical Magazine* under the erroneous name *Azalea indica*, from a plant grown by a James Vere. Until the publication of Wilson's *Monograph* (1921) it was known by that name or as R. *indicum*, but the true R. *indicum* is confined to Japan and has flowers with only five stamens; it also differs in its relatively narrower, acute leaves. Wilson observes that up to about 1845 forms of R. *indicum* were more plentiful in gardens than those of R. *simsii*, but that from 1850 onwards the former rapidly dropped out of cultivation, their place being taken by the latter, which also usurped their name. The so-called Indian

Azaleas derive mainly from R. *simsii* and are raised in vast quantities every year by Belgian and Dutch growers for indoor decoration during the winter months.

R. *simsii* in its wild form is rare in gardens and of course very tender. At Wakehurst Place, Sussex, there is a plant raised from seeds collected by Forrest, but under what number is not known. Most of the seeds of R. *simsii* sent home by Forrest appear to have come from cultivated plants. In the Wakehurst specimen, which received an Award of Merit on May 23, 1933, the flowers are bright rose, nearly 3 in. across, larger than in wild plants; perhaps a hybrid.

R. SINOGRANDE Balf. f. & W. W. Sm. [PLATE 93

An evergreen shrub or a tree up to 35 ft high, the young shoots silvery grey, very stout, and up to 1 in. thick. Leaves oval or oblong, occasionally obovate, rounded at both ends, ordinarily 10 to 20 in. long, 6 to 12 in. wide, at first grey scurfy above, ultimately dark green and glabrous, silvery grey beneath with a closely appressed scurf, not downy or hairy in the ordinary sense of those words; midrib very prominent beneath as are also the fourteen to sixteen pairs of roughly parallel veins springing from it; stalk very stout (up to ½ in. thick) 1 to 2 in. long. Flowers produced in April in a racemose truss of twenty to thirty, and about 9 in. wide; pedicels about 1½ in. long, densely woolly. Calyx woolly, fringed with small teeth. Corolla bell-shaped, fleshy, dull creamy white to soft yellow, marked with red patches at the base, 2 in. wide, eight- to ten-lobed, the lobes ¾ in. wide, notched. Stamens eighteen or twenty, downy towards the base, shorter than the corolla. Ovary covered with reddish down; style glabrous; stigma ⅖ in. wide. *Bot. Mag.*, t. 8973. (*s.* Grande)

R. *sinogrande* was discovered by Forrest in 1912, growing at 11,000 ft on the western flank of the Shweli–Salween divide, latitude 25° 20′ N. The plants were in fruit and from them the species was introduced to gardens (F.9021). In this area, on the borders between Burma and mid-Yunnan, R. *sinogrande* is at the south-eastern extremity of its area. From here it ranges along the mountains between the Salween and the eastern branch of the Irrawaddy to some way north of 28° and is also found east of the Salween in this latitude. Most of Forrest's later sendings are from this northeastern corner, where Burma, China and Tibet adjoin. Westward it ranges across the upper Irrawaddy to the Delei valley in the Mishmi Hills, Assam, but its western limit is uncertain.

'R. *sinogrande* sometimes forms forests single-handed. We passed through whole glades of its gnarled and twisted branches, when its pale yellow globes were alight and shining brightly under the dark canopy of leaves. Some of the trunks were twenty-four inches round. . . . One advantage about R. *sinogrande* is the lateness of its new growth. The great spear-headed buds burst in July, and even in August one can pick out the trees a mile away by the plumes of silver foliage shooting up from ruby-red tubes' (Kingdon Ward, *Plant Hunting on the Edge of the World*, p. 277, in reference to R. *sinogrande* in the Mishmi Hills).

Botanically this is the eastern counterpart of R. *grande*, differing in the eglandular ovary and pedicels and the shorter and stouter style. In leaf it is much the finer species and in that respect the most splendid and remarkable of all rhododendrons, or indeed of all woody plants hardy in this country. In the Cornish woods, where it first faced the English climate, leaves 2½ ft long and 1 ft or more wide have been produced on young plants. It first flowered at Heligan in Cornwall in May 1919. It grows fastest and has attained the largest size in the Atlantic zone, but in woodland gardens south of London it is perfectly at home and flowers just as well as in the milder parts. It is nearly hardy and in some forms completely so. In the Windsor collection some plants were cut to the ground by the freezing winds of February 1956, but others were unharmed or almost so, and none was actually killed (*R.C.Y.B. 1957*, p. 62).

R. *sinogrande* was awarded a First Class Certificate when shown by G. H. Johnstone, Trewithen, Cornwall, on March 9, 1926. Four years earlier, Dame Alice Godman had shown a truss from a plant grown under glass at South Lodge, Sussex, and the species had then received an Award of Merit as a tender rhododendron. The plant was a gift from J. C. Williams of Caerhays and also provided the truss figured in the *Botanical Magazine*.

var. BOREALE Tagg & Forr.—Described as having rather more leathery and smaller leaves than in the type and flowers soft yellow throughout without markings or pale yellow with a crimson blotch at the base. Introduced by Forrest in 1922 (F.21750). It is sometimes referred to as the 'northern form' of *R. sinogrande* (it was collected in latitude 28° 18′ N.), but Forrest's 20387, introduced the previous year, came from still farther north and is not mentioned in the description of var. *boreale*.

R. SMIRNOWII Trautv.

A sturdy evergreen shrub 4 to 12 ft high in cultivation, usually wider than it is high, but described in the wild as a tree-like shrub 15 to 20 ft high; young shoots thick, and clothed with a soft white felt. Leaves narrowly oblong, tapered at the base, blunt at the apex, 4 to 7 in. long, 1 to 2 in. wide, thick and leathery, dark green, soon becoming glabrous above; lower surface covered with a thick, soft felt, at first almost pure white, finally pale brown; stalk ¼ to ¾ in. long. Flowers produced during May or June in fine trusses 4 to 6 in. through; pedicels 1 to 1½ in. long, slightly downy. Calyx very small, with five rounded lobes. Corolla bright purplish rose 2 to 3 in. across, broadly funnel-shaped, the five rounded lobes with beautifully frilled margins. Stamens ten, downy at the base. Ovary clad with white wool; style glabrous. *Bot. Mag.*, t. 7495. (*s. Ponticum ss.* Caucasicum)

Native of north-east Asiatic Turkey, especially around Artvin on the river Coruh, where it reaches to the tree-line; it is not certain whether it also occurs in bordering parts of Russia. It was discovered by Baron Ungern-Sternberg in 1885 and introduced to Kew the following year by way of St Petersburg. The species is distinct in the very thick white felt on the lower surface of its leaves, resembling in this respect *R. ungernii* and species of the Argrophyllum subseries of the Arboreum series. It is perfectly hardy, and would be more valued if it had come from China. Some plants distributed as *P. smirnowii* are *R. ungernii*.

R. *smirnowii* and *R. ungernii* are of botanical interest as relict species, more closely allied to east Asiatic rhododendrons than to their neighbours. *R. ponticum* and *R. caucasicum*.

R. SOULIEI Franch.   [PLATE 91
R. *cordatum* Lévl.

An evergreen bush 5 to 10 ft high; young shoots purplish, they and flower-stalks glandular and viscid. Leaves 2 to 3½ in long, 1 to 2 in. wide; broadly ovate, with a heart-shaped or truncate base and a blunt, glandular tip, of a distinct glaucous, somewhat metallic hue, quite glabrous on both surfaces; stalk glandular when young, ½ to ¾ in. long. Flowers in a terminal cluster, about six in each, opening in May; pedicels 1½ to 2 in. long. Calyx up to ¼ in. long, glandular at least on the margins of the lobes, sometimes throughout. Corolla very open and saucer-shaped, five- or six-lobed, soft rosy pink or white flushed with pink, 2 to 3 in. across. Stamens eight or ten. Ovary glandular; style glandular to the tip. *Bot. Mag.*, t. 8622.   (*s.* Thomsonii *ss.* Souliei)

Native of W. Szechwan; discovered by the French missionary Soulié near Kangting (Tatsienlu) and introduced by Wilson in 1903 when collecting for Messrs Veitch and also cultivated from the seeds he sent a few years later, during his first expedition for the Arnold Arboretum. Some of the plants raised at Kew flowered when only four years old. It is a very hardy rhododendron, best planted in open woodland or slight shade, as it needs plenty of light if it is to flower freely. It is also one of the most beautiful, with flowers of exquisite shape and colouring set off by foliage of a rich sea-green. It has been awarded a First Class Certificate on three occasions. The first went to a plant 9 in. high, shown by Messrs Veitch on May 18, 1909; flowers bright rose suffused on a paler ground. The second was given to a form with flowers of a deeper pink, shown from Exbury on May 19, 1936, under the name 'Exbury Pink'. The third award was to 'Windsor Park', shown by the Crown Estate Commissioners, Windsor Great Park, on May 22, 1951; truss of nine flowers, white with a pink flush deepening at the margins, and with a small crimson blotch at the base of the three upper lobes.

R. PURALBUM Balf. f. & W. W. Sm.—Flowers pure white, otherwise not differing botanically from R. *souliei*. It was introduced by Forrest in 1913 from the mountains in the north-east of the Yangtse bend, and was discovered by him. A plant from the original introduction (F. 10616) flowers freely in the Edinburgh Botanic Garden, but the species is rare in gardens.

R. SPERABILE Balf. f. & Farrer

An evergreen shrub 3 to 9 ft high of stiff habit; young shoots clothed with loose and (at first) white wool and glandular bristles. Leaves lanceolate or narrowly elliptic, sharply pointed, 2 to 4 in. long, ½ to 1¼ in wide, dark green and becoming glabrous above, covered beneath with a thick loose wool which is at first dull white, later reddish brown, and persists till the leaf falls; stalk ¼ to ½ in. long, woolly and glandular like the young shoot. Flowers in a terminal hemispherical truss 3 in. wide, opening in May. Calyx small, shallowly five-lobed, glandular; flower-stalk ⅝ in. long, woolly and glandular. Corolla bell-shaped, clear scarlet, about 1½ in. long and wide, five-lobed. Stamens ten, 1 to 1¼ in. long, glabrous. Ovary slender, tapered, thickly clothed like the lower part of the style with glandular hairs. *Bot. Mag.*, t. 9301. (*s.* and *ss.* Neriiflorum)

R. *sperabile* was discovered by Farrer and Cox in 1919, growing at 10,000 ft in a ravine below the Hpimaw pass in north-east Upper Burma and was introduced by them (Farrer 888); later sendings by Forrest were from the same area. According to the collectors' field notes it varies in the colour of its flowers from scarlet-crimson to deep crimson, and also in habit, from compact to leggy, but is always comparatively dwarf, and this is also true of cultivated plants, which are normally less than 6 ft high.

R. *sperabile* is hardy in the woodland gardens of Sussex and flowers freely. It is not so fine a species as R. *neriiflorum*, but the dwarfest and most compact forms deserve to be propagated. It received an Award of Merit when shown by Lionel de Rothschild, Exbury, on May 5, 1925 (from Farrer 888).

A vigorous and tall-growing form of R. *sperabile* was introduced by Kingdon Ward in 1926 from the Di Chu valley on the borders between Assam, Tibet, and Burma (KW 7124).

var. WEIHSIENSE Tagg & Forr.—Leaves relatively narrower, less lanceolate, sometimes elongate elliptic, with a paler and thinner indumentum. Introduced by Forrest from the Mekong–Salween divide west of Weihsi. It grows taller than the typical form and is of rather sparse habit. The name var. *chimiliense* was given to Forrest's 26478, from the Chimi-li pass on the Nmai–Salween divide, but the name was apparently never published. In some of the cultivated plants from this batch of seed the leaves are almost glabrous beneath.

R. SPERABILIOIDES Tagg & Forr.—Resembling the above in general appearance this differs in having no glands on the ovary, leaf-stalk, and young shoots. The stamens also are hairy at the base. Flowers of various shades of crimson, borne in trusses of six to ten flowers, the corolla 1 to 1½ in long. A native of the Tsarong region of S.E. Tibet on the Salween–Kiuchiang divide; discovered by Forrest and introduced by him in 1921. It occurs at higher altitudes than R. *sperabile*—12,000 to 13,000 ft—and is always of dwarf habit in cultivation, to about 4 ft high. It received an Award of Merit on April 4, 1933, when shown from Exbury.

R. SPICIFERUM Franch.

R. *pubescens* Balf. f. & Forr.

A small shrub up to 6 ft high; young stems slender, scaly and clad with whitish down interspersed with longer, bristly hairs. Leaves mostly lanceolate to narrowly so, or narrow-oblong, ½ to 1½ in. long, up to ⅜ in. wide, acute to obtuse or rounded at the apex, mucronate, margins revolute, dark green above, paler beneath, clad on both sides with the same mixture of scales and two types of hair seen on the young stems, but the upper surface becoming more or less glabrous. Flowers two or three together in clusters from the uppermost leaf-axils of the previous year's shoots, opening in March or April; pedicels about ¼ in. long, hairy and scaly. Calyx with five short, sometimes very short and indistinct, lobes. Corolla varying from pink to almost white, widely funnel-shaped, about ½ in. long and ⅜ in. wide at the mouth, scaly outside. Stamens ten, exserted, filaments usually hairy at the base. Ovary downy and scaly; style glabrous, or downy at the base. *Bot. Mag.*, t. 9319.   (*s.* Scabrifolium)

Native of the drier parts of Yunnan and of S.W. Szechwan and Kweichow; discovered by Père Delavay near Yunnan-fu in 1891. In 1918 Forrest collected a specimen in the Muli area of S.W. Szechwan from which Sir Isaac Bayley Balfour described *R. pubescens*, now included in *R. spiciferum*. But the first introduction was apparently by Kingdon Ward, also from the Muli area, in 1921. It is closely allied to *R. scabrifolium*, differing in its much smaller and relatively narrower leaves. It is a pretty species, slightly tender and best grown in a sunny sheltered position. Like all the members of the Scabrifolium series it is found wild in open situations or light woodland in regions of comparatively low rainfall.

The Award of Merit was given on April 19, 1955, to the clone 'Fine Bristles', with white flowers suffused with varying shades of Persian Rose; it was shown by the Crown Estate Commissioners, Windsor Great Park.

R. SPINULIFERUM Franch.

R. duclouxii Lévl.; *R. fuchsiaeflorum* Lévl.; *R. scabrifolium* var. *pauciflorum* Franch.

An evergreen shrub 3 to 8 ft high, the young shoots covered with pale hairs and bristles. Leaves lanceolate or oblanceolate, pointed at the apex, wedge-shaped at the base, 1½ to 2¼ in. long, ½ to ¾ in. wide, somewhat hooded and puckered above, with a few hairs near the margin, scaly and hairy beneath;

RHODODENDRON SPINULIFERUM

stalk ¼ in. long. Flowers in clusters, terminal and from the upper leaf-axils, opening in April; pedicels downy, about ¼ in. long. Calyx very short, downy. Corolla tubular, usually brick-red, about 1 in. long and ½ in. wide, the five ovate lobes being erect or pressing inwards round the ten glabrous stamens which protrude about ¼ in. beyond them. Ovary and base of style downy. *Bot. Mag.*, t. 8408. (*s.* Scabrifolium)

Native of Yunnan, China; discovered by Delavay, and introduced to France by Maurice de Vilmorin in 1907, thence to Kew in 1910. The fears at first expressed as to its probable tenderness have not been borne out by experience. At Kew it has proved to be quite hardy. In the tubular shape of the corolla, which narrows rather than expands towards the mouth, the species resembles R. *keysii*.

R. STAMINEUM Franch.

R. *pittosporaefolium* Hemsl.

An evergreen shrub 6 to 15 ft high; young shoots glabrous, slender, brown. Leaves clustered at the end of the twig, narrowly oval to oblanceolate, abruptly but sharply pointed, tapered at the base, of stiff texture, 2 to 4 in. long, 1 to 1½ in. wide, dark shining green above, paler beneath, quite glabrous: stalk ¼ to ½ in. long. Flowers fragrant, produced in April or May in clusters of three or four, each cluster springing from an axil of one of the leaves which are crowded near the end of the shoot. Calyx with five glabrous, narrow, bluntish lobes up to ⅛ in. long; flower-stalk ¾ in. long. Corolla white, stained with yellow on the three upper lobes, funnel-shaped with a slender tube, spreading into five recurved lobes, and 1 to 2 in. wide. Stamens ten, 1½ to 2 in. long, standing out far beyond the corolla, with some white down near the base. Ovary glabrous or slightly downy; style rather longer than the stamens and quite glabrous. *Bot. Mag.*, t. 8601. (*s.* Stamineum).

Native of western and central China; discovered by Père Delavay in 1882 in N.E. Yunnan, near the border with Szechwan. Wilson collected seeds in Hupeh for Messrs Veitch in the autumn of 1900, and a plant raised from these flowered at Caerhays in 1911. He reintroduced it in 1910, during his second expedition for the Arnold Arboretum, this time from Mt Omei in W. Szechwan. According to Wilson it is a low-level rhododendron, growing at 4,000 to 6,000 ft, and usually found in hot, moist valleys among other shrubs, most of them evergreen.

R. *stamineum* is the type of an interesting series, further discussed on page 588. It received an Award of Merit as a shrub for the cool greenhouse when exhibited by the Crown Estate Commissioners, Windsor Great Park, on May 24, 1971, but there is a plant at Wakehurst Place, Sussex, 10 ft high in a sheltered place.

R. STEWARTIANUM Diels.

R. *aiolosalpinx* Balf. f. & Farrer; R. *nipholobum* Balf. f. & Farrer

An evergreen shrub up to 10 ft high, young shoots glabrous. Leaves obovate to oval, 2 to 4½ in. long, more or less rounded at both ends, grey-green above, undersurface covered with a powdery indumentum or with a thin veil of hairs; stalk about ¼ in. long. Flowers in trusses of three to seven, opening in February, March, or April. Corolla tubular-campanulate, 1¾ in. long and wide, with five rounded, notched lobes; the colour, according to Farrer, ranging from 'cream and pure white through all flushes and shades of pink to rich deep rose'; another collector found plants with 'scarlet red' flowers, and others are described as 'deep crimson'. Stamens ten, downy at the base. Ovary glandular; style glabrous. (*s.* and *ss.* Thomsonii)

Native of N.E. Burma and of bordering parts of S.E. Tibet and N.W. Yunnan, with its greatest concentration in the mountains between the Salween and the upper eastern Irrawaddy, from 26° 20′ N. to about 28° 50′ N.; discovered by Forrest in 1904; introduced by Farrer and Cox in 1919 from the Chimi-li and simultaneously by Kingdon Ward from Imaw Bum, a few miles farther west. Forrest sent numerous batches of seed during the 1920s, some from the Chimi-li but mostly from farther north. Kingdon Ward's 8294 from the Mishmi Hills, Assam, is near to R. *stewartianum*.

R. *stewartianum* first flowered in the spring of 1930 at Exbury, Logan, and Bodnant, and received an Award of Merit when shown from the first-named garden on March 20, 1934. It is remarkably variable in the colour of its flowers and Farrer found, in one area, plants growing together bearing flowers of nearly all the shades mentioned above. In some plants the colour is deepest near the margin of the corolla, paling downwards. Although quite hardy, R. *stewartianum* flowers too early to be of value for most gardens—in some years it is in full bloom in February.

R. ECLECTEUM Balf. f. & Forr.—Allied to R. *stewartianum*, but with the leaves always glabrous beneath except for the sometimes hairy midrib. Also, in its typical state, it is very easily distinguished by its almost sessile, obovate leaves, slightly cordate at the base; in the original description their shape was likened to that of a Jargonelle pear. It appears to be a native mainly of the region from the Mekong–Salween divide around Ka-kar-po westward to upper Burma but has also been collected in S.W. Szechwan. The variation in colour is as remarkable as it is in R. *stewartianum*. Perhaps the finest, and certainly the most distinct, are those with pure white flowers, with blackberry-coloured nectar-pouches and anthers. Such is Kingdon Ward's 6869, from the Seinghku valley, north-west upper Burma. His 6900, from the same area, has flowers of a deep glowing pink. Unfortunately it is just as early-flowering as R. *stewartianum*.

var. BELLATULUM Tagg—Leaves with distinct petiole, more or less oblong, rounded or obtuse at the base.

var. BRACHYANDRUM (Balf. f. & Forr.) Tagg R. *brachyandrum* Balf. f. & Forr.—Flowers deep rose or crimson.

R. STRIGILLOSUM Franch.

An evergreen shrub or small tree up to 20 ft high, the young shoots and leaf-stalks clothed thickly with stiff, pale, gland-tipped bristles, $\frac{1}{6}$ in. long, which persist partially through the first winter. Leaves narrowly oblong-lanceolate, slender pointed, heart-shaped at the base, 3 to 6 in. long, $\frac{3}{4}$ to $1\frac{1}{2}$ in. wide, dull green and glabrous above, clothed with brown hairs beneath, especially on the midrib; stalk $\frac{1}{4}$ to $\frac{5}{8}$ in. long. Flowers borne in March, sometimes in February or April, in terminal trusses of up to twelve, on bristly stalks about $\frac{1}{2}$ in. long. Calyx rim-like. Corolla rich red, sometimes paler or even white, tubular-campanulate, $1\frac{1}{2}$ to 2 in. long and wide, unspotted, with dark nectar-pouches at the base. Stamens ten, glabrous. Ovary densely clad with gland-tipped bristles; style glabrous. *Bot. Mag.*, t. 8864. (*s.* Barbatum *ss.* Maculiferum)

A rare native of W. Szechwan, known only from Mt Omei, the Wa-shan, and around Pao-hsing-hsien; discovered by the French missionary David in 1869; introduced by Wilson for Messrs Veitch in 1904. It is a striking plant, easily recognisable even when out of flower by its narrow, drooping, bristly leaves. It is hardy in a sheltered position, but flowers too early in the year to be suitable for general planting. The colour of cultivated plants is usually a rich red. It received an Award of Merit when shown from Bodnant on February 27, 1923.

R. SULFUREUM Franch.

R. *commodum* Balf. f. & Forr.; R. *theiochroum* Balf. f. & W. W. Sm.; R. *cerinum* Balf. f. & Forr.

An evergreen shrub 2 to 4 ft high; young shoots sprinkled with glands. Leaves leathery, oval, tapering to a short stalk at the base, abruptly pointed and with a mucro at the apex, $1\frac{1}{2}$ to 3 in. long, $\frac{3}{4}$ to $1\frac{1}{2}$ in. wide, dark dull green and glabrous above, glaucous and with numerous small scales beneath. Flowers closely packed in compact terminal clusters of four to eight, opening in April. Calyx scaly, deeply five-lobed, the lobes $\frac{1}{6}$ in. long, rounded at the end; flower-stalks $\frac{1}{2}$ to $\frac{2}{3}$ in. long, scaly. Corolla rather flat and open but bell-shaped at the base, about 1 in. wide, bright yellow, faintly spotted inside, scaly outside, five-lobed, the lobes roundish ovate, $\frac{3}{8}$ in. wide. Stamens ten, $\frac{3}{8}$ in. long, densely clad with white hairs at the base; anthers large, reddish brown. Ovary scaly; style glabrous, $\frac{1}{4}$ in. long, abruptly bent over. *Bot. Mag.*, t. 8946. (*s.* and *ss.* Boothii)

A native of the rainier parts of N.W. Yunnan, and of bordering areas of upper Burma, on the mountains between the upper Irrawaddy and its tributaries and the Salween; discovered by Père Delavay on the Tali range in 1886; introduced by Forrest in 1910. It grows mainly at 10,000 to 12,000 ft. on moist, shady cliff-ledges, mossy rocks, etc., or occasionally as an epiphyte on the trunks and branches of trees. Although far removed from it geographically, it is allied to R. *boothii* from the borders between Bhutan and Assam. And it is interesting that R. *dekatanum* Cowan, a species not in cultivation, was found in an area not far from the type-locality of R. *boothii*, yet is very closely allied to R. *sulfureum* (*R.Y.B. 1948*, p. 65).

R. *sulfureum* first flowered at Caerhays in April 1920. Most forms are tender, but a plant at Borde Hill in Sussex has lived in a sheltered place for at least thirty years. Plants with flowers of a vivid pure yellow are very striking, and the smooth brown bark is another attraction. R. *sulfureum* received an Award of Merit when shown by Lord Stair, Lochinch, Wigtonshire, on April 6, 1937.

R. SUTCHUENENSE Franch.

R. *praevernum* Hutch.; R. *sutchuenense* var. *geraldii* Hutch.; R. × *geraldii* (Hutch.) Ivens

A stout, evergreen shrub eventually 10 ft high; young shoots very thick (½ in. or rather more in diameter), covered with a greyish floss. Leaves 6 to 10 in. long, 1½ to 2½ in. wide, tapering at both ends, more gradually towards the base, dark green and glabrous above, paler and also glabrous beneath except for the sometimes downy midrib; stalk 1 in. long, stout, yellowish, and wrinkled. Flowers produced in March in terminal clusters 6 to 8 in. across, up to ten in each; pedicels about 1 in. long. Calyx very small glabrous, with five broad, abruptly pointed lobes. Corolla five-lobed, open bell-shaped, about 3 in. across, rosy lilac with purple spots on the upper side, and sometimes blotched at the base (commonly so in wild plants). Stamens twelve to fifteen, downy near the base; anthers very dark. Ovary and style glabrous. *Bot. Mag.*, t. 8362. (*s.* Fortunei *ss.* Davidii)

Native of W. Hupeh and E. Szechwan; described from specimens collected by Père Farges 1891–4. It was introduced to Britain by Wilson, who sent seeds to Messrs Veitch in 1900 and 1901, and it first flowered in their nursery in 1919, when 2 ft high. In 1907 Wilson sent a further supply of seed to the Arnold Arboretum, which was widely distributed.

According to Wilson, R. *sutchuenense* is common in western Hupeh at 4,500 to 7,000 ft, always found in mixed woods, often in the shade of evergreen oaks or in the company of thin-stemmed bamboos. It is one of the most striking of the Chinese rhododendrons and, like so many of Wilson's introductions, is well adapted to our average climate, needing only moderate shade and shelter. Plants from the original seed have made massive bushes wider than high and still make annual growths almost 1 ft long in a good season. The flowers are often destroyed by frost, but on a large bush the buds expand over such a long period, and are borne so profusely, that there is nearly always some display.

R. *sutchuenense* varies somewhat in the marking of the corollas, though no more so than in many other species. According to Wilson, plants with a wine-coloured blotch at the base are commoner in the wild than those in which it is merely spotted. A plant with blotched flowers was exhibited by Gerald Loder of Wakehurst Place on February 24, 1920, and was given botanical status by Hutchinson as var. *geraldii*, on the grounds that the type had unblotched flowers. A similar form received an Award of Merit when exhibited by the Misses Godman, South Lodge, Sussex, in 1945. A rather more distinct variant, raised from Wilson seeds and cultivated at Kew, was given specific rank by Hutchinson as R. *praevernum*. In this the leaves are rather narrower than in the type, more tapered at the base, and glabrous on the midrib beneath (not downy as in the type); the flowers are blotched. At the time, rhododendron growers were sceptical about this species, remarking that some of their plants from the original seed were intermediate between typical R. *sutchuenense* and R. *praevernum*. It is here regarded as part of the normal variation of the species.

R. TAGGIANUM Hutch.

An evergreen shrub 6 to 7 ft high; young shoots scaly. Leaves oblong-elliptical, tapered at both ends, 3 to 6 in. long, 1 to 2 in. wide, glaucous and with numerous tiny dark scales beneath; stalk ½ to 1 in. long, not grooved. Flowers usually three or four in a cluster, very fragrant. Calyx large, ⅝ to ¾ in. long, deeply five-lobed, the lobes oval, ⅓ to ½ in. wide; flower-stalk ¾ in. long, very scaly. Corolla pure glistening white except for a pale yellow blotch at the base inside, funnel-shaped, five-lobed, 3 to 4 in. long and wide. Stamens ten, 2 in. long, downy on the lower half. Ovary densely scaly; style as long as the stamens, scaly on the lowest third. Seed-vessel 2 in. long, glandular, the calyx persisting at the base. *Bot. Mag.*, t. 9612. (s. Maddenii ss. Megacalyx)

This beautiful species was discovered by Forrest in 1925 on the western flank of the Nmai Hka–Salween divide, upper Burma, growing as a shrub 6 to 7 ft high on the margins of open conifer forest and among scrub at 10,000 to 11,000 ft. He introduced it in the same year. Subsequently Kingdon Ward found it farther west in the Seinghku valley and in the Adung valley nearby, where it makes dense thickets along the river bank at 6,000 ft.

R. *taggianum* first flowered in the Edinburgh Botanic Garden in May 1930 (under glass), the plant, which had been raised from Forrest's 1925 seed, being then only 18 in. high. It has to be treated as a greenhouse shrub over much of the country, but is grown out-of-doors in a few favoured gardens in the Atlantic zone. A plant shown by the Marquis of Headfort on April 5, 1932, received an Award of Merit. It had been brought into early flower under glass. It was given a First Class Certificate on April 13, 1943, when shown by Murray Adams-Acton. At Brodick in the Isle of Arran, where it grows in the open, its normal flowering time is late May.

R. *taggianum* is very closely allied to R. *lindleyi*, but with a more eastern distribution. It differs in having the calyx-lobes without marginal hairs, and in other minor characters.

R. TALIENSE Franch.

An evergreen shrub up to 10 ft high in the wild, sometimes taller, with stout shoots, tomentose when young. Leaves up to 4 in. long, ¾ to 1½ in. wide, oblong-ovate to lanceolate, pointed at the apex, roundish to slightly cordate at the base, dark green above and glabrous when mature, underside coated with a dense, tawny felt; petiole about ½ in. or slightly more long, felted. Flowers in a compact terminal cluster of up to fifteen, opening in April or May; pedicels up to ⅞ in. long, densely tomentose. Calyx about 1/10 in. long. Corolla funnel-campanulate, about 1½ in. long, creamy yellow or creamy white, often flushed with rose and marked with crimson spots, five-lobed. Stamens ten, hairy in the lower third. Ovary and style glabrous. (s. and ss. Taliense)

R. *taliense* was discovered by the French missionary Delavay in the Tali range, Yunnan, and described in 1886, and was introduced by Forrest from the same area in 1910, possibly earlier. A rhododendron found by Wilson in W. Szechwan, of which seed was sent in 1908, is probably R. *taliense*. It is a rare species in gardens and of little ornament, but as the type of the Taliense series it deserves mention. From other members of the Taliense subseries it is distinguished by the densely felted leaf-stalks and flower-stalks.

R. TANASTYLUM Balf. f. & Ward

An evergreen shrub varying from 8 to 20 ft high in the wild; young shoots soon becoming glabrous. Leaves elliptic-lanceolate or oblanceolate, tapered about equally towards both ends but terminated by a short slender point, 3 to 5½ in. long, 1 to 1¾ in. wide, glabrous and green on both surfaces; stalk ½ to ⅝ in. long. Flowers borne during May in a racemose cluster of about eight; pedicels about ¾ in. long. Calyx a mere wavy rim. Corolla tubular-campanulate, 2 in. long, 1½ in. wide, deep crimson with darker spots, five-lobed, the lobes notched. Stamens ten, glabrous or slightly downy at the base; ovary and style glabrous, the latter much longer than the stamens and standing out well beyond the corolla. (*s.* and *ss.* Irroratum)

Native of the Yunnan–Burma borderland westward through upper Burma to the Mishmi Hills, Assam, and the region of the Tsangpo gorge; also of Thailand; discovered by Kingdon Ward above Hpimaw, upper Burma, and introduced by Farrer and Cox five years later from the same locality, where it grows at about 8,000 ft. In the typical form the flowers are crimson or crimson-scarlet, but other colours have been recorded by Kingdon Ward and Forrest in their field notes, e.g., 'black crimson', 'light or dark amethyst purple', or 'morose purple'. It is found at altitudes between 6,000 and 11,000 ft and is tender in some forms. It is not of much ornamental value, even the crimson forms having a hint of magenta in their colouring.

R. KENDRICKII Nutt.—This imperfectly known species was described by Nuttall in 1853 from a specimen collected by his nephew Thomas Booth in the Assam Himalaya, just east of the Bhutan frontier. The type-specimen is of foliage and fruit only, and no plant has been traced which is known for certain to have been raised from the seed Booth collected. The amplified description of R. *kendrickii* in *Notes Roy. Bot. Gard. Edin.*, Vol. 10, pp. 107–8, is based mainly on specimens collected by Cooper in Bhutan. The leaves are leathery, relatively narrow, being up to 6 in. long but not much over 1 in. wide, with wavy margins, glabrous beneath except for flock on the midrib. Truss dense, many-flowered. Corolla pink and spotted in the Cooper specimens, but dark red and unspotted in Cox and Hutchison 416, collected in 1965 in the Apa Tani valley, some 120 miles east of the type-locality (the specimen under this number perfectly matches the type in foliage). Ovary sparsely hairy, sometimes glandular.

In 1924 Kingdon Ward collected seed in the Tsangpo gorge of a rhododendron which, from the fruiting specimen, was identified as R. *kendrickii*, under which name the seed was distributed (KW 6284). However, a plant raised from this seed by Sir John Ramsden at Bulstrode Park was described by Cowan in 1936 as a new species—R. RAMSDENIANUM. It is very near to R. *kendrickii*, however.

R. TELMATEIUM Balf. f. & W. W. Sm.

An evergreen shrub of erect habit up to 3 ft high; young shoots very scurfy. Leaves elliptic-lanceolate, tapered about equally to both ends, $\frac{1}{4}$ to $\frac{1}{2}$ in. long, $\frac{1}{10}$ to $\frac{2}{16}$ in. wide, dull dark green above, pale brown below, very scaly on both sides; stalk $\frac{1}{16}$ in. long. Flowers solitary, in pairs or threes, opening in April or May. Calyx about $\frac{1}{16}$ in. long, scaly. Corolla widely funnel-shaped, $\frac{1}{2}$ in. wide, five-lobed, rosy purple, the lobes more or less scaly up the centre outside. Stamens normally ten, sometimes less, downy towards the base. Ovary scaly; style glabrous, overtopping the stamens. (s. Lapponicum)

Native of S.W. Szechwan and bordering parts of Yunnan; discovered by Forrest and introduced by him from the Chungtien plateau in 1914. It belongs to a group of the Lapponicum series in which the undersides of the leaves have a close covering of brownish or greyish scales dotted with darker, larger, stalked scales. It is a very hardy species, suitable for the rock garden, but not among the best of the series.

A rhododendron scarcely differing from R. *telmateium* was found by Ludlow and Sherriff in a dry zone of the Tibetan Himalaya.

R. DIACRITUM Balf. f. & W. W. Sm. R. *pycnocladum* Balf. f. & W. W. Sm.— Very near to R. *telmateium*, but with the leaves oblong or oblong-elliptic. The type is from the Chungtien plateau.

R. DRUMONIUM Balf. f. & Ward—Leaves similar to those of R. *diacritum*. Style slightly shorter than the stamens. Otherwise very like R. *telmateium*. The type, collected by Kingdon Ward below the Chungtien plateau, was a dwarf carpet-forming shrub, but Forrest's 13768 from the same area came from plants 2 to 2$\frac{1}{2}$ ft high.

R. TEMENIUM Balf. f. & Forr.

A shrub 2 to 5 ft high in the wild; young stems usually more or less covered with bristly hairs. Leaves short-stalked or almost sessile, oblong or oblong-elliptic or oblong-obovate, 1$\frac{1}{4}$ to 3 in. long, $\frac{3}{4}$ to 1 in. wide, rounded and mucronate at the apex, rounded or broad-cuneate at the base, of leathery texture, almost glabrous above, undersides papillose, glabrous on mature leaves except for a few floccose hairs. Flowers in terminal clusters of four to six, opening in April or May. Calyx variable in size, sometimes rim-like, sometimes $\frac{3}{8}$ in. long, coloured like the corolla, which is in some shade of red, fleshy, tubular-campanulate, 1$\frac{1}{4}$ to 1$\frac{1}{2}$ in. long, five-lobed. Ovary tomentose and glandular. (s. Neriiflorum ss. Sanguineum)

Like other members of the confusing R. *sanguineum* complex, R. *temenium* is a native mainly of the Salween–Kiuchiang and Salween–Mekong divides in the Tibetan region of Tsarong and bordering parts of Yunnan. It resembles R. *aperantum* in the glabrous and papillose undersurface of the leaves, but that species is nearly always of dwarf habit, the stems are not bristly, and the leaf-bud scales are persistent (deciduous in R. *temenium*). It comes from alpine elevations and makes a compact, hardy bush.

subsp. ALBIPETALUM Cowan—Flowers white. Introduced by Rock.

subsp. CHRYSANTHEMUM Cowan—Flowers yellow. Ovary tomentose, but not glandular. Introduced by Rock. The clone 'Cruachan', raised from his no. 22272, received an Award of Merit on April 22, 1958, and a First Class Certificate in 1964, on both occasions when shown by Mrs K. L. Kenneth, Tich-an-Rudha, Ardrishaig; the flowers are sulphur-yellow. The original plant has since died. The subsp. GILVUM Cowan is similar, but the ovary is glandular.

subsp. GLAPHYRUM (Balf. f. & Forr.) Cowan R. *glaphyrum* Balf. f. & Forr. —Flowers cream or rose or a blend of the two. Ovary eglandular. Introduced by Forrest.

subsp. POTHINUM (Balf. f. & Forr.) Cowan R. *pothinum* Balf. f & Forr.— Like typical R. *temenium*, but with the ovary devoid of glands. Introduced by Forrest.

R. TEPHROPEPLUM Balf. f. & Forr.
R. deleiense Hutch. & Ward.; *R. spodopeplum* Balf. f. & Farrer

A small evergreen shrub 1 to 4 ft high; young shoots scaly. Leaves oblong-lanceolate to oblong-obovate, rounded or pointed at the mucronate apex, mostly tapered at the base, $1\frac{1}{4}$ to 5 in. long, $\frac{1}{2}$ to $1\frac{3}{4}$ in. wide, sprinkled with tiny black glands above, glaucous and very scaly beneath; stalk $\frac{1}{6}$ to $\frac{1}{4}$ in. long. Flowers opening in April or May in a truss of three to nine; pedicels $\frac{3}{8}$ to $1\frac{1}{8}$ in. long. Calyx deeply five-lobed, the lobes more or less scaly, membranous, $\frac{1}{4}$ in. long, rounded. Corolla funnel-shaped, 1 to $1\frac{5}{8}$ in. long and wide, varying from pale pink to rosy crimson and crimson purple, sometimes almost white, five-lobed, the lobes roundish ovate. Stamens ten, slightly downy at the base. Ovary densely scaly, deeply grooved; style scaly towards the base, sometimes for more than half its length. *Bot. Mag.*, t. 9343.   (*s.* Boothii *ss.* Tephropeplum)

R. *tephropeplum* was discovered by Farrer in 1920, a few months before his death. He found it on the Chawchi and Maguchi passes, between the Nmai Hka and the Salween, 'abundant on rocks and cliffs, forming wide and often procumbent masses'. The synonymous name R. *spodopeplum* is founded on a specimen he collected the same season on the crags of Shing Hong. It was introduced by Forrest in the following year from farther north on the same divide, where the Nmai Hka becomes known as the Taron or Kiu-chiang. Subsequently it was found to have a wide range to the westward, through upper Burma and the Mishmi Hills to the eastern end of the Himalaya. ·

R. *tephropeplum* is a very variable species. In habit it may be dwarf and compact, or laxly branched and up to 6 ft high. The flowers range in colour from almost white through clear pink to magenta pink, and there is also variation in size of leaf and in the number of flowers in each truss. The most noteworthy introductions are as follows:

Forrest 26431, from cliffs and rocky ledges on the Nmai Hka–Salween divide, at 11,000 ft. According to the field note, the plants had almost pure white flowers, which is true of some of the garden plants raised from this batch of seed.

Forrest 25572 and 25714, from screes and rocky slopes at 13,000 to 14,000 ft, on the Salween–Kiuchiang divide around 27° N. Plants 2 to 3 ft high, with rose-coloured flowers.

Kingdon Ward 8165. This is the type-collection of R. *deleiense*, now included in R. *tephropeplum*, but originally distinguished from it by the larger leaves and more numerously flowered inflorescence. It is a comparatively dwarf and compact form with flowers of a deep purplish rose, hardy, and usually not flowering until early May. It was found by Kingdon Ward in the Delei valley, Assam, in 1928, on rocky ridges and in thickets, at 8,000 to 9,000 ft.

KW 6794, from the Seinghku valley, north-west upper Burma, a compact form with flesh-pink to white flowers. KW 6834, a sparsely branched form with rose-purple flowers, is from the same valley.

KW 6303. This was found by Kingdon Ward in November 1924 in the Tsangpo gorge at the eastern end of the Himalaya, growing 6 to 8 ft high in *Abies* forest. A large-leaved form.

KW 20844, a dwarf form introduced by Kingdon Ward during his last expedition to Burma in 1953. It is in cultivation in the Savill Garden, Windsor Great Park.

Eight years after it was introduced, Lionel de Rothschild wrote of R. *tephropeplum* 'There is something distinctive about this dwarf which is difficult to describe. The shape and habit and foliage is not particularly striking, but it is so friendly, so lavish in distributing its little clear coloured flower heads at every possible point at which they can be produced that you cannot help taking to it at first sight.' Two years later he added: 'My opinion of *Rhododendron tephropeplum* increases with each new variety of the species that I see in flower' (*New Flora and Sylva*, Vol. 1, p. 163, and Vol. 4, p. 9). Although its flowers and expanding buds may be killed by frost it is winter hardy and needs only a sheltered position and shade from the hottest sun; in too much shade it becomes leggy and the flowers take on a bluish magenta tinge.

R. *tephropeplum* received an Award of Merit when shown from Bodnant on April 30, 1929, and again on April 30, 1935, as R. *deleiense*, shown by Lord Swaythling, Townhill Park, Hants.

R. THAYERIANUM Rehd. & Wils.

An evergreen shrub up to 12 ft high in the wild; young shoots sticky and downy. Leaves crowded at the end of the shoot in a cluster of as many as twelve or more, leathery, oblanceolate, tapered abruptly to a finely pointed apex and gradually towards the stalk, which is $\frac{1}{3}$ to $\frac{1}{2}$ in. long; they are 2½ to 8 in. long, $\frac{3}{8}$ to 1¼ in. wide; bright green and ultimately glabrous above, covered beneath with a very close yellowish-brown felt. Flowers borne around midsummer, ten to sixteen in a terminal raceme the main-stalk of which is 1 to 1½ in. long, glandular; the individual flower-stalks 1½ to 2 in. long, slender, sticky with glands. Calyx cupped, with five glandular roundish lobes $\frac{1}{6}$ in. long. Corolla five-lobed, funnel-shaped, about 1¼ in. long and a little more wide, opening pink, turning white, with bands of rosy red running lengthwise. Stamens normally ten, their white stalks downy on the lower half, about 1 in. long; anthers pale brown. Ovary and style very glandular. *Bot. Mag.*, t. 8983. (*s.* Arboreum *ss.* Argyrophyllum)

This species was discovered by Wilson in the Mupin area of W. Szechwan during his second expedition for the Arnold Arboretum in 1910. He found it in fruit, and the corollas were known only from withered remains until a plant raised from his seeds flowered at Caerhays in 1922. The rather loose trusses of flowers, which open in June and July, are delicately tinted and very charming. This is a very well-marked species, especially in its long narrow leaves which persist on the branches for four or five years; in the long slender flower-stalks which give the truss its loose appearance and a diameter of 6 in.; and in the sticky, glandular character of the young parts. It grows wild in woodlands. The Thayer family after whom it is named is an old and well-known one whose ancestral home is at Lancaster in Massachusetts. They generously supported the earlier Chinese expeditions.

R. THOMSONII Hook. f.

An evergreen, glabrous shrub up to 14 ft high and more in diameter in the Cornish gardens. Leaves roundish oval, 2 to 4 in. long, two-thirds as wide, round at the apex except for a short, abrupt tip, and rounded or slightly heart-shaped at the base, dark green above, blue-white or glaucous green below; stalk about ¾ in. long. Flowers borne in March or April, six to ten in a loose terminal cluster; pedicels up to 1 in. long. Calyx ½ to ¾ in. deep, rarely shorter, cup-shaped, often tinged with red. Corolla bell-shaped, fleshy, rich blood-red, 2 to 3 in. across, five-lobed. Stamens ten, glabrous. Ovary and style glabrous. *Bot. Mag.*, t. 4997.   (s. and ss. Thomsonii)

Native of the Himalaya as far west as Nepal; introduced by J. D. Hooker in 1850 from Sikkim, where it grows at 10,000 to 13,000 ft. It first flowered in 1857 with Messrs Methven of Edinburgh, who had taken a scion from one of their seedlings and grafted it on R. *ponticum*.

R. *thomsonii* is hardy at Kew, but needs a sheltered position, and even then its flowers and young growths are very liable to injury by late frost. In more favoured gardens it is magnificent, and really deserves a place even in a garden with the climate of Kew, since it makes a handsome specimen and the flowers are so splendid that a display one year in three is ample return for the room it occupies. It received an Award of Garden Merit in 1925.

Crossed with other species, R. *thomsonii* has given rise to some of the finest and best known hybrid grexes, notably Luscombei (with R. *fortunei*), Shilsonii (with R. *barbatum*), and Cornish Cross (with R. *griffithianum*), 'Ascot Brilliant' is an old hybrid between R. *thomsonii* and a hardy hybrid, raised by Standish over a century ago; more recent commercial hybrids with R. *thomsonii* as one parent are 'Sir John Ramsden' and 'J. G. Millais'.

var. CANDELABRUM (Hook. f.) C. B. Cl.   R. *candelabrum* Hook, f.—Flowers paler than in the typical variety. Calyx smaller. Ovary glandular. Described from Sikkim.

var. PALLIDUM Cowan—Flowers rose-pink. Calyx large. Ovary glandular. Described from specimens collected by Ludlow and Sherriff in the Tibetan Himalaya.

R. LOPSANGIANUM Cowan—Allied to R. *thomsonii*, but not so tall-growing, and with smaller flowers and leaves. The leaves are markedly papillose beneath and the calyx is small, not forming a distinct cup. Described in 1937 from specimens collected by Ludlow and Sherriff in the Tibetan Himalaya and introduced by them. It is named after the then Dalai Lama of Tibet.

R. VISCIDIFOLIUM Davidian—In describing this species in 1966, Davidian remarks that it agrees with R. *thomsonii* var. *pallidum* in some respects, differing in the copper-red flowers, the small calyx, and the tomentose or glandular ovary. The leaves are glandular and sticky beneath, whence the specific epithet. It was discovered by Ludlow, Sherriff, and Taylor in the Tibetan Himalaya on the Lo La and was introduced by them in 1938. It is in cultivation at Glenarn in Dunbartonshire.

R. TOSAENSE Makino
R. *komiyamae* Makino

A semi-deciduous, twiggy azalea usually from 3 to 8 ft high; young shoots very slender, clothed with appressed, flattened, forward-pointing hairs, of a grey or greyish-brown colour. Leaves lanceolate to oblanceolate, $\frac{1}{3}$ to $1\frac{1}{2}$ in. long, $\frac{1}{16}$ to $\frac{2}{5}$ in. wide, toothless, furnished on both surfaces with appressed hairs; stalk very short. Flowers in clusters of two to six, or solitary, on short pedicels. Calyx very small, clad with white hairs. Corolla funnel-shaped, about $1\frac{1}{2}$ in. wide, lilac-purple. Stamens five to ten, shorter than the corolla, downy at the base. Ovary bristly; style glabrous. Seed-vessel egg-shaped, $\frac{1}{3}$ in. long, covered with appressed hairs, the calyx persisting at the base. *Bot. Mag.*, n.s., t. 52. (*s.* Azalea *ss.* Obtusum)

Native of S. Japan, on Shikoku, Kyushu, and the southern part of the main island; also of some mountains farther to the north-east, west of Mt Fuji. It reached this country through the Arnold Arboretum, to which Wilson sent seeds from Shikoku in 1914. He wrote of it: 'I have seen a few flowers, but the colour is not attractive, though doubtless in spring when covered with blossoms, the plant would have a charm of its own.' It is in fact a very pleasing species, but more than one plant is needed if it is to make an effective display. It is hardy in woodland south of London, but uncommon in cultivation. As in most members of the Obtusum subseries, the upper leaves on the annual shoots (the so-called summer-leaves) are much smaller than the 'spring-leaves' borne lower on the shoot, which are mostly shed in winter.

R. *komiyamae*, included in R. *tosaense* by Rehder, is recognised as a distinct species by Japanese botanists, differing in having flowers with ten stamens against normally five in R. *tosaense* in the narrow sense. Plants of this nature are said to be confined to two mountains to the west of Mt Fuji.

R. TRICHANTHUM Rehd.
R. *villosum* Hemsl. & Wils., not Roth

An evergreen shrub up to 18 ft high; branchlets slender, scaly, and clothed with pale bristles $\frac{1}{8}$ in. long. Leaves scattered on the vigorous shoots, clustered at the end of weaker ones; ovate or oblong, pointed, rounded or tapered at the base, 2 to $3\frac{1}{2}$ in. long, $\frac{3}{4}$ to $1\frac{1}{4}$ in. wide; upper surface sparsely scaly, downy about the midrib, and freely sprinkled with pale, long bristles; lower surface more scaly but less bristly, and downy only on and about the midrib; stalk ⅛ to ¼ in. long, bristly. Flowers in May or June in clusters of three to five, borne on bristly pedicels about ½ in. long. Calyx minute, hidden in bristles. Corolla funnel-shaped, about 1¾ in. wide, light to dark purple, bristly on the tube outside and scaly. Stamens ten, hairy towards the base. Ovary bristly and scaly; style glabrous. *Bot. Mag.*, t. 8880.   (*s.* Triflorum *ss.* Augustinii)

Native of W. and S.W. Szechwan at altitudes of up to 11,000 ft, said to be a very common species, especially in woodland, where it forms dense thickets; introduced by Wilson in 1904. It is a very distinct species in the bristliness of its various parts, and quite handsome in its darker-coloured forms. It is hardy in a sheltered position.

The Award of Merit was given on June 8, 1971, to the clone 'Honey Wood', exhibited by Major A. E. Hardy, Sandling Park, Kent.

R. TRICHOCLADUM Franch. [PLATE 92

R. *xanthinum* Balf. f. & W. W. Sm.; R. *brachystylum* Balf. f. & Ward

A deciduous or partly evergreen shrub up to 5 ft high, with usually stiff erect branchlets, clothed their first and part of their second year with long, pale bristles. Leaves oblong to obovate and oval, often rounded at the apex, 1 to 1½ in. long, ⅓ to ¾ in. wide, dark dull green and glabrous except for a few bristles above; scaly beneath with bristles on the midrib when young; margins bristly. Flowers as many as five in a terminal compact cluster, open in May. Calyx five-lobed, the lanceolate lobes ⅙ in. long, fringed with long bristles; flower-stalk ½ to ¾ in. long, scaly and very bristly. Corolla open and flattish, 1 to 1¼ in. wide, yellow tinged with green, woolly in the throat, slightly scaly outside, five-lobed, the lobes rounded. Stamens ten, scarcely ½ in. long, downy towards the base, anthers brown. Ovary scaly; style glabrous, abruptly bent over. *Bot. Mag.*, t. 9073.   (*s.* Trichocladum)

Native of N.W. Yunnan westward through upper Burma to the eastern Himalaya; discovered about 1884, by the Abbé Delavay; introduced by Forrest in 1910. R. *trichocladum* is no great beauty, its growth being curiously stiff; still its soft yellow, flatly open flowers have some attractiveness. Forrest found it at 11,000 ft altitude and upwards and it is quite hardy. Flowers frequently open in autumn.

R. *trichocladum* is the oldest of a small group of species all resembling it in general aspect and distinguished from it and from each other by secondary characters such as the amount of bristles and scales on the pedicels and calyx, the size of the latter, the presence or absence of hairs on the upper surface of the leaf. Of possibly greater significance is the length and thickness of the style. Even in a single collecting there is variation in the characters at present considered to be of specific value. The following are perhaps the commonest in cultivation, though few are met with outside the gardens where they were raised from the wild seed:

R. MELINANTHUM Balf. f. & Ward—This was described from a specimen collected by Kingdon Ward in 1913 in one of the high valleys of the Ka-kar-po range, Mekong–Salween divide, and was introduced by him in the same year (KW 406). He also collected seed of what is supposed to be R. *melinanthum* in November 1922 on the Taru Tra, N.E. Burma, during his journey across the upper feeders of the Irrawaddy (KW 5849). R. *melinanthum* differs from R. *trichocladum* mainly in the smaller calyx not fringed with hairs, and the longer style (*Bot. Mag.*, t. 8903). It is usually said that R. *melinanthum* is the best of this group because of its deep-yellow flowers, but a plant has been noted of a particularly pleasing colour which does not agree at all with R. *melinanthum*, though grown under that name. It is quite near to R. *trichocladum*.

The others must be dealt with more shortly. R. CHLORANTHUM Balf. f. & Forr. resembles R. *melinanthum* in having a small unfringed calyx, but according to the original description the style is shorter and the leaves less scaly beneath. R. MEKONGENSE Franch. is but a less hairy version of R. *trichocladum*. It was included in it by Bayley Balfour but later resurrected. R. OULOTRICHUM Balf. f. & Forr. scarcely differs from R. *trichocladum*; it is in cultivation from seed collected by Farrer and Cox in 1919 on the Burma–Yunnan frontier. R. RUBRO-LINEATUM Balf. f. & Forr. takes its name from one of the specimens included in it, whose flowers were described by Forrest as creamy yellow lined and flushed with rose on the outside; this came from the Tali range. But another specimen, from farther north, is credited with canary-yellow flowers. The specimens differ from R. *trichocladum* in being very much less hairy, and in having the calyx-lobes much reduced. Red pigmentation in the flowers is also to be seen in some forms of R. *trichocladum*.

For two more distinct species of the Trichocladum series, see R. *lepido-stylum* and R. *viridescens*.

R. TRICHOSTOMUM Franch.

R. *sphaeranthum* Balf. f. & W. W. Sm.; R. *ledoides* Balf. f. & W. W. Sm.; R. *radinum* Balf. f. & W. W. Sm.; R. *trichostomum* var. *ledoides* (Balf. f. & W. W. Sm.) Cowan & Davidian; R. *trichostomum* var. *radinum* (Balf. f. & W. W. Sm.) Cowan & Davidian

An evergreen shrub 1½ to 4 ft high, usually of rather lax habit; young shoots slender, covered with a mass of scurfy overlapping scales, mixed with which are whitish hairs. Leaves linear-lanceolate, narrow-oblong or narrow-lanceolate, ⅜ to 1⅜ in. long, 3/16 to 5/16 in. wide, narrowed at both ends, dull green and sometimes scaly above, paler and with a thick scurf of scales beneath; stalk about ⅛ in. long. Flowers in May, densely packed, ten to twenty or even more in a hemispherical cluster 1 to 1½ in. wide; pedicels up to 3/16 in. long, usually shorter. Calyx minute (about 1/12 in. long). Corolla white, pale pink, or rose-coloured, fading with age, about ⅜ in. long and ½ in. wide, with a tubular base about ¼ in. long which is hairy inside and expands at the mouth into five lobes, outside of corolla sometimes scaly. Stamens five, hidden away in the tube of the corolla, their filaments glabrous or downy. Ovary scaly; style very short, glabrous. *Bot. Mag.*, t. 8831. (*s.* Anthopogon)

Native of Yunnan and W. Szechwan at altitudes of up to 13,000 ft, usually on open rocky slopes or in pinewoods; discovered by Père Delavay in the mountains above Lankiung, north of Tali. It was probably introduced by Wilson from W. Szechwan in 1908, but the cultivated plants mostly derive from Forrest's sendings from 1913–14 onwards, and from those of Kingdon Ward and Rock.

R. *trichostomum* is perhaps the most ornamental of the Anthopogon series and is also of taller and laxer growth than any of the other commonly cultivated species. It is slightly tender in some forms, but is out of place in woodland and should be given a fairly sunny position. In the past fifteen years it has received Awards of Merit on four occasions: May 20, 1960, to clone 'Sweet Bay' (from F.20480); May 22, 1972, to clone 'Lakeside'; both shown by the Crown Estate Commissioners, Windsor Great Park; May 24, 1971, to clone 'Quarry Wood'; and May 22, 1972, without clonal name; both plants shown by Mr and Mrs Martyn Simmonds, Quarry Wood, Newbury.

A plant raised at Edinburgh from Wilson's 1208 (the type-collection of R. *sargentianum*) proved to be distinct and was named R. *hedyosmum* by Balfour. It is now merged with R. *trichostomum* or treated as a variety of it—var. *hedyosmum* (Balf. f.) Cowan & Davidian. The material depicted in *Bot. Mag.*, t. 9202, as R. *hedyosmum* represents not the original plant but a seedling of it, grown by E. J. P. Magor of Lamellen, Cornwall. This plant does not belong to R. *trichostomum* in any form, differing in its much larger calyx.

R. TRIFLORUM Hook. f.

An evergreen shrub 6 to 10 ft high with glabrous, red, peeling bark; young shoots slender, glaucous, scaly. Leaves ovate-lanceolate, rounded at the base, sharply pointed, 2 to 3 in. long, 1 to 1¼ in. broad, bright green and glabrous above, glaucous and thickly furnished with scales beneath; stalk ¼ to ⅓ in. long. Flowers fragrant, opening in May and June, usually in threes, at the end of the shoot when young growths are pushing. Calyx small, shallowly undulated; flower-stalks ½ to ⅞ in. long. Corolla pale yellow spotted with green, with a short funnel-shaped tube and five spreading oblong lobes giving the flower a diameter of 1½ to 2 in., scaly outside. Stamens ten, ½ to 1 in. long, downy towards the base; ovary scaly; style longer than stamens, glabrous.   (s. and ss. Triflorum)

Native of the eastern Himalaya; discovered by J. D. Hooker in the Sikkim Himalaya in 1849 and introduced by him. It is not a showy plant, although the flowers are interesting in their unusual colour. The red, semi-transparent, loose bark is also attractive with sunlight behind it. It is hardy.

var. MAHOGANI Hutch.—This was found by Kingdon Ward in the Tibetan province of Kongbo, near Tsela Dzong on the Tsangpo, growing with the typical state. 'Another rhododendron which grew here to perfection was R. *triflorum* and its dark variety, which I called the "Mahogany Triflorum" (K.W. 5687). In the valley it is a small compact scrubby plant with lemon-yellow flowers; but on these sheltered tree-clad slopes it formed a large bush 12 or 15 ft high with reddened flowers which were especially beautiful when the light shone through them. . . . The flowers vary from pale yellow—the typical R. *triflorum* colour—to salmon pink, mahogany, burnt sienna, and other tones. Moreover, the bushes were smothered in bloom and are as hardy as anything' (Kingdon Ward, *The Riddle of the Tsangpo Gorges*, p. 44). This variety sounded promising, but proved a sad disappointment when it first flowered in gardens. 'Was the dingy horror under the number KW 5687 shown in the Triflorum Class, was this the Mahogany Triflorum we have so anxiously awaited?' (G. H. Johnstone in his Report on the Rhododendron Show for 1931).

R. BAUHINIIFLORUM Watt ex Hutch.—Very closely allied to R. *triflorum* but with more widely expanded flowers. Native of Assam in the Naga Hills and Manipur; discovered by Sir George Watt in 1881-2 but probably not introduced until Kingdon Ward sent seeds from Mt Japvo in 1928. It is a finer species than R. *triflorum* and almost as good as R. *lutescens*, besides being very much later-flowering. There is a fine clump in the Savill Garden, Windsor Great Park, which is about 10 ft high and was in flower in the fourth week of May in 1973.

R. TSCHONOSKII Maxim.

R. *trinerve* Franch.; *Azalea tschonoskii* (Maxim.) O. Kuntze

A semi-evergreen azalea 2 ft or perhaps more high, with rather horizontal branches, the young shoots covered with appressed, dark brown, linear bristles pointing towards the end of the shoot. Leaves in a tuft at the end of the twig, $\frac{1}{3}$ to $1\frac{1}{2}$ in. long, $\frac{1}{6}$ to $\frac{5}{8}$ in. wide, oval, tapering and pointed, upper surface dull, dark green, lower one pale, both covered with bristly hairs. Flowers produced two to six together, each on a bristly stalk so short that the flower is almost hidden in the tuft of leaves. Calyx minute, covered with bristles. Corolla white, about $\frac{1}{2}$ in. across, funnel-shaped. Stamens five. Ovary densely clad with brown bristles; style glabrous. (s. Azalea *ss*. Obtusum)

Native of Japan, Sakhalin, and Korea; introduced by Maries in 1878. This curious little azalea is only worth cultivating for the orange-red of its fading leaves. The flowers are insignificant.

R. UNGERNII Trautv.

An evergreen shrub or small tree up to 20 ft high in the wild; young shoots downy. Leaves narrow oblong, 3 to 6 in. long, one-third as wide, tapering at the base, the apex ending in a short, abrupt point; glabrous above, but covered beneath with pale brownish wool; stalk $\frac{3}{4}$ in. long. Flowers in large trusses 6 in. through, opening in July; pedicels up to $1\frac{5}{8}$ in. long, hairy and glandular. Calyx-lobes five, lanceolate, covered with glandular hairs. Corolla broadly bell-shaped, with five rounded, slightly notched lobes, white to pale rose, $1\frac{1}{2}$ to 2 in. across. Stamens hairy at the base. Ovary glandular; style glabrous. *Bot. Mag.*, t. 8332. (s. Ponticum *ss*. Caucasicum)

Native of the Artvin region of N.E. Asiatic Turkey and of bordering parts of Russia (Adzaria), at 2,500 to 6,000 ft; introduced to cultivation in 1886 by way of St Petersburg, having been discovered by Baron Ungern-Sternberg in the previous year. It was discovered and introduced at the same time as R. *smirnowii*, with which it has been much confounded. The leaves are much longer than in that species, up to almost 9 in. long on wild plants, and are abruptly narrowed at the apex to a mucronate tip (obtuse in R. *smirnowii*), the lobes of the corolla are not frilled, and the calyx-lobes are much longer. It is also taller-growing in the wild. It is hardy in Britain, but not so fine a species as R. *smirnowii*.

R. UVARIIFOLIUM Diels

R. *niphargum* Balf. f. & Ward; R. *dendritrichum* Balf. f. & Forr.; R. *monbeigii* Rehd. & Wils.

An evergreen shrub 15 to 25 ft high; young shoots stout and as much as ⅜ in. thick, grey-downy. Leaves stout and leathery, obovate or oblanceolate, blunt or almost rounded at the apex, long-tapered at the base; 3 to 10 in. long, 1½ to 2¾ in. wide, dark green and soon glabrous above, covered beneath with a close white, grey, or fawn felt; stalk ½ to 1 in. long. Flowers in a compact rounded truss of ten to fifteen, opening in spring. Calyx very small. Corolla bell-shaped, five-lobed, 1½ in. long, rosy white to pale rose, with a crimson blotch at the base and similarly coloured spots on the upper side. Stamens ten, minutely downy at the base, white with dark brown anthers, ovary slender, glabrous or with a little down, tapered at the top to the glabrous style. *Bot. Mag.*, t. 9480. (*s.* Fulvum)

R. *uvariifolium* is a species of wide range, from the Yungning area, on the borders between N.W. Yunnan and Szechwan westward to the region of the Tsangpo bend at the eastern end of the Himalaya, at altitudes of 7,000 to 13,000 ft. It was discovered by Forrest in 1904 on the ascent from the Yangtse to the Chungtien plateau and introduced by him in 1913. It is closely allied to R. *fulvum*, which has a less woolly brown or yellow tomentum.

The Award of Merit was given on April 13, 1965, to the clone 'Yangtse Bend', exhibited by the Royal Botanic Garden, Edinburgh.

R. VACCINIOIDES Hook. f.

R. *sinovaccinioides* Balf. f. & Forr.

A small, compact, evergreen shrub often found wild on trees growing as an epiphyte, or on rocks and only a few inches high. Shoots thickly set with leaves and rough with wart-like glands the first year, densely furnished with stalked glands the second. Leaves obovate to oblanceolate, with a notched, mucronate apex, tapering to a stout winged stalk, ½ to 1¼ in. long, ¼ to ⅓ in. wide, glabrous except for a few scattered scales. Flowers solitary or in pairs, terminal. Corolla pink or white tinged with pink, tubular at the base, ⅕ in. long, spreading at the mouth into five rounded lobes each ⅕ in. long, with scattered glandular scales outside. Stamens ten, hairy on the middle part only. Ovary scaly, tapered at the apex into a short stout style. Seeds with a long tail at each end. *Bot. Mag.*, t. 9407B.

Native of the eastern Himalaya, Assam, upper Burma, N.W. Yunnan and bordering parts of S.E. Tibet; discovered by J. D. Hooker in Sikkim and introduced by him in 1850, but the seedlings soon died off. It is of no value for gardens, the flowers being even smaller than they are in R. *micranthum*, but is of interest as a member of the section Vireya, characterised by the long-tailed seeds, which has its main distribution in Malaysia, New Guinea, and the Philippines. In Sleumer's classification it belongs to the subsection Pseudovireya, of which it is the type-species. The Vaccinioides series, as defined in *The Species of Rhododendron*, comprises those members of this subsection which occur in the Sino-Himalayan region, Formosa and the Philippines (and includes one species—R. *vidalii*—which is considered by Sleumer to belong to the typical subsection of Vireya).

R. VALENTINIANUM Forr. ex Hutch.

An evergreen shrub 3 or 4 ft high; young shoots densely bristly and scaly beneath the bristles. Leaves oval inclined to oblong, 1½ to 2 in. long, ¾ to 1 in. wide, pale green and bristly above, nearly covered with tawny scales beneath, margins bristly; leaf-stalks ⅛ to ½ in. long, bristly and scaly. Flowers two to six in a close terminal cluster. Calyx ⅓ in. long, five-lobed, the lobes oblong, scaly outside and densely woolly-hairy on the margin. Corolla bright yellow, between funnel- and bell-shaped, about 1½ in. long, five-lobed, densely scaly outside. Stamens ten, with white hairs at the lower part; anthers pink. Ovary and base of style scaly. *Bot. Mag.*, n.s., t. 623. (*s.* Maddenii *ss.* Ciliicalyx)

R. *valentinianum* was discovered by Forrest in 1917 on the Shweli–Salween divide, Yunnan, near the border with Burma, growing in open scrub at 11,000 ft. In a note accompanying the original description, Sir Isaac Bayley Balfour remarked on the affinity between this species and the Himalayan R. *ciliatum*, but there are many differences apart from the obvious one of flower-colour, notably that the leaves are smaller in R. *valentinianum* and densely scaly beneath.

R. *valentinianum* is a charming species, but, although winter-hardy, it is bud-tender and is really seen to best advantage in a cool greenhouse except in the milder parts. Grown out-of-doors it needs a well-lighted position, otherwise it sets little flower-bud and becomes lanky in habit. It received an Award of Merit in 1936 when shown from Bodnant.

R. FLETCHERIANUM Davidian—Fairly closely allied to R. *valentinianum*, but differing in the leaves being green and sparsely scaly beneath, with shallowly crenate margins, the more widely funnel-shaped corollas and bristly-hairy ovaries. The flowers are paler yellow, and the habit more erect. *Bot. Mag.*, n.s., t. 508. It is allied to R. *ciliatum*—more closely than is R. *valentinianum*—but differs in flower-colour, the crenate leaves and narrower calyx-lobes. It was discovered by Dr Rock in 1932, growing on the Sola La in the Yunnan–Tibet borderland, at 13,500 to 14,000 ft, and introduced by him (Rock 22302). It was grown in gardens as Rock's form of R. *valentinianum* until named and described as a new species in 1961.

R. *fletcherianum* is hardy, but flowering as it does in March or April the display is often ruined by frost. It needs a sheltered position, but one where it receives abundant light. Award of Merit April 14, 1964, when shown by E. H. M. and P. A. Cox, Glendoick, Perthshire (clone 'Yellow Bunting', with primrose-yellow flowers).

R. VASEYI A. Gray
Azalea vaseyi (A. Gray) Rehd.

A deciduous azalea, attaining heights of 12 to 15 ft in the wild, bushy. Leaves linear-oval, very tapering at both ends, 2 to 4 in. long, ½ to 1½ in. wide, at first sparsely bristly, becoming glabrous; upper surface lustrous, hairy on the midrib and at the edges; stalk ¼ in. or less long. Flowers produced before the leaves in

RHODODENDRON VASEYI

early May, four to eight together in a terminal cluster; pedicels up to ⅝ in. long, glandular. Calyx very small. Corolla clear pale pink, with a short, bell-shaped base, the limb about 1½ in. across, with five oblong lobes, the upper three spotted with reddish brown at the base. Stamens normally seven, sometimes five or six. Ovary glandular; style sometimes with a few glands near the base. *Bot. Mag.*, t. 8081. (*s.* Azalea *ss.* Canadense)

Native of the mountains of western North Carolina; discovered by G. R. Vasey on Balsam Mountain in 1878; introduced to Kew in 1891. It is placed in the same group as the rhodora, R. *canadense*, but Rehder considered that its nearest relative is the Japanese R. *albrechtii*. It is a better garden plant than either, being very hardy, free-flowering, and without any fads, growing well in full sun even on quite poor sandy soils. It can readily be raised from seeds, which it ripens in plenty; seedlings with white flowers sometimes occur—f. ALBUM Nichols.

The Award of Merit was given in 1969 to the clone 'Suva', exhibited by Edmund de Rothschild, Exbury, on May 19. The species as a whole received an Award of Garden Merit in 1927.

R. VEITCHIANUM Hook.

An evergreen shrub up to 12 ft or so high in the wild, often epiphytic; young branchlets scaly, without bristles. Leaves leathery, narrowly obovate or elliptic-obovate, obtuse and acuminate at the apex, narrowed to the base, 2 to 4 in. long, ⅜ to 1¾ in. wide, scaly above when young, permanently scaly beneath, the scales spaced about their own diameter apart or slightly more widely; petiole up to ½ in. long. Flowers in terminal trusses of up to five, on scaly stalks about ⅜ in. long. Calyx very short, often with a few slender hairs on the margin, scaly near the base. Corolla five-lobed, widely funnel-shaped, 2½ to 3 in. long, more in width, white, slightly tinged with green outside, the lobes (in the type) with crinkled margins, scaly on the outside, mostly on the upper (adaxial) side of the tube, which is also slightly downy on the outside near the base. Stamens ten, downy towards the base. Ovary scaly; style scaly near the base. *Bot. Mag.*, t. 4992. (*s.* Maddenii *ss.* Ciliicalyx)

Native of the mountains of lower and central Burma, Thailand, and Laos; introduced by Thomas Lobb for Messrs Veitch from the mountains east of Moulmein and first exhibited by them in May 1857. In the plant shown the corolla-lobes were strongly crinkled, but this is probably not a characteristic of the species as a whole. Seeds from self-pollinated flowers produce many plants with smooth-edged lobes, which used to be known in gardens as var. *laevigatum*. Some plants are intermediate, with undulated lobes.

R. *veitchianum* is too tender to be grown outdoors even in the mildest parts of the country. It is mentioned here only because it is one of the oldest members of the Ciliicalyx subseries, in which other, closely allied and somewhat hardier species will probably be included when the group is revised. Its flowering time under glass is late spring and early summer.

R. CUBITTII Hutch.—Near to R. *veitchianum*, but with the young stems somewhat bristly and the leaves oblong or oblong-lanceolate, bristly on the margins. The corolla is more richly coloured, being deep pink outside along the ribs, white or light pink inside, with a flare of brownish-crimson or orange-yellow markings. It is also near to R. *formosum*, but in that species, as in R. *veitchianum*, the leaves are oblanceolate to obovate, and the corolla is scaly all over on the outside, whereas in R. *cubittii* there are only a few scales on the adaxial side. *Bot. Mag.*, t. 9502. This species was described from a small scrap collected by G. Cubitt in the Bhamo Division of northern Burma in 1909, and was otherwise unknown until exhibited from Trengwainton, Cornwall, in March 1935, when it received an Award of Merit. The plant there, which still exists, had been planted against a garden wall two years previously, and was then 6 ft high and more in width. Although tender, R. *cubittii* is grown outdoors in several other gardens in the milder parts (see *Journ. R.H.S.*, Vol. 86, fig. 94). It is one of the finest members of the Maddenii series, with beautifully formed flowers, slightly crisped at the margin, and a smooth purplish-brown bark. The F.C.C. was given in 1962 to clone 'ASHCOMBE', exhibited by the Crown Estate Commissioners, Windsor Great Park.

R. INAEQUALE (C. B. Cl.) Hutch. R. *formosum* var. *inaequale* C. B. Cl.— Near to R. *veitchianum*, but the leaves are narrowly elliptic, oblong-elliptic, or oblanceolate-elliptic, mostly less than $1\frac{1}{2}$ in. wide, the calyx is downy, the corolla has a large yellow or chartreuse blotch on the inside, and the fruit is obliquely ellipsoid to obliquely oblong-ovoid, not cylindric as in R. *veitchianum. Bot. Mag.*, n.s., t. 295. Native of Assam, discovered by Griffith in 1837 on the Kollong Rock in the Khasi Hills and described from fruiting specimens collected by Hooker and Thomson in the same locality thirteen years later. The flowers were not known until Kingdon Ward introduced the species from Mt Japvo in the Naga Hills in 1927 (KW 7717). It is also in cultivation from seeds collected by Cox and Hutchison in the Khasi Hills in 1965. It is tender, but perhaps hardier than R. *veitchianum*.

R. TARONENSE Hutch.—This imperfectly known species was described from a specimen collected by Kingdon Ward in November 1922 in the valley of the Taron (Kiuchiang), on the borders between Yunnan and north-east Burma. The flowers were not fully expanded, which may explain the shortness of the corolla-tube in the dried specimen (only $\frac{3}{4}$ in. long). Whether this species is in cultivation it is impossible to say. The plant at Exbury, which received a First Class Certificate when shown as R. *taronense* in 1935, is also figured in *Bot. Mag.*, n.s., t. 1, and was raised from Forrest's 27687. The field-specimen under this number has been identified as R. *taronense*, but the Exbury plant really agrees much better with R. NOTATUM Hutch., described from Kingdon Ward specimens collected in the Seinghku valley and Nam Tamai valley in N.W. upper Burma. However, the two species—R. *taronense* and R. *notatum*—are doubtfully distinct, and both are included in R. *veitchianum* by Sleumer.

R. VENATOR Tagg

An evergreen shrub up to 10 ft high in the wild; young shoots and leaf-petioles covered with gland-tipped bristles intermixed with white floccose hairs. Leaves oblong-lanceolate to oblong-oblanceolate, tapered or abruptly narrowed to a mucronate tip, rounded or heart-shaped at the base, upper surface medium green, glabrous at maturity, underside pale green, glabrous except for scattered stellate hairs on the midrib and main veins; petiole stout, $\frac{1}{2}$ to $\frac{5}{8}$ in. long. Flowers borne in May or June in a compact truss of about ten; pedicels about $\frac{1}{2}$ in. long, glandular-bristly and hairy. Corolla deep red, tubular-campanulate, about $1\frac{1}{2}$ in. long, fleshy, with five dark nectar-pouches at the base. Stamens ten. Ovary conoid, clad with branched hairs and gland-tipped bristles; style hairy at the base.

R. *venator* was discovered by Kingdon Ward in the Tsangpo gorge, S.E. Tibet, in November 1924. 'In swampy places there grew a spreading untidy shrub with more or less ascending branches—one of the "Irroratum" series with blood-red flowers (KW 6285). This plant we saw henceforth almost daily, and it was especially abundant in the swamps round Pemakochung, where it took on almost the appearance of mangrove' (*Riddle of the Tsangpo Gorges*, p. 201). He saw only a few precocious trusses but plants flowered in several gardens in 1933 and the species was described in the following year. It was reintroduced from the type-locality by Ludlow, Sherriff, and Elliot in 1946–7.

R. *venator* is of some value as a hardy red-flowered species, blossoming after the main danger of frost is past, and not taking up much room. But the habit is rather straggly. It is at present placed in the Parishii subseries of the Irroratum series, but its relationships are uncertain. Dr Cowan suggested that it was nearer to R. *floccigerum* in the Neriiflorum series.

R. *venator* received an Award of Merit when shown from Bodnant on May 23, 1933 (a form with orange-scarlet flowers).

R. VERNICOSUM Franch.

R. *adoxum* Balf. f. & Forr.; R. *lucidum* Franch., not Nutt.; R. *euanthum* Balf. f. & W. W. Sm.; R. *rhantum* Balf. f. & W. W. Sm.; R. *sheltonae* Hemsl. & Wils.; R. *araliaeforme* Balf. f. & Forr.

An evergreen shrub said occasionally to be 15 to 25 ft high in the wild; but considerably less at present in cultivation; young shoots glabrous. Leaves glabrous, oval to oblong-ovate, rounded at the base and abruptly narrowed to a mucro at the apex, 2½ to 5 in. long, about half as much wide; dull green above, rather glaucous beneath; stalk ¾ to 1¼ in. long. Flowers not fragrant, opening in May in rather loose trusses of about ten. Calyx small, fleshy, being only an unequal-sided development of the flower-stalk, which is about 1 in. long and glandular. Corolla widely funnel-shaped, 2½ in. wide, pale clear rose, seven-lobed. Stamens fourteen, glabrous. Ovary densely glandular, the style also densely furnished over its whole length with dark red glands. *Bot. Mag.*, tt. 8834, 8904–5. (s. and ss. Fortunei)

Native of Szechwan and Yunnan, where it is widely distributed; discovered by the French missionary Soulié about 1889 west of Kangting (Tatsien-lu); introduced by Wilson in 1904, and also cultivated from seeds sent later by Forrest, Kingdon Ward, Rock, and Yu. It is allied to R. *decorum* but can always be distinguished from it (and from other members of the Fortunei subseries) by the remarkable red glands on the style.

R. *vernicosum* is somewhat variable. Four species are sometimes referred to as 'geographical forms' of R. *vernicosum* and maintain a shadowy existence, though all four were considered as synonymous with R. *vernicosum* by Dr Cowan. Of these, R. *araliaeforme* was described from specimens collected by Forrest in Tsarong province, S.E. Tibet, and the plants cultivated under this name were from seeds he sent home from this area in 1919; the plants called R. *euanthum* and R. *rhantum* were from seeds collected in the Lichiang range; and R. *sheltonae* is the name by which the Wilson introduction from W. Szechwan was originally known.

The specific epithet, which means 'varnished', seems very unfitted for a dull-leaved plant like this. But a varnished appearance can be developed by heating the surface of the leaf, which is, probably, what had been done when drying the original specimens on which Franchet based his description.

R. *vernicosum* is a beautiful and quite hardy species. Some forms do not flower until May and these are the best for frosty gardens. The Award of Merit was given in 1964 to clone 'Loch Eck', when exhibited from the Younger Botanic Garden, Benmore, Argyll, on April 14. The clone 'Sidlaw' received a Preliminary Commendation when shown by E. H. M. and P. A. Cox on May 19, 1969.

R. VERRUCULOSUM Rehd. & Wils.

An evergreen, erect-branched shrub described as growing up to 3 ft high in the wild, but sometimes taller in cultivation; young shoots rough with scales. Leaves elliptic, up to ¾ in. long, about half as wide, slightly glaucous green and thickly set with shining yellow scales above, more sparsely scaly beneath; stalk about ⅛ in. long. Flowers usually solitary, with a very short scaly stalk. Calyx shorter than the corolla-tube, deeply five-lobed, the lobes blunt, oval-oblong, sparsely scaly, usually fringed with weak hairs. Corolla about 1 in. wide, purple or blue-purple, with or without scales on the outside, hairy in the throat. Stamens seven or eight, with purple filaments; anthers yellowish. Ovary densely scaly; style purple, glabrous. (s. Lapponicum)

Native of W. Szechwan; discovered by Wilson in 1908 at altitudes of 10,000 ft and upwards. It is a very hardy species, allied to R. *impeditum*, but taller and not flowering until May. Forms with the corolla not scaly outside would in fact run down to R. *impeditum* in the key in *Species of Rhododendron*, which is badly out-of-date. R. *verruculosum* received an Award of Merit when shown by Col. S. R. Clarke, Borde Hill, Sussex, on May 24, 1932.

R. VILMORINIANUM Balf. f.
R. *augustinii* var. *album* Hort.

An evergreen shrub of erect habit probably up to 8 ft or more high; young shoots slender, downy. Leaves lanceolate, slenderly pointed, 1 to 2½ in. long, ⅓ to ¾ in. wide, dull dark green and downy on the midrib above, scaly below; leaf-stalk ⅙ to ¼ in. long, furnished with a few long bristles. Flowers opening in May, two to four in a terminal cluster. Calyx very small, five-lobed, the larger lobes ¹⁄₁₀ in. long, scaly; flower-stalk ⅓ in. long. Corolla shortly tubed, 1½ in. wide, yellowish white with brownish spots on the upper side; scaly outside. Stamens ten, the longest 1¼ in. long, all with a tuft of white down near, but not at, the base of the white stalks; anthers exposed, crimson. Ovary scaly with a fringe of white hairs at the top; style glabrous, greenish yellow, except where it joins the ovary. (s. Triflorum ss. Yunnanense)

Native of China, probably from E. Szechwan, and collected by Farges; raised c. 1898 from seed by de Vilmorin at Les Barres. It is the plant distributed by Chenault of Orleans as "R. Augustinii album", but is of course easily distinguished from R. *augustinii* at any time by the absence of the line of down on the midrib beneath that is so distinctive a character of that species. R. *vilmorinianum* is best marked by the yellowish scales and their occurrence outside the corolla-tube, by the down on the shoots and upper surface of the midrib, and by the bristles on the leaf-stalk.

R. VIRGATUM Hook. f.
R. *oleifolium* Franch.; R. *sinovirgatum* Balf. f., *nom. inedit.*

An evergreen shrub up to 8 ft high in the wild, with slender branches covered when young with brown scales. Leaves 1 to 3 in. long, ⅜ to almost 1 in. wide, narrow-elliptic or oblong-lanceolate, tapered or somewhat abruptly narrowed at both ends, dark green, glabrous and sometimes scaly above, underside paler green, sometimes slightly glaucous, sprinkled with shining brown scales; leaf-stalk ⅛ to ¾ in. long. Flowers produced in April singly or in pairs from the upper-most leaf-axils on the previous season's growths, bud-scales persisting during flowering and concealing the pedicels, which are up to ⅜ in. long. Calyx shortly five-lobed, usually scaly. Corolla funnel-shaped, ¾ to 1½ in. long, with five rounded, spreading lobes, varying in colour from white to various shades of purple or rose, scaly and usually more or less downy on the outside. Stamens ten, downy. Ovary scaly; style downy in the lower half or glabrous, sometimes scaly. *Bot. Mag.*, tt. 5060, 8802. (*s.* Virgatum)

R. *virgatum* is a species of wide range, from E. Nepal, through Sikkim (where J. D. Hooker discovered it in 1849) as far east as Yunnan, where Delavay collected the type of R. *oleifolium* around 1884. It was introduced by Hooker in 1850 and reintroduced by Forrest (as R. *oleifolium*) in 1906. There have been several sendings since then, the most recent being by the University of North Wales expedition to E. Nepal (B. L. & M. 298).

Although it has been found as high as 12,500 ft, R. *virgatum* is not a very hardy species and is mainly confined in the wild to elevations of 7,000 to 10,000 ft, and prefers open, dry sunny places or thin pine woodland. It is uncommon in cultivation.

R. *virgatum* is the only member of the series to which it gives its name. Of the two species once grouped with it, R. *oleifolium* is now considered to be synonymous and R. *racemosum* has been transferred to the Scabrifolium series. From that series R. *virgatum* differs in having the flowers solitary in each leaf-axil, or at the most in pairs. The glabrous leaves distinguish it from all members of that series except R. *racemosum* and R. *hemitrichotum*, and they have the leaves glaucous beneath; in R. *virgatum* the leaves are green beneath.

R. VIRIDESCENS Hutch.

An evergreen shrub up to 6 ft high in cultivation; young stems bristly at first. Leaves broad-elliptic, obovate or oblong-obovate, up to 1⅞ in. long and 1 in. wide, rounded at the apex, rounded-truncate at the base, glaucous when young, upper side pale sea-green on mature leaves, glabrous, under-side paler, sparsely scaly, margins and petioles bristly at first, later almost glabrous; petioles up to ¼ in. long. Flowers opening in June, borne in terminal trusses of four or five; pedicels ½ to ⅝ in. long, bristly and scaly. Calyx with ovate to roundish lobes, about 1/12 in. long, bristly and scaly. Corolla five-lobed, broadly funnel-shaped, about 1½ in. wide, yellowish green or lemon-yellow, sometimes tinged with red on the margin, the upper lobes marked with green spots, sparsely scaly outside. Stamens ten, the upper five about half as long as the lower set. Ovary densely scaly; style curved, glabrous. (*s.* Trichocladum)

R. *viridescens* was described in 1933 from a plant at Exbury, raised from Kingdon Ward's 5829, collected on the Doshong La at the eastern end of the Himalaya. The seed under this number was distributed as R. *trichocladum*, to which R. *viridescens* is closely allied, though it differs horticulturally in its persistent leaves and late-flowering. The wild-collected specimens and some from cultivated plants have the pedicels, leaf undersurface, and petioles hairy, but in the type and in some garden plants, the hairs are less evident or lacking. It is quite an attractive species both in flower and foliage, and received an Award of Merit when shown by E. H. M. and P. A. Cox, Glendoick Gardens Ltd, Perth, on June 27, 1972 (clone 'Doshong La').

R. VISCOSUM (L.) Torr.
Azalea viscosa L.

A deciduous shrub of bushy habit eventually 6 to 8 ft high, with twiggy branches, hairy when young. Leaves thinly arranged along the shoot or in a tuft of five or six at the end, obovate, 1 to 2 in. long, tapering to a short stalk at the base; dark green and glabrous above, paler and bristly along the midrib beneath; margins bristly. Flowers produced during June and July at the end of the previous year's shoots, six to twelve together in a cluster. Calyx small, and like the slender flower-stalk, glandular-hairy. ¾ in. long, curved, hairy. Corolla white or pink, 1 to 1¼ in. long, the lower half is a narrow tube often more highly coloured, the upper half five expanded oblong lobes ¾ in. long. The whole corolla, but especially the tubular part, is covered with sticky hairs. Stamens exserted. Ovary clad with usually gland-tipped bristles; style longer than the stamens, downy in the lower part.   (*s.* Azalea *ss.* Luteum)

Native of eastern N. America; introduced in 1734, and still one of the most delightful of garden shrubs because of its late blossoming and its exquisitely fragrant flowers. It is the reputed parent, or one of the parents of a great number of garden azaleas. Loddiges in their catalogue for 1836 gave a list of one hundred and seven varieties, which, according to Loudon, were hybrids or varieties of R. *viscosum*. The identity of many of these old varieties is lost, but some are still to be obtained under their old names. Relatively few, however, show any viscosum 'blood', but rather that of R. *periclymenoides* and R. *calendulaceum*. The viscosum group at the present time is, as a matter of fact, a rather limited one, but is well distinguished by the lateness in flowering, strong fragrance, and the viscous blossoms.

var. GLAUCUM (Ait.) Torr. *Azalea viscosa* var. *glauca* Ait.—The swamp honey-suckle is variable in the wild, more especially in the colour of the flowers and leaves. This is its most distinct variety, with pure white, fragrant flowers, and leaves blue-white on the lower, or sometimes on both, surfaces. A very charming shrub, flowering late like the type.

Other variants are described by Rehder in *A Monograph of Azaleas*, pp. 160–5. On the variability of R. *viscosum* Dr Henry Skinner writes: 'From the dwarf, twiggy and semi-evergreen bushes of the marshes of South Carolina to the tall, grey-leaved and large-flowered shrubs of the pond margins of Cape Cod, the Swamp azalea is much more changeable than its sister of the Gulf coast [R. *serrulatum*]. . . . It seems certain that not a little of the trouble is due to R. *viscosum* and *arborescens* having met on occasion in the northern states. . . . In some of these northern swamps genes have been so freely exchanged between these two species that nomenclatural assignment of present populations becomes virtually impossible' (*R.C.Y.B. 1957*, p. 28).

R. SERRULATUM (Small) Millais *Azalea serrulata* Small—Closely related to R. *viscosum*, which it replaces from mid-Georgia south to Florida and west to south-eastern Louisiana. According to Rehder its distinguishing characters are the red-brown branchlets, the leaves of firmer texture, finely but distinctly serrated at the margin, and the longer corolla-tube (about twice as long as the lobes, against one-and-a-half times as long in R. *viscosum*). It is remarkable for flowering very late in its natural habitat, but is of no importance for British gardens.

R. WARDII W. W. Sm.

R. *croceum* Balf. f. & W. W. Sm.; R. *gloeoblastum* Balf. f. & Forr.; R. *oresterum* Balf. f. & Forr.; R. *prasinocalyx* Balf. f. & Forr.; R. *astrocalyx* Balf. f. & Forr.

An evergreen shrub up to 15 or 20 ft high in the wild; young shoots sometimes glandular, otherwise glabrous. Leaves thinly leathery, glabrous, varying in shape from nearly orbicular to ovate, oblong-elliptic or oblong, rounded to obtuse at the apex, rounded, truncate or somewhat cordate at the base, 1¼ to 4¾ in. long, 1 to 2½ in. wide, dark or medium green above, paler, sometimes rather glaucous, beneath; petiole ⅜ to 1¼ in. long. Flowers in a loose terminal truss of up to fourteen, opening in May; pedicels up to almost 2 in. long, usually glandular. Calyx five-lobed up to ½ in. long, usually glandular. Corolla five-lobed, cup-shaped to saucer-shaped, up to 2½ in. across (exceptionally to 3 in. across), pure yellow, sometimes with a crimson blotch inside at the base. Stamens ten. Ovary conoid, glandular; style glandular from base to tip. *Bot. Mag.*, n.s., t. 587.   (s. Thomsonii ss. Souliei)

R. *wardii* is a species of wide range, from S.W. Szechwan westward through N.W. Yunnan to S.E. Tibet, in the provinces of Tsarong, Kongbo, and Takpo, but has not been reported from Burma. It occurs at 10,000 to 14,000 ft, in open thickets or occasionally as undergrowth in coniferous forest or deciduous woodland. It was discovered by one of the French missionaries, but was first validly described from specimens collected in 1913 by Kingdon Ward and by Forrest, both of whom sent seeds in that year. The former found it on the Doker La and around Atuntze, in the north-western corner of Yunnan; the latter 120 miles farther east, in the mountains of the north-east Yangtse bend. There have been many further sendings since then, the most recent being by Ludlow and Sherriff shortly before and after the second world war.

From R. *souliei* and R. *puralbum*, its nearest allies, R. *wardii* differs only in the colour of its flowers. From R. *campylocarpum* to which it is also nearly related, it can be distinguished by the style being glandular throughout and by the shallower corolla, but in some plants from Ludlow and Sherriff seeds the corolla is rather deeper than is typical for this species. It also resembles R. *campylocarpum* in the range of flower-colour, from pale creamy yellow, lemon, or sulphur to deep primrose, and in the frequent presence of a crimson or maroon blotch at the base of the corolla.

R. *wardii* is perfectly hardy near London and needs only light shade. Some of the strains introduced by Ludlow, Sherriff, and Taylor are valuable for the small garden, or one where late frosts are frequent, as they flower late in May and are of bushy compact habit, besides being beautiful in flower. All the seed collected came from the Tibetan Himalaya near Molo (*c.* 94° E.), some of it from as high as 13,000 ft.

Several forms of R. *wardii* have received Awards of Merit:

April 27, 1926, as R. *croceum*, flowers lemon-yellow, and as R. *astrocalyx*, flowers bright yellow with a small crimson flash (both shown by A. M. Williams, Werrington Park, Cornwall);

May 19, 1931, as R. *wardii* KW 4170, flowers bright yellow, green-flushed, raised from seeds collected by Kingdon Ward in the Muli area of S.W. Szechwan in 1921 (Lionel de Rothschild, Exbury);

May 5, 1959, as R. *wardii* "Ellestee", probably from seeds collected by Ludlow, Sherriff, and Taylor, flowers clear yellow with a deep crimson blotch (Collingwood Ingram, Benenden, Kent);

May 20, 1963, as R. *wardii* 'Meadow Pond', from Ludlow, Sherriff, and Elliot 15764, flowers primrose-yellow with a deep crimson blotch (Crown Estate Commissioners, Windsor Great Park).

R. LITIENSE Balf. f. & Forr.—Closely allied to R. *wardii* and, like it, having the style glandular to the tip; differing in the always oblong leaves, markedly glaucous beneath, and in the rather smaller, less saucer-shaped corollas. For a discussion of the taxonomic position of this species see *R.Y.B. 1951–2*, p. 157. It is a native of N.W. Yunnan, discovered and introduced by Forrest. Award of Merit, May 19, 1931, when shown by Lionel de Rothschild, Exbury, and a First Class Certificate in 1953 on the same date.

R. WASONII Hemsl. & Wils.

A sturdy evergreen shrub 2 to 5 ft high; young shoots thick, stiff, greyish white at first. Leaves narrowly oval or ovate, pointed, mostly rounded at the base, 2 to 3 in. long, 1 to 1½ in. wide, of hard leathery texture, ultimately glabrous and dark green above, clothed beneath with a close, rusty-brown down which becomes very dark on the two-year-old leaves; stalk ¼ to ½ in. long. Flowers produced in March and April in a terminal truss of six to ten. Corolla bell-shaped, 1¼ to 2 in. wide, creamy white or lemon-yellow, sometimes shaded with rose, or wholly rose-coloured, always spotted with crimson; five-lobed, the lobes overlapping. Calyx very small; flower-stalk ½ to 1 in. long, both white with down. Stamens ten, about ½ in. long, downy at the base; anthers dark brown; ovary clothed with white down; style as long as the corolla, glabrous, pale yellow. *Bot. Mag.*, t. 9190.   (*s.* Taliense *ss.* Wasonii)

Native of W. Szechwan, China; discovered and introduced in 1904 by Wilson, who observed that it is 'a common-low-growing species partial to rocks in forests'. It is a hardy, slow-growing species, with handsome foliage, with flowers, in the best form, of a clear, pale yellow, blotched at the base.

var. RHODODACTYLUM Hort. R. *rhododactylum* Balf. f., *nom. inedit.*—Flowers white, lined with pink. Raised from Wilson's no. 1876. Award of Merit, March

27, 1923, when shown from Bodnant, as *R. rhododactylum*. For this name see *Rhodo. Soc. Notes*, Vol. II, p. 258.

R. WATSONII Hemsl. & Wils.

An evergreen shrub or small tree, sometimes 30 ft high in the wild; young shoots stout, often ⅝ in. in diameter, scurfy white when young, becoming yellowish. Leaves oblanceolate to obovate, abruptly narrowed at the apex to a short point, tapered at the base to a thick, winged, yellowish stalk that is up to 1 in. long and ½ in. wide, 6 to 9 in. long, 2 to 4 in. wide, dark dull green and glabrous above, covered beneath with a pale, very close scurf; midrib broad and yellow above. Flowers produced from February to April in trusses of twelve to eighteen blooms and about 6 in. wide. Calyx small, $\frac{1}{12}$ in. long, with even triangular teeth; flower-stalks 1 to 1½ in. long, thinly downy. Corolla bell-shaped, 2 in. wide, nearly as deep, seven-lobed, white with a small purple blotch at the base. Stamens fourteen, shorter than the corolla, their white stalks downy towards the base. Ovary and style glabrous. (*s.* Grande)

Native of W. Szechwan; discovered by Wilson in 1904 and introduced by him. It is a little-known species, rare in cultivation, which is placed in the Grande series, of which it is an aberrant member, differing from all the other species, except *R. peregrinum*, in its glabrous ovary; the petiole is very short, with the decurrent base of the blade forming a wing on either side, as in *R. praestans*. During his second expedition for the Arnold Arboretum Wilson collected seed from trees 25 to 30 ft high, with trunks 2 to 2½ ft in girth.

R. PEREGRINUM Tagg—Near to *R. watsonii*, but with the leaves rounded to subcordate at the base and the petiole up to 1 in. long. It occurred as a rogue among plants of *R. galactinum* raised by E. J. P. Magor of Lamellen, Cornwall, from Wilson's 4254, collected in W. Szechwan on the Panlanshan, during his second expedition for the Arnold Arboretum.

R. WEBSTERIANUM Rehd. & Wils.

An evergreen shrub up to 3 ft high, with erect branches and young shoots densely covered with glistening, yellowish-grey scales. Leaves ovate to elliptical, blunt-ended, ¼ to ¾ in. long, half as wide; dark green and scaly above, thickly covered beneath with yellowish-grey scales. Flowers usually solitary, rarely in pairs or threes. Calyx deeply five-lobed, the lobes about ⅛ in. long, oval, scaly down the centre, fringed with hairs. Corolla rosy-purple, about 1 in. wide, with a short tube (hairy inside) and five rounded oval lobes ⅜ in. long, not scaly. Stamens ten, downy close to the base; anthers yellowish. Ovary scaly, conical, $\frac{1}{12}$ in. long; style glabrous or sometimes slightly scaly or downy towards the base, slightly longer than the stamens. (*s.* Lapponicum)

Native of W. Szechwan at altitudes of up to 15,000 ft; introduced by Wilson in 1908. It is a perfectly hardy species of no special merit, now uncommon in cultivation.

R. WEYRICHII Maxim.

R. *shikokianum* Makino

A deciduous azalea, described as often tree-like in habit in the wild, 3 to 15 ft high (Wilson); young shoots clothed with forward-pointing hairs, becoming brown and nearly glabrous the second year. Leaves obovate, ovate, or diamond-shaped, usually acutely pointed; distributed along vigorous shoots but often produced in a whorl at the end of shorter twigs, 1½ to 3½ in. long, 1 to 2¼ in. wide, pale green and soon glabrous above, greyer green and rather conspicuously veined beneath; stalk ¼ to ½ in. long, downy only when young. Flowers produced two to four together in a terminal cluster. Calyx very small, hairy. Corolla about 2 in. wide, of a rather dull rich red, funnel-shaped at the base, with five spreading lobes. Stamens six to ten, usually glabrous. Ovary densely clothed with erect, pale, reddish hairs; style usually glabrous. *Bot. Mag.*, t. 9475. (*s.* Azalea *ss.* Schlippenbachii)

Native of S. Japan, in Kyushu, Shikoku, and the Kinki district of the main island; also of the Korean island of Quelpaert; introduced by Wilson in 1914 to the Arnold Arboretum. Plants raised from seed obtained from that institution in 1915 flowered in May 1921 at Kew, where the species has proved fairly hardy in a sheltered place. It is most nearly akin to R. *reticulatum*, but is well marked by the colour of the flowers which may be termed rich brick-red and as distinct among azaleas as that of R. *griersonianum* is among rhododendrons proper.

R. AMAGIANUM (Makino) Makino ex Nemoto *Azalea amagiana* Makino— Closely related to R. *weyrichii*, but with thicker leaves, lustrous above, the base of the midrib beneath and the petiole white-tomentose; they are commonly rhombic in outline and relatively rather broader than in R. *weyrichii*. The flowers are often more than 2 in. wide and are borne in July after the leaves have expanded. *Bot. Mag.*, n.s., t. 379. It is a local species, confined to Mt Amagi and Mt Hijane in Idzu province; introduced to Britain in the late 1930s. It is hardy but needs light shade at least in southern England. A mature specimen of this azalea is a wonderful sight when in flower. The colour is a soft shade of true scarlet, with darker spotting on the upper lobe. Award of Merit July 6, 1948, when shown by Lord Aberconway, Bodnant.

R. SANCTUM Nakai—This, another native of Japan, is very closely allied to R. *amagianum*, but the flowers are rose-coloured and are borne earlier, in May or June. Like R. *amagianum* it is a local species, found wild only in the mountains south-east and south-west of Nagoya.

R. WIGHTII Hook. f.

An evergreen shrub or small shrubby tree, with stout, tomentose young stems. Leaves very leathery, dark green, 6 to 8 in., sometimes more, long, 2½ to 3 in. wide, oblong-elliptic, or broadest slightly above or below the middle, obtuse or abruptly acuminate at the apex, rounded to truncate at the base, glabrous above when mature, underside covered with a close, continuous indumentum varying in colour from fawn or grey to cinnamon-brown; petiole up to 1 in. long, tomentose. Inflorescence a terminal truss of up to twenty flowers; rachis variable in length, sometimes 2 in. long; pedicels up to 2¾ in. long. Calyx minute. Corolla campanulate, up to 2 in. long, pale yellow, spotted with crimson on the upper lobe and sometimes with a crimson blotch at the base, five-lobed. Stamens ten, downy towards the base. Ovary tomentose; style glabrous. *Bot. Mag.*, t. 8492. (s. Lacteum)

Native of the Himalaya from Nepal to some way east of Bhutan; discovered by J. D. Hooker and introduced by him in 1850. It is a common species in the inner valleys, forming thickets of considerable extent at 12,000 to 14,000 ft. It is not an easy plant to cultivate and early this century was still an exceedingly rare plant in gardens. The best-known example grew in the garden of Miss Clara Mangles at Littleworth near Farnham, and the species received an Award of Merit when she exhibited a truss on May 14, 1913. It is now established in cultivation, but uncommon, though quite hardy. It bears some resemblance to R. *lacteum*, but in that species the flowers are usually of a much richer colour and unspotted, and the leaves are relatively wider. In cultivated plants the truss of R. *wightii* tends to be rather lax, though this is not a character of the species as a whole. The flowering time of R. *wightii* is April or May.

R. WILLIAMSIANUM Rehd. & Wils.   [PLATE 94

An evergreen shrub up to 4 or 5 ft high, of rounded shape and usually wider than high, keeping close the ground, densely and intricately branched; young shoots slender, glaucous, thinly furnished with gland-tipped bristles. Leaves orbicular to ovate, usually heart-shaped at the base, 1 to 2 in. long, at first bronzy, finally dark green above, glaucous beneath; stalk ⅓ to ⅝ in. long, purplish when young, glandular-bristly. Flowers two to (rarely) four in a loose terminal cluster, opening in April. Calyx minute, glandular at the margin; flower-stalk ¾ to 1¼ in. long, glandular. Corolla bell-shaped, 2¼ in. wide, soft rosy red, five- (rarely six-) lobed, the lobes notched; stamens ten, 1¼ in. long, glabrous; style overtopping the stamens and, like the ovary, sparsely set with stalked glands. *Bot. Mag.*, t. 8935. (s. Thomsonii ss. Williamsianum)

Native of W. Szechwan, China; discovered and introduced by Wilson in 1908; he describes it as very local and occurring only in isolated thickets on the cliffs of Wa-Shan. It was later found on Mt Omei by Chinese botanists, growing in similar habitats. According to Fang, the plants there have rather larger leaves than in the typical form and up to fourteen stamens.

This species is named in honour of J. C. Williams of Caerhays and is one of the most distinct as well as beautiful of Chinese rhododendrons. It flowers when quite small, attracting notice then by the curiously disproportionate largeness of the flowers. It is quite hardy at Kew, but is slow-growing and dwarf. In more favoured gardens it makes dense hemispherical bushes not only attractive for its delicately coloured blossom but also for bronzy young foliage. Easily increased by late summer cuttings. It must be regarded as indispensable to any collection of rhododendrons. Its only fault is that both the flowers and the young growths are often killed by frost, but despite that it must be planted in an open, sunny position. Given the protection of a tree-canopy it does not set flower-bud and loses its characteristic shape.

R. *williamsianum* has proved to be a potent parent, imparting a compact habit and a short rounded leaf to its offspring in the most diverse crosses. All the hybrids between it and other species are charming, though some are inclined to be shy-flowering. Several crosses between R. *williamsianum* and Hardy Hybrids are now available, raised in Holland and Germany. See further in the section on hybrids.

R. WILSONIAE Hemsl. & Wils.

An evergreen shrub up to 6 or 7 ft high, with glabrous, slender branches. Leaves narrowly oval or oval-lanceolate, 2½ to 4½ in. long, 1 to 1¾ in. wide; narrowly tapered at the base, acuminate at the apex, glabrous on both surfaces, rather glossy above, pale beneath, the texture leathery or even hardish; stalk up to ½ in. long. Flowers slightly fragrant, produced singly from a scaly bud in the axil of each leaf at the end of the shoot, four or six in all; pedicels ¾ to 1 in. long, glabrous. Calyx five-lobed, the lobes curiously diverse in length, some being quite short, others linear and up to ½ in. long. Corolla flesh-pink, about 2 in. across, funnel-shaped at the base, deeply five-lobed, the upper lobe spotted with brown. Stamens ten, hairy at the base. Style and ovary glabrous, the latter long and slender. (*s.* Stamineum)

Native of central China; discovered by Wilson in the Patung district of W. Hupeh, where it grows in rocky places with other shrubs and trees at 5,000 to 6,500 ft, and introduced by him in 1900 when collecting for Messrs Veitch. It first flowered in 1912 at Caerhays. R. *wilsoniae* is a rather tender species, but has grown at Wakehurst Place, Sussex, for many years in a fairly exposed position, and is 10 ft high there. It received an Award of Merit as a shrub for the cool greenhouse when shown by the Crown Estate Commissioners, Windsor Great Park, on March 30, 1971.

R. WILTONII Hemsl. & Wils.

An evergreen shrub 5 to 12 ft high; young shoots clothed with a thick, brown wool. Leaves obovate, tapered at the base, abruptly narrowed at the apex to a short tip, 2 to 4 in. long, ¾ to 1¼ in. wide, glossy green and deeply wrinkled above, thickly clothed beneath with brown wool; stalk about ½ in long. Flowers in clusters of about ten in April or May, on woolly pedicels up to 1 in. long. Corolla white or pink, speckled or blotched inside with crimson, bell-shaped, 1¼ in. deep, rather more wide, the five lobes almost erect. Stamens ten, shorter than the corolla, downy towards the base. Ovary covered with pale brown wool; style quite glabrous. *Bot. Mag.*, t. 9388. (*s.* Taliense *ss.* Wasonii)

Native of W. Szechwan, known from Mt Omei, the Washan, and the Mupin region; discovered by Wilson and introduced by him in 1904, for Messrs Veitch, and also cultivated from his no. 4264, collected during his second expedition for the Arnold Arboretum. With its striking leaves, on which the line of every vein is deeply etched, it is one of the most easily recognised of all rhododendrons. It is worth growing for these alone, but is also attractive in its flowers. It received an Award of Merit when shown by Edmund de Rothschild, Exbury, on March

30, 1957 (flowers white with a crimson blotch, flushed with pink on the outside).

R. XANTHOCODON Hutch.

An evergreen shrub or small tree in the wild. Leaves elliptic or oblong-elliptic, rounded and mucronate at the apex, rounded to broad-cuneate at the base, 1¼ to 3 in. long, 1⅜ to 1⅞ in. wide, dull green and sparsely scaly above, densely scaly and glaucous green beneath; stalk about ½ in. long. Flowers opening in May, in terminal trusses of five to ten; pedicels up to ⅞ in. long. Calyx small, shortly lobed, densely scaly. Corolla creamy yellow or soft yellow, unspotted, tubular-campanulate, 1 to 1½ in. long, with five slightly spreading lobes. Stamens ten, downy at the base. Ovary scaly; style glabrous. (s. Cinnabarinum)

R. *xanthocodon* was discovered by Kingdon Ward out of flower in July 1924, growing on the Nam La, a pass in S.E. Tibet under Namcha Barwa, the mountain which dominates the great bend of the Tsangpo river. He collected seeds in the autumn (KW 6026) and the species was described some ten years later after it had flowered at Bodnant. Unfortunately, Dr Hutchinson placed it in the Triflorum series, thus obscuring its affinity, which is with R. *cinnabarinum* and R. *concatenans*. It differs from both in having the leaves scaly above, and in its narrow-campanulate corollas, and from the former also in the colour of the flowers and their smaller size. That is true at least of the type-plant. But other plants raised from KW 6026 approach R. *cinnabarinum* in the shape of their corollas, and it may eventually prove that the presence or absence of scales on the upper surface of the leaves is not a reliable character.

R. *xanthocodon* is perfectly hardy in a sheltered place and makes a tall, laxly branched shrub. The colour of the flowers varies somewhat, but is always a pleasant and uniform shade of yellow.

R. CONCATENANS Hutch.—This, another of Kingdon Ward's discoveries, was described in 1935 from a plant at Nymans in Sussex, raised from his seed no. 5874. He found this species (which he nick-named 'Orange Bill') in June 1924, growing in a tanglewood of rhododendrons on a steep slope above the torrent that runs from the Doshong La to the Tsangpo, and gathered seed in the following autumn. 'But I had a really desperate time getting seed of it. It grew, as I say, well up the steep slope and often out of reach on the cliffs above. I went after it on October 22nd during a heavy snowstorm and got a few capsules. On October 26th I tried again; by this time the bushes were well snowed up, but I got some more seed, and it is a relief to think that the seeds are germinating, considering the awful strain on my temper while struggling in that accursed cold muddle' (*Riddle of the Tsangpo Gorges*, p. 113).

R. *concatenans* is closely allied to R. *cinnabarinum*, indeed it is nearer to it than is R. *xanthocodon*. It differs in the shorter, campanulate corolla and, in the typical state, in its apricot-yellow flowers. A feature of the Kingdon Ward introduction is that the young leaves are verdigris-coloured and remain glaucous above for several months. As in R. *cinnabarinum*, they are without scales on the upper surface. R. *concatenans* is a hardy species, flowering in late April or May; it is best placed in a fairly sunny position, as the characteristic leaf-colouring is not developed in shade, or at least is less vivid. *Bot. Mag.*, n.s., t. 634. It received a First Class Certificate when shown from Nymans on May 8, 1935.

R. concatenans was reintroduced by Ludlow, Sherriff, and Taylor in 1938 from the Lo La, some ninety miles to the south-west of the type-locality (L.S. & T. 6560). A plant raised from the seeds by Collingwood Ingram at The Grange, Benenden, Kent, produced flowers described as Chinese Coral suffused red-orange inside, brighter red outside. It received an Award of Merit when exhibited by him in 1954 under the clonal name 'Copper'. According to the field note, the wild plants had apricot-coloured flowers.

R. XANTHOSTEPHANUM Merrill
R. aureum Franch., not Georgi

An evergreen shrub 4 ft and upwards high; young shoots sprinkled with scales. Leaves ovate-lanceolate to oblong-lanceolate, usually pointed, tapered at the base, 1½ to 3½ in. long, ⅜ to 1⅛ in. wide, dark glossy green and soon glabrous above, glaucous and closely pitted with tiny glistening scales beneath; stalks ¼ to ½ in. long. Flowers opening in May in clusters usually of three to five. Calyx deeply five-lobed, the lobes rounded, more or less scaly like the flower-stalk which is ¼ to ½ in. long. Corolla funnel-shaped, about 1 in. long, five-lobed, scaly outside, of varying shades of yellow (rich, bright, or tinged with green). Stamens ten, rather longer than the corolla, downy at the base. Ovary densely scaly as is the style also towards the base. *Bot. Mag.*, t. 8882.   (s. Boothii ss. Tephropeplum.)

Native of Yunnan and the Tsarong province of S.E. Tibet westward through upper Burma to the eastern end of the Himalaya; discovered by Delavay about 1886 in the Tali range, Yunnan; introduced by Forrest in 1910. It occurs at mostly 8,000 to 11,000 ft, in thickets on rocky slopes and cliffs or at the edge of torrents. As a rule it is a bushy shrub in the wild up to 6 ft high, but Kingdon Ward found it 15 ft high in the gorge of the Taron (Kiuchiang). It is allied to *R. tephropeplum*, differing in the colour of its flowers. In *R. sulfureum* of the Boothii subseries the flowers are yellow but they are wider and the style is bent, whereas in *R. xanthostephanum* it is straight. It is a rather tender species, needing a sheltered position.

The Award of Merit was given on May 15, 1961, to clone 'Yellow Garland', exhibited by the Crown Estate Commissioners, Windsor Great Park. This was raised from Forrest 21707, collected on the Salween-Kiuchiang divide in 1922.

R. AURITUM Tagg—Near to *R. xanthostephanum*, but flowers creamy white, slightly tinged with pink and calyx-lobes strongly reflexed. It was described in 1934 from a garden plant raised from Kingdon Ward's seed no. 6278, collected 'blind' in November 1924, during his exploration of the Tsangpo gorge at the eastern end of the Himalaya, and was reintroduced from the same locality by Ludlow, Sherriff, and Elliot in 1946-7. Kingdon Ward's field note reads: 'Shrub of 6-10 ft semi-erect, the branches flopping over unless supported, forming a thick bush. Bark peeling, exposing a smooth copper-red stem. Truss 5-7 flowered. Abundant on gneiss cliffs and boulders in open situations along the river bank. . . .' It is hardy in mid-Sussex, but not of much beauty.

R. YEDOENSE Maxim.

R. yedoense is the name given by Maximowicz in 1886 to a double-flowered garden form of an azalea that grows wild in Korea. Unfortunately this azalea was not described as a species until many years later and must therefore be treated as a variety of its own cultivated offspring:

var. POUKHANENSE (Lévl.) Nakai *R. poukhanense* Lévl.; *R. coreanum* Rehd.— A deciduous or nearly deciduous azalea 3, 4, or occasionally up to 6 ft high; young shoots clothed with appressed bristles. Leaves lanceolate, oval-lanceolate, or oblanceolate, pointed, tapered at the base to a stalk $\frac{1}{8}$ to $\frac{1}{6}$ in. long, $1\frac{1}{2}$ to 3 in. long; both surfaces bristly, especially at the margins. Flowers fragrant, produced in April and May usually two to four together in a terminal cluster; Flower-stalk $\frac{1}{8}$ in. long, bristly. Calyx five-lobed; the lobes ovate, about $\frac{1}{4}$ in. long, very bristly, especially on the margins, green. Corolla rosy purple, funnel-shaped, $1\frac{1}{2}$ in. long, rather more wide, five-lobed, freely spotted on the upper lobes. Stamens ten, about as long as the corolla, downy on the lower third; anthers purple. Ovary bristly; style $1\frac{1}{4}$ in. long, usually glabrous. *Bot. Mag.*, n.s., t. 455 (*s. Azalea ss.* Obtusum)

Native of Korea; introduced to the Arnold Arboretum by J. G. Jack in 1905, thence to England in 1913. It flowered at Kew in April 1914. Although now known by the above varietal name, it is a genuine wild type and according to Wilson is the common azalea of Korea from about the latitude of the capital, Seoul, southward, but is uncommon on Poukhan-san from which it derives its name. 'It is partial to open country and on grassy mountain slopes and in thin Pine-woods it forms dense matlike masses from a few inches to a yard high . . . but in thickets the plants are more loosely branched and often two metres high' (*Monograph of Azaleas*, p. 66). It also occurs on Daghelet Island (Quelpaert). It is perfectly hardy at Kew. The plant which provided the material figured in the *Botanical Magazine* is from a plant there raised from seeds collected in Korea by Mr Moorcraft in 1951, while serving with the British forces. The flowers in this form are rosy pink, but more commonly they are a vivid shade of lilac purple.

R. yedoense var. *poukhanense* received an Award of Merit when shown by Capt. Collingwood Ingram, Benenden, Kent, on April 11, 1961 (flower-colour described as Mauve).

The double-flowered type of the species is also known as 'Yodogawa', and was introduced to Europe from Japan in 1884.

R. YUNNANENSE Franch. [PLATE 96

R. chartophyllum Franch.; *R. pleistanthum* Balf. f.; *R. aechmophyllum* Balf. f. & Forr.; *R. suberosum* Balf. f. & Forr.

A semi-evergreen or nearly deciduous shrub, ultimately 8 to 12 ft high; stiffly and somewhat thinly branched; young wood slightly scaly. Leaves narrowly oval or obovate, $1\frac{1}{2}$ to 3 in. long, $\frac{1}{2}$ to $\frac{3}{4}$ in. wide, tapering at both ends, ciliate and sometimes sparsely bristly when young, bright green above, paler beneath, slightly scaly on both sides; stalk ¼ in. or less long. Flowers produced in one or more clusters at the end of the previous year's shoots during the latter half of May, each cluster consisting of four or five flowers. Corolla 1½ to 2 in. across, widely funnel-shaped, white, pale blush, pale rose, or pale lavender, with a flare of brown, crimson, or sometimes greenish spots. Stamens ten, hairy at the base. Ovary scaly, style glabrous. *Bot. Mag.*, t. 7614.   (*s.* Triflorum *ss.* Yunnanense)

Native mainly of Yunnan and S.W. Szechwan, but extending into bordering parts of S.E. Tibet and upper Burma and also found in Kweichow. It was discovered by the French missionary Delavay and introduced by him to Paris in

RHODODENDRON YUNNANENSE

1889. Messrs Veitch had plants in their Coombe Wood nursery by 1894, presumably raised from seeds obtained from Paris and one of these, received from Veitch, first flowered at Kew in 1897. Later, seeds were sent from China by Forrest, Kingdon Ward, and Rock, and the present garden stock mainly descends from these. In the wild R. *yunnanense* grows mainly in open places and seems, judging from Forrest's field notes, to be partial to streamsides. Its altitudinal range is remarkably wide: Forrest's collections from the Tali range were mostly from around 9,000 ft, a comparatively low altitude for that part of Yunnan, but around Atuntze, near the inner border of the rhododendron zone, he found it at 13,000 to 14,000 ft.

This very charming species is quite hardy, apart from a tendency to bark-split after late frost, when grown in an isolated position. Being by nature a thicket-forming shrub, and of rather gaunt habit on its own, it is best planted in a clump of several individuals or mixed with other scaly-leaved species of the same habit. It varies in the colour of its flowers, but the pure white or blush-tinted forms are really the most characteristic and most desirable. There is also great variation in the colour of the speckling, from light brown or green to crimson. It is easily raised from cuttings, but no clones have been named, which is surprising, considering what a variable species it is.

R. *yunnanense* received an Award of Merit on May 19, 1904, when shown from the Glasnevin Botanic Garden, Dublin; and an Award of Garden Merit in 1934.

R. HORMOPHORUM Balf. f. & Forr. R. *chartophyllum* Franch. f. *praecox* Diels—This is really only a form of R. *yunnanense* with the leaves almost completely deciduous, in the sense that they are almost all shed by the time the new ones develop. Introduced by Forrest, and better known by the synonymous name. The wild plants are sometimes up to 9 ft high or, at the other extreme, have prostrate main stems creeping among or under stones and rocks, with erect branchlets only 1 to 1½ ft high; cultivated plants are usually dwarfer and denser than in R. *yunnanense*. Award of Merit May 18, 1943, to a white-flowered form, leafless at flowering time, the foliage turning red in autumn, shown by Lord Digby, Minterne, Dorset.

R. RIGIDUM Franch. R. *caeruleum* Lévl.; R. *eriandrum* Lévl. ex Hutch.; R. *hesperium* Balf. f. & Forr.; R. *rarosquameum* Balf. f.; R. *sycnanthum* Balf. f. & W.W. Sm.—This species, better known as R. *caeruleum*, is allied to R. *yunnanense*, differing mainly in its quite glabrous, bluish-green leaves, glaucous green beneath. The flowers vary in colour from lilac or rosy pink to white, and are more or less spotted. It is fairly widely distributed in Yunnan and is said to be common in the north-eastern part of the province. The most admired form has white flowers, borne in May, and was introduced by Dr Rock under his no. 59207; it received an Award of Merit when exhibited by Lionel de Rothschild, Exbury, on May 16, 1939.

R. ZALEUCUM Balf. f. & W. W. Sm.
R. *erileucum* Balf. f. & Forr.

An evergreen shrub found by collectors varying from 6 to 30 ft high; young shoots scaly. Leaves oval-lanceolate, wedge-shaped to rounded at the base, usually sharply pointed, 1½ to 3 in. long, ⅜ to 1¼ in. wide; dark green and with a few scales above, very glaucous or bluish white and scaly beneath, the scales well apart from each other; stalk ⅛ to ⅓ in. long. The margin of the leaf is fringed with hairs when young, but most of them fall away. Flowers produced in March or April from the end of the shoot and the axils of the terminal leaves in umbels of three to five, slightly fragrant; flower-stalk ⅖ in. long, scaly. Calyx small, shallowly bowl-shaped, with a few hairs on the margin. Corolla rosy white, 1 to 1⅝ in long, funnel-shaped at the base, expanding at the mouth into five oval rounded lobes, scaly all over the outside. Stamens ten, slightly downy

towards the base. Ovary scaly; style glabrous. *Bot. Mag.*, t. 8878.   (*s.* Triflorum
ss. Yunnanense)

Native of N.W. Yunnan and bordering parts of upper Burma; discovered by
Forrest in 1912 on the Shweli–Salween divide and introduced by him in that
year. The most striking character of this rhododendron is the intensely glaucous
white undersurface of the leaves, due to a coating of wax. Although the flowers
are typically white or pink, plants with flowers coloured as in R. *ponticum* were
found by Farrer and Cox in Burma (Farrer 980), and a yellow-flowered form
was introduced by Kingdon Ward in 1953 from the Triangle between the two
branches of the upper Irrawaddy. Having a wide altitudinal range, from 6,000
to 13,000 ft, it is variable in hardiness, but Forrest's original introduction was
perfectly hardy. R. *zaleucum* is unusual among its allies in that it sometimes grows
as a small tree in rain-forest; as a general rule the species of the Yunnanense
subseries prefer more open habitats.

R. *zaleucum* received an Award of Merit when shown by Col. S. R. Clarke,
Borde Hill, Sussex, on May 24, 1932 (flowers mauve-pink, slightly spotted).

R. ZEYLANICUM Booth ex Cowan

R. *rollissonii* Hort., not (?) Lindl.; R. *nobile* Hort. ex Lindl., not Wall.; R. *arboreum* of
many authors in part, not Sm.; R. *arboreum* var. *zeylanicum* Millais; R. *nilagiricum sens.*
Stapf in *Bot. Mag.*, t. 9323, in part

An evergreen shrub or tree said to attain almost 70 ft in the wild; young
stems stout, glandular-downy when young. Leaves leathery, elliptic or elliptic-
oblong, 2 to 5 in. long, 1¼ to 2 in. wide, obtuse at the apex, rounded or truncate
to slightly cordate at the base, dark green and bullate above, clad beneath with
a yellowish or rust-coloured, woolly indumentum, which is rather sticky to the
touch owing to the presence of stalked glands amongst the hairs, margins
strongly revolute; stalk stout, up to ¾ in. long. Inflorescence as in R. *arboreum*;
pedicels ⅜ to ½ in. long, glandular. Calyx small, irregularly five-lobed, densely
glandular on the margin. Corolla rich scarlet, about 1¾ in. long. The flowering
time is April–May, i.e., later than in R. *arboreum*. *Bot. Mag.*, t. 7696. (*s.* and *ss.*
Arboreum)

Native of Ceylon at 6,000 to 8,000 ft; introduced in the 1830s. Its original
habitat was in the zone of temperate forest, of which vestiges still remain,
and on the mountain summits, where it formed dwarf forest. At the present
time it also occurs as isolated specimens in the patana grasslands, which are at
least in part the result of the burning of the primaeval forest. One such specimen,
growing on the golf-course at Nuwara Eliya, was 35 ft in height and spread
and 9¾ ft in girth below the lowest branch, when measured in 1926 (C. Ingram,
Gard. Chron., Vol. 80, p. 289 and fig. 134).

In the last century R. *zeylanicum* was commonly grown under the name R.
rollissonii, and this would be the correct name for the species were it not that
there is some doubt concerning the identity of the rhododendron described and
figured under that name in 1843 (*Bot. Reg.*, Vol. 29, t. 25). At the end of the last
century it was grown at Kew under the name R. *kingianum*, in the belief that it
had been raised from seeds collected by Sir George Watt in Manipur, and that

it was the rhododendron for which he had proposed that name. But Dr Cowan later pointed out that the plant in question is obviously R. *zeylanicum* and that it does not in the least resemble the Manipur rhododendron, of which Sir George Watt's drawing and detailed manuscript description have been preserved (*Notes Roy. Bot. Gard. Edin.*, Vol. 19 (1936), p. 161). But see further below.

Although closely related to R. *arboreum*, the Ceylon rhododendron is well distinguished from it by its relatively broader, bullate leaves, and by the presence of glands on their undersurface. It is uncommon in cultivation, but grows quite well, though slowly, in the milder parts and even seeds itself. The most notable specimens are at Stonefield and Arduaine in western Scotland. The latter is about 20 ft high, on eleven stems, and was raised from seeds brought from Ceylon in 1898 (*R.C.Y.B. 1964*, pp. 10–11; *1966*, p. 35).

R. *zeylanicum* and R. *nilagiricum* are discussed by Dr J. M. Cowan in *Notes Roy. Bot. Gard.*, Vol. 19 (1936), pp. 157–66.

R. NILAGIRICUM Zenker R. *arboreum* var. *nilagiricum* (Zenker) C. B. Cl.; R. *arboreum* of many authors, in part, not Sm.—Closely related to R. *zeylanicum*, differing in its narrower leaves without glands on the undersurface, and in its tomentose, not glandular, pedicels and calyx, the latter very small. Flowers scarlet, crimson, or pink. Native of S.W. India; described from the Nilgiri Hills and also found in the Anaimalai and Palni Hills, farther south. Whether R. *nilagiricum* and R. *zeylanicum* should be regarded as distinct species is debatable. If they are to be united, as they were by Dr Stapf (*Bot. Mag.*, t. 9323), then the name for the combined species would be R. *nilagiricum*, which has long priority. But Cowan, in the article alluded to above, considered that they should be kept separate, remarking, however, that they are more closely allied to each other than either is to R. *arboreum*.

The rhododendron figured in *Bot. Mag.*, t. 4381, as R. *nilagiricum* is not that species but R. *arboreum*.

R. KINGIANUM Watt ex W. Watson R. *arboreum* var. *kingianum* Hook. f.—The name R. *kingianum* was proposed by Sir George Watt for a rhododendron found by him on Ching Sow, Manipur, in 1882, the original specimen of which is preserved in the Kew Herbarium (Watt 6535). He also sent seeds to Kew, and a plant raised from these was described by Sir Joseph Hooker in 1900 under the name R. *arboreum* var. *kingianum* (*Bot. Mag.*, t. 7696). Cowan, in the paper referred to above, takes the view that R. *kingianum*, i.e., the plant raised at Kew, is R. *zeylanicum*. If this judgement is correct, two possibilities have to be considered: that Hooker was in error in supposing that the plant he described was raised from the seeds collected by Watt; or that R. *zeylanicum* occurs in Manipur. The latter possibility is far from unlikely. Numerous species of the eastern Himalaya and neighbouring mountains occur on the hills of peninsular India and Ceylon, or are represented there by closely related forms. Watt's 6535 is certainly near to R. *zeylanicum* in the shape and indumentum of its leaves (but perhaps even nearer to R. *nilagiricum*), and similar specimens have been collected in the Khasi Hills of Assam. The identity and status of R. *kingianum* is therefore best left in abeyance until the whole R. *arboreum* complex has been studied as a whole.

THE HYBRIDS

INTRODUCTION

In this section an attempt has been made to give a reasonably comprehensive account of the hybrids of *Rhododendron* available to growers at the present time. The hybrids have always outnumbered the species in gardens, and it was felt by the editors that to ignore them would greatly lessen the value of this revised edition. The hybrids (including azaleas) currently in commerce number over a thousand and it is obviously impossible to include them all. Hybrids listed by only one nurseryman have been excluded unless they have received an award or have such obvious merits that they are certain to become more widely available. Space has been given to hybrids of historical interest and to certain old hybrids which, though no longer in commerce, are still to be found in gardens. The descriptions are in the main based on living material, and we are most grateful to the garden owners and managers who have helped to make this possible. Descriptions of some of the older hybrids are taken from the manuscript notes compiled by Arthur Ivens, kindly made available by Messrs Hillier. Mr Ivens' meticulous descriptions, mostly quite as detailed as those given to species by botanists, have also proved most valuable for verifying the identity of certain Hardy Hybrids whose correct name was in doubt. Some descriptions are drawn from those published by the Royal Horticultural Society when the hybrid received an award. The historical notes are the product in the main of research in the files of *The Gardeners' Chronicle* since 1841, and study of original descriptions in horticultural publications. But the two volumes on *Rhododendron* by J. G. Millais are the souce of much information on the hybrids raised in the late 19th century and the early part of the present century. Millais was the chronicler of the rhododendron world of his time, and these two volumes, cumbersome and rather carelessly compiled though they are, are a storehouse of interesting information, and a monument to the intelligent affection that the genus *Rhododendron* has inspired in so many of its devotees.

NOMENCLATURE OF HYBRIDS.—For the most part hybrids in the genus *Rhododendron* have been named in the same way as other perennial plants. The names of Hardy Hybrids, most azaleas, etc., indicate clones, i.e., plants propagated vegetatively and derived from a single mother-plant. These names are usually 'fancy' names, but some of the older hybrids (and a few later ones) bear clonal names in Latin, e.g., 'Album Elegans' and 'Everestianum'. The standard practice worked well enough for commercial hybrids, few of which were primary crosses and mostly were of unrecorded or at least undeclared parentage. But the hybrids raised in private gardens from the early years of this century onwards were the result of deliberate crosses and therefore of known parentage. These came to be named according to the system already in use among orchid breeders, by which the products of a cross receive a collective 'fancy' name, which remains constant no matter how many times or where the cross is made, and any seedling of the cross worthy of distinction is given a clonal name, also in the vernacular, which belongs solely to it and its vegetatively propagated progeny. A group of seedlings and clones having a common parentage came to be known as a 'grex' (Latin for herd or flock), a term also borrowed from the orchidists.

As an example of this system, in the modified form that came into force in the 1950s, we may take the hybrid between *R. dichroanthum* and *R. griersonianum* originally made at Bodnant. The 'grex-name' for this cross is Fabia. Named clones from this cross are Fabia 'Minterne Apricot' (raised at Minterne), Fabia 'Roman Pottery' (raised at Embley Park) and several others. A confusing feature of this system of nomenclature, as it has been applied to rhododendrons, is that the collective or grex-name may also be used in a clonal sense. Thus the name 'Fabia', as distinct from grex Fabia, would belong to the clone, if any, descended from the plant which received an Award of Merit when shown by the raiser in 1934 as *R.* Fabia simply. Fabia, the example so far used, is a straight cross between two species, but many registered grexes have a hybrid as one parent, e.g., the famous Naomi grex, which has four species in its parentage, and a few are the result of hybrid with hybrid crosses, e.g., the Jalisco grex, also a compound of four species.

The system of nomenclature discussed here was first adopted by Lionel de Rothschild in 1931 and became the official method of naming rhododendron crosses when the Rhododendron Stud Book was issued in 1934 (in the Year Book of the Rhododendron Association for that year). Its abandonment was officially proposed in a note published in the *Rhododendron and Camellia Year Book* for 1956 (pp. 156–9), and put into effect around 1959, since when only clonal names have been accepted for registration by the Royal Horticultural Society, which is the International Registration Authority for *Rhododendron*. However, most of the important interspecific crosses were named as grexes, and the system was applied retrospectively to some earlier ones, so there is an inheritance of well-established grex-names that cannot now be conveniently abandoned. If a name is stated in the International Register to be a grex-name it is so treated in the descriptions that follow, and the formula-name, i.e., the statement of parentage, is placed immediately after it; grex-names are given without inverted commas, to avoid confusion with clonal names. In the formula, the parents are given in alphabetical order, as is now customary; the old convention, by which the seed-parent was given first, is impracticable, since in many cases it is not known which way round the cross was made, and some crosses have been made both ways.

Considering the size of the genus, and the amount of hybridising that has been done, it is at first sight surprising how very few interspecific crosses bear valid botanical names. The explanation is that botanical names for garden hybrids are usually acquired fortuitously; commercial hybrids in some groups were given Latin names by their raisers, and if these were supported by an adequate description, they came to be accepted as botanically valid. However, in *Rhododendron* the 'Latin phase' of naming was a short one (virtually all hybrids raised after 1850 bear 'fancy' names) and in any case the vast majority of interspecific crosses were named according to the system discussed above, and consequently bear names such as Ángelo, Fabia, and Elizabeth. In the interests of consistency, the few crosses that bear valid botanical names are included in this section, instead of being treated with the species as in previous editions, and their names are given as in the *International Rhododendron Register*. Thus *R.* × *praecox* Carr., the valid botanical name for *R. ciliatum* × *R. dauricum*, is given as Praecox and in effect regarded as a grex-name that happens to be in Latin instead of in the vernacular.

Another method of naming hybrids is the condensed formula, e.g., Oreocinn as a substitute for *R. oreotrephes* × *R. cinnabarinum*. This method was used by Edward Magor of Lamellen for his hybrid grexes, and the results were treated with derision by his fellow rhododendron breeders, who with good reason prided themselves on choosing elegant and memorable names for their crosses. Some of the Magor names were indeed most uncouth—Smirnauck and so on—but his son Major Walter Magor has recently pointed out that this system of naming was actually proposed by no less an authority than Sir Isaac Bayley Balfour of the Royal Botanic Garden, Edinburgh (*R.C.Y.B. 1966*, p. 135). The same method was used by a few other breeders, though on a lesser scale, and has now been abandoned.

AWARDS.—As throughout this work, the abbreviation A.M. stands for the Award of Merit, and F.C.C. (a higher award) for First Class Certificate, both being granted by the Royal Horticultural Society. The abbreviations A.M.T. and F.C.C.T. indicate the equivalent awards given to rhododendrons and azaleas after trial in the garden of the Royal Horticultural Society at Wisley in Surrey (or at Exbury in Hampshire in the case of a few early trials). Before 1923, rhododendrons and azaleas were judged by the Society's Floral Committee. In 1924 this was divided into two subcommittees, and to subcommittee B (Floral B) was entrusted the judging of ornamental trees and shrubs, and 'botanical species'; its first chairman was Gerald Loder of Wakehurst Place, Sussex. After the formation of the Rhododendron Association the judging of rhododendrons and azaleas was transferred to a joint committee of the Association and the Royal Horticultural Society, which started work in 1931. Shortly after the second world war, the Rhododendron Association was dissolved and its functions transferred to the Rhododendron Group of the Royal Horticultural Society. At the same time the Rhododendron Joint Committee became a Standing Committee of the Society and since 1953 has also judged camellias.

RHODODENDRON HYBRIDS

In a horticultural sense the rhododendrons are those members of the genus *Rhododendron* which are not classified as azaleas or azaleodendrons. Botanically, they fall into two major groups—the lepidote (scaly) and elepidote (non-scaly) rhododendrons—which are just as distinct from each other as either is from the azaleas. Hybrids between the two groups (lepidote–elepidote crosses) are rare, and only one, 'John Marchand', is described here; several have in fact been raised, but have presumably not been ornamental or vigorous enough to be worth propagating. The elepidote rhododendrons (subgen. *Hymenanthes*) cross readily among themselves, except that 'elephant–mouse' crosses are generally not successful. Lepidote hybrids, of which only a few hardy ones existed early this century, are now quite numerous, and some are valuable garden plants, e.g., the various dwarf and medium-sized blues resulting from crosses between *R. augustinii* and members of the Lapponicum series; and dwarf yellows such as 'Chink' and 'Chikor'; and the Lady Chamberlain and Lady Rosebery grexes; and the old Praecox. The prevalence of polyploidy among the lepidotes inhibits crossing to some extent, but hybrids between the various subgenera into which the lepidotes have been divided by Sleumer are frequent and the plants vigorous: examples are Praecox (subgen. *Rhododendron* × subgen. *Rhodorastrum*); Multiflorum (subgen. *Rhododendron* × subgen. *Pseudorhodorastrum*); and 'Chink' (subgen. *Rhododendron* × subgen. *Pseudazalea*).

In the historical notes below, the Hardy Hybrids and 'Species Hybrids' are discussed separately, but in the descriptive section all the rhododendron hybrids are treated together. It can be assumed that any hybrid raised by one or other of the Waterer firms in the last century is in the Hardy Hybrid category.

HARDY HYBRIDS

These could be defined as a group of nursery-bred rhododendrons, mostly many generations removed from the wild parents, which are very hardy, flower mostly in late May or June, tolerate exposure and full sun, and bear firm, upright, many-flowered trusses in a wide range of colouring. They owe their toughness to members of the Ponticum series, but the colouring of all but the white, mauve, and light rosy-pink sorts comes mainly from *R. arboreum*, and the dense, many-flowered truss of this species has also helped to give the Hardy Hybrids their distinct floral characters.

The first of the parental species to arrive—*R. maximum*—was introduced by Peter Collinson from America in 1736 but it remained a very rare plant in Britain for more than three decades after that. The next parent of the Hardy Hybrids—*R. ponticum*—was introduced, according to Aiton, in 1763, but apparently did not come into commerce until some time between 1775 and 1780. From then on there was the possibility of hybridisation between the two. It is said that many intermediates had sprung up by 1806, but the only recorded deliberate cross between the two was the white-flowered 'Smithii Album', raised by William Smith of Norbiton.

The third of the Pontic–American species—*R. catawbiense*—was brought from its remote home in the Roan Mountains by the Frasers, father and son, in 1809, and with its arrival the history of the Hardy Hybrids could be said to have begun. According to Michael Waterer it was crossed at Knap Hill with a rosy form of *R. maximum* in 1811, which is not impossible, since it is known that the Frasers brought home plants. Crosses were also made, or occurred spontaneously, with *R. ponticum*. The result was a numerous swarm of late-flowering rhododendrons in shades of blush, light pink, and mauve. Several of these are still cultivated, e.g., 'Everestianum', 'Album Elegans', and 'Roseum Elegans' (of which the Knap Hill nursery had large standards by 1864, said to be half-a-century old).

These Pontic–American hybrids, deriving as they do from three closely related species, had no great potentialities for development. But in 1825 a long-awaited event took place—the first flowering of the Himalayan *R. arboreum*. This first introduction was of a blood-red form, and it seems to have flowered almost simultaneously in several gardens. At any rate, all the foundation-crosses were figured and described in the same year—1831. For these see Altaclerense, Russellianum, and Smithii. They were, however, only the first stage in a breeding programme the ultimate aim of which was to combine the colouring of the blood-red *R. arboreum* with the hardiness and late-flowering of the Pontic–Americans. In themselves the first-crosses were far from this ideal, for they flowered much too early and were not wholly hardy. The first step was to reinforce the Pontic–American influence by crossing back the Arboreum hybrids onto hardy parents. At Highclere, the pollen of Altaclerense was put on 'Lee's Dark Purple', a late-flowering form or hybrid of *R. ponticum*, and also on *R. maximum*, the result being seedlings ranging in colour from pink or rose to deep crimson or deep purple. These were flowering by 1863. Standish had started crossing at Bagshot about 1838, and one of his first efforts, a hybrid between Altaclerense and *R. catawbiense*, named 'Blandyanum', was exhibited in 1847. By the early 1850s many such hybrids were offered by Standish and Noble and the two Waterer firms, flowering towards the end of May. In 1855 Waterer of Bagshot put into commerce 'John Waterer' and 'Mrs John Waterer'—the first hybrids from *R. arboreum* that were really late-flowering (early to mid-June). At about the same time this firm distributed 'Lady Eleanor Cathcart', with pink flowers heavily blotched as in a pelargonium. What was probably the original plant was 12 ft high in 1856, which suggests an origin not much later than 1836. It is usually supposed to be the result of a straight cross between *R. arboreum* and *R. maximum*, but something that seems to have been very similar was raised at Highclere from *R. maximum* crossed with Altaclerense.

By the 1860s the stream of Hardy Hybrids was in full spate, and most of the varieties still known today made their appearance in that or the next two decades. Although many hybrids were raised by the continental breeders, those that have survived are nearly all of English origin. The greater success of the English breeders is shown by a list of recommended varieties published by Édouard André in his book *Plantes de Terre de Bruyères* (1864). These are classified into two sections: the English group, very hardy near Paris; and the Belgian group, half-hardy near Paris. A probable reason is that the English nurserymen had pushed their crossing further. Standish and Noble had flowered fourth-generation seedlings by 1855 and were getting seedlings into flower in four years by grafting their tops on *R. ponticum*. At that rate of crossing, the hybrids that came into commerce in the 1870s may have been seven or eight generations removed from the first-crosses of *R. arboreum*, It has also been said that the continental breeders used mainly *R. maximum* as the hardy basis for their hybrids, while the English relied more on *R. ponticum* and *R. catawbiense*. According to Standish and Noble the first-cross between *R. arboreum* and *R. maximum* did not flower at Highclere until the plants were twenty-six years old, and they stated that hybrids with the blood of *R. maximum* in them were also slower to flower than those deriving from *R. ponticum* and *R. catawbiense*. Still, *R. maximum* was certainly used in England to some extent—sufficiently, at any rate, to have imparted to so many of the hybrids its prominent flare of speckles.

The breeders never really achieved their aim of putting the glowing red of the best *R. arboreum* onto a late-flowering, hardy plant, for even the reddest of the old Hardy Hybrids have a blue basis to the flower, as might be expected from their ancestry. The effect of blending *R. ponticum* and its two American allies with the Himalayan *R. arboreum* was a proliferation of unexpected new characters for the breeder to work on. For example, the brownish or yellowish markings on the upper (posterior) lobes shown by the European and American parents, especially by *R. maximum*, are darkened and intensified in many of the hybrids, and become independent of the ground-colour of the corolla. At the other extreme, the corolla may be quite unspotted, a character that apparently first appeared in the old Belgian hybrid 'Concessum'. Many of the hybrids that became popular were throw-backs which owe little or nothing to *R. arboreum*—for example, 'Lady Grey Egerton', with its near-blue flowers, and the many whites with a large brown or yellow flare deriving from *R. maximum*.

A species not so far mentioned in connection with this group is *R. caucasicum*. Crossed with *R. arboreum* this gave rise to Nobleanum and various dwarfs bred primarily for forcing. As these flower very early they are really the antithesis of what the breeders of the Hardy Hybrids were aiming at, though as plants they are perfectly hardy. There are, however, several hybrids showing the influence of *R. caucasicum* which do not flower until May, e.g., 'Prince Camille de Rohan' and 'Chev. Felix de Sauvage', of continental origin, and the common 'Cunningham's White' (which also shows the influence of *R. ponticum*). The late-flowering 'Madame Carvalho' also has the blood of *R. caucasicum* in it, judging from its upright, crowded pedicels.

By 1900 the development of the old-style Hardy Hybrid had more or less run its course, though a few were put into commerce this century, e.g., 'Mrs P. D. Williams' and 'Mrs T. H. Lowinsky'. The appearance of the famous 'Pink Pearl' in 1897 marked the beginning of a new race of hybrids, created by crossing some of the older sorts with the Himalayan *R. griffithianum*, which had been introduced by Hooker in 1850 and first flowered in this country in 1858. This species had two qualities of interest to the breeder—the great size and beautiful shape of its flowers—and one important disadvantage—its great tenderness. James Mangles, further mentioned below, was the leading advocate of *R. griffithianum*, and in 1881 he prophesied that it would be the progenitor of hybrids as varied and popular as those that nurserymen of an earlier generation had raised from such unpromising material. The first attempt in this direction of which there is any record was made by Mr Scott for the Lawson Company of Edinburgh, about 1869, using 'John Waterer' as the hardy parent. Some of the hybrids were flowering by 1877 and were said to be very fine, but the firm apparently never propagated them. Some were sold (Mangles had one); the rest were dispersed when the firm was wound up in 1888. The first hybrid of *R. griffithianum* to receive an award was Mangles' own cross between it and *R. ponticum*, named 'Alice Mangles', which received a First Class Certificate in 1882, but seems to have been lost. Three years later Messrs Veitch received the same award for 'Manglesii', named in honour of Mangles, who had died the previous year at the age of fifty-two. This, too, was a first-cross, the other parent being an old white-flowered hybrid of *R. catawbiense*. Mangles himself had made similar crosses, a few of which had borne their first flowers by the time he died, but these did not reach commerce until long after the arrival of 'Pink Pearl' on the scene. Among them are 'Beauty of Littleworth', 'Isabella Mangles', and 'Dawn's Delight'; see also 'Loder's White'.

After the appearance of 'Manglesii', nothing further of note occurred in this field until Messrs Waterer of Bagshot showed 'Pink Pearl', which was not only the first second-generation hybrid from *R. griffithianum* and the first to have the typical Hardy Hybrid truss, but also one of the very few hybrids of that species of any description to have been exhibited up to that time. This no doubt explains the astonished delight that it evoked. Early this century the same firm put out several other hybrids from *R. griffithianum*, e.g., 'Alice', 'Corona', and 'Mrs E. C. Stirling', all fine rhododendrons, but since then the development of this class of Hardy Hybrid has been mainly the work of Dutch nurserymen. L. J. Endtz and Co. raised a third generation by crossing 'Pink Pearl' with various older hybrids such as 'Stanley Davies' and 'Doncaster', the result being a number of hybrids in the style of 'Pink Pearl' of which at least one—'Souvenir de Dr S. Endtz'—is generally considered to be an improvement on its parent and might by now have supplanted it in the British market had it been more adroitly named. The firm of M. Koster and Sons took a different line. They used first-generation hybrids of *R. griffithianum* such as 'George Hardy' (thought to be one of the parents of 'Pink Pearl'), and the similar 'Coombe Royal'—and crossing these with Hardy Hybrids raised many well-known rhododendrons, e.g., 'Betty Wormald', 'Mrs Lindsay Smith', 'Mrs G. W. Leak', and 'Mrs Charles E. Pearson'. These had flowered by the end of the first world war and the last two mentioned were named after the wives of members of the delegation of the Horticultural Trades Association which visited Holland in the spring of 1919.

Another set of hybrids deriving from crosses with *R. griffithianum* was made by Otto Schulz in 1890 in the glasshouses that supplied material for the artists of the Royal Porcelain Factory, Berlin. The other parents used, with the exception of 'Prince Camille de Rohan', are not known in this country, and it may be, judging from the results, that some were only two or even one generation removed from *R. arboreum*. In 1896 all the seedlings that had flowered, some 200 in all, were bought by the Dutch nurseryman C. B. van Nes, but proved to be hopelessly tender in his nursery at Boskoop. However, some were named and put into commerce for the British market, reaching this country before the first world war or shortly after it. The best known of this set are 'Queen Wilhelmina', 'Princess Juliana', 'King George', 'Lord Swaythling', 'Mrs A. M. Williams', and 'Geoffroy Millais'. Like most other first-crosses from *R. griffithianum*, these hybrids really need woodland conditions, especially 'Queen Wilhelmina', a lovely but decidedly tender April-flowering rhododendron. In 1898 van Nes embarked on a large-scale breeding programme, in which the Schulz seedlings were crossed with Hardy Hybrids, mostly of British origin. According to Millais, who visited the van Nes nurseries in 1921, some 250,000 seedlings were raised. This may be an exaggeration, but obviously there must be enormous wastage in such hybrid-on-hybrid crosses, with the Ponticum series entering into the parentage on both sides. At any rate, only 250 plants were kept for further trial, and of these thirty-two had been named by 1929 (see the note by C. B. van Nes and Sons in the *Year Book of the Rhododendron Association* (1929), pp. 137–42). The most famous of these is 'Britannia', and it is interesting to note that this rhododendron has the same parentage as 'Earl of Athlone', 'Unknown Warrior', and 'C. B. van Nes', all being the products of a cross between 'Queen Wilhelmina' and 'Stanley Davies'. 'Britannia' has in turn given rise to 'Kluis Sensation', a fine red-flowered hybrid raised by Messrs Kluis of Boskoop.

The early breeders, as already mentioned, had set great store by lateness of flowering: a hybrid, to be reckoned as hardy, had to flower not earlier than the last week in May. Many of the hybrids from *R. griffithianum*, however, do not conform to this criterion. The Schulz hybrids sent out by van Nes are, of course, the result of first-generation crosses, and have never been classed as Hardy Hybrids. But even the second-generation hybrids raised from them by van Nes mostly flower in early or mid-May and some, for example 'Earl of Athlone', are classified in the R.H.S. *Rhododendron Handbook* as 'C', meaning hardy only in sheltered and warm gardens. It could be said that with the introduction of the blood of *R. griffithianum* into the trade-hybrids the distinction between them and the hybrids raised by private growers began to be blurred. Other Asiatic species, hitherto ignored by the commercial breeders, now began to be used. John Standish had already produced 'Ascot Brilliant', a hybrid of *R. thomsonii* flowering around the end of April, and later in the century Messrs Waterer of Bagshot used the same species in their breeding, one of the results being the splendid 'J. G. Millais', which flowers at about the same time as 'Ascot Brilliant', and 'Sir John Ramsden'.

Another species that began to be used towards the end of the 19th century was *R. fortunei*, which began to spread into gardens after 1859. The nurseryman George Paul used a selected form of this species known as 'Mrs Butler' (or 'Mrs Charles Butler') and crossed it with various Hardy Hybrids. He raised altogether some 1,000 plants, which were hailed by William Watson of Kew as the beginnings of a new race, as well they might have become had not their début almost coincided with that of 'Pink Pearl', The Paul hybrids mostly flowered early in May, and many had a lax truss which gardeners of the time, accustomed to the compact trusses of the Hardy Hybrids, found too floppy. The firm of Messrs W. C. Slocock has been more successful with *R. fortunei*. Their 'Lavender Girl' (q.v.) flowers late and has the truss of a Hardy Hybrid, but inherits from *R. fortunei* its distinctive foliage.

R. campylocarpum, introduced by Hooker in 1850, was ignored by the commercial breeders of the last century, but has been used to some extent during the last sixty years to produce yellow-flowered rhododendrons in the style of the older Hardy Hybrids, e.g., 'Goldsworth Yellow' and the Zuyder Zee group. For the use of other species, introduced this century, see pp. 825–8.

Species Hybrids

The Hardy Hybrids are the result of intensive breeding through many seed-generations from a limited number of species, three of which—the related *R. ponticum*, *R. catawbiense*, and *R. maximum*—are not in themselves of much beauty. Except for some of the oldest that happen to have been preserved, they are remote in appearance from any of the parent species, and could never be mistaken for anything but what they are— vegetable artifacts, bred for the market. The hybrids now to be considered are collectively the result of what might be termed *extensive* breeding. Some 120 species of lepidote or elepidote rhododendrons— mainly the latter—have been used in crossing by one breeder or another and, even if those that have been used out of curiosity or because its pollen happened to be available, are eliminated from the total, it remains very large, and embraces virtually every series into which these species are classified. By no means all these hybrids are first-generation crosses, but even the most complex that have so far been raised are only two generations removed from the wild ancestors. The tendency has, in other words, been to breed outwards, adding more and more species to the brew, rather than to explore in depth the potentialities of a limited number of species, as the old hybridists, with so much less material at their disposal, were forced to do.

Mostly the species hybrids have been raised in private gardens by wealthy rhododendron enthusiasts, who were able to follow their own whims, or their own ideals of beauty, without any thought for the general usefulness or the commercial viability of their products. Nevertheless, they produced some of the loveliest of hardy shrubs, many of which are now available in commerce.

Many hybrids were raised at Highclere near Newbury in the time of the second Earl of Carnarvon, who was Vice-President of the Horticultural Society from 1829 until his death in 1833. The most famous of these is Altaclerense (q.v.), but numerous azalea and azaleodendron crosses were also made. The Highclere breeding was supervised by J. R. Gowen (*d*. 1862), who even by some of his contemporaries was thought to be the Earl's head gardener. He was in fact a man of independent means, who served as a member of the Council of the Horticultural Society for several years and later became, first its Secretary (1845–50) and then its Treasurer (1850–5). Lindley had named the orchidaceous genus *Govenia* after him as early as 1831, and he is also commemorated by *Cupressus goveniana*, introduced to the Society's garden during the period of his secretaryship.

The Earl of Carnarvon was no doubt inspired by his brother, the Hon. and Rev. William Herbert, Rector of Spofforth in Yorkshire and later Dean of Manchester, a man of remarkable gifts, classical scholar, linguist, and naturalist, but best remembered as a botanist with two important works to his credit—a monograph on the Amaryllidaceae and a classification of the genus *Crocus*. He was also one of the first experimental hybridisers. His 'Hybridum' is mentioned in the section on Azaleodendrons, under Fragrans. He also made an apparently successful cross between *R. dauricum* and *R. ponticum*, named by him *R. Aprilis*, which is of interest as the first recorded hybrid between a lepidote and an elepidote rhododendron.

After 1850 the scope of the hybridiser was greatly increased by the introduction of new species from the Himalaya, including five of the most used parents—*R. griffithianum*, *R. thomsonii*, *R. campylocarpum*, *R. cinnabarinum*, and *R. ciliatum*. Most of these had flowered by 1860 and two years later James Bateman of Biddulph Grange in an article in the *Gardeners' Chronicle* remarked that hybrids between them were beginning to appear—'the first fruits, doubtless, of a splendid and abundant harvest still to come'. But there was a darker side, he added, for 'as the products of the hybridisers' skill multiply amongst us, all traces of the original forms will inevitably disappear from our gardens, and nowhere, but in their native Himalayas, will the species be seen as they started into being at the fiat of the Almighty!' In saying that new Himalayan hybrids were beginning to appear he probably had in mind the hybrids from *R. ciliatum*, for it was primarily this species and the other, more tender members of the Maddenii series that attracted the attention of the commercial breeders. The nurseryman Isaac Davies had his famous Praecox (*R. ciliatum* × *R. dauricum*) in flower by 1858, only eight years after the seed collected by Hooker in Sikkim had been distributed. It was quickly followed by Veitch's 'Princess Alice' (*R. ciliatum* × *R. edgeworthii*), which had received a First Class Certificate in the year Bateman made his comments. However, the harvest he predicted was slow to ripen. Apart from *R. griffithianum* and the species of the Maddenii series, Hooker's introductions from Sikkim seem to have been of little interest to commercial breeders, but some first-crosses were made in private gardens.

The most active of the amateur hybridists in the latter part of the 19th century was James Mangles of Valewood, near Haslemere (1832–84), known, according to Millais, as 'the High Priest of the Rhododendron cult'. As already mentioned, he was the first to advocate the use of *R. griffithianum* in crossing, and himself raised many hybrids from it, few of which had flowered by the time of his death at the age of fifty-two. Some, for example the beautiful 'Isabella Mangles', remained at Valewood, the rest (some probably still in seed-pans) were moved to Littleworth Cross near Farnham, the home of his brother Henry Mangles, who died in 1908, and his sister Miss Clara Mangles, who outlived Henry by twenty-three years. Since Henry too was a hybridist and had a Himalayan House at Littleworth, the attribution of some of the hybrids exhibited by him and later by his sister is uncertain. Some, notably 'Rose Mangles' of the Royal Flush grex and the famous azaleodendron 'Glory of Littleworth', were almost certainly raised by Henry, though his brother is always given the credit. Millais, the historian of the Rhododendron world of his day, seems to have been unaware that Henry ever existed. His first visit to Littleworth was apparently in 1915, and he may have assumed that when Miss Mangles referred to 'my brother' she meant James.

Among the Cornish gardens that received Hooker's Sikkim seed was Tremough, near Penryn, the property of the Shilson family. Here several Himalayan crosses were made towards the end of the 19th century, of which the best known—*R. griffithianum* × *R. arboreum*—bears the grex-name Beauty of Tremough. The first hybrid between *R. barbatum* and *R. thomsonii* was also made there (Shilsonii). The head gardener at Tremough was Richard Gill (1849–1927), who later set up his own nursery on land leased to him by the Shilson family, which developed into the famous firm of R. Gill and Sons. Other first-crosses of Himalayan species were made at Penjerrick by Samuel Smith, who became head gardener there in 1889. Among his hybrids were *R. campylocarpum* × *R. griffithianum* (Penjerrick) and *R. griffithianum* × *R. thomsonii* (Cornish Cross). The second Lord Aberconway wrote interesting accounts of the work of these two men, which will be found in *The Rhododendron Society Notes*, Vol. III, pp. 186–9 and 252–5.

Some six years after Hooker's Sikkim seed had been distributed, the first of the Chinese rhododendrons arrived (all the Chinese species hitherto introduced had been azaleas or azaleastrums). This was *R. fortunei*, the parent in the first or second generation of many famous hybrids. One of the first to use it was John Luscombe of Coombe Royal, near Kingsbridge in Devon, a garden once famous for its citrus fruits, which were grown against high retaining walls and protected during winter by lath-blinds. Luscombe crossed *R. fortunei* with *R. thomsonii* (Luscombei) and, like Mangles, raised some hybrids from *R. griffithianum* crossed with Hardy Hybrids, of which 'Coombe Royal' is probably one. A poor form of *R. fortunei* growing in the Temperate House at Kew was mated there with *R. griffithianum* by W. Binder in 1875. But the far more illustrious form of this cross was made by Sir Edmund Loder, Bt, at Leonardsleee, Sussex, in 1900. He was born in 1849—an auspicious time, for it was in the autumn of that year that Hooker harvested the seed of the Sikkim rhododendrons which became for Sir Edmund a lifelong interest, though not an exclusive one. As a young man he cultivated alpines, and later brought together at Leonardslee what was then perhaps the most comprehensive collection of conifers in the British Isles (the catalogue was published in the *Gardeners' Chronicle* for 1919). Apart from Loderi, he raised several other fine hybrids, and was one of the first gardeners to grow outdoors near London many rhododendrons and azaleas hitherto deemed suitable only for the milder parts or for greenhouse decoration.

By the time Sir Edmund Loder died in 1920 a new era in rhododendron history had opened. Between 1900 and 1910 Wilson introduced some sixty new species from Hupeh and W. Szechwan, most of which had flowered by 1920, and the first of many more Forrest introductions from Yunnan and bordering parts had arrived. Altogether, from 1915 to 1975, around 100 species of rhododendron (in the narrow sense) have been used in hybridising that were not available to the 19th-century breeders. At the same time, the crossing of rhododendrons has been carried out on an ever-increasing scale since the second decade of this century, and there is no end in sight.

Considered in their role as parents of hybrids, the 20th-century introductions can be roughly classified as follows:

1. FORTUNEI SERIES—To this series, represented in the latter half of the 19th century by *R. fortunei* and *R. griffithianum*, was now added *R. discolor*, closely allied to *R. fortunei*, but of larger size and with the valuable quality of flowering late. Some sixty-five registered crosses have been made with it, of which about a third have received awards. *R. decorum*, another ally of *R. fortunei*, has also been used, but with much less success. Wilson's *R. calophytum*, a very distinct member of this series, has produced some fine hybrids, but they are too bulky, and mostly too early flowering, for the majority of gardens.

2. THOMSONII SERIES—In the typical subseries there is no rival to *R. thomsonii*, nor in the Campylocarpum subseries to *R. campylocarpum*, both of them Himalayan species introduced by Hooker in the middle of the last century. But *R. wardii*, with yellow, widely cup-shaped flowers, has been of almost equal importance to *R. campylocarpum* as a parent of yellow-flowered hybrids, and the similar *R. litiense* was used to good effect by Francis Hanger at Wisley. *R. wardii* was introduced from Yunnan by Forrest and by Kingdon Ward; its ally the pink-flowered *R. souliei*, introduced by Wilson, has not so far produced any hybrid of real worth. Wilson's main contribution to this series is *R. williamsianum*, the parent of many dwarf and medium-sized hybrids, none more lovely than it, but some making better plants for the average garden.

3. NERIIFLORUM SERIES—Twentieth-century introductions such as *R. discolor* and *R. wardii* are related to species cultivated earlier, but the Neriiflorum group was unknown in gardens until the second decade of this century. *R. neriiflorum*, *R. haematodes*, *R. forrestii*, and *R. sanguineum* subsp. *didymum* are responsible for most of the dwarf and medium-sized red-flowered hybrids, while *R. dichroanthum*, almost unique among rhododendron species (as distinct from azaleas) in its orange or salmon-coloured flowers, has produced hybrids in a range of attractive and unusual shades.

4. IRRORATUM SERIES—The typical subseries has been little used in crossing, but the Parishii subseries, which is really entitled to independent rank, contains some splendid red-flowered species which, unlike most reds, do not open their trusses until late May or June. Unfortunately, they are either, like *R. elliottii*, definitely tender, or like *R. eriogynum*, the species most used, on the borderline of hardiness. Most of the hybrids of *R. elliottii* were raised at Exbury, or by Francis Hanger after he left Exbury for Wisley, but the finest of them are on the tender side. The hybrids from *R. eriogynum*, the best known of which are Romany Chal and Tally Ho, are hardier but not really suitable for cold gardens.

5. R. GRIERSONIANUM—This remarkable species is confined to a small area on the borders between Yunnan and Burma, and is not closely allied to any other elepidote rhododendron. Yet it crosses readily even with Hardy Hybrids, and has, for the breeder, the valuable quality of producing hybrid seedlings that set bud abundantly when only four or five years old, even when the other parent is slow to flower when raised from seed. No other species has been so frequently crossed as *R. griersonianum*: some 155 hybrids registered up to 1968 have it as one parent, of which 48 have received awards, most of them red-flowered. It is a potent parent, passing on to its first-generation offspring its characteristic long-pointed bud-scales and trumpet-shaped flowers.

6. R. AURICULATUM—Once grouped with *R. griersonianum*, this species, introduced by Wilson, is the parent of several late-flowering hybrids, of which the best known are the Polar Bear and Argosy grexes.

7. R. YAKUSHIMANUM—Since about 1950 this species (q.v. under *R. degronianum*) has been so much used in breeding that it may in time rival *R. griersonianum* in the number of hybrids it has parented. The great charm of the two Wada clones comes from a subtle combination of characters which cannot be communicated to their offspring, but they have valuable qualities for the breeder none the less—hardiness, dwarf, compact habit, a comparatively late flowering season, a good truss and handsome foliage. Starting in 1951 with crosses of *R. yakushimanum* with Hardy Hybrids and 'Fabia Tangerine', Messrs Waterer of Bagshot have carried out a complex project of hybridisation and selection which has involved selfing and intercrossing the first generation of seedlings (see further in *Rhododendrons 1974*, pp. 50–3, and for earlier reports *R.C.Y.B. 1959*, pp. 102–3, and *R.C.Y.B. 1962*, pp. 97–9). Arthur George has raised crosses between *R. yakushimanum* and hybrids, including his own 'Springbok', a

hybrid between *R. griersonianum* and *R. ponticum*. These hybrids, many of great promise, are still rather scarce at present (1975), all the named varieties being clones that have to be vegetatively propagated. Other hybrids of *R. yakushimanum* are with species, e.g., 'Streatley', raised by T. H. Findlay for the Crown Estate Commissioners.

8. LEPIDOTE SPECIES—In the last century, scaly-leaved species and hybrids were few and the majority were tender; of the hardy hybrids, the commonest were Praecox and the various crosses between the alpine roses and *R. minus* or *R. carolinianum*. Since the 1930s, however, thanks to the introductions of Wilson, Forrest, and Kingdon Ward, and the work of private hybridisers, there is now a varied choice of dwarf and medium-sized scaly-leaved hybrids. The most widely grown are the crosses between *R. augustinii* and purple-flowered members of the Lapponicum series. Perhaps the finest, or at least the most satisfactory for cold gardens, are Blue Diamond, Blue Tit, and 'Saint Merryn', but there are many others in the same style.

There are a fair number of yellow-flowered species scattered through the lepidote series, but the hybrids from them are fewer than might be expected. In theory *R. lutescens* or *R. bauhiniiflorum*, crossed with the two yellow-flowered members of the Lapponicum series, should have given rise to a set of hybrids comparable to the Blue Diamond group. But no such crosses have been recorded. Indeed, almost the only hybrid of *R. lutescens* that has been raised, and the best known in gardens, is Lionel de Rothschild's Bo-peep, the other parent of which is *R. moupinense*, introduced by Wilson. Yellow Hammer, raised at Caerhays, is the only other of the pre-1939 yellow lepidote hybrids that is widely cultivated; it unites Wilson's *R. flavidum* with Forrest's *R. sulfureum*. In recent years several excellent dwarf and hardy yellows have been raised: see 'Chink', 'Chikor', 'Curlew', and 'Princess Anne'.

A very distinct group, containing some of the finest rhododendron hybrids, derives from crosses between the variable *R. cinnabarinum* and *R. maddenii*, in which the influence of the second parent, obvious in the F1 hybrid, has been diluted by back-crossing with *R. cinnabarinum* (or by crossing with *R. concatenans*, a very close ally of *R. cinnabarinum* introduced by Kingdon Ward). See Royal Flush, Lady Chamberlain, Perseverance, Comely, and 'Trewithen Orange'. Another set of *R. cinnabarinum* hybrids stems from crosses between it (or *R. concatenans*) with members of the Yunnanense subseries of the Triflorum series: see 'Peace', Alison Johnstone, and Oreocinn.

R. moupinense, already mentioned as a parent of Bo-peep, has given, from a mating with *R. ciliatum*, one of the finest of all lepidote hybrids—Bodnant's Cilpinense; with Praecox, the old hybrid of *R. ciliatum* and *R. dauricum*, it has given 'Tessa' and 'Tessa Roza'; and with *R. sulfureum* Golden Oriole.

The Maddenii series does not mate readily with other lepidotes. Most of the hybrids of the typical subseries, which is highly polyploid, are with the uniformly hexaploid Cinnabarinum series. The species of the Ciliicalyx subseries that have given most hybrids with other series are the small-flowered *R. ciliatum*, *R. burmanicum*, and *R. valentinianum*; *R. fletcherianum*, recently separated from the latter, has so far been crossed only with *R. ludlowii* (see 'Curlew'). In general, the lepidote species are less indulgent to the hybridiser than the elepidotes and seemingly unpredictable in their breeding behaviour. Their greater botanical diversity, and the prevalence of polyploidy, are no doubt the main reasons for this, but other genetic factors may be involved.

Many, perhaps the majority, of the best-known hybrids raised in private gardens in the 1920s and 1930s were first-generation crosses between species, while the remainder, except towards the end of this period, had a species as one parent. When a hybrid was used in crossing it was mostly Loderi, more used as a parent than any other rhododendron except *R. griersonianum*, or one of the Cornish hybrids combining various Himalayan species. Indeed, one of the interesting features of hybridisation since the coming of the Wilson and Forrest species has been the enduring importance of the older Himalayan introductions. The Naomi, Carita, and Yvonne grexes, three of Lionel de Rothschild's best-known crosses, owe nothing to rhododendron introductions of this century, the component species being all Himalayans introduced by Hooker, and *R. fortunei*. The parentage of the famous Lady Chamberlain and Lady Rosebery grexes is also purely Himalayan. Matings between Hardy Hybrids and species started in the last century, when *R. griffithianum* and *R. fortunei*, as already mentioned, were the species most used, and crosses of the same type, using more recent introductions, have been made frequently since 1920. Lionel de Rothschild's cross between 'Corona' and *R. williamsianum*—the Bow Bells grex—is a well-known example, but for the most part the matings have had red-flowered plants on both sides. Lionel de Rothschild introduced from France a hybrid of *R. maximum* which he called 'Moser's Maroon' and used it with species to produce some of his best-known hybrids. More recent examples are the Hobbie hybrids, mentioned below.

Towards the end of the 1930s breeders began to make hybrid-with-hybrid crosses, using recent productions. For example, Bodnant's Bartia is a cross made in 1936 between Portia, raised there ten years earlier, and the Cornish Barclayi; five species are involved, representing five series, all of them red-flowered except *R. griffithianum* (Portia is *R. neriiflorum* (*euchaites*) × *R. strigillosum*; both it and Bartia have received awards, but apparently neither is in commerce). Another example is Lionel de Rothschild's famous Jalisco cross (q.v.), made shortly before the second world war. Since the 1950s this type of crossing has been used quite frequently, but the parentage is often simpler than it appears to be at first sight. Thus T. H. Findlay's 'Queen Elizabeth II', not yet in commerce, has six species in its parentage, but these belong to only two series—Fortunei and Thomsonii—which are known to blend well in crossing. Many of the most successful hybrids raised in Britain in recent years continue, however, to be F1 species-hybrids, e.g., 'Blewbury', 'Streatley', 'Chikor', 'Curlew', and 'Pink Pebble', or have a species as one parent. Complex crosses, especially if Hardy Hybrids are involved in the parentage or if the component species are ill-matched, are beyond the scope of most breeders, owing to the large number of seedlings that have to be flowered if something worthwhile is to be obtained.

The first to cross the 20th-century introductions was J. C. Williams of Caerhays (1861–1939), who was also the mentor of Lionel de Rothschild during his apprenticeship as a hybridiser. 'I was visiting Caerhays for the first time and the owner asked me what crosses I had made; when I told him, to my intense surprise, he told me to burn the lot. Needless to say, I did not follow his advice, but, needless to say also, I have done it since. They were made between hybrids of the old Waterer Rhododendrons and naturally in nearly every case reverted to the *ponticum*. . . . He also advised me to study the Mendelian theory and to follow the system that the orchid growers have used with such success' (L. de Rothschild, *Y.B. Rhod. Ass. 1933*, p. 71). Many of the Wilson rhododendrons first flowered at Caerhays, and the cross between *R. discolor* and *R. griffithianum* was first made there in 1913. Caerhays seems to have been one of the few private gardens to receive seed from Forrest's 1910 expedition, and two species introduced in that year, crossed with Wilson species, gave what have since become among the most widely grown of species hybrids—Blue Tit and Yellow Hammer. But the most fruitful of J. C. Williams's crosses was Royal Flush, seedlings from which, given to Lionel de Rothschild, were used by him to produce the Lady Chamberlain and Lady Rosebery grexes, perhaps the most famous of all the Exbury hybrids.

Another pioneer in using the Wilson and Forrest introductions was E. J. P. Magor of Lamellen, who received Chinese seed and seedlings from J. C. Williams. In 1916 he crossed two Forrest introductions to produce Prostigiatum, and in 1919 flowered Oreocinn, which unites the Himalayan *R. cinnabarinum* with Wilson's *R. oreotrephes*. The Stud Book reveals Magor to have been a rather indiscriminate hybridiser, but he produced some fine rhododendrons none the less. Those just mentioned are in commerce, and so too is 'Gilian', a fine clone of the Cornish Cross grex, and the beautiful 'Lamellen'. He also raised 'Saint Tudy' and 'Saint Breward'.

However, these two Cornish gardens were ahead of others only by a matter of four or five years. Hybridisation started at Bodnant and at Exbury around 1920, and in these two gardens were made more than two-fifths of all the crosses listed in the current edition of the Stud Book (published in the second part of the R.H.S. *Rhododendron Handbook*). The garden at Bodnant in Denbighshire was founded in 1875 by H. D. Pochin (*d.* 1895), 'an enthusiast in gardening, with an accurate knowledge of trees, shrubs and all hardy plants' (*Gard. Chron.*, Vol. 21 (1884), p. 207). Rhododendrons were evidently not among his interests, for few were planted, but the original garden was rich in other ericaceous plants and had a comprehensive collection of the conifers available at that time, many of which still exist. Pochin's daughter Laura, who inherited from her father both the garden itself and his love of plants, had married in 1877 Charles McLaren, created Baron Aberconway in 1911. Her husband had little interest in horticulture, and the Bodnant garden as it exists today was designed and planted, with her active encouragement, by their son Henry McLaren (1879–1953), one of the most gifted plantsmen of his generation, who became President of the Royal Horticultural Society in 1931, three years before his father's death, and was succeeded in that position by his son, the present Lord Aberconway. He endowed the garden and presented it to the National Trust in 1949.

The first Chinese and Himalayan rhododendrons were planted at Bodnant in 1909, and to these were later added the harvest of Forrest's and Kingdon Ward's expeditions. The breeding of rhododendron hybrids started in 1920 and was the work of Frederick C. Puddle, who had made a name for himself as an orchid breeder before he came to Bodnant as head gardener in 1918. He retired in 1947 and was succeeded by his younger son Charles Puddle. Somewhat fewer crosses were made at Bodnant than at Exbury, and mostly they were on different lines. The Bodnant reds get their colouring mainly from the Neriiflorum series and the Cornish Himalayan hybrids; less use was made than at Exbury of *R. eriogynum* and *R. elliottii*. The Bodnant hybrids, too, and especially the later ones, are on the average of smaller stature than those raised at Exbury. No use was made of *R. discolor*, partly because the second Lord Aberconway disliked the throat-marking that this species imparts to its hybrids, and little use of any of the larger species and hybrids.

Lionel de Rothschild (1882–1942) was the son of Leopold de Rothschild, whose two London gardens, at Gunnersbury Park and Gunnersbury House (run in tandem, each with its own head gardener), were known for their orchids, which Lionel de Rothschild later bred at Exbury with considerable success, and for such diverse plants as roses, water-lilies, and scented-leaved pelargoniums. The cultivation of fruit under glass was another speciality, and the Japanese Garden at Gunnersbury House, created by the brilliant head gardener there, James Hudson, was famous in its time (Hudson's lecture on it to the Royal Horticultural Society in 1905 was illustrated by slides made from photographs taken by Lionel de Rothschild, a keen photographer in his youth). In view of his later achievements it is appropriate that the young Lionel, at the age of twenty-four, should have deputised for his father as host to the geneticists and plant breeders who visited the two Gunnersbury gardens during the International Hybridisation Conference of 1906. Even at that time he was interested in gardening (in the lecture referred to Hudson had termed him 'an enthusiastic patron of horticulture'), but it was only after he bought the Exbury property on the Solent in 1919, two years after his father's death, that he found scope for his energies and talents as a gardener. During the next twenty years he created a great woodland garden and embarked on a project of rhododendron hybridisation which has never been equalled in quantity or diversity. Lionel de Rothschild was adventurous in his use of parents. In no other garden were *R. elliottii* and *R. lacteum* used so much and to such good effect; he was one of the first to see the potentialities of *R. wardii* as a parent, and used it to produce his famous 'Hawk Crest'. Having ample space to fill in the Exbury woods, he could use as parents such large species as *R. discolor*, *R. calophytum*, and *R. auriculatum*, and it could be said of many of the Exbury hybrids that, with their subtle colouring, they look better in woodland than in the open garden, even though they do not actually need sheltered conditions. Still, Lionel de Rothschild produced some of the loveliest of rhododendrons, and his achievement was very much a personal one, for he decided himself what crosses were to be made. He was also an authority on the species of *Rhododendron*, and the founder and President of the Rhododendron Association, which was replaced in 1945 by the Rhododendron Group of the Royal Horticultural Society.

The Exbury hybrids (which include many azaleas as well as rhododendrons) have been more widely distributed commercially than those of any other private garden, and some are now as well known in the United States as they are in this country. From 1934, the head gardener at Exbury was Francis Hanger (1900–61), who in 1946 became Curator of the Royal Horticultural Society's Garden at Wisley, and raised some fine hybrids there, such as the Constable grex, 'Emerald Isle', and 'Billy Budd'. Hanger's predecessor at Exbury was Arthur Bedford, who had succeeded James Hudson as head gardener at Gunnersbury House, where he had previously been foreman, and came to Exbury after the Gunnersbury estate was sold in 1925.

Hybrids were raised in many other gardens between the wars, but nowhere on such a scale as at Exbury and Bodnant. Indeed, breeding was carried on to some extent in most of the larger collections and many excellent hybrids are still to be seen in them which have never been distributed commercially. Hybrids of a type similar to those bred in private gardens have also been raised in nurseries, notably by Messrs Slocock, and more recently, at the Glendoick and Hydon nurseries. During the past few decades, thanks to the efforts of Sir Eric Savill and Mr T. H. Findlay, the Crown Estate Commissioners have been carrying on in Windsor Great Park the traditions of the great private collections of pre-war years. It has not been possible to do full justice in this work to the hybrids raised at Windsor, since so many of the finest have been named and received awards since the late 1960s and have not yet been reproduced in commercial quantities; but some of the earlier ones available in the trade are described below. One of the few private gardens where hybridisation is still carried on is Tremeer in Cornwall, where Lt-Gen. Harrison has produced several hybrids that will prove of value in small gardens, such as 'Saint Merryn' and 'Pink Pebble'. Collingwood Ingram, whose cherry hybrids are so well known, has also made many rhododendron crosses since the 1930s, but at present only his 'Sarled' is readily available in commerce. Two promising hybrids raised by him are 'Carolyn Hardy' and 'Oporto', both of which received an Award of Merit in 1967.

In recent years the dwarf hybrids raised by Dietrich Hobbie in Germany have become quite common in the trade, and several have received awards after trial at Wisley. Herr Hobbie's property is situated at Linswege in Oldenburg, between the Ems and the Weser, where very severe winters are not infrequent, but the soil, being mostly pure peat several feet deep, is naturally favourable to rhododendrons. Inspired by what he had seen at Exbury and in the Cornish gardens, Herr Hobbie started hybridising in 1939; by 1958 he had made 600 crosses, and planted out a quarter of a million seedlings. The Hobbie clones now in commerce have *R. forrestii* or *R. williamsianum* as one parent and a Hardy Hybrid as the other. They have proved to be very floriferous and trouble-free. For further information, see the article by Dietrich Hobbie in the *Year Book* for 1959.

DESCRIPTIONS

ALADDIN (*auriculatum* × *griersonianum*).—Flowers up to 14 in a loose truss; pedicels clad with white, glandular hairs. Corolla up to $4\frac{1}{2}$ in. wide, funnel-shaped with a slender base, salmon pink with a deeper coloured throat. Leaves oblong-elliptic, acute, narrowed to a slightly cordate base, thinly brown-hairy beneath. A large shrub, flowering late June or early July. (Crosfield. A.M. 1935.)

Mention may be made here of another late-flowering cross between *R. auriculatum* and a red-flowered species. This is the LEONORE grex, with *R. kyawii* as the other parent. The cross was made at Exbury and also at Borde Hill and Werrington. There is an example at Kew near the Rhododendron Dell, which was flowering beautifully in July 1974.

ALBATROSS (*discolor* × Loderi).—A beautiful group of hybrids resembling Loderi in their huge, fragrant, seven-lobed corollas varying in colour from almost white to delicate pink from deeper coloured buds, while the influence of *R. discolor* shows in their tall growth, in their later flowering (from end-May but mainly in June), and often in the pronounced green or maroon ray in the throat (see *Rothschild Rhododendrons*, pl. 58). The best known clones are 'EXBURY ALBATROSS' (F.C.C. 1935), flowers blush pink with a brownish ray in the throat; and 'TOWNHILL ALBATROSS', raised by Lord Swaythling, with flowers described as Fuchsia Pink at the edges, paler in the centre (A.M. 1945).

'ALBUM ELEGANS'.—Truss compact, with about 16 flowers. Corolla at first tinged with mauve, opening white with a flare of greenish yellow, funnel-shaped, about $2\frac{1}{4}$ in. wide. Medium size, vigorous. Early June. An old hybrid of *R. catawbiense*. (Waterer, Knap Hill, before 1847.) 'ALBUM GRANDIFLORUM' is similar, but the flowers are up to 3 in. wide, flatter, slightly frilled, with a brownish-green flare.

'ALICE'.—Truss conical, with 14 to 18 flowers. Corolla broadly funnel-shaped, about $3\frac{3}{4}$ in. wide, rosy pink fading to blush at the centre of the lobes, unspotted. Calyx regular, with strap-shaped lobes to $\frac{1}{2}$ in. long. Mid- to late May. (Waterer, Bagshot. A.M. 1910.) It is said to be a seedling of 'Pink Pearl', but is quite distinct in its unspotted flowers and is also rather laxer and more erect; also perhaps not quite so free-flowering. It is named after Mrs Gomer Waterer.

ALISON JOHNSTONE (*concatenans* × *yunnanense*).—Flowers up to ten in a loose truss. Corolla funnel-shaped with a tubular base, yellow or greenish yellow at first, becoming apricot pink, about 1½ in. wide at the mouth. In the form that received an Award of Merit in 1945 the corolla is unmarked, but in some plants there are two bands of speckles inside. April. (G. H. Johnstone, Trewithen.)   [PLATE 97

ALTACLERENSE (*arboreum* × (*catawbiense* seedling × *ponticum*)).—This foundation-cross, from which many of the pink- and red-flowered hardy hybrids are derived, was made at Highclere, the seat of the Earl of Carnarvon, in 1826, by J. R. Gowen. The seed-parents were specially forced plants from a cross between R. *ponticum* and a selected seedling of R. *catawbiense*. The pollen came from a truss off the plant of R. *arboreum* at The Grange, Alresford, which had flowered for the first time in the previous year. 1800 seedlings were raised and the bulk distributed to private gardens and nurseries in England and Scotland. Of those retained at Highclere, one flowered in 1831, and was figured and described in the *Botanical Register* for that year (t. 1414).

Whether any of the plants originally distributed from Highclere still exist it is impossible to say. Having a hybrid as one parent, the plants must have varied, some inclining to Smithii, others to Russellianum (qq.v.).

AMOR (*griersonianum* × *thayerianum*).—Truss lax, with about ten flowers. Corolla funnel-campanulate, 2½ to 3 in. wide, pale pink with a red throat, slightly speckled on the upper lobe. Leaves oblanceolate, acute, with a skin-like indumentum. June. (Stevenson, Tower Court. A.M. 1951.) A charming rhododendron of moderate size.

ANGELO (*discolor* × *griffithianum*).—This cross was first made by J. C. Williams of Caerhays, who called it 'Cornish Loderi', R. *discolor* being closely related to R. *fortunei*, which, with R. *griffithianum*, is the parent of the Loderi grex. The cross was later made at Exbury by Lionel de Rothschild, and by A. G. Soames of Sheffield Park. Angelo resembles Loderi in its flowers, but they are borne later, at the end of May or early June, and usually have more pronounced markings in the throat. The plants grow taller, to about 25 ft. In the form which received the Award of Merit in 1935 when shown from Exbury, the flowers were described as 5¼ in. wide, wavy-edged, delicately tinged with pink, marked with reddish brown in the throat. Leaves 6 to 8 in. long, including the short, stout petiole (the last a *discolor* character). In 'EXBURY ANGELO' (F.C.C. 1947) the flowers are white, with green throat markings. In 'SOLENT QUEEN', another Exbury clone, the flowers are pale rose fading to white (A.M. 1939). 'SHEFFIELD PARK ANGELO' has white flowers with greenish-yellow markings in the throat (A.M. 1950; *R.C.Y.B. 1950*, fig. 40). The Angelo clones are essentially plants for woodland gardens and need a sheltered, half-shaded position.   [PLATE 98

'APRIL GLOW' (formerly 'April Shower').—Flowers seven to ten in the truss. Corolla campanulate, 1½ to 1¾ in. wide, frilled, red in the bud, opening deep pink, somewhat darker on the reverse. Leaves oval, rounded at the base, up to 3¼ in. long, reddish when young. May. Low, dense habit ('Wilgen's Ruby × *williamsianum*; A. C. van Wilgen, Holland).

'ARBUTIFOLIUM'.—Flowers about 12 in a racemose cluster; rachis about 1 in. long. Corolla rosy pink, slightly spotted, tubular-funnel-shaped, $1\frac{1}{8}$ in. wide, scaly outside, downy inside at the base. Style slightly downy in the lower part; stigma yellow. Calyx very small, the lobes being less than $\frac{1}{8}$ in. long. and much shorter than the ovary, with a few hairs at the edge. Leaves $1\frac{1}{4}$ to 2 in. long, up to $\frac{7}{8}$ in. wide, more or less elliptic, equally narrowed at both ends, leathery, dark dull green above, purplish in winter, covered beneath with brown scales among which are scattered larger, darker scales. A dense, dwarf shrub to about 4 ft high, more in width, flowering in June.

A hybrid of unknown history, usually considered to be R. *ferrugineum* × R. *minus*; it was in cultivation under its present name in 1833, but was first described by Rehder in 1904. It is useful for its late flowering and fairly common in collections. The rhododendron sent out by Dutch nurseries as "R. *punctatum*" and occasionally sold in garden-centres in this country is very similar to 'Arbutifolium'. Its name has recently been altered to 'PUNCTA', to avoid confusion with R. *punctatum* Andr., which is a synonym of R. *minus*. A hybrid with, probably, the same parentage as 'Arbutifolium' is 'HAMMONDII', distinguished by its narrower leaves, up to $1\frac{3}{4}$ in. long and $\frac{1}{2}$ in. wide.

A related hybrid is 'MYRTIFOLIUM', raised by Loddiges before 1828 from R. *minus* crossed with R. *hirsutum*. It differs from 'Arbutifolium' in having leaves that are not so dark a green and slightly glossy, more tapered at the apex, somewhat hairy at the edge when young, densely scaly beneath, the larger, darker type of scale being more numerous and more closely spaced; in the larger calyx about half as long as the ovary; and in the taller, laxer habit.

Also to be mentioned here is 'LAETEVIRENS' ('Wilsonii'), of unknown origin, which was considered by Rehder to be the result of a cross between R. *ferrugineum* and R. *carolinianum*, a species closely related to R. *minus*. It has longer leaves than any other hybrid of this group, $2\frac{1}{2}$ in. long, $\frac{3}{4}$ in. wide, and also larger flowers, the pale rose corolla being up to $1\frac{1}{4}$ in. wide. It flowers in late May or early June and makes a dense leafy bush up to 5 or 6 ft high. Rehder named it R. × *laetevirens* on the grounds that its garden name, R. *Wilsonii*, had been validly published for a hybrid between R. *ciliatum* and R. *glaucum*.

'ARMISTICE DAY'.—Truss rounded with 10 to 14 flowers. Corolla shaped more or less as in 'Britannia', crimson-scarlet, about 3 in. wide. Calyx with narrow lobes. Leaves lanceolate, about 6 by $2\frac{1}{4}$ in. Lax habit. May. (Van Nes.)

'ARTHUR BEDFORD'.—Truss compact, with 14–16 flowers. Corolla funnel-shaped, $3\frac{1}{4}$ in. wide, lavender with a deep brownish-red flare. Leaves oblong-elliptic, to $6\frac{1}{2}$ in. long, with purplish petioles. Tall, fairly compact, vigorous. Late May or early June. (Lowinsky, before 1935, distributed from Exbury. F.C.C.T. 1958.) Arthur Bedford was for some years head gardener to Lionel de Rothschild at Exbury.

ARTHUR J. IVENS (*houlstonii* × *williamsianum*).—Flowers about five in the truss. Corolla widely campanulate, up to $3\frac{1}{4}$ in. wide, deep rose in the bud, opening Persian Rose with two small crimson marks at the base. Filaments of stamens white. Style glandular throughout. Leaves oblong-ovate, to $2\frac{3}{4}$ in. long, $1\frac{1}{2}$ in. wide. Low-growing and compact, wider than high. (A. J. Ivens, for Messrs Hillier; cross made 1932. A.M. 1944.) Arthur Ivens was for many years nursery manager to Messrs Hillier.

'ARTHUR OSBORN'.—Flowers about six in the truss; pedicels clad with white, glandular hairs. Corolla funnel-shaped, about 2½ in. wide, dark red. Leaves oblong-lanceolate, to 3½ in. long, with a fawn indumentum beneath. Open, dwarf habit. June. (*griersonianum* × *sanguineum* subsp. *didymum*; Royal Botanic Gardens, Kew.) One of the best late-flowering rhododendrons for a small garden. The name is given as clonal only in the *International Register*, but the cross was made in other gardens. A clone of the same parentage is 'NUT-MEG'.

'ASCOT BRILLIANT'.—Flowers 10 to 16 in the truss. Corolla funnel-campanulate, about 2 in. wide, bright crimson red, with black speckling on the upper lobes. Calyx-lobes up to ¼ in. long, often tinged with red. Leaves elliptic, to about 4½ in. long, slightly glaucous beneath. Medium size, rather lax habit. Late April or early May. (Standish, before 1862.) A hybrid of R. *thomsonii* crossed with some hardy hybrid, and probably the first ever to have been raised from that species. It is very free-flowering.

AURORA (Kewense × *thomsonii*).—Flowers eight to ten in a broad, lax truss. Corolla funnel-shaped with a narrow tube, 5- or 6-lobed, 3¾ in. wide, rosy pink (Neyron Rose), with slight speckling in the throat, nectaries crimson. Calyx ¾ in. wide. Leaves intermediate between those of the parents. A tall, very vigorous shrub. April. Raised by Richard Gill in his nursery at Tremough, Cornwall, but named by Lionel de Rothschild. A.M. 1922. It is so similar to the best forms of Luscombei that it has even been suggested that Gill used R. *fortunei*, not Kewense, in making this cross (*Rhodo. Soc. Notes*, Vol. III, p. 188). The cross was later re-made at Bodnant.

The BRINCO grex (Loderi × *thomsonii*) is virtually the same as Aurora, but no plant of any note has emerged from it.

The ADELAIDE grex is the result of a back-cross of R. *thomsonii* onto Aurora, made at Exbury. The plants show the influence of the species in the foliage and the large calyx, but the flowers are in larger trusses, and the corollas funnel-campanulate, about 3½ in. wide, blood-red. A.M. 1935.

AVALANCHE (*calophytum* × Loderi).—Flowers fragrant 12 to 14 in the truss; pedicels rosy red. Corolla funnel-shaped, 4 in. wide, 6- or 7-lobed, pure white with three lines of speckles in the throat uniting into a blotch at the very base. Tall-growing, to some 20 ft. Early April. Rothschild. The description is of clone 'Avalanche' (A.M. 1934; F.C.C. 1938). In other forms of the cross the flowers are delicate pink (*Rothschild Rhododendrons*, pl. 18). The clone 'ALPINE GLOW', with pink-flushed flowers, received an A.M. in 1938.

A similar hybrid—CALFORT—was raised by Collingwood Ingram from R. *calophytum* crossed with R. *fortunei*. In the plant at Wisley the corollas are 3¾ in. wide, faintly tinged pale lilac, with a heavy maroon blotch breaking into speckles. Leaves narrowly oblong-elliptic. Calfort received an A.M. in 1932, and the same award was given in 1967 to the clone 'BOUNTY', also raised by Collingwood Ingram.

AZOR (*discolor* × *griersonianum*).—Flowers about eight in a lax truss. Corolla trumpet-shaped, 7-lobed, about 3 in. wide, pink, speckled on the upper lobe, deep red in the throat. Style glandular-hairy in the lower part; stigma red. Leaves dull green, oblong-elliptic or oblanceolate, 7 in. long, 2 in. wide.

Tall-growing. June. The cross was made originally at Tower Court, but later repeated in other gardens. The plant described here is a good average member of the grex, but some plants have bluish-pink flowers. The best clone is 'AZOR SISTER', from Tower Court (F.C.C.T. 1960).

'BAGSHOT RUBY'.—Flowers 14 to 18 in a rounded truss, on glandular-downy pedicels. Corolla widely funnel-shaped, about 1¾ in. across, ruby-red, upper lobe with a flare of dark brown spots on a lighter ground. Stamens with whitish or pinkish anthers. Style reddish, with a dark crimson stigma. Medium size. Late May or early June. (Waterer, Bagshot. A.M. 1916.)

BARCLAYI ('Glory of Penjerrick' × *thomsonii*).—This cross, made at Penjerrick early this century, unites R. *thomsonii* with R. *arboreum* (blood-red) and R. *griffithianum*. Several plants were raised, of which some were propagated, the best known clone being 'ROBERT FOX' (A.M. 1922). The truss has about eight flowers. Corolla blood-red, with black nectaries, shaped as in R. *thomsonii* and also inheriting from that species the large calyx, coloured like the corolla. Leaves obovate, abruptly short-acuminate, about 5 in. long, half as wide. It is hardy, but flowers very early—late March or early April.

'BARON SCHROEDER'.—Flowers about 20 in a large, dense truss. Corolla widely funnel-shaped, 2½–3 in. wide, dark reddish purple with a flare of yellowish green on a white ground at the base of the central lobe. Stamens and style crimson. Leaves rather narrow, 5 by 1⅜ in. Moderate growth, dense habit. Early June. (Waterer, Bagshot.) Named after Baron Sir Henry Schroeder, Bt (*d.* 1910), one of the leading orchid-growers of his time and a benefactor of the Royal Horticultural Society, who made a substantial contribution to the building of the Old Hall. He preferred to be known by his German title.

'BARONESS HENRY SCHROEDER'.—Flowers about 20 in the truss, on brownish-red glandular pedicels. Corolla 2½ in. wide, white flushed with magenta pink, fading to pure white, with a flare of deep crimson speckles. Medium size. Late May or early June. (Waterer, Bagshot.) There is a clump of this hybrid on the Broad Walk at Kew. The F.C.C. of 1883 belongs to a hybrid of R. *javanicum*, raised by Messrs Veitch and given the same name.

'BARONESS LIONEL DE ROTHSCHILD'.—Flowers about 16 in a dense, rounded truss. Corolla widely funnel-shaped, 2¾ in. wide, deep crimson at the margins, lighter at the centre, with a greenish-brown flare on a light ground. Anthers dark brown. Stigma crimson. Leaves lanceolate, 5½ by 1¼ in., deep green and rather bullate above, thinly brown-felted beneath. End May. (Waterer, Bagshot, before 1880.)

'B. DE BRUIN'.—Flowers about 20 in a shapely conical truss. Corolla funnel-campanulate, 2¾ in. wide, dark rich scarlet spotted black on the upper lobe. Stamens conspicuously white-hairy. Style and ovary glabrous. Early to mid-June. A fine colour, but poor foliage and straggly habit. The name is believed to commemorate Bas de Bruin, a member of the firm M. Koster and Sons, not Baron de Bruin, as stated in the *International Register*. But it was raised by A. Waterer at the Knap Hill Nursery.

'BEAUTY OF LITTLEWORTH'.—Flowers 15 to 18 in a large conical truss. Corolla widely funnel-campanulate, 4½ in. wide, white from mauvish-pink buds, speckled with purplish red on the upper lobe. Style glabrous. Leaves elliptic to 8 by 3¼ in. A tall, vigorous grower. May. F.C.C. This splendid hybrid is quite hardy, needing only shelter from wind and slight shade. In woodland it is apt to grow so fast that it becomes lanky and the young growths are so long that they bend under their own weight. Like the more famous 'Loder's White', it is the creation of J. H. Mangles of Valewood, Haslemere; after his untimely death in 1884 it passed to his brother and sister, who lived at Littleworth Cross near Farnham, and received an F.C.C. when shown by the former in 1904. The same award was given to it in 1953 after trial at Wisley. It is a hybrid of R. *griffithianum*, probably crossed with a white-flowered Hardy Hybrid.

BEAUTY OF TREMOUGH (*arboreum* × *griffithianum*).—This cross was made in several Cornish gardens, but the named clones, with the exception of 'John Tremayne', raised at Heligan, were mainly the creation of Richard Gill, who was head gardener to Henry Shilson of Tremough, and later set up his own nursery there. Using a blood-red form of R. *arboreum* he raised and distributed many seedlings, some of which were named and propagated, notably: 'BEAUTY OF TREMOUGH' (F.C.C. 1920); 'GLORY OF PENJERRICK' (A.M. 1904); 'GILL'S TRIUMPH' (A.M. 1906); and 'GILLII' (A.M. 1919). However, these hybrids are not really satisfactory outside the milder parts and are not further dealt with here.

'BEEFEATER'.—Flowers about 22 (sometimes a few more) in a flat-topped truss. Corolla fleshy, tubular-campanulate, 3 in. wide, with broad, rounded lobes, Geranium Lake, finely speckled near the base of the upper lobes, nectaries dark crimson. Stigma red. Anthers black. Leaves dull green above, undersides bright green with traces of flock, 8 by 2½ in. May. A back-cross of R. *elliottii* onto Fusilier (*elliottii* × *griersonianum*), raised in the R.H.S. Garden at Wisley. F.C.C. 1959. The truss is excessively large and poorly formed.

'BETTY WORMALD'.—Flowers 10 to 12 in a tall truss; rachis 3 to 3¾ in. long; pedicels to 2¼ in. long. Corolla 3 to 4 in. wide, broadly funnel-shaped, slightly frilled, Tyrian Rose at the edge, paling towards the centre, with heavy brownish-crimson speckling on the upper lobe, nectaries red. Style upswept, with a dark red stigma. Leaves dark green, to 7 by 2½ in. Medium height. Late May. (Koster and Sons, before 1922, from 'George Hardy' crossed with a red hybrid. F.C.C.T. 1964.) Of the 'Pink Pearl' type, but with larger, more vividly coloured flowers. 'MARINUS KOSTER', also raised by Koster and Sons, is very like 'Betty Wormald'. F.C.C.T. 1948.   [PLATE 99

'BIANCHI'.—Flowers about 18 in the truss on upright pedicels. Corolla 2 in. wide, almost bowl-shaped, pale pink, with crimson or green speckling on and below the central lobe. Anthers mauve. Style pale pink with a crimson stigma. Leaves elliptic, dull dark green. A charming old hybrid, now very rare. There is an authentic plant in Mr Frederick Street's garden at West End, near Woking, and a matching one, of large size, at Grayswood Hill, Haslemere. For its history see F. Street, *Hardy Rhododendrons* (1954), pp. 74–6, and *Gard. Chron.*, Vol. 132 (1952), p. 66.

BIBIANI (*arboreum* × 'Moser's Maroon').—Flowers about 14 in a dense rounded truss. Corolla tubular-campanulate, dark red with brown spotting. Leaves elliptic, acute, dull green above, brownish or silvery beneath, about 6 by 2 in. April. (Rothschild. A.M. 1934.) A perfectly hardy though rather early-flowering hybrid, showing strongly the influence of R. *arboreum*. There is an example 15 ft high in the Rhododendron Dell at Kew.

'BILLY BUDD'.—Flowers 10 to 12 in a dense, flat-topped truss. Corolla tubular-campanulate, 2 in. wide, lobes broad and shallow, Turkey Red. Pedicels, calyx ovary and style all glandular. Leaves elliptic, slightly wavy at the margin, with traces of floccose tomentum beneath. May. (R. *elliottii* × May Day; R.H.S. Garden, Wisley. A.M. 1957.)

BISKRA (*ambiguum* × *cinnabarinum* var. *roylei*).—Flowers pendent, in trusses of about eight. Corolla widely tubular-funnel-shaped, about 1½ in. long, 2 in. wide, vermilion. April. Tall-growing. (L. de Rothschild, 1934. A.M. 1940.)

'BLANDYANUM'.—Flowers up to 25 in a dense hemispherical truss; pedicels densely glandular. Corolla narrowly funnel-shaped, 3 in. wide, rosy crimson with a few black spots on the centre lobe. Style glabrous, rosy crimson, stigma purple. Ovary white-felted. Calyx glabrous, membranous. Leaves elliptic to oblanceolate, 5½ by 2¼ in. obtuse at the apex, cuneate at the base, thinly brown-felted beneath; petiole grey-felted. A dense, rounded shrub. Mid-May. An old hybrid, raised by Standish and Noble, from R. *catawbiense* pollinated by Alta-clerense, and therefore composed of R. *arboreum*, R. *catawbiense* (two doses) and R. *ponticum*. They received a Silver Knightian Medal for it in 1848.

'TOWARDII', which sprang from the same cross as 'Blandyanum', was named after the foreman at Bagshot Park, under whom Standish had worked before he set up his own nursery. Judging from a plant at Kew, the foliage is quite as handsome as Standish and Noble claimed, the leaves being dark green and broad-elliptic. But the colour of the flowers is a dark bluish pink and not pleasing. It is probably no longer in commerce.

'BLEWBURY'.—Flowers up to 20 in a compact truss. Corolla campanu-late, about 1½ in. wide, white, spotted with reddish purple on the upper side. Leaves narrow-elliptic, about 3½ in. long and 1 in. wide, rather rigid, dark green above, clad beneath with a thin brown indumentum, recurved at the margin, midrib impressed above. Late April or early May, compact and probably not more than 5 ft high (*anhweiense* × *roxieanum*; Crown Estate Commissioners). A charming hybrid of great individuality, taking after R. *roxieanum* but probably making a better garden plant. A.M. April 30, 1968.

BLUE DIAMOND (*augustinii* × Intrifast).—Flowers four or five per truss. Corolla almost flat with a short tube, deep violet-blue, about 1¾ in. wide. Leaves elliptic, subacute, up to 1⅜ by ⅝ in. April. Taller growing than most of the R. *augustinii* × Lapponicum series hybrids, to about 7 ft or so high, but of dense habit. (Crossfield. A.M. 1935. F.C.C. 1939, to a better coloured form than the one previously shown.)

This is a variable grex. The plant described above is probably the same as the 'F.C.C. form' but there is another clone in commerce with relatively much wider leaves, broad-elliptic, roundish at the apex, dark mat green. This has attained 7 ft in 18 years in poor dry soil and sets flower-bud on every shoot, though in the same garden both Bluebird and Blue Tit seldom flower well.

'BLUE PETER'.—Flowers about 15 in a conical truss. Corolla funnel-shaped, strongly ridged, about 2¾ in. wide, with frilled margin, Cobalt Violet fading to almost white at the centre, with coarse speckling on the upper lobe. Stamens very unequal, conspicuously white-hairy at the base. Late May. (Waterer, Bagshot. A.M. 1933. F.C.C.T. 1958.) A fine near-blue hybrid. As always, the lighter centre enhances the colouring of the flowers when seen from a distance.

BLUE TIT (*augustinii* × *impeditum*).—Flowers two or three per cluster, of which more than one is usually borne at the end of each shoot. Corolla pale lavender-blue, about 1½ in. wide, with faint brownish speckles on the upper lobe. Leaves light green, broadish elliptic, obtuse, to about 1 in. long. Dense habit, attaining 4 by 6 ft in 15 years. (J. C. Williams, 1933.) A charming hybrid, but usually flowering rather patchily, on the strong shoots only.

The AUGFAST grex (*augustinii* × *fastigiatum*) is related to Blue Tit, but the flowers are darker in colour and borne somewhat later. It is also taller-growing. The cross was made by E. J. P. Magor, who named it, later by Messrs Hillier and Messrs Reuthe.

BLUEBIRD (*augustinii* × *intricatum*).—Flowers four or five in a small cluster. Corolla almost flat, 1½ to 2 in. wide, with a short tube, rich violet-blue. Leaves mostly elliptic, acute or subacute, up to 1¼ in. long, rather yellowish green when young, in one clone almost chlorotic. April. Low, spreading habit. (Aberconway, 1930. A.M. 1943.) BLUESTONE, also raised at Bodnant, is a backcross of Bluebird with R. *augustinii*.

'BODDAERTIANUM'.—Flowers 18 to 22 in a dense truss; pedicels glandular, to 1 in. long. Calyx variable, rim-like or with linear lobes to ¼ in. long. Corolla funnel-shaped, 2½ in. wide, pink-flushed at first, becoming white, with a flare of maroon-purple spots reaching from the middle of the centre lobe into the throat. Style glabrous. Ovary glabrous except for a few scattered hairs. Leaves narrow, oblong-elliptic, acute, 7 by 1½ in., coated beneath with a very thin indumentum. A large shrub resembling R. *arboreum* in habit. Late April or early May. A very striking, perfectly hardy rhododendron with a long season of flower.

As pointed out by A. J. Ivens in his manuscript note on this hybrid, the parentage R. *arboreum* × R. *campanulatum* usually given for it is unlikely. He suggests R. *arboreum* crossed with R. *ponticum* (white-flowered forms on both sides) and this seems very likely, though the latter may have been a hybrid of R. *ponticum*, not the pure species. In this connection it is significant that a hybrid very similar to what is now known as 'Boddaertianum' was in cultivation until recently under the name R. 'Smithii Album', and that Smith of Norbiton is known to have crossed R. *arboreum* with R. *ponticum* (see R. 'Smithii'). But judging from the illustration in *The Garden*, Vol. 75 (1911), p. 264, 'Smithii Album' had larger flowers and fewer in the truss than 'Boddaertianum'.

The history of 'Boddaertianum' is not known for certain, but it is said to have been raised by van Houtte and to have been known originally as 'Gloire d'Anvers' (*Gard. Chron.*, Vol. 132 (1952), p. 55).

BONITO (*discolor* × Luscombei).—Truss with about 15 flowers on stalks 1½ in. long. Corolla about 5 in. wide, funnel-shaped, pink in bud, opening white flushed with pink, with brown and rose markings on upper side of throat. A tall, vigorous shrub. Late May-early June. (Rothschild.) A.M. 1934. A commercial clone differs from the A.M. plant in having greenish-yellow markings in the throat.

BO-PEEP (*lutescens* × *moupinense*).—Flowers solitary or in twos. Corolla pale creamy yellow, deeper in the bud, with two lines of darker speckles, broadly funnel-shaped, about 2 in. across. March. A loose bush to about 4 ft high. (Rothschild, 1934. A.M. 1937.) A charming hybrid which unfortunately does not quite coincide in flowering time with Praecox.

'BOULE DE NEIGE'.—Flowers in a dense hemispherical truss; flower-bud scales persistent. Corolla funnel-shaped, 2¼ in. wide, white, freckled with a few brown and green spots on the upper lobe. Ovary white-felted, Calyx very small. Leaves elliptic to obovate, 4 by 2 in. Dense, fairly dwarf habit. Mid-May. (*caucasicum* × *catawbiense* hybrid; Oudieu, 1878.) This hybrid is valued in the north-eastern USA for its great hardiness and excellent habit; it was available in commerce in Britain until recently. It bears some resemblance to 'Cunningham's White', but has broader leaves and a denser truss.

BOWBELLS ('Corona' × *williamsianum*).—Flowers about six in a lax truss. Corolla pale bright pink from deeper-coloured buds, slightly red-speckled, broad funnel-campanulate, 2¾ in. wide. Leaves ovate, obtuse, cordate at base, petiole purplish; young growths bright bronze coloured. May. Erect habit, usually under 6 ft high, but old plants in woodland at Exbury are taller; some plants in gardens appear to belong to a dwarf, compact clone. (Rothschild, 1934. A.M. 1935.) This remains one of the best hybrids raised from R. *williamsianum*.

BRIC-A-BRAC (*leucaspis* × *moupinense*).—Flowers in threes. Corolla milky white, not or very slightly spotted, about 2 in. wide, similar in shape to that of R. *leucaspis* and with the style deflexed as in that species. Anthers brownish red. Leaves leathery, elliptic-obovate, about 2 in. long, veiny but lustrous above. February or March. It is of dwarfer, denser habit than R. *moupinense*, which it resembles less than the other parent (Rothschild, 1934. A.M. 1945.)

'BRITANNIA'.—Flowers 10 to 14 in a conical truss. Corolla with a broad bell-shaped tube (gloxinia-shaped) and a spreading slightly wavy limb, 3 in. wide, soft pinkish scarlet with deeper-coloured nectaries, almost unspotted. Leaves up to 9 in. long and 3½ in. wide in shade. Late May or early June. ('Queen Wilhelmina' × 'Stanley Davies'; Van Nes. A.M. 1921; F.C.C.T. 1937.) After half a century in our gardens, 'Britannia', raised in Holland, remains one of the most popular hybrids and is still, perhaps, the best scarlet of its class. Grown in a well-lighted position it makes a compact bush, but shade from the hottest sun is advisable, since the foliage, naturally a rather yellow-green, becomes more so in a hot position. On the other hand, in too much shade it becomes lax, and develops large leaves which are apt to be broken off by wind.

BROCADE (? × *williamsianum*).—Flowers about six in the truss, on glandular-hairy pedicels. Corolla campanulate, 5- or 6-lobed, 2¼ in. wide, blush-white shaded rose-pink. Leaves oblong ovate, dark green, rather rigid, up to 3 in. long, on reddish-brown slightly glandular petioles. April. Compact habit, to about 5 ft. (Rothschild.) A pretty rhododendron and also a puzzling one. The other parent was recorded in the Exbury stud-book as 'Vervaeniana'—an ever-green greenhouse azalea. Even if such a cross were possible, it cannot have been responsible for this hybrid.

'BROUGHTONII'.—Flowers up to about 20 in a pyramidal truss. Corolla funnel-campanulate, deeply lobed, rosy crimson shading to paler on the three upper lobes, with dark spotting on all the three upper lobes. Leaves fairly glossy, elliptic to narrow-oblanceolate, to about 10 in. long and 3 in. wide, cuneate at the base. A very large and dense shrub, up to 20 ft or even more in height, Mid- to late May. An old hybrid, deriving mainly from R. *arboreum* and R. *maximum*, raised before 1853. It somewhat resembles 'Cynthia', but the longer, relatively narrower leaves distinguish it, as well as many other characters, e.g. the wider zone of spotting and the paler centre of the corolla.

'BUTTERFLY'.—Flowers 10 in a loose truss on pale green pedicels 2 in. long. Corolla with a short tube and widely spreading limb, butterfly-shaped, 3 in. wide (narrower transversely), pale creamy yellow, heavily speckled with crimson. Erect, open habit. Early May. (*campylocarpum* × 'Mrs Milner'; Slocock. A.M. 1940.) Very pretty, aptly named, but needs a fairly sunny position if it is to flower freely.

CAREX (*fargesii* × *irroratum*).—Flowers about ten in a lax truss. Corolla campanulate, 7-lobed, 3 in. wide, pale lilac-pink, darker on the reverse, with some maroon spotting inside, mostly on the upper lobes. Style white, red-glandular to the tip. Calyx ¼ to ⅜ in. wide, glandular. Leaves about 4 in. long, half as wide, broad-elliptic, rounded at both ends. A tall bush. April. A spontaneous hybrid of R. *fargesii*, of which the other parent was probably R. *irroratum*, raised at Exbury. A.M. 1932. Two other clones have been named 'CAREX WHITE' and 'CAREX BLUSH'.

CARITA (*campylocarpum* × 'Naomi').—Flowers 10 or 11 in a lax truss on pedicels almost 2 in. long. Corolla pink in the bud, opening pale yellow, with greenish or brownish speckling in the throat, five-lobed. Leaves elliptic, 5 to 6 in. long, 3 in. wide. (Rothschild, 1935.) This description is from a plant at Exbury probably of the clone that received the A.M. in 1945. But the grex is variable in flower-colour, as might be expected from the parentage. In 'CARITA INCH-MERY' the corollas are pink with a straw-pink centre, mostly six-lobed. In 'GOLDEN DREAM' they are deeper yellow than in the A.M. clone. These and others are portrayed in *Rothschild Rhododendrons*, pl. 7. A clone in commerce has corollas translucent white, pink-tinged, at the edges, pale primrose at the centre of the lobes (mostly six in number); buds buff-pink. The Carita grex flowers end-April or early May, and the plants grow to about 15 ft in height.

CARMEN (*forrestii* × *sanguineum* subsp. *didymum*).—Flowers three per truss. Corolla deep blood-red, campanulate, almost 1½ in. wide. Leaves broad elliptic-obovate, about 1¾ in. long, dark green. Dwarf to 2 ft or so, more in spread. April or early May. (Rothschild, 1935.) Best planted where the sun can enliven the colour of its flowers.

'CAUCASICUM PICTUM'.—Truss dense, with about 12 flowers on erect pedicels. Corolla pink at first, later white flushed with pink, with a dense brownish-crimson flare, lobes angled, frilled. Leaves oblanceolate, about 5 in. long, reticulate above as in R. *caucasicum*. Late April or early May. A dense bush to about 8 ft. A hybrid of R. *caucasicum*, listed by Standish and Noble in 1853.

'C. B. VAN NES'.—Flowers 12 to 14 in a loose truss. Corolla campanulate, 2⅜ in. wide, with broad, overlapping lobes, slightly wavy at the edge, glowing crimson-scarlet, with a few dark spots on the upper lobes. Leaves oblong-elliptic, up to 5 in. long and 1¾ in. wide, dull, deep green above. Compact habit. Late April or early May. A sister seedling of 'Britannia'.

'CETEWAYO'.—Flowers about 12 in a small, dense truss. Corolla dark plum-coloured (Beetroot Purple), campanulate, about 2 in. wide. Stamens dark, with whitish anthers. Late May-early June. (Waterer, Knap Hill, before 1883. A.M.T. 1958.) '. . . a large bush has all the melancholy dignity of a superb prune mousse' (J. Russell, *Rhododendrons at Sunningdale*, p. 42).

CHASTE (*campylocarpum* × 'Queen of the May').—Flowers in a bun-shaped truss of about 12. Corolla pale yellow with crimson feathering in upper part of throat, about 3¼ in. wide; lobes truncate, overlapping. May. (Crosfield.) A fine but uncommon hybrid. The commercial clone is described.

'CHEVALIER FELIX DE SAUVAGE'.—Flowers up to 20 in a dense truss. Corolla deep rosy pink with a prominent dark eye, funnel-campanulate, 2¼ in. across, frilled at the edge. Leaves to 5 in. long, 2 in. wide, elliptic, recurved. Dense habit. A hybrid of R. *caucasicum* raised on the Continent around 1870, flowering late April or early May. 'PRINCE CAMILLE DE ROHAN' is similar, but the flowers are paler pink and the leaves relatively narrower, about 5½ by 1⅝ in. It was raised by Waelbrouck, secretary of the Conseil Communal of Ghent, and put into commerce by Verschaffelt in 1855. The prince admired it in his nursery, so it was named after him.

'CHIKOR'.—Flowers up to six in a truss. Corolla with a cup-shaped limb and tubular base, 1 to 1½ in. wide, soft yellow, with slight deeper spotting. Dwarf, compact habit. Late April–early May. A lovely, very free-flowering hybrid between R. *chryseum* and R. *ludlowii*, raised by E. H. M. and P. A. Cox, Glendoick. F.C.C.T. 1968.

CHINA (*fortunei* × *wightii*).—Flowers up to 17 in a loose conical truss. Corolla creamy white with a red mark in the throat, about 3½ in. wide. A vigorous shrub of medium size. May. (Slocock. A.M. 1940; A.M.T. 1948.) In 'CHINA A', from the same cross, the flowers are more yellow and slightly smaller.

'CHINK'.—Flowers up to five in the truss. Corolla pale primrose, wide funnel-shaped, about 1½ in. wide, with greenish-yellow speckling at the base of the central lobe and below the upper sinuses. Calyx small, edged with long silky hairs. Leaves elliptic, apiculate, to 1¾ in. long, edged with sparse long hairs. March. Low-growing and bushy. (*keiskei* × *trichocladum*; Crown Estate Commissioners, Windsor. A.M. 1961.)

'CHIONOIDES'.—Flowers about 14 in a dense truss. Corolla white from a creamy bud, with a greenish-yellow flare, funnel-shaped from a broad base, 1⅞ in. wide. Style scarcely expanded at the apex. Late. Compact, moderate growth. (Waterer, Bagshot, before 1865.) See F. Street, *Hardy Rhododendrons*, p. 95, and *Gard. Chron.*, Vol. 132 (1952), p. 205.

CHOREMIA (*arboreum* × *haematodes*).—Flowers about ten in the truss. Corolla dark scarlet, waxy, tubular-campanulate, about 2 in. wide; calyx petaloid. Leaves stiff, oblanceolate or elliptic, dark green and glossy above, coated beneath with a plastered pale indumentum. April. Excellent dense habit. (Aberconway. A.M. 1933. F.C.C. 1948.)

'CHRISTMAS CHEER'.—Flowers about eight in the truss on erect, reddish pedicels; bud-scales of inflorescence persistent. Corolla funnel-shaped with a broad base, 1¾ in. wide, frilled at the edge, pink in the bud and when first open, fading to blush but darker outside on the ridges, with pale red or greenish speckles running from the base of the two upper sinuses into the throat. Stamen-filaments white. Style deep pink. Ovary oblong-conoid, white-hairy. Leaves medium green, brown beneath from a very fine close indumentum, elliptic to narrow-obovate, rather narrowly cuneate at the base. April.

The plant described here belongs to a clone in commerce as 'Christmas Cheer', which is said to attain about 6 ft in height. It is doubtfully the same as the large plants in the R.H.S. Garden at Wisley and in the Savill Garden under this name. The latter is 15 ft high. It is possible that these are the true 'Christmas Cheer', and that the dwarfer plant is the same as 'Silberaad's Early Pink', of which there is a detailed description in the Ivens Manuscript, drawn up in 1930, which seems to agree with the plant described above in every respect.

Another hybrid in this group is 'ROSA MUNDI', which was probably raised by Standish and Noble. This differs from the plant described above in its dark green leaves and in its still dwarfer habit—only 2 or 3 ft high in twenty years.

CILPINENSE (*ciliatum* × *moupinense*).—Inflorescence two- or three-flowered. Corolla broad funnel-shaped, 2¾ to 3 in. wide, pale pink shading to a deeper colour at the edges, with two lines of crimson speckles. Calyx-lobes edged with long hairs. Leaves bright green, glossy, reticulate, elliptic to slightly obovate, to 2 in. long. March–April. (Aberconway, 1927. A.M. 1927. F.C.C. 1968.) The description is of a commercial clone, which does not usually exceed 3 ft in height, but much more in width. A lovely hybrid, nearer to R. *ciliatum* than to the other parent. There are other forms, however, some with smaller, whiter flowers.

CINNKEYS (*cinnabarinum* × *keysii*).—Flowers from terminal and upper axillary buds, forming a many-flowered multiple truss. Corolla about 1½ in. long, waxy, tubular, light red with soft yellow lobes. Late May–early June. Erect habit, to 10 ft or even more. (Magor, cross made 1917.) In 'MINTERNE CINNKEYS', raised by Lord Digby, the flowers have pale red lobes. A.M. 1951. This was probably raised from R. *keysii* var. *unicolor*.   [PLATE 100

'COLONEL ROGERS'.—A hybrid between R. *falconeri* and R. *niveum*, with larger flowers than in the latter, mauve at first but paling to white as they age. It is probable that the original plant was the one mentioned by Millais in 1917 as growing in the garden at Riverhill, Sevenoaks, Kent. The cross is believed to have occurred in other gardens.

COMELY (*concatenans* × 'Lady Chamberlain').—This cross was made originally at Bodnant, but the clones that have so far received awards were raised in other gardens. These are:

—'GOLDEN ORFE'.—Flowers about seven in the truss. Corolla similar to that of R. *concatenans* in shape, i.e., tubular-campanulate and rather short, 2 in. long and wide, orange-yellow (Nasturtium Orange, 25C). Raised at Tower Court, Ascot, and taken to Tremeer, Cornwall, by Mrs Stevenson after her remarriage to Gen. Harrison. A.M. 1964. It is in commerce.

—'DAYAN'.—This was raised at Exbury by Edmund de Rothschild, and received an A.M. in 1967; described in *R.C.Y.B. 1968*, p. 231.

'CONCESSUM'S MASTER'.—Dense truss of about 16 flowers. Corolla almost saucer-shaped, 3 in. wide, Rose Bengal, paling to almost white at the centre. June. An old hybrid probably so called because superior to the still older 'CONCESSUM', which was raised in Belgium and shown by Standish and Noble in 1854.

CONROY (*cinnabarinum* var. *roylei* × *concatenans*).—Flowers pendent, about six in the truss. Corolla tubular-campanulate, 2 in. long, 1½ in. wide, fleshy, light orange tinged with pink. Leaves elliptic, dark green, 3 in. long. Medium sized. May. (Aberconway. A.M. 1950.)

A similar hybrid is 'CAERHAYS PHILIP', in which the parent on the *cinnabarinum* side was var. *blandfordiiflorum*. The corollas are yellow, more open than in the A.M. form of Conroy, 2½ in. wide. Raised at Caerhays by the Hon. Charles Williams and Charles Michael. A.M. 1966.

'CONSTABLE'.—Truss open, with about 20 flowers. Corolla funnel-campanulate, about 3 in. wide, in a pleasing shade of greenish yellow, with reddish markings in the throat. Late April–early May. (Hawk 'Jervis Bay' × *litiense*; R.H.S. Wisley. A.M. 1961.) *R.C.Y.B. 1962*, fig. 35.

'CONSTANT NYMPH'.—Truss dense, dome-shaped, with 12 to 14 flowers. Corolla widely funnel-shaped, to 4½ in. wide, waved and slightly frilled at the margin, white, flushed with light purple at the centre of the lobes. Late May. (*campanulatum* × 'Purple Splendour'; Waterer, Knap Hill, intr. 1955. A.M.T. 1971.)

CORNISH CROSS (*griffithianum* × *thomsonii*).—Flowers six to nine in a lax truss. Corolla funnel-campanulate, about 4 in. wide, upper lobe and throat beneath it crimson, rest of corolla paler crimson, especially at the centre of the lobes, overall effect two tones of crimson pink. Calyx large, irregularly lobed, coloured like the corolla, about 1 in. wide. Leaves elliptic to obovate, broadly obtuse, to 10 in. long, 3½ in. wide. Late April–early May. To about 12 ft high. Bark peeling, pinkish brown. 'Cornish Cross' was the name given to plants raised by Samuel Smith at Penjerrick, from a cross made about 1920, propagated and distributed by Messrs R. Veitch. But the same cross had been made at the end of the 19th century by Sir John Llewellyn, Bt, of Swansea and received an A.M. when shown by him under the name 'PENGAER' in 1911. In 'EXBURY CORNISH CROSS' (A.M. 1935) the flowers are brighter and more evenly crimson than in the plant described above. Smith had used a not outstanding form of R. *thomsonii* and a R. *griffithianum* raised at Penjerrick; in the Exbury cross, the F.C.C. form of R. *griffithianum* was used (*Rothschild Rhododendrons*, p. 67 and pl. 31; *Rhodo. Soc. Notes*, Vol. III, pp. 254–5).   [PLATE 101

Another fine clone of Cornish Cross is 'GILIAN' (A.M. 1923). It was raised by E. J. P. Magor, who originally gave the parentage as R. *campylocarpum* × R. *griffithianum* but later became convinced that he must have misrecorded the cross. His son Major Walter Magor tells us his father was eventually quite satisfied that 'Gilian' is a form of Cornish Cross. The flowers are rich crimson red, fading at the centre as they age.

CORNUBIA (*arboreum* × Shilsonii).—This cross was made by S. Smith, head gardener to R. Barclay Fox, Penjerrick, in 1901. The seed-parent was a blood-red *arboreum*. Shilsonii is a hybrid between R. *barbatum* and R. *thomsonii*, so the cross brings together the three great red-flowered Himalayan rhododendrons. It was named 'Lilianii' at Penjerrick, but half of the 400 or so seedlings raised were made over to Messrs Gill, who named their share 'Cornubia'. The plants are variable in the shade of red of their flowers, but the influence of R. *arboreum* shows in the compact, hemispherical truss; the corollas are larger than in that species, 2 to 3 in. wide. The foliage usually has the texture of R. *arboreum*, but varies in size. The flowering time is late winter or early spring. A.M. 1912 (flowers blood-red).

'CORONA'.—Flowers 10–11 in a pyramidal truss, the rachis 4 in. or slightly more long. Corolla funnel-shaped, limb cup-shaped owing to the overlapping lobes, 2 in. or slightly more wide, ground colour blush-pink, heavily overlaid Coral Pink, which is the predominant colour of the flower when seen from a distance. Compact habit, moderate growth. Late May. (Waterer, Bagshot. A.M. 1911.) A charming, most distinct hybrid, needing slight shade in the drier parts. 'PETER KOSTER' somewhat resembles 'Corona', but the corolla is slightly speckled and the rachis is only half as long. (M. Koster and Sons; 'Doncaster' × 'George Hardy'.) It is possible that 'George Hardy' or similar hybrid was one parent of 'Corona' also.

'CORRY KOSTER'.—Flowers about 16 in a conical truss; rachis 3 in. long. Corolla at first buff-pink, becoming light pink shading to white at the edges, spotted brown-crimson on the upper lobe, funnel-shaped, about 3 in. wide, margins frilled. Moderate growth. Late May. (M. Koster and Sons, 1909.) Probably a hybrid of 'Chev. Felix de Sauvage'.

'COUNTESS OF ATHLONE'.—Truss conical, with about 15 flowers. Corolla funnel-shaped, 3½ in. wide, with overlapping lobes, wavy-edged, pale mauve with greenish-yellow markings near the base of the upper lobe. Medium growth. Late May. (C. B. van Nes and Sons, 1923; 'Catawbiense Grandiflorum' × 'Geoffroy Millais'.) A pleasing colour, but corolla poorly shaped and truss too large.

'COUNTESS OF DERBY'.—A hybrid of 'Pink Pearl', differing in the much larger truss, 10 in. wide, large flowers (4 in. wide), of a deeper, cleaner pink. Leaves dull greyish green. The other parent is 'Cynthia'. (Sunningdale Nurseries, 1913 A.M. 1930.)

'COUNTESS OF HADDINGTON'.—Flowers fragrant, up to six in a cluster. Corolla tubular-funnel-shaped, 2¾ in. wide, white flushed with lilac pink, yellow in the throat at first. Calyx leafy, divided almost to the base, lobes almost ½ in. long, spreading. Leaves elliptic-lanceolate, obtuse, up to 4 in. long, light green above, margins ciliate. Of rounded, fairly dense habit, to about 6 ft high and wide. April. (*Journ. R.H.S.*, Vol. 88 (1963), fig. 38; *Gard. Chron.*, suppl. ill., May 19, 1888.) F.C.C. 1862, when shown by the nurseryman R. Parker of Tooting, and said in the original description to be a hybrid raised 'from R. *dalhousiae*'. There can be little doubt that R. *ciliatum* is the other parent. Indeed, J. H. Mangles, who was well informed on such matters, wrote in 1881 that R. *ciliatum* was the seed-parent (*Gard. Chron.*, Vol. 15, 2nd ser., p. 108). Once established it should survive most winters in a sheltered place in southern England.

'COUNTESS OF SEFTON'.—Flowers about four per truss, fragrant. Corolla funnel-campanulate with spreading lobes, $3\frac{1}{2}$ in. wide, white, with red spotting in the upper part and stained red outside when first open. Calyx with shallow, rounded lobes, edged with long, white hairs. Leaves elliptic, bullate, glossy, densely scaly beneath. Low growing and fairly compact. A hybrid between R. *edgeworthii* and R. Multiflorum (*ciliatum* × *virgatum*), raised by Isaac Davies of Ormskirk, Lancs, shortly before 1879. The results of the cross varied, and altogether six of the seedlings were named and propagated, of which the best were said to be 'Countess of Derby' and 'Lady Skelmersdale', but 'Countess of Sefton' seems to be the only one to have survived, at least under its original name. Short descriptions were given in *Gard. Chron.*, 2nd ser., Vol. 12, p. 201 (1879). 'Countess of Sefton' is almost hardy, and should survive most winters in a sheltered place in southern England.

COWSLIP (*wardii* × *williamsianum*).—Flowers about five in a lax truss on glandular red-tinged pedicels. Corolla cup-shaped, 3 in. wide, pink in the bud, becoming ivory white with a slight tinge of pink, streaked with red at the base below the centre lobe. Style glandular to the apex, with a red stigma. Leaves broadly oblong-elliptic, rounded at the apex, cordate at the base, about $2\frac{1}{2}$ in. long. Compact and fairly dwarf. April or early May. (Aberconway. A.M. 1937.)

CROSSBILL (*lutescens* × *spinuliferum*).—Flowers about three in each truss. Corolla funnel-campanulate, about 1 in. long and wide, pale yellow, stained red outside, with two bands of yellow-green speckles inside. Stamens and style exserted, the latter about $1\frac{1}{2}$ in. long, upcurved. April. The cross was made at Caerhays and later repeated at Exbury.

CUNNINGHAMII.—Flowers up to 24 in a compact truss. Corolla broad-campanulate, about $2\frac{1}{4}$ in. wide, white with a flare of dark purple markings and crimson nectaries. Leaves oblanceolate, to $6\frac{1}{4}$ in. long and almost 2 in. wide, acute, deep green and rather bullate, clad beneath with a brown tomentum. A large, compact shrub. Early May.

This hybrid was made by George Cunningham, Oakvale Nursery, Liverpool, in the 1840s. The above description, based on the Ivens Manuscript, agrees with the original accounts and figures (*Gard. Mag. Bot. Hort.* (1851), t. 16; Paxton's *Flow. Gard.*, Vol. I (1850), p. 81 and t. 16, as R. *cinnamomeum* var. *cunninghamii*). So, too, does the hybrid grown under the name 'George Cunningham'. The parentage of Cunninghamii is R. *arboreum* var. *cinnamomeum* crossed with 'late white Maximum' (seed-parent).

The R. *cunninghamii* of K. Koch is probably 'Cunningham's White' (q.v.), which is quite a different hybrid.

'CUNNINGHAM'S ALBUM COMPACTUM'.—Flowers about 14 in a dense truss, from persistent bud-scales. Corolla funnel-shaped, 2 in. wide, white with greenish-brown markings at the base of the upper lobe. Leaves narrow-elliptic, to 4 in. long and only just over 1 in. wide, rigid, dull green above, clad beneath with a brown indumentum. Compact habit, to about 6 ft high. May.

A hybrid of R. *caucasicum*, believed to have been raised in the 1830s or 1840s at Cunningham's Comely Bank Nursery, Edinburgh, with a white-flowered R. *arboreum* as the pollen-parent. According to a letter to Kew (1909) from J. Fraser, then co-proprietor of this nursery, one-third approximately of the seedlings from this cross take after R. *caucasicum* in habit, and vary in colour from white to pale yellow. This hybrid has been confused with 'Cunningham's White', which has quite different foliage. It was apparently also known in the last century as 'Cunningham's Dwarf White'.

'CUNNINGHAM'S BLUSH'.—Similar to 'Cunningham's White' (see below) but flowers up to 14 in the truss and the corollas tinted with pink even when fully open and with darker speckling. The two may well have come from the same seed-pod. It is an uncommon but quite pretty rhododendron, attaining 12 ft or so in height. There are two clumps of it at Nymans in Sussex, in the Heather Garden.

'CUNNINGHAM'S SULPHUR'.—A compact bush with pale yellow flowers, very near to R. *caucasicum* in its botanical characters, raised by Cunningham and Fraser, Comely Bank Nurseries, Edinburgh, at the end of the last century and sent out originally as "R. *sulphureum*". According to J. Fraser, in the letter to Kew referred to under 'Cunningham's Album Compactum', it was raised from R. *caucasicum* pollinated by a white-flowered R. *arboreum*.

'CUNNINGHAM'S WHITE'.—Flowers about eight in a lax truss, on ascending pedicels 1⅜ to 1⅝ in. long. Corolla funnel-shaped, about 2 in. wide, tinted light mauve when opening, becoming pure white with fine speckling of yellow, brown or purple on the upper lobe. Leaves dark green, oblanceolate, 4 in. long. A compact shrub, usually not more than 10 ft high, flowering early to mid-May. It is a hybrid between R. *caucasicum* and R. *ponticum album*. A very similar plant, figured in *Bot. Mag.*, t. 3811, was raised by Veitch and is of the same parentage (assuming that Veitch's R. *ponticum albiflorum* was the same as the plant used by Cunningham). Many of the so-called varieties of R. *ponticum* grown in the early part of the last century were hybrids.

'Cunningham's White' is one of the commonest of the old hybrids, especially in the North and Midlands. In a letter to Kew, received early this century, James Smith of the Darley Dale Nurseries stated that this hybrid thrives well in a limestone district, in evidence of which were the large number of thriving plants planted by his firm near Buxton. It has been recommended for covert planting in place of R. *ponticum*, probably because it is less aggressive. Being easily propagated by cuttings, and very hardy, it has been used as a stock, especially on the Continent and for rhododendrons intended for export to the colder parts of North America. Even the greenhouse azaleas are said to grow well on its roots.

'CURLEW'.—Flowers solitary, or in twos or threes. Corolla wide-campanulate, 2 in. wide, light yellow, marked with greenish brown in the upper part of the throat. Calyx deeply lobed, long ciliate, lobes to ¼ in. or slightly more long. Leaves dark green, narrow-obovate to obovate, about 1½ in. long. Dwarf, spreading habit, to about 1 ft high. May. A lovely hybrid raised by Peter Cox, from R. *ludlowii* crossed with R. *fletcherianum* 'Yellow Bunting'. F.C.C. 1969, when exhibited by Glendoick Gardens Ltd.

'CYNTHIA' ('Lord Palmerston').—Flowers up to 24 in a pyramidal truss on pedicels to 2 in. long. Calyx-lobes oblong, acute or truncate at the apex. Corolla funnel-shaped, ribbed, about 3 in. wide, deep rose-pink with darker spotting on the upper lobes (mostly confined to the central one). Stamen-filaments pink.

Leaves oblong elliptic to slightly obovate, broadly obtuse at the apex, about 6½ in. long and 2⅝ in. wide. May.

'Cynthia' was exhibited by Charles Noble in 1862 under the name 'Lord Palmerston' and was presumably raised by Standish and Noble before the dissolution of their partnership in 1856. It is one of the largest and most vigorous of the old hybrids, attaining a height of 25 ft (or even more in a sheltered place). It was slow to gain recognition but in the early decades of this century it was second only to 'Pink Pearl' in popularity. Unfortunately, it is not a good mixer, the flowers having a strong hint of magenta in their colouring.

'DAIRY MAID'.—Flowers about 12 in a dense truss, on red-tinged pedicels. Corolla funnel-campanulate, 2 to 3 in. wide, creamy yellow with a red mark in the throat. Compact habit. Early May. (*R. campylocarpum* × hardy hybrid; Slocock. A.M. 1934.)

DAMARIS (*campylocarpum* × 'Dr Stocker').—The following description is of 'DAMARIS LOGAN', the clone by which this cross is mainly represented in commerce: Truss with 10 to 12 flowers on glandular pedicels 1½ to 2 in. long. Corolla campanulate, clear bright yellow (Dresden Yellow), 2½ to 3 in. wide. Leaves bright green, oblong-elliptic, 5 by 1¾ to 2 in., showing the influence of R. *caucasicum* in their veiny upper surface. Dense growth, medium height. Late April or early May. One of the finest yellows. (K. McDouall, Logan, Wigtonshire, before 1931. A.M. 1948.)

The cross was first made by E. J. P. Magor of Lamellen, and named by him after his youngest daughter. The plant that first flowered with him had primrose yellow flowers in a flat truss of six, resembling those of 'Mrs Kingsmill' but deeper in colour (*Rhodo. Soc. Notes*, Vol. III, p. 52). The cross was also made at Townhill and by Messrs Hillier.

'DAME NELLIE MELBA'.—Flowers about 12 in a conical truss; rachis 2½ in. long. Corolla widely funnel-shaped, 3½ in. across, rich pink, darker on the tube outside and paling inside towards the centre of each lobe, with two bands of brownish-crimson spots. Leaves dark green and glossy, up to 7 in. long, 2¼ in. wide. A vigorous hybrid, flowering late April or early May, finely coloured. A.M. 1926. It was raised by Sir Edmund Loder at Leonardslee, but named and distributed by Lionel de Rothschild. It is a hybrid between a blood-red form of R. *arboreum* and 'Standishii'. Nevertheless, it seems to be quite hardy.

DAMOZEL ('A. W. bright rose' × *griersonianum*).—Truss lax but well shaped, with about 14 flowers; pedicels, calyx and outside of corolla with white, curled hairs. Corolla 3 to 4 in. wide, funnel-shaped, deep crimson pink (between Claret Rose and Delft Rose), speckled on all lobes. Leaves dull green, oblanceolate, acute, 7½ by 2 in. Fast growing but of rather sprawling habit. Mid- to late May. (Rothschild, 1936. A.M. 1948.) The description is of a commercial clone, which seems to be different from the A.M. form.

'DAVID'.—Flowers 15 to 19 in a dense truss. Corolla campanulate, 2¾ in. wide, margins slightly frilled, deep blood-red (near Cardinal Red or Currant Red), with black embossed spotting below the central lobe. Style and stamen-filaments white. Leaves dark dull green, oblong-elliptic, 6–7 in. long. Medium growth. May. A fine deep red, one of the best of its colour, raised by F. J. Rose

for Lord Swaythling at Townhill Park, from 'Hugh Koster' pollinated by
R. *neriiflorum* (whose influence does not show at all).

'DAWN'S DELIGHT'.—Flowers in a lax truss of about ten; rachis almost
3 in. long. Corolla campanulate with a spreading limb 4¼ in. wide, frilled at the
edge, vivid rosy red in bud, becoming delicate pink, paling at the centre, with
a few large speckles, banded red outside. Leaves oblanceolate, 7¼ by 2½ in. May.
A lovely hybrid of medium size, raised by J. H. Mangles, which was taken to
Littleworth Cross after his death in 1884 and received an Award of Merit when
shown from there by his sister Miss Clara Mangles, in 1911.

Another Mangles hybrid that may be mentioned here is 'DAPHNE DAF-
FARN', which is uncommon, but represented at Kew in the Rhododendron
Dell. The flowers are in dense, rounded trusses of up to 20; the corollas are
slightly less than 3 in. wide, slightly frilled of a beautiful shade of pink shading
to paler in the centre. The original plant at Valewood is figured in *Gard. Chron.*,
September 20, 1930 (suppl. ill.).

DAYDREAM (*griersonianum* × Lady Bessborough).—Flowers about 12 in a
lax truss. Corolla trumpet-shaped, 3 in. wide, rather crumpled, Carmine Rose
(52C) with redder speckling and much darker coloured in the throat, eventually
fading to straw-yellow or dirty white, but the throat and flare remaining red.
Tall. Early May. (Rothschild. A.M. 1940.)

'DIANE'.—Truss compact with eight to ten flowers. Corolla broad-campanulate, 3 in. wide, primrose, paler at the margin, with crimson markings in the
throat. Style stout with a pale green stigma. Late April or early May. (Koster.
A.M.T. 1948.)

'DIPHOLE PINK'.—Flowers about twenty in the truss. Corolla 3 in. wide,
funnel-shaped, deep rosy pink with orange-brown speckling. Late May or early
June. (Waterer, Bagshot. A.M. 1916.) Still one of the best late-flowering pinks.
There is a clump of this hybrid at Kew on the Broad Walk.

'DONCASTER'.—Flowers about 15 in the truss. Corolla funnel-shaped, 3 in.
wide, dark red with a flare of black spots. Easily recognised even when out of
flower by its dark green, elliptic-obovate leaves, which are rather wavy-edged,
slightly concave above, and apparently edged with lighter green owing to the
exposure of the pale underside, and by their pinkish or reddish petioles; also
by its dwarf, spreading habit. Late May or early June. It is one of the reddest
of the old hybrids but, as in all of this type, there is a blue base to the colour
which shows up as the flower ages. It was raised at Knap Hill before 1885.

'HUGH KOSTER' somewhat resembles 'Doncaster' in flower and foliage,
and is a hybrid of it, but the corollas are rather lighter in colour, and the style
and stamen-filaments are white, not pink as in 'Doncaster'. It is also taller, but
still of bushy habit. (Koster and Sons. A.M.T. 1933.)

'DR A. W. ENDTZ'.—Flowers 12 to 14 in a rounded truss. Corolla 4 in.
wide, frilled, deep lilac-pink. Medium size, compact habit. Late May. (*catawbiense* hybrid × 'Pink Pearl'; L. Endtz and Co., before 1927.)

'DR STOCKER'.—Flowers five to eight in the truss, on ascending, clustered
pedicels. Corolla broadly funnel-campanulate, 3 in. wide, creamy white with a
brownish-green flare. Leaves glossy, light green, reticulate above, oblong-
elliptic, 5½ by 2 in. Fairly dwarf, spreading habit. Late April. A hybrid between

T A S—EE

R. griffithianum and some form of *R. caucasicum*, or possibly 'Cunningham's Sulphur'. A.M. 1910, when shown by Dr Stocker of Avery Hill, Kent. It was raised by his head gardener G. Abbey and put into commerce by Messrs Veitch of Exeter in 1910.   [PLATE 102

'DUCHESS OF CONNAUGHT'.—Flowers about 20 in truss. Corolla spreading funnel-shaped, 3 in. wide, white, mauve-tinged at first, with a large yellow flare and some brown speckling. Anthers pale purple. Calyx well developed, with membranous, pink-edged lobes. Leaves oblanceolate, 5 to 6 in. long. One of the old white-flowered hybrids from *R. maximum*.

'DUCHESS OF PORTLAND'.—Flowers 12 to 14 in a conical truss, on erect pedicels. Corolla campanulate, 2 in. wide, lobes not spreading much, folded at first along the centre line and appearing pointed, white with a small crimson mark in the upper throat. Leaves rather thin, oblanceolate, 6 by 2 in., with a thin cobwebby indumentum beneath. April. A compact, medium-sized plant, one of the finest whites, but Frederick Street has pointed out that it is a martyr to rhododendron fly. A.M. 1906. It was raised by Fisher, Son, and Sibray from *R. barbatum* crossed with 'Handsworth Early White'. This parentage has been disputed, for obvious reasons, but the foliage strongly suggests that it is correct.

'DUCHESS OF TECK'.—This hybrid, raised by Messrs Waterer of Bagshot at the end of the last century, was little known until recently reintroduced to commerce. The corollas are lilac-pink at the edge, almost white at the centre, with a conspicuous flare of brown spots. Compact habit. June.

'DUCHESS OF YORK'.—Flowers fragrant, 10 to 12 in a lax truss. Corolla almost 3 in. wide, trumpet-shaped, five- to seven-lobed, rosy pink, with a flare of light green spots. Stamens mostly abortive. Foliage recalling that of *R. fortunei*. Medium growth. End May. A.M. 1894. This is one of many hybrids raised by G. Paul at the end of the last century from *R. fortunei* crossed with hardy hybrids. It was once hoped that they, and others of similar parentage bred by Luscombe of Coombe Royal, would be the foundation of a new race of hardy hybrids, but most have remained little more than names in the stud-book, and have not been used in breeding further varieties. But more successful hybrids with the same formula were raised later, the best known being 'Lavender Girl' (q.v.).

DUKE OF CORNWALL (*arboreum* × *barbatum*).—This group is uncommon outside the milder parts of the country and also scarce in commerce. In 'DUKE OF CORNWALL', which is the 'type' of this grex, the flowers are lustrous dark scarlet-crimson, spotted black on the upper lobes, borne in April; leaves dark green, glossy, 10 in. long, 2 in. wide, glabrous beneath. A.M. 1907. Other clones are 'DUCHESS OF CORNWALL', with flowers of a beautiful shade of crimson, in a dense truss of 12 to 15, borne in early spring. The leaves are clad beneath with a white indumentum. Also 'EDMONDII', for which see Millais' *Rhododendrons*, pp. 79, 120 and 2nd series p. 123; 'TRELAWNY' (see *Journ. R.H.S.*, Vol. 61 (1936), p. 223; A.M. 1936); and 'JOHN HOLMS' (see *Journ. R.H.S.*, Vol. 83 (1958), p. 38; A.M. 1957).

'WEREI' is a seedling of *R. arboreum* raised at Penjerrick, of which the pollen-parent is probably *R. barbatum* (and certainly not *R. thomsonii* as was stated when it received an A.M. in 1921). The flowers are a very pleasing shade of salmon-pink, borne in April. The plants known as R. *barbatum* var. *carneum* are also probably hybrids between that species and R. *arboreum*.

'EARL OF ATHLONE'.—Flowers up to 20 in the truss. Corolla tubular-campanulate, 2¾ in. wide, with erect, overlapping lobes, vivid blood-red, with two faint lines of black speckles in the tube. Style stout, white, abruptly up-turned at the apex; stigma green. Leaves dull medium green, elliptic-obovate, 4 to 5 in. long. Of rather straggly habit and not a strong grower. Late April or early May. ('Queen Wilhelmina' × 'Stanley Davies'; van Nes. F.C.C.T. 1933.)

'EARL OF DONOUGHMORE'.—Flowers 10 to 15 in the truss; rachis 2 in. long—pedicels glandular. Corolla Spinel Red (54A), darker in the throat, funnel-shaped, about 4 in. wide. Style stout, red, glabrous. Leaves oblanceolate, dull green, to 7½ in. long. May. A hybrid raised in Holland by M. Koster and Sons from R. *griersonianum* crossed with ('Mrs L. A. Dunnet' × Hardy Hybrid). It is best grown in almost full sun, as it is inclined to sprawl in shady woodland.

'EILEEN'.—Flowers 16 in the truss. Corolla 3 in. wide, blush with a broad edge of pink (66D) and a flare of yellow on the lower part of the central lobe. Style white; stigma pale red. Medium growth. Early June. (Waterer, Bagshot.)

ELEANORE (*augustinii* × *desquamatum*).—Inflorescence four- or five-flowered. Corolla shaped as in the parents, about 3 in. wide, amethyst-violet, slightly spotted. A tall, vigorous shrub. Late April or early May. (Rothschild.) There is also a paler form, which appears to be the one that received the A.M. in 1943.

ELISABETH HOBBIE ('Essex Scarlet' × *forrestii*).—Flowers about five per truss, on glandular pedicels 1 in. long. Corolla campanulate, 2 in. wide, Turkey Red. Style and stamen-filaments red. Leaves elliptic to obovate, 2 to 3 in. long, rounded at the apex, glossy, lateral veins impressed. May. (Dietrich Hobbie, Linswege, Germany.) Many plants were raised from this cross. The plant described above is from a commercial clone, and is bushy and very vigorous, with excellent foliage. 'SCARLET WONDER', which belongs to this grex, is similar in flower-colour and foliage, but is dwarfer and more spreading. Two others in the same style as 'Scarlet Wonder', and said also to be 'Essex Scarlet' × R. *forrestii*, are 'BADEN-BADEN' and 'BAD EILSEN'.

ELIZABETH (*forrestii* × *griersonianum*).—Flowers six to nine in the truss, on glandular reddish pedicels. Corolla obliquely funnel-shaped, 2¾ to 3 in. wide (somewhat larger on plants grown in shade), scarlet, slightly speckled, nectaries dark red. Stamens with red filaments and black anthers. Leaves medium green, slightly rugose, oblong to oblong-obovate, obtuse, 2½ to 3½ in. long; petioles reddish. April. (Aberconway, 1933. A.M. 1939; F.C.C. 1943.)

This is perhaps the finest of the hybrids raised by F. C. Puddle at Bodnant and, if habit and foliage as well as flower are considered, the finest of all the smaller hybrids. Its only fault is its early flowering. As an example of its growth may be taken a plant growing on the north side of a beech hedge at the top of a dry wall, which in eighteen years has spread to 10 ft in both directions and is 3 ft high at the back, sloping to the top of the dry wall and beyond it at the front. Sister plants in woodland, put in at the same time, are much laxer in growth and 6 ft high. 'JENNY', a clone of this grex, has drooping, self-layering outer branchlets and is good for a bank where it can spread at will. The flowers are a trifle smaller.

'ELSA CRISP'.—Flowers 14 to 18 in a conical truss. Corolla funnel-shaped from a broad base, 3 in. wide, delicate pink (pale Rose Bengal) at the edge, paling at the centre of each lobe and in the throat, with slight crimson speckling on the lower part of the centre lobe. Anthers pale brown, tinged with pink, filaments white. Style white, sharply upswept at the tip, with a dark red stigma. Early June. (Waterer, Bagshot.) Said to be a seedling of 'Mrs E. C. Stirling'.

ELSAE.—This is a hybrid of unknown origin and parentage, thought to be a cross between R. *grande* and either R. *falconeri* or, as Millais thought, R. *hodgsonii*. The flowers are ivory white with a crimson blotch in the throat, campanulate, borne in large trusses of about 20; leaves up to 1 ft long, dark green and reticulate above, with impressed laterals, clad beneath with a woolly brown tomentum which tends to wear away, exposing the felted under-layer. In the *Notes* of the Rhododendron Society, Vol. III, p. 115, the provenance is given as 'Raised by the Hon. John Boscawen and given to G. Carlyon of Tregrehan'. The Hon. J. T. Boscawen was Rector of Lamorran, in the grounds of Tregoth-nan, the property of his brother the sixth Viscount Falmouth. It is perhaps of relevance that in 1877 Boscawen showed to the Scientific Committee of the R.H.S. a 'splendid' truss of campanulate waxy white flowers from a 'fine tree' at Tregothnan, which Dr Hooker, who was in the chair, pronounced to be R. *argenteum* [R. *grande*] crossed with R. *lanatum*. This may well have been the original 'Elsae', even though the parentage suggested by Hooker does not seem very likely.

Despite the uncertainty about the parentage of 'Elsae', the name is used in the International Register as the collective name for crosses between R. *grande* and R. *hodgsonii*. Hybrids of this parentage were raised at Clyne Castle, Swansea, with flowers in various shades of pink or mauve, and one of these received an Award of Merit when shown by Adm. Heneage-Vivian in 1940 (as "Elsae Clyne").

'ELSPETH'.—Flowers eight to ten in the truss. Corolla campanulate, 2¾ in. wide, vivid red in the bud, the colour lightening as the flower opens and gradu-ally turning to cream, but the edges often remaining red for some time, giving a picotee effect. (*campylocarpum* × hardy hybrid; Slocock. A.M. 1937.)

'EMERALD ISLE'.—Flowers about nine in a loose truss. Corolla 4 in. across, widely campanulate, greenish yellow, deepening in the throat. May (Idealist × Naomi; R.H.S. Gardens, Wisley.) A.M. 1956. A product of the same cross is 'NEW COMET', which has light yellow flowers shaded with pink. A.M. 1957.

'ESSEX SCARLET'.—Flowers 16 to 20 in a compact truss. Corolla funnel-campanulate, 3 in. wide, rich crimson-scarlet with a heavy black flare, lobes wavy. Leaves narrow-elliptic. Upright, vigorous growth. June. A.M. 1899 when shown by G. Paul's nursery. Unusually late-flowering for a hardy hybrid of such an intense colour. It is a parent of the Elisabeth Hobbie grex.

ETHEL (F. C. Puddle × *forrestii*).—Truss with about six flowers on stout reddish pedicels. Corolla tubular-funnel-shaped, about 2 in. long and wide, deep scarlet. Leaves oblanceolate, 3½ by 1¼ in., dark green and glossy, lateral veins slightly impressed above. Dwarf, spreading habit. April. (Aberconway,

1934. F.C.C. 1940.) The F. C. Puddle grex is R. *griersonianum* × R. *neriiflorum*, but the influence of the former species, so potent in first-generation crosses, scarcely shows in this hybrid. It is one of the best low-growing reds, attaining 3 by 6 ft in 15 years or so.

'EVERESTIANUM'.—Flowers about 20 in a dense truss. Corolla widely funnel-shaped, about 3 in. across, with broad-ovate, frilled lobes, rosy lilac, paler in the centre, with a flare of yellowish-green spots. Style mauve; ovary glandular-downy. Leaves oblong-elliptic to oblong-obovate, 4¼ by 2 in. Dense habit. End May or June. It is remarkable that this hybrid, raised at the Knap Hill nursery before 1843, is still widely available in commerce today. Yet even in 1853 it was referred to as 'an old but very fine kind', which suggests that it may have arisen very soon after the introduction of R. *catawbiense* in 1809. It is a hybrid between that species and either R. *maximum* or (R. *maximum* × R. *ponticum*).

EXMINSTER (*campylocarpum* × *thomsonii*).—This uncommon hybrid was raised at Penjerrick and named by Messrs R. Veitch of Exeter, who put it into commerce and received an A.M. for it in 1923. The corollas are campanulate, cream-coloured heavily flushed with pink; inflorescence with five or six flowers. Foliage intermediate between those of the parents. The cross was made in other gardens.

FABIA (*dichroanthum* × *griersonianum*).—This cross has been made in many gardens, with differing results according to the form of R. *dichroanthum* used, but no two plants are exactly alike in colour even when raised from the same seed-pod. The inflorescence is lax, with seven to ten flowers. Corolla funnel-shaped, 2½ to 3 in. wide, with a large coloured calyx, usually in blended shades of orange and pink. Leaves dark green or medium green, more or less elliptic, to 5 in. long, with a light coloured indumentum beneath. The height varies, some clones being 3 to 4 ft high, others taller, but all are compact. Flowering time late May or June. The plants are very hardy and will stand full sun, though slight shade is better.

In the form that received the A.M. when shown from Bodnant in 1934 the flowers were described as bright scarlet. In 'TANGERINE', one of the best clones and also raised at Bodnant, they are soft vermilion shading to a pinker colour at the edge, and orange in the throat. 'ROMAN POTTERY', raised by J. Crosfield at Embley Park, has flowers described as pale orange with coppery lobes. In 'FABIA TOWER COURT', a dwarf clone, they are 'soft orange pink, with a deep rose flush at the tips' (*Rhododendrons at Sunningdale*, p. 53).

MOHAMET (*dichroanthum* × *eriogynum*) resembles the Fabia grex, but the corolla has a broader base. It is less hardy and not so good. Raised at Exbury.

'FAGGETTER'S FAVOURITE'.—Flowers slightly fragrant, 11 to 13 in a dome-shaped truss with an unusually long rachis. Corolla 6- or 7-lobed, funnel-shaped, 3¾ in. wide, deep pink in the bud, opening creamy white flushed with Phlox Pink, with two lines of brownish-green speckles in the throat. Style with large green stigma. Compact habit, medium size, fast-growing. A chance hybrid of R. *fortunei*. A.M.T. 1955. Mr Faggetter was rhododendron foreman at the Goldsworth Nurseries of Messrs Slocock, where this hybrid was raised.

FAIRY LIGHT (*griersonianum* × 'Lady Mar').—This Exbury hybrid has never received an award, but is useful for its moderate growth and late flowering (June). The corolla is clear rich pink, darker in the throat and with slight red speckling on the upper lobe, the outside of the tube bright red.

'FASTUOSUM FLORE PLENO'.—Flowers 15 to 17 in a broad truss. Corolla funnel-shaped, 2 to 2¾ in. wide, most of its stamens converted into extra petals or staminodes, pale bluish mauve with a golden-brown or greenish flare. Leaves oblong obovate, 5 by 2 in., dull green. Late May or early June. A large, compact shrub, raised on the continent before 1846 and still one of the most valuable of all rhododendrons. The colour is nearly blue in some lights. Very near to R. *catawbiense*. A.G.M. 1928.

FITTRA.—See under R. *racemosum*.

'FLORIADE'.—Flowers 14 to 20 in a large truss. Corolla campanulate, 3½ to 4 in. wide, deep crimson with a heavy brown flare and dark crimson nectaries. End-May. A hybrid of recent introduction, raised in Holland by Adrian van Nes.

FORTUNE (*falconeri* × *sinogrande*).—This hybrid, raised by Lionel de Rothschild at Exbury, received an F.C.C. when shown in 1938. The flowers are borne up to thirty together in a splendid truss 7 in. high and 9 in. wide. The corolla is clear yellow with a crimson mark at the base. The leaves resemble those of R. *sinogrande* in their glossy upper surface, but the indumentum is thicker and darker (*Rothschild Rhododendrons*, pls. 15 and 16).

'FRAGRANTISSIMUM'.—Flowers deliciously fragrant, three or four in each truss; pedicels scaly, glabrous except for a few scattered hairs. Corolla widely funnel-shaped, 3 to 4 in. wide, pure white except for a yellowish tinge in the throat. Stamens hairy at the base only. Style scaly in the lower half, with a green stigma. Calyx variable in size, up to ¼ in. long. Leaves varying from ovate-elliptic and acute to obovate and obtuse, up to 3½ in. long, upper surface somewhat rugose, covered at first with brown crisped hairs, later more or less glabrous, dullish medium green, lower surface pale green, scaly, the scales spaced from almost contiguous to about three times their own diameter apart. A tender hybrid of lax habit, from R. *edgeworthii* crossed with R. *formosum*, grown outdoors in the milder parts. It is possible that there is more than one clone under the name 'Fragrantissimum', since the cross has certainly been made more than once, and the name may have been used in a collective sense. The original 'Fragrantissimum' received an F.C.C. when shown by the nurseryman Rollisson in 1868.

The same cross, made by Rinz of Frankfurt-am-Main, is named SESTER-IANUM. This form received an F.C.C. when shown by Messrs Veitch in 1862.

'FRANCIS B. HAYES'.—Truss conical with about 16 flowers. Corolla funnel-shaped, 2½ in. wide, mauve in the bud, pure white when fully open, with an intense, rather sharp-edged flare of black and maroon on the upper lobes. Medium size. June. (Waterer, Bagshot.) The blotch is very much darker than in 'Sappho'. F. B. Hayes (*d.* 1884) was a native of Boston, USA. He had a large collection of rhododendrons on his estate at Lexington, Mass.

'FRANK GALSWORTHY'.—Truss compact, rounded, with 16 to 20 flowers. Corolla funnel-shaped, 2½ in. wide, deep reddish purple with a large yellowish flare. Late May or early June. (Waterer, Knap Hill. A.M.T. 1960.)

'FURNIVALL'S DAUGHTER'.—Flowers about 15 in a compact, rounded truss. Corolla funnel-shaped, 3½ in. wide, lobes broad and rounded at the apex, especially the centre lobe, which is about as wide as long, delicate pale pink with a large flare of dull crimson. Calyx-lobes pinkish, to ⅜ in. long, reflexed. Style white with a pink stigma. Leaves elliptic-obovate, up to 6½ in. long, about half as wide. Late April or early May. (Knap Hill. F.C.C.T. 1961.) A seedling of 'Mrs Furnivall'.   [PLATE 103

FUSILIER (*elliottii* × *griersonianum*).—Flowers about 10 in the truss, on glandular pedicels to 1 in. long. Calyx dark brownish red, shallowly lobed, rather spreading. Corolla fleshy, tubular-funnel-shaped, about 3 in. wide, soft scarlet with darker nectaries. May. Tall and vigorous. Rather tender. (Rothschild. A.M. 1938; F.C.C. 1942.)

'GALACTIC'.—Flowers up to 22 in a dense truss on stout pedicels up to 1¾ in. long. Corolla campanulate, 3½ in. wide, pale primrose, darkening in the tube, with crimson pencilling at the base. Stigma greenish yellow. Leaves up to 9 by 3½ in., oblanceolate, clad beneath with a plastered indumentum. Tall. March–April. A fine hybrid raised by Lionel de Rothschild at Exbury from Avalanche × R. *lacteum*. See *Rothschild Rhododendrons*, pl. 35. A.M. 1964, F.C.C. 1970.

'G. A. SIMS'.—Flowers 14 to 16 in a compact truss. Corolla funnel-campanulate, 2¾ in. wide, blood-red with a flare of black spots. Rather spreading and straggling habit. Late May or early June. (Waterer, Knap Hill. A.M.T. 1972.) The flowers are darker than in 'Doncaster', also raised at Knap Hill.

GAUL (*elliottii* × Shilsonii).—Flowers about 20 in a compact truss. Corolla 2 in. wide, tubular-funnel-shaped, deep red, with a cup-shaped calyx of the same colour. (Rothschild. A.M. April 18, 1939.) A fine red, not suitable for cold gardens.

'GAUNTLETTII'.—This hybrid was raised by V. N. Gauntlett and Co. of Redruth, Cornwall, at the end of the last century and continued to be sold by them under this name after they moved to Chiddingfold, Surrey, in 1905–6. In their catalogue 101, which appeared early in the 1930s, they give 'White Pearl' as a synonym of 'Gauntlettii', thus implying that Messrs Cutbush had renamed their hybrid and obtained an Award of Merit for it (see 'White Pearl'). However, they probably obtained this misinformation directly or indirectly from Millais' work on rhododendrons, in which he asserted that 'Gauntlettii' and 'White Pearl' were one and the same, when in fact there is little doubt that the latter was simply the trade-name given to 'Halopeanum', raised in France.

No authentic plant of 'Gauntlettii' has been seen, but judging from the photograph reproduced in Messrs Gauntlett's catalogue the corollas appear to be nearer to funnel-shaped than to campanulate, thus differing from 'White Pearl'.

'GEOFFROY MILLAIS'.—Flowers 14 in a tall truss; rachis 4½ in. long. Corolla wide campanulate, 4 in. wide, lobes broad, slightly wavy, pink in the bud, opening white, with a ray of brownish-red markings, flushed with crimson on the reverse. Style pinkish with a crimson stigma, glandular in the lower half. Leaves elliptic, 6½ by 2⅛ in. One of the Schulz hybrids, raised at the Porcelain Factory, Berlin, around 1890, and distributed by van Nes. A fine white, in the same style as 'Manglesii' and 'White Pearl'. A.M. 1922.

'GEORGE HARDY'.—Flowers 12 to 14 in a conical truss; rachis 2¾ to 3¾ in. long; pedicels to 2 in. long, glandular. Calyx large, reddish, very irregularly lobed, some lobes ovate, others oblate. Corolla short-campanulate, to 3¾ in. long, lobes longer than tube, rosy in the bud, opening white with crimson markings mainly confined to the centre lobe; nectaries not coloured. Style glandular at the base. Leaves dark green, oblong-lanceolate, to 6 in. long. Medium growth. Late May. A quite handsome hybrid, standing full sun, mentioned here because it is probably a parent of 'Pink Pearl'. It is a hybrid of R. *griffithianum* crossed with some hardy white, and is believed to have been raised by J. H. Mangles at Valewood, Haslemere. According to Millais, it was put into commerce by Messrs Waterer of Bagshot.

There are many hybrids of similar character to 'George Hardy', difficult to distinguish one from another. 'MANGLESII' was raised by Messrs Veitch at their Coombe Wood nursery. It received an A.M. when shown by them in 1885 and was named in memory of J. H. Mangles, who had died the previous year. It is from a cross between R. *griffithianum* and either 'Album Elegans' or 'Album Grandiflorum'. It is a more demanding plant than 'George Hardy', needing shade and shelter; the flowers are similar, but the style is glandular to the tip. 'COOMBE ROYAL' was probably raised by Luscombe of Coombe Royal, Kingsbridge, Devon, and received an Award of Merit when shown by Messrs R. Veitch of Exeter in 1900. Plants seen under the name are very like 'George Hardy', but with fewer, larger flowers on a shorter rachis. Another in this group is 'STANDISHII'. This is not the same as the old hybrid of that name raised by Standish and Noble from Altaclerense crossed with a hybrid between R. *ponticum* and R. *maximum*, and named in 1850. But Standish may well have experimented with R. *griffithianum* in the later years of his life. A plant in the Knap Hill nursery under this name differs from 'George Hardy' in having corollas with coloured nectaries and two lines of speckles (in 'George Hardy' they are all in one group).

GLADYS (*campylocarpum* × *fortunei*).—Flowers about 10 in a loose truss. Corolla widely funnel-shaped, 6-lobed, 3½ in. wide, pale cream with a few purple markings. Leaves oblong-ovate, 4 in. or slightly more long, 2 in. wide. Late April or early May. This description, from the 'Ivens Manuscript', is of the original 'Gladys', which received an A.M. when shown by Lord Swaythling of Townhill Park in 1926. It was raised, according to this source, by Brig.-Gen. Clarke of Chilworth Manor, near Southampton, not by Col. S. R. Clarke of Borde Hill, as stated in *Journ. R.H.S.*, Vol. 52, p. lii, though this cross was made at Borde Hill also. Three years before 'Gladys' was exhibited by Lord Swaythling, the cross was made in his garden by F. J. Rose, using R. *campylocarpum* "var. *elatum*" and a selected form of R. *fortunei*. The plants first flowered in 1931, and a group of trusses from them was a feature of the Rhododendron Show of that year. The colours ranged from cream to deep pink. On the same occasion an Award of Merit was given to 'MARY SWAYTHLING', presumably one of this set, in which the flowers are primrose-yellow with no markings.

'GLADYS ROSE' received an A.M. when shown by the Crown Estate Commissioners in 1950. This has flowers in a lax truss of about nine; corolla ivory-yellow, darker on the upper lobe, flushed pale pink and also pink in the bud. It was raised at Townhill (see above).

The cross using R. *campylocarpum* "var. *elatum*" was also made by Messrs W. C. Slocock and the results, varying in colour, were given the grex-name LETTY EDWARDS, the individual plants being distinguished by numbers. But the clonal name 'Letty Edwards' is now attached to the clone which received an F.C.C. after trial at Wisley in 1948. This has flowers in trusses of ten to twelve, corolla widely funnel-shaped, pale primrose shaded deeper on the upper lobe and in the throat, unmarked except for faint greenish-yellow speckling in the throat.

GOLDEN HORN (*dichroanthum* × *elliottii*).—Flowers about seven in the truss on glandular-downy pedicels. Calyx fleshy, enlarged, coloured like the corolla, which is campanulate, about 2½ in. wide, orange in the bud, opening deep salmon-pink blending with orange and mottled with brown. Leaves oblanceolate, to 5 in. long, obtuse, dull green above, bright green on the underside beneath a thin brown indumentum. Low-growing and compact. Late May or early June. (Rothschild.) The description is of the clone 'Golden Horn' (A.M. 1945). In 'PERSIMMON' the corolla is deep, glowing red speckled with black dots, and the calyx is smaller (*Rothschild Rhododendrons*, pl. 11).

GOLDEN ORIOLE (*moupinense* × *sulfureum*).—Trusses mostly three-flowered; inner bud-scales crimson. Corolla tubular-funnel-shaped, about 2 in. wide, resembling that of R. *sulfureum* but of a beautiful shade of clear light yellow (Dresden Yellow). Leaves elliptic, obtuse, about 2 in. long. Stems cinnamon-brown, peeling. A small shrub of erect habit. March. (J. C. Williams.) This description is of the clone 'GOLDEN ORIOLE TALAVERA' (F.C.C. 1963), for which a white-flowered R. *moupinense* was used (*R.C.Y.B. 1964*, pl. 3). 'GOLDEN ORIOLE BUSACO', from a pink-flowered form of that species, has the corollas primrose-yellow suffused with pale pink, with some crimson spots on the upper lobes. Both are lovely and probably hardy, but flower too early for most gardens.

'GOLDFORT'.—Flowers about 12 in the truss. Corolla funnel-shaped, 3 in. wide, 5- to 7-lobed, pink in the bud, opening pale primrose tinged with apricot, speckled with green in the throat. Style glandular in the lower half, with a greenish stigma. Late April or early May. (*fortunei* × 'Goldsworth Yellow'; Slocock.)

'GOLDSWORTH CRIMSON'.—Flowers 12 to 16 in a compact truss. Corolla funnel-shaped, 3½ in. wide, lobes broadly rounded at the apex, bright red, fading towards the centre and darker on the reverse, upper lobe speckled with black. Medium size, of fairly compact, spreading habit. Early May. ('Doncaster' × *griffithianum* hybrid; Slocock. F.C.C.T. 1971.)

'GOLDSWORTH ORANGE'.—Flowers in a lax truss of up to ten; pedicels bright green. Corolla funnel-shaped with a broad base, 6- or 7-lobed, fleshy, yellow, lobes paler than tube and tinged with pink, upper part of throat with a broad band of greenish-brown speckles. Low, spreading habit. June (*dichroanthum* × *discolor*; Slocock. A.M. 1959.)

'GOLDSWORTH YELLOW'.—Flowers up to 16 in the truss on ascending pedicels. Corolla funnel-campanulate, 2½ in. wide, undulated at the margin, lobes at first angled owing to infolding at the tips, buff-pink in the bud becoming pale creamy yellow but pink-tinged at first, especially on the ridges outside, speckled brown in the upper part of the throat. Leaves medium green, reticulate above, mostly oblong-obovate, to 5 in. long. Moderate height, spreading habit. End April or early May. A.M. 1925, when shown by Messrs W. C. Slocock. Millais published the name 'Goldsworth Yellow' in the first volume of his *Rhododendrons* (1917), p. 38, and gives the history of the plant in his second volume, p. 103. According to his version, the original was bought in the winding-up sale of Veitch's Coombe Wood nursery (1913–14). But he also records that Messrs Slocock made the cross R. *caucasicum stramineum* × R. *campylocarpum* before 1917, and this is a likely parentage for 'Goldsworth Yellow'.

Although many yellow-flowered hardy hybrids have been raised since, 'Goldsworth Yellow' remains one of the most useful, as it stands full sun and does not flower unduly early.

'GOMER WATERER'.—Flowers about 20 in a handsome rounded truss. Corolla wide funnel-shaped, 3 in. wide, mauve in the bud, opening white flushed with mauvish pink at the edges, with a flare of yellowish brown on the upper lobes. Leaves dark green, very leathery, elliptic or slightly obovate, to 5 in. long. Moderate, dense growth. Early June. (Waterer, Bagshot. A.M. 1906.) A tough, wind-resistant rhododendron, but with beautiful flowers.

'GRAND ARAB' ('The Grand Arab').—Flowers 15 in a compact, conical truss; rachis 1 in. long. Corolla funnel-shaped, 2 in. wide, magenta-crimson with slight black spotting at the base of the centre lobe. Style crimson, glabrous. Ovary densely white-felted. Calyx with shallowly triangular, glandular-ciliate lobes. Leaves narrowly elliptic, tapered at both ends, 4 by 1¾ in., clad beneath with a scarcely visible indumentum. It makes a well-shaped bush to 10 ft or slightly more high. Early May. An old hybrid of R. *arboreum*. Nothing is known of its origin, but it was listed by John Waterer in 1854. In the following year he put into commerce the much later flowering 'John Waterer' and 'Mrs John Waterer', but 'Grand Arab' has persisted in cultivation, especially in the North and Midlands.

GRENADIER (*elliottii* × 'Moser's Maroon').—Flowers about 12 in a globular truss; rachis about 1½ in. long. Corolla funnel-campanulate, of waxy texture, 3 to 3½ in. wide, deep red, with dark nectar-pouches and some dark speckling on the upper lobes. Leaves dark green, elliptic, with a loose tomentum beneath. Tall and vigorous. June. This is one of the finest hybrids raised by Lionel de Rothschild from R. *elliottii*, but in common with other late-flowering hybrids of the Parishii group it is slow to ripen its growths, which may be damaged by autumn frosts. It received a First Class Certificate in 1943.

GROSCLAUDE (*eriogynum* × *haematodes*).—Flowers up to 10 in a lax truss on stellate-hairy pedicels. Calyx irregular, large, coloured like the corolla, which is campanulate, 2½ in. wide, fleshy and glossy, deep scarlet-red, with some black speckling. Leaves to 4½ in. long, rounded at the apex, dull green, coated beneath with a brown indumentum. Compact and fairly dwarf. June. (Rothschild. A.M. 1945.) It flowers later than the May Day grex, from which it differs in the shape of the corolla and other characters.

HALCYONE (Lady Bessborough × *souliei*).—Flowers about seven in a lax truss. Corolla bowl-shaped, 3½ in. wide, rosy pink in bud, opening white flushed with pink, heavily lined and speckled with darker pink. Leaves similar to those of R. *souliei*, from which it also derives the shape of its corolla. Medium growth. May. (Rothschild.) The description is from a commercial clone, which flowers well even where R. *souliei* never sets a flower-bud. In 'PERDITA' (A.M. 1948) the corolla is less spotted and pinker (*Rothschild Rhododendrons*, pls. 51–2).

'HANDSWORTH EARLY WHITE'.—Flowers about ten in the truss on erect pedicels. Corolla funnel-shaped, 2 in. wide, pink in the bud, opening white, almost unmarked. Leaves narrowly oblong-elliptic to oblanceolate, 5–7 in. long. Compact and low-growing. March or April. (Fisher, Son and Sibray.) A hybrid of R. *caucasicum*.

HARRISII (*arboreum* × *thomsonii*).—This cross was first made about 1880 in Lord Swansea's garden at Singleton near Swansea by his head gardener Harris, who later set up his own nursery. The original plants were up to 25 ft high when Millais saw them in 1915. The cross was later made at Caerhays with better results and the plants from this cross are usually treated as a separate grex under the name RED ADMIRAL. It was also made at Penjerrick, where it was named TREGEDNA. These hybrids are as early flowering as R. *arboreum*, and not common outside the milder parts. The flowers are fewer in the truss than in R. *arboreum*, with a more pronounced calyx, and vary in colour from crimson to blood-red. The leaves are usually (to the naked eye) glabrous beneath, relatively broader than in R. *arboreum* and usually obtuse at the apex.

HAWK ('Lady Bessborough' × *wardii*).—This well-known Exbury hybrid unites two yellow-flowered members of the Thomsonii series—R. *campylocarpum* and R. *wardii*—with the tall-growing, late-flowering R. *discolor* of the Fortunei subseries. Lionel de Rothschild made the cross twice. The first batch, which started to flower about 1940, had R. *wardii* KW 4170 as its parent, and its best known clone is 'JERVIS BAY'. This has about 10 flowers to the truss. The corolla is widely funnel-shaped, 3 in. across, primrose-yellow with a deep red eye. It received an A.M. in 1951. 'CREST', which received an F.C.C. in 1953, is from the repetition of the cross. The flowers are about twelve in the truss. The corolla is very widely funnel-campanulate, 4 in. across and 1½ in. deep, with seven rounded lobes, a lovely clear primrose-yellow shading to deeper below the upper lobes, unmarked except for faint streaking at the very base of the throat (*Rothschild Rhododendrons*, pl. 23).

'Crest' is so different in its flowers from those of the first batch that it has been suggested that some other form of R. *wardii* was used as the parent. Or it may be that mere chance decreed that the combination of characters seen in 'Crest' appeared in the second and not in the first batch. The seven lobes come from R. *discolor*, but KW 4170 ('Lemon Bell' as Kingdon Ward called it), with its unblotched corolla, has asserted itself over the other two parents—R. *campylocarpum* "var. *elatum*", with its red eye, and R. *discolor*, which usually imparts a streaked throat to its offspring. 'Crest' is generally acknowledged to be the finest yellow-flowered hybrid yet raised, but may in time be supplanted by its offspring, of which a number have already received awards. See the note by T. H. Findlay in *R.C.Y.B. 1967*, pp. 73–4.

The clonal name 'HAWK' is linked in the *International Register* to the form that received an Award of Merit when shown from Windsor by the Crown Estate Commissioners in 1949. Whether the plants in commerce as 'Hawk' are of this clone it is impossible to say. The foliage in the Hawk grex is mostly oblong-elliptic and obtuse, truncate or slightly cordate at the base, up to about 7 in. long. The plants flower in late April or May and attain a height that varies somewhat with the clone.

Using 'Crest' as one parent, T. H. Findlay has raised a number of fine hybrids for the Crown Estate Commissioners, Windsor, which are not yet generally available (1975). The following have received awards and been described in the *Rhododendron and Camellia Year Book* (the second parent is given in brackets): 'ARBORFIELD' (× 'Loderi Julie'), A.M. April 30, 1963, *R.C.Y.B. 1964*, p. 134 and fig. 54; 'BINFIELD' (× 'China A'), A.M. May 5, 1964, *R.C.Y.B. 1965*, p. 166 and fig. 41; 'QUEEN ELIZABETH II' (× Idealist), A.M. May 2, 1967, *R.C.Y.B. 1968*, p. 133 and fig. 6, see also *R.C.Y.B. 1969*, p. 109; 'THEALE' (× Penjerrick), A.M. May 3, 1966, *R.C.Y.B. 1967*, p. 166 and plate 6; 'WARFIELD' (× Jalisco), A.M. May 18, 1970, *R.C.Y.B. 1971*, p. 185 and fig. 66.

Another hybrid from 'Crest' is 'CARA MIA', raised by Edmund de Rothschild at Exbury from a cross with 'Aurora'; A.M. May 3, 1966, *R.C.Y.B. 1967*, p. 163 and fig. 37.

'HELENE SCHIFFNER'.—Flowers 12 to 14 in a compact hemispherical truss 3 to 4 in. wide. Calyx almost nil. Corolla funnel-shaped, about 2 in. wide, mauve in the bud, becoming a singularly pure and hard white, unmarked or with very faint brown markings. Leaves dark green, glossy, lanceolate to oblanceolate, up to 5 in. long, about 1¾ in. wide. Dwarf spreading habit to not much more than 5 ft. Late May. F.C.C. 1893, when shown by the nurseryman Seidel of Stiesen near Dresden. A remarkable rhododendron, easily recognised by the glaring whiteness of its flowers and its comparatively dwarf habit. It seems to have the 'blood' of both *R. ponticum* and *R. caucasicum* in it. The name is usually incorrectly given as "Hélène Schiffner".

'HOLLANDIA' ('G. T. Streseman').—Flowers about 14 in the truss. Corolla slightly frilled, about 3 in. wide, carmine pink, shading to paler at the centre of the lobes, with brown speckling on the centre lobe. Leaves elliptic to oblanceolate, dark sea-green. May. ('Charles Dickens' × 'Pink Pearl'; L. J. Endtz and Co.) This is not the same as the hybrid which received an A.M. in 1925. The latter was raised by M. Koster and Sons, and had bluish-mauve flowers with a mustard-coloured flare.

'HUGH WORMALD'.—Flowers about 18 in a large, pyramidal truss. Corolla funnel-shaped, 2¾ in. wide, bright cerise pink with a dark brown flare on the upper lobe, the other lobes with a white stripe down the centre. (Koster.) Admired by Millais but now uncommon (Millais, *Rhododendrons*, 2nd series, pl. fac. p. 58).

HUMMING BIRD (*haematodes* × *williamsianum*).—Inflorescence with four or five flowers. Calyx large, spreading, coloured like the corolla, which is open campanulate, 2¼ in. wide, carmine-pink, fleshy, unspotted. Leaves elliptic or roundish elliptic, rigid, about 1½ in. long, rich green above, paler and thinly coated beneath; petioles brownish red, bristly-glandular. Compact habit. April or early May. (J. C. Williams.) A pretty rhododendron in flower, with good foliage. 'ELIZABETH LOCKHART' is a sport from this raised by Prof. R. D. Lockhart of Aberdeen, in which the young foliage is dark chocolate brown, and even the mature stems, leaf-blades and petioles are deeper than normal. The flowers too are darker than normal, near to Indian Lake.

'ICECREAM'.—Flowers 12 to 14 in a dome-shaped truss. Corolla funnel-shaped, 3½ in. or slightly more wide, light pink with a white throat, spotted with olive on the upper lobe. Compact habit. Late May or early June (Slocock). A.M.T. June 2, 1960. It is the result of a complex cross involving three species— R. *dichroanthum*, R. *decorum*, and R. *discolor*—and a Hardy Hybrid.

IDEALIST (Naomi × *wardii*).—Flowers about 12 in the truss on purplish pedicels 2 in. long. Corolla saucer-shaped, 4 in. wide, 5- to 7-lobed even in the same truss, buff-pink in the bud, opening pale primrose, with a pinkish flush at first, and with two bands of light red streaking below the upper lobes. Leaves oblong elliptic, to about 5 in. long, half as wide, broadly obtuse at the apex; petioles stained purple. Medium size. May. (Rothschild. A.M. 1945.) The description is made from a commercial clone. A lovely hybrid, related to the Carita grex, but with a shape of flower inherited from R. *wardii*.

The cross was later repeated at Exbury and some of the seedlings were sent to the Knap Hill nursery, from which 'VIENNA' was selected and registered in 1962.

IMPEANUM (*hanceanum* × *impeditum* (*fastigiatum*?)). Flowers about five in each inflorescence. Corolla rotate, about 1¼ in. wide, 'beautiful deep lilac' in the F.C.C. plant, but paler in some plants. Leaves dark green, glaucous beneath, elliptic or oblong-ovate, to ¾ in. long. A densely branched, low-growing shrub. May. (Kew; introduced 1932. F.C.C. 1934.) Useful for its late flowering. It is almost certain that R. *fastigiatum* was used, not R. *impeditum*.

IMPI (*sanguineum* subsp. *didymum* × 'Moser's Maroon').—Flowers 10 to 12 in small trusses; pedicels dark red, white-hairy. Corolla funnel-shaped, 2¼ in. wide, deep vinous red (brilliant red in transmitted light). Anthers dark red. Medium growth, erect habit. June. (Rothschild. A.M. 1945.)

INAMORATA (*discolor* × *wardii*).—Flowers about eight in a lax truss on plum-coloured pedicels. Corolla suphur-yellow, bowl-shaped, about 3 in. wide, with a red mark at the base. A vigorous hybrid taking after R. *discolor* in its foliage and late-flowering (June) and after R. *wardii* in its flowers. It was raised by Lionel de Rothschild at Exbury and received an Award of Merit on June 27, 1950, but its normal flowering time is early in the month.

INTRIFAST (*fastigiatum* × *intricatum*).—This hybrid is really so near to R. *fastigiatum* that for garden purposes it could be regarded as a good form of it, with exceptionally blue young foliage. It is of dense mounded habit, to about 2 ft. (Lowinsky.)

Another hybrid of R. *fastigiatum* is PROSTIGIATUM, raised by E. J. P. Magor, of which the other parent is R. *prostratum*, a member of the Saluenense series. It is a dwarf, twiggy shrub with deep violet-blue flowers 1 in. across, produced in twos or threes, and sea-green leaves about ¾ in. long, densely scaly beneath. A.M. April 8, 1924.

'ISABELLA MANGLES'.—Flowers about 12 in the truss on pedicels to 2¼ in. long. Corolla campanulate, with a short, broad tube and spreading limb, about 4 in. wide, slightly wavy at the edge, rosy pink, paling towards the centre of the lobes and deeper outside, becoming creamy white before it falls.

Leaves oblong–elliptic, to 6½ by 2¾ in. Early May. This is one of the finest creations of J. H. Mangles and doubtless the result of crossing R. *griffithianum* with some hardy hybrid. It grows and flowers well at Kew, where there are plants 10–12 ft high, but is uncommon outside collections.

'IVERY'S SCARLET'.—Flowers 12 to 14 in a dense truss. Calyx very small, glandular. Corolla campanulate, 2½ in. wide, deep vivid red, speckled on the three upper lobes. Leaves narrowly oblong-elliptic, tapered at both ends, rich green above, underside paler, dull green, with a prominent midrib. Slender habit, to about 15 ft. May. A very handsome hybrid from blood-red R. *arboreum*, gaining its late flowering and hardiness from, probably, R. *ponticum*. It was raised at the middle of the last century by the nurseryman Ivery of Dorking. Millais, who much admired it, gives its subsequent history in his *Rhododendrons*, p. 120. It needs a sheltered place, but is quite hardy and flowers over a long period. Most large collections have it, but it is scarce in commerce.

'JACKSONII'.—Flowers 12 to 14 in a dense truss; bud-scales persistent. Corolla widely funnel-campanulate, frilled and undulated, 2¼ in. or slightly more wide, bright pink, red on the ridges outside, speckled with crimson in the upper part of the throat, the speckles most numerous below the centre lobe. Style and stamen-filaments white. Calyx very small. Leaves oblong-oblanceolate to oblong-elliptic, with 16 to 18 pairs of veins, about 4 by 1¾ in., dull medium green above, covered beneath with a close brown indumentum. Low, spreading habit. Flowering time normally April, starting in March in a mild season and sometimes delayed until late April or early May.

A hybrid deriving mainly from R. *arboreum* and R. *caucasicum*. It was distributed by Smith's Darley Dale nursery in Derbyshire towards the end of the last century, but was probably raised by William Jackson and Co. of Bedale, Yorks, who in 1845 were asking 10/6 to 63/- per plant for 'R. Jacksonii', without description. The name apparently came to be used by them in a collective sense, since in 1861 they were offering 'R. Nobleanum, Jacksonii and varieties, including scarlet, crimson, blush and shaded salmon . . .' The price was then £5 a hundred. Probably Smith's 'Jacksonii', i.e., the plant now commonly cultivated under this name, was perpetuated because of its unusually bright colouring, and the ease with which it can be propagated by layers. There is another hybrid in cultivation as 'Jacksonii' which is quite different from the one here described and more like a form of Nobleanum. And to add to the confusion, the true 'Jacksonii', as it is now reasonable to call it, was also distributed as R. 'Venustum', and is described under that name by Millais in the first volume of his *Rhododendrons* (1917), p. 119. According to him, plants on their own roots could be obtained from the Derbyshire nurserymen at sixpence to a shilling each, according to size.

JALISCO ('Dido' × 'Lady Bessborough').—This cross, made by Lionel de Rothschild and registered in 1942, involves four species: R. *decorum*, R. *dichroanthum*, R. *discolor* and R. *campylocarpum*. Some of the seedlings from this cross were given by Rothschild to King George VI for the Windsor collection, which explains why the three best-known clones received their awards when exhibited by the Crown Estate Commissioners, Windsor Great Park. These are:

—'JALISCO ECLIPSE'.—Flowers up to ten in a lax truss, on red-tinged pedicels. Corolla 7-lobed, tubular-funnel-shaped, about 3½ in. wide, pale yellow, darker in the tube, with several lines of deep crimson speckles in the tube merging into a blotch at the base. Calyx thick and fleshy, pale yellow, irregular, to ¼ in. long. A.M. 1948. In 'JALISCO ELECT', which received an A.M. on the same occasion, the corolla has less heavy markings in the throat, and the calyx is spreading, about 1½ in. wide. The most admired clone is 'JALISCO GOSHAWK', in which the influence of R. *dichroanthum* is less apparent. The calyx is small and not fleshy. The corolla is funnel-campanulate, about 4¾ in. wide, clear yellow (Mimosa Yellow), with crimson markings in the throat. (*R.C.Y.B. 1955*, fig. 41). The only clone from a plant retained at Exbury that has so far received an award is 'JALISCO JUBILANT', with up to 14 flowers in the truss, corolla red in the bud, opening buttercup yellow, deeper in the throat; calyx irregular, up to 1 in. long (A.M. 1966; *R.C.Y.B. 1967*, p. 7). 'EXBURY JALISCO' has not yet received an award, but is said to be at least as fine as 'Jalisco Goshawk'.

The Jalisco clones flower towards the end of May or in June and are of moderate size.

Clones of Jalisco have been crossed at Windsor with Fusilier and two of the resulting hybrids have received awards: 'GRILSE', A.M. May 20, 1957, *R.C.Y.B. 1958*, p. 109; and 'WINKFIELD', A.M. May 19, 1958, *R.C.Y.B. 1959*, p. 138.

'JAMES BURCHETT'.—Flowers 15 to 18 in a dense truss. Corolla 5- to 7-lobed, funnel-shaped, 3 to 3½ in. wide, white flushed with pale mauvish pink at the edge, with a brownish-green flare extending from the throat to the base of the upper lobes. Anthers off-white, mauve-tinged. Stigma small, brownish green. Leaves dark green, elliptic, 8 by 2½ in. Dense habit, moderate size. Late June. (Slocock. A.M.T. 1960.) A valuable, free-flowering hybrid of R. *discolor*.

'J. G. MILLAIS'.—Flowers about 14 in the truss. Corolla funnel-campanulate, 3 in. wide, deep glowing red (near Turkey Red), speckled with dark crimson, mainly on the upper lobes but slightly marked on the lower lobes also. Ovary glabrous. Leaves dark green, 5 by 2 in. Late April or early May. (Waterer, Bagshot.) One of the finest of the early flowering reds, vigorous, hardy, making a shapely specimen to about 15 ft high, sometimes even taller. Named after the well-known gardener, artist and naturalist (*d.* 1931), author of one of the major works on rhododendrons, of which he had a large collection in his garden at Compton's Brow, Horsham, Sussex. Messrs Waterer let him have a plant in 1914 'and when it flowered in 1915 many of my friends considered it to be the finest early-flowering hybrid they had ever seen'. The parentage is said to be 'Ascot Brilliant' crossed with 'Pink Pearl'.

'J. H. VAN NES'.—This hybrid, with R. *griffithianum* in its ancestry, has beautiful flowers, the corolla being almost bowl-shaped and of firm texture, soft red, paling at the centre. But it is said to be bud-tender.

'JOHN BARR STEVENSON'.—Truss up to 7 in. across, with 14 to 16 flowers on pedicels up to 1¾ in. long. Corolla 3¼ in. wide, broad-campanulate, lemon-yellow with a reddish-purple mark in the throat. Leaves broad-elliptic, 6 by 2½ in. April (*lacteum* × 'Logan Damaris'). Raised by J. B. Stevenson at Tower Court and distributed by Maj.-Gen. Harrison, Tremeer, Cornwall.

'JOHN MARCHAND'.—Flowers three or four in the truss. Corolla campanulate, 2 in. wide, deep rosy pink. Calyx rim-like, edged with stalked glands, which are also present on the stems and pedicels. Leaves elliptic, rigid, apiculate, 1½ in. long, 1 in. wide, glabrous above, with scattered branched hairs beneath. Dwarf habit. March (*moupinense* × *sperabile*). This interesting lepidote–elepidote cross was made by John Marchand for Messrs Wallace of Tunbridge Wells. All the seedlings were bought by Collingwood Ingram of The Grange, Benenden, Kent. 'It proved a very good buy for, without exception, every one of those tiny seedlings has grown into a charming bushy shrub, always abundantly floriferous and equally happy in either sun or shade' (C. Ingram, *R.C.Y.B. 1967*, pp. 12–13 and plate 1). 'John Marchand' received an Award of Merit on March 22, 1966.

'JOHN WALTER'.—Flowers about 20 in a dense truss. Corolla funnel-shaped, 2¼ in. wide, bright crimson with some brown markings, margins slightly frilled. Ovary glabrous or almost so. Leaves elliptic to obovate, 4 in. long, almost half as wide, rounded at the base, rather concave above, with traces of brown tomentum on the petiole and midrib. Dense habit. Early June. (Waterer, Bagshot.) An old hybrid, put into commerce before 1860 and related to 'John Waterer'.

'JOHN WATERER'.—Flowers about 16 in the truss on short glandular pedicels. Corolla funnel-shaped, 2¾ in. wide, crimson, speckled with brown, crimped at the edges. Ovary and style glabrous. Leaves lanceolate, 5 by 1¼ in., clad beneath with a thin indumentum. Moderate size. Mid- to late June. This old hybrid, still quite common, is of interest as one of the first really late-flowering hybrids deriving from R. *arboreum*. It was put into commerce, together with 'Mrs John Waterer' (q.v.), in 1855. It is interesting that in both these hybrids the ovary is glabrous or almost so, which suggests that R. *ponticum* enters into their parentage. In the International Register 'John Waterer' is said to be R. *arboreum* crossed with R. *catawbiense*. This statement is certainly erroneous (see Russellianum), but R. *catawbiense* may have played its part.

'JOSEPH WHITWORTH'.—Flowers about 16 in a dense truss. Corolla widely funnel-shaped, 3½ in. across, dark purple-lake, heavily speckled with black on all lobes. Calyx well developed, with triangular or strap-shaped lobes. Leaves elliptic to slightly obovate, dark green with a greyish tinge, 6 to 7 in. long, about half as wide. Dense habit. Early June. (Waterer, Bagshot, before 1864.) The colour is too dark to be pleasing, but the foliage and habit are good. Named after the Midlands industrialist and philanthropist, later knighted, who lived at Stancliffe, Darley Dale (*d.* 1897).

KARKOV (*griersonianum* × Red Admiral).—Truss compact, globular, with about 16 flowers. Corolla funnel-shaped, 3½ in. wide, crimped and wavy at the edge, carmine-rose. Leaves narrow-elliptic, 6 in. long. Medium size. May. (Rothschild. A.M. 1947.)

'KATE WATERER'.—Flowers about 17 in a hemispherical truss. Corolla funnel-shaped, 2⅝ in. wide, with broad, overlapping lobes, rosy crimson passing to clear rose, with a flare of bright green markings on a white ground. Compact, symmetrical habit. June. (Waterer, Bagshot, before 1876.) One of the best of the old hardy hybrids, very free-flowering.

KIEV (*elliottii* × Barclayi).—Truss flat-topped, lax, with eight to ten flowers;

pedicels glandular. Corolla tubular-campanulate, very thick and fleshy, 2½ to 3 in. long, width variable (2 in. in the sample seen, 4 in. according to the A.M. description), deep blood red, speckled all over inside except at the very base. Stamens with red filaments and black anthers. Leaves elliptic, 6½ by 3 in.; petioles tinged bronzy purple. Tall-growing. May. (Rothschild. A.M. 1950.) The colour is striking but the truss is poorly formed. Rather tender and suitable only for woodland.

Another Exbury hybrid from R. *elliottii* is the KILIMANJARO grex, the other parent of which is a plant of the Dusky Maid grex (R. *discolor* × 'Moser's Maroon'). This has a rounded truss of about 18 flowers. Corolla funnel-shaped, deep red (Currant Red), speckled, 3½ in. wide. Medium size. Late May or early June. F.C.C. 1947 (*Rothschild Rhododendrons*, pl. 33).

'KLUIS SENSATION'.—Flowers 14 to 18 in a rounded truss. Corolla broadly funnel-shaped, 3½ in. wide, slightly frilled, crimson-scarlet, shading to a lighter colour in the centre, spotted dark red on the upper lobe. Leaves dark green above, much paler beneath, tending to be concave above, 7 in. long. Early June. (A. Kluis 1946.) A fine red, free-flowering hybrid.

'KLUIS TRIUMPH'.—Flowers 12 to 16 in a dome-shaped truss. Corolla campanulate with a spreading limb, 2½ in. wide, coppery red, spotted dark red on the central lobe. Leaves dull green, narrow-oblong, slightly concave above, with pinkish petioles. Late May, i.e., slightly earlier than 'Kluis Sensation'. (A. Kluis, 1946. F.C.C.T. 1971.) An unusual and pleasing colour.

'LADY ALICE FITZWILLIAM'.—Flowers very fragrant, in twos or threes. Corolla funnel-shaped, 4 in. wide, white, faintly stained with yellow in the throat and pinkish on the reverse along the ridges. Style scaly in lower half. Calyx-lobes ovate, ⅛ to ¼ in. long, fringed with silky hairs. Leaves oblong-elliptic or slightly obovate, acuminate, about 2½ in. long, dark green and rugose, pale beneath. When this rhododendron received an F.C.C. in 1881 it was said to be one of the numerous hybrids between R. *ciliatum* and R. *edgeworthii*, which appears to be the correct parentage. It is almost hardy on a wall, and that is the best place for it, the habit being very lanky. It flowers in May and makes the most glorious displays even in gardens near London.

LADY BERRY ('Rosy Bell' × Royal Flush).—Flowers pendent, about five in the truss. Corolla fleshy, tubular-campanulate, 3 in. long, 2½ in. wide, Rose Opal inside, the outside Jasper Red, paling on the lobes. Calyx rim-like. Leaves sea-green, oblanceolate, 4 by 1½ in. Medium size. May. (Rothschild. A.M. 1937, F.C.C. 1949.) A beautiful but tender hybrid, showing the influence of R. *cinnabarinum* very strongly. The F.C.C. clone is described (R.Y.B. *1949*, fig. 1). The cross is a surprising one, considering that the parents of 'Rosy Bell' are both diploid and give no obvious sign of their presence. Were it not that this hybrid is given as the seed-parent one would have supposed that the cross was made the other way about, and that the pollen of 'Rosy Bell' had caused Royal Flush to set seed apomictically. The latter is a hybrid between two highly polyploid species.

LADY BESSBOROUGH (*campylocarpum* "var. *elatum*" × *discolor*).—Flowers about 10 in a loose truss. Corolla 7-lobed, funnel-campanulate, 3½ in. wide, pale buff-pink in the bud, opening ivory-white, throat speckled with crimson below the upper lobes and somewhat darker in tone than the limb. Style glandular almost to the tip. Leaves oblong-elliptic, dull green, to 6 in. long. Tall. Late May or early June. (Rothschild. F.C.C. 1933.) One of the best known Exbury hybrids, deriving its colouring from R. *campylocarpum* and its large size, seven-lobed corolla, foliage and late-flowering from R. *discolor*. The plant described here is probably of the F.C.C. clone. In 'ROBERTE' the flowers are delicate salmon-pink, fading to yellowish at the centre of each lobe (F.C.C. 1936).

The A. GILBERT grex, raised by T. H. Lowinsky, is of the same parentage as Lady Bessborough, though a different form of R. *campylocarpum* was probably used. A.M. 1925.

LADY CHAMBERLAIN (*cinnabarinum* var. *roylei* × Royal Flush, orange form).—The influence of R. *cinnabarinum* predominates in this group of hybrids, which is the result of a back-cross between it and R. *cinnabarinum* × R. *maddenii*, the parentage of Royal Flush. They could almost be regarded as superior forms of R. *cinnabarinum*, but no doubt derive their larger flowers from the R. *maddenii* element. In 'EXBURY LADY CHAMBERLAIN' (F.C.C. 1931) the flowers are four or five to the truss, with a ground colour of orange-red, shading to paler on the lobes and tinged with rose on the outside. Other clones have been named, in various shades of orange blended with pink, most of which are available in the trade. The cross was also made at Bodnant ('BODNANT YELLOW', F.C.C. 1944), but in this case a different form of R. *cinnabarinum* was used. [PLATE 104

The hybrids of the Lady Chamberlain grex flower in May. They are perhaps rather less hardy than R. *cinnabarinum* and need a sheltered but only slightly shaded position. They are of slender, upright habit, to 8 ft or so.

The LADY ROSEBERY cross is the same as that which produced the Lady Chamberlain grex, except that the pink-flowered form of Royal Flush was used. The resulting plants are usually regarded as forming a separate grex. In the typical clone the corollas are 2½ in. long, 1¾ in. wide, rather deeply lobed, crimson outside on the tube, pinker on the lobes, pink within. F.C.C. 1932. There are other clones in this sub-grex, differing slightly in colour. All are beautiful.

'LADY CLEMENTINE MITFORD'.—Flowers 16 to 18 in a compact truss. Corolla widely funnel-shaped, 3 in. wide, peach-pink, paling to blush along the centre of each lobe, with a flare of brownish or greenish markings, which become redder at the edge of the flare. Style and stamen-filaments white, anthers pinkish. Ovary glabrous. Leaves mostly narrow-obovate, dark green, to 5½ in. long, finely tomentose when young. A large, dense shrub. Early June. (Waterer, Knap Hill.) An old hybrid that still holds it own. It received an Award of Merit (after trial) in 1971, about a century after it was first introduced.

'LADY DE ROTHSCHILD'.—Flowers about 16 in a large truss; rachis 3 in. long; pedicels up to 2 in. long, glandular. Corolla widely funnel-shaped, 3½ in. across, white, with a flare of blackish crimson. Rather leggy habit. June. (*griffithianum* × 'Sappho'; Waterer, Knap Hill. A.M. 1925.)

'LADY DECIES'.—Flowers up to 20 in a dense truss. Corolla widely spreading, almost flat, nearly 4 in. across, lilac-mauve shading to white in the centre, with a flare of bright yellow. Late May or early June. (Waterer, Bagshot, before 1922.)

'LADY ELEANOR CATHCART'.—Flowers 12 to 15 in a rounded truss, on purplish-red, glandular pedicels. Corolla funnel-campanulate, about 2¼ in. wide, light rose with a narrow, dark maroon flare, often likened to that of a pelargonium. Stamens white with yellow anthers. Style glabrous, pale green with a red stigma. Leaves felted when young, oblanceolate, to 4½ in. long, 1¾ in. wide, dull dark green above, rusty beneath. A very large shrub. June. This famous hybrid was put into commerce by John Waterer of Bagshot in 1854 or possibly a year or so earlier, at 21/- a plant—a high price for those days. In 1853 the plant in the nursery was heavily cut to supply graft-wood, but three years later it starred in the Regent's Park Exhibition, when a plant was shown 12 ft high, which suggests an origin not much later than 1836. At Highclere, hybrids which appear to have been similar to 'Lady Eleanor Cathcart' were raised by fertilising *R. maximum* with the pollen of Altaclerense (which had first flowered there in 1831). Some of the Highclere seedlings were flowering by 1843, the best 'pale vermilion and splendidly spotted'. But the same cross may well have been made by John Waterer. 'LADY ANNETTE DE TRAFFORD', from Knap Hill, resembles 'Lady Eleanor Cathcart', but the flowers are paler pink and the leaves relatively broader. 'LADY LONGMAN' is a hybrid between 'Lady E. Cathcart' and 'Cynthia', raised at the Sunningdale Nurseries by Harry White, their manager, before 1930. The flowers are bright rosy crimson, much more intensely coloured than in 'Lady E. Cathcart', and with a darker flare.

'LADY GREY EGERTON'.—Truss dense with about 20 flowers. Corolla 2¾ in. across, funnel-shaped, pale lilac, paling towards the centre, with a ray of light brown speckles situated towards the base of the centre lobe and running into the throat. Stamens and style coloured more or less like the corolla; stigma pale brownish pink. Leaves obovate, rounded at both ends. Mid-June. (Waterer, Knap Hill.) A lovely hybrid, but the colour of the flowers seems to vary slightly with the weather or perhaps with soil conditions. Sometimes it is spoilt by an excessive infusion of pink. It is named after the wife of Sir Philip Grey Egerton, a member of the Council of the R.H.S. around the middle of the last century and a friend of R. S. Holford of Westonbirt.

'LADY PRIMROSE'.—Flowers 10 to 12 in a fairly compact truss. Corolla funnel-shaped, with spreading lobes, about 2 in. wide, greenish yellow in the bud, opening clear sulphur yellow, speckled with red in the throat below the centre lobe. Leaves similar to those of *R. campylocarpum*. Dense habit, medium size. Late April or early May. (Slocock. A.M. 1933.) Although not highly rated, this is an attractive rhododendron.

LADYBIRD ('Corona' × *discolor*).—Flowers in dense trusses. Corolla widely funnel-campanulate, 3½ in. across, wavy at the margin, coral-pink with a darker mark in the throat. Leaves dark green and glossy, 7 by 3 in. Tall and vigorous. Late May or early June. (Rothschild. A.M. 1933.)

LAMELLEN (*campanulatum* × *griffithianum*).—Flowers about eight in a racemose truss; rachis 4 in. long. Corolla open-campanulate, 3½ in. wide, with broad lobes, lilac in the bud, opening pure white, with slight speckling. Style glabrous with a large green stigma. Ovary slightly glandular. Leaves 6½ by 2¾ in., elliptic, veins impressed above, obtuse to subacute at the apex, truncate to cordate at the base. April. An interesting hybrid raised by E. J. P. Magor of Lamellen, uncommon in gardens. The description is from a plant growing at Grayswood Hill, Haslemere.

'LANGLEY PARK'.—Flowers 10 to 14 in the truss on erect, pale green pedicels. Corolla campanulate, of firm texture, not much spreading at the mouth, 2 in. long and 2¾ in. wide, deep glowing red, slightly speckled, nectaries darker red. Stamens with white filaments and red anthers. Style white, stout. Leaves narrow-elliptic, 6 by 1¾ in., up-folded along the midrib. Compact, medium size, mid-May. It is interesting that this fine red hybrid is a sister-seedling of 'Britannia', both having been raised by C. B. van Nes from 'Queen Wilhelmina' crossed with 'Stanley Davies'.

'LANGWORTH'.—Flowers about 16 in a conical truss. Corolla funnel-shaped, 4 in. wide, margins slightly waved, white, streaked with brown in the throat, with green spotting on the upper lobe. Vigorous, spreading habit. Late May. (*fortunei* × 'Sappho'; Slocock. A.M.T. 1962.)

'LASCAUX'.—Flowers about eight (sometimes more numerous) in a flat-topped truss. Corolla tubular-funnel-shaped, 1¾ in. long, 2½ in. wide, Barium Yellow, faintly speckled on the upper lobes and with red marks inside at the base. Calyx petaloid, irregular, its lobes up to 1 in. long. Medium size. June. ('Fabia' × *litiense*; R.H.S. Garden, Wisley. A.M. 1954.)

LAURA ABERCONWAY (Barclayi × *griersonianum*).—Flowers about nine in a loose truss. Corolla funnel-shaped, 3½ in. wide, margins slightly frilled, Geranium Lake. Leaves lanceolate, thick and leathery, dark green above, yellowish green beneath. Medium size. May. (Aberconway. F.C.C. 1944.) An uncommon, beautifully coloured rhododendron, uniting the Chinese R. *griersonianum* with three Himalayan species (R. *arboreum*, R. *griffithianum* and R. *thomsonii*).

'LAVA FLOW'.—Flowers four or five in the truss; outer bud-scales dark red. Corolla rich scarlet, trumpet shaped, 2¾ in. wide, speckled, especially on the upper lobes, glandular hairy on the outside. Anthers black. Leaves elliptic, subacute and apiculate, about 3 in. long, dull above, clad beneath with a buff powdery indumentum. Mid- to late June. Bushy habit. An interesting and finely coloured hybrid raised at the Sunningdale nurseries from R. *griersonianum* crossed with KW 13225. The second parent is an unidentified member of the Neriiflorum series, said to resemble R. *sanguineum* subsp. *didymum* except in having brilliant scarlet flowers (*Rhododendrons at Sunningdale*, p. 31). 'GLOWING EMBER' is of the same parentage and from the same raiser.

'LAVENDER GIRL'.—Flowers fragrant, 12 to 18 in the truss, on brownish-red pedicels. Corolla funnel-shaped, seven-lobed, 3¼ in. wide, pale pinkish mauve (Roseine Purple) on a chalky white ground, paling to almost white in the centre, with two bands of brownish streaks in the upper half of the throat. Style greenish white. Leaves oblanceolate, 7½ by 2⅞ in. Vigorous, spreading but dense habit. May. (*fortunei* × 'Lady Grey Egerton'; Slocock. F.C.C.T. 1967.) A handsome and very useful rhododendron, associating well with the deciduous azaleas.

'LEE'S SCARLET'.—Flowers about ten in the truss on upright, glandular pedicels. Corolla campanulate, frilled, deep crimson-pink with a bright red blotch at the base and speckled in the lower half. Style very stout, with a dark red stigma. Very early flowering, often starting before Christmas. A curious hybrid of unknown origin.

'LEONARD MESSEL'.—Flowers three to five in the truss, on pedicels up to 1 in. long. Corolla tubular-campanulate, $\frac{7}{8}$ in. long, 1 in. wide, with ovate lobes, pale yellow, lightly spotted with brown. Calyx about $\frac{3}{16}$ in. long, deeply lobed, scaly. Leaves 2$\frac{3}{8}$ by almost 1 in., oblong-elliptic, bright green and glossy above, dull pale green beneath. A natural hybrid of R. *brachyanthum*, raised at Nymans from seeds collected by Kingdon Ward in the wild, probably in the Seinghku valley, N.W. Burma. A pretty shrub, taller than R. *brachyanthum*, flowering in May. A.M. 1966.

'LEONARDSLEE GILES'.—Flowers 12 in a large, dome-shaped truss. Corolla funnel-shaped, 4$\frac{3}{4}$ in. wide, pink in the bud, opening pink, fading to white, with slight brown speckling on the upper lobes. Anthers greyish brown, filaments white. Style white with a crimson stigma. Leaves elliptic, 9 by 3$\frac{1}{2}$ in. Late April or early May. A hybrid between R. *griffithianum* and 'Standishii' raised at Leonardslee. A.M. 1948, when shown by the Misses Godman of South Lodge.

'LIONEL'S TRIUMPH'.—Flowers about 18 in the truss on long, red-tinged pedicels. Corolla campanulate, 4 in. across, clear soft yellow, flushed with pink at the edges and blotched and speckled with crimson in the throat. April. A magnificent hybrid raised by Lionel de Rothschild at Exbury which first flowered in 1954, twelve years after his death, and received an A.M. when exhibited in that year. The parentage is R. *lacteum* × 'Naomi'. It is still scarce in commerce. In 1967 the same award was given to the clone 'HALTON'; see *R.C.Y.B. 1968*, p. 232.

'LITTLE BEN'.—Flowers up to eight in the truss. Corolla tubular-campanulate, 1$\frac{1}{2}$ to 2 in. wide, glowing blood-red. Calyx petaloid, variable in size, coloured more or less like the corolla. Leaves ovate to elliptic, rounded at both ends, up to 3$\frac{1}{2}$ in. long, half as wide. Dwarf, to about 2$\frac{1}{2}$ ft in height, spreading. Late March or April. A very free-flowering hybrid, raised by C. Scrase-Dickins of Coolhurst, Horsham, from R. *neriiflorum* pollinated by R. *forrestii*. F.C.C. 1937. He also raised 'LITTLE BERT', with R. *forrestii* as the seed-parent, the pollen-parent in this case being the form of R. *neriiflorum* known as R. *euchaites*. A.M. 1939. Lower-growing than 'Little Ben', with darker, relatively narrower leaves, and red bud-scales.

LODAURIC (*auriculatum* × Loderi).—Flowers fragrant, about seven in the truss, on stout, glandular pedicels; rachis almost 2 in. long. Corolla broadly funnel-shaped, 5 in. wide, 6- or 7-lobed, white, with two lines of brownish-crimson markings in the tube. Style red-glandular to the tip, with a large, pale green, discoid stigma. Leaves intermediate between those of the parents. Tall. Late June or early July. (Crosfield, 1939.) 'ICEBERG', of the same parentage, was raised by Messrs W. C. Slocock and received an A.M. in 1958. This has more numerous flowers per truss. A merit of this cross is that the flowers do not burn in the sun—a fault that mars the Polar Bear grex.

LODERI (*fortunei* × *griffithianum*).—This magnificent hybrid, of which there are many forms, was raised by Sir Edmund Loder, Bt, of Leonardslee, Sussex, at the beginning of this century. The seed-parent was a good form of R. *for-*

tunei in his own collection. The pollen came from a particularly fine plant of R. *griffithianum* in the greenhouse of his neighbour F. D. Godman of South Lodge. He made this cross twice and a high proportion of the offspring had large flowers and leaves, the rest being too near to R. *fortunei*. He also made the reverse cross, but with less success, since the pollen-parent (R. *fortunei*) predominated in the offspring, only a few plants showing Loderi-characters (Millais, *Rhododendrons* (1917), p. 178). The first seedlings flowered in 1907 and several had been named by 1910, when William Watson of Kew visited Leonardslee and saw them in flower. In the following year he gave the botanical name R. *Loderi* to the results of the cross (*Gard. Chron.*, Vol. 50 (1911), p. 31). Altogether some 100 seedlings were planted out, some of which did not flower until after Sir Edmund's death in 1920.

The flowers of Loderi are fragrant and borne nine to twelve together in a tall, rather open truss, on a rachis 2 to 3½ in. long. Corolla six- or seven-lobed, up to 6 in. or even slightly more wide, funnel-shaped with a broad tube, varying slightly according to the clone from white to blush or light pink, but always pink in the bud, with or without slight brownish or greenish markings in the throat. Style glandular, with a green knob-like stigma. Calyx well developed, irregularly lobed. Leaves elliptic, 8 to 12 in. long, glabrous, medium green, with a tendency in some clones to become chlorotic between the main lateral veins; petioles usually stained with plum-purple on the upper side. Many clones have been named, of which the following have received awards, but all those in commerce are worthy of cultivation, and really the differences between them are not great.   [PLATE 105

—'DIAMOND'.—White, with slight markings in the throat. F.C.C. 1914. This and 'Pink Diamond' were the first of the group to be exhibited.

—'JULIE'.—White suffused with sulphur. Raised at Townhill Park from a cross between two forms of Loderi. A.M. 1944.

—'KING GEORGE'.—Blush-tinted at first, becoming pure white, 6 in. wide, unmarked in the throat apart from two faint bands of green. F.C.C. 1970.

—'PINK DIAMOND'.—Light pink, holding its colour well. F.C.C. 1914.

—'PRINCESS MARINA'.—Flowers of good substance, 12 in the truss, pale pink fading to white. The result of a cross between 'King George' and 'Sir Edmund', raised at Leonardslee by Sir Giles Loder, Bt. A.M. 1948.

—'SIR EDMUND'.—Blush, veined with pink when first open, mostly six-lobed. The original plant flowered some years after Sir Edmund Loder's death in 1920. A.M. 1930.

—'SIR JOSEPH HOOKER'.—White with a slight blush tinge and very faint greenish or greyish markings in the throat, about 12 in the truss. A.M. May 21, 1973. Quite as fine as 'King George'.

—'VENUS'.—At first deep pink, fading to lighter pink, with faint green markings in the throat. The original plant is at Exbury but was raised at Leonardslee. One of the finest clones, recommended for an Award of Garden Merit.

An article by Sir Giles Loder on the clones of Loderi and its hybrids will be found in the *Rhododendron Year Book* for 1950, pp. 16–19.

The Loderi group are exceptionally vigorous and free-flowering rhododendrons, needing shelter and slight shade if they are to be seen at their best. In time they will attain a height of about 25 ft. The normal flowering time is about mid-May.

Sir Edmund Loder was not the first to raise hybrids between R. *fortunei* and R. *griffithianum*. The cross was made at Kew in 1875, and from the single pod obtained several plants were raised, to which William Watson gave the collective name R. *Kewense* in 1888. He stated the parentage to be R. *griffithianum* × R. *hookeri*, but there seems to be really no doubt that the second parent was R. *fortunei*. When describing R. *Loderi* twenty-three years later Watson remarked that Sir Edmund Loder was convinced that this was the case and had made his cross with the purpose of proving that he was right.

The Kew plants all had blush-white flowers except for one, which had pink flowers and was named R. *Kewense roseum*. In 1907 the nurseryman George Paul showed a form of R. *Kewense* with blush-tinted flowers, which, according to Millais, he had himself raised, and the cross was apparently made by other nurserymen before Loderi came on the scene. How many clones there are under the name Kewense, and whether or not they descend from the Kew plants, it is impossible to say. A common commercial clone seems to be rather less demanding than the Loderi clones, perhaps because the leaves are smaller. The flowers are white with a slight flush of pink, with two lines of green or brown markings in the throat, mostly five-lobed, and the calyx is larger than in the Loderi clones.

'LODER'S WHITE'.—Flowers about 12 in a large conical truss. Corolla widely funnel-shaped, 4 in. wide, wavy at the margin, mauvish pink in the bud, opening pure white (but retaining for some time a suggestion of pink when the plant is grown in shade), very lightly speckled. Anthers pale brown; filaments white. Stigma reddish brown. Leaves elliptic to slightly obovate, 7¾ by 3 in., dark medium green above, light green beneath. A vigorous shrub attaining 10 to 15 ft in height and more in width. Mid- to late May. It is perfectly hardy and can be grown in full sun, as at Kew, where there is a clump on the Broad Walk. But it is happier perhaps in slight shade and the flowers are more delicately coloured when not fully exposed to the sun.

Millais wrote of this hybrid: 'No one who loves beautiful shrubs can pass a plant of Loder's White in flower without halting to admire it, for there is a quality about the exquisite flowers, set off so superbly by the dark foliage, that places it quite in the first rank of good things. . . . Cornish gardeners, who enjoy a galaxy of fine things, and are not superabundant in their praises, consider Loder's White the best hybrid Rhododendron ever raised, not even excepting Loderi, and no doubt many agree with them.'

Millais' account of the history of this hybrid is as follows: J. H. Mangles of Valewood, Haslemere (who died in 1884), sent a number of hybrid rhododendron seedlings to his friend F. D. Godman of South Lodge. One proved to be so outstanding when it flowered that he gave scions to his neighbour Sir Edmund Loder of Leonardslee for grafting. Many plants were raised, and some were sent by Sir Edmund to gardens in Cornwall, where the hybrid became known as Loder's White. Mangles himself is usually supposed to have raised it, but according to Millais the consignment he sent to South Lodge also contained some hybrid seedlings raised by Mr Luscombe of Coombe Royal. It is a hybrid of R. *griffithianum*, though possibly not of the first generation. The other parent is not known. It was once said to be R. *arboreum album*, but that is only a guess and a bad one at that. It received an Award of Merit in 1911 when shown by Messrs Reuthe and an Award of Garden Merit twenty years later.

'LORD ROBERTS'.—Flowers about 20 in a dense truss. Corolla funnel-shaped, 1¾ to 2¼ in. wide, dark crimson on a bluish base which shows up as the flowers fade, with a flare of dark spots on the upper lobe. Stamens with conspicuously hairy filaments and bluish anthers. Style reddish with a dark crimson stigma. Medium size, July. It is believed to have been raised by Messrs Fromow of Chiswick, who exhibited it as a new rhododendron in 1900. The older 'THE WARRIOR', raised by John Waterer before 1867, is similar but the corollas are spotted on the lower lobes also.

'LORD SWAYTHLING'.—Flowers about 12 in the truss. Corolla funnel-shaped, 3½ in. wide, with stout ridges, bright red in the bud, opening pink inside but with the brighter colour of the bud persisting for some time on the reverse, speckled inside in two lines below the central lobe. Style red at the top, with a large green stigma. Vigorous, narrow habit. Late April or early May. This is one of the hybrids of R. *griffithianum* raised by Schulz at the Porcelain Factory, Berlin, at the end of the last century, and was put into commerce by C. B. van Nes (see further in introductory note). A.M.T. 1954. It is hardy but flowers early and needs a sheltered place.

LUSCOMBEI (*fortunei* × *thomsonii*).—Flowers up to 12 in a loose truss; rachis variable in length even on the same plant, to about 1½ in. long. Corolla funnel-shaped with a broad tube, 3 to 4 in. wide, usually 6- or 7-lobed, rosy pink, nectaries darker, usually with some lines of speckles in the throat. Calyx well developed, irregularly lobed, usually pale green, but coloured like the corolla in one clone. Leaves up to 6½ in. long, about half as wide, broad-elliptic or obovate, rounded at the apex, usually slightly cordate at the base; petioles usually plum-coloured.

The cross between R. *fortunei* and R. *thomsonii* was first made by Thomas Luscombe of Coombe Royal, Kingsbridge, Devon, who was among the first gardeners to flower both these species. Some twelve or fourteen plants from the cross had flowered by 1881, only three of them good, and there were then some hundreds still to flower (H. J. Mangles in *Gard. Chron.*, Vol. 15 (1881), p. 363). The name R. *Luscombei* was given by William Watson in 1892 to a plant at Kew, almost certainly one of the original seedlings. Luscombe also gave a plant to Veitch's Coombe Wood Nursery, which was apparently propagated and distributed under the name R. *Devoniense*. The finest forms of Luscombei are those raised by Sir E. Loder at Leonardslee, of which 'PRIDE OF LEONARDSLEE' is a named clone. Another superior form is 'LUSCOMBEI SPLENDENS', with flowers 4 in. wide, deep rose. The original plant was given by H. J. Mangles to Frederick Godman of South Lodge, Sussex, and is thought to have been raised by Luscombe, though Mangles himself is known to have repeated the cross in his garden at Valewood.

As usually seen in gardens, Luscombei is a large and vigorous shrub of dense habit, attaining 15 ft in height and twice that in width. Although represented in all the older collections it is no longer common in the trade and has never received an award in any of its forms, possibly because it is better as a garden plant than it is in the truss.

'MADAME ALBERT MOSER'.—Flowers 14 to 20 in the truss. Corolla funnel-shaped, 3 to 3½ in. wide, slightly wavy at the margin, mauve, with a large flare of orange-yellow. Style with a pale red stigma. Leaves oblong-elliptic, 7 by 2 in. Late May. A.M.T. 1954. A most handsome and unusual rhododendron, of which there is an old specimen in the Knap Hill nursery. 'MADAME JULES PORGES' is similar, but the flare is greenish brown, heavily embossed, the stigma is pale brown and the leaves are relatively broader and sometimes obovate, about 5 by 2½ in.

'MADAME CARVALHO'.—Flowers 16 in a conical truss. Corolla widely funnel-shaped, 2¾ in. wide, white flushed with mauve and with a flare of yellowish-green markings. Filaments of stamens white, anthers grey. Style dull white. Leaves oblong-obovate, 4 by 1¾ in. Dense habit, medium size. June. (Waterer, Bagshot, 1867.)

'MADAME DE BRUIN'.—Flowers about 20 in a dense, conical truss. Corolla 2¾ to 3 in. wide, funnel-shaped with a rather angular limb, brilliant cerise-red, paler towards the centre, slightly speckled. Leaves light green, oblong-obovate, 4 to 5 in. long, acute. Medium size. Late May or early June. (M. Koster, 1904.) A remarkably bright and clear colour for a hardy hybrid.

'MADAME FR. J. CHAUVIN'.—Flowers 10 to 12 in a lax truss. Corolla funnel-shaped, deep pink paling to soft pink, with a dark red blotch in the throat. Late May–early June. (Koster, 1916.) A hybrid of *R. fortunei*. A.M.T. 1933.

'MANDERLEY'.—Flowers up to 10 in the truss. Corolla about 2½ in. wide, dark red, spotted darker on the centre lobe. Leaves reddish when young. Low, spreading habit. May. A recent introduction, raised in Holland from 'Scandinavia' × Fabia (*Dendroflora*, No. 3 (1966), p. 74).

'MARCHIONESS OF LANSDOWNE'.—Flowers about 14 in a compact truss. Corolla broadly funnel-shaped, 2¾ in. wide, pale magenta-pink with a very dense almost black flare on the central lobe, appearing to have been burnt on with a poker, and with some speckling on the adjacent lobes. Leaves rather small, about 3 in. long. Compact habit. July. (Waterer, Bagshot, before 1879.)

'MARCIA'.—This hybrid is a back-cross of *R. campylocarpum* onto 'Mary Swaythling' (*R. campylocarpum* × *fortunei*) and therefore bears a quite strong resemblance to that species. The flowers number about ten in each truss; corolla soft yellow, about 3 in. wide, five-lobed, with slight crimson streaking at the base. Stigma dark red. Leaves ovate, 3½ by 2 in., whitish beneath. Late April or early May. Only one plant was raised—by F. J. Rose for Lord Swaythling, at Townhill Park. F.C.C. 1944.

MARILOO ('Dr Stocker' × *lacteum*).—Truss with 15–20 flowers, on red pedicels. Corolla broad-campanulate, 4 in. wide, slightly frilled, pale cream, sometimes tinged with crimson on the reverse along the three upper lobes and with markings of the same colour within. Leaves broad elliptic, mat green, 8½ by 3¼ in., lateral veins impressed above. (Rothschild.) The description is of the clone 'MARILOO EUGENIE' (A.M. 1950). In 'MARILOO GILBURY' (A.M. 1943) the corollas are creamy pink, striped with crimson on the reverse down the centre of the lobes. In the original clone—'MARILOO'—the flowers are soft yellow, green-tinged at first (*Rothschild Rhododendrons*, pl. 29). The Mariloo clones flower in April and need a sheltered position.

'MARS'.—Flowers 12–14 in a dense truss. Corolla between funnel-shaped and saucer-shaped, with relatively broad, rounded lobes, pure deep red without shading or spots. Calyx rim-like. Stamen-filaments hairy almost throughout, with off-white anthers. Leaves elliptic, obtuse, 6 by 2¼ in. Compact, spreading. May. (Waterer, Bagshot. A.M. 1928, F.C.C. 1935.) A fine red, with unusually shaped flowers, said to be a hybrid of 'Corona'. The statement in the *International Register* that it was raised before 1875 is the result of confusion between this and an early hybrid of R. *arboreum*, raised by Lee of Hammersmith before 1843, and also called 'Mars'. The hybrid here described was a novelty in 1928.

MATADOR (*griersonianum* × *strigillosum*).—Truss with 9 to 12 flowers; pedicels and calyx densely covered with long, erect, glandular hairs. Corolla funnel-campanulate, 2½ in. wide, scarlet with darker nectaries, speckled on the upper lobes. Style bright red. Anthers black. Leaves thinly woolly beneath, oblong-elliptic, acute, 6 by 1¾ in.; petioles with erect, glandular hairs. Medium size. Late April or early May. (Aberconway. F.C.C. 1946.) A fine red, with distinctive foliage. The cross was also made at Exbury and it may be that the plant described is of that provenance and slightly different from the F.C.C. clone.

'MAXIMUM TRIUMPHANS'.—Flowers about 14 in a dense hemispherical truss; rachis ⅞ in. long. Corolla campanulate, slightly over 2 in. wide, crimson, slightly brown-spotted in the tube, nectaries brown-red. Style glabrous. Ovary white-felted and somewhat glandular. An old hybrid, deriving mainly from R. *arboreum* and R. *maximum*, which probably originated in the 1840s, and was still in commerce until recently. According to A. J. Ivens, to whose manuscript notes we are indebted for the above description, there are (or were) fine specimens at Townhill Park and Embley Park in Hampshire. 'They are not tall, but exceedingly dense, forming banks of hoary foliage which is an ideal foil for the richly coloured flower-trusses.'

MAY DAY (*griersonianum* × *haematodes*).—Flowers about eight in a lax truss; pedicels with erect, crisped hairs, not glandular. Corolla funnel-campanulate, 3 in. wide, scarlet, speckled within, mainly on the central lobe. Anthers black. Style and stigma red. Leaves mat-green, oblanceolate, 6 by 1½ in., clad beneath with a light brown indumentum. Usually not more than 5 ft high. Late April or early May. (A. M. Williams. A.M. 1932.) A thoroughly good garden plant, hardy, flowering freely and not too early. The cross was also made at Bodnant, Exbury and Borde Hill, so the plant described above, from a commercial clone, may not represent the original cross. Some plants have a petaloid calyx, and there is some variation in size of leaf and size and colour of flower.

IBEX (*griersonianum* × *pocophorum*) is similar to May Day and no better. It possibly grows taller, however.

'MICHAEL WATERER'.—Truss compact, with about 15 flowers, on glandular pedicels. Corolla funnel-shaped, 2¼ in. wide, crimson-red with a black flare. Stamen-filaments rosy crimson. Style brighter red. Leaves narrowish elliptic, acute. It has attained 15 ft in the Rhododendron Dell at Kew but is normally of moderate size and fairly compact. End May or early June. (Waterer,

Bagshot, before 1969.) There is a clump of this hybrid on the Broad Walk at Kew.

'MIDSUMMER'.—Flowers about 13 in a compact truss. Corolla widely funnel-shaped, 2¾ in. wide, bright rosy pink with a V-shaped flare of ochre-yellow spots. Anthers mauve, filaments white. (Waterer, Bagshot.) One of the latest to flower of the old hardy hybrids, sometimes even at the beginning of July.

'MOERHEIM'.—Truss few flowered. Corolla 1⅛ in. wide, widely funnel-shaped, lavender-mauve tube about ¼ in. long, Calyx deeply lobed, about 3/16 in. long. Leaves medium green, glossy, elliptic, sometimes broadly so, to about ⅞ in. long, scaly on both sides. Dwarf and compact, vigorous. March or early April. Raised in Germany and originally distributed as "R. *impeditum* 'Moerheimii'".

'MOERHEIM PINK'.—Flowers five to eight in a compact truss, on green pedicels. Corolla 3 in. wide, between cup-shaped and funnel-shaped, 5- or 6-lobed, slightly frilled, Neyron Rose, deeper outside along the ridges. Leaves elliptic, subacute to acute, to 2¾ in. long, dull green. May. An attractive, fairly dwarf hybrid of R. *williamsianum* raised by Dietrich Hobbie in Germany. A.M.T. 1972.

MOONSHINE ('Adriaan Koster' × *litiense*).—This cross was made in the R.H.S. Garden at Wisley by Francis Hanger, in an effort to produce a hardy yellow of compact habit with a full, upstanding truss. It was made in 1946, and the first of the batch to flower, named 'Moonshine', received an A.M. in 1952. This, however, was surpassed by 'MOONSHINE SUPREME', which received the same award in the following year. This has the flowers in a fine conical truss, on ascending pedicels. Corolla campanulate, 3½ in. wide, primrose-yellow. Leaves elliptic, 4 in. long, lateral veins slightly impressed. Compact habit. Late April or early May. Another named clone in this grex is 'MOONSHINE GLOW'. For the history of this cross, see: *Journ. R.H.S.*, Vol. 81 (1956), p. 486.

MOONSTONE (*campylocarpum* × *williamsianum*).—Flowers about six in a lax truss; pedicels glandular. Corolla broad-campanulate with more or less erect lobes, 2½ in. wide, ivory coloured with a slight red mark at the base inside. Style glandular to the tip. Compact and fairly dwarf. April. (J. C. Williams.) There are also forms with pink flowers.

'MORNING CLOUD'.—Flowers 15 to 18 in a compact, rounded truss. Corolla 2¼ in. wide, white flushed with pink, with greenish-yellow markings in the throat. Leaves narrow-elliptic, dark green above, covered beneath with a brown woolly tomentum. Low-growing and compact. May. A hybrid between R. *yakushimanum* and 'Springbok' (*griersonianum* × *ponticum*); raised at the Hydon Nurseries, Godalming, A.M. May 24, 1971. Other clones from this cross have been named 'Hydon Ball', 'Hydon Dawn', and 'Hydon Glow'.

'MOSER'S MAROON'.—Flowers about 16 in the truss, on dark crimson pedicels. Corolla funnel-shaped, 2⅜ in. wide, dark maroon crimson, with black spots on the centre lobe, hairy in the throat. Style red, glandular. Young leaves brownish, as if varnished above, coated beneath with cobwebby hairs; mature leaves dull green above, brownish green beneath, 6 by 2⅝ in.; stems purplish. Lanky habit. Early June. A remarkable rhododendron, evidently the result of hybridisation combined with a mutation similar to that which produced 'Elizabeth Lockhart' (q.v. under Humming Bird). It was raised by Moser of Versailles, but named by Lionel de Rothschild, and received an Award of Merit when shown by him in 1932. According to information given by the raisers to Messrs Hillier in that year, it is the same as the hybrid they called 'Marcel Moser', though it is not the same as what is grown in Holland under that name. It is a parent of some of the best-known Exbury hybrids.

'MOUNT EVEREST'.—Flowers slightly fragrant, 10 to 12 in a well-formed truss; rachis 2½ to 3 in. long. Corolla 2¾ in. wide, funnel-shaped, purest white, with slight brownish or maroon pencilling in the throat. Style glabrous, with a green or yellow stigma. Calyx small, scarcely lobed. Leaves elliptic, 5½ by 2¼ in. A vigorous shrub of medium size. May. (Slocock, 1930. F.C.C.T. 1958.) One of the finest white-flowered rhododendrons.

'MRS A. C. KENRICK'.—Truss conical, with 12 to 16 flowers. Corolla funnel-shaped, 3 in. wide, slightly wavy at the edge, rosy pink, fading to paler at the centre, with slight crimson speckling on the upper lobes. Medium size. Early June. (M. Koster and Sons (?) A.M. 1925.)

'MRS A. M. WILLIAMS'.—Flowers about 10 in a compact truss. Corolla funnel-shaped, 3 in. across, wavy at the margin, bright crimson-scarlet (near Cardinal Red), spotted dark brown on the upper lobe. Low-growing and compact (the plant in the Wisley Trials was 6 ft high and 15 ft wide in 1954). Early May. Raised by Otto Schulz at the Porcelain Factory, Berlin, at the end of the last century, from R. *griffithianum* crossed with some hardy hybrid and put into commerce by C. B. van Nes and Sons in the 1920s. F.C.C.T. 1954. It is said to be quite hardy.

'MRS ANTHONY WATERER'.—Flowers about 14 in the truss. Corolla widely funnel-shaped, lobes broadly rounded at the apex, overlapping, white, slightly flushed with pink or mauve and with a large flare of yellow to brown markings on the central lobe. Calyx variable, some lobes to ⅜ in. long. Style white with a small red stigma. Leaves elliptic, light green. Medium size. Early June. (Waterer, Knap Hill, before 1915.)

'MRS A. T. DE LA MARE'.—Flowers slightly fragrant, 12 to 14 in a lax truss. Corolla funnel-campanulate, five-lobed, 4 in. wide, pale pink in bud, opening pure white with a dense flare of green speckles in the throat that become sparser and greenish brown towards its edge. Compact, spreading habit. May. ('Sir Charles Butler' × 'White Pearl'. A.M.T. 1958.) A beautiful white, with a pronounced green eye. The first-named parent is a form of R. *fortunei* or near to that species. The other, probably the same as 'Halopeanum', is a hybrid of R. *griffithianum*.

'ADMIRAL PIET HEIN' is of the same parentage but has mauvish flowers without any pronounced marking in the throat, though the central lobe is lightly speckled. A.M.T. 1957.

'MRS C. B. VAN NES'.—Flowers about 12 in the truss. Corolla widely funnel-shaped, 3½ in. across, bright crimson in the bud, opening rich pink, darker on the reverse, with inconspicuous markings. Compact habit. Mid-May. A hybrid of 'Princess Juliana' raised by C. B. van Nes.

'MRS CHARLES E. PEARSON'.—Flowers 10 to 12 in a compact, dome-shaped truss; rachis 1½ in. long. Corolla 4 in. wide, broadly funnel-shaped, mauve in the bud, opening very pale lavender, sometimes with a deeper flush at the edge, becoming pure white for a time before falling, spotted with chestnut on the upper lobes. Anthers pale purplish pink. Style white with a red stigma, glandular at the base. Leaves medium green, glossy, elliptic, 5½ by 2¼ in. Moderate size. Late May or early June. ('Catawbiense Grandiflorum' × 'Coombe Royal'; Koster, cross made 1909. F.C.C.T. 1955.) A beautiful rhododendron, resembling 'George Hardy', 'Beauty of Littleworth', etc., in general aspect, but with icy mauve flowers. It is named after the wife of C. E. Pearson, v.m.h. (*d.* 1929), a partner in the firm of J. R. Pearson and Sons of Lowdham, Notts, founder of the Horticultural Trades Association and a member of the R.H.S. Floral Committee for forty years.

'MRS DAVIES EVANS'.—Flowers 16 to 20 in a dense globular truss. Corolla almost flat when fully open, 3 in. wide, frilled, deep mauve with a white, speckled patch on the central lobe. Stamens with large white anthers. Medium size. Late May. (Waterer, Knap Hill, before 1915. A.M.T. 1958.) A hybrid of great charm and character.

'MRS FURNIVALL'.—Flowers 10 to 14 in a compact truss. Corolla funnel-campanulate with a short tube, 3 in. wide, light rosy pink, with a heavy flare of dark brown and crimson markings. Leaves drooping, elliptic to oblong-obovate, 4 by 1¾ in., rounded at the apex. Medium size. Late May or early June. (Waterer, Knap Hill, around 1920. F.C.C.T. 1948.) One of the finest and most popular of hardy hybrids, though now rivalled by its offspring 'Furnivall's Daughter'. It is sometimes confused with 'Mrs G. W. Leak', but that flowers a fortnight earlier, has different leaves, the corollas have coloured nectaries, and the ovary is densely glandular (sparsely hairy in 'Mrs Furnivall').

'MRS G. W. LEAK'.—Flowers about 12 in a conical truss. Corolla widely funnel-shaped, 3½ in. across, light pink, shading to deeper on the three upper lobes, and with a heavy flare of brown and crimson markings; nectaries deep crimson. Leaves dull green, elliptic, 7¼ × 2⅝ in. Medium size, fairly compact, erect habit. Mid-May. ('Chevalier Felix de Sauvage' × 'Coombe Royal'; Koster 1916. F.C.C.T. 1934.) It is named after the wife of G. W. Leak, who was manager of R. H. Bath Ltd, Wisbech, early this century. This handsome rhododendron derives its markings from the first-named parent, which is a hybrid o R. *caucasicum*, and its large flowers and truss from the second, a hybrid of R. *griffithianum*.

'MRS J. C. WILLIAMS'.—Flowers 16 to 20 in a globular, compact truss. Corolla funnel-shaped, 3½ in. wide, lobes much overlapped, white, slightly tinged with pink at the margins, with a rather small reddish-brown flare. Stigma red. Anthers pale brown. Compact, rather spreading habit. Late May or early June. (Waterer, Knap Hill. A.M.T. 1960.)

'MRS J. G. MILLAIS'.—Truss with about 14 flowers. Corolla widely funnel-shaped, almost flat, upper lateral lobes not much overlapped by the central, white, with a flare of solid yellow. Style greenish white, stigma red. Anthers pale mauve. Ovary glabrous. June. (Waterer, Knap Hill.)

'MRS JOHN CLUTTON'.—Truss conical, with 15 to 18 flowers. Corolla widely funnel-shaped, 2¾ in. wide, pinkish mauve in the bud, opening pure white, with a small flare of greenish or reddish-brown marking. Dense habit, medium size. (Waterer, Knap Hill. F.C.C. 1865.) In the last century this was ranked as one of the best whites.

'MRS JOHN KELK'.—Flowers 14 in a compact rounded truss. Corolla funnel-shaped, 2 in. wide, lobes much rounded at the apex, rose-pink, paler at the centre, with a small flare of brownish-crimson spots. Leaves oblong-obovate, lined and puckered longitudinally, with traces of brown indumentum beneath. Compact, rather low-growing. Mid- to late June. (Waterer, Bagshot.)

'MRS JOHN WATERER'.—Flowers about 18 in a well-formed truss. Corolla funnel-shaped, slightly over 2 in. wide, deep rose, with a flare of dark crimson markings. Stamen-filaments densely hairy, purplish red. Ovary glabrous. Leaves stiffly leathery, oblong-elliptic, more or less acute, slightly convex on each side of the midrib. Very tall and vigorous. Mid- to late June. This, with 'John Waterer', is one of the first of the really late-flowering hybrids from R. *arboreum* and was put into commerce in the same year—1855—by the Bagshot firm. It is still of value for screening, owing to its large size and toughness.

'MRS LINDSAY SMITH'.—Flowers about ten per truss. Corolla 5- or 6-lobed, funnel-shaped with a rather broad tube, 3¾ to 4¾ in. long, lobes over-lapping, mauve in the bud, opening white with a slight mauvish tinge, and with a flare of brown, crimson or greenish speckles. Leaves elliptic, lateral veins impressed above. Lank habit, vigorous. Late May. ('Duchess of Edinburgh' × 'George Hardy'; Koster 1910. A.M.T. 1930.) A beautiful flower, but ugly habit.

'MRS LIONEL DE ROTHSCHILD'.—Truss fairly compact, with about 16 flowers. Corolla 3 to 3½ in. wide, funnel-shaped, white edged with apple-blossom pink and with dark crimson spotting on the upper lobe. Medium height. June. (Waterer, Knap Hill. A.M. 1931.) A free-flowering rhododendron, with R. *griffithianum* in its ancestry.

'MRS MARY ASHLEY'.—Truss lax, with about eight flowers. Corolla funnel-campanulate, 3 in. wide, Phlox Pink at the edges, creamy pink in the centre, with a red mark in the throat and slight speckling. Leaves elliptic, 5 by 2⅛ in. Medium height. Early May. (Slocock.) A pleasing but uncommon hybrid.

'MRS P. D. WILLIAMS'.—Flowers 15 to 17 in the truss; pedicels with spreading, curled hairs. Corolla widely funnel-shaped, about 3½ in. across, ivory white with a flare of brown spots on a yellow ground. Leaves dark green, oblanceolate, 5 to 6 in. long, 1½ to 1¾ in. wide. Medium height. Early June. (Waterer, Knap Hill. A.M.T. 1936.)

'MRS PHILIP MARTINEAU'.—Flowers about 14 in a rounded truss. Corolla funnel-shaped, 3½ in. wide, with overlapping lobes, rose-pink with a flare of yellow brown on a light pink ground. Anthers mauve. Style red. Leaves oblong-obovate, dark green, rounded at the apex. Tall-growing. Early June. (Waterer, Knap Hill, F.C.C.T. 1936.)

'MRS R. S. HOLFORD'.—Flowers 15 to 20 in a conical truss. Corolla funnel-shaped, 3 to 3½ in. wide, salmon-pink, with darker spotting on the upper lobe. Medium size. June. (Waterer, Knap Hill, before 1866.) A hybrid of

R. *catawbiense*, with beautifully coloured flowers. Named after the wife of the founder of the Westonbirt Arboretum.

'MRS T. H. LOWINSKY'.—Flowers about 14 in a dense truss. Corolla 3 in. across, widely funnel-shaped, upper lobes much overlapped, mauve in the bud, tinged with that colour at first, fading to white, but in some seasons retaining a pinkish-mauve flush until they fall, central lobe with a very large and conspicuous brown-orange flare. Leaves dark green, broad-elliptic to slightly obovate, to 4¼ in. long, half as wide. Medium size. Late June. (Waterer, Knap Hill, before 1917.) A delightful, very free-flowering and distinct rhododendron, whose flowers are usually described as 'orchid-like'. It has R. *ponticum*, R. *maximum* and R. *catawbiense* in its make-up, and seems to be related to 'Mrs P. D. Williams'. It has been confused with 'Mrs Tom Lowinsky', which was raised by T. H. Lowinsky and received an A.M. in 1919. This is a very tender rhododendron, three-quarters R. *griffithianum*, being a hybrid between that species and 'White Pearl'. The hybrid described here has never received an award, nor much publicity, though it has become in recent years one of the most popular rhododendrons.

'MRS TOM AGNEW'.—Flowers about 16 in the truss. Corolla widely funnel-shaped, 2¾ in. across, upper lateral lobes not overlapped by the central, mauve-pink in the bud, opening pure white, with a conspicuous flare of yellow-brown on the central lobe, which becomes redder towards the base and sometimes extends onto the adjoining lobes. Calyx with long, narrow lobes. Leaves small, oblanceolate. Tall. June. (Waterer, Bagshot, before 1877.) There is a clump of this hybrid at Kew on the Broad Walk. In some seasons it flowers late in June with the young growths.

'MRS WILLIAM AGNEW'.—Flowers 16 to 18 in a compact truss. Corolla widely funnel-shaped, 3¼ in. across, pale magenta pink, paling to blush at the centre of each lobe, slightly speckled with yellow at the base of the central lobe. Anthers fawn. Style pale pink with a brownish stigma. Tall. Early June. (Waterer, Bagshot.)

MULTIFLORUM (*ciliatum* × *virgatum*).—Flowers produced from terminal and upper axillary buds, mostly in pairs from each bud. Corolla funnel-campanulate, 1½ to 2 in. wide, with overlapping lobes, hairy and slightly scaly on the outside, rosy pink in the bud, opening light mauvish pink. Leaves elliptic, oblong-elliptic or oblong-lanceolate, medium green, reticulate and glossy above, to 2½ in. long. Low spreading habit. Stems brown, peeling. April. This cross was made and named before 1868 by Isaac Davies of Ormskirk, Lancs, who also raised Praecox. F.C.C. 1870. The Davies plants were said to be white-flowered, but they seem to have been used for forcing under glass, which is apt to bleach the colour. Or the cross may have been repeated later, with different results. Multiflorum is hardy but bud-tender and may lose branches after a hard spring frost. It is prettiest in the early stages of flowering, when the pink buds and mauve open flowers make a delightful combination.

'MUM'.—Flowers about 18 in a dense truss. Corolla widely funnel-shaped, with broad lobes, the centre lobe overlapping the upper laterals and often reduplicated, mauve-pink in the bud, opening white with a yellow flare, and with two dark crimson spots at the base of the two upper sinuses. Anthers mauvish.

Style white, glabrous, green at the apex, stigma dark, scarcely expanded. Ovary glandular. June. It is very near to R. *maximum* and it has even been suggested that it is the same as the old hybrid known as 'Maximum Album'. It was distributed by Messrs Waterer of Bagshot at the end of the last century.

NAOMI (Aurora × *fortunei*).—This famous Exbury hybrid is the result of mating R. *fortunei* with a hybrid which is itself one-quarter R. *fortunei*, and shows the influence of that species in the form of the corolla, which is basically funnel-shaped but usually with a pronounced tube; in the delicate pink colouring of some of the clones and also the yellowish ground-colour of many of them, which shows up in the tube especially; in the fragrance of the flowers; and in hardiness of the plants. R. *griffithianum*, working in its usual unobtrusive way, has enlarged the corolla and, with R. *fortunei*, raised the number of lobes to six or seven. The form of the truss is also the contribution of these two species. R. *thomsonii* is responsible for the deeper pink colouring of some of the clones, such as 'Naomi Glow' and, with R. *griffithianum*, for the usually pronounced calyx; some clones also show its influence in their relatively broad leaves. The following are the best known clones:

—'NAOMI'.—Flowers 10 in the truss. Corolla funnel-shaped with a narrow tube, 3¾ in. wide, 7-lobed, soft lilac mauve shading to greenish yellow in the tube, where there are faint brownish crimson markings. Style glandular at the base. Leaves elliptic to oblong-obovate, 6¼ by 2¾ in., obtuse. A.M. 1933.

—'EXBURY NAOMI'.—Flowers about 14 in the truss. Corolla 4 in. wide, with a ground-colour of biscuit-yellow, tinged with pink, especially on the edges, and deep pink in the bud. Style glandular to the tip, with a large dark green stigma. Leaves oblanceolate, 8½ by 2¾ in.

—'NAOMI GLOW'.—Flowers 10 in the truss. Corolla 3¼ in. wide, 6- or 7-lobed, vivid pink with crimson markings in the throat. Style stout, glandular to the tip. Leaves oblanceolate, obtuse, 6½ by 2¾ in.

—'NAOMI NAUTILUS'.—Corolla widely spreading, frilled, 4 in. wide, rose passing to cream in the centre. Leaves obovate, obtuse, 5½ by 2½ in. A.M. 1938.

—'NAOMI STELLA MARIS'.—This is apparently rather similar to 'Naomi Nautilus', but was not properly described when it received an F.C.C. in 1939.

—'NAOMI PINK BEAUTY'.—Corolla of a beautiful shade of pink, shading slightly to creamy pink at the centre, with some crimson markings in the tube.

The Naomi clones are hardy, and flower at the end of April or in May. The original plants at Exbury are now 15 to 18 ft high and almost as much in spread, furnished to the ground. Many are depicted in *Rothschild Rhododendrons*, pls. 12, 14, 64.

'NEW MOON'.—Flowers 11–12 in the truss. Corolla funnel-shaped from a broad base, 6-lobed, pale pink in the bud, flushed with pink when first open, becoming white, tinged with yellow in the upper part of the throat and with slight streaking there. Style almost straight, with a small green stigma. May. (*fortunei* × *campylocarpum* hybrid; Slocock. A.M.T. 1953.)

'NIMBUS'.—Flowers fragrant, about eight in the truss; rachis 2½ in. long. Corolla 7-lobed, funnel-shaped from a broad base, 4 in. wide, pure white when fully expanded. Leaves elliptic, leathery, 7½ by 3 in. Vigorous, upright habit.

Late May or early June. ('Snow Queen' × Cornish Loderi; Waterer, Knap Hill. F.C.C.T. 1967.) Cornish Loderi is the same cross as Angelo, i.e., R. *discolor* × R. *griffithianum*.

NOBLEANUM (*arboreum* × *caucasicum*).—This well-known cross unites the great Himalayan tree rhododendron with the dwarf R. *caucasicum* from the Caucasus and bordering parts of Turkey. The cross was made many times, with differing results, according to what forms of the species were used. Since the original 'Nobleanum' is known only from the portrayal of a single corolla it is best to give a generalised description. Flowers twelve to twenty in a compact truss, opening during winter or early spring, sometimes as early as December; rachis up to 1 in. or slightly more long; bud-scales more or less persistent at flowering time; pedicels up to 1 in. or slightly more long, usually glandular and downy. Corolla funnel-shaped or funnel-campanulate, about 2 in. wide, sometimes larger, variable in colour from deep crimson to light pink, or bi-coloured pink or white (or wholly white in the forms deriving from white-flowered R. *arboreum*). The corolla is always in some degree speckled—either on the lobes (mainly on the upper lobes), or in other forms below the sinuses. Ovary white-felted; style glabrous with a crimson or brownish-crimson stigma. Leaves elliptic, oblong or oblanceolate, 5 to 7 in. long, variable in width, dull medium or dark green above, underside clad with a thin brown tomentum or, in at least one clone, burnished silver. The habit is as variable as the flowers and foliage, some forms being low and dense, others tall-growing.

The first recorded cross between R. *arboreum* and R. *caucasicum* was made in 1829 by William Smith of Norbiton, using the latter species as the seed-parent. One plant flowered in 1835 when 8 in. high, and was described and figured by Sweet under the name R. *venustum* (*Brit. Fl. Gard.*, 2nd series, t. 285). The flowers were rich pink, paler at the edge, marked all over with red spots, with 'wavy and crumpled' lobes. In the same year two forms from the same cross, made at the Knap Hill Nursery, were figured in *Bot. Reg.*, t. 1820. The plate is mainly devoted to a form named by Lindley R. *pulcherrimum*, with pink corollas fading to paler at the centre, and pink spotting on the upper lobes. The plant named R. *Nobleanum* is represented on the same plate by a single corolla, described as 'deep and brilliant rose'. The history of this famous name, as given by Gerald Loder, is as follows: 'The older Anthony Waterer used to tell the story of how one day when he was a boy J. C. Loudon and a Mr Noble were paying his uncle Michael Waterer a visit, [and] he was sent from the lunch table for a truss of a hybrid rhododendron just then in flower for the first time. It was there and then named R. Nobleanum, but whether the gentleman was connected with then firm of Standish and Noble is not known.' (*Rhodo. Soc. Notes*, Vol. II, p. 252.) It may be added that the firm of Standish and Noble did not exist at that time; the visitor is hardly likely to have been Standish's future partner Charles Noble, who did not retire until 1898.

There can be no doubt that the cross was made by other nurserymen. The best forms have been propagated vegetatively, but seedlings were also sent out. According to a letter preserved at Kew, the firm of Cunningham and Fraser used to repeat the cross whenever they needed a new stock of plants for sale, using the red-flowered or white-flowered R. *arboreum* according to which form of Nobleanum was required. Whether the original clone of Nobleanum is still in commerce it is impossible to say, as the name soon came to be used in a collective sense. As for R. *venustum*, Sweet said that Smith had a good stock of it, which can only have meant that he had plenty of seedlings from the cross. Another of the Smith seedlings, then 1–2 ft high and grown by the nurseryman Rollisson, was named R. *caucasico-arboreum* by Maund and Henslow in 1840 (Maund's *Botanist*, Vol. IV, t. 157). It was similar to the type, but clearly not the same. The hybrid commonly grown as 'Nobleanum Venustum' at the present time has corollas with inconspicuous spotting, pink paling to white at the centre. It makes a low spreading shrub up to 6 ft high and often starts to flower in December. A hybrid grown in Cornish gardens as 'Nobleanum Venustum' is again different. It is discussed by Millais in *Rhododendrons* (1917), p. 119. Two plants at Kew received originally as R. *venustum* agree with the type in having the corollas distinctly speckled but represent two different clones. However, there is really no reason why all these different forms should not descend from one or other of the Smith seedlings.

The common white-flowered form of Nobleanum has narrow leaves and rather small flowers with greenish-yellow spotting. 'HEATHERSIDE BEAUTY', of uncertain parentage, is to be preferred as an early-flowering hardy white.

A rhododendron whose flowers are produced in the dead of winter and are destroyed by frost more often than not might seem to have little claim to a place in gardens. Yet Nobleanum received an Award of Garden Merit in 1926 and few rhododendrons are better known to the public at large. Unlike many other early-flowering rhododendrons it is perfectly hardy and growths are produced late enough for them to escape damage by frost in most seasons. Also, the flowers open over a long period, so even if most of the trusses are spoilt, some will usually escape. If the weather be exceptionally favourable, no tree gives such a brilliant display in the first two months of the year, and for this reason a few examples are worth growing. If possible, a spot sheltered by trees from the north and east should be given them.

See also 'Jacksonii' and 'Christmas Cheer'.

NOTE. Nobleanum is used here as the name for the R. *arboreum* × R. *caucasicum* hybrids since it is the established name and is accepted by the *International Register*. The correct botanical name, however, is R. × PULCHERRIMUM Lindl. (syns. R. *venustum* Sw. (1835), not Salisb. (1796); R. *caucasico-arboreum* Maund and Henslow). Rehder adopts R. *caucasico-arboreum*, on the grounds that the name R. *pulcherrimum*, though published earlier, is not supported by a botanical description.

NORMAN SHAW ('B. de Bruin' × *discolor*).—Flowers 14 in a fairly dense truss. Corolla funnel-shaped, 5- to 7-lobed, slightly frilled, Bengal Rose, paling when fully open and gradually shading to paler at the centre of each lobe, with two lines of speckles in the throat. Anthers white, tinged with pink. Style pale pink or white, stigma brown. Tall-growing. Mid- to late June. (Rothschild. A.M. 1926.) A useful late-flowering rhododendron. The cross was re-made by A. J. Ivens for Messrs Hillier.

'OLD PORT'.—Flowers about 15 in the truss. Corolla widely funnel-shaped, about 2½ in. across, dull wine-red with blackish crimson markings. Style and stamen-filaments crimson. Calyx very small. Leaves glossy, shaped more or less as in R. *catawbiense*, of which it is a hybrid. Medium size, dense habit. Mid-June. (Waterer, Knap Hill, before 1865.)

OREOCINN (*cinnabarinum* × *oreotrephes*).—Flowers about seven in a loose truss. Corolla tubular-campanulate 1½ to 2 in. wide, lilac pink with two lines of brown markings. An attractive hybrid raised by E. J. P. Magor before 1919, the year it first flowered. It flowers freely in May and grows to about 10 ft.

Magor also crossed R. *cinnabarinum* with R. *yunnanense* (Yunncinn grex). He judged the result to be inferior to Oreocinn, but the Yunncinn cross was repeated at Bodnant and produced the clone 'YOUTHFUL SIN', which received an Award of Merit in 1960.

'OUDIJK'S SENSATION'.—Flowers five to seven in the truss. Corolla funnel-campanulate, 3 in. wide, undulated at the margin, Rose Bengal, darker in the bud and on the reverse, speckled with crimson on the lower part of the upper lobe. Leaves oblong-elliptic, to about 4 in. long and half as wide, with a pronounced cusp at the apex; petiole dark red. An attractive hybrid of recent introduction, flowering in May. It belongs to the NORDENEY grex ('Essex Scarlet' × *williamsianum*), raised by Dietrich Hobbie, and was put into commerce by Le Feber and Co.

'PAULINE'.—Flowers 15 to 17 in the truss. Corolla funnel-shaped, 3 in. wide, vivid crimson-pink (near Delft Rose), with black markings mainly confined to the centre lobe, merging into a black blotch in the throat. Style pink, with a small dark red stigma. Leaves dark green, 6 by 2 in. Vigorous, compact habit. Late April or early May. (T. H. Lowinsky, distributed by L. de Rothschild. A.M.T. 1957.)

'PEACE'.—Flowers seven or eight in the truss. Corolla broadly funnel-shaped, 1¾ in. wide, greenish yellow in the bud, opening creamy white, but more yellow on the reverse and on the central lobe. Late April. (*concatenans* × *rigidum* (*caeruleum album*); Aberconway. A.M.T. 1946.) The description is made from a plant at Kew growing in full sun by King William's Temple. In the A.M. description the flowers are said to be flushed with rose externally, so it may be that the Kew plant represents an earlier form of the cross, called 'Lemon Bill', also raised at Bodnant. At any rate, the Kew plant is very beautiful.

PENJERRICK (*campylocarpum* × *griffithianum*).—Flowers slightly fragrant, six to nine in a lax truss on usually red-tinged pedicels 1¼ to 2 in. long. Corolla pendent, campanulate, up to 4 in. wide, with broad lobes, varying in colour according to the clone: ivory-white, pale yellow, sometimes flushed with pink, or pure pale pink, nectaries often coloured crimson. Leaves glossy, dark or medium green above, grey-green beneath, obtuse at the apex, slightly cordate at the base, 5 to 6 in. long, half as wide. Tall, rather sparsely branched shrubs, flowering in April.

This hybrid, considered by some to be the most beautiful of all, has been raised in many gardens, but the best known are the 'Penjerricks of Penjerrick', which were bred by Samuel Smith, the head gardener there for many years. The second Lord Aberconway greatly admired the Smith plants and procured some of the surplus for Bodnant, where they still grow (*Journ. R.H.S.*, Vol. 76 (1951), pp. 259–61; *Rhodo. Soc. Notes*, Vol. III, pp. 253–4). Penjerrick is available from nurserymen in various shades, but none of this set has received a clonal name.

The first gardener to make the cross between R. *campylocarpum* and R. *griffithianum* was H. J. Mangles of Valewood, Haslemere. After his death the seedlings were taken to the garden of his brother and sister at Littleworth Cross, and one of these, named 'Mrs KINGSMILL', received an A.M. in 1911, when shown by Miss Mangles. This was said in the original description to have creamy white flowers, though what is sometimes seen under the name at the present time has light yellow flowers with green pedicels. Apparently another of the Mangles seedlings was known as 'Mrs Randall Davidson', but whether this was ever propagated it is impossible to say, nor has any authentic description of it been traced.

PERSEVERANCE (*cinnabarinum* var. *roylei* × 'Lady Chamberlain').—'Lady Chamberlain' being itself three-quarters R. *cinnabarinum*, this hybrid comes even nearer to that species. There is apparently only one clone from the original cross, which was made by Murray Adams-Acton and registered in 1942. The corollas are bright apricot inside and on the lobes, the tube coral-pink on the outside. It is very hardy and free-flowering. The same cross was made at Exbury, the result being 'REVLON', with flowers carmine on the outside, said to be very fine but still scarce in commerce. A.M. 1957. Both flower somewhat later than 'Lady Chamberlain'.

'PHALAROPE'.—This is a clonal selection from hybrids between R. *davidsonianum* and R. *pemakoense*, raised by Peter Cox and distributed by Glendoick Gardens Ltd. In the plant seen, which may not be the clone 'Phalarope', the flowers are produced from both the terminal and upper axillary buds, making a cluster of about ten. Corolla mauvish pink, unspeckled, 1½ to 1¾ in. wide. Leaves narrow-obovate or narrow-elliptic, 1 to 1¼ in. long. A small, neat bush, very free-flowering in late April or early May.

'PHILIP WATERER'.—Flowers 12 to 15 in a conical truss; rachis 3 in. long. Corolla almost flat, about 4½ in. wide, wavy at the margins, soft rose with darker veins, unspeckled. Stamens pale rose with greyish anthers. Style stout, rose-coloured, with a pale yellow stigma. End-May or early June. (Waterer, Bagshot. A.M. 1924.) A striking hybrid, which has 'Mrs E. C. Stirling' as one parent.

'PICOTEE'.—Flowers in a dense globular truss of about 14. Corolla 2 in. wide, white, with a narrow edge of lilac-pink, with slight speckling near the lower edges of the central lobe. Anthers white, flushed with pink. Moderate size. Late May or early June. (Waterer, Knap Hill.) Pretty and unusual.

'PINK CHERUB'.—Flowers 15 to 20 in a dense, rounded truss. Corolla funnel-shaped, 2 in. wide, wavy at the margin, lilac-pink (67D), paling to white in the centre, with greenish-yellow speckling on the upper lobe. Leaves dark dull green, 5 by 1½ in. Dwarf, compact habit. Late May. (R. *yakushimanum* × 'Doncaster'. A.M.T. 1968.) This is one of the hybrids of the Yakushima rhododendron raised by Messrs Waterer Sons and Crisp and recently put into commerce.

'PINK DRIFT'.—Flowers about three per truss, each truss at the end of a short twig. Corolla 1 in. wide, rotate, pale mauvish pink. Leaves dull olive-green, mostly acute, to about ⅞ in. long; terminal buds brown. Dwarf, dense and twiggy. May. (*calostrotum* × *scintillans*; H. White, Sunningdale Nurseries.) The flowers could be better coloured, but they are borne in great profusion, and the foliage and habit is excellent.

'PINK PEARL'.—Flowers about 18 in a large conical truss; rachis 3 in.

long; pedicels 1 to 1¾ in. long, glandular. Corolla broadly funnel-shaped, 3¾ to 4 in. wide, slightly waved at the edge, soft pink passing to a bluer shade as the flowers age and becoming almost white before they fall, speckled with brown on the upper lobes. Stamen-filaments and style pinkish. Anthers mauve. Calyx-lobes short, roundish. Vigorous; reasonably compact when grown in sun. A.M. 1897; F.C.C. 1900; A.G.M. 1952.

This famous hybrid was raised by John Waterer and Sons of Bagshot and first exhibited by them at the Temple Show in 1896. Of its parentage, F. G. Waterer wrote in 1903: 'There has been a great deal of discussion as to its parentage, and although I do not in the present article intend to give its immediate parents, we can say that it was raised from the results of crossing two hardy hybrids, and is not, as has been said, a direct *Aucklandii* seedling; yet it throws back to that strain' (*Fl. and Sylva*, Vol. 1, p. 272). It is now generally accepted that the hybrid of R. *griffithianum* used was 'George Hardy' (q.v.) and that the other parent was 'Cynthia' or 'Broughtonii', probably the former.

More than three-quarters of a century after it made its appearance 'Pink Pearl' is still one of the most popular of rhododendrons. The fashion now is to disparage it, but discriminating judges of an earlier generation admired it very much. Despite its sumptuous truss it is a very tough and hardy rhododendron, and free-flowering almost to excess, even when young. Its greatest fault is that the flowers, beautifully coloured when they first expand, fade to an impure shade of pink. For all that, it is best grown in almost full sun, since in the degree of shade that might suit more demanding hybrids the pink tends to 'blue' and the habit of the plant becomes ungainly.

Less well-known than 'Pink Pearl' is its branch-sport 'MOTHER OF PEARL', in which the flowers are pale mauvish pink in the bud when first open, becoming pure white. It received an Award of Merit in 1930. Another branch-sport from 'Pink Pearl' is 'TOPSVOORT PEARL', raised in Holland.

For an interesting article on 'Pink Pearl' and its progeny by Frederick Street, see *R.Y.B. 1950*, pp. 61–71 (reprinted in his *Hardy Rhododendrons* (1953), Chap. 5).

'PINK PEBBLE'.—Flowers four or five in the truss on reddish, glandular pedicels. Corolla between bell- and bowl-shaped, 2 in. wide, vivid crimson in the bud, opening rosy pink inside, darker on the reverse. Anthers dark brown. Style glandular to the tip with a small green stigma. Compact habit. Mid-May (*callimorphum* × *williamsianum*; Lt-Gen. Harrison, Tremeer, Cornwall, 1954). Unlike many species-hybrids from R. *williamsianum*, this is very free-flowering when young, and also has the merit of making its young growth late. A.M. May 20, 1975.

POLAR BEAR (*auriculatum* × *diaprepes*).—Flowers fragrant, eight to ten in a lax truss. Corolla tubular at the base, widely expanded at the mouth where it is about 4½ in. across, seven-lobed, pure white, with green speckling in the throat merging into a green blotch at the very base. Leaves soft green, whitish beneath, mostly oblong-elliptic or elliptic, slightly cordate at the base, up to 1 ft long and 4 in. wide on strong shoots, excluding the petiole. Very vigorous and eventually a tree. Late July or August. (Stevenson 1926. F.C.C. 1946.) Apart from being too large for most gardens, this hybrid has two faults: the corollas are of rather flimsy texture and tend to brown badly in hot weather; and the foliage is too light in colour to serve as a foil to the flowers. Although hardy, it needs a sheltered position, where it will make growths 1½ ft long in a damp summer (but such growths come from sterile shoots, not from below flower-trusses).

The ARGOSY grex is the result of crossing R. *auriculatum* with R. *discolor*, which, like R. *diaprepes*, is a member of the Fortunei subseries flowering late, but earlier than that species. 'ARGOSY SNOW WHITE' received an A.M. in 1938 when shown by Messrs Waterer of Bagshot. It flowers in July and has shorter leaves than Polar Bear. The cross was originally made and named at Exbury.

PRAECOX (*ciliatum* × *dauricum*).—Flowers in twos and threes from buds clustered at the ends of the shoots. Corolla widely funnel-shaped, 1½ to 1¾ in. across, of a beautiful rosy purple. Leaves more or less persistent through the winter, dark glossy green and sparsely bristly above, lower surface paler, scaly. A shrub of compact habit, to 4 or 5 ft. February or March. (Isaac Davies, Larkfield Nursery, Wavertree, nr Liverpool, cross made 1853.)

The history of this lovely hybrid is that in 1853 Isaac Davies, who later moved his nursery to Ormskirk, put the pollen of R. *ciliatum* onto R. *dauricum* (not the other way about, as wrongly stated in the *International Register*). This is the first recorded use in hybridising of R. *ciliatum*, which had been introduced by Hooker in 1850 and first flowered in 1851 or 1852. The hybrids were flowering by 1858 and exhibited in the following year.

Flowering so early in the spring, R. Praecox can be a sad disappointment in low-lying gardens, where its flowers or buds are cut almost every year by frost. Yet there are many gardens south of London with good air-drainage where it is almost as reliable in its display as the snowdrop or winter aconite.

Two of the seedlings raised by Isaac Davies were distinct enough to be named separately. One was 'PRAECOX SUPERBUM', of which nothing is known except that it eventually turned out to be almost deciduous. The other was 'PRAECOX RUBRUM'. This was mentioned in the original description of Praecox and was later figured in *Garden*, Vol. 38 (1890), t. 761. The flowers are darker than in the typical form.

It is recorded that in 1874 Messrs Veitch had a plant in their Coombe Wood Nursery known as 'PRAECOX GRANDIFLORUM'. It is possibly the same as 'EARLY GEM', which received a First Class Certificate in the same year. This was said to be useful for forcing and was described four years later in *Gard. Chron.*, 1878, p. 336. It was said to be a backcross of R. Praecox onto R. *dauricum*, though from the characters given it would seem to be nearer to R. *ciliatum*.

Probably of the same parentage as Praecox is 'EMASCULUM'. This has the flowers solitary or in pairs at the end of the shoot. Corolla 1½ to 2 in. wide, pale lilac-purple, unspotted. Calyx scarcely lobed, scaly. Stamens none or aborted. Style glabrous. It grows to about 6 ft high and flowers some two or three weeks later than Praecox—in March and early April. Nothing is known of its origin, but according to William Watson it was grown by Messrs Veitch in their Coombe Wood nursery as "R. *amoenum*".

'PRINCESS ALICE'.—Flowers deliciously fragrant, mostly in threes on stout white-hairy pedicels about ¾ in. long, almost ⅛ in. thick. Corolla funnel-campanulate with a spreading slightly wavy limb, about 3 in. wide, white, tinted pale rose at first, barred with pink on the reverse along the ridges. Calyx green, lobes obtuse, to about ½ in. long. Leaves dark green, slightly rugose, elliptic-obovate, narrowed to an acuminate apex, up to 4 in. long (on plants grown under glass). Dwarf, lax habit. May. A hybrid between R. *ciliatum* and R. *edgeworthii*, raised by Messrs Veitch, and awarded a First Class Certificate in 1862. Since then the cross has been repeated in other gardens, e.g., by Mangles at Valewood, and at Leonardslee. As might be expected from the parentage, it is only slightly tender and should survive most winters near London on a sheltered wall, though usually grown as a conservatory plant.

This hybrid is named after the Princess Alice, daughter of Queen Victoria, who died in 1878.

'PRINCESS ANNE'.—Flowers up to ten in the truss; rachis about 1 in. long. Corolla funnel-shaped, 1¼ in. wide, pale clear yellow, greenish outside and with green markings near the base of the upper lobes. Stamens exserted, with brown anthers. Style longer than the stamens, with a small green stigma. Leaves light green, reticulate, up to 1¾ in. long. Late April or early May. Dwarf, compact habit (*hanceanum* × *keiskei*; Messrs Reuthe, Keston, Kent). A beautiful hybrid, flowering at a season when a dwarf yellow is needed to set off the later Lapponicums.

'PRINCESS JULIANA'. Flowers eight to ten in the truss, slightly fragrant. Corolla campanulate, with a short, broad tube and spreading much-frilled limb, 3¾ in. or slightly more wide, pale rose, fading at the centre, not speckled. Leaves dull green, acute, to 7 in. long. Low, spreading habit. May. One of the Schulz hybrids, raised at the Porcelain Factory, Berlin, around 1890 and distributed by C. B. van Nes. A.M. 1910.

'PROF. HUGO DE VRIES'.—Similar to 'Pink Pearl', of which it is a hybrid, but its corollas hold their colour better and are darker in the bud; and the leaves are relatively broader, obovate, to 5½ in. long and 2⅜ in. wide. Botanical differences are that the stamens are stouter with anthers about 3/16 wide, against ⅛ in. in 'Pink Pearl', and the ovary is more sparsely glandular. It flowers towards the end of May. It was raised by L. J. Endtz and Co. of Boskoop, and received an A.M. in 1921. The parentage was given by the raisers as 'Pink Pearl' × 'Doncaster', which is surprising, since there is scarcely any difference, even botanical, between 'Prof. Hugo de Vries' and 'Countess of Derby', which is 'Pink Pearl' × 'Cynthia'. But 'Countess of Derby' is a more compact grower than 'Prof. Hugo de Vries' and flowers later, in early June.   [PLATE 106

'PROMETHEUS'.—Truss compact with 18 flowers on brownish-crimson pedicels. Corolla widely funnel-shaped with a short broad tube, 2⅜ in. wide, rosy crimson, brighter on the reverse, speckled with black on the central lobe. Tall, rather lax. Early June. (C. Noble.)

'PTARMIGAN'.—Flowers in twos or threes. Corolla with a short tube and spreading limb, 1⅛ in. wide, white. Anthers dark brown. Style scaly at the base. Calyx scaly and ciliate. Leaves more or less elliptic, to 1⅛ in. long, densely scaly on both sides. Dwarf, spreading. April. (*leucaspis* × *microleucum*; P. Cox, Glendoick. F.C.C. 1965.) Very free-flowering.

'PURITY'.—Flowers about 12 in the truss. Corolla widely funnel-shaped, 2 in. across, lobes rounded at the apex and overlapping, milk-white with a small greenish-brown flare. Leaves narrow-elliptic about 3½ in. long, 1 in. wide, dull green. Medium size. Early June. Probably raised at Knap Hill in the last century. There is an example in the Rhododendron Dell at Kew.

'PURPLE EMPEROR'.—Flowers 17 to 20 in a dome-shaped truss. Corolla widely funnel-shaped, 3 in. across, wavy at the margins, deep purple, paling towards the centre, with black speckling on the centre lobe. Anthers off-white. Leaves elliptic, acute. Early June. (Waterer, Knap Hill. A.M.T. 1953.)

'PURPLE SPLENDOUR'.—Flowers about 15 in a fine, full truss. Corolla broadly funnel-shaped, 3 in. wide, strongly ribbed, wavy-edged, deep purple with a flare of black markings, Anthers yellow, filaments pinkish. Leaves blackish green and reticulate above, oblong-elliptic to about 6 in. long, varying in width from 2 to 2½ in., acute to obtuse at the apex; flower-buds often surrounded by reduced leaves or leafy bud-scales. Compact, medium size, vigorous. Late May to mid-June. (Waterer, Knap Hill, before 1900. A.M. 1931.) A splendid rhododendron of the most sumptuous colouring. R. *ponticum*, R. *maximum* and R. *catawbiense* all enter into its ancestry.

'PURPUREUM GRANDIFLORUM'.—Flowers about 14 in the truss. Corolla widely funnel-shaped, 3 in. across, undulated at the margin, violet-purple, with rather inconspicuous green speckling low on the centre lobe. 'PURPUREUM ELEGANS' is similar, but the flowers are darker purple, with a ray of brown markings on a lighter ground. They are both old hybrids of R. *catawbiense* crossed probably with a dark form of R. *ponticum*, raised at Knap Hill before 1850. Both show the influence of the former in their foliage, and of the latter in their colouring and glabrous ovaries. Another very old dark purple rhododendron is 'LEE'S DARK PURPLE', which has royal purple corollas with a flare of greenish brown or ochre speckles. Unlike the previous two hybrids, this has a well-developed calyx, which suggests that R. *maximum* enters into its ancestry. It is possible that this is the same as 'Lee's Late Purple', which was used at Highclere as a parent before 1844.

'PYGMALION'.—Flowers about 16 in the truss on reddish-brown pedicels. Corolla widely funnel-shaped, 3 in. wide, crimson-scarlet with a black flare and some crimson markings on the lower lobes. Anthers dark chocolate, on crimson filaments. End-May or early June. (Waterer, Bagshot. A.M.T. 1933.) It bears a slight resemblance to 'Doncaster' but is much taller and more vigorous.

QUAVER (*leucaspis* × *sulfureum*).—Flowers four to six in a loose truss. Corolla widely funnel-campanulate, 1 in. wide, pale greenish yellow. Calyx ⅜ in. long, deeply lobed. Leaves elliptic, 2¼ in. long, 1⅜ in. wide, glossy above, glaucous and scaly beneath. Dwarf. Late March or early April. (Rothschild. A.M. 1968.)

QUEEN OF HEARTS (*meddianum* × 'Moser's Maroon').—Truss with about 16 flowers. Corolla funnel-shaped 3 in. wide, deep crimson-scarlet with a flare of black spots. Calyx red, deeply lobed. Leaves broad-elliptic to slightly obovate, showing the influence of R. *meddianum*. May. (Rothschild. A.M. 1949.)

'QUEEN SOURIYA'.—Flowers fragrant, ten in a dome-shaped truss. Corolla widely funnel-shaped, 3½ in. wide, wavy at the margin, pink in the bud, opening cream flushed with lilac-pink and with a pale amber-yellow flush in the throat. Vigorous and fairly tall. May. (*fortunei* hybrid; Slocock. A.M.T. 1957.)

'QUEEN WILHELMINA'.—Flowers about eight in the truss. Corolla campanulate, $3\frac{1}{2}$ in. wide, deep red in the bud, opening a beautiful rosy scarlet, fading to rosy pink, almost devoid of markings. Moderate size. Flowering time variable, sometimes quite early in April, usually late April or early May. Medium size. A superbly coloured hybrid, raised by Schulz at the Porcelain Factory, Berlin, around 1890 from R. *griffithianum* crossed with a hardy hybrid, and distributed by C. B. van Nes. It is rather tender and flowers too early for most gardens, but grows well in several gardens in the south of England.

RACIL (*ciliatum* × *racemosum*).—Flowers arranged as in R. *racemosum*, i.e., from upper axillary as well as terminal buds, one to three from each bud and forming a cluster of up to 20 flowers in all. Corolla pale pink, funnel-campanulate, about 1 in. wide. Calyx with long hairs at the edge, scaly. Leaves obovate, obtuse, coloured more or less as in R. *ciliatum*, $2\frac{1}{2}$ by $1\frac{3}{8}$ in. Erect, to about 5 ft. April. There appear to be several clones of this rather dull hybrid; the description is of one in commerce. The Award of Merit was given in 1957 to clone 'Halbury'.

RED CAP (*eriogynum* × *sanguineum* subsp. *didymum*).—Flowers six to eight in the truss; pedicels glandular and floccose. Corolla campanulate, $1\frac{1}{2}$ to 2 in. wide, dark red. Style red at the apex, with a dark stigma. Leaves narrowly oblong-obovate to almost elliptic, $3\frac{1}{4}$ by $1\frac{1}{4}$ in., medium green and fairly glossy above, coated beneath with a pale woolly tomentum. Of semi-dwarf, rather open habit. Late June or early July. This cross was made by J. B. Stevenson at Tower Court, also at Borde Hill, Exbury, and Townhill Park. The A.M. was given in 1945 to 'TOWNHILL RED CAP', when shown by Lord Swaythling, but the description given above is from a plant at Borde Hill. There is probably little variation in this grex, which is inferior to the Arthur Osborn grex, from which it differs in the campanulate corolla.

REMO (*lutescens* × *valentinianum*).—Flowers from terminal and uppermost axillary buds, one or two from each bud. Corolla tubular-funnel-shaped, $1\frac{3}{4}$ in. wide, clear light yellow, with two lines of deeper speckles in the upper part. Calyx-lobes scaly and ciliate, lanceolate. Leaves elliptic, $2\frac{1}{4}$ in. long, acute to acuminate at the apex, edged with scattered hairs, sparsely scaly on both sides. Low growing. April. (Stevenson.) It is rather tender.

'ROBERT KEIR'.—Flowers 14 in a full, rounded truss. Corolla funnel-campanulate with a spreading limb, mostly seven-lobed, $3\frac{1}{4}$ in. wide, at first creamy white overlaid with pink, at length ivory-white with a yellow flush in the throat. Leaves broad-elliptic, rounded and apiculate at the apex, about 8 in. long, half as wide. April. (*lacteum* × 'Luscombei'.) This fine hybrid was raised at Tower Court, and is named after Robert Keir, who was for many years head gardener there, first to J. B. Stevenson and later to Mrs Stevenson. A. M. 1957.

ROMANY CHAL (*eriogynum* × 'Moser's Maroon').—Flowers about 12 in a lax truss; pedicels downy and sparsely stellate-hairy. Corolla campanulate, $2\frac{3}{8}$ in. wide, deep glowing red with markings on the upper lobes. Anthers black. Style red with a black stigma. Calyx crimson, with ovate, reflexed lobes. Leaves oblong-elliptic, 5 in. long, dull green, thinly brown-tomentose beneath. Vigorous, eventually making a tall pyramid. Late June. (Rothschild. F.C.C. 1937.) A splendidly coloured hybrid, at its best in light woodland. There is a fine group in the Valley Gardens, Windsor Great Park.

ROMANY CHAI (*griersonianum* × 'Moser's Maroon') is similar to Romany Chal, but the colour of the flowers is not quite so good, and the corolla is funnel-shaped at the base. It is perhaps rather more hardy.

'ROSEUM ELEGANS'.—Flowers about twenty in a rounded truss. Corolla funnel-shaped, 2⅝ in. wide, rosy lilac, with a small brown flare. Ovary purplish brown, almost glabrous. Early June. An old hybrid of R. *ponticum*, raised at Knap Hill and still in commerce.

'ROSY BELL'.—Flowers about five per truss. Corolla campanulate, about 1¾ in. wide, appleblossom-pink, unmarked. Calyx lobed to the base, with spreading, ovate segments about ⅜ in. long. Leaves elliptic, acuminate, tapered at the base, up to 2 in. long and ¾ to 1 in. wide. Dwarf, rather spreading habit. Late April or early May. (*ciliatum* × *glaucophyllum*; Isaac Davies, 1882. A.M. 1894, when exhibited by Kew.) A delightful hybrid, whose display is sometimes spoilt by frost.

The hybrid between R. *ciliatum* and R. *glaucophyllum* was also raised by Thomas Nuttall before 1859 and is figured in *Bot. Mag.*, t. 5116, under the name R. *wilsonii*. which Nuttall chose to commemorate his friend W. Wilson the crypto-gamist.

A back-cross of R. *glaucophyllum* onto Rosy Bell was raised by T. C. Thacker of Knowle, Warwickshire, and has been named 'ARDEN BELLE'. It resembles the former closely, differing in its greener more glossy foliage.

The hybrid GRIEVEI is usually supposed to be of the same parentage as 'Rosy Bell', but the International Register gives it as *ciliatum* × *virgatum*, i.e. the same as Multiflorum. It was raised by James Grieve (*d.* 1924), who also bred the well-known apple named after him. He set up his own nursery at Pilrig in 1896, but apparently raised this hybrid earlier, while working for Messrs Dickson and Sons of Edinburgh.

ROYAL FLUSH (*cinnabarinum* × *maddenii*).—This hybrid, raised by J. C. Williams at Caerhays shortly before 1917, is best known as a parent of Lady Chamberlain and Lady Rosebery. The seed-parent was R. *cinnabarinum* var. *roylei* and the pollen-parent an early-flowering form of R. *maddenii* grown at Heligan and known as 'Heljackii'. The seedlings bore lapageria-like flowers in shades of orange-yellow or pink and are decidedly bud-tender. What is usually called the 'orange form' of Royal Flush is a lovely plant with fleshy, tubular-campanulate flowers buff-yellow inside with an orange throat, orange-pink out-side. The cross had previously been made at Littleworth Cross, near Farnham, by Henry A. Mangles (*d.* 1908) and the plants were grown in the greenhouse there by his sister Miss Clara Mangles (*d.* 1931); several were named, but apparently only 'ROSE MANGLES', with pink flowers, went into commerce.

'ROYAL PURPLE'.—Flowers about 12 in a compact truss. Corolla widely funnel-shaped, 2½ in. wide, violet-purple with a slight orange flare on a paler ground. Stamen-filaments coloured like the corolla, with purplish anthers. Style crimson, with a dark red stigma. Ovary glabrous, dark chocolate-brown. Leaves dark green, acute. June. A handsome hybrid raised at the Sunningdale Nurseries in Charles Noble's time. See *Rhododendrons at Sunningdale*, p. 46.

'ROZA STEVENSON' ('Roza Harrison').—Flowers 10 to 12 in the truss. Corolla saucer-shaped, mostly seven-lobed, 4½ in. wide, pale lemon-yellow, deeper at the centre. Leaves oblong-elliptic, obtuse, about 5 in. long and half as wide. Late April or early May. A lovely hybrid raised by Mr and Mrs Stevenson at Tower Court from Loderi 'Sir Edmund' × *wardii* KW 5736. It received an F.C.C. in 1968, when exhibited by Kew under the name 'Roza Harrison'. The name commemorates one of the most knowledgeable of rhododendron enthusiasts (*d.* 1967), who with her husband J. B. Stevenson, built up the famous Tower Court collection of species, much of which was later moved to the Valley Gardens, Windsor Great Park. Eleven years after Mr Stevenson's death she married Major-General Harrison, but the name given by Kew was altered later to the one she bore when the plant was raised.

RUSSAUTINII (*augustinii* × *russatum*).—Flowers in terminal trusses of four or five, sometimes supplemented by trusses from the upper leaf-axils. Corolla 2 in. across, rich near-blue, fading to almost white in the centre, downy in the tube. Stamen-filaments coloured like the corolla, style paler. Calyx well developed, variable in size and form, up to ¼ in. long. Leaves elliptic or oblong-elliptic, 1¼ to 2 in. long, obtuse. Late April. This cross was made by Sir John Ramsden before 1936, possibly also in other gardens. The description is made from a particularly fine clone grown at Grayswood Hill, which won a first prize in the Rhododendron Show of 1972 when exhibited from Nymans. In other forms the corollas are speckled and smaller. Russautinii is of erect habit, to about 5 ft.

—'ILAM VIOLET' is the only clone so far named. It has flowers of a deep violet-purple and was raised by Edgar Stead of New Zealand, using a hybrid he himself raised between R. *augustinii* and its var. *chasmanthum* as one parent, and a good form of R. *russatum* as the other. All the seedlings had pale blue flowers except the one he named 'Ilam Violet' (*R.Y.B. 1947*, p. 47).

The cross between R. *augustinii* and R. *russatum* was also made by J. B. Stevenson at Tower Court and named AZAMIA. For this the good form of R. *russatum* once known as R. *cantabile* was used.

RUSSELLIANUM (*arboreum* × *catawbiense*).—Flowers numerous in a dense truss, on downy pedicels about 1 in. long. Corolla campanulate, bright rosy red, unspotted, with darker nectaries. Calyx very small. Leaves thick and leathery, oblong, abruptly acute at the apex, rounded at the base, somewhat convex above from the recurving of the margins, felted beneath, 4 to 9 in. long; petioles 1 in. long, woolly at first, becoming glabrous. This foundation-cross was made by the nurseryman Russell of Battersea and was described and figured by Sweet in 1831 (*Brit. Fl. Gard.*, Vol. I (2nd series), t. 91). It is therefore contemporaneous with Altaclerense (q.v.). The cross was no doubt made in other places, just as the Smithii cross was repeated many times. A clone of Russellianum still in commerce is 'SOUTHAMPTONIA', distributed by Rodgers' Red Lodge Nursery and probably raised there. This agrees well with the original Russellianum except that the flowers are Tyrian Rose with a lighter centre, slightly speckled. The flowers are in trusses of about seventeen and open in April or early May.

The same cross, using a white-flowered form of R. *arboreum*, was made by Iveson for the Dowager Duchess of Northumberland at Syon House, London, and one form is figured in *Bot. Mag.*, t. 4478 (1849) under the name R. *Clivianum*.

This had white pink-flushed flowers spotted on all the lobes but most densely on the centre lobe.

'SAINT BREWARD'.—Flowers from terminal and upper axillary buds, forming a compact, globular truss. Corolla about 2 in. wide, rotate-funnel-shaped, deep violet-blue. Stamen-filaments pale blue. Stigma pale pink. Leaves softly downy on both sides, mostly elliptic, acute, about 2 in. long. Late April or early May. A dense bush attaining eventually a height of 6 to 8 ft. A hybrid of R. *augustinii* raised by E. J. P. Magor of Lamellen, Cornwall, and distributed by Maj.-Gen. Harrison. F.C.C. 1962. 'SAINT TUDY', also raised at Lamellen, is similar.

'SAINT MERRYN'.—Flowers in trusses of two to four. Corolla widely funnel-shaped, 1 in. wide, deep violet-blue. Stamens coloured like the corolla, with black anthers. Style and stigma crimson. Leaves glossy, about ¾ in. long, obtuse. Late April or early May. A charming hybrid raised by Maj.-Gen. Harrison from 'Saint Tudy' × R. *impeditum* A.M. 1970. 'BLUE STAR' is from the same raiser and of the same parentage.

'SAPPHIRE'.—Flowers about four in the truss. Corolla about 1⅜ in. wide, pale purplish blue shading to paler at the centre. Calyx-lobes narrowly triangular, acute. Leaves elliptic, obtuse, about ½ in. long. Of rounded but not very dense habit. April. A hybrid of R. *impeditum* raised by Frank Knight when he was at the Knap Hill nursery. The pollen came from a sprig of 'Blue Tit', given to him as a button-hole when it was first exhibited by Caerhays in 1931 (*Journ. R.H.S.*, Vol. 94, p. 122). 'MAYFAIR', another seedling from the cross, flowers two weeks later, has darker, bluish foliage, and is denser in habit.

'SAPPHO'.—Flowers about 15 in a dome-shaped truss. Corolla widely funnel-shaped, about 3 in. across, centre lobe of lower flowers often duplicated, mauve in the bud, opening white, with a heavy flare of purple overlaid with black. Stamens ten to twelve, with white filaments. Style variable in length, sometimes shorter than the longest stamens, sometimes slightly longer. Medium size, of rather leggy habit. June. (Waterer, Knap Hill, before 1867, but the same name had been used earlier for a hybrid with rosy crimson flowers.) One of the best-known and most likeable of the older hardy hybrids. When the centre lobe is duplicated, as it often is on the lower flowers of the truss, the extra lobe also carries a flare (see W. Watson, *Rhododendrons and Azaleas*, pl. III). [PLATE 107

'HYPERION', also raised at Knap Hill and still grown there, is rather like 'Sappho', but the corollas are flatter, 3½ in. wide, flushed with mauve, and the flare extends onto the two upper laterals, whereas in 'Sappho', in the normal five-lobed corolla, it is confined to the centre lobe.

SARITA LODER (*griersonianum* × Loderi).—Flowers about eight in the truss (9 to 11 in the A.M. clone); rachis 3 in. long, brownish; pedicels 1¾ in. long, dark brownish red, sticky from stalked white glands. Corolla seven-lobed, widely trumpet-shaped, soft pink shaded paler. Stamen-filaments red. Style glandular, red; stigma dark reddish brown. A tall shrub. Early June or late May. A fine hybrid raised by Lt.-Col. Giles Loder, The High Beeches, Handcross. There are still many plants there, up to 20 ft high, varying greatly in colour. Some have paler flowers than on the plant described here, which grows at Wisley and appears to be similar to the A.M. clone of 1934.

SARLED (*sargentianum* × *trichostomum*).—Flowers about seven in the truss. Corolla tubular with a spreading limb, ½ in. wide at the mouth, tube about $\frac{7}{16}$ in. long, slightly scaly on the outside of the lobes, shell-pink in the bud, opening almost pure white, but with a slight flush of pale brownish pink in the tube. Leaves ⅝ to ¾ in. long, glossy and reticulate. Dwarf, to about 2 ft high, much more in width. Late May. A very free-flowering and vigorous hybrid raised by Collingwood Ingram, The Grange, Benenden, Kent, only now becoming widely available in commerce. The description is based on a plant from the late Miss Davenport-Jones, who distributed this hybrid from the mid-1950s onward. In order to mate the two species 'I was obliged to go down on all fours and employ a watchmaker's glass to see what I was doing. I cannot honestly say that the seedlings from this effort have proved any more beautiful than either of their parents, but I can say they are very definitely more vigorous and consequently easier to grow and to propagate' (C. Ingram, *R.C.Y.B. 1967*, p. 14).

The form of *R. trichostomum* used in this cross was previously known as *R. ledoides*, whence the grex-name Sarled.

'SCANDINAVIA'.—Flowers 14 to 18 in a dome-shaped truss. Corolla open-funnel-shaped, Cardinal Red (near 53B) on a ground of rose-red (58B), with black speckling on the upper lobe. Bushy. Late May or early June. ('Hugh Koster' × 'Betty Wormald'; M. Koster and Sons. A.M.T. 1950.)

SETA (*moupinense* × *spinuliferum*).—Flowers from terminal and upper axillary buds, about seven in all on the plant seen. Corolla tubular-funnel-shaped, 1¼ to 1½ in. long, about 1 in. across, white or pinkish at the base, shading to bright crimson on the lobes. Anthers chocolate-coloured. Style greenish white with a crimson stigma. Leaves lanceolate to elliptic, up to 2 in. long, margins recurved, obtuse to subacute at the apex, rather stiff, midrib beneath pale, yellowish. A small erect shrub to about 5 ft. March or April. (Aberconway. A.M. 1933. F.C.C. 1970.) Quite a pretty hybrid, of unusual appearance, which has been recommended for an Award of Garden Merit.

'SEVEN STARS'.—Flowers 12 to 14 in a lax truss. Corolla funnel-shaped, 2 in. wide, light magenta pink in the bud, opening white, flushed with light pink along the centre of the lobes. Leaves oblanceolate or narrow-obovate, 4 in. or slightly more long. Compact habit, ultimate size unknown. Late April or early May. (R. *yakushimanum* × Loderi 'Sir Joseph Hooker'; Crown Estate Commissioners. A.M. 1967.)

SHILSONII (*barbatum* × *thomsonii*).—Flowers about 14 in a loose truss. Corolla campanulate, 2½ in. wide, of waxy texture, blood-red, with darker coloured nectaries. Stamens white, glabrous or almost so. Style rather thick, glabrous. Calyx petaloid, irregular, up to ⅜ in. long. Leaves dark green, 4½ by 2¾ in., apiculate at the apex, cordate at the base. A tall shrub to 15 ft or so. April. The cross was first made by Richard Gill while he was head gardener to Henry Shilson of Tremough, Cornwall, and received an Award of Merit when shown from there in 1900. The Gill cross had the reputation of being hard to grow well, but the cross was remade by Sir Edmund Loder at Leonardslee in Sussex, with better results, and probably in other gardens too. At any rate, what is now grown as 'Shilsonii' is a good grower, quite hardy, taking after *R. thomsonii* in its foliage and the form of its flowers, but the latter are of a purer red than in

R. *thomsonii*. The description is from a plant in Mr Hillier's collection at Jermyns House near Romsey.

'SIGISMUND RUCKER'.—Flowers about 12 in the truss. Corolla funnel-shaped, 2¼ in. wide, coloured a strange shade of magenta-crimson (71B), with heavy black spotting. Style purplish red, with a small dark red stigma. Ovary dark brownish green, glabrous. Leaves elliptic. Medium size. (Waterer, Knap Hill.) An old hybrid now rarely seen. It is named after a well-known amateur gardener of the last century (*d.* 1875), who had a collection of orchids and ferns in his garden at Wandsworth.

'SIR CHARLES LEMON'.—Flowers about ten per truss; rachis ¾ in. long; pedicels ½ in. long, clad with short hairs. Corolla campanulate, 2½ in. wide, white, with purplish spotting on the upper lobes, extending into the throat. Stamens sparsely hairy at the base, with brown anthers. Style glabrous. Ovary oblong-conoid, with a few crisped hairs. Calyx obsolete. Leaves oblong-elliptic, to 6 in. long, main veins deeply impressed above, undersurface clad with a vividly coloured rusty-red tomentum, not extending to the midrib, which is prominent, pale green. A large shrub or small tree. April. Although sometimes placed under R. *arboreum* the almost glabrous ovary shows that it cannot belong to that species. Lionel de Rothschild, who pointed this out, suggested that it is a hybrid between R. *arboreum* var. *cinnamomeum* and R. *campanulatum*, which seems very likely (*Y.B. Rhod. Ass. 1934*, pp. 108-9). The original plant grew at Carclew in Cornwall, where it was planted in the time of Sir Charles Lemon (*d.* 1868). Millais, in his first volume (1917), gives the size of the original specimen as 30 ft in height and 27 yds round. Assuming that the same plant is referred to, which seems almost certain, it was 10 ft high in 1874, and grown under the name R. *cinnamomeum* (*Journ. Hort.*, Vol. 27, n.s., p. 403). It is reputed to have been raised from seeds collected in the Himalaya by Hooker, but even so, that would be no argument against its hybrid origin, since such hybrids may well occur in the wild.

'Sir Charles Lemon', both in foliage and flower, is one of the finest of rhododendrons, though its full beauty is revealed only after it attains a fairly large size,

SIREN (Choremia × *griersonianum*).—Flowers about ten in a lax truss. Corolla funnel-shaped from a broad base, 2½ in. wide, scarlet, with slight speckling, especially on the three upper lobes. Anthers black. Stigmas red. Calyx coloured like the corolla, irregularly lobed, up to 1½ in. long. Leaves dark green, narrow-oblong, to 6½ in. long, clad beneath with a pale tomentum. Medium size, to about 8 ft. Late April or May. (Aberconway. A.M. 1942.) A fine scarlet rhododendron, with a strikingly large calyx, derived from R. *haematodes*, one of the parents of Choremia.

SIR FREDERICK MOORE (*discolor* × St Keverne).—Flowers slightly fragrant, about 15 in a large compact truss. Corolla funnel-shaped from a broad base, seven-lobed, 3 to 4 in. wide, slightly frilled at the margin, light pink, with conspicuous speckling of brown or crimson in the upper part of the throat. Style pale green with a large pale red stigma. Leaves up to 7 in. long and 2 in. wide. A large vigorous shrub. Late April or early May. (Rothschild, 1935. A.M. 1937, F.C.C.T. 1972.) A beautiful hybrid with flowers of a clear pink.

It is remarkably hardy considering that St Keverne is a hybrid between R. *griffithianum* and R. *zeylanicum* (R. *kingianum* Hort.). It is named after a former Director of the Glasnevin Botanic Garden.

—'CHARLOTTE DE ROTHSCHILD', which belongs to this grex, was named recently and received an A.M. in 1958.

SIR JOHN RAMSDEN ('Corona' × *thomsonii*).—Flowers about ten in a dome-shaped truss. Corolla widely funnel-shaped, 3 in. across, red in the bud and stained with that colour on the reverse, inside flushed and veined pink on a creamy white ground. A vigorous, free-flowering shrub to 12 ft or more. May. (Waterer, Bagshot. A.M. 1926. F.C.C.T. 1955.) Named after Sir John Ramsden, Bt, of Bulstrode Park, Bucks. An attractive hybrid, similar to Cornish Cross.

SMITHII (*arboreum* × *ponticum*) syn. 'Cornish Early Red'.—Flowers about 20 in a dense truss, on glandular pedicels. Corolla campanulate, slightly undulated at the edge, rosy purple, almost crimson, heavily speckled, mostly on the upper lobes. Stamens hairy in the lower half. Style glabrous; ovary 'rusty'. Leaves oblong or elongate, acute, viscid and hairy beneath when young, becoming glabrous.

The above is based on Sweet's original description, made from a plant that flowered in 1831. The cross had been made both ways by William Smith, who at that time was still gardener to the Earl of Liverpool at Coombe Wood House, Kingston-on-Thames, but later set up his own nursery at Norbiton nearby. Since Altaclerense also first flowered in 1831 it is likely that the two crosses were made at the same time, i.e., in 1826. The Smithii cross was later made in other places, e.g., by Rogers' Red Lodge Nursery, Southampton; by Rendall of St Austell, Cornwall; by Davis of Hillsborough, Co. Down (who around the middle of the last century was offering layers 12 to 15 in. high at £3 10s a hundred); and no doubt in other gardens.

Smithii is not much planted at the present time and may not even be in commerce. But it has the distinction of growing to a greater size than any other rhododendron in this country. The examples given by Millais in his first volume (1917) were: Leonardslee, Sussex, 80 years planted, 25 ft high and 3½ ft in girth at 5 ft; Tregothnan, Cornwall, 30 ft high, 8 ft in girth at ground level, dividing into three stout branches at 3 ft; Carclew, Cornwall, a tree 35 ft high, 5 ft in girth at 4 ft; also a very large specimen at Saltwood in Kent.

Smithii is perfectly hardy and flowers in late April or early May. Having been raised so many times it is variable, according to the forms of the two parents used. And it may be that the *ponticum* used was not pure, but one of its early hybrids with R. *maximum*. A. J. Ivens, in his manuscript notes, provided two descriptions, both agreeing very well with Sweet's except that in one plant (at Embley Park) the ovary is glandular-downy (as it may have been in the type), while in the other (from Rogers' nursery) it is almost glabrous.

'SNOWFLAKE'.—Flowers in a conical truss. Corolla widely funnel-shaped, 3 in. across, with rounded lobes, white with a flare of brownish-green speckles, and with a red mark at either side at the base of the two upper sinuses. Anthers large, pale pink. Style white, expanded into a large stigma. Leaves elliptic, acute, 5½ by 2 in. Medium size. June. (Waterer, Knap Hill, before 1875.)

SNOW QUEEN ('White Pearl' ('Halopeanum') × Loderi).—Flowers fragrant,

12 to 15 in a conical truss; rachis and pedicels reddish. Corolla funnel-shaped, 3¾ to 4 in. wide, five-lobed, flushed with pink in the bud, opening pure white with a small red mark and a few speckles in the throat. Leaves dark dull green, 8 by 2½ in. Tall and vigorous. May. This fine hybrid was raised at Leonardslee in Sir Edmund Loder's time and put into commerce by the Knap Hill Nursery, who got their stock from J. G. Millais. It is very much in the style of Loderi, but easier to grow successfully. Millais gave the name 'Snow Queen' to one particular plant, which he thought to be distinct from other plants from the cross, so the name is strictly clonal only, not a grex-name as stated in the *International Register*. Millais, incidentally, gives the parentage as 'Gauntlettii' × Loderi. See 'White Pearl' and 'Gauntlettii'.

'SOLEIL D'AUSTERLITZ' ('Sun of Austerlitz').—Flowers up to 30 in a dense truss; pedicels only ½ in. long, gladular. Corolla broad-campanulate, 2¼ in. wide, crimson shading to paler in the tube, slightly spotted at the base of the centre lobe. Style stout, glabrous. Ovary white felted. Leaves silvery beneath, recalling those of R. *arboreum*. A dense, compact shrub, broader than high. April or early May. This hybrid is usually called 'Sun of Austerlitz', but John Waterer had it in 1852 under its French name; also 'Charles Truffaut', which is known to have been raised by Bertin at Versailles, before 1851. It is a hybrid of R. *arboreum*.

'SONGBIRD'.—Inflorescences from terminal and axillary buds, forming bunches of as many as 20 flowers at the ends of the shoots. Corolla rotate, 1⅛ in. wide, hairy in the throat, deep violet-blue. Stamen-filaments densely hairy at the base. Calyx well developed, with lobes up to ¼ in. long, densely ciliate. Leaves glossy, elliptic, obtuse, about ¾ in. long. April. An excellent dwarf shrub, raised by the late Sir James Horlick, Bt, from 'Blue Tit' crossed with R. *russatum*, whose influence shows in the deep colouring of the flowers, the large calyx, and the hairy middle of the corollas, to which both the stamens and the corolla itself contribute. A.M. 1957.

'SOUTHERN CROSS'.—Flowers fragrant, about ten in a compact truss. Corolla widely funnel-shaped, 4½ in. across, wavy at the margin, white with a pink flush deepest on the upper lobes, with throat-markings of yellowish brown. Leaves dull dark green, 8 by 2½ in. Strong-growing. June. A hybrid between R. *discolor* and 'Lodauric Iceberg', raised by A. F. George and distributed by Hydon Nurseries. It was highly commended after trial at Wisley. Other clones of the same parentage are 'Gipsy Moth', 'Northern Star', 'Starcross', and 'Veldstar'.

'SOUVENIR DE DR S. ENDTZ'.—Flowers about 16 in a dome-shaped truss. Corolla widely funnel-shaped, up to almost 4 in. across, deep rosy pink in the bud, opening pink, shading to paler in the centre, speckled with crimson and brownish crimson on the upper lobes, nectaries crimson. May. ('John Walter' × 'Pink Pearl'; L. J. Endtz and Co. A.M. 1924. F.C.C.T. 1970.) One of the best of the derivatives of 'Pink Pearl', with flowers of a purer and richer pink and differing also in the dome-shaped truss and the presence of coloured nectaries in the corolla. It is also of more compact habit.

'SOUVENIR OF ANTHONY WATERER'.—This hybrid, raised at Knap Hill, is in commerce and described as having salmon-pink flowers with an orange flare.

'SOUVENIR OF W. C. SLOCOCK'.—Flowers about 12 in a compact truss. Corolla funnel-campanulate, 3 in. wide, buff-pink in the tight bud, expanding bud and corolla when first open cream-coloured flushed with pink, becoming ivory with a pink flush, with crimson speckling on a paler ground. Compact habit. May (*campylocarpum* hybrid; Slocock, before 1928.)

SPINULOSUM (*racemosum* × *spinuliferum*).—This hybrid was first made at Kew, later at Bodnant and twice at Exbury, the second time using Forrest's dwarf form of R. *racemosum*. The flowers are borne in terminal and axillary inflorescences, as in R. *racemosum*, but the corollas are more tubular, with protruding stamens, and the leaves are larger than in that species. The dwarf Exbury form is considered to be the best. In this the corollas come near to R. *spinuliferum* in their colouring and the leaves are up to 3 in. long, dark green above. A.M. 1948. In the form that received the same award when shown from Wisley in 1944 the flowers are white shading to pink at the tips of the lobes. This probably represents the Kew cross.

STANLEYANUM (*arboreum album* × *campanulatum*).—R. *stanleyanum* appears to be the first name of specific form given to a known hybrid between R. *arboreum* and R. *campanulatum*. This was raised by the nurseryman Whalley, of Fairfield Nurseries, Liverpool, and is described in *Gard. Chron.* (1851), p. 197. The description is sufficient to show how different this hybrid was from 'Boddaertianum', which is supposed, almost certainly wrongly, to be R. *arboreum* × R. *campanulatum*. Another known hybrid between these two species is 'COMTESSE FERDINAND VISART', raised by Van Houtte from R. *arboreum* var. *cinnamomeum*, and figured in *Fl. des Serres*, Vol. 9, t. 935. See also 'Sir Charles Lemon'.

'STANLEY DAVIES'.—Flowers about 16 in a compact truss, on whitish-green pedicels. Corolla wide-campanulate, 2½ in. wide, dark glowing red but with a slight blue tinge when seen in diffused light, paling to almost white at the base of the throat and with black markings mostly confined to the centre lobe. Stamens densely hairy towards the base, with bluish-purple anthers. Leaves lanceolate to oblong-obovate, 5 by 2 in. Medium size, bushy. Late May or early June. This hybrid was distributed by Messrs Clibrans of Altrincham, who exhibited it at an R.H.S. Show in 1912, but was probably raised by Isaac Davies of Ormskirk, who certainly bred hardy hybrids, though he is best known for his lepidote hybrids, such as Praecox. It is still available in commerce, and was used by the Dutch breeders, its most famous offspring being 'Britannia'.

'STARFISH'.—Flowers about nine in a conical truss. Corolla flat, almost 4 in. across, edges of lobes undulated and recurved, soft pink shading to white at the centre, with markings of crimson and brown. Late May. (Waterer, Bagshot, before 1922.) A curious rhododendron with star-shaped flowers, said to be a seedling of 'Mrs E. C. Stirling'.

'STRATEGIST'.—Flowers about 15 in the truss. Corolla funnel-shaped, 2 to 2⅜ in. wide, with broad lobes, rosy pink, paling at the centre, with light speckling of crimson and olive-green on the centre lobe. Anthers mauve, filaments white. Style dull crimson. Leaves broadly oblong-elliptic, 5 by 1⅞ in., rounded at the base. Tall-growing. June. (Waterer, Bagshot.)

'STREATLEY'.—Flowers about nine in a lax truss. Corolla widely campanulate, 2 in. wide, deep rosy pink in the bud, opening white flushed with pink, lightly speckled with red. Leaves dark green, elliptic, somewhat convex above, with an impressed midrib. Dwarf habit (*aberconwayi* × *yakushimanum*; Crown Estate Commissioners). A. M. May 5, 1964. An interesting hybrid, not unlike R. *yakushimanum* in foliage, but with differently shaped flowers. Another seedling from this cross, so far unnamed, is taller, with broader leaves.

'SUSAN'.—Flowers about 12 in the truss; pedicels almost glabrous. Corolla funnel-shaped, 3 to 3½ in. wide, five-lobed, Amethyst Violet (81D), the three upper lobes somewhat darker than the two lower, heavily speckled with maroon. Leaves dark green, elliptic, thinly felted beneath when young, later greenish brown there, 5½ by 2½ in. A large shrub of compact habit, vigorous. May. This hybrid is as fine in foliage as it is in its flowers, which are near to blue in some lights. It is a pity that there are not six hybrids as good, flowering at fortnightly intervals from the beginning of May. It is perfectly hardy, but needs slight shade. Unfortunately, its history is not fully known. It was raised by P. D. Williams of Lanarth, Cornwall, and originally known as 'Williams' Campanulatum Hybrid', but later named 'Susan' and put into commerce by Messrs W. C. Slocock. It received an Award of Merit in 1948 and an F.C.C. in 1954, both after trial (the A.M. of 1930 belongs to a quite different hybrid, raised at Nymans and also called 'Susan'). It is near to R. *campanulatum*, but it is difficult to believe that it is a hybrid between that species and R. *fortunei*, as stated by Lionel de Rothschild, and later in the *International Register*.

SUSSEX BONFIRE (Cornish Cross × *haematodes*).—Truss six- to eight-flowered. Corolla campanulate with a spreading limb, 2½ in. wide, dark blood-red, with dark nectaries. Calyx petaloid, to ¾ in. long, coloured like the corolla. Leaves dark green, more or less elliptic, glabrous, to 4 by 2 in. Medium size. Late April or early May. (Loder. A.M. 1934.) The description is made from a commercial plant, of little merit, as the flowers are too dark and rather lustreless. In the Borde Hill form of the cross, the flowers are a lighter and brighter red, and the leaves lighter green. But such variation is only to be expected when such a variable hybrid as Cornish Cross is used as a parent.

'SWEET SIMPLICITY'.—Truss rounded, with 18 to 20 flowers. Corolla funnel-shaped, 2½ to 2¾ in. wide, white edged with delicate pink, with olive-green markings on the upper lobes. Anthers pale yellow. Ovary reddish green, glandular and downy. Leaves 6½ by 2½ in., dark green and fairly glossy. Medium size. Compact habit. June. (Waterer, Bagshot, before 1922. A.M.T. 1970.) A charming hybrid, not unlike 'Lady Clementine Mitford', but whiter in the centre, and with less conspicuous markings.

TALLY HO (*eriogynum* × *griersonianum*).—Flowers 9 to 14 in a fairly compact truss, on glandular pedicels. Corolla funnel-campanulate, about ½ in. wide at the base, 2¾ to 3½ in. wide across the limb, vermilion or scarlet, with darker spotting, especially on the three upper lobes. Anthers dark brown, filaments coloured like the corolla. Style tomentose and glandular almost to the tip. Calyx variable, even in the same truss, up to ⅜ in. long. Leaves dull medium green above, under-surface lighter and glossy, coated with a pale brown floccose tomentum still partly persisting on the year-old leaves, oblong-elliptic, mostly 4 to 6 in. long, 1½ to 1¾ in. wide, but sometimes up to 9½ in. long and 2⅞ in. wide, or even longer (in the Leonardslee form). It is a moderately compact shrub, to about 10 ft, more in width. Late May or June.

This fine hybrid was raised at Embley Park (seed-parent *griersonianum*) and at Leonardslee (seed-parent *R. eriogynum*), and received an F.C.C. when shown simultaneously from these two gardens on May 27, 1933. The cross was also made at Exbury. The above description is made from several plants, all very much alike; even the variation is size of leaf may be due to position. Lionel de Rothschild, who also made the cross, said he could see no difference between the three forms. As neither parent shows much variation, this is not surprising. Tally Ho is well represented in the woodland gardens of Sussex, but might not be satisfactory in cold gardens, as it is rather bud tender and subject to bark-split.

A back-cross of Tally-Ho with *R. eriogynum*, raised in the R.H.S. Garden at Wisley, received an A.M. in 1959 under the name 'ROSENKAVALIER' The back-cross with *R. griersonianum* has also been made.

'TED WATERER'.—Truss with about 12 flowers. Corolla almost flat, about 3¼ in. wide, rosy mauve at the edge, paling at the centre, with a flare of yellowish to brownish-green markings. Anthers purple, filaments white. June. (Waterer, Bagshot. A.M. 1925.)

TEMPLE BELLE (*orbiculare* × *williamsianum*).—Truss about five-flowered. Corolla campanulate, about 2 in. wide, usually six-lobed, soft pink. Style glabrous. Leaves roundish, about 2½ in. long and almost as wide, cordate at the base. A dwarf dense bush. April. This hybrid was raised at Kew around 1916 and later by F. Rose for Lord Swaythling at Townhill Park. In the Townhill cross, about one-fifth of the plants proved to be even taller and more vigorous than *R. orbiculare*. The rest were typical Temple Belle (*R.Y.B. 1949*, p. 95).

TESSA (*moupinense* × Praecox).—Flowers about three per truss. Corolla funnel-shaped, 2 in. wide, purplish pink, spotted with crimson on the upper lobes. Leaves up to 2 in. long and half as wide, elliptic, somewhat concave beneath. Of comparatively dwarf, rather open habit. Early spring, usually in March. (Stevenson. A.M. 1935.) In 'TESSA ROZA' (A.M. 1953) the flowers are deeper, more rosy pink. This hybrid is really very different from Praecox, with which it is usually compared, and shows the influence of *R. moupinense* strongly in its foliage and in its larger flowers. Being less twiggy, it does not smother itself in flowers as Praecox does.

'THE BRIDE'.—Flowers in a compact truss of 14 to 16; inflorescence bud-scales persistent. Corolla funnel-shaped, about 2½ in. wide, pure white, with greenish spotting on the upper lobe. Stamen-filaments white. Style white; ovary dark green, glandular. Leaves light green, oblong-elliptic, to 4 in. long, 1⅜ in. wide, tapered at the base. Medium size, compact habit. Late May. This hybrid is believed to be the same as one raised by Standish and Noble in their Bagshot nursery, before 1850, by selfing a hybrid between *R. caucasicum* and a white-flowered form of *R. ponticum*. In point of fact, they called this plant 'Bride', not 'The Bride', and said it had variegated foliage, but the two may well be the same. At any rate, the plant here described is clearly a hybrid of *R. caucasicum*. According to Frederick Street, it is very subject to attack by rhododendron bug.

'THE HON. JEAN MARIE MONTAGU'.—Flowers about ten in the truss. Corolla funnel-campanulate, 2¾ in. wide, deep scarlet-crimson (near Cardinal

Red), with some black speckling. Leaves oblanceolate to elliptic, 7½ by 2½ in. Medium size. May. (C. B. van Nes.)

'THE MASTER'.—Flowers about 12 in a large truss, on glandular pedicels. Corolla seven-lobed, funnel-shaped from a broad base, 4 in. wide, with undulated lobes, delicate pink on a creamy ground, with crimson and brown speckling in the throat merging into a prominent blotch at the very base. Style glandular in the lower half or almost to the tip, with a green stigma. Leaves oblong-obovate elliptic, obtuse, medium-green, with pinkish petioles. Tall-growing. May. (Slocock, A.M.T. 1966.) In a lecture given in 1964, the raiser himself said of this hybrid: 'When King George came round the Chelsea Show and saw this thing, as big as a quart pot, he said "Well, Mr Slocock, I will wait; let me know when you have got the Headmaster." So large I think it is almost vulgar; how it arrived, I do not know. It came from "China" × "Letty Edwards" officially. Neither of these have huge trusses. . . . All I can say is, the bees must have got there first, but I would love to know what flower they visited on the way.' (*Journ. R.H.S.*, Vol. 89 (1964), p. 413). He later suggested it might be a tetraploid (*R.C.Y.B. 1970*, p. 23).

'THE QUEEN'.—Flowers 10 to 12 in a dome-shaped truss. Corolla widely funnel-shaped, 3 in. across, with broad, rounded lobes, mauve in the bud, opening pale mauve shading to white at the centre, with a small orange flare on the centre lobe. Anthers mauve, filaments white. Style sharply upswept at the apex, with a crimson stigma. Leaves dull, dark green, tapered to an acute apex, cuneate at the base. Large, bushy. June. This hybrid was shown by Charles Noble in 1864 and put into commerce three years later, but was probably raised before the dissolution of his partnership with Standish (1856). The parentage was said to be 'Album Elegans' crossed with some other light-coloured hybrid.

'THE QUEEN MOTHER'.—Flowers in trusses of nine or ten; pedicels ⅞ in. long, clad with red glandular hairs. Corolla wide-campanulate, 2 in. broad, deep rosy pink in the bud, opening white flushed with pink, darker on the reverse. Style white, covered with red glands. Leaves elliptic, up to 3½ in. long. Late April (*aberconwayi* × Halcyone; Crown Estate Commissioners). A.M. April 30, 1968.

THOMWILLIAMS (*thomsonii* × *williamsianum*).—Flowers about six in an open truss. Corolla wide-campanulate, clear rosy magenta. Leaves up to 2½ in. long, almost as wide, cordate at the base. Dense, fairly dwarf habit. April or early May. This cross was made by E. J. P. Magor at Lamellen, also at Bodnant, and received an Award of Merit when shown from the latter garden in 1935. It makes a neat specimen, but takes after R. *williamsianum* in refusing to flower freely unless grown in a sunny place.

'THUNDERSTORM'.—Flowers 18 in a compact, dome-shaped truss. Corolla 2¼ to 2¾ in. wide, dark red, speckled on the centre lobe. Anthers and filaments white. Leaves dark green, glossy, elliptic to narrow-obovate, cuneate at the base, 7 by 2½ in. Medium size. Late May or early June. (Slocock. A.M.T. 1955.) It is not unlike 'David' in its flowers, but the foliage is quite different.

'TORCH'.—Flowers six to ten in the truss on brownish pedicels. Corolla widely funnel-shaped from a broad base, five- or six-lobed, 4½ in. wide, bright crimson shading to orange-scarlet on the upper lobes and in the throat, where there is a heavy blotch of dark brown-crimson, nectaries dark crimson. Style pink, with a red stigma. Leaves oblong-oblanceolate, to 8½ by 3 in. Medium size. May. ('Britannia' × Sarita Loder; Messrs Slocock.)

TORTOISESHELL ('Goldsworth Orange' × *griersonianum*).—There are several clones in this grex, raised by Messrs Slocock, of which the following have received awards:

—'CHAMPAGNE'.—Flowers 11 to 14 in the truss; pedicels covered with simple and stellate hairs. Corolla funnel-shaped, 3¼ in. wide, pale yellow at the edge, where there is a slight pink tinge, deepening to richer yellow in the throat and along the centres of the three upper lobes, which are very faintly speckled. Anthers dark crimson. Calyx cup-shaped, irregularly lobed. A.M.T. 1967. In 'TORTOISESHELL WONDER' (A.M. 1947) the corollas are uniform salmon-pink. The flowering time of this grex is June and the plants are medium sized to tall.

'TREASURE'.—Flowers solitary, in twos or threes. Corolla campanulate, about 2 in. wide, crimson-pink (51A). Leaves 1 to 1½ in. long, roundish, slightly cordate at the base, bright green, not glossy; petioles purplish. Late April or early May. Dwarf, congested habit. This hybrid was raised by J. J. Crosfield of Embley Park, Hants, in the 1930s but has only recently become widely available.

'TREWITHEN ORANGE'.—Flowers about five in the truss. Corolla campanulate with a spreading limb, lobes rounded, extending about one-third or slightly more towards the base, soft orange with a slight suffusion of pink. A beautiful hybrid raised by George Johnstone of Trewithen from *R. concatenans* crossed with (*R. cinnabarinum* var. *blandfordiiflorum* × *R. maddenii*). The second parent, named Full House and also raised at Trewithen, is really the same cross as Royal Flush, except that different forms of *R. cinnabarinum* and *R. maddenii* were used. 'Trewithen Orange' flowers in April and received an F.C.C. in 1950. In 1967 the A.M. was given to the clone 'GEORGE JOHNSTONE', raised at Trewithen and exhibited by Collingwood Ingram, Benenden, Kent.

'UNIQUE'.—Flowers up to 14 in a dense truss, on short, glandular pedicels. Corolla funnel-campanulate, 2½ in. wide, pink in the bud, opening ivory flushed with pink, yellower in the throat. Anthers pale brown. Stigma red. Leaves broad-elliptic or sometimes slightly obovate, 3¾ by 1¾ in., obtuse, darkish medium green above, paler beneath. Late April or early May. A hybrid of dense, almost dwarf habit, making a shapely specimen when young, and remaining compact even when old, if grown in a sunny position. It is a hybrid of *R. campylocarpum*, raised by Messrs W. C. Slocock. A.M.T. 1934. F.C.C. 1955. A hybrid of the same name was raised by Messrs Wallace, but is uncommon and probably not in commerce.

VALASPIS (*leucaspis* × *valentinianum*).—Flowers about four in the truss, on stout pedicels. Corolla widely spreading, 2 in. wide, scaly outside, pale creamy yellow. Calyx almost ½ in. long, lobed almost to the base. Leaves broad-elliptic, to 2 in. long, glossy above, glaucous beneath, ciliate. Dwarf, open habit. April. (Aberconway. A.M. 1935.)

VANESSA (*griersonianum* × Soulbut).—Flowers in a lax truss, on glandular pedicels. Corolla trumpet-shaped, 3 in. wide, clear soft pink, with dark crimson nectaries, throat deeper coloured than the limb, with two lines of speckles. Style glandular to the tip. Leaves oblong-oblanceolate, to 7 in. long, dark green and glossy. May. (Aberconway, cross made 1924. F.C.C. 1929.) There appear to be three clones at least of Vanessa in commerce. The one described above is 'Vanessa B'. In 'Vanessa A', which is probably the F.C.C. clone, the corolla is more heavily speckled. 'VANESSA PASTEL' is rather more distinct; the corolla has a cream ground-colour, but is flushed with pink at the edge and the throat is red. F.C.C. 1971.

Vanessa is of interest as the first hybrid of *R. griersonianum* to be exhibited at an R.H.S. Show, but many followed in the next few years. The Vanessa clones flower in May, are of moderate growth, and quite hardy.

'VISCOUNT POWERSCOURT'.—Flowers 14 in a dense truss. Corolla funnel-shaped, 2⅝ in. wide, margins wavy, deep rosy pink, with a conspicuous flare of black markings on the centre lobe. Anthers pale brown, filaments rosy mauve. Style pale rose; ovary glabrous. Leaves elliptic to oblanceolate, acute, to 4 in. long. Moderate growth. June. (Waterer, Bagshot, before 1888. A.M. 1906.) One of the old dark-eyed hybrids that are now again becoming popular.

'VULCAN'.—Flowers about ten in a dome-shaped truss. Corolla funnel-shaped, 2⅝ in. wide, wavy at the margin, bright red (near 45D). Medium size, compact habit. May. ('Mars' × *griersonianum*; Waterer, Bagshot, 1938. A.M.T. 1957.) This is an example of the use of *R. griersonianum* to produce hardy hybrids in brighter and cleaner shades of red than any of the older sorts, which derived their colouring from *R. arboreum*. An earlier example, from the same raisers, is 'BONFIRE', which is *R. griersonianum* crossed with a hybrid between *R. discolor* and 'Mrs R. G. Shaw'. This received an A.M. as early as 1933, when the original seedling was exhibited in a pot, bearing one truss, and 18 in. high. The cross had been made in 1928. The flowers in 'Bonfire' are geranium-red, speckled on the centre lobe, borne in conical trusses. It grows taller than 'Vulcan', and flowers in May.

WHITE GLORY (*irroratum* × Loderi).—Flowers about 15 in the truss. Corolla funnel-shaped, five- or six-lobed, pure white except for faint crimson speckling in the throat Leaves elliptic, rather rigid. A very beautiful white, but flowering too early for most gardens (March or early April). It was raised at Leonardslee and received an A.M. when shown from there by the Dowager Lady Loder in 1937.

'WHITE PEARL' ('Halopeanum').—Flowers 9 to 12 in a tall truss; rachis 2¼ to 3½ in. long; pedicels 1½ to 2 in. long. Corolla campanulate with a spreading limb, about 3½ in. wide, rosy pink in the bud, opening pure white, except for some crimson speckling on the centre lobe and the five crimson nectaries at the base. Style glabrous; ovary sparsely glandular-downy. Calyx up to ¼ in. long, with broad, obtuse lobes, concave on the outside. Leaves dark green, glossy, oblanceolate to elliptic, cuneate at the base, 8½ by 2 in. Tall. May.

'White Pearl' received an A.M. when shown by Messrs Cutbush of Barnet in 1906. According to the *International Register* it is the same as 'Halopeanum', and there seems to be little doubt that this is the case. 'Halopeanum' was the result of a spontaneous cross between *R. griffithianum* and some hybrid of *R. arboreum* (probably with *R. maximum*). It occurred in the garden of Mons. Halopé of Cherbourg, and planted outside survived the hard winter of 1894-5. It was described and figured in *Revue Horticole* the following year and put into commerce in 1897. Messrs Cutbush appear to have been the agents of M. Koster and Sons of Holland, and may well have obtained the plants from them, renaming the hybrid to increase its appeal and gain for it some reflected glory from 'Pink Pearl'. The description given above is from a plant on Battleston Hill in the R.H.S. Garden at Wisley. See further under 'Gauntlettii'.

'White Pearl' is a quite handsome, hardy white, with striking deep green, glossy foliage, but there are others of the same character which are superior.

'WHITE SWAN'.—Flowers 16 to 18 in a conical truss. Corolla widely funnel-campanulate, 4 in. or slightly more wide, wavy at the margin, pale pink at first, becoming pure white except for green markings in the throat below the centre lobe. Style with a large green stigma. Tall. May. (*decorum* × 'Pink Pearl'; Waterer, Bagshot. A.M.T. 1937. F.C.C.T. 1957.)

'WILLBRIT'.—Flowers five to eight in the truss. Corolla campanulate, deep pink, 3 in. wide. Leaves ovate, cordate at the base, 1¾ to 3¼ in. long, reddish when young. Compact rounded habit. Late May. A member of the Ammerlandense group ('Britannia' × *williamsianum*), raised by Dietrich Hobbie and put into commerce by Le Feber and Co., Holland, in 1964. The cross has also been made at the Boskoop Experimental Station, Holland, and three clones named, of which 'KARIN' is said to be the best (*Dendroflora*, No. 3, p. 52).

'WINDLESHAM SCARLET'.—Flowers 12 to 15 in a dome-shaped truss. Corolla 3 in. across, wide-campanulate, wavy and frilled at the margin, dark crimson (53B/C), speckled with black on the upper lobe. Late May. ('Britannia' × 'Doncaster'; Messrs Fromow, Windlesham, raised *c*. 1930. F.C.C.T. 1971.)

'WINDSOR LAD'.—Flowers 16 in the truss, on stout, bright green pedicels. Corolla widely funnel-shaped, 3 in. wide, lilac-coloured (81B or C), with a large green-yellow flare on a lighter ground. Leaves oblanceolate. Late May or early June. (Waterer, Knap Hill.)

WINSOME (*griersonianum* × Humming Bird).—Flowers four to six in lax trusses. Corolla funnel-shaped from a broad base, about 2¼ in. wide, pure soft pink (Neyron Rose), slightly speckled on the centre lobe, nectaries scarlet. Anthers black. Style pink, darkening at the apex, with a small stigma. Leaves bronze-coloured when young, more or less elliptic, 3½ in. long, clad beneath with thin, pale wool. Dwarf. May. (Aberconway. A.M. 1950.)

YELLOW HAMMER (*flavidum* × *sulfureum*).—Flowers from terminal and upper axillary buds, mostly in pairs from each bud. Corolla tubular-campanulate, about ⅞ in. long and ¾ in. wide, downy on the outside, soft yellow. Leaves about 1½ by ½ in., darkish green, scaly beneath. Moderately dwarf, to 5 or 6 ft, taller in woodland. March or April, but a fair proportion of the flower-buds opening in autumn. A very popular hybrid, raised by J. C. Williams of Caerhays Castle, Cornwall, before 1931.

YVONNE ('Aurora' × *griffithianum*).—Flowers about 11 in the truss; rachis 2½ in. long. Corolla widely funnel-campanulate, about 4 in. across, pink in the bud, opening ivory-white with a pink flush. Style with a large green stigma. Calyx green, shallowly and obscurely lobed. Leaves 6 in. long, half as wide. (Rothschild.) The description is of 'Yvonne Opaline', which was the first to be exhibited, and received an A.M. in 1931. In 'YVONNE PRIDE' the flowers are creamy white with a red eye (A.M. 1948). The Yvonne cross is related to Loderi, but with an infusion of R. *thomsonii* through 'Aurora'. The only other species involved is R. *fortunei*. The plants need a sheltered position and flower in late April or early May.

'ZUIDERZEE'.—Flowers about 16 in a compact truss; pedicels less than 1 in. long. Corolla wide-campanulate, 3 in. across, creamy yellow, spotted with red on the upper lobes and with some streaking in the throat. Leaves elliptic, obtuse, lateral veins impressed above, 5 by 2½ in. Bushy and slow-growing. May. (*campylocarpum* hybrid × 'Mrs Lindsay Smith'; M. Koster and Sons. A.M.T. 1936.)

Similar hybrids, of the same parentage and from the same raiser, are: 'ADRIAAN KOSTER', 'DIANE' (A.M.T. 1948), and 'HARVEST MOON' (A.M.T. 1948). Similar too is 'JERSEY CREAM', raised by J. J. Crosfield, Embley Park, but for this R. *campylocarpum* itself was used.

M. Koster and Sons also crossed a hybrid of R. *campylocarpum* with R. *caucasicum*, the result being 'CANARY' (1920). According to H. J. Grootendorst, the flowers are clear yellow but the habit poor and the foliage yellowish green (*Rhod. en Azal.*, p. 63). More recently, the same firm has put into commerce 'ALICE STREET', the result of a cross between 'Diane' and R. *wardii*. It is a fine hardy yellow, with large, bowl-shaped flowers, but is scarce in commerce.

AZALEODENDRONS

The name 'Azaleodendron' was coined by Rodigas in 1892 for hybrids between the Japanese azalea R. *japonicum* (the *Azalea mollis* of gardens) and various Hardy Hybrid rhododendrons, raised at Ghent a few years previously (see further below). The following year it was taken up by Dr Masters as a sectional name under *Rhododendron*. In Rehder's classification of the genus, all the azaleas are grouped in a single subgenus (*Anthodendron*), and all the remaining species (except the azaleastrums), in another subgenus (*Eurhododendron*). The azaleodendrons, being hybrids between these two major groups, were given the rank of a separate subgenus— subgen. *Azaleodendron* (Rodigas) Rehd. In modern classifications, Rehder's two main groups (*Eurhododendron* and *Anthodendron*) are split into two or more subgenera but as it happens, all the known azaleodendrons, with the exception of the Hardijzer group, are of similar parentage to the type of the subgenus *Azaleodendron*, being crosses between (in modern nomenclature) the subgenera *Azalea* and *Hymenanthes*, and therefore constitute a single subgenus, for which the name *Azaleodendron* continues to be valid. Attention is called to this fact since it is often assumed that the term 'azaleodendron' is merely a horticultural coinage of no botanical standing, when in fact it is only invalid when used as a generic name.

In the last century numerous azaleodendrons were raised, of which few survive, no doubt because the majority lacked vigour. Those still grown mostly have ugly foliage and are tolerated only because of their striking flowers. Considering how many azaleodendrons were raised in the last century, Lionel de Rothschild's failure in breeding them is interesting. For two years running he crossed any hybrid rhododendron he had in flower with four different types of azalea, making the crosses both ways—fifty or sixty crosses each year all told. From these he got one pod of seed and raised three seedlings, which had not flowered at the time he wrote (*Y.B. Rhod. Ass. 1934*, pp. 113–14). There is no further record of these, so presumably they were worthless.

Most of the azaleodendrons in cultivation are described below. The Belgian hybrids to which the name *Azaleodendron* was first applied seem mostly to have dropped out of cultivation, except for 'DR MASTERS', not seen, described as having rosy flowers tinted with lilac, heavily spotted on the upper lobe. They were raised by van der Meulen from *R. japonicum* crossed with hardy hybrids, including 'Prince Camille de Rohan' and 'John Waterer'.

HARDIJZER GROUP

Although it would be reasonable to term these hybrids 'azaleodendrons' in the horticultural sense, they are of quite different parentage to those discussed above, one parent being the lepidote *R. racemosum*, the other a Kurume azalea. In Sleumer's classification the former is placed in the subgenus *Pseudorhodorastrum*; the latter belongs to the subgenus *Tsutsia*. See further under 'Ria Hardijzer'.

DESCRIPTIONS

AZALEOIDES.—The name R. *azaleoides* starts in a French work—Dumont de Courset's *Botaniste Cultivateur*, Vol. III (1811). The plant described had come from England, and there is little doubt that it was the hybrid raised at Thompson's nursery at Mile End, near London, from R. *ponticum* pollinated by some azalea—possibly R. *periclymenoides* (*nudiflorum*). It is figured in Andrews' *Botanical Repository*, t. 379 (1804), under the name R. *ponticum* var. *deciduum*, though R. *azaleoides* was apparently the name used for the hybrid by the nursery. At any rate, Sims stated in 1822 that Thompson had four varieties under the name R. *azaleoides*, one of which had scented flowers. This name has been a source of confusion, since it was used more or less in the same sense as the modern term 'azaleodendron' and applied later to other hybrids of this character. The azaleodendron described in previous editions of this work under the name R. *azaleoides* is most probably a hybrid between R. *viscosum* and R. *maximum* and, as Rehder pointed out, does not resemble the Thompson plant figured by Andrews. Whether the original R. *azaleoides* is still in cultivation it is impossible to say.

'BROUGHTONII AUREUM' ('Norbitonense Broughtonianum').—Truss 4 in. wide, with eight to sixteen flowers on downy stalks 1 to 1½ in. long. Calyx-lobes pale green, of unequal length, oblong. Corolla 2½ in. wide, of a beautiful soft, primrose yellow, with reddish-brown spots in the upper part. Stamens ten. Leaves narrowly obovate or oblong, 2 to 6 in. long, ¾ to 1¾ in. wide, dark dull green above, pale green and prominently net-veined beneath, covered with pale down on both sides. An almost evergreen shrub eventually 6 ft high. Late May or early June.

Similar to this is 'SMITHII AUREUM' ('Norbitonense Aureum'), which differs in having the leaves very glaucous beneath; its flowers too are of a paler colour and not so flat and open; the flower-stalk is longer and more slender, and the calyx-lobes somewhat narrower. 'Broughtonii Aureum' is the better shrub—more beautiful and growing better.

These two azaleodendrons seem to be the only two that have survived of the 'Norbiton Hybrids' (R. *norbitonense* André), also known as 'Smith's Yellow Rhododendrons'. They were raised by William Smith, who had been gardener to the Earl of Liverpool at Coombe Wood House, near Kingston-on-Thames, and around 1830 set up his own nursery a mile or so away on Norbiton Common. He was one of the most adventurous hybridisers of his day, his best known production, apart from his yellow azaleodendrons, being the cross between R. *arboreum* and R. *ponticum* named after him, various Indian azaleas, and one of the first 'lepidote × elepidote' crosses. He died before 1846 and was succeeded by J. B. Smith.

The first of Smith's 'yellow rhododendrons' were raised around 1830 and three were shown in the Ghent Exhibition in 1839 'au grand étonnement des amateurs'. A second and larger set was raised in the late 1830s. At least nine were raised in addition to the two described here and all these are listed and described by the French horticulturalist André in 1864. 'Smithii Aureum' is the best documented of the set. It was figured in 1842 in Paxton's *Magazine of Botany* and is the result of a cross between R. *molle* (*Azalea sinensis*) and Smith's own white-flowered hybrid between R. *ponticum* and R. *maximum*. The original plant was bought by Lucombe and Pince of Exeter, who distributed the clone under the name R. *aureum* (*Gard. Chron.* (1843), p. 425). The parentage of 'Broughtonii Aureum' is not recorded, but in view of its similarity to 'Smithii Aureum' it is likely to have been of the same parentage. Watson's assertion, in *Rhododendrons and Azaleas* (1911), that 'Broughtonii Aureum' was raised at Broughton in Peebles-shire was the result of an uninspired guess. The well-known dendrologist F. R. S. Balfour of Dawyck, in the same county, took the trouble to make enquiries at Broughton when the first edition of this work was being prepared, and found no memory or record of there ever having been a nursery there. The name 'R. Broughtonianum' appears in André's list of the Smith azaleodendrons, and there is little doubt that the name commemorates Sir J. D. Broughton, who had a garden at Kingston not far from Smith's nursery and held the entire stock of many of his azalea hybrids, which he bought as seedlings after they had first flowered (*Gard. Chron.* (1842), p. 743). Two azaleas were also named after him, one by Smith, another by Jackson, also of Kingston.

According to André, many of the Smith azaleodendrons were introduced to France by Paillet, and became the vogue in the years 1845–50, when they were 'le sujet de toutes les conversations horticoles et de tous les soins des cultivateurs'. But the fashion passed when it was found that the plants were of poor constitution and sparse in their foliage. Andre's account is to be found in his book

Plantes de Terre de Bruyères, published in 1864. At that time he was already Chief Gardener of the City of Paris, at the age of twenty-four.

FRAGRANS.—Flowers very fragrant, in clusters of twelve to twenty; pedicels ¾ to 1 in. long, glandular. Calyx-lobes linear-triangular, ⅛ to ¼ in. long. downy and glandular. Corolla funnel-shaped, about 1¼ in. long and wide, white at the centre, deeply and unequally tinged at the edge with purplish lilac, downy outside and in the throat. Stamens ten, very hairy at the base, Leaves persistent except in hard winters, oblanceolate, 2 to 4 in. long, ½ to 1½ in. wide, tapering gradually to the base, more abruptly to the short point, dark glossy green above, glaucous beneath, quite glabrous when mature. A slow-growing bush, eventually up to 6 ft high and more in width, flowering in June or early July.

A hybrid of the azalea *R. viscosum,* crossed with *R. maximum, R. ponticum,* or *R. catawbiense,* or with a hybrid involving two of these species. Many crosses of this type were made in the first half of the 19th century, and the resulting hybrids all had flowers in some shade of lilac or purple with a white centre, and many were fragrant. *R. periclymenoides (nudiflorum)* was also used, with similar results. The plant here described, which may be one of several very similar clones, has also been known as *R. odoratum* and, wrongly according to Rehder, as *R. azaleoides.* It agrees well with a hybrid grown in gardens under the name *R. fragrans* as early as 1835, which was figured in *Bot. Mag.,* t. 3454, as 'R. *maximum hybridum'.* Sir William Hooker renamed it thus in the belief that it was the same as the hybrid between 'the common white glaucous-leaved azalea' and *R. maximum,* which was raised by the Rev. William Herbert at Spofforth, and was figured in *Bot. Reg.,* t. 195 (1817), under the name *R. hybridum.* The present plant and the two depicted in these works certainly agree quite well. Later, in 1843, the name *R. fragrans* was used by Paxton for an azaleodendron raised by the nurseryman Chandler of Vauxhall some twenty-five or thirty years previously (*Paxton's Mag. Bot.,* Vol. X, p. 147, t.). The seed-parent was said to have been *R. catawbiense,* though it may in fact have been *R. ponticum.* However, this plant was said to be very dwarf and compact, with the leaves 'a little wrinkled and destitute of much glossiness'. This does not sound like the plant here described, which is more likely to be the same as *R. hybridum.* That at any rate was Rehder's opinion (*Monogr. Azaleas* (1921), p. 190), but in view of the uncertainties as to the history and parentage of the *R. fragrans* of gardens it seems better to adhere to the familiar name.

Also in cultivation is 'GOVENIANUM', which may represent a single clone. It resembles the plant described in most respects, including the glaucous undersurface of the leaf, but the flowers are of a darker shade, and the calyx-lobes narrower and more strap-shaped. The hybrid described by Sweet in 1828 under the name *R. Gowenianum* was raised by Gowen at Highclere from either *R. viscosum* or *R. periclymenoides* pollinated by a hybrid of *R. ponticum* and *R. catawbiense* (*Brit. Fl. Gard.,* t. 263 (1828)). But it is possible that the plant now cultivated is the result of some unrecorded cross made by Gowen, similar to that made by the Rev. William Herbert, who was the brother of the second Earl of Carnarvon, the owner of Highclere and patron of Gowen.

Gowen also made a cross at Highclere in 1825 between *R. periclymenoides* and *R. catawbiense* (pollen-parent), from which 97 plants were raised; the best was named 'Carton's Rhododendron' by Lindley, after the head gardener there

(*Bot. Reg.*, t. 1449 (1831)). This was given botanical status by de Candolle as R. *cartonianum* (syn. R. *cartoni* Bean).

'GALLOPER LIGHT'.—Flowers about twelve in a rather loose truss, on glandular-downy pedicels. Corolla 2 in. wide, funnel-shaped, strawberry pink on a cream base, with a yellow flare in the upper part, the pink coloration fading as the flower ages. Leaves semi-deciduous, rugose, dark green. A hardy vigorous hybrid of unknown parentage, growing to 6 ft high. Late May or early June. It received an Award of Merit when shown by Lionel de Rothschild in 1927 but was raised at the Knap Hill Nursery, not at Exbury.

'GEMMIFERUM'.—Flowers in a dense truss 3 in. across, on sticky, downy pedicels. Corolla funnel-shaped, 1¼ in. long and wide, of a more or less uniform purplish rose. Calyx-lobes ⅛ in. long, linear, hairy on the margins. Leaves 2 to 3½ in. long, 1 to 1½ in. wide, obovate to oval, downy beneath when young, becoming glabrous with age, dark glossy green above, pale green beneath, margins recurved. It makes an evergreen bush of rather loose habit up to 6 ft high, flowering in May or early June. Of unknown origin and parentage. Rehder suggests it might be a hybrid between the azalea R. *prinophyllum* (*roseum*) and R. *catawbiense*.

'GLORY OF LITTLEWORTH'.—Truss compact, hemispherical, with fifteen to eighteen flowers; rachis 2¼ in. long; pedicels 1 to 1½ in. long, glandular-downy. Corolla 2 in. wide with a slender tube, fragrant, cream fading to milky white, with a large blotch of coppery orange spots. Stamens six to eight. Leaves oblong-lanceolate with impressed laterals. Late May or early June. A lovely but rather demanding plant, not often seen in good condition. It received an Award of Merit on May 23, 1911, when shown by Miss Clara Mangles of Littleworth Cross near Farnham and was almost certainly raised there by her brother Henry Mangles (*d.* 1908), who, like his brother James Mangles (*d.* 1884), was a keen hybridiser.

'NELLIE'.—Flowers about twelve in a hemispherical truss, on glandular pedicels. Corolla funnel-shaped with a narrow tube, almost 2½ in. wide, with a large yellow blotch, glandular on the outside, lobes wavy and somewhat recurved. Stamens ten. Leaves semi-deciduous, up to 4 in. long and 1½ in. wide. June. Raised by Harry White at the Sunningdale Nursery. Probably R. *occidentale* is the azalea-parent.

'RIA HARDIJZER'.—Flowers crowded in a pseudo-terminal cluster, made up of several distinct axillary inflorescences, each with about three flowers, on white-hairy pedicels. Corolla funnel-shaped, 1 in. or slightly more wide, deep pink, slightly speckled in the throat. Stamens variable in number, more than five. Ovary clad with ascending white hairs. Leaves elliptic to slightly obovate, ¾ to 1 in. long, scaly beneath, the upper ones persistent, the lower ones deciduous. Dwarf, compact habit. Two other hybrids in this group, with similarly coloured flowers are: 'HARDIJZER BEAUTY', which is more robust than the preceding, with leaves up to 2 in. long, and with more flowers in the total cluster—up to sixty (A.M.T. May 12, 1970); and 'MARTINE', similar to 'Hardijzer Beauty' but of dwarfer habit with smaller leaves; the ovary is scaly.

These interesting hybrids were raised by P. W. Hardijzer in Holland and put into commerce by W. Hardijzer and Co. One parent is R. *racemosum* and the other a Kurume azalea, the influence of the first showing in the inflorescence and the presence of scales on one or more parts, and of the latter in the presence on the stems of appressed, strigose hairs of the type characteristic of the Obtusum subseries (subg. *Tsutsia*), and the reduced number of stamens. These hybrids are not azaleodendrons in the botanical sense. They represent a distinct hybrid subgenus, so far unnamed.

'TORLONIANUM'.—Flowers about twelve in a dome-shaped truss. Corolla funnel-shaped, 1¾ in. or slightly more wide, rosy lilac with a conspicuous orange blotch, tube narrow, downy inside and out. Calyx-lobes linear, ciliate. Stamens nine. Leaves persistent, elliptic, glossy and reticulate above. Medium size. Late May. Of unknown parentage and origin, raised before 1845. Rehder suggests it is *R. calendulaceum* crossed with *R. catawbiense*.

AZALEA HYBRIDS—DECIDUOUS

These azaleas all derive from species of the subseries Luteum of the Azalea series, which in modern classifications ranks as a subgenus of *Rhododendron* (subg. *Azalea*, also known as subg. *Pentanthera*). Of the component species all are American except *R. luteum*, the Pontic azalea, and two closely allied species from E. Asia, *R. molle* and *R. japonicum*. The hybrids that have resulted from the mingling of these are all that garden shrubs should be—hardy, undemanding, sun-tolerant, and colourful. Mostly the flowers are fragrant (except in the Mollis azaleas) and in many of them the leaves colour well before they fall. The season of the deciduous azaleas starts early in May with the Mollis hybrids and lasts until about the third week in June, when the later Ghents and Knap Hills are in flower.

GHENT AZALEAS

The Ghents are the oldest of the hybrid deciduous azaleas and could be regarded as the counterpart of the earliest hybrid rhododendrons, which derive from *R. maximum*, *R. catawbiense*, and *R. ponticum*. Like these they are the result of crossing species of eastern North America with their one European relative, in this case the Pontic azalea, *R. luteum*, and therefore owe nothing to the Himalaya nor to Eastern Asia. Which American species were used is not known, but *R. calendulaceum*, *R. periclymenoides*, and *R. viscosum* were certainly among them. Some may be purely American in parentage, especially the later flowering sorts. It is probable that most of the present commercial stock derives from the crosses made by the Belgian baker P. Mortier of Ghent in the 1820s and 1830s, which soon entered the trade and had reached Britain by 1831. In his 1836 catalogue, Loddiges of Hackney listed seventy-two 'Hybridae Belgicae', among them two still cultivated today—'Gloria Mundi' and the well-known 'Coccinea Speciosa'. Ghent-type crosses were also made at Highclere by Gowen for the Earl of Carnarvon, and of these Loddiges offered twenty-four, but none of the names appears in any modern list. It is also said that Ghents were raised in some British nurseries early in the last century, which may be so. But a list of those cultivated in the Knap Hill Nursery in 1852 contains seven names—a third of the total—that also occur among the Belgian hybrids offered by Loddiges, and not one that suggests an English origin.

Despite the large number of Ghents that were raised and named in the last century, a search through the horticultural literature of the Victorian period provides no confirmation for the statement often made that they were popular garden plants at that time. On the contrary, writers in the 1870s refer to them as uncommon. Millais, writing almost half-a-century later (1917), made the same observation. At the present time they are quite overshadowed by the large-flowered modern hybrids. This is a pity, for the Ghent azaleas are valuable garden plants, strong-growing and trouble-free, and mostly giving vivid autumn colour. Their small flowers render them more suitable for natural plantings than the large-flowered hybrids.

An interesting character of the Ghent azaleas (and of later hybrids deriving from them) is that seedlings occasionally occur in which the stamens are converted into petals. Since the stamens are always five in number and alternate with the corolla-lobes, the result is a fairly symmetrical 'hose-in-hose' flower. The best known of these double Ghents is 'Narcissiflora'. There is another group with double flowers of similar form known as RUSTICA FLORE PLENO. These were put into commerce by Charles Vuylsteke of Loochristi, near Ghent, in 1888, and are usually supposed to be the result of crossing double Ghents with Mollis azaleas. Like the Mollis azaleas they were intended primarily for forcing, and had the advantage that their flowers lasted longer. The best known of this group is 'Norma'.

MOLLIS (MOLLIS–SINENSIS) AZALEAS

The Mollis azaleas, as they are usually called, derive mainly from *R. iaponicum*, the only Japanese member of the Luteum subseries, which in the last century was generally known as *Azalea mollis*, but its Chinese relative, then known as *Azalea sinensis*, enters into the parentage of some varieties, As pointed out in the section on the species, the name *Azalea mollis* was wrongly used, for it belonged properly to the Chinese azalea, which therefore takes the name *R. molle* (Bl.) Wils., while the Japanese species (the *Azalea mollis* of 19th-century gardens) becomes *R. japonicum*. The purist should therefore call the group the Japonicum or Japonicum-Molle azaleas, but the traditional nomenclature is accepted by the *International Register*. It is in any case erroneous to refer to these azaleas as × Molle hybrids, as is sometimes done, since this implies that *R. molle* (the former *Azalea sinensis* of gardens) is the dominant parent, which is certainly not the case.

The Mollis group owes its origin to the great Belgian nurseryman Louis van Houtte, who had named some twenty varieties by 1873. It is usually said that he obtained his stock from Siebold's nursery at Leyden in Holland, which had obtained *R. japonicum* (*Azalea mollis*) from Japan in 1861. It seems to have been overlooked that van Houtte stated that his new azaleas were the result of thirty years of breeding, which, if true, means that their origin goes back to the early 1840s and that according to some authorities *R. japonicum* was introduced by Siebold in 1830. The wide colour-range of the twenty original varieties certainly suggests a long period of breeding. *R. japonicum* commonly bears orange-red or flame-red flowers in the wild, rarely yellow. The van Houtte varieties ranged in colour from lemon- and buff-yellow through rose and salmon to orange and salmon-red. Furthermore, the beautiful 'Chevalier de Reali' has very fragrant flowers, whereas those of *R. japonicum* are almost scentless. It is also of possible significance that van Houtte had an azalea, called by him *Azalea sinensis alba*, which, as Rehder suggested, seems to be a hybrid between *R. molle* and *R. viscosum*. The pale yellow varieties put out by van Houtte may well have derived from this, and possibly some of the others.

By the late 1870s the Mollis azaleas had become important commercial plants but, like most of the azaleas grown in the last century, they were looked on primarily as subjects for the decoration of house or conservatory, bought or lifted from the reserve border, in early winter, potted up and forced into flower. 'Those who have not seen the thousands—the acres—of these plants in the grounds at Gendbrugge can form no conception of the magnitude of the trade in them—trade which extends to all the nations of the civilised world' (*Journ. Hort.*, Vol. 33 (1877), p. 449).

The group was soon taken up and further developed by the Dutch nurserymen, and it was also a Dutch firm—M. Koster and Sons—who first put into commerce varieties that are known to have been the result of crossing *R. japonicum* with *R. molle*, though, as just pointed out, there is a distinct possibility that the original van Houtte varieties had 'Chinese' blood in them. The Koster varieties, which were actually raised by another Dutch grower, were first put into commerce in 1892, and many others followed before the end of the century. Other Dutch breeders also used the Chinese as well as the Japanese azalea, but there has been so much intercrossing between the varieties that it is now no longer possible to differentiate between those that are colour-forms of *R. japonicum* and those that are in some degree hybrid in origin (H. J. Grootendorst, *Rhododendron en Azalea's* (1954), pp. 112–18).

In the work just cited, Mr Grootendorst gives interesting information concerning the propagation of Mollis azaleas by seeds. Of the varieties described here, 'Babeuff' (the original clone only) comes fairly true from seed when isolated. 'J. C. van Tol' is a hybrid between a red and yellow form, and throws three-quarters red and one-quarter yellow when selfed. Of these, the yellows breed true but are poor growers; the reds in the second generation give one-third true-breeding reds, while the other two-thirds resemble the original 'J. C. van Tol' in their genetic make-up. These are the Mendelian ratios to be expected when red is dominant over yellow. In the course of their breeding, M. Koster and Sons discovered that if certain selected Mollis azaleas are crossed, the progeny is more or less uniform in colour, and it is therefore possible, by repeating the cross annually, to produce quantities of seedling azaleas true to colour. The first Mollis azalea to be propagated in this way was 'Koster's Brilliant Red', which was therefore not originally a clone. But some of the seedlings have since been propagated vegetatively, so that the name now covers several similar but not identical clones. Other Dutch nurseries now produce such line-hybrids, but the seedlings are usually sold to colour, without a distinguishing cultivar name.

Although the Mollis azaleas were originally sent out as plants for forcing, they were being grown in the open ground at Kew by the end of the 19th century and are now little used for their original purpose. Since the second world war they have had to compete with the Knap Hill and Exbury azaleas, but are still widely grown and well represented in commerce. For the most part their flowering time is in the first half of May, which means that their display is at risk in frosty gardens, but that, and their lack of fragrance, are their only faults. They are very hardy, of good habit, and do not grow much over 4 or 5 ft high. Full sun is best for them but they will stand slight shade. The most characteristic colours in this group are in the orange, flame, and red part of the spectrum, and at their best are of a truly remarkable brilliance.

KNAP HILL AZALEAS

The Ghent azaleas are the result of crossing the small-flowered, long-tubed species of eastern North America with their European relative. The Mollis azaleas unite the two larger flowered, short-tubed species of eastern Asia. The Knap Hill azaleas, as usually defined, are an omnium gatherum of hybrids that derive from both the Pontic–American and the east Asiatic species and also have another character in common, namely that they all have in their ancestry azaleas bred in the Knap Hill Nursery in the time of the two Anthony Waterers, father and son, who are therefore the founders of the group, though few of the clones now in commerce were actually raised by them.

The history of the Knap Hill group goes back to the middle of the last century, when Anthony Waterer and his partner set out to improve the Ghents by crossing them with the Chinese azalea *R. molle*, formerly known as *Azalea sinensis*. In 1861 the *Gardeners' Chronicle* reported: 'Some fine seedlings have been obtained, with blooms of large size and possessing great richness and variety of colour. They also have the good property of being late bloomers. Though among them orange and flame-coloured tints prevail, yet one we remarked had a crimson top petal and the rest rose; equally remarkable combinations of colour were also to be met with in other sorts' (*Gard. Chron.* (1861), p. 531).

By the end of the century there were seedlings with flowers over 3 in. across, but none of these 'improved Ghents' was ever named and propagated, with the exception of 'Nancy Waterer', which is usually classified as an ordinary Ghent. A possible reason for this neglect is that from the early 1870s the British market was flooded with the Belgian and later the Dutch Mollis hybrids, which had flowers quite as large and vividly coloured as the Waterer azaleas and fulfilled the prevailing demand for 'forcing' plants. At that time, there seems to have been little demand for Ghents, improved or otherwise. Taste began to change early in this century, and the merits of the deciduous azaleas as garden plants began to be appreciated. The Knap Hill Ghents were now in demand, but the plants sent out were seedlings. The younger Anthony Waterer, who succeeded in 1896, carried on his father's work but, being of ample means and somewhat eccentric, he never bothered to exploit it commercially. The best of the Knap Hill azaleas never left the nursery in his lifetime, and the gardening public at large had no notion of what he and his father had achieved. 'The colours have always been remarkable: the crimson deep and solid, the scarlets brilliant as a new hunting coat, the yellows attaining the colour of rich Guernsey butter, the oranges bright with crimson filaments to the anthers, and of course there were beautiful pinks and whites' (*Rhodo. Soc. Notes*, Vol. II, p. 274). So wrote P. D. Williams of Lanarth after the younger Anthony's death in 1924. He and his cousin J. C. Williams of Caerhays were favourites of Anthony Waterer and received some of his prized seedlings. Lionel de Rothschild also acquired some before 1924, but the Knap Hill azaleas did not reach the trade until 1930, when much of the stock was sold to other nurserymen, and many years passed before any became available to the public. Since the second world war, the Knap Hill Nursery has resumed hybridising and put out many new varieties, and other growers have also developed the Knap Hill breed.

The Exbury strain of the Knap Hill azaleas demands special mention, since it has developed to the stage where it is surely entitled to independent rank. About 1921 Lionel de Rothschild acquired from Anthony Waterer an azalea named 'George Reynolds' which had butter-yellow flowers of very large size. Curiously enough, it is very uncharacteristic of the Knap Hill breed, being nearer to a Mollis–Sinensis hybrid than to a Ghent, which may explain why Anthony Waterer was willing to part with it. This was crossed at Exbury with some unnamed Knap Hill azaleas with orange flowers, and one of the seedlings from this cross received an Award of Merit in 1934 under the name 'Hotspur'. A few years after Anthony Waterer's death, Lionel de Rothschild acquired a financial interest in the Knap Hill Nursery and was therefore in a position to draw on its resources. He also used true *R. molle*, raised from seeds collected in China by Forrest and by Rock. Discarding all but the best seedlings, and crossing only within the various colour-groups, he produced a splendid strain that owes as much to his efficiency and sound judgement as it does to the work of the Anthony Waterers. It is doubtful whether any Boskoop nurseryman, breeding for a competitive market, could have achieved as much as this amateur did in such a short space of time. Further details concerning the Exbury azaleas will be found in *The Rothschild Rhododendrons*, pp. 36–7 and plates 39–48. Many Exbury clones have been named and received awards, but the greater part of those in cultivation are seedlings supplied to colour, of which large quantities have been exported to the United States.

The Knap Hill group of azaleas are mostly of moderate growth, to about

5 ft. The young foliage in many clones and seedlings is bronze-tinted, and many also give excellent autumn colour. The flowers are more or less fragrant, larger than in the Ghents, sometimes much larger, and the tube of the corolla is generally longer than it is in the Mollis type of azalea. The influence of *R. molle* is often shown by a flare of discrete markings, while others have the solid flare characteristic of the Ghents. The group as a whole, including the Exbury strain, is a very large one and is open-ended, for new sorts are being named all the time. Here it is possible to mention only those that have received awards and are available from more than one nurseryman. It should also be mentioned that in this group seedlings are available in the trade, sold to colour, which are often only marginally inferior to named clones.

OCCIDENTALE HYBRIDS

R. occidentale is closely related to the East American members of the Luteum subseries, having the white flowers of *R. viscosum* but in other respects being near to *R. calendulaceum*. But being a native of western North America it was introduced later—around 1851 by William Lobb for Messrs Veitch. This was apparently a poor form (the species is very variable). However, the elder Anthony Waterer, probably through his American friends, introduced a finer form in the 1870s, for which he received a Botanical Certificate in 1886. Being very late-flowering it had potentialities as a parent and was crossed at Knap Hill with Ghent azaleas, presumably of the improved type then being bred there. By 1890, there were numerous seedlings of this new race in the nursery, with flowers ranging from white through cream to pink and deep pink, fragrant, with unusually long tubes. They flowered very late—some at the end of June and in early July. These azaleas went into commerce, but those known to Millais (1917) were mainly white, and ranged in flowering time from June 1 to July 15. These were seedlings. Apparently no named clones were distributed, but 'Mrs Anthony Waterer' (F.C.C. 1892) should probably be regarded as one of these Occidentale hybrids, rather than as a member of the Knap Hill group. It may be that the two groups were interbred in the time of the younger Anthony Waterer, for some of the white-flowered Knap Hill and Exbury azaleas seem to have *R. occidentale* blood in them. 'Albicans', also raised at Knap Hill, was said to be a hybrid between *R. occidentale* and *R. molle*. It received an Award of Merit in 1894 when shown from Syon House, but seems to have been lost.

The Occidentale hybrids now in commerce consist mainly of a group of rather similar clones raised by M. Koster and Sons of Holland by crossing *R. occidentale* with Mollis–Sinensis azaleas in 1895. See 'Delicatissima', Exquisita', 'Graciosa', and 'Superba'. All are lovely, with delicately coloured fragrant flowers, borne in late May or early June, and growing to 5 or 6 ft high, but are best kept away from more brightly coloured azaleas. See also 'Bridesmaid' and 'Irene Koster'.

DESCRIPTIONS

'ADRIAAN KOSTER'.—Deep pure yellow (Mollis; M. Koster and Sons, 1901). One of the few self-coloured yellows in the Mollis group, and probably the best.

'ALBATROSS'.—White with a pink tinge on the reverse, wavy at the margin (Knap Hill, 1941). A.M.T. May 26, 1953.

'ALICE DE STUERS'.—Salmon-pink suffused with orange-pink; flare orange (Mollis; M. Koster and Sons). A.M.T. May 11, 1959.

'ALTACLARENSE'.—This name belongs properly to a hybrid between R. *molle* (*Azalea sinensis*) and a late flowering form of R. *viscosum*, raised at Highclere and figured in *Bot. Reg.* (1842), t. 27. It had white flowers, flushed with pink at the edge, spotted with yellow on the upper lobe and with a tinge of yellow in the throat. It must have been similar to 'Daviesii' (q.v.), which has the same parentage. The azalea grown at the present time as 'Altaclarense' is quite different and evidently not of the same parentage. The flowers are soft yellow with a deeper flare, and with an orange-pink flush on the upper lobes which fades as the flower ages. It received a First Class Certificate in 1862, when shown by Lee of Hammersmith, and was said to be *Azalea sinensis* × Ghent azalea. An excellent azalea, giving good autumn colour. It does not fall into any established category, but in appearance and flowering time it is nearer to the Mollis azaleas than to the Ghents, with which it is grouped in the International Register.

'Altaclarense' is said to be the same as 'Aurea Grandiflora', of which the nurseryman William Young of Milford held the entire stock in 1859 (*Gard. Chron.* (1859), p. 891). The parentage of this was stated by Young to be *Azalea sinensis* × *Azalea pontica* (i.e., R. *molle* × R. *luteum*).

For 'Altaclarense Sunbeam' see 'Sunbeam'. For azaleas deriving from 'Altaclarense' see 'Mrs Oliver Slocock' and 'Christopher Wren'. Another, apparently not yet in commerce in Britain, is 'GOLDEN FLARE', raised in Holland and highly rated there.

'AMBER RAIN'.—Buttercup-yellow with an orange flare (Knap Hill–Exbury). A.M. May 19, 1958.

'ANNABELLA'.—Golden yellow flushed orange-rose (Knap Hill–Exbury, 1941).

'APPLE BLOSSOM'.—Pure soft rose (Mollis; K. Wezelenburg and Son). Highly rated in the Boskoop Trials of 1966.

'BABEUFF'.—Apricot with an orange flare. Compact erect habit (Mollis; Gebr. Kersbergen, 1918).

'BALLERINA'.—White, very large, frilled at the edge, with a small, conspicuous orange flare (Knap Hill–Exbury).

'BALZAC'.—Deep orange with a darker, redder tube; flare flame-coloured (Knap Hill–Exbury). A.M. May 29, 1934 (*Rothschild Rhododendrons*, plate 43).

'BASILISK'.—Deep yellow, flushed with salmon-pink outside and on the margins; lobes frilled; flare deep orange (Knap Hill–Exbury). A.M. May 29, 1934.

'BERRYROSE'.—Salmon-pink with a tube of deep red; flare yellow (Knap Hill–Exbury). A.M. May 29, 1934.

'BRAZIL'.—Bright tangerine; lobes frilled (Knap Hill–Exbury).

'BRIDESMAID'.—White with a yellow flare; buds pale greenish yellow. Leaves bright green. Dense habit (Occidentale Hybrid; Waterer, Bagshot).

'BYRON'.—Double, 2 in. wide, white, outer lobes tinged with Carmine Rose (Rustica fl.-pl.; C. Vuylsteke, 1888). A.M.T. May 11, 1953.

'CECILE'.—Salmon-pink, darker pink in the bud, with a yellow flare (Knap Hill–Exbury). A beautiful azalea, recommended for an Award of Garden Merit.

'CHEVALIER A. DE REALI'.—Lemon-yellow in the bud, opening soft yellow, but the original colour retained for a time on the centre of each lobe; flare slightly darker yellow (Mollis; L. van Houtte, 1875).

'CHRISTOPHER WREN'.—Yellow, the two upper laterals flushed with orange pink; flare deep yellow (L. J. Endtz and Co.). A fine, vigorous azalea, believed to derive from 'Altaclarense'. It flowers at the same time as the Mollis azaleas.

'COCCINEA SPECIOSA'.—Tangerine red, upper lobe yellower, 1½ to 1¾ in. wide, tube slender, scarlet-crimson. A very old Ghent, listed by Loddiges in 1836, and still common in cultivation, recommended in 1968 for an Award of Garden Merit. It is of widely spreading habit and flowers in early June.

'CORNEILLE'.—Double, white flushed with pale pink, petaloids white, tube bright red at the base, its upper part and the outside of the limb pink (Ghent; C. Vuylsteke).

'CORONATION LADY'.—Salmon-pink with an orange-yellow flare (Knap Hill; Waterer, Bagshot). A fine azalea, raised from 'Cecile'.

'DAVIESII'.—Buds buff-yellow, pink at the tips; open flowers 2 in. wide, at first creamy white flushed with pink, becoming pure white, slightly frilled, especially on the upper lobe; tube slender, it and the ribs of the limb covered with stalked glands. Leaves glaucous. Dwarf suckering habit. Late May or early June. An exquisitely beautiful azalea, raised by Isaac Davies of Ormskirk, Lancs, before 1879, from R. *molle* (*Azalea sinensis*) crossed with R. *viscosum*. Davies also raised 'AVALANCHE', of the same parentage, but with pure white flowers.

'DAYBREAK'.—Orange-yellow suffused with bright red; flare orange (Knap Hill; Waterer, Bagshot). A.M.T. May 19, 1966.

'DELICATISSIMA'.—Soft yellow in the bud, opening cream with a slight tinge of pink, about 2¼ in. wide; flare yellow, not conspicuous. Fragrant (Occidentale Hybrid; M. Koster and Sons, 1901). 'MAGNIFICA' is similar but less creamy.

'DEVON'.—Vivid blood-red, flushed with orange on the upper lobe, fragrant, 1¾ to 2 in. wide. Excellent autumn colour (Knap Hill; Slocock). A.M.T. May 22, 1952. 'SATAN', raised at Knap Hill and distributed by Messrs Slocock, is similar.

'DIRECTEUR MOERLANDS' ('Golden Sunlight').—Golden yellow with a faint olive-brown flare (Mollis; raised in Holland).

'DOUBLE DAMASK'.—Double, creamy white, fragrant (Knap Hill).

'DR M. OOSTHOEK'.—Deep orange-red, with a darker flare (Mollis; raised in Holland). A.M.T. May 20, 1940. The best of its colour, recommended for an Award of Garden Merit.

'EVA GOUDE'.—Sulphur-yellow, almost self-coloured, fragrant (Knap Hill, 1951). Beautifully coloured, but a weak grower.

'EXQUISITA'.—Creamy white, flushed with pink, especially on the upper lobes, flare orange, margins frilled. Fragrant (Occidentale Hybrid; M. Koster and Sons, 1901.) F.C.C.T. May 30, 1968.

'FANNY' ("Pucella").—Deep purplish rose, 1¾ in. wide; tube red; flare orange. A Ghent azalea of unknown origin, very free-flowering in mid- or late May, of an unusual colour that clashes with most pinks and reds. The International Register gives 'Pucella' as its correct name—surely a corruption of 'Pulchella'? It is possibly the same as 'Pulchella Roseola', described in the Register as 'pinkish mauve, yellow blotch'.

'FARALL YELLOW'.—Deep yellow with a flare of buttercup-yellow (Knap Hill; M. Haworth-Booth). A.M.T. 1957.

'FLORADORA'.—Light orange with a flare of brownish spots (Mollis; M. Koster and Sons). A.M. 1911.

'FRANS VAN DER BOM'.—Light apricot orange with darker markings on the upper lobe (Mollis; M. Koster and Sons, 1892).

'FREYA'.—Double, 1½ in. wide, shell-pink tinged with deeper rosy pink (Rustica fl-pl.; Vuylsteke). A.M. 1897; A.M.T. May 11, 1953.

'GEORGE REYNOLDS'.—Deep yellow, 3½ in. wide, with a flare of orange spots. Raised at Knap Hill and acquired by Lionel de Rothschild, this is a parent of the famous Exbury strain of the Knap Hill azaleas. It received an Award of Merit when shown from Exbury on May 19, 1936. *Rothschild Rhododendrons*, plate 47.

'GIBRALTAR'.—Rich orange-red, frilled, in a large truss (Knap Hill–Exbury, 1947).

'GOG'.—Orange-red (Knap Hill, before 1927, distributed by Messrs Slocock). An azalea of exceptional vigour, colouring well in the autumn.

'GOLDCREST'.—Chrome-yellow with a flare of darker yellow, fragrant. Early (Knap Hill). A.M.T. May 11, 1953.

'GOLDEN EYE'.—Vermilion red with a large tangerine flare (Knap Hill). A.M.T. May 22, 1952.

'GOLDEN ORIOLE'.—Bright yellow with a darker flare, fragrant. Very vigorous and free-flowering. Early (Knap Hill).

'GOLDEN SUNSET'.—Light yellow tinged with orange-red in the bud and when first expanded; flare orange (Knap Hill–Exbury, distributed by Waterer, Bagshot). A.M. May 22, 1956.

'GRACIOSA'.—Soft yellow at first, becoming white, tinged with pink at the edge; large orange flare (Occidentale Hybrid; M. Koster and Sons). A.M. 1908.

'HAMLET'.—Orange tinged with pink, with a darker flare (M. Koster and Sons). A.M.T. May 23, 1936. Although classed as a Mollis it flowers later than most members of that group.

'HARVEST MOON'.—Clear primrose-yellow with a slightly darker flare (Knap Hill; Slocock). A.M.T. May 26, 1953. A lovely azalea but not a strong grower. It associates well with the rhododendron 'Purple Splendour'.

'HOMEBUSH'.—Double, about sixteen in dense, rounded trusses, deep carmine-pink, about 1½ in. wide. Raised at the Knap Hill Nursery before 1925 and distributed by Messrs Slocock. A charming azalea, similar to the Rustica Florepleno group. A.M.T. May 31, 1950. Numerous doubles, mostly with fragrant flowers, have been raised recently at Knap Hill by Donald Waterer, and were named in 1974.

'HORTULANUS H. WITTE'.—Bright orange-yellow (Mollis; M. Koster and Sons).

'HOTSPUR'.—Flame-red with a yellow flare, about 4 in. wide (Knap Hill–Exbury; 'George Reynolds' × Waterer's orange seedling). A.M. May 29, 1934. Other seedlings were raised from this cross, similar in size and shape of flower, but of different colouring. Two of these, 'Hotspur Orange' and 'Hotspur Red', are sometimes sold as 'Hotspur' simply. *Rothschild Rhododendrons*, pp. 33–4, 105, plate 48.

'IRENE KOSTER'.—White, flushed crimson pink, but the central lobe almost white, with a yellow flare, 2¼ in. wide; tube crimson pink. Very fragrant (Occidentale Hybrid; Koster and Co.). According to H. J. Grootendorst, seedlings were originally distributed under this name.

'J. C. VAN TOL'.—See p. 911.

'KLONDYKE'.—Deep golden yellow, suffused salmon-red; buds orange and yellow (Knap Hill–Exbury, 1947).

'KNAP HILL RED'.—Brilliant red (Knap Hill, 1948).

'KOSTER'S BRILLIANT RED'.—Bright orange-red (Mollis; M. Koster and Sons). Seedlings were originally sent out under this name, so there is some variation among the clones.

'LADY ROSEBERY'.—Crimson with an orange flare, about 2¼ in. wide; trusses compact, with up to thirty flowers (Knap Hill, raised by Anthony Waterer II, introduced 1944).

'LAPWING'.—Creamy yellow suffused with pink and with a deeper yellow flare, fragrant, 2 in. wide. Early (Knap Hill, 1935). A.M.T. May 11, 1953.

'MARION MERRIMAN'.—Chrome-yellow, flushed darker yellow, flare orange-yellow, six-lobed, truss with up to thirty flowers. (Knap Hill; raised by Anthony Waterer II and named the year after his death). A.M. 1925; A.M.T. May 31, 1950.

'MRS ANTHONY WATERER'.—Creamy white, about 2 in. wide, with a yellow flare and pink tube, very fragrant. Late. Good autumn colour. Raised at the Knap Hill Nursery, 1886. F.C.C. May 25, 1892. This is one of the elder Anthony Waterer's hybrids of R. *occidentale* (see p. 914).

'MRS OLIVER SLOCOCK'.—Orange-yellow flushed terra-cotta. A hybrid between the yellow 'Altaclarense' and a Mollis azalea, raised by Messrs W. C. Slocock. A.M. May 9, 1933. A fine azalea, usually classified as a Mollis.

'MRS PETER KOSTER'.—Scarlet, with a flare of brownish orange (Mollis; M. Koster and Sons). A.M.T. May 11, 1953.

'NANCY WATERER'.—Soft rich yellow, 2 in. wide, with a deeper flare (A. Waterer, Knap Hill; in commerce 1880). A beautiful, vigorous azalea, which received no award when it first appeared but has now been recommended for an Award of Garden Merit. It is usually classed as a Ghent, but is probably one of the first results of the elder Anthony Waterer's attempts to improve the Ghents by crossing them with R. *molle* (*Azalea sinensis*).

'NARCISSIFLORA' ('Narcissiflora Plena').—Flowers double, well formed, beautiful soft yellow, 1½ in. wide, with a tube 1 in. long. Narrow habit. Bronze autumn colour. A fine azalea of unique colouring, excellent for the small garden. It is a Ghent, near to R. *luteum*, raised by L. van Houtte, before 1871. F.C.C. 1879. F.C.C.T. May 29, 1923. 'BARTHOLO LAZZARI' is similar but not so good.

'NORMA'.—Double, buff-pink, the upper lobe in some flowers marked with a slight orange flare; petaloids also buff-pink, but sometimes white with a yellow stain, both colours occurring in the same truss (Rustica fl.-pl.; Vuylsteke). A.M.T. 1959. In the year the award was given, the plant in the trials was flowering from May 9, but the usual flowering time for 'Norma' is mid- to late May. It is vigorous and very free-flowering.

'PALLAS'.—Vermilion ageing to pink, with a yellow flare on the upper lobe, 2 in. wide; bud and tube dark red (Ghent, before 1875). Tall growing.

'PERSIL'.—White with a buttercup-yellow flare, 2¼ in. wide; trusses compact, with up to twenty flowers. Raised in the Knap Hill Nursery and distributed by Messrs Slocock. Although classed as a Knap Hill, it is near to the Ghents.

'PHOEBE' ('Phébé').—Double, sulphur-yellow with a darker tube (Rustica fl.-pl.; C. Vuylsteke, 1888).

'QUEEN EMMA' ('Koningin Emma').—Deep apricot-orange (Mollis; K. Wezelenburg and Son). A fine azalea that has never received an award in Britain, though highly rated in Holland. It is named after the grandmother of Queen Juliana of the Netherlands.

'REDSHANK'.—Tangerine-orange, flushed with red; trusses with fifteen to twenty flowers, sometimes more (Knap Hill, 1947). A.M.T. May 26, 1953.

'SANG DE GENTBRUGGE'.—Rich tangerine-scarlet with a deep orange flare; tube yellow and pink (Ghent; L. van Houtte, 1973).

'SILVER SLIPPER'.—Creamy white with a yellow flare; bud, opening flower and its tube tinged with pink; fragrant (Knap Hill–Exbury, distributed by Waterer, Bagshot, 1948). A.M.T. June 7, 1962; F.C.C.T. 1963.

'SPEK'S BRILLIANT'.—Bright orange-scarlet with a deeper flare (Mollis; Jan Spek). The true variety is a clone, but seedlings are sometimes sold under the name.

'SPEK'S ORANGE'.—Bright orange with a greenish flare (Mollis; Jan Spek). F.C.C.T. May 26, 1953. As suggested by the date of the award, this clone is late-flowering for a Mollis azalea.

'STRAWBERRY ICE'.—Light flesh-pink, veined and flushed with deeper pink; flare yellow; truss with twenty or more flowers (Knap Hill–Exbury, distributed by Waterer, Bagshot). A.M.T. May 31, 1962. Recommended for an Award of Garden Merit.

'SUNBEAM'. (Altaclarense 'Sunbeam').—Chinese yellow flushed apricot, with a tangerine blotch (M. Koster and Sons, 1895). A.M.T. May 16, 1962. A hybrid of the yellow 'Altaclarense', usually classed as a Mollis.

'SUN CHARIOT'.—Golden yellow with a flare of deeper yellow (Knap Hill–Exbury, distributed by Waterer, Bagshot). F.C.C.T. May 31, 1967. One of the finest yellows in the Knap Hill group, flowering in late May or early June.

'SUPERBA'.—Buff-pink in the bud, opening white flushed with pink, becoming pure white, margins frilled; flare yellow, large, occupying most of the central lobe (Occidentale Hybrid; M. Koster and Sons, 1901).

'SYLPHIDES'.—Pale pink with a flare of buttercup-yellow (Knap Hill). A.M.T. 1957.

'TOUCAN'.—Corolla widely expanded, cream, fading to white, pink-tinged at the margins, flare large, yellow, fragrant (Knap Hill, 1941).

'UNIQUE'.—Orange-yellow in the bud, opening deep buff-yellow flushed with orange, upper lobe deep yellow. The very large trusses, up to fifty flowers, are composed of a terminal cluster supplemented by axillary ones (Ghent; in cultivation 1864). A.M.T. May 22, 1952.

'VISCOSEPALUM'.—Flowers very fragrant, twelve to fourteen in the truss; pedicels densely glandular. Buds buff at the tips with a green tube, opening ivory white with a small yellow flare, $1\frac{3}{4}$ in. wide, tube sticky with stalked glands. A hybrid between R. *molle* (*Azalea sinensis*) and R. *viscosum*, raised at the Knap Hill Nursery before 1842. The original plant is 9 ft high and 21 ft in spread. 'Viscosepalum' is much nearer to R. *viscosum* than is 'Daviesii', which has the same parentage but is more richly coloured and not so glandular.

'WHITETHROAT'.—Pure white, double, $1\frac{1}{2}$ in. wide, in trusses of about eight (Knap Hill, 1941). A.M.T. May 19, 1962.

'WILLEM HARDIJZER'.—Porcelain Rose flushed with scarlet; flare orange (Mollis; W. Hardijzer and Co.). A.M.T. May 28, 1969.

'WRYNECK'.—Sulphur-yellow, flushed pink at the margins; flare yellow (Knap Hill).

AZALEA HYBRIDS—EVERGREEN

The hybrids in this group derive from species of the Obtusum subseries (subgenus *Tsutsia*), and are sometimes known as Japanese azaleas and aptly so, since the oldest of the hybrids arose in the gardens of Japan several centuries ago, and the parental species are mainly natives of Japan. The term 'evergreen' is not entirely apposite for these azaleas, for mostly the leaves produced at the beginning of the growing season—the so-called 'spring leaves'—are dropped in the autumn, and the winter furnishing consists of the later-formed 'summer leaves', which are mostly smaller and thicker than the early ones. The amount of leafage retained depends partly on the clone, partly on the climate and the season.

It is only since the beginning of this century that evergreen azaleas have been cultivated out-of-doors in Britain to any extent, and their present popularity is of quite recent date. The number now available in commerce is considerable, and hybrids bred in Europe and the United States now outnumber the old Japanese garden varieties. The hybrid evergreen azaleas as a whole do not lend themselves to a coherent system of classification, several of the groups recognised in modern works being really no more than miscellaneous assemblages of hybrids that happen to have been raised by the same breeder. But the Kurume azaleas form a well-marked group, and the Indian azaleas, although of diverse parentage, have a common history in that they were bred for indoor decoration.

INDIAN AZALEAS

The first evergreen azalea to reach Europe was *R. indicum*, which was introduced to Holland in the 17th century and subsequently lost. Linnaeus, who knew it only from the figure in a Dutch work, gave it the name *Azalea indica*, which in gardens came to be used indiscriminately for all the evergreen azaleas then known. The first of these to become established in gardens was *R. simsii*, introduced to Britain about 1808, which is in fact closely allied to *R. indicum* and was identified with it by the botanists of the time. *R. simsii* is a native of China and tender in most forms. The evergreen azaleas that followed, although brought from Canton nurseries, were of Japanese origin. They were: the form of Mucronatum (q.v.) with white flowers, which was generally known as 'Indica Alba' and later as 'Old White', and is probably what is now grown as typical *R. mucronatum*. This came in 1819 and was followed by 'Phoeniceum' (q.v.) in 1824. By the mid-1830s William Smith of Norbiton had already raised seedlings or hybrids from these early introductions, which are said to have stimulated interest in the group. Finally, in the early 1830s several forms of *R. indicum* arrived, of which the sportive 'Variegatum' was probably the most important as a parent.

In the 1840s and 1850s these 'Indian azaleas', as they were then known, became popular plants for the greenhouse and for indoor decoration, 'to adorn mansions at routs, balls, and other festive occasions' (as a contemporary writer put it). Many new varieties were raised in nurseries and private gardens from seed of the original introductions, of which many were no doubt hybrids, either spontaneous or deliberately made. The peak of the flowering season was then early May, not much earlier than the natural flowering time of these plants. Forcing does not seem to have been practised much in Britain at that time, and there were at that time no azaleas that could be reliably forced into flower by Christmas (or earlier), as many of the modern race can be. One of the best forcers was, curiously enough, 'Indica Alba'—the *R. mucronatum* of present-day gardens—which quite late in the last century was still forced commercially as a cut-flower. Another used for the same purpose was 'Fielder's White', probably a seedling of 'Indica Alba', which was raised at Enfield early in the 1840s, and continued to be grown, even on the Continent, long after the Belgian greenhouse azaleas had supplanted the other English varieties.

The old Indian azaleas bred in Britain have long since been lost here, but a few were imported to the USA soon after they entered commerce and are still grown there in the south-east. Among those listed by Lee are: 'Fielder's White'; Todman's 'Flag of Truce' and 'Prince of Orange', raised in a garden by Clapham Common, London; and 'Iveryana', raised Ivery of Dorking (*The Azalea Book* (1958), pp. 201–5 and plates 44 and 46). These deserve to be reintroduced, if only for sentimental reasons, all having originated here more than a century ago.

Around 1860 the English Indian azaleas began to be eclipsed by the forerunners of the great race of Belgian Indians and by the 1880s had all but disappeared from lists of recommended varieties. The early history of these continental varieties is apparently unknown, but the breeders were presumably working on the same lines as the English nurserymen and using the same material. The new kinds that came into commerce in ever-increasing numbers after 1860 are thought to have been derived predomi-nantly from *R. simsii* and to a lesser extent from *R. scabrum* (through 'Phoeniceum'). There seems to be little doubt that a major part in their formation was played by the three forms of *R. simsii* which Robert Fortune found in a Shanghai nursery and sent to Standish and Noble in 1851. These were 'Vittata', 'Vittata Punctata', and 'Bealii', all with white flowers variously striped or flecked and the first two perhaps representing two forms of a single sportive clone. Whether Standish and Noble ever put these into commerce in Britain is not certain, but it is surely significant that they showed 'Bealii' in Paris in 1853, and that all three introductions were first figured, as early as 1854, in Belgian publications. By 1864 'Vittata Punctata' had become the most used forcing variety in the Paris area, but in Britain their arrival seems to have passed almost unnoticed.

No doubt owing to the predominance of *R. simsii* in their ancestry, the modern greenhouse azaleas are tender and would not have called for mention here were it not that they have been used to some extent in the breeding of hardy sorts. The first to attempt this seems to have been William Carmichael, mentioned below under 'Mrs Carmichael'. Crossing various greenhouse azaleas with 'Amoenum' he raised several hybrids which he hoped would found a new race to rival the hardy rhododendrons. Some proved to be indeed quite hardy, but ironically they were also found to be excellent forcers and were never much used for their intended pur-pose. In more recent times Indian azaleas were used in breeding by Lionel de Rothschild at Exbury and by B. Y. Morrison at Glenn Dale, USA. Some of the Japanese Satsuki azaleas also have Belgian Indica azaleas in their parentage.

Kurume Azaleas

This numerous race was bred at Kurume, an inland town in Kyushu, which is the southernmost of the four main islands of Japan. The ancestral forms, it is said, were brought early in the 19th century from sacred Mt Kirishima, and from them seedlings were raised and propagated by Motozo Sakamoto. On his death the collection passed to Kijiro Akashi, who developed the race and is said to have raised most of those in cultivation. The azaleas of Mt Kirishima, according to Wilson, are very variable in the size and persistence of their leaves, and also in their flowers, which 'vary a little in size, in degree of fragrance and greatly in colour; the most common shades are rosy mauve to magenta, but salmon and salmon-red are plentiful; pink, scarlet and crimson are rather rare. Plants bearing white flowers are occasionally found'. The two species that grow on the mountain are R. *kiusianum* and R. *kaempferi*, and it is now thought that the polymorphism of the Kirishima azaleas is due to hybridisation between them. Some of the Kurume azaleas show the influence of R. *kaempferi* quite strongly, but others, especially those with white or pale pink flowers, are very different from authentic R. *kiusianum* as grown in this country, yet show no influence of R. *kaempferi*. There appears to be some other element in the race, and it is suggested that this may be R. *sataense* (see further on page 697).

In the 19th century Kurume was remote from the main horticultural centres, and its azaleas were scarcely known, even in Japan itself, but early in this century a few reached Europe through the Yokohama Nursery Company, and others were imported by Dutch nurserymen. Among these were two of the most famous: 'Hinomayo' and 'Hinodegiri'. Apart from these, the Kurumes grown in Britain belong to the 'Wilson Fifty', so called because they were selected from Asahi's collection by the great plant-collector E. H. Wilson when he visited Kurume in 1918. Two sets of these fifty varieties (out of the 250 then grown) were bought by him for the Arnold Arboretum, where they were propagated and further distributed. See further in: Rehder and Wilson, *Monograph of Azaleas* (1921), pp. 34–8; Wilson, *Plant Hunting*, Vol. II, Chap. XLIX; Lee, *The Azalea Book* (1958), pp. 136–42. Wilson gave English names to his Fifty, which are not translations from the Japanese but invented by him. They are rarely used, the Japanese names being more memorable, even if difficult to pronounce correctly.

Wilson considered the Kurumes to be 'the loveliest of all Azaleas'. Yet they are not widely grown, partly because they are supposed to be tender, partly, perhaps, because they have to compete with more garishly coloured, larger-flowered azaleas bred in Europe and America. A few are definitely tender, but these have mostly dropped out of commerce; the rest are hardier than generally supposed, though like many other evergreen azaleas they may suffer damage from frost when young. The flowers are small, but borne in wonderful profusion in late April or May. In several varieties the calyx is petaloid, i.e., converted into a sort of outer corolla, coloured and marked like the true corolla. Although the result of several generations of breeding, they have retained the dense and comparatively dwarf habit of their wild ancestors. They tolerate full sun, and woodland conditions are quite alien to their nature. Nowhere in Britain can Kurume azaleas be seen in greater number than in Windsor Great

Park, where there is an extensive planting in the Valley Gardens and a smaller collection in the Savill Garden.

MODERN HYBRIDS

Until the 1920s, the only evergreen hybrid azaleas suitable for outdoor cultivation in this country had been bred in the gardens of Japan—the only exception being the few hybrids from 'Amoenum' such as those raised by William Carmichael. At the present time, the majority of the hybrids commonest in gardens were sent out by Dutch nurserymen. The most valuable of these were raised by P. M. Koster of Koster and Co. by crossing *R. kaempferi* (seed-parent) with 'Malvaticum' (q.v.) The seedlings were sold in 1921 to C. B. van Nes and Sons, who put them into commerce. They take after *R. kaempferi* in their habit; and also in their foliage, except that the spring leaves mostly have impressed veins, as in the pollen-parent. The flowers of this group range in colour from orange through pink to reddish purple, and are very freely borne in May. Many give brilliant and long-lasting autumn colour. The orange-coloured varieties, such as 'Anny' and 'Alice', unfortunately share with *R. kaempferi* the bad quality of fading rapidly in sunny weather—a tendency that can to some extent be mitigated by growing the plants in light shade. The same is true of 'John Cairns', another Koster hybrid from *R. kaempferi*, the other parent of which is uncertain. This was put into commerce by L. J. Endtz and Co.

The so-called Vuyk hybrids were raised by A. Vuyk, founder of the firm Vuyk van Nes. He raised a number of seedlings from various evergreen azaleas pollinated by the Mollis azalea 'J. C. van Tol'. The offspring show no sign at all of the influence of the latter, and it is now thought that its effect was to induce the seed-parents to set seed apomictically. At any rate, this, rather than self-pollination, is the explanation put forward by H. J. Grootendorst in his work *Rhododendrons en Azalea's*, to which we are indebted for information concerning the Dutch hybrids. The best known of this set are the lovely 'Palestrina', the seed-parent of which was a Malvaticum–Kaempferi hybrid; and 'Beethoven' (seed-parent 'Maxwellii'). For other Vuyk hybrids see 'Prinz Bernhard', 'Vuyk's Scarlet', and 'Vuyk's Rosy Red'.

Lionel de Rothschild made a few crosses between evergreen azaleas, with his usual success. The best known—'Leo', 'Eddy', 'Naomi', and 'Pippa'—are all hybrids of *R. kaempferi* and among the best of their class. It is frequently stated that de Rothschild made much use of the Formosan *R. oldhamii* as a parent, but it is pointed out in *The Rothschild Rhododendrons* that he used it only once, to produce Bengal Fire (q.v.).

The Glenn Dale Azaleas are the result of a massive hybridisation carried out by B. Y. Morrison at the Plant Introduction Station, Glenn Dale, Maryland, USA, between 1935 and 1940. Altogether 70,000 seedlings were raised from crossings between a wide diversity of species and hybrids, and some 450 clones were eventually selected and named (see further the article by Mr Morrison in *R.Y.B. 1951–2*, pp. 14–18; and Lee,

The Azalea Book (1958), pp. 153–4 and 237–76). These hybrids were selected for use in a region with much warmer summers than ours, but several are succeeding well in Britain, and some have received awards after trial at Wisley. The hybrids raised by J. B. Gable, a nurseryman of Stewartstown, Pennsylvania, are also of diverse parentage. For these see Lee, op. cit., pp. 152–3 and 235–7. Of the Gable hybrids 'Rosebud' and 'Stewartstonian' are now well established in Britain.

It is not possible to give more than a selection of the evergreen hybrid azaleas cultivated in Britain, but it is hoped that all those mostly widely available in commerce have been included, to which have been added a few that have shown promise in recent trials at Wisley. The evergreen azaleas are certainly a valuable race, especially for labour-saving gardens, as they lend themselves to thicket-planting, But their winter-foliage is far from decorative for the most part, and their colouring is of limited range. In the following descriptions the number of flowers per truss is not given, as it is nearly always small, from one to four.

DESCRIPTIONS

'ADDY WERY'.—Corolla about 1½ in. wide and long, of a rather hard shade of bronzy red, with deeper speckling in the upper part. Leaves glossy. Compact habit (Kurume azalea 'Suetsumu' × 'Malvaticum'; H. den Ouden, Holland). A.M.T. May 5, 1950.

'ANNY'.—Corolla orange-red, about 2¼ in. wide, faintly speckled. Calyx-lobes about ¼ in. long, mostly obtuse, sometimes acute (R. *kaempferi* × 'Malvaticum'; C.B. van Nes and Son, 1920). 'ALICE', from the same raiser and of the same parentage, is similar, but the colour is indeterminate, the upper part of the corolla being crimson, shading to orange.

'ASA-GASUMI' ('Rosy Morn').—Flowers solitary or in pairs. Corolla 1¼ in. wide, Neyron Rose, scarcely spotted. Calyx petaloid, large, misshapen (Kurume; Wilson No. 14).

'ATALANTA'.—Corolla 2¼ in. wide, near Mallow Purple, but duller than in 'Pippa' (q.v.). Slight coarse, dark speckling on the upper lobe. Style and stamens white. Low growing (R. *kaempferi* × 'Malvaticum'; C. B. van Nes). Inferior to 'Pippa'.

'AZUMA-KAGAMI' ('Pink Pearl').—Corolla 1½ in. wide, pale carmine rose (52D), paling in the throat, with faint speckling. Style and most of stamens malformed, some of the latter slightly petaloid. Calyx large, petaloid, coloured like the corolla. Dense habit (Kurume; Wilson No. 16). There is another azalea in cultivation as 'Azuma-Kagami', which is similar to the plant described but has a more deeply lobed corolla, some of the lobes being almost free. It is also of more open, twiggier habit. The plant described is very hardy and free-flowering.

'BEETHOVEN'.—Corolla 2¾ in. wide, lilac mauve (78B) with faint speckling, lobes undulated but not frilled (Vuyk van Nes; said to be a hybrid of 'Maxwellii'). One of the best purples.

'BENGAL BEAUTY'.—Corolla Neyron Rose with darker speckling, 2 in. wide, margins slightly wavy. Calyx with lobes up to ¼ in. long. Early June. Compact habit (R. *kaempferi* 'Daimio' × R. *simsii*; M. Haworth-Booth). A.M.T. June 3, 1966. Of recent introduction, valuable for its late flowering and holding its colour well. Another clone with flowers in a 'browner' shade of pink has been named 'FINAL BLUSH'.

BENGAL FIRE (*kaempferi* × *oldhamii*)—This hybrid, raised at Exbury, shows the influence of the second parent in its conspicuously hairy young leaves and stems. The flowers are about 1¾ in. wide, and in one clone are dark orange-red, in another lighter and brighter. It is hardy once established and attains about 6 ft.

'BETTY'.—Corolla near Neyron Rose (58C/D) shading to darker along the centre of each lobe, rather narrowly funnel-shaped, about 1⅜ in. wide, with a dark red style and stamen filaments. Calyx-lobes short and broad, obtuse. Upright habit. May. (*kaempferi* × 'Malvaticum'; C. B. van Nes). One of the best pinks in this group. It is sometimes grown under the name 'Kathleen'. What is believed to be the true 'Kathleen' has flowers of a similar but more uniform colour, with slight darker speckling near the base of the centre lobe. The style and filaments are pale pink, and the calyx-lobes are large and spreading, up to ¼ in. long. It belongs to the same group as 'Betty' and is of similar habit.

'BLAAUW'S PINK'.—Flowers hose-in-hose. Corolla 1½ in. wide, salmon-pink (38A) but a little darker at the edge and paling at the centre, with slight spotting. Stamens partly petaloid. Calyx almost as long as corolla and of the same colour (J. Blaauw and Co., 1953).

'CAMPFIRE'.—Flowers hose-in-hose. Corolla bright red (53D), slightly speckled, wavy at the margin, 1¾ in. wide. Calyx almost as large as corolla. Late May. Low, dense habit (Gable, USA). It was sent to the Wisley trials from Holland as "Hino-scarlet" and is described under that name in R.C.Y.B. *1970*, p. 195.

'CHIPPEWA'.—Corolla 2½ in. wide, salmon-pink with a redder blotch on the upper lobes. Late June. Low, spreading habit (a hybrid of R. *indicum*; Bobbink and Atkins, USA).

'EDDY'.—Corolla 2½ in. wide, funnel-shaped from a broad base, with heavy, dark speckling on the upper lobes, margins slightly waved. Stamens nine. Persistent leaves dark green, up to 2 in. long. May. Tall, to about 7 ft (R. *kaempferi* × Indian azalea 'Apollo'; Rothschild). A.M. 1944.

'FAVORITE'.—Corolla 1½ in. wide, vivid crimson-pink, slightly waved at the margin. Bright green, glossy leaves. Early May. Dense habit (R. *kaempferi* × 'Hinodegiri'; C. B. van Nes). Very free-flowering.

'FLORIDA'.—Corolla 2½ in. wide, red shaded vermilion with darker speckling on the upper lobes, semi-double owing to the conversion of the stamens into irregularly shaped mostly large extra lobes. Low growing. Late May (Vuyk van Nes). Bud-tender; flowers ugly in form, but of vivid colour.

'FORSTERIANA'.—Flowers hose-in-hose. Corolla 1¼ in. wide, campanulate, near Currant Red (47B). Style and stamens abnormal. Late May or early June. Low and dense (Otto Forster, Lebenhof, Austria, before 1892). A hybrid of 'Amoenum', hardy but poorly coloured. Mention may be made here of another of Forster's hybrids, the once very common 'HEXE', which is the result of a cross between 'Amoenum' and the Indian azalea 'Duc de Nassau', raised in 1878. Being of dwarf habit and easily raised from cuttings, it was a very popular pot plant early this century, and was also used as a stock for grafting the Indian azaleas. The flowers are hose-in-hose, rosy crimson, 1¾ in. wide. A.M. 1907. The name 'Hexe' has been wrongly used for a quite different azalea, which is vigorous, late-flowering, and has semi-double flowers with a normal calyx.

'FRIEDA'.—Corolla light purple with reddish markings, 1½ in. wide; tube slender. Calyx very small, with obtuse lobes. May. To about 5 ft (a hybrid of R. *kaempferi*; C. B. van Nes, 1952). Very free-flowering.

GUMPO.—The so-called Gumpo azaleas are usually listed under R. *simsii* var. *eriocarpum* (Hayata) Wils. (for which see under R. *indicum*). Whatever may be the status of the wild plants placed under this variety, the Gumpo azaleas, which came from a Japanese nursery, are near to R. *indicum* and are best treated as a horticultural group of uncertain taxonomic position. All are of low, spreading habit, building up to 2 ft or slightly more in height, and mostly differ from typical R. *indicum* in their darker, blunter leaves. In common with that species they flower late, in early June. In 'GUMPO WHITE' the corolla is pure white, frilled, about 2 in wide; stamens five, with brown anthers. 'GUMPO RED', as seen in British gardens, has flesh-pink flowers with darker staining on the upper lobe, not 'salmon rose' as stated in the catalogue of Mr Wada, who distributed these Gumpo azaleas from his Hakoneya Nursery before the second world war. It is possible that this pale pink form is the result of propagating a branch-sport of the original 'Gumpo Red', since a plant has been seen on which one twig bore flowers agreeing with Wada's description. The corollas in 'Gumpo Red', as seen, are waved and frilled, about 2¼ in. wide; stamens five, with dark anthers. The true 'GUMPO FANCY' has not been seen; it was described by Wada as having pink flowers edged with white. 'JITSUGESUSE', another member of this group, has Mallow Purple flowers, speckled on the upper lobe. All the Gumpo azaleas are said to be rather tender.

'HATSUGIRI'.—Corolla about 1 in. wide, magenta-purple. Calyx normal. Leaves dark green, oblanceolate. Low, dense habit, 2 to 3 ft high, much more in width. Late April or early May. A Kurume azalea closely related to 'Amoenum' but with a normal calyx, differing from most Kurumes in its dull darkish green leaves. Very hardy and free-flowering. F.C.C.T. May 12, 1969.

'HINODEGIRI' ('Red Hussar').—Corolla 1 in. or slightly more wide, with a slender tube, bright red (53B), deepening in the throat. Calyx normal. Leaves light glossy green, the upper (persistent) ones obovate, up to ⅝ in. long. Late April or early May. Fairly compact habit, eventually 4 or 5 ft high (Kurume; Wilson No. 42). A.M.T. 1965. One of the best known of the Kurumes, not quite hardy. It had been introduced before Wilson sent it.

'HINOMAYO' (properly 'Hinamoyo').—Flowers solitary or in pairs. Corolla 1¼ in. wide, Phlox Pink, slightly speckled in the throat. Calyx normal. Leaves light glossy green, the upper ones mostly oblanceolate-spatulate. Dense habit, eventually 5 ft high (Kurume). A.M. 1921; Award of Garden Merit 1954. The most popular of the Kurume azaleas and one of the hardiest, already established in gardens before the introduction of the 'Wilson Fifty'. The flowers are of such a clean shade of pink, and produced in such abundance that the effect of a large group growing in full sun is rather overpowering. It is prettier as an individual specimen or small colony, and flowers quite well in dappled shade. It is one of the most deciduous of the Kurumes, regularly shedding most of its summer leaves, at least in colder gardens, but perfectly bud-hardy. For an interesting note on this azalea by K. Wada, see *R.C.Y.B. 1970*, pp. 181–3, where it is pointed out that the correct Japanese name is 'Hinamoyo'.

'IMA-SHOJO' ('Fascination').—Corolla ⅞ in. wide, deep red (Turkey Red); anthers pale, conspicuous. Calyx-segments mostly petaloid, but short and narrow, so the flower is not hose-in-hose. Leaves dark green and glossy, unusually short, even the spring leaves being mostly ¾ in. or less long. Very dense habit (Kurume; Wilson No. 36).

'IROHAYAMA' ('Dainty').—Corolla mauvish pink at the edge, white in the throat, unspeckled or almost so, about 1½ in. wide. Style and filaments white. Calyx normal. Dense habit, up to 5 ft (Kurume; Wilson No. 8). A.M. 1952.

'JOHN CAIRNS'.—Corolla 1¾ to 2 in. wide, deep brownish scarlet with darker speckling on the upper lobes. Leaves colouring well in the autumn, the persistent ones deep bronze throughout the winter. Dense habit to about 5 ft high and wide (*R. kaempferi* hybrid; L. J. Endtz and Co.). Award of Garden Merit 1952.

'KIMIGAYO' ('Cherub').—Corolla tubular-campanulate, 1 to 1½ in. wide, Phlox Pink, white in the throat. Dwarf (Kurume; Wilson No. 15). A.M.T. 1952.

'KIRIN' ('Daybreak').—Corolla 1¼ in. long, with deep, oblong lobes, silvery pink (55B), darker outside. Calyx petaloid, with laciniated lobes, coloured like the outside of the corolla (Kurume; Wilson No. 22, but introduced earlier). One of the prettiest of the Kurumes but not quite hardy. It is sometimes sold by florists in late winter as a pot-plant.

'KIRITSUBO' ('Twilight').—Corolla light rosy mauve, deeper at the edges, about ½ in. wide, with a long tube. Calyx normal in some flowers, in others partly petaloid. Dense habit (Kurume; Wilson No. 24).

'KORAN-YUKI'.—Corolla 1¼ to 1½ in. wide, with a short slender tube abruptly widening into the limb, scarlet. Stamens and style long-exserted. Calyx variable, partly petaloid. Dense twiggy habit. Of the Kurume type, introduced from Japan to the Tower Court collection.

'KURE-NO-YUKI' ('Snowflake').—Corolla 1½ in. wide, white with a faint greenish flare. Calyx petaloid, white, lobes mostly strap-shaped, almost as long as corolla. Compact, dwarf habit (Kurume; Wilson No. 2). Very hardy and free-flowering. A.M.T. 1952.

'LEO'.—Corolla orange-pink (41B/C), 1½ in. wide, with slight purple spotting on the upper lobes. Upper leaves obovate, rounded and mucronate at the apex. Low spreading habit. Late May or early June. A pleasingly coloured hardy, very free-flowering azalea, raised at Exbury.

'MALVATICUM'.—This azalea was found by the Dutch firm of Koster and Co. in a consignment of 'Hinodegiri' received from Japan early this century. It had large, mauve flowers with seven to nine stamens, and was probably a hybrid of 'Hinodegiri' (or possibly of R. *kaempferi*), the other parent almost certainly being some form of Mucronatum. It proved to be very hardy, and was used as a parent in breeding the large race of Malvaticum–Kaempferi hybrids (see page 924). It is doubtful whether what is in commerce as 'Malvaticum' is really the true clone.

'MARIE'.—Corolla 2½ to 2¾ in. wide, vivid cerise-pink. Calyx petaloid, coloured like the corolla, but some lobes green at the edge. Leaves rather thick. Erect habit, to about 6 ft. May (R. *kaempferi* × dark red Indian azalea; Rothschild). A very striking but rather tender azalea. 'LOUISE' is of the same parentage and said to be somewhat hardier. It has bright red flowers, and received an Award of Merit in 1939.

'MARTHA HITCHCOCK'.—Corolla 2½ to 3 in. wide, slightly frilled, white with a margin of magenta, self-coloured on strong shoots, speckled with reddish brown on the upper lobes. Leaves dull, dark green. Late May or early June. Low spreading habit, to about 4 ft high (Mucronatum × 'Shinnyo-no-tsuki'; Glenn Dale, USA). A.M.T. June 1, 1972. Lee, *The Azalea Book*, plates VI and 51. The second parent of this hybrid derives partly from R. *indicum*, partly from R. *simsii* (through 'Elizabeth', one of the many sports of the famous Indian azalea 'Vervaeneana').

'MAXWELLII'.—Corolla funnel-shaped, 2¾ in. wide, 2 in. long, Rose Bengal (57C) with heavy brown speckling on the upper lobes. Calyx-lobes awl-shaped, spreading, ⅝ in. long, acute. Leaves rather thin, hairy on both sides, up to 2 in. long. Late May. Low-growing. It is a plant of Japanese gardens, introduced early this century. See further under 'Phoeniceum'.

'MOTHER'S DAY'.—Corolla 2¼ in. wide, with overlapping lobes, crimson (53B), speckled near the bases of the upper lobes. Calyx green with obtuse lobes. Stamens seven, petaloid in some flowers or with petaloid excrescences at the tip. Leaves glossy darkish green, bronze-tinted in winter, broad-elliptic, obtuse, up to 1 in. long or slightly more on strong shoots. Late May. Low spreading habit (Auguste van Hecke, Belgium). F.C.C.T. May 27, 1970.

'MRS CARMICHAEL'.—This azalea, which received a First Class Certificate in 1877, was one of the hybrids from 'Amoenum' raised by William Carmichael (1815–1904), who was trained in the Edinburgh Botanic Garden under William M'Nab and served as head gardener to the Prince of Wales at Sandringham 1863–73. They were distributed by B. S. Williams of Holloway. 'Mrs Carmichael', the other parent of which was the Indian (greenhouse) azalea 'Stella', has deep purplish-rose flowers with a darker blotch, and is half-hardy (Millais). It seems to have dropped out of cultivation in this country, but is a parent of some of the American Glenn Dale hybrids.

MUCRONATUM.—Flowers solitary, in twos or threes; pedicels hairy, sometimes slightly glandular. Corolla widely funnel-shaped, 2½ in. wide, white. Stamens eight to ten. Ovary with long, straggly hairs. Calyx-lobes lanceolate, up to about ⅜ in. long. Spring leaves deciduous, dull green, rather thin, ovate-lanceolate to lanceolate, 1 to 2½ in. long, ⅜ to ¾ in. wide, hairy on both surfaces;

summer leaves smaller, thicker, persistent. May. A spreading shrub, usually seen under 4 ft high, but attaining 10 ft in the milder parts.

Mucronatum is a plant of Japanese gardens, also cultivated in China, whence it reached Britain in 1819. Under the names *Azalea indica alba* or *A. ledifolia* it was cultivated as a pot-plant in the last century but gradually spread into the open garden once it was found to be hardy. When Millais published the first volume of his work on rhododendrons (1917) Mucronatum was still a scarce plant out-of-doors, but was grown in quantity at Leonardslee and South Lodge, as well as in the south-west (where Sir Charles Lemon of Carclew was growing it outside as early as the 1830s). It is quite hardy, stands full sun, and is very pretty at the end of May when covered with its pure white fragrant flowers. In the 1840s and 1850s other white-flowered varieties were raised from it, but there seems to be little doubt that what is grown as ordinary *R. mucronatum* in this country is the original 'Indica Alba' of greenhouses, which later became known as 'Old White'. See further on p. 921.

The taxonomic status of Mucronatum is a controversial matter. Wilson considered it to be no more than a white-flowered form of R. *ripense*, and accordingly treated it as a species, under which he placed the wild prototype as a variety— R. *mucronatum* var. *ripense* (Makino) Wils. But H. Hara the Japanese authority considers that Mucronatum is part of a garden swarm deriving from R. *ripense* and R. *macrosepalum*, and in some degree from R. *scabrum* and R. *kaempferi* also (*R.Y.B. 1948*, pp. 122–4). However, what is grown in this country as R. *mucronatum* is certainly very near to R. *ripense*, but apparently some forms cultivated in Japan show the influence of R. *macrosepalum* quite strongly. The cultivar-name Mucronatum should therefore probably be regarded as indicating a group of horticulturally similar clones, differing slightly from each other in their botanical characters. The botanical synonymy of Mucronatum is: R. *mucronatum* (Bl.) G. Don; *Azalea mucronata* Blume; *Azalea ledifolia* Hook.; R. *ledifolium* (Hook.) G. Don; *Azalea indica* var. *alba* Lindl.; *Azalea rosmarinifolia* Burmann; R. *rosmarinifolium* (Burmann) Dipp., not Vidal.

Two named clones in the Mucronatum group are 'NOORDTIANUM' and 'BULSTRODE'. The former was introduced to Belgium towards the end of the last century. It has larger flowers and leaves than ordinary Mucronatum and narrow, acute calyx-lobes ¾ in. long. For further details, see K. Wade's note in *R.C.Y.B. 1968*, pp. 144–5. 'Bulstrode' was received by the Sunningdale Nurseries from Bulstrode Park as 'Oomurasaki', which clearly it is not (J. Russell, *Journ. R.H.S.*, Vol. 74, p. 148). The flowers are large, beautifully shaped, and have a slight yellow-green eye. For the true 'Oomurasaki', see under 'Phoeniceum'.

Other members of this group are 'LILACINUM', with mauve flowers; 'FUJIMANYO', with rosy-purple double or semi-double flowers (R. *mucronatum* f. *plenum* (Sims) Wils.); and 'SHIROMANYO' (R. *mucronatum* f. *narcissiflorum* (Planch.) Wils.), with double white flowers. The two double forms were introduced to cultivation in the last century, and are mentioned by Millais (1917) as being grown out-of-doors in this country, but seem to have dropped out of commerce.

For another member of the Mucronatum group, see 'Sekidera'.

'NAOMI'.—Corolla 2¼ in .wide, soft salmon-pink, paler in the centre, slightly speckled with red on the upper lobes. Open habit, to 5 or 6 ft eventually. Late

May or early June. A hybrid of R. *kaempferi* raised at Exbury. It is quite hardy, with flowers of an unusual and attractive colour.

'ORANGE BEAUTY'.—Corolla 1½ to 1¾ in. wide, slightly frilled, soft scarlet (43C), speckled on the upper lobes. Leaves glossy, light green. Low bushy habit, rarely more than 3 ft high but more in width. Late April or early May (R. *kaempferi* × 'Hinodegiri'; C. B. van Nes). F.C.C.T. 1958. A well-known and valuable azalea, flowering unfailingly. It is best in slight shade as the flowers fade rather quickly in hot sunny weather.

'PALESTRINA'.—Corolla white, about 2 in. wide, with green markings at the base of the three upper lobes. Spring leaves bright green, up to 2 in. long, with impressed veins; persistent leaves darker, up to 1 in. long. An erect shrub, building up to a conical bush about 4 ft high, very free-flowering in May. It was raised in Holland from a Malvaticum–Kaempferi hybrid and shows strongly the influence of Mucronatum, which is one of the parents of 'Malvaticum'. It is puzzling that there is another clone grown under the name 'Palestrina' which has somewhat smaller flowers with less conspicuous markings, shorter leaves and a horizontal habit. There is also a difference in botanical characters. The flowers of the plant described above have seven or eight stamens and a hairy style; in the horizontal, small-leaved plant, which is nearer to R. *kaempferi*, the stamens number five and the style is glabrous. The latter, at least in a cold garden, is much the finer of the two, being more floriferous, a better grower and with neater, brighter green winter foliage.

'PHOENICEUM'.—This azalea with reddish-purple flowers, now only of historical interest, was introduced to Britain in 1824, and was at one time much used as a stock for grafting the Indian azaleas, also, to some extent, as a parent in their breeding. Its taxonomic status is uncertain, but Wilson considered it to be either a form of R. *scabrum*, a native of the Ryukyus, or a hybrid between it and R. *mucronatum* (which he regarded as a good species). The botanical name R. *phoeniceum* was first published by G. Don in 1834, but two years earlier an azalea raised by William Smith of Norbiton and said to be a hybrid of 'Phoeniceum', had been named R. *pulchrum* by Sweet. Wilson considered this to be not a hybrid but simply a seedling variant of 'Phoeniceum', and in consequence the name R. *pulchrum* Sweet has been used for this 'species'. But no useful purpose is served, either botanical or horticultural, in subjecting these complex garden productions to orthodox taxonomic treatment. R. *scabrum*, R. *macrosepalum*, and R. *ripense* have been cultivated in Japanese gardens for several centuries and have given rise to a swarm of hybrids and forms of which 'Phoeniceum' and similar azaleas are a part. For clones usually placed under R. *pulchrum* see 'Maxwellii' and 'Tebotan'. Another member of this group is 'OOMURASAKI', with large, rosy purple flowers heavily spotted on the upper lobes (R. *pulchrum* var. *calycinum* (Lindl.) Rehd.). This was introduced by Fortune from China, and again later from Japan, but is apparently not in commerce at the present time.

'PIPPA'.—Corolla Petunia Purple, slightly speckled on the upper lobes, 2½ in. wide, with rather narrow lobes. Stamens eight, their filaments coloured like the corolla. Style reddish. Mid-May. Low, spreading, open habit. A beautiful azalea, raised by Lionel de Rothschild, obviously deriving partly from R. *kaempferi*; as in some other hybrids of this species the tube is translucent, giving a yellow glow to the centre of the flowers and brightening its colour. 'Pippa' also shows the influence of Mucronatum, especially in its foliage. R. *oldhamii* does not enter into its parentage, as erroneously stated in the International Register. It is superior to 'Atalanta', which differs in its slightly deeper less pure colouring, white style and filaments, and mostly five stamens; also in its denser habit.

'PORT KNAP'.—Corolla ¾ to ⅞ in. wide, with a short tube and spreading limb, Phlox Purple. Early May. Low, spreading habit. Raised at the Knap Hill Nursery. A.M.T. May 13, 1958. It is near to R. *kiusianum*.

'PRINS BERNHARD'.—Corolla 2 in. wide, Geranium Lake, slightly speckled with brown on the upper lobes. Low spreading habit. May (Vuyk van Nes). Others from the same raiser and of similar type are: 'PRINSES JULIANA', with soft orange flowers in late May or early June, low growing; and 'KONINGIN WILHELMINA', vermilion red.

'PURPLE TRIUMPH'.—Corolla 2¼ in. wide, slightly waved at the margin, Cyclamen Purple. Spreading habit. May (Vuyk van Nes).

'RASHOMON' ('Meteor').—Corolla 1¼ in. wide with a short tube, scarlet. Calyx well developed, with oblong, obtuse lobes. Dense habit, eventually 5 ft high (Kurume; Wilson No. 37).

'ROSEBUD'.—Corolla 1¾ in. wide, Phlox Pink (62B), double, most of the stamens being converted into petals or staminodes. Calyx enlarged, up to ⅝ in. deep, green, or partly or wholly coloured like the corolla. Late May or early June. Spreading habit, ultimate height uncertain (Gable, USA). A charming azalea with truly double flowers, after the style of R. *indicum* 'Balsaminiflorum'. A.M.T. 1972. 'LORNA', from the same raiser and of the same parentage, is similar. The two parents, both Gable hybrids not commonly available in this country, involve between them five species.

'SAOTOME' ('Peachblossom').—Corolla rosy pink (55C), 1¼ in. wide, tube ½ in. long. Anthers maroon-crimson. Style green (Kurume; Wilson No. 21).

'SEKIDERA'.—Corolla 3 in. wide, funnel-shaped, pure white and light purple speckling on the upper lobes. Stamens seven or eight. Calyx-lobes up to 1 in. long, acute; pedicels and edge of calyx-lobes glandular. Low, spreading habit. May. A lovely azalea, not completely hardy. It belongs to the same complex of Japanese garden hybrids as Mucronatum, but is near to R. *macrosepalum*.

'SHIN-SEKAI' ('Old Ivory').—Corolla 1 in. wide with a slender tube ½ in. long, and narrow, spreading lobes, creamy white, tube deeper coloured. Style contorted. Calyx irregularly petaloid. Dwarf and compact (Kurume; Wilson No. 3, but introduced earlier). A.M. 1921; A.M.T. 1952. Hardy.

'SILVER MOON'.—Corolla 2½ in. wide, white faintly spotted with yellowish green on the upper lobes, slightly waved at the margins. Compact habit, attaining probably 4 ft or so in height. Early June, A.M.T. 1973. A promising azalea of recent introduction, flowering later than the white Mucronatum and 'Palestrina'. It is one of the many clones raised at Glenn Dale, USA, from a complex cross: (Mucronatum 'Lilacinum' × 'Willy') × ('Mrs Carmichael' × 'Willy').

Another white of the same parentage, also late-flowering but of lower more spreading habit, is 'SWANSONG', A.M.T. 1972.

SIR WILLIAM LAWRENCE.—This name was given by Lionel de Rothschild, apparently as a grex-name, to hybrids raised by him from R. *kaempferi* crossed with 'Hinodegiri' (the cross which, in Holland, produced 'Orange Beauty'). What is usually offered by nurserymen as 'Sir William Lawrence' has flat-faced flowers of a pale shade of Rose Bengal, becoming whiter and translucent at the centre, quite unspotted, 2 in. or slightly more wide, opening in early June. This azalea cannot be of the parentage given for Sir William Lawrence, but presumably came from Exbury originally. It is possibly a hybrid of R. *simsii*. The plant that received an Award of Merit in 1958 as 'Sir William Lawrence' after trial at Wisley has pink flowers with maroon spotting, produced around mid-May.

'SPLENDENS'.—Corolla 1 to 1½ in. wide, funnel-shaped with a narrow tube, deep rosy pink with a redder centre. Calyx normal. Low, spreading habit. Late May or early June. A hybrid between 'Amoenum' and some form of R. *indicum*, free-flowering and quite pretty. Something very like it is in commerce under the incorrect name 'Caldwellii'. The type 'Caldwellii' had hose-in-hose flowers.

'STEWARTSTONIAN'.—Corolla 1½ in. wide, deep brownish red (47A), slightly darker in the throat. Stamen-filaments and style red, the latter long-exserted. Leaves glossy, the upper ones obovate to almost rounded, bronze in winter. May. Rather like 'Addy Wery'. Raised by J. B. Gable, Stewartstown, USA, whence the name, which is often wrongly given as "Stewartsoniana".

'SUGA-NO-ITO' ('Betty').—Corolla 1½ to 1¾ in. wide, soft shell-pink, paler in the throat with six pale reddish-brown speckles on the upper lobes. Calyx-lobes elongate and partly petaloid (Kurume; Wilson No. 31). Hardy. According to Lee (*The Azalea Book*, p. 139), the correct name for this azalea is 'Kumo-no-ito'.

'TAKASAGO' ('Cherryblossom').—Corolla 1¼ in. wide, light shell-pink, slightly deeper at the edge, with pale crimson speckling on the upper lobes. Calyx irregularly petaloid, coloured like the corolla. Not quite hardy (Kurume; Wilson No. 11).

'TEBOTAN'.—Corolla double, Mallow Purple, with about eleven segments and a denser cluster of tiny green leaves at the centre. Allied to 'Phoeniceum', it has long been cultivated in Japanese gardens, and could be looked on as the counterpart among azaleas of the cherry 'Fugenzo'. It is said to be rare in Japan, but in 1919 Wilson obtained a plant for the famous Holm Lea collection in Massachusetts (*Gard. Chron.*, Vol. 73 (1923), p. 255). According to him the azalea that used to be sold by Japanese nurserymen as 'Tebotan' is really 'Fujimanyo' (q.v. under Mucronatum). The true 'Tebotan' is cultivated in the Savill Garden and received an Award of Merit when shown by the Crown Estate Commissioners on May 21, 1962. Unfortunately the name 'Tebotan' was altered to 'Violet Cloud' in *Journ. R.H.S.*, Vol. 87, p. 521, but is perfectly valid as a cultivar-name.

'UKAMUSE' ('Princess Delight').—Corolla 1½ in. or slightly more wide, salmon-pink, paler in the throat, with darker speckling on the upper lobes.

Calyx irregularly petaloid. Stamen-filaments and style white (Kurume; Wilson No. 47). Hardy.

'VIDA BROWN'.—Flowers mostly solitary. Corolla 1¾ in. wide, crimson, with a large petaloid calyx. Low, spreading habit. Late May or early June. Raised by C. E. Brown and put into commerce by Messrs Stewart, Ferndown, Dorset. A.M.T. 1960.

'VUYK'S ROSY RED'.—Corolla 2¾ to 3 in. across, widely funnel-shaped from a broad base, Neyron Rose, with a brighter red flush in the throat and on the outside, slightly speckled on the upper lobes. Stamens eight or nine, their filaments pink. Style red. Low growing. Late May or early June. (Vuyk van Nes, 1954.) A.M.T. May 31, 1962. Crossed with an unnamed seedling, this has produced 'MAHLER', with Petunia Purple flowers speckled on the upper lobes, borne in the first half of June.

'VUYK'S SCARLET'.—Flowers solitary or in pairs. Corolla funnel-shaped from a broad base, of firm texture, lobes frilled, overlapping, bright crimson (not scarlet), with some darker spotting in the upper part. Low, spreading habit. Early May (Vuyk van Nes, 1954). One of the best and most reliable of the ever-green azaleas. F.C.C.T. May 10, 1966.

'WILLY'.—Corolla 2¼ in. or slightly more wide, clear rosy pink. Style yellow-ish white, reddish at the tip. Calyx-lobes relatively broad, obtuse or rounded at the apex, glossy. Leaves mostly deciduous, in some years turning bright red before they fall; the persistent ones bronze in winter. It makes a fairly dwarf flat-topped bush, usually not more than 4 ft high. Mid-May (R. *kaempferi* × 'Malvaticum'; C. B. van Nes). Very hardy and free-flowering, the best of its group for cold gardens.

There are several other Malvaticum–Kaempferi hybrids similar to 'Willy' in colour, and, for the average garden, just as good, e.g., 'FEDORA' (F.C.C.T. 1960), 'JEANETTE' (A.M.T. 1948), 'HENRIETTE', and 'IVETTE'. The last-named is easily distinguished by its calyx, some of whose lobes are very long and partly petaloid. But many others of the same colouring were distributed and could no doubt still be found. See also 'Betty'.

ADDITIONAL NOTES

THE WATERERS*

In the year 1723 Thomas Waterer of Woking came to live in Knap Hill where he became tenant of a copyhold property known as Ryde Heron. It is not yet known how and when his descendants took to horticulture. We do know, however, that his grandson Michael Waterer I (1745–1827) inherited the property in 1794, that his tenancy was confirmed in 1796 and that in that year he was described as a nurseryman of Woking. The first Michael Waterer founded the Knap Hill Nursery and today the office of the present company is situated a mere three or four hundred yards from Ryde Heron.

During his lifetime, about the year 1810 and possibly earlier, rhododendrons were growing in the Nursery and it is recorded that seedlings were raised from

* Contributed by Mr Donald Waterer.

a cross between R. *catawbiense* and a deep rose-coloured R. *maximum*. An aged specimen, traditionally the 'old original' R. *catawbiense* of 1810, is still living in the Nursery today. If the elder Michael was responsible for this cross, it was his eldest son, Michael Waterer II (1770–1842), who took the seedlings under his wing, cared for them and thereby founded the 'Waterer Hybrid Rhododendrons'.

Having managed the Knap Hill Nursery for some years, the younger Michael became in January 1809 his father's 'co-partner in the art and mystery of a nurseryman'. He came into full control of the Nursery on the death of his father in 1827 and was able to immerse himself in the production of hybrid rhododendrons and azaleas. The *Gardeners' Magazine* wrote in 1834, 'The stock of standard Rhododendrons is most valuable, and we are persuaded that if a number of them were taken up and put into baskets or tubs and exposed for sale in London, they would be eagerly purchased by the possessors of small gardens. Since this was written Mr Waterer has adopted this idea and has sent some most splendid specimens of Kalmia latifolia to the Horticultural Society's Show at Chiswick Garden for which he obtained a Silver Medal on the 10th. June.' Michael had in fact already shown azaleas and rhododendrons in Regent Street in 1832 and on two other occasions at the Horticultural Society's Garden in 1834.

In 1841 he held his first private exhibition in the King's Road, Chelsea, with all the success foreseen by the *Gardeners' Magazine*. In November 1842 he was a victim of the cholera epidemic. In the spring of that year his hybrid rhododendrons and azaleas had been praised highly both at his Knap Hill Nursery and at his second private exhibition in the King's Road, Chelsea. In 1829, aware no doubt of the rapidly increasing importance of the main road from London to Portsmouth and Exeter, he had bought the late John Taylor's Nursery at Bagshot. This property he left to his brother John Waterer I (1784–1868). His Knap Hill Nursery he left to his youngest brother Hosea Waterer I (1793–1853).

There was a brief attempt by the brothers John and Hosea to work together. This was short-lived. John Waterer I had a Nursery in the King's Road, Chelsea, as well as at Bagshot. In the spring of 1843 he held a private exhibition at his King's Road Nursery while, more or less at the same time, Hosea Waterer held the third private exhibition from Knap Hill, also in the King's Road. Both displays were highly praised.

During the years 1844–6 no Waterer exhibitions were reported in the King's Road and it may be assumed that this was a period of dichotomy in which the Bagshot firm was acquiring individuality. Both firms were among the earliest exhibitors at the Botanic Garden in Regent's Park and continued to show there for very many years. In 1847 Hosea Waterer returned to the King's Road and the *Pictorial Times* had an illustration of his large marquee with paths and beds filled with rhododendrons and azaleas.

In 1850 the *Gardeners' Chronicle* reported, 'The Woking and Bagshot American plants are the world's wonder. The marvellous exhibitons made by Mr. Hosea Waterer and the Bagshot growers have excited much curiosity as to the where and how such results are attained.' It referred also to 'Mr. Hosea Waterer, the greatest of these cultivators'.

Hosea was a protagonist of the truly hardy, late-flowering hybrid rhododendrons. In 1851 he maintained that nine-tenths of the so-called hardy hybrids of that time were early bloomers. 'Hence,' he complained, 'the disappointment which we in common with many others witness nearly every spring.' In the 1860s it was observed that Dean Herbert and Henry Burn, having crossed R. *arboreum* with R. *catawbiense* and other late-flowering kinds, had unfortunately used R. *arboreum* as the female parent. The progeny of these crosses had flowered too early. Hosea Waterer had crossed R. *arboreum* with R. *catawbiense*, using the latter as the female parent and with the result that the seedlings had flowered later at a time when spring frost was not likely to be seriously damaging. 'The whole race at Knap Hill and Bagshot,' it was maintained, 'have sprung from this judicious crossing which, in a commercial point of view, has evidently been most satisfactory.'

John Waterer shared his brother's views and it is to him that we owe R. 'Lady Eleanor Cathcart', 'Mrs John Waterer', and 'Joseph Whitworth', all of which are still in commerce.

In 1853 Hosea Waterer I died leaving the Knap Hill Nursery to his nephews Anthony Waterer I (1822–96), son of his auctioneer brother James of Chertsey and Robert Godfrey, son of his sister Elizabeth. These two men had already been working in the Nursery for some years. The partners presented in 1856 an exhibition of their plants at Ashburnham House in connection with Cremorne Gardens. The tent was 365 ft long and 95 ft wide. The private view was attended by members of the Royal Family. There was a raised platform at one end of the tent and 'wander where we will we are never beyond the sound of music both vocal and instrumental'. Presumably this was the event which gave rise to a rumour many years later that the Chelsea Flower Show had its origins in the Waterer Shows.

In 1861 Waterer and Godfrey were crossing hardy Azaleas with 'the best orange-yellow Chinese sort'. The seedlings had large flowers with great richness and variety of colour. Thus were laid the foundations of the Knap Hill Strain of azaleas into which, a few years later, the blood of R. *occidentale* was introduced.

This splendid partnership lasted until 1867 when Robert Godfrey, suffering from ill health, withdrew from the firm and Anthony became sole proprietor. John Waterer I of Bagshot died in 1868 having increased the size of his Nursery from 30 acres to more than 200. He was the last of the three remarkable brothers, pioneers and men of vision. It was unfortunate that, in attempting to dispose of his property fairly among his four sons, he gave insufficient thought to the fact that a large part of his fortune lay in real estate and that, as a result, dissension arose among his sons culminating in a famous case at law, Waterer-*v.*-Waterer.

His third son, John Waterer II (1826–93), determined to maintain the Bagshot Nursery as a family concern, was obliged to raise a very large mortgage which was not redeemed in his lifetime. In spite of this burden he produced a large number of successful hybrid rhododendrons, among them R. 'Gomer Waterer' and R. 'Pink Pearl', to this day the most renowned of all rhododendrons. Some doubt has been expressed that he was in fact the raiser. Among the papers of his son, Gomer Waterer, there is this note. 'My father raised this plant and I always understood him to say it was a seedling from R. George Hardy crossed with R. Broughtonii, but as in those days they did not make a note of the crosses they made, I do not guarantee this as accurate. What I do know definitely is that he raised it.' During the 1950s his grandson was shown an old rhododendron at Littleworth raised by Mangles and reputed to be the 'original' Pink Pearl, but this was not the famous Pink Pearl of commerce.

At Knap Hill the years 1860–90 saw the production of many splendid hybrid rhododendrons and it is remarkable how many of them are still leading varieties today. Anthony Waterer I admired the blotched or spotted upper petal inherited mainly from R. *maximum* which, in his opinion, gave form and substance to the flower. His younger son Hosea Waterer II (1852–1927) emigrated to America and settled in Philadelphia and it was no doubt with his help that Anthony was able to ship 1,500 hybrid rhododendrons to America and to exhibit them in flower at the Centennial Exhibition of 1876 in Philadelphia. The success of this exhibit was such that a spark of interest in rhododendrons in the USA was fanned into flames. The plants were bought by Professor Charles Sargent, a staunch friend of the family, and by H. H. Hunnewell and were planted at Brookline, Mass., and Wellesley, Mass. Anthony had selected mainly hybrids of R. *catawbiense* for this venture. These were the first of a series of 'iron-clad' hybrids which he raised primarily for the American market, and which were likely in his opinion to withstand the rigours of winter in the Eastern States. Several of them were named for members of Professor Sargent's family.

The hybridising of azaleas which had started at Knap Hill in the 1820s was carried out with great success by Anthony Waterer I. Thousands of seedlings were raised year after year from which selections and fresh crossings were made. Having seen a seedling flower and having assessed its merit his interest in it ceased. He was concerned with the constant improvement of his strain of seedlings and consequently very few of his azaleas were named and vegetatively propagated.

During the second half of the 19th century the standard of cultivation in both the Knap Hill and Bagshot Nurseries was extremely high. Meticulous attention was paid to land drainage, to soil fertility, and to the eradication of disease. The Waterers of those days were firm believers in the principle, 'If thine eye offend thee, pluck it out.' Eagle-eyed, they were quick to perceive and to burn any plant which was 'not right'. They were blessed with a plentiful supply of devoted labour which supported their endeavours with loyalty and skill. The high degree of skill and concentration was remembered with envy and wonder in later years. Not the least of their blessings were armies of women for whom flower-picking in June was one of the year's greatest pleasures. The two Nurseries were visited annually by thousands of people from all parts of the world and great efforts were made to exhibit in many parts of England as well as in London rhododendrons and azaleas brought to perfection in flower and foliage.

When John Waterer II died in 1893 it was learned that the Bagshot Nursery had become a Limited Company. His sons John Waterer III (1865–1948) and Gomer Waterer (1867–1945) were appointed managers. A career in the army for Gomer Waterer had been thwarted by a threat of blindness. He left Wellington prematurely and received successful treatment for his eyes in Weimar. In order to boost the trade of the Bagshot firm he had paid the first of many successful visits to the USA in 1892. A year later he transported about 50 rhododendrons, 7 to 9 ft tall, and 150 smaller ones to the Andorra Nursery in Philadelphia where he supervised their preparation for the Chicago Exhibition.

Azaleas did not interest him particularly. He was governed by great enthusiasm for the breeding and cultivation of hardy hybrid rhododendrons and many of his hybrids are in constant demand today. If his suspicion of the hardiness of some 'modern' hybrids seemed excessive, it should be remembered that he was nurtured in the tradition of Hosea Waterer I for whom any hybrid rhododendron which flowered at a time when spring frost would ruin its flowers with monotonous regularity was a 'so-called Hardy Hybrid'. This was a tradition which has helped so many of the Waterer hybrids to survive with flying colours into the second half of the 20th century.

Gomer Waterer was a talented showman and to him must be given the credit for launching Pink Pearl in 1897 and for having made it a best-seller by 1902. His efforts to bring increased trade to the Bagshot Nursery were successful but unfortunately the spectre of his grandfather's will remained to haunt him. In 1914 the Bagshot Nursery ceased to be a family business. His interest in rhododendrons continued at Bagshot in collaboration with Percy Wiseman until 1931 and thereafter at Knap Hill with Robert Jenkinson and Frank Knight. He died at Knap Hill in 1945.

Anthony Waterer II meanwhile was improving his strain of azaleas and his hybrid rhododendrons were remarkable. The latter were stamped with extraordinary individuality. He admired the work of the Moser family at Versailles and was a frequent visitor to their Nursery. It may well be that some of Anthony's hybrids owe part of their individuality to material obtained from that great firm and to ideas formulated on French soil. Today the two Anthonys, father and son, are remembered as a composite personality—'Old Anthony'. Frederick Street has referred to the 'collective anonymity' of the Waterers and, indeed, there is no hard-and-fast line between the work of one generation and the next.

Anthony Waterer II was a bachelor. When he died in 1924 Hosea Waterer II inherited Knap Hill and returned from America to manage it. He showed some of his brother's named Knap Hill azaleas and rhododendrons at the Royal Horticultural Hall in 1926. He died the following year and his American sons sold the business to the present Knap Hill Nursery Ltd in 1931.

STANDISH AND NOBLE

The firm of Standish and Noble is often mentioned in connection with the Hardy Hybrids, though only one—'Cynthia'—has retained its popularity and even that is not characteristic of the group. The senior partner—John Standish—was a Yorkshireman, born in 1814. He served his garden apprenticeship at Bowood, Wilts, where his father was forester to the Marquess of Lansdowne, and later became foreman at Bagshot Park under Andrew Toward. Some time in the 1830s he set up his own nursery at Bagshot and became known as a breeder of calceolarias. Other groups in which he made crosses at some time or another in his career, apart from rhododendrons, were clematis, gladioli, phlox, peas, and grape-vines. But the hybrid that first brought him fame, and really launched him on his career, was his cross between *Fuchsia* 'Globosa' and *F. fulgens*, the latter being a species of recent introduction whose taxonomic status as a member of the genus *Fuchsia* had been disputed by some botanists. Through this cross he made the acquaintance of the great John Lindley, the leading horticultural botanist of his day, and the two became friends.

Charles Noble entered into partnership with Standish in 1847, but unfortunately nothing can be ascertained about his early life. In the following year Robert Fortune set out for China on an expedition the primary purpose of which was to introduce the tea-plant to India, but it was arranged, probably through Lindley's influence, that Standish and Noble should handle Fortune's sendings of ornamental trees and shrubs—a remarkable *coup*, considering that Standish was then aged only thirty-four and Charles Noble probably even younger. Two azaleas were sent to them by Fortune—the famous 'Amoenum' and R. *indicum* 'Crispiflorum', but the richest fruits belonged to other genera (*Clematis lanuginosa*, *Mahonia bealei*, *Skimmia reevesiana*, etc.).

In 1850, these two young men published an interesting note on the hybridisation of rhododendrons, which gives the parentage of several of their crosses— or rather of Standish's crosses, for most of the work must have been done by him much earlier, probably starting while he was still at Bagshot Park. The remarkable range of woody plants that they were able to offer is shown by their advertisement in the *Gardeners' Chronicle* for September 10, 1853 (pp. 578–9). This includes, among the rhododendrons, many hybrids raised by the firm, none of which has survived in commerce. Of more interest is the offer of plants raised from the seed that Hooker had sent from Sikkim three years previously; twenty-four Sikkim rhododendrons could be bought for from five to ten guineas the set.

The Standish and Noble partnership lasted only ten years—'two suns could not shine in the same horizon' is said to have been Standish's explanation for the breach. The dissolution took place in the autumn of 1856, and shortly afterwards Noble announced that he was setting up a nursery of his own near Sunningdale station—the present Sunningdale Nurseries. Standish retained the Bagshot nursery until 1864, but a few years previously he had acquired 80 acres of barren land near Ascot, where he set up a completely new establishment—the Royal Nurseries of John Standish and Co. The new nursery was still in preparation when he staged his famous exhibit at the R.H.S. Show on June 5–6, 1861, of the plants sent to him by Fortune from Japan. They had arrived only a few days previously, but 'were as fresh and healthy-looking as though they had all their lives been revelling in the pure air of Bagshot, and had never known the discomforts of a long sea voyage'. The plants included *Sciadopitys verticillata* and the normal green-leaved *Aucuba japonica* in both its male and female forms. After his removal to Ascot, Standish put out the rhododendron hybrid 'Ascot Brilliant', still common in cultivation. There are also some white-flowered hybrids of R. *griffithianum* in gardens under the name 'Standishii' which were probably raised by him at Ascot. He died in 1875, and most of the information given here comes from the obituaries published in the horticultural press, and from various notes, announcements, and advertisements in the *Gardeners' Chronicle* for the years 1846–64. Little is known of Charles Noble's career after he left Standish, but he carried on a large and successful business at Sunningdale and retired in 1898. Like many other nurserymen of his time and later, he seems to have suffered from the pressures of urban development. On three occasions he had to auction stock, or sell it off at bargain prices because rented land had to be given up or, in 1865, because it was needed for the construction of two new public roads and a new railway-line. An account of the Sunningdale Nurseries in Charles Noble's time will be found in *Gard. Chron.*, Vol. 18 (1882), p. 596.

RHODOTHAMNUS   ERICACEAE

A genus of two species bearing a superficial resemblance to some lepidote rhododendrons, but more closely allied to *Phyllodoce*, with which it
has formed an intergeneric hybrid (see × *Phyllothamnus*). Another close
ally is *Kalmiopsis* of western N. America; indeed, the relationship is so
close that the only species of *Kalmiopsis* (*K. leachiana*) was transferred to
Rhodothamnus by the American botanist Copeland.

R. CHAMAECISTUS (L.) Reichenb.   [PLATE 110
Rhododendron chamaecistus L.

A low or semi-prostrate evergreen shrub, rarely more than 1 ft high; young
shoots minutely downy, but almost hidden by the closely set leaves. Leaves
almost without stalks, narrowly oval, ¼ to ½ in. long, half or less than half as
wide, tapered at both ends, edged with conspicuous bristles, otherwise glabrous
and glossy green on both sides. Flowers produced during April at the end of the
twigs, two to four in each cluster. Corolla pale, clear rose, spreading, 1 to 1¼ in.
wide, the five lobes ovate, rounded half as deep as the corolla; calyx ½ in. wide,
the five lobes linear-ovate, pointed, covered like the stalk (which is ½ in. long)
with gland-tipped hairs. Stamens ten, glabrous, ½ in. long; anthers very dark
purple. Seed-vessel globose, hairy, many-seeded, with the sepals persisting at the
base.

In the words of Reginald Farrer, R. *chamaecistus* is 'the joy and glory of the
Dolomites and all the South-eastern limestones'. Its south-western limit is in the
Bergamo pre-alps, east of Lake Como; in the north-west it reaches into southern
Bavaria; its eastern limit is in Slovenia and Lower Austria. It is absent from
Switzerland.

Farrer contrasted this lovely species with 'the coarse and clownish Alpenrosen',
and indeed there is no Sino-Himalayan rhododendron that surpasses it in ele-
glance or in purity of colouring. It is uncommon in cultivation and often reported
to be difficult, though it has thrived and flowered profusely on rock gardens in
soils ranging from pure peat to mortar rubble. It needs a sunny position, but
artificial protection may have to be given in spring to save its flowers from destruc-
tion by frost. Plants dug up in the wild (illegally, for the species is protected)
are difficult to establish. Cuttings taken in late summer can be rooted, though
not readily. Seeds provide another means of increase; they ripen very quickly—
by midsummer—and are said to germinate best in full light.

The second species of *Rhodothamnus* is R. SESSILIFOLIUS P. H. Davis.
Surely one of the most remarkable plant discoveries of recent years, this species
was found growing in N.E. Anatolia within the area of the relict species *Orphanidesia* (*Epigaea*) *gaultheriodes* and was described in 1962. It is closely allied to
R. *chamaecistus*, though separated from it by a distance of almost 1,500 miles.

RHODOTYPOS   ROSACEAE

A genus of a single species, closely allied to *Kerria* and once often called '*Kerria japonica alba*' in gardens. It is easily distinguished from that genus by its opposite leaves, four petals and white flowers. The generic name refers to the rose-like flowers.

R. SCANDENS (Thunb.) Makino
Corchorus scandens Thunb.; *R. kerrioides* Sieb. & Zucc.

A deciduous shrub growing about 6 ft high; branches erect; young shoots glabrous. Leaves opposite, ovate, long-pointed, 2½ to 4 in. long, half as much wide, upper surface dark green and soon becoming glabrous, undersurface

RHODOTYPOS SCANDENS

paler and hairy, prominently parallel-ribbed, the margins deeply, irregularly, and sharply toothed. Flowers solitary at the end of short twigs, 1¼ to 2 in. across, pure white; petals four, rounded, with a short claw; calyx four-lobed, the lobes leaf-like, hairy, toothed, persisting until the fruit is ripe. Fruits about the size of small peas, shining, black, clustered above the calyx. *Bot. Mag.*, t. 5805.

Native of China, and perhaps Japan; introduced in 1866. It is a very hardy plant, and quite easily propagated by cuttings made of moderately soft wood and placed in brisk bottom heat. Its flowers are at their best in May and June, but they continue to expand up to the end of July.

RHUS   SUMACH   ANACARDIACEAE

A large genus of shrubs, small trees, or climbers, with ternate or pinnate leaves, found in most temperate regions of the globe, and occasionally in the tropics. About a dozen species are grown in the open air in the British Isles, but several others (such as *R. succedanea*) can be cultivated in Corn-wall and similar places. Individually the flowers of the sumachs are small and of little beauty, being greenish, yellowish, or dull white, but in a few species the panicles are sufficiently large and the flowers white enough to give a pleasing effect. In some species the fruits are handsome, but, on the whole, their value in gardens is in the size and autumn colouring of the foliage. The leading characters of the genus are the alternate leaves and usually dioecious flowers, the five-lobed calyx (which adheres to the fruit), the five petals, the one-celled ovary with three styles, and the usually globose fruit, either glabrous or hairy, containing one bony seed.

The juice of several species, notably *R. radicans* and *R. vernix*, is exceedingly acrid and poisonous to many people, but care should be taken in pruning or making cuttings of any of the species. *R. verniciflua* yields the famous lacquer of Japan. The leaves of several species have also an economic value either for dyeing or tanning, and the fruits of some, such as *R. succedanea* and *R. verniciflua*, give a wax used for candle-making.

The cultivation of all the sumachs is simple. They do not require a very rich soil except when they are grown purely for size of foliage as *R. typhina* (q.v.) and *R. glabra* sometimes are. Where autumn colour is desired, ordinary garden soil without added manure is sufficient. Like many other trees with soft wood and a large pith, they are subject to the attacks of the 'coral-spot' fungus (*Nectria cinnabarina*). Branches so attacked should be cleanly cut off and burnt, the wound coated with tar. Most can be propagated by root-cuttings, and seed is often available.

R. AROMATICA Ait.

R. canadensis Marsh., not Mill.; *Toxicodendron crenatum* Mill.; *R. crenata* (Mill.) Dipp., not Thunb.

A low, spreading, deciduous shrub 3 to 5 ft high; shoots downy or almost glabrous. Leaves aromatically fragrant when bruised, trifoliate, with a common stalk ½ to ¾ in. long. Leaflets not stalked, the side ones broadly ovate, the terminal one the largest, obovate, and 1½ to 3 in. long, the side ones about half as big; all coarsely toothed, lower surface downy, becoming glabrous. Flowers yellowish, in dense roundish clusters ½ to ¾ in. across, produced in April at the end of short stalks on the shoots of the preceding year. Fruits red, hairy, about the size of small red currants.

Native of eastern N. America; introduced in 1759. It is a variable species, but is probably represented in cultivation only by the typical variety, described above. It is rather pretty in spring, when its twigs are clothed with the abundant yellow flowers, and its scented foliage is handsome and distinct.

R. TRILOBATA Torr. & Gr. R. *aromatica* var. *trilobata* (Torr. & Gr.) A. Gray—Leaves smaller, the leaflets ½ to 1 in. long, the terminal one often fan-shaped, with a few comparatively large lobes. They are unpleasantly scented, and the shrub is sometimes known as 'skunk bush'. The flowers are greenish. It has a more western distribution than R. *aromatica*, in the Rocky Mountains, British Columbia, California, etc., and extends into Mexico.

R. CHINENSIS Mill.

R. javanica of many authors, not L.; *R. osbeckii* [DC.] Carr.; *R. semi-alata* Murr.

A small deciduous tree, sometimes 20 ft or more high, with a short trunk and a rounded gauntly branched head; branchlets yellowish, downy; winter-buds brown, velvety. Leaves pinnate, varying in size according to the vigour of the plant, ordinarily from 8 to 15 in. long, and composed of seven to thirteen leaflets, between each pair of which the common leaf-stalk is winged. Leaflets stalkless, oval, usually 2½ to 4 (occasionally 6) in. long, and about half as wide, pointed, the margins conspicuously round- or sharply toothed, the under-surface covered with velvety down. Flowers in a large, terminal panicle 8 or 10 in. long and wide, yellowish white, produced in August. Fruits small, orange-coloured.

R. *chinensis* is widely spread in Asia, throughout the Himalaya (from Hazara in the west to Bhutan in the east), Assam, upper Burma, Siam, Indo-China, throughout China to Korea, Japan, and Formosa, and it has also been found in Sumatra. Miller grew the species from seeds received from Paris in 1737, but the plants were destroyed in the winter of 1740, and it was probably not established in cultivation in Britain until the 1870s. R. *chinensis* varies in the degree of winging of the leaf-rachis and the name var. ROXBURGHII (DC.) Rehd. has been given to plants where the leaf-rachis is not or only slightly winged.

As a flowering plant R. *chinensis* is one of the handsomest of the sumachs, although it does not bloom so freely here as on the Continent. It may be cut down annually like R. *glabra* 'Laciniata'. In some places it colours brilliantly in the autumn.

R. COPALLINA L.   DWARF SUMACH

A deciduous shrub rarely more than 4 ft high in this country, but said to become a small tree 25 to 30 ft high in the southern United State; branchlets covered with a fine reddish down. Leaves pinnate, composed of nine to fifteen (occasionally more) leaflets, the common stalk being winged on both sides between the leaflets, which are stalkless (or the basal ones shortly stalked), lanceolate, 2 to 3½ in. long, rarely toothed, dark glossy green above, paler and downy beneath, the lower leaflets the smallest. Flowers greenish yellow, unisexual, produced in crowded pyramidal panicles 4 to 6 in. long, 3 to 4 in. wide, the female panicle normally the smaller. Fruits bright red, hairy.

Widely spread in eastern N. America, this species varies considerably in a wild state. The form cultivated in Britain is, no doubt, the shrubby northern one. American writers describe it as being of singular beauty, its foliage dying off a rich reddish purple which, with the scarlet fruits of the female tree, gives a charming combination of colour. It flowers in July and August. Introduced to England and cultivated in the Fulham Palace grounds in 1688. Distinct because of its entire leaflets and winged stalk.

R. CORIARIA L.   TANNER'S OR ELM-LEAVED SUMACH

A deciduous or semi-evergreen shrub 2 to 10 ft high; young branchlets densely brown-hairy. Leaves up to 7 in. long, with mostly nine to fifteen leaflets (occasionally more numerous); rachis winged, at least between the upper leaflets; leaflets elliptic to ovate, obtuse, rarely lanceolate and acuminate, up to 2 in. long and 1 in. wide, coarsely toothed, hairy on both sides, more densely so beneath. Inflorescence a narrow, dense panicle about 4 in. long, sometimes longer, produced in July or August. Flowers unisexual or hermaphrodite, yellowish green. Fruits globose, $\frac{3}{16}$ to ¼ in. wide, purplish brown, hairy.

A species of wide distribution, from the Canary Islands and Madeira through the Mediterranean region to the Caucasus and Afghanistan. Although introduced to Britain in the 17th century and fairly common in gardens early in the last century, it is now very uncommon. It has little claim to consideration as an ornamental, but is of interest as the lectotype of the genus *Rhus* and as the species to which the vernacular name 'sumach', of Arabic origin, properly belongs. It is also the only species of *Rhus* native to the mainland of Europe (the mainly N. African R. *pentaphylla* Desf., and R. *tripartita* (Ucria) Grande of N. Africa and S.W. Asia both extend to Sicily but no farther). It is a characteristic plant of the Mediterranean *maquis*, and in S.E. Europe is also found in deciduous brushwood communities and pubescent oak woodland, with *Fraxinus ornus*, *Pyracantha coccinea*, etc. The leaves and stems of sumach contain an important tanning and dyeing material, used in powdered form to produce Cordoba and Morocco leathers.

R. *coriaria* is probably hardy in a sunny place and well-drained soil, and might thrive best in eastern England. The leaves on wild plants are said to colour red in the autumn.

f. HUMILIOR Nic.—A dwarf form, smaller in all its parts. Plants once grown at Kew had roundish, deeply toothed leaflets. Described from Italy.

R. GLABRA L.

A deciduous, usually dioecious shrub, from 4 to 6 (rarely 10) ft high, with glabrous leaves and branches. Leaves pinnate, about 12 to 18 in. long, composed usually of from fifteen to twenty-nine leaflets, which are oblong-lanceolate, shallowly to rather deeply toothed, 2 to 4½ in. long, ½ to ¾ in. wide, glaucous beneath. Flowers mostly unisexual, closely packed in a dense pyramidal panicle 4 to 10 in. long, the stalks covered with red down. Fruits the size of large shot, packed like the flowers in a dense panicle, and covered with soft crimson hairs. They remain long on the plant after the leaves have fallen.

Native of N. America, where in some parts it is almost a weed; also of Mexico. It is nearly allied to R. *typhina*, and is very similar in its handsome fruit, but differs in the glabrous young wood and leaves, and its purely shrubby habit. The foliage turns a bright, rich red. Flowers in July and August.

cv. 'LACINIATA'.—One of the handsomest of hardy foliage plants, the leaflets being deeply cut so as to make the leaf almost or quite doubly pinnate. Its greatest beauty is obtained by cutting it hard back every spring, and thinning down the young shoots to one or two, thus obtaining broad feathery leaves 3 ft long, very striking in their autumn colour.

'Laciniata' is an older variety than its counterpart in R. *typhina*. It was discovered in the USA near Philadelphia by Elias Durand and was introduced to Britain from France in 1865.

P. × PULVINATA Greene *P.* × *hybrida* Rehd.—A natural hybrid between *P. glabra* and R. *typhina* occurring in the wild with the parents. Stems at first downy; leaflets downy on the veins beneath. Some plants grown as R. *glabra* belong here.

R. MICHAUXII Sarg.

R. *pumilum* Michx., not Meerburgh

A low, diciduous shrub up to 3½ ft high, spreading by means of underground suckers; stems erect and rather stout, covered with short hairs. Leaves pinnate, 8 to 12 in. long, dull green; leaflets usually nine to fifteen, ovate or oblong, 1½ to 3 in. long, rounded and slightly oblique at the base, the terminal one the largest, with a winged stalk, the upper surface hairy, the lower one covered with a dense, yellowish down, the margins coarsely toothed. Panicle erect, terminal, hairy, 6 to 8 in. high, half as much wide; flowers ⅛ in. wide, densely arranged, petals greenish yellow; calyx covered with grey down. Fruits nearly round, ⅛ in. in diameter, scarlet, very downy.

Native of the S.E. United States; first discovered by Michaux towards the end of the 18th century. For about one hundred years it was lost sight of, but was again discovered and reintroduced to cultivation. It was sent to Kew in 1901 from the Biltmore Arboretum, USA, and flowered the same year. According to some authorities it is very poisonous, perhaps the most poisonous of American sumachs, but I have spoken with Americans who regard it as harmless.

R. POTANINII Maxim.

R. henryi Diels; *R. sinica* Hort., and of some authors, not Diels

A deciduous tree up to 30 ft high, with a rounded head of branches; young shoots glabrous or minutely downy. Leaves from 10 to 16 in. long, composed of seven, nine, or eleven leaflets, which are oblong to oblong-lanceolate, obliquely rounded or broadly tapered at the base, tapered at the apex to a fine point, 2½ to 5 in. long, 1 to 1¾ in. wide, margins entire or sparsely toothed, glabrous and dark green above, but with a tuft of hairs at the base of the midrib and on the short stalk. Flowers small, produced in June on terminal pyramidal downy panicles 3 to 7 in. high, the main and secondary flower-stalks as well as the sepals covered with brown down; the greenish-white petals are also downy outside, and about ⅛ in. long. Fruits rich red, downy, about the size of peppercorns, densely packed in drooping panicles.

Native of China in the provinces of Kansu, Shensi, Shansi, Honan, and Hupeh; discovered by Potanin in Kansu in 1885, three years later by Henry in Hupeh; introduced by Wilson in 1902 when collecting for Messrs Veitch. It makes a quite handsome small or medium-sized tree, sometimes many-stemmed, and usually colours red in the autumn. But it rarely flowers or fruits in this country.

Among the largest recorded specimens are: Kew, *pl.* 1908, 40 × 5 ft (1967); Wakehurst Place, Sussex, 58 × 7½ ft at 3 ft (1964); Westonbirt, Glos., in Clay Island, 55 × 5 ft at 2 ft (1966).

R. potaninii received an Award of Merit in 1932, for its foliage and autumn colour. The young plant exhibited in 1909 under the name *R. sinica*, which received the same award, was probably *R. potaninii*.

R. PUNJABENSIS Brandis—*R. potaninii* is closely related to this species, which in its typical state is a native of the N.W. Himalaya as far east as Kumaon. *R. punjabensis* has more hairy stems and foliage, but otherwise the two species scarcely differ. Rehder recognises a variety of *R. punjabensis* in China—var. SINICA (Diels) Rehd. & Wils., differing from the Himalayan type in having the upper part of the rachis slightly winged and in the usually fewer and more sessile leaflets. *R. potaninii* is supposed to differ from this variety in being more glabrous, in having the leaflets distinctly stalked and in its unwinged leaf-rachis. But the differences are not at all clear-cut, and certainly *R. potaninii* cannot be reliably distinguished from *R. punjabensis* var. *sinica* by the differences given by Rehder in the key on p. 542 of the present (second) edition of his *Manual*. It is possible that *R. punjabensis* var. *sinica* is in cultivation in Britain from Wilson 275, collected during the first expedition for the Arnold Arboretum but, if so, it is probably by this time grown as *R. potaninii*.

R. RADICANS L.   POISON IVY

R. toxicodendron of many authors, in large part, not L.

A deciduous shrub, either climbing or loosely spreading in habit, the climbing form attaching itself to rocks, walls, trunks of trees, etc., by means of aerial roots like those of the ivy, and frequently reaching to a considerable height; the bushy form up to 8 or 9 ft high. Leaves always composed of three leaflets, the side ones very shortly stalked, the end one with a stalk ½ to 1¼ in. long, the common leaf-stalk 2 to 4 in. long. Leaflets very variable in size, shape, and toothing, broadly ovate to obovate, pointed, sometimes quite entire, often coarsely and irregularly notched at the margin, and either glabrous or slightly downy beneath. The terminal leaflet is always the largest, and from 2 to 5 in. long, the lateral ones about two-thirds as large. Flowers dull white, ⅛ in. across, on slender panicles 1½ to 2½ in. long, often unisexual, the sexes sometimes separated. Fruit a round, whitish drupe, ¼ in. wide, smooth or downy. *Bot. Mag.* t. 1806.

The poison ivy is very abundant in N. America and Mexico. As a garden plant its chief value is in the beautiful red tints of its autumn foliage. It was cultivated by Compton, Bishop of London, at Fulham, in the 17th century. The poisonous effects of the sap—a yellowish milk-like fluid which soon turns black on exposure —have long been known. As long ago as 1623, the author of the *Historye of the Bermudaes* referred to them. On the skin of many persons, but far from all, the sap produces blisters and eczema-like eruptions, which are exceedingly painful and persistent. The supposed active principle, 'toxicodendrol', is insoluble in water, and it is of no use to attempt to remove it from the skin by ordinary washing. The best-known remedy to apply is an alcoholic solution of sugar of lead (lead acetate), and the sooner it is used on the affected parts the more effective it is. So serious are the effects of the rhus poison on some people that the plant should never be grown where anyone unaware of its dangerous properties could come in contact with it. Even in England I know of a man who had been making cuttings of it for propagation, who was kept in hospital for several months through the almost corrosive effects of the sap. It is said that the symptoms are sometimes recurrent, and that on some persons the eruptions break out annually at the same time of year, but with decreasing virulency. This phenomenon, extraordinary if true, does not appear to have been conclusively established, although the testimony of patients is on record who aver that they have had second and third attacks, although they have never been near the plant after the first. In my experience mere contiguity to the plant without touching it will not induce skin poisoning, although when in flower the escaping pollen appears to have evil effects, especially on the eyes, in N. America.

There is one other property of this remarkable plant to which attention may be drawn. This is the indelibility of its juice when applied to linen. It produces a quite ineradicable stain, and is, in fact, one of the best possible marking inks available.

var. RYDBERGII (Small) Rehd. *R. rydbergii* Small—A small, non-climbing, sparsely branched shrub, spreading by underground runners. Leaves clustered at the ends of the shoots, glabrous except for the usually downy veins beneath; terminal leaflet broad-ovate to almost orbicular, abruptly acuminate. Native mainly of the western USA and British Columbia, but also reported from the east.

R. DIVERSILOBA Torr. & Gr.—Usually a shrub. Leaflets rounded to obtuse at the apex, or abruptly narrowed to an acute point, the terminal one lobed or sinuate. Western N. America. It is just as poisonous as *R. radicans*.

R. TOXICODENDRON L. POISON OAK.—A sparsely branched shrub spreading by suckers. Petioles and undersides of leaflets velvety-pubescent; leaflets elliptic or rhombic-ovate, variously lobed. Native of the south-eastern USA in the coastal plain. The name R. *toxicodendron* has been wrongly applied to R. *radicans*.

R. ORIENTALE (Greene) Schneid. *Toxicodendron orientale* Greene; *T. radicans* subsp. *orientale* (Greene) Gillis; R. *ambigua* of some authors, not (?) Lav. ex Dipp.; *Ampelopsis japonica* Hort., in part—A native of Japan, Sakhalin, the Kuriles, China, and Formosa, very closely allied to R. *radicans*, differing in its hispid fruits. This rhus, which is just as poisonous as its American relative, was once grown in nurseries and gardens under the wrong and misleading names "*Ampelopsis hoggii*" and "*A. japonica*", which are properly synonyms of the Japanese creeper *Parthenocissus tricuspidata*.

R. SUCCEDANEA L.   WAX TREE

A deciduous tree up to 30 or 35 ft high. Leaves pinnate, up to 1 ft in length; leaflets usually nine or eleven but sometimes as many as fifteen, ovate-oblong (often obliquely so), narrowed to a long point, not toothed, 2 to 4½ in. long, ⅝ to 1¼ in. wide, shortly stalked, glabrous on both surfaces. The midrib usually runs nearer one side of the blade than the other and from it proceed, almost at right angles, ten to twenty pairs of thin veins. The leaves have a glossy, often purplish hue. Flowers very small, yellowish, produced in slender panicles 3 to 5 in. long that come in the crowded leaf-axils near the end of the shoot, the whole forming a thick cluster of blossom there. Fruits ⅜ in. broad, globose to rather kidney-shaped, borne in pendulous clusters, the seed and its waxy covering enclosed by a thin, smooth, yellowish-brown skin.

A species of wide distribution, from the Himalaya to Japan, Formosa, and Malaysia. In Japan it used to be much cultivated in the southern islands for the sake of the wax or tallow obtained from the fruits. This wax was used for making candles and was a principal source of artificial light in Japan until the importation of petroleum from America and Russia. Seeds appear to have first been introduced from Japan to France in 1862. It is scarcely hardy at Kew although it may survive for several years in a sheltered place. The leaves of plants grown in pots open with a pale bronzy tint and turn a lovely soft red colour before falling, and the species will no doubt be well worth cultivation in our warmer counties for its autumnal beauty.

R. TRICHOCARPA Miq.

Toxicodendron trichocarpum (Miq.) Kuntze

A deciduous tree of slender habit, 20 to 25 ft high, or sometimes a bush 5 to 12 ft high. Leaves 12 to 20 in. long, with thirteen to seventeen leaflets, which are broadly ovate, entire, 1½ to 2½ in. long, largest towards the apex of the leaf, very downy on both sides. Flowers in slender, downy, long-stalked panicles, inconspicuous. Fruit a large, yellowish, prickly drupe, which is not fleshy and sheds its outer coat when ripe.

Native of Japan, where it is common throughout the country, of the S. Kuriles, Korea, E. and Central China; introduced to the USA from Japan by Prof. Sargent, and thence to Kew a few years later; reintroduced by Wilson from Japan in 1914 and from Korea in 1918. Although often a tree in the wild,

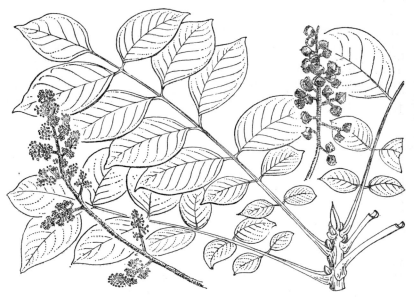

RHUS TRICHOCARPA

it is usually seen in gardens as a sparsely branched, slow-growing shrub 5 to 8 ft high. Although the species is said to be dioecious, this form produces large clusters of fruits, most of which are fertile. They may of course be the result of apomixis. On plants grown in a sunny place the leaves colour brilliant orange or scarlet in the autumn. Although perhaps less venomous than R. *radicans* and its immediate allies, this species belongs to the same group and should be handled with caution.

R. TYPHINA L.   STAG'S-HORN SUMACH

R. *hirta* Sudw., not Engl.

A deciduous, small tree of gaunt, flat-topped habit, occasionally 25 or more feet high; branchlets thick, very pithy, yielding when cut a copious, yellowish-white, thick juice, soon turning black and hard on exposure; all the young bark is covered with short, dense, reddish hairs. Leaves pinnate, 1 to 2 ft long, consisting of from about thirteen to twice as many leaflets, which are oblong-lanceolate, 2 to 4½ in. long, ½ to 1 in. wide, long-pointed, toothed, covered with brownish hairs when young, nearly or quite glabrous by autumn (the stalk remaining downy). Female flowers crowded in a dense, pyramidal, very hairy panicle 4 to 8 in. long; male flowers (which are borne on separate plants) greenish, and on a bigger, more open panicle. Fruits closely packed in dense panicles, and covered thickly with crimson hairs.

Native of eastern N. America, and cultivated in England since the reign of James I. The female plant is one of the handsomest of sumachs, for, added to its finely coloured fruit clusters, its leaves acquire in autumn rich shades of orange, red, and purple. The male plant, which colours its leaves too, is sometimes known as "R. *viridiflora*". This tree succeeds remarkably well in some of the murkiest of London suburbs. It is sometimes used as a fine-foliaged summer shrub, grown in a group, and cut back every spring almost to the ground, the young shoots being afterwards reduced to one or two. Given liberal treatment at the root, erect stems 5 or 6 ft high with leaves up to 3 ft long will be produced, the leaflets correspondingly large.

cv. 'DISSECTA' ('*Laciniata*').—Leaflets very handsomely cut (R. *typhina* var. *laciniata* Manning ex Rehd., not Wood; R. *typhina* f. *dissecta* Rehd., R. *typhina* var. *filicina* Sprenger).

'Dissecta' was found at the end of the last century by J. W. Manning, a nurseryman of Reading, Massachusetts, who propagated and distributed it as R. *typhina laciniata*, but this name had been used earlier for another variant (see below). Besides being a beautiful foliage plant, it colours brilliantly in the autumn. A.M. 1910.

f. LACINIATA (Wood) Rehd.—Leaves and bracts more or less laciniate; inflorescence often partly transformed into contorted bracts. A monstrous form said to be fairly common in the wild. Not to be confused with 'Dissecta', often known as 'Laciniata'.

R. VERNICIFLUA Stokes   VARNISH TREE
R. vernicifera DC.; *R. vernix* Thunb., not L.

A deciduous tree up to 60 ft high in China, of erect, slender habit when young. Leaves pinnate, 1 to 2 ft long, with seven to thirteen leaflets which are broadly ovate, the largest 6 or 7 in. long, half as much wide, sometimes obliquely heart-shaped at the base, shortly stalked, velvety downy beneath, especially on the sixteen to thirty veins. Flowers yellowish white, small and inconspicuous, produced during July in a cluster of lax, branching panicles from the leaf-axils near the end of the shoots, the largest panicles 10 in. long by 6 in. wide. Fruits about the size of small peas, yellowish.

A native of the Himalaya and China, but cultivated and possibly native in other parts of E. Asia and Malaysia. This is the tree which yields by incision the famous varnish or lacquer of Japan. As a tree for the garden it is desirable for its noble foliage. The fruits also are ornamental, but are not produced by all trees, since this species is partly dioecious, and in this country do not normally contain ripe seed; they are borne in long, lax panicles. An oil is expressed from the fruit in China, etc., which is used in candle-making.

Wilson collected seeds in China in 1907 from trees growing truly wild in the mountains. Plants raised from them grew faster when young than the Japanese trees which previously were the only representatives of the species in gardens, but there seems to be no difference in overall rate of growth, nor in hardiness.

R. *verniciflua* belongs to the Toxicodendron group and its sap can cause severe blistering.

The following examples have been recorded: Kew, *pl.* 1898, 35 × 4½ ft (1967); *pl.* 1902, 50 × 4 ft (1967); *pl* 1908, 41 × 2¾ ft (1967); Wakehurst Place Sussex, 55 × 6 ft (1973); Westonbirt, Glos., *pl.* 1939, 42 × 2¾ ft (1966); Hergest Croft, Heref., 50 × 3¾ ft (1961); Stanage Park, Radnor, 49 × 6¼ + 5¾ ft (1970); Edinburgh Botanic Garden, *pl.* 1908, from W.259, 44 × 3¼ ft (1970) and 34 × 3¾ ft (1967); University Botanic Garden, Cambridge, 53 × 5¼ ft (1969); National Botanic Garden, Glasnevin, Eire, 50 × 4¼ ft (1966).

R. SYLVESTRIS Sieb. & Zucc.—Allied to R. *verniciflua* but a smaller tree, or a large shrub, which does not yield varnish. The leaflets are shorter, 1¾ to 4 in. long, but despite that have more numerous veins, mostly in eighteen to twenty-five pairs, which are consequently set very much closer together than in R. *verniciflua*. It is a native of Japan, E. and Central China, and Korea; it was in cultivation in France by 1881 but was probably not introduced to Britain until later. Even now it is uncommon in this country, but is available in commerce. The leaves usually colour red in the autumn.

R. VERNIX L.   POISON SUMACH
R. *venenata* DC.

A small deciduous tree up to 20 ft high, with a trunk 15 to 18 in. thick, usually much smaller in England, and often breaking near the ground into two or three stems; branchlets glabrous and grey. Leaves pinnate, with purplish stalks, quite glabrous except when young; leaflets nine to thirteen, 2 to 4 in. long, one-third as much wide, ovate or obovate, entire. Flowers ⅛ in. across, greenish yellow, produced on thin, slender panicles 4 to 8 in. long from the leaf-axils of the current season's growth. Fruits the size of a peppercorn, yellowish white, and hanging in a cluster of graceful panicles from near the end of the branchlets.

Native of the eastern United States; cultivated in England since early in the 18th century. Few of the sumachs are more beautiful than this in their autumn tints, the foliage putting on brilliant shades of orange and scarlet before it falls. Yet it is not much grown in this country, and perhaps wisely so, for it is one of the most dangerous hardy trees in cultivation, owing to the toxic properties of its sap—even, it is said, of its exhalations! The latter may be doubtful; but all that has been said as to the need of care in dealing with R. *radicans* applies with equal, if not greater, force to this species. It appears with both that persons in a state of perspiration are most susceptible to their effects. It flowers in July, and the fruit often remains throughout the winter.

INDEX

As the general arrangement of this work is alphabetical it has not been considered necessary to index names which appear in their proper sequence. The following is an index of 'popular' or English names; of the more important synonyms which, in accordance with the usual practice, are given in italics; and of a number of trees and shrubs which are not described in their alphabetical order but under related plants.

The attention of the reader is called to the glossary of botanical terms on p. 112, and to the glossary of nursery terms on p. 54 of Vol. I of this edition. The plates are listed on pp. xiii–xvi; the line drawings on pp. xi–xii